The Complete
Garden Guide

TIME
LIFE
BOOKS

Alexandria, Virginia

PART I

PHOTO GALLERY

GARDEN DESIGN

PLANTING AND MAINTENANCE

KITCHEN GARDENING

PART IV

REFERENCE

A Garden Sampler

No matter what type of garden you desire—a cool woodland retreat, a backyard kitchen garden, or a fragrant showstopper of roses— your personal imprint is an important part of the design. While the gardens you see in books or magazines may evoke a particular style or theme and follow accepted design principles, invariably something of the designer's personality comes through that makes the garden uniquely his or her own.

Your house and surroundings might indicate a certain style, but in the end the choice is yours. You may opt for an entryway garden that reflects the architecture of your home, while saving backyard or side gardens for a more personalized touch. Or you might take elements of one style and mix them with compatible elements of another. For example, the owner of the stone cottage near Philadelphia at left opted for a formal design yet filled the beds with plants that evoke a colorful cottage garden. For a planting guide to each of the gardens in this section, see pages 58-77.

A love of the Provence region of France was the inspiration behind this northern California garden. Cool grays and greens were purposely selected to suggest a sunny Mediterranean landscape; mounds of French and English lavender and sprays of deep pink Erysimum (wallflower) provide harmonious waves of color. Reflecting the undulating rhythm of the border planting, a stepped pathway of rounded Colorado River-washed stones leads to the back entrance of the house, which is flanked by olive trees. The massive Plectostachys at the entrance to the path (lower left) began as a small 1-gallon container plant; it owes its healthy growth both to careful pruning and to the addition of turkey manure to this garden's sandy loam.

9

Reminiscent of an Early American dooryard planting, this delightful Maine garden of herbs, vegetables, and flowers combines such traditional elements as a straight path—leading here to a bench instead of a door—a profusion of plants, and a fence enclosure with an unusual location: The garden is installed on the site of an abandoned clay tennis court. The plants were carefully chosen and arranged to maximize color, texture, and fragrance and to provide a bounty for the kitchen as well. Tall Phlox paniculata in striking pink welcomes a visitor entering the path, which is lined with 'Lemon Gem' marigolds. Feathery yellow-headed dill off to the left of the walkway fronts raspberry brambles, while purplish blue bellflowers and lilies in pale pink and yellow create a pleasing combination on the right.

10

Perfect for quiet reflection and restoration of the spirit, this Japanese-inspired garden near Boston borrows the elements of a traditional rock-and-water planting. A stream, defined by well-placed fieldstone, encircles an island bed dominated by a simple, evocative ornament. But rather than rely on a few strategically placed and perfectly manicured plants, the gardeners have indulged their desire for lush flowers and foliage, including in the mix Spiraea japonica 'Little Princess' (foreground), Geranium endressii, and a variety of ferns, along with colorful splashes of azalea and iris, a magnolia, and a Japanese maple.

12

Swimmers in this pool in Phoenix, Arizona, might think themselves afloat in the midst of a prairie meadow— except that this planting is composed of wildflowers native to the desert. Scarlet flax, purple arroyo lupine, and California poppies combine with Indian fig, prickly pear, and saguaro to rim the edge of a man-made oasis, providing privacy for sunbathers as well as sanctuary for the quails, doves, hummingbirds, owls, hawks, and butterflies that flock to this inviting, low-maintenance garden.

The glossy dark green leaves and large blush pink flowers of the vigorous 'New Dawn' rose adorn a pergola in this elegant Alabama garden. Leading the eye upward, the climber helps frame the view of the bench beyond, beckoning visitors to that part of the garden. A low hedge of Camellia hiemalis sets off the walkway beneath the pergola, while the bright green foliage of 'Nastarana' rose adds a lively note to the foreground. A tall Ternstroemia hedge describes the garden's boundary and provides a handsome background for the white bench.

High walls and a bright blue gate enclose this Santa Barbara, California, garden, making a private haven and an enchanting transition from the outside world to the house. The long-stemmed fragrant flowers of English lavender (left foreground) lean over a Mexican evening primrose, whose pale pink petals surround bright yellow stamens. Spilling onto the tile walk is a drift of Mexican fleabane sprinkled with dainty pink-and-white daisylike flowers. Enormous upward-branching rosemaries flank the gate in the wall, which is adorned with a brilliant red trumpet creeper.

19

Masses of blue catmint highlight the vivid red of Jupiter's-beard, used sparingly as a color accent in this low-maintenance New Mexico perennial garden. In the background, the contrasting golden columbine also appears more intense against the cool tone of the catmint. By allowing the bright yellow to leap forward in the mind's eye, this combination and placement of colors makes the garden seem more lushly planted.

White baby's-breath and yellow beggar-ticks spill onto the stone walk in front of an antique fence and gate, softening this formal entryway garden in Seattle. Along with pink petunias and the white trumpets of variegated nicotiana, the plants were chosen both for their pleasing color contrasts and their dainty forms, which accent the Victorian setting. Low, deep green mounds of common thrift and other foliage plants unite the composition.

Set against the lush green backdrop of a tall thuja hedge, a medley of foliage plants supply a breathtaking exhibition of colors, sizes, forms, and textures as they sweep alongside a pebble walk in Washington State. Irregular repetitions of yellow-leaved hakonechloa and arching spires of Chinese silver grass, combined with plantings such as the mounded 'Jackman Blue' rue, add color and textural excitement when the flowering plants are not blooming. When they are, the garden is punctuated by splashes of flowering orange alstroemeria, pink geraniums, and yellow daylilies, a composition tied together by interweaving vines of clematis bearing indigo blossoms.

23

The owner of this delightful backyard garden, which is visible from her kitchen and living room windows, wanted a cutting garden that would still look lush after she collected her bouquets. By densely planting colonies of annuals that thrive in the northern California climate, she is guaranteed blooms from summer until fall. The daisylike blossoms of cosmos in delicate pink and bold magenta, a planting of fluffy white snow-on-the-mountain, and a few rose pink hybrid cactus dahlias dominate one side of the stepping-stone path. On the other side, feathery red-violet celosia, pink cleome, and two perennial salvias—cobalt blue Salvia guarantica and pale blue S. uliginosa—provide a tangle of tantalizing blooms.

The dependable annuals dominating this Portland, Oregon, front yard ensure continuous bloom from midsummer to first frost. Snowy white sweet alyssum edges a bed that includes lemon yellow signet marigolds, pink zonal geraniums, multi-hued zinnias, and tall, bright yellow African marigolds. Sculpted pines and evergreen shrubbery provide the framework for the garden.

An artful blend of plants makes this small Virginia garden appear larger than it is. For a bold look and continuous color, the owners turned to such annuals as the two massive castor bean plants near the corner of the walkway. The maroon foliage of hybrid polka-dot plants creates a pool of deep color amid the greenery. Rose-pink verbena (foreground) and yellow lantana add textural contrast and continuous bloom.

Contrasting textures and harmonious greens combine to form a foliage border in Pennsylvania that is anything but dull. Fan-leafed hyacinth bean, which covers the rustic fence, and the feathery foliage of daphne and cleome provide a beautiful textural backdrop for the dramatically veined, broad leaves of 'Striata' canna and its bold orange blossoms. Silvery mounds of dusty-miller and tall white orbs of cleome add a luminous glow. Touches of yellow marigolds and purple Brazilian verbena pull the planting together and spark color interest.

The owners of this timber-and-mortar cottage in Virginia wanted to add interest without obscuring the architecture. The 6-foot-tall plume poppies framing the doorway make a dramatic vertical statement, while their huge, deeply lobed, blue-green leaves act as a light foliage screen along the walls. The plume poppy's invasive growth habit is held in check by equally aggressive purple coneflower and pink wild sweet William.

This verdant Pennsylvania shade garden offers color and interest throughout the year, yet requires little maintenance. A river of fern moss (Thuidium delicatulum), interrupted by mounded deep green islands of haircap moss (Polytrichum communa), provides year-round cushiony green paths through this north-facing, gently sloped site. Located under a canopy of deciduous trees, borders of easy-care dwarf evergreen shrubs, evergreen ground covers, and ferns are highlighted throughout the growing season by pockets of seasonal flowers such as dwarf Japanese iris, Phlox stolonifera (creeping phlox), and Lobelia cardinalis (cardinal flower), providing color from March through October.

Plants that can withstand harsh waterside conditions are the key to the success of this lush Bridgehampton, New York, garden located on a pond near the Atlantic Ocean. Proclaiming the start of the summer season, a red Oriental poppy adds drama to the scene. Deep pink and bright white, salt-tolerant rugosa roses are just beginning to produce blossoms that will continue through late summer, when the clumps of daylilies flanking the poppy will commence their own spectacular show of color. The thin, willowy stems of phragmites at the rear of the 4-foot-wide border will last into winter. Although the garden is a full 80 feet long, it requires only an hour a week of care—namely, weed pulling. Once a year, in spring, the garden is top-dressed with rotted manure. Should the need arise, an underground watering system augments the local rainfall, which usually measures a generous 45 inches a year.

Overlooking Long Island Sound and Manhattan, this large New York coastal garden blends evergreens, grasses, and perennials that tolerate wind and salt spray. A wide stand of rudbeckia just beginning to show its golden flowers is the backdrop for a low juniper spilling gracefully over a boulder; at the boulder's base, several clumps of annual 'Daybreak Mix' gazania have burst into bloom. Farther back, tall, arching maiden grass mixes with pastel clumps of 'Blue Lacecap' hydrangea and 'Betty Prior' shrub roses, here in their July splendor. For added protection from the elements, the garden receives a thick layer of cedar-bark mulch that is refreshed every 18 to 24 months. The plot is watered by an automatic irrigation system, so the gardener's most demanding chore is deadheading.

A surprising variety of textures, shapes, and colors abound in this sun-scorched Arizona garden, where a scant 7 inches of rain fall in a year. Many of the plants are imports that are well adapted to the American desert: The Cape marigold, with its white daisylike flowers, and the bright yellow bulbine (foreground) are from South Africa, and the medicinal aloe, bearing tall stalks topped by bright orange blossoms, is native to North Africa. American desert natives include ocotillo, a shrub with tall, unbranched stems (upper left); rounded bunnyears cactus; and pinkish purple desert penstemon and moss verbena. Along the fence at the rear of the garden is a mass of tall, yellow-blooming brittlebush.

The plants in this informal Maryland garden were selected to withstand steamy summer temperatures, erratic periods of drought, and winter lows that regularly approach zero. Shrubs ranging in hue from the blue-green of the blue spruce at the center of the border to the deep green of the San Jose holly at the back give the scene a cool feel. The owners spend just 2 hours each week maintaining the garden.

A rainbow of color, this Richmond, Virginia, garden was designed to stand up to the area's high heat and humidity. 'Pink Gumpo' azaleas, reddish orange gaillardias, and feathery rose-pink astilbes blooming among hostas and other foliage plants add bright color in spring. Later, annuals and daylilies keep the garden in bloom through October. After spring planting, only an hour's worth of cleanup is required each week to maintain the quiet elegance.

37

A night garden such as this one in Alabama is the perfect solution for gardeners who are often away from home during the daylight hours. Cool and inviting, the white, green, and silver tones cast a pale glow in the evening or on a moonlit night. The luminous effect is created by a variety of perennials, including summer-blooming daisylike Japanese asters (far right foreground) and airy stalks of rose campion (right, center of border), which flower among dense silver and green foliage for up to 9 months of the year. Although the lines of the borders are formal, they are softened by an overhanging edging of velvety gray-leaved lamb's ears, mingled with white pansies and snow-in-summer.

39

Designed in the tradition of a romantic English border, this striking California garden provides color throughout the year. Spiky purple Mexican bush sage, purple Peruvian verbena, and pink gloxinia penstemon contribute to the cascade of color. Roses and herbs are planted among the perennials to create interesting textures while maintaining color harmony and progression. For all of its showy good looks, this garden requires relatively little attention: Dead flower heads are removed once a week, and the entire garden is fertilized once a month. The plants are also mulched with redwood shavings to which nitrogen has been added.

41

Late-season color abounds in this Washington State garden, where flowers bloom from mid-July to late October. The large bronze-purple leaves of canna make a regal backdrop for the simple beauty of low-growing, daisylike dahlias. Towering sunflowers and a carpet of pink geraniums complete the arresting combination.

To extend the life of this Pennsylvania border, the owners chose cultivated dahlias with an array of flower forms, including cactus, water lily, anemone, and decorative. Blooming from summer to late fall, the dahlias offer a colorful display when many other bedding plants are waning or have stopped flowering for the season.

This problematic slope in Washington State was transformed into a lovely hillside border punctuated by summer bloomers. Dense umbels of showy, deep blue Agapanthus 'Bressingham Blue' (African lily) stand out in bold contrast to golden mounds of orange coneflower, slender trumpets of Cape fuchsia, and lemon yellow daylilies. Vigorous summer-flowering tubers, the African lilies bloom throughout the season, preferring full sun but tolerating partial shade. Their large clumps of fleshy, straplike leaves provide handsome fill-in foliage even when the plants are not in flower.

Designed to thrive under the hot Virginia sun, this terraced bed is highlighted with clusters of dazzling lilies. These Asiatic hybrids—orange 'Milano' and creamy white 'Roma'—are hardy and easy to grow. Best planted in groups of three or more, they have an erect growth habit and flower heads that add an exotic touch to the garden.

45

Wet feet aren't a problem for swamp roses (Rosa palustris), which arch gracefully over a quiet pool in this Texas garden; unlike other roses, they can thrive right at the water's edge. Here, the pool not only reflects the plant's graceful shape but also serves to display its delicate fallen petals. R. palustris blooms for 6 weeks or longer in this garden, emitting a sweet scent when the buds first open. The rose's pink color is intensified by the yellow-and-green foliage of the variegated canna. With its dark, smooth bark, flowing lines, and oval hips that appear after flowering, the swamp rose provides four-season interest in the garden.

This garden in Pennsylvania is a classic example of the formal jardin potager, or kitchen garden. The foursquare layout features symmetrical beds separated by paths that beckon visitors to stroll and enjoy the plantings up close. Sown successively from late winter through spring, 'Red Salad Bowl' and 'Green Joe' lettuce forms frilly borders around container-grown topiaries of rosemary in the foreground. Other edible plants include 'Pagoda' parsley in the far right corner and two potted sweet bay trees along the side. Neatly clipped barberry, low-growing thyme, and plantain lilies edge the garden, while a tall topiary of English ivy stands at the center. Wrought-iron benches add to the traditional feel of the garden.

Interweaving 'Ruby Red' and bright green 'Black-Seeded Simpson' lettuce adds a whimsical touch to this Virginia garden in spring. Laced among the lettuce are 'Sugar Snap' peas growing in wire cages and 'Cherry Belle' radishes.

A rustic arch draped with 'Scarlet Runner' beans and a wall of tomatoes trained on high stakes add vertical interest to the formal layout of this Long Island kitchen garden. The birdbath at its center echoes the wells that were often the focus of kitchen gardens of the past.

50

A Victorian-style fence surrounds this long rectangular plot in Pennsylvania, which is divided into four beds by neatly manicured grass pathways. A tall, lush cone of vining 'Blue Lake' green beans thrives in the bed in the foreground, along with a large patch of 'Clarimore' zucchini, three varieties of green peppers, and blue-leaved 'Premium Crop' broccoli. Across the path is a small cutting garden where white 'Mt. Fuji' phlox, thinleaf sunflower, 'Autumn Sun' rudbeckia, and the bright orange-and-gold blossoms of 'Whirlybird Hybrids' nasturtium provide a vivid focal point. Culinary herbs occupy the bed in the far corner, and vegetables fill the fourth bed. The wrought-iron bench and the standard roses on either side of it reinforce the period look.

Intensively planted in fall for harvest over the mild California winter, cool-weather vegetables and annuals—some with edible flowers—make a dense, colorful patchwork. Rot-resistant redwood boards contain the double-dug raised beds, which are replenished before every planting with compost.

Ornamental kale and billowy sweet alyssum decorate a rock retaining wall in a terraced five-level vegetable garden in Santa Barbara, California. Beyond the wall are 'Green Ice' lettuce, young filet bean plants, and 'Silver Queen' corn.

54

This imaginative island garden overflowing with vegetables, herbs, and flowering ornamentals is the focal point of a front yard in California. Dominated by imposing, bold-leaved 'Purple Sprouting' broccoli, the vegetables in the bed's center contribute a variety of shapes, heights, textures, and foliage colors. They also act as a foil for the alluring burst of bright purple pansies, red and yellow Persian buttercups, and dainty white paludosum daisies in the foreground. The narrow brick path beckons strollers and also provides easy access for tending the plants.

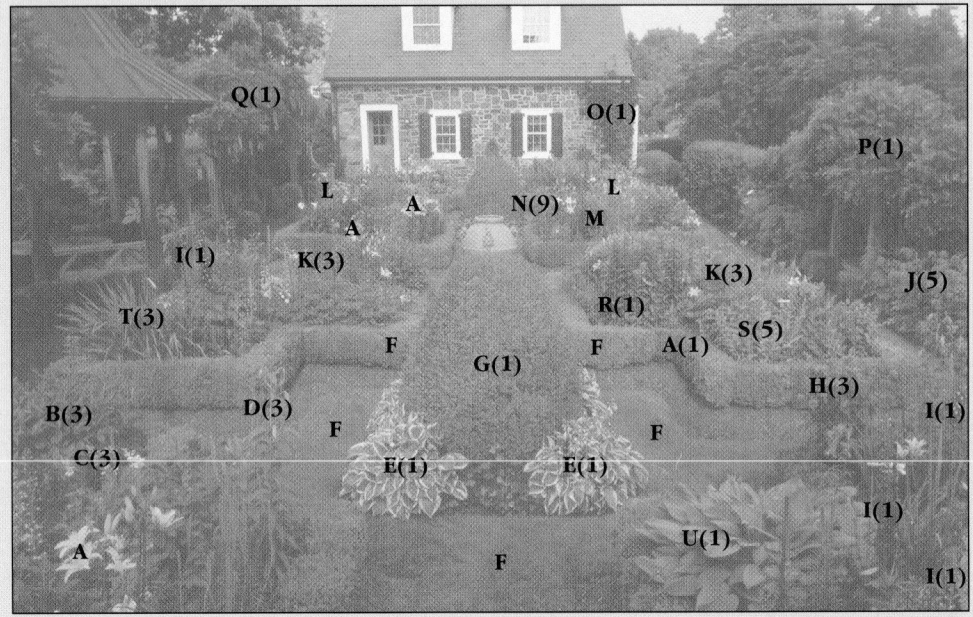

pages 6-7

A. *Lilium 'Luxor'* (lily) (many)
B. *Paeonia officinalis*
(peony) (3)
C. *Filipendula ulmaria*
(queen-of-the-meadow) (3)
D. *Lilium speciosum*
'Rubrum' (showy
Japanese lily) (3)
E. *Hosta fortunei 'Francee'*
(plantain lily) (2)
F. *Buxus sempervirens*
'Suffruticosa'
(edging boxwood) (many)

G. *Buxus sempervirens*
'Arborescens' (boxwood) (1)
H. *Monarda didyma*
(bee balm) (3)
I. *Delphinium elatum*
'Pacific Giants'
(candle larkspur) (4)
J. *Astilbe thunbergii*
'Straussenfeder' (astilbe) (5)
K. *Astilbe chinensis* var.
taquetii 'Superba' (astilbe) (3)
L. *Achillea filipendulina*
'Gold Plate'
(fern-leaf yarrow) (many)
M. *Liatris spicata*
'Kobold Rose'

(button snakewort) (many)
N. *Lilium tigrinum*
(tiger lily) (9)
O. *Hedera helix*
(English ivy) (1)
P. *Wisteria sinensis*
(Chinese wisteria) (1)
Q. *Castanea dentata*
(American chestnut) (1)
R. *Phlox paniculata*
(summer phlox) (1)
S. *Lilium 'Apollo'* (lily) (5)
T. *Iris ensata*
(sword-leaved iris) (3)
U. *Hosta fortunei 'Aoki'*
(plantain lily) (1)

pages 8-9

A. *Plectostachys serphyllifolia* (1)
B. *Erysimum* (wallflower) (2)
C. *Digitalis* (foxglove) (3)

D. *Chamaerops humilis* (European fan palm) (1)
E. *Olea europaea* (common olive) (2)
F. *Solanum jasminoides* (potato vine) (1)
G. *Lavandula angustifolia* (English lavender) (1)

H. *Lavandula dentata* (French lavender) (3)
I. *Salvia leucantha* (Mexican bush sage) (3)
J. *Erigeron karvinskianus* (fleabane) (1)
K. *Verbascum bombyciferum* (mullein) (1)

NOTE: The key lists each plant type and the total quantity needed to replicate the garden shown. The diagram's letters and numbers refer to the type of plant and the number sited in an area.

pages 10-11

A. *Phlox paniculata*
(summer phlox) (4)
B. *Anethum graveolens*
(dill) (many)
C. *Antirrhinum majus
'Rocket Mix'* (snapdragon) (24)
D. *Delphinium* (larkspur) (1)
E. *Digitalis purpurea 'Foxy
Hybrids'* (common foxglove) (12)

F. *Tagetes 'Lemon Gem'*
(marigold) (60)
G. *Rubus* sp. (raspberry) (21)
H. *Lathyrus odoratus*
(sweet pea) (20)
I. *Campanula lactiflora*
(milky bellflower) (3)
J. *Lilium Asiatic hybrids*
(lily) (15)

K. *Papaver* sp. (poppy) (12)
L. *Lilium* x *aurelianense
'Golden Splendor'*
(aurelian lily) (15)
M. *Pinus strobus*
(white pine) (1)
N. *Prunus pensylvanica*
(wild red cherry) (1)

pages 12-13

A. *Spiraea japonica
'Little Princess'* (spirea) (2)
B. *Geranium endressii*
(Pyrenean cranesbill) (2)
C. *Magnolia stellata*
(star magnolia) (1)

D. *Acer palmatum 'Bloodgood'*
(Japanese maple) (1)
E. *Cedrus atlantica* (Atlas cedar) (1)
F. *Pieris japonica*
(lily-of-the-valley bush) (2)
G. *Rhododendron 'Hinodegiri'*
(azalea) (7)
H. *Rhododendron 'Polar Bear'* (4)

I. *Rhododendron 'Hinocrimson'* (3)
J. *Athyrium filix-femina*
(lady fern) (2)
K. *Iris ensata* (sword-leaved iris) (4)
L. *Athyrium goeringianum*
(Japanese fern) (2)
M. *Iris cristata* (crested iris) (3)

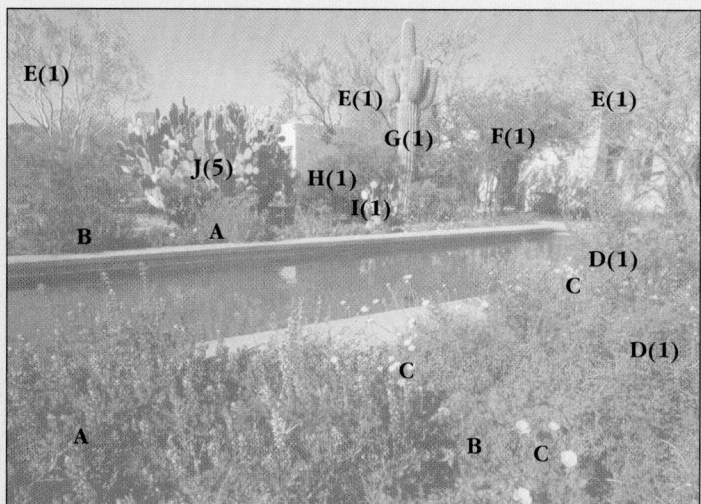

pages 14-15

A. *Lupinus succulentus*
(arroyo lupine) (many)
B. *Linum grandiflorum*
'Rubrum' (scarlet flax) (many)
C. *Eschscholzia californica*
(California poppy) (many)
D. *Larrea tridentata*

(creosote bush) (2)
E. *Olneya tesota*
(desert ironwood) (3)
F. *Acacia farnesiana*
(sweet acacia) (1)
G. *Carnegiea gigantea*
(saguaro) (1)

H. *Lycium fremontii*
(wolfberry) (1)
I. *Opuntia violacea*
var. *santa-rita*
(purple prickly pear) (1)
J. *Opuntia ficus-indica*
(Indian fig) (5)

pages 16-17

A. *'Nastarana', noisette*
(rose) (2)
B. *Camellia hiemalis* (4)
C. *Ophiopogon japonicus*
(mondo grass) (12)
D. *Vinca rosea* (periwinkle) (9)
E. *'White Pet', polyantha*
(rose) (1)

F. *'New Dawn', large-flowered*
climber (rose) (8)
G. *Salvia 'Victoria Blue'*
(sage) (6)
H. *Cycas revoluta*
(sago palm) (2)
I. *Ternstroemia* sp. (6)

J. *'American Beauty', hybrid*
perpetual (rose) (1); *'Reine des*
Violettes', hybrid perpetual
(rose) (1); *'Rosa Mundi', gallica*
(rose) (1); *'Gruss an Teplitz',*
bourbon (rose) (1)

NOTE: The key lists each plant type and the total quantity needed to replicate the garden shown.
The diagram's letters and numbers refer to the type of plant and the number sited in an area.

pages 18-19

A. *Lavandula angustifolia 'Hidcote Giant'* (English lavender) (7)
B. *Oenothera berlandieri* (evening primrose) (9)
C. *Erigeron karvinskianus* (fleabane) (5)
D. *Alyssum* spp. (many)
E. *Salvia leucantha* (sage) (2)
F. *Rosmarinus officinalis* (rosemary) (6)

page 20

A. *Nepeta* x *faassenii* (catmint) (8)
B. *Centranthus ruber* (red valerian) (5)
C. *Aquilegia chrysantha* (columbine) (9)
D. *Pinus edulis* (pinyon) (1)
E. *Hemerocallis 'September Gold'* (daylily) (4)
F. *Aronia melanocarpa* (chokeberry) (4)
G. *Populus tremuloides* (quaking aspen) (4)

pages 20-21

A. *Nicotiana langsdorffii 'Variegata'* (2)
B. *Tagetes x 'Striped Marvel'* (2)
C. *Tagetes 'Lemon Gem'* (2)
D. *Petunia integrifolia* (3)
E. *Gypsophila paniculata* (1)

F. *Chamaecyparis pisifera 'Plumosa Compacta'* (2)
G. *Armeria maritima 'Sea Thrift'* (2)
H. *Fuchsia x 'Checkerboard'* (1)
I. *Bidens ferulifolia*

'Variegata' (1)
J. *Fragaria x 'Pink Panda'* (1)
K. *Liatris spicata* (1)
L. *Hibiscus moscheutos 'Lady Baltimore'* (1)

pages 22-23

A. *Cotinus 'Velvet Cloak'* (1)
B. *Clematis x durandii* (2)
C. *Agapanthus 'Bressingham White'* (3)
D. *Sedum spectabile 'Meteor'* (1)
E. *Helleborus x sternii 'Blackthorn Hybrids'* (1)
F. *Onosma alboroseum* (1)
G. *Hakonechloa 'Aureola'* (3)

H. *Ruta 'Jackman's Blue'* (2)
I. *Artemisia x 'Huntington Botanic'* (1)
J. *Alstroemeria Ligtu Hybrids* (3)
K. *Hemerocallis 'Happy Returns'* (6)
L. *Achillea 'W. B. Child'* (1)
M. *Geranium x 'Mavis*

Simpson' (1)
N. *Stachys byzantina 'Silver Carpet'* (1)
O. *Miscanthus sinensis 'Variegatus'* (2)
P. *Salvia guaranitica* (1)
Q. *Thuja 'Pyramidalis'*
R. *Hydrangea anomala* ssp. *petiolaris* (1)

NOTE: The key lists each plant type and the total quantity needed to replicate the garden shown. The diagram's letters and numbers refer to the type of plant and the number sited in an area.

pages 24-25

A. *Cleome hasslerana*
'Lavender Queen', 'Pink Queen',
'Rose Queen' (5)
B. *Zinnia elegans cv.* (3)
C. *Salvia guaranitica* (1)

D. *Celosia argentea* (2)
E. *Lobularia maritima* (2)
F. *Chrysanthemum x*
morifolium (2)
G. *Cosmos bipinnatus*
'Sensation Mix' (6)
H. *Euphorbia marginata* (3)

I. *Tithonia rotundifolia* (1)
J. *Dahlia cv.* (1)
K. *Rosa 'Meidiland Red'* (1)
L. *Salvia uliginosa* (1)

NOTE: *The key lists each plant type and the total quantity needed to replicate the garden shown.*
The diagram's letters and numbers refer to the type of plant and the number sited in an area.

A. *Acer palmatum* (1)
B. *Rhododendron 'Vulcan'* (1)
C. *Tagetes erecta cv.* (many)
D. *Photinia x fraseri* (many)
E. *Zinnia elegans cv.* (many)
F. *Tagetes erecta 'Lulu'* (many)
G. *Pelargonium x hortorum 'Blues'* (8)
H. *Lobularia maritima* (many)
I. *Pinus mugo var. mugo* (1)
J. *Pseudotsuga menziesii* (1)
K. *Hydrangea macrophylla* (1)
L. *Pinus densiflora 'Umbraculifera'* (2)

pages 26-27

A. *Ricinus communis* (1)
B. *R. communis 'Carmencita'* (1)
C. *Berberis thunbergii 'Aurea'* (1)
D. *Yucca filamentosa 'Golden Eagle'* (1)
E. *Sedum x 'Autumn Joy'* (4)
F. *Hosta 'Gold Standard'* (1)

G. *Nicotiana alata 'Nikki'* (3)
H. *Tradescantia pallida 'Purple Heart'* (3)
I. *Lantana camara 'Flava'* (2)
J. *Digitalis purpurea 'Shirley Hybrids'* (14)
K. *Iris sibirica 'Flight of Butterflies'* (1)
L. *Verbena 'Sissinghurst'* (2)

M. *Coreopsis verticillata 'Moonbeam'* (6)
N. *Berberis thunbergii 'Crimson Pygmy'* (1)
O. *Ceratostigma plumbaginoides* (3)
P. *Spiraea japonica 'Limemound'* (1)
Q. *Centranthus ruber* (3)

R. *Achillea x 'Moonshine'* (4)
S. *Spiraea japonica 'Little Princess'* (1)
T. *Hemerocallis 'Stella d'Oro'* (3)
U. *Hypoestes phyllostachya* (3)
V. *Rosa 'The Fairy'* (1)
W. *Miscanthus sinensis 'Variegatus'* (1)
X. *Rosa 'Betty Prior'* (1)

pages 28-29

A. *Verbena bonariensis* (many)
B. *Senecio vira-vira* (10)
C. *Daphne x 'Carol Mackie'* (2)
D. *Cleome 'Helen Campbell'* (many)

E. *Dolichos lablab* (3)
F. *Elymus glaucus* (2)
G. *Calendula officinalis*
(volunteer seedlings)

H. *Dahlia 'David Howard'* (2)
I. *Canna x generalis 'Striata'* (3)
J. *Dahlia 'My Love'* (3)
K. *Pyrus* (1)

page 29

A. *Macleaya cordata* (9)
B. *Echinacea purpurea*
'Bright Star' (5)

C. *Liatris spicata* (2)
D. *Phlox maculata*
'Alpha' (6)

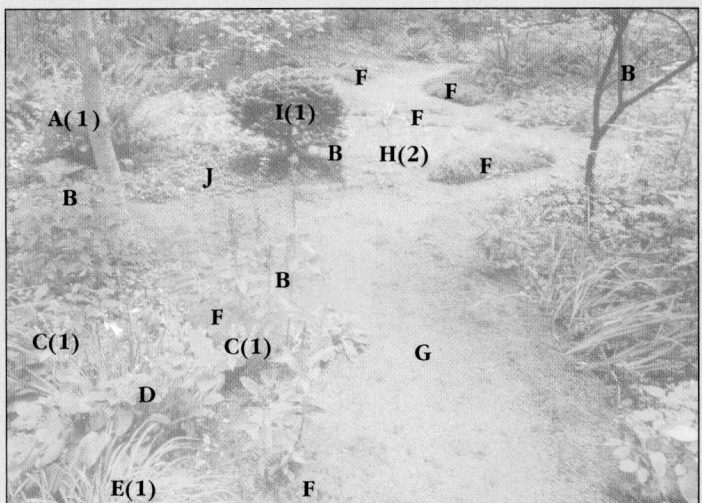

pages 30-31

A. *Polystichum acrostichoides* (1)
B. *Lobelia cardinalis* (many)
C. *Scutellaria integrifolia* (2)
D. *Hosta sp.* (many)

E. *Iris gracilipes* (1)
F. *Polytrichum communa* (many)
G. *Thuidium delicatulum* (many)

H. *Gentiana scabra* (2)
I. *Chamaecyparis obtusa 'Nana'* (1)
J. *Phlox stolonifera* (many)

page 32

A. *Rosa rugosa* (2)
B. *Papaver orientale* (1)
C. *Hemerocallis fulva 'Europa'* (7)

D. *Hibiscus moscheutos* (1)
E. *Phragmites communis* (6)

NOTE: The key lists each plant type and the total quantity needed to replicate the garden shown.
The diagram's letters and numbers refer to the type of plant and the number sited in an area.

pages 32-33

A. *Gazania 'Daybreak Mix'* (3)
B. *Juniperus chinensis 'Nana'* (5)
C. *Pinus mugo* (1)
D. *Rudbeckia fulgida 'Goldsturm'* (8)

E. *Ilex glabra 'Compacta'* (2)
F. *Hibiscus 'Lord Baltimore'* (1)
G. *Miscanthus sinensis 'Gracillimus'* (3)

H. *Amelanchier x 'Cumulus'* (1)
I. *Hydrangea 'Blue Lacecap'* (3)
J. *Rosa 'Betty Prior'* (4)
K. *Alyssum 'Carpet of Snow'* (7)

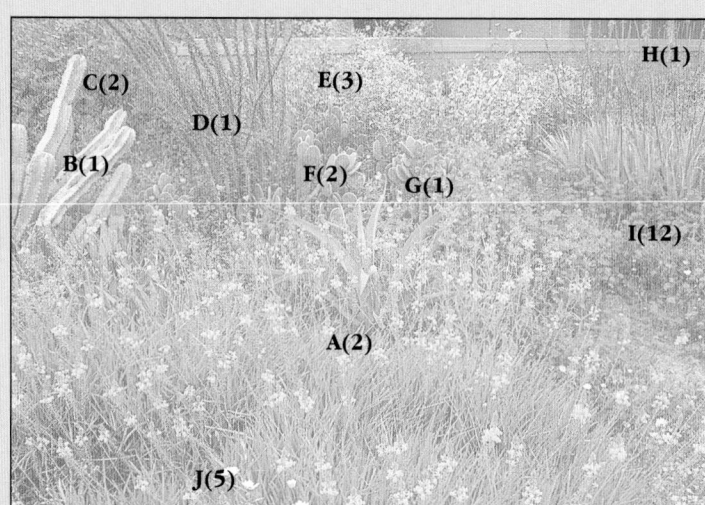

pages 34-35

A. *Bulbine caulescens* (2)
B. *Cereus hildmannianus* (1)
C. *Simmondsia chinensis* (2)
D. *Fouquieria splendens* (1)
E. *Encelia farinosa* (3)

F. *Opuntia microdasys* (2)
G. *Penstemon parryi* (1)
H. *Aloe barbadensis* (1)
I. *Verbena tenuisecta* (12)
J. *Dimorphotheca sinuata* (5)

pages 36-37

A. *Liriope 'Silver Dragon'* (36)
B. *Picea pungens 'Hoopsii'* (1)
C. *Rhododendron 'Koromu Shikibu'* (5)

D. *Ilex x attenuata 'Foster #2'* (2)
E. *Ilex 'San Jose'* (1)
F. *Zelkova serrata* (1)

G. *Ligularia dentata* (3)
H. *Impatiens wallerana* (6)
I. *Hosta undulata 'Albo-marginata'* (6)

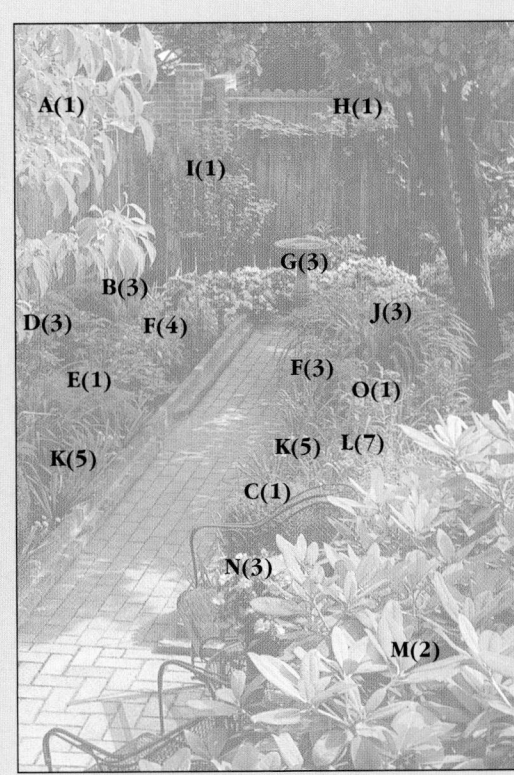

page 37

A. *Cornus florida* (1)
B. *Astilbe simplicifolia 'Bronze Elegans'* (3)
C. *Buxus sempervirens* (1)
D. *Paeonia lactiflora 'Sarah Bernhardt'* (3)
E. *Coreopsis verticillata 'Moonbeam'* (1)
F. *Salvia farinacea 'Victoria'* (7)
G. *Rhododendron 'Pink Gumpo'* (3)
H. *Rosa 'Blaze'* (1)
I. *Hibiscus syriacus* (1)
J. *Hemerocallis 'Hyperion'* (3)
K. *Tagetes erecta 'Primrose Lady'* (10)
L. *Lilium regale* (7)
M. *Rhododendron 'Spring Dawn'* (2)
N. *Impatiens 'New Guinea hybrid'* (3)
O. *Gaillardia sp.* (1)

NOTE: *The key lists each plant type and the total quantity needed to replicate the garden shown. The diagram's letters and numbers refer to the type of plant and the number sited in an area.*

pages 38-39

A. *Lychnis coronaria 'Alba'* (12)
B. *Campanula latiloba*
(C. persicifolia) 'Alba' (3)
C. *Salvia greggii 'Alba'* (1)

D. *Viola 'Crystal Bowl'* (18)
E. *Asteromoea mongolica* (18)
F. *Stachys byzantina* (24)
G. *Senecio 'New Look'* (2)

H. *Cerastium tomentosum* (4)
I. *Veronica spicata 'Icicle'* (3)
J. *Phlox maculata*
'Miss Lingard' (6)

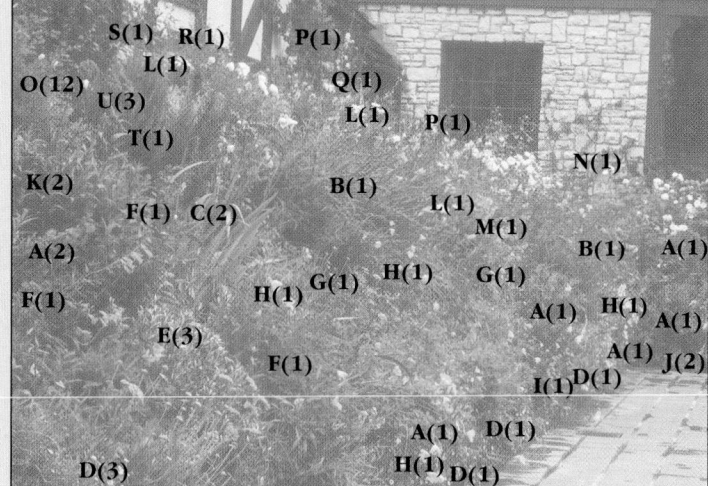

pages 40-41

A. *Penstemon gloxinioides*
'Firebird' (7)
B. *Salvia leucantha* (2)
C. *Iris 'Babbling Brook'* (2)
D. *Erigeron karvinskianus* (6)
E. *Convolvulus cneorum* (3)
F. *Verbena peruviana* (3)
G. *Dianthus caryophyllus* (2)
H. *Oenothera berlandieri* (4)

I. *Lobelia erinus* (1)
J. *Stachys byzantina* (2)
K. *Penstemon gloxinioides*
'Midnight' (2)
L. *Chrysanthemum maximum* (3)
M. *Penstemon gloxinioides*
'Apple Blossom' (1)
N. *Rosa sp.*
'Cl. First Class Prize'(1)

O. *Aquilegia x hybrida*
('McKana Hybrids') (12)
P. *Rosa sp. 'The Reeve'* (2)
Q. *Rosa sp. 'Fair Bianca'* (1)
R. *Rosa sp. 'Mary Austin'* (1)
S. *Rosa sp. 'Graham Thomas'* (1)
T. *Rosmarinus officinalis* (1)
U. *Limonium perezii* (3)

A. *Helianthus annuus 'Autumn Beauty'* (5)
B. *Canna x generalis 'Red King Humbert'* (4)
C. *Dahlia hybrid* (5)
D. *Geranium x riversleaianum 'Mavis Simpson'* (1)
E. *Sedum x 'Autumn Joy'* (4)

pages 42-43

A. *Pyrus cv.* (1)
B. *Cleome spinosa 'Helen Campbell'* (12)
C. *Dahlia cv.* (5)
D. *Salvia uliginosa* (4)
E. *Dahlia 'Snow Country'* (3)

F. *Dahlia 'David Howard'* (4)
G. *Daphne x burkwoodii 'Carol Mackie'* (2)
H. *Senecio vira-vira* (6)
I. *Bidens ferulifolia 'Golden Goddess'* (10)

J. *Dahlia 'Gerry Hoek'* (9)
K. *Verbena bonariensis* (4)
L. *Agastache mexicana 'Toronjil Mirado'* (2)
M. *Dolichos lablab* (3)
N. *Canna x generalis 'Striata'* (3)

NOTE: The key lists each plant type and the total quantity needed to replicate the garden shown. The diagram's letters and numbers refer to the type of plant and the number sited in an area.

pages 44-45

A. *Helianthus decapetalus* (1)
B. *Artemisia*
'Huntington Garden' (2)
C. *Agapanthus*
'Bressingham Blue' (10)

D. *Hemerocallis cv.* (3)
E. *Achillea ageratum*
'W. B. Child' (3)
F. *Phygelius capensis* (1)

G. *Rudbeckia fulgida*
'Goldsturm' (6)
H. *Hemerocallis 'Corky'* (4)

page 45

A. *Lilium 'Roma'* (3)
B. *Lilium 'Milano'* (9)
C. *Veronica austriaca*
'Crater Lake Blue' (2)

D. *Tagetes erecta 'Inca Gold'* (9)
E. *Achillea*
'Coronation Gold' (3)

F. *Antirrhinum majus*
Wedding Bells Series (6)
G. *Cosmos bipinnatus*
'Seashells' (4)

pages 46-47

A. *Pontederia cordata* (1)
B. *Canna sp.* (3)
C. *Iris Louisiana Hybrids* (6)
D. *Salvia farinacea* (12)

E. *Rosa palustris* (1)
F. *Lonicera sempervirens* (1)
G. *Myriophyllum aquaticum* (1)

NOTE: The key lists each plant type and the total quantity needed to replicate the garden shown. The diagram's letters and numbers refer to the type of plant and the number sited in an area.

pages 48-49

A. 'Green Ripple' English ivy
B. Hen-and-chickens
(*Sempervivum* sp.)
C. 'Red Salad Bowl' lettuce
D. 'Albus' white creeping thyme
E. Joseph's-coat
(*Alternanthera ficoidea*)

F. 'Elegans' Siebold plantain lily
G. 'Green Joe' lettuce
H. Rosemary
I. 'Crimson Pygmy' barberry
J. Japanese painted fern
K. 'Telecurl' English ivy
L. Sweet bay tree (*Laurus nobilis*)

M. 'Argenteus' common thyme
N. 'Pagoda' parsley
O. Boxwood
P. English ivy

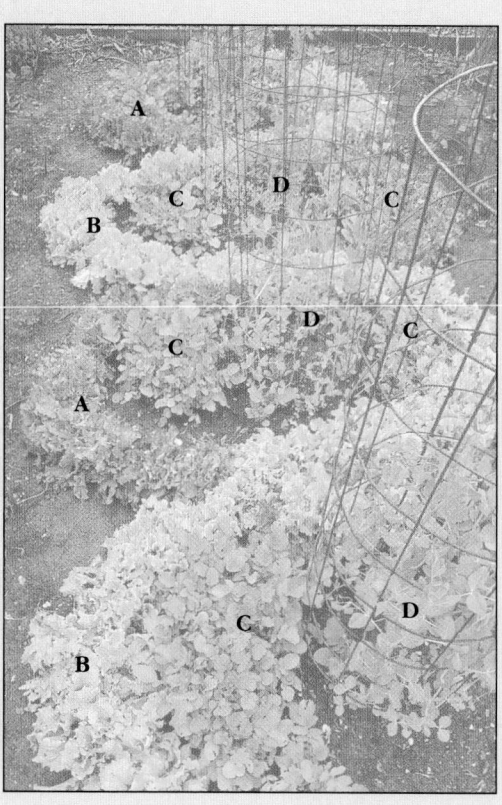

page 50

A. 'Ruby Red' lettuce
B. 'Black-Seeded Simpson' lettuce
C. 'Cherry Belle' radish
D. 'Sugar Snap' peas

pages 50-51

A. 'Lavender Lace'
Chinese wisteria
B. 'Joseph's Coat' climber rose
C. Nasturtium
D. 'Hidcote' English lavender
E. Italian flatleaf parsley
F. Sweet basil

G. Purple basil
(Ocimum basilicum cv.)
H. Common sage
I. 'Silver Carpet' lamb's ears
J. Common thyme
K. 'Truly Yours' geranium
L. Purple sage

M. 'Early Girl', 'Big Boy', and
cherry tomatoes
N. Wild marjoram
O. Green bell pepper
P. Cucumber
Q. Rhubarb
R. 'Scarlet Runner' beans

pages 52-53

A. Wisteria
B. Thin-leaf sunflower
(Helianthus decapetalus)
C. 'Autumn Sun' rudbeckia
D. 'Mt. Fuji' phlox
E. 'Blue Lake' green beans
F. 'Roc d'Or' yellow beans
G. 'Clarimore' zucchini
H. 'Ariane', 'Nory Charm',
and 'Purple Bell' peppers

I. 'Premium Crop' broccoli
J. 'Whirlybird Hybrids' nasturtium
K. 'Tres Fin Maraichiere' endive
L. Rose
M. 'Cayenne', 'Texas Joe Parker',
'Jalapeño', and 'Sweet Banana'
peppers
N. 'Rosa Bianco' and 'Agora'
eggplants
O. 'Haricots Verts' filet beans

P. Sorrel
Q. Lovage
R. Lemon balm
S. 'Oakleaf' lettuce
T. 'Ruby' Swiss chard
U. 'Paros' Swiss chard
V. Arugula
W. 'Pink Mist'
pincushion flower

page 54

A. Snapdragon
B. Johnny-jump-up
C. 'Rocambole' garlic, French shallots, 'Italian Red Bottle' and 'Walla Walla' onions
D. Pinks
E. Marigold
F. 'Buttercrunch' lettuce

G. 'Jewel Hybrids' nasturtium
H. Petunia
I. 'Rouge d'Hiver' lettuce
J. Arugula
K. Ornamental kale
L. 'Four Seasons' lettuce
M. 'Romanesco' and 'Premium Crop' broccoli

N. 'Yukon Gold' potato
O. 'Scarlet Nantes' carrot
P. 'All-America' parsnips
Q. 'Ruby' Swiss chard
R. 'Finocchio' bulbing fennel
S. 'Bounty Shelling' and 'Old Spice' peas
T. 'Scarlet Ball' turnip

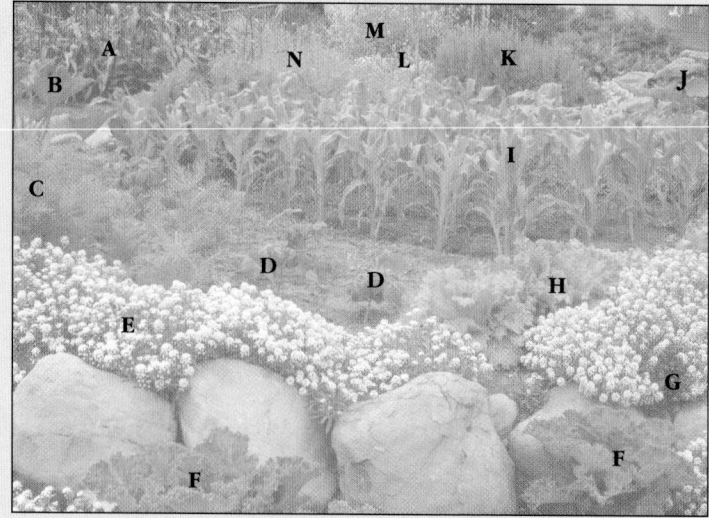

pages 54-55

A. 'Early Sunglow' corn
B. 'Green Comet' broccoli
C. 'Sensation Hybrids' cosmos
D. Filet beans
E. 'Carpet of Snow' sweet alyssum

F. 'Nagoya' ornamental kale
G. 'Crystal Palace' lobelia
H. 'Green Ice' lettuce
I. 'Silver Queen' corn
J. 'Richgreen' zucchini
K. Lavender

L. 'Red Ace' beet
M. Arugula
N. Dittany-of-Crete *(Origanum dictamnus)*

A. 'Tecolote Giants Red' Persian buttercup
B. 'Tecolote Giants Yellow' Persian buttercup
C. Sweet alyssum *(Lobularia maritima)*
D. Paludosum daisy *(Chrysanthemum paludosum)*
E. 'Blue Princess' horned violet
F. 'Universal Antique Mix' pansy
G. Marguerite *(Chrysanthemum frutescens)*
H. 'Touchon' carrot
I. 'Green Sprouting' broccoli
J. 'Sugar Snap' peas
K. 'Slo Bolt' cilantro
L. 'Joy Choi' pak-choi
M. 'Black-Seeded Simpson' lettuce
N. Wallflower *(Erysimum 'Bowles' Mauve')*
O. 'Chioggia' beets
P. 'Burpee's Golden' beets
Q. 'Purple Sprouting' broccoli
R. Euryops daisy *(Euryops pectinatus 'Viridis')*
S. 'Beverly Sills' bearded iris
T. Curly parsley

NOTE: The key accompanying each garden diagram identifies the plants by letter.

CHAPTER ONE

Designing Your Garden

There is much more to designing a flower garden than selecting your favorite plants and putting them in the ground. Before you touch your trowel, you must ask yourself how you intend to use the garden and how you would like it to look. Most important, you must get to know the property itself.

The Berkeley, California, garden at left strikes a fine balance between style and practicality, demonstrating how plants and landscape elements can work together to create a cohesive design. The lush plantings of pink-flowered fleabane, spiky lavender, and the common garden pole bean lead the eye upward to take in the wood trellis and the garden gate. The trellis serves as both a boundary and a backdrop for the plants, while the gate's window breaks the horizontal line and offers a glimpse of what lies beyond. In the foreground, a sundial reinforces the geometric design of the garden's structural elements.

On the following pages you'll learn how to create your own design—one that makes the most of your property and fulfills your fondest dreams for a garden of beautiful blooms.

Planning for Outdoor Living

Your garden should make as important a contribution to your home life as your house, and its design deserves the same careful attention given your interior decor. Like your house, the garden can be a source of pleasure and relaxation. It can express your interests and tastes. And by projecting beauty and interest to the passing public, it can be an asset to your community.

To design such a space successfully, follow the steps that landscape architects do. First, ask yourself some questions to determine your wants and expectations for a garden. Next, take a discerning look at your property. Then, assess the potential for improvement—what can be upgraded, what should be replaced, what is fine just as it is. Finally, decide on a style *(pages 92-95)*. At that point you are ready to plan—first the hardscape (terraces, walkways, and the like), then the plant choices and the planting arrangement.

Executing a good garden design takes time. A garden will evolve as it matures, changing character as plants grow taller and broader. While this is going on, your needs and interests may change as well. At some point you may have to hire a profes-sional for difficult jobs such as earth grading or tree removal. You might also need to implement your design in stages so you don't break your budget. Fortunately, the design process does not have to be rushed. You can give yourself plenty of time to make the right choices. Begin by asking a basic question:

What Is a Garden?

A garden is fundamentally a humanized outdoor space, an idealized form of the natural landscape. The term *garden* can mean a discrete planting, such as a perennial border or a vegetable patch. At other times it can refer to an entire property as the object of a comprehensive garden design.

A garden can occupy various locations in relation to the house. It can be located on a remote part of the property, as might be typical of a vegetable or cutting garden. Or it can be adjacent to the house—a kind of outdoor room. And, of course, it can encompass all the grounds, including the house itself.

In summer (far left), a climbing rose scrambles up an arched trellis gateway in this Connecticut garden, drawing the eye also to the tall stand of globe thistles and deep orange Asiatic lilies surrounded by a sweep of English lavender. The fine foliage of Artemisia and Dianthus adds texture and cooling shades of green to the scene. In winter (left), the underlying plant framework of the garden emerges, including the hedge of evergreen eastern hemlocks that marks the border.

In practice, most properties are made up of more than one garden, each in its own space, according to its use. The individual gardens are then linked into a whole by a unifying network of pathways and sightlines.

Rewards of a Good Design

By linking all parts of your property with the house, a well-designed garden will increase your living space. Various areas will become cherished parts of daily life as places to entertain, play, or relax in comfort and safety. The sense of security afforded you by your house will extend to the surrounding property.

The character of your neighborhood can be a starting point for design decisions. You may want to block a sightline to a neighbor's property or frame a distant view. The style of your house and the history of your area are other possible cues. To complement a 19th-century southern farmhouse, for example, a dooryard flower garden surrounded by a white picket fence, with a stone path leading from fence to door, might be just right. Or you may be influenced by the local ecology, choosing plants to either attract or repel wildlife.

But your garden could also be designed to satisfy less tangible impulses—to create a mood, conjure up memories, or express certain ideals. You might be inspired by the soft feel of pine needles underfoot or the fluttering of swarms of

butterflies on a butterfly bush. Such ideas can be the beginning of a highly satisfying garden plan.

Deciding What You Want

Your first step is to assemble a wish list of attributes for your garden. For most people, the top priority is year-round interest. It is a good idea to study your site first in winter to get the clearest idea of its structural framework—the hardscape, made up of imposed features such as walks and fences; and the softscape, composed of trees, shrubs, and ornamental grasses. Another important criterion for most gardeners is conservation—of energy, money, and natural resources. This means devising a plan that minimizes mowing, watering, fertilizing, weeding, and pruning, and choosing plants that have proved themselves.

Although the design of your house will directly affect the design of your garden, you should also consider the garden's effect on the house. Shade trees, for example, can reduce the cost of cooling your house. On the other hand, some plants can be destructive and should be grown away from the house. A wisteria vine, for example, can pull down your gutters. And tree limbs overhanging your roof can come crashing down in a storm.

Consult the other members of the family who will be using the garden. What kind of play area will the children want? Do you want a cook's garden with fruits, vegetables, and herbs? Also consider the kinds of pets you have and what their impact may be on a garden.

If you have particular horticultural goals, look for suitable places to realize them—a stony slope for a rock garden, a soggy area for a bog garden, a south- or east-facing wall for an attached greenhouse. The site itself will suggest intriguing possibilities to add to your wish list.

Assessing Your Property

The next step is to make an informal survey of your property. Eventually, you will need to make detailed sketches and keep a record of your observations *(page 85),* but at this stage you should only be taking an overall look at the site.

Start beyond its boundaries. From here you will see the public face of your property. Walk or drive past and try to look at the site with the eyes of someone encountering it for the first time. Is the house open to view or shrouded by trees? Is the entryway welcoming or obscured by shrubs? What kind of impression does the garden make, and is it

harmonious with the architecture of the house?

Ask your neighbors for permission to walk your boundary line from their side, and look at your house from their point of view. From here you'll see what privacy screening you may want or need. Then go inside your house and look out each window and door. From this vantage point, you'll see opportunities to feature certain sightlines. Inspecting the grounds from upstairs windows is particularly revealing of patterns that are not otherwise apparent. Areas visible from important viewpoints such as a picture window in the living room or the window over the kitchen sink are obvious spots for a garden.

The view from a door might reveal a destination—an inviting, sun-dappled bench, for example—and the passage toward it should begin with a comfortable transition space to the outdoors, such as a wide landing with a pathway leading to a patio or to another part of the garden. You might decide that it is worth enlarging a window or replacing a small door with wider French doors to give the house better views to the garden.

Developing Focal Points

As you explore the views on your property, you will discover eye-catching spots you may wish to feature. These will be the focal points on which to base your garden design.

Focal points occur wherever sightlines intersect. They usually lie within the property but sometimes occur beyond it. In the front of the house, for instance, the focal point is the entranceway, where the strong vertical lines of the front door meet the horizontal of the threshold. In a landscape, a focal point will exist where the curve of a path disappears around a row of shrubs or the corner of a house. It could also be an imposing feature beyond your boundaries—a graceful tree or a pond, perhaps.

The sightline leading to a focal point is known as an axis, and your garden may have more than one. An axis creates movement in the garden, inviting the eye to follow it to the focal point. Together, axes unify the design by linking the viewer to all its parts. These links can be strengthened in several ways. First, a focal point itself will become more prominent if an object or a plant is placed there, or if it is framed or enclosed. Also, an axis will be accentuated if a pathway is built along it and the line enhanced with plantings. For instance, the focal point of a view from a patio might be a small flower bed. Adding a flagstone walk from the patio to the bed and framing the view

The metal wall sculpture at the rear of this elegant circular terrace garden in New Orleans provides a dramatic focal point that beckons a visitor. Twin pillars topped with geraniums, as well as the potted palms at the entrance, frame the view and strengthen the axis.

with a pair of vertical shrubs or an arched trellis will create a unified arrangement.

Moving through the Garden

Just as you surveyed your property from the vantage points of the street and the house, you should also stroll through the garden itself to find existing or potential focal points. These will become stopping places, and the sightlines leading to them will become pathways.

You can best create this delightful effect by establishing a series of spaces, or rooms, that are either open or closed, beginning with the enclosed space of the house, moving away from the house, and then back again. For example, a network of axes might start from the living room, conveying the visitor through sliding glass doors to the deck, then across a lawn to an intimate shade garden with a hammock under a tree, then over to a sunny, open vegetable garden, and finally back to an herb garden beside the kitchen door.

A garden subdivided into such separate rooms, each with its own character, is both inherently interesting and functional. As in a house, each space has its own purpose: A sunny corner near a hedge might be a retreat; the open lawn, a playing field; the patio, a place for dining alfresco.

How you or your visitors move through the garden—the route you take and what you see along the way—will affect your experience of it. You can determine whether someone strides along quickly or lingers to admire the view. For instance, a walk along a narrow, winding path bordered with interesting flowers is likely to be slower than one along a straight, wide path crossing a lawn. Gates at transition points and steps built into a sloping path also affect the pace of your walk, forcing you to slow down and take in the scene.

Finally, it is the stopping places—a deck, patio, walled courtyard, clearing, or shady bench overlooking a view—that lend a garden a feeling of shelter and restfulness. Be sure to have several such stops on your garden journey, and keep them separate and distinct so that they are a pleasure to rediscover each time you arrive.

Although the meandering gravel path in this Los Angeles garden is its "official" walkway, steppingstones interplanted with sweet alyssum allow for the human tendency to create shortcuts. The low, drystone wall provides an appealing spot for garden strollers to sit and rest, while a decorative birdbath and garden urn create interesting focal points along the way.

Highlighting a Property's Strengths and Weaknesses

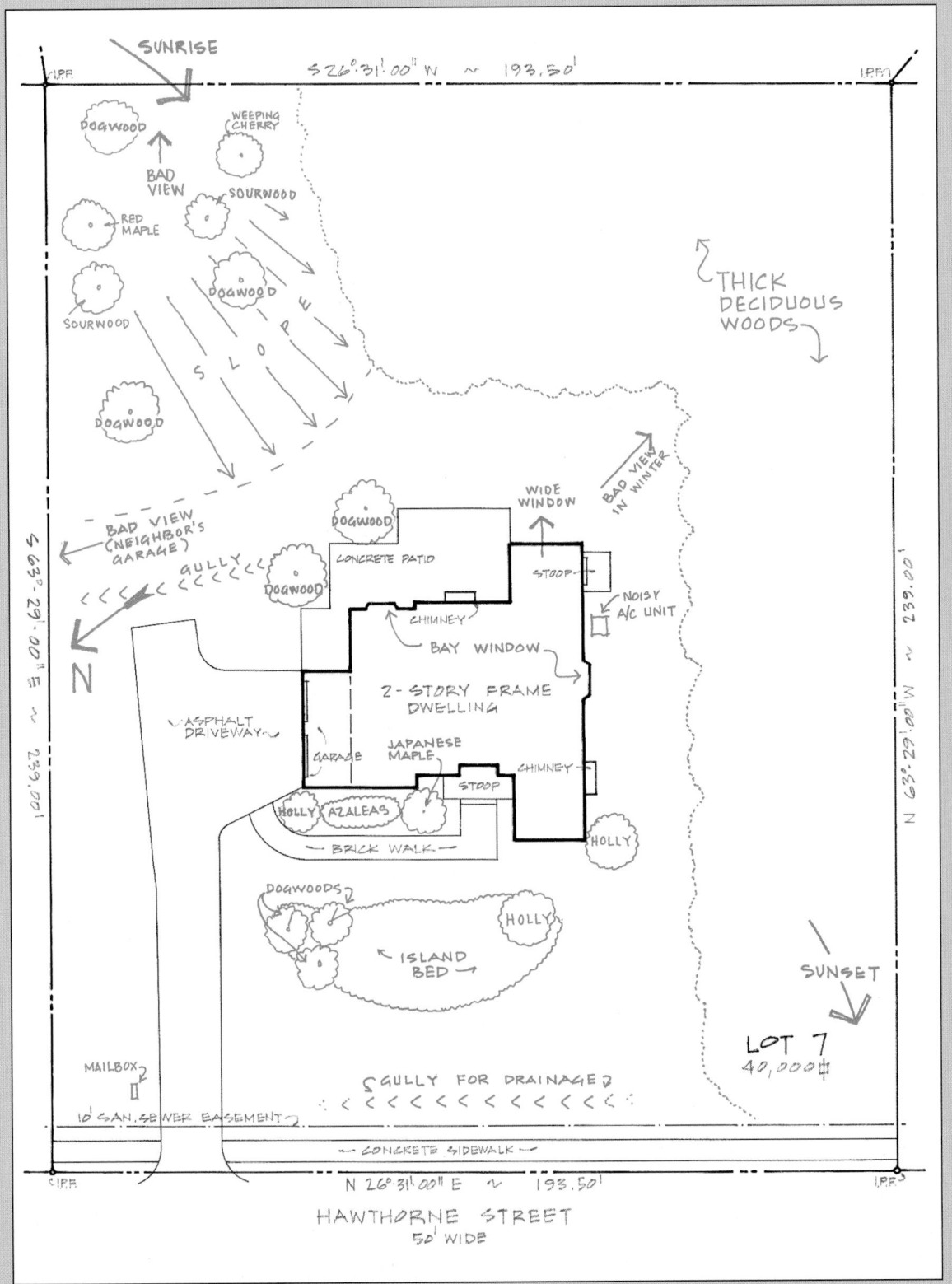

On a property-survey plat serving as a base map, the homeowner has used red ink to indicate existing plantings and record notes on topography, views to emphasize or screen, and possible drainage problems. The assessment reveals minimum landscaping but plenty of potential for an outstanding garden on this nearly one-acre property. Two obvious problems demand attention: The overgrown woods to the south and west take up considerable space and loom over the house to such an extent that it is not even necessary to mark on the map the oppressive shade they cast. Another target for major redesign is the steep slope in the eastern corner, planted with randomly scattered trees.

The Principles of Design

The cottage-like feel of this house in southern California, painted Colonial blue with white shutters, is matched by the plain picket fence and backyard border of 'Heritage' climbing roses, pinks, pansies, and Mexican bush sage. A path of irregular paving stones and a venerable shade tree complete the picture.

Historically, gardeners have relied on certain widely accepted conventions of design to organize the landscape around them. These visual guidelines evoke a feeling of order and harmony in what might otherwise seem an ungovernable wilderness. Properly applied, design principles unify the landscape while maintaining interest by juxtaposing contrasting elements. Thus your garden plan might include a cool oasis at the wooded edge of your property balanced by a sunny kitchen garden closer to your house. Or within a single perennial bed you may choose a unifying color contrasted with a variety of plant textures and forms.

Unity

The first governing principle of garden design is unity—the perception that all the elements of the garden have coalesced into a coherent composition. These elements include the materials and plants used to build a garden and their positions relative to each other.

You can achieve unity in several ways. First, the house and the garden should complement each other in style. For example, a Federal house typically would be surrounded by a formal garden *(pages 92-93)*. Further, the materials of the house and the garden should be similar. If a house is built of brick, unity is furthered when the garden walls are also brick. By the same token, a rustic wooden house is enhanced by a wooden fence.

The materials you use should also be compatible with the land itself. In a seaside garden on a granite shore, for example, you might use a similar rough stone for the retaining walls. You might even incorporate some large stones into the design of a flower border.

Another approach to establishing unity is to repeat an existing line, form, texture, or color in

your design. You could mirror the curve of a dramatically arched doorway in the contour of a flower bed or the rounded edge of a patio. Repeating a foliage or flower color is a familiar device to tie together the design of a border. Such visual rhythms, as with musical rhythms, carry you from one point to another in a composition.

And, of course, you strengthen the unity of your design by providing strong focal points to orient the parts of your garden to one another.

Simplicity

As a rule of thumb, you should strive to keep your design as simple and straightforward as possible. Too much ornamentation, too many focal points, too great a variety of plants and other materials can create an impression of disorder and confusion. Even if you're designing a garden that is meant to perform many different functions, try to keep it simple. A successful design will provide a unifying structure for all the elements in your landscape, from open areas for entertaining and

playing to shady glades and backyard herb gardens. You can separate each garden area with screening plants and provide clear pathways or transitional areas that allow you to move easily from one part of the landscape to another.

Proportion and Scale

Proportion is the size relationship among parts of a whole—the dimensions of a single tree, for example, seen against an entire grove. Scale is the measurement of one object or space in relation to another. In a garden, we relate the size of objects and spaces primarily to the size of our bodies. By that measure, alpine plants in a rock garden are tiny and a redwood tree is huge.

Designers understand that the principles of proportion contribute to the mood of a garden. For example, a garden will feel cramped and constrained if enclosed within disproportionately high vertical elements such as buildings, walls, or fences. A planting of small trees and shrubs in a city garden surrounded by apartment buildings

The contrast between the bright openness of the lawn and the darkness of the shady patch under the river birch adds weight and dimension to the streamside plantings in this Charlottesville, Virginia, garden. Cheerful splashes of yellow 'Hyperion' daylilies glow next to the dark Hosta sieboldiana 'Elegans'. The stream itself cuts through the greensward like a shiny black ribbon.

87

would help counteract the looming effect of the tall buildings. On the other hand, if your garden reaches out in a vast expanse from your house, a space enclosed within vertical human-scale elements—a trellis, wall, or hedge—would provide a welcome sense of intimacy and security.

Human scale is not the only measuring stick in matters of proportion. For example, the flowers in a border are usually arranged by height, with the tallest in the back and the shortest in the front. Likewise, your house is an important determinant of scale; nearby trees and structural elements should be in proportion to the size of your house.

When designing your garden, keep in mind that the size of an object is also relative over distance. This can be a useful tool for manipulating space. The farther an object is from the viewer, the larger it must be to stand out clearly. For a perennial border at the back of your property to make an impact from your deck, for example, it should be at least half as wide as the distance between the deck and your garden.

Study the relative size of every object and plant in your garden to find a balance that pleases you. You will notice that the combinations you like will tend to be harmonious—composed of related forms, textures, and colors.

Harmony and Contrast

A good garden design is based on a balance between harmony and contrast. Closely related colors, comparable textures and forms, and similar qualities of line blend together like the musical tones that make a harmonious chord. If objects or plants are too much alike, however, they may tend to blend together and lose their distinction. It is best to set up contrasting groupings of plants so that they complement each other. Textural contrasts are particularly effective in a predominantly single-color garden. In a shady foliage garden, for example, lacy fern fronds and astilbe offset smooth-leaved hosta and the upright spears of iris.

When planning your garden, keep in mind that too much contrast may seem chaotic and jumbled,

A meandering gully of river stones in this Greenwich, Connecticut, garden mimics a stream as it flows through a lawn and around an embankment of dwarf mountain pine and lily-of-the-valley bush. The illusion is furthered by the granite rocks and the spikes of Siberian iris, recalling water-loving yellow flag. This streambed has a practical function as well; it is also used as a drainage channel.

The Delights of Water

A water feature such as a pool, fountain, or stream adds a cooling touch to the landscape and can be a decorative focal point as well. The soothing trickle of water masks unwanted background noises and evokes a touch of the countryside even in the heart of the city.

If you don't have a natural water feature on your property, it is relatively easy to build one *(pages 125-127)*. You can simulate a stream or waterfall by using a simple recirculating pump to draw water from a pool to a higher point where it will run down in a rivulet. The pool below, in Missouri, is built to look like a stream flowing through rocky outcrops at a meadow's edge. Dotting the rocks are colorful native plants such as yellow Ozark sundrops and rosy poppy mallow. Pink prairie phlox and lance coreopsis, behind the phlox, also do well in the fast-draining, rocky soil.

This pool's irregular shape, rough materials, and native plants harmonize with the naturalistic design of this garden. In a more formal garden, a rectilinear, round, or oblong pool accented by a simple arrangement of water lilies or a central fountain can act like a glistening mirror. If you lack the space for such a pool, try a wall fountain that trickles a stream of water into a basin.

while too little contrast can seem monotonous. Begin by juxtaposing open and enclosed areas. Think of your garden as space, and the structures and blocks of plantings as solid elements within that space. Balance the proportion of empty and solid spaces and carefully plan how they will flow together and connect.

Similarly, the alternations of light and shade in the garden create an interesting contrast. They can be used to subdivide the space into discrete areas, each with its own purpose, such as a shady deck for reading and relaxing, a sunny area for a swimming pool, or a dappled woodland for strolling. At night, skillfully arranged artificial lighting can carve out still other spaces in the garden.

Harmony and contrast also figure in the selection and arrangement of plants. Most important for the purposes of design is a plant's form, or habit. Most plants are round, prostrate (or carpeting), vase shaped, arching, conical, or columnar. Plants of different forms can be combined to create a coherent and interesting design. In a dry garden, for example, a mound of mountain marigold and a silvery, horizontal mat of snow-in-summer may be used to offset the upright forms of agave and cactus.

But don't omit the other senses from your planning. The contrast between the feel of grass and that of moss along a woodland path, the sudden fragrance of a rosebush in bloom, and the gentle sound of a gurgling fountain help enrich the garden experience.

Natural Patterns

With gardens that are ornamental versions of the natural landscape, it is logical to look to nature for basic shapes when designing them. One of these shapes is the meandering stream. This is a sweeping curve that repeats itself and often includes clusters of vegetation on the outward side of each arc or on an island within the stream. In a garden, such a shape could be used for pathways, beds, and even a deck or patio, mimicking the place in nature where a blockage in a stream has widened it into a pool.

There are rarely any hard edges or boundaries in the natural world. Areas of contrasting texture are more likely to merge into each other. You might think of this principle when you blend the edge of a patio into a lawn, perhaps by using sections of flagstone matching those of the patio to begin a pathway

In this San Francisco terrace garden attached to a one-story house, a eucalyptus tree provides midsummer shade. The white 'Alister Stella Gray' rose will reach only to the roof, and the musk rose 'Ballerina', between the chairs, grows just high enough to waft its fragrance to anyone seated there.

Several visual tricks in this Massachusetts garden—bright colors and large foliage up front, a mirroring symmetry to strengthen the archway focal point, and a tapering lawn—suggest a large plot leading into the woods. In fact, it ends just behind the row of hemlocks.

onto the lawn. Or, as a transition to a woodland, you could plant a small grove of trees just at the edge of the woods.

In nature, plants and rocks tend to cluster. Do the same with your arrangements, whether you have a group of trees at a focal point, perennials in a bed, rocks in a rock garden, or bulbs naturalized in a lawn. The clusters will eventually merge into drifts and come into contact with one another.

Finally, plants in nature grow at different levels. This establishes a layered pattern that you can mimic in your garden. Tall trees will create a top layer or canopy. Under this canopy, you can plant smaller shade-tolerant trees and shrubs typical of a shady understory. At the lowest level will be flowers and ground covers. Such a design is inherently unified and harmonious.

To create the illusion that a small garden is larger than it really is, designers use a variety of optical tricks. If you have a small or awkwardly shaped lot, one or more of these design tips might work for you.

• Place large objects in the foreground and small ones at a distance. For example, front your patio with large planters and place smaller pots at a focal point at the back. Decrease the size of paving blocks as they recede to the rear.

• Group plants by size and texture. Position those with large leaves in the foreground and those with finer foliage toward the back.

• Simulate the perception that parallel lines converge toward a focal point by slightly tapering a pathway, lawn, or pool so that it narrows at the far end.

• Use a hedge, trellis, or bed to partially block the view to a focal point.

• Subdivide your garden and make strong transitions from one space to another.

• For an illusion of greater depth, plant bold, hot-colored flowers in the foreground and cooler pastels toward the rear of the garden.

Garden Styles

A garden may have a certain character or style, just as houses do. Styles have historical associations, but they are also influenced by regional cultures and growing conditions. Your first consideration should be to keep the style of your garden in harmony with that of your house. Next, take into account climate, soil, and the lay of the land. In fact, many popular garden styles have developed over the years specifically to address regional environmental conditions.

But the style you choose should not be the result of practical considerations alone. It should reflect your taste, your sense of beauty, and your desires. Thus you might decide to have one style of garden in the front yard—a formal one, perhaps—and a totally different look for the side or back yard, where you entertain or where your children play. The garden types described here are only a sample of the range of possibilities.

Formal and Informal Gardens

A house with a strong classical design calls for the strong axes and crisply defined focal points of a formal garden. Building materials such as brick or stone block look appropriate in a formal setting. Formal gardens are boldly geometric in structure. Straight lines, simple curves, precise angles, and sharp edges all contribute to a formal feeling. Symmetrical pairings mirroring each other and framing a central feature (such as two roses pruned into standards flanking a garden sculpture); carpet planting of a single type of plant; and ornate pruning are all elements of a formal design.

Despite this rigidity, formal gardens come in great variety and include rose and herb gardens, flower beds arranged like mosaics, water gardens that reflect the sky in yet another kind of symmetry, and walled vegetable gardens called potagers. Their strong ground plans are easy to read, and they retain a presence even in winter's landscape.

If you like the formal look but only up to a point, you can soften the formal geometry with a cascade of wisteria or a climbing rose on a wall or with a naturalistic planting of herbaceous perennials that billows over a border's straight edge. This softening of the formal style became the basis for the traditional English cottage garden, typically a charming, informal mix of annual and perennial blossoms set within a well-defined garden space.

During Colonial times, American houses had cottage or dooryard gardens that were similar to their English cottage counterparts, with a profusion of flowering plants blooming in beguiling disarray on either side of the front door and along the front of the house. Today, a more structured version of the dooryard garden has become the most popular American landscape style—an informal garden with a somewhat loose, natural appearance featuring irregular or compound curves. But this is not laissez-faire gardening. The style calls for crisply defined beds forming a strong ground pattern. Planting arrangements, though not usually symmetrical, are carefully balanced. Brick, stone, and concrete effects borrowed from the house are built into paths and walls.

The axes and focal points in an informal garden are subtler and the patterns less regular than in a formal arrangement. They may exist naturally on your land, needing only a little emphasis from you to bring them out. Or a focal point might be implied by making a clearing in a line of trees, and the axis leading to it may be no more than an irregularly spaced line of shrubs.

In addition, the method for framing a focal point by bracketing it will be more naturalistic than in a formal garden. For example, rather than balancing two identical clipped shrubs on either side of a focal point, you might achieve an informal balance with a small conifer and a clump of soft foliage to one side and a large rock on the other. The two masses may be equivalent in visual weight, but their textures and forms are quite different.

Japanese-Inspired Gardens

The Japanese-style garden blends some of the principles of formal design—strong, clean lines, for example—with the asymmetry of the informal garden. Each element is carefully chosen to achieve an exquisite effect—a rock is placed just so, a tree is sited to weep over a pool and be reflected in the water, the sinuous motion of a stream is captured in the flowing bends of a path.

The plants and building materials in a Japanese garden reflect a fine attention to detail and are generally kept to a small scale. The emphasis is on the texture and form of plant foliage, rock, and wood, with occasional splashes of flower color.

Enclosed by a low hedge of Japanese holly, this Atlanta, Georgia, parterre—four rectangular beds laid out in a carpetlike pattern—lends a formal accent to the stone steps leading up to the back garden. Wall germander outlines the central beds, which are filled with red wax begonias surrounding a pot of trained ivy.

Regional Gardens

Regional garden designs reflect local climate and growing conditions. They incorporate native plants best suited to that environment and include structural elements, such as walls and water features, that temper the effects of the weather.

Desert gardens thrive in extremes of drought and heat. A desert is not hot all year round, but it is dry, with annual rainfall of less than 10 inches. Plants grow low to the ground, and trees are spaced widely to conserve water. A desert garden follows that model, using plants like prickly pear, ocotillo, and spiky yucca. Trees such as carob, acacia, and common olive have deep taproots to reach underground water, and cast cooling shade. High courtyard walls and sun-screening trellises help moderate the heat and glare.

Mediterranean gardens are a variation on the desert garden. Originating in the arid climate of Spain, North Africa, and the eastern Mediterranean, they have transplanted easily to California and the American Southwest. Suited to contemporary, stucco, or Spanish-style houses, these gardens nestle in the shelter of a courtyard or an atrium. The plantings can be lush, featuring exotically colored and scented tropical trees such as citrus, banana, and palm, all surrounding a central fountain. Vines such as jasmine and bougainvillea climb the garden's walls, and ferns, hibiscus, oleander, and bird-of-paradise grow in pots and raised beds.

Landscape Plants for Specific Styles

Formal

TREES
Acer
(maple)
Cedrus
(cedar)
Cupressus sempervirens
(Italian cypress)
Fagus sylvatica
(European beech)
Magnolia
(magnolia)
Picea
(spruce)
Quercus
(oak)

SHRUBS
Berberis thunbergii
(Japanese barberry)
Ilex crenata
(Japanese holly)
Ilex vomitoria
(yaupon)
Prunus laurocerasus
(cherry laurel)
Rosa hybrids
(hybrid roses)
Taxus baccata
(English yew)

VINES
Rosa
(climbing hybrid rose)
Wisteria
(wisteria)

GROUND COVERS
Calluna vulgaris
(heather)
Hosta
(plantain lily)

Informal

TREES
Acer rubrum
(red maple)
Acer saccharum
(sugar maple)

SHRUBS
Euonymus alata
(winged spindle tree)
Lagerstroemia indica
(crape myrtle)
Rhododendron
(rhododendron)
Rosa rugosa
(rugosa rose)
Syringa
(lilac)

Japanese

TREES
Acer palmatum
(Japanese maple)
Malus floribunda
(Japanese flowering
crab apple)
Pinus densiflora
(Japanese red pine)

SHRUBS
Chaenomeles
(flowering quince)
Juniperus
(juniper)
Pieris japonica
(lily-of-the-valley bush)
Pinus mugo
(dwarf mountain pine)

VINES
Wisteria floribunda
(Japanese wisteria)

GROUND COVERS
Liriope muscari
(big blue lilyturf)

*Acer rubrum
(red maple)*

Woodland Gardens

Wherever it might appear, a woodland garden consists of the same two elements: a number of large trees to create an overhead canopy, and a succession of underlayers—smaller trees, shrubs, and ground-level plants like wildflowers, ferns, and mosses. To create a successful design, reduce the natural abundance of a woodland to a few simple elements. Build in a clearing to let in light for the less shade-tolerant plants and to bring about a contrast of light and dark. But make sure a few saplings are interspersed among the older trees to ensure successive generations of shade trees. Then make

a path through the garden to take you from place to place and to keep visitors from trampling delicate plants. If you choose plants that produce berries and flowers to create a habitat for wildlife, after a time you will develop a self-sustaining environment that requires little further effort.

Meadow and Prairie Gardens

While woodland gardens provide a shady oasis, wildflower meadow and prairie gardens are open, sunny, and alive with color and texture. They also are more precarious, requiring periodic mowing to prevent unwanted saplings from taking over and to allow desirable seedlings to become established. These gardens work especially well as transition areas between the more structured part of the garden and the openness of the surrounding countryside. Plant mixtures for meadows and prairies will vary according to soil and rainfall, but all will require full sun. You can purchase seed mixes suited to your area from seed companies. These mixes will include annual and perennial wildflowers, such as daisies, sundrops, butterfly weed, and Texas bluebonnet. The annuals should reseed themselves after the first year. Also included will be native bunch grasses like switch grass, big bluestem, and little bluestem. Bulbs planted in broad swaths also naturalize well in a wild meadow.

A North Carolina garden sets the simplicity of the Japanese style within a Western border and lawn. Plants indigenous to Japan, such as red laceleaf Japanese maple, multicolored Houttuynia cordata, and two varieties of Japanese cedar, harmonize beautifully. The shape of the pyramidal rock, for example, is echoed in the smaller cedar 'Bandai-Sugi'.

Composing with Color

You can ensure maximum year-round interest in your garden by weaving threads of seasonal color throughout its beds and borders. The first step is to sketch out color ideas on paper, so that when you are ready to plant you will be able to create a sense of unity throughout the garden. Your personal preferences will guide you in your initial choice of colors. You may lean toward hues from the warm end of the spectrum, such as red, orange, and yellow, rather than the cool end, which includes the greens, blues, and violets. Perhaps you prefer delicate tints over strong shades, and harmonious blendings over bright contrasts. Before you make any final decisions, however, there are a number of other things you must consider.

Color, Light, and Mood

How colors appear in your garden will depend on two factors: whether a planting is located in sun or shade, and the way light changes from morning to night and through the seasons. Pastels stand out in the soft light of early morning or evening, for example, and fairly glimmer in the shade, but their pale presence is lost in bright midday sun, where strong, bright colors like reds and oranges do best. Colors that glow warmly in autumn light, such as bronze or purple, may look drab on hazy summer days or in the cold glare of winter.

One way to plan for successful seasonal colors is to observe the hues nature reveals over time. Spring is a symphony of pastel-blooming trees, shrubs, and bulbs, followed by deeper tints of blue, yellow, and pink as summer gets under way. Late summer is dominated by highly saturated colors—vibrant yellow, Day-Glo orange, hot red, deep pink, fuchsia, and violet. By contrast, fall is cloaked in muted shades of gold, bronze, rust, plum, and purple.

Certain color groupings will create different moods in the garden. Try planting pink, purple, or blue pastels interspersed with neutral whites and grays for a cooling and soothing effect. A garden theme mixing the neutral colors with various shades of green will create a cool retreat in the heat of summer. To add a little warmth, introduce soft creams and buttery yellows to the mix.

If you want a more vibrant atmosphere, choose strong yellows, golds, oranges, and reds. But use red with care; it is the most dominant color in the spectrum and can be overpowering. A backdrop of dark green foliage can tone down even the brightest reds, but a bright green background will make the reds pop out even more.

Color and Space

Through creative placement of colors, you can define spaces and change perspectives in a garden design. Cool colors lengthen distances; warm colors make them appear closer. Your choice of color groupings, therefore, should be based on the perspective you want to achieve.

Setting the landscape afire with its glowing orange-red fall foliage, a katsura tree (Cercidiphyllum japonicum) stands out from the subtler lime yellow coloring of Hydrangea anomala ssp. petiolaris (climbing hydrangea) and Idesia polycarpa (iigiri tree).

Anchored by a Colorado blue spruce, drifts of Zinnia elegans 'Sun Red', orange Helichrysum bracteatum 'Bright Bikini' (strawflower), pink Phlox maculata 'Alpha' (wild sweet William), and yellow Lilium 'Citronella' put on a dazzling summer show. In the foreground, a broad green drift of Sedum spectabile 'Brilliant' (showy stonecrop) completes the planting.

When planning beds and borders close to the house, consider how you can accentuate or complement the color of the roof, sides, or trim with foliage and flowers. Also, select herbaceous plants with colors that will tie in with those of adjacent small shrubs, ground covers, and larger plantings. This way, you will maintain a unified color theme.

You can also choose flower colors to attract butterflies and hummingbirds, which favor strong pinks, reds, yellows, and oranges. (Hummingbirds prefer tubular flowers; butterflies, flat and cup-shaped flowers.) To reduce the potentially overwhelming visual impact of these bright colors, use white flowers or dark green, gray, and variegated foliage to separate vivid pinks and reds from equally intense yellows and oranges.

Color from Bulbs and Annuals

To color your landscape from late winter into fall, be sure to include masses of small- and large-flowering bulbs in your design. Select different varieties that bloom simultaneously or those whose bloom times coincide with those of other flowering plants. For example, create a pleasing contrast by teaming up spring-blooming yellow tulips with blue forget-me-nots or with deep blue grape hyacinths. Or, for a harmonious combination, plant purple pansies next to pale lavender crocuses.

Many summer- and fall-flowering bulbs, such as lilies, dahlias, and begonias, bloom for several weeks and will brighten your beds and borders with a rich tapestry of hues ranging from deep pink to brick red, from apricot to bronze. For a blooming sequence that lasts from late winter through fall, plant a sunny border with a mixture of bulbs and perennials—daffodils, Siberian irises, flowering onion, peonies, daylilies, dahlias, rudbeckias, perennial phlox, asters, and chrysanthemums.

Because of their long bloom periods, which can span three seasons, annual bedding plants are good additions to planting schemes that focus on color. Choose their colors carefully, though, so that they will continue to complement the perennials and bulbs in the bed. You can also plant annuals to cover bare spots in the early years of a garden and to fill gaps between shrubs and trees.

Color in the Shade

Areas dominated by trees and shrubs are typically shady, and many varieties of annuals, perennials, and bulbs can brighten these shadowy spots.

Begin with late-winter and early-spring bulbs that bloom before deciduous trees leaf out to block the sun. Snowdrops, crocuses, squill, Grecian windflowers, and daffodils are early bloomers that will naturalize into colorful masses.

For the rest of the growing season, fill spaces that receive partial or dappled shade with brightly colored, long-lasting, shade-tolerant perennials such as astilbe, foxglove, spurge, cardinal flower, alumroot, Virginia bluebells, monarda, St.-John's-wort, and red valerian *(Centranthus ruber)*. The most reliable annual for a shady nook is *Impatiens wallerana* (busy Lizzie). If you'd like to draw attention to a planting of dark green shrubs, illuminate them with a grouping of white or pastel flowers, such as impatiens, columbine, lily of the valley, primrose, and bleeding heart.

Foliage Plants

Flowering plants bring a rainbow of colors to a border or bed, but herbaceous foliage plants also have their place. By no means confined to green, the foliage colors of these plants range all over the rest of the spectrum. Used in contrast with the blooms surrounding them, they can turn a merely pleasing border into a visual feast.

The texture of the foliage, which can vary from fine to coarse, also plays a major role. When foliage plants of different texture and shape are planted next to each other, for example, they add a dramatic dimension to the design. Ferns are a good example of plants with fine and feathery foliage. The leaves range in color from dark green to bright green, but one, *Athyrium nipponicum* 'Pictum', is dramatically edged in silver. Other fine, feathery-leaved plants include astilbe, *Artemisia* x 'Powis Castle', goatsbeard, *Perovskia* (Russian sage), yarrow, and *Dicentra eximia* 'Luxuriant'.

A good combination for a shade garden is to plant ferns beside smooth-leaved hostas. Depending on the variety, hosta leaves may be small and narrow or large and flat; tinted with blue, cream, yellow, chartreuse, or dark green; variegated with spots and stripes, or one intense solid color.

Other winning texture combinations include furry silver-gray lamb's ears planted with spiky gray-green or green *Santolina;* the large, glossy, purple leaves of *Heuchera micrantha* 'Palace Purple' with the fragile, feathery leaves of achillea; the thick, vertical, sword-shaped leaves of *Yucca filamentosa* with the small, rounded leaves of *Sempervivum* (houseleek); and the narrow, stiff leaves of ornamental grasses with the low-growing lacy foliage of *Astilbe chinensis* 'Pumila'.

A medley of shade-loving plants, their low-growing, rounded habits broken by spiky leaves and filigrees of flowers, receives morning sun and then dappled shade in this east-facing Oregon garden.

Finalizing Your Plan

When you are ready to commit your final planting plan to paper, you'll need to keep in mind how large each plant you choose will grow and how far and how fast it will spread. It takes about 3 years for most herbaceous perennials to spread into drifts, and 5 years for many shrubs to reach maturity. Depending on the growth rate of trees (slow, moderate, or fast), it can take anywhere from 8 to 20 years for them to reach significant size. You'll need to consider whether the trees you have in mind will eventually branch out so broadly that they'll turn your sunny garden into a shady one.

If you're planting slow-growing trees and shrubs, it's important to select a combination of evergreen and deciduous species that will continue to complement each other at maturity. Careful planning in the beginning will save you from the unpleasant and possibly expensive task of removing major plantings after several years of growth because they are crowding each other or simply no longer look good together.

Spacing shrubs to allow for future growth need not leave your garden looking bare and uninteresting during its first few years. To create fullness, you can interplant with perennials, annuals, and filler bulbs, such as tulips, hyacinths, or lilies. And once the shrubs start spreading, it's a simple matter to relocate the herbaceous plants as needed.

Planning for Seasonal Interest

To create a garden that provides four seasons of interest, you will need a mixture of plants, including some that are visually appealing throughout the year and others that bloom in different months. Before you break ground, your paper plan should indicate which plants produce long-lasting foliage or flowers and which overlap their blooming cycles.

Perhaps the surest way to formulate a successful year-round planting plan is to superimpose on your base map a different tissue overlay for each season. Indicate on each overlay which features—bloom color, leaf texture, distinctive bark, berries, and the like—will be prominent at which locations during that season.

Noting life cycles of flowers, trees, and shrubs will allow you to group plants to advantage. For

In this Connecticut garden, tulips and daffodils share a bed with perennials that will help disguise the bulbs' fading foliage. At the far end, a scarlet Japanese maple contrasts pleasantly with the pastel purple blossoms of a Higan cherry, while a backdrop of rhododendrons provides year-round greenery and the promise of summer flowers.

Tracking the Growth of a New Garden

A new bed, if properly planted, *will show a lot of bare ground. In the bed at right, widely spaced astilbes thrust up white spires beneath a young Korean mountain ash tree. Three red Japanese barberry shrubs and a dwarf hinoki false cypress have space for modest growth, while the pink-flowered sedums, variegated hostas, and tiny ajuga plants require more room.*

By the third year, the astilbes have filled in, *the sedums have spread widely, the hostas have doubled in size, and the ajugas have put out runners in all directions, thickening into a ground cover. The canopy of the Korean mountain ash has expanded 3 to 5 feet, while the barberries and false cypress have yet to reach mature size.*

The bed has attained a pleasing fullness by the fifth year. While the shrubs show steady but compact growth, the mountain ash continues to expand at 2 feet or so a year, toward its maximum size of 40 feet tall with a canopy 25 feet wide. The astilbes, sedums, and hostas require little maintenance or division, which means this bed need not be disturbed for many years to come.

example, when daffodils have finished blooming, you will want their withering leaves out of view. The best way to accomplish this is to grow them in the midst of colorful foliage or tall swaths of annual or perennial flowers, which will come into full growth just as the bulb foliage begins to fade.

Although annuals have a life cycle of just a few months, they create a continuous flow of color from late spring to summer's end. Some, such as impatiens, scarlet sage, pot marigold, zinnia, cleome, cosmos, and zonal geranium, keep on producing blooms until they are killed by a hard frost. Overlapping with these warm-weather favorites are late-summer perennials, which also carry their colorful flowers until nipped by cold temperatures.

You can plan for even more fall color by choosing deciduous shrubs and trees with leaves that take on intensely brilliant hues and by planting perennials such as asters, *Sedum* x 'Autumn Joy' (stonecrop), goldenrod, *Chrysanthemum* x *morifolium* (florist's chrysanthemum), Japanese anemone, *Caryopteris* (bluebeard), *Colchicum autumnale* (autumn crocus), *Colchicum speciosum* 'Album' (showy autumn crocus), *Rosa* Meidiland varieties, and ornamental grasses.

Brightening Winter Months

In the winter, when trees and shrubs have dropped their fiery leaves, you can still enjoy ample color in the various shades of evergreen foliage, tree and shrub bark, berries, dried grasses, and the seed heads of some perennials and shrubs. The bark of certain deciduous trees, such as birch, eastern sycamore, and *Stewartia pseudo-camellia* (Japanese stewartia), and the shiny leaves of holly, bull bay, and ivy will delight your eye after most herbaceous plants have gone dormant for the winter.

By late winter, small-bulb shoots are already pushing their way out of the soil. The delicate snowdrops are among the first to bloom, quickly followed by crocuses and other small bulbs and by the blossoming of shrubs such as witch hazel, forsythia, and *Prunus mume* (Japanese flowering apricot). From then on there is no stopping the show of spring-flowering squill, hyacinths, daffodils, and tulips. And if you have planned carefully, you can enjoy the sequential blooms of rhododendron species, flowering cherries, magnolias, dogwoods, lilacs, viburnums, and a host of other blooms that creep over the ground, wind their tendrils up fences, and blossom overhead.

Putting in the Plants

Begin with the largest trees, which involve the greatest amount of digging and the most extensive trampling on surrounding soil. Because cultivated soil is easily compacted, don't till any soil for planting smaller shrubs and herbaceous plants until you are sure you no longer have any need to walk on it. After the large trees are in, add medium-size shrubs and trees. Follow this stage by planting small decorative specimens, dwarf shrubs, perennials, vines, and ground covers and other filler plants, such as bulbs, annuals, and herbs.

When planting small shrubs, place them in groups of two, three, or even five if space allows. If they are slow growing, shrubs can be sited fairly close together to form a mass that makes a strong impression; you can also plant them farther apart at regular intervals to impart rhythm and continuity to a bed or border. Perennials look better when they are planted close to one another in groups of three or five; but if the plants are young, leave ample room between them. Annuals are more effective when planted in drifts or massed along the edges of a border. It doesn't matter if they crowd one another. Avoid planting flowers singly at random intervals, where their impact would be lost.

In this East Hampton, New York, garden, low-growing bird's-nest spruce, bloodleaf Japanese maple, and variegated hinoki false cypress (far right) furnish year-round interest. The ground-hugging lady's-mantle combined with the large ribbed leaves of hosta, the tall spires of foxtail lily, and the lacy heads of hydrangea contribute more seasonal texture. 'Just Joey' roses, 'Johnson's Blue' geraniums, and other perennials provide weeks of color.

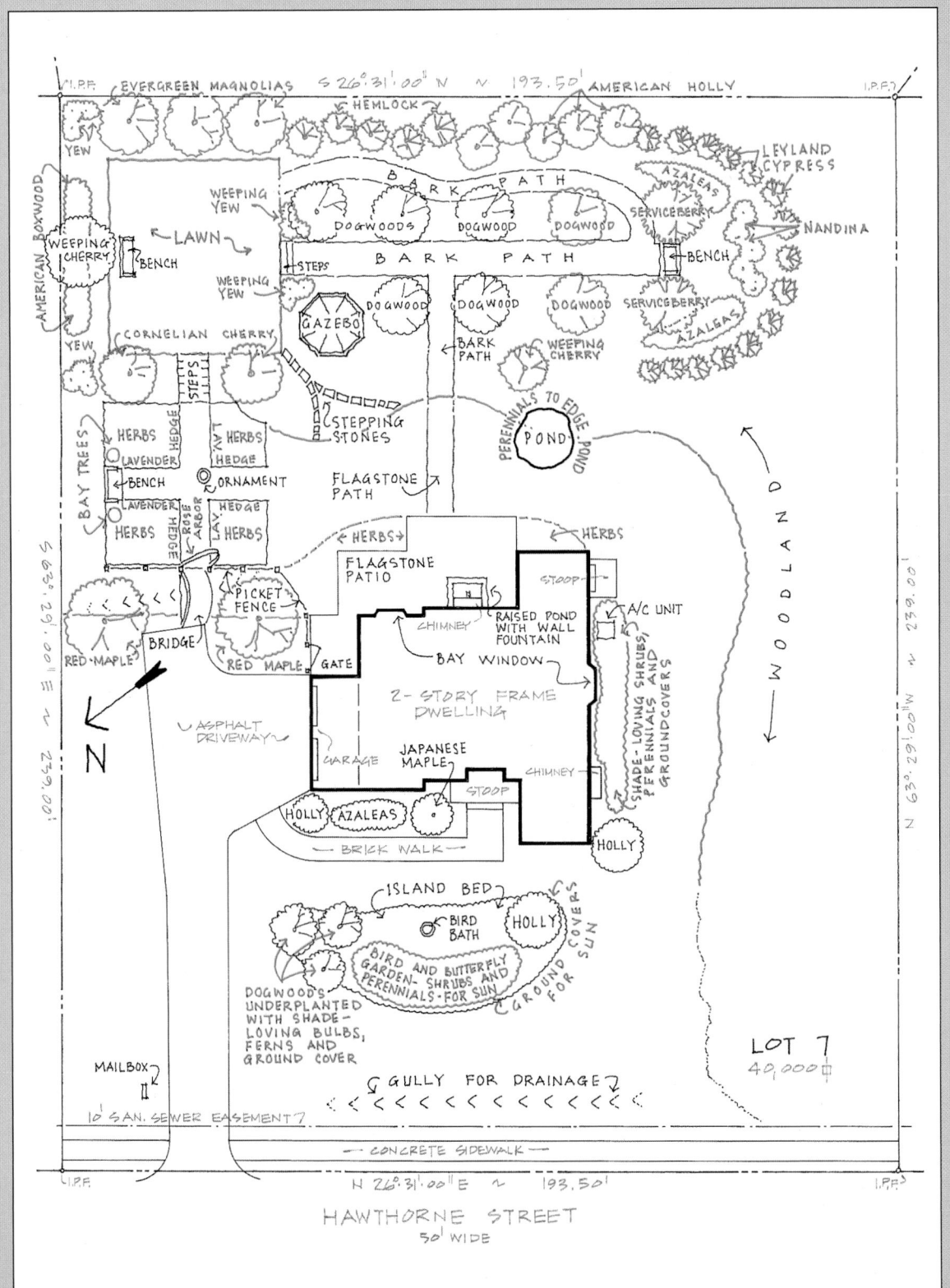

The final phase of this sample garden design is to impose a planting plan on the property map. The map now shows in black ink the regrading and transplanting to be done, and the installation of hardscape elements—such as a brick path and a flagstone patio—the gardener has chosen. Using green ink, she has laid out an ambitious project that will probably take several years to complete. Included are a screen of ornamental trees along the rear property line, a foliage cul-de-sac in the south corner, a lawn framed by shrubs and ornamental trees on the new terrace in the east corner, a formal herb garden, a mixed shade border on the southwest side of the house, and a bird-and-butterfly garden in the existing bed at the front of the house.

CHAPTER TWO

Furnishing Your Landscape

Adding hardscapes and other landscape features requires careful consideration and thoughtful planning. Whether it's pathways, lighting, terraces, or pools, the decorative elements of a garden should not only be stylish and beautiful but functional as well.

The Montchain, Delaware, garden at left strikes a fine balance between style and practicality, demonstrating how decorative elements can work with the landscape to create a cohesive design. In this informal, wooded landscape, two pools cut into a gently sloping hill simulate a natural, stone-edged pond and waterfall. Brightly colored, sun-loving Hemerocallis (daylilies) are planted in masses at the pool's far edge, while in the foreground, pink clematis, allium, daylilies, and lantana border a small terrace overlooking the landscape. A sculpture placed atop a large boulder provides a unique finishing touch to this garden's natural setting.

Pathways and Pavings

Paths and walkways create physical links between one place and another. In working them into your garden plans, keep in mind that no matter where they go or what they are made of, walkways should be compatible with the style of your house and with your landscape.

Start by deciding where you want the walkways to begin and end. Stroll around your property, examining its dimensions and contours. Do your design ideas lend themselves to pathways that follow a straight line, as in a formal garden? Or are meandering routes more appropriate, paths that induce the visitor to stop here and there along the way?

Take plenty of time in your exploratory walk through the garden, following natural routes from place to place. Once you've chosen the likeliest lines for your paths to follow, wait for a good heavy rain to come along, and then go out and check drainage patterns along and adjacent to these lines. Improperly positioned walkways can act like dams, exacerbating drainage problems.

In general, heavily traveled walkways, such as those leading to the house from the front sidewalk or the driveway, should be formal in design and constructed from hard, durable materials like concrete, brick, unglazed tile, or stone. They should follow straight lines and right angles or simple curves, and their edges should be well defined. For safety's sake, all walkways should have smooth but nonslick surfaces, and, ideally, they should be wide enough—4 to 5 feet across—for two people to walk abreast comfortably.

Informal Paths

Informal styles are usually chosen for less traveled paths, such as those leading into and through the garden, and can be constructed with softer paving materials. Such paths often have a meandering quality, but they can take any form you want them to. Merely setting out stone slabs in an irregular pattern through your garden will create a simple walkway and add visual interest. A winding gravel path with wood rounds set into the gravel at intervals would not only be aesthetically pleasing

The path in this New Hampshire garden is paved with long rectangular stones set in a zigzag pattern; within the frame they create are multicolored cobblestones and round and diamond-shaped concrete slabs. Simple plantings, including a compact Rhododendron 'Ramapo' and an arborvitae hedge, line one side of the path; yellow shrubby cinquefoil spills over from the other.

but would also encourage a leisurely stroll. Informal paths are usually narrower than main walkways—from 2½ to 3 feet wide—but should still be wide enough for you to traverse comfortably with garden equipment. For an even more informal look, you can soften the effect of paving materials by letting plantings spill onto them. Place small mound-forming plants like moss, thyme, or alyssum around paving stones to add texture, beauty, and softness to the surface.

Selecting Pavement Styles

When choosing a hardscape material, keep in mind the mood it will contribute to your overall design. But equally important are such practical matters as cost and ease of installation and main-tenance. If you don't have a lot of time to devote to plant care, you may want to invest in an intricate paving pattern or a mosaic tile that will act as a focal point, and then put in plants and ground covers that virtually look after themselves. If, on the other hand, you have considerable time for gardening, select a simple garden paving material and offset it with glorious flower borders.

Weather is another practical matter to consider. Some paving materials are more susceptible than others to damage by frost or hot, baking sun. And some, such as smooth concrete, tile, wood, brick, and stone, can be slippery when wet.

When you've worked out the practical questions, it's time to consider aesthetics. Look at the style and colors of your house and at the colors and textures of your present plantings, then decide how you want your pathways to fit in with them.

The gray stones of this Berkeley, California, pathway take a backseat to the Dianthus 'Rose Bowl', thrift, and Dalmatian bellflowers that grow between them. Geraniums and Santa Barbara daisies offer a profusion of blooms, while spotted dead nettle, lamb's ears, and Siberian iris add texture and lushness.

Making a Natural Fieldstone Pathway

Using only a shovel, you can build an informal pathway of natural fieldstone. This material, an unquarried stone, fits in well with rustic, naturalistic landscape designs. The one drawback is that the stones are heavy, so it's best to have your local stone yard or quarry deliver them and deposit them beside the site of the pathway.

Choose randomly sized stones that are flat on top and large enough to tread upon comfortably. Then experiment with different arrangements, mapping out a route that is underlain by firm soil. Working along the route, but before you have begun digging, set the larger stones in place to get the general shape of the path. Then fill in the gaps with smaller stones. Leave a natural stepping distance between large stones laid in a line—about 18 inches. If your path is curved, set a large stone at the points where the path bends, to serve as stopping areas. Vary the size of the stones, and try to match shapes of adjoining stones so that their sides align fairly well.

To set a steppingstone path of large, widely spaced stones, dig a hole for each stone, add a little builder's sand or stone dust (available where you buy the fieldstone), and position the stone in the hole. Adjust the material underneath the stone and replace the soil around it until the stone is firm and stable. For a path of closely set stones, follow the directions below for laying the stones in a trench.

1. Before you dig your trench, do a practice run by laying the stones down in a pattern that's both comfortable to walk on and aesthetically pleasing. Once you have settled on a workable path, dig a trench 5 to 6 inches deep and spread a 3-inch-deep bed of builder's sand or stone dust over it. Then lay the stones in place, aligning their irregular sides as much as possible.

2. When the stones are set in the trench, fill the spaces between them with soil. To keep the stones from tilting or wobbling, make sure at least two-thirds of the thickness of each is encased firmly in the soil. Then wet the soil with a fine spray of water. If the soil settles, add more. The surface of the stones should stand slightly higher than ground level. Plant grass or a ground cover between the stones or sweep builder's sand between them (left).

Paving Materials

The possibilities for paving are almost limitless. Your choices range from such hard materials as brick, concrete, flagstone, fieldstone, granite, tile, and wood to softer materials, including loose aggregates such as gravel, cobbles, crushed rock, woodchips, or bark chips. And, of course, you can combine hard and soft materials very successfully.

Stone works especially well in naturalistic settings; you can find it in many sizes and in both regular and random shapes. In making a choice, remember that different types of stone vary in durability, slipperiness, and resistance to frost damage. Tiles—both terra cotta and the more durable high-fired types—though relatively expensive are highly decorative, conveying a feeling of elegance. Tile is a poor choice, however, in climates where cycles of freezing and thawing occur, because wide cold-weather temperature fluctuations can cause it to crack. Remember, too, that in the rain, glazed tiles are more slippery than unglazed types.

Wood is a versatile paving material and conveys a warmth difficult to achieve with a harder material such as concrete. Woods that can be left to weather naturally, such as red cedar, cypress, and redwood, can be especially attractive. Although easy to install and fairly inexpensive, wood pavings will eventually decompose. You can extend their life somewhat by installing them in a way that allows for ventilation on the underside.

Loose Aggregates

Gravel is a popular choice among loose-aggregate paving materials. Inexpensive and easy to install, it is especially useful in spots where a less porous paving might create or worsen a drainage problem. Some maintenance is required, however. You'll need to rake gravel periodically, because it gets squeezed out of place when walked on. Your pathway will also require an edging to keep the migrating gravel from spilling over onto plantings.

Gravel tends to refract and absorb light, which can help soften the appearance of the entire garden. Remember, though, that gravel may look a bit boring when used exclusively, so plan to interrupt the line of a simple gravel path by introducing other paving materials at random, such as stone pavers or wood rounds.

The same holds true for other visually neutral materials, such as woodchips. It is best to combine them with other, more intricate-looking pavers. And no matter what type of loose-aggregate material you use, be sure to place layers of newspaper under it to help control weeds.

Patterns and Textures

As you plan your walkways, consider the roles that color, pattern, and texture play in the appearance of your garden. Simple, neutral paving works best with complex planting schemes. If your garden is filled with flowers, for example, brick might clash with red, pink, or orange blooms. Consider using gravel or flagstone and save brick for areas where the focus is on evergreens or foliage.

You can use pattern and texture in paving to convey various moods. Woodchips used together with steps created from landscape timbers, for example, lend a quiet, woodland feel. Wood planks set in a base of gravel give a more dynamic feeling—the mixture of textures, patterns, and materials keeps the eye moving.

Straight lines that run away from a particular viewpoint intensify a sense of direction and depth, whereas lines that cross the field of vision create a sense of breadth. Patterns that have a static quality—regular, symmetrical shapes such as squares, circles, and hexagons, for example—can help create a restful effect. Use them in places where you might want guests to linger. If you do choose a static arrangement, pay attention to the size of your paving units. A broad expanse of small units can create a fussy or dull appearance.

Edgings

There are several good reasons for bordering your pathways with some sort of hard edging. First, if you pave a path with a soft material such as gravel, bark, or woodchips, you will need some sort of edging to contain the material and prevent it from spreading out onto the surrounding ground and thinning out on the path until bare earth shows through. Second, if the path cuts across the lawn, edging will serve the dual purpose of keeping the turf grass within bounds and providing a hard surface for the wheels of your lawn mower as you mow the edge of the lawn.

You will find a variety of edgings at home stores. Brick can be set on edge or on end, for example. You can also buy stone or concrete pavers or concrete sections designed to be set end to end. For rustic or woodsy landscapes, pressure-treated 4-by-4 or 6-by-6 timbers and uncut stone work well.

Paving with Brick

Brick comes in many colors, shapes, and textures, and adds warmth and interest to virtually any landscape. It can be arranged in a variety of different patterns and looks equally appropriate in formal and informal settings. It is also durable and easy to work with.

In selecting a specific brick, first consider your climate. Where frost occurs, look for brick designated SX, which means it will resist the effects of freezing and thawing. Then select a brick texture: Some have smooth, sleek surfaces and sharp edges, whereas others are more porous, with rounded edges.

The way in which you lay the brick can create moods. A running pattern—used alone *(photo below)* or in combination with a stacked bond pattern—conveys fluidity and movement. By contrast, a basket-weave pattern gives a feeling of containment.

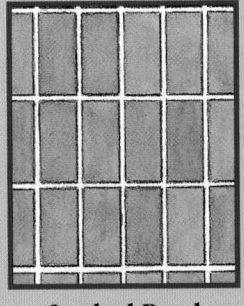

Stacked Bond

Herringbone

Basket Weave

Diagonal Herringbone

Running and Stacked Bond

Entrances and Exits

The journey through your garden should be punctuated by entrances and exits that not only provide access to its spaces but also organize them. As points of arrival and departure between house and garden and within the garden itself, they will unite the separate parts of your property and set the stage as you move from one area to the next.

The Front Entry

Because your front door is the first destination for visitors, the passage to it should allow clear access from the front sidewalk without sacrificing privacy. Paradoxically, this passageway can seem more inviting if it is fronted by a hedge or a fence. An enclosure around the front of your property conveys a sense of shelter from the outside world. A gate or a trellised archway will frame the view to the house and help direct visitors to the front door.

For the shape and dimensions of your front pathway, look to the style of your house and the contours of your land. Keep the design simple, and use appropriate materials and scale. But don't forget the practicalities. The front door should be visible and the path direct. Look closely to find natural traffic patterns: People and pets will instinctively take the shortest route to a destination, crossing over lawns and even through hedges to get there. (For more on pathways, see pages 106-107.)

From House to Garden

When guests walk out of your house on their way to the garden, whether through a front, side, or rear door, the area outside the door should give them the impression of linking the interior with the exterior. This space can be as small as a doorstep or as large as a patio or deck. It can incorporate elements that are extensions of the house— lighting, furniture, even an awning or a roof. At the same time, it can introduce elements of the garden, such as a small pool, a climbing rose, or clusters of plants in decorative containers.

The transition from one space to another

Extending an entranceway welcome almost to curbside, a Los Angeles garden fills the strip of earth between the sidewalk and the road with Tulbaghia violacea (society garlic), Geranium incanum, and a red-flowered Leptospermum scoparium (New Zealand tea tree). In many gardens, such island beds are the only locations in full sun. Before planning a sidewalk garden, find out if your municipality has height restrictions on sidewalk plantings.

within the garden can be marked or signaled in several ways. The subtlest is a change in the materials underfoot. For example, the transition from lawn to a woodchip path can mark the entrance to a woodland. A gravel walkway that becomes a concrete sidewalk may indicate an exit from the garden to the driveway. More obvious are the portals created by open or gated passages, standing free or as part of a hedge or fence. The simplest is a passage between two shrubs at either side of a pathway. More elaborate would be an archway or pergola. A picket or wrought-iron gate will give the visitor a glimpse of the space beyond, whereas one of solid wood, if tall enough, will block the view and make the entrance a surprise.

A picket gate mounted on rough-hewn posts has been embellished by a rustic archway of interwoven boughs. The style fits in with the informal pebbled path leading to the utility area of this southern California garden. Wild lilac, snakebeard, and 'Bonica' shrub roses edge the pathway.

Choosing Openness or Privacy

The impression made by the entrance to your house can be altered with a few simple landscaping changes, depending on the design of the house. A dramatic front door or a handsome roofline may call for an arrangement that boldly displays them. On the other hand, you may want more screening if, for example, you have large windows that look out on the street.

The house below is fronted by an open expanse of lawn, its foundation softened by a line of shrubbery. Vertical accent shrubs flank the entranceway and strengthen it as a focal point. To a visitor, such an exposed design may seem imposing, if not slightly forbidding. Curtains or shutters in the windows are needed to maintain a sense of privacy.

Planting a screen of trees and a hedge creates a sheltering enclosure in front of this house. The trees block upper-window sightlines from the street. Indoors, the house is bright because curtains can be left open. Outdoors, the hedge-enclosed space feels more intimate and inviting to a visitor than an open space would.

Places for Stopping and Viewing

Nestled against the side of a small gatehouse in this Atlanta, Georgia, garden, a bed of boxwood, peonies, ferns, and ivy makes a tranquil resting place at the edge of a walled flagstone terrace. The formal gateway, crowned with an evergreen arch, announces the beginning of an excursion into the garden.

Whether you seek a cozy spot to rest after an afternoon of planting and pruning or a vantage point from which to admire the perennials in bloom, your garden should include places to stop, rest, and reflect. Benches have long been used along the garden path as popular stopping places, but you can create a number of other arrangements as well. A hammock swinging from a venerable old tree, an outdoor table and chairs, or a seat built into an arbor will all add individuality and style to your garden.

Patios and decks are something of a middle ground between the house and the garden. They allow a comfortable transition between indoors and outdoors, and can be treated as an extra "room" in which to relax and entertain. Because of its proximity to the house, a patio should be built of materials that complement the house. A brick house might have a brick or colored concrete patio, for example, and a clapboard house, a patio surface of flagstone or terra-cotta tile.

Decks extend out over the property and can be used to deal with difficult gradients, such as a site too steep for walking or even for steps. With their elevated vantage point, they also offer a unique view of the garden. And the materials typically used to construct decks—pressure-treated pine, redwood, and cedar—work well aesthetically with the design and building materials of most houses.

Planting Arrangements

Your garden design can include beds of spectacular plantings arranged to be stopping places at the ends of pathways or along their length—

especially when the spot is equipped with a bench for restful viewing. With plantings calculated to provide interest through a long season of growth, these stopping places will maintain their appeal for much of the year.

An Elevated Perspective

If an overlook, such as a balcony or an accessible rooftop, is part of your property, it can become the visitor's ultimate destination. From there, an appealing view of your garden or of a distant vista can be a delightful surprise.

Roof gardens and balcony plantings can be part of your overall garden design. If the view from your overlook is less than captivating, you can minimize it by creating a focal point within the roof garden or screen offending views with a simple garden structure such as a latticework trellis.

Designing a roof garden is always a challenge. Your plants will generally grow in large containers or planters, which must be designed to allow for adequate drainage. The drain water must, in turn, be effectively channeled off the roof. Also keep in mind that the soil mix must be light enough to be supported by the roof once the plants are in place. One technique to ensure safety is to position heavy plantings directly over the supporting pillars of the structure.

Balconies are interesting places to experiment with container gardening. Make sure you take note of the growing conditions before you make plans—sun angles and the direction and strength of the wind will affect your plant choices.

Depending on the size of your balcony, you may be able to grow climbing vines against the building walls for green cover as well as have annual and perennial plantings for seasonal interest. Before you move any containers onto the balcony, however, find out how much weight it can safely support.

An arbor made of ginkgo trees supports the weight of a fragrant climbing white Rosa soulieana. Such a sheltered stopping place provides shade and seclusion and even some protection from a light summer rain in this East Hampton, New York, garden. The white-edged leaves of the variegated hostas thriving in its corners pick up the white of the blossoms.

Trees for Shade

Abies
(fir)
Aesculus hippocastanum
(common horse chestnut)
Betula
(birch)
Cedrus atlantica
(Atlas cedar)
Cladrastis lutea
(American yellowwood)
Cornus florida
(flowering dogwood)
x *Cupressocyparis leylandii*
(Leyland cypress)
Fagus
(beech)
Koelreuteria paniculata
(golden-rain tree)
Liquidambar
(sweet gum)
***Magnolia grandiflora* 'Bracken's Brown Beauty'**
(southern magnolia)
Magnolia stellata
(star magnolia)
Malus floribunda
(Japanese flowering crab apple)
Picea
(spruce)
Pinus strobus
(eastern white pine)
***Prunus subhirtella* 'Pendula'**
(Higan cherry)
Quercus phellos
(willow oak)
Stewartia pseudocamellia
(Japanese stewartia)
Tilia
(linden)
Tsuga
(hemlock)
Ulmus
(elm)
Zelkova
(zelkova)

Enclosing the Garden

The fences, walls, and gates you place around the outskirts of your property and at the boundaries of its internal "rooms" should act like picture frames, defining and showcasing the space within. But these elements must be useful as well as beautiful. On the practical side, walls and fences enclose your property, provide protection and privacy, act as windbreaks, and muffle street sounds. Walls generally make more formidable barriers than fences because they are usually made of such weighty, permanent materials as poured concrete, stone, or brick. Fences can be solid structures, too, but they are typically constructed of wood in decorative, open patterns. They offer less privacy but let in more light and air.

Walls and fences play a major role in garden design because of the strong vertical dimension they impose. They also provide wonderful planting

opportunities. A wall might double as a support for a raised bed; a fence might serve as a trellis for climbing flowers or vines.

You can also use walls and fences to espalier shrubs and ornamental trees: The patterns created by flowers, fruit, and seasonal foliage color will ornament the structure as well as enliven the garden. Even the simplest of planting strategies—for example, just setting a few containers of flowers at its base—will add interest to an expanse of wall or fence.

An important focal point in either a wall or a fence is its gateway. An attractive or unusual garden gate serves not only as a passageway but also as an accent in its own right, framing a view within or beyond the garden. Gates can add ornamental interest, focus the eye, and break up the solid line of a garden boundary.

By their bulk, weight, and strength, walls contribute a sense of stability and permanence to your landscape. The most common building materials for walls are concrete block, poured concrete, brick, and stone. If you decide on a stone

Bright red bougainvillea (left) crests a concrete wall in this garden in Rancho Santa Fe, California. Echoing the tawny hues of the surrounding desert, the wall also serves as a backdrop for a profusion of native plantings, including Agave, Sedum, Aconitum, and Euphorbia.

Living Garden Boundaries

Hedges are a lovely natural alternative to walls and fences. But remember that some trees and shrubs can take 10 years to grow to a useful height for a hedge. One tree that is ideal for this purpose is x *Cupressocyparis leylandii,* a handsome, fast-growing tree with a columnar habit. In cool, temperate climates, choose from such evergreens as *Viburnum tinus* 'Spring Bouquet', *Prunus caroliniana* 'Bright 'n' Tight', *Rhododendron* 'Fragrantissimum', *Euonymus japonica, Pieris, Taxus, Buxus, Pyracantha, Thuja, Spiraea, Ilex crenata,* and *Prunus lusitanica.* For tropical gardens, *Griselinia* and *Olearia* perform well, as does a ficus hedge like the one at right.

If you prefer a flowering hedge, forsythia is inexpensive and easy to grow. And if you want roses, both *Rosa rugosa* and *R. eglanteria* make beautiful informal hedges that produce not only blooms but also bright rose hips in the fall.

A Gallery of Wooden Fences

Wooden fences can range from the simple to the ornate. Slats can be diagonal, horizontal, or vertical; picket fences can have various intervals between pickets and tops that are pointed or rounded, spearheaded, or double- or triple-saw-toothed. The look of the fence will also be affected by the finish. Unfinished wood creates a rustic appearance as it ages. Or, if you prefer, you can stain the wood or paint it.

Pressure-treated pine is the least expensive fence wood that offers resistance to insects and decay. But typical pressure-treated pine fencing will often be poorly cured and subject to warping, and it will have knots, holes, and splits. Furthermore, it will be considerably darker than untreated pine and may have a greenish cast from its chemical treatment. Thus, it will not weather handsomely if it is left unfinished. If the design of your fence will be intricate, opt for redwood, cypress, or cedar, which are more expensive but are better choices when fine workmanship is required and appearance is a priority.

**Concave-topped
Double Picket**

Interwoven Slat

wall, select a stone that will help merge the style of your house with the landscape. Keep in mind that stone can be either dry-laid or mortared in place. If you choose brick or concrete block, you have the further option of building with pierced brick or block, which will make your wall a bit more like a screen, allowing a limited amount of air and light to pass through.

To decide on a building material, you must first consider the purpose of the wall, which will, in turn, help you select its location, height, and length. If, say, you want a barrier to prevent children and small dogs from wandering into the street, you may need a wall only 3 feet high. If you want to keep out intruders or large animals, you'll need a wall at least 6 feet high.

Remember that a wall will become a prominent feature in your garden. The strong line it introduces might not necessarily fit best along the property line, so experiment with various possible positions.

Doing It Yourself or Contracting Out

Some walls have heavier work to do than merely enclosing the perimeter of your property. For these, you will have further choices to make.

If you want to build a retaining wall, for example, you may need to consult a professional about materials, siting, and design before tackling the job. Something as relatively uncomplicated as a dry-laid retaining wall made of stone—or even broken chunks of sidewalk—can be an efficient way to control erosion on a slope or to change grade. But you must be sure your wall will withstand the downhill pressure of soil and water.

In a few locales a retaining wall as low as 18 inches is subject to building regulations concerning construction methods and form—although in most jurisdictions the code doesn't apply unless the wall is at least 3 feet tall. It's best to hire a contractor if the wall you want will be tall enough to come under the local code. And if you are planning a wall with a height of 6 or more feet, or one that will run near the property line, make sure you're clear on local height and setback restrictions.

Adorning a Wall with Plants

The right plantings, of course, can provide the perfect finishing touch for a stone wall. Consider installing succulents or rock plants such as alyssum or campanula in the crevices to help soften the look of the wall. Espaliered apple or pear trees can lend year-round interest and interrupt the unbroken expanse of a high wall. Vines with long, supple branches can do the same for a long, low wall. Good choices include *Euonymus fortunei* (winter creeper) and *Campanula poscharskyana* (Serbian bellflower).

To support vines or espaliered limbs, drill holes in the wall at mortar intersections, hammer in expandable steel plugs, and screw in steel eyes.

Prominent wooden posts interrupt the expanse of latticework fencing that encloses this Long Island, New York, garden. The open design of the fence allows air to circulate and affords a sense of privacy that is enhanced by the plants— sage, strawberries, phlox, and hibiscus— growing in borders and containers alongside it. Red 'Queen Elizabeth' roses and the pale pink blooms of the climbing rose 'Compassion' spill over the top of the fence at intervals, breaking its horizontal line.

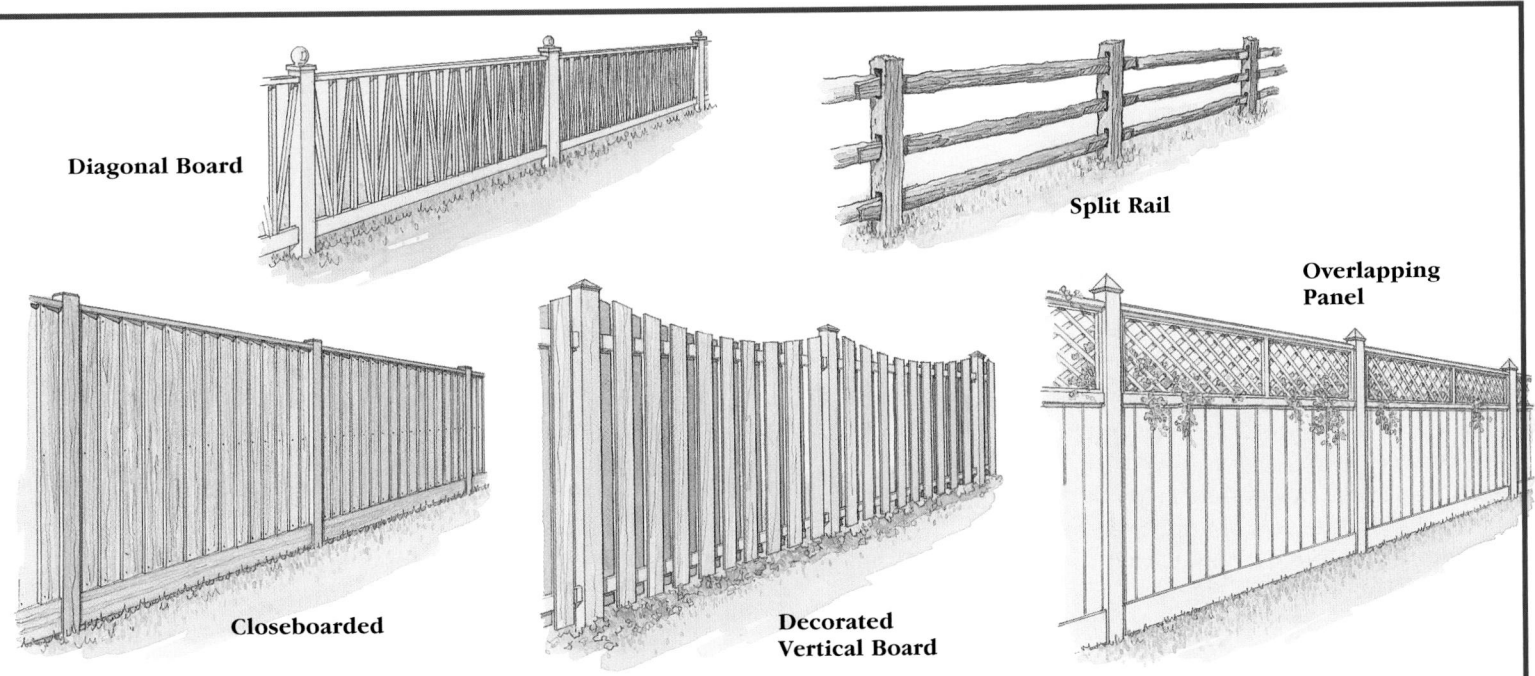

Diagonal Board

Split Rail

Closeboarded

Decorated Vertical Board

Overlapping Panel

Then string braided metal wires through the eyes in any pattern you like, and attach the growing stems to the wires with plastic ties.

Fences

Fences, like walls, should serve as far more than boundary markers. They offer almost limitless opportunities for introducing pattern and texture as well as vertical and horizontal interest.

Fences are generally less imposing, easier to install, and less expensive than walls. And they can, like walls, lend unity to your landscape if you use construction materials that harmonize with the overall style of your house and complement your garden. The more formal the look of the garden, the more architectural the fence should be.

Choosing a Fence Design

Decide in the planning stages how much privacy you want. Depending on style and design, fences may offer substantial privacy or virtually none at all. Fences of interwoven slats or louvered wood, for example, let in limited light and air, leaving you quite enclosed within your garden. A louvered fence is a good choice for encircling a patio, as it offers a degree of ventilation, filters sunlight, and softens wind. You can paint a louvered fence, stain it, or allow it to age naturally.

Open fence styles like lattice and wrought iron are more for decoration than privacy, although they can serve as effective psychological barriers against casual intrusions. They also make wonderful mounting surfaces for a variety of plantings and allow good ventilation. Lattices made of vinyl look good, last longer than wooden ones, and are available in several colors. Wrought iron has a quiet, distinguished look that is particularly suited to urban areas. And a split-rail fence, often made from untreated wood, is so open that it merges your property with the surrounding landscape.

Picket fences blend easily with a variety of house styles, and can look just right in the city or in rural and suburban settings. When painted white, they are bright and cheerful additions to the landscape. But white fences look their best when freshly painted, so keep time and maintenance requirements in mind when you choose a finish. If you don't want the obligation of repeated upkeep, consider a dark stain for your picket fence—it will give a more formal appearance with far less maintenance.

Before you install a fence, find out about local regulations regarding allowable fence heights. In many places the height limit is 42 inches for front-yard fences and 6 feet for backyard fences. If you are not sure of the exact location of the property line, contact a surveyor when building a fence on a boundary. You may want to position the fence a few inches inside the line to be sure of avoiding legal entanglements with touchy neighbors.

Gates

Gates can be plain and sturdy or highly detailed and ornamental. They can be either traditional or contemporary in style but work best, of course, when the design and materials of the gate are coordinated with the dominant architecture of the property. Because a gate is the focal point of a wall or fence—or even of a dense hedge—it can communicate a certain style or feeling. A solid wooden gate with a lattice design on top, for example, suggests openness without sacrificing privacy. A white wooden gate placed midway along a brick wall and decorated with climbing roses lends color and charm. And a wrought-iron gate looks elegantly formal at the entrance to a Victorian-style home. Whatever type of gate you choose, you can add ornamental interest with catches, hinges, and locks that enhance the overall effect.

Anchoring Wooden Fence Posts

To delay rot, set fence posts in concrete. First dig a posthole deep enough to set one-third the total length of the post belowground. Then place a flat stone in the hole to act as a base. Insert the post, then pour in and tamp down 4 to 6 inches of gravel. Fill the hole with concrete 2 to 3 inches at a time, tamping it in as you go. Use a level to make sure the post is vertical. To allow for expansion, cut two pieces of plywood into wedges that are several inches long, as wide as the post, and an inch thick; coat them with motor oil, then position them on either side of the post as you pour the concrete. Remove them after the concrete dries and fill the spaces with sand or tar.

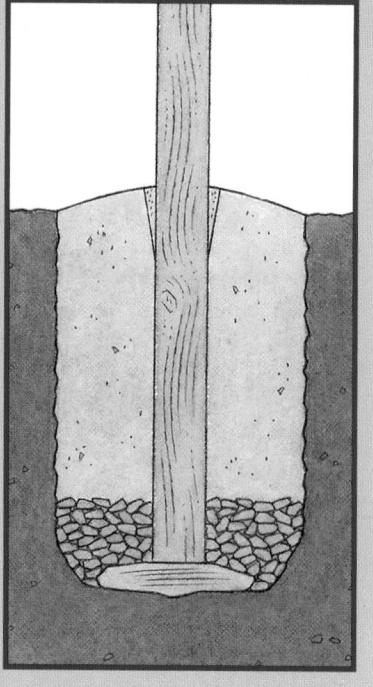

Accessories for the Garden

A mossy stone bench surrounded by Trillium ovatum (coast trillium) and T. sessile (toadshade) and overhung with blossoms of a Rhododendron yakusimanum 'Ken Janek' provides a spot to sit and contemplate this woodland walk in Oregon.

Decorative elements such as containers, statuary, benches, and sundials can help you create a garden that's more than just a pretty collection of plants. Thoughtfully selected and placed, outdoor decorative pieces can create a focal point, complement foliage and flowers, define boundaries, provide smooth transitions between plantings, and increase the area available for cultivation. Before you select your garden decorations, make sure you know your garden well, and let its size, style, and purpose guide you. Classical statues look appropriately imposing in a formal garden with well-defined beds; a stone frog hiding under parsley sprigs might better suit a kitchen garden.

Container Gardening

Containers, a favorite of the city gardener with limited space for cultivation, come in many shapes, sizes, and materials. Filled with annuals or perennials, they can go almost anywhere to brighten an existing plant bed or to extend your growing area on patios, decks, balconies, sidewalks, and even walls. People confined to wheelchairs or those for whom bending and kneeling are difficult may find containers a pleasing gardening alternative to

Making a Log Planter

A fallen tree trunk can be recycled into a distinctive wooden planter that will hold a mixture of perennials and annuals. First, dig out the center of the log to a depth of about a foot, then cut a V-shaped groove from the center opening out to one end of the log; this will provide drainage. Fill the hole with an appropriate soil mix, then plant easy-care varieties such as begonias, hostas, impatiens, or bulbs.

Place one or more logs around a patio or along a garden path; or place your log planter in a less structured setting. Set several small boulders around the log to stabilize it and help it blend with its setting.

working in the ground. Containers can also become garden focal points or accents if they have a striking shape or texture.

Be sure to choose containers that will suit their contents. If you want to highlight your plantings, simple containers are best. If, on the other hand, you wish to feature a lovely pot, choose a simpler plant. And if an outdoor container is to hold perennials, be sure it is large enough to keep freezing temperatures from reaching the roots.

Choosing Containers

Pick a container that is the correct size and weight for your plant and your purposes. If you are hanging plants from a ceiling or wall, lightweight plastic planters or a wire-and-moss arrangement may be best. Heavier trees and shrubs need to be based in sturdy tubs or barrels so that they are not blown over by a strong wind. And always locate your containers where they're not too difficult to reach for watering.

Anything from a wheelbarrow to an old sink can be turned into a container for plants. Most of the containers available commercially are made of terra cotta, wood, plastic, cast stone, or concrete or fiberglass molded to look like stone.

Terra cotta works well in both formal and informal settings, and its neutral color harmonizes with almost any color of flower or foliage. But it may not stand up to repeated freezing and thawing, and glazed terra cotta is even less resistant to fluctuating hot and cold temperatures.

Wood containers, such as barrels or tubs, are unaffected by frost and can be treated to resist rot. They look better in casual settings and, because they are available in large sizes, are often used for permanent plantings such as ornamental fruit trees, juniper trees, and some varieties of cypress, azalea, and rhododendron. Small wooden boxes are attractive underneath windows, on porch or deck railings, or along the perimeter of a patio. You can paint them for added visual interest.

Because plastic and composite containers start to look shabby relatively quickly, it's best to limit their use to annuals. Petunias, impatiens, geraniums, and snapdragons will flourish in a plastic container hung from the porch ceiling. Plastic is

Vinca 'Little Bright Eyes', Cleome 'Royal Queen', Zinnia elegans 'Bouquet White', and Artemisia schmidtiana 'Silver Dust' surround this New Jersey garden's sundial in summer. In winter, the absence of flowers will bring out its elegant form even more strongly.

available in a variety of colors. Green and other neutral colors are a safe bet with any planting; white containers quickly show scratches and dirt.

Cast-stone and concrete containers are appropriate for both formal and informal gardens. They resist damage from rain, snow, and freezing temperatures. Plan the placement of a large stone container carefully—once it is filled it will be difficult to move. Some fiberglass containers look like stone but are much lighter.

Decorative Details

Garden ornaments can make a garden uniquely your own. Adornments help set a garden's tone, be it whimsical, understated, formal, practical, or sentimental. An ornament might be a focal point, or you might tuck one in an out-of-the-way corner to be discovered unexpectedly.

Heavy stone objects like urns look best in a formal garden with well-defined paths. In this sort of setting you might use an obelisk or a sundial on a pedestal as a centerpiece. A fragrant herb garden would be a prime location for a conical beehive shape; small stone sculptures of dogs, cats, frogs, rabbits, turtles, or gnomes are popular additions to a woodland garden.

Ornaments of all sorts are available in gardening stores and through catalogs, but if you're creative, you can turn almost anything into a garden decoration. Birdbaths and old birdcages are an inviting touch. Or if an old weather vane or lantern appeals to you, try it out. After all, it's your garden.

Seating

Before you choose seating for your garden, consider these questions: Will a seat at a given location serve as a brief rest spot, an afternoon lounging retreat, or a vantage point from which to view a certain portion of the landscape? Will the seating be permanent, or will you want to shift it as the sunlight fades and the seasons change?

A bench or chair for the garden is more than just a place to sit; it can be used as a decoration as well. Various kinds of seats are available in a range of sizes, materials, and colors. The challenge is to make sure that your seat, bench, or swing harmonizes with its surroundings. A formal scrolled-iron bench, for example, may look out of place among plant containers created from rusted milk pails and weathered wine cases.

In formal gardens, stone benches might be used to define boundaries between cultivated

beds; they can also work in tandem with such stone ornaments as statues, vases, and urns to contribute to the stately tone of such gardens.

You might also place a bench at the end of a path, grass alley, or arbor to provide a visual focal point and a convenient resting place after a stroll in the garden. Cast-iron furniture looks at home in a formal setting, while rustic twig furniture adds a homey touch to a more informal garden. Wicker and rattan contribute an exotic flavor to many settings; they will survive longer if they are somewhat protected from the elements.

Traditionally, garden furniture has been green, white, or black. White contrasts most sharply with the surrounding foliage; green blends more smoothly with the varied tints of leaves, bushes, and grasses; and black is the most stately. But many colorful alternatives are now available.

The owner of this Los Angeles garden, not Mother Nature, provided the large flat-topped stone on which to sit and enjoy the scenery. Set atop flagstones among plumes of rose fountain grass, feather grass, and drifts of sweet alyssum, the stone seat also provides a visual transition between the two plant groupings.

121

Vertical Garden Structures

Vertical elements—trellises, arbors, pergolas, lath houses, and gazebos—can be the most interesting and decorative structures in your garden. They create design interest in the landscape by leading the eye upward. And, like the walls or fences that enclose your garden, they strengthen its sense of composition by framing what lies beyond them.

Whether simple or elaborate, vertical landscape elements perform practical as well as aesthetic functions. They can provide shade for plants and people, sheltered spots for seating, and alcoves or other places for repose. They can serve as focal points. They can provide niches for container plants or act as supports on which to train climbing flowers and vines.

Vertical elements should be aesthetically pleasing, blending with your overall garden design and the architectural style of your house. When planning for these elements, keep in mind that unless the vertical structure supports an evergreen climber, over the long winter the framework of your arbor or pergola will be clearly visible.

Construction materials used for vertical elements include wood, stone, brick, metal, and wrought iron. You can also fashion appealing rustic structures from willow twigs or grapevines

gathered in your own garden or a nearby field.

While vertical structures can add greatly to the visual impact of your garden, they are also capable of overpowering it if installed without forethought. One such architectural element goes a long way, so exercise restraint. As with any garden structure, a vertical one should be proportioned to match the scale of the garden and home so that it complements and does not overwhelm the landscape.

Freestanding Structures

Pergolas, arbors, trellises, and gazebos are usually ornamental—even fanciful—elements within the garden. An arch or a pergola can resemble a piece of sculpture, beautiful in its own right and enhanced even further by the adornment you choose for it. Beyond their aesthetic appeal, freestanding garden structures provide shade along with privacy and protection—all without sacrificing light or air. They make wonderful supports for all manner of plantings. A trellised archway draped with wisteria or fragrant roses makes a lovely frame for a garden pathway. Keep in mind that your plantings should be in proportion to the size of your structures. Small, wispy climbers may look skimpy, or even sickly, when grown on a large, bold frame such as a pergola. On the other hand, heavy vines such as Japanese wisteria will overwhelm a more delicate trellis. In either case, prune your plantings regularly to control their growth.

Pergolas and Arbors

Pergolas—elongated structures of columns supporting a sturdy, overhead gridwork of wood rafters—are bold, linear affairs. Traditionally, they function as covered walkways and should therefore lead somewhere, connecting one area to another or perhaps just ending a garden stroll at a seat or ornament. Plan the location of a pergola with care—it will take up considerable room. You might build one over a patio as an extension of your house, or locate it as a freestanding unit at a distance from the house, creating a garden retreat.

Pergolas originated as frameworks for such climbing plants as grapevines. *Vitis vinifera* 'Purpurea' and the hybrid 'Brant' provide wonderful color on a pergola in the fall. Other climbing vines also do well on pergolas.

Arbors, with their graceful arches and enclosed seats, are generally less imposing than pergolas. An arbor can be used to create a private nook off the beaten path, a quiet spot for resting or reading, or for just enjoying your garden in solitude. If you

An arched trellis laden with pink clematis beckons visitors to pass beneath it and into the Salem, Oregon, garden beyond. Along with the fence, the trellis acts as both a focal point and a garden divider. A border hedge of boxwood lines the walkway, and white hawthorn blooms in front of the fence.

Making a Rustic Trellis

Fashioning your own trellis from flexible grapevines or willow twigs is not difficult and can lend a pleasant rustic touch to an informal garden design. To make a trellis like the one shown below, first construct a rectangular frame of sturdy branches— cedar, maple, walnut, or sycamore—by nailing the pieces of wood together to form posts and crosspieces. Then bend flexible grapevines or willow shoots so that they arch over the frame, and attach them to the supporting pieces with twine or plastic ties.

Wind additional grapevines around the crosspieces for a decorative touch. Then prop your finished trellis against a garden wall or fence and train climbing roses, vines, or even vegetables to scurry up it.

design it so that it faces a lovely view in the garden or occupies a particularly warm and sunny spot, you'll be sure to enjoy it to the fullest. Arbors are usually associated with climbing plants—classically, grapes and roses. Train them to climb up the sides of the structure and cascade over the top.

Trellises

A trellis acts like a screen, creating a partial barrier that provides a measure of shade, shelter, and privacy but never completely blocks out air and light. A traditional trellis has panels of wood latticework that can either stand freely or abut a wall, a fence, or the side of a house. If you incorporate a seating area into your trellis, it can provide a wonderful spot for just relaxing.

Traditionally, trellis panels are made from a grid of perpendicular wood slats attached to a frame. The design of the trellis can be simple or intricate, incorporating a variety of arches and posts. You can build a trellis from decay-resistant woods such as redwood, cypress, or cedar that weather naturally into a handsome hue over the years. If you use pine, however, it should be pressure-treated;

otherwise, you will have to treat it with a preservative and either stain or paint it to prevent rotting.

Although a trellis primarily serves as a plant support, don't mask the underlying wood pattern with too much vegetation. Try to balance the style and intricacy of your trellis design with the habit and vigor of your climbing and twining plants. If your trellis has a tightly woven crisscross pattern, for example, it's better to use a light, airy climber like clematis than a larger-leaved climber, which would look too heavy.

Gazebos and Lath Houses

A gazebo is a roofed and often elevated pavilion that serves as a kind of ornate freestanding deck and gives a whimsical focus to the garden. It is usually circular, square, or octagonal, with low latticework sides that often support pretty flowering vines. A lath house is similar to a pergola in form but much more lightly constructed. Its main purpose is to create dappled shade rather than to support climbing plants, though it can bear light herbaceous vines.

This pergola constructed over a patio in Santa Barbara, California, creates a garden room for outdoor relaxation. The chairs and the table, with its tree-trunk pedestal, echo the natural look of the pergola. Juniper shrubs flank the structure, and Laurentia fluviatilis 'Blue Star Creeper' fills the spaces between the flagstones.

Rock Gardens and Water Features

Adding rock gardens or water features to your property is not a simple undertaking; it requires thoughtful planning to make the finished elements look as if they belong in a particular spot. Yet nothing compares with the topographical texture, color, variety, and focus these features bring to a garden, to say nothing of the elegance they impart.

If a rock garden is high on your list of wants, you should first candidly assess whether it will look natural in its setting. Don't try to impose one on a region lacking natural rock formations. And remember that once it is set in place, a rock garden is not easily rearranged, so before you undertake any heavy lifting, prepare carefully. Concentrate first on the overall design for placement of the rocks, as this task will be more demanding than that of drawing up a planting plan.

Begin by sketching a design on paper. If your garden will be larger than a few square yards, work out a schedule for building it—perhaps in stages over several seasons. Good drainage is important,

so avoid low, wet places. A possible exception to a location with good drainage is a spot on a slope with a drainage problem that might be solved or at least ameliorated by installing a rock garden.

As you create your design, take advantage of existing features—rock formations, a mound or rise, or shrubs that will provide background. If your garden already contains a single large rock or an attractive collection of them, use these as your starting point.

Adding Elevation

If your rock garden will be large, include minor grade changes in your plan—stones and rocks generally look best in layers, just as they occur in nature. Choose stones that are flat and wide and are native to your area.

If you'd like a sloping rather than a vertical rise in elevation, place each succeeding tier of stones

Fluffy white double arabis tumbles downward through the grade changes in this upstate New York rock garden, finding a foothold in gravelly patches along the way. Composed of native granite stones in various shapes and sizes, the man-made outcrop provides a home for pink phlox, golden Aurinia, and shade-tolerant Ajuga.

several inches back from the one beneath it. Position each stone to slant downward toward the rear so rainwater will seep back among the stones.

Installing a Water Feature

Planning for a water feature begins with assessing its purpose. Will it be a dominating feature in your landscape or brighten a hidden corner? From what spot on your property would you like to view it? How will it fit into the rest of your garden plan? What wildlife do you expect to attract? Do you want to have fish? If your landscaping style is informal, you might want to simulate a natural pond. Such a free-form basin requires considerable space. If you prefer straight lines and geometric patterns, a formal pool with a fountain or a piece of sculpture might suit you best. Given its shape, a formal pool will most likely require a concrete bottom and sides—and, in most cases, installing these is a job for a contractor.

For the health of your pool, choose a site that receives direct sunlight for at least 3, and preferably 6, hours each day. Containers that hold less than 100 gallons, however, do need shade in the middle of the day to prevent overheating of the water, which could be fatal to fish and plants. Avoid low places where runoff might collect under your

The lush textures of a full-blown summer morning are reflected in the dark, velvety waters of this garden pond in Birmingham, Alabama, where bog plants, water lilies, and other aquatics thrive in submerged containers. Potted caladiums and ferns complete the cheerful setting and tie the water garden to the soft lawn beside it.

pond and damage concrete or masonry during freezes and thaws. If possible, avoid overhanging trees, whose falling leaves could pollute the water.

As you plan your pond, consider the visual effect you want to create. The color of the pond liner—the sheet of waterproof material laid along the bottom and sides to serve as the actual container for the water—is important. A dark liner intensifies reflections and creates a mirrorlike effect; a light liner cuts down reflections and invites the observer to look deeply into the pond.

Building the Pond

If your pond is not of Olympic proportions and does not require concrete, you can probably do the work yourself—or at least oversee it. Lay out the shape of the pond in any design you choose, using a garden hose or a rope. To line an irregularly shaped pond, you'll need a strong synthetic-rubber liner at least 45 millimeters thick. Its length and width should be the same as that of your excavation plus twice the maximum depth.

You might wish to plan for both a shallow area in your pond where birds can drink and a deeper one that will provide fish with cool temperatures and security. Depending on the climate, the depth of your pond should vary from a minimum of 4 inches to a maximum of 3½ feet. Dig two or three tiers in your pond, finishing with a shelf around the perimeter to lodge the coping stones that will form the edging of the pond and anchor the lining in place. Line the excavation with sand, carpet padding, or even newspapers to protect your pond liner from being punctured by sharp stones or roots. Lay the liner in the excavation and weight the edges with brick or stone coping.

Fill the pond with water and let it stand at least 1 week to reduce the chlorine levels before you introduce any fish or plants. In a well-balanced pond—one stocked with oxygenating grasses—algae growth will be restrained and the pond will remain reasonably clean. Bog plants and flowering aquatics will thrive along with water lilies submerged in widemouthed pots.

Avoid stocking the pond with more fish than the miniature ecosystem can support. To prevent a buildup of toxic ammonia and solid waste, you will probably need a filtration system. A pond of a capacity of less than 1,000 gallons needs only a small pump to circulate at least half the water every hour through a filter box and up to a fountain that aerates the water. You can purchase effective systems that use either biological, mechanical, or chemical means of filtering.

TIPS FROM THE PROS

Making a Pond Self-Sustaining

A new pond is likely to become cloudy with algae at first, because its natural chemical balance, its microorganisms, and the plant populations you put in need time to establish themselves. To keep unicellular algae—the floating cloudy stuff—under control while that process takes place, you can use a commercial algicide. However, don't try to get rid of all the mosslike algae that clings to the sides of the pond. It may be unsightly, but it is also useful to the health of your water garden. And natural scavengers, especially snails and tadpoles, will graze on it and help keep it in check.

To maintain a good ecological balance in the pond, include the following elements:
- One bunch of submerged plants for each 1 to 2 square feet of pond surface. Small ponds (fewer than 100 square feet in surface area) and those that receive a great deal of sun will need a higher ratio of plant material than larger and shadier ones.
- Floating leaf plants to cover roughly 50 percent of the pond's surface.
- One scavenger fish for each 1 to 2 square feet of pond surface.
- Up to 20 gallons of water for each 4-inch fish.

Lighting Your Garden for Utility and Beauty

Bathing the evening landscape with the glow of soft light will add hours of enjoyment, as well as increase the security of your garden. Whether your plans call for decorative lanterns along a garden path, entranceway lampposts, recessed lights in walls or steps, or dramatic accent lights, the key is to use soft, low-wattage lighting for a more natural effect.

Safety First

You'll need to plan your lighting scheme so that it not only shows off your plantings to best advantage but also helps your guests avoid bumping into objects or tripping on steps or walkways. At a minimum, you should focus the lighting on paved surfaces. Ankle-level lights along the edges of pathways, for example, will deflect light downward, both illuminating the walkway and lending a flattering glow to plants and flowers bordering the path. You should also install lighting in or alongside steps, on walls, or underneath railings to help people see where they are walking, and illuminate pools, decks, and patios for safety as well as for aesthetic reasons.

Advanced Lighting Technology

If you thought you needed an electrician or a landscape architect to install lighting in your garden, think again. The advent of low-voltage outdoor lighting systems has changed all that. Operating at 12 to 24 volts of electricity instead of the 120 volts that household fixtures require, these lighting systems are inexpensive to install, maintain, and use. No permits are required, the cables don't need to be heavily protected and buried, and the only special equipment you need is a step-down transformer to reduce your household current to the correct voltage. Do-it-yourself lighting kits, complete with the transformer, are available at most garden centers. Many of these kits also come with timing devices to turn the lights on and off automatically.

Another advancement in garden lighting has been the introduction of new, smaller bulbs. These bulbs are more energy efficient than older models and can cast light with laserlike accuracy or great subtlety, giving you a choice of design effects not previously available.

Types of Installations to Choose From

Garden lights range in type from freestanding lamps and lanterns to ground-level path lights, recessed step lighting, floodlighting, and accent lighting. In regions that receive plentiful sunlight, small, pagoda-shaped, solar-powered walk lights require no wiring and can be placed at any sunny spot in the garden.

Lighting fixtures are made of all types of materials—plastic, cast brass, bronze, copper, steel, aluminum, granite, and stone. As a rule of thumb, outdoor lights should be inconspicuous—it is their effect, not their design, that should have the greatest impact on your garden. Of course, some fixtures are meant to be decorative, such as lampposts at the entrance to a path or lanterns to frame a gate. But ideally, your lighting plan will be designed so that, once installed, the fixtures will be virtually unnoticeable during the day. Placing fixtures high in trees is one way of hiding them while at the same time creating intriguing shadows and diffusing the light (box, opposite).

Bulbs of clear, white light can be used anywhere in the landscape. Color filters are usually reserved for illuminating water features; overuse of colored lights can create a garish effect. Yellow lights, however, are good for discouraging mosquitoes and other flying insects.

All fittings must be grounded for safety; and cables, above- or belowground, must be weather- and childproof. Of course, installations in wet spots and pools must use submersible fixtures.

Using Lighting to Create an Effect

To achieve the effect you want, think about what parts of the garden you wish to illuminate—not only what must be lit for safety reasons, but which structural accents, trees, or shrubs you want to highlight for aesthetic reasons. Take a powerful flashlight outdoors and shine it in various directions, playing up light and shadow to see where lighting will have the best impact. You will most likely have to use trial and error to find the right lighting scheme for your property. A simple change in the location, intensity, angle of beam, or the number of lights you use can dramatically affect the outcome.

For the most natural look, it is better to err on the side of caution; overlighting will give an artificial look to your plants. Instead of installing one or two powerful lights, use five or six low-wattage ones for a softer, warmer glow.

Plants to Light Up the Night

White blooms are particularly lovely at night. Under soft illumination, flowers like *Phlox paniculata* 'Mount Fuji', *Nicotiana alata*, and *Ipomoea alba* appear to float above their dark greenery. Plants with silver or variegated leaves also produce a beautiful effect under night lighting. Since white flowers tend to be more heavily scented than brightly colored ones, planting jasmine or lily of the valley along the edge of a pathway or along steps will provide a wonderful perfume to add to the pleasure of your nighttime garden strolls.

Artful Highlighting

Lights can be positioned to illuminate objects in your garden in dramatic or subtle ways, allowing you to showcase trees, shrubs, and ornaments. Whether you wish to highlight a particular plant feature or perhaps imitate moonlight, you can find a fixture and a mounting position to create the desired effect. Some of the methods shown here require a wall as a backdrop; others rely solely on clever positioning of the lights. Modern lighting fixtures are easily moved, making it simple to change the lighting scheme when desired.

Silhouetting: *If a small tree or shrub with attractive symmetry or unusual form is growing in front of a wall, you can feature it by placing a light behind the plant to show it in full relief.*

Shadow lighting: *Another treatment for a tree or shrub in front of a wall is to aim a light source at the plant from the front. The light will do double duty, both illuminating the plant and casting its form in shadow against the wall.*

Downlighting: *Mounting soft, diffuse lighting at least 20 feet up in a tree will allow the light to filter down, imitating a gentle moonlight effect. This can also be a particularly subtle and evocative way of illuminating ground cover or a walkway beneath trees.*

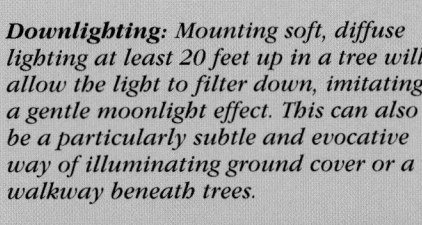

Uplighting: *Placing light sources in front of your trees and angling them upward highlights bark and foliage, accentuating textures and shapes.*

Crosslighting: *Placing fixtures high in trees so that beams of light cross each other will accentuate depth and texture, highlighting the three-dimensional forms of your plantings and softening shadows falling within the combined beams.*

CHAPTER THREE

Designing with Plants

By the time you sit down to choose the plants for your garden, you will already have a picture in your mind—and a plan on paper—based on the style of the garden you want, the purpose behind the design, the size of your property, and any plants already in the ground.

Once your basic garden plan has been determined, you will need to select plants whose forms, textures and colors complement your design and blend in with the surrounding landscape. In the Ashton, Maryland, garden at left, an archway adorned with a blush-pink tea rose leads the eye upward and beyond, into the surrounding woodland. Plantings of bright yellow-green Japanese barberry highlight the dark cerise blooms of a single antique rose, 'Belle de Crecy'.

On the following pages you'll learn how to make selections based on the entire panoply of plants—beginning with the garden's most stalwart members, the trees and shrubs. With an understanding of basic design principles and a palette of carefully chosen plants, you can create a garden that both unifies and enhances your entire landscape.

Laying Down the Framework

The structure of a garden is formed by its trees and shrubs. They serve as visual linchpins that hold the entire planting scheme together. Some may already be growing on your property and are sited just where you want them; others may need transplanting to fit into your design. In addition, you will unquestionably want to put in a number of new shrubs and trees—both deciduous and evergreen. If you select these plants carefully for shape, winter silhouette, and visual density, they will create shade, accent focal points, define spaces, provide backdrops, and screen out unwanted views.

But there is much more to garden design than just these architectural plants. Evergreen ground covers and small areas of lawn, for example, will help balance the design of your garden. Like trees and shrubs, they are permanent elements in the landscape. Vines also have a part to play: They can climb walls and fences or stand in for a shrub in a narrow space. Ornamental grasses, too, can partially fill the role of shrubs. While not as permanent as woody plants, they will provide interest for 10 or 11 months of the year. Tall varieties can be used as focal points, and smaller, weeping specimens are ideal for planting around a patio or a pond.

The most prominent of all these garden inhabitants are the trees that tower over the landscape and give your garden its fundamental character. Large trees that flourish in full sun not only bestow generous amounts of shade but also lend an air of maturity to even a newly installed garden. Because such trees link your property with the surrounding land, it's a good idea to choose species similar to those growing nearby, which are likely to be native or adapted types.

Deciduous trees are the best choice for providing shade next to the house. In summer their leafy canopies block out the sun and naturally cool your

This house and garden in Washington, D.C., are shielded from the scorching summer sun by midsize deciduous trees. Twelve river birches and two each of dogwood, redbud, and serviceberry create dappled light and ideal growing conditions for the ivy, sweet woodruff, wild ginger, and other shade-loving plants growing in this formal space.

home's interior; in winter the bare branches allow the sun to brighten and warm the rooms. To create shade for a bed or border, choose deciduous species with fine-textured foliage or an open habit that will cast dappled shade. Avoid trees with shallow roots, such as silver and Norway maples and American sweet gum, because they will outpace the roots of smaller plants in the competition for growing room, moisture, and nutrients. If space is limited, use small varieties of ornamental trees that won't overwhelm the house or the landscape or require constant pruning to restrain their size. Install cultivars of dogwood, Japanese maple, sassafras, birch, and hawthorn in groupings of three or more to screen an area from late afternoon sun.

Keep your intended location in mind when choosing trees. For example, don't plant fruiting types near a deck, patio, or walkway, where the dropping fruits will make a mess underfoot and may stain stonework, decks, or outdoor furniture.

Accent Plants

An easy way to create anchors or focal points is to plant individual accent trees and shrubs—also known as specimens. Some specimen trees and shrubs add color to a planting design with spring or summer flowers or brilliantly hued fall foliage, while others capture interest with such features as textured bark, twisted limbs, or distinctive leaves.

A tree with contorted or sculptural lines will take on a more dramatic appearance if it rises from a ground cover or a sward of green grass. The simplicity of the setting will allow you to focus on the strong lines of a trunk or spreading branches. To maintain this feeling of openness when planting a specimen tree in an island bed, surround it with plants that grow only a few feet tall.

You can also place two specimen plantings in such a way that they call attention to each other. Plant low-growing *Acer palmatum* 'Dissectum Atropurpureum', for example, in the same bed with *Cedrus atlantica* 'Glauca' (Atlas cedar). In winter, the weeping leafless branches of the maple will set off the cedar's pale bluish green needles.

An accent tree can also be used as a focal point in front of an evergreen hedge or a fence or to soften a corner of the house. But take care not to overwhelm the scene with an unusually large or excessively showy selection. Your accent tree should match the scale of its surroundings.

Flowering Sargent cherries and blue pansies are among the plants that provide springtime color in this Charlottesville, Virginia, garden. Rounded boxwood, the long horizontal line of the wall, and garden steps linking the upper and lower gardens make a striking, year-round composition.

TREE AND SHRUB SHAPES

Columnar Plants	Type/Growth Pattern	Height	Zones
Acer platanoides 'Columnare' (Norway maple)	fast-growing deciduous tree	40-50 ft.	4-9
Acer rubrum 'Columnare' (red maple)	fast-growing deciduous tree	40-50 ft.	3-7
Ginkgo biloba 'Princeton Sentry' (maidenhair-tree)	slow-growing deciduous tree	50 ft.	4-8
Malus 'Sentinel' (crab apple)	fast-growing deciduous flowering/fruiting tree	15-20 ft.	4-8
Pinus sylvestris 'Fastigiata' (Scotch pine)	fast-growing needled evergreen tree	25-40 ft.	2-8
Rhamnus frangula 'Columnaris' (alder buckthorn)	fast-growing deciduous flowering/fruiting shrub	12 ft.	2-8

Pyramidal Plants	Type/Growth Pattern	Height	Zones
Oxydendrum arboreum (sourwood)	slow-growing deciduous flowering tree	25-30 ft.	5-9
Pseudolarix kaempferi (golden larch)	slow-growing needled deciduous conifer	30-50 ft.	6-8
Quercus palustris (pin oak)	fast-growing deciduous tree	50-80 ft.	2-9
Sciadopitys verticillata (Japanese umbrella pine)	slow-growing needled evergreen tree	40-80 ft.	4-8
Thuja occidentalis 'Pyramidalis' (American arborvitae)	moderate-growing evergreen shrub	10-20 ft.	3-8

Fan/Vase Plants	Type/Growth Pattern	Height	Zones
Amelanchier canadensis (shadblow serviceberry)	fast-growing deciduous flowering/fruiting tree	6-20 ft.	4-9
Cercis (redbud)	moderate-growing deciduous flowering tree	20-30 ft.	4-9
Magnolia x *soulangiana* (saucer magnolia)	moderate-growing deciduous flowering/fruiting tree	20-30 ft.	4-9
Prunus x *blireiana* (blireiana plum)	moderate-growing deciduous flowering tree	25 ft.	5-8
Salix matsudana 'Tortuosa' (dragon-claw willow)	moderate-growing deciduous tree	35 ft.	4-9

Weeping/Arching Plants	Type/Growth Pattern	Height	Zones
Buddleia alternifolia/ *B. davidii* (butterfly bush)	fast-growing deciduous flowering shrub	6-10 ft.	5-9
Fagus sylvatica 'Pendula' (weeping beech)	moderate-growing deciduous tree	40 ft.	4-7
Forsythia x *intermedia* 'Spring Glory' (golden-bells)	fast-growing deciduous flowering shrub	6 ft.	5-9
Pyrus salicifolia 'Pendula' (willow-leaved pear)	moderate-growing deciduous flowering tree	25 ft.	5-7
Tsuga canadensis 'Pendula' (Canada hemlock)	slow-growing needled evergreen tree	20 ft.	2-8

Broad-Spreading Plants	Type/Growth Pattern	Height	Zones
Aesculus parviflora (bottlebrush buckeye)	fast-growing deciduous flowering shrub	15 ft.	4-8
Castanea mollissima (Chinese chestnut)	moderate-growing deciduous tree	30-60 ft.	4-9
Cephalotaxus harringtonia (Japanese plum yew)	slow-growing needled evergreen shrub	20 ft.	6-9
Crataegus x *mordenensis* 'Toba' (hawthorn)	fast-growing deciduous flowering/fruiting tree	25 ft.	4-9
Photinia x *fraseri* (Fraser photinia)	fast-growing evergreen flowering/fruiting shrub	10-15 ft.	8-9

Rounded Plants	Type/Growth Pattern	Height	Zones
Aesculus x *carnea* 'Briotii' (red horse chestnut)	slow-growing deciduous tree	40 ft.	3-7
Amelanchier arborea (downy serviceberry)	moderate-growing deciduous flowering/fruiting tree	20 ft.	4-9
Buxus sempervirens (common boxwood)	slow-growing evergreen shrub	15 ft.	5-8
Chaenomeles speciosa (flowering quince)	medium-growing deciduous flowering/fruiting shrub	2-10 ft.	4-8
Malus 'Coralburst'; *M.* 'Snowdrift' (crab apple)	moderate-growing flowering/fruiting tree	8-20 ft.	3-8
Raphiolepis indica (Indian hawthorn)	fast-growing evergreen flowering/fruiting shrub	5 ft.	9-10

Plant Features as Accents

When trees with fine and feathery foliage are sited alongside trees bearing large, bold leaves, they create a pleasing contrast, adding variety and texture to beds of massed plantings. Tree foliage comes in many shapes, sizes, and textures, including the heart-shaped leaves of *Cercis canadensis* 'Forest Pansy' (eastern redbud), the fan-shaped leaves of maidenhair-tree, and the large compound leaves of *Aesculus parviflora* (bottlebrush buckeye). For gracefully long leaves, look to sourwood. If you want foliage of a finer texture, consider the feathery foliage of *Sambucus racemosa* 'Plumosa Aurea' (European red elder), threadleaf Japanese maple, and evergreens such as *Chamaecyparis* (false cypress) and Atlas cedar.

Flowering and fruiting ornamentals provide double pleasure. In the spring or summer they produce lovely blooms, and in the fall, colorful foliage and fruits. Among the best examples are two trees, Washington hawthorn and *Prunus maackii* (Amur chokecherry), and several shrubs, including shadblow and *Viburnum dilatatum* (linden viburnum). You can get the same effect with a number of plants that may be shaped as either shrubs or small trees: kousa dogwood, *Sorbus alnifolia* (Korean mountain ash), golden-rain tree, *Stranvaesia davidiana* (Chinese stranvaesia), pomegranate, and *Prunus* x *blireiana* (blireiana plum).

Shrubs that produce both showy flowers and strikingly colored leaves include *Pieris japonica* 'Red Mill', *Nandina domestica* 'Nana Purpurea', Oregon grape, and witch alder. These plants can be chosen to harmonize or contrast with the house trim or a facade of brick or stained wood siding. If nestled against a backdrop of evergreen plantings, they will stand out even more dramatically.

Some deciduous trees and shrubs continue to provide interest in the winter with shaggy, mottled, corky, or richly colored bark or with gnarled, twisted, knotted, or multiple trunks or branches. Those with the most striking bark are 'Heritage' river birch, *Acer palmatum* 'Senkaki' (coral bark maple), Amur chokecherry, *Salix alba* 'Britzensis' (coral bark willow), *Pinus bungeana* (lace-bark

Perfuming the air with their delicate flowers, Lonicera heckrottii (goldflame honeysuckle) and Trachelospermum jasminoides (star jasmine) climb an arbor in Columbia, South Carolina. The jasmines were planted against the adjoining fence—a good 10 feet away on either side of the arbor—and have worked their way onto the support over the years.

pine), *Platanus occidentalis* (eastern sycamore), and Amur cork tree. The eastern sycamore has an intriguingly shaped trunk, as does *Crataegus* x *mordenensis* 'Toba' (hawthorn). And *Corylus avellana* 'Contorta' (Harry Lauder's walking stick) grows strikingly twisted branches.

Focusing on Evergreens

A planting design that features the shapes, textures, and colors of evergreen trees and shrubs will ensure year-round structural interest. But be careful not to overuse evergreens, which can give a dark, heavy feel to your garden. It's best to strike a balance between the weight of evergreens and the airiness of deciduous ornamentals.

Evergreens range in shape from miniature cones to tall pyramids, from neat mounds to weeping giants. Their foliage also varies dramatically: It may be needled or broad-leaved, with needle tex-tures ranging from soft and feathery to coarse and stiff, from glossy and prickly to smooth and silky. Broad-leaved varieties might be long and droop-ing, small and round, or narrow and pointed. Col-ors run the gamut from palest to darkest green, as well as blue-green, blue-gray, silvery blue, or varie-gated yellow and green or cream and green.

Some evergreen shapes and foliage textures are suited to particular landscape styles. For example, the loose, irregular forms of broad-leaved rhodo-dendrons, *Pieris japonica*, and mountain laurel go well in a woodland garden or a shaded formal gar-den. The stiff, pyramidal shape of Colorado blue spruce, the cone-shaped *Sciadopitys verticillata* (Japanese umbrella pine), and the almost perfectly rounded littleleaf boxwood add formality to a de-sign. The rangy shapes of x *Cupressocyparis ley-landii* (Leyland cypress) and deodar cedar are at home in an informal garden, while the irregular but compact hinoki false cypress and Atlas cedar are equally suited to a formal or an informal design.

Dwarf evergreens are good choices for a rock garden, and can give shape and weight to any loose arrangement of foliage and flowers. Good choices include *Ilex cornuta* 'Carissa', *Ilex crenata*, *Picea abies* 'Nidiformis', *Picea glauca* 'Conica', *Rhododendron* 'Moonstone' and *R.* 'Ramapo', and *Taxus baccata* 'Repandens'. For vertical accents, plant taller evergreen varieties such as cedar, English holly, bull bay, Norway spruce, and Douglas fir. They will stand out dramatically when surrounded by low or round shapes.

Plants for Screening

Hedges are the workhorses of the garden. They not only serve as stately backdrops for herbaceous borders, they can also provide privacy, block undesirable views, and muffle street noises. They can direct the flow of traffic in a garden and lead the eye toward a focal point. They can be planted to form intimate, enclosed garden rooms, and they can give structure to a flat, featureless expanse of lawn. A row of shrubs or trees can also act as a windbreak, keeping the house and garden warmer. When planted near a vegetable garden, a windbreak can create a warmer microclimate, shielding tender young plants and extending the growing season.

When you buy trees and shrubs for hedges or windbreaks, keep in mind both aesthetics and utility. If you wish to complement a formal garden design, choose stiff varieties or those that lend themselves to close clipping for a hedge; floppy or arched varieties are best for an informal garden. And be sure the mature size of the varieties you choose is appropriate for the location.

You can manipulate the sense of space on your property through the height of your hedges: Masses of tall, dense evergreens will make an area look smaller; a hedge of low shrubs or open and airy deciduous trees will create an expansive effect.

A hedge of fast-growing evergreens will screen an unsightly view or object. A more natural-looking alternative, however, would be to install a mixed selection of evergreens in clumps. To block unwelcome sightlines projecting from your neighbors' upper windows, consider a combination of tall columnar or pyramidal evergreens and twiggy deciduous trees such as hornbeam or *Pyrus calleryana* (Callery pear), whose high canopies will put the screening where you most need it.

If your property is large and deep, you can form a multilayered screen by planting tall trees behind lower-growing shrubs, or slow-growing evergreens on the boundary and fast-growing deciduous trees

inside. When the purpose of a hedge is to delineate property lines without producing a closed-in look, deciduous shrubs can be very effective. Make sure, however, that such an installation fits in with the garden's overall design. To create a barrier that keeps your pets in and those of your neighbors out, plant fruiting shrubs that bear thorns or prickly leaves, such as barberry, hawthorn, rose, firethorn, or holly. These plants have the added benefit of providing food for wildlife.

Vines

The fastest way to block an ugly view or create a sense of privacy is to install a fence or trellis and grow a perennial vine on it. This almost instant barrier makes a good alternative to the dense shade and screening offered by a mid-size hedge. It can also enclose a space that is too small or narrow for trees or shrubs. Few vines, however, are evergreen, and many deciduous ones die back or need cutting back annually. And some varieties, such as trumpet vine, yellow jessamine, *Akebia quinata* (five-leaf akebia), *Actinidia chinensis* (kiwi fruit), and Japanese wisteria, are such sturdy, heavy growers they need pruning regularly to keep them from getting out of hand or even pulling down the structure they are growing on.

Most of these vines must be trained to climb a support, or be secured to it with wire or twine. Other fast growers, such as clematis, climbing hydrangea, cross-vine, *Polygonum aubertii* (China fleece vine), and star jasmine, twine and grip with tendrils. Vines that climb with extreme ease and cling to any vertical surface with suction roots include *Hedera colchica* 'Dentata' (Persian ivy), Boston ivy, Virginia creeper, *Euonymus fortunei* (winter creeper), and *Ficus pumila* (climbing fig).

Ornamental Grasses

With their graceful foliage and fluffy plumes, perennial ornamental grasses add form and texture to the landscape for most of the year. And their nodding seed heads and rustling leaves provide appealing sound and movement during the winter, when most of the garden is in the doldrums. Varieties range in height from 6 inches to 14 feet. The shorter varieties, such as *Carex morrowii* 'Aurea Variegata' (variegated Japanese sedge), *Arrhenatherum elatius* var. *bulbosum* (bulbous oat grass), *Festuca amethystina* (large blue fescue), and *Hakonechloa macra* 'Aureola' (golden variegated hakonechloa), make striking

EVERGREEN SHRUBS AND TREES
Abelia x *grandiflora* (glossy abelia)
Berberis julianae (wintergreen barberry)
Chamaecyparis lawsoniana 'Allumii' (Port Orford cedar)
x *Cupressocyparis leylandii* (Leyland cypress)
Euonymus alata (winged spindle tree)
Ilex x *altaclarensis* 'Wilsonii' (altaclara holly)
Ilex aquifolium (English holly)
Ilex x *attenuata* 'Fosteri' (Foster holly)
Juniperus chinensis (Chinese juniper)
Juniperus occidentalis (Sierra juniper)
Juniperus virginiana 'Skyrocket' (red cedar)
Ligustrum japonicum (waxleaf privet)
Pittosporum (pittosporum)
Prunus caroliniana 'Bright 'n' Tight' (Carolina cherry laurel)
Taxus (yew)

DECIDUOUS SHRUBS AND TREES
Carpinus betulus (European hornbeam)
Forsythia (golden-bells)
Viburnum (arrowwood)

VINES
Clematis armandii (Armand clematis)
Gelsemium sempervirens (yellow jasmine)
Hydrangea anomala ssp. *petiolaris* (climbing hydrangea)
Jasminum mesnyi (primrose jasmine)
Jasminum nudiflorum (winter jasmine)
Lonicera sempervirens (trumpet honeysuckle)
Rosa 'Cécile Brunner' (rose)
Wisteria (wisteria)

Capitalizing on Ornamental Grasses

Most ornamental grasses need not be divided for propagation; they are fast spreading or self-seeding. But like many other herbaceous perennials, they may start to look straggly and die off in the center after years of growth. When they do, it's time to divide them. Do this in early fall so the plants can reestablish themselves before the onslaught of winter; otherwise, wait until midspring.

There are many creative uses for divided clumps. Install low- to mid-height grasses to control erosion on a slope, to replace a lawn, or to screen the base of a deck. They also add diversity in sunny herbaceous borders.

Use medium and tall varieties in place of shrubs to create a hedge. Where it may cost a small fortune to edge a sizable property with shrubs or trees, tall perennial grasses are an inexpensive and fast-growing alternative.

If space is limited, you can plant a compact, slow-growing variety, such as *Miscanthus sinensis* 'Gracillimus' (maiden grass), *Carex morrowii* 'Aurea Variegata' (variegated Japanese sedge), or *Hakonechloa macra* 'Aureola' (golden variegated hakonechloa).

Consider planting some of the smaller grass varieties in containers so they can decorate your front entrance, deck, or patio. To keep the roots from freezing in extremely cold weather, you may have to overwinter the pots in a garage or cool basement.

---

combinations when planted as edging companions to low-growing creeping ground covers.

Among those grasses that grow to a middle height are *Pennisetum alopecuroides* (fountain grass), *Calamagrostis acutiflora* 'Stricta' (feather reed grass), *Cortaderia selloana* 'Pumila' (dwarf pampas grass), and *Miscanthus sinensis* 'Purpurascens'. The taller grasses, which can be planted as a privacy screen, include *Cortaderia selloana* (pampas grass), *Miscanthus sinensis* (eulalia), and *Erianthus ravennae* (Ravenna grass).

The leaf colors of most ornamental grasses range from creamy yellow to bright green. Some types have variegated hues, and others—including such low-growing species and cultivars as *Festuca ovina* var. *glauca* (blue fescue), *Imperata cylindrica* 'Red Baron' (Japanese blood grass), *Ophiopogon planiscapus* 'Nigrescens' (black mondo grass), and *Carex elata* 'Bowles' Golden' (Bowles' golden sedge)—are distinctively colored.

Ornamental grasses are not only visually appealing but also desirable as fast-growing plants with minimal cultural requirements. In most regions they require no watering or fertilizing and will grow in poor soils. However, perennial varieties will need cutting back once a year in very early spring, before they start to send up new shoots.

Although ornamental grasses spread by root systems and seeds, they are easy to control. Simply remove the young volunteers, taking care to remove all roots, as soon as they germinate in late summer or the following spring.

Lawns and Meadows

A lawn—even a small one—can be an asset to a garden. It will set off the house and separate the beds from the borders and the driveway. It will serve as a tranquil foil for the diversity of surrounding plants and garden elements. And it can provide a place for relaxation and play. Turf grass, however, needs constant attention. So you might want to consider replacing part of your lawn with an evergreen ground cover or converting some of it to a sizable island bed planted with a combination of small trees, shrubbery, and ground covers.

One of the most colorful and carefree kinds of open expanses is one that has been converted from a lawn into a wildflower meadow. Planted with native annuals and perennials, it requires no feeding or watering and need be mowed only once a year. It also provides food and shelter for butterflies, bees, and beneficial insects. In putting in a meadow, you will want to plant a variety of native flowers. Perennial wildflowers that are good in a wide variety of meadow environments include goldenrod, milkweed, aster, rudbeckia, *Echinacea purpurea* (purple coneflower), tansy, sunflower, yarrow, *Oenothera caespitosa* (twisted evening primrose), *Ranunculus* (buttercup), oxeye daisy, wild bergamot, *Phlox paniculata* (garden phlox), and *Liatris* (gay-feather). Although annual or biennial wildflowers such as *Centaurea cyanus* (cornflower) and Queen Anne's lace die at the end of

The weeping green foliage of Pennisetum alopecuroides (fountain grass) softens the lines of the stonework and creates an intimate seating area in this garden near Baltimore. In the background, the golden foliage of Calamagrostis acutiflora 'Stricta' (feather reed grass) adds warmth and privacy to the scene.

their flowering season, they also work well in a carefree meadow environment. Because they self-seed prolifically, they will return year after year with almost the same certainty as perennials.

A Ground-Cover Carpet

Offering dense growth, year-round color, and interesting texture, ground covers make a fine alternative to turf grass. They can also define, separate, or unify portions of the landscape. When choosing a ground cover to replace an area of lawn, look for a type that meets your needs for speed of growth, ability to withstand light foot traffic, tolerance for sun or shade, and seasonal flower or foliage colors.

Ground covers that will accept moderate foot traffic include *Thymus praecox* (creeping thyme), wintergreen, ivy, winter creeper, bearberry, *Ajuga reptans,* and periwinkle. For shady areas, choose pachysandra, *Chrysogonum virginianum* (gold-enstar), *Lamium maculatum* (spotted dead nettle), *Potentilla verna* (spring cinquefoil), or *Ophiopogon* (lilyturf). Ground covers that spread quickly in full sun and are effective in controlling erosion on a slope include *Verbena peruviana* (Peruvian verbena), *Hypericum calycinum* (creeping St.-John's-wort), *Cerastium tomentosum* (snow-in-summer), *and Chamaemelum nobile* (Roman chamomile). One of the best ground covers to grow in moist or wet ground, whether sunny or shady, is *Lysimachia nummularia* (loosestrife). If the soil is moist and well drained, plant Corsican mint.

Annuals for Accent

Among the many reasons to grow annuals—length of bloom period, ease of care, minimal expense—perhaps the most compelling is that you can choose from an enormous variety of colors. During their short life spans, annuals produce seed so rapidly that hybridizers have been able to tinker with them endlessly, introducing new colors far more quickly than is possible with other types of plants.

The temporary nature of annuals also allows you to experiment with compositions and color schemes that are more daring than any you might be willing to undertake with your more permanent plantings. You can let your imagination run wild with the lavish selection of annuals that are available for your garden.

The Mixed Border

Annuals bring a vitality to the mixed border. If your garden is newly planted, their colors and shapes can supply eye-catching contrasts and harmonies during the time it takes for perennials and shrubs to fill out and mature. For example, soft pink *Diascia barberae* and a pale blue cultivar of *Lobelia erinus* contrast soothingly with the large, lustrous dark green leaves of Oregon grape or the simple blue-green to gray-green foliage of *Daphne mezereum.* Tall pink *Cleome hasslerana* can supply height at the back of the border and pull the composition together by repeating tints of pink.

If it's bold color you like, try yellow and crimson 'Double Madame Butterfly' snapdragons with a smattering of 'Giant Double Mixed' zinnias in red, scarlet, orange, and golden yellow. Low-growing clusters of white *Iberis umbellata* nestled among the fiery hues will help temper them.

Other annuals combine marvelous color with a flower shape so distinctive that they are worthy of a spot in the most prominent border. Perfectly at home among showy perennials are the jewel-like red-orange blooms of *Emilia javanica,* which look like miniature paintbrushes atop wiry 2-foot

Blazing red Salvia splendens 'Hot Shot' sizzles around 'Ultra White Madness' petunias, deep purple Salvia farinacea 'Rhea', and the coarse foliage of rose daphne (right), igniting this Pacific Northwest garden with hot color.

'Raspberry Rose' and 'Jolly Joker' pansies and pink and peach 'Oregon Rainbow' Iceland poppies (below) brighten the front of this mixed border in Oregon. Pink and creamy white spires of Digitalis purpurea 'Excelsior' and ruby blooms of 'Red Charm' peony are shaded by a backdrop of white, yellow, and salmon azaleas.

stems; the quill-petaled, urn-shaped, rose red flowers of *Cirsium japonicum,* which hover 2 feet above dark green spiny leaves; and the enormous sunburst-shaped pink, lavender, or white flower clusters of cleome, which float on 3- to 4-foot stems. When designing with such striking flowers, plant each species together in large groups, weaving in drifts of gray-leaved plants such as *Stachys byzantina* (lamb's ears), *Artemisia, Senecio,* and *Santolina* to soften the color scheme.

Some annuals with distinctive blooms have forms that are equally elegant. Consider *Lavatera trimestris* (rose mallow), which grows 3 feet tall and wide. Its densely branching stems, large, cup-shaped pink or white flowers, and lower leaves that resemble those of a maple blend in effortlessly with border regulars such as iris, lady's-mantle, bergenia, and old-fashioned shrub roses. In a border with big, downy, early-summer-blooming peonies, rose mallow can carry the flower show from midsummer to early fall.

Annuals that have sparse foliage are at their best when mated with plants that have abundant leaves. Stiff stands of easy-to-grow *Verbena bonariensis,* with its pale lilac-colored flat-topped blooms, pair well with lemon yellow daylilies, whose slender,

Four beds filled with pansies—yellow 'Crown Cream', purple 'Blue Perfection', and peach, red, and pink 'Imperial Antique Shades'— square off at the intersection of paths in a Virginia garden. Perennial orange 'Harvest Moon' Oriental poppies rise above the symmetrical arrangement.

arching leaves mask the strong but spindly stems of the verbena. The verbena offers summer color long after the perennial's petals have dropped. Simply pull up the stalks of the daylilies once they turn dry and brown, and leave the foliage intact to provide a green backdrop for the verbena.

The Annual Border

Simple borders composed of only a few judiciously chosen flowering plants often have the greatest impact. *Cuphea ignea,* an eye-catcher whose abundant scarlet cigar-shaped flowers have black-and-white tips resembling cigar ash, forms a compact foot-high mat of color; place it before soaring red-blooming cannas with their curled, wide-bladed leaves to create a pleasing contrast in form and a harmony of color. An ideal backdrop for this marriage would be a yellow-green hedge of *Philadelphus coronarius* 'Aureus' (mock orange) or tall, woody layers of fast-growing green-leaved *Spiraea prunifolia* (bridal wreath).

For a tall border with a tropical effect, try combining gold, yellow, and apricot cannas with the 5-foot stems of *Abelmoschus manihot* (sunset hibiscus), a Brazilian native whose large, fragile-looking flowers come in shades of pale to buttery yellow with maroon centers. To create a striking border in limited space, pair the red-plumed form of *Celosia cristata* (feather amaranth) with deep yellow marigolds and golden-hued calendulas. In back of the combination, plant a fountain of *Miscanthus sinensis* 'Zebrinus', a perennial ornamental grass whose 5- to 6-foot-tall arching, straplike leaves display horizontal bands of creamy yellow and green.

Color Massing

Probably the easiest way to make the most of annual color is to plant a solid mass of a single variety that has especially striking blossoms. Choose an area of your yard that you want to highlight, and plant enough of the annual variety to make a bold statement. Because dramatic shocks of color dominate the area in which they're placed, resist the temptation to repeat the bold planting all around your property—or else the sheer numbers of the one color will overwhelm the viewer and lose its impact.

No matter how stunning the hue of an individual bloom, however, a stretch of unbroken color tends to tire the eye. Masses of color look best in out-of-the-way settings seen briefly and from a distance. The far corner of your backyard or the side wall of your garage is ideal; a mass of color in such removed, even remote, locations comes as a pleasant surprise when the viewer's eye discovers it. And you can extend the pleasure for months by changing the planting as the growing season progresses—replacing an expanse of fading summer-blooming purple petunias, for instance, with the fall flowers of lemon yellow chrysanthemums.

Design Bedding

Compact, profusely blooming annuals are ideal for decorative plantings called design beds, where the creative range is limited only by the gardener's imagination. These plantings can be simple, composed of, say, deep yellow *Rudbeckia hirta* 'Double Gold' blooming behind neat, squat mounds of pink, white, and red 'Prince', 'Princess', and 'Gaiety' *Dianthus chinensis,* all planted in a free-form island in your lawn. Or the beds can be formal, tracing strict geometric lines or neatly defined shapes.

If you prefer the ornate, try fashioning a circle

Low-growing orange and russet nasturtiums and white candytuft edge an Oregon bed layered with red and pink zinnias and deep gold marigolds and capped by radiant yellow sunflowers. The hedge runs along the edge of the yard, hiding a busy road from view.

How to Keep Annuals Blooming All Season Long

Once an annual has formed seeds, its life cycle is over and the plant stops producing flowers. For this reason, you'll need to prune off spent flowers before they go to seed if you want your annuals to bloom continuously through the season. In addition, cutting back plants that have become tall and scraggly encourages new, leafy growth. Pruned stems usually form new flower buds within 2 to 3 weeks.

Cut main stems just above a leaf or pair of leaves *(left)*. The joint where the leaf or leaves emerge from the stem is the place from which side shoots will grow. Make a clean cut with pruning shears, removing about one-third or more of the stem. This will

stimulate branching and the production of new flowers throughout the summer *(right)*.

Salvia, zinnias, and most annuals with daisylike blooms take readily to this degree of pruning. Trailing and soft-stemmed annuals—such as nasturtiums, petunias, portulaca, and sweet alyssum—that have grown shabby-looking benefit from a more drastic treatment that removes all but a few inches of leafy stem. For annuals with decorative seedpods, such as love-in-a-mist, and those whose seed you plan to collect, stop cutting back at least 2 months before the first fall frost to give them time to mature.

bed divided into four equal pie-like slices of color by flagstone paving. Within the structured bed, plant scarlet geraniums in opposite quadrants and bright blue petunias in the other two; soften them by ringing the perimeter of the bed with the bronzy-leaved 'Early Splendor' cultivar of *Amaranthus tricolor* and by planting an outermost rim of silver *Senecio cineraria* (dusty-miller).

The fancier the bed's design, the more formal its appearance. Beds in the shapes of rectangles, circles, and half-moons can be any size that suits your property, but for a large-scale bed, avoid the overused combination of a solid block of one color edged with another color. A mass of blue ageratum skirted with pink wax begonias or yellow marigolds is rescued from the realm of the ordinary when clusters of other varieties that grow or can be trimmed to the same uniform height are interspersed among the rim plantings. Hybrid petunias in violet, blue, and yellow are easy-care annuals that respond well to trimming in such a design.

When planting an edging or a row in a formal design, situate your annuals so that you achieve a lush, unbroken line. Planted single file or on a straight grid, the row will be pocked with unsightly holes. Instead, arrange the plants in a zigzag, or for wider perimeters, position them in slanted, overlapping rows three, four, or five plants deep.

Less formal bedding designs reflect the planting patterns of a border: bands of color interwoven throughout the groupings of plants. A delightful annual bed for a somewhat dry spot in your yard might combine two popular annuals—yellow and white snapdragons and cream and peach-colored common nasturtiums—with the lesser known *Linaria maroccana* (Moroccan toadflax), whose blooms resemble small snapdragons, and lacy-leaved *Foeniculum vulgare* 'Purpureum' (bronze fennel). Choose white and yellow toadflax and group it near a mass of the snapdragons for a contrast in scale; repeat the pairing as space allows, placing the taller fennel in the middle of the bed and letting the nasturtiums wander throughout.

Multicolored Annuals

Among the most interesting annuals are those that display contrasting colors on a single bloom in zoned, striped, and spotted patterns. Pansies, for example, have been bred to produce symmetrical blotches, with as many as three colors on one flower. Some petunias have bicolored designs in red, purple, blue-violet, or pink with white stripes that look like the spokes of a wheel. The beautiful funnel-shaped flowers of *Salpiglossis sinuata*

(painted tongue) carry velvety swatches of purple, red, and brown with overtones of white, yellow, and pink, with prominent veining in dark, contrasting shades. The genus *Dianthus,* which includes sweet William and *D. chinensis* (China pink), comprises virtually all types of variegation. In one prevalent type, called picotee, petals sport a thin outer margin in a color that contrasts with the rest of the blossom. Impatiens, wax begonia, and *Nicotiana alata* hybrids are just a few of the many annuals that can have picotee markings.

An ideal plant to blend with multicolored flowers is *Cynoglossum amabile* (Chinese forget-me-not), renowned for its exquisite clear blue color. For early-spring display in Zones 7 through 10, sow Chinese forget-me-nots in late summer and early fall with creamy yellow, dusty pink, and purplish many-toned blooms of 'Imperial Antique Shades' pansies. Add the delicate pastels of the multicolored *Papaver rhoeas* 'Mother of Pearl' (corn poppy); each bloom boasts shades of gray, lilac, peach, and palest pink that blend together like a parfait. For summer bloom in cooler areas, sow Chinese forget-me-nots in early spring with hybrid verbena 'Peaches and Cream' and apricot, peach, lavender, and salmon *Clarkia amoena* (farewell-to-spring), which features speckled and picotee markings.

In this northern California garden, the pink blossoms of the shrub rose 'Bonica' reconcile the potentially clashing colors of two annual vines—hyacinth bean, with its flat, red-violet seedpods, and common morning-glory, with blue-violet trumpet-shaped flowers.

In this Missouri border, yellow 'Castle Series' celosia spotlights the fuchsia and red blooms of 'Cut and Come Again' zinnias and round 'Globosa Mix' gomphrena. Pale blue 'Belladonna' delphiniums contrast with orange butterfly weed in a composition that spans the spectrum.

Annuals with Multicolored Blooms

Abelmoschus spp.
(abelmoschus)
Agrostemma githago
(corn cockle)
Alcea rosea
(hollyhock)
Antirrhinum majus
(snapdragon)
Arctotis stoechadifolia
(African daisy)
Callistephus chinensis
(China aster)
Chrysanthemum carinatum
(chrysanthemum)
Clarkia amoena
(farewell-to-spring)
Cosmos bipinnatus
(cosmos)
Dahlia hybrids
(dahlia)
Dianthus barbatus
(sweet William)
Dianthus chinensis
(China pink)
Digitalis spp.
(foxglove)
Gazania rigens
(treasure flower)
Impatiens spp.
(impatiens)
Layia platyglossa
(tidytips)
Linaria maroccana
(Moroccan toadflax)
Lobelia erinus
(lobelia)
Mimulus x *hybridus*
(monkey flower)
Mirabilis jalapa
(four-o'clock)
Nemesia strumosa
(nemesia)
Nemophila menziesii
'Pennie Black'
(baby-blue-eyes)
Papaver rhoeas
(corn poppy)
Pelargonium spp.
(geranium)
Petunia x *hybrida*
(petunia)
Rudbeckia hirta
'Gloriosa Daisy'
(gloriosa daisy)
Salpiglossis sinuata
(painted tongue)
Tropaeolum spp.
(nasturtium)
Viola spp.
(pansy)

Note: The abbreviation "spp." stands for the plural of "species"; where used in lists it means that many, but not all, of the species in a genus meet the criterion of the list.

Alcea rosea (hollyhock)

Heat-Tolerant Annuals

Annuals are unequaled when it comes to landscaping around paved driveways, brick paths, stone terraces, concrete walls, and a variety of other hard or rocky surfaces, known collectively as hardscapes. Hardscapes pose special challenges for plants growing close to them. For one thing, they absorb and radiate heat: On a sunny summer day a blacktopped driveway or stuccoed wall can significantly raise the temperature in the immediate area, so anything planted nearby must be reliably heat tolerant. Also, soil that is close to buildings or pavement may contain high levels of minerals deposited by water that has first washed over these surfaces. And driveways are sources of chemical pollution in the form of oily runoff and vehicle exhaust fumes.

Fortunately, there are many heat-loving, poor-soil-tolerant annuals that flourish unfazed in these locales. In addition, the microclimates created by hardscapes often enable you to grow more kinds of plants than would otherwise be possible under the normal conditions of your property. The warm environment created by a stone patio with a southern exposure, for example, might allow tender annuals to do well in a region where summers are short and cool.

Assessing Your Hardscapes

When planning any garden, you'll get the best results if you consider the conditions of the site and choose plants that are best suited to them. This is especially true of hardscape locations, which may be dramatically affected by patterns of light and shade, heat, and traffic. Start by noting how many hours of sunlight the site receives. Be aware that the amount may vary widely from one spot to the next. That's because vertical hardscapes such as walls and buildings can block light, forming pools of shade in the midst of sun. Bear in mind, too, that the heat given off by pavement or other hardscape surfaces will cause the sur-

Sweet alyssum, purple pansies, silver dusty-miller, and white geraniums fill the beds of this California garden in the spring. The alyssum guards the pansies from contact with heat-retaining gravel and also softens the straight lines and sharp corners created by the bricks. Pink geraniums make a grand focal point in the stone planter.

Undaunted by a sultry Virginia summer, purple blooms of verbena overflow their raised planter. The dry heat produced by the bricks enclosing the bed is increased by a brick sidewalk beneath. But with regular watering the verbena—descended from plants native to the Americas—is thriving.

rounding soil to dry out faster than normal. In addition, walls can keep rainfall from reaching the ground adjacent to them. Plan on watering plants in these areas more often, and for added insurance, use annuals that are especially drought resistant. A thick layer of mulch will also help keep the soil cool and moist. For plants that prefer the conditions around your hardscapes, check the encyclopedia that begins on page on 608.

Last, look at the size and use patterns of walkways and driveways. Broad paths and lightly used hardscapes have the room to accommodate annuals that sprawl over their borders. On the other hand, narrow, heavily traveled hardscapes—the paths to back or side doors, for instance—are best edged with upright plants that won't spill onto the walkway and get trampled. Varieties of *Tagetes* (marigold), *Begonia* (wax begonia), and *Senecio* (dusty-miller) are just a few candidates for tight situations. The list at right features upright plants as well as plants with a sprawling habit.

Choosing the Right Plants

Bare hardscapes seem to cry out for the beauty annuals can bring. Grow the plants in beds and borders along patios, terraces, and decks. If space is narrow, try planting a mixed-color variety of a bushy annual such as *Salvia splendens* (sage) or *Zinnia elegans* (common zinnia) that will grow 8 to 12 inches tall. If you have room for a wide swath of color, place low-growing, compact plants such as *Gazania* species and *Ageratum houstonianum* (flossflower) along the edges of the hardscape and larger accent plants—*Zinnia angustifolia* (narrowleaf zinnia) or *Kochia scoparia* (burning bush), for example—behind them.

You need not restrict the beauty to the perimeter of your hardscape. For a weed-inhibiting carpet of blossoms in the midst of a sunny patio where foot traffic is light, plant *Portulaca grandiflora* (moss rose) and *Lobularia maritima* (sweet alyssum) between the pavers. Just remove any grass or weeds, and then fill the spaces with a fast-draining soil that contains 1 part gardener's sand for every 2 parts topsoil. Sow seeds in the soil or set out seedlings, and water lightly. And in your search for hardscape plants, don't overlook herbs. Many, such as basil and sweet marjoram, will like the hot, dry microclimate furnished by sunny hardscapes.

On sloping terrain alongside a flight of stone or

concrete steps, plant annuals that are naturally sprawling. They will drape gracefully on the incline, whereas more-upright species will tend to lean uphill or downhill in their efforts to resist gravity. Raised flower beds with sides of brick or other stonework are also pretty when dressed with these trailing plants to soften their edges.

If a wall runs beside your driveway, patio, or walk, with a narrow strip of land separating the two hard surfaces, try planting *Cobaea scandens* (cup-and-saucer vine) or *Ipomoea* species (morning-glory) along the wall's base. These robust climbers should form lush upper growth in a relatively short period of time.

Like other hardscapes, a rock garden creates a special microclimate, since its stones absorb heat and block precipitation and wind. Rocks also help maintain moisture in the soil below them by shading it from the sun—and by returning water to the soil at night as humidity condenses on their cool surfaces and seeps into the ground. For these

reasons, well-chosen plants in rock gardens often require little maintenance.

In general, the most appealing rock gardens include a combination of small, mounded plants and sprawlers that can be trained over the edges of the rocks, brightening the surfaces with their flowers and foliage. Petite flowering annuals are well suited to the task because their small roots adapt to the confined spaces between stones and to the shallow soil on rocky outcrops. Also, they are ideal for providing color and interest in the hot season, when many perennials fade.

Spreading *Phlox drummondii* (annual phlox), brightly colored *Brachycome iberidifolia* (Swan River daisy), and dwarf varieties of *Cheiranthus cheiri* (English wallflower) are just a few annuals that thrive in sunny rock gardens. If your site is partially shaded, try snapdragon-like *Collinsia heterophylla* (Chinese houses) or delicate *Exacum affine* (German violet). The lee side of a partially shaded rock may be moist and chilly enough

Nestled between pavers on a southern Pennsylvania patio, Portulaca grandiflora (moss rose) self-sows from year to year. Blooms stay open through the day, providing maximum beauty in a cheerful mix of bright colors that hug the ground at heights of about 6 inches. The flowers do tend to attract bees, so barefooted visitors should beware.

to let cool-loving *Iberis* species (candytuft) and *Nemophila menziesii* (baby-blue-eyes) bloom all summer long.

If you have a naturally rocky area on your property, try planting it with annual wildflowers that are native to your locale or from regions with comparable climates. Natives often self-sow, and they also blend well with the other aspects of the landscape where they evolved. Talk to your local Cooperative Extension Service or check catalogs that sell seeds and young plants specifically for your region to find the right annual wildflowers for your rock garden.

To plant rock-garden annuals, create pockets of well-draining soil, using 2 parts topsoil to 1 part gardener's sand. If the site is partially shaded and you're installing plants that prefer fertile soil, add 1 part compost or leaf mold and 1 part peat moss to the mix as well. Either sow seeds or transplant seedlings into the spaces. Once the seedlings are a few inches high, spread a mulch of shredded bark around them to keep the soil cool and moist.

Heat-loving annuals add a touch of softness to the stone surfaces in a walled niche in Connecticut (above). Red-violet Petunia integrifolia surrounds the base of the center sculpture, while tall white Nicotiana alata, which self-sows from year to year, brightens the entire space.

Petite yellow Dahlberg daisies, open-faced Gaillardia aristata 'Burgundy', spiky Salvia coccinea 'Lady in Red', and orange California poppies flourish through the summer in the rocky Missouri garden at left. The limestone chunks bordering the raised bed prevent rainwater from draining through the soil too quickly.

149

The Many Styles of Perennial Gardens

This Pennsylvania garden uses the symmetry of an arbor to impose formality on its plantings of dark violet Salvia x superba, pale violet Nepeta, pink Dianthus deltoides, and blue oat grass. The bench provides an eye-level focal point against the backdrop of the towering hedge.

As you search for an appropriate style for your perennial garden, the possibilities will be almost endless. You might wish to recreate all or part of a garden fondly remembered from childhood, or one seen on a memorable vacation. Your inspiration might come from a fictional garden in a favorite novel, or from a particular time in history: perhaps the plantation gardens of the South, the wildflower meadows of Texas, the mission gardens of California, or the prairie landscapes of the Midwest. Or your model garden could have a horticultural theme—a rock garden, a cutting garden, and a shade garden are examples.

Be careful not to design a garden that will be too difficult for you to construct, plant, and take care of. A 200-foot double border—one that flanks both sides of a walkway or driveway—on an English country estate is magnificent to see, but it takes hundreds of hours, great professional expertise, and a lot of money to install the border and maintain it in peak condition. Similarly, a serene Japanese garden you may once have admired most likely required major earth working, backbreaking placement of stones, and meticulous pruning of trees and shrubs to achieve its stylistic simplicity and grace.

Garden Ideas to Borrow

Countless gardeners before you have wrestled with making gardens, and their successes—the

results of their hard work and imaginations—are evident in the pages of gardening books and magazines. These are great resources when it comes time to plan your own garden. You can also look for ideas in the gardens of friends and neighbors, and in public gardens, which are useful to study because they give a true measure of how well specific plants will grow in your area.

Use these gardens for inspiration—to borrow an idea or two or mix and match a few plant combinations—but resist the urge to copy them plant for plant. Tempting as it might be to simply duplicate a planting that appeals to you, even if you were to succeed at recreating one of these elaborate productions, you would rob your garden of its own character and deprive yourself of the satisfaction of creating something unique.

Nor is it necessary to recreate a whole landscape to capture its essence. Some pairings of columbine and Solomon's-seal in your own shady corner might be just enough to remind you of the plantings along a woodland path. Likewise, a single mature lavender plant in a terra-cotta container placed just so on the patio might be all that is necessary to conjure up the appealing look of an entrance to a French country inn.

Choosing Your Design Framework

One thing you will want to decide on from looking at other gardens is your design framework—whether you prefer your garden to be formal or informal, or a mixture of both. These are loose concepts; what is formal to you might seem quite relaxed or even chaotic to a neighbor. Clearly, however, some gardens are laid out in an orderly manner, with straight, architectural lines, while other gardens use plants in a more casual style.

Within both formal and informal design frameworks, you can choose from a number of different garden styles. Perennials will have a major role regardless of the style you select. They form such a rich and diverse family of plants that they can fit comfortably into virtually any planting scheme.

The mossy path curving through this informal shade garden evokes a woodland scene. Framed by a blanket of mondo grass, the path meanders through a thicket of white foamflower, and, in the foreground, purple phlox and a variegated variety of Solomon's-seal.

The daisies, delphiniums, poppies, and snapdragons of this garden are grouped tightly in a color plan of blues, pinks, and whites, with yellow added as an accent. Such a jumble of plants in rich, vibrant colors is the essence of the cottage garden style.

Perennials for a Cutting Garden

Achillea
(yarrow)
Allium
(flowering onion)
Aster
(aster)
Campanula
(bellflower)
Chrysanthemum
(chrysanthemum)
Coreopsis
(tickseed)
Delphinium
(delphinium)
Digitalis
(foxglove)
Echinacea
(purple coneflower)
Echinops
(globe thistle)
Eryngium
(sea holly)
Gaillardia
(blanket-flower)
Gypsophila
(baby's-breath)
Heliopsis
(false sunflower)
Iris
(iris)
Lavandula
(lavender)
Liatris
(gay-feather)
Paeonia
(peony)
Phlox
(phlox)
Rudbeckia
(coneflower)
Solidago
(goldenrod)
Thalictrum
(meadow rue)
Veronica
(speedwell)

Formal Gardens

Generally, the mark of a formal garden is the straight line—in its paths, pools, borders, hedges, and even in the way a view is directed along an axis, or sightline. In the most formal gardens, spaces are crafted into open-air rooms by the use of walls or hedgerows. Often, columns of marble, stone, wood, or even living trees are used to suggest walls. In classical gardens, the formality is reinforced through symmetry, with one side of the garden mirroring the other.

Most such elements would overpower the typical suburban garden, of course, but it is possible to have formality on a more intimate scale. You might put in a small knot garden—so called for its knotlike shape—where you arrange the beds in a balanced geometric pattern with, perhaps, brick walkways in between the plantings. The beds in a knot garden can be curved or have squared corners, and are usually edged in miniature boxwood.

The same general color scheme and some of the same plants used in the cottage garden at left appear in this perennial border in Atlanta, Georgia. However, this garden's neat edging of brick and the layers of plants rising against a vertical backdrop— the clipped hedge—give it a more elegant and formal aspect.

However, some gardeners in warmer climates outline the edges of the beds with perennials and herbs, including lavender, germander, and rosemary, instead of using the evergreen shrubs.

You might choose to adopt an even more subdued level of formality, using a patio's straight edge as the boundary of your garden, for example, or choosing to plant perennials in borders instead of in beds with a freer form. A simple curve with a fixed radius can lend a formal air to a border in a way that a winding curve will not.

Without changing the outlines of a rectangular garden plot, you can either enhance or soften its air of formality by your choice of plantings. If you prefer the less formal, plant the garden's straight borders with perennials of different colors and with a relaxed form that will creep over the edges of the border. On the other hand, if order and regularity are to your liking, you could lay out a neat pathway through the plot with a mass planting, on both sides, of a graceful perennial like *Nepeta* (catmint) or a showy one like peony.

Informal Gardens

Curving lines and asymmetry are the key characteristics of the informal garden. The landscape is no less crafted than in a formal garden, but the borders, if there are any, might take a rambling course alongside a lawn. Often, the plantings are in beds rather than borders, the walkways are curved rather than straight, and trees and shrubs are located randomly and pruned only for their health, not to conform to a particular shape.

Cottage Gardens

One of the most popular and enduring styles is the cottage garden, whose air of rustic domesticity may be a better match for a suburban property than would a grand, classically formal garden. The cottage garden's origins lie in the old-fashioned villages of England, where the occupants of small thatched- or tile-roofed cottages filled their gardens with annuals and perennials. These were species plants—not today's highly developed cultivars and hybrids, which usually cannot reproduce themselves faithfully from seed. The old plants set seed freely, however, perpetuating themselves and producing a riot of color amid a rambling growth of foliage—and, best of all, requiring little care from the owner.

In the late 19th and early 20th centuries, some of England's leading gardeners developed a style

based on the cottage garden but refined to a high level of sophistication. They took pains to design herbaceous borders that would bloom in rolling waves of color throughout the summer months.

The American cottage garden so in favor now lies somewhere between its two predecessors. Crafting color schemes and choosing plants for their foliage, form, and ease of care—as well as their flowers—are more important to today's gardeners than to those who tended the appealing but unruly tangle of plants dominating the early dooryard gardens. Even so, today's standards are not as rigid or demanding as those that produced the refined English border. The variety of plants to choose from is different, too, with a greater reliance on hardy perennials that are distinctly American, such as daylilies and rudbeckias.

Cutting Gardens

Nothing announces serious gardeners—or a serious love of flowers—more than choosing to grow

The rocket larkspurs, irises, and daisies in this wide perennial flower bed remain accessible to the gardener, whose design included a maintenance path made of woodchips.

A handsome fence adds strength and completeness to this border, which includes pale yellow Achillea 'Moonshine' (foreground), reddish Alstroemeria, and tall, lilac-colored Verbena bonariensis. Without such backdrops, which define the plants' shapes and highlight their colors, some borders might lose their visual impact and become harder to see.

a cutting garden. There, plants are raised for the sole purpose of producing beautiful blooms for indoor arrangements. Although the cutting garden is less common in the American landscape than other garden styles, it deserves a second look.

Again, perennials are an ideal ingredient, especially long-stemmed plants like delphinium, solidago, and iris. Most will not rebloom, as cut annuals do, but they will present an array of flowers throughout the growing season if enough different kinds are planted.

Traditionally, the cutting garden occupies its own bed or beds away from the main garden; plants grow in well-spaced rows, allowing the gardener to reach them easily. Even a small area, about 10 by 10 feet, will yield hundreds of blooms in a season. But if space is at a premium, you can grow flowers for cutting in between plants in the vegetable plot or within display beds and borders.

Perennial Borders and Beds

The two most common ways to display perennials are in a border or a bed. The border typically forms the edge of a garden space and lies next to a vertical element—a wall of the house, a fence, or a hedge, for example.

The width of the border can vary, but it is an important factor in choosing plants. In a conventional border, the rule of thumb is that no plant should be taller than one-half the width of the space. If your border is a thin strip of ground between a wall and a sidewalk, for example, the scale of the perennials you place there should be modest—perhaps a row of petite plants such as candytuft, threadleaf coreopsis, or ajuga.

One advantage of the border garden is that its vertical element offers a handsome backdrop for the flowers. A white fence or wall, for instance, spotlights the color and form of the plants growing in front of it. Be careful, though, of color clashes, particularly against red brick walls, where bold red or orange blooms might be jarring.

A flower bed doesn't have the visual anchor that is inherent in a border; it often takes the form of a free-floating island. But the bed does valuable service: It can direct views across a lawn, and spotlight such landscape features as decks, patios, and swimming pools. Also, a bed might be the only place on your property where you can grow perennials in the full sun that most require.

There are pitfalls to watch out for, however, if you decide to create island beds. Islands must be large enough to hold their own in an overall design. Even if they are large, they might need the

added visual weight of some shrubs or small trees so they won't be overshadowed by imposing elements—such as the house—that are nearby.

Both borders and beds, if they are broad enough, will need maintenance paths—narrow, hidden trails that give you access to plants without the risk of your stepping on them or compacting their soil. In a bed, you might create a path from woodchips or river stones that, from a distance, is hidden by plant foliage. In a border, your path might run between the back of the plantings and the wall or hedge backdrop. Apart from the access it affords you, the path will also improve air circulation among the plants and prevent lingering dampness that might cause fungal infections.

Borders and beds also benefit from edging, especially if the adjacent ground is a lawn. Brick, stone, or concrete pavers laid just 6 to 12 inches wide will keep the lawn mower away from the plants and keep the plants from smothering the grass as they flop forward. Edging also acts as a unifying element for the whole plant display.

The deep pink hardy geranium and the catmint at the front of this perennial border (above) spill forward but, thanks to an edging of paving stones, remain well clear of the lawn. The line of stones also sharpens the formality of the border.

An Explosion
of Perennial Choices

Selecting plants to fit your garden style is the most challenging and rewarding aspect of perennial gardening. The complexities of selecting perennials for their bloom colors, their shapes, and their foliage and textures can appear overwhelming. But by taking a systematic approach and learning all you can about the plants and how they might look in your garden, you can become a master.

The whole idea of composing with herbaceous plants can be a new one for many home gardeners. In the past, gardeners were able to find beauty in only a limited range of old-fashioned species of such perennials as daylilies, hostas, peonies, bearded iris, and phlox. Shrub borders were old favorites, as were foundation plantings of broad-leaved evergreens and a well-trimmed lawn. Color was achieved by planting a few perennials, some spring-blooming bulbs, flowering trees, shrubs, and, especially, beds of bright, cheery annuals.

In recent years, gardeners have found—in mail-order catalogs and local nurseries alike—a sumptuous and sometimes bewildering array of perennials. At the same time, a distinct type of perennial garden plant, the ornamental grass, has gone from being a relative unknown in the garden to a sought-after addition to any planting, particularly given the development of many fine cultivars.

The enduring popularity of perennials has changed the face of the American garden. In an age when people want beauty and color in their garden but have little time to nurture it, well-chosen perennials provide ready solutions. Diverse and versatile, perennials can be used in any

A drift of Echinacea purpurea, the purple coneflower, shows up nicely against a backdrop of unfinished fenceboards (right). Lending a different character to the species is a cultivar called E. purpurea 'Alba', or white purple coneflower (above), which can be used in a color scheme where purple would clash. Echinacea purpurea is one of many enduring species that have been bred to produce new colors.

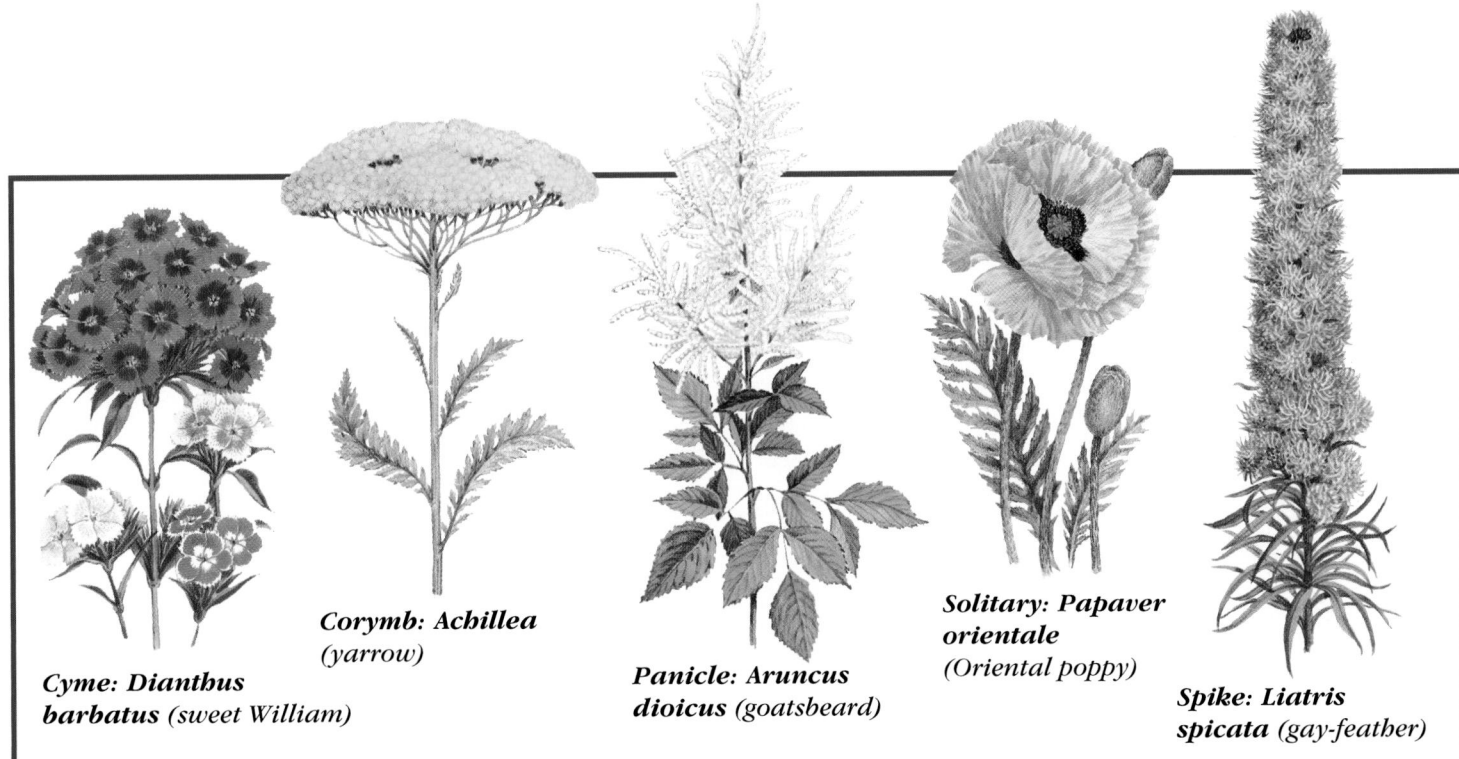

Cyme: Dianthus barbatus (sweet William)

Corymb: Achillea (yarrow)

Panicle: Aruncus dioicus (goatsbeard)

Solitary: Papaver orientale (Oriental poppy)

Spike: Liatris spicata (gay-feather)

A Variety of Flower Heads

The flower heads of perennials (inflorescences) can be grouped into several types, each lending its particular character to a plant and even influencing the length of its blooming season. Spikes, for example, generally have a long season, as the tiny individual flowers open in sequence from bottom to top. Other factors also influence the duration of flowering, such as the speed of pollination, the number of blooms produced, and the durability of the petals. Besides the inflorescences shown above, perennial flowers also take the form of racemes, such as *Polygonum bistorta* 'Superbum'; umbels, such as *Asclepias tuberosa*; and heads, such as *Echinacea purpurea*.

setting but are particularly well suited to looser, more natural landscape styles. Many are also able to withstand climatic extremes and troublesome pests and diseases.

If you do not have a ready source of free perennials from gardening friends or relatives eager to divide mature plants, or if you can't take advantage of low-cost perennials from garden-club plant sales, your initial investment in perennials can be high. But with your expenditure comes the chance to create landscapes full of color and vitality using plants that require relatively little care. You'll also save the money you would spend on replacing annuals year after year, and in a fairly short period of time you'll have mature plants from which to propagate new ones.

Choosing Perennials for Color

The most important task perennials perform in the garden is enlivening the landscape with color. It is this decorative factor that places the well-designed perennial bed or border at the heart of any garden plan.

If you consciously choose a color scheme for a part or all of your perennial garden, it is best to start not with a specific plant in mind but with a particular color or colors. Once you decide on an all-white garden, say, or a grouping of soft yellows, white, and blue, you can select plants that will fall into those color bands and bloom throughout the growing season. (For information on perennials and other plants organized by color, see the Color Guide to Herbaceous Plants beginning on page 604.) Interplanting foliage perennials that echo the selected hues—silvery foliage plants in an all-white garden, for instance—or that provide a buffer of green between potentially clashing colors will help tie the entire arrangement together.

One color is virtually unavoidable in the garden—green. But green comes in many different shades and tints. (Shades are colors darkened by black, such as deep purple from violet; tints are colors that have been lightened by white, such as pink from red.) The careful selection of the right quality of green will enhance your color scheme.

Mixing and Matching Colors

Red, yellow, and blue are the primary colors on the color wheel. *When equal amounts of two primary colors are mixed, secondary colors—orange, green, and violet—result. A primary color mixed with an adjacent secondary hue creates a third level of colors. Colors said to be harmonious share a portion of color; contrasting colors do not.*

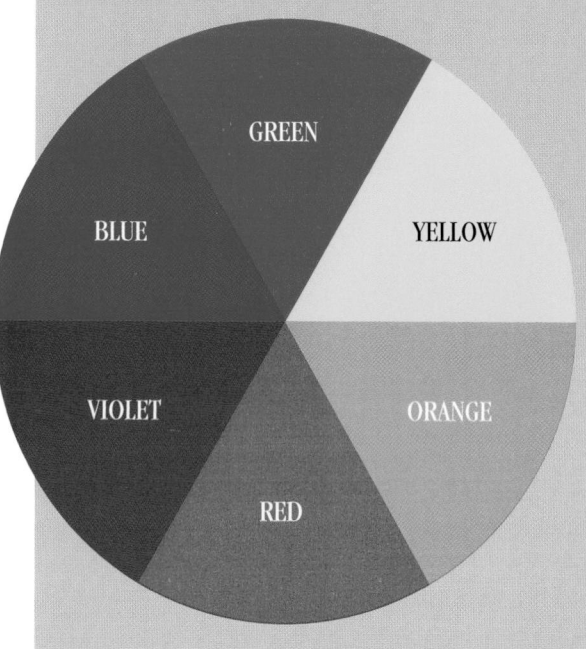

In the planting above, the gardener has used the neutral gray foliage of Stachys byzantina to link the harmonious colors of Veronica 'True Blue' and the pink-flowered cranesbill, Geranium x oxonianum 'Claridge Druce'.

For example, the mauve-pink *Dianthus plumarius* 'Agatha' blends well with its own blue-green foliage but would be jarring when paired with the yellow-green fringes of *Hosta fortunei* 'Aureomarginata'. Successful pairing of colors is made much simpler if you understand the basics of the color wheel.

Using the Color Wheel

Different versions of the color wheel have been devised over the years, some reflecting the great scientific lengths to which color theory has been taken. However, most gardeners rely on the simple, standard version that starts with the three primary colors—red, yellow, and blue.

An equal mix of two primary colors produces one of the three secondary colors. Hence orange is a mix of yellow and red and lies between them on the wheel; violet appears between red and blue; and green lies between blue and yellow. Mixing primary colors with their adjacent secondary colors yields the further gradations yellow-orange, red-orange, red-violet, blue-violet, blue-green, and yellow-green.

Conventional wisdom holds that the most pleasing color combinations are either contrasting, meaning that they stand directly opposite each other on the color wheel, or harmonious, found next to each other on the wheel and sharing a common pigment. A contrasting color combination might be blue and orange, violet and yellow, or red and green. Harmonious pairings include green and yellow-green, red-orange and orange, or blue-violet and blue.

Tints and shades, as well as blends of different colors—mauve, for example, which combines red and violet—add more variables. So do such elements as the amount and strength of the light the plants receive (pastels show up better in low light, bright colors look better in full sun), how well the flower's petals reflect light, and the tendency for light colors to appear to come forward toward

The robust blooms of the popular daylily Hemerocallis 'Bejeweled' *team with the dainty pink flowers of* Achillea 'Rose Beauty' *to produce a striking monochromatic effect (above).*

Coming from opposite sides of the color wheel, *the rich blue of* Nepeta mussinii *and the pale yellow, umbrella-shaped blossoms of* Achillea 'Moonshine' *demonstrate the striking combinations that are possible with the use of contrasting colors (below).*

the viewer's eye and for dark colors to recede.

Clearly, with all these factors to consider, it is easy to become bogged down in the complexities of color. The best course is to use the color wheel to follow the basic rules of creating contrasting and harmonious color groupings but to let your garden plants, your eye, and your taste have the final say. If you occasionally create combinations that simply don't work well together, you won't be the first gardener to make a mistake. Keep in mind that you can always move perennials from one spot in the garden to another if you don't like the results.

Marrying Cool and Hot Colors

Besides combining plants for harmony or contrast, it is generally considered preferable to group cool colors such as violets, blues, and off-whites together. Such combinations work particularly well in those areas that receive filtered light or partial shade, where there will be no glaring sun to wash out the lighter hues. Within this family of cool colors you can use yellows or reds to create accents, but for a better blending consider a red leaning toward violet rather than toward orange, and yellows that are lemon and pastel, not the pure and brilliant yellow of some achilleas or euphorbias, for example.

A garden of hot colors—reds, oranges, and pure yellows—works best in beds or borders that receive full sun. Here, you can have fun with fiery-colored varieties of such plants as geums,

The robust, coarse-veined leaves of Hosta sieboldiana create a bold contrast in size and texture when placed next to the delicate foliage of Saxifraga stolonifera (strawberry saxifrage). Texture can provide visual interest in a garden well after the flowers have faded.

poppies, daylilies, and gaillardias. Be careful with rich colors such as magenta, blue-violet, or purple, however; they sometimes create a strident note in a bed or border unless they are somehow tempered. One way to handle such dominant colors is to isolate them in a separate bed where their brilliance will not overshadow more subdued colors. If you lack the space for this, try planting them in partial shade (if they are suited for these conditions), which will reduce their impact. When viewed in shadows, colors that were once overpowering or garish will softly glow.

Foliage is another important component of color in the perennial garden. It might not present itself as vividly as flowers, but it lasts much longer. A color scheme of reds, purples, and grays, for instance, might be constructed of the gray foliage of artemisia and one of the purple-leaved varieties of heuchera with coral red flowers. For a color combination of violet, yellow-green, and gray, you might plant *Stachys byzantina* (lamb's ears) between *Alchemilla mollis* (lady's-mantle), lavender, and euphorbia. Note that the neutral color gray is of immense value in the perennial garden: It calms the colors around it and ties them together.

Planning for Texture and Mass

Plant foliage not only contributes color, it also gives the garden texture and mass. Many perennials are grown principally for their foliage, among them hostas, artemisia, lamb's ears, epimedium, santolina, and lamium. A number of others—ajuga, lady's-mantle, and Solomon's-seal, for example—produce foliage at least as valuable as their flowers. Even such prominent flowering plants as Japanese and Siberian iris, ligularia, acanthus, and blackberry lily display handsome leaves along with their blooms.

The fineness or coarseness of the leaves gives a plant its texture. Just as light colors seem to pop out and dark hues recede, a coarse-textured plant leaps forward into view and a fine-textured one retreats. With careful attention to the placement of fine-textured plants, for example, you can create an illusion of depth in a small garden.

More important, you can add interest to your garden by carefully positioning plants of varying textures. A coarse-leaved plant like ligularia would have greater visual impact set against the fine foliage of veronica than if it were next to an equally big-leaved plant like hosta.

If a plant's character comes from its leaf and flower texture, then its overall shape, or mass, dictates its stature. Mature miscanthus grass, for example, though it is fine in texture, may grow 6 feet high and 4 feet across—the size of a large shrub. Wild ginger, on the other hand, though it has coarse foliage, grows only a few inches high.

Just as you should think about associations of different colors and textures in planning your garden, you should also consider mass. For example,

a flowering mound of phlox will look more imposing when given space to show off than when it is surrounded by other perennials of similar bulk.

Putting It All Together

With all these components in mind, it is time to put your planting ideas down on paper. Assemble those ideas first according to the colors, textures, and shapes you have decided on, and then select plants that will provide them. For a long border or bed, you should work in short sections, keeping in mind that the most pleasing designs have some unifying element, such as a repeated pattern of color, a progression of color, or a recurring plant.

A perennial garden should present itself in layers—tall plants at the back, medium ones in the middle, and smaller ones up front. There are exceptions, of course: You might plant a tall perennial like macleaya at the front of a border to serve as an accent at a strategic spot. In island beds, which are viewed from all sides, the layering generally moves from the center outward in all directions. And in a garden seen from inside the house as well as outside, you would not want tall plants blocking the view of the rest of the flowers.

It is best to plant in odd numbers—threes, fives, sevens—so that identical plants are not rigidly grouped and can flow easily into and among the others. You can give structure to a bed through the regular and rhythmic placement of bulkier perennials or drifts of plants, and then fill in gaps with buffers like gray-leaved neutrals or other foliage plants. By limiting the types of plants and planting individuals en masse, you will achieve a garden with less variety in color but with a simple, strong, and effective design.

Finally, as you combine plants, consider scale. A bear's-breech, with its tall flower spikes and coarse leaves, would be a minor accent in a long border; next to a patio, however, it would dominate the scene. Within the confines of a small garden in the city or in the suburbs, or in the small gardens of larger properties, it is usually best to limit the use of large-scale plants.

The gentle undulation of this California perennial border is achieved by combining plants of similar mass. A fan of Iris 'Victoria Falls' and the compact mounds of deep purple Spanish lavender, spiky English lavender, and fleabane echo the shapes of the background shrubs and provide a transition to the creeping thyme in the foreground.

Designing with Bulbs

Gardeners today use bulbs with abandon, incorporating them into traditional beds and borders *(page 166)* and using them as colorful accents in combination with other plants. Bulbs shine in these settings. Yet there is something undeniably satisfying about all-bulb groupings, with their rich, simultaneous burst of color—especially in spring, when the rest of the garden is just beginning to stir. With such unlimited design choices, it's often a good idea to create a plan on paper first, to help you see how you might include bulbs in your garden. (See pages 100-103 for details on finalizing your plan on paper.)

The Elements of Design

The star-burst shape of spiky Eryngium (sea holly) beautifully echoes the open trumpet form of 'Golden Pixie' lilies. Strengthening the combination is the contrast between the lily's golden yellow color and the sea holly's lavender-blue.

Just as certain homes lend themselves to particular styles of gardens—a Federal-style brick house, for instance, with its elements of balance and symmetry, seems an apt setting for a formal garden—certain plants lend themselves to particular styles of planting. The garden surrounding such a house would likely have tidy beds of uniform plantings, outlined in straight edges and simple curves. The bulbs chosen would have simple, strong forms and compact blooms, and they would be closely grouped to create the effect of a stunning carpet of color. Tulips, hyacinths, and daffodils, placed in upright, soldierly formations and edged with annuals, make good formal plantings.

Since different types of bulbs bloom at different times you can highlight certain parts of the formal garden as the seasons progress. For example, in the early spring you can brighten the entrance to the front door and the path leading to it with a mass planting of early-blooming crocuses. As the weather warms up, shift attention to a pool or a slope edged with a bank of blooming lilies and allium or perhaps to a shady bench flanked by groupings of caladium and calla lilies. On a shady terrace, arrange large pots of colorful begonias.

The grounds around a simple frame house might be planted in mixed drifts of bulbs that would multiply over the years. Such an informal approach is characterized by irregular curves and asymmetrical shapes. A cluster of lilies, for example, might be balanced by a dwarf conifer on one side and a stand of low-growing blue fescue grass on the other.

An informal garden plan could also include naturalized plantings—drifts of robust species able to spread on their own from year to year. Such plantings might be started at the edge of a lawn, along a woodland floor, or around trees or shrubs. A rock garden made of randomly spaced stones set into a hillside also expresses a natural, informal look when planted with bulbs. Depending on the space, you could plant delicate-looking bulbs, such as scillas or allium, or larger bulbs such as daffodils or tulips *(pages 170-171)*. Just be sure to keep the planting in scale; you don't want the tall bulbs to dwarf the small ones.

Of course, your garden style may also combine some formal and informal elements. Deliberate contrast can be effective—a jewel-like formal bed, say, next to a naturalized woodland shade garden. But keep proportions in mind; plant large plants in large places, small plants where they can be isolated and featured.

Choosing Bulbs for Color

Deciding on a color scheme will help organize your choice of bulbs. Bulbs come in nearly every color you could want, from whites and the palest tints to the richest, most saturated hues. For vivid, energetic arrangements select plants in contrasting colors, such as yellow and violet, orange and blue-violet, or red and yellow. To create a more relaxed and peaceful mood, appropriate for an informal garden, consider harmonious color combinations such as blue-violet and mauve or shades of plum and rose. Remember, however, that these are guidelines, not hard and fast rules. If your heart is set on a particular color scheme, give it a try; your garden should reflect your tastes and your imagination. And part of the beauty of bulbs is that they can be lifted and moved easily.

Bulbs can contribute color to your garden as accent plants or in broad swaths. For example, a small group of *Allium giganteum,* with large purple globes on 4-foot stems, would highlight the foliage of a nearby planting of *Heuchera* 'Palace Purple' (alumroot) and the flowers of blooming *Lavandula* (lavender). But if you plant the allium in large bands among ornamental grasses and the rich yellow flowers of a few *Achillea* 'Coronation Gold' (yarrow), the contrast in colors and the scale of the planting will make the allium stand out from the other plants.

It is generally best to cluster like colors together and to group the clusters next to each other to make patterns. An exception might be when you combine different colors of the same type of bulb—a spring bed of *Anemone blanda* (Greek anemone) in blue, white, and pink, for example, can be quite cheery.

White-flowered bulbs such as tulips can be quite striking when planted as part of an all-white garden, especially when paired with the creamy-edged leaves of *Hosta* 'Northern Halo' and other silvery foliage plants. They are also useful to break up overly dominant color patterns or subdue strident colors. Plan for about a fourth of your bulbs at any given time to be white: crocus, narcissus, or tulip in spring; lily or dahlia in summer. In a shady location, the natural light-reflecting qualities of white flowers attract the eye and brighten shadowy curves and corners. In fact, whites and pale hues show up best in shady locations and at twilight.

Yellow is another color that makes a beautiful accent. A proportion of one yellow bloom to about three violet or blue ones creates a vivid combination. Green, a steady presence in the garden, forms a bridge between the two colors. Yellow also harmonizes with orange, a tricky hue to weave into a color scheme.

Texture and Form

Although color is a bulb's dominant attribute, the texture and overall shape of the plant can also add to the garden design. To begin with, there can be enormous variations in flower heads. Parrot tulips, for example, have developed ragged-edged petals that are wildly mottled in color. Lilies exhibit a wide range of trumpet shapes. Other lilylike flowers, such as the *Gloriosa superba,* have a lacy, airy quality.

Polianthes tuberosa 'Dangerous Pleasures' (tuberose)

Scented Bulbs

Amaryllis belladonna
(belladonna lily)
Convallaria majalis
(lily of the valley)
Crinum americanum
(swamp lily)
Crocus biflorus
(Scotch crocus)
Crocus imperati
(crocus)
Cyclamen
(Persian violet)
Eucharis
(Amazon lily)
Freesia
(freesia)
Galanthus
(snowdrop)
Gladiolus callianthus
(gladiolus)
Hyacinthus
(hyacinth)
Hymenocallis
(spider lily)
Iris
(iris)
Leucojum vernum
(spring snowflake)
Lilium
(lily)
Lycoris squamigera
(magic lily)
Muscari
(grape hyacinth)
Narcissus
(daffodil)
Pancratium
(sea daffodil)
Polianthes tuberosa
(tuberose)
Puschkinia scilloides
(striped squill)
Scilla
(squill)
Sternbergia lutea
(winter daffodil)
Trillium
(wake-robin)
Tulipa
(tulip)

Bulbs yield some of the largest and tallest of all flowers, such as the 9-inch-wide "dinner-plate" dahlia and the equally extraordinary *Eremurus himalaicus* (Himalayan desert-candle), with a flowering stalk reaching as high as 9 feet. These giants never fail to make an impression. On the other hand, the miniature detailing of a *Cyclamen coum* or the dangling bells of a *Fritillaria meleagris* require a close inspection for the viewer to fully appreciate their delicate form.

Decorative Foliage

A few bulbs are grown solely for their interesting foliage. Notable is the caladium, whose heart-shaped leaves are speckled and striped in pink, red, lavender, and white. A common houseplant, caladium is frost-tender but will do well in a shady, moist spot in the garden. The gigantic elephant's ear, or *Colocasia esculenta,* also thrives in shady and damp conditions.

Many flowering bulbs also have attractive foliage, which gives the plants interest after their blooms fade. Some cannas, for example, have purplish leaves, and the foliage of *Canna* x *generalis* 'Pretoria' has startling green-and-gold variegation. Several small tulip cultivars—'Red Riding Hood', 'Cape Cod', and 'Oriental Splendor', to name a few—have red-striped leaves. And *Tulipa aucheriana* has wavy-edged leaves that radiate from its short stem.

The foliage of flowering bulbs such as arum, oxalis, and cyclamen, when planted in masses, makes a beautiful ground cover. And in Zones 8 to 10, agapanthus, clivia, and canna foliage is evergreen, preserving their position in the garden throughout the year.

For most bulbs, however, foliage is viewed as the price a gardener must pay to enjoy the beauty of the flower. It takes some ingenuity to deal with the sprawl of daffodil foliage or the withering of allium or hyacinth leaves. With careful planning, though, you can take advantage of the emerging foliage of perennials to disguise the bulbs' progressively unsightly leaves. Ferns, for example, come into leaf just as snowdrops, crocuses, and winter aconites are fading. *Astilbe* (false spirea), *Epimedium* (bishop's hat), *Paeonia* (peony), and Siberian iris are also good camouflage.

A Bulb for Every Season

Once you have settled on the bulbs and colors you like, select for bloom season. The flowering glory of most bulbs is brief—2 to 3 weeks. The encyclopedia beginning on page 608 will help you pick bulbs that bloom when you want them to and in the colors and shapes you prefer. Happily, many bulbs of the same genus bloom at different times. So if you love tulips, you can extend their presence in the garden for months by planting early-spring-blooming species tulips, followed by Triumph and Darwin tulips, which flower in mid-spring, and finishing with single and double late varieties, which will carry you into summer.

The Bewitchment of Scent

The scents exuded by bulb flowers range from lemony to sweet. Scent evolved to attract pollinators, and the fragrance emitted by some lilies and narcissus may seem overpowering at times. By contrast, the delicate perfume of small spring bulbs such as crocuses, scilla, and snowdrops may be hardly noticeable. Most fragrant bulb flowers come in white, pale pink, mauve, or yellow, and their petals are waxy, like those of hyacinth, tuberose, and lily. To get the most enjoyment from scented bulbs, plant them in a border close to where you walk, near the front entrance to your house, or near a patio or window.

Practical Considerations

Any garden design has to take into account the growing requirements of plants. With a few exceptions, bulbs prefer soil with a more or less neutral pH of about 7.0, and good drainage. Generally, spring bloomers such as daffodils require a dry period in the summer, when they are dormant. Cyclamen, trout lily, and other woodland bulbs need protection from hot summer sun. Plants that evolved in mountain meadows—crocuses and tulips are examples—can tolerate a good baking.

Meeting these requirements is made easier by the use of companion plants. Shrubs and perennials not only conceal the long spindly stems of tall bulb plants such as lilies—and, of course, help hide withering bulb foliage after flowering—but their roots also take up excess moisture in the soil. And later, when the bulbs are dormant, perennials shade the ground and moderate soil temperature.

You'll want to bring all these variables together when you create the detailed map of your garden design *(page 103)*. For example, a hard-to-mow slope might be just the place for a rock garden or a drift of naturalized bulbs. A diagram also helps you keep track of where your bulbs are planted.

Showy deep blue Agapanthus 'Bressingham Blue' (African lily) stands out in bold contrast to golden mounds of orange coneflower, slender trumpets of Cape fuchsia, and yellow daylilies in this Washington State garden. Vigorous summer-flowering tubers, the African lilies bloom throughout the season.

Bulbs in the Bed and Border

Beds and borders are the building blocks of most garden designs. These self-contained plantings give the garden its shape and character, and afford the gardener an opportunity to combine plants in myriad ways, using color, form, and texture for maximum effect. The strong hues of flowering bulbs have an immediate and vivid impact in such a setting. Indeed, many of the more formal bulbs that produce uniform shapes and colors, such as tulip, iris, narcissus, and hyacinth, look most at home in a bedding display.

Use a bed or border to position plants where they can best be appreciated—along a walkway or near an entrance, around a pool or patio or a garden bench. Beds and borders are a versatile way of organizing your plants for viewing, presenting lovely vistas from afar or up close.

Cultivating a Bed or Border

Beds and borders also allow you to group your plants according to their growing requirements. They are the part of the garden where you can most easily focus your cultivation efforts to im-prove soil texture and fertility specifically for the plants you have chosen.

Bulb experts agree that the most important factor for success in growing bulbs is your soil's drainage. The soil must allow water to percolate away from the bulbs, but it also must contain enough compost or other organic matter to hold nutrients and to retain sufficient moisture to keep the bulbs from drying out completely. In a bed or border you can prepare the soil to meet those needs and thus protect your sometimes considerable investment in growing stock.

Serving a Purpose

Although they share a common purpose in the garden, beds and borders accomplish it slightly differently. A border forms the edge of a garden space and usually lies along a vertical element—a fence, a hedge, or a wall. The vertical element serves as a backdrop to set off the plants, which are typically laid out with the tallest at the back and the shortest in front and are generally viewed from the front only. A bed, on the other hand, is often a freestanding area visible from all sides. It can be geometric or irregular in shape and surrounded by lawn, ground cover, or even gravel.

A bed must be in proportion to the space around it—neither so small that it fades from view at a modest distance nor so large that it overpowers its surroundings. On a small lot, you can give a bed of limited size more visual weight by adding shrubs or small trees, or by mounding earth to form a raised bed (left). The height of the plants should be proportional to the width of the plot. As a general guideline, no plant should be taller than one-half the width of the space. And when designing either a bed or a border, be sure to give yourself enough room to move around the plantings to perform routine maintenance chores.

Formal Beds and Borders

Bulbs in massed plantings make spectacular formal designs. Expect to plant the bulbs rather densely in a formal bed—inches apart—and to think of the planting as a one-season affair, good for drawing attention to an area for a short period of time. Try, for example, a spring bed of clusters of pink, red, and yellow tulips, surrounded by an edging of vivid blue grape hyacinths. Other good edging plants include pansies, impatiens, rock cress, candytuft, primroses, coleus, or ornamental kale. Forget-me-nots are a traditional foundation

---

TIPS FROM THE PROS

Making a Mounded Bed

One way to make your bulb bed more visible from a distance is to create a gentle hillock or mound. The extra elevation adds dimensional interest and increases the color impact you will get from plants of similar height—for example, a grouping of tulips and daffodils. In addition, the eye will naturally be carried to the top of the mound, where you can place a special feature—a dwarf shrub with an interesting shape, perhaps, or a large ornamental rock.

Besides its decorative appeal, a mounded or raised bed is an ideal location for bulbs because you can easily mix up your own soil recipe on the site to ensure that it will have good drainage.

To make a raised bed, pile topsoil at least a foot high, so there will be enough to envelop completely the roots of your plants. A few artfully arranged rocks will help keep the soil in place until the plants can establish a root system. Depending on your preference for a formal or an informal arrangement, the raised bed can be centered within an available space on your property or given an off-center position. Orient the slope of the bed to the point from which you will view it.

A line of nodding 'Ice Follies' daffodils leads to a cascading white wisteria in this formal San Francisco garden. Extending the white theme, creamy tulips and a snowy azalea glow against dark masonry walls.

The flowing curves of this informal early-spring border burst with colorful naturalized bulbs, including crown imperial, emerging scilla, and a variety of daffodils. Interspersed are ivory and purple pansies and primulas to fill in the bare spots.

plant for bulb displays, creating a misty blue haze through which the bulbs grow.

You might want to experiment with a single-color scheme. For an all-white spring garden, plant *Crocus vernus* 'Snowstorm', *Narcissus* 'Thalia' and 'Mount Hood', *Hyacinthus orientalis* 'L'innocence', *Anemone blanda* 'White Splendor', *Leucojum aestivum,* and *Tulipa* 'Ivory Floridale' and 'White Dream'.

A summer bed could have clusters of red or yellow canna with a central group of red and yellow gladiolus, surrounded by mixed dahlias. For accents, try marigold, petunia, lobelia, and alyssum.

Informal Plantings

In contrast to the uniformity of a formal bed, an informal planting should offer some surprises. Give it an irregular, asymmetrical shape, and choose a wider variety of plants.

Consider, for example, creating dramatic pairings of bulbs with trees and shrubs. Blue-flowered bulbs such as scilla, muscari, and chionodoxa can create a beautiful effect when clustered in a ring around the base of a white-barked birch or small flowering cherry. Bulbs also combine well with spring-blooming shrubs—witch hazel and forsythia are two excellent examples.

Certain shrubs benefit from a screen of plants around their bare stems. For example, a hedge of lilacs, such as *Syringa* x *chinensis,* looks better with a skirt of bulbs and ferns at the beginning of the year. A succession of early-spring bulbs such as snowflakes and snowdrops, followed by crocuses and winter aconites, will finish blooming just as the dark red and pale green fronds of the maidenhair fern and the royal fern begin unfurling at the base of the lilacs. The ferns will then fill out to mask the bulbs' dying foliage.

Pastel tulips in an informal bed or border can pick up the pale blue of a *Wisteria* or lilac or the pink of spirea. Position them in front of glossy green *Ilex* (holly) or the deep maroon foliage of *Berberis thunbergii* 'Rose Glow' (barberry), and the tulips will shine. Dark purple tulips pair well with the burgundy in a cut-leaf *Acer palmatum* (Japanese maple). Their waxy blooms create a stimulating contrast with the lacy maple foliage.

Similarly, bold, waxy hyacinth flowers contrast with the fine, delicate blossoms of arabis, goldentuft, and myosotis. While hyacinths are at their best massed in a formal bed, they can serve as a good accent dotted among other plants, and their perfume is a bonus.

A specimen tree or shrub anchoring a bed can be accented with a group of bulbs. The number of bulbs should vary with the mature size of the variety chosen—a dozen daffodils, tulips, or hyacinths, for example; half a dozen large fritillaries, lilies, or galtonias; or minor bulbs in groups of three to four dozen.

Going for a Large Effect

Whether your bedding plot is formal or informal, you can strengthen its impact by choosing bulbs for height. The white-veined green leaves of an elephant's ear, for example, would contrast dramatically with the spiky foliage of a yucca or with an upright temple juniper. Or place an immense *Dahlia imperialis* next to a mass of burgundy-leaved cannas and a vining gloriosa lily.

Lilies are generally tall plants with long, relatively bare stems. They combine well with plants that rise to conceal those stems. Low grasses work well, as do dwarf conifers. For example, plant copper-colored *Lilium* x *dalhansonii* with blue-gray *Pinus flexilis* 'Glauca Pendula' (limber pine). The purple bells of a 'Betty Corning' clematis climbing over such a pair would make a stunning display.

Other tall bulb plants include *Fritillaria imperialis, Camassia, Cardiocrinum giganteum,* the tender *Watsonia,* and the giant *Canna iridiflora*—all of which grow to more than 4 feet tall in the right conditions.

Managing Bulb Foliage

Since bulb leaves should not be cut back until they are withered and brown, you'll need various planting strategies to hide them as they decline. Daffodils, for example, develop a floppy habit, especially as their foliage yellows in the sun. Plant them with hostas, daylilies, peonies, leopard's-bane, astilbe, ferns, and grasses—perennials that emerge in time to hide the homely daffodil leaves. Or put them at the base of flowering shrubs or among ground covers such as ivy, vinca, or low-growing cotoneaster, allowing you to tuck the daffodil leaves out of sight.

Crocus foliage is shorter and thus not so troublesome, getting conveniently lost among low ground covers such as vinca, sedum, bugleweed, euonymus, ivy, and carpet junipers. Do not plant

Towering Lilium 'Golden Splendor' and the smaller white 'Gypsy' shine among the pastel pink of filipendula and the blue of campanula in this Oregon garden. Clipped box bushes anchor the corner of the bed.

crocuses with pachysandra, however; it will smother the bulbs and cause them not to return.

Another way to hide withering bulb foliage is to plant annuals such as pansy, iberis, and *Lobularia maritima* (alyssum) among the bulbs just before the latter start to grow. Since the roots of annuals are shallow, the growing bulbs will find a way through them. The annuals will remain in flower through the summer, attracting attention away from the withering bulb leaves.

The foliage of certain autumn-flowering bulbs appears in the spring, long before the flowers arrive, and can be a nuisance if you have not planned for it in your garden design. Fall-blooming crocus and cyclamen have tidy, decorative leaves that add interest to the scene, but the foliage of the belladonna lily and colchicum is broad and floppy and should be tucked unobtrusively among other plants, such as hostas, in the spring.

Orange-trumpeted Asiatic hybrid lilies and purple-petaled columbine burst from a rock-edged bed in Idaho. Low-growing, plum-colored oxalis climbs between the stones.

Bulbs for Specific Conditions

MOIST SOIL
Caladium
(angel-wings)
Camassia quamash
(camassia)
Canna
(canna)
Convallaria majalis
(lily of the valley)
Eranthis hyemalis
(winter aconite)
Erythronium americanum
(dogtooth violet)
Fritillaria meleagris
(checkered lily)
Lilium superbum
(Turk's-cap lily)
Narcissus cyclamineus
(daffodil)

SHADE
Achimenes
(magic flower)
Anemone blanda
(Greek anemone)
Arum italicum
(painted arum)
Begonia
(begonia)
Clivia miniata
(Natal lily)
Convallaria majalis
(lily of the valley)
Crocus tomasinianus
(crocus)
Cyclamen
(Persian violet)
Erythronium americanum
(dogtooth violet)
Eucharis grandiflora
(Amazon lily)
Fritillaria
(fritillary)
Galanthus
(snowdrop)
Hyacinthoides hispanica
(Spanish bluebell)
Iris xiphioides
(English iris)
Leucojum aestivum
(summer snowflake)
Lilium candidum
(Madonna lily)
Lycoris squamigera
(magic lily)
Muscari
(grape hyacinth)
Oxalis spp.
(shamrock)
Zantedeschia
(calla lily)
Zephyranthes
(zephyr lily)

Note: The abbreviation "spp." stands for the plural of "species." Where used in lists it means that many, but not all, of the species in a genus meet the criterion of the list.

The nodding bells of Hyacinthoides hispanica seem to splash their way gaily past the mossy rocks in an Oregon garden in April. Bright pink arabis flows through a crevice alongside.

Bulbs for the Rock Garden

A rock garden reproduces on a small scale the growing conditions of the mountain plants known as alpines. These tough little plants can thrive in pockets of gritty soil sandwiched among rocks in wind-scoured heights.

Located on a terraced slope or in a natural outcrop, a rock garden is a sheltered environment that provides plants with a variety of microclimates. Those areas shaded by the rocks are shadowy and cool, while those in full sun are warm and sheltered. The rocks protect the plants from wind, keep their roots cool, and channel water to them. In winter the rocks absorb the sun's heat by day and release it at night, moderating root-damaging temperature fluctuations in the soil. And adding a coarse gravel mulch helps keep the plants' crowns and leaves from rotting.

Tailoring the Soil for Bulbs

Alpines are usually planted in a mixture of garden soil, sand or grit, and leaf mold. Additional coarse grit will create the pockets of quick-draining soil favored year round by iris, crocus, narcissus, oxalis, and tulip. To mature well, iris, calochortus, and brodiaea plants need rapid drainage in summer. By adding more humus to the mixture, you can give erythronium, cyclamen, and anemone the rich, moisture-retentive soil they need. You can also apply water and food as needed. For example, anemone and colchicum like extra water in summer; erythronium and fritillaria need extra fertilizer.

Nestling such early-spring bloomers as *Iris reticulata,* species tulips, and crocus against rocks will give them shelter and warmth. The periods of shade the rocks provide will give cyclamen, fritillary, galanthus, oxalis, and scilla a needed respite from the summer sun.

Showcasing Smaller Bulbs

A rock garden has just the right scale for those smaller bulbs that might get lost at ground level

170

Species Tulips: Tiny but Tough

Species tulips like these *Tulipa bakeri* 'Lilac Wonder' naturalize easily in a sunny spot. Natives of the Mediterranean, they bloom very early in spring in Zones 5 to 7; *T. clusiana* even grows in Zone 9. With multiple flowers on each stem, species tulips look best in an uncrowded position in a rock garden. They combine well with other bulbs that bloom at the same time—*Pulsatilla vulgaris, Adonis vernalis,* or bulbous iris. Evergreen dwarf shrubs, such as *Ilex crenata* (Japanese holly), *Chamaecyparis obtusa* (Hinoki false cypress), and *Arctostaphylos uva-ursi* (bearberry), also make good companions.

among larger plants. The rocks help set off the plants. For instance, elevated in a terraced rock garden and silhouetted against dark stones, the pale blue, purple-veined petals of *Crocus speciosus* stand out. And because the plants are elevated, the scents of species tulip, crocus, narcissus, iris, and grape hyacinth more easily reach your nose. Rock gardens for hardy spring and summer bulbs like *Allium cyaneum* and *Lilium cernuum* can be as small as 3 square feet. A larger garden would be appropriate for ixia, freesia, romulea, brodiaea, babiana, or bletilla. They generally grow from 12 inches to 18 inches high.

Bulbs for the Mixed Rock Garden

Bulbs combine handily in rock gardens with dwarf shrubs and perennials, which discreetly cover the spots left bare when the bulbs go dormant. Low-growing, mat-forming herbs such as thyme, mint, and oregano protect the bulbs from splashing mud. They also provide ground-covering greenery for colchicum or *Cyclamen hederifolium,* which bloom without foliage in the fall.

Look for drought-tolerant plants that prefer fast-draining soil. Dwarf evergreens and other small shrubs such as heather, daphne, dwarf cotoneaster, ground-cover azalea, and blue spruce offer excellent possibilities for combinations with bulbs. The bulbs' upright form rising through these sprawling plants makes an interesting and colorful contrast.

Finally, choose companion perennials for color: pinks and white from saxifrage, arabis, phlox, primula, and pink; blues and lavender from bellflower, gentian, and mint; yellow and orange from dwarf aster and chrysanthemum in the fall. The silver-blue foliage of blue fescue is a good foil for brightly colored bulbs. In a shady, damp spot, plant small astilbe, fern, and hosta.

Designing with Roses

An arbor blanketed with 'Cl. First Prize' and 'Abraham Darby' serves as a threshold between rose beds with such beauties as deep red 'Chrysler Imperial' and a cutting garden beyond. The formality of this Long Island garden is emphasized by the straight lines of a trim yew hedge, low edgings of boxwood, and a wide brick walk.

With their multitude of colors, shapes, and sizes, roses exist for almost any garden situation. In choosing the plants that bring the most beauty into your garden, you'll be considering the hues of both flower and foliage, the texture of the leaves, and even the winter charm of hips. But it is the form of the plant that will help you decide how best to use it. Plump shrubs make sumptuous hedges, stiffly elegant bushes are for formal beds, tall climbers enliven a trellis or fence, and low growers blanket the ground—and these are only some of the ways to introduce roses into your landscape.

For many gardeners, the thought of a rose garden conjures up an image of upright bushes neatly arranged inside a formal, geometric frame of dense, clipped greenery. This stately, even spare, look can be magnificent, showcasing the beautiful long-stemmed blooms of hybrid teas such as the deep red 'Mister Lincoln' or the pale yellow 'Elina' and grandifloras such as the elegant pink 'Queen Elizabeth'. If growing roses for cutting and exhibiting in competitions is your goal, devote space solely to these showy types, and—because hybrid teas and grandifloras are typically scant on leaves—enclose the bed with a low hedge of yew, holly, or boxwood to contribute foliage to the overall picture. A protective barrier of greenery also creates a pleasant microclimate for roses, shielding them from strong winds and shading the soil to slow the rate of evaporation. Partial afternoon shade will help keep the blossoms looking their best longer and preserve their fragrance.

If you're planning a large traditional garden, plant a network of several rose beds, divided by paths of brick, stone, or turf grass. The straighter the paths and the more symmetrical their arrangement, the more formal your rose garden will look. And any number of special touches can be added. For variety in height, try planting climbers and ramblers, trained along arches and tripods. Ornaments such as urns, a sundial, or statuary will give the garden a sense of whimsy, dignity—or whatever personality you wish to convey.

Hedges: Double-Duty Roses

Roses can also play a substantial role outside of the formal setting. Define the perimeter of your property with species roses; separate one area from another with teas and shrubs; edge a walkway with miniatures or clustering floribundas. The floribunda 'Betty Prior', for example, makes a lush yet tidy hedge to guide visitors to your front door. Plant a single row of 'Betty Prior' 3 feet apart and keep the bushes trimmed to shorter than 5 feet. Unlike 'Betty Prior', modern shrub roses such as pink 'Bonica' and the snow white hybrid rugosa 'Blanc Double de Coubert' spread out and form a loosely cascading hedge. Use these shrubbier roses as a transition between the patio and the lawn or as a low screen to block the view of your neighbor's yard. Planted in staggered rows about 2½ feet apart, the shrubs create an impenetrable barrier of thorny canes and foliage. Roses suitable for both formal and informal hedges are listed on page 175.

Woody Shrubs and Roses

If you have room for only one hedge, try combining evergreen shrubs with roses. In moist, well-drained soil in the hot southeastern United States,

Upright and vase shaped in habit, the floribunda 'Iceberg' rises to 5 or 6 feet and spreads only slightly, making it an ideal rose for use as an open hedge. Its plush, pure white 3-inch flowers offer a textural contrast to this driveway of concrete pavers in southern California.

Roses and Herbs: Sharing a Gardening Heritage

Roses and herbs have made ideal garden companions for centuries. The oldest known gallica and the first rose known to be cultivated for medicine and perfume, *Rosa gallica officinalis*—'Apothecary's Rose'—shared a bed with fragrant herbs and, in time, with other roses in the enclosed walls of medieval monastery gardens. For hundreds of years, essences were distilled from the plants and combined into conserves, syrups, balms, and ointments that were used for treating ailments ranging from lung and liver disorders to headaches and hangovers. These mixtures contained the petals of gallicas and their citrus- and clove-scented damask descendants such as 'York and Lancaster' and 'Celsiana', vitamin-rich hips of rugosas, and such pungent herbs as lavender and chamomile.

Today, a garden of herbs and roses is still an enticing blend of function and beauty. Herbs may be grown for their culinary and possible medicinal value, and their powerful aromas help keep insects and pests away from prized roses. In addition, the striking foliage of such plants as gray-green santolina, silvery artemisia, and lacy-textured tansy offers an ideal foil for roses' showy blooms. Bushy herbs like germander also have a place, forming short, dense hedges of tiny, glossy green leaves, which add a sober note to the heady tumble of color and fragrance. In planting roses and herbs together in your own garden, you can create anything from a casual cottage version, with roses spotted here and there, to a dramatic setting that echoes the walled gardens of the past, like the Atlanta, Georgia, garden shown above.

Traditionally, roses were awarded the prime sites within a walled garden, surrounded by low hedges outlining island beds in ornamental shapes. In the garden above, the narrow, walled space is divided into three main diamond-shaped beds, each defined by a clipped hedge of true dwarf box and ground-hugging marjoram. At the rear of the garden, a rustic pergola draws the eye upward to a stand of trees beyond the garden wall. A weeping rose standard, 'The Fairy', adds a vertical dimension to each bed, and underplantings of herbs and vegetables fill the areas inside the hedges. At left center, a potted standard lemon verbena and a rosemary topiary echo the upright form of the roses and relieve the strict symmetry of the patterns, creating a garden that is lush yet orderly, and a feast for the senses.

plant *Photinia* x *fraseri* (Fraser photinia), whose new foliage is tipped with red, and *Raphiolepis indica* 'Springtime' (Indian hawthorn), which forms stiff mounds of dark green foliage, behind 'Buff Beauty' and 'Mrs. Dudley Cross' to get a gorgeous living fence. 'Buff Beauty' is a fragrant hybrid musk with 2-inch pale apricot blooms that grows to 6 feet, and 'Mrs. Dudley Cross'—a 4-foot tea rose that does especially well in warm climates—has smaller, pink-tinged yellow flowers. The photinia grows quite straggly if left untamed and should be pruned to 6 feet, while the Indian hawthorn tops out at 6 feet and needs only occasional shaping.

Farther north, alternate cool-climate needled and broad-leaved evergreens with the hardy silvery pink rugosa 'Frau Dagmar Hartopp', pruned to 4

'Bonica'

Beside a trickling fountain in this garden in Vancouver, British Columbia, apricot 'Leander' blooms mingle gently with the off-white peony 'Coral Sunset'. The blue foliage of common rue, the pure green leaves of a pink shrub rose, and the glossy evergreen foliage of a cherry-laurel hedge bring the soft tints into sharper focus.

feet in height and width. *Picea pungens* 'Montgomery', a spruce with a bluish cast that forms a dwarf pyramid, and *Ilex glabra* 'Compacta' (dwarf inkberry), with dark green foliage and black berries in fall, will complement the rugosa's flashy passage to winter as its foliage turns deep maroon, then golden yellow, and its large hips ripen to red.

Color Schemes for Beds and Borders

Get the most out of your roses' vibrant color display by placing them in beds and borders with other flowering plants. The opportunities to compose a stunning picture of color and form are infinite; just make certain that the companions you choose share the same cultural conditions required by most roses—fairly acid, well-drained, loamy soil, and plenty of sunlight and water.

Tall or spiky plants such as lilies, hollyhocks, and foxgloves complement the arching or rounded shapes of rosebushes. Low-growing plants, including annual 'Carpet of Snow' sweet alyssum and candytuft, conceal the bare, twiggy ankles of hybrid teas—and they produce white flowers that go with roses of any color. When combining roses with other colorful plants, keep in mind that pleasing arrangements are usually harmonious—composed of colors that are within the same color family—or contrasting—meaning that the colors are from the opposite side of the color spectrum. The

Recommended Roses for a Hedge

Formal Hedges

UNDER 3 FEET
'Cécile Brunner'
'La Marne'
'Marie Pavié'
'Nearly Wild'
'White Pet'

3 TO 5 FEET
'Archduke Charles'
'Autumn Damask'
'Betty Prior'
'Carefree Beauty'
'Elina'
'French Lace'
'Iceberg'
'Old Blush'
'Olympiad'

TALLER THAN 5 FEET
'John Cabot'
'Penelope'
'Queen Elizabeth'

Informal Hedges

3 TO 5 FEET
'Ballerina'
'Belle Poitevine'
'Blanc Double de Coubert'
'Bonica'
'Erfurt'
'Hansa'
'Sea Foam'

TALLER THAN 5 FEET
'Belinda'
'Cl. Pinkie'
R. glauca
R. palustris
R. rugosa alba
'Simplicity'
'Will Scarlet'

vivid magenta flowers of *Geranium psilostemon*, for example, harmonize well with the perfumed deep pink bourbon 'Madame Isaac Pereire'. As an added bonus, the rose acts as a brace for the tall geranium.

Since roses come in virtually every color except blue, try pairing them with perennials and annuals in tints or shades of blue or violet. The yellow-pink blooms of the hybrid tea 'Peace' or the bright pink trusses of the bourbon 'Louise Odier' rising above the pale blue, cloudlike flowers of *Nigella damascena* (love-in-a-mist)—a self-sowing annual—paints a portrait of soothing pastels. For more drama, plant the clear yellow shrub 'Graham Thomas' with deep violet 'Black Knight' delphiniums. If you want truly eye-popping color, pair 'Playboy'—whose blooms are splashed with orange, yellow, and scarlet—with blue-violet flower stalks of *Nepeta* x *faassenii* (catmint) and *Salvia* x *superba* 'May Night' (sage). If the combination seems too garish, add bright yellow 'Moonshine' achillea to temper the mix.

The Many Tones of White

White roses come in creamy tones tinged with yellow—the climbing tea 'Sombreuil' is one example—and blush tones flushed with the lightest tints of pink, such as 'Celestial', an alba. When placed amid delicate pastel flowers of pink and apricot, these near-white roses seem to deepen the tints of their neighbors. And in a garden of hot colors—orange, scarlet, fiery red—a mass of pure white roses is a refreshing respite.

For a cool midsummer display, plant white 'Frau Karl Druschki', using a technique called pegging to create a low habit and encourage prolific blooms. Back the rose with the sculpted foliage of sea kale and its lacy mounds of dainty white flowers, then let tall, steel blue spherical flower heads of *Eryngium* x *tripartitum* (three-lobed eryngium) lean on the sea kale for support.

The large floribunda 'Iceberg' helps make a gleaming white statement when it is combined with the almost translucent white cups of *Campanula persicifolia alba* (white bellflower) and a pure white cultivar of fireweed, *Epilobium angustifolium* 'Album'. In back of this trio—which will bloom from early summer through fall—plant a tall stand of the big-leaved foliage

Saucer-shaped semi-double pink blooms of the floribunda 'Simplicity' contrast merrily with sunny yellow bearded iris. At upper right, the deep blue spikes of rocket larkspur and white and lilac dame's rocket add a sedate note to the cheery scene.

The Whitest Roses

'Alba Semi-plena'	*R. rugosa alba*
'Blanc Double	'Sally Holmes'
de Coubert'	'Sea Foam'
'Boule de Neige'	'Silver Moon'
'Fair Bianca'	'Snow Bride'
'Frau Karl Druschki'	'Sombreuil'
'Iceberg'	'White Meidiland'
'Irresistible'	'White Pet'
'Lamarque'	
'Linville'	
'Madame Alfred	
Carrière'	
'Madame Hardy'	
'Madame Legras	
de St. Germain'	
'Madame Plantier'	
'Marie Pavié'	
'Nastarana'	
R. banksiae banksiae	

'Frau Karl Druschki'

of *Macleaya cordata* (plume poppy), which should reach at least 7 feet by July, lending an otherworldly quality to the luminous landscape.

Bicolored/Multicolored Roses

Not all rose blooms are one solid color. Apricot-and-salmon 'Party Girl' and yellow-and-red 'Rainbow's End', for instance, are blends, which means that varying degrees of each color merge in the blooms. A bloom can also be striped, blotched, or mottled with separate colors, or there may be an "eye" of a second color at its center. The oldest striped rose of record, 'Rosa Mundi', a sport of the gallica 'Apothecary's Rose', has pale pink blooms blotched with the vivid pink of its parent. Alternate plants of 'Rosa Mundi' and 'Apothecary's Rose' for an enchanting hedge or border.

'Camaieux', with crimson, purple, and lilac stripes on a creamy background, is at home with solid-colored flowers such as the wine red and pink hybrids *Penstemon campanulatus* 'Garnet' and 'Evelyn'. The colors of the two penstemons match the rose's stripes, but the shape of their blooms is tubular, making for a pleasing contrast in form against the roundness of the rose. Add white foxglove to complement the red and pink.

TIPS FROM THE PROS

Companions Worth Cultivating

Pair roses and ornamental grasses for a sensational-looking garden, says Mike Shoup, founder of the Antique Rose Emporium in Brenham, Texas. Ornamental grasses come in many colors, to be combined with roses of all hues, and their graceful, linear growth habit—tufted, mounded, arching, and upright—offers a refreshing counterpoint to the more rounded shapes of rosebushes and their blooms. To delight the eye with a planting composed of varying forms, textures, and colors, try the following combinations:

- Tufted, fine-textured, icy blue *Festuca ovina* var. *glauca* 'Blaufuchs' with soft pastels such as light pink 'Old Blush' and 'Cécile Brunner', rose pink 'Duchesse de Brabant', and pink-apricot 'Perle d'Or'.

- Arching, burgundy-leaved *Pennisetum setaceum* 'Rubrum' (purple fountain grass) with yellow-pink 'Lafter', 'Dr. Eckener', and yellow 'Graham Thomas' for dramatic contrast.
- Metallic blue *Panicum virgatum* 'Heavy Metal' (switch grass) and *Elymus arenarius* 'Glaucus' (blue Lyme grass) with mauve 'Reine des Violettes' and 'Cardinal de Richelieu', bright pink 'Betty Prior', and rose pink 'Nearly Wild'.
- Tall *Miscanthus sinensis* 'Morning Light' (Japanese silver grass), whose slender green leaves have a narrow margin of clear white, with red shrub rose 'John Franklin' and in front of climbers such as bright pink 'Zéphirine Drouhin' and dark red, tiny-leaved 'Red Cascade'.

'Gruss an Aachen' and Helictotrichon sempervirens (blue oat grass)

Wildflowers for Every Garden

The brilliant pink flowers and willowlike leaves of Epilobium angustifolium—called fireweed because it is one of the first plants to germinate after a fire—make a delicate tracery against a house in Crested Butte, Colorado. Fireweed can be invasive, but a less vigorous white variety is well behaved in a perennial bed.

It is very likely that you are already growing wildflowers in your garden. Many of the old standbys of the traditional herbaceous borders that have long been the hallmark of English gardens trace their ancestry to North America. Such plantings would be far poorer without New World asters, wild indigos, columbines, lupines, coneflowers, coral bells, phloxes, and their progeny.

In many instances, the plants have been changed through selection and breeding. When horticulturists find a truly outstanding individual and want to reproduce it, they do so vegetatively, from cuttings or tissue culture. That way, the results will be clones, identical to the mother plant. (On the other hand, when plants are grown from seed, the results are often unpredictable.) These cloned plants are called *cultivars*—short for "cultivated variety." Cultivars usually possess some distinctive quality—a long flowering period, an unusual color, small stature, or handsome foliage. They are not necessarily better than seed-grown plants, but they *are* predictable, identical, and, therefore, uniform in appearance. This is a great advantage in formal gardens.

A Formal Setting for Wildflowers

There are many types of formal gardens, from small island beds to intricate parterres. All, however, are guided by the geometric principles of scale

and proportion. Shorn hedges, well-defined planting beds, and the use of symmetry are all typical of formal gardens.

Formal gardens are most often designed to reflect the architecture of a formal house. When the owner of a Georgian-style house chooses straight-edged, geometric beds and neatly clipped hedges, it is because these features enhance the simple, elegant lines of the house. Next to a brick path, mass plantings of a discreetly hued cultivar such as the pale, creamy-yellow *Coreopsis verticillata* 'Moonbeam' (threadleaf coreopsis) enclosed by a clipped hedge of dwarf edging boxwood yields a neat, tailored look that harmonizes with more formal architectural styles.

Wildflowers for Beds and Borders

The predictability of cultivars also makes them good choices for traditional perennial beds and borders because a particular color, height, or width is a given. Gardeners design such ornamental plantings around specific color schemes, so being able to count on a particular shade is all-important. For example, in a pink to purple border that is meant to be soothing, the vivid scarlet of *Lobelia cardinalis* (cardinal flower) would be jarring. The darker wine of its cultivar 'Ruby Slippers', however, adds just the right touch of color.

Of course, cultivars are not the only natives suitable for perennial borders. Dozens of others, often not as well known, serve beautifully. *Baptisia alba* (white wild indigo), a midborder star, has clusters of pea-like flowers for nearly a month in spring and remains a neat 30-inch shrub until frost. Also for the midborder is golden threadleaf coreopsis, which adds tiny flowers and airy volume. Like its better-known, shorter cultivars 'Zagreb' and 'Moonbeam', it blooms for weeks on end, carrying the border through the summer.

Designing for a Natural Look

When gardens take inspiration from nature rather than from architectural or traditional styles, they almost seem to have evolved on their own. Rather than being geometric in form, the beds in such gardens flow and curve, following the natural contours of the land. Slopes, stands of trees, and the banks of streams or creeks are good places to site free-form beds, where they will also save on maintenance by eliminating the need to mow.

The gardener augments this less constrained look by placing plants in irregular groups of mixed textures and varying sizes and heights. If shrubs are combined with the herbaceous plants, they should reflect the diversity found in nature; fewer than half should be evergreen. And save the task of regular shaping for some other part of the garden. Instead, allow deciduous shrubs like the native *Callicarpa americana* (beautyberry), with its long, arching stems and purple berries, to grow into their natural shapes.

Lively in form but restrained in color, the boltonia in the foreground above enhances the monochromatic color scheme of a formal garden in Potomac, Maryland. Blooming from late summer into fall, its airy flowers contrast with the thick, plush texture of the lamb's ears that edge the border.

The Versatility of Ornamental Grasses

Most herbaceous plants change with the seasons, tying the garden to the natural world, but the ornamental grasses do it with exceptional flair. In summer their graceful forms serve as cool green and blue fillers when planted in natural drifts, providing a subtly textured background for the shifting colors of perennials and annuals. Throughout fall and winter, the grasses remain standing, turning shades of almond, russet, tan, and gold. Grasses also bring year-round movement and sound to the garden as they sway and rustle in the wind.

A *purple verbena and a yellow hymenoxys nestled between its trailing stems bask in the center of a wide walkway leading through a southern California garden (left). Planted in pockets between the paving stones, these perennials enjoy a cool root run (cool soil) and, simultaneously, the good air circulation and full sunlight they need for optimum growth.*

Prairie wildflowers cover a sunny slope in the Wisconsin garden at left. In midsummer the white spires of Culver's root are surrounded by black-eyed Susans and pink bee balm. Later in the season, the feathery plumes of goldenrod will dominate. After frost the slope is peppered with the dark round seed heads of the black-eyed Susans.

tus. If form is paramount in a planting scheme, consider dividing this grass every 2 years, since it may lose its neat outline with age.

Two other evergreen or semievergreen grasses are *Muhlenbergia capillaris* (pink muhly) and *Deschampsia caespitosa* (tufted hair grass). Found growing in moist, rich soil in the Southeast, pink muhly makes a 1½-foot clump of extremely fine-textured leaves surmounted in fall by airy panicles of pink flowers that are lovely when backlit by the afternoon sun. *Muhlenbergia rigens* (deer grass) is another delicate-looking species suitable for dry-climate gardens in the West.

In silhouette, tufted hair grass is similar to muhly grass, but its foliage is a darker green. Its delicate flowers open green, then change to buff, gold, or a purplish bronze, depending on the cultivar. One of the few ornamental grasses that tolerate shade, it is lovely juxtaposed against ferns and hostas or massed as a ground cover in a woodland garden.

Tall Grasses

Prairie grasses attaining heights of 4 feet and more are ideal for the back of a sunny border, but they needn't be relegated solely to supporting roles. If you have a pool in your garden, the slim, graceful leaves of *Panicum virgatum* (switch grass), *Sorghastrum nutans* (Indian grass), or *Andropogon gerardii* (big bluestem) would make elegant reflections on its surface. Placed in front of a dark broad-leaved evergreen such as the native *Ilex glabra* (inkberry), any of these grasses presents a striking contrast of color and texture. If you juxtapose them with the red berries of *Aronia arbutifolia* (chokeberry) or the scarlet autumn leaves of *Itea virginica* (Virginia sweetspire), for instance—the composition fairly sparkles.

The height and mass of these grasses equip them to serve as architectural elements within the garden. To turn an area of lawn open to public view into a private seating area, partially surround it with clumps of grass planted in a sinuous curve or, for a more formal look, in an L shape. Because a tall grass reaches its mature size about 3 years af-

The Low-Growing Grasses

The arching leaves of grasses spilling onto a paved terrace, driveway, or walk make a pretty edging. Among the low-growing grasses suitable for this purpose are *Sporobolus heterolepis* (prairie dropseed), whose ⅟₁₆-inch-wide emerald green leaves form a fountainlike hummock. Prairie dropseed grows well in dry soil, as does the dwarf evergreen *Festuca ovina* var. *glauca* (blue fescue). Sometimes no more than 6 inches in height, blue fescue has dome-shaped tufts of needlelike leaves that color best in full sun and dry soil. Its dense, mounded form makes this grass a striking accent among trailing plants in a rock or trough garden. For textural contrast, mass blue fescue in front of the flattened, leathery pads of a prickly pear cac-

ter planting, the new garden room it defines will assume its character sooner than it would if shrubs were used.

Along a property line, a tall grass makes a low-key three-season herbaceous hedge that is cut to the ground by late winter to make way for new growth. A less restrained, more colorful alternative is to embellish the leafy screen with stately wildflowers. Choose a mix of annuals, biennials, and perennials ranging in height from 3 to 6 feet or more: *Helianthus maximiliani* (Maximilian sunflower) and *H. annuus* (common sunflower); *Ipomopsis rubra* (standing cypress), with brilliant red flowers that are magnets for hummingbirds; goldenrods; a dusky purple *Vernonia* (ironweed); yellow-flowered *Agastache nepetoides* (giant hys-

sop); or splashes of blue from *Baptisia australis* (blue wild indigo). Your choices will depend not only on growing conditions but also on the space available. A useful guideline is to limit the height of the tallest plant to no more than half of the width of the planting.

Meadows and Prairies

Whether growing in hedges, beds, or borders, ornamental grasses interplanted with colorful wildflowers evoke prairies or meadows. *Prairie*, the French word for meadow, denotes the complex, grass-dominated, treeless ecosystem that once covered much of the central United States and

Canada. The special, untamed beauty of an expanse of flowering plants and grasses in a treeless clearing has caught the eye and won the heart of many a gardener.

Even though most people notice the flowers first, grasses are the major component of a prairie, making up more than 50 percent of its biomass. Such proportions account for the subtle, color-flecked green of the prairie, compared with the intense color of a conventional bed or border. If the grasses tone down the brilliance of the flowers, they also help to hide their demise. And in winter when other herbaceous plants have withered, grasses add volume and a tawny presence.

A pleasing possibility for the gardener who yearns for a bit of the prairie but has a small yard is a "pocket meadow," which is simply a prairielike mixture of flowering plants and grasses scaled down in height and mass to suit the space. By choosing plants that stay under 3 feet tall, a gardener can create a meadow in as few as 60 to 100 square feet.

A pocket meadow looks best when it is framed with a fence or shrub border as a background. In front, a path or a row of a grass with a mounding habit, such as prairie dropseed, gives it a finished edge. Another option is to mow a curving path through the meadow. Even in a small space where the plants are only hip high, a path gives the illusion of greater depth. It also allows whoever walks on it the wonderful sensation of being surrounded by a miniature ecosystem alive with the sound and sight of insects drawn to the flowers.

Establishing a pocket meadow is not substantially different from planting a border. Within the allotted space, intersperse grasses and flowering plants at intervals of a foot or so. Position flowering plants in irregular drifts. Even though the end product will appear to have evolved naturally, the young plants require care. Mulch the meadow well, and keep it watered and weed free while the plants establish themselves.

A cooling sight on a hot July day in Milwaukee, a man-made garden pond (below) features the cupped blossoms of a nonnative water lily. Natives include the dark green fringe of sedge in the foreground and two clumps of dark green arrowhead that offer a vertical accent to the water lily's flat, round leaves.

Shade Gardening with Style

The lacy blue foliage of *Dicentra eximia* (fringed bleeding heart) daintily accents the broad, powdery-surfaced leaves of Hosta 'August Moon' and yellow-edged H. 'Golden Tiara'. The bright new growth on the tips of the spiky yew echoes the golden tones of the hostas, completing the shady vignette.

Just as a flowering garden changes from month to month and from season to season as plants bloom and fade, a shady foliage garden also presents a series of new faces over time. Spring-blooming bulbs, growing in the sunlight that filters through the bare branches of deciduous trees, can give way to winter-dormant perennials known for their appealing foliage, such as hostas, astilbes, ferns, and daylilies. The fresh leaves of these plants will conceal those of the spent bulbs and will remain attractive throughout the summer.

Keeping company with the perennials can be a mixture of evergreen and deciduous shrubs. To form a tapestry that will engage the eye through the growing season and beyond, combine shrubs that have contrasting leaf colors and textures. Vivid fall color is assured if you choose shrubs such as *Amelanchier canadensis* (shadblow serv-

iceberry), a large plant that turns brilliant orange-red; *Aronia* (chokeberry), showing red in fall; or *Hamamelis mollis* (Chinese witch hazel), *H. vernalis* (American witch hazel), or *H. virginiana* (common witch hazel), with yellow autumn color.

In cold climates, evergreens enhance the shade garden's winter appeal. Yew, boxwood, rhododendron, *Pieris,* and holly are among the many shrubs that remain green year round. In addition, a number of perennial foliage plants manage to survive above ground during the winter. Some, such as *Polystichum setiferum* (soft shield fern) and *P. lonchitis* (northern holly fern), become large enough to assume the design role of a small shrub.

To alleviate bare ground during the winter months, plant evergreen ground covers such as *Ajuga* (bugleweed), pachysandra, *Mazus reptans,* and *Heuchera* (alumroot).

Combining Foliage Plants

Once you've decided which foliage plants to include in your shade garden, your next step is to fit them into a harmonious design. As you plan your garden's layout, take time to consider each plant's form, texture, mature height, and color. If you will be including flowering plants in the design, plan for them as well.

The form, or shape, of a plant is often its most noticeable feature. When small plants have distinctive forms, mixing them together willy-nilly can create a discordant design. To unify a composition, group three or more of one type of plant together and arrange clusters of perennials in naturalistic drifts that flow through the garden. If you are planting a shady border, occasionally repeat the pattern of plants to create a visual rhythm. The exception to planting in groups occurs when you want to use one dramatic plant as a specimen.

Sometimes a plant whose greatest virtue seems to be its ability to complement others in a harmonious grouping can also make a powerful statement when mass-planted on its own. *Polygonatum biflorum* (small Solomon's-seal), for example, is delightful combined in a woodland garden with *Trillium* (wake-robin), *Smilacina* (false Solomon's-seal), ferns, and *Mertensia virginica* (Virginia bluebells). Yet when it is mass-planted, its arching stems form an impressive display. Likewise, a mass planting of a hosta cultivar with a low-growing habit can prove a dramatic variation on a ground cover.

Marrying Foliage Textures and Colors

Juxtaposing plants of different textures can create fascinating effects in your garden. For an intriguing composition, try mixing fine-leaved plants with those that have larger, coarser leaves. A broad-leaved hosta paired with a feathery fern, for example, or the straplike foliage of daylilies or *Liriope* (lilyturf) with the heart-shaped foliage of *Epimedium* (barrenwort) creates an appealing contrast.

Color adds yet another dimension to plant pairings. Use accents of gold, lime green, or bluish green to enrich a combination, or use gold or variegated leaves where you need a flash of light. For example, the yellow-green and bronze-purple varieties of the Japanese barberry shrub *(Berberis thunbergii)* create a vivid pairing in light shade, with the darker foliage seeming to recede behind the brighter leaves. In fact, you can visually enlarge a shady spot by placing dark or cool-colored foliage toward the back of the garden, where it will subtly blend into the shadows. If a cozier space is what you want, put brighter-colored foliage in the back; it will appear to leap forward, foreshortening the distance.

Demonstrating how a shady border can depart from the traditional floral emphasis of a sunny one, this planting in Vancouver, British Columbia, features a pleasing mix of leafy perennials. The Solomon's-seal in back arches over the hostas and maidenhair ferns in front, adding height and movement to the design.

Designing with Shade-Tolerant Herbaceous Plants

Although most shade-tolerant herbaceous plants are grown primarily for their bloom, many of them also have lovely foliage. And because such plants are generally shallow rooted, they are ideal for shade gardens, where competition with the roots of trees and shrubs is often intense.

Cimicifuga (bugbane) sends up beautiful plumelike flower spikes in summer, but its ferny foliage is equally attractive during the rest of the season. A tall plant that will tolerate partial shade, bugbane should be placed in the back of flower borders or on the fringes of woodlands. For the edge of a path or in a rock garden, consider *Corydalis lutea* (yellow corydalis), a low-growing, clumping plant with gray-green fernlike leaves. Its delicate yellow flowers will persist through most of the growing season if it is kept well watered.

Other flowering perennials with fine, feathery foliage include bleeding heart, astilbe, *Aruncus* (goatsbeard), and *Aquilegia* (columbine). For interesting contrast, try mixing them with the strappy leaves of shade-tolerant daylilies, the large heart-shaped leaves of *Begonia grandis* (hardy begonia), or the geranium-like foliage of *Alchemilla* (lady's-mantle).

If you're looking for a plant to light up a dark spot or act as an accent, combine variegated *Pulmonaria saccharata* (Bethlehem sage) with the deep purple leaves of *Heuchera micrantha* 'Palace Purple'. Another heuchera with striking foliage is *H. americana* 'Garnet' (rock geranium), which has a geranium-shaped leaf with apple green margins and deep purple veins.

The Wide World of Hostas

Hostas, also known as plantain lilies, are an astonishingly varied group of plants, the majority of which prefer shade. They grow in most of North America, although they are less successful in regions that don't get winter chill or are extremely arid. Because of the diversity of size, texture, and color in this genus, there is a hosta to meet almost any landscape requirement. Some grow only a few inches tall with petite leaves; others have large paddlelike leaves and grow to a substantial 36 inches tall and wide. *Hosta fortunei* 'Gold Standard', a chartreuse-leaved cultivar edged with dark green, makes clumps that grow to a width of 5 feet or more. Foliage color among hostas

ranges from bright yellow, gold, and creamy white, usually in the form of variegation, to the entire spectrum of greens and blues. Leaves can be long and thin, broad and round, oval, heart shaped, or pointed. Foliage textures vary as well, from smooth to deeply ribbed.

Hostas adapt to a variety of growing conditions; they thrive in both dry and wet locations. The yellow varieties tend to do best when their shade is no more than partial; those with blue foliage usually prefer more time in the shade. While hostas are easy to propagate by division, a single clump can grow in the same place for several years.

Petasites japonicus var. giganteus 'Fuki' (giant butterbur) blankets a New Jersey border with leaves that can grow up to 4 feet in diameter. In early spring this spreading perennial produces cones of daisylike, pale yellow flowers before the large leaves appear.

Mining Hostas' Assets

Put hostas to work in your shade garden. Edge a path or walkway with midsize cultivars such as *H.* 'So Sweet', which has green leaves with white margins and very fragrant flowers; 'Golden Tiara', with long heart-shaped green leaves edged in gold; or the cream-edged *H. undulata* 'Albo-marginata'.

Create a striking ground cover by mass-planting small hostas such as *H.* 'Kabitan', a narrow, gold-leaved variety, or *H.* 'Ginko Craig', a green-and-white beauty. Although hostas don't spread by means of runners like traditional ground covers, you can space the clumps so that the leaves overlap to completely cover the ground. For spring color, plant early-blooming daffodils between the hostas; the hosta foliage will appear just as the daffodils are fading.

Large hostas perform well as foundation plantings, in mixed-flower borders, or as specimen plants. Giants—as tall as 3 feet and 5 feet or more across—include the blue *H. fortunei* var. *hyacinthina*; *H. sieboldiana* 'Elegans', a blue-green cultivar; *H.* 'Sum and Substance', prized for its 2-foot-wide heart-shaped chartreuse leaves; and *H.* 'Blue Angel', which has striking, heart-shaped, deeply ridged blue leaves.

Experiment with hostas and other plants to create exciting color and texture combinations. Plant a broad-leaved hosta such as *H. sieboldiana* 'Frances Williams' next to a feathery *Athyrium filix-femina* (lady fern). Or combine *H.* 'Gold Edger', a chartreuse-leaved cultivar, with a variegated ivy that picks up the same yellow-green color. Equally eye-catching is a collection of different hostas that echo and accent one another's colors and forms. Don't be afraid of trial and error. Hostas are sturdy, and you can move them around without much damage if they don't marry happily.

Ferns: Prehistoric Wonders

Ferns are another group of adaptable and intriguing shade performers. There are ferns suited to just about any garden condition, from full sun to deep shade, from wet conditions to dry, and from alkaline to acid soil. The less fussy ones will put up with whatever situation they are given. *Thelypteris noveboracensis* (New York fern), for example, prefers damp, acid soil and light shade but will tolerate fairly dry conditions, neutral soil, and medium shade.

The diversity of ferns provides the shade gardener with a wealth of choices. There are creepers that make excellent—although sometimes invasive—ground covers. *Dennstaedtia punctilobula*

Mass plantings of colorful hostas brighten shady areas of the garden where grass will not survive. Cultivars encircling a tree are (counterclockwise from top) H. 'Kabitan', H. x tardiana 'Blue Wedgewood', H. 'Antioch', H. fortunei 'Francee', and H. sieboldiana 'Elegans'.

(hay-scented fern), for example, will quickly fill a space with its 30-inch-tall fronds. It tolerates wet or dry conditions and deep shade. Other good ground covers include *Gymnocarpium dryopteris* (oak fern), *Polypodium aureum* (rabbit's-foot fern), and *Polypodium glycyrrhiza* (licorice fern).

Designing with Ferns

To create a soft, lacy effect in your garden, choose a genus with dainty foliage, such as one of the many maidenhair ferns. Depending on the species, these ferns form dense clumps ranging in height from 8 to 20 inches. One of the best is the hardy *Adiantum pedatum* (northern maidenhair). For a splash of color, add the purple-and-silver *Athyrium nipponicum* 'Pictum' (painted lady fern).

Ferns are particularly attractive when planted around woodland ponds and along streams. Delicate, aerial ferns grow happily at the water's edge and will quickly naturalize, softening the shoreline. *Osmunda cinnamomea* (cinnamon fern), *O. regalis* (royal fern), and *Dryopteris marginalis* (marginal shield fern) are ideal for such settings.

Ferns as Woodland Companion Plants

In woodland gardens, combine ferns with rhododendrons, azaleas, and delicate woodland flowers. Members of the genus *Dryopteris,* also known as fancy ferns, have finely cut rich green foliage that rises from a central crown; they mix admirably with trillium, bleeding heart, phlox, and primrose.

A diminutive woodlander, growing just 4 inches tall, is the oak fern. It looks especially charming mixed with *Linnaea borealis* (twinflower), *Claytonia virginica* (spring beauty), and *Dicentra cucullaria* (Dutchman's-breeches). When the Dutchman's-breeches foliage dies back in early summer, the fern can fill in the gap.

Because of their striking foliage and forms, ferns make excellent accents in a shady flower bed or border. Good candidates for this role include many *Dryopteris* species. And *Asplenium nidus* (bird's-nest fern) also does the trick with thin, leathery, tonguelike fronds that will grow an impressive 4 feet high in warm, humid conditions.

In cooler zones, *Matteuccia* (ostrich fern) is a good choice. With its erect feathery fronds that stand 3 feet tall and resemble a shuttlecock, this fern makes a dramatic display. Combine it with spring-flowering bulbs or woodland flowers, or let a clump of the ferns make a showing on their

A dependable shade performer, Athyrium filix-femina (lady fern) grows to a height of 3 feet and thrives in moist soil. The wild species, shown above in its springtime glory, often looks tired and tattered by summer's end; try one of its hybrids, such as A. filix-femina 'Victoriae', instead.

In this Seattle shade garden, northern maidenhair ferns (Adiantum pedatum)—also known as five-finger ferns—display their "fingers" against leathery spears of Asplenium scolopendrium (hart's-tongue fern). Overarching fronds of Polystichum munitum (western sword fern) add weight to the design.

The dark olive shade of the broad, crinkled *Heuchera* (alumroot) leaves accentuates the dark ribs of *Athyrium nipponicum 'Pictum'* (painted lady fern) in the St. Louis, Missouri, shade garden at left. The fern's silvery fronds add streaks of light to the composition.

Hairy leaf buds known as fiddleheads mark the early appearance of Osmunda cinnamomea (cinnamon fern). As the season progresses, the fiddleheads unfurl into fertile cinnamon-colored fronds, later to be joined by sterile green fronds.

own. For evergreen ferns, try the flat, swordlike fronds of *Polystichum acrostichoides* (Christmas fern), which grow to a length of 24 inches, and the equally substantial *P. setiferum* (soft shield fern).

A Perfect Match: Ferns and Rocks

Tiny, shallow-rooted ferns are ideal for growing in rock gardens, on the earthen risers of garden steps, and even in the crevices of walls. In fact, the warmth radiated by a wall may create a microclimate that enables you to grow a fern that is only borderline hardy in your zone. For such spots, try *Cystopteris fragilis* (fragile fern), which is much tougher than its name suggests; *Polypodium virginianum* (rock polypody), which will grow happily in just 2 inches of soil; the 6-inch-tall *Asplenium trichomanes* (maidenhair spleenwort), or *A. scolopendrium* (hart's-tongue fern), with its crinkled, tongue-shaped fronds.

In a shady, moist rock garden, plant *A. rhizophyllum* [also classified as *Camptosorus rhizophyllus*] (walking fern). It especially appreciates limestone rocks. An intriguing miniature for Zone 10 is the spreading *Selaginella kraussiana* (mat spike moss), which grows only half an inch tall.

Caladiums

The brightly colored heart- or arrowhead-shaped leaves of caladiums come in a beautiful silvery white that is veined with dark green, or in striking mixtures of pink, green, and cream. Well suited to shrub and flower borders as well as containers, caladiums grow in clumps about 12 inches tall and will thrive in either full or partial shade. They prefer evenly moist but well-drained soil, and their favorite weather condition is hot and humid; they are hardy perennials only to Zone 10. Caladiums do produce flowers, but they are so undistinguished that connoisseurs generally remove them, along with spent foliage, to encourage more leaf production. The broad, colorful leaves make caladiums a delightful foil next to any lacy green plant, including ferns, columbine, and astilbe. Use the silvery varieties in front of deep green plants such as yew; they will shimmer in contrast.

Coleus

Like caladiums, coleus will grow as a perennial in very warm regions but in colder climes must be

189

Nestled comfortably around rocks and beneath a blooming mountain laurel, dainty sweet woodruff and spotted lungwort (lower left), glossy wild ginger (lower right), and the blue-green arrowhead-shaped leaves of astilbe (right), create an arresting combination of perennials in this Connecticut garden.

treated as an annual. Coleus flaunts a wide range of foliage colors, including solids or mixtures of salmon, pink, red, maroon, chartreuse, yellow, and bronze. Dwarf varieties grow to about 6 inches tall, with leaves as small as an inch long; others may reach 36 inches, with leaves from 3 to 6 inches long. Leaf texture may be velvety to crinkled, with smooth, scalloped, or serrated edges.

Put the dwarf varieties to work in the front of a shady border. The larger varieties look handsome combined with tall ferns, which help isolate the multiple bold colors. Because of the diversity of color and textures, coleus is an excellent plant to combine with other shade plants to create your own unique plant marriages. Try a pink-leaved coleus next to the deep purple foliage of *Heuchera micrantha* 'Palace Purple', or combine a red or maroon specimen with a blue hosta.

Coleus does best in indirect light or light shade. Pinch back the stems in early summer to encourage bushy growth, and remove the inconspicuous flower spikes that emerge throughout the summer. This will help the plant focus its energy on foliage production.

You can create an unusual specimen by training a potted coleus as a standard. Remove side growth to encourage the plant to grow a tall stem and to leaf out on top. The plants are easy to propagate from cuttings in either water or a rooting medium, so you can reproduce your present inventory—and even increase your supply—by taking cuttings in autumn and overwintering them indoors.

Woodland Foliage Plants

A woodland setting is a shade gardener's paradise, for this is the natural habitat for many of the shade-loving species. It presents a classic opportunity to create a foliage garden that is not only in tune with nature but also complements it by adding a measure of order and design. Many woodland plants have an exquisite but ephemeral bloom season; their foliage is the dominant feature for the rest of the growing season. Think in terms of massing and combining plants to produce a pleasing flow of foliage color and texture in the woods.

Ornamental Grasses for Shade

Although the list of ornamental grasses for full shade is not long, you should be able to find something to meet your needs. One of the best is *Hakonechloa macra* 'Aureola' (golden variegated hakonechloa), shown above tucked in next to a hosta and beneath a blue spruce. Hardy in Zones 5 to 9, it grows in clumps 16 inches tall and 18 to 24 inches wide. Other grasses that do well in full shade include *Carex* (sedge) and *Deschampsia caespitosa* (tufted hair grass). For partial shade, try *Miscanthus sinensis* 'Variegatus' (eulalia) or *Chasmanthium latifolium* (northern sea oats). *Liriope* (lilyturf) works well along shady borders.

Some of the woodland plants, such as Virginia bluebells, *Dicentra*, and Dutchman's-breeches, have pretty foliage and flowers in spring, but then die back in early summer. Combine them with plants such as columbine, ferns, hostas, and Solomon's-seal, which will fill in the bare spots created by the summer-dormant woodland plants.

For a fascinating foliage mix, combine *Trillium erectum* (purple trillium), with its whorl of three leaves on a 6- to 18-inch tall stem; *Tiarella cordifolia* (foamflower), which spreads over the ground by runners; *Sanguinaria* (bloodroot), another colonizing plant with rounded, shallow-lobed pale green leaves; *Viola* (violet); Solomon's-seal; and *Clintonia borealis* (corn lily), which grows clusters of oval leaves about 6 inches long.

Another attractive woodland composition is achieved by joining purple trillium with *Asarum canadense* (wild ginger), a ground cover with velvety heart-shaped medium green leaves, and *Aquilegia canadensis* (wild columbine). Equally admirable—and unusual—is *Podophyllum* (May apple). On each stem is one broad, deeply lobed leaf that opens each spring like an umbrella. The foliage carpets the ground until midsummer, when it withers and dies back. As an encore to the May apple, interplant *Galium odoratum* (sweet woodruff). It doesn't mind the deep shade under the May apples, and it will provide a pretty green cover when they are gone. For information on which woodland species will do best in your area, contact local botanical gardens, arboretums, nursery and garden centers, and local plant societies.

The mottled magenta-and-lime-green foliage of a St. Louis, Missouri, planting of Coleus 'Bellingrath Pink' assumes the role of a floral accent next to the lacy bluish green leaves of Pelargonium denticulatum (fern-leaf geranium).

191

CHAPTER FOUR

Successful Garden Plans

Your garden, as well as your home, reflects your personal idea of beauty. If you prefer modern styles, you may design a garden that has strongly defined lines and bold-colored plants. On the other hand, if you're a romantic at heart, you may choose to create an evocative, fragrant garden, such as the small lavender garden at left. But whatever its style, every garden requires a plan to make it work.

This chapter will show you how to select, place, and maintain plants for a wide range of garden designs. From waterwise gardens to backdoor cutting gardens, you'll learn, step by step, how to create a workable, easily maintained design. Each basic plan is accompanied by two alternate plans for the same garden site. The alternates may reflect regional variations, different environments, or simply alternative approaches to plant selection. Armed with these flexible plans you can easily create a garden that reflects your personal sense of style.

Create Your Own Cottage Garden

One of the most popular gardening styles is the charming, informal cottage garden. The cottage garden's origins lie in 15th-century English villages, where the occupants of small, rustic cottages filled their gardens with a colorful mix of flowers, herbs, and vegetables. The garden provided much of the cottager's daily necessities: medicinal teas, herbal balms and insect repellents, and fresh vegetables for the soup pot.

Today's American-style cottage garden relies on a mix of low-maintenance annuals, perennials, and self-sowing biennials. The casual, densely planted style is perfectly suited to today's busy gardener. Close plantings shade the ground, reducing weeding and watering chores. The occasional removal of spent flowers and unwanted seedlings will keep your garden looking its best.

While the cheerful tumble of flowers in a cottage garden looks casual, the effect takes planning. The mix of annuals, biennials, perennials, and woody plants shown here produces a colorful tapestry that peaks in early summer. Alternate designs on the next two pages focus on a garden of easy-going plants that self-sow from year to year, creating changing color combinations, and an all-summer garden that offers something new to anticipate throughout the growing season. Any of these three gardens is suited to the picket-fenced front yard of a true cottage, but they are all adaptable to any sunny spot in your landscape. Whether it is nestled outside the kitchen door, fronts a patio, or is tucked between the house and garage, the cottage garden should be located for both ease of use and beauty.

Luxurious Floral Abundance

The cottage garden at left relies on old-fashioned biennial sweet Williams, foxgloves, and wallflowers for its nostalgic appeal and early summer bloom. Annual blue bachelor's-buttons and brilliant nasturtiums begin in midsummer and flower into fall. The foliage of perennial lamb's ears and Siberian irises add structure all summer. The bougainvillea provides a flowery backdrop and enclosure that is the essence of the cottage style. It is hardy only in Zone 10, and gardeners in other zones can achieve similar results with clematis or a climbing rose.

In keeping with the spirit of true cottage gardening, this one has a variety of useful plants. Lamb's ears, bachelor's-buttons, and spireas dry well for flower arrangements, and nasturtium blossoms add peppery flavor to salads.

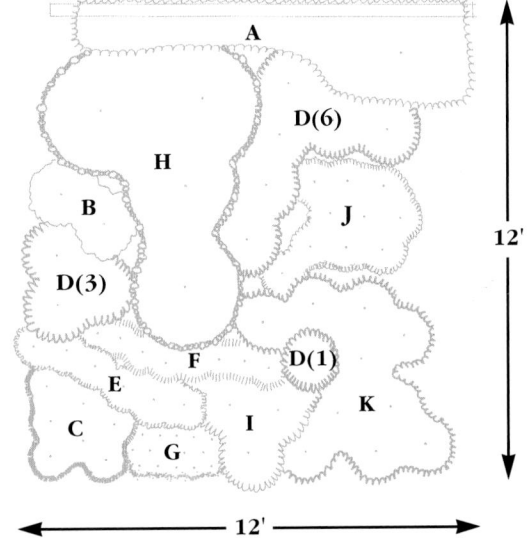

Plant List

A. Bougainvillea x buttiana (bougainvillea) (1)
B. Centaurea cyanus (bachelor's-button) (2)
C. Dianthus barbatus (sweet William) (7)
D. Digitalis purpurea (foxglove) (10)
E. Erysimum 'Bowles Mauve' (wallflower) (6)
F. Iris sibirica (Siberian iris) (8)
G. Papaver nudicaule (Iceland poppy) (15)
H. Spiraea x bumalda 'Lime Mound' (spirea) (4)
I. Stachys byzantina (lamb's ears) (3)
J. Tropaeolum majus (nasturtium) (10)
K. Salvia x superba 'May Night' (violet sage) (10)

◆ How to Plant This Garden ◆

1. Sow Iceland poppies in spring.

2. Plant bougainvillea in early spring, close to a support.

3. Sow bachelor's-buttons and nasturtiums directly in the ground in spring; plant violet sage after the last frost.

4. Plant lamb's ears, Siberian irises, and spirea in midspring.

5. Start sweet Williams, foxgloves, and wallflowers outdoors from seed in midsummer. Transplant into the garden in early fall.

Aftercare and Maintenance
• Deadhead spent flowers to keep the plants blooming.
• Water Siberian irises regularly during dry spells.

A Cottage Garden of Self-Sowing Flowers

The annuals, biennials, and perennials that contribute the bulk of summer color in this cottage garden range from 3-inch English daisies to 6-foot hollyhocks. Once planted, they perpetuate from self-sown seed, needing only a rigorous thinning in spring to give each plant room to develop.

Certain permanent plant fixtures provide continuity and structure for the effervescent display of summer flowers, such as beautybush, a large shrub with soft pink late-spring flowers; 'Dropmore Scarlet' honeysuckle, a woody vine with fragrant summer blooms; 'Lavender Lassie' shrub rose; and rhubarb, a long-lived perennial that produces edible red stalks in spring and decorative foliage all summer. These four cold-hardy plants need a period of winter dormancy and will not grow well in subtropical climates. All require full sun and well-drained soil to perform well.

In addition to flowers for generous bouquets, this cottage garden produces rhubarb stalks for pies and conserves, pot marigold petals to add golden color to stocks and soups, and feverfew leaves to brew into an astringent tea that is a traditional headache remedy. This garden also will yield rose petals for cake decoration or to dry for potpourri, small sunflower seeds for songbirds, honeysuckle blossoms to attract hummingbirds, and hollyhocks for children to fashion into dolls.

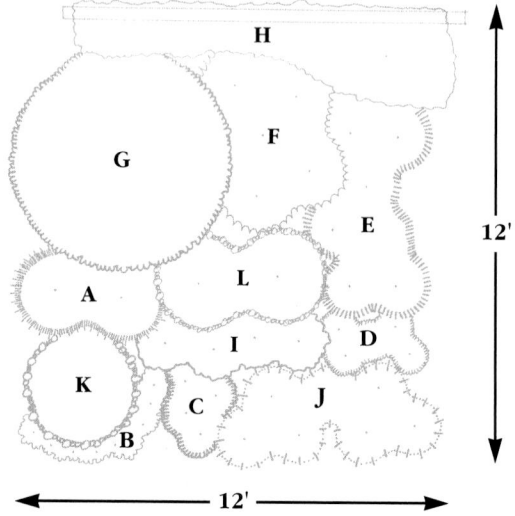

Plant List

A. *Alcea* 'Country Romance Mix' (hollyhock) (2)
B. *Bellis perennis* (English daisy) (9)
C. *Calendula officinalis* (pot marigold) (4)
D. *Chrysanthemum parthenium* (feverfew) (5)
E. *Cleome hasslerana* 'Colour Fountain' (spider flower) (7)
F. *Helianthus* x *multiflorus* 'Flore Pleno' (perennial sunflower) (5)
G. *Kolkwitzia amabilis* (beautybush) (1)
H. *Lonicera* x *brownii* 'Dropmore Scarlet' (honeysuckle) (1)
I. *Lychnis coronaria* (rose campion) (4)
J. *Papaver rhoeas* (Shirley poppies) (7)
K. *Rheum rhabarbarum* 'Valentine' (rhubarb) (1)
L. *Rosa* 'Lavender Lassie' (shrub rose) (2)

◆ How to Plant This Garden ◆

1. Double dig the garden site.

2. Plant beautybush, shrub rose, and honeysuckle in early spring or fall. Plant honeysuckle 1 foot from trellis. Add plenty of compost to generous holes for root systems.

3. In early spring, plant rhubarb with the crowns 1 to 2 inches below the surface. Add soil gradually to fill in the hole as plants grow.

4. Sow Shirley poppies and pot marigold seeds in early spring. Thin plants to 8 to 10 inches apart.

5. Sow spider flower seeds in midspring. Thin to 10 to 12 inches.

6. Set out the remaining plants in midspring. Water after planting.

Aftercare and Maintenance
• *Remove old wood from beautybush, shrub rose, and honeysuckle in late winter or early spring.*

A Cottage Garden for All-Summer Bloom

The plants in this cottage garden provide a succession of bloom, beginning with the early-summer flowers of lavender chives and multi-colored columbines shown here, and finishing the season with the last huge, rosy blossoms of Clematis 'Dr. Ruppel' in early fall. This is a pink-and-blue garden, with white highlights provided by the fragrant early blooms of a mock orange shrub and the graceful late-summer spires of gooseneck loosestrife. Most of the plants are long-lived perennials that flower each summer with minimal care. The annual cosmos and globe amaranth are exceptions, but both self-sow reliably and require only the removal of unwanted seedlings each spring. All these plants will do well in mild to very cold climates; this is not a garden for subtropical or tropical locales. Plant this garden in full sun in loamy, well-drained garden soil, amended with several inches of compost. Position it where it will be convenient to snip a few chives for cooking or to assemble an impromptu bouquet. Its long-blooming season and beautiful combinations of colors and forms qualify this cottage garden for a highly visible location, such as near a patio or front entrance.

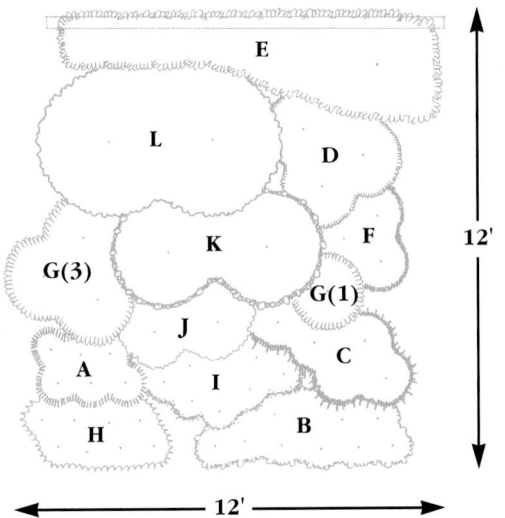

Plant List

A. *Allium schoenoprasum* (chives) (6)
B. *Aquilegia* 'Music Series' (columbine) (10)
C. *Artemisia absinthium* (wormwood) (5)
D. *Campanula lactiflora* 'Pritchard's Variety' (bellflower) (3)

E. *Clematis* 'Dr. Ruppel' (clematis) (1)
F. *Cosmos bipinnatus* 'Versailles Series' (cosmos) (3)
G. *Delphinium* 'Blue Bird' and 'Galahad' (delphinium) (4)
H. *Dianthus barbatus* (sweet William) (8)

I. *Gomphrena globosa* (globe amaranth) (8)
J. *Lysimachia clethroides* (gooseneck loosestrife) (2)
K. *Paeonia* 'Sarah Bernhardt' (peony) (2)
L. *Philadelphus* 'Belle Etoile' (mock orange) (2)

◆ How to Plant This Garden ◆

1. Plant mock orange *in early spring, leaving room for it to reach its full 6-foot spread.*

2. Plant clematis *in early spring, providing a support to climb.*

3. Plant chives, columbines, *wormwood, bellflowers, delphiniums, and loosestrife 2 feet apart.*

4. Plant sweet William seedlings *in midspring, 1 foot apart.*

5. Sow cosmos and globe amaranth *in midspring, raking lightly over seeds. Thin to 10 to 12 inches apart.*

6. Plant peonies *in late summer with their eyes (buds) no more than 1 to 2 inches below the soil's surface. Add straw mulch the first winter to prevent frost heaving.*

Aftercare and Maintenance
•Restrain invasive loosestrife by pulling up unwanted stems. Dig and divide every 2 to 3 years.

Create Your Own Formal Garden

Formal gardens are best known for their strong lines, balanced geometric designs, and classical sense of beauty and repose. The formal garden is often built along a central axis oriented to the house. Minor axes may intersect the central axis, and decorative focal points such as an urn or a pool can punctuate these axes. There may be an oval or rectangular garden "room" at the end of an axis, with walls composed of stone, clipped hedges, or a line of narrow trees.

The choice of plants in a formal garden and the way they are cultivated reflect a planned consistency of line and effect. Ornate pruning, carpet planting of a single type of plant, and flower beds laid out in carefully proportioned designs are typical of formal design. Unlike the casual profusion of the cottage garden, the variety of plants is kept to a minimum. Geometric-shaped beds are neatly outlined by carefully clipped hedges. These can be filled with densely spaced annuals to create solid blocks of color, or a few carefully chosen perennials for a long-lasting formal design. All the formal parterre gardens shown here and on the following pages begin with a strong framework of neat, angular, hedge-bordered beds and brick walkways following a straight axis. The parterre on this page consists primarily of foliage plants, giving it a year-round permanence. The alternate designs *(pages 200 and 201)* incorporate fragrant herbs or flowers for color and plant variety.

The Elegance of Simplicity

Straight lines and a clear central axis make this formal garden easy to lay out. The lines and symmetrical beds draw attention to the central hexagon, the main focal point. An urn at the end of the central axis provides another focal point, drawing your gaze to the distant view.

Simple plant choices of dwarf boxwood and yew border the self-contained beds. In the traditional manner, both plants are sheared into round or rectangular forms, but their contrasting leaf shapes, textures, and shades of green sharply accent one another. The variegated foliage of the geranium provides further subtle color, while its pink blossoms echo the warm hues of the patterned brick walkway that unifies the design.

Simplicity, restraint in the use and number of colors, and carefully orchestrated geometry—characteristics of all formal gardens—are the keys to this successful plan.

◆ How to Plant This Garden ◆

1. In the early fall, plant yews in the central and rear beds. Plant boxwoods along the edges, spacing them 9 to 12 inches apart for a dense border.

2. In the spring, plant geraniums in even rows, spaced at 1-foot intervals. Keep them 2 feet away from the base of the shrubs. Cover soil surface with a finely ground mulch of compost, bark, or leaf mold to preserve soil moisture.

3. Water all plants at planting time. Water yews and boxwoods regularly until well established.

Aftercare and Maintenance
• Keep plants evenly moist until they are established, then water when the surface dries.
• As soon as growth begins, clip boxwoods and yews to promote rapid branching and fullness. Do not allow them to grow beyond their planned height.
• Deadhead geraniums regularly. Trim stems periodically to keep plants compact.

Plant List

A. Buxus microphylla 'Compacta' (boxwood) (36)
B. Pelargonium x hortorum (zonal geranium) (80)
C. Taxus baccata (English yew) (9)

C(6) C(2) A(2) B(62) A(10) A(6) 32' C(1) A(18) B(18) 23'

A Formal Garden with Fragrant Herbs

A thick, 4-foot-tall sheared privet hedge serves as a dramatic backdrop for this fragrant herb-and-flower garden. The privet, a deciduous shrub, frames the garden with its rich green, lance-shaped leaves in summer. In winter, it takes on a striking architectural appearance while maintaining the garden's formal lines.

A low border of clipped lavender cotton makes a compact, fresh-scented edging for the beds. Echoing its silvery foliage, a tall, unclipped English lavender stands at the center of the bed. The dark purple spires of lavender contrast boldly with the tiny, yellow button-flowers of lavender cotton. Sweet William, a reliable, self-seeding biennial, and mass plantings of cool white ageratum complete the garden's elegant color scheme.

Plant List

A. Ageratum boustoni-anum 'Neptune White' (ageratum) (62)
B. Dianthus barbatus (sweet William) (12)
C. Lavandula angustifolia 'Hidcote' (English lavender) (3)
D. Ligustrum vulgare 'Lodense' (privet) (9)
E. Santolina chamae-cyparissus (lavender cotton) or **Lavandula angustifolia** 'Dwarf Blue' (English lavender) (74)

◆ How to Plant This Garden ◆

1. In the fall, plant privets *1½ feet apart, mixing several inches of compost into clay or sandy soils.*

2. In the spring, after the last frost, improve the soil *in each herb bed by mixing in 2 inches of compost—more if soil is clay.*

3. Plant each bed, *crowding ageratums and sweet Williams (every 6 to 8 inches) for a fast, finished look.*

4. Position English lavender and lavender cotton *1 foot apart. At planting, pinch tips of herbs to encourage a bushier habit.*

5. Regularly water all plants. *Keep soil moist until growth begins.*

Aftercare and Maintenance
• *To maintain a full, dense hedge,* *prune the privets after their sweet-smelling blooms fade.*
• *Water sweet Williams and ageratums when soil surface begins to dry out, directing the water with a hose or can.*
• *Water privets and lavenders when soil is dry to 1 inch beneath the surface.*
• *Deadhead ageratums and sweet Williams regularly for a longer season of bloom and a tidy, compact appearance.*
• *In cold climates, overwinter English lavender in pots indoors, or plant new seedlings each spring.*
• *In spring, in all but the warmest climates, prune winter-damaged growth of both English lavender and lavender cotton and reshape them into low, compact mounds.*

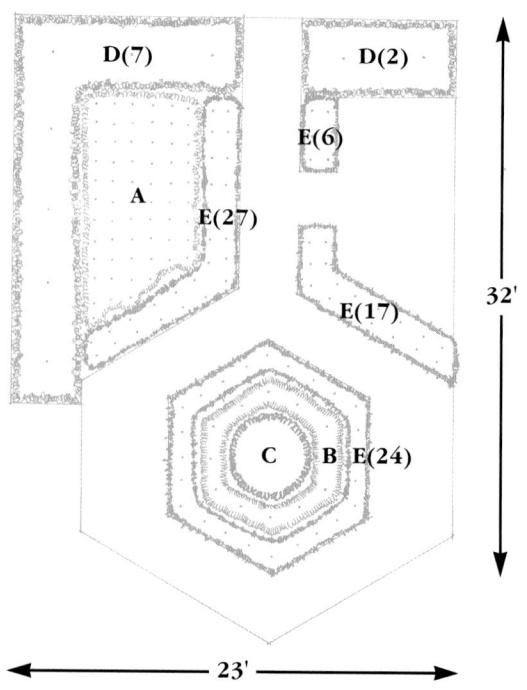

A Formal Flower Garden

The hedge-lined parterre in this plan is restricted to a limited palette of flowers and hues, although a larger variety could be used with an equally striking effect. The pastel rose and New Guinea impatiens add an elegant touch of color to the composition. For a brighter color scheme consider substituting lemon-yellow marigolds and a yellow shrub rose for the pastels used in this plan.

The low 'Kobold' barberry hedge brings further color to this garden through several seasons. New foliage is intensely green, deepening by summer, and in autumn the leaves take on a handsome yellow cast tinged with red. The barberry edging may be pruned for precise formality, as shown here, but left alone it naturally forms neat mounds approximately 2 feet tall.

The dense background hedge 'Sarcoxie' euonymus requires periodic shearing to maintain its shape and size. Its glossy, dark green leaves with whitish veins are a perfect foil for the delicate tints of the 'Lilac Rose' impatiens. Their placement draws the viewer's eye naturally to the garden's center, where the fragrance of the 'Tiffany' rose mingles with that of the surrounding 'Monarch White' pinks to create a sweet-and-spicy centerpiece.

C(7) **C(2)**

A(2)

D A(10)

A(6)

32'

E B A(18)

23'

◆ How to Plant This Garden ◆

1. In fall, plant wintercreeper euonymus and barberries 1½ feet apart in soil amended with compost.

2. Plant the rose in a hole at least 18 inches deep and wide. Mix in several shovelfuls of compost and a handful of bone meal. Set the bud union at ground level in warm climates, and 1 to 2 inches below ground in cold regions.

3. Plant pinks and New Guinea impatiens in spring after danger of frost has passed. Amend soil with 2 inches of compost or leaf mold.

4. Water all plants well after planting. Mulch with shredded bark.

Aftercare and Maintenance
• Deadhead roses to promote continuous bloom. Remove dead, diseased, or damaged canes in early spring.
• Keep floral beds moist throughout the growing season. Fertilize on a regular basis with a balanced, all-purpose fertilizer.

Plant List

A. Berberis thunbergii 'Kobold' (barberry) (36)
B. Dianthus 'Monarch White' (pinks) (18)
C. Euonymus fortunei 'Sarcoxie'

(winter creeper euonymus) (9)
D. Impatiens x 'Lilac Rose' (New Guinea impatiens) (62)
E. Rosa 'Tiffany' (hybrid tea rose) (1)

Create Your Own Fragrant Garden

While colorful gardens please the eye, fragrant gardens evoke many fond memories—from the sweet peas of childhood gardens to the clean smell of linens freshened with lavender sachets.

Some of the most fragrant plants are the old, subtly colored species. While these richly scented antiques have shorter blooming periods than modern hybrids, they are relatively hardy and easy to maintain. Unfortunately, many newer cultivars often sacrifice fragrance for bigger, bolder blossoms and a longer blooming period.

Enjoying fragrant plants depends as much on their location in the garden as on careful selection. To prevent even the most intense fragrance from wafting away in the breeze, try enclosing your garden with fences, walls, or tall plants that provide a windbreak. Try planting some of your favorite fragrant species in containers or raised beds near entrances, below bedroom windows, or beside decks and patios, where you will notice them easily. Highly scented, old-fashioned flowers like heliotrope, spicy cottage pinks, and some roses are well suited to containers.

The following gardens are carefully laid out for fragrance as well as beauty. In the purple-and-white garden shown opposite, fragrant herbs and shrubs combine to create an enchanting scene and bouquet. If you prefer sweeter, headier scents, or have a passion for old roses, consider the alternate gardens on the following pages. The first is composed of a variety of roses for a garden filled with traditional fragrance and form. The second is less traditional in its plant selection but equally rich in fragrance.

An Aromatic Blend of Herbs and Shrubs

Gardeners in temperate climates can enjoy the perfumes that pervade the garden shown here. The design includes a weathered gray perimeter fence that helps hold in the honeyed scents of the tall butterfly bush and 'Iceberg' floribunda rose. The feverfew, catmint, and lavender will release their perfume as visitors stroll along the brick paths and brush against their foliage.

Easy to grow in average soil, these low-maintenance plants develop casual arching branches and sprawling mounds, softening the garden's somewhat formal design. With their subtle colors, billowing forms, and evocative scents, these plants create a restful retreat you'll savor all summer long.

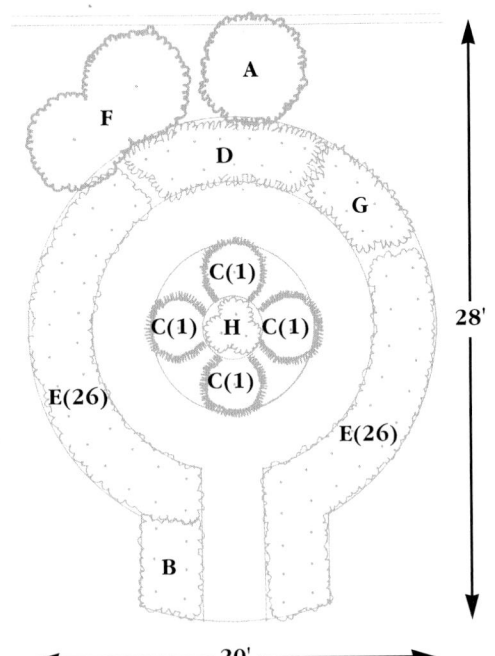

Plant List

A. *Buddleia davidii* 'Lochinch' (butterfly bush) (1)
B. *Chrysanthemum parthenium* (feverfew) (6)
C. *Lavandula angustifolia* 'Hidcote' (lavender) (4)
D. *Lychnis coronaria* 'Alba' (rose campion) (12)
E. *Nepeta* x *faassenii* (catmint) (52)
F. *Rosa* 'Iceberg' (floribunda rose) (2)
G. *Salvia* x *superba* (violet sage) (7)
H. *Santolina chamaecyparissus* (lavender cotton) (3)

◆ How to Plant This Garden ◆

1. In a porous potting mix, plant lavender cotton *with the rootball at the same level as in its container.*

2. Plant catmints *1 foot back from the walkway. Space lavenders evenly around the central bed, and set sages 12 inches apart.*

3. Plant butterfly bush *2 feet from the fence and mulch well.*

4. Plant rosebushes *so bud union is at ground level in warm regions and 2 inches deep in cold ones.*

5. In spring, plant feverfews *and rose campions in full sun.*

Aftercare and Maintenance
• Pinch growing tips of butterfly bush to encourage bushiness.

A Fragrant Garden Based on Roses

Perhaps no garden is more intensely fragrant than one filled with antique roses. The companion herbs shown here, with their sprawling mounds of scented foliage, complement the roses' casual look. All of the plants featured in this garden are relatively easy to maintain and will thrive in average, well-drained soil.

The circular design of this garden gives easy access to all of the plants, allowing close-up appreciation of the spicy gallica rose 'Camaieux' and even the climbing 'Dr. J. H. Nicolas'. Most antique roses flower only once in early summer, but the raspberry-scented 'Madame Isaac Pereire' blooms again in the fall. Complementing the white and pink roses, catmint, sage, and purple-hued English lavender spill along the path and out of their containers, inviting you to brush up against their aromatic leaves.

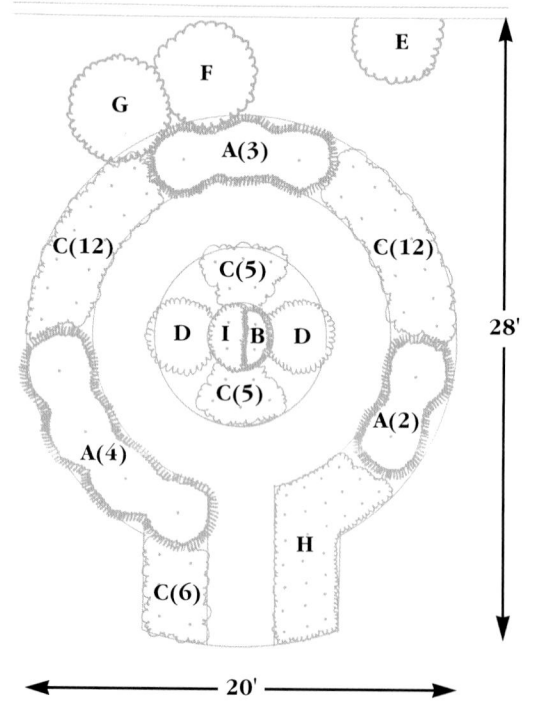

Plant List

A. *Lavandula angustifolia* 'Grosso' (English lavender) (9)
B. *Lavandula stoechas* ssp. *pedunculata* (Spanish lavender) (2)
C. *Nepeta* x *faassenii*

(catmint) (40)
D. *Rosa* 'Camaieux' (gallica rose) (2)
E. *Rosa* 'Dr. J. H. Nicolas' (climbing rose) (1)
F. *Rosa* 'Madame Hardy' (old garden rose) (1)

G. *Rosa* 'Madame Isaac Pereire' (bourbon rose) (1)
H. *Rosa* 'Popcorn' (miniature rose) (27)
I. *Salvia officinalis* (garden sage) (2)

◆ How to Plant This Garden ◆

1. Fill a container with a porous potting mix. *Plant garden sage and Spanish lavender plants close together for a full look.*

2. Dig holes for roses *18 inches wide and just deep enough to accommodate the roots. Spread roots out and cover with fine, compost-rich soil. Water roses well.*

3. Plant English lavender *at even intervals in the areas shown.*

4. Plant catmints *1 foot back from the walkway and 1 foot apart.*

Aftercare and Maintenance
• *Water roses monthly with a fish emulsion solution.*
• *Feed roses a balanced fertilizer in early spring and again in summer.*
• *In spring, add a deep layer of compost mulch around roses.*
• *Control vigorous 'Madame Isaac Pereire' by removing the largest canes every few years in winter.*
• *Divide sages every few years.*

A Sweet-and-Spicy Garden

Spring fragrance gets off to an early start in this garden planted with spicy-scented viburnum. Old-fashioned purple dame's rocket follows with its soft evening aroma. By early summer the potent fragrance of tall, arching mock orange penetrates every corner. Madonna lilies and pinks add their own sweet-and-spicy scents from early to midsummer.

This garden is at the peak of bloom from late spring to early summer. The Peruvian daffodils and 'David' phlox provide midsummer fragrance and color, and the low carpets of pink-and-white flowering thyme continue blooming until frost. They release a delightfully spicy fragrance if you brush by their foliage.

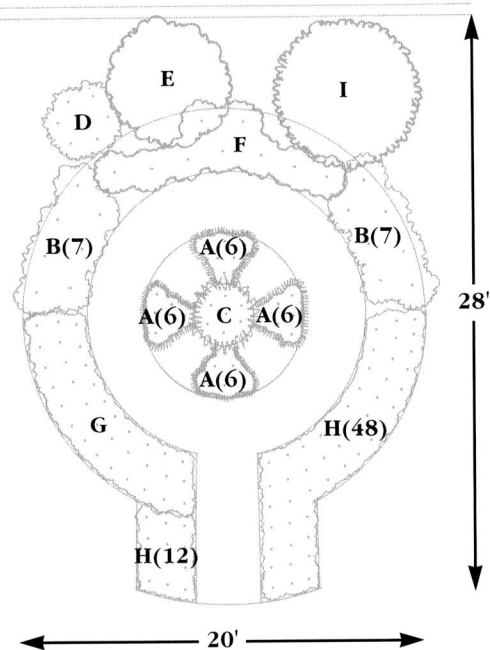

◆ How to Plant This Garden ◆

1. In early summer set three to five bulbs of Peruvian daffodils in loose potting soil in the urn with their tips 1 inch below the surface.

2. Dig a hole slightly wider and as deep as mock orange and Burkwood viburnum rootballs. Loosen the soil on the sides of the holes and spread out any circled roots before covering them with soil.

3. Plant Madonna lilies while the bulbs are dormant in late summer, covering them with no more than 2 inches of soil. Water well.

4. Sow seed for dame's rockets when the soil has warmed in the spring. The plants will bloom the following year. For faster bloom, set out bedding plants, allowing 1 to 2 feet of space between plants for expansion and air circulation.

5. Plant thyme 1 foot apart and 8 inches back from the walkway.

6. Plant garden phlox 2 feet apart.

Aftercare and Maintenance
• *North of Zone 8, lift Peruvian daffodil bulbs after foliage yellows. Dry the bulbs and store upside down with roots still attached.*
• *Prune mock orange annually after bloom, removing the oldest, weakest stems at the base of the plant.*
• *Divide garden phlox every 2 to 3 years.*

Plant List

A. Dianthus 'Bath's Pink' (pinks) (24)
B. Hesperis matronalis (dame's rocket) (14)
C. Hymenocallis narcissiflora (Peruvian daffodil) (7)
D. Lilium candidum

'Cascade Strain' (Madonna lily) (7)
E. Philadelphus coronarius (mock orange) (1)
F. Phlox paniculata 'David' (garden phlox) (9)

G. Thymus serpyllum 'Albus' (mother of thyme) (34)
H. Thymus serpyllum 'Coccineus' (mother of thyme) (60)
I. Viburnum x burkwoodii (Burkwood viburnum) (1)

Create Your Own Secret Garden

Whether set deep within a wooded glade or enclosed by the green walls of an outdoor room, a garden can be a peaceful hideaway. Your leafy retreat may be an oasis of cool shade and bubbling water where you can rest on a hot summer day, or perhaps a small dining area in a walled enclosure covered with rambling roses and clematis vines.

Whether made of brick, stone, lattice, or hedging, walls help define a secret garden. Sheared hedges such as hawthorn, holly, box, yew, privet,

or hornbeam create a more formal enclosure than vine-covered walls, but either style provides a sense of privacy. You can complete the structure of your outdoor room with a living carpet of grass or creeping thyme.

To create a secluded room, follow the plan here. If you prefer an abundance of old-fashioned flowers, or would like your garden to reach its peak later in the summer, then consider the two alternate plantings that follow.

Structuring a Garden Room

In the garden pictured opposite, you will find an inexpensive and quick way to create a secluded garden room. Instead of building a costly fence or wall, install sturdy stands of latticework planted with 'New Dawn' climbing roses. You won't have to wait 10 years for the new hedge to mature; you should feel comfortably enclosed in this private retreat in about 3 years. The rose-covered lattice walls will block out most views beyond the garden's confines, providing a pleasant seclusion and insulating your private bower.

This garden is not large, but it is rich enough in detail to seem a world of its own. A garden seat furnishes a place to rest and to appreciate the many plants springing up among the paving stones. The rustic path draws attention to the fragrant edging plants. Sharp scents of thyme and oregano blend with spicy pinks and the sweet perfume roses.

Color plays a role in the garden's look. Golden flowers of tree lupine and feverfew contrast with purple-flowered thyme, while pink roses and foxgloves complement the garden's abundant green foliage. Gardeners north of Zone 8 can substitute 'Father Hugo' roses for the tree lupines.

As your garden grows and its plants mature, you can change the room's decor by trying out new varieties of your favorite bedding plants or tucking a variety of different herbs in between the paving stones.

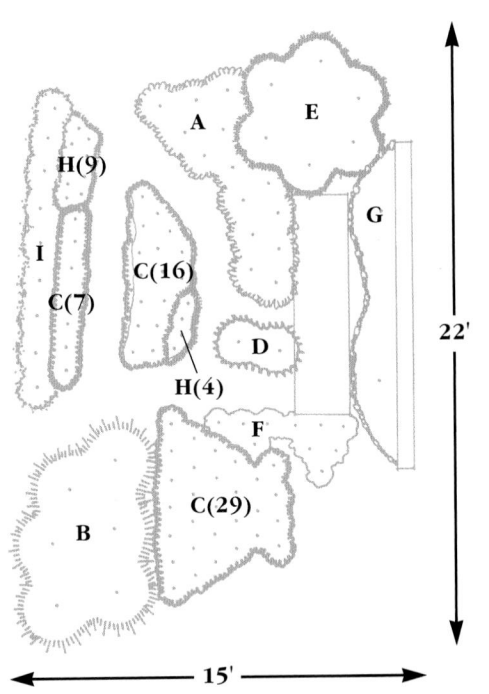

Plant List

A. Anemone hupehensis (Japanese anemone) (14)
B. Chrysanthemum parthenium 'Aureum' (feverfew) (6)
C. Dianthus deltoides 'Flashing Light' (maiden pinks) (52)
D. Digitalis purpurea (common foxglove) (2)
E. Lupinus arboreus (tree lupine) (7)
F. Origanum onites 'Aureum' (pot marjoram) (10)
G. Rosa 'New Dawn' (climbing rose) (2)
H. Sisyrinchium bellum (California blue-eyed grass) (13)
I. Thymus praecox (thyme) (9)

◆ How to Plant This Garden ◆

1. Amend soil with compost.

2. Work an all-purpose granular fertilizer into the site, following package directions. Water well.

3. In the early fall or spring, plant roses 1 foot from the base of a trellis. Loosely tie canes to the trellis with soft twine.

4. Allow 1 foot of space around each lupine and foxglove, but cluster other plants closer together.

5. Slip the marjorams and pinks in between paving stones, blending colors so that they are evenly dispersed over the area.

Aftercare and Maintenance
• Continue to tie rose canes to the lattice as they grow, arching canes to promote flowering stems.
• Trim herbs annually to 2 to 3 inches to keep them compact; replace them every other year.

A Hideaway Among Old-Time Flowers

Whether it is the lure of nostalgia or romance, planting a secret garden filled with old-fashioned flowers recalls a simpler time. Lovely clematis shelters this garden from the bustling world beyond. The abundant, vigorously growing vine quickly covers the trellis in a dense screen of foliage and flowers.

Red valerians give long-lasting color to the garden, and their pinkish red panicles above gray-green foliage make beautiful cut flowers. Drifts of catmints add a bright blue accent to the composition, while a small clump of carmine-hued pinks sweetly scent the air.

The hortensia hydrangea blossoms abundantly—enough to cut a few stems to dry for colorful, long-lasting arrangements.

The daylilies and evening primroses provide masses of yellow blooms in late spring and early summer that yield to the bright white flowers of 'Miss Lingard' phlox later in the season.

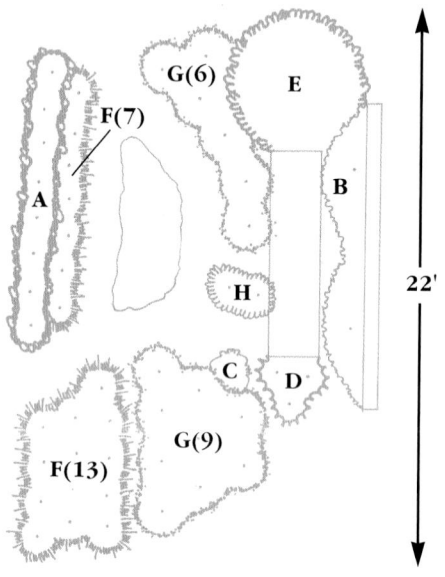

◆ How to Plant This Garden ◆

1. Dig several inches of compost into the soil and work in a balanced granular fertilizer. Water well.

2. After the last frost in spring, plant evening primroses, red valerians, Allwood pinks, lemon daylilies, catmint, and thick-leaf phlox.

3. Plant clematis about 1 foot in front of the base of the trellis. Cover the soil with several inches of mulch to shade its roots.

4. Allow 5 feet of space at the side of the bench for the hydrangea.

Aftercare and Maintenance
• In spring, cut back the hortensia hydrangea stems to the ground, or as high as 18 inches if you prefer a taller shrub.
• Tie clematis to the lattice with soft twine as stems grow. Cut out all dead clematis wood in early spring. Cut stems back to the topmost pair of large buds.
• Deadhead red valerians and thick-leaf phlox frequently to induce more flowers and prevent rampant self-sowing.
• Remove faded flowers and foliage from the plants to add to your compost pile.

Plant List

A. Centranthus ruber (red valerian) (8)
B. Clematis 'Bees Jubilee' (clematis) (2)
C. Dianthus x allwoodii (Allwood pinks) (1)
D. Hemerocallis lilioasphodelus (lemon daylily) (3)
E. Hydrangea macrophylla 'Nikko Blue' (hortensia hydrangea) (1)
F. Nepeta x faassenii (catmint) (20)
G. Oenothera tetragona 'Fireworks' (evening primrose) (15)
H. Phlox carolina 'Miss Lingard' (thick-leaf phlox) (2)

A Secret Garden for Late-Summer Repose

In the heat and glare of deepest summer, a hidden retreat filled with flowers and fragrance is a most welcome resting place. Butterflies flutter around a fragrant, white-flowered buddleia, while jasmine scrambles over the trellis, filling the garden with a sweet scent. For cooler climates, try substituting a hardy, fast-growing vine such as sweet autumn clematis or coral honeysuckle in place of the jasmine.

The blue-gray foliage and white flowers that light up this garden room for evening enjoyment also seem to cool it down on hot August days. Quiet lavenders and catmints produce mounds of pale, scented foliage and bluish purple flowers, while the strap-shaped leaves and lilac-blue sprays of lily-of-the-Nile arch gracefully above. Spiky Adam's-needle and its towering blooms supply a touch of drama matched only by the silvery sheen of the wormwood foliage.

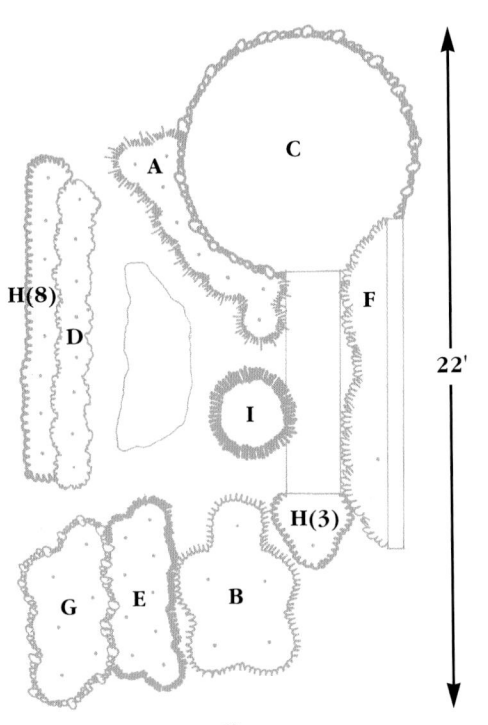

Plant List

A. Agapanthus Headbourne Hybrids (lily-of-the-Nile) (8)
B. Artemisia absinthium 'Lambrook Silver' (wormwood) (5)
C. Buddleia davidii 'White Bouquet'
(butterfly bush) (1)
D. Campanula carpatica 'Blue Chips' (Carpathian bellflower) (8)
E. Calamintha nepeta (calamint) (9)
F. Jasminum officinale (jasmine) (2)
G. Lavandula angustifolia (English lavender) (6)
H. Nepeta x faassenii 'Six Hills Giant' (catmint) (11)
I. Yucca filamentosa (Adam's-needle) (1)

◆ How to Plant This Garden ◆

1. Amend the entire site with a thick layer of compost.

2. In cold climates, plant lilies-of-the-Nile in pots.

3. Plant the yucca in the background, where its sharp leaves will be out of the way.

4. Water all plants well to keep the soil continuously moist.

5. Cover all the planting beds with 2 inches of fine bark or chopped-leaf mulch.

Aftercare and Maintenance
• If soil is poor, apply an all-purpose fertilizer in midspring and again in early summer. Water well after fertilizing.
• Deadhead butterfly bush to encourage bloom into autumn. Cut stems to the ground in spring.
• Cut lily-of-the-Nile flower stems to the base after blooms fade.
• In spring, trim catmints to a small mound.
• Overwinter the potted plants indoors.

Create Your Own Evening Garden

The silvery foliage and cool white flowers of the evening garden will continue to be enjoyed long after sunset. With few color contrasts, the garden is fresh and serene by day, while at night it brightens even the darkest corner. For gardeners who spend their days away from home, a garden composed of white-flowering or night-scented plants offers a pleasurable setting for dining or relaxing after a busy day.

Some evening gardens rely on a foundation of blue-gray or variegated foliage plants for their brightening effect, while others consist largely of white-flowering plants. Pale foliage reflects evening light, often from countless tiny hairs that cover the leaves of some species. White blossoms glow resplendently in moonlight, especially those with large or doubled petals.

Garden rooms on patios or in sheltered corners of the landscape are especially pleasant in the evening. They provide a sense of privacy and seclusion. A garden room may also provide a setting for tender, container-grown plants that need protection in cool climates.

If you are drawn to delicate, flowering exotics, you may want to try the white-flowering plant combinations illustrated here. Alternate gardens on the following pages include an evening garden consisting only of plants with silvery foliage, and one composed of fragant flowers that give off their scent after dark.

A White Garden Room

The evening garden featured here is a dazzling display of both tender and hardy white-flowering plants. The tiers of raised beds and rows of tall pots lift the floral bouquets, creating levels of reflected evening light. Elevated beds bring interesting features, such as the clustered flowers of the primroses and the fluted petals on cyclamen, into close view.

The neatly sheared row of boxwood provides an effective backdrop for dozens of sparkling pansies and clearly accents the gardenia and the exotic-looking calla lily.

The tender plants in this collection—primrose, cyclamen, gardenia, and calla lily—can be grown in cool-weather climates only in planters and containers, as they are here. Potting mixes provide excellent drainage, and containers allow the plants to be moved inside for protection during winter. The hardier ivy and boxwoods remain in place year round to provide welcome color.

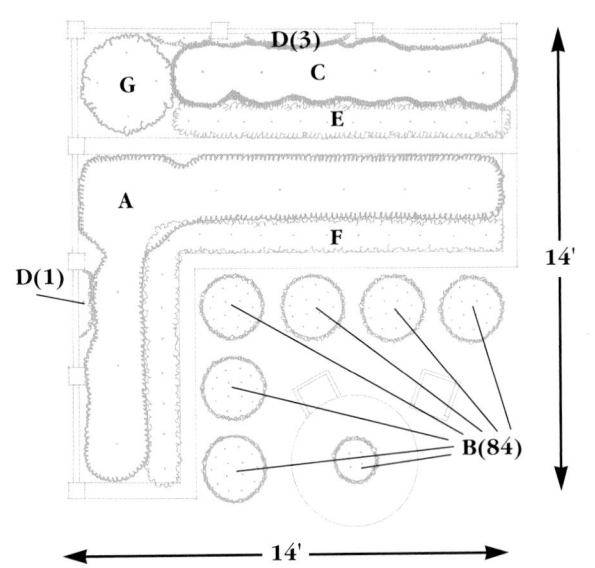

Plant List

A. Buxus sempervirens 'Suffruticosa' (dwarf boxwood) (9)
B. Cyclamen persicum (florist's cyclamen) (84)
C. Gardenia jasminoides (gardenia) (6)
D. Hedera helix
(English ivy) (4)
E. Primula malacoides (fairy primrose) (12)
F. Viola x wittrockiana (pansy) (18)
G. Zantedeschia aethiopica (calla lily) (5)

◆ How to Plant This Garden ◆

1. Plant the ivy close to the trellis.

2. Amend soil with compost before planting the gardenias.

3. Set the boxwood plants 8 inches apart in the raised bed.

4. Plant florist's cyclamens in tubs approximately 8 inches apart.

5. Loosen soil and set the calla lily rhizomes 2 inches deep.

Aftercare and Maintenance
• *Mulch gardenias with compost.*
• *Clip the boxwoods to 6 inches at planting, then trim regularly once they are established.*
• *Lightly fertilize pansies, florist's cyclamens, and primroses every 2 weeks during blooming season.*
• *Water the calla lilies lightly until leaves appear, then increase watering, and feed weekly. Store the rhizomes in sawdust in a cool location over the winter.*

A Silver-Gray Garden

This evening garden, suitable for a temperate climate, relies on unusual silver-gray and variegated foliage for its striking effect. The 'Silver Carp' lamb's ears and nearly white dusty-millers, the brightest foliage in the garden, provide a frosted effect in evening light. Male *Actinidia kolomikta* vines produce showy heart-shaped leaves touched with white and pink. This is a relative of the edible kiwi, and with a female actinidia nearby, will produce edible grape-size fruits. Also dramatic are the gray-green, thistlelike leaves of the cardoon, which can grow up to 8 feet long.

Although foliage predominates, white flowers are also a feature in this evening garden. Small blossoms float on the sturdy rose campion stems, while tall, narrow clusters of the Adam's-needle tower above its dramatic swordlike leaves.

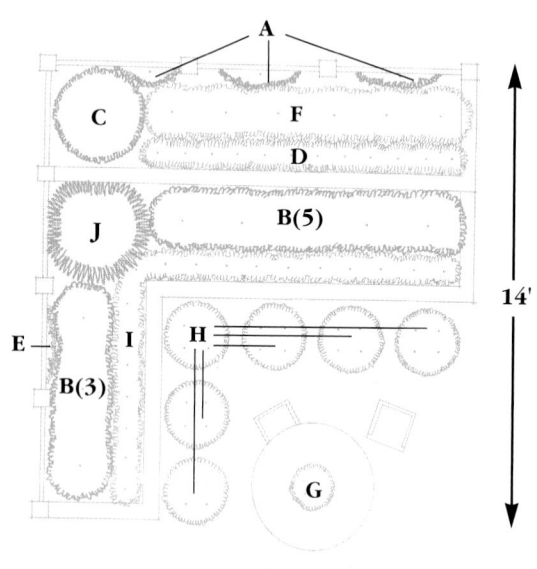

Plant List

A. *Actinidia kolomikta* (actinidia) (3)
B. *Artemisia absinthium* 'Lambrook Silver' (wormwood) (8)
C. *Cynara cardunculus* (cardoon) (1)
D. *Eryngium bourgatii* (sea holly) (12)
E. *Hedera helix* 'Eva' (English ivy) (1)
F. *Lychnis coronaria* 'Alba' (rose campion) (6)
G. *Nephthytis afzelii* (nephthytis) (1)
H. *Senecio cineraria* 'Cirrus' (dusty-miller) (24)
I. *Stachys byzantina* 'Silver Carpet' (lamb's ears) (18)
J. *Yucca filamentosa* 'Golden Sword' (Adam's-needle) (1)

◆ How to Plant This Garden ◆

1. Position Adam's-needle and cardoon *where their sharp leaves will be out of the way.*

2. Plant actinidias *in front of a support, at least 5 feet apart.*

3. Crowd dusty-millers together, *leaving only a few inches between plants.*

4. Plant wormwoods *at the same depth* as they were in their containers, and 18 inches apart.

5. Plant nephthytis *in a pot when night temperatures stay above 40°.*

6. Set sea hollies *6 to 12 inches apart, being careful not to disturb the long taproots during planting.*

Aftercare and Maintenance
• *Mulch plants with shredded bark to keep soil moist. Keep mulch 1 to 2 inches away from plant stems to prevent rot.*
• *Tie actinidia stems to trellis during the growing season. Prune hard in the winter to restrict their vigorous growth.*
• *Trim dusty-millers regularly to prevent them from becoming leggy.*
• *In spring, prune wormwoods to within 6 inches of the ground.*

A Garden of Evening Scent

At dusk, when most gardens appear to rest, a garden of fragrant flowers like the one shown here imparts a sensory parade. The light vanilla scent of pinkish white clematis hangs in the evening air. Winter daphne's heady aroma perfumes the air in spring. Climbing sweet peas and tall summer-sweet along the patio walls supply a privacy screen in summer that also holds in their light fragrances. As shown here, by early fall, white, waxy tuberoses release their potent perfume, and evening light is reflected from their tall, spikelike wands.

Blooming from spring through fall, heliotrope, sweet alyssum, and pincushion flower offer a constant invitation to this garden. 'Defiance' verbena closes the season with its scarlet flowers in autumn.

All of the plants here thrive in containers filled with a loose, rich potting mix. These combinations produce spreading masses of foliage and flowers that reliably fill the evening garden with several seasons of beauty and light fragrance.

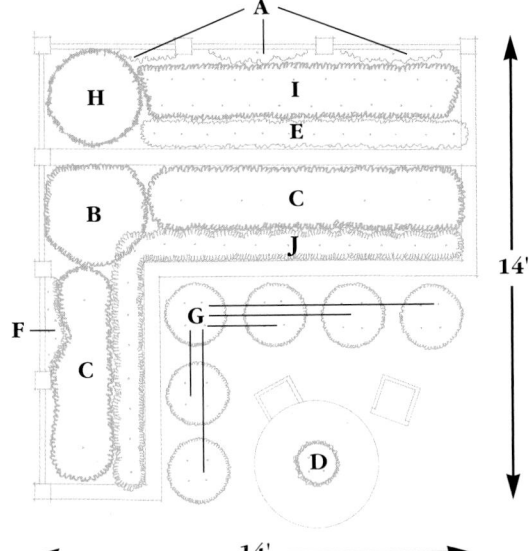

Plant List

A. Clematis montana 'Elizabeth' (clematis) (3)
B. Clethra alnifolia 'Hummingbird' (summer-sweet) (1)
C. Daphne odora 'Aureo-marginata' (winter daphne) (8)
D. Dianthus x allwoodii (Allwood pinks) (4)
E. Heliotropium arborescens 'Marine' (heliotrope) (12)
F. Lathyrus odoratus 'White Supreme' (sweet pea) (6)
G. Lobularia maritima 'Snowcloth Improved' (sweet alyssum) (24)
H. Polianthes tuberosa 'The Pearl' (tuberose) (37)
I. Scabiosa atropurpurea 'Mixed Doubles' (pincushion flower) (21)
J. Verbena x hybrida 'Defiance' (verbena) (18)

◆ How to Plant This Garden ◆

1. Set the clematis, winter daphnes, and summer-sweet in soil to the tops of their rootballs.

2. Plant the pincushion flowers and heliotropes 8 to 10 inches apart in rows in front of the clematis.

3. Sow seed of fast-growing sweet peas in front of the trellis, 4 inches apart and covered with ½ inch of soil.

4. Sow seed of alyssum on top of soil, as they require light for germination.

5. Set the tuberoses 4 to 6 inches apart in rows, or plant six in a 12-inch pot. Cover them with 2 inches of soil.

6. Plant Allwood pinks in an 8-inch pot; plant verbenas in front of the winter daphnes 8 inches apart.

Aftercare and Maintenance
• Prune summer-sweet in early spring. Keep it evenly moist.

Create Your Own Patio Garden

A patio expands the living area of your house and becomes an outdoor space that connects the indoors with the garden. It also provides a place where people can sit, with room for an arrangement of potted plants or edging beds that bring a part of the garden close to the house.

Gardening in containers allows you to move plants into sun or shade as necessary or to group plants with diverse cultural needs for visual effect. Tall containers and raised beds also protect garden plants from pets and children.

Groups of pots and planters can display favorite plant collections close to your house or patio, with easy access for garden maintenance. Terra cotta, which ages from orange to brick red, is an attrac-tive, practical material for patio containers. It allows air to penetrate to plant roots and provides excellent drainage, critical for potted plants. Wooden tubs and half barrels are rustic alternatives, while stoneware and metal urns contribute a more artistic touch. But bear in mind that container plants tend to dry out faster than garden plants, so you must be vigilant about watering them.

You may want to begin container gardening with the easy-care ornamentals shown in the garden opposite. The alternate plan on the next page adds a few edibles such as basil and strawberries. The tender plants in the second alternate garden *(page 217)* are most suitable for a partially shaded site in a warm or coastal climate.

A Country Look for an Urban Patio

The patio garden at left is informal and full of variety, and its scale is appropriate for a small backyard. The garden features a mix of annuals and perennials in a charming array of pots. The interplay of flowers and foliage will continue to decorate this garden over several seasons, provided plants get off to a good start in a rich soil mix that is kept evenly moist.

Wooden and terra-cotta planters spill over with a profusion of grasses, herbs, bulbs, and flowers. Crimson-leaved fountain grass plays counterpoint to the garden's emerald leaves and golden blooms, while sweet alyssum and elegant foxgloves offset the Johnny-jump-ups, sweet violets, and lemon balms.

Lilies, which need some winter cold to promote blooms, are planted in a ground-level bed along the low brick retaining wall. The plant-crowded containers in the foreground and on top of the wall sustain the illusion that the garden and its patio are one.

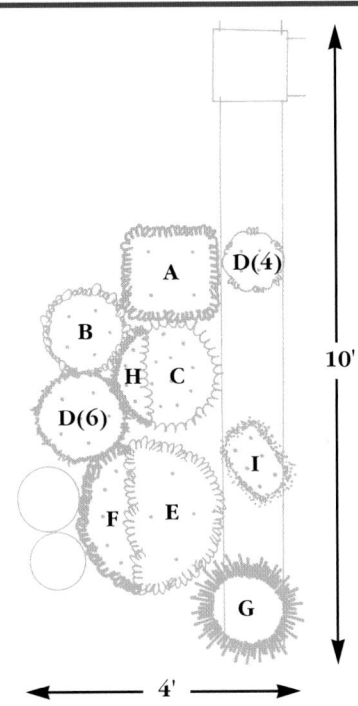

Plant List

A. *Digitalis purpurea* (common foxglove) (4)
B. *Galium odoratum* (sweet woodruff) (6)
C. *Lilium* (Asiatic hybrid lily) (10)
D. *Lobularia maritima* 'Snowdrift' (sweet alyssum) (10)
E. *Melissa officinalis* (lemon balm) (4)
F. *Ocimum basilicum* (common basil) (5)
G. *Pennisetum setaceum* 'Rubrum' (crimson fountain grass) (1)
H. *Viola odorata* (sweet violet) (6)
I. *Viola tricolor* (Johnny-jump-up) (6)

10'

4'

◆ How to Plant This Garden ◆

1. In the fall or early spring, plant lily bulbs 8 inches deep in the garden, or grouped in a 10-inch pot.

2. Plant crimson fountain grass in a container wider and deeper than its rootball. Use a knife to cut any wrapped roots.

3. Plant alyssum, lemon balm, and basil in the ground in Zones 9 or 10, or in 10- or 12-inch pots suitable for either indoors or out.

4. Plant Johnny-jump-ups in spring. They are a self-seeding annual; once planted, they'll show up in other places in following years.

5. Plant sweet violets in the ground or in 8-inch pots for easy rearranging.

6. Tuck foxgloves in next to the lilies.

Aftercare and Maintenance
• Fertilize and mulch lilies when they begin to grow.
• Pinch the growing tips of basil to promote fullness. Use the leaves to flavor salads.

A Container Garden of Annuals and Edibles

This small garden nook is a delightful mix of flowering ornamentals and edibles in a variety of attractive and unusual containers. The rich blend of purple basil with the vibrant yellows, pinks, and oranges of the annuals is at its peak when the garden is in full summer bloom.

Variegated houttuynias and nasturtiums are good choices in this colorful patio garden. The pale splotches in their foliage highlight the bright red-and-orange nasturtium blooms as well as the Transvaal daisies. They also combine well with the yellow Dahlberg daisies and black-eyed Susans.

In this garden, purple basil and Swiss chard are charming as ornamentals but, like the strawberries, are also welcome in the kitchen.

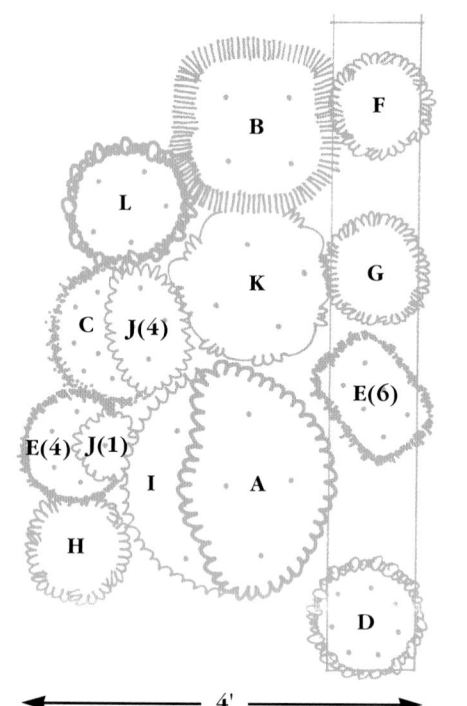

Plant List

A. Beta vulgaris 'Rhubarb' (Swiss chard) (4)
B. Canna x generalis (dwarf canna) (4)
C. Dyssodia tenuiloba (Dahlberg daisy) (7)
D. Fragaria 'Ozark Beauty' (garden strawberry) (8)
E. Gazania rigens 'Sunshine' (treasure flower) (10)

F. Gerbera jamesonii 'Dwarf Frisbee Pink' (Transvaal daisy) (1)
G. Gerbera jamesonii 'Dwarf Frisbee Scarlet' (Transvaal daisy) (1)
H. Gerbera jamesonii 'Dwarf Frisbee Yellow' (Transvaal daisy) (1)
I. Houttuynia cordata 'Chameleon'

(houttuynia) (3)
J. Ocimum basilicum 'Purple Ruffles' (common basil) (5)
K. Rudbeckia hirta 'Rustic Dwarfs' (black-eyed Susan) (4)
L. Tropaeolum majus 'Alaska' (garden nasturtium) (6)

◆ How to Plant This Garden ◆

1. Start seed indoors in early spring for Dahlberg daisies, black-eyed Susans, Swiss chard, and basil. Set out transplants after all danger of frost has passed.

2. Sow nasturtium seed outdoors in a container about 1 to 2 weeks after the last frost.

3. Set strawberries with their crowns above the soil surface and their roots spread out below.

4. Since Transvaal daisies are difficult to grow from seed, plant nursery seedlings. Keep their crowns above the soil level.

Aftercare and Maintenance
• For continued flowering and fruit pro-

duction, pick strawberries frequently and remove runners.
• Keep container plants well watered but not soggy; hot, windy weather can cause them to dry out quickly.
• Remove the leaves of daisies and Swiss chard that become ragged with age.
• To stimulate continued flowering, regularly deadhead flowers and cut them for indoor use.

A Shady Patio for Tender Plants

This patio sits in partial shade, creating a cool, lush setting for tender, moisture-loving plants. Plants whose colors may seem muted in direct sunlight appear richer in the soft, dappled light of this garden.

The shadiest areas of the garden are best for the colorful foliage of caladium and Japanese fern. The hydrangea, tuberous begonias, Johnny-jump-ups, lobelias, and sweet cicely all flower more profusely in brighter light. Catching partial sunlight in the front, lobelia adds brilliant blue highlights, and 'Little Bunny' pennisetum waves bright bottle-brush clusters above wispy leaves.

All of these luxuriant and shade-loving plants grow best in soil amended with leaf mold or compost. Keep them well fed and slightly moist, and they'll reward you with richly colorful foliage and a summer-long display of flowers.

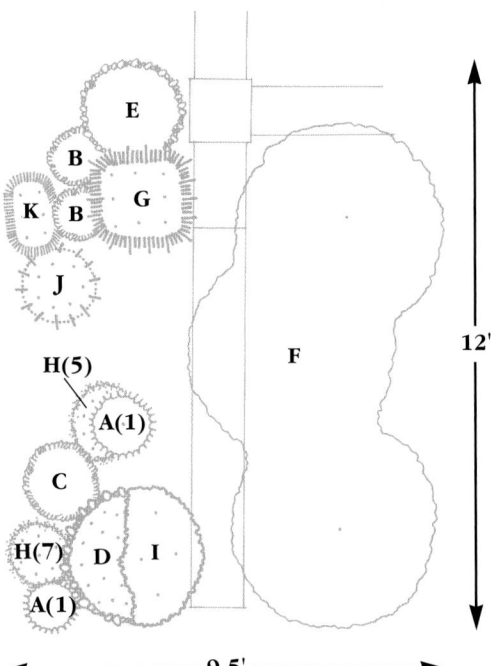

Plant List

A. Athyrium nipponicum 'Pictum' (Japanese painted fern) (2)
B. Begonia x tuberhybrida 'Nonstop' (tuberous begonia) (2)
C. Begonia x tuberhybrida 'Skaugum' (tuberous begonia) (1)
D. Caladium x hortulanum

(caladium) (15)
E. Fuchsia x hybrida 'Estelle Marie' (fuchsia) (1)
F. Hydrangea arborescens 'Annabelle' (hydrangea) (3)
G. Iris pallida 'Variegata' (sweet iris) (9)
H. Lobelia erinus 'Riviera Blue Splash'

(edging lobelia) (12)
I. Myrrhis odorata (sweet cicely) (4)
J. Pennisetum alopecuroides 'Little Bunny' (Chinese pennisetum) (8)
K. Viola tricolor (Johnny-jump-up) (6)

◆ How to Plant This Garden ◆

1. Start begonia and caladium tubers *indoors in early spring. Transplant outside after all danger of frost has passed.*

2. Plant lobelias and Johnny-jump-ups *close together for a massed effect.*

3. Loosen soil *to 8 inches for sweet irises. Set the rhizomes close to the surface of the soil.*

4. Set fuchsia, Japanese painted ferns, *and pennisetums in pots with the tops of the rootballs at the soil surface.*

5. Plant hydrangeas *1 to 1½ feet from the base of the wall.*

Aftercare and Maintenance
• *Feed caladiums, tuberous begonias, and fuchsias every 2 weeks with a fish*

emulsion or other liquid fertilizer.
• *To encourage foliage on caladiums, remove any flowers that appear.*
• *Keep tuberous begonias and fuchsias evenly moist but not wet.*
• *Withhold water from begonias and caladiums when foliage fades in the fall. Dry tubers outdoors before storing in a frost-free place over the winter.*

Create Your Own Garden for a Small Yard

Although limited in space, small yards have the potential for becoming showplaces for favorite plants. If you have a small yard or a confined yet promising space to personalize with plants, you can do so with creative and surprising results.

When designing your small garden, consider the potential for vertical expansion. Without taking up precious bed space, many versatile and exciting plants can grow up hedges, walls, fences, trellises, and even trees. You can also train shrubs or small trees to grow flat against a vertical element using the technique called espalier, by which their trunks and branches are encouraged to conform to a supporting framework.

Manipulating space can make your yard look larger than it actually is. Adjust the scale and boundaries of your site by installing raised beds or by varying the height of your fence. For example, a low fence, as in the garden design shown opposite, allows you to see over it to the larger landscape beyond and appropriate its expanse. Even a small slice of a borrowed view adds a sense of spaciousness. A meandering path or a small center oval of lawn can also create the illusion of space.

If you are a novice gardener, you may want to begin with the simple plan shown on this page. If you like the challenge of managing a broader plant palette, try one of the two alternate plans on the following pages, which include more perennials and shrubs.

A Private Garden

In this seaside garden plan, the fence provides a sense of privacy and shields the plants from the wind and the ocean's salt spray. An angular layout with a patterned brick path opens onto a small patch of lawn that extends to a herbaceous border at the far end. The boxwood hedge lined with sweet alyssum repeats the shape of the walk and thus helps define the garden's somewhat formal character.

The boxwoods and other evergreens provide year-round interest, while annual and perennial flowers offer seasonal color and texture. Trees and a tall hedge rise above the fence, expanding the horizon. The low-flowering plants emphasize the contrasting levels, their colors carefully selected to harmonize with the deep, earthy rose of the bricks. All of these plants do well in average soil conditions inland or along a seashore.

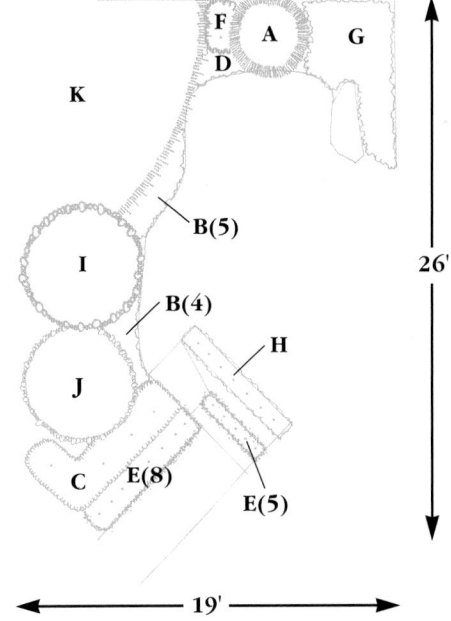

Plant List

A. *Artemisia ludoviciana* (western mugwort) (1)
B. *Browallia speciosa* 'Marine Bells' (bush violet) (9)
C. *Buxus sempervirens* 'Suffruticosa' (dwarf boxwood) (5)
D. *Dianthus deltoides* 'Ruber' (maiden pinks) (2)
E. *Lobularia maritima* (sweet alyssum) (13)
F. *Malva alcea* var. *fastigiata* (mallow) (2)
G. *Oenothera erythrosepala* (evening primrose) (11)
H. *Oenothera speciosa* (evening primrose) (7)
I. *Rosa rugosa* 'Blanc Double de Coubert' (rugosa rose) (1)
J. *Rosa* 'Sexy Rexy' (rose) (1)
K. *Taxus baccata* (English yew) (1)

◆ How to Plant This Garden ◆

1. In spring, after danger of frost, *dig compost into the soil.*

2. Set boxwoods *1 foot apart at approximately the same depth as in their containers.*

3. Plant western mugwort *in a 1-gallon pot; keep soil evenly moist.*

4. Plant roses, *keeping bud unions just above ground in warm climates and 1 to 2 inches below ground in colder areas.*

5. Sow sweet alyssum seed, *or set out bedding plants from cell packs.*

6. Plant annuals: *bush violet,* maiden pinks, and evening primrose.

Aftercare and Maintenance
• *Trim boxwood hedge to 1½ feet regularly during growing season.*
• *Shear sweet alyssums before seeds set to keep compact and prevent self-sowing.*

Midsummer Bloom in a Small Yard

Although small, this yard includes a diverse collection of plants that display a variety of colors and forms. The shortest plants, dwarf zinnias and low-growing, evergreen maiden pinks, provide bright accents of color. Taller, but still only 10 inches high, 'Little Miss Muffet' Shasta daisies produce 2- to 3-inch-wide creamy white flowers with sunny yellow centers. In late spring, 'Abbotswood Rose' campion brings a new form to the garden with a compact, showy mound of bright pink blooms. After the flowers fade, gray-green clumps of foliage harmonize all summer with spiky silver stems of Russian sage.

Evergreen germander makes the most of limited space in this yard. Small, even at maturity, it easily can be kept as a 1-foot-high hedge. Although this garden is at its peak in midsummer, compact dwarf blue spruce provides form and color that maintains interest throughout the seasons.

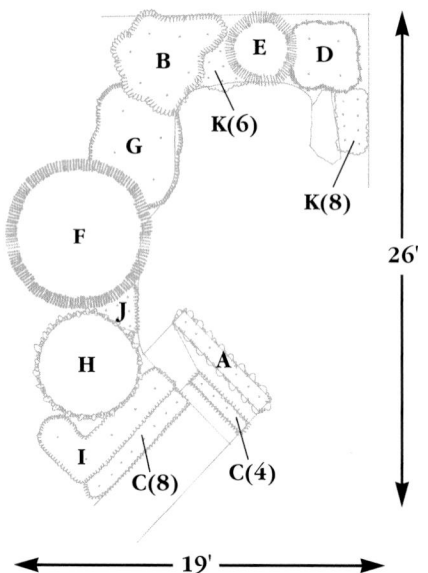

Plant List

A. *Chrysanthemum* x *superbum* 'Little Miss Muffet' (Shasta daisy) (7)
B. *Delphinium* 'Chelsea Star' (delphinium) (8)
C. *Dianthus deltoides* (maiden pinks) (12)
D. *Lychnis* x *walkeri* 'Abbotswood Rose'

(campion) (4)
E. *Perovskia atriplicifolia* (Russian sage) (1)
F. *Picea pungens* 'Fat Albert' (Colorado blue spruce) (1)
G. *Potentilla fruticosa* 'Abbotswood' (cinquefoil) (4)

H. *Rosa rugosa* 'Rosea' (rugosa rose) (1)
I. *Teucrium chamaedrys* (germander) (5)
J. *Veronica spicata* 'Blue Charm' (speedwell) (6)
K. *Zinnia* Thumbelina Series (zinnia) (14)

◆ How to Plant This Garden ◆

1. Set the dwarf blue spruce and the rose in the ground at the same depth as they were in their containers, preferably in full sun.

2. Dig in a 3-inch layer of compost before planting daisies, delphiniums, pinks, campions, Russian sage, speedwells, and zinnias.

3. Locate campions, delphiniums, Russian sage, and speedwells behind the lower-growing daisies, pinks, and zinnias.

4. Add a 1-inch layer of compost to beds for germanders and cinquefoils.

Aftercare and Maintenance
• Keep the spruce moist but not wet, since it cannot tolerate dry soil.
• Pinch the main buds on delphiniums when the plants are 5 inches tall.
• Leave hips on the rose for brilliant fall color.
• Deadhead Shasta daisies throughout the growing season to encourage more blooms and keep plants compact.

A Small Yard in Pink and Yellow

Rich pinks and yellows create a cheerful, bright design for this small yard. The strong, sculptural lines of a pyramidal yew are complemented by sprays of variegated 'Morning Light' grass and the compact, free-flowering polyantha rose, 'The Fairy'. The edges of the brick pathway are softened with low-growing lemon thyme, a fragrant herb that gives off a fresh scent when touched. 'Golden Showers' azalea bears peach-yellow, vanilla-scented blooms. 'Wargrave Pink' cranesbill is planted nearby, with complementary salmon-pink flowers that bloom from early summer through fall. Festive red, pink, orange, yellow, and white blooms of 'Bright Bikini' strawflowers light up this summer garden and make long-lasting dried flowers to enjoy throughout the year.

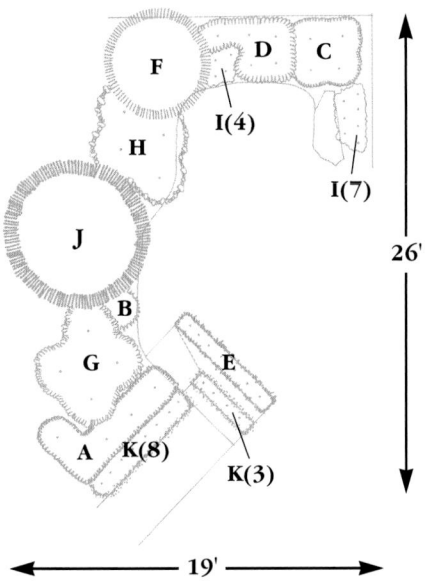

Plant List

A. *Berberis thunbergii* var. *atropurpurea* (Japanese barberry) (5)
B. *Coreopsis rosea* (pink tickseed) (1)
C. *Coreopsis verticillata* 'Moonbeam' (tickseed) (4)
D. *Geranium endressii* 'Wargrave Pink' (cranesbill) (5)
E. *Helichrysum bracteatum* 'Bright Bikini' (strawflower) (7)
F. *Miscanthus sinensis* 'Morning Light' (Japanese silver grass) (1)
G. *Rhododendron* 'Golden Showers' (azalea) (4)
H. *Rosa* 'The Fairy' (polyantha rose) (4)
I. *Tagetes* 'Antigua Gold' (marigold) (11)
J. *Taxus* x *media* 'Hatfieldii' (Hatfield's yew) (1)
K. *Thymus* x *citriodorus* (lemon thyme) (11)

◆ How to Plant This Garden ◆

*1. **Prepare a planting bed** for each azalea by incorporating several shovelfuls of peat moss into an area twice the width of the rootball. Plant at the same depth as in the container.*

*2. **Add well-rotted manure or compost** to beds before planting the roses and barberry plants. Check their rootballs for tightly wrapped roots. Loosen or cut the roots free before planting.*

*3. **Loosen the soil in beds** before planting the yew, Japanese silver grass, tickseeds, strawflowers, thymes, and marigolds. Leave 10 feet for the yew to spread and 8 feet for the grass.*

Aftercare and Maintenance
• Mulch azaleas with chopped leaves. Replenish the mulch annually. Avoid cultivating around their shallow roots.
• Trim polyantha roses in late winter after the second year to shape the plants. Trim deadwood anytime.
• Shear tickseed plants toward the end of summer to encourage a second flush of bloom.
• Cut clumps of Japanese silver grass to the ground in late winter.

Create Your Own Entryway Garden

The entryway garden should be planned to enhance the architecture of your house. Formal, traditional houses call for symmetrical plantings while less formally designed homes are complemented by well-laid-out, asymmetrical gardens. While the style of the architecture dictates the main lines of the entryway garden plan, your climate, setting, and personal preferences leave plenty of room for creative design. The most formal entryway garden, for instance, may be softened with summer flowers, while a small clipped hedge can add just the right balance of control to an exuberant mix of blooms.

The plants for your entryway garden should look good in all seasons. In every region, it is important to include some plants that will provide color and shape throughout the year, connecting your home with the landscape and preventing a bare, out-of-season look. Plants with evergreen foliage are especially valuable for this purpose.

A welcoming setting for any entry must have a broad, easily negotiated path to the door. While plants can cover its edges, they shouldn't spill more than several inches into the walkway.

If privacy is important, an entry design may include a hedge or fence that is large and thick enough to shield the house from passersby without creating a forbidding barrier to friends.

The design here, suitable for the Northeast, Midwest, and mid-Atlantic regions, combines casual, colorful bloomers and a tidy but not overly formal hedge. The effect is easygoing but controlled. For a more romantic look in the Southeast, consider the alternate design on the following page. Or, to create an oasis in the Southwest, you might try the planting described on page 225.

Extending a Traditional Welcome

The combination shown here of shrubs, vines, and flowers for a sunny front entrance in a temperate region has a traditional look that suits this colonial-style house. A handsome boxwood hedge flanks the front door, providing year-round symmetry and matching the lines of the low white fence at the beginning of the path.

The formal effect is softened by a seemingly random scattering of annuals lining the pathway. Morning-glories along the fence rails, perennial lilies, and delicate Queen Anne's lace reinforce the unpretentious period charm of the house.

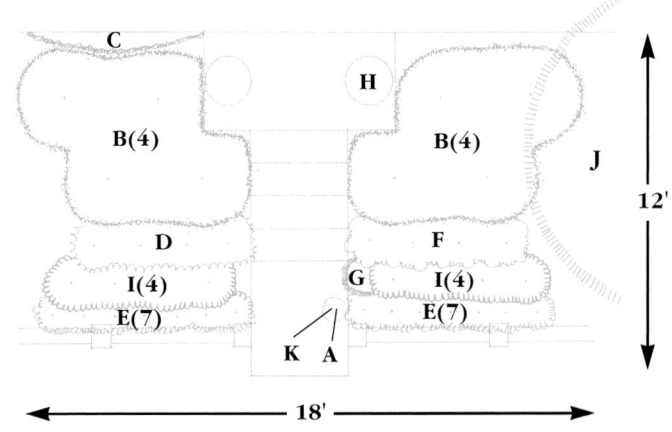

◆ How to Plant This Garden ◆

1. Create a rich, well-drained site by digging 2 inches of compost into the soil.

2. Dig 12-inch-deep holes for lily bulbs. Spread roots and fill, covering the top of the bulbs with 9 inches of soil.

3. Plant the trumpet creeper on a strong trellis 24 inches from the house. Gently tie the main stems onto the trellis. Next, plant the yew and boxwoods.

4. Sow morning-glories, Queen Anne's lace, and zinnias in deeply worked soil. Keep soil moist until germination.

5. Grow geraniums in containers.

6. Plant snapdragons and rose campion in a sunny spot.

Aftercare and Maintenance
• In colder climates, screen boxwood with burlap to protect it from winter damage.
• Divide the coneflowers every 4 years.
• Top-dress established lilies with compost or well-rotted manure each fall.

Plant List

A. Antirrhinum majus (snapdragon)
B. Buxus spp. (boxwood) (8)
C. Campsis radicans (trumpet creeper) (1)
D. Daucus carota var. carota (Queen Anne's lace) (4)
E. Ipomoea tricolor (morning-glory) (14)
F. Lilium spp. (lily) (4)

G. Lychnis coronaria (rose campion) (1)
H. Pelargonium x hortorum (zonal geranium) (1)
I. Rudbeckia laciniata 'Goldquelle' (coneflower) (8)
J. Taxus cuspidata (Japanese yew) (1)
K. Zinnia elegans (zinnia)

An Entryway Garden for the Sultry South

This lush, romantic garden suits the gardening style of the Southeast. This region favors durable plants that must be tolerant of the heat and humidity common in the South, and must do well in either full or partial sun. Such plants also provide year-round interest in a region where the gardening season never really ends.

Golden-rain tree is a colorful focal point, with bronze or shrimp pink spring foliage and languid, graceful clusters of yellow blooms all summer. The shiny green gardenia hedge scents the entry from summer into early winter and requires little upkeep. Heat and humidity intensify its rich, sweet scent. Occasional pruning keeps it blooming freely at a 4- to 6-foot height. The clematis vine softens the hard lines of the building with purple summer blooms that give way in fall to picturesque, feathery, silver seed heads.

Deceptively modest-looking lilyturf may be the most hardworking plant in this garden. Its evergreen foliage provides year-round structure to the garden and sets off the other flowers, including long-blooming Peruvian lilies and tender black-eyed Susan vines, which must be replaced annually.

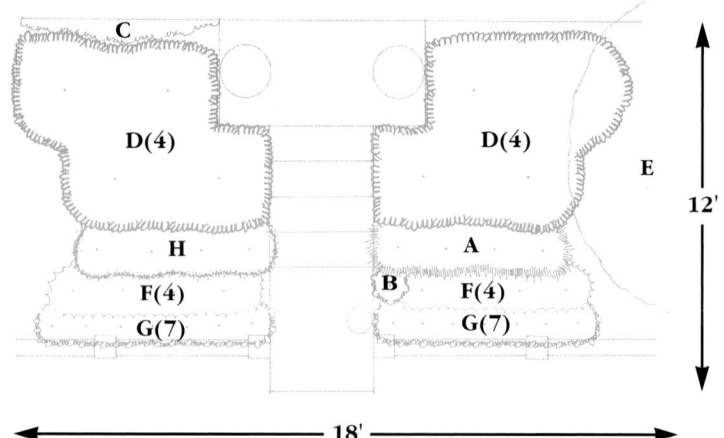

Plant List

A. *Acanthus dioscoridis* (lesser bear's-breech) (4)
B. *Alstroemeria aurantiaca* 'Lutea' (Peruvian lily) (1)
C. *Clematis* x *jackmanii* (Jackman clematis) (1)
D. *Gardenia jasminoides* 'August Beauty' (common gardenia) (8)

E. *Koelreuteria paniculata* (golden-rain tree) (1)
F. *Liriope muscari* 'Variegata' (variegated blue lilyturf) (8)
G. *Thunbergia alata* 'Susie' (black-eyed Susan vine) (14)
H. *Trachelium caeruleum* 'Violet Blue' (blue lace flower) (4)

◆ How to Plant This Garden ◆

1. Prepare the site *by digging in 1 to 2 inches of compost to a depth of 2 feet to increase the root depth, making the plants more drought-resistant.*

2. Plant the golden-rain tree *in spring in a bowl-shaped hole as deep at its center as the rootball. Before planting, loosen soil out to the branch spread of the tree.*

3. Grow Peruvian lilies, *lesser bear's-breech, black-eyed Susan vine, gardenias, and lilyturfs under the golden-rain tree.*

4. To plant the Peruvian lilies, *spread the tubers and cover with 2 inches of soil.*

5. After planting clematis *and garde-*

nias, cover soil with 3 inches of mulch.

Aftercare and Maintenance
• *Mulch the gardenias with compost to protect the roots, and add organic matter to the soil. If leaves turn yellow, the soil may be too alkaline. Test and adjust pH.*

An Entryway Garden for the Sundrenched Southwest

If you garden in the Southwest, you need plants that thrive in this region's hot, dry conditions. You may also have to contend with alkaline soil that is unfriendly to many plants. The region's brilliant sunshine and low rainfall call for plants whose colors and forms can hold their own in such a challenging environment.

This entryway, planted with shades of blue and green, makes a cool oasis from the hot sun. Evergreen Texas mountain laurel, with its showy violet blooms, and the white flowers of star jasmine both offer appealing fragrance while soothing the eye with lush, green foliage.

The soft, hazy effect of the sea lavender's tiny blossoms is balanced by purple coneflowers and nasturtiums, whose bright colors are powerful enough to withstand the glare of the sun.

In autumn, the evergreen cotoneaster is bright with orange berries that will, along with the seed heads of the coneflower, feed the birds of winter. The fernlike leaves of yarrow and the plumes of crimson fountain grass add soft texture and bright color. All these plants grow well in these demanding conditions and reward minimal care with an abundance of colorful blooms.

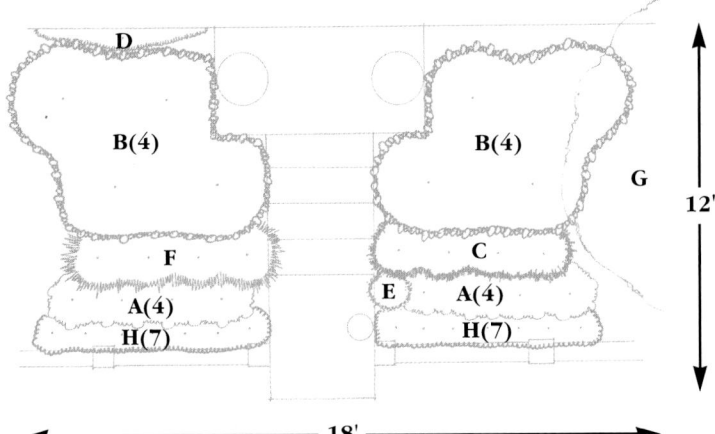

Plant List

A. *Achillea millefolium*
'Sulphur Beauty'
(common yarrow) (8)
B. *Cotoneaster congestus*
(Pyrenees cotoneaster) (8)
C. *Echinacea purpurea*
(purple coneflower) (4)
D. *Jasminum multiflorum* (star jasmine) (1)

E. *Limonium latifolium*
(sea lavender) (1)
F. *Pennisetum setaceum*
'Rubrum' (crimson fountain grass) (4)
G. *Sophora secundiflora*
(Texas mountain laurel) (1)
H. *Tropaeolum majus*
'Climbing Mix'
(garden nasturtium) (14)

◆ How to Plant This Garden ◆

1. Test the soil and, *if it is alkaline, adjust with powdered sulfur to bring it closer to neutral.*

2. Spread amendments and compost, *working them into the soil.*

3. Plant Texas mountain laurel and cotoneaster first. *Container specimens of cotoneaster will transplant easily.*

4. Train the star jasmine vines, *planted 18 inches from the house, on wires.*

5. Next, plant the crimson fountain grass, *followed by the sea lavender and drifts of yarrow and purple coneflower.*

6. Plant nasturtium seed *1 inch deep in full or part sun.*

Aftercare and Maintenance
• *Divide the yarrow every 3 years.*
• *Unlike most fountain grasses, crimson fountain grass does not self-seed. Propagate by dividing large clumps.*

Create Your Own Driveway Edging

Of all areas in a home landscape, the driveway is the most frequently used and is also the place where visitors may form their first impression of the home. But making a driveway attractive and welcoming poses a special set of problems. Surrounding plants must survive exhaust fumes, salt runoff from roads and walks, extra heat reflected by paving in summer, occasional trampling, and perhaps abuse from snow-removal equipment.

Driveway landscaping also presents a unique visual problem. Most driveways consist of a large, flat area. Surrounded by equally flat lawn or ground covers, the scene can seem open and barren. The solution is to introduce vertical elements—trees, shrubs, ornamental grasses, and flowers—with a variety of forms, textures, and colors to soften and contrast with that commanding slash of driveway.

The realities of gardening around a driveway rule out delicate or demanding plants and those that look less than presentable at anytime during the growing season. Fortunately, there are still plenty of excellent choices that meet these challenging criteria.

The plan shown here combines sturdy perennials that perform well in full sun or partial shade and could be worked into a planting of existing shrubs and trees. The alternate shrub garden that follows is especially low in maintenance requirements and offers attractions for all seasons. The other alternate planting, an annual driveway garden for full sun, provides the most colorful effect.

Tough Plants That Soften Hard Lines

The durable flowering perennials in this design all have a long period of bloom and foliage that remains attractive throughout the growing season. They will do fine in full sun, but will also bloom well with as little as 4 hours of sun a day. In fact, the astilbe is happiest in partial shade; with more sunlight it requires extra water. In summer, the garden is sheltered from drying winds by a high hedge at the back. A low rock wall between the plants helps shield them from the occasional wayward tire for an enduring roadside existence—except for the lilies. Tuck the lilies into a safe spot, as shown here. In winter, the plants retreat to ground level or below, thus escaping the rough treatment of errant snowplows and the weight of high-piled snow.

◆ How to Plant This Garden ◆

1. Till the soil 12 to 15 inches deep and work in 2 to 3 inches of compost to improve drainage and moisture retention.

2. Plant lily bulbs with 9 inches of soil over the bulb tip.

3. Plant astilbes and coral bells in a lightly shaded, moist spot.

4. Locate remaining plants in a spot with at least 8 hours of sun.

5. Mulch all plantings with a light layer of shredded bark.

Aftercare and Maintenance
• Spray Shasta daisies with a strong jet of water from a hose to rid plants of aphids or spider mites in summer.
• Spot-water astilbes weekly to keep soil evenly moist during dry weather.
• Deadhead chamomile throughout the growing season to keep it blooming all summer.

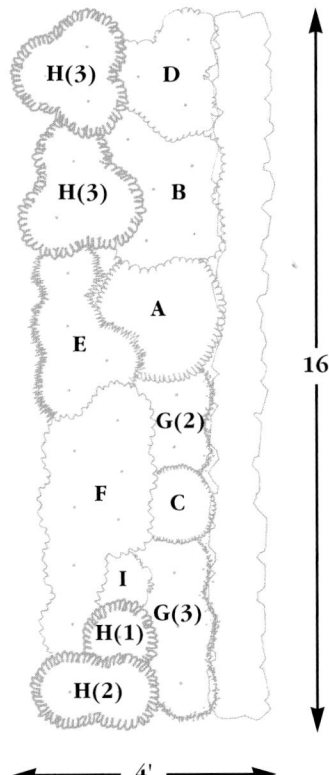

Plant List

A. *Artemisia ludoviciana* var. *albula* 'Silver King' (wormwood) (1)
B. *Astilbe* x *arendsii* (astilbe) (5)
C. *Chamaemelum nobile* (chamomile) (1)
D. *Chrysanthemum* x *superbum* (Shasta daisy) (3)
E. *Coreopsis lanceolata* (lance-leaved coreopsis) (4)
F. *Hemerocallis citrina* (citron daylily) (7)
G. *Heuchera sanguinea* (coral bells) (5)
H. *Lilium* cv. (Asiatic hybrid lily) (9)
I. *Stachys byzantina* (lamb's ears) (1)

A Driveway Planting with Shrubs

This driveway edged with shrubs looks good year round with minimal attention. The shrubs give permanent structure to the landscape, unlike perennials and annuals that disappear by late fall in most cold climates. Once established, these slow-growing plants need little more than an annual pruning and mulching to look their best. Shrubs such as these are big enough to complement a large driveway, whereas small plants may look lost unless planted in great masses.

This shrub garden works best in mild-winter areas in Zones 5 through 8. Several species, including cinquefoil, cotoneaster, and juniper, are hardy in much colder zones. This plan includes two shrubs, a hydrangea species and cinquefoil, that will grow to reasonable size and bloom well even if cut to the ground each winter.

The garden emphasizes seasonal interest, from the spring flowers of weigela to the evergreen junipers that brighten the winter landscape.

Plant List

A. *Chionanthus virginicus* (white fringe tree) (2)
B. *Cotoneaster dammeri* 'Royal Beauty' (bearberry cotoneaster) (1)
C. *Hibiscus syriacus* 'Woodbridge' (rose-of-Sharon) (4)

D. *Hydrangea macrophylla* 'Domotoi' (bigleaf hydrangea) (2)
E. *Juniperus horizontalis* 'Hughes' (creeping juniper) (1)
F. *Kerria japonica* 'Pleniflora' (kerria) (1)
G. *Potentilla fruticosa*

'Katherine Dykes' (cinquefoil) (6)
H. *Spiraea japonica* 'Little Princess' (Japanese spirea) (3)
I. *Weigela florida* 'Variegata Nana' (dwarf variegated weigela) (2)

◆ How to Plant This Garden ◆

1. Assess the amount of sun and shade in your garden site.

2. In spring, plant white fringe trees in a sunny spot. Prepare a hole as deep as the rootball at the center. Loosen soil beyond the edges of the hole and work in compost.

3. Plant spirea, cotoneaster, juniper, and cinquefoil in sunny sites, and hydrangea, rose-of-Sharon, weigela, and kerria in part shade.

Aftercare and Maintenance
• *Prune hydrangea immediately after flowering, since it blooms on the previous season's wood.*
• *Prune cotoneaster and juniper if they need shaping.*

A(1)
I
G
B
F
H
C
E
A(1)
D
16'
4'

A Driveway Planting with Annuals

Spring brings a clean slate and the opportunity to try new color combinations in this garden. The annuals here produce maximum color and bloom throughout summer and early fall. While this planting is an excellent choice for cold-climate areas where the space around the driveway may be piled high with snow, a driveway garden of annuals is also sensible for situations such as a summer cottage or rental.

The plants have been chosen to grow to a variety of heights, avoiding the frequent pitfall of monotonous flatness in annual plantings. All withstand pollution, salty breezes, and residual road salt in the soil, and none require especially fertile soil, so preparing the bed and planting is fast and easy.

All of these plants grow well in the heat of summer and full sun, except the pot marigolds, which may falter. If they do, cut them back to rebloom as the weather cools, providing color through the first light frosts of fall.

Plant List

A. *Calendula officinalis* 'Prince' (pot marigold) (7)
B. *Catharanthus roseus* 'Bright Eye' (periwinkle) (9)
C. *Celosia argentea* var. *cristata* 'Amazon' (celosia) (4)
D. *Cosmos bipinnatus* 'Sensations Pink' (cosmos) (6)
E. *Cosmos bipinnatus* 'Sensations White' (cosmos) (3)
F. *Gomphrena globosa* 'Strawberry Fields' (globe amaranth) (5)
G. *Salvia farinacea* 'Strata' (mealy-cup sage) (11)
H. *Senecio cineraria* 'Cirrus' (dusty-miller) (3)
I. *Verbena* x *hybrida* 'Imagination' (verbena) (10)

16'

4'

◆ How to Plant This Garden ◆

1. Assess your site to be sure it has at least 6 hours of sun per day to encourage flowering.

2. To prepare the site, till 2 to 3 inches of compost into the soil. Rake soil smooth.

3. Sow seeds of calendula and cosmos after the last frost. Cover with a ¼-inch layer of soil and keep moist. Thin so seedlings are 12 inches apart.

4. Plant periwinkle, celosia, globe amaranth, sage, dusty-miller, and verbena seedlings after last frost.

5. Keep soil moist until plants are growing. Mulch when seedlings are 3 to 4 inches tall, keeping mulch 1 inch from plant stems.

Aftercare and Maintenance
• Pinch tips of sage, globe amaranth, and cosmos when plants are about 12 inches high to make them bushy and full.
• Lightly fertilize all plants in early summer.

Create Your Own Garden of Varied Light

It is best, if possible, to plant tall deciduous trees, such as maples and oaks, on the south side of your property. In the summer, they will provide welcome shade and channel fresh breezes toward the house, while in winter, warming sunlight will shine through their bare branches.

Observing the time of day when parts of your garden are in sun and shade will help you understand your site and ensure the success of your garden plan. On a site plan, mark sun and shade patterns in your garden for each season over a year. Date your drawings and note both morning and afternoon light. You may discover that the amount of sun your garden receives is affected by the shadows of houses and trees on neighboring properties. Using this information, you can create successful designs or make plans to cut down or prune some trees to create new sunny spaces.

If you have a wet and wooded or otherwise partly shaded spot, you might choose the garden featured here. Its perennials do well in moist, rich soil, and their colors add brightness to the dappled sunlight. Or use the first alternate planting on the following page; it features flowers, such as phlox and goatsbeard, that also fare well in sunny sites. If your location is partly shaded but the soil is dry, the second alternate planting (*page 233*) will produce the best results.

F(5)
A G(13)
F(6) G(3) D
B(2)
F(5)
B(2)
C
E(6)
E(3) H

15'

14'

Plant List

A. Allium giganteum (giant onion) (5)
B. Astilbe x arendsii (astilbe) (4)
C. Astilbe thunbergii 'Straussenfeder' (astilbe) (1)
D. Clethra alnifolia 'Hummingbird' (summersweet) (3)
E. Hakonechloa *macra* 'Aureola' (golden variegated hakonechloa) (9)
F. Iris ensata (sword-leaved iris) (16)
G. Primula florinadae (Tibetan primrose) (16)
H. Rodgersia pinnata 'Superba' (rodgersia) (1)

A Garden for a Moist, Shaded Site

The garden opposite combines an interesting mix of moisture- and shade-loving perennials in a wide range of textures and forms. A wide, grassy path rambles through patches of dappled light, leading to a pond partially hidden by landscaped banks, while perennials spill onto the path.

Japanese irises thrive in this garden, standing in wet soil at the pond's edge. Their flat flowers and clumps of broad, swordlike leaves make a dramatic contrast with the fluffy, pointed panicles of the astilbes nearby.

If you have enough room, you may want to add a dramatic clump of variegated hosta. A birdhouse or two on poles will provide nesting sites for songbirds, adding a lively note to your garden.

◆ How to Plant This Garden ◆

1. Test your soil before planting irises, which require acid-to-neutral conditions. If soil is alkaline, apply powdered sulfur or iron sulfate (1 ounce to 2 gallons of water). Plant irises in the spring at the same depth they were growing in their containers.

2. Locate astilbes in sheltered sites with morning sun and giant onions in sunny spots. Dig several shovelfuls of compost into the bed at planting time.

3. Plant rodgersia, Tibetan primrose, summersweet, and golden variegated hakonechloa in moist soil for best growth.

Aftercare and Maintenance
• *Check soil acidity regularly during the growing season. Amend as needed.*
• *Divide irises when they become overcrowded and do not flower as abundantly.*
• *Water astilbes regularly to keep soil moist.*

A Native Wildflower Garden in Dappled Shade

This garden combines some of the most beautiful native and naturalized wildflowers with conventional perennials. Their blossoms of pink, red, blue, and white brighten the area, and their contrasting plant forms add structure to the path after the garden has bloomed. Together, these plants create a cool, restful mood in the garden as they adapt to sun and dappled shade. With this flexibility, you can plant them in an area already lightly shaded by the high canopy of deciduous trees and lower shrubs, or you can site them near newly planted trees that do not yet cast much shade. The plants were chosen for their ability to thrive in the moist conditions found by the pond.

Plant List

A. Aquilegia caerulea (Rocky Mountain columbine) (6)
B. Aruncus dioicus (goatsbeard) (2)
C. Asclepias incarnata (swamp milkweed) (6)
D. Aster novae-angliae (New England aster) (4)
E. Cimicifuga racemosa (black cohosh) (1)
F. Dicentra eximia 'Snowdrift' (wild bleeding heart) (11)
G. Filipendula rubra (queen-of-the-prairie) (2)
H. Iris versicolor (blue flag) (3)
I. Lobelia cardinalis (cardinal flower) (7)
J. Phlox paniculata 'Cotton Candy' (perennial phlox) (4)
K. Phlox paniculata 'Mt. Fuji' (perennial phlox) (3)

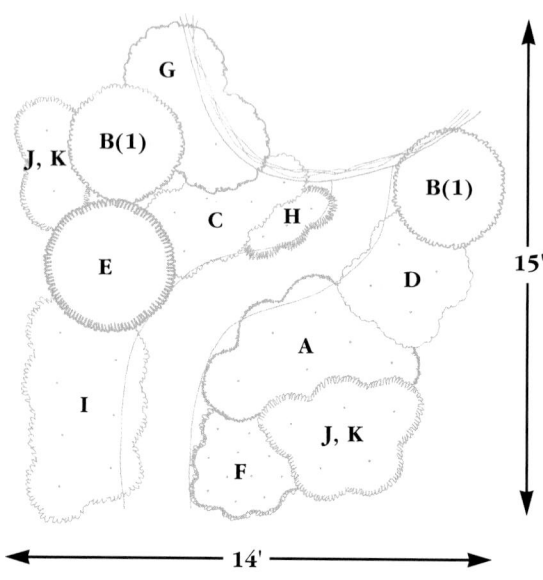

15'

14'

◆ How to Plant This Garden ◆

1. Plant queen-of-the-prairie, goatsbeard, and swamp milkweed close to the water's edge in a bright spot.

2. Site blue flag in a sunny area in damp soil or water to a maximum of 6 inches deep.

3. Plant Rocky Mountain columbines and New England asters in a raised or sloping spot where soil drains.

4. Before planting phlox, amend soil with compost or aged manure. Space approximately 2 feet apart for good air circulation.

5. Place cardinal flower and black cohosh where their tall, showy spikes become focal points. Both plants do best in acid soil amended with leaf mold.

6. Scatter wild bleeding heart in the shadiest spots, but away from standing water. Add leaf mold to the soil to keep it moist and rich.

Aftercare and Maintenance

• Dig and divide blue flags and queen-of-the-prairie in the fall every 2 to 3 years.
• Pinch back asters twice before midsummer for denser, more compact plants. Divide clumps every 2 to 3 years.
• Divide phlox every 2 to 3 years in early fall, keeping the strong outer divisions. In spring, thin the clumps to five or six stems to improve air circulation.
• Covering cardinal flowers with a light straw mulch after the ground freezes in winter protects them in cold climates.
• Leave the seedpods on the Rocky Mountain columbines intact to encourage reseeding and to attract birds.
• Fertilize all plants lightly each spring after growth begins.

A Dry Garden in Partial Shade

Here is a colorful garden that uses plants suited to a dry, partly shaded site. The plants may not grow as tall or as lush as those found in more moist and fertile conditions, but they are equally attractive, with agapanthus and speedwell adding vertical contrast. This planting borders a crushed stone walk leading to a red brick patio. The dark reddish brown colors of this hardscape allow the rich floral blues and yellows to assume prominence, with white and pink tones emerging as sharp accent colors.

Dry soil in shade can be a difficult place to garden successfully. Therefore, before you plant your garden, double dig the soil and enrich it with large amounts of moisture-retentive materials such as compost, leaf mold, and manure. This work will pay off in moister soil and stronger plants.

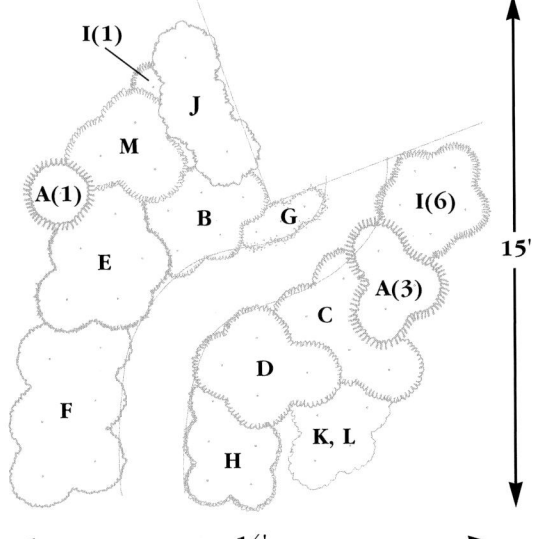

Plant List

A. Agapanthus africanus (agapanthus) (4)
B. Alchemilla mollis (lady's-mantle) (5)
C. Campanula medium 'Alba' (Canterbury bells) (4)
D. Campanula medium 'Caerulea' (Canterbury bells) (4)
E. Centaurea macro- cephala (knapweed) (5)
F. Dennstaedtia punctilobula (hay-scented fern) (6)
G. Hyacinthoides hispanica (Spanish bluebell) (3)
H. Geranium sanguineum 'Album' (cranesbill) (5)
I. Iris foetidissima (scarlet-seeded iris) (7)
J. Rudbeckia hirta 'Goldilocks' (black-eyed Susan) (3)
K. Tradescantia x andersoniana 'Osprey' (spiderwort) (2)
L. Tradescantia x andersoniana 'Zwanberg Blue' (spiderwort) (2)
M. Veronica longifolia (speedwell) (3)

◆ How to Plant This Garden ◆

1. Plant clumps of Canterbury bells every spring to bloom the following year.

2. Plant black-eyed Susans, ferns, knapweeds, speedwells, and spiderworts in drifts.

3. Add compost to soil before planting lady's-mantle, cranesbill, and iris.

4. In Zones 7 to 10, plant agapanthus in the ground. In colder climates, sink potted plants in the ground.

5. In fall, plant Spanish bluebell bulbs 3 inches deep in mild climates and 6 inches deep in colder regions. Spread them in drifts running through neighboring plants.

6. Apply a pine bark mulch to preserve soil moisture.

Aftercare and Maintenance
• To promote strong, compact growth in knapweeds, spiderworts, and speedwells, apply a balanced fertilizer sparingly once a month to midsummer.
• Cut back spiderwort and geranium foliage in midsummer if it becomes untidy.
• Sow biennial Canterbury bells the following spring to promote earlier and more abundant blooms.
• Lift and overwinter the potted agapanthus indoors.

Create Your Own Hillside Shade Garden

Beautifying a partly shaded bank presents several challenges for gardeners. Variations in steepness, degrees of shade, drainage, and soil quality play critical roles in developing a solid cover that will flourish on the hillside throughout the year. Fortunately, a wide array of low ground covers and shrubs, as well as perennials and vines, is available to survive difficult conditions and even help control erosion.

The effect of such a garden can be dramatic. Even though flower color is sometimes limited in shady gardens, combinations featuring variegated foliage add brightness. Interesting leaf shapes that cast shadows in dappled sun provide striking patterns of light and color as well.

When selecting plants for shade, look for contrasting foliage textures. Combine plants with large, leathery leaves, grasslike spikes, and finely fringed leaf margins. These will become the focal points around which you can add less striking plants that work hard to cover and stabilize the slope. Ivy or other hardy vines and ground covers, such as periwinkle or spurge, are good examples.

Your garden site may be like the one featured here, which has slow drainage and stays moist after heavy rainfall. If your site features well-drained soil, consider the first alternate planting on the following page; but if you have a site with drier, poorer soil, the shade garden plan *(page 237)* will be more suited to your needs.

A Far-East Feel

The Oriental pavilion at the top of the shaded slope shown opposite gives this garden a contemplative aura and underscores the quiet harmony of the plant combinations. Like a Chinese landscape painting, this garden design draws your gaze up the winding path to the hilltop and invites you to scale the path for a view from the crest. Springtime visitors who make the effort will be rewarded with a tapestry-like view of the flowering shrubs.

Moisture-loving rhododendrons and azaleas offer splashes of welcome color in the spring against vivid green foliage that persists for most of the year. Masking the bare lower stems of the larger shrub behind are masses of large, puckered hosta leaves. They add contrasts in color and texture, anchoring the sloping landscape and providing a sense of balance to the base of this design.

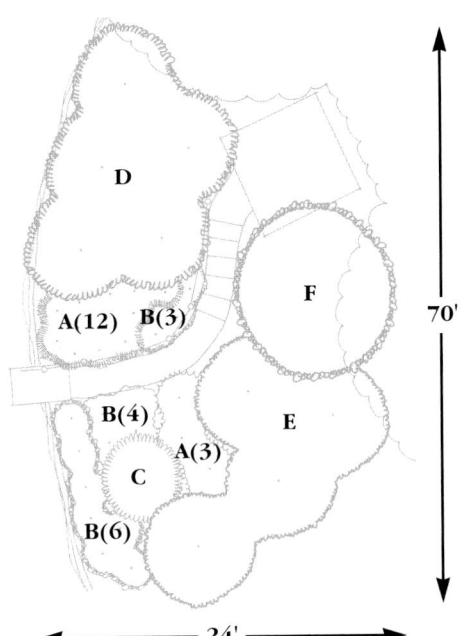

Plant List

A. *Aquilegia flabellata* **var.** *pumila* (dwarf blue columbine) (15)
B. *Hosta* 'Big Boy' (hosta) (13)
C. *Hosta sieboldiana* (hosta) (1)
D. *Rhododendron* Gable Hybrids 'Karen' (azalea) (5)
E. *Rhododendron* Leach Hybrids 'Bali' (rhododendron) (4)
F. *Rhododendron smirnowii* (Smirnow rhododendron) (1)

◆ How to Plant This Garden ◆

1. Plant azaleas and rhododendrons *in light to medium shade at the top of the slope in holes 2 feet deep and wide. Fill holes, mixing two to three shovelfuls of organic matter with soil. Protect soil around the shrubs with a layer of pine bark mulch.*

2. Locate hostas in partial shade *at the bottom of the slope, where moisture is constant. Enrich soil in their planting area with compost or leaf mold.*

3. Tuck columbines into shaded areas *around the bases of shrubs. Crowd them together for a mass effect. Add mulch between plants.*

Aftercare and Maintenance
• *Monitor soil moisture on the slope; irrigate fast-draining areas.*
• *Apply acid fertilizer to azaleas and rhododendrons in the spring.*
• *Divide hostas after 6 to 8 years.*

A Rich Hillside of Blooms and Foliage

Many plants prosper in the shady, rich, well-drained soil of this hillside woodland setting. The design features plants notable for their striking foliage as well as for their blooms. Both the barrenwort and the viburnum have reddish-tinted leaves early in the growing season and more dramatic color in the fall. The glossy mountain laurel foliage reflects the filtering sunlight and adds color with early summer blooms. Most dramatic of all, the ligularia spreads its broad leaves near the base of the slope. It will become the central landscape feature when its towering spires of yellow flowers emerge in late summer. Nearby ostrich ferns, Japanese anemones, and yellow globeflowers complete the woodland scene.

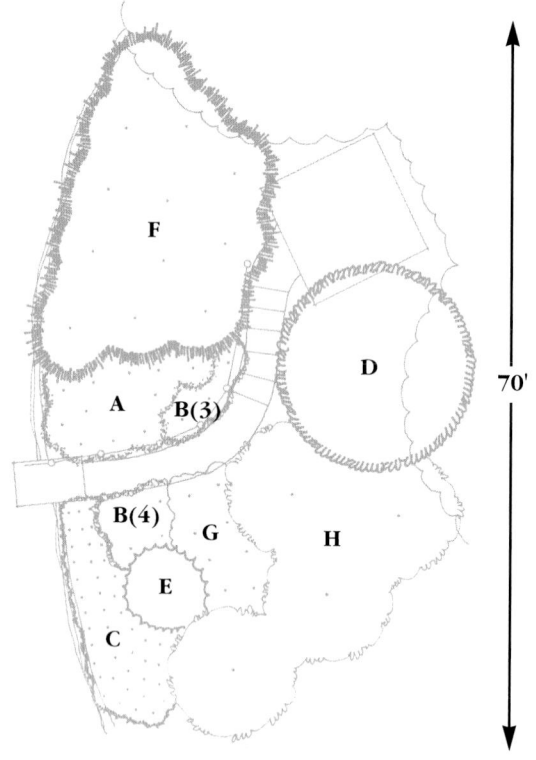

Plant List

A. *Anemone* x *hybrida* 'Whirlwind' (Japanese anemone) (12)
B. *Aquilegia canadensis* (wild columbine) (7)
C. *Epimedium* x *versicolor* (barrenwort) (46)

D. *Kalmia latifolia* 'Fuscata' (mountain laurel) (1)
E. *Ligularia* x *przewalskii* 'The Rocket' (ligularia) (1)
F. *Matteuccia pennsylvanica* (ostrich fern) (12)

G. *Trollius europaeus* 'Lemon Queen' (globeflower) (6)
H. *Viburnum trilobum* 'Bailey Compact' (American cranberry bush viburnum) (4)

◆ How to Plant This Garden ◆

1. In spring or early fall, plant mountain laurel and viburnums in loosened, unamended soil to encourage their roots to spread. Mulch with chopped leaves.

2. In spring or very early fall, install the remaining plants in soil amended with compost. Plant ligularia in a spot with naturally damp soil. If plants are potbound and have circled roots, loosen them with your fingers or slice the rootballs with a knife, then spread roots out in the planting holes.

3. Water well after planting. Apply a 1- to 2-inch layer of bark mulch between the plants.

Aftercare and Maintenance
• Replenish the mulch layer around the shrubs and perennials annually.
• Water ligularia regularly, keeping soil moist to wet. Keep ostrich ferns moist.

• For an added bonus of summer-long color, underplant the viburnums with shade-loving annuals such as impatiens, begonias, or coleus.
• Collect and crush dried seedpods of columbines. Sprinkle seed where more plants are needed.
• If leaf miner attacks foliage of columbine, remove affected leaves immediately and discard.

A Garden for a Dry, Shady Slope

Dry, shady conditions that appear only seasonally in parts of a property may exist year round under evergreen trees and shrubs. Despite such difficult garden conditions, it is still possible to create an attractive landscape. The garden illustrated here features trees, shrubs, and perennials that will thrive in partial shade to create an interesting four-season landscape.

Spring- and early summer-flowering wild columbine and fairy-lantern in the lower reaches of the garden give way to summer mallow blossoms and the fall color of decorative Indian currants midway up the slope. Glossy evergreen holly grape foliage and bright red-osier dogwood stems add winter interest, while the red cedar provides a year-round presence with its density and texture.

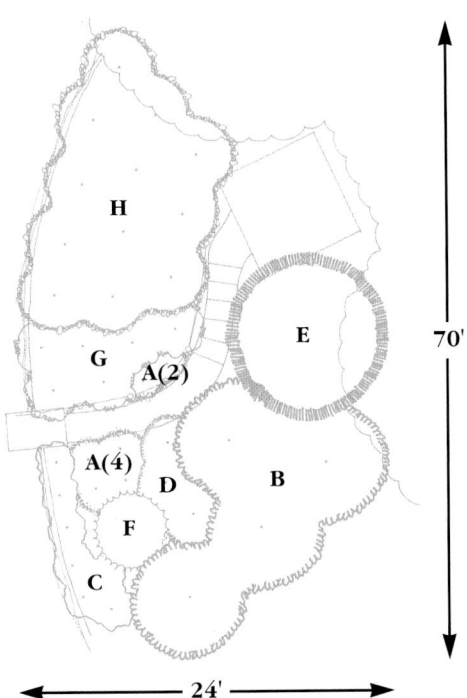

70'

24'

Plant List

A. *Aquilegia canadensis* (wild columbine) (6)
B. *Cornus sericea* (red-osier dogwood) (4)
C. *Disporum smithii* (fairy-lantern) (7)
D. *Filipendula vulgaris* 'Flore Pleno' (dropwort) (3)
E. *Juniperus virginiana* 'Hillii' (red cedar) (1)
F. *Mahonia aquifolium* 'Compacta' (holly grape) (1)
G. *Malva alcea* (hollyhock mallow) (6)
H. *Symphoricarpos orbiculatus* 'Foliis Variegatus' (variegated Indian currant) (12)

◆ How to Plant This Garden ◆

1. Plant dropworts, *red-osier dogwoods, red cedar, holly grape, and Indian currants in spring or early fall. Once established, they tolerate dry conditions, but must receive water frequently after planting and during their first year.*

2. Dig a 2- to 3-inch layer *of compost or leaf mold into the soil before planting the columbines and fairy-lanterns.*

3. Water entire planting site thoroughly, *then cover with a 2- to 4-inch layer of organic mulch. Be sure to keep the mulch 2 to 3 inches away from the trunks of the trees, the bases of the shrubs, and perennial stems.*

Aftercare and Maintenance
• *Replace the mulch annually in the spring to control weeds, regulate soil temperature, and retain soil moisture.*
• *Water the garden every 2 to 3 weeks to prevent soil from drying out completely.*
• *Deadhead fading mallow blooms to encourage a redisplay of color.*
• *Thin out suckers that arise around Indian currants to keep the plants in bounds.*

Create Your Own Waterwise Garden

Perhaps your community restricts the amount of water you can use in summer, or you are concerned about conserving natural resources. Maybe you live in a hot, dry climate like the Southwest, or you travel in summer and have little time for watering lawn and flowers. Whatever the reason, xeriscaping—the practice of combining drought-adaptive plants with thrifty water use—makes good sense.

Principal elements of waterwise gardening include little or no turf grass, use of native species when possible, and minimal paving to reduce runoff. Digging deep into the soil and amending it with organic matter such as rotted manure, compost, and leaf mold will increase the soil's water-retention capacity. If you can't redig your whole garden, then top-dress the existing beds, add organic matter when you plant, or mulch heavily. Where organic mulches are not available or would be too expensive, crushed stone makes

an effective mulch for a xeriscape garden. The sun's heat warms the stones by day, and water condenses on them in the cool of night, increasing the amount of moisture that enters the soil.

The choice of plants is one of the most important factors in xeriscaping. Plants native to or compatible with your environment will be tougher and less prone to disease and insect damage. Regular maintenance will help control weeds and insects that compete with your garden plants for moisture and nutrients.

The design on this page features a southwestern garden abounding in cacti, which require minimal water or care once established. The first alternate planting focuses on drought-resistant perennials that can be planted in most zones; the second shows a garden laid out according to the varying water needs of different groups of plants, a principle that can be applied in any location. All are gardens for full sun.

Southwestern Cactus Garden

The plants in this garden evolved in the dry climate of the Southwest and can cope with the harshness of a hot desert. This plan combines the cacti in an arrangement of columns, spheres, and clusters to arrive at a pleasing contrast of forms, textures, and colors. All the plants have been given enough space to achieve their mature size, but the amended soil allows for closer spacing than in their natural desert environment, dramatizing the juxtaposition of forms and creating a strikingly artistic whole.

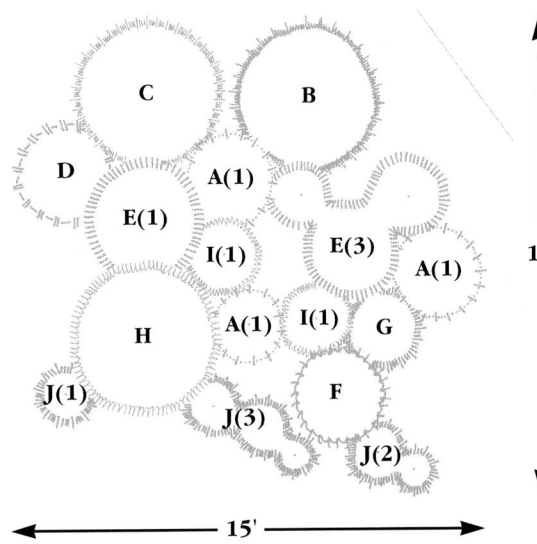

Plant List

A. *Agave victoriae-reginae* (century plant) (3)
B. *Cephalocereus senilis* (old-man cactus) (1)
C. *Cereus hildmannianus* (curiosity plant) (1)
D. *Cleistocactus strausii* (silver-torch) (1)
E. *Echinocactus grusonii* (golden barrel cactus) (4)
F. *Echinocerus* sp. (hedgehog cactus) (1)
G. *Ferocactus pilosus* (fishhook cactus) (1)
H. *Parodia magnifica* (parodia) (1)
I. *Rebutia albopectinata* (crown cactus) (2)
J. *Uebelmannia flavispina* (Uebelmannia) (6)

◆ How to Plant This Garden ◆

1. Dig a planting area deep enough to accommodate a 3- to 4-inch layer of coarse gravel topped by 1 foot of soil mix made of half loam and half sand or grit. Wet soil gently with spray from a hose.

2. To protect yourself from sharp spines, wrap folded

burlap around plants that need moving.

3. Pack soil mix around plants. Stake tall plants until established.

4. Leave room for clump-forming cacti (silver-torch, parodia, and fishhook) to spread.

5. Mulch soil with granite chips up to the crowns of the plants. Moisten the soil, and shade the plants with burlap until established.

Aftercare and Maintenance
• Water cacti only when dry; remove dust with hose spray.

A Drought-Resistant Perennial Garden

Suitable for a wide range of climates, this garden is perfect if you travel often or have little time to spend watering. Many of these tough, low-maintenance perennials are actually native wildflowers or cultivars of wildflowers that combine ornamental leaves or flowers with the sturdiness of native plants. The garden is really a small, refined version of the American prairie, and includes ornamental grasses to underscore the theme. Be sure to buy nursery-grown specimens rather than plants taken from the wild.

Yarrow, black-eyed Susan, and tickseed provide informal bouquets, and the sturdy rugosa rose produces attractive red hips after its white flowers fade. All these plants thrive in full sun and average, well-drained soil.

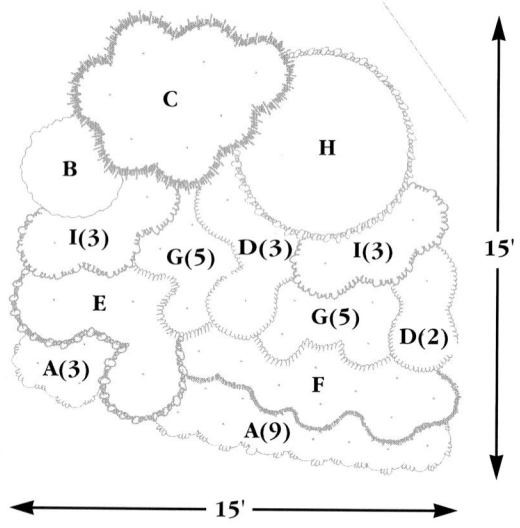

Plant List

A. *Achillea millefolium* (yarrow) (12)
B. *Baptisia australis* (blue false indigo) (1)
C. *Calamagrostis acutiflora* 'Karl Foerster' (feather reed grass) (8)

D. *Coreopsis verticillata* 'Moonbeam' (tickseed) (5)
E. *Euphorbia griffithii* 'Fireglow' (spurge) (3)
F. *Gaillardia* x *grandiflora* 'Golden Goblin'

(blanket-flower) (9)
G. *Linum perenne* (perennial flax) (10)
H. *Rosa rugosa* 'Alba' (rugosa rose) (1)
I. *Rudbeckia hirta* (black-eyed Susan) (6)

◆ How to Plant This Garden ◆

1. Spread 2 inches of compost over the soil, work in to a depth of 12 inches, and rake smooth.

2. Plant false indigo 4 feet from other plants.

3. Arrange remaining perennials in loose, natural-looking drifts. Space tickseed, spurge, blanket-flower, and flax 1 to 1½ feet apart. Space others 2 feet apart.

Aftercare and Maintenance
• Deadhead self-seeding tickseed to encourage more blooms. Near the end of the growing season, shear back to keep it neat.
• Divide yarrows, blanket-flowers, and black-eyed Susans every 2 to 3 years.
• Apply a 2- to 3-inch-deep layer of mulch to keep weeds down. Reapply as necessary.
• Prune roses to shape in the spring. Once plants are established, remove the oldest canes and any winter damage each spring.

A Garden Zoned by Water Needs

This drought-tolerant garden is designed according to the water needs of the plants. Grouping plants with similar needs for moisture makes gardening easier and reduces maintenance time, even where water availability is not an issue. Here, the cosmos, coneflowers, Russian sage, and asters at the back and sides of the garden are quite drought resistant. Those requiring more moisture, such as lamb's ears, baby's-breath, mullein, and cinquefoil, are placed at the front of the garden where they are easily accessible for watering. This garden of annuals and perennials could work well if part of the site is close to a water source and other parts are difficult to reach.

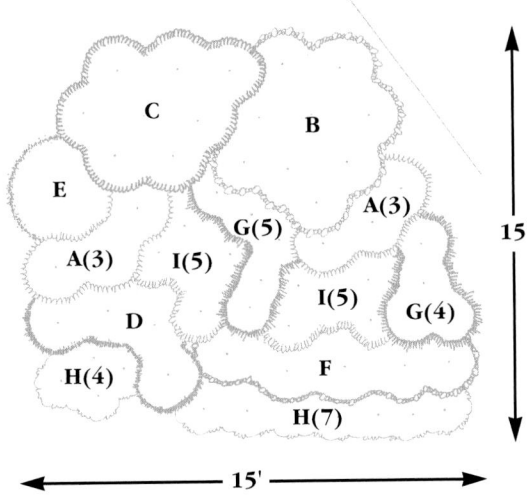

Plant List

A. Aster novae-angliae 'Harrington's Pink' (New England aster) (6)
B. Cosmos bipinnatus 'Versailles White' (cosmos) (9)
C. Echinacea purpurea (purple coneflower) (8)
D. Gypsophila paniculata 'Perfecta' (baby's-breath) (4)
E. Perovskia atriplicifolia (Russian sage) (1)
F. Potentilla nepalensis 'Miss Willmott' (cinquefoil) (5)
G. Salvia x superba 'East Friesland' (violet sage) (9)
H. Stachys byzantina (lamb's ears) (11)
I. Verbascum phoeniceum 'Pink Domino' (purple mullein) (10)

◆ How to Plant This Garden ◆

1. Prepare the garden site by double-digging soil to a depth of 2 feet. Dig 2 to 3 inches of compost into the top layer of soil when returning it to the bed. The extra digging promotes longer plant roots and more efficient water use.

2. Sow cosmos seeds after the last frost, covering them with a thin layer of soil, and gently pat down. Sprinkle with water daily until seeds germinate.

3. Plant perennial asters, purple coneflowers, baby's-breath, cinquefoil, lamb's ears, Russian sage, and violet sage in groups for clumps of color. Space baby's-breath and Russian sage 3 feet apart, all others 2 feet apart.

Aftercare and Maintenance
• Pinch 2 to 3 inches of tip growth from asters during early summer in cool climates and midsummer in hot climates to encourage branching.
• Cut Russian sage to 6 inches in early spring to encourage new growth and abundant flowers.

Create Your Own Bird and Butterfly Haven

A garden is a natural stopping point for hummingbirds, songbirds, and butterflies attracted to the food, water, and shelter that home landscapes provide. With careful planning, you can attract a variety of birds and butterflies to your backyard. Be sure to include an array of nectar-rich blooms in summer, brightly colored berries and fruits in the fall and winter, nesting sites safe from prowling predators, and both high and low sheltering foliage. Your hard work will be rewarded with a built-in garden pest control system, and pollinators aplenty for your seeding and fruiting plants. You will also have a setting that gives you and

your family hours of pleasurable garden viewing and interest.

Bright colors are the signal that attracts birds and butterflies into your garden in search of energy-giving nectar. Explosive bursts of vivid reds, oranges, yellows, pinks, and some blues lure them best. The predominantly red-and-orange garden opposite caters to hummingbirds; the one on the following page offers a home to a variety of songbirds; the subsequent garden gives food and shelter to butterflies. You can put in a garden to attract one type of winged creature, or plants from each plan to create a habitat for all three.

Attracting Hummingbirds

Pendant flowers with tubular blooms are hummingbird favorites. Mass plantings of fiery orange Peruvian lily in this warm-climate garden will draw in the hummers, as will red rose campion and bold yellow tickseed. The protective canopy of the western redbud offers them a sheltered observation point,

if and when they should come to rest. In addition, the birdbath in the middle of the garden provides drinking water and a bathing spot. Because these tiny fliers are drawn to water, consider installing an ornamental pool or a cascading waterfall.

For gardeners in the Northeast, a reliable substitute for the western redbud is its hardier eastern relative, *Cercis canadensis*. Other cold-hardy hummingbird favorites include bee balm, honeysuckle, and *Campsis*. You can also draw hummingbirds right to your house with trailing petunias and fuchsias in hanging pots.

Plant List

A. *Alstroemeria aurantiaca* (Peruvian lily) (29)
B. *Brugmansia* x *candida* (angel's-trumpet) (2)
C. *Cercis occidentalis* (western redbud) (1)
D. *Coreopsis lanceolata* (lanced-leaved tickseed) (30)
E. *Gazania rigens* (treasure flower) (23)
F. *Lychnis coronaria* (rose campion) (20)

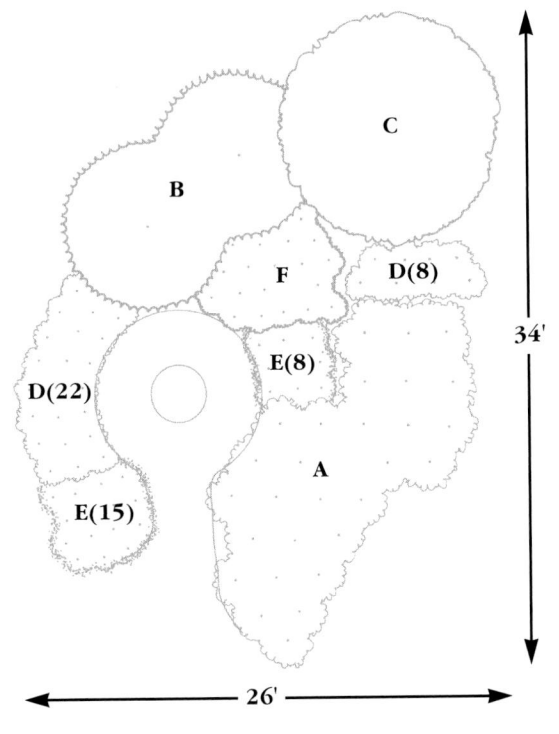

◆ How to Plant This Garden ◆

1. Plant western redbud in a hole as deep as the rootball and twice as wide. Stake during the first growing season.

2. Plant Peruvian lily tubers 1 foot apart on mounded soil in planting holes. Cover with 2 inches of soil. Water well.

3. Set tickseeds 12 to 15 inches apart in a section of unamended soil. Water well.

4. Cluster rose campions 8 to 10 inches apart.

5. Set low-growing treasure flowers close together to provide a

quick, attractive ground cover.

6. In warm climates, plant angel's-trumpets in full sun or partial shade; in cold climates, plant them in a 5-gallon container for overwintering indoors.

Aftercare and Maintenance
• Avoid overwatering western redbud, since it is native to regions with dry summers.
• Mulch Peruvian lilies in winter in Zones 6 and 7 to protect them from heavy frost. Dig up and store indoors in colder regions.

A Songbird Garden

Songbirds bring beautiful sound and color to the garden year round. Fortunately for the bird-loving gardener, they are easy to attract.

In the garden illustrated here, shrubs make up most of the songbird's nesting and feeding habitat, providing protective cover, food, and shelter for insects, and ample supplies of fall berries. Serviceberry bears white flowers followed by sweet, juicy, blackish purple fruit. This shrub grows to 20 feet tall and spreads vigorously from the base by erect sucker growth. Its attractive yellow-and-gold fall color gives it an extra season of interest in your garden.

Arrowwood viburnum, another colorful shrub, spreads 6 to 15 feet wide and grows nearly as tall. Birds flock to its blue-black fruit, which appears in late September through October. This tough, useful plant adapts to many soil conditions and brings reddish purple fall color into the garden.

Low-growing 'Coral Beauty' cotoneaster produces many attractive coral-red berries. It makes a wonderful evergreen ground cover with its glossy foliage and abundant fruit.

Brilliant scarlet cardinal flowers and bee balm both provide a middle level of color at 3 feet high from summer to fall. The cardinal flower's lance-shaped leaves are often tinted a reddish bronze. The birdbath provides songbirds with essential water for drinking and bathing. Be sure to clean it regularly.

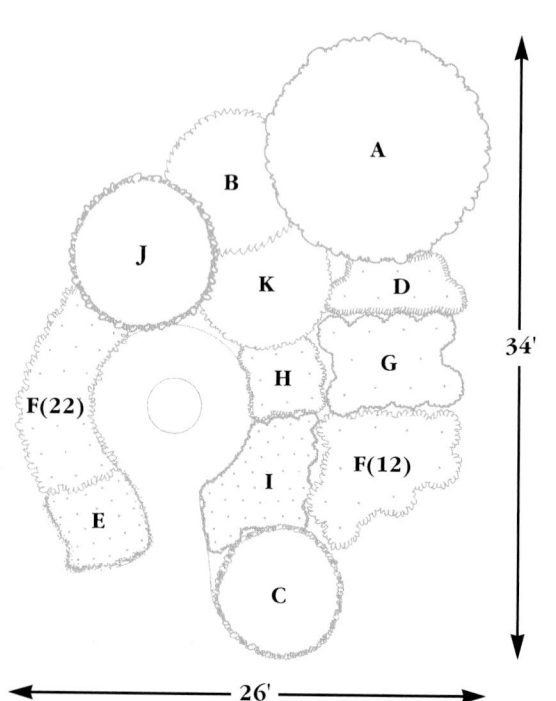

Plant List

A. *Amelanchier canadensis* (serviceberry) (1)
B. *Aronia arbutifolia* (red chokeberry) (1)
C. *Cotoneaster dammeri* 'Coral Beauty' (bearberry cotoneaster) (1)
D. *Lobelia cardinalis* (cardinal flower) (7)
E. *Mimulus* Malibu Series (monkey flower) (25)
F. *Monarda didyma* 'Gardenview Scarlet' (bee balm) (34)
G. *Solidago sphacelata* 'Golden Fleece' (goldenrod) (11)
H. *Tagetes* 'Crackerjack' (African marigold) (9)
I. *Tagetes patula* 'Naughty Marietta' (French marigold) (39)
J. *Viburnum dentatum* (arrowwood viburnum) (1)
K. *Viburnum trilobum* 'Compactum' (American cranberry bush) (1)

◆ How to Plant This Garden ◆

1. Plant arrowwood viburnum 3 feet from path. Plant red chokeberry, bearberry cotoneaster, and American cranberry bush in sun for maximum fruit production.

2. Locate serviceberry, monkey flowers, and cardinal flowers in the dampest area of the garden.

3. Cluster bee balms 1 foot apart.

4. Plant goldenrods and marigolds 8 inches apart in the driest areas.

Aftercare and Maintenance
• Leave faded flowers on the plants to form berries and seeds that will help attract birds.

A Butterfly Garden

The happy lilt of songbirds is a welcome sound in any garden. Fortunately for the bird-loving gardener, songbirds are easy to attract and will provide year-round color and melody.

Microclimate is important when planning a butterfly garden. The garden illustrated here is situated in a sunny spot, a necessity for butterflies that need the sun to warm their wings for flight. Butterfly bush, summer-sweet, and glossy abelia, all flowering shrubs, not only feed butterflies, but also act as windbreaks to protect them from harmful gusts. Butterfly favorites such as 'Fantasy Mix' petunias, rosy perennial Jupiter's-beard, 'Brilliant' showy stonecrop, butterfly weed, and pincushion flower bloom from midsummer to early fall.

Planting a variety of native meadow plants, such as asters, butterfly bush, and Joe-Pye weed, also assures colorful butterfly blooms and foliage through fall.

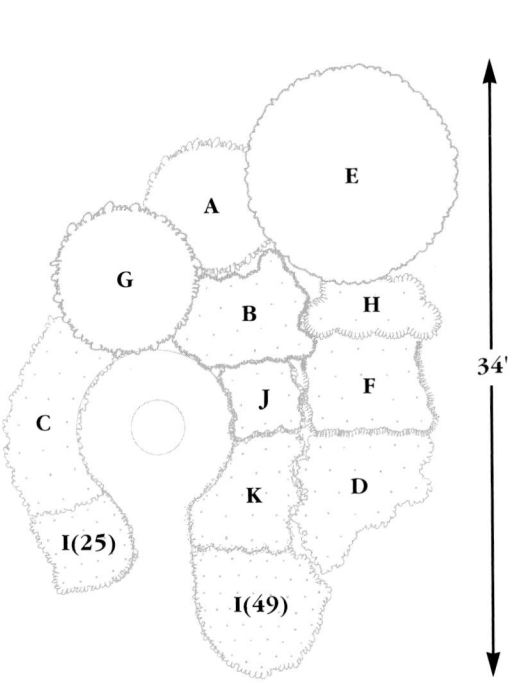

34'

26'

Plant List

A. Abelia x grandiflora (glossy abelia) (1)
B. Asclepias tuberosa (butterfly weed) (20)
C. Aster x frikartii 'Mönch' (Frikart's aster) (22)
D. Aster novae-angliae 'Purple Dome' (New England aster) (22)

E. Buddleia davidii 'Pink Delight' (butterfly bush) (1)
F. Centranthus ruber (Jupiter's-beard) (19)
G. Clethra alnifolia 'Rosea' (summer-sweet) (1)
H. Eupatorium maculatum

(Joe-Pye weed) (7)
I. Petunia x hybrida 'Fantasy Mix' (garden petunia) (74)
J. Scabiosa caucasica 'Pink Mist' (pincushion flower) (9)
K. Sedum spectabile 'Brilliant' (showy stonecrop) (18)

◆ How to Plant This Garden ◆

1. Plant summer-sweet, glossy abelia, and butterfly bush in ordinary well-cultivated soil.

2. Amend soil with organic matter before planting asters, Jupiter's-beard, Joe-Pye weed, petunias, pincushion flowers, and stonecrop.

3. Plant butterfly weed in unamended soil.

Aftercare and Maintenance
• Place large, flat stones in birdbath to allow safe access to water for butterflies.
• Water regularly, keeping soil moist until plants are established.
• Deadhead butterfly bush to prolong bloom into fall; cut stems halfway back in spring.

Waves of Color from Spring to Fall

Gardeners dream of a sequence of blooms and colorful foliage that will transform their landscape into a continuously evolving display. With the right combination of plants, you can step into your garden almost anytime and be surrounded by waves of color. To create such color succession, go beyond the use of annuals and perennials and include bulbs, vines, shrubs, and trees.

Bulbs bring primary hues, soft pastels, and even variegated colors in spring and summer. You can select annuals to fill in when perennials are just beginning to sprout in spring and to obscure yellowing leaves as the perennials die back in autumn. Deciduous trees, shrubs, and vines provide year-round interest, with their sculptural woody structures becoming most noticeable during winter. Some of the shrubs and trees add berries, varied leaf color, and seasonal blooms to ensure an always-changing picture.

Often you can find creativity in simplicity. For example, you can extend the flowering season by taking advantage of the full range of a single genus. Daffodils, tulips, peonies, lilies, and daylilies are all available in varieties that flower early and late, throughout the growing season.

For a splash of spring color, follow the garden plan on this page. This design offers gently rolling waves of blue and white blooms that thrive in partial shade. For a display of spring and late-summer color in a sunny site, consider the first alternate plan of several early- to late-blooming plants. Or fill your garden with contrasting color from spring to frost with the second alternate planting of pink, purple, and yellow blooms.

A Sequence of Blooms for Shade

Shade can work to your advantage. A mix of newly planted and established trees and undulating drifts of cool colors create the shady garden shown here. The flowering plants, which flourish in the dappled light of the trees, are framed by the rich green lawn and conifer foliage. All of the plants thrive in well-drained average to rich soil.

The pendant flower clusters of the Carolina silverbell illuminate the darkest corner of the garden in midspring. Waves of cool blue forget-me-nots carpet the garden floor with tall, bright tulips popping through. Peonies take center stage in late spring with their spectacular blooms. Wall rock cress and columbine will continue to flower into summer.

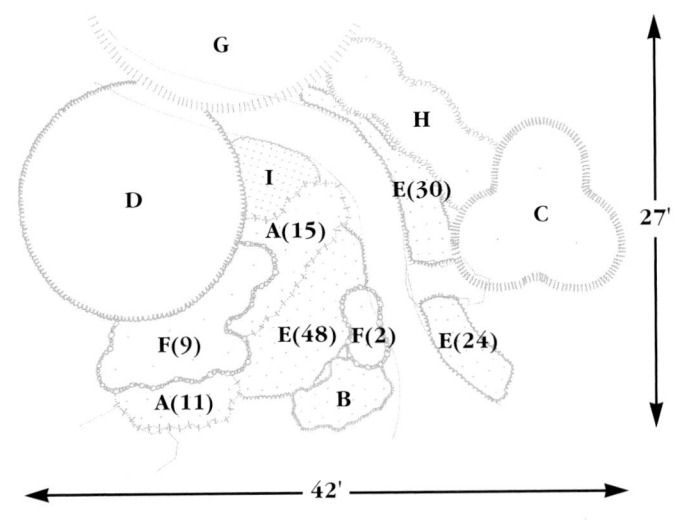

Plant List

A. Aquilegia vulgaris (columbine) (26)
B. Arabis caucasica (wall rock cress) (23)
C. Chamaecyparis pisifera 'Filifera aurea' (goldthread false cypress) (3)
D. Halesia carolina (Carolina silverbell) (1)
E. Myosotis sylvatica (forget-me-not) (102)
F. Paeonia lactiflora (garden peony) (11)
G. Pinus strobus (eastern white pine) (1)
H. Syringa x persica (Persian lilac) (3)
I. Tulipa Darwin Hybrids (tulip) (92)

◆ How to Plant This Garden ◆

1. Mix a spoonful of bone meal into each 8-inch-deep planting hole before planting hybrid tulip bulbs about 8 inches apart.

2. Set out peonies with their eyes 2 inches below the soil surface. Peonies planted too deeply may not bloom.

3. Set wall rock cress rosettes in a checkerboard pattern and plant 6 inches apart.

4. Plant Carolina silverbell, eastern white pine, Persian lilac, and goldthread false cypress in holes as deep as the rootball and twice as wide.

5. Plant forget-me-nots with columbine in a moist, shady spot.

Aftercare and Maintenance
• Cut tulip stems as the petals begin to drop. Leave fading foliage to replenish the bulb's food supply.
• Deadhead garden peonies to encourage more robust growth.

A Garden of Spring and Fall Color

If you travel in the summer or have little time for garden care, this planting may be for you. It maximizes color with an artful combination of early- to late-blooming plants, including different cultivars of daffodils and lilies, whose sequential blooms prolong the flowering season. A temperate climate and well-drained soil in full sun are ideal for these plants. Various lilies bloom from early to late summer, while 'Wide Brim' hosta adds handsome variegated leaves. The chrysanthemums, dwarf euonymus, and hydrangea imbue the garden with autumn color.

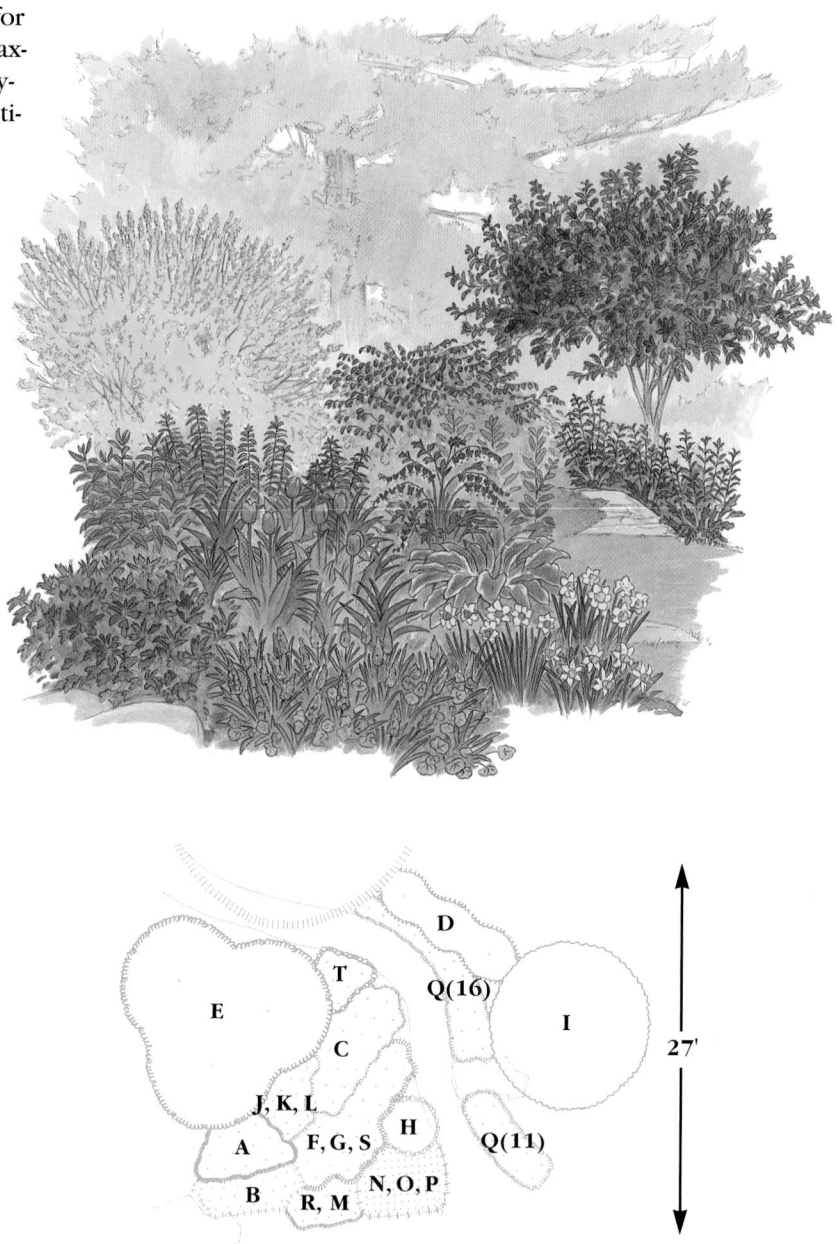

Plant List

A. Campanula persicifolia 'Telham Beauty' (peachleaf bellflower) (12)
B. Chrysanthemum x morifolium 'Shades of Autumn' (chrysanthemum) (22)
C. Dicentra spectabilis (bleeding heart) (17)
D. Euonymus alata 'Compacta' (winged euonymus) (3)
E. Forsythia x intermedia (forsythia) (3)
F. Hemerocallis 'Hyperion' (daylily) (11)
G. Hemerocallis 'Lacy Queen' (daylily) (10)
H. Hosta 'Wide Brim' (hosta) (1)
I. Hydrangea paniculata 'Grandiflora' (peegee hydrangea) (1)
J. Lilium 'Amber Gold' (lily) (3)

K. Lilium lancifolium var. splendens (tiger lily) (5)
L. Lilium mackliniae (lily) (6)
M. Muscari armeniacum (grape hyacinth) (90)
N. Narcissus 'Ice Follies' (daffodil) (35)
O. Narcissus 'Jack Snipe' (daffodil) (35)
P. Narcissus 'Kilworth' (daffodil) (35)
Q. Scabiosa caucasica 'David Wilkie' (pincushion flower) (27)
R. Tropaeolum 'Double Dwarf Jewel Series' (nasturtium) (16)
S. Tulipa 'Pine Diamond' (tulip) (100)
T. Veronica spicata (speedwell) (6)

◆ How to Plant This Garden ◆

1. In the fall, plant daffodils and tulips *at a depth three to four times the diameter of the bulb. Plant grape hyacinths 3 inches deep. Set lily bulbs in holes at a depth two times the diameter of the bulb.*

2. Set daylily crowns *no more than 1 inch below soil.*

3. Sow nasturtium seed *or set out seedlings after the last frost.*

4. Plant forsythia, *winged euonymus, and hydrangeas in holes as deep as the rootballs and twice as wide.*

5. Plant bellflowers, *speedwell, pincushion flowers, and chrysanthemums* in groups. Plant bleeding hearts and hostas in the shadiest garden spot.

Aftercare and Maintenance
• *Tuck fading tulip and daffodil leaves under nearby foliage.*
• *Deadhead lilies regularly throughout summer.*

A Garden of Continuous Color

This garden plan creates a three-season color symphony from spring through fall. In spring, the large double pink flowers of *Prunus serrulata* harmonize with crocus, tulip, iris, primrose, and horned violet. In a summer show of yellow and orange, golden Marguerite, 'Golden Showers' azalea, and long-blooming Stella de Oro daylily are set off by spurge's grayish evergreen foliage. Summer-blooming perennials, including 'Rose Queen' sage, Russian sage, and astilbe, add touches of lilac and pink. The composition closes in autumn, as the flowering cherry's red leaves are set off by the Colorado blue spruce, more daylily blossoms, and spurge.

This plan places late-blooming perennials and annuals that flower all summer long next to early-blooming bulbs, so summer foliage discreetly covers the wilting leaves of the spring bloomers. Thus, daylilies will hide crocus leaves, petunias will overtake primroses, spurge will replace browning iris leaves, and violet sage will mask the dormant tulips.

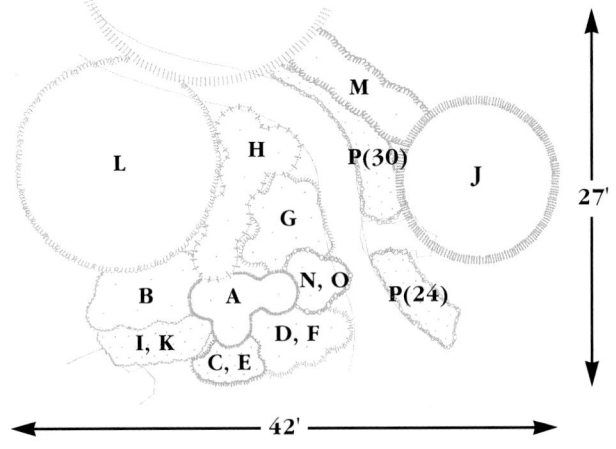

Plant List

A. Anthemis tinctoria 'Moonlight' (golden Marguerite) (4)
B. Astilbe x arendsii 'Finale' (astilbe) (6)
C. Crocus spp. (crocus) (24)
D. Euphorbia characias spp. wulfenii (spurge) (5)
E. Hemerocallis 'Stella de Oro (daylily) (14)
F. Iris reticulata 'Harmony' (iris) (70)

G. Kniphofia 'Shining Sceptre' (torch lily) (3)
H. Perovskia atriplicifolia (Russian sage) (5)
I. Petunia x hybrida 'Total Madness Mix' (common garden petunia) (24)
J. Picea pungens 'Fat Albert' (Colorado blue spruce) (1)
K. Primula denticulata (drumstick primrose) (24)

L. Prunus serrulata 'Kwanzan' (Japanese flowering cherry) (1)
M. Rhododendron Weston Hybrids 'Golden Showers' (azalea) (3)
N. Salvia x superba 'Rose Queen' (violet sage) (3)
O. Tulipa 'Beauty Queen' (tulip) (6)
P. Viola cornuta (horned violet) (54)

◆ How to Plant This Garden ◆

1. Plant cherry, azaleas, and Colorado blue spruce in spring.

2. In the fall, plant crocuses 2 to 3 inches deep, tulips 6 to 8 inches deep, and irises 3 to 4 inches deep.

3. Wear gloves when planting spurge, because its white sap can irritate skin.

Allow at least 3 feet of space around its planting site.

4. Plant horned violets when frosts are light. After the last frost in spring, plant torch lilies, astilbes, Russian sage, golden Marguerites, petunias, drumstick primroses, violet sage, and daylilies.

Aftercare and Maintenance
• After the first frost, cut Russian sage to about 6 inches high, removing all old stems. Protect with winter mulch and remove it in spring.
• Keep soil moist around astilbes and azaleas.
• Deadhead astilbes, daylilies, torch lilies, petunias, and sage as needed.

Create Your Own Winter Garden

For some gardeners, winter is a dull, colorless season, a time to retreat indoors and dream of spring. But with a little planning, you can create a garden to provide visual pleasures through the frigid months. Choose plants that provide color and texture with evergreen foliage, beautiful bark, or colorful berries.

Evergreen trees and shrubs are the backbone of any frost-to-thaw garden. From spring to fall, they provide a soothing green background for more colorful annuals and perennials. But after the frost kills the last of the fall flowers, the evergreens are still there to remind you of spring and summer. By choosing a variety of evergreens with different foliage colors, you can also add shades of blue and gold to your winter plantings.

Some deciduous trees and shrubs, too, can offer winter beauty, in their colorful stems, fruits, and berries. Many ornamental grasses are also wonderful in winter, with their graceful, arching foliage and fluffy seed heads. You can even experience fragrance in your winter garden; a few shrubs blossom during the colder months, and their sweetly scented flowers bring a touch of spring to the crisp winter air.

The garden featured opposite relies on evergreen foliage and brightly colored berries to liven up the winter landscape. The first alternate garden highlights plants that are best suited for winter in southern gardens. The second showcases tough, cold-hardy plants to entice northern gardeners outdoors during the dull winter months.

Welcome Winter Color

This winter garden would fit perfectly in an outlying corner of your property. A sunny, well-drained site with slightly acid soil is ideal for all these plants. The broad central path will encourage you to stroll through the plantings often to admire the bright red berries of the American holly, cotoneaster, and flowering dogwood. An extra dividend of this garden is in watching the winter birds that will come to eat the berries. Even when the berries are gone, you'll still enjoy the beautiful horizontal branching structure of the dogwood and the cotoneaster. The purple foliage of the wintercreeper euonymus complements the bright green leaves of the holly and the 'Pfitzerana' juniper, as well as the gold-marked, blue-green branches of the compact 'Gold Star' juniper.

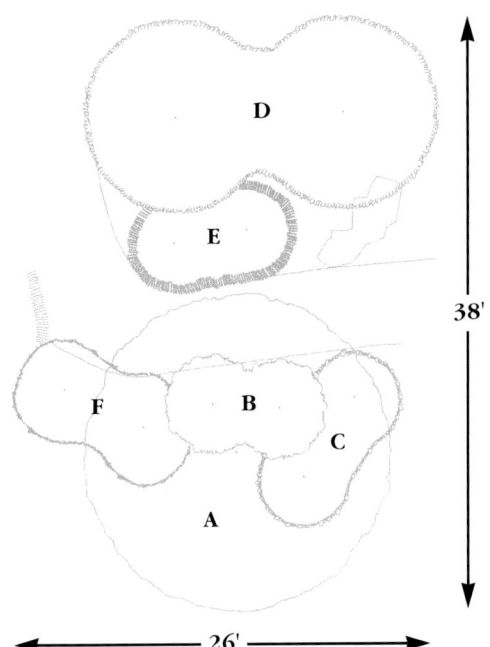

Plant List

A. Cornus florida (flowering dogwood) (1)
B. Cotoneaster horizontalis 'Compacta' (cotoneaster) (2)
C. Euonymus fortunei 'Colorata' (winter creeper euonymus) (2)
D. Ilex opaca 'Brilliantissima' (American holly) (2)
E. Juniperus chinensis 'Gold Star' (Chinese juniper) (2)
F. Juniperus chinensis 'Pfitzerana' (Chinese juniper) (2)

38'

26'

◆ How to Plant This Garden ◆

***1. Spread a 2- to 3-inch layer** of compost or leaf mold over the whole planting area, and work it into the top 8 to 12 inches of soil.*

***2. Plant one male** and one female holly tree, spaced 8 to 10 feet apart. Only the female tree will produce berries, but it needs a male tree nearby for pollination to occur.*

***3. In a sunny spot,** plant flowering dogwood.*

***4. Allow about 4 feet between** the junipers and the cotoneasters, and 4 to 6 feet between the wintercreepers.*

Aftercare and Maintenance
• Mulch to a depth of 2 to 3 inches. Keep mulch clear of the plants' trunks

or stems to prevent rot.
• Prune young hollies in winter as needed; use the trimmings for decorations.
• Prune dogwood lightly to develop shape.
• If junipers start to get leggy, cut the longest shoots back to a branch union. Prune in late spring or early summer.

A Garden for Mild Winters

Southern gardeners may experience milder winters than their northern counterparts, but they still welcome plants that add interest to the off-season. Gardeners in mild climates can enjoy such winter-blooming shrubs as wintersweet and winter daphne. Besides producing pretty flowers at this somewhat barren time of year, these shrubs also perfume the air.

Once the flowers lure you out into the garden, you'll stay to admire the steely blue foliage of the dwarf Colorado blue spruce, the red buds and berries of the skimmia, and the arching evergreen leaves and fluffy seed heads of the pampas grass. Worth admiring, too, is the smooth, dark red bark of the Sargent cherry. It grows quickly and, with proper pruning, will provide a canopy high enough to walk under.

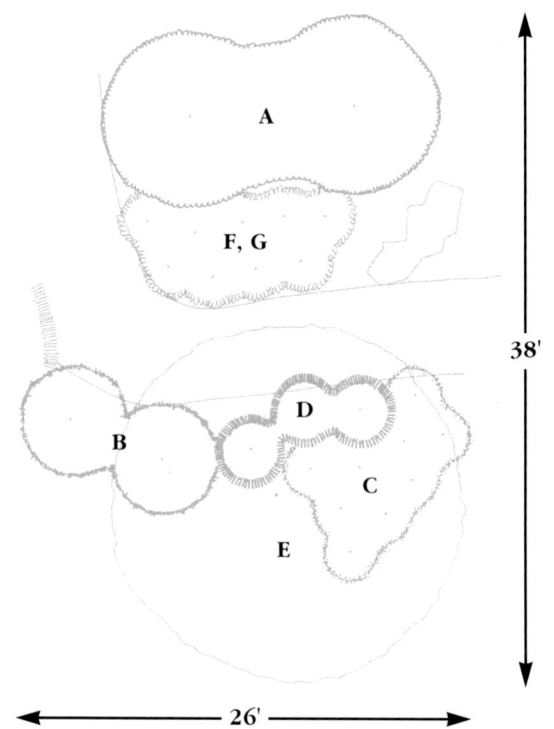

◆ How to Plant This Garden ◆

1. Plant in early to midspring *so plants will have a chance to get established before winter. Loosen soil over the entire site and work in a 2- to 3-inch layer of compost.*

2. Dig a hole *for the Sargent cherry that is as deep as the rootball and twice as wide.*

3. Plant both male and female skimmias. *The females will produce berries only if males are there for pollination.*

4. Space skimmias and winter daphnes *2 feet apart within their clumps. Allow 5 feet between spruces, 8 feet between pampas grasses, and 6 to 8 feet between*

wintersweets to accommodate their spread. Cut roots that circle the rootball or spread them out when planting.

Aftercare and Maintenance
• *Spread a 2- to 3-inch layer of mulch, such as shredded bark or bark chips, to control weeds and keep the soil moist. Keep mulch 2 to 3 inches from plant trunks and stems.*
• *Each spring, pull back the mulch around winter daphnes and add a 1-inch layer of compost or leaf mold, then replace the mulch.*
• *To keep wintersweets bushy, prune one or two of the oldest stems to the ground after they have finished flowering.*
• *Cut pampas grasses to the ground in late winter.*
• *Water regularly to keep the soil evenly moist.*

Plant List

A. Chimonanthus praecox (wintersweet) (2)
B. Cortaderia selloana 'Pumila' (pampas grass) (2)
C. Daphne odora (winter daphne) (9)
D. Picea pungens 'Glauca Globosa' (dwarf Colorado blue spruce) (3)
E. Prunus sargentii (Sargent cherry) (1)
F. Skimmia japonica 'Nymans' (skimmia) (4)
G. Skimmia japonica 'Rubella' (skimmia) (5)

A Winter Garden for the North

Northern gardeners need all the help nature offers to make it through the raw winter days. With its mix of evergreen foliage, attractive bark, and fabulous fruits, this colorful garden is the perfect remedy for cold weather.

All of the plants in this garden are hardy to at least Zone 5, and many thrive well into Zone 3. Whether you view your garden from the comfort of your house or slog through the snow to get closer, you'll be warmed by the winter colors of the rose, with its large, orange-scarlet hips, which are echoed on the other side of the path by the small, glossy, bright red fruits of the crab apple. The young shoots of the red-osier dogwood add another touch of welcome color. Color and form alike come from the silvery blue, scalelike foliage of 'Blue Vase' juniper, which stands out beautifully against the broader, dark green to purplish leaves of 'Olga Mezitt' rhododendrons. Add the attractive dried flower heads of peegee hydrangea, and you'll have a planting that's packed with cold-season interest.

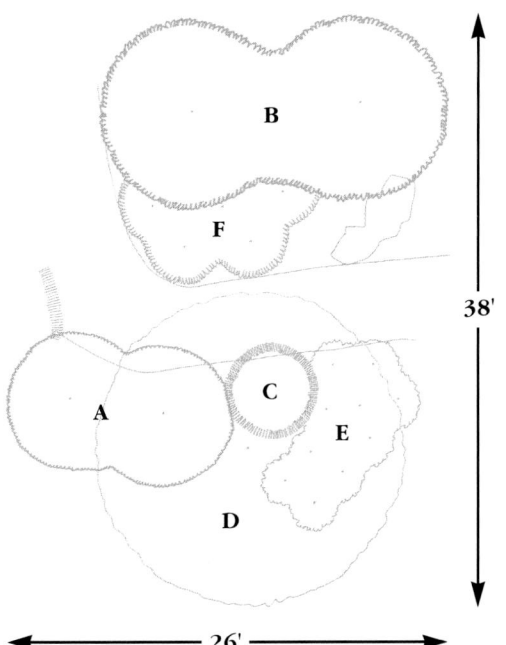

38'

26'

◆ How to Plant This Garden ◆

1. Prepare the site *and set plants out in early to midspring so they'll have a chance to get established before the first winter.*

2. Add compost or leaf mold *to the dogwood planting holes to enrich the soil.*

3. If any of the container-grown shrubs *shows a mass of circling roots when you remove the pot, use a knife to make a few vertical slits around the rootball. This will encourage cut roots to grow out into the surrounding soil.*

4. Set rhododendrons *about 2 feet apart and roses about 2 to 3 feet apart. Allow 4 to 6 feet between dogwoods and 8 to 10 feet between peegee hydrangeas.*

Aftercare and Maintenance
• Apply a 2- to 3-inch layer of bark mulch over the bare soil.
• Cut all stems of peegee hydrangeas to just above the ground in late winter for best flower display, or trim off the lowest branches to encourage a treelike form that shows off the ridged bark.
• Prune roses in late winter to remove one-third of the oldest canes. Also shorten the remaining canes by about one-third. Wear gloves to protect your hands from the prickly stems.
• Starting 2 to 3 years after planting, prune dogwoods in early spring to promote new growth. Cut one-third to one-half of the stems to the ground each year, or cut all stems to the ground every other year.

Plant List

A. *Cornus sericea*
(red-osier dogwood) (2)
B. *Hydrangea paniculata*
'Grandiflora' (peegee hydrangea) (2)

C. *Juniperus chinensis*
'Blue Vase' (Chinese juniper) (1)
D. *Malus* 'Donald Wyman'
(crab apple) (1)

E. *Rhododendron* 'Olga Mezitt' (rhododendron) (10)
F. *Rosa rugosa* 'Albo-plena' (rugosa rose) (5)

Create Your Own Four-Season Garden

Think of your four-season garden as a roomlike enclosure of small trees and tall shrubs framing the walls and supplying the "furniture," larger trees providing a canopied roof, and a floor carpeted with lawn and beds of herbaceous plants. The plants in this "room," must have year-round presence to hold the design together. You'll need a balance of deciduous and evergreen plants that complement one another in shape, substance, and mood. Then fill in with plants that display their best in all the different seasons.

Begin your planning in winter. The evergreens, and the deciduous shrubs and trees stripped of their foliage, will reveal the inherent structure of your garden. You may find that many of your plants already have seasonal strengths of their own—brightly colored berries, fascinating bark patterns, or dormant foliage that whispers and shivers in the breeze. You may only need to move plants around to play their winter colors, textures, and forms against each other.

Then embellish the winter framework with plants from the garden opposite, shown in early summer, or from the two alternate gardens that follow. The first alternate planting makes use of the quiet contrasts of shrubs and ornamental grasses. The second features heaths and heathers for coastal climates or areas with acid soil.

Interest Through the Seasons

The garden illustrated here artfully mixes conifers, small deciduous trees, shrubs, and flowering perennials for a rich, ever-changing effect. Colorado blue spruce, rich green savin juniper, and the plume-like foliage of Japanese cedar supply the strongest structural elements that carry the garden year round.

Silhouetted against the evergreen backdrop in winter are the lower-growing deciduous trees that make their impact in summer. The decorative leaves of Japanese maple glisten from spring until they drop in the fall, and accent the bright red blossoms of red buckeye in midspring and the perky yellow flowers of broom in summer.

Filling in along the central path, peonies are the star performers in spring, but they also carry bright green color into summer and burnished hues into fall. Variegated hosta leaves introduce summer-long color and textural interest and underscore the tall, sturdy spikes of iris.

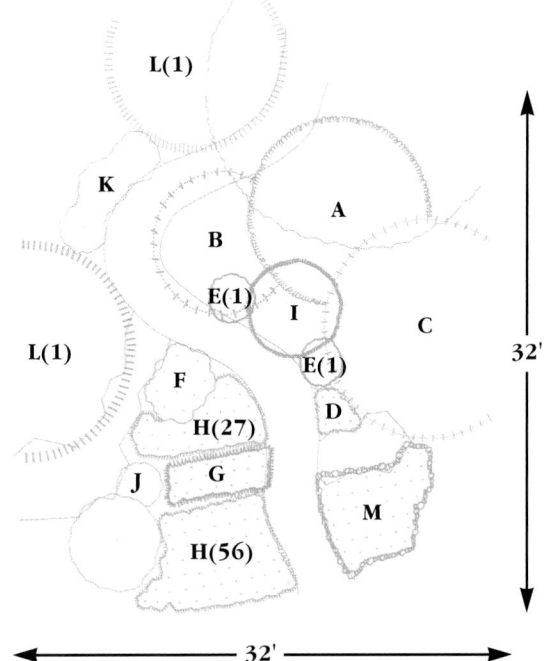

Plant List

A. *Acer palmatum* 'Atropurpureum' (Japanese maple) (1)
B. *Aesculus pavia* (red buckeye) (1)
C. *Cryptomeria japonica* (Japanese cedar) (1)
D. *Cytisus decumbens* (broom) (8)
E. *Hosta fortunei* 'Aureo-marginata' (variegated hosta) (2)
F. *Hosta fortunei* 'Francee' (variegated hosta) (10)
G. *Iris germanica* (bearded iris) (21)
H. *Iris sibirica* (Siberian iris) (83)
I. *Juniperus sabina* (savin juniper) (1)
J. *Paeonia lactiflora* 'Beersheba' (garden peony) (1)
K. *Paeonia lactiflora* cv. (garden peony) (3)
L. *Picea pungens* 'Glauca Hoopsii' (Colorado blue spruce) (2)
M. *Sedum sieboldii* (stonecrop) (43)

How to Plant This Garden

1. In mild climates, *plant trees, shrubs, and perennials in the fall. In cold regions, plant in the spring as soon as the soil has warmed.*

2. In fall, *set peony roots on mounds in planting holes. Spread roots, keeping the eyes no more than 1 to 2 inches below the soil surface.*

3. Plant bearded irises in sun, *keeping rhizomes partially uncovered.*

Aftercare and Maintenance
• *Replenish organic mulch annually as it biodegrades.*

A Garden of Shrubs, Grasses, and Perennials

Tall, rustling flame grass stands as a sentinel in this garden, ever-present, but in changing colors. In summer, its silvery flowering plumes rise above wispy green leaves. By autumn, however, the grass develops the burnished orange and purplish tones shown here. Flame grass continues to stand as the garden's focal point during winter, when its tones mellow.

Sturdy evergreens—a pendant hemlock and a bulky juniper—provide structural weight and contribute to the changing seasonal colors. The deep, dark greens of the juniper and mugo pine make the silvery blue fescue look even bluer, and late in the season their green color softens the harsh winter landscape.

Flowering heartleaf bergenia, bright pink catchfly, and rich blue plumbago scatter pockets of floral color throughout the year. Masses of daffodils and daylilies create a constantly varying stream of color from spring through autumn.

In fall, orange fothergilla foliage stands out, while the flame grass provides brillant color. The reddish foliage of brilliantly blue-flowered heartleaf plumbago takes on a rusty brown cast, and the waxy leaves of bergenia turn glossy red.

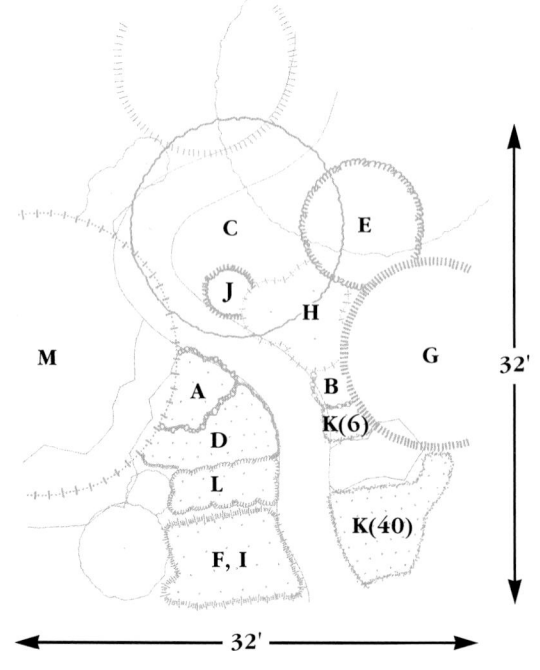

Plant List

A. *Bergenia cordifolia* 'Silberlicht' (heartleaf bergenia) (8)
B. *Ceratostigma plumbaginoides* (plumbago) (1)
C. *Cornus mas* (cornelian cherry) (1)
D. *Festuca ovina* var. *glauca* 'Elijah Blue' (blue fescue) (26)
E. *Fothergilla major*

(fothergilla) (1)
F. *Hemerocallis multiflora* (Mayflower daylily) (21)
G. *Juniperus virginiana* 'Hillii' (red cedar) (1)
H. *Miscanthus sinensis* 'Purpurascens' (flame grass) (3)
I. *Narcissus* cv. (daffodil) (50)

J. *Pinus mugo* var. *mugo* (mugo pine) (1)
K. *Silene* x 'Longwood' (catchfly) (46)
L. *Tricyrtis formosana* var. *stolonifera* 'Amethystina' (toad lily) (10)
M. *Tsuga canadensis* 'Pendula' (weeping Canada hemlock) (1)

◆ How to Plant This Garden ◆

1. In cold climates, *plant red cedar, pine, and cornelian cherry in spring. Plant in the fall in warm climates.*

2. Plant fothergilla *in acid soil.*

3. Set rootballs of flame grass *and blue fescue at the same depth as in their containers.*

4. Plant daylilies in spring or fall, *setting them in holes 2 feet apart.*

5. Set catchflies and heartleaf bergenias *in clumps with individual plants 8 to 10 inches apart.*

6. Plant plumbagos in the spring, *after the last frost.*

7. In the fall, *plant daffodils in 8-inch-deep holes.*

Aftercare and Maintenance
• *Tuck fading daffodil foliage under the arching daylily leaves.*
• *Mark the location of plumbagos to avoid damaging them in spring.*

A Garden of Heaths and Heathers

This garden provides a dramatic year-round spectacle of colors and variety. Heaths and heathers make perfect all-season companions to broadleaf evergreens and conifers. In spring, the dark green foliage of spring heath is draped with bright red flowers, while in late summer, pale lilac blossoms adorn the golden mounds of heather.

The vertical shapes of 'Crippsii' false cypress and arborvitae are set off by the rich, spreading blue-green mantle of juniper and bright green spray of wintercreeper euonymus. 'Blue Emerald' phlox adds to the spring show with a colorful blue carpet of flowers across the garden. Variegated sedge, hellebore, and yucca supply a sharp textural contrast to the plump, red fruits of holly and cornelian cherry that punctuate the muted winter landscape.

This garden plan is best suited to cool, humid coastal climates, but it can be enjoyed in most mild climates if you supply moist, acid soil.

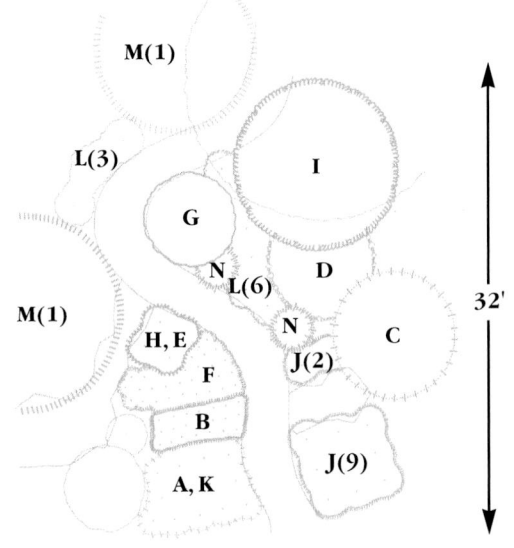

Plant List

A. *Calluna vulgaris* 'Blazeaway' (heather) (13)
B. *Carex morrowii* 'Variegata' (sedge) (21)
C. *Chamaecyparis* 'Crippsii' (false cypress) (1)
D. *Cornus mas* (cornelian cherry) (1)
E. *Dryopteris erythrosora* (wood fern) (4)
F. *Erica carnea*

'Myretown Ruby' (spring heath) (25)
G. *Euonymus fortunei* 'Greenlane' (winter creeper euonymus) (1)
H. *Helleborus* x *hybridus* (hellebore) (16)
I. *Ilex* 'Sparkleberry' (holly) (1)
J. *Juniperus horizontalis* 'Mother Lode' (juniper) (11)

K. *Muscari armeniacum* (grape hyacinth) (300)
L. *Phlox subulata* 'Blue Emerald' (phlox) (9)
M. *Thuja occidentalis* 'Elegantissima' (arborvitae) (2)
N. *Yucca filamentosa* 'Color Guard' (yucca) (2)

◆ How to Plant This Garden ◆

1. Plant false cypress, junipers, winter-creeper euonymus, yuccas, and arborvitae so that the tops of the rootballs are just below the soil.

2. To ensure berry production by Ilex 'Sparkleberry', which is a female, plant I. 'Apollo', a male, within 100 feet.

3. Add large quantities of moist compost or peat moss to the soil before planting heaths and heathers. Mulch

with additional compost or peat moss after planting.

4. Plant sedges, ferns, hellebores, grape hyacinths, phlox, and cornelian cherry in a well-drained site.

CHAPTER FIVE

Planting Your Garden

Savvy gardeners know that some of the most important work done in the garden is the effort that goes into preparing the soil. What it takes to grow robust plants—like the tea and hybrid tea roses and verbena filling the front yard of this Independence, Texas, home—is a fertile, loamy soil that supplies them with the air, water, and nutrients that keep them growing strong. Knowing how to enrich your soil will go a long way toward achieving your goal of a beautiful, healthy garden.

In addition to cultivating your soil, understanding how your plants should be placed in the ground will help ensure that they survive and thrive in the garden. Peonies, for example, perform best when their roots are planted with the buds only an inch or two below the soil's surface—shallow enough for them to experience a necessary period of chill, but not so shallow they might freeze. Whether you purchase your plants in containers or as bare roots will also determine how they should go into the ground. On the following pages, you'll learn how to plant a variety of garden flowers.

Readying New Ground to Receive Plants

The first steps toward creating a new garden—deciding on the site and settling on the design—take you only so far: After that it's time to go outdoors and mark off your plot *(below),* begin preparing the soil, and choose your plants.

Good soil preparation is the single most important factor in growing beautiful, healthy plants of all kinds. To properly ready the soil in your garden you must first understand it. Does the soil drain well? Although some plants thrive in soil that remains continuously moist or is dry, most require good drainage. Look at the soil texture and color, and the health of plants that may already be growing in it. Is the soil heavy clay or loose sand? Is it poor or fertile? Adding organic amendments will condition the soil and fertilizer can replenish its nutrients.

Other factors, including light and exposure, will affect how your garden grows. For example, most perennials and roses prefer full sun, meaning at least 6 hours a day with 4 of those in the after-noon. But a lush garden is still possible even if your site has full or partial shade; it all depends on the plants you choose. The Plant Selection Guide on pages 590-593, as well as the Encyclopedia of Plants that begins on page 608, can help you select the plants best suited to your garden's conditions.

Investing some initial time and effort in cultivating and fertilizing the soil in your beds, improving areas of poor drainage, and choosing and siting your plants correctly will pay off handsomely later in vigorous growth and abundant blooms. Remember, many of your plants are going to be in the ground for a long time, and there will never be another opportunity to start them out right.

Appraising Your Soil

Bringing your soil to the point where it's ready for planting means first knowing its present condition. You should make at least a rough determina-

Outlining Your Garden Plot

For a plot with a curving edge, use a garden hose to outline the perimeter, matching the bed's size to the dimensions shown on your garden plan. Then mark the perimeter with powdered lime or by cutting into the soil alongside the hose with a garden spade.

For square corners, first stake off one side of the bed. Then set a peg 3 feet from the first stake and tie a string to it; mark the string at a point 5 feet from the peg. Tie a string to the first stake and mark it at 4 feet from the stake. Cross the two strings at the marks. Set a third stake at that point, creating a right angle at the first stake.

The 3:4:5 ratio used to find the right angle at left, which can be used with a garden plot of any size, demonstrates that a triangle with its three sides in the proper ratio will have a right angle opposite the longest side.

Preparing the Ground without Digging

Some professional gardeners have devised a way of preparing a plot of land for gardening virtually without turning a single spadeful of soil. The method, called smothering, holds obvious advantages for the home gardener who wants to cultivate a relatively large piece of ground, for which the labor of digging, or even using a power tiller, would be great.

Smothering consists simply of covering up unwanted vegetation to deprive it of light until the plants die—a period of about 3 months. Once the covering is in place and the process has begun, you don't even have to wait the full time before you plant. You can cut down through the cover—indeed, you need never remove it—to put in your plants, which will begin growing while the grass and most weeds around them are dying.

If your chosen garden plot is covered with sod, mow the grass as low as possible, then cover the area with sheets of old newspaper. But take care not to use papers with colored inks, which can deposit harmful chemicals in the soil. A covering three or four sheets thick should be enough to do the job; overlap the edges a few inches to ensure that all sunlight is blocked out. Then cover the newsprint with a layer of leaves or other organic mulch about 1 foot deep, which will weigh down the paper, improve the appearance of the plot, and eventually decompose and add humus to the soil.

Smothering woody plants and persistent weeds will require a heavier covering—perhaps a layer of cardboard or a thickness of 30 or so sheets of newspaper, followed by the mulch. Any weeds that are strong enough to survive smothering can be destroyed by digging them out.

---

tion of the soil's texture—that is, the relative amounts of clay, silt, and sand particles that make up most of the mineral content of soil.

Soil with a high percentage of clay or silt is likely to be quite dense and compact, allowing little space for air and growing plant roots to penetrate and for water to slowly percolate and drain away. If you dig into these soils with a spade, they feel heavy; clay soil will also stick to the blade, making it difficult to turn and break up.

At the other end of the scale, sandy soil is so loose and porous that it cannot retain moisture or nutrients and offers plant roots little to grab onto. It feels coarse and gritty in your hand and does not clump together well.

The soil with the best texture is loam. A mixture containing roughly 20 percent clay and 40 percent each of silt and sand, loam is easy to work, holds water and nutrients well, and allows air to reach plant roots. Loam also has an ideal soil structure, which is determined by how well the soil particles cling together and in what shapes. The best structure is one in which the soil is friable—meaning that the particles form small, irregularly shaped, slightly moist clumps or crumbs that hold together well but will break up easily in your hand. Soil with this ideal structure contains countless small spaces that conduct air, water, and nutrients to plant roots.

Another factor you should take into account when analyzing your soil is its acidity or alkalinity—the pH level—which you can measure using an inexpensive tester available at garden shops and home centers. Most plants will flourish in soil ranging from somewhat acid—a pH of about 5.8—to slightly alkaline, or just above the neutral level of 7; it is in this range that soil nutrients become most available to the plants. Should the soil test excessively acid, you can raise its pH by working in a quantity of dolomitic limestone. If it is too alkaline, an application of sulfur will bring it to the desired level of acidity.

Soil Fertility

Three chemical elements are essential to plant growth—nitrogen, phosphorus, and potassium—and these all occur naturally in soil. Responsible for strong roots and healthy leaf, stem, flower, and fruit development, these elements, as well as traces of secondary elements, are the products of decaying organic matter. Compost, well-rotted cow manure, and leaf mold—soil made up chiefly of decayed vegetable matter, particularly leaves—are good sources of organic matter, and working them into the soil of your new garden may well provide all the fertilization the plot needs during its first year.

Soil Amendment of Choice

If you had to select one all-purpose soil amendment that would both improve soil structure and supply nutrient-rich organic matter, the choice would undoubtedly be compost. Compost is made up of rotted plant materials such as grass clippings and fallen leaves, fruit and vegetable scraps from the kitchen, aged livestock manure, sawdust, newsprint, and any number of other organic ingredients. It also contains a teeming population of living organisms and microorganisms, who do the work of breaking down the raw materials into the black, moist, crumbly humus.

Building a Compost Pile

A well-made compost pile is an ideal habitat for microorganisms, providing the food, water, air, and warmth they need to grow and reproduce at top speed. A thriving population quickly converts ordinary wastes from kitchen and garden into an invaluable fertilizer and soil conditioner.

The microorganisms need a balanced diet of carbon and nitrogen. Fibrous materials such as dry leaves, straw, and sawdust provide plenty of carbon, while nitrogen is furnished by green materials such as grass clippings, wastes from the vegetable garden or flower bed, and kitchen scraps (vegetable or fruit only).

To start a compost pile, spread a layer of brown fibrous material several inches deep and at least 3 feet wide and 3 feet across on bare soil. Add a layer of green material and

sprinkle it with soil or a commercial compost activator to introduce microorganisms. Water until the materials are sponge damp. Continue in this fashion until the layered pile is at least 3 feet high—the size necessary to generate sufficient heat. Turn the pile once or twice a week with a garden fork to aerate it and rid the center of excess moisture. Water as needed to keep the pile slightly moist. The compost is ready to use when it is dark and crumbly.

The three-bin composter shown below can produce a large, steady supply of compost. The decomposing pile in the center bin is flanked by a newly assembled pile *(right)* and a bin containing finished compost *(left)*. Wire mesh on three sides and the gaps between the slats on the bin's front help keep the pile aerated. The slats are removable, making it easy to turn the pile. Several smaller compost bins are shown on the next page.

Compost is almost a panacea for imperfect soils. If a soil is loose and sandy, generous additions of compost will pull it together and make it crumbly, so that water, nutrients, and plant roots can get a good foothold. If the soil is heavily compacted clay, compost will loosen and lighten it. As a fertilizer, finished compost provides a good balance of 2 parts nitrogen to 1 part each of phosphorus and potassium. And if it is made from a large variety of materials, compost will contain a healthy balance of trace elements as well. Even the best soil can benefit from periodic additions of compost to help maintain its structure and replenish its supply of nutrients.

Choosing a Fertilizer

Although compost adds nutrients to the soil, you may need to add fertilizer periodically to meet the needs of particular plants or to help replenish depleted nutrients. Fertilizers take two forms—organic and inorganic. Organic fertilizers are derived from animal or vegetable matter. Examples include compost, cottonseed meal, blood meal (from slaughtered cattle), and finely ground bone. Many gardeners prefer organic fertilizers because they are manufactured by environmentally friendly methods, don't harm important soil microbes,

Decomposing waste occupies one of the two cinder-block bins at left; the other stores finished compost. The spaces between the blocks allow air to circulate. You can mortar the blocks at the back and the sides of the bins, but leave the front blocks free so you can withdraw the compost.

A Compost Bin to Suit Your Needs

Even the simplest compost bin keeps decomposing wastes tidy and compact. And as long as you have the right mix of ingredients and enough of them, it will generate the heat needed to ensure speedy composting. For freestanding compost piles or those in open bins, you should start with a pile measuring 3 feet wide, deep, and high. For the ready-made bins available at garden and home centers, simply fill them according to the manufacturer's instructions.

Each of the composters shown here can be easily constructed or purchased for less than a hundred dollars. Some require manual forking and turning of the debris pile, while others need little or no attention from the gardener.

To create the bin at right, wrap a length of hardware cloth 4 feet wide and 12 feet long around two stakes hammered into the ground. Secure the ends of the hardware cloth with wires. To turn the compost pile, unfasten the cylinder, reposition the stakes adjacent to the loose pile, reassemble the cylinder, and fork in the pile.

The plastic barrel composter at left is designed to produce finished compost in a month or less. The barrel rests on rollers; turning a handle rotates the barrel and aerates the contents thoroughly. Finished compost is removed through a hinged door on the barrel; a finished batch must be removed before starting a new one.

A compact plastic compost bin like the one at left is an excellent choice where space is limited. Fresh waste material can be added continually to the top of the bin while older material is decaying to finished compost. Compost is retrieved from the pull-out drawer at the bottom of the bin. Enough air enters the pile through the large slots to supply the decay microorganisms completely, making it unnecessary to turn the pile.

Breaking Ground for the Garden

1. Shave off any sod with your garden spade, *cutting through the soil horizontally. Use the surplus sod to fill in bare spots on your lawn, or shake off the loose soil and save the remaining material for the compost pile. If your plot is large—and you're not in a hurry to plant—you may choose to smother the grass (page 261).*

2. To work the soil, drive your spade all the way into the soil at 4-inch intervals; *toss each slice of loosened soil forward and use the blade to break it up. Be careful not to step on the broken soil, which might compact it into a dense, unworkable mass.*

3. Use a spading fork to work amendments into the broken-up soil. *Choose from such amendments as compost, rotted cow manure, limestone, peat moss, and other materials as needed to ready the soil for your plants.*

and don't leave chemical residues. They also work a little slower than their inorganic counterparts, lessening the chance of burning plant roots if you happen to overfertilize.

Inorganic fertilizers are products of the petrochemicals industry. On the plus side, they tend to be faster acting and easier to use. However, they can leach out of soils quickly, requiring repeated applications that over time can become expensive. The most significant disadvantage of chemical fertilizers is that they can damage the many beneficial microorganisms that live in the soil.

Either type of fertilizer may be sold as a so-called complete fertilizer, its packaging indicating the percentages of nitrogen, phosphorus, and potassium—always in that order—that it contains. The percentages may sometimes be labeled N-P-K, the chemical symbols for these elements. A 5-10-5 fertilizer, for example, contains 5 percent nitrogen, 10 percent phosphorus, and 5 percent potassium, plus small or trace amounts of other chemicals; the remainder is inert filler. A product labeled 10-10-10 is called a balanced fertilizer. One labeled 0-20-0 is a single-nutrient fertilizer, in this case an all-phosphorus product called a superphosphate.

As a rule, perennials need relatively little fertilizer compared with the amount needed by annuals and roses. But because perennials stay in the ground for so long, they may benefit from judicious applications of fertilizer from time to time. For more information on fertilizing particular types of plants, see pages 294-295.

Cultivating the Soil

Many professional gardeners recommend digging and amending the soil for a garden in the fall, covering it with a mulch to hold in moisture and prevent weeds, and then waiting until spring to begin planting. During the wait the soil will settle, and winter frosts and thaws will cause it to expand and contract, improving its structure by breaking it into smaller clumps.

In areas of the country where the summers are hot and dry, it is often best to work the soil in spring and let it lie until fall. If you are too impatient to let a growing season slip by, however, it is still important to give your cultivated plot at least several weeks to begin settling before you plant it.

Make sure the soil is slightly moist before you dig; otherwise you risk destroying the soil's structure. If the ground is too wet, digging will pack the soil into a dense mass that blocks the movement of water, air, and roots. If the ground is dry, the digging may cause it to disintegrate into a powder.

To determine if your soil is ready for digging, turn over a spadeful and break up a clod. If the

264

clod comes apart easily, you can proceed. If it sticks stubbornly together or can be formed into a ball in your hand, it is too wet; wait a few rainless days and try again. If the clump of soil crumbles to dust, it is too dry; soak the entire plot, then let it drain for 3 or 4 days before you begin digging .

Reasons for Double Digging

The technique called double digging involves digging up and amending a layer of topsoil about 12 inches deep and then loosening and amending to an equal depth the layer of subsoil beneath it.

Professional gardeners differ on the importance of double digging. Some say it is unnecessary extra work, that you can have a fine garden without it. Others say it gives the plants plenty of loosened soil in which to sink their roots—which in the case of some perennials can grow to a depth of 24 inches. Still other gardeners don't even stop at conventional double digging. After removing the topsoil and amending it, they do not merely loosen the subsoil, they dig it up and amend it thoroughly, put the original topsoil back where the subsoil was, and put the former subsoil on top.

Personal preferences aside, many experts agree that if your soil is a heavy clay with poor drainage, it is important to double dig. If you have better soil, double digging may not be absolutely necessary but will probably return a dividend in more robust, more extravagantly blooming plants.

The Deluxe Treatment: Double Digging

1. Beginning at one end of the garden plot you have laid out, remove any sod covering as shown opposite. Then dig a trench about 1 foot wide and as deep as the blade on your spade, running from one side of the plot to the other. Remove the topsoil and heap it in a cart or wheelbarrow. Thoroughly loosen the layer of exposed subsoil with a spading fork and work in the appropriate soil amendments. Do not remove the subsoil.

2. Dig out another trench next to the first one, moving the loosened topsoil over to cover the amended subsoil of the first trench. Work amendments into this topsoil. Then loosen and amend the subsoil in the second trench. Repeat the process for each succeeding trench until the last one. Then amend the topsoil reserved from the first trench and use it to fill the last one.

Planting Annuals

Annuals are good choices for any landscape, and if you're a novice gardener, they make for an easy and immediately gratifying introduction to gardening. Starting out can be as simple as sowing seeds directly into the ground and then watching what happens, or pushing aside some soil and setting in young bedding plants purchased from your local nursery or garden center.

If you're an experienced gardener who enjoys devoting more time and effort to a project, you can spend delightful hours poring over mail-order nursery catalogs, choosing between the countless beautiful varieties of annuals pictured and described there. You can also get seeds started indoors before spring arrives, then wait for the perfect day to transplant them to the garden. Here and on the next two pages, you'll learn all you need to know about the three techniques for getting your annual garden started—indoor sowing, transplanting, and direct-seeding.

Starting Seeds Indoors

Some annuals have tiny seeds that may be lost if sown outdoors. Others need a long time to grow before they flower. If you want annuals such as zinnias, geraniums, and verbena blooming in your garden as early as possible—and you want to ensure the highest rate of germination for your seeds—get them going in the protected, controlled environment of your home. Seeds can be started indoors in winter so that young plants will be ready to put into the ground in spring.

Purchase a soil mix that has been specifically formulated for starting seeds. Wet the mix completely and let it sit for a few minutes until the water is thoroughly absorbed; then fill seed flats to a depth of about 3 inches. If you don't want to use flats, you can also use individual plastic pots or even small plastic cups or cartons you may find around your house. Simply clean them well first and poke a few drain holes in the bottom.

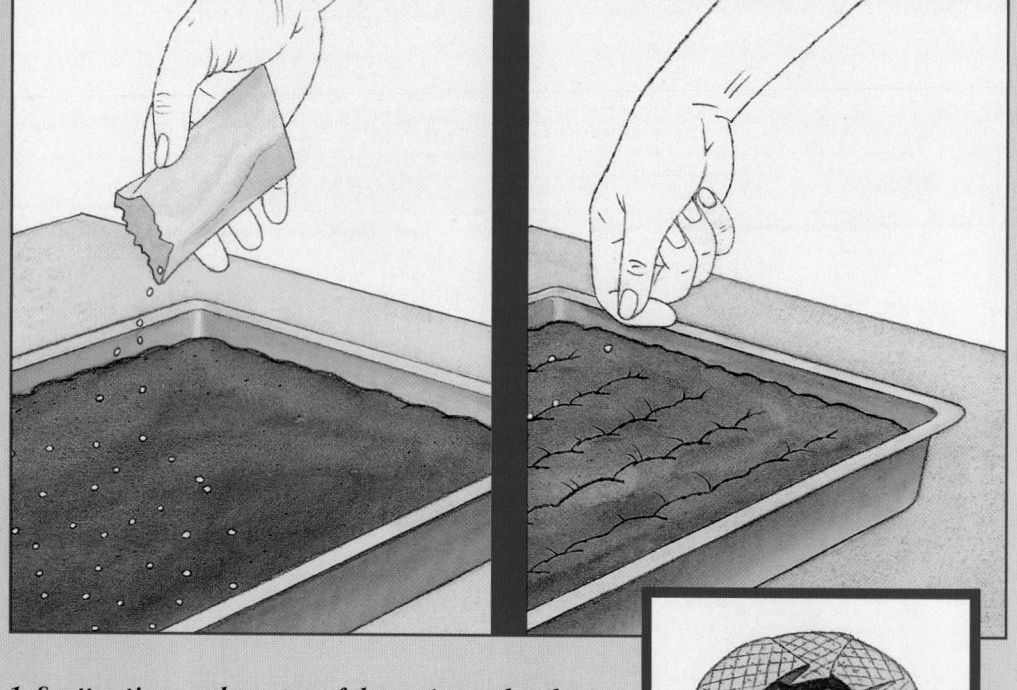

1. Scatter tiny seeds on top of the moistened soil mix (above); place larger seeds one by one in ¼-inch furrows, spaced ½ inch apart (above, right). If the seed-packet directions indicate, cover the seeds with a thin layer of soil. Alternatively, gently press the seeds into a wet peat pot as shown at right. Then set the flats or peat pots under grow lights on a warm, bright but indirectly lit window sill, or in a darkened setting, according to seed-packet instructions. All seedlings should be placed in a well-lit spot once they become visible.

2. Keep the soil mix moist by watering gently and then covering the flat with a clear, thin plastic bag supported by metal hoops (above). You can use clothes hangers for the hoops. Seal the bag with a twist tie to maintain high humidity. After the shoots are plainly visible, remove the plastic covering. Continue watering to keep the soil moist but not soaked; overwatering can cause damping-off, a disease that kills seedlings.

After sprouting in a well-lit greenhouse window, these flats of annual seedlings await transplanting to larger containers. The robust scarlet and yellow potted marigolds were started at an earlier date and are ready to be hardened off and planted in the garden.

Annuals to Start Indoors

Ageratum houstonianum
(flossflower)
Asclepias spp.
(bloodflower)
Browallia speciosa
(browallia)
Cardiospermum halicacabum
(balloon vine)
Coleus x hybridus
(coleus)
Dianthus spp.
(pink, sweet William)
Eustoma grandiflorum
(tulip gentian)
Impatiens spp.
(impatiens)
Lagurus ovatus
(hare's-tail grass)
Petunia x hybrida
(petunia)
Salvia spp.
(sage)
Torenia fournieri
(wishbone flower)

Note: The abbreviation "spp." stands for the plural of "species"; where used in lists it means that many, but not all, of the species in a genus meet the criterion of the list.

4. Two weeks before transplanting— *which should be done once the danger of frost is past—move your plants to a cold frame to acclimate them to outdoor conditions, a process known as hardening off. Open the frame during the day to maintain proper air circulation and to keep plants from getting too much heat under the glass; close it at night. If you don't have a cold frame, place the seedlings outside a few hours each day, gradually lengthening the exposure time.*

3. After the seedlings produce a second set of leaves *(their first true leaves), use a plant marker or similar instrument to separate and lift each one out of the flat (above, left). Hold each seedling by its leaf (it can grow a new leaf, but not a new stem) and place it in a peat pot or other container filled with moist, sterile potting soil. Position the seedling in a hole the size and depth of its tiny root system. Gently tamp the soil without injuring the stem (above, right). Place the pots on a tray to be set under grow lights or near a warm, sunny window. Keep the plants well watered.*

267

Transplanting Annuals

Before transplanting seedlings to your garden, take time to ready their new home. If you're preparing a new flower bed, dig in an inch or two of organic matter such as leaf mold or compost before planting. This will improve drainage and supply the young plants with nutrients. If you're adding annuals to an existing bed, use a hand cultivator to loosen the soil and add a slow-release dry fertilizer, using the amount recommended on the package. Transplant your annuals on a cool, cloudy day or in the late afternoon so that the flowers are not stressed by sun and heat.

1. With a trowel, dig a hole slightly larger and deeper than the plant's rootball. *Water the plant thoroughly and allow the excess to drain away. Then gently remove the plant from its cell pack or other container by turning it upside down and easing the plant out. With a cell pack, support the plant with one hand, then gently press your thumb against the bottom of the pack to push the plant out (right).*

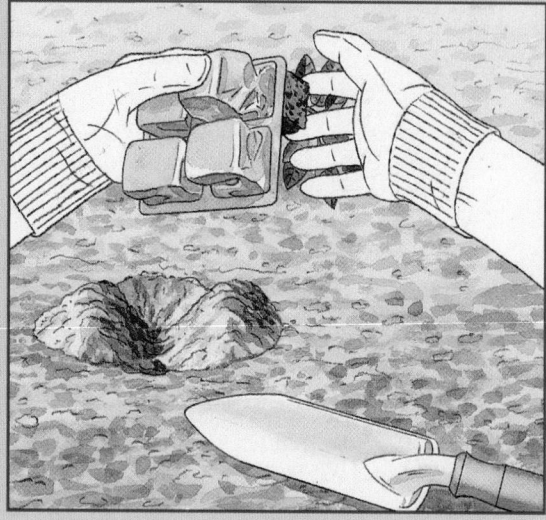

2. Use your fingers to gently loosen the roots at the bottom and sides of the plant's rootball (right). *If the plant is extremely root-bound, use a knife to slice partway into the rootball, then fluff the roots apart. For plants in peat pots, gently tear off the lip or the top part of the pot (far right), then set the pot in the ground; this will help the pot's soil retain moisture.*

3. Set the plant into the hole with the base of its stem slightly below the rim. *Return the soil to the hole and firm it around the plant, creating a slight depression around the plant's stem to direct water there. Water thoroughly and mulch with an organic material such as shredded bark, making sure the mulch doesn't touch the stem.*

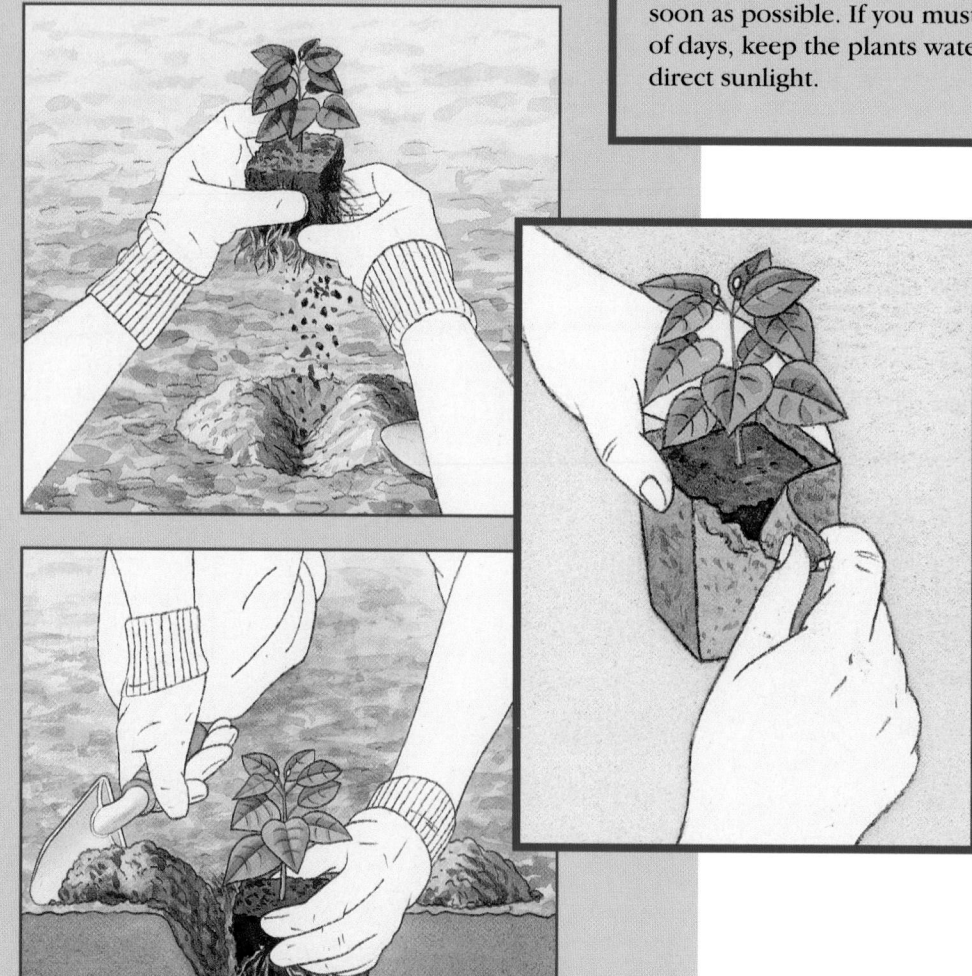

Choosing Bedding Plants

If you want flowers in a jiffy and haven't the time or the inclination to start them from seed, most home and garden centers stock a selection of popular annuals that can immediately go into the ground. These reasonably priced annuals typically come in cell packs that hold anywhere from two to eight plants. Larger specimens are also available but will cost more.

For healthy, long-lasting flowers in your garden, look for compact plants that have many shoots and good bud development but few to no blooms. Leaves should be deep or bright green; avoid plants with blemishes or yellowing leaves. Gently lift or remove annuals from their containers to check that they are not root-bound, and inspect both the soil and the plant for damage from pests and disease. The soil should be dark and moist to the touch, not dry or soaked. Avoid leggy plants.

Healthy annuals will outgrow their containers quickly, so plant your purchases as soon as possible. If you must wait a couple of days, keep the plants watered and out of direct sunlight.

Direct-Seeding

The simplest way to start annuals is by sowing seeds directly into the soil of the garden—and there are, in fact, a number of annuals that prefer to be direct-seeded *(list, right)*. To prepare a seedbed, first clear all vegetation from a patch of ground and amend the soil to a depth of 8 inches with 1 to 2 inches of compost or other organic matter. Break up any soil clumps with a spading fork, and smooth the bed with a tined rake.

You can sow seeds in one of two ways. The easiest is to scatter them on the prepared bed; if planting small seeds, mix some sand in before scattering to prevent them from massing together. The second method, described below and used for a more controlled effect, involves only slightly more effort. With the handle of a rake, draw furrows in the seedbed that are 1 inch deep—or as deep as the seed packet instructs. Follow the packet's recommendation for spacing between furrows, which will vary depending on the species.

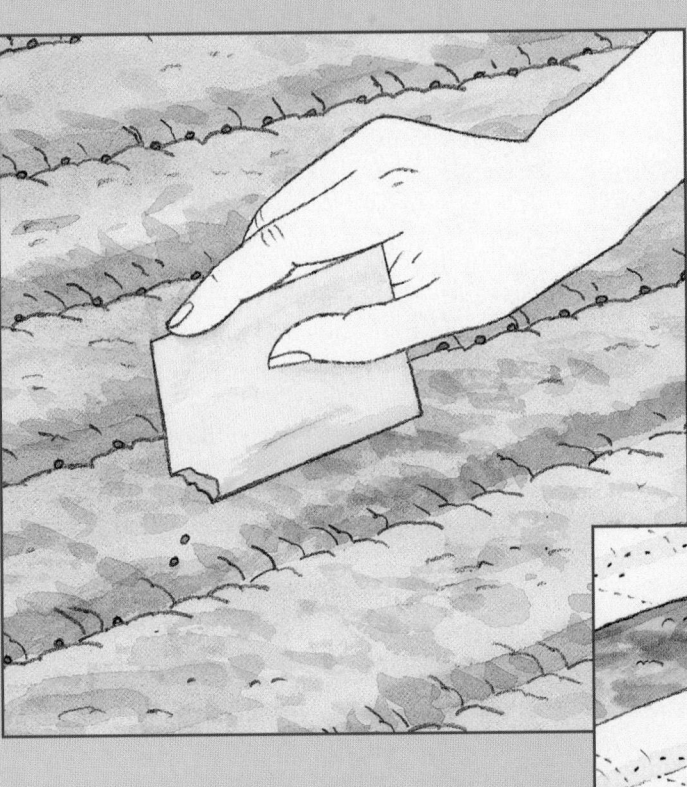

1. Sprinkle the seeds out of the packet evenly into the furrows, *sowing about four seeds for every plant you plan for. Cover the seeds with a thin layer of soil, if the seed packet calls for it. To sow very tiny seeds like basil (inset, below), line the furrow with white, unscented toilet paper so that you can easily see their number and distribution. The paper will disintegrate. Lightly tamp the seedbed's surface with a rake to press the seeds gently into the ground; mist or water lightly with an adjustable spray nozzle to dampen the bed, and water daily thereafter so that the ground does not dry out.*

2. After a week or 10 days, when the seedlings begin to crowd one another, *thin the crop by cutting off three out of four seedlings just above the stem's base. Cut out the weakest seedlings, retaining only those with the stoutest stems and the greenest leaves. When the seedlings are around 4 inches high, pinch back the plant's top growth with your thumb and index finger. This will encourage side branching of new stems and will stop the plant from growing too leggy in its first few weeks. Continue to keep the flower bed well watered, and put down an organic mulch after the annuals are well established, usually 6 to 8 weeks later.*

Annuals to Direct-Seed

Adonis aestivalis
(pheasant's-eye)
Agrostemma githago
(corn cockle)
Borago officinalis
(borage)
Callistephus chinensis
(China aster)
Centaurea cyanus
(bachelor's-button)
Cirsium japonicum
(rose thistle)
Clarkia **spp.**
(clarkia, godetia)
Consolida ambigua
(larkspur)
Cucurbita **spp.**
(gourd)
Emilia javanica
(tassel flower)
Eschscholzia californica
(California poppy)
Foeniculum vulgare
(fennel)
Gypsophila elegans
(baby's-breath)
Lavatera trimestris
(rose mallow, tree mallow)
Mentzelia **spp.**
(mentzelia)
Moluccella laevis
(bells of Ireland)
Nigella damascena
(love-in-a-mist)
Papaver **spp.**
(poppy)
Perilla frutescens
(beefsteak plant)
Phacelia campanularia
(California bluebell)
Phaseolus coccineus
(scarlet runner bean)
Phlox drummondii
(annual phlox)
Reseda odorata
(mignonette)
Sanvitalia procumbens
(sanvitalia, creeping zinnia)
Silene **spp.**
(campion, catchfly)
Silybum marianum
(blessed thistle)
Tropaeolum majus
(common nasturtium)
Zinnia **spp.**
(zinnia)

Note: The abbreviation "spp." stands for the plural of "species"; where used in lists it means that many, but not all, of the species in a genus meet the criterion of the list.

Planting Perennials

Perennials are long-lived plants that must be given room and time to grow and flourish. This means that a newly planted perennial bed or border may look somewhat skimpy its first year, even after the plants are established.

Achieving Flowers the First Year

Many perennials, especially first-year seedlings and those that were planted with bare roots, will not bloom until their second year in the garden. If you have your heart set on seeing abundant flowers the first year, however, you can do several things to make that happen while waiting for your fledgling perennials to mature.

One option is to plant annuals among the perennials. If you have left the proper amount of space between the young perennials, you will have plenty of room to interplant colorful annuals without disturbing the roots of the long-term inhabitants. Annuals that tend to reseed, such as marigolds and snapdragons, should be deadhead-ed as flowers fade to prevent unwanted seedlings the following year, to encourage abundant bloom, and to keep the plants tidy.

If you are willing to pay higher prices for your plants, you can buy container-grown perennials that are large enough to bloom the year you plant them. A third option is to plan your garden to include *Rudbeckia fulgida* 'Goldsturm', *Coreopsis verticillata* 'Moonbeam', *Hibiscus moscheutos* hybrids, or several other perennial varieties that bloom nicely their first year in the ground. If none of these flowers appeals to you, you can get your garden started with plants donated by friends who have divided their overgrown perennials and now have more healthy, mature plants than they know what to do with. These too will flower the year you plant them, if you can get them into the ground before their normal bloom time.

Finally, and perhaps most gratifying of all the possibilities, you can make sure that flowering perennials of all kinds show up in your garden the first year by filling the beds and borders with plants that you yourself have nurtured for a year or more in a separate nursery bed.

Planting Depths for Bare-Root Perennials

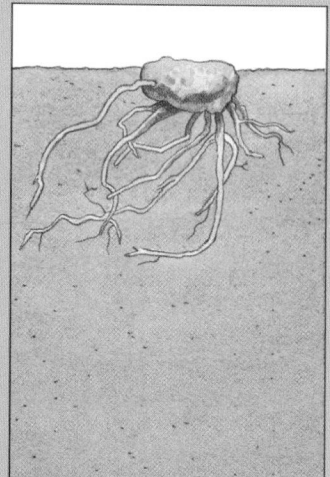

Perennials that grow from rhizomes, such as iris and bergenia, should be planted with the roots below ground and the rhizome's surface just emerging from the soil.

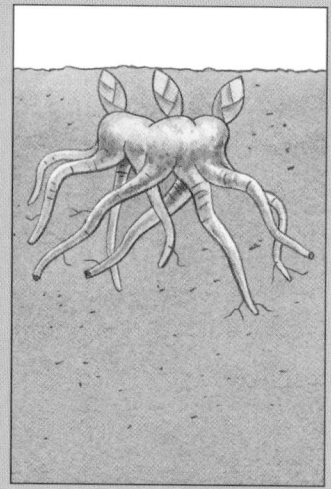

Plant peonies with the tips of the buds just below ground level if your area has mild winters, and up to 2 inches below the surface if you live in the North.

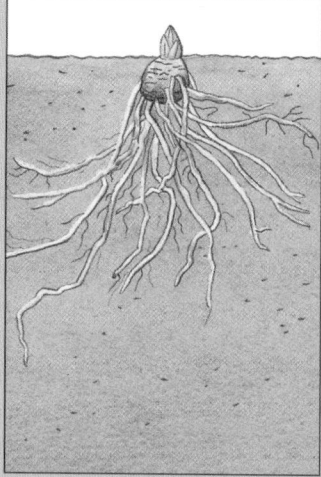

More than half of all perennials (including hostas, above) do best when planted so that the crown—where the roots and the stem meet—is flush with the soil surface.

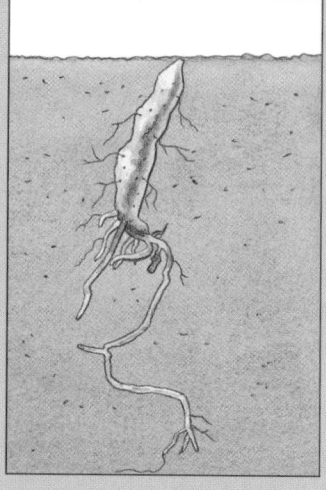

Plant daylilies (Hemerocallis) and other plants with a fleshy main root or taproot with the taproot straight up and down and the bud just below ground level.

270

Planting Bare-Root Perennials

Unwrap the plant and check its roots, *clipping off any that are damaged or diseased (left). Place the plant in a bucket of water to keep the roots wet while you dig a hole as deep and as wide as the plant's longest roots. Form a cone of soil in the hole high enough to hold the plant at the proper level. Place the plant atop the cone, gently spreading out the roots (above). Fill in the rest of the soil, tamp down, water generously, and mulch.*

Planting a Nursery Bed

Setting aside a small plot of ground—perhaps a 10-by-10-foot area—for a nursery bed can pay dividends both in the quality and beauty of your perennial garden and in the money you save by raising your own stock. Almost any sunny spot will do for most perennials; a part of the vegetable garden or an out-of-the-way area behind the garage would be ideal. And the space can be compact because you can set the plants in neat rows and much closer together than you would in the garden. With a nursery bed you can buy one plant each of as many varieties as you are interested in and watch them grow and flower. In a year, stem cuttings *(pages 316-317)* can be taken from some perennials to propagate additional plants. In a few years, others can be divided to produce the number of new plants you want.

In the meantime, you will have a chance to learn the plants' behaviors—whether they spread too fast; require staking; respond well to your property's climate; demand little attention or much care; and, perhaps most important, produce flowers of the color, size, and shape you expected. You also can judge how the colors, flower shapes, and foliage types of different plants work next to each other before taking the trouble to establish them in your garden.

Planting Container-Grown Perennials

Dig a hole slightly larger than the plant's rootball. *Then tap the bottom of the pot to loosen the plant and slide it out. With your fingers, fluff out the roots. If the plant is severely root-bound, use a knife to cut an inch or two into the rootball from its base.*

Without disturbing the top of the rootball, *carefully pull apart the two lower sections and gently tease loose as many roots as possible with your fingertips. Take care not to break the rootball apart.*

Place the plant in the prepared hole, *spreading the roots out all around (left). Make sure the base of the plant is level with the surrounding soil. Fill the hole with soil, tamp it down, then water the plant thoroughly and mulch.*

Where and When to Plant

Even with a garden plan to guide you, there still remains the process of actually placing individual plants for best effect. To achieve a natural, unforced look, start with an area you have marked off for a single variety, and try to site the plants randomly rather than in a straight line or some other rigid formation. It also helps to work with an odd number of plants—three, five, or seven is best.

Allow enough space between the plants to afford them room to grow and to enjoy good air circulation—important for preventing lingering dampness in flowers and foliage, which can lead to disease. Perennials that are difficult to transplant successfully when mature, such as peonies and wild (false) indigo, should be given even more space to spread out than other plants.

As a rule, bare-root perennials should be planted at a time that will give them a chance to establish themselves before they have to face extremes of weather. This means, usually, in the spring or

fall. Most larger, container-grown plants can be planted anytime during the growing season and into the fall.

Late-season bloomers such as asters, phlox, and chrysanthemums should be planted in the spring. They need time to become firmly rooted before they can direct their energy toward flowering later in the season. For the same reason, Oriental poppies, peonies, and other early-blooming perennials should be planted in the fall for flowering the following spring. Hostas, pachysandra, and other foliage plants can be planted anytime, because their flowers are not their main attraction.

In regions colder than Zone 6, limit the planting of bare-root perennials to the spring so that the plants will have the summer and fall to establish deep roots before cold weather sets in. Container-grown plants, however, will tolerate fall planting well if you follow up with a mulch of pine needles or salt hay to protect the roots from extreme cold over the winter.

Conversely, in the warmest zones it is best to plant bare-root perennials in the fall, giving them

Delphiniums and foxgloves give way to yellow chamomile, dahlias, and violet sage at the front of this new 7-by-20-foot Maine border. Planted in ready-to-bloom condition, these perennials were grown first in the gardener's own nursery bed. Annuals and biennials fill the bed's bare spots with color.

A member of a vast and hardy genus, this Hemerocallis 'Cherry Cheeks', with its 6-inch flowers on 28-inch stalks, will flourish in almost any soil. Daylilies are robust spreaders, but they are not invasive. To keep them in check, divide daylilies about every 3 years.

Holding Bare-Roots for Planting

Occasionally a spring shipment of bare-root plants arrives from the mail-order nursery before the soil has thawed and dried out enough to cultivate. If that happens, or if for some other reason you are unable to put the plants into the ground immediately, it is essential to keep their roots moist and covered. Even the best care won't preserve bare-root perennials out of the soil for more than about 2 weeks, however. If you are delayed in planting beyond that time, pot the plants temporarily in a good growing medium such as moist sawdust, moist finished compost, or leaf mold, and set them in a cool, shady spot. You won't need to worry about the plants' roots drying out, and, in addition, potting helps get growth under way.

Another method for holding plants until you are ready to plant them in the garden is "heeling in." An acclimatization process, heeling in is recommended only if the cold weather—and any chance of hard frost—has passed.

To heel in plants, you need to find a sheltered spot outdoors. Dig a narrow, shallow trench and lay the plants across it so that their crowns are at ground level and their roots are spread out in the trench. The plants can be placed side by side—spacing does not matter. After positioning the plants, water the roots, cover them with soil, and gently tamp the soil in place. This not only will keep your bare-root plants alive but will also give them a head start on becoming accustomed to outdoor living. Remember, though, that this is only a temporary procedure and that when the plants show signs of growing, you must dig them out and put them into the garden or nursery bed without delay.

Planting Tips

Planting can be hard work, but you need not do it all in one day. Have the soil ready for the plants before you dig the holes; to keep roots from drying out, unpot, unwrap, or unearth each perennial just before you place it in the hole. If you are cultivating a new bed, loosen and amend the soil as needed. When putting new plants into an existing bed, mix some fertilizer into the soil before digging planting holes. Use a product that blends organic ingredients such as dehydrated manure, blood meal, bone meal, and sunflower meal with minerals such as phosphate and potassium.

time to take hold before the heat of summer arrives. Container-grown plants will tolerate planting in the spring if they are protected by a good mulch, which will shield the roots from the effects of extreme heat by moderating ground temperatures. But to avoid rot, take care that the mulch does not touch the crown, stem, or any low-growing leaves of the plants.

Planting in midsummer is not recommended, but if you must do it, water the soil a few days before you dig so that it will be slightly moist. After planting, water the site well, apply mulch, and keep the plants shaded from the sun for the first few days. Whatever the season, your perennials will have an easier time of it if you plant them on an overcast day.

Planting Bulbs

When choosing a planting site for your bulbs, you first need to consider the area's light and temperature. Early-flowering bulbs such as snowdrop, winter aconite, spring snowflake, endymion, spring cyclamen, and crocus can be planted beneath deciduous trees and shrubs, whose bare branches in the first weeks of spring do not block the sun's rays. Areas that receive partial shade (3 to 4 hours of full sun) work well for wild and dwarf daffodils, snowflake, windflower, winter aconite, meadow saffron, and trout lily. The bulbs of late-flowering daffodils, Dutch hyacinths, and tulips take longer to mature and must be planted in full sun in northern regions.

Summer-blooming bulbs such as cannas and dahlias require at least 6 hours of full sun to develop strong stems and large blooms. When planting these bulbs in the spring, take care that they won't be in the shade cast by a building or under the dense canopy of a tree later in the season. And in southern states where the sun is very hot at noon, flowers that bloom from late spring through

DEPTH AND SPACING OF FALL-PLANTED BULBS

SOIL DEPTH

Plant spring-blooming bulbs and hardy summer-blooming bulbs in late summer to late fall, depending on the specific variety. This chart gives the recommended planting depth and spacing for a number of bulb varieties.

1 "

Eranthis (winter aconite)
2-3 inches apart

2 "

**Crocus vernus
(Dutch crocus)**
2-3 inches apart

**Anemone blanda
(windflower)**
2-3 inches apart

**Muscari
(grape hyacinth)**
3 inches apart

3 "

**Chionodoxa
(glory-of-the-snow)**
2-3 inches apart

**Iris reticulata
(dwarf iris)**
2-3 inches apart

4 "

**Allium aflatunense
(ornamental onion)**
4-6 inches apart

5 "

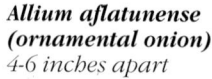

6 "

**Iris hollandica
(Dutch iris)**
6 inches apart

7 "

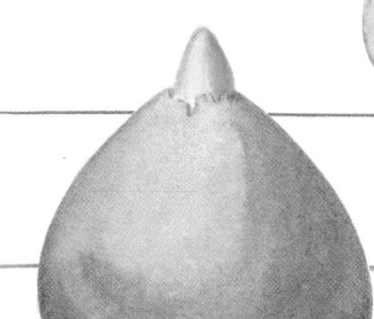
Tulipa (tulip)
6 inches apart

Narcissus (daffodil)
4-6 inches apart

8 "

the summer months will last longer if they are planted in a part of the bed that receives filtered sun in the afternoon. Bulbs planted in a warm, protected southern exposure next to a building or wall will bloom earlier than those planted in an unprotected northern exposure.

Preparing the Soil

After you've decided on a spot for your bulbs, get to know your soil type. Most bulbs require soil that holds moisture—but not too much. Heavy clay is lethal to bulbs because it can become sodden and rot them. Be wary of sandy soils as well, since they can drain water away too fast. Loam, a crumbly combination of clay, sand, silt, and organic matter, is the ideal. (*Fritillaria meleagris* and several types of Siberian and Japanese iris are the exceptions to this rule—they prefer moist soil.)

If your soil has too much clay or sand to allow proper drainage, improve it by adding organic matter, such as compost, shredded leaves, or ground pine bark, or commercial composted sewage sludge. Peat moss will do the job, although it doesn't last as long. For heavy clay, add sand to the amendments to further loosen the soil.

Besides improving drainage, organic matter will add nutrients and help maintain a pH of 6.0 to 7.0, the slightly acid to neutral level preferred by most bulbs. If your soil's pH is below 5.9, you will also need to add lime. The amount of lime needed

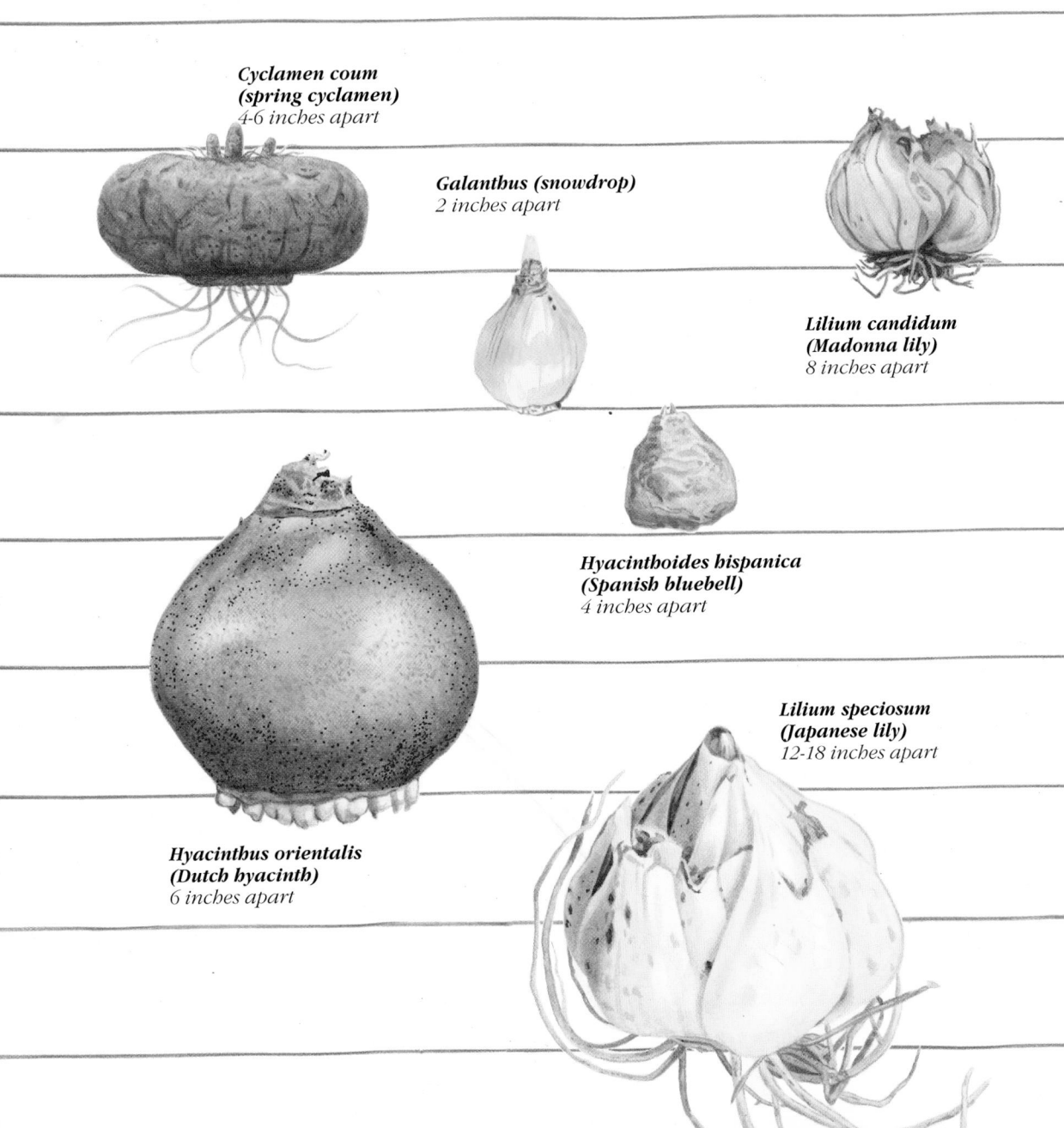

**Cyclamen coum
(spring cyclamen)**
4-6 inches apart

Galanthus (snowdrop)
2 inches apart

**Lilium candidum
(Madonna lily)**
8 inches apart

**Hyacinthoides hispanica
(Spanish bluebell)**
4 inches apart

**Hyacinthus orientalis
(Dutch hyacinth)**
6 inches apart

**Lilium speciosum
(Japanese lily)**
12-18 inches apart

will depend on your soil type and its pH reading.

Work the soil to a depth of 10 to 12 inches for large bulbs and 6 to 8 inches for smaller bulbs; remove rocks, old roots, and weed clumps. For soil that is in good condition, cover the bed with a 1-inch layer of organic matter; if major improvement is in order, spread several inches of organic matter over the plot and dig it into the soil.

If you are preparing the bed at least several weeks before planting, you can also dig in a slow-release fertilizer such as a 9-9-6 or a low-nitrogen 5-10-20; these chemical granules need time to break down or they will burn the bulbs. If you are planting at the same time you are preparing the bed, avoid fertilizer burn by enriching the soil with compost and an organic fertilizer rather than a synthetic one. Several organic formulas that are specially suited for bulbs are available at your local garden center. Refer to the package to determine the correct application rate. If a test of your soil indicates adequate phosphorus, you can get by with putting down a top dressing of compost and fertilizer rather than digging them in.

Planting Your Bulbs

A rule of thumb for planting most bulbs is to dig a hole 3 times as deep as the bulb is high. However, depth varies with soil type: In lighter soils, bulbs can be planted an inch or so deeper; in heavy soils, prepare a shallower hole and top with several

DEPTH AND SPACING OF SPRING- AND SUMMER-PLANTED BULBS

SOIL DEPTH

Plant tender summer-blooming bulbs in late spring to early summer, and hardy fall-blooming bulbs as soon as they are available in late summer. This chart gives the recommended planting depth and spacing for a number of bulb varieties.

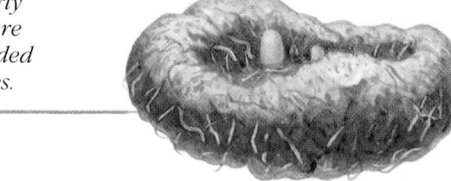

Begonia x tuberhybrida (tuberous begonia)
10 inches apart

1"

Ranunculus asiaticus (Persian buttercup)
4 inches apart

2"

Crocosmia (montbretia)
6 inches apart

Gladiolus callianthus (Ethiopian gladiolus)
5 inches apart

3"

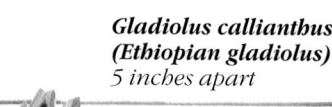

Canna x generalis (canna lily)
16 inches apart

4"

5"

Zantedeschia aethiopica (calla lily)
10-12 inches apart

6"

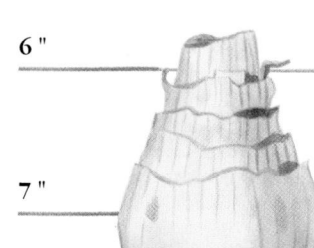

7"

Galtonia candicans (summer hyacinth)
6-8 inches apart

8"

inches of organic mulch. Exceptions include the Madonna lily, tuberous begonia, and *Hippeastrum* (amaryllis), which are always planted close to the surface. Refer to the charts below and on pages 274-275 for specific spacing and planting depths for the different bulb species.

When planting many bulbs in a new bed where the soil is loose and crumbly, a small trowel is the best tool for the job *(pages 278-279)*. If you're planting bulbs in an established bed among perennials and shrubs, use a shovel to loosen the soil in small areas and a trowel to dig individual planting holes. If the soil is not compacted, a hand-held hollow bulb planter *(page 279)* can be used to remove plugs of earth. Dig several inches below where the bulb will rest, and work in organic matter or a slow-release synthetic fertilizer at the rate of 1 tablespoon per square foot. If you use a synthetic, prevent damage to the bulbs by covering the fertilized layer with untreated soil up to planting depth before placing the bulbs in the holes. Position the bulbs with their pointed ends up; plant flat tubers of anemones and cyclamens sideways.

Cover the bulbs with soil, tamp it down, and water the planting thoroughly. Mulch the entire bed—new or established—with 2 to 4 inches of shredded pine bark, pine needles, or shredded leaves to control weed growth, retain moisture, and moderate soil temperature.

To keep track of the bulbs after they are planted and after the foliage has died back, you may want to mark their location. Metal labels have tabs that

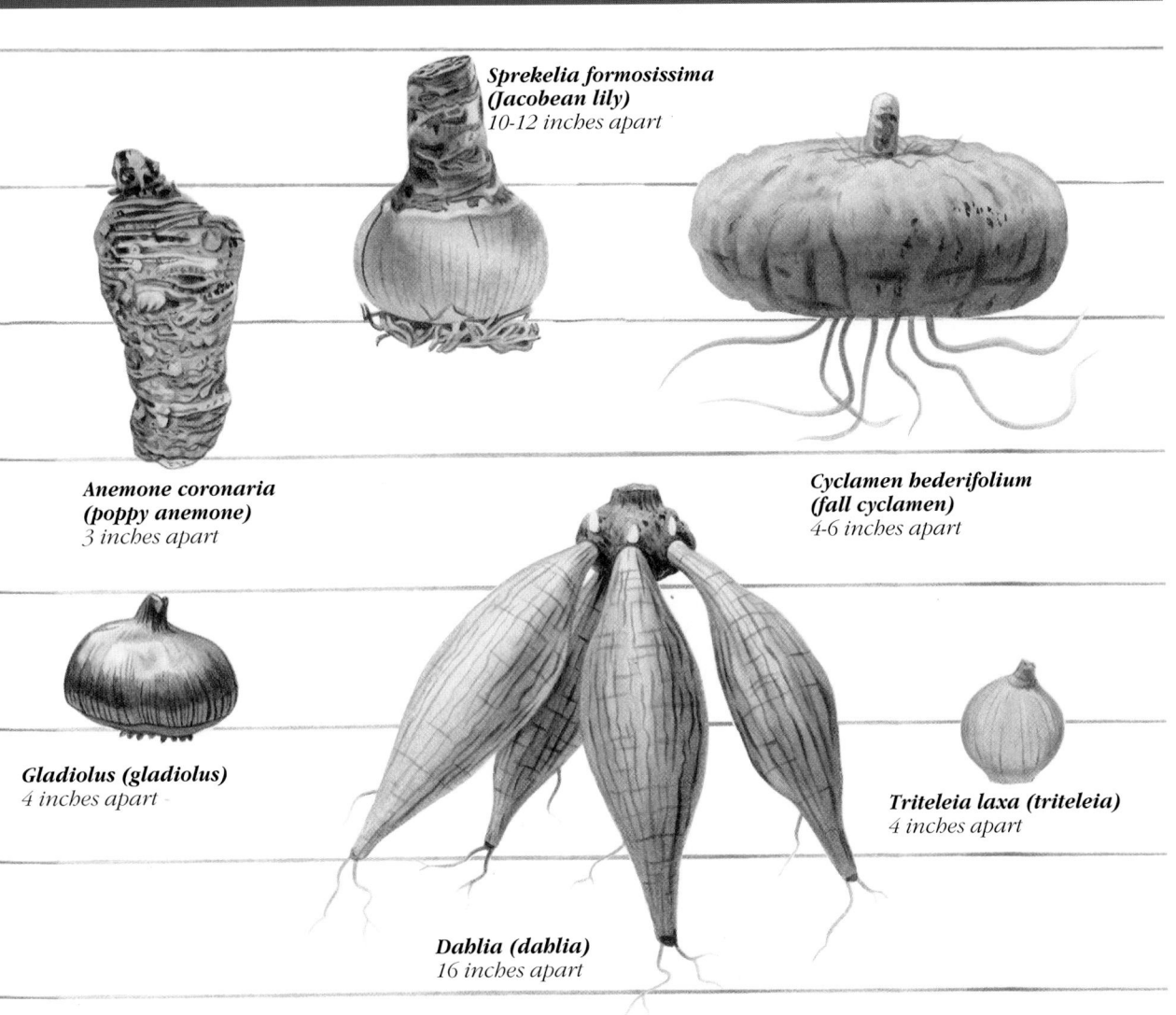

Sprekelia formosissima (Jacobean lily)
10-12 inches apart

Anemone coronaria (poppy anemone)
3 inches apart

Cyclamen hederifolium (fall cyclamen)
4-6 inches apart

Gladiolus (gladiolus)
4 inches apart

Triteleia laxa (triteleia)
4 inches apart

Dahlia (dahlia)
16 inches apart

Nestled among evergreens at the base of a fountain, purple Crocus speciosus 'Artabir' adds a pocket of color to a backyard Virginia garden. Plant the hardy autumn-flowering bulbs in late summer for blooms 6 to 8 weeks later.

southern areas, as late as December. Hardy summer-blooming bulbs are usually planted in the fall. They can be planted in late spring with other flowering perennials, but in the North they may not get established sufficiently to bloom the same year.

Tender summer-blooming bulbs can't be planted until the soil temperature reaches 65° to 70°F, because they will rot if planted in cold, wet earth. Some, such as caladium and tuberous begonia, should be started indoors in spring, 3 to 4 weeks before the last frost date, so they have several inches of growth before they're moved outdoors. Canna and dahlia benefit from being started indoors in northern areas where summers are short.

Use flats filled with an enriched potting mix containing peat moss. If you are starting caladium and begonia tubers, soak them in tepid water to remove the wax coating that is applied to prevent them from dehydrating during transit. If you are planting caladiums, encourage them to produce many leaves by breaking off the primary shoot.

Arrange the tubers in the potting mix, cover them with another inch of it, and place the flats in a sunny window. Water regularly to keep the mix barely moist, and feed the growing plants every 2 weeks with a diluted fish or seaweed liquid fertilizer. Plant the tubers outdoors when they have sprouted several inches of foliage and the soil temperature is 70°F.

For a continuous show of color over several weeks, combine bulbs that bloom at different times. If your combinations include both large and small bulbs, plant them in layers. First dig a rectangular hole 12 inches deep. Loosen the soil in the bottom of the hole, mix in a slow-release bulb food, and top with a layer of unfertilized soil to bring the depth of the prepared trench up to about 8 inches. Place large bulbs in the bottom and cover with 4 inches of soil. Next, set the smaller bulbs in the trench and fill to the top with soil. Tamp it down and water thoroughly, then cover with a layer of mulch.

Bulbs that can be layered include dwarf iris over early daffodils or early to midspring tulips, squill over late-spring ornamental onion, windflower over early to midspring daffodils, muscari over mid- to late-spring tulips, and crocus over early to midspring hyacinths.

If you're interplanting similar-size bulbs that bloom at different times in the spring, dig an area to the required depth and alternate the bulbs, placing them as close together as possible. Bulbs with sequential bloom times that can be planted at the same depth include late-blooming daffodils and ornamental onion, crocus and muscari, and dwarf iris and windflower.

can be marked with permanent ink, and their two pin legs keep them securely anchored in the ground. Vinyl markers are also good because they can be cut, are flexible, and won't break in the cold. Or you can use labels made of sturdy plastic, which are pointed at one end for insertion into soft earth.

When to Plant

Hardy spring-blooming bulbs require a chilling period and should be planted in early fall. This gives them time to develop a good root system before the ground freezes. In northern areas the best planting time may be as early as September; in

Tools for Planting Bulbs

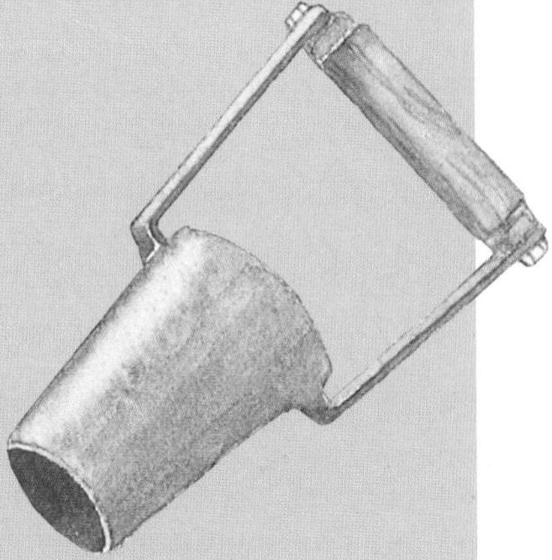

A _hand trowel_ is the perfect tool for quick planting of bulbs in loose soil. Using what is called the stab-pull method, plunge the trowel into the ground, pull the soil toward you, and drop the bulb into the hole. Then remove the trowel, let the soil fall back over the bulb, and tamp it down. Use a small trowel with a pointed end, called a dibble, when planting in narrow spaces, such as between the rocks in a rock garden.

A _long-handled bulb planter_ works well in prepared soil; use a heavy-duty version when planting in hard earth. By standing on its footrests, you can push the serrated-edged cylinder into the ground with the weight of your body. The planter's 30-inch shaft eliminates bending, and the mower-style handle allows you to twist the digger and remove the soil plug in the 9-inch-long hollow cylinder.

Protecting Bulbs from Animals

Many small rodents are fond of tulip and crocus bulbs. To outwit them, place chipped stones at the bottom of the planting hole, position the bulb, and sprinkle more stones around it to reach but not cover the pointed tip. Fill in with soil.

_Larger rodents—chipmunks and squirrels among them—_also find tulip and crocus bulbs a tasty treat and will dig them up before the ground freezes. In the West, gophers can quickly destroy entire plantings. One way to prevent such foraging when putting in bulb beds is to plant in wire baskets. Dig a trench and line the bottom and sides with metal hardware cloth. Lay the bulbs on top, cover with several inches of soil, and tamp down. A top dressing of well-aged cow manure or commercial composted sewage sludge will further repel pests. Bulbs not bothered by rodents include daffodils, squills, glory-of-the-snow, and snowdrops.

Planting Roses

Roses grow best in rich, loamy, well-drained, slightly acidic soil that holds water and nutrients well and allows air to reach plant roots. To achieve such a combination, you'll probably need to amend your soil with both organic and inorganic materials. If the overall quality and texture of your soil is generally inferior for growing roses, you'll want to work on the entire bed. If the soil is in good shape, you can focus your attention on the roses' planting holes. Either way, soil preparation takes time, but it can mean the difference between roses that limp along from year to year and those that are long-lived, with lush growth and opulent blossoms.

Using Soil Amendments

There is an array of organic and mineral amendments to help bring your soil to peak condition. To improve drainage in tightly compacted clay soil or help sandy soil retain moisture, incorporate organic materials such as peat moss, leaf mold, ground-bark mulch, well-rotted manure, or compost. As an added bonus, these amendments also provide plant roots with some of the nutrients they need and help keep soil pH in the slightly acid range preferred by roses. Just be sure that any organic

With their clusters of pink blossoms dancing at the tips of gently arching stems, 'Ballerina' hybrid musk roses create a lovely informal hedge in this Houston, Texas, garden. The plants are closely spaced to create a continuous line of color but allow enough room for maintenance.

matter you dig into the soil is well decomposed—it should be dark, crumbly, and earthy smelling.

Mineral amendments include gypsum, which helps to loosen heavy clay soils and lower the pH of alkaline soil. Coarse sand, perlite, vermiculite, and pumice are other mineral amendments that improve soil by adding bulk and changing texture. Do not use vermiculite in heavy clay, however, since it tends to absorb and retain water. The amount of mineral amendments you use will depend on your particular soil. Organic material, in any case, should make up about one-quarter of your total soil volume.

Roses prefer a pH level of around 6.5. To determine the pH level of your soil, you can pick up an inexpensive testing kit at any garden center. Or, for a more detailed analysis, take a soil sample to your local Cooperative Extension Service or to a private laboratory. Either way, aim to test and amend the soil a few months before putting your roses into the ground—in the late fall before spring planting, for example—so that the pH balance has a chance to adjust properly.

If your soil is too acidic, you can raise the pH by adding dolomitic limestone. Work it into the top 6 inches of soil and then water. Your soil type will dictate how much lime to apply—sandy soils generally require the least amount of lime to raise the pH level by one point; clayey soils need more. Since too much lime can burn tender roots, start out cautiously, digging in no more than 5 pounds of lime per 100 square feet of area. Then wait a month or so before retesting your soil and adding more lime, if needed.

To lower the pH of alkaline soil, dig in iron sulfate, ground sulfur, or gypsum, following package directions. Use a maximum of 2 pounds per 100 square feet per application, then wait a month and retest. Experts recommend lowering or raising your soil's pH level no more than one point per year. Since extremely alkaline soil can be difficult to alter, you may want to consider growing your roses in raised beds or containers as an alternative.

Preparing the Rose Bed

Gardeners once believed that planting new roses in a bed where other roses had grown would result in "rose sickness"—reduced vigor caused by the depletion of trace elements in the soil or vestiges of root diseases left in the soil by the old plants. Experts now agree that as long as the soil is amended to replenish nutrients or replaced if there has been disease in a particular spot, there's no reason to avoid repeated plantings in the same bed.

To ready a bed for planting, begin by removing any existing sod. Then, with a hoe, dig about 16 inches down into the soil, removing any large rocks. If you're willing to spend extra time with the soil, consider double digging *(page 265)*. Although this technique involves digging up and amending 24 inches of soil rather than the usual 12 inches, many rose gardeners think the added work is worth the payoff in more and larger blooms. Whether or not you double dig, add all of your amendments during the digging phase. This is also the best time to add bone meal or another source of phosphorus—at 3 to 4 pounds per 100 square feet—to promote healthy root growth. Unlike the other major nutrients, phosphorus is difficult to supply to roots once plants are established. You can also include a granular fertilizer if you are preparing the bed about a month before planting; the idle weeks before you plant will give the fertilizer time to blend with the soil.

Spacing Between Roses	
Type of Rose	**Planting Distance**
Miniatures	1–1½ ft.
Hybrid Tea, Grandiflora, & Floribunda Bushes *Compact and average varieties*	2–2½ ft.
Hybrid Tea, Grandiflora, & Floribunda Bushes *Tall varieties*	2½–3 ft.
Low-Growing Shrubs	3–4 ft.
Standards	4 ft.
Shrubs	4–6 ft. or half of expected height
Climbers & Ramblers *Trained horizontally*	8–10 ft.

Spacing for a Lush Hedge

To achieve the lushest possible effect with medium-sized hedges (3 to 5 feet tall), plant your roses in staggered rows. Although the size and growth habits of your particular variety should determine the distance to be kept between plants, if you aim for 1½ to 2 feet of space, you will create a dense feel and still have enough room between the plants to perform maintenance chores.

Planting a Bare-Root Rose

Before planting your bare-root rose, do the following: Rinse the plant under a hard stream of water from a garden hose to clean off any bacteria or fungal spores. Then immerse the rose in a bucket of water for at least 1 hour and no more than 24 hours to replenish the plant's moisture. Never leave the rose soaking more than a day, or the plant may die. Using a pair of sharp shears, prune off any broken or injured roots just above the point of the injury, and cut back any canes that are damaged or are the diameter of a pencil or less. Set the plant aside, keeping it in water until you are ready to transfer it to the planting hole.

1. Dig a planting hole at least as wide and as deep as the spread of the plant's roots. *If you haven't already prepared the soil, add the necessary amendments to the soil removed from the hole. Next, return enough of the improved soil to the hole to form a cone-shaped mound; this will serve as a support for the plant.*

2. Lay a spade across the hole to mark ground level, *then set the plant on top of the mound, spreading its roots out evenly all around. Allowing for changes as the soil settles, adjust the height of the mound so that the plant's bud union will be just above ground level in climates where temperatures do not drop below 20°F, or 1 to 2 inches below ground level in colder climates.*

3. Fill the hole about halfway with soil *and tamp it down gently with your hands; this removes air pockets around the roots. Fill the hole with water and allow it to drain. Then fill the hole to the top with soil and water once more. Check to see that the bud union remains at the proper level; if not, add or remove soil as necessary.*

4. Mound additional soil around the bottom of the plant *and up to within 3 inches of the tops of the canes; this will keep them from drying out while the plant is getting established. Check every 2 to 3 days for new growth. When buds sprout, usually after about 2 weeks, gradually and gently remove the soil mound with water from a garden hose or with your fingers. Loosen the plant's nametag so that it does not constrict the cane as it grows.*

Planting a Container-Grown Rose

A container-grown rose can be planted any time from early spring to midfall, as long as the ground is not frozen or waterlogged and the plant has enough time to establish itself before frost occurs. Choose a day that is overcast, with no wind or direct sun to dry canes and roots. If you must plant on a sunny day, wait until late afternoon to spare the plant the midday sun. If the rose has been sitting in a sunny location while waiting its turn for planting, this precaution is unnecessary.

1. Dig a hole slightly wider than the container and, if your soil has been prepared, of equal depth. If the soil is unprepared, dig 6 inches deeper and add amendments to the removed soil; return about 6 inches of soil to the hole. Then loosen the plant from the sides of its container by gently inserting a trowel in a few places around the pot. Take care not to disturb the roots.

2. Support the plant at its base and invert the container to slide it out; if the plant won't slide out on its own, press on the bottom of the container, or carefully cut away the pot from around the plant. Keeping the soil intact and without disturbing the roots, position the plant in the hole.

3. Add or remove soil as necessary to be sure that the rose's bud union is at the correct position for your climate. Typically, the nursery establishes the correct position when it pots the plant; you should only have to keep the soil surface of the rootball flush with the edge of the planting hole. Fill in the hole, tamping soil around the roots to remove air pockets. Water the plant thoroughly, add more soil if necessary, and spread a layer of mulch around the plant. Keep the rose well watered until it is established.

Spacing Your Plants

Spacing between rose plants is determined by climate, growth habits, and the visual effect you want to achieve *(chart, page 281)*. However, a few rules always apply. Most important, never crowd your plants. Crowding hampers air circulation and makes it more difficult for you to move around between your plants to tend them. Second, arrange plants so you can avoid as much as possible having to step into the bed, since walking on the bed compacts the soil.

When to Plant

The climate in your area and whether your rose is bare-root or container grown will determine the best time for planting. Ideally, bare-root roses should be planted as soon as you receive them—in late winter in areas where temperatures remain above freezing year round; in early spring or late fall where winter temperatures remain above 0° F; and in midspring where winters are extremely cold. Before you plant, make sure all danger of hard frost has passed and that the ground is neither hard or frozen nor soggy and waterlogged. Container-grown roses may be planted anytime from early spring to midfall. If you plant during hot weather, however, be sure to keep the rose well watered for the first 6 weeks.

If you intend to plant your bare-root roses within a few days of receiving them, keep them wrapped in their shipping materials and place them in an unheated but frostproof location, such as a garage or shed. But if it will be 2 weeks or more before you plant, you must heel the roses in. To do this, dig a shallow V-shaped trench, lay the plants side by side in the trench, and add just enough moist soil to cover the roots. This will insulate the plants and keep them from becoming dehydrated. If you must wait awhile before planting container-grown roses, keep them in a warm, sunny spot out of the wind, and keep the soil moist.

CHAPTER SIX

Maintaining the Garden

If soil is properly prepared and planting is done correctly, a garden should require relatively little upkeep. The one shown at left, in Los Angeles, was designed with the region's dry climate in mind: It is filled with many heat- and drought-tolerant plants and is mulched with gravel to conserve water.

Watering, fertilizing, and mulching give plants the moisture and nutrients they need to thrive, while staking, pruning, and weeding keep a bed looking tidy. Dividing overgrown plants keeps them healthy and increases your stock, and checking your plants for pests and diseases can help keep trouble at bay. (See the Troubleshooting Guide, pages 576-583, for descriptions of common pests and diseases.)

In areas of the country where the ground alternately freezes and thaws, winter's approach calls for putting down a protective mulch. But whatever the winter weather, most perennials should be cut to the ground at the end of the growing season. Roses also benefit from pruning and winter protection (pages 304-309), while spent annuals can simply be discarded in the compost pile.

Mulching and Weeding

The work required to keep a garden well mulched pays off handsomely. Besides helping to create the best growing conditions for your plants, a mulch minimizes watering and weeding chores and gives beds and borders a finished look.

Organic Mulches versus Stone

Mulches best suited to the home garden include numerous organic materials—shredded bark, cocoa shells, woodchips, and leaves, among others— and one inorganic material—stone. Stone mulch is available in different forms, most commonly as gravel, crushed rock, or stone chips. Another useful inorganic mulch is the long-lasting, porous synthetic material called landscape fabric. While it is an effective weed blocker, landscape fabric is unat-

tractive and should be covered with a decorative mulch *(opposite)* if used in a bed or border. If you use the fabric on a steep slope, however, don't cover it with another mulch—the loose pieces of mulch would likely be washed downhill by rain.

Both organic and stone mulches slow the evaporation of soil moisture and keep soil temperatures fairly cool and steady. Organic mulches are especially effective shields against heat—on a 100°F day, the soil beneath a 3-inch layer of mulch may be as much as 30°F cooler than the air above. Organic mulches also improve the soil as they decay, creating humus. Because they decompose, however, they have to be replenished regularly.

Stone mulches have the virtue of permanence. And only 1 inch of rock or gravel may be enough to cover the soil beneath your plants. But there are drawbacks. When spread under a deciduous tree, for example, the mulch makes fallen leaves

Unfit for brewing because they were roasted too long, these coffee beans were put to work as an eye-catching mulch in a Seattle, Washington, garden.

An expanse of fine stone chips provides a handsome setting for sand phlox, a spring-blooming native perennial that thrives in fast-draining sandy or rocky soil. The heat and light a stone mulch reflects help keep foliage dry, reducing the likelihood of crown rot in susceptible plants.

difficult to rake up. It can also become hot enough in bright sun to raise the air temperature by 10°F or more, and the stones themselves can burn any plant stems they touch. In addition, sunlight hitting pale-colored stones can produce an unpleasant glare. And finally, the very permanence of stone means that it doesn't improve soil structure.

Choosing and Applying a Mulch

Looks, longevity, site, and price are all factors to consider when selecting and using organic mulch. Using one type of mulch throughout the garden will give it a uniform appearance, but combining materials is also an option: A serviceable but unsightly layer of newspapers, ground corncobs, or ground sugarcane stalks can be concealed beneath a more appealing top dressing of chunks of bark or pine needles. Avoid using peat moss as a mulch, however. Although it's a good soil amendment, when placed on top of the soil peat moss blows around, is hard to rewet when it dries out, is a fire hazard, and is expensive to boot.

There are no hard-and-fast rules about how deeply you should mulch. Soil type must be taken into account; a loose, sandy soil, for instance, dries out more quickly than clay soil and consequently needs a thicker layer of mulch. The density of the mulch itself is important—the coarser and airier it is, the deeper you can apply it. Be careful, however, not to use a mulch so dense that little air and water can pass through it into the soil.

Whatever material you choose, lay it thickest between plants, tapering it down to soil level within an inch or two of the base of the plants. Avoid piling up mulch against trunks or stems lest it encourage pests and diseases. As a rule of thumb, use a 1- to 2-inch layer for a mulch with particles measuring ½ inch in diameter. Particles ranging from ½ inch to an inch or so should be spread at least 2 to 3 inches deep, and dry leaves, pine needles, and woodchips deeper still. If the woodchips are fresh, mix each cubic yard with 3 pounds of controlled-release nitrogen fertilizer before you lay down the mulch. Otherwise, microorganisms in the woodchips will draw nitrogen from the soil.

If weeds continue to appear, you've probably skimped on mulch and should add more. But if slugs and snails are a problem, additional mulch may draw still more of them. In such cases, it's better to use a combination of landscape fabric and a thin covering of mulch. Plan on renewing bark and leaf mulches annually. Woodchips can last 2 years and pine needles up to 3 years.

Laying Landscape Fabric in an Existing Bed

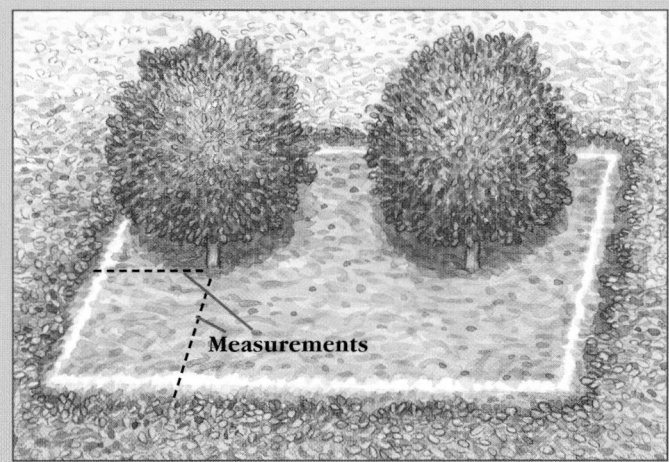

Measurements

1. Use lime to outline the area that is to be mulched, then remove any weeds and debris from around the plants. Measure the bed's length and width to determine how many lengths of fabric to cut, allowing for a 4- to 6-inch overlap between adjoining sections. Correctly position the fabric in an area adjacent to the bed. Next, measure the distance from a plant's center to the two closest edges of the bed that form a right angle. Transfer this measurement to the fabric and mark the point where the two lines intersect.

2. Cut from one edge of the fabric to the point where the two lines intersect, then make a series of radiating cuts around it (above). The cuts should equal the radius of the plant's trunk or stem cluster, plus about 3 inches.

3. Slip the fabric around each plant, then fold the pie-shaped wedges under to make a neat circle. When all of the sections of fabric are in place, cover them with a decorative mulch such as woodchips or pine needles.

Using an Onion Hoe

A lightweight onion hoe that is well sharpened and properly wielded requires little effort to use. To sever a weed just below ground level, position the blade a few inches above the soil *(inset)* and pull it toward you in a shallow arc. In tight spots, turn the hoe sideways and use one of its narrow edges to slice off a weed. A blade used in rocky soil will need more frequent sharpening than one used in sandy soil. This chore is easily accomplished with a sharpening file called a bastard mill file, which you stroke over the blade.

Using a Dandelion Digger

Working when the soil is moist, *thrust a long-handled dandelion digger into the ground deep enough to reach the tip of a weed's root (inset). Then push down on the tool's handle to pry the weed out. Examine the root; if it isn't intact, dig out the portions that broke off to prevent regrowth.*

In those climates where the ground alternately freezes and thaws in winter, apply a winter mulch to newly planted beds after the soil has frozen to keep the temperature constant. The best choices are airy materials such as pine boughs, straw, and salt hay, laid down over what remains of the growing-season mulch.

When Weeds Appear

Although keeping soil mulched is an excellent preventive, no garden is completely free of weeds. Perennial weeds are a worse problem than annual ones. Their more extensive root systems are harder to dig out, and any fragments left behind may grow anew. Use a digging fork with ground ivy, Bermuda grass, and other perennial weeds that have wide-spreading runners; a narrow-bladed dandelion digger *(left)* is best for weeds with deep roots such as Canada thistle and dandelion. An onion hoe works well for cutting larger shallow-rooted annual weeds, including chickweed. For weeds in spots that are hard to get at with a digging tool, try pouring boiling water on them.

Working the garden with a hoe to destroy weeds is an art that becomes easier with practice. Hold the hoe so that the blade cuts through the soil in a shallow arc, going no deeper than about an inch below the surface. Avoid turning over soil clods; this may expose buried weed seeds and encourage resprouting. And above all, hoe regularly. Annual weeds may be killed quickly, but perennial weeds may take repeated cutting.

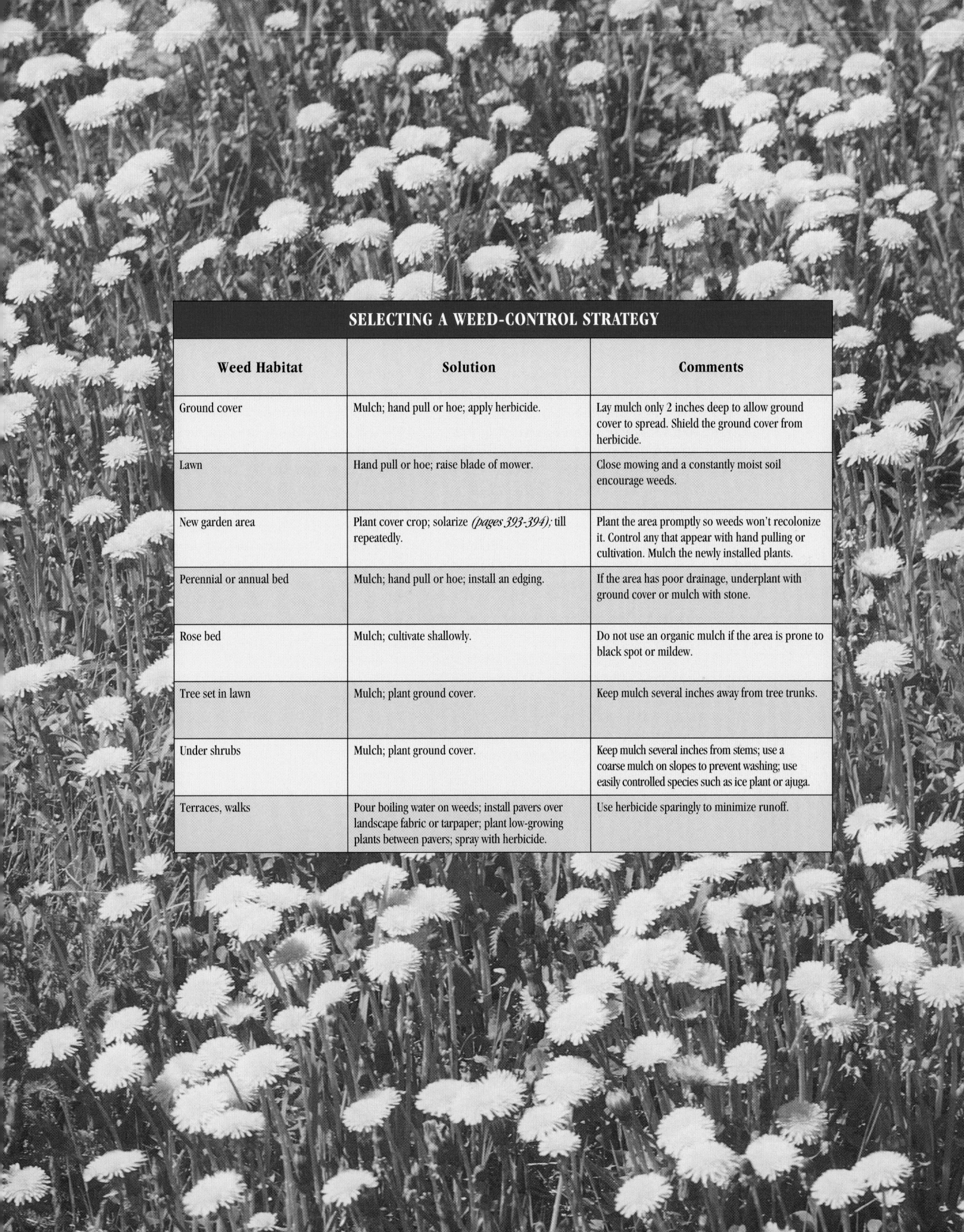

SELECTING A WEED-CONTROL STRATEGY

Weed Habitat	Solution	Comments
Ground cover	Mulch; hand pull or hoe; apply herbicide.	Lay mulch only 2 inches deep to allow ground cover to spread. Shield the ground cover from herbicide.
Lawn	Hand pull or hoe; raise blade of mower.	Close mowing and a constantly moist soil encourage weeds.
New garden area	Plant cover crop; solarize *(pages 393-394)*; till repeatedly.	Plant the area promptly so weeds won't recolonize it. Control any that appear with hand pulling or cultivation. Mulch the newly installed plants.
Perennial or annual bed	Mulch; hand pull or hoe; install an edging.	If the area has poor drainage, underplant with ground cover or mulch with stone.
Rose bed	Mulch; cultivate shallowly.	Do not use an organic mulch if the area is prone to black spot or mildew.
Tree set in lawn	Mulch; plant ground cover.	Keep mulch several inches away from tree trunks.
Under shrubs	Mulch; plant ground cover.	Keep mulch several inches from stems; use a coarse mulch on slopes to prevent washing; use easily controlled species such as ice plant or ajuga.
Terraces, walks	Pour boiling water on weeds; install pavers over landscape fabric or tarpaper; plant low-growing plants between pavers; spray with herbicide.	Use herbicide sparingly to minimize runoff.

The Prudent Use of Herbicides

When mechanical methods of weed control fail despite your best efforts, you may decide the problem is severe enough to warrant using a herbicide. If you do, be sure to choose the right product and use it responsibly, for your own sake and for the sake of the environment.

Choosing a Herbicide. There are two basic types of herbicides for the home garden—preemergent herbicides, which prevent seeds from germinating, and postemergent herbicides, which kill plants that are actively growing. Postemergents work in one of two ways. One kind kills foliage on contact and is a good choice for annual weeds. The other kind, called systemic, is drawn into the plant's tissues, disrupting natural functions and destroying the plant from within. Use systemic herbicides on herbaceous perennial weeds or woody weeds; a contact herbicide may cause damage but fail to kill them.

The Importance of Labels. A herbicide label indicates the types of plants for which the product is formulated, when and how to apply it, and the period of effectiveness. Such information is vital. For instance, if you sow seeds in a bed recently treated with a preemergent herbicide that persists in the soil for months, the seeds won't germinate and you will have wasted your time and money. (See the guide to reading herbicide labels below, left.)

Taking Site and Weather into Account. If a weed is growing among ornamental plants, you'll need to protect them from the chemical. Don't use a granular herbicide on a slope, since it is likely to wash downhill and do unintentional damage. Be especially cautious with herbicides near a vegetable garden, drainage field, wetland, stream, or garden pool; the chemicals can drift or wash onto other plants, kill fish, or pollute water supplies. You also need to exercise care in the root zone of a tree or shrub, which can be harmed if the roots absorb a systemic herbicide.

Never apply herbicides when it is rainy or windy; wait until a dry, calm day.

Heeding Precautions. While working with herbicides, don't drink, smoke, eat, touch your face, or use the bathroom. Keep pets and children away from treatment areas. (Follow this precaution if a neighbor's property is sprayed, whether by the homeowner or by a commercial service.)

Before you fill a sprayer with herbicide, test the nozzle's spray pattern with plain water so you'll know how to aim; for a ready-mixed spray product, spray newspaper to check the pattern. For liquids that are diluted before application, avoid disposal problems by preparing only a small quantity; if necessary, mix a second batch to finish the job. The herbicide should wet the foliage and stems well without dripping; using an excessive amount increases the risk of environmental damage.

To check a granular herbicide spreader's rate of application, mark out a measured area on a driveway or sidewalk and run the spreader over it. Sweep up and measure the herbicide, and adjust the spreader if necessary.

When finished, rinse all equipment with three changes of water. Wash your clothes and take a shower. Store the herbicide in its original container, preferably under lock and key.

Reading a Herbicide Label

Herbicide labels, which are regulated by the Environmental Protection Agency, contain information that will help you choose the right product for the job and use it properly. For the best results, read the entire label and follow the instructions to the letter. A typical label includes the following kinds of information:

- **Uses.** Plants that the herbicide controls; may also list plants on which the herbicide should *not* be used. Areas where the product can safely be used; other areas where it should *not* be used, such as near vegetable gardens or water sources.
- **Cautions and Hazards.** Specific dangers to users and the environment; emergency procedures to follow in case of accidents with the herbicide.
- **Directions for Use.** Dilution formulas as necessary; amount to use per unit area; details of application, such as appropriate methods and equipment, and weather conditions not conducive to safe use; clothing and safety wear, such as goggles.
- **Contents.** The product's chemical name and its chemical formula; the common name; percentages of ingredients in the formulation.
- **Storage and Disposal.** Specific directions for correct handling of the container and any unused portions.

Watering and Fertilizing

Water droplets deposited by a sprinkler's low-pressure spray linger on this daylily blossom. Overhead watering has the advantage of rinsing plants clean of dust and pollutants, but soaker hoses can also be used in perennial beds. For optimum flowering, keep the plants well watered during the period that they are forming flower buds and are just starting to produce blooms.

Proper watering and fertilizing of your plants will keep them growing robust and strong. Plants are most demanding while they're becoming established—a year or so for perennials, twice as long for shrubs and trees. Give new plantings relatively light, frequent waterings and monitor for signs of stress, such as drooping or dull-looking leaves. The soil should dry out slightly between waterings so that oxygen can reach plant roots.

As plants mature, progressively deeper and less frequent watering is called for. This encourages the roots to penetrate far into the soil, where they can tap into moisture reserves and come through dry spells in good condition. Established plantings of drought-tolerant trees, shrubs, and perennials may need only minimal watering during such periods—or even none at all, depending on the soil's structure. A good rule of thumb, though, is to moisten soil to a depth of 12 inches two to three times a month for woody plants, and every 7 to 10 days for herbaceous plants. Roses need at least an inch of water each week during the growing season, and at the height of summer—when roses are in full flower and the days are at their hottest—

they may need an inch of water every other day. For bulbs, normal rainfall usually provides enough moisture. However, if you experience a long period of dry weather during the bulbs' active growth periods, give them at least 1 inch of water a week.

Even though plants in the shade do not face harsh, moisture-evaporating sun, rainfall may be prevented from reaching them by tree foliage or high walls, and the rain that does get through is often soaked up by competing tree roots. As a result, you can't assume that even ample rainfall has met your shade plants' moisture needs, so check the plants regularly. Water them as needed, making sure they receive about an inch of water every 7 to 10 days in a long, slow soaking.

The Best Watering Methods

Watering large areas with a hand-held, high-pressure hose is a waste of time because so much of the water runs off instead of sinking into the soil. Moving hoses and sprinklers from place to place is tedious work as well. For the best results with the least effort, consider a system of low-flow, low-pressure hoses and delivery devices that is custom tailored to your site. These systems can be installed above ground or buried, and not all of them require installation by a professional. Some can be easily put together by the homeowner from materials available in a local garden center (shown in the box at right) and can be ready to operate in just a few hours.

First off, there are two basic ways to apply water to your garden: by sprinkling or by soaking. Sprinkling works well with perennials and ground covers, especially those that thrive in a humid environment. The overhead action helps wash dust and pollutants from foliage, and it also discourages undesirable insects such as spider mites. Roses and bulbs—plants that are prone to fungus diseases—will benefit most from watering with a soaker hose, which supplies a slow, steady flow of water directly into the soil. Soaker hoses are also preferable for areas prone to summer drought such as California, Texas, and other arid spots, and for those flower beds too narrow to be sprinkled without a lot of waste.

Testing Soil Moisture

To determine how well a watering regimen delivers moisture to the root zone of your plants, use a soil auger *(below)* to collect a sample of earth. The auger, basically a hollow cylinder with a handle and a window cut in one side, is pushed into the ground vertically, twisted to free a core of soil, then pulled out at an angle, window side up. Feel the soil; if only the top few inches are moist, adjust your watering regimen to get deeper penetration.

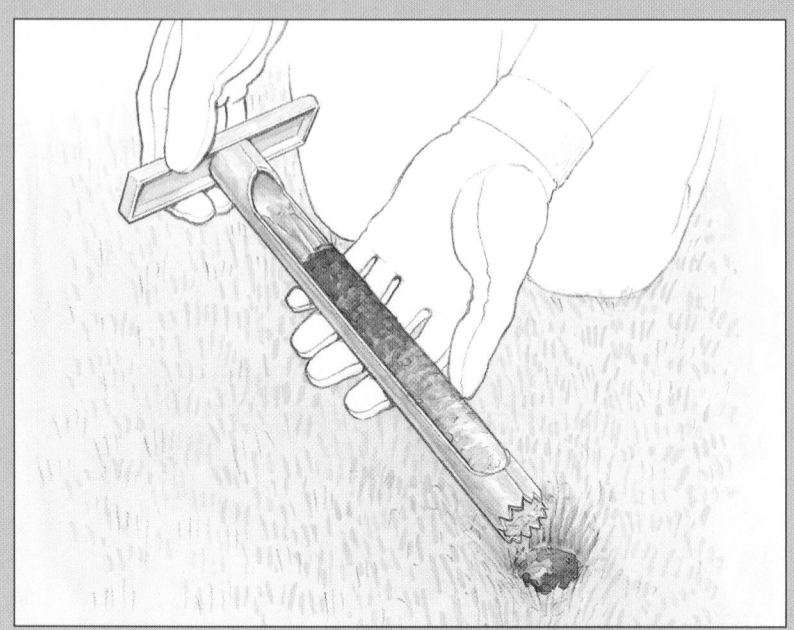

An Off-the-Shelf Irrigation System

At a very reasonable cost, you can put together an irrigation system using garden hoses, soaker hoses, sprinklers, timers, and other accessories widely available at garden centers and hardware stores. The property illustrated at right has a series of setups that are arranged to suit a variety of plantings in different parts of the garden. Except for two garden hoses that need to be moved into position when it is time to water, the irrigation system can be left in place year round.

The system uses two different kinds of soaker hose. One has metal fittings at each end that are identical to those of a conventional garden hose. The other kind allows the gardener maximum flexibility in customizing an irrigation system because it is cut to the lengths appropriate for particular areas.

The various pieces of the system are joined with specially designed tubular fittings. Virtually any layout can be assembled. In the example shown here, a timer—either electronic or mechanical—is attached to each of the three outdoor faucets supplying water to the garden.

The system supplies different areas as follows:

• The backyard lawn and most of the surrounding perennial border are irrigated simultaneously by a single impulse sprinkler, which is stored beside the house between waterings, along with the garden hose *(brown)* that supplies it. A soaker hose with brass fittings on its ends *(green)* is operated off the same faucet via a Y-connector and waters the back of the border, to the left of the lawn.

• Custom-cut lengths of soaker hose are placed in a ring around each of the trees planted behind the garage *(red)*, and are joined by tubular connectors to nonporous supply pipes *(blue)*.

• The garden hose *(brown)* running from the faucet beside the driveway does double duty, supplying the backyard trees and the hedge flanking the driveway. Two-part metal couplings at either end of the hose make the hose easy to connect and disconnect.

• A Y-connector attached to the faucet on the front of the house allows the sunny street-side perennial bed and the shrubs in the partly shaded side yard to be watered independently with soaker hoses *(green)*.

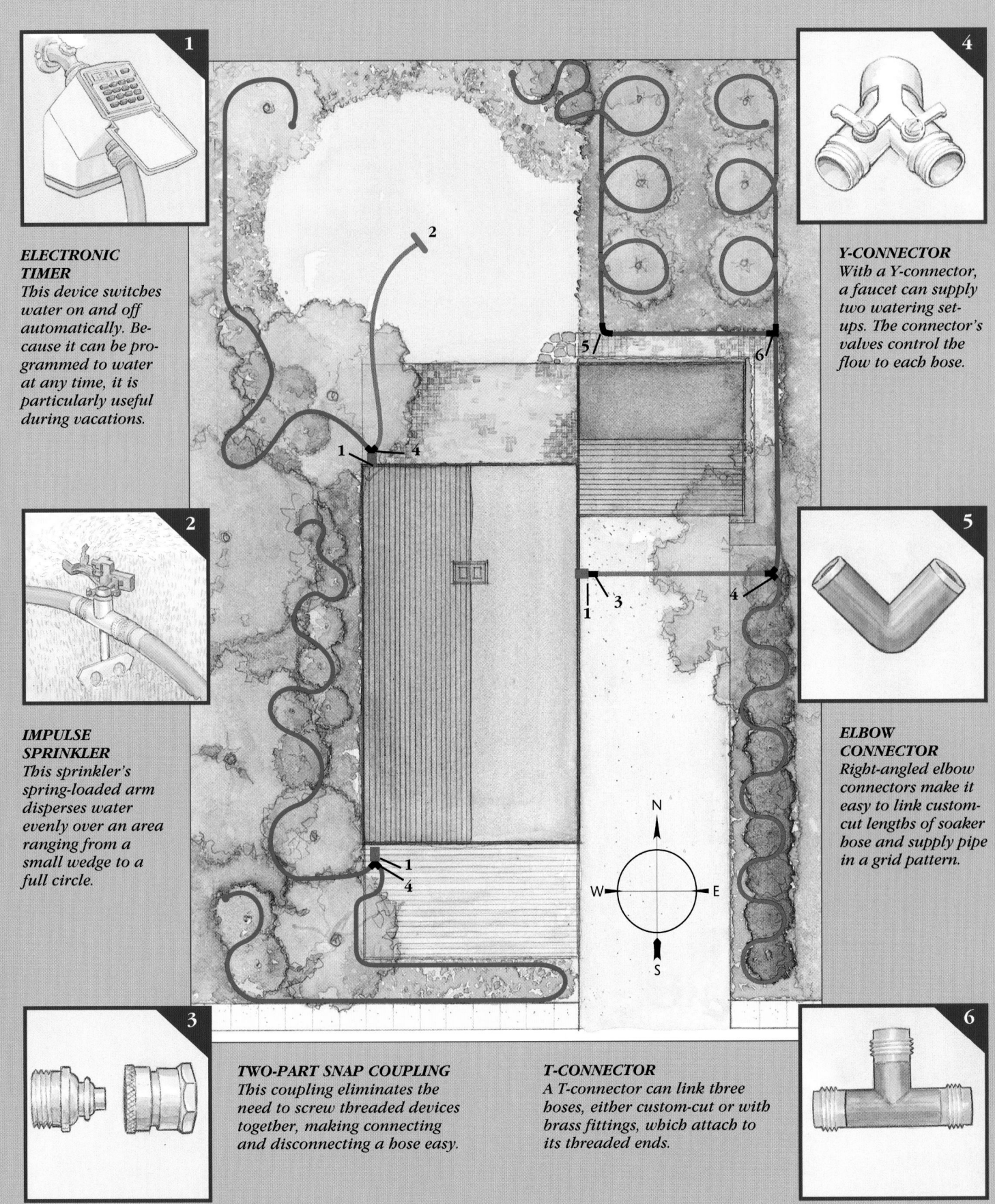

1

ELECTRONIC TIMER
This device switches water on and off automatically. Because it can be programmed to water at any time, it is particularly useful during vacations.

2

IMPULSE SPRINKLER
This sprinkler's spring-loaded arm disperses water evenly over an area ranging from a small wedge to a full circle.

3

TWO-PART SNAP COUPLING
This coupling eliminates the need to screw threaded devices together, making connecting and disconnecting a hose easy.

T-CONNECTOR
A T-connector can link three hoses, either custom-cut or with brass fittings, which attach to its threaded ends.

4

Y-CONNECTOR
With a Y-connector, a faucet can supply two watering set-ups. The connector's valves control the flow to each hose.

5

ELBOW CONNECTOR
Right-angled elbow connectors make it easy to link custom-cut lengths of soaker hose and supply pipe in a grid pattern.

6

In fact, a major disadvantage of sprinklers is that they can waste water, especially if the pressure isn't appropriate to the soil. For clay, where water runoff is a problem, pick a sprinkler that has a low—or slow—delivery rate. A sprinkler with a higher delivery rate suits a sandy soil, providing a fast soaking that minimizes evaporation.

Whatever the soil type, a sprinkler head should produce droplets rather than a fog or mist. (The easiest time to check a sprinkler's output is when it is illuminated by the low, slanting rays of an early-morning or late-afternoon sun.) In addition, the droplets should be emitted at a low angle; sprayed high into the air, water is more likely to drift out of range of the garden or evaporate. All told, as much as 50 percent of the output of an ill-chosen and ill-used sprinkler can go to waste.

Fertilizing for Best Results

In addition to regular moisture and the nutrient boost they gain from decaying organic mulch, your plants will likely benefit from a well-timed dose of fertilizer. For perennials, one application of organic fertilizer just before the growing season

begins will usually be enough. Supplement that with a second application in midsummer or early fall if plants show stunted growth, yellowing leaves, or small, sparse flowers. As an alternative to using a granular fertilizer on a flagging perennial, give the plant a quick, temporary boost by sprinkling or lightly spraying its leaves with a liquid infusion of seaweed or fish emulsion.

Fertilizing should be done with a light hand, especially in the case of chemical fertilizers, which can burn a plant's tender roots. In addition, a nitrogen-rich fertilizer, whether chemical or organic, can cause excess vegetative growth and, as a consequence, make staking necessary *(pages 296-298)*. Be especially sparing with chemical fertilizers late in the season, since a burst of growth then may not have time to mature and will be damaged by winter cold.

Giving Roses a Boost

The simplest way to boost a rose's diet is to use a commercial fertilizer sold as a "rose food." These dry, granular products contain a combination of natural organic materials, which provide nutrients

Watering a Slope

The chart at right shows how a garden's contours and its soil type—sandy, loamy, or clay—affect the rate of water absorption. A sandy, level area, for instance, can absorb up to 1.7 inches of water per hour. But on a sandy 10 percent slope—one whose elevation rises 1 foot for every 10 feet of run—only 1.02 inches are absorbed; the remainder runs off before it can soak into the ground. When the slope increases to 20 percent, the maximum amount of water absorbed in an hour falls still further, to 0.68 inch.

To give a slope a proper soaking without excessive runoff, apply water more slowly than on level ground. In addition, water the top of the slope more heavily than the bottom, since as much as half of that water may move downhill, either on the surface or underground. If you're using soaker hoses, minimize runoff by laying them across the slope.

SOIL TYPE	INCHES OF WATER ABSORBED PER HOUR ON THREE GRADES		
	LEVEL	*10% SLOPE*	*20% SLOPE*
SANDY	.5"-1.7"	.3"-1.02"	.2"-.68"
LOAMY	.25"-1.0"	.15"-.6"	.1"-.4"
CLAY	.1"-.2"	.06"-.12"	.04"-.08"

over a period of time, and inorganic chemicals, which deliver nutrients right away. In general, you'll want to feed your roses before they come out of dormancy in the early spring and again about 2 months before the first expected frost date. (See pages 584-585 for zone and frost date maps.) In warm climates where frost isn't a threat, though, you can feed your plants late in the season for a burst of autumn bloom.

Give roses that bloom repeatedly an additional dose of fertilizer after their first bloom cycle. If you want to grow the largest blooms possible on repeat-blooming modern roses, you may fertilize every month during the growing season, up to the frost cutoff date. Check the fertilizer label, however, for instructions on when and how often to apply a specific product.

Roses growing in containers need more frequent feeding than plants in the ground because the near daily watering they require tends to leach nutrients out of the soil. Your best bet with these plants is to cut the recommended dosage of rose food in half and apply it twice as often. You may also use an appropriate liquid fertilizer—a complete chemical formula mixed with water and typically applied every 2 weeks.

Fertilizing Bulbs

Although bulbs contain their own food supply for the next season's blooms, feeding them each year with commercial fertilizers ensures stellar performances. Fertilize established beds in mid- to late fall when the bulbs are sending out good root growth and before the ground starts to freeze. Use a 9-9-6 slow-release synthetic sprinkled over the ground at the rate of 1 pound per 100 square feet of surface area.

If your bulbs are in a mixed herbaceous bed that has been fertilized regularly, these additional feedings aren't necessary. Also, soils that have been amended with organic materials such as compost, shredded leaves, shredded bark, or aged manure don't need regular, additional fertilizing. Instead, layer compost around the plants in the spring and put down mulch in the fall. If the soil was not amended at planting time, periodic top-dressing with organic-rich materials will create nutrient-laden, moisture-retentive, loamy soils.

A Quick Plant Pick-Me-Up

To give your plants a quick temporary boost, spray a diluted liquid fertilizer, such as manure or compost "tea" or fish emulsion, directly onto the plants' leaves, which will absorb the nutrients quickly. Or pour the fertilizer onto the soil so that it soaks down to the plants' roots.

To make manure or compost tea, first fill a bucket two-thirds full of water. Add manure or compost to bring the water level to the top of the container, and steep for a day or two. Alternatively, put the manure or compost in a cheesecloth or burlap bag and soak it in the water as you would a tea bag. Then, either removing the bag or leaving the solid material at the bottom of the bucket, pour off the liquid into another container and dilute it with more water to the color of weak tea. Never use manure tea full strength; it can burn your plants. (To use the tea in small amounts, dip off what you need and dilute it.) Pour about 1 pint of manure or compost tea around each plant, or pour it into a clean sprayer and spray the leaves thoroughly on both sides. Since manure and compost teas are good sources of nitrogen, this tonic will be especially welcomed by plants with leaves that are yellowing or turning bluish purple underneath or by those that are showing spindly or stunted growth. Plants that bloom throughout the season may benefit from a spritz of fertilizer every 2 weeks or so during flowering.

After globes of silver-lilac flowers have faded, the broad blue-green leaves of Allium karataviense (ornamental onion) will continue to add interest to this perennial border for several weeks. Properly fed, watered, and left undisturbed, clumps of ornamental onions will flower and multiply for 10 seasons or more.

Staking Plants to Add Support

The majority of plants have stems that are strong enough to remain erect when their blossoms open. Nevertheless, you may find that in some cases—with perennials in particular and with some bulbs—you will need to devise simple supports to keep your plants standing upright and the garden looking orderly.

Why Plants Fall Over

In general, plants over 2 feet in height are more likely to need staking for suppprt, especially those plants with large, heavy blossoms; bulbs such as dahlias, turberous begonias, and some gladiolus and lilies fall into this category. A severe thunderstorm can easily flatten such top-heavy plants to the ground and snap off the blooms. In addition, recently planted perennials that haven't had time to develop sturdy stems may need temporary support until they become established.

Sometimes, however, an apparent need for staking may actually indicate a separate problem. Weak stems, for example, may be a sign that the plants need better care. In the case of an old, overgrown clump of perennials, dividing the plants may be the best solution *(pages 310-315)*. Other common sources of trouble include overwatering and a soil oversupplied with nitrogen and lacking in phosphorus and potassium.

Location plays a role as well. Plants exposed to wind will be more susceptible to toppling than those in a sheltered spot, and a sun-loving plant set in the shade may grow lanky and lean toward the light. In either case, transplanting when the plants are dormant should solve the problem.

Staking Methods

When staking is necessary, choose a method that is appropriate to the plant's growth habit. Use

Three Ways to Stake

For a single-stemmed plant, *use a stake about three-fourths the mature plant's height. Loop twine around the stem balfway up and tie it to the stake (left). When the plant is about two-thirds grown, add another loop of twine above the first one. Add a third tie at the base of the flower head when it is about to bloom (far left).*

When a bushy plant is several inches tall, *cut four or five stakes to the height of the mature plant's foliage and drive them into the ground (below). Loop twine from stake to stake 6 to 8 inches above the ground. When blooms appear, add a tier of twine just below the flowers.*

The foliage and blossoms of blue bellflowers and white feverfew hide the bamboo stakes that keep them from sprawling (left). In the photograph below, a framework of twiggy branches is barely visible beneath a stand of yellow yarrow.

To stake a fine-textured perennial such as baby's-breath (above), *choose several twiggy branches about 6 inches shorter than the plant's mature height and sharpen their ends. Push the branches into the ground around the plant, angling them toward its center.*

single stakes to brace the unbranched stems of tall perennials such as pompon, cushion, and decorative chrysanthemums and the delphinium illustrated on the following page. Single staking is also appropriate for gladiolus, dahlias, and other heavy-bloomed bulbs. Bamboo canes, a half-inch in diameter and painted green, are perfect for blending in with the foliage of a fully grown plant, although steel stakes, sometimes coated with dark green plastic, are also available.

Push the support gently into the ground beside the plant's stem; if the stem's natural inclination is to bend a little, angle the stake to follow it. For bulbs, place the stake in the planting hole next to the bulb when you are planting it. Use twine, which may be green or tan colored, to tie the plant's stem to its support—or you may use raffia fiber, paper- or plastic-coated thin wire, or green-tinted plastic gardening tape, which is slightly elastic. Knot the twine around the stake, securing it tightly, then loop the twine loosely around the plant so that it does not constrict the stem.

For dense, bushy perennials such as heliopsis, Shasta daisies, and peonies, you can buy wire hoops or frames at garden centers. These supports are circular, square, or rectangular in shape, with three or four long legs. When the clump of growing foliage is about a foot tall, place the support over the plant and push its legs several inches into the ground until the frame is at the height of the plant growth.

A homemade frame of twine and stakes *(page 296)* is just as effective and much less expensive than wire hoops. For groups of spiky plants such as delphiniums, you may choose to stake them on a frame rather than tie each stem individually. Simply use four or five canes that are about three-fourths as tall as you expect the plant to grow, and push them into the ground around each cluster. As flowers begin to bloom, tie twine to the stakes at height intervals of 12 inches and weave it among the stems.

For staking bushy plants and for baby's-breath and other fine-textured plants, try using twiggy branches *(page 297)*. Birch, oak, buddleia, and vitex are good choices.

When to Stake

The key to successful, unobtrusive staking is planning ahead. Put the stakes in place early in the season, while the plant is still growing upright and before flower buds appear. As the plant fills out, its foliage will hide the stakes *(page 297, top)*.

TIPS FROM THE PROS

André Viette, an internationally known horticulturist and past president of the Perennial Plant Association, grows more than 3,000 varieties of perennials at his nursery in Fishersville, Virginia. He doesn't stake any of them. Weak stems, he says, are often the product of improper watering and fertilizing. Viette recommends watering deeply, rather than lightly and more frequently, and favors organic fertilizer *(pages 294-295)* that is high in phosphorus and low in nitrogen.

Other ways expert gardeners avoid staking their plants include:
- Cutting back tall-growing perennials such as asters when they are about half grown to limit their ultimate height.
- Planting a support of strong-stemmed annuals such as larkspur among newly planted perennials with still-floppy, immature stems.
- Designing a perennial border to have a cottage-garden look, suitable for plants with sprawling, informal growth habits.
- Choosing tall perennials with sturdy stems that don't need staking. This group includes:

Aconitum napellus (monkshood)	*Echinacea purpurea* (purple coneflower)	(narrow-spiked ligularia)
Artemisia lactiflora (white mugwort)	*Hemerocallis cultivars* (daylily)	*Macleaya cordata* (plume poppy)
Aruncus dioicus (goatsbeard)	*Iris sibirica cultivars* (Siberian iris)	*Miscanthus sinensis cultivars* (eulalia)
Astilbe x *arendsii* 'Professor Weilen' (astilbe)	*Liatris pycnostachya* (gay-feather, blazing star)	*Perovskia atriplicifolia* (Russian sage)
Dictamnus albus (gas plant)	*Ligularia stenocephala* 'The Rocket'	

Perennials That Need Staking

TALL FLOWER STEMS: Single Stakes

Chrysanthemum (pompon, cushion, decorative)
Delphinium (*elatum* hybrids)
Digitalis (foxglove)

BUSHY PLANTS: Stakes and Twine or Twiggy Branches

Anchusa azurea 'Dropmore' (bugloss)
Aster novae-angliae (New England aster)
Campanula lactiflora (milky bell-flower)

Centaurea montana (cornflower)
Chrysanthemum maximum (Shasta daisy)
Chrysanthemum morifolium (florist's chrysanthemum)
Chrysanthemum nipponicum (Nippon daisy)
Chrysanthemum parthenium (feverfew)
Clematis heracleifolia 'Davidiana' (clematis)
Gaillardia x *grandiflora* (blanket-flower)
Helenium autumnale 'Bruno', 'Riverton Beauty' (sneezeweed)
Helianthus x *multiflorus* (sunflower)

Heliopsis (false sunflower)
Paeonia lactiflora (peony)
Salvia azurea ssp. *pitcheri* (sage)
Solidago (goldenrod)
Thalictrum delavayi (Yunnan meadow rue)
Thalictrum rochebrunianum (lavender mist meadow rue)
Thalictrum speciosissimum (dusty meadow rue)

FINE-TEXTURED PLANTS: Twiggy Branches

Achillea millefolium (yarrow)

Clematis integrifolia 'Caerulea' (clematis)
Coreopsis grandiflora 'Badengold', 'Mayfield Giant' (tickseed)
Gypsophila paniculata 'Bristol Fairy', 'Perfecta' (baby's-breath)
Limonium (sea lavender, statice)
Linum (flax)
Physostegia (false dragonhead)
Veronica latifolia 'Crater Lake Blue' (speedwell)

'Fanfare' Delphinium

Enhancing the Bloom

Applying a handful of special pruning methods at the right time and to the right plant will increase the number of blooms or the size of the blooms your plants produce. Such techniques—including pinching, thinning, disbudding, deadheading, and cutting back—help keep a plant looking its best and direct energy that would otherwise be spent on seed production into creating more flowers.

Many plants benefit from a combination of the pruning methods. When delphiniums are in bloom, for example, deadheading, or removing faded blossoms, prolongs the display. When flowering stops, cutting back the stalks to the rosette of leaves at the base of each plant makes the plants look tidy and often stimulates a second flowering.

Why Deadhead?

Removing flowers as they begin to fade is an important garden chore, and not for appearance alone. Some perennials, such as pincushion flower and Stokes' aster, may stop blooming if they aren't attended to promptly, and a hybrid perennial allowed to go to seed may in time be crowded out by its less desirable offspring. Deadheading also stimulates some roses—hybrid teas, grandifloras, floribundas, and repeat-blooming climbers—to produce another round of flowers. Cut away the old blooms throughout the growing season, stopping several weeks before the first

Pinching Stem Tips

Using your fingers, pinch off emergent stem tips just above the topmost unfurled leaves. The net result will be three or four new branches, smaller but more plentiful flowers, and a stockier plant. This technique works well with plants that can develop numerous stems and buds, and that look attractive when bushy. Chrysanthemums can be pinched two or three times, up until the flower buds develop.

Perennials to Pinch

Anaphalis
(pearly everlasting)
Anthemis
(golden marguerite)
Artemisia
(wormwood)
Aster
(aster)
Boltonia
(boltonia)
Centaurea
(cornflower)
Chrysanthemum maximum
(Shasta daisy)
Chrysanthemum morifolium
(florist's chrysanthemum)
Chrysanthemum nipponicum
(Nippon daisy)
Echinacea
(purple coneflower)
Erigeron
(fleabane)
Eupatorium
(boneset)
Gaillardia
(blanket-flower)
Gillenia
(bowman's root)
Heliopsis
(false sunflower)
Nepeta
(catmint)
Perovskia
(Russian sage)
Phlox paniculata
(summer phlox)
Physostegia
(false dragonhead)

Deadheading Spent Flowers

For perennials with flowers at the tips of leafy stems, cut just below the fading flowers (right) to stimulate new buds. For plants with leafy flower stems and a rosette of leaves at the base of the plant, cut back to just above the topmost unopened bud. If there are no buds, cut the stem off just above the foliage rosette. For perennials with bare stems, cut off close to the ground to encourage new growth.

Perennials to Deadhead

Achillea
(yarrow)
Anthemis
(golden marguerite)
Armeria
(thrift, sea pink)
Campanula
(bellflower)
Centaurea
(cornflower)
Chrysanthemum maximum
(Shasta daisy)
Chrysanthemum morifolium
(florist's chrysanthemum)
Delphinium
(delphinium)
Digitalis
(foxglove)
Echinops
(globe thistle)
Eupatorium
(boneset)
Gaillardia
(blanket-flower)
Heuchera
(alumroot)
Lobelia
(cardinal flower)
Nepeta
(catmint)
Penstemon
(beardtongue)
Phlox paniculata
(summer phlox)
Platycodon
(balloon flower)
Salvia
(sage)
Scabiosa
(pincushion flower)
Sidalcea
(false mallow)
Stokesia
(Stokes' aster)
Verbena
(verbena)
Veronica
(speedwell)

Deadheading Rhododendrons

The gorgeous blossoms of frothy pink Rhododendron 'Centennial Celebration' suggest the rewards that can be gained by a little tinkering with a plant's growth processes.

Pinching off spent rhododendron flowers can double or triple the number of blossoms next year as well as make the bush more compact. Remove dead blossoms and developing seed pods by bending the woody stem, just above where new buds are forming, and pulling gently until it snaps (below). With the seed pods gone, growth will be concentrated in the new buds. After a few weeks, when the buds have grown out about 4 inches, pinch off the last inch or so of that growth to encourage more shoots to sprout (bottom).

frost—you wouldn't want to promote any new growth that would be vulnerable to the cold.

Not all plants require deadheading. Species, antique, and shrub roses, as well as climbers that bloom once per season, don't need this treatment. And neither do the blossoms of linums, geraniums, and penstemons, which fall off by themselves. Other plants, such as rudbeckia and 'Autumn Joy' sedum, have ornamental seed heads that enliven a garden through the fall and provide interest into the cold months of winter.

Pinching Plants to Stimulate Blooming

Perennials that bloom in midsummer or later and annuals such as coleus and most vines benefit from having their stem tips pinched back early in the growing season. In response to pinching, a stem produces several new branches that together may yield double or even triple the number of blooms on an unpinched stem. The technique makes plants shorter and more compact—and, in the case of perennials, less likely to need staking.

Pinching done early in the growing season has little or no effect on a plant's blooming schedule. If, however, you want to delay a plant's flowering, pinching in midsummer is desirable. The technique is not appropriate for spring perennials, however, because these plants don't have enough time to form new flower buds before their blooming season comes to an end.

Thinning for Larger Flowers

If you'd prefer fewer but larger flowers to an abundance of smaller ones, you can prune away up to a third of a plant's stems, cutting them off at the base. Perennials that bloom in midsummer should be thinned in early spring, and fall bloomers in midsummer. As with pinching, this method isn't suitable for spring bloomers—it merely reduces the number of flowers, with no payoff in size.

Thinning is particularly useful for restoring the display of phlox, sunflower, and rudbeckia that are several seasons old and that, if left unattended, would likely produce a dense mass of stems with undersized blooms. And in addition to rejuvenating a plant's blooming, thinning improves its form, opens its center up to more light, and reduces the risk of disease by improving air circulation. When a plant is heavily thinned, it sends up more vigorous growth from its roots.

Disbudding for Showy Blooms

For peonies, chrysanthemums, and other perennials whose flower buds appear in groups, removing all but the central bud yields a single blue-ribbon blossom. However, this showy flower is likely to make the stem so top-heavy that staking is required *(pages 296-298)*. For a different effect, pinch off the central bud but leave the side buds, which will develop into a spray of flowers.

For exhibition-size blooms on hybrid tea roses and grandifloras, pinch off any buds that sprout below the top, or terminal, bud *(box, right)*. Do this when the buds are tiny, because later disbudding will leave black scars on the stem.

On floribundas and miniature roses, which produce clusters of blossoms, pinch off the terminal, or central, bud in a cluster. Ordinarily, the terminal bud blooms first, then fades and leaves a hole in the cluster just as the adjacent buds are opening up. For prettier sprays that bloom together, remove the terminal bud as early as possible. The other blooms will fill in the space and be more uniform in size. Disbudding is not necessary for antique (old garden) roses, shrub roses, species roses, climbers, and polyanthas.

Cutting Back for Better Shape and Bloom

Cutting back simply means shortening a stem or branch to stimulate new growth, usually from the vegetative bud located just below the point where the branch or stem was pruned. You can steer the new growth in a particular direction—from the center of the plant outward, for example—by choosing where to make your cuts.

This pruning technique may be undertaken at two different times in a perennial's growing cycle, and for different reasons. In both cases, all of the plant's stems should be reduced in height by one-third to one-half. Performed early in the growing season, cutting back results in shorter plants that bloom later than usual. Carried out later in the season, as soon as a plant stops flowering, the shearing stimulates the growth of new foliage and, in the case of catmint, bellflowers, and many other perennials, a second wave of bloom. Refer to the chart on pages 302-303 for more information on when and how to prune specific plants. For particulars on pruning roses, see pages 304-308.

Encouraging the Most Beautiful Blooms

By disbudding, deadheading, and fertilizing your roses, you can spur them to produce abundant blooms that are even more gorgeous than usual. Removing certain buds affects the size or proportion of remaining buds and the flowers that follow; deadheading stimulates the plant to bloom again sooner than it otherwise would. A good diet ensures that the plant has the nutrients it needs to put on a spectacular show.

DISBUDDING *Grasp the cane securely and with your fingers gently pinch off all buds that sprout on the sides of the cane (right). Do this as soon as these lateral buds appear. If the rose is a type that produces clusters of blooms, pinch off the terminal, or center, bud to get blooms of equal size in the spray.*

DEADHEADING *After a bloom has passed its peak, use a clean pair of pruning shears to cut the stem and remove the flower. Make the cut at a 45° angle on the cane, ¼ inch above the highest outward-facing leaf bearing five leaflets (left). The dormant bud seated on the cane at the base of the leaf will grow into a new shoot and produce a bloom within 6 weeks.*

FEEDING *Water the soil thoroughly around the plant. The next day, measure an appropriate fertilizer according to the package directions, pull the mulch away from the plant to expose the soil, and sprinkle the fertilizer around the drip line—the area beneath the outermost leaves. Use a trowel to dig the food into the top 2 inches of soil (right). Last, sprinkle the soil with water to dissolve the nutrients and start them seeping into the soil.*

The perennials, shrubs, and vines listed below can be trimmed or pruned at strategic times during the year to encourage more blooms and produce shapelier plants. Perennials are deadheaded, pinched back, or cut back at intervals during the growing season to discourage seed production and encourage reblooming. Shrubs and vines can be thinned, which involves cutting an old branch or stem back to where it started as a bud or to the ground, or you can give them a heading cut, which removes part of a branch back to a bud or leaf node. Some shrubs and vines benefit from deadheading, and can be encouraged to produce new, flower-bearing branches by cutting them back hard in early spring. In all cases, timing is crucial: Prune shrubs that flower in early spring after they finish blooming; shrubs that flower later, which bloom on new spring growth, should be pruned in late winter or early spring.

		BLOOM SEASON	WHEN TO PRUNE	THIN OUT	PINCH BACK	DEAD-HEAD	COMMENTS
PERENNIALS	*Achillea* (yarrow)	summer				✔	cut back for second flowering
	Anaphalis (pearly everlasting)	late summer to fall			✔		
	Anthemis (golden marguerite)	midsummer to early fall			✔	✔	cut back for second flowering
	Armeria (thrift)	spring to summer				✔	
	Aster x *frikartii* (Frikart's aster)	early summer to fall				✔	
	Boltonia (boltonia)	late summer to frost	early summer		✔		pinch back for compact growth
	Campanula (bellflower)	early to midsummer				✔	
	Centaurea (cornflower)	spring to summer			✔	✔	
	Centranthus (red valerian)	summer					cut back for second flowering
	Chrysanthemum x *morifolium* (florist's chrysanthemum)	late summer to frost	spring to midsummer		✔	✔	pinch back every 3 weeks to midsummer
	Chrysanthemum x *superbum* (Shasta daisy)	spring to fall			✔	✔	
	Delphinium (delphinium)	summer				✔	cut back for second flowering
	Dianthus (pink, carnation)	spring to summer				✔	shear mat-forming types to promote compact growth
	Digitalis (foxglove)	spring to summer				✔	
	Echinacea (coneflower)	summer			✔		
	Echinops (globe thistle)	summer				✔	cut back for second flowering
	Erigeron (fleabane)	summer			✔		
	Eupatorium (boneset)	summer			✔	✔	
	Gaillardia (blanket-flower)	summer to fall			✔	✔	
	Gillenia (bowman's root)	spring to summer					
	Heliopsis (false sunflower)	midsummer to fall			✔		
	Nepeta (catmint)	summer			✔	✔	cut back for second flowering

		BLOOM SEASON	WHEN TO PRUNE	THIN OUT	PINCH BACK	DEAD-HEAD	COMMENTS
PERENNIALS	*Penstemon* (cardinal flower)	spring to fall			✔	✔	cut back for second flowering
	Perovskia (Russian sage)	summer			✔		
	Phlox paniculata (summer phlox)	spring to fall			✔	✔	cut back for second flowering
	Platycodon (balloon flower)	summer			✔	✔	
	Scabiosa (pincushion flower)	summer				✔	
	Stokesia (Stokes' aster)	summer				✔	cut back for second flowering
	Veronica (speedwell)	spring to summer				✔	cut back for second flowering
SHRUBS	*Buddleia* (butterfly bush)	summer	early spring			✔	cut to 12 inches to rejuvenate
	Caryopteris (bluebeard)	summer to fall	early spring				cut to 12 inches to rejuvenate
	Forsythia (forsythia)	early spring	after flowering	✔			cut branches in winter for indoor forcing
	Halesia (silver bell)	midspring	after flowering				
	Hibiscus (rose of Sharon)	summer to fall	early spring				head back to 2 or 3 buds in spring for larger flowers
	Hydrangea (hydrangea)	summer	early spring	✔			head back in midsummer for second flowering
	Philadelphus (mock orange)	early summer	after flowering	✔			cut to 12 inches to rejuvenate
	Potentilla (bush cinquefoil)	summer to frost	late winter	✔			
	Rhododendron (rhododendron)	spring	after flowering		✔	✔	snap off spent blooms; pinch back new growth a few weeks later
	Spiraea (spirea)	spring to summer	after flowering	✔			cut to 8 inches to rejuvenate
	Syringa (lilac)	spring	after flowering	✔		✔	cut to 3 feet to rejuvenate
	Weigela (weigela)	spring	after flowering	✔			
VINES	*Campsis* (trumpet creeper)	late summer	spring				head back summer growth to 3 or 4 buds
	Clematis (spring-blooming clematis)	spring	after flowering				cut back old vines
	Clematis (fall-blooming clematis)	summer to fall	early spring				head back to 3 or 4 buds
	Lonicera japonica (Japanese honeysuckle)	summer	early spring				head back to 3 or 4 buds
	Wisteria (wisteria)	midspring	end of summer/ early spring				cut summer growth to 2 inches; cut end tips in spring

Pruning Roses

Pruning is a necessary chore for many plants, but roses above all others. Sooner or later, any unpruned rose—even a species or low-maintenance shrub rose—will grow lanky, and flower production will gradually diminish as older canes become exhausted. Neglected, unpruned roses are also more vulnerable to pests and diseases, and can eventually die if left untended. Pruning not only protects the plant's health, it also encourages strong root development and stimulates growth. Well-trimmed plants are attractively shaped, their flowers are bigger and more abundant, and their canes are stronger and more vigorous.

What to Prune Away

How and when roses are pruned varies according to the type of rose in your garden, the growth habits you hope to encourage, and where you live. But there are some general approaches to

pruning you'll need to know before tackling your particular plants. First, you should examine the base of the rose for suckers—canes growing up from the rootstock, below the bud union. If left unchecked, these can overwhelm and eventually kill the grafted cultivar. Clipping them off at ground level is an exercise in frustration, however; they will only grow back. You must remove them as close to the bud union as possible.

Next, look for dead, diseased, and damaged canes; they will appear blackened and withered. Cut the canes back to healthy white or pale green pith, or back to the bud union if no healthy tissue is visible. It is also a good rule of thumb to remove any cane thinner than a pencil, including small, twiggy shoots with fewer than five leaves; if they appear too weak to support blossoms, remove them. Canes growing in awkward directions—into the center of the plant or into tangles where they will rub against each other and become damaged—are also candidates for pruning. Cutting

Roses That Need Little Pruning

'Ballerina'
'Belle Poitevine'
'Blanc Double
    de Coubert'
'Bonica'
'Boule de Neige'
'Erfurt'
'Frau Dagmar
    Hartopp'
'Gabrielle Privat'
'Hansa'
'Henry Hudson'
'Jens Munk'
'La Marne'
'Linda Campbell'
'Max Graf'
'Mrs. B. R. Cant'
'Nearly Wild'
'Nozomi'
'Pinkie'
'Red Cascade'
R. banksiae
    banksiae
R. palustris
'Roseraie de l'Hay'
'Sea Foam'
'The Fairy'
'Thérèse Bugnet'
'White Meidiland'

'Hansa'

Pruning a Hardy Rose

Hardy roses include such antique varieties as damasks, gallicas, centifolias, albas, and mosses, as well as shrub roses and some species roses. These tend to be robust plants that require less pruning and care in general. Nevertheless, all hardy roses benefit from a spring cleanup that includes trimming away dead, diseased, or damaged canes; canes too thin and weak to support flowers; and any crossing canes or canes growing into the center of the plant. Hardy roses benefit as well from an overall shaping to improve the appearance of the plant. Pruning all the longer canes back by one-third will give the bush a well-tended, healthy look; it will also promote outward growth and abundant blossoms. Make the cuts in late spring, after the rose has flowered.

A. Cut off dead canes and those more than 4 years old at the bud union (left). Cut back diseased or damaged canes to healthy wood ¼ inch above an outward-facing bud, or, if there is no healthy tissue, to the bud union. Use loppers for canes over ½ inch in diameter and make clean, angled cuts.

B. When two canes are entangled or rubbing against each other, cut away the smaller of the two. Prune below the point of contact and about ¼ inch above an outward-facing bud; this will direct new growth away from the center of the plant.

C. Cut spindly stems that are too weak to support blossoms—generally those thinner than a pencil—back to a junction with a larger, healthier cane.

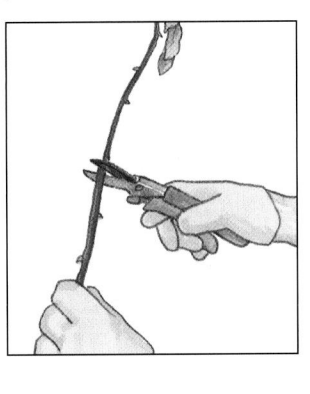

D. To give the plant an overall full, rounded shape, cut off one-third of the overall length of the longer canes. Cut off the tips of all other canes to stimulate growth.

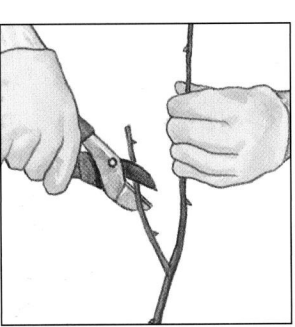

E. To increase plant fullness and encourage the production of more blossoms, cut lateral growth down to an outward-facing bud, pruning as much as one-third of the length of the cane.

How to Remove Suckers

Suckers—those canes that sprout from the rootstock below the bud union—are aptly named since they drain energy from the rootstock and can overcome and kill the cultivar if they are not removed. You can easily identify suckers: They are thinner and paler than the cultivar and display a different leaflet pattern. Do not cut suckers off at ground level, as this stimulates growth just as pruning does. Instead, dig gently down to where the sucker attaches to the rootstock and pull it away, taking care not to disturb the plant.

them away will not only improve the appearance of the rose and avoid further injury to canes, it will also open up the center of the plant to air and light, which will help prevent disease.

How Much to Prune

Once the initial pruning of unwanted wood is complete, further cuts are usually made to stimulate growth, or to give your rose an overall shaping. Shaping typically takes the form of light, moderate, or hard pruning.

Light pruning, usually performed on antique, species, and shrub roses, involves cutting back the ends of most canes by no more than one-third. In fact, some gardeners cut away just the tips of canes on species roses and low-maintenance shrubs. Grandifloras and floribundas should also receive this type of light pruning if abundant blooms are desired. But if your species and shrub

Pruning a Modern Rose

1. Cut off dead canes and those more than 4 years old at the bud union. Cut back diseased or damaged canes to healthy white or pale green pith (inset), or, if no healthy tissue can be found, to the bud union. Next, remove canes that are crossed and those smaller than a pencil in diameter. Thin out any canes growing toward the center of the plant. Make all cuts at a 45° angle ¼ inch above an outward-facing bud.

2. Decide whether you wish to do moderate or hard pruning. If hard pruning is your goal, remove all but three or four healthy canes, leaving them no more than a foot long (below). This will yield large, show-type blooms. For moderate pruning, leave six to 12 canes at about one-third of their original height, or 1 to 2 feet. This will produce abundant, slightly smaller blooms and a fuller rosebush. In deciding how to prune, remember that modern roses with an upright habit look best if pruned to an urn shape, with canes growing evenly outward and upward.

roses begin to grow leggy under this regimen, prune some of the main canes back by one-third and the rest back by about two-thirds to bring them back to a healthier, fuller shape.

Moderate pruning is generally practiced on modern roses with an upright habit and where a larger, fuller plant is desired. Remove all but six to 12 canes, and cut back the remaining canes to a length of 1 to 2 feet. Practice moderate pruning if you are inexperienced or unsure about the growth habits of your roses. Severe, or hard, pruning is practiced on hybrid teas and grandifloras when show-quality blooms are desired. In this case, all but two to four canes are removed; those left should be cut to a length of between 6 and 12 inches, or up to 18 inches with grandifloras. In northern climates, where roses can be badly damaged during the winter, plants may need hard pruning in spring. In milder climates, hard pruning may restore a weakened, neglected plant to health.

Making a Cut

Before making a cut, look for a healthy bud that is just beginning to swell and that faces in the direction in which you want the new shoot to grow. Generally this will be facing outward on the cane, but in some cases you may wish to encourage growth toward the center of a leggy, spreading plant. Make a clean, sharp cut at a 45° angle ¼ inch above, and in the same direction as, the bud. The angled cut ensures that rainwater will run off the stem rather than collect as it would in a flat cut. And some experts believe that such a cut, by exposing more of the cane to the air, will help it heal more quickly.

Tools for Pruning

You will need three cutting tools for pruning roses: pruning shears, long-handled loppers, and a pruning saw. Bypass pruning shears, which have curved, scissor-action blades, are the best for all-purpose work such as removing canes, flowers, and leaves. Avoid anvil shears, which have a straight blade that strikes against a blunt surface: They can crush delicate rose canes and leave them vulnerable to pests and diseases. Anvil shears should be used only on wood that is completely dead.

Long-handled loppers have short, heavy-duty blades useful for cutting canes that are too thick for pruning shears, or that are difficult to reach. For woody canes that are too thick even for lop-

Pruning Climbers and Ramblers

To prune ramblers and once-blooming climbers, wait till after they flower so as not to remove potential flowering buds. Cut off old, woody canes at the bud union (above), and remove all weak, diseased, or overlong canes. Cut flowering shoots back to four or five sets of leaves.

Prune repeat-blooming climbers while they are dormant, in late winter or early spring. Remove suckers; dead, diseased, or damaged canes; and weak new growth. Prune out the oldest canes, keeping three or four vigorous young canes; trim these back to promote even distribution of buds. If you tie long young canes horizontally to a support, pointing their ends downward, you will encourage lateral growth and more blooms.

pers, use a pruning saw with large teeth and a long, thin, curved blade.

Keep all of your pruning tools sharp and clean. Dull blades make jagged cuts and can even tear the canes, creating entry points for infestation. Disinfect pruning tools after each use with rubbing alcohol or a solution made from 1 part household bleach to 9 parts water.

As important as the right tools for the job are the right clothes. Be sure to wear gloves—thick leather ones are best—so that you can grasp thorny stems properly to make the cleanest cuts. And when you need to reach into the spiky interior of a plant, you'll appreciate having on long sleeves and pants.

The Right Time of Year to Prune

In general, the best time to prune is just as the plant's dormancy period ends—when you see buds beginning to swell on the plant but before active growth has begun. In mild climates, dormancy may end in late winter—as early as January—or in early spring; in locations with severely cold winters you may have to wait until April. In any event, you must be sure the threat of a late freeze has passed. Some gardeners wait to prune their roses until forsythia is in bloom.

The timing and extent of pruning is also determined by the type of roses in your garden. Hybrid tea roses, grandifloras, floribundas, miniatures, and standard roses should all receive a hard pruning in early spring before the onset of new growth. Since these roses bloom on new wood, pruning is necessary to stimulate the growth of new canes and ensure an abundance of blooms. Antique roses and shrub and species roses may require no more than a hygienic pruning in spring to remove dead, diseased, or damaged canes. If the plants have become unshapely, however, wait until after their flowers have faded to prune them back within bounds. There are exceptions to this rule: Hybrid perpetuals, hybrid musks, noisettes, Chinas, repeat-blooming damasks and portlands, old garden tea roses, and moss roses bloom on new wood, so if they require shaping up, it should be done in early spring.

Ramblers and once-flowering climbers bloom on growth from the previous year, so early-spring pruning should involve nothing more than the removal of dead wood. Wait until the plants have finished blooming to perform any shaping that needs to be done. Prune repeat-blooming climbers while they are dormant—in late winter or early spring.

After spring pruning is finished, keep your plants well watered. Pruning induces new growth, and water is crucial to maintaining it.

In summer, deadheading is all that's necessary. But if you are cutting roses for flower arrangements, make the same type of cut you use when pruning—angled, and ¼ inch above a bud. Stop deadheading and cutting blooms a month before the first expected frost to avoid winterkill of new growth.

Fall pruning is undesirable in most climates, except to cut back very long canes. But in areas where winter temperatures drop to between 10° and 15° F for as long as 2 weeks at a time, hybrid roses will need pruning after the first frost. Cut them down to three to six canes, and shorten each cane to 1 to 2 feet. Then protect the roses from the extreme cold *(opposite)*.

Pruning a Standard Rose

Begin pruning a standard, or tree, rose by removing suckers, which in this case grow not only from the rootstock but along the trunk. Pull them from the rootstock, and cut them as close as possible to the trunk. Remove undesirable canes, twiggy stems, and canes that rub or grow into the plant center (right). Next, depending on the cultivar, trim to produce either a round, symmetrical shape or a loose, cascading one. Aim for even spacing and uniform cane length, leaving four to six canes pruned to about 12 inches (far right). Prune only to outward-facing buds.

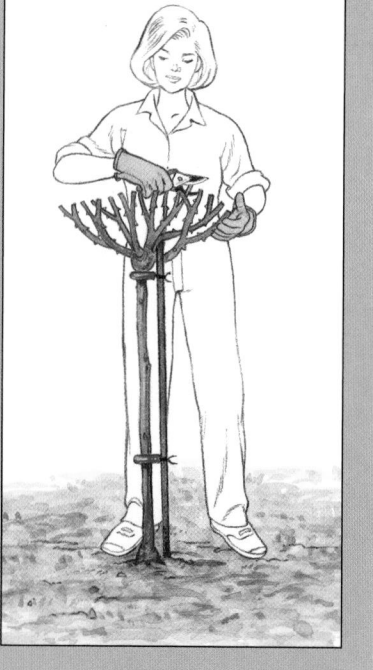

Winter Protection

In late summer to midfall, reduce watering and stop deadheading and applying nitrogen fertilizers, both of which spur new growth. Where temperatures drop to between 10° and 15°F for 2 weeks at a time, you can protect most roses by heaping material around the plant's base *(far right)*. Where temperatures drop below zero, bury the entire plant *(below)*; this is especially important for tree roses. To insulate climbers, remove them from their support and tie the canes loosely with twine. Dig a trench, lay the canes in it, and cover with soil and organic mulch. Add more mulch after the ground freezes. Do not start winter protection too soon; the increased warmth may produce new growth that will be hurt by a sudden chill.

1. After the first frost, cut back all canes to 1 to 2 feet. This helps the plant conserve energy and eliminates the parts that are the weakest and likeliest to suffer damage in a freeze. It also eliminates the possibility of injury caused by canes whipping against each other in the wind.

2. In climates where winter temperatures drop periodically into the teens or go as low as 10° to 15°F for 2 weeks at a stretch, surround rosebushes with imported soil, mulch, or leaves. Pile the insulating material up around the plant and between the canes to a height of 6 to 12 inches above the bud union. Then spread a layer of straw, loose leaves, peat moss, or ground bark over the mound.

4. Next, fill the cage to the top with leaves, straw, or ground bark. Make sure not to pack the insulating material too tightly; wet, matted leaves can harbor disease. Avoid removing the cages too early at winter's end—a late-spring freeze can be fatal to a newly exposed rose. After the last freeze, gently remove the leaves or straw and carefully scrape away the earth mound covering the canes. Rinse the canes with a light spray of water.

3. If winter temperatures regularly drop below 0°F, or if extended frigid weather is predicted, mound soil around the base of the plant to a height of 6 to 12 inches above the bud union. Then form a cage from chicken wire or tar paper stapled together, and place it around your rose. To secure the cage, pack another few inches of earth around its base.

Propagating Perennials
by Division

Most herbaceous perennials enthusiastically colonize their surroundings, spreading new roots and shoots outward every year. Though their stems and leaves may die back each fall, the roots are dormant through the winter, then thrust out new growth in both roots and shoots every spring. Perennials are slow to mature, and generally spend more than one season growing roots and foliage before they bloom or propagate in any other way. This is the vital habit distinguishing them from the annuals, which throw their energy into growing fast, blooming, and scattering seed in the single season before they die.

Because nurseries have to work with nature's timing, the perennials they propagate and sell must be carefully tended for a year or more before coming to market. This makes perennials a costly crop for nurseries—one reason they carry higher prices than annuals. If you are growing perennials in your garden, however, propagation is already taking place. To propagate your own plants, you have only to take charge of the process.

The dusty pink blooms of Sedum telephium 'Autumn Joy' turn russet in the fall, then last through the winter as eye-catching seed heads. Trouble free if grown in well-drained soil, sedums are easy to propagate by division or from stem cuttings (pages 316-317).

Dividing to Increase Plants

The simplest propagation practice in perennial gardens is division, which takes direct advantage of the plants' tendencies to spread. Division is simply separating young, already rooted offshoots from mature perennials and placing them elsewhere in the garden. The independent plants produced are called divisions, or slips. New plants created by this method develop the same growth traits and flower color as the originals, so you can confidently fill flower beds with your favorites. Another bonus from division is that most slips establish themselves quickly and bloom the same season or the following one.

Dividing for Healthy Plants

Division is also a means of maintaining your mature perennial plantings; many perennials look their best only when regularly divided. Gaillardias and chrysanthemums tend to deteriorate at their centers, while growing actively around the edges. You may wind up with unsightly, dead-looking patches in the midst of your lovely blooming clumps unless you dig the plants out, trim old growth away, and reset new growth in its place.

Other perennials, such as rudbeckia, outgrow their spaces, crowd their neighbors, and make the whole flower bed more susceptible to disease. Division of such plants thins the invaders, permits air to circulate through the bed once more, and lets you develop a colorful new border with your fledgling plants elsewhere in the garden.

Division is also the easiest way to keep some of the shorter-lived perennials growing in your garden year after year. Members of the genus *Dianthus*—sometimes called pinks—generally last only a few years. You must replace the plants with offspring if you want to keep these popular plants growing in your garden.

When to Divide

Although a few plants, like the globe thistle and the gas plant, will remain the same size in the same place for years, they are exceptions in the world of perennials. Most genera actively grow outward from their centers as they deplete soil nutrients there and develop new roots away from the plants' centers. This pattern produces a natural crisis, and when it arrives, perennials send out clear distress signals. These include a dead, woody portion at the center of the clump, fewer blooms, and fewer stems emerging in the spring. Crowns or rhizomes may be forced out above the surrounding soil, and a plant may grow so large that there is no air space around it in the bed. The remedy is division.

Perennials in need of division should be tackled while they are dormant or growing vegetatively, not when they are preparing to bloom. For most plants, this means early spring to early summer, as soon as the growing crowns can be seen. (Exceptions include plants like doronicum, primrose, iris, and other early-spring bloomers, which should be divided after flowering.) When performing any divisions, work on a cool, cloudy day—it helps keep the plants' roots moist while they are exposed to the air.

How to Begin

Division starts at the roots of the plant, since offshoots must have their own roots already formed if they are to live on their own. The root systems of perennials fall into several categories—fibrous, fleshy, and rhizomatous.

Most perennials have fibrous roots. These resemble slender, outspread fingers, and grow relatively close to the soil surface. A few plant types, most notably *Hemerocallis* (daylily), have thick, fleshy roots that can closely intertwine. Another handful of perennials, including iris, grow from rhizomes—hard, tuberous stems planted just below the soil's surface.

Choose your division method to match the root type of your plants *(list of plants, above; division methods, pages 312-315)*. For every method, the overall procedure is the same: Gather your tools and prepare replanting sites ahead of time; work fast; protect roots from drying out; and pamper the slips while they acclimate.

Plants Recommended for Division

FIBROUS ROOTS:
Acanthus (bear's-breech)
Achillea (yarrow)
Ajuga (bugleweed)
Alchemilla (lady's-mantle)
Allium (flowering onion)
Amsonia (bluestar)
Anchusa (bugloss)
Anemone (windflower)
Arabis (rock cress)
Arenaria (sandwort)
Armeria (thrift, sea pink)
Artemisia (wormwood)
Aruncus (goatsbeard)
Astilbe (astilbe, false spirea)
Brunnera (brunnera)
Campanula (bellflower)
Centaurea (knapweed)
Delphinium (delphinium)

Dianthus (pinks)
Dicentra (bleeding heart)
Doronicum (leopard's-bane)
Geranium (cranesbill)
Geum (avens)
Hosta (plantain lily, funkia)
Iris sibirica (Siberian iris)
Lamium (dead nettle)
Ligularia (golden-ray)
Limonium (sea lavender, statice)
Lobelia (cardinal flower)
Lychnis (catchfly, campion)
Monarda (bee balm)
Nepeta (catmint)
Oenothera (sundrop, evening primrose)
Phlox paniculata (summer phlox)
Polygonum (smartweed, knotweed)
Potentilla (cinquefoil, five-finger)

Primula (primrose)
Pulmonaria (lungwort)
Rudbeckia (coneflower)
Sedum (stonecrop)
Smilacina (false Solomon's-seal)
Solidago (goldenrod)
Stachys (lamb's ears)
Stokesia (Stokes' aster)
Thalictrum (meadow rue)
Tricyrtis (toad lily)
Trollius (globeflower)
Veronica (speedwell)
Viola (violet)
FLESHY ROOTS:
Hemerocallis (daylily)
Kniphofia (torch lily, tritoma)
RHIZOMES:
Bergenia (bergenia)
Iris (iris)

Regular division necessary for health of plants.

Before beginning the actual work of dividing, consider both the parent plant and your intentions for the offspring. Do you want to populate the garden with many shoots, even if some will not bloom this year? Or do you want to turn last year's single clump into three distinct blooming plants? Or is your aim to rejuvenate the parent by maintenance division, whether or not you end up with more individual plants? Starting out knowing what you want will shorten the handling time for the plants—and the less time they're out of their natural element, the better.

Ready the soil in the area where you will put the new divisions, so that they can go into the ground immediately. Preparation should include adding a soil amendment such as compost, peat, or sand as necessary to ensure good drainage and improve soil structure. Judging by the size of the parent plant, allow plenty of space around the hole you dig for each new shoot, so that the plant will not be crowded when it is mature. If the ground is not wet from a recent watering or rain, be sure to water anything you plan to divide at least an hour before you start working.

Making the Cut

The simplest way to divide a perennial with a healthy center is to slice off the new growth from the sides with a spade or sharp knife, leaving the main clump undisturbed in the ground. This is also a good way to handle invasive plants that seem to have no recognizable center. Cut so that each section of new growth includes one or two visible growing crowns or shoots, and an intact portion of root. Daylilies, phlox, centaurea, and bleeding heart are among those you can divide this way. If a plant looks poorly at the center, or if you want many divisions, dig it out of the bed, using the technique shown below.

Both your new divisions and the parent plants require a little extra care after the main procedures are complete. Set the new divisions into prepared holes, spreading out the roots and positioning the crowns at ground level, not below. Press soil firmly over the roots, eliminating air pockets and giving the roots good contact with the soil. If you have lifted the parent plants from the soil, take this opportunity to work up the soil there, too, and add compost to the holes before resetting the plants in them.

If you are dividing in late summer or fall, when perennials have full complements of foliage, prune back the stems and leaves of plant divisions by about half after planting. This restores balance to the plant, giving the smaller root system less top growth to nourish and reducing water loss through respiration. If you are dividing in early spring, before the plants have developed much top growth, cutting back is unnecessary.

Water all your new plantings thoroughly and keep the soil moist for the next few days. Providing shade from full sun for a week also helps—an old lawn chair or pruned-off evergreen branches strategically placed can intercept the scorching

How to Divide Perennials with Fibrous Roots

While the main goals of division are to separate offshoots for distribution and to rejuvenate aging perennials, keeping all the plants healthy and growing afterward is a major concern. Give them the best chance to thrive by minimizing root damage, preserving a balance between the top growth and the roots, and treating new transplants tenderly after separation and moving.

The tools for division will vary with the type of plant you're working on, but you probably already have the equipment on hand. You'll need a spade or a shovel for digging large clumps and a trowel for small, shallow-rooted ones; a bucket of water or a hose for rinsing soil off the roots; and an old kitchen knife or cross-bladed shears. Wet burlap is useful to cover dug-up plants when you're not working on them.

Keep spades, knives, and shears sharp so you can make clean cuts. Having all the equipment at your fingertips before you start speeds the operation and spares the plants unnecessary stress.

1. *Dig deeply around the plant with a sharp shovel or spade, along a line below the tips of the foliage. Don't use a fork for this job—it is too likely to sever roots. To test whether you have freed the root mass, grasp the foliage at its base and rock the plant gently. Dig deeper anywhere roots are still holding on.*

2. *Lift the plant carefully from the ground, supporting the roots with your hands (left). Shake and rinse off the soil until you can clearly see the roots and the crowns—where roots join stems. Cut out and discard any old, woody tissue, rotted soft tissue, or areas of insect damage on roots or foliage.*

312

rays. Because the smaller root systems of divisions are especially vulnerable to drought in dry spells and to frost-heave damage in winter, protect them with ample mulch through their first seasons.

Divisions well established in their transplant locations will soon show new growth. When they do, they should share in your normal maintenance procedures, including fertilizing and pinching back to encourage bushy growth. If it's still early in the growing season, you may well see blooms this year on the newly divided plants of most genera.

Dividing Fleshy-Rooted Plants

Hemerocallis (daylily), *Kniphofia* (torch lily), and a few other perennials grow from fleshy root-stocks, which tangle together underground and can be more difficult to separate than fibrous roots. Where the plant clumps are large and unwieldy, some experts recommend dividing them as they stand in the flower bed *(page 314)*. This approach may cause some foliage and root damage, but daylilies bounce back very quickly; most divisions that have two or three fans of foliage will take hold and bloom happily the next season. To divide smaller clumps of daylilies, dig them up completely, as you would fibrous-rooted perennials. Wash and examine the roots before cutting them apart; slice off any soft, rotted tissue and discard it in the compost pile.

Replant your fleshy-rooted divisions in holes that you have prepared; spread the roots out horizontally and press the soil firmly around them. To minimize water loss through respiration, trim off half of the foliage on each fan. Keep the new plants well watered for the first few days while they adjust to their new spot.

Dividing Rhizomatous Perennials

Bearded iris and bergenia grow from rhizomes—stems that grow horizontally underground and

3. Separate the plants into smaller clumps. Some roots—like those of primroses or Siberian iris—can be pulled apart by hand, as at left above. Some, like those of phlox, can be teased apart with a hand fork. For solid, tangled roots use a knife, *spade, or other sharp instrument to separate stubborn masses (above, right). Cut down among the roots to divide the various growing crowns and stems. Each division should have a growing crown or two and some fibrous roots attached. After* *you have severed your divisions, examine each one again, removing any dead or rotted sections. It's a good idea to thin out matted roots; this will stimulate strong new root growth. Trim off broken or very long roots.*

Three Ways to Divide Daylilies

Daylilies—the most widely grown of the fleshy-rooted perennials and the most frequently divided—spread exuberantly from single, original plantings to form densely packed clumps. Although they keep blooming even when crowded, you'll have even more of a good thing after you divide them *(below)*.

The best time to work on daylilies is in early fall, after flowering has finished for the season, but well before frost. Before digging up any plants, prepare holes in which to replant the divisions. Obviously, you will have to cut roots inside a clump, but as you dig to free the edges, keep clear of the roots by digging around the clump just outside the leaf tips. A sharp edge on your shovel or knife makes the job a bit easier on both you and the plant.

Large clumps of daylilies can be divided right in the ground. Plan your cuts so that each division will include one to three foliage fans and the root tissue below. Drive a sharp spade or shovel down firmly between the fans, cutting through the roots (below). Then dig up the sections, working from the outside of the clump toward the center.

To shave outer fans off the edges of a large clump without disturbing or replanting the lilies at the center, angle the spade as you drive it in between fans, keeping one to three fans in each group (below). Go deep enough to cut the roots, then dig around and under the cut sections and lift them away from the sides of the main clump.

To divide small clumps of daylilies, dig them out of the ground with a spade or shovel, digging in a wide circle just outside the foliage tips to avoid roots. Lift the entire clump from the hole, supporting the center of the clump as you lift. Rinse hardened soil from the roots, then cut them apart with a sharp knife, or divide them with your spade as they lie on the ground (below).

store nourishment that is drawn in through small feeder roots. Irises in particular show their need for division and renewal by diminished bloom. Really crowded specimens of both iris and bergenia will push their rhizomes up out of the soil, sometimes causing the plant to keel over, pulling exposed rhizomes completely out of the soil.

The best time to divide rhizomatous plants is after they have bloomed. Because rhizomes lie close to the surface, they are easy to dig up with a garden fork or spade, but you must loosen the soil thoroughly to minimize breakage of the feeder roots. Some rhizomes are prone to rot and to infestation by root maggots. Before you dig, sterilize your tools in a solution of 1 part chlorine bleach to 10 parts water; once you've dug up a rhizome, dip it in the bleach solution as well. Use a sharp knife to divide the rhizomes, and shears to trim the foliage. Replant the divisions in shallow, trenchlike holes that have soil mounded up in the center. Spread the feeder roots out evenly over the mounds of soil.

Layering to Form New Roots

Another strategy for dividing some perennials is to encourage a plant to form roots where none exist—along stems—and then separate the root-studded stem as a new plant. This is done by an old-fashioned technique called layering. Layering lets you create divisions during the growing season while leaving plants in place in their beds—even while they bloom. And it takes almost none of your valuable gardening time.

Plants that respond well to layering include

those with creeping stems or stems that are upright but flexible and long enough to be bent to the ground without breaking. *Dianthus, Geranium, Campanula, Arabis,* and *Phlox subulata* are all good candidates.

The best time to begin the rooting process is spring, as soon as stems have grown to several inches long. Start with a plant that has some space in the bed around it, since you will be staking the stems down on the soil. You may need to pin down the stems if they are too firm to stay down obediently; fence staples, hairpins, or a small rock will usually do the job.

Choose an outer stem and trim off all but the top few leaves. Bend the stem down to the soil surface so that the leafless part touches the ground. Loosen the soil there and bury the stem about 2 inches deep, pinning it in place if necessary. Keep the stem tip, with its remaining leaves, above the ground, staking it to hold it erect. Water the area thoroughly and mulch to help keep the moisture in. If you want more rooting stems, you can repeat this treatment all the way around the plant, if the plant and the surrounding space are large enough. Once you've positioned the stems, all you have to do is keep the layered area moist while you wait for roots to form along the buried section of stem.

How long the rooting takes will vary according to climate and the type of perennial you're layering. Even while stems are staked and buried, their tips may bloom for you. It is easiest to leave the whole setup alone, if you can, until the next spring. Then dig up the rooted stems, sever them below the roots, and plant the new individuals as you would any other rooted division.

Dividing and Planting Rhizomes

Since a rhizome is a specialized form of stem growing horizontally underground, it needs gentle uprooting and careful replanting. The technique is shown here with iris rhizomes.

Use these same steps to divide bergenia, but don't trim back its foliage, as shown in Step 3; instead, remove a couple of leaves entirely before replanting the rhizome.

 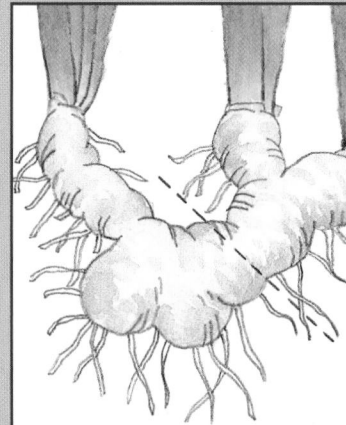 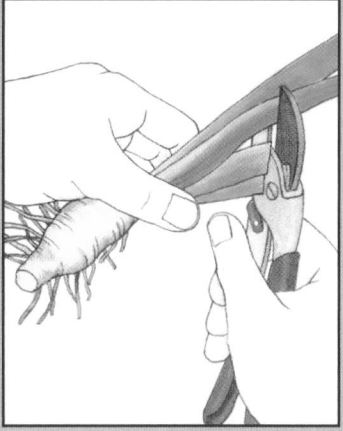 

1. Loosen the soil thoroughly around the plants and lift the rhizomes with a garden fork (above) or shovel, taking care not to break tender feeder roots. Shake or rinse the soil off and examine the rhizomes for damage. If you find iris-borer holes, rotted spots, or dried-out hollows, cut off and discard these areas.

2. Separate the rhizomes, starting with those that split into sections naturally in your hand. Cut others apart with a sharp, clean knife, separating V-shaped pieces and preserving the feeder roots. Dip the divided rhizomes in the diluted bleach solution and let them dry briefly in the shade before you replant.

3. Trim the foliage fans to a third of their height, or about 4 inches long, to reduce respiration and water loss while the divisions adjust. You can give the plant a more natural look by angling the cuts and by making the outer leaves shorter than the center leaf. Remove any foliage that is withered or diseased.

4. Set divided rhizomes on soil mounded in the middle of prepared holes, with the fans parallel and the feeder roots spread over the mounds; the tops of the rhizomes should just peek through at the soil surface. Tamp 2 to 4 inches of soil firmly over the feeder roots and water the area well.

Propagating Perennials through Stem Cuttings

Dividing your perennials at the roots is not the only way to produce exact replicas of them. Cuttings taken from the stems or side shoots of a wide range of plants can be encouraged to form roots and become independent plants. These new plants almost always bloom in the very next growing season.

Stem cuttings are a good means of getting offspring from a plant that doesn't need dividing, from one that you don't want to dig up, or (with the owner's permission) from one that doesn't belong to you. And plants that are hard to divide because they grow from taproots, like lupines or wild indigo, are good candidates for stem-cutting propagation. Perhaps you want a great many more of some specimen. Dividing the roots of that special chrysanthemum might yield only four rooted pieces, whereas stem cuttings could give you perhaps 20 rooted sections to transplant.

Stem cutting is also a good fallback procedure for the gardener who missed the proper time to propagate perennials by division: Cuttings can be taken almost anytime the plants are growing strongly, although it's best to take them either before or after flowering.

Of course, like every other method, this one has its drawbacks as well as its advantages. It is more labor-intensive than propagation by simple division. Cuttings require lots of attention from you; in the early stages, you may need to check them several times daily. Stem cutting is also a long-term proposition—it may take several months from the time you cut stems to when you set the new perennials in their permanent beds. In addition, fungus disease flourishes among cuttings, lowering the success rate—in some batches, every one of your leafy babies may mysteriously wilt and die. But with care and attention to details, you can multiply your stock of a fine plant many times over by cultivating stem cuttings.

TIPS FROM THE PROS

Secrets of Successful Stem Cutting

Experts suggest the following strategies for bringing stem cuttings to transplant size. Though even professional nurseries suffer losses, their methods can help you get good results.

1. Choose strong, healthy plants to cut from. A plant stressed by poor conditions or insect damage, or weakened by disease, is a poor risk.

2. Work quickly: Cut only a few stems at a time and process them completely before cutting another batch.

3. Work in clean conditions. Scrub all your equipment with a diluted bleach solution—10 parts water to 1 part bleach —including the containers you will use for planting the stem cuttings.

4. Use a rooting hormone and a spray compound (Wilt-Pruf is one) to reduce moisture loss through leaf respiration.

5. Set plants to root in several separate containers rather than in one large one. This prevents wholesale disaster if you happen to overwater or underwater the container, and it inhibits the spread of disease from one group of cuttings to another. (Plastic dishpans make good rooting containers; they are easy to handle and have good depth.)

6. Provide bottom heat from an electric plug-in cable or mat (available at nurseries and garden centers).

7. Watch over your cuttings once they're prepared. You may need to attend to them more than once a day.

Preparations for Cutting

Before making your stem cuttings, there are a few things you'll need to do. Several hours ahead of time, water the plants well so the stem tissue will be firm. Then mix up a solution of 10 parts water to 1 part bleach and use it to wash a sharp cutting knife, a cutting board, your work surface, and the containers that will hold the stem cuttings. Flats can hold quite a few cuttings, as can dishpans, but you can also use individual plastic pots or even small plastic cups or cartons you may find around your house. Simply clean them well first and poke a few drain holes in the bottom. Next, fill the containers with a 4-inch layer of a sterile growing medium: A commercial blend or a 50/50 mix of perlite and vermiculite works well. Don't use houseplant potting soil or topsoil, and don't use soil brought in from the garden. Water the sterile medium until it is well moistened but not soggy.

Each container will need an incubator tent to cover the planting and keep in moisture, so have on hand plastic food wrap or large clear plastic bags. Also gather wooden or wire supports—pencils work nicely—to insert at the rims of the containers; so the plastic won't rest on the cuttings.

Once you've gathered all the necessary materials, examine your plants for erect but bendable stems. As you snip off these stems, put them into a moistened plastic bag to keep them damp while you are working.

All-Important Follow-Up

Place your containers of cuttings in a bright but shaded location—under a large tree is a good place in the summer. Temperatures of 65° to 75°F are ideal. Cuttings taken late in the season may need bottom heat from an electric mat or cable, available at nurseries and garden centers, to encourage them to root.

Check the containers regularly, opening each plastic tent at least once a day for air flow. If large drops of water appear on the plastic, punch a few small air holes. If the surface of the planting medium feels dry or any cuttings shrivel, carefully add a little water without disturbing the cuttings. If any leaves drop, remove them immediately; they may be hosts for disease organisms. If an entire cutting dries up, remove it as well.

Roots should form in 3 to 4 weeks, or even sooner. New growth on the foliage tips indicates roots are developing, as does resistance to a gentle tug on the tops of the cuttings. When roots have formed, remove the plastic covers and allow the plants to harden off—become accustomed to the outdoor conditions—for several days before you transplant them.

Transplant rooted cuttings directly into flower beds if frost is still several weeks away. If the growing season has ended, leave small plants together in the container, but give them some shelter—a cold frame or a heavy mulch if your climate is mild. If the cuttings have grown large, separate them into individual pots before sheltering them. Rooted cuttings can safely be planted with other perennials the next spring.

How to Propagate from Stem Cuttings

1. Locate a number of strong plant stems. *Then, using a sharp, clean knife or cross-bladed plant shears, slice off a few 5- to 6-inch segments, making slanting cuts about ¼ inch below a leaf joint or node. Trim off the lower leaves, leaving a rosette of leaves at the top of each cutting. Place the cuttings in a moistened plastic bag.*

2. Pour some commercial rooting hormone powder onto a piece of paper. *Following the manufacturer's instructions, dip the cut end of each stem into the powder. Do not dip the stems into the container, as this could contaminate the powder. Tap off any excess and lay the stems aside.*

3. Use a pencil to make holes at least 3 inches deep in the planting medium; *space the holes far enough apart so the leaves of the cuttings won't touch. Set the cuttings in the holes, pressing soil around each stem so it stands upright. Add wooden or wire supports to the rim of your container, and wrap the pot with plastic sheeting to seal in humidity. Tape down the plastic or tuck it underneath the container. Make sure the plastic doesn't touch the cuttings or the soil surface.*

Perennials to Propagate from Stem Cuttings

Amsonia (bluestar)	(plumbago)	***Eupatorium*** (boneset)	(lavender)	***Phlox paniculata*** (summer phlox,
Anthemis (chamomile)	***Chrysanthemum*** (chrysanthemum)	***Helenium*** (sneezeweed)	***Linum*** (flax)	garden phlox)
Arabis (rock cress)	***Clematis*** (clematis)	***Helianthus*** (sunflower)	***Malva*** (mallow)	***Physostegia*** (false dragonhead)
Aster (aster)	***Delphinium*** (delphinium)	***Heliopsis*** (false sunflower, oxeye)	***Monarda didyma*** (bee balm)	***Salvia*** (sage)
Baptisia (wild indigo)	***Dianthus*** (pinks)	***Iberis*** (candytuft)	***Nepeta*** (catmint)	***Sedum*** (stonecrop)
Boltonia (boltonia)	***Echinops*** (globe thistle)	***Lamium*** (dead nettle)	***Perovskia*** (Russian sage)	***Verbena*** (verbena, vervain)
Ceratostigma	***Erigeron*** (fleabane)	***Lavandula***	***Phlox divaricata*** (wild blue phlox)	***Veronica*** (speedwell)

Propagating True Bulbs

Most gardeners are familiar with growing plants from seeds they order through catalogs or buy at the nursery and increasing their number of plants by sowing seeds gathered from the original stock. The process of creating new plants from seed is termed sexual propagation, because the seeds originate from reproductive plant parts that are fertilized through pollination.

Since true bulbs produce viable seed, they can be propagated by this method. But the wait for bulbs to grow to maturity from seed may require more patience than you—and many other gardeners—possess. Tulips and daffodils, for example, can take up to 4 or 5 years to flower from seed, and hyacinths may take even longer. Furthermore, cultivars and hybrids that have been propagated from seed are susceptible to reverting to earlier forms in their genealogy. The resulting plants may not give you the exact look you were expecting from your flowers.

Starting from Seed

If you can commit yourself to a long-term proposition, the best approach to propagating true bulbs from seed is to sow a different variety of seed every year. Although the first crop will take years to come into flower, after that your waiting will be over. Each year a different planting will add its blooms to the existing bulb show.

Despite the long wait, propagating by seed is the best choice for a few true bulb genera, including Scilla, simply because they don't easily lend themselves to other propagation methods. Planting scilla seed will give you flowers in 3 to 4 years.

Nevertheless, for most true bulbs it's far easier and more reliable to propagate asexually—by dividing the bulbs and then planting their offsets. Some bulbs, such as daffodils, have large offsets that will flower as early as the first season.

Separating True Bulbs

After the foliage has turned brown, dig the bulbs up in their naturally formed clumps. Taking care not do damage the roots, brush away clinging soil *(below, left)*. Discard any injured, diseased, or rotted bulbs. Ease the daughter bulbs away from the mother bulb *(below, right)*, making sure each one includes a portion of the basal plate. The smallest, youngest bulbs may still be firmly attached to the mother. If they do not separate easily, leave them in place and allow them to mature for another year or two. Dust the separated mother and daughter bulbs with a fungicide such as garden sulfur and replant.

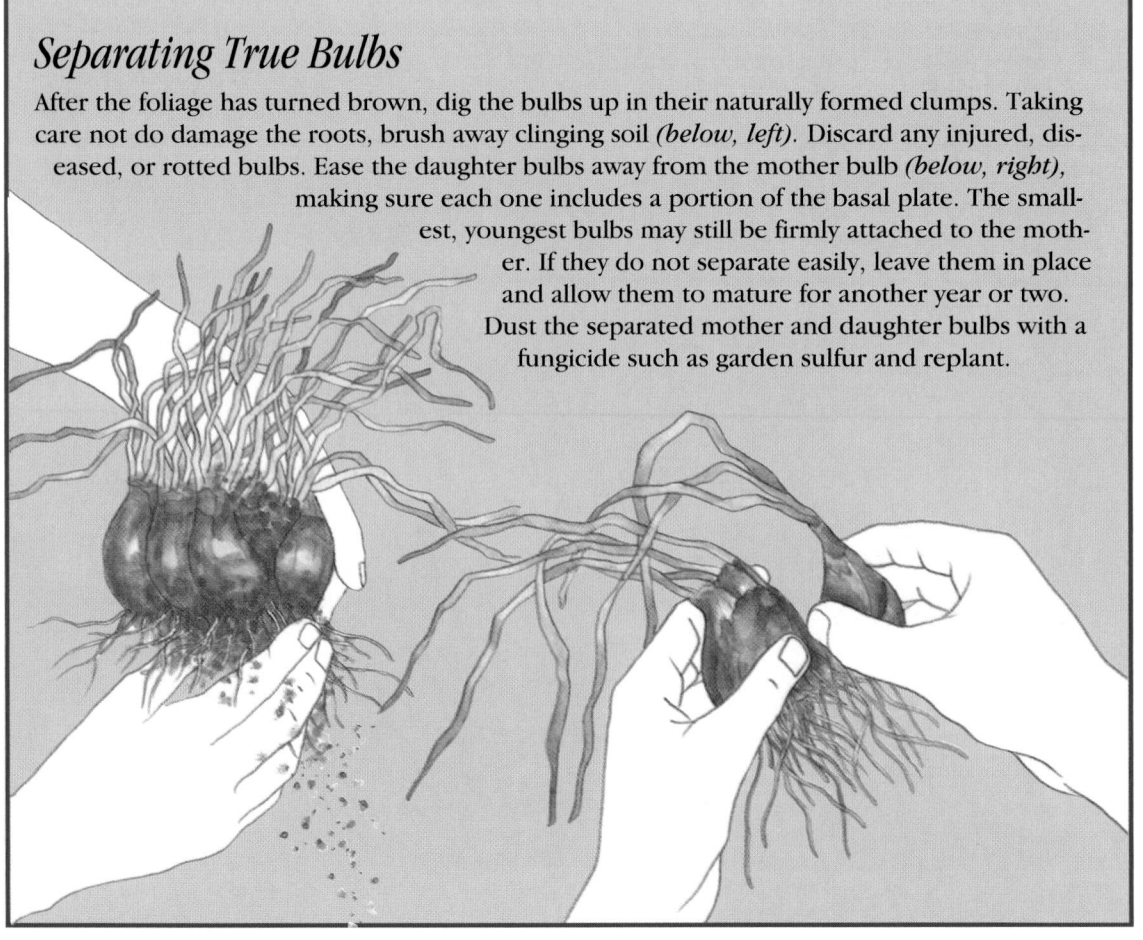

When and How to Divide Bulbs

The correct time for digging and dividing true bulbs depends on the growth habit of the plant. Most should be dug after their foliage has withered but while it still remains in place to show the location of the bulbs. If the foliage is not too far gone, it might even serve as a handle to help lift the bulbs. An exception is *Galanthus* (snowdrop), which should be dug immediately after flowering.

If you plan to propagate several varieties of bulbs, it's a good idea to mark the foliage with an indelible pen while the plants are still in flower. That way, you'll be able to identify the bulbs later when all the withered, brown leaves look more or less the same.

Choose only healthy, disease-free plants for propagation. Dig the bulbs carefully with a spading fork, making sure not to damage them; cuts and bruises can give rise to rot. Imbricate bulbs such as lily and fritillary, which have scales but no papery outer covering, are especially fragile and vulnerable to injury. Gently brush away any clinging soil and carefully separate the bulbs as shown in the box at far left.

Different Treatment for Different Bulbs

In general, hardy bulbs such as tulips and daffodils can be dug, divided, and replanted all in one operation. Tender summer bulbs, such as *Zephyranthes* (zephyr lily) and *Chlidanthus* (delicate lily), should be dug in fall, separated, stored over the winter, and planted in spring.

Once they are divided, sort the bulbs according to size—small, medium, or large. You can plant the largest ones in the garden to flower the following year. Medium-sized bulbs can also go directly into the garden, but they may or may not bloom the following year.

The smallest bulbs will need further growing before they are mature enough to bloom. It's best

Rising above tiny blue Myosotis sylvatica (forget-me-not) blossoms, these gloriously hued Dutch irises stand about 18 inches tall. One of the few irises that grow from bulbs, not rhizomes, the plants can be propagated by seed or by division.

Selected True Bulbs

Allium
(onion)
Amaryllis belladonna
(belladonna lily)
Calochortus
(mariposa lily)
Camassia
(camass)
Chionodoxa
(glory-of-the-snow)
Crinum
(spider lily)
Eucharis grandiflora
(Amazon lily)
Eucomis
(pineapple lily)
Fritillaria
(fritillary)
Galanthus
(snowdrop)
Galtonia
(summer hyacinth)
Habranthus
(habranthus)
Hippeastrum
(amaryllis)
Hyacinthoides
(hyacinthoides)
Hyacinthus
(hyacinth)
Hymenocallis
(spider lily)
Ipheion
(spring starflower)
Iris
(iris)
Lachenalia
(Cape cowslip)
Leucojum
(snowflake)
Lilium
(lily)
Lycoris
(spider lily)
Muscari
(grape hyacinth)
Narcissus
(daffodil)
Nerine
(nerine)
Ornithogalum
(star-of-Bethlehem)
Oxalis
(sorrel)
Puschkinia
(striped squill)
Scilla
(squill)
Sprekelia formosissima
(Jacobean lily)
Sternbergia
(winter daffodil)
Tulipa
(tulip)
Vallota
(Scarborough lily)
Zephyranthes
(zephyr lily)

to plant them in a nursery bed to allow them to develop a bit before planting them in the garden.

Lily bulblets and bulbils, too, should be planted out in a nursery bed to mature *(right)*. Separate the bulblets from the mother bulb and the bulbils from the stem in late summer, about 6 weeks after flowering, and then replant the mother bulb in the garden.

Nursery Beds

Immature bulbs, bulblets, and bulbils will do best in more carefully arranged growing conditions than you would use for full-sized bulbs. The prime consideration is good drainage. Another is freedom from competition with larger plants for moisture and nutrients. Still another is the need to grow in a situation where the baby bulbs' tiny, grasslike sprouts will not be mistaken for unwanted grass or weeds and pulled out.

The arrangement that meets all these needs perfectly is a nursery bed. Set aside a small, sunny, out-of-the-way piece of ground devoted exclusively to young plants. Here, without excessive effort, you can cultivate and amend the soil for ideal drainage and fertility.

Because the plants you start here will be transplanted as soon as they are mature enough, you can grow them relatively close together and in rows without worrying about aesthetics. And because you know that those wisps of vegetation that appear in the bed may well be something you planted, there's less danger you'll uproot them.

Water the bed amply to encourage good growth. Take pains to weed it carefully in the autumn, because when new shoots begin to emerge the following spring you may find it difficult to weed without jeopardizing them.

As soon as winter weather arrives, mulch the ground to moderate changes in the temperature of the soil. Otherwise, the expansion and contraction of earth that alternately freezes and thaws could heave the tiny bulbs out of the ground.

Allow the plants to grow for a year or two in the nursery bed; at the end of that time they should be ready to go into the garden. Dig them after the foliage dies back and plant where desired.

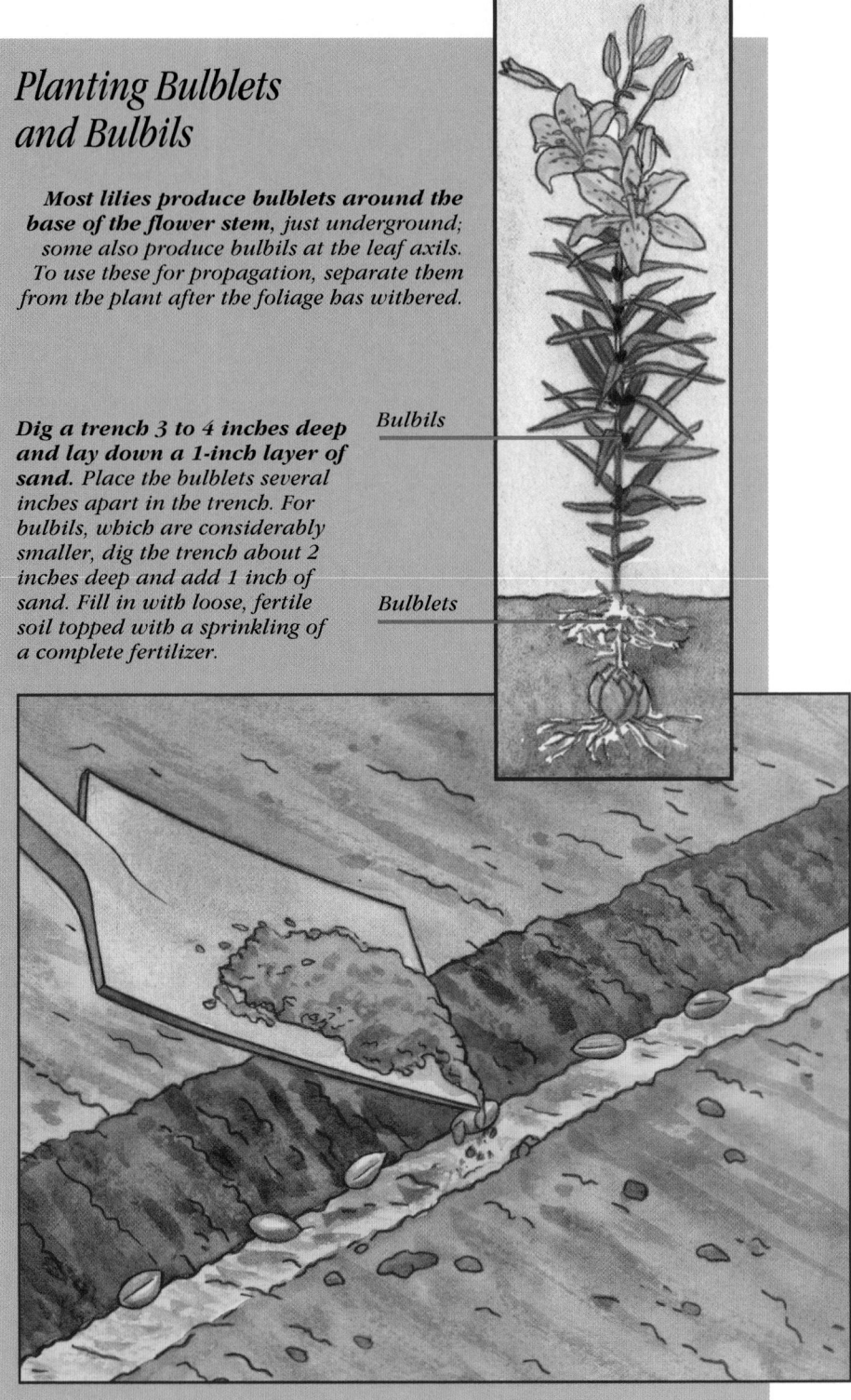

Planting Bulblets and Bulbils

Most lilies produce bulblets around the base of the flower stem, just underground; some also produce bulbils at the leaf axils. To use these for propagation, separate them from the plant after the foliage has withered.

Dig a trench 3 to 4 inches deep and lay down a 1-inch layer of sand. Place the bulblets several inches apart in the trench. For bulbils, which are considerably smaller, dig the trench about 2 inches deep and add 1 inch of sand. Fill in with loose, fertile soil topped with a sprinkling of a complete fertilizer.

Bulbils

Bulblets

Lilies That Produce Bulblets and Bulbils

BULBLETS:

Lilium auratum
(gold-banded lily)
L. henryi
(Henry lily)
L. lancifolium
(tiger lily)
L. longiflorum hybrids
(Easter lily)
L. regale
(regal lily)

L. speciosum
(showy Japanese lily)
L. Asiatic hybrids
(lily)
L. Oriental hybrids
(lily)
L. trumpet hybrids
(lily)

BULBILS:

L. lancifolium
(tiger lily)
**L. Asiatic hybrid
'Enchantment'**
(lily)

Scaling to Propagate Lilies

Most lily bulbs look something like artichokes, being made up of a series of overlapping fleshy scales that grow out in a spiral formation from a central, flowering axis. All of the scales are attached to the bulb's basal plate, but they grow in a loose configuration, and the outer ones can easily be removed without cutting and without harming the remaining bulb. This characteristic allows lilies and a few fritillaries—especially *Fritillaria imperialis*—to be propagated by a special technique called scaling. (Most fritillaries, which are composed of very few scales, may be destroyed in the process.)

Planted in a proper medium, at the right temperature, the scales will form bulblets at their base. These can be planted in turn, just like the bulblets from the underground portion of the stem of a growing lily bulb. Each scale will produce at least one bulblet, and each bulblet, potentially, will grow into a mature bulb. You can use scaling to supplement the bulblets and bulbils that grow naturally on lilies, particularly for varieties that produce few offsets. Scaling before you plant an expensive lily variety also helps ensure survival to the next generation—and protects your investment—should the original die during its first year, as sometimes happens.

How to Scale

Bulbs can be scaled at any time—even when you've just brought them home from the nursery. However, because lily and fritillary are hardy bulbs, meant to stay in the ground over winter, most bulblets produced by scaling will need to experience a period of chilling before they can begin to sprout. Therefore, the best time to scale is in late summer or early autumn, which will allow time for the bulblets to emerge and then be refrigerated for several months before you plant them out in the garden in the spring. Also, completing the operation by autumn will give the parent bulb time to reestablish itself after you replant it, before winter sets in.

Brightening a garden in Washington, D.C., orange Fritillaria imperialis (crown imperial) and its purple-hued cousin, F. persica, both can be propagated by growing bulblets on scales removed from the original bulbs.

Propagation by Scaling

Scales will produce bulblets quite readily, but there are some minimum requirements for success. The scales will do best planted in a flat containing coarse vermiculite or a combination of coarse sand and peat moss. Keep the medium moist and the temperature between 60° and 70°F. The top of the refrigerator or a warm cupboard is a good place to keep the flat; light does not matter. After the bulblets emerge and the necessary chilling has taken place, plant them, with scales attached, in a nursery bed. Place the scales upright so that the tips of the scales are about 1 inch below ground and 6 inches apart.

1. Dig the bulb and gently remove the soil, *taking care not to damage the roots. Cut off the top growth to about 6 to 8 inches.*

2. Carefully pull off several outer scales, *discarding any that are unhealthy, broken, or otherwise damaged. Rinse them, let them dry on newspaper, and dip them—and the wounded areas of the bulb—in a fungicide. Replant the bulb immediately; it will bloom normally again the next spring.*

3. Plant the scales upright, *about half to two-thirds submerged, in a flat filled with a suitable medium. Slip the flat into a plastic bag propped up with small sticks to protect the scales. Inspect occasionally for adequate moisture or rot.*

4. After 6 weeks, *check one scale for bulblets with roots. Leaving the flat in plastic, chill over winter and plant the scales in spring.*

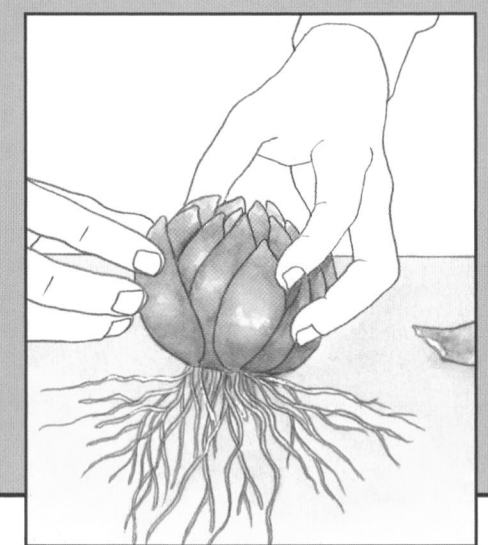

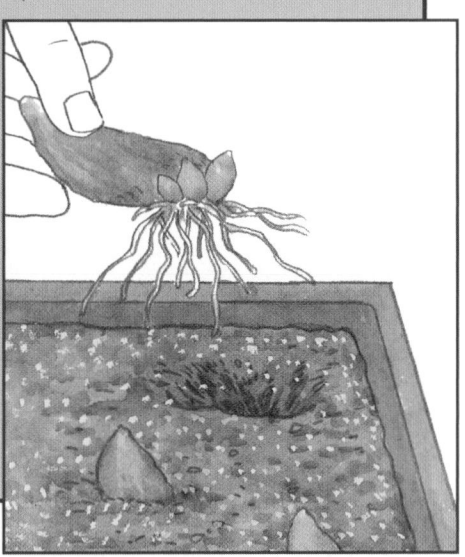

Choose the plants you'd like to scale, and mark them while they are still in flower. When the time is right, dig the bulbs carefully and remove and plant the scales as described above. Scales from most lilies will produce bulblets in 6 to 8 weeks; trumpet lilies will take about 12 weeks.

The newly emerged bulblets will be ready for chilling once they reach ¼ inch or more in height. You can accomplish the chilling in one of two ways. The first option is to do your initial planting of the scales in a cold frame in the garden, where the emerging bulblets will remain to be chilled over the winter, or, once the bulblets have reached the proper size, you can place them in your refrigerator. They should be kept at 35° to 40°F—the temperature range in most refrigerators—for 2 months or longer.

If you keep them in the refrigerator, wait until the proper spring planting time to set them out in the garden. Don't remove the bulblets from the withered scales, as the tiny bulbs are fragile and easily damaged; also, the scales can still provide some nourishment to the bulblets after they are in the ground. Allow the bulblets to grow over the summer, then dig them up and replant them the following fall; set them at a depth of 6 inches and about 4 to 6 inches apart.

Propagating Corms

Like other bulbs, cormous plants can be propagated from seed. Indeed, gladiolus produces abundant seed, is easy to grow from seed, and may bloom the first year. *Ixia, Sparaxis,* and *Tritonia* should bloom from seed within 2 years; *Babiana, Crocosmia, Tigridia,* and *Watsonia* within 3 years; *Crocus* and *Colchicum* in 3 or more years.

Still, unless you are growing only species, not cultivars or hybrids, the easiest and most reliable way to increase your stock of most cormous plants is to grow them from the corms and cormels they produce. For example, although hybrid gladiolus grows well from seed, the flowers that emerge may be throwbacks. Gladiolus also produces many cormels, however, which grow into clones of the original plant. So if you want your favorite gladiolus hybrids to reappear year after year, use this method to reproduce them.

Propagating from Cormels

Obtain cormels by lifting the desired plant when the foliage has withered but is still visible. Remove the cormels as illustrated at left and replant the mother corm in the garden.

In most climates, the cormels of gladiolus, freesia, and watsonia must be stored over the winter before being set out. And because their blooms will not appear until the second or third year, you will have to lift and store them once or twice more before they flower.

Prepare a shallow trench in a nursery bed and plant the cormels 1½ to 2 inches deep and 2 to 3 inches apart. In their first year, they will produce narrow, grasslike foliage. If need be at the end of the season, dig hardy corms such as crocus and replant them farther apart.

Separating Cormels

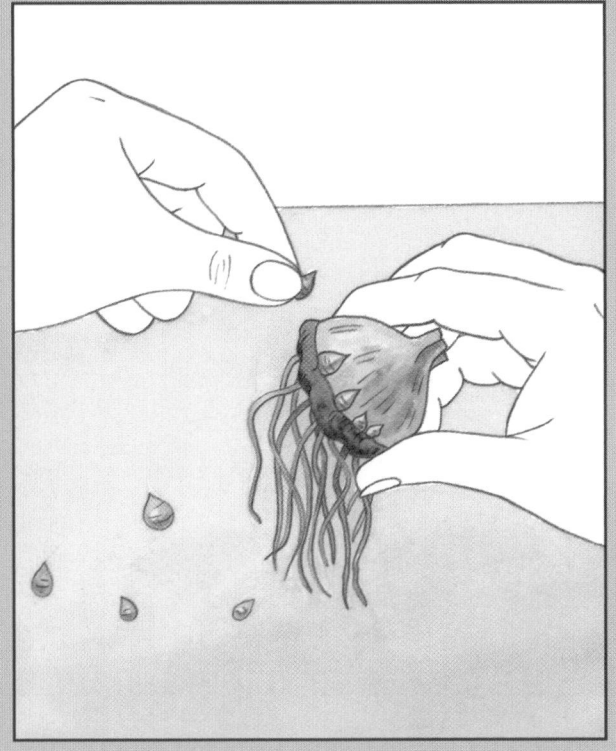

When propagating with cormels from a tender plant, such as the gladiolus hybrid above, wait until fall before digging. By then the mother corm has died, the daughter corm is fully mature, and cormels have emerged. Dry the new corm as quickly as possible, then gently pull off the cormels. Place the corm in a paper bag filled with dry peat moss and store over winter in a cool area such as a basement or garage. Sort the cormels by size and store them similarly. Plant them in a nursery bed in spring after all danger of frost has passed. If the plants you are propagating are hardy, you can simply lift them when the foliage has died, separate the cormels, and replant both corm and cormels immediately.

Crocus 'Snow Beauty' (crocus)

Propagating Tubers and Rhizomes

Some tuberous and rhizomatous plants can be started from seed. Seeds of dahlia and tuberous begonia, for example, are readily available through nursery catalogs. Or you can collect seeds from plants in your garden, though you run the risk of ending up with a different—and perhaps inferior—new generation. A tuber such as caladium, for example, grown solely for its strikingly colored foliage, may produce a good deal of undesirable variation when grown from seed.

Dahlia and tuberous begonia, if propagated from seed, require a long growing season to begin to flower. In all but the warmest regions, if the plants are to have time to flower the first year, the seeds must be started indoors in late winter, then planted out after the weather has warmed.

You will have a longer wait before you see flowers from other tubers and rhizomes started from seed. *Achimenes* (orchid pansy), anemone, begonia, belamcanda, corydalis, ranunculus, and *Zantedeschia* (calla lily), won't bloom until the second year, and *Gloriosa* may take even longer. If you don't want to wait that long, your alternative is asexual propagation techniques that are appro-

priate to tubers and rhizomes, such as division or stem cutting.

Asexual Propagation

The need to lift and store tender plants such as canna, dahlia, and tuberous begonia offers a convenient opportunity to propagate them asexually, by division. However, the process is a bit more invasive than that of separating true bulbs or plucking bulblets or cormels.

Instead of producing neatly sectioned or self-contained offsets that practically come off in your hand, tubers and rhizomes must be separated by force. Some tubers do grow offsets, but even these are firmly attached to the main body. To divide them, you must cut them into pieces.

Nevertheless, division is a faster, easier, and more foolproof way to increase your stock of

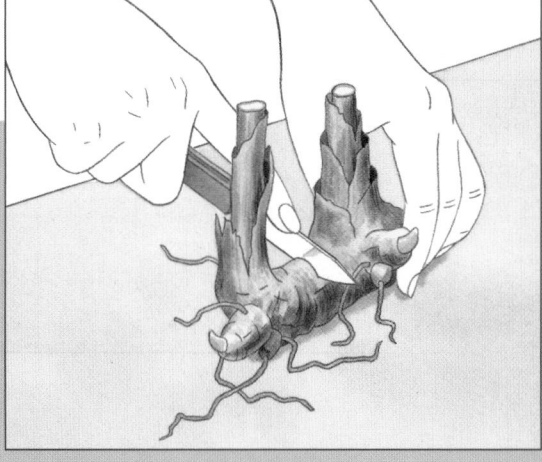

Dividing Tubers and Rhizomes

In dividing a dahlia tuber (below), cut it so that each section includes a portion of the root, a slice of the crown, and a growth bud. The buds, which are located around the crown, have been exaggerated for clarity in this illustration. Dip the cut surfaces in a fungicide and plant as described in Chapter 5.

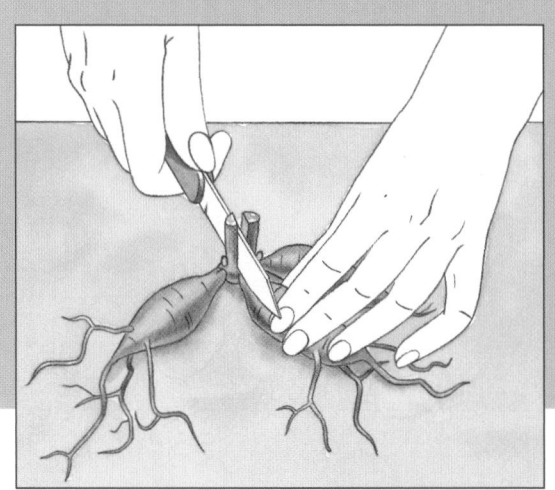

These striking blooms of the Dahlia cultivar 'Cherry Drop' demonstrate that asexual propagation from your own stock of tubers and rhizomes can be a reward for the eye as well as the pocketbook.

these plants than growing them from seed. The divided pieces usually will produce flowers their first year in the ground. And the offspring will be exact duplicates of the originals.

Dividing Tubers and Rhizomes

To propagate them successfully, you must make sure to cut the tuber or rhizome so that each piece contains one or more growth nodes. These will appear on the tops of tubers and along the tops or sides of rhizomes.

Use a sharp knife sterilized in a solution of 1 part household bleach to 10 parts warm water. Dip the knife in the solution after each cut. If you are dividing tender plants that were lifted and stored for the winter, do your cutting just before spring planting. Hardy plants should be dug when the foliage has died back, divided, and replanted.

Before replanting, allow the cut pieces to heal for 2 days in a warm place. During that time, a callus will form over the cut, protecting the tuber or rhizome from rot once it is planted in the soil.

Plant the divided pieces in the garden, following the planting instructions for different genera shown in Chapter 5. The pieces cut from tender

bulbs will bloom later that season; those cut from hardy bulbs will bloom the following year.

Propagating from Stem Cuttings

Both dahlia and tuberous begonia produce branching plants and can be propagated by stem cutting. Pick plants that are the best examples of the hybrids or cultivars you wish to reproduce. Tag your choices early in the growing season and switch to better ones should any originals falter.

There are two ways to obtain stems for rooting. One is to cut them directly from desired varieties in your garden when the plants are in full growth. Use a sterilized knife to cut 4 to 6 inches off the growing end of a stem, making sure that the cut piece has a terminal bud or growth node, for further vertical growth, and intact nodes in the axils of its lowest set of leaves, for root growth. Make your cut just below the lowest leaves. You can also take a cutting from farther down on a stem; just be certain that you include at least two sets of leaves with growth nodes in their axils.

Whether you cut from the tip of a stem or farther down, follow the instructions on pages 316-317 to root the stem cuttings.

Place tuberous begonias (left) in a warm, bright location to promote emergence of the eyes, or growth points. Cut a large tuber into 2 or 3 divisions, each of which must contain an eye. Dust the pieces with a fungicide and let them callus over for 2 days before planting.

Canna rhizomes, like the one at left, must be stored over winter from Zone 7 northward. In early spring, remove the rhizomes from storage and discard any withered or diseased ones. Cut so that each section contains a growth node and roots. Pot the sections or plant in the garden, depending on your climate.

CHAPTER SEVEN

Problem-Solving Garden Techniques

There are a host of techniques that can help you solve common problems in the garden. Even if you've selected suitable plants for your site, you may find that the drainage problem is too severe or the soil too poor for the plants to thrive. Or perhaps your plants are constantly flattened by the wind. Or maybe your flowers aren't blooming as they should.

The Charlottesville, Virginia, garden at left is a good example of a difficult site transformed by a problem-solving technique. By building a raised bed to support a variety of shade-loving plants, the owners overcame problems with drainage as well as with compacted soil around tree roots.

On the following pages are descriptions of various garden techniques, ranging from terracing for hard-to-work slopes to container gardening for small spaces. Armed with this information, you can change a bare or dull site into a garden you'll be proud of.

Terracing for Hard-to-Work Slopes

Working a garden situated on a hill can be a discouraging prospect. However, by building a few steps, or terraces, that cut across the slope, a resourceful gardener can transform a troublesome landscape into a multilevel spectacle of imagination and beauty. Terraces are essentially miniature retaining walls, and installing them on a slope will not only enhance your property's appearance but also solve any problems with erosion and water runoff caused by the natural terrain.

Bluestone granite rocks support terraces bisected by a brick walkway. The tiered slope displays begonias, catharanthus, and red geraniums amid a background of hostas, ferns, and other perennial foliage.

When to Terrace

Deciding whether to terrace a hillside depends on several factors. First, how steep is your incline?

You don't need to take formal measurements; just consider how difficult it is to perform your gardening chores. Does standing on the hill require some extra effort? If the slope is covered with grass, is mowing it unduly tiring? Does the mower slip out of your control? If you cannot work easily on the hill, then terracing may be the perfect solution for you.

If your slope is excessively steep, you may want to consult a professional landscape architect, who can quickly determine whether terracing is advisable. Your property may require sturdy retaining walls or banks instead, especially if you live in an area that experiences severe rains and mud slides. Other options for steep inclines include holding the slope back with ground covers *(box, page 331)*

and planting shrubs and trees into the side of your slope *(box, page 331)*.

Making a Terracing Plan

Terraces can be built of stone, railroad ties, landscaping timbers, or bricks. Choose a buttressing material that suits your garden design; for instance, you might select bricks for a formal effect, or railroad ties if you want a more rustic look.

The number of terrace steps you should install will depend on the slope's length, or run. The dimensions of your terraces—how high they will stand and how deep you make them—will vary with the run and the height, or rise, of the slope. How wide you make the terraces depends on the site and the amount of planting you'd like to do. In any case, all the terraces should be uniform in size. As a rule, terraces should be at least 1 foot deep, that is, 1 foot from the terrace's front edge to the rise where the next terrace begins. For visual definition and stability, each terrace should be

at least 5 inches but no more than 12 inches high. Because they drain so well, terraces may dry out too fast if they are higher than 12 inches. Also, you don't want to be climbing and working on steps more than a foot tall. Terraces with 8-inch rises and 2-foot depths work well on most slopes. To calculate the rise and run, see the box below.

As you develop your terracing plan, take into account any features such as trees and shrubs that presently exist on the slope. Can they be included

How to Size Your Terraces

Calculating the number of terraces your slope can accommodate and their dimensions is a matter of simple arithmetic. First you need to measure the rise (height) and the run (horizontal length) of your slope. For the rise, have a helper hold a 2-by-4 board horizontally, with one end resting on the top of the slope, as shown below. Check to see if the board is level. Then measure the vertical distance from the ground at the foot of the slope to the board. Measuring from one end of the board, mark off that distance. To calculate the run, reverse the position of the board so that it stands upright at the foot of the slope, and measure the horizontal distance from the top of the slope straight across to the point on the board that corresponds to the slope's rise. For a slope with a more gradual rise, measure the slope in increments and add the resulting figures together.

Next, divide the rise measurement by the height you want each terrace to be. For example, if the rise is 32 inches and you want terraces 8 inches high, divide 32 by 8, for a result of 4 steps. To find the depth of each terrace, divide the run measurement by the number of steps you want to build. If the run is 96 inches, divide 96 by 4; your terraces will be 24 inches, or 2 feet, deep. The numbers rarely work out this neatly, but you can adjust the measurements an inch or two to come up with some usable dimensions.

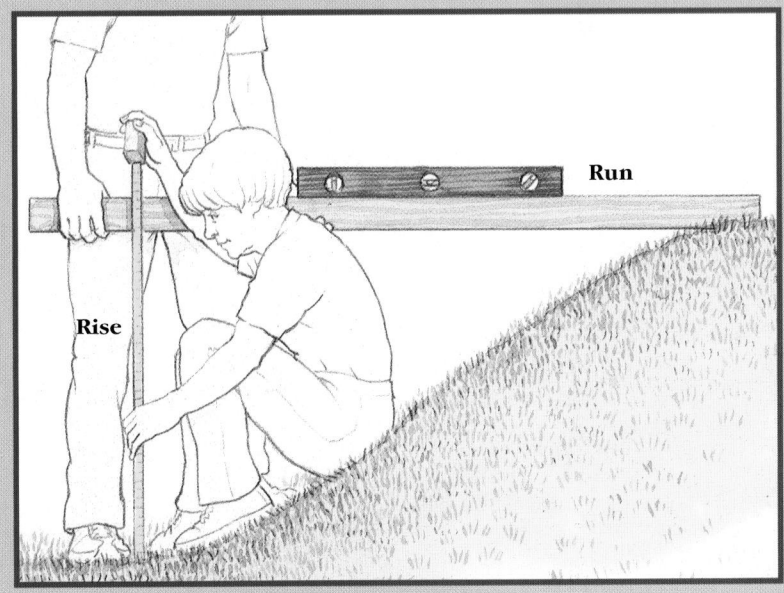

Building a Stone Terrace

One of the easiest ways to build terraces is to construct the tiers with large stones, which are available at local quarries and are relatively inexpensive. Select stones with at least one flat side; you'll place this side up so that the top edges of all the terraces look uniform.

Before starting your first tier, clear the slope of existing plants, including any sod. If there are any trees, it's best to build the terraces around them. Deep-rooted trees pose less of a problem than shallow-rooted ones, whose roots extend just below the ground surface and interfere with construction. If you have shallow-rooted trees, you may want to consider alternatives, such as building raised beds around the trunks or planting some kind of ground cover.

1. At the foot of the slope, measure off the width of the first terrace and drive a stake into the ground at either end. *Mark the height of the terrace on each stake. Stretch a string between the two stakes at the marked points. Use a line level or lay a carpenter's level lightly across the string to make sure that the guideline is exactly horizontal.*

2. Start laying the stones for the first terrace. *If necessary, scoop out some soil with a trowel to fit large or irregularly shaped stones neatly and solidly into the earth. Build up the rows of stones until the terrace wall lines up with the string. To ensure drainage, pour coarse gravel behind the stones until it reaches about three-quarters of the height of the terrace.*

3. Fill in the first terrace by scraping soil from farther up the slope *and shoveling it behind the stones until the entire terrace is at the right height. Make sure the terrace is flat by laying a carpenter's level across it, as shown above. Use a measuring tape to check that the terrace is as deep as you planned.*

4. Move the stakes and string to mark the position and height of the next terrace. *Lay stones as described in Step 2, then pour in gravel and level off the terrace with shovelfuls of earth. Repeat the process until you have terraced the entire slope. Amend the soil and let it settle for a few days before planting.*

in the terrace structure, or do they need to be removed? Large trees and shrubs are best left in place, since removing them could exacerbate erosion or runoff problems. Also, if the incline descends toward your house, plan on leaving a flat area at the bottom. This will keep water that is running off the terraced hill away from your foundation. An added benefit of this open space is that it may allow more daylight to enter your home. Planting ground covers or shrubs along the outer embankments of your terraces will also decrease runoff and erosion.

Preparations for Planting

When selecting plants for the terraces, look for low-growing types that creep or form mounds. Plants that cascade create a lovely display and also help unite the levels of the terraced area. Good choices are creeping phlox *(Phlox stolonifera)* or moss phlox *(P. subulata)*, creeping juniper, sedums with trailing stems, small-leaved ivies, and herbs such as thyme. Mounded plants such as winter jasmine, prostrate abelia, and dwarf cutleaf stephanandra (lace shrub) help soften the edges of the terraces without obscuring them.

As is true for any new garden bed, you will need to work the soil in each of your terraces before planting. Amend it as necessary, keeping the soil level 1 to 2 inches below the top edge of the border. This prevents soil from being washed over the front of the terrace during heavy rains.

Planting Trees

A slope provides the opportunity to nurture a lovely tree or shrub in a spot you may not otherwise be inclined to plant. Too often trees and shrubs tilt aimlessly off the sides of steep slopes, but you can avoid this problem with proper planting. First, dig a hole deep enough so that the top of the rootball is flush with the uphill side of the slope. Fill in the hole and mound soil on the downhill side of the rootball until the entire rootball is well covered. Make a water basin for the trunk by building up a rim

of earth around the top of the mound. Then cover the area with mulch and water slowly but thoroughly. If you plant a tree on a very steep incline, you may want to stake it from the uphill side.

Planting Ground Covers

Planting an erosion-controlling ground cover on a slope is sometimes the best option, especially on a short, steep drop. If you choose creeping juniper or another low-lying woody shrub whose branches grow horizontally, consider laying down landscape fabric to control weeds *(left)*. Avoid using the fabric, however, if you select a ground cover such as vinca or ivy that roots as it grows.

Clear the slope of existing vegetation, and if grass abuts the edges, install mowing strips. Then lay panels of landscape fabric across the slope; overlap the lengths by 4 to 6 inches. To hold the fabric in place, stake it with bent wire. Measure and mark the correct spacing for your plants and cut Xs into the fabric at the marks. Dig holes large enough to accommodate the rootballs, then plant. Do not cover the fabric with chunky mulch; heavy rains may cause it to slide down the incline.

Solving a Drainage Problem

If the site you've chosen for a new garden is generally suitable but suffers from poor drainage, you can consider several remedies. One is to diligently double dig the selected plot, thoroughly loosening the heavy subsoil and then amending it until it drains nicely.

If the drainage problem persists, perhaps because the site is underlaid with a layer of impervious soil (hardpan), you might want to create a simple drainage system (*below*). This approach works well when the soggy ground lies fairly close to a potential runoff area, such as a gutter, a roadside ditch, or a low-lying spot on your property where you can dig a catchment basin.

However, the drainage may be so poor that you have no hope of improving it except at great expense. One indication that you have such a problem is if water pools in an area after a rain and takes more than an hour or two to drain; another is if the soil is still soggy 12 to 24 hours after a rain. In either case, you can still have your garden where you want it, in the form of a raised bed. By creating your own soil for the bed, with perfect texture, structure, pH, and fertility, you can avoid not only a drainage problem but other site problems as well.

A raised bed can be any size or shape you wish, although its widest point should be no more than about two arm's lengths; otherwise, you might have difficulty reaching into the center of the bed from either side. The bed can be a simple, neat raised island of topsoil dug and mounded up from the surrounding ground. Or it can be bordered by a frame made of landscaping timbers, redwood or cedar planks, logs, bricks, cinder blocks, or stones.

Drying Out a Wet Patch

1. Working from the wet area toward a nearby street, dig a trench 12 to 18 inches wide and 1 foot deep at the start. As you dig, gradually increase the depth to about 18 inches at the outlet end so that water drains in the right direction.

2. If you lack an outlet to a street, dig a dry well to serve as a basin for your drainage ditch: Dig a pit about 3 feet deep at a low spot. Fill it with water three times and monitor it; all water should be gone 1 hour after the last fill. Then fill the basin with gravel up to the point where the ditch joins it.

Set off simply but handsomely with weathered planks, this raised bed of spiky larkspur, yarrow, daisies, and lamb's ears scintillates with color and robust growth. The plants flourish in an environment unaffected by problems with drainage, soil structure, or pH.

3. Lay a bed of gravel in the ditch and install a perforated drainpipe over it. *If your system empties into a dry well, extend the pipe a few inches into the well (above). Cover the pipe inlet with a piece of woven landscape fabric to screen out silt, sand, and stones.*

4. Cover the drainpipe with a layer of gravel, *and bring the level of gravel in the dry well up even with it. Cut out strips of landscape fabric as wide as the ditch and lay them over the gravel to keep overlying soil from sifting down and clogging the openings in the pipe.*

5. Fill in the ditch and the dry well with topsoil, *mounding the soil over them to allow for settling. Finally, go back to the original zone of poor drainage and build up the area with topsoil, contouring the surface to slope gently in the direction of the drainpipe.*

333

Planting Under Trees

It is possible to install flower beds under large shade trees without building a raised bed, but you'll have to take several factors into consideration: How much light and rain can penetrate the tree's canopy of leaves? How thick and shallow are the tree roots? Even if enough light and rain reach the soil, shallow tree roots can be an almost prohibitive problem. Tree roots do not grow straight down into the earth, as is commonly believed; they grow in the top 18 inches of soil, spreading out far beyond the drip line. Roots can quickly invade flower beds and sap all the water and nutrients from them. Maples, sycamores, and beeches are among the worst offenders, and planting beneath them almost always ends in disappointment. Some trees, however, such as oaks and conifers, have deeper-growing roots and can coexist well with other plantings. And beds planted beneath small trees—with a mature height of under 20 feet—typically do well, since such trees have smaller, less invasive root systems.

If you find relatively root-free areas under trees where you can place plants, you are in luck; some of the most beautiful landscape scenes are made up of lush plants that thrive and look their best in the shade of handsome trees.

Planting Amid Tree Roots

To grow herbaceous plants at the foot of a mature tree, the soil must be relatively free of roots—unless you are willing to cut away some roots, a method of last resort. To find out how dense the roots are, push a shovel into the ground. If the blade is stopped by a mesh of roots, move to a new spot and try again until the shovel penetrates at least as deep as the length of the blade.

If you must chop through a major root, take care not to overstress the tree. Don't cut away more than about 10 percent of the total root network, and have the crown pruned back a proportionate amount. After you finish digging, place landscape mesh around the perimeter of the hole to slow down encroachment by new root growth from the tree.

Always check the drainage of the soil in such a site. Dig a hole twice as wide and deep as the rootball you are planting and fill it with water. If the water doesn't drain away after 15 minutes, either improve the drainage *(below)* or put in plants that tolerate boggy conditions.

To speed drainage, dig the hole 4 inches deeper than twice the depth of the rootball and line the bottom with 4 inches of pebbles. Cover the pebble layer with 4 inches of soil mix made up of 1 part original soil, 4 parts compost or humus, and 1 part pebbles. Set the crown of the plant slightly above the soil level and fill with soil mix. Tamp down firmly, water and tamp down again, then cover with mulch.

Container Gardening for Small Spaces

Gardening in containers is the ideal solution when growing space is limited. Container plants can go almost anywhere to extend your growing area on patios, decks, balconies, sidewalks, and even walls. Since they aren't planted in the ground, you don't have to worry about poor or compacted soil, a common problem in small urban gardens. And perhaps best of all, potted plants can be moved around or replanted to suit your immediate needs.

Choosing Containers

Your plants will thrive in almost any type of container as long as it has a hole at the bottom for drainage. Experienced container gardeners prefer large, deep containers because they allow for a more diverse planting and because they don't need to be watered as often as small or shallow pots.

When choosing your containers, take into consideration where they'll be spending most of their time. Plastic pots hold moisture better than clay ones and, if placed in shadier spots, should be monitored to make sure the soil doesn't stay too wet. Pots and boxes made of clay, which is porous, provide good air circulation and drainage—and for this very reason need to be watered frequently so that the soil doesn't dry out. Use them anywhere, but check the soil daily if they receive full sun. Wooden tubs provide superior protection from both heat and cold and will do well anywhere; they'll need to be replaced eventually, though, because they rot. And if you want to use a copper pot, put your plants in another container placed inside the copper one, since most plants find the metal poisonous.

A large clay pot of pink Swan River daisies anchors the many fragrant container plants lining these porch steps in Washington State. The casual yet artful display includes an intriguing array of geraniums, such as the cultivars 'Persian Queen', with chartreuse foliage and magenta flowers; 'Wilhelm Langguth', with variegated leaves; and 'Lady Plymouth', a scented variety. The grouping is accented by the white-throated blue flowers of Nolana and the tiny purple blossoms of heliotrope.

335

The combination of annuals and perennials creates an impression of movement in this Portland, Oregon, container garden (left). Annuals include yellow Bidens, tall yellow Verbascum, silvery-green-leaved Helichrysum petiolare, and red and fuchsia Cosmos. Perennials Astrantia major, with white flowers, and spiky Phormium tenax complete the display.

Single containers can add sparkle to any number of spots around your property. A large, elegant pot on your front step or a rustic one on a deck or balcony will both brighten and distinguish your home. Even a container placed among your bed or border plantings will add interest and dimension.

A container that isn't itself impressive can be brought to life with trailing plants, whose flowers and leaves will cover the sides. Sweet alyssum, baby-blue-eyes, or portulaca, with their draping foliage, will hide an unattractive concrete block, for instance. On the other hand, a pretty pot might be filled exclusively with an upright variety to highlight the container as well as its occupants.

Choosing Plants

Thanks to their shallow roots, vigorous growth, and prolific blooms, annuals are perfect for planting in containers. Colorful and versatile, annuals seem to take on a new character when they're planted in an attractive pot and given a place where their beauty can be enjoyed up close.

Some of the most beautiful arrangements combine different annuals with a variety of habits, colors, and foliage interest. Mix various flowering plants—some trailing and some tall and spiked—with light- and dark-colored foliage, such as pale dusty-miller and purple-toned basil, in sunny spots, or pair them with multihued coleus and polka-dot plants in partial shade. Annual grasses, including red or purple *Pennisetum* (fountaingrass), provide a nice change from flowers and are especially suitable in contemporary settings. Even a vegetable or two, like a purple eggplant or a red pepper, can add drama near summer's end.

When choosing your plants, match their size at maturity with the scale of the pot. An upright plant shouldn't rise more than about one and a half to two times the height of

Spikes of Pennisetum setaceum (fountain grass) arch over low-growing Setcreasea pallida (purple-heart) in this late-summer container planting in Maryland (right). A nearby pot of herbs helps brighten the gray deck.

Tuberous Begonias

Tuberous begonias (*Begonia* x *tuberhybrida*) have an upright or trailing habit and simple or compound blooms, and come in every color but blue. Although many gardeners treat them as potted annuals, these summer favorites are actually tender bulbs.

Start the tubers indoors in flats several weeks before the last frost date. When the shoots are 3 inches tall, move them to containers filled with a commercial potting-soil mix. Space three or four tubers concave side up in the container, 2 to 3 inches apart, with the top of the tuber at the soil line. For a hanging basket, choose a cascading form. Upright begonias, like the bright red varieties at left, are better suited to pots on the ground.

Tuberous begonias prefer partial to full shade. They thrive in cool and moist, but not soggy, soil. Keep them well fertilized and provide plenty of water throughout the season for maximum bloom.

the container, or the overall look will be top-heavy. Also, consider your plants' growth habits: Those that are especially dense and bushy, such as wax begonias and impatiens, are best grown by themselves rather than with other species if your container is small.

For visual impact, arrange several containers together. Try combining contrasting flower colors, for example, by placing a tub of golden *Calendula officinalis* (pot marigold) next to deep blue *Centaurea cyanus* (bachelor's-button). Or simply cluster pots blooming with assorted varieties of marigolds or geraniums. Usually, three or four medium-size containers look better than a large tub surrounded by small pots.

Hanging Baskets

Your container plants need not be confined to ground level. In fact, nothing shows off a trailing or spreading plant like a basket suspended from above. Hanging plants do need a little more care than those in other containers, however. Because they are meant to be seen from the bottom as well as the top, they require more grooming to stay attractive. And because hanging plants are exposed to air on all sides, they dry out faster than other plants. In particular, moss-lined wire baskets *(pages 338-339)*, which have no solid sides to hold moisture, need a great deal of water and should be placed out of the harsh sun.

Planting and Caring for Container Plants

Before you plant your container, decide on the arrangement if you're using different varieties. The tallest plants should go in the center or the back, the trailers around the rim, and the medium-sized bushy and upright plants in between. Be sure the plants you've chosen all prefer similar light and soil conditions.

Your pot should be at least 8 inches deep. Place a layer of rocks, gravel, or pottery shards in the bottom to keep the drainage holes clear of soil. Then fill the container to within 2 inches of the top with a potting-soil mix from a garden center or nursery, or with a homemade version. A soil composed of equal parts topsoil, compost, and vermiculite will do nicely.

Use healthy young plants that you've purchased or grown from seed. Remove the plants

Making a Moss-Lined Basket

A moss-lined hanging basket is typically fashioned from a simple wire frame and lined with sphagnum moss, both purchased from a garden center. This simple container is perfect for displaying lush foliage and colorful blossoms from all sides. Water the basket every day to maintain a fresh and vibrant show of blooms.

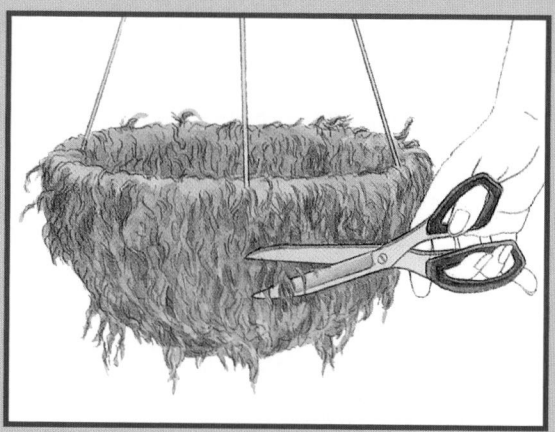

1. Soak the moss in water to make it pliable; squeeze out the excess moisture. Place it in a basket frame (left) and press it into an even 1-inch layer, adding or removing moss as necessary.

2. Cover up any wire showing on the outside of the basket by pressing additional moss around it. Next, attach the wire hanger, hang the basket, and trim any dangling moss with scissors to achieve a neat but natural appearance (above). In a separate bucket, mix enough commercial potting-soil mix to fill the basket, adding a few handfuls of peat moss to help retain moisture. Then cover the bottom of the basket with some of the soil mixture.

Hanging under a leafy arbor, a moss-lined wire basket overflows with hot pink Impatiens wallerana and dangling blooms of tender perennial fuchsia. Both plants prefer the partial shade and humid atmosphere of their Seattle home.

from their cell packs or pots, and gently spread apart the bottom of the rootball. Using a small trowel, dig a hole slightly bigger than the roots and position the plant, distributing its roots evenly in the space. Fill the hole with soil, pressing it firmly in place. Group plants closer together than you would in an outdoor garden. Water the container, and cover the soil with a bark mulch or sphagnum moss to help hold in moisture.

Sun, wind, and drought can be the mortal enemies of container plants because they dry them out quickly. Infrequent watering can kill your potted plants, and irregular watering will stress them, leaving them vulnerable to pests and diseases. To protect outdoor container plants that dry out quickly, water them daily—more often during the height of summer—and move them to sheltered locations during very hot weather. When watering, wet the soil thoroughly and avoid wetting the leaves, which can invite disease.

Although frequent watering is essential, it tends to leach nutrients out of the soil. Keep your plants supplied with vital minerals by feeding them regularly with a commercial liquid fertilizer that contains an equal balance of potassium, phosphorus, and nitrogen; too much nitrogen will encourage leafy growth at the expense of blooms. If you water several times a week, use the fertilizer at half strength and apply it every 2 weeks or so.

Rosy pink petunias flank this container garden, which hangs from a fence in a seaside Delaware town. Planted in a commercially available "hay basket," the garden also features white African daisies, trailing yellow Bidens, and blue Salvia farinacea 'Victoria'.

3. Use a pencil to poke a hole through the moss near the bottom of the basket. *Remove a seedling from its cell pack and insert it through the hole (above), firming the moss around it on the outside. Repeat to make a row around the basket, then cover the roots with soil. Continue planting in rows to within 2 inches of the top of the basket. Then plant a few seedlings at the top of the basket (right), and water.*

Planting in Window Boxes

A window box of annuals pleases the eye from both inside and outside the house. Geraniums are a favorite for window boxes, but you may want to experiment with combinations of unusual varieties of flowers and foliage to enliven a scene that may be growing too familiar.

When attaching boxes to your windows, keep in mind that they are heavy. Mount them securely with bolts or brackets, and check them yearly to make sure the hardware hasn't weakened from rusting. Also remember that if your boxes hang inside the drip line of the house, they may not get much rainfall. This—along with drying winds and the warmth from the house—means they will need diligent watering, although a mulch of shredded bark will help retain some moisture. On the plus side, the extra heat allows early planting in spring and extends the fall blooming season.

Solving Wind-Related Problems

One factor that is easy to overlook when you're designing a planting is the impact of wind. Moving air can be highly beneficial to your plants, cooling them in hot weather and reducing the incidence of insects and diseases that sultry, stagnant air encourages. However, in a garden that is excessively windy, the cooling and drying effects may become so intensified that plants are harmed. Such damage is most severe when wind is combined with either freezing winter weather or summer drought.

Some broadleaf evergreens, including rhododendrons and camellias, are especially vulnerable to winter winds because they retain their foliage year round. (Deciduous plants are nearly impervious to winter winds, since they shed their leaves.) When sunshine warms a broadleaf evergreen, moisture is drawn out of its foliage. As long as the ground isn't frozen, the roots can replace the lost moisture. When the ground freezes, however, sun and wind together can remove so much moisture

A slope rimmed with a windbreak of Pfitzer junipers and smothered by Algerian ivy protects this California terrace. Dwarf strawberry trees and pastel pansies ring the terrace.

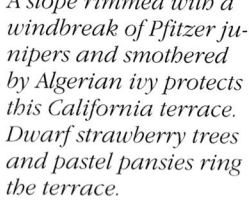

that the plant suffers damage. The leaves turn brown and, if the desiccation is really severe, the plant dies.

A microclimate well suited to broadleaf evergreens is a bed against the north wall of a house or on the shady side of a tall hedge, either of which serves as shelter from the drying effect of the winter sun. You can create a microclimate in which a substantial portion of a garden will be shielded from cold winds by planting a windbreak. A windbreak is also in order if persistent winds in summer exacerbate drought. In either case, determine the prevailing direction of the wind and, as nearly as possible, plant the windbreak at a right angle to it *(opposite, top)*.

If large shade trees on your property prevent air from circulating around nearby plants, you may want to consider creating a wind channel. This involves removing the lower branches of the trees so that the wind can reach the plants, thus keeping them cool and well ventilated *(opposite, below)*.

Planting a Windbreak

A wall of evergreens—eastern red cedars in this illustration—protects an area equal to at least double the height of the trees from damaging winds *(below, right)*. The long arrows trace the path of the wind that is deflected up and over the windbreak. Wind also blows through the trees, whose branches and foliage dissipate its force and slow it down, as indicated by the short arrows on either side of the trees. A solid wall of stone or brick makes a poor barrier against wind, producing strong eddies on the sheltered side that are harmful to plants. For an effective windbreak, plant two or three staggered rows of closely spaced trees *(inset)*; the junipers shown here are set 5 to 6 feet apart.

Evergreens for Windbreaks

Abies concolor
(Colorado fir)
Cedrus atlantica
'Glauca'
(blue Atlas cedar)
Juniperus scopulorum
(western red cedar)
Juniperus virginiana
(eastern red cedar)
Picea abies
(Norway spruce)

Picea pungens
(Colorado spruce)
Pinus strobus
(eastern white pine)
Pinus sylvestris
(Scotch pine)
Pseudotsuga menziesii
(Douglas fir)
Thuja occidentalis
'Nigra'
(American arborvitae)

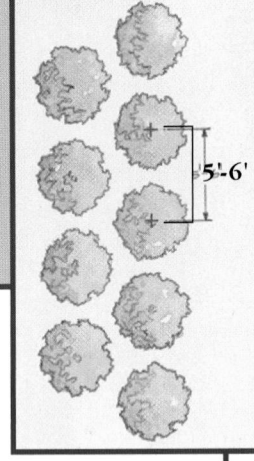

Clearing a Wind Channel

Removing the lower branches of large trees that impede air circulation—a process known as limbing up—allows a cooling breeze to flow into a garden. In the diagram at right, a pair of scarlet oaks has been limbed up to the level of the roof line. The dotted line indicates the extent of the growth that was pruned away. Good ventilation is particularly desirable in hot, humid climates, making the garden more livable and creating better growing conditions for plants.

Shade Trees to Limb Up

Acer rubrum
(red maple)
Cladrastis kentukea
(yellowwood)
Nyssa sylvatica
(black gum)
Quercus coccinea
(scarlet oak)

Quercus phellos
(willow oak)
Quercus rubra
(red oak)
Sophora japonica
(Japanese pagoda tree)
Tilia cordata
(littleleaf linden)

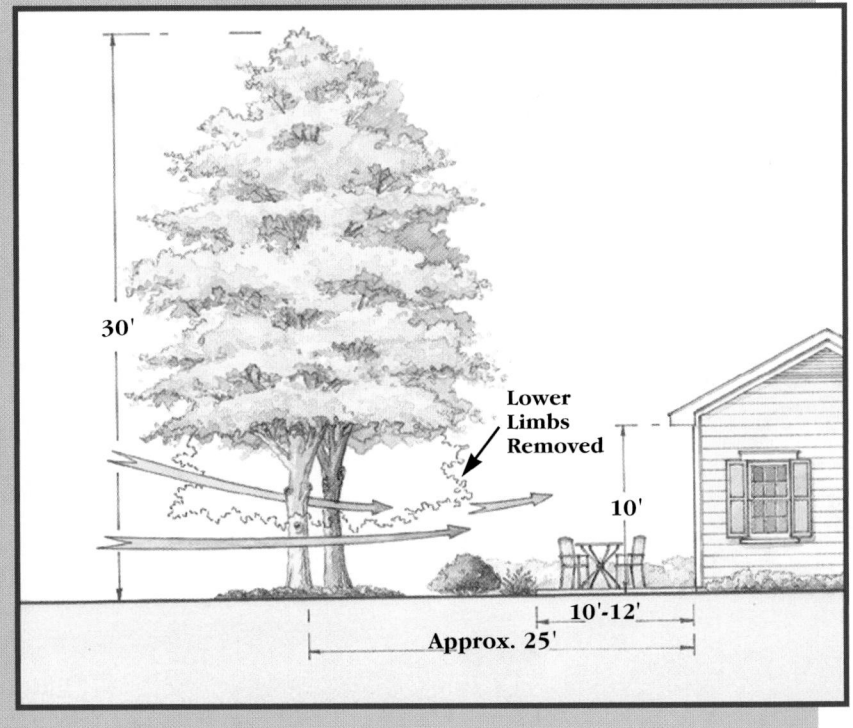

Limiting Your Garden Water Needs

Undemanding plants in this easy-care garden include Tilia cordata, the ornamental grass, Miscanthus sinensis 'Gracillimus' and barberry. Low-growing Juniperus 'Blue Rug' provides an attractive, low-maintenance groundcover.

Watering is the most important gardening chore, and one that hardly any gardener can trust to nature alone. Erratic rainfall patterns or extended droughts during the growing season are the rule rather than the exception for most of the United States *(map, page 344).*

When it comes to water, working with nature is far more rewarding and less complicated than trying to outwit it. And, if you design your garden to make it not only beautiful but also as self-sufficient as possible, you can reduce the time you spend on watering and on maintenance in general. This sensible, less adversarial approach to gardening is called xeriscaping.

The Xeriscape Approach

Xeriscaping is a term that derives from *xeros*—the Greek word for dry and also the botanical term for drought—and from *landscape*. This new way of thinking about gardening originated in the semi-arid West in the early 1980s, but it is equally applicable to virtually every part of the United States.

There are seven basic guidelines for establishing a water-thrifty garden, all of which make good gardening sense:

- Plan and design comprehensively, taking your area's climatic conditions into account at every stage.
- Analyze your garden's soil and improve it to increase water retention.
- Create lawn areas of manageable sizes and shapes, and plant them with grasses that are suited to the climate.
- Select plants that are well adapted to your area and group them according to their water needs.
- Irrigate efficiently by applying the right amount of water at the right time, and by using the right equipment for the task.
- Use mulches to keep the soil moist and cool and to reduce the growth of weeds.
- Adopt routine maintenance practices that conserve water. These include mowing turf grass high, weeding regularly so that ornamental plants don't compete with weeds for moisture, and fertilizing sparingly.

The Benefits of Xeriscaping

Efficient watering, in itself a timesaver, also has timesaving consequences. Because the excessive growth that often results from overwatering is curtailed, a plant's need for nutrients—and therefore the need for fertilizer—is reduced. Also curbed is the production of excessively soft, waterlogged tissue that is prone to attack by insects, so fewer applications of pesticides may be necessary. And since efficient irrigation practices concentrate water where ornamental plants need it most instead of applying it wastefully to the whole garden, another consequence is fewer weeds. Weed seeds that germinate readily in moist soil have difficulty surviving the xeriscape garden's generally drier conditions.

The April display put on by a mixed planting of drought-tolerant perennials and shrubs includes (clockwise from lower right) pink-and white-flowered Santa Barbara daisies; Jerusalem sage, with yellow flowers; the pink Mexican evening primrose; sweet pea shrub, with small pinkish purple blooms; yellow daylilies; and a pale-flowered, stiffly upright westringia.

Drought Potential in the Continental United States

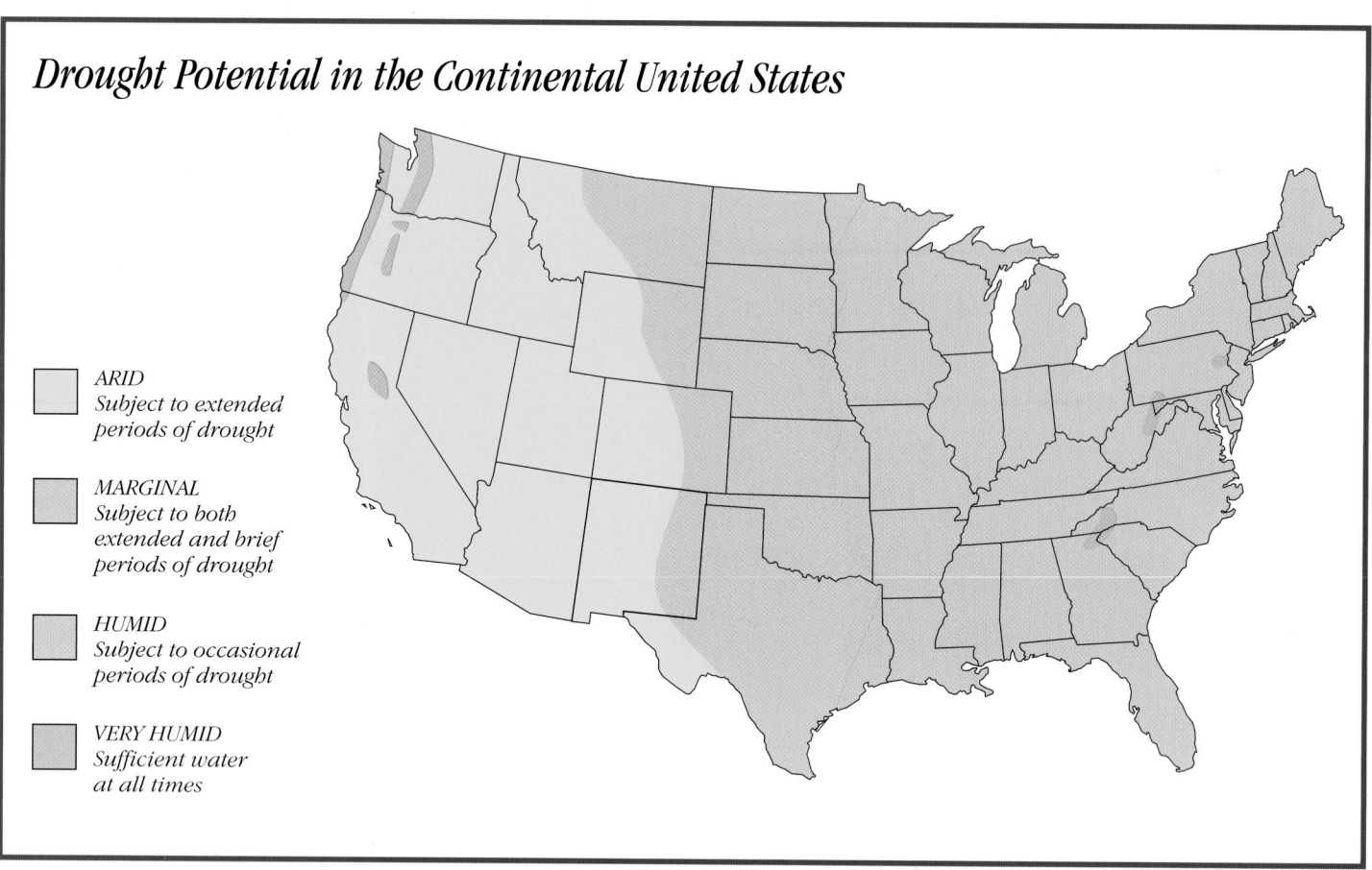

ARID
Subject to extended periods of drought

MARGINAL
Subject to both extended and brief periods of drought

HUMID
Subject to occasional periods of drought

VERY HUMID
Sufficient water at all times

Besides the practical benefits of xeriscaping, there are aesthetic ones as well. When there's a good match between plants and their environment, there's a much better chance of strong, healthy growth and a fine display of flowers. In addition, a well-designed xeriscape remains in good condition even in the heat of summer, when more conventional landscapes frequently look parched and droopy.

Getting Started

Converting your garden to a xeriscape doesn't necessarily mean starting over, a prospect that is daunting to most gardeners. It may simply mean taking a close look at your garden's moisture supply and demand and replanting an area or two where those factors are out of balance. For instance, you may decide to plant daylilies or creeping mahonia on a steep, dry bank where keeping turf grass in decent condition has been a losing battle. Or you might remove the solitary but thirsty rosebush growing in the midst of trailing lantana, which blooms less profusely with frequent waterings.

Water-thrifty plants such as Russian sage, core-

opsis, cotoneaster, catmint, and yucca are classic choices for a xeriscape. But there's no reason to restrict yourself solely to plants that tolerate drought. High-maintenance, water-demanding varieties can be part of a xeriscape without a burdensome amount of work as long as you plant them together instead of scattering them about (*opposite*).

Creating Zones

Grouping plants with similar cultural and maintenance needs—a procedure known as zoning—is one of the surest ways offered by the xeriscape approach to cut work time in the garden. The major factor in dividing a garden into zones is water. You'll want to consider how convenient it is to irrigate different parts of your garden and whether you'll do it manually or with an automatic system. And, since the water-retentive capacity of soil varies greatly according to its structure and organic content, you'll need to familiarize yourself with your soil. Other factors to assess include soil pH and the distribution of light and shade.

Unless a garden is unusually large, three zones—for high, moderate, and low water use—

344

In the northern California hillside garden at left, rose-pink sea thrift and white and pale blue Douglas irises bloom luxuriantly during the dry season.

should suffice. The fewer zones you have, the easier watering will be. Too many zones also increase the chance of giving less thirsty plants too much water, which harms plants as much as not enough water. When you are blocking out your garden's zones and considering plant choices, keep these guidelines in mind:

- Limit the number of different kinds of plants.
- Keep lone specimen plants to a minimum.
- Group plants in well-defined beds.
- Link zones by using transitional plants that tolerate different moisture levels.
- Use patios and other paved areas to separate zones. Place drought-resistant plants next to pavement, which heats up in sunlight and causes the soil to dry out faster.

Sites for High Water Use

You may want to put your oasis, or zone of high water use, in an area close to the house, where plants will be both easier to water and harder to overlook. If your ground slopes, you can take advantage of water's natural downward flow and place moisture-loving plants near the foot of the slope. Alternatively, site these plants in partial shade, which will shield them from heat and direct sunlight and help reduce their water needs. But be flexible: If the best place for water- and sun-loving favorites such as roses lies at the periphery of your yard, and if you are willing to spend the extra time and effort it will take to maintain them, then situate the oasis zone there.

CHAPTER EIGHT

Coping with Garden Pests

Insects are everywhere, in astonishing variety and equally astonishing numbers—worldwide, there are some 2 million species. Fortunately, only about 1,000 of these qualify as pests. Moreover, fewer than a dozen species are likely to feed destructively on the plants growing in a particular garden. For the knowledgeable gardener, controlling that handful of pests is a manageable business rather than an unending battle.

This chapter describes fundamental good-gardening practices and smart plant selection, both of which help keep pest problems to a minimum. Learning to recognize undesirable insect species is essential, as is the ability to identify beneficial creatures such as the cardinal at left, shown feeding her offspring one of the garden's most voracious pests— a tomato hornworm. Once you know the enemy, you can choose from among an array of control methods, from handpicking caterpillars off plants to spraying with pesticides. If you decide to use chemicals, follow the recommendations in this chapter to ensure your personal safety and the health of your garden.

Creating a Pest-Resistant Garden

No matter what you do in your garden, insects will always be among the creatures sustained by its elements—soil, mulch, water, turf, the compost pile, the flowering annuals and perennials, the shrubs and trees. How you approach the ones that can eat their way through your thoughtfully chosen plants is an important matter. Whatever steps you take against the destructive few will also affect the garden's benign creatures, from invisible soil microbes to pest-eating ladybird beetles to the songbirds that enliven the scene.

Tolerance in the Garden

The most sensible course is to accept insects, including the pests, as a fact of garden life. Trying to eradicate them with a chemical assault is a losing battle. More important, such an aggressive approach is environmentally unsound.

A corollary of tolerating a varied population of insects is learning to live with imperfection. Tolerating a certain amount of pest damage is fundamental to the environmentally friendly philosophy of pest control known as Integrated Pest Management, or IPM. It calls for using a variety of cultural, physical, biological, and chemical methods that work together to keep the damage done by pests at an acceptable level while preserving the overall health of the garden environment.

When you practice the cultural measures described on the following pages, you do not compromise the attractiveness of your garden. On the contrary, the basics of good gardening are also the basics of sensible pest control. Providing good growing conditions has two significant advantages: Your plants will be far more likely to reach their full potential in beauty, and they will be healthy. By keeping your plants strong and vigorous, you will maximize their natural ability to withstand pests and diseases.

Doing the Essential Groundwork

The single best guarantee that your plants will be healthy is soil of the highest quality. For the most complete picture of your garden's soil, have it professionally tested. When the soil is reasonably dry, dig up samples to about 4 inches deep from several spots around the garden. Combine them and send about 1 pint of the mixture to your local Cooperative Extension Service or any private soil-testing lab. The results will reveal your soil's pH level, available nutrients, the presence of organic matter, and the soil's texture, determined by the proportions of sand, silt, and clay particles it contains. The ideal soil type is loam—a crumbly, loose combination of sand, silt, and clay that drains well and contains sufficient organic matter, nutrients, air, and water.

You may be lucky enough to have loamy soil. It's more likely, however, that you'll need to amend your soil to bring it closer to the ideal. A heavy clay soil must be amended to let air, water,

---

How to Buy a Healthy Plant

Follow these guidelines when you purchase new plants, to avoid importing problems into your garden:

- Shop at a garden center or nursery known for the quality of its plants, the expertise of its salespeople, and a fair return policy in case a plant proves unsatisfactory.
- Check a plant for the presence of pests and for pest damage, such as webs or egg masses on stems or leaves, or holes chewed in the leaves. Be sure to examine the undersides of the foliage.
- Look for foliage with good color and form. Reject plants that show wilting, curling, spotting, or yellowing.
- Carefully lift a container plant out of its pot to check that roots are white and moist, not brown or soggy. They should fill the soil ball but not encircle it.
- Look for plants that have good branch structure, with no broken stems or bark wounds.
- Choose plants with full, healthy buds or, if the growing season has begun, new foliage and stems.

Drawing on Nature's Diversity

A garden abounding with plants of different kinds—exotics, natives, perennials, annuals, broadleaf evergreens, conifers, flowering shrubs and trees—is far less vulnerable to devastating infestations of pests than a garden designed with a more restricted plant palette. Selecting a garden's principal furnishings from only a handful of plant families—roses, boxwood, iris, and dogwood, for instance—is risky business, since an equally small handful of pest species has the potential to devastate your entire garden.

In short, the closer a garden comes to monoculture, the more it is deprived of the protective mechanisms that exist in natural plant communities, which are characteristically rich in species. A garden like the one shown here is attractive to pest predators such as birds, beneficial insects, lizards, and toads. It supplies many different food sources such as nectar, pollen, fruit, and seeds over a long season. And its range of trees, shrubs, and herbaceous plants of varying sizes and densities creates habitats for a variety of species. With good planning, the elements that make the garden beautiful will also discourage pests, and at no environmental cost.

The Myth of Companion Planting

Many gardeners wouldn't think of planting a vegetable garden without including lots of aromatic plants reputed to keep insect pests away from their crops. Nevertheless, research suggests that this so-called companion planting doesn't deserve the faith that gardeners place in it. It is true that certain plants hinder the proliferation of undesirable organisms. For instance, it has been shown that marigolds can control pest nematodes, tiny worms that live in soil and infest plants. The problem is that the marigolds suppress the nematodes only when the plants are spaced so densely that there is virtually no room left in the garden for a food crop. The pest-repelling abilities of other favorite companion plants have been tested under controlled conditions and have been just as disappointing.

and nutrients penetrate it more easily and reach plant roots. To lighten clay, mix it half-and-half with coarse sand or organic matter such as peat moss or compost. These materials can also be used to improve the structure of dense, silty soil, which, like clay, is prone to waterlogging. In light, porous, sandy soils, water drains away quickly and takes plant nutrients with it. The solution in this case is to dig in clayey topsoil or an organic material such as composted manure to improve the soil's capacity to hold moisture.

It is also important to keep your soil's pH within a healthy range. Most plants will grow well in soil that is slightly acid, with a pH between 6 and 7. When the pH is too high or too low, plants aren't able to draw essential nutrients from the soil, and as a result they grow poorly. You can correct a soil that is too acidic by digging in dolomitic limestone, which is alkaline. When a soil is too alkaline, on the other hand, use iron sulfate to increase its acidity. Test your soil's pH every year or two to be sure that it remains within a desirable range.

Supplying Nutrients

A soil test will also reveal whether your soil provides enough of the three nutrients essential for healthy plant growth—nitrogen, phosphorus, and potassium. Garden fertilizers are labeled to show what percentage they contain of each of these elements, and the numbers are always arranged in the same order. Thus a fertilizer designated "12-4-4" is by weight 12 percent nitrogen, 4 percent phosphorus, and 4 percent potassium; the remaining 80 percent is made up of inert fillers.

You have a choice of using either a chemical fertilizer, which is manufactured or mined, or an organic fertilizer, which is derived from plant or animal material. The two types are equally nourishing to plants and equally convenient to use. However, the organic fertilizers have an important advantage: The nutrients they contain are released gradually over a period of time. Chemical nutrients, by contrast, are often immediately available to the plants, increasing the risk of burning plant roots if you happen to overfertilize.

Not all plants thrive on the same regimen of nutrients. The nitrogen-rich diet that turf grasses demand, for instance, would stimulate rapid, floppy growth if it were applied to herbaceous perennials, making them targets for aphids. A general-purpose fertilizer will suffice for most plants, but be sure to accommodate those plants that have special needs.

Plants to Suit the Site

Choosing the plants that will fulfill your vision for your garden is an intensely personal, aesthetic exercise—and an eminently practical one as well. As you're making decisions on such matters as flower season and color, the height of a shade tree, or the combination of foliage textures for a mixed hedge, you will want to compare each plant's cultural requirements with the general conditions your garden offers. You'll also want to identify any microclimates on the site, such as a sunny corner sheltered from winter winds.

In creating a profile of your garden conditions, you'll need to consider several things:

- The hardiness zone of your area, based on the average minimum temperature.
- Temperature and humidity in summer. Are nights cool or hot? Plants adapted to cool nights often do poorly where summers are muggy.
- The average amount of rainfall and its distribution over the course of the year. If your area has dry spells lasting 2 weeks or so, as much of the United States does during summer, drought-tolerant plants would be likely candidates for your garden.
- The hours of sun and shade that different parts of the garden receive in different seasons of the year, and the quality of that shade—dappled or dense?
- Soil composition, acidity, and drainage in various parts of the garden.

Once you have collected this information, you can determine whether there is a good match between a plant's cultural requirements and your garden's environment. What you learn from your analysis may also help explain why certain plants in your garden, or in nearby gardens that are similar to yours, have flourished while others have grown poorly or died.

Pest-Resistant Plants

In addition to a plant's visual appeal and its ability to thrive in your garden, you will want to consider how vulnerable it is to pests. Some species are naturally resistant to pest damage, and in some cases horticulturists have developed new hybrids and cultivars offering such resistance. Some popular pest-resistant deciduous shrubs and small trees are listed on page 352.

Plants actively counter pests with a variety of mechanical and physiological measures. Two examples of mechanical, or physical, defenses are tough outer membranes that prevent insect pests from feeding on leaves or pods, and needlelike thorns that discourage browsing animals, such as deer. (See pages 380-381 for a list of deer-resistant plants.) A covering of hairs on stems and leaves, which on some plants can be sticky, traps pests that land on them and prevents the insects from feeding. Physiological defensive tricks include releasing toxic or repellent compounds to deter

pests. Oak trees, for example, contain bitter-tasting compounds called tannins that thwart bark beetles and boring insects, and geraniums contain a chemical that paralyzes Japanese beetles.

Plants are classified according to the degree of resistance they possess. "Immune" means that a plant cannot be harmed by a particular pest; "resistant" identifies plants that are rarely infested by specific pests and suffer only minor damage if they are attacked; "tolerant" describes a plant that is subject to infestation but does not suffer any permanent damage. Finally, the word "susceptible" is a red flag for gardeners because it indicates that a plant is highly vulnerable to one or more pests. There are also species and cultivars that are innately resistant to disease *(lists, pages 388-389).*

Native Plants, Native Pests

Plants that grow naturally in your geographical area can usually be counted on to perform reliably in the garden, since they are adapted to the prevailing climate and soil. Many of these native species are also resistant to native pests. Over eons of coexistence, plants that evolved effective defenses against the indigenous pests were more likely to succeed than their susceptible cousins.

Parrotia persica (Persian parrotia) adds a touch of yellow to this lush autumnal garden. Naturally resistant to pests, it can withstand attacks that would cause serious damage to more vulnerable trees.

351

Not all natives are trouble free, however. In the eastern United States, for example, native cherries are often beset by ugly masses of tent caterpillars, while some of the exotic species imported from Asia are less attractive to these pests. And, of course, every part of the country has its share of imported pests, and native plants have no defense against these.

For information on ornamentals native to your area, contact your local Cooperative Extension Service. Numerous mail-order nurseries also specialize in native plants, and more and more retail nurseries are stocking natives. See the box on page 348 for buying guidelines.

Maintenance Practices That Foil Pests

Proper techniques for watering, fertilizing, and sanitation keep a garden growing well and also help fend off pests and diseases. How often you need to water depends on the amount of precipitation your garden receives and on soil type—sandy soils dry out quickly, clayey soils more slowly. To determine whether it's time to water, check the soil's moisture level by digging down 3 to 4 inches with a trowel or soil auger; if the top 1½ to 2 inches are dry, the garden is due for a watering.

In the absence of sufficient rainfall, a rule of thumb is to provide at least 1 inch of water per week, dispersed slowly and evenly during one long soaking. When plants are watered deeply at long intervals instead of frequently and lightly, they develop tougher outer layers that protect them from moisture loss and discourage pests from feeding. In addition, root systems are encouraged to grow downward to soil levels that retain moisture. As a result, the plants develop a greater tolerance for drought. For additional information on good watering practices, see page 390.

A 2- to 4-inch layer of organic mulch such as shredded bark or compost will help conserve soil moisture, suppress weeds and, especially when compost is used, provide a slow-release source of plant nutrients. Mulch also helps keep the soil rich in the microorganisms that break down fallen leaves, dead animals, and other kinds of organic matter into humus—the single most vital ingredient of high-quality soil.

Weeds compete with ornamentals and vegetable crops for space, light, water, and nutrients. And since weedy areas frequently harbor crickets, grasshoppers, slugs, snails, stink bugs, and other pests that damage plants, eliminating weeds eliminates a source of trouble.

Clear garden beds of spent flowers, fallen leaves and fruit, weeds, and other debris that could harbor pests, and add them to the compost pile. In the case of diseased plant materials or weeds that have gone to seed, dispose of them in the trash or incorporate them into a compost pile that gets hot enough to render them harmless—at least 140°F.

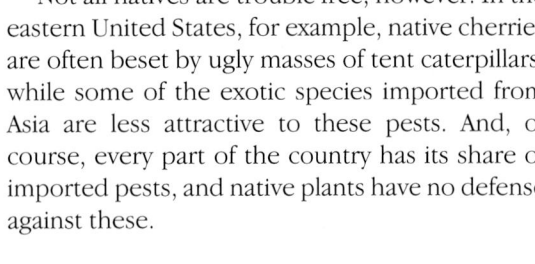

Pest-Resistant Shrubs and Trees

DECIDUOUS FLOWERING SHRUBS

Abeliophyllum distichum
(white forsythia)
Acanthopanax sieboldianus
(five-leaf aralia)
Berberis thunbergii
(Japanese barberry)
Buddleia davidii
(butterfly bush)
Calycanthus floridus
(Carolina allspice)
Caragana arborescens
(Siberian pea shrub)
Chionanthus virginicus
(fringe tree)
Clethra alnifolia
(sweet pepperbush)
Cytisus scoparius
(Scotch broom)
Deutzia gracilis
(slender deutzia)

Deutzia x *rosea*
(deutzia)
Enkianthus campanulatus
(red-veined enkianthus)
Euonymus alata
(winged euonymus)
Forsythia x *intermedia*
(border forsythia)
Fothergilla major
(large fothergilla)
Hippophae rhamnoides
(sallow thorn)
Hypericum prolificum
(shrubby St.-John's-wort)
Jasminum nudiflorum
(winter jasmine)
Philadelphus **spp.**
(mock orange)
Potentilla fruticosa
(bush cinquefoil)
Spiraea **spp.**
(bridal wreath)
Stewartia ovata

(mountain camellia)
Symphoricarpos **spp.**
(coralberry, snowberry)
Viburnum sieboldii
(Siebold viburnum)
Weigela florida
(old-fashioned weigela)

Note: The abbreviation "spp." stands for the plural of "species"; where used in lists it means that many, but not all, of the species in a genus meet the criterion of the list.

ORNAMENTAL TREES LESS THAN 30 FEET HIGH

Carpinus caroliniana
(American hornbeam)
Cornus mas
(cornelian cherry)
Elaeagnus angustifolia
(Russian wild olive)
Franklinia alatamaha
(franklinia)
Koelreuteria paniculata
(golden rain tree)
Lagerstroemia
'Natchez', 'Biloxi', 'Muskogee'
(crape myrtle)
Magnolia stellata
(star magnolia)
Myrica pensylvanica
(bayberry)
Parrotia persica
(Persian parrotia)
Pistacia chinensis
(Chinese pistachio)
Stewartia pseudocamellia
(Japanese stewartia)
Styrax japonicus
(Japanese snowbell)

Deutzia x *rosea* (deutzia)

Identifying Insect Pests

Sometimes even a culturally pest-resistant garden comes under attack by insects. If they inflict damage on your plants that is beyond your threshold for tolerance, you will want to deal with them quickly and effectively. To do this, you must first identify the insects, then choose an appropriate method of control. Since every pest-control method involves time, effort, money, and environmental risk, it's important to have a good understanding of the several types available—physical, biological, and chemical *(pages 359-375)*—before you make your choice.

This may seem like a straightforward approach, but it all hinges on a somewhat complex task—correct identification of a pest and its stage in the life cycle. Identification is easier with a basic understanding of insect anatomy *(right)*. Since the aim is not to eliminate every creeping creature in your garden, learning about anatomy and life cycles will also help you distinguish between the pest insects and the beneficials *(pages 364-369)*. Most beneficial insects feed on pests or use them as hosts for their young. In this way, they are a naturally assertive biological control, keeping pest populations in check.

One key to avoiding major pest problems is to monitor your garden regularly. This means checking your plants weekly for signs of pests and pest damage. At the height of the growing season, you may want to check as often as once a day if possible.

Keep a garden diary. When you see pest damage, record the date, the approximate number of leaves or plants infested, and the location of the damage on the plant. If you can see the pest, note the type of insect, if you know it, and how many there are; this will help you detect changes in the population from day to day or from week to week. Also make note of any unusual environmental conditions such as unseasonable temperatures, drought, or extra rainfall; these can affect pest populations as well as the plants themselves.

Remember, too, that not all plant damage can be blamed on pests. Nutritional deficiencies, diseases, or environmental stresses such as pollution can weaken a plant. But if your once-thriving plants are failing and you can rule out stress, soil problems, and weather-related hardships, chances are that pests are to blame.

With any pest problem, 90 percent of the solution lies in identifying the culprit. The clearest evidence you can get is to observe the insect feeding on your plant. If you can't see the pest, however, you will have to base your diagnosis on the damage it has done *(page 354)*.

Whatever region, climate, or zone you live in, you face a fairly limited number of insect pests. Learn to recognize the usual suspects by anatomy, habit, and damage pattern. When examining insects, it's useful to look at them through a hand-held 10-power magnifying lens, the kind available for around 15 dollars through well-stocked garden centers or mail-order

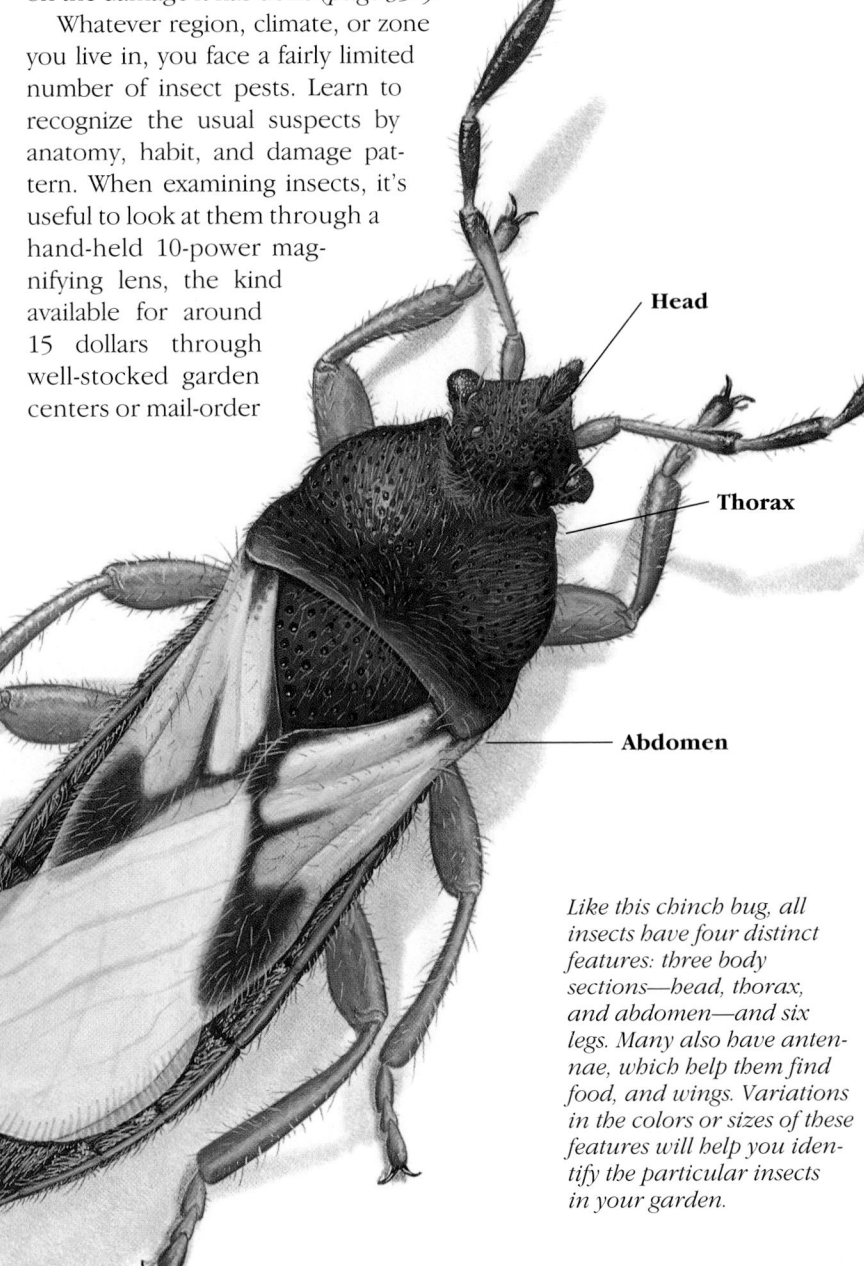

Head

Thorax

Abdomen

Like this chinch bug, all insects have four distinct features: three body sections—head, thorax, and abdomen—and six legs. Many also have antennae, which help them find food, and wings. Variations in the colors or sizes of these features will help you identify the particular insects in your garden.

Common Plant Pests

Identifying the damage pests inflict on your garden is often a confusing task. However, there are some telltale indications that will quickly enable you to zero in on your plants' attackers. The havoc wreaked by several of the more commonly found insect pests and insect relatives is illustrated below.

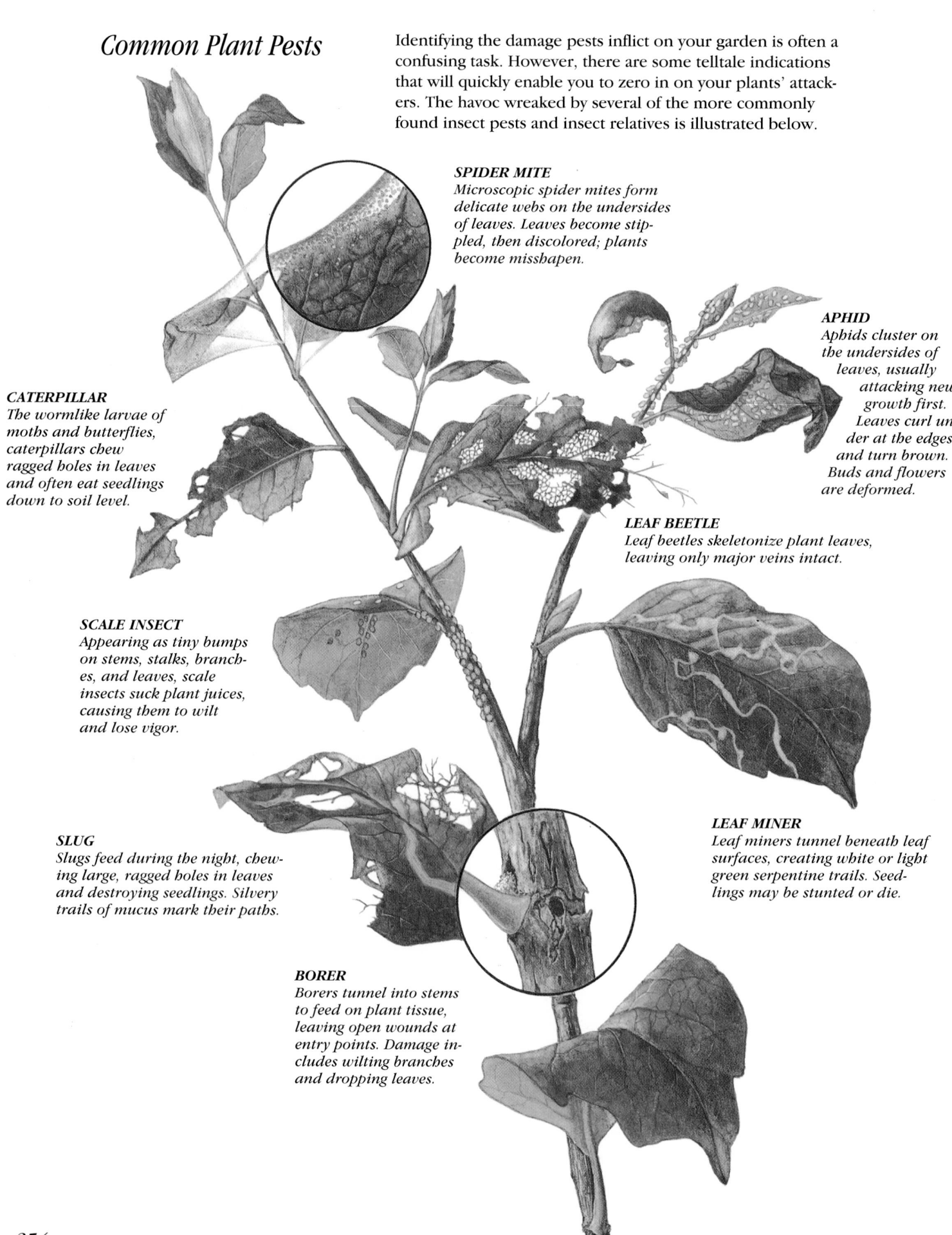

SPIDER MITE
Microscopic spider mites form delicate webs on the undersides of leaves. Leaves become stippled, then discolored; plants become misshapen.

APHID
Aphids cluster on the undersides of leaves, usually attacking new growth first. Leaves curl under at the edges and turn brown. Buds and flowers are deformed.

CATERPILLAR
The wormlike larvae of moths and butterflies, caterpillars chew ragged holes in leaves and often eat seedlings down to soil level.

LEAF BEETLE
Leaf beetles skeletonize plant leaves, leaving only major veins intact.

SCALE INSECT
Appearing as tiny bumps on stems, stalks, branches, and leaves, scale insects suck plant juices, causing them to wilt and lose vigor.

LEAF MINER
Leaf miners tunnel beneath leaf surfaces, creating white or light green serpentine trails. Seedlings may be stunted or die.

SLUG
Slugs feed during the night, chewing large, ragged holes in leaves and destroying seedlings. Silvery trails of mucus mark their paths.

BORER
Borers tunnel into stems to feed on plant tissue, leaving open wounds at entry points. Damage includes wilting branches and dropping leaves.

Many insect pests have markings and body shapes similar to those of beneficial insects, and even the most knowledgeable gardener will have to take a closer look to tell plant friend from foe. It is especially easy to confuse the destructive Mexican bean beetle *(far left, bottom)* with the helpful ladybird beetle *(far left, top)*. The trick is to count spots: The number will vary from one ladybird beetle to another, but all Mexican bean beetles have exactly 16 spots. In the case of the destructive peach tree borer moth *(bottom left)* and the digger wasp *(top left)*, a beneficial that preys on caterpillars and other pests, the difference lies in body contour: The troublesome moth has a thick middle, while the wasp has a narrow waist.

catalogs. Once you've become familiar with the local troublemakers, any newcomer will be obvious to your trained eye.

Many people lump all garden creatures that creep, crawl, and fly into a single category, called bugs. True bugs, however, are only one of the 28 orders in the class Insecta, and account for just a tiny fraction of the more than 2 million insect species. All insects, bugs included, share a unique anatomy: They have three body sections—head, thorax, and abdomen—and six legs, arranged in three pairs *(page 353)*. An insect body is exoskeletal—that is, the skeleton is on the outside, much like a suit of armor—and most are less than ¾ inch long. Some insects have antennae, which they use for smelling or tasting. Most insects have one pair of compound eyes, one on either side of the head; many have additional, simple eyes, on the upper part of the face. They have no lungs but breathe through tiny holes along the sides of the body, taking in oxygen directly to various internal organs. Much of an insect's internal equipment is geared toward reproduction.

Most insects also have wings. Their ability to fly lets them travel great distances, especially if drawn by an attractive host plant. This, coupled with their prodigious reproductive powers, explains how pest populations can explode overnight. Insect life cycles are short, allowing some species to produce 25 generations in a season; many lay eggs by the hundreds. This is another reason to deal quickly with any pest infestation.

Feeding Habits as Evidence

Insects live to eat, and they do so in a variety of ways. Some chew, some suck, and some bore through leaves, roots, stems, and even thick tree bark. As you become better acquainted with different pests and their habits, you'll quickly recognize the damage they create and be able to match it to the offending pest.

Sucking insects such as aphids, cicadas, leafhoppers, lace bugs, psyllids, and whiteflies feed on a plant by inserting a feeding tube in a leaf and sucking the juice out. This causes the leaves to discolor and eventually fall off. Chewing insects eat holes in the leaves, stems, and flowers of plants, marring their appearance. Among the chewers are beetles, caterpillars, crickets, grasshoppers, and weevils.

Borers, the other large group of insect pests, eat away at the insides of plants through feeding tunnels. Borers are hard to detect because you can't see them until the damage is done, when plants yellow and wilt or, in more advanced cases, branches and stems die back. This group includes bark beetles, tree borers, stalk borers, and wood wasps.

When you see the insects themselves in your garden, their numbers are another clue to their identity. Most pest insects tend to act in groups when they attack a plant. By contrast, most of the beneficial insects are predators that feed on the pests, so they usually appear in smaller numbers in your garden.

Knowing When an Insect Becomes a Pest

Other clues to identifying insect pests lie in knowing which plants they attack and at what stage of their life cycle they act as pests. For example, the sod webworm and the tomato hornworm are both larval stages of moths, and feed on grass and tomato plants, respectively. These and other pest species inflict damage only as larvae; in other species, the adult is the pest, and in a few species, the insect is damaging in all of its life stages. For instance, blister beetles inflict damage only as adults (the larvae are actually considered beneficial), while weevils attack plants from the larval stage through adulthood.

Knowing the life-cycle stages in which a pest feeds on your plants will help you spot a troublemaker more quickly, because you'll know what kind of creature—adult or larva—to be looking for. Complete identification of your pest will also help you apply the most effective control at the life stage—dormant, larval, or adult—when the pest is most susceptible to attack.

Metamorphosis: Simple or Complete

On their way to adulthood, insects not only grow, they also undergo a transformation called metamorphosis. This transformation can be either simple or complete. In simple metamorphosis *(right)*, insects such as aphids, crickets, and plant bugs alter very little as they grow from eggs to adulthood. This contrasts with complete metamorphosis *(far right)*, in which insects such as beetles, butterflies, and wasps experience drastic physical changes before emerging as adults.

Unlike animals that nurture their eggs until they hatch, insects commonly lay their eggs and leave them to gestate on their own. Insect eggs come in many shapes and sizes, and because they are independent, they are often covered with a protective layer of tiny hairs or a shellaclike coating. The eggs are normally laid on or near the plants or host insects that will provide food for the nymphs or larvae. Some insects lay eggs singly; most deposit them in batches ranging from 50 to hundreds of eggs.

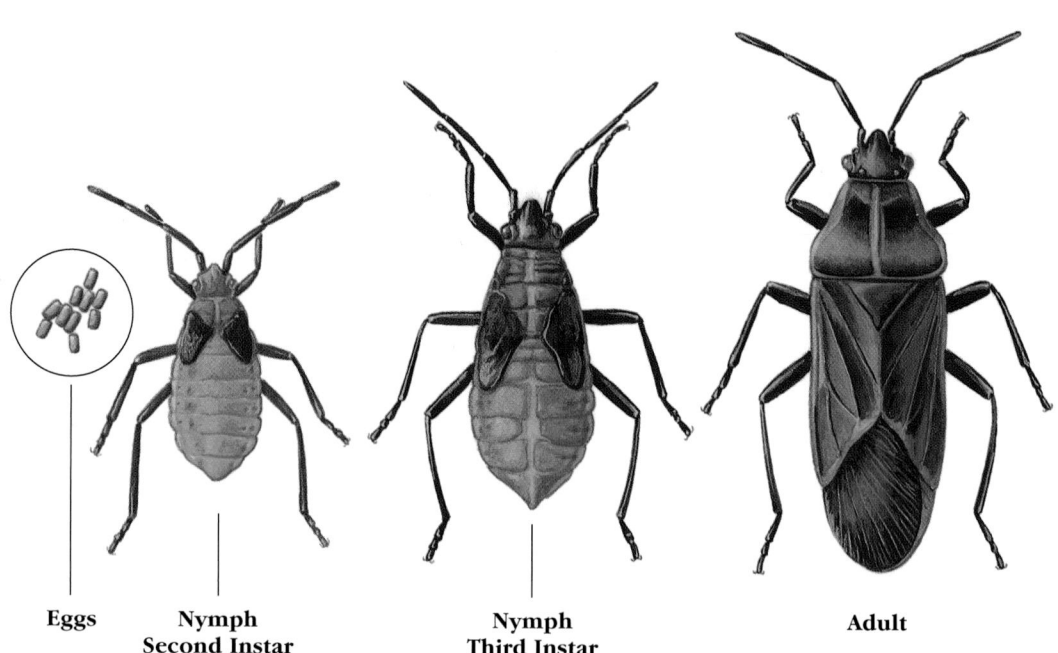

Eggs   **Nymph Second Instar**   **Nymph Third Instar**   **Adult**

Some insects, like the box elder bug shown above, develop by simple metamorphosis, changing little as they grow. Emerging from nearly microscopic eggs laid on leaves or in small crevices in the ground, the immature insects, or nymphs, are each covered with a rigid shell, or exoskeleton. As a nymph grows, its exoskeleton becomes too tight, forcing the nymph to shed, or molt, its outer layer and grow a larger one. Immediately after a molt, the insect is soft bodied and pale, but within a couple of hours, the new exoskeleton hardens and begins to take on color. Typically, an insect's development involves four to eight molts, or instars. A box elder bug undergoes five instars during its early life.

Insect Relatives

Insects are often grouped with certain other garden pests and beneficials that seem related but belong to no insect order. These include spiders and mites—known by their four pairs of legs—as well as centipedes, millipedes, slugs, snails, and roundworms. These so-called insect relatives have feeding habits similar to those of the insects inhabiting your garden. As with insects, you'll want to take care not to eliminate them indiscriminately, since not all are harmful. (Mammal pests include moles, gophers, mice, squirrels, rabbits, woodchucks, and deer. They can devastate a garden within hours and obviously call for control methods that differ from those for insect pests. See pages 376-381.)

Snails and Slugs

Snails and slugs hide during the day and feed on low-hanging leaves and fruits at night or on overcast or rainy days. They prefer damp soil in a shady location and are most damaging in summer, especially in wet regions or during rainy years. For details on coping with these elusive garden pests, see box on page 362-363.

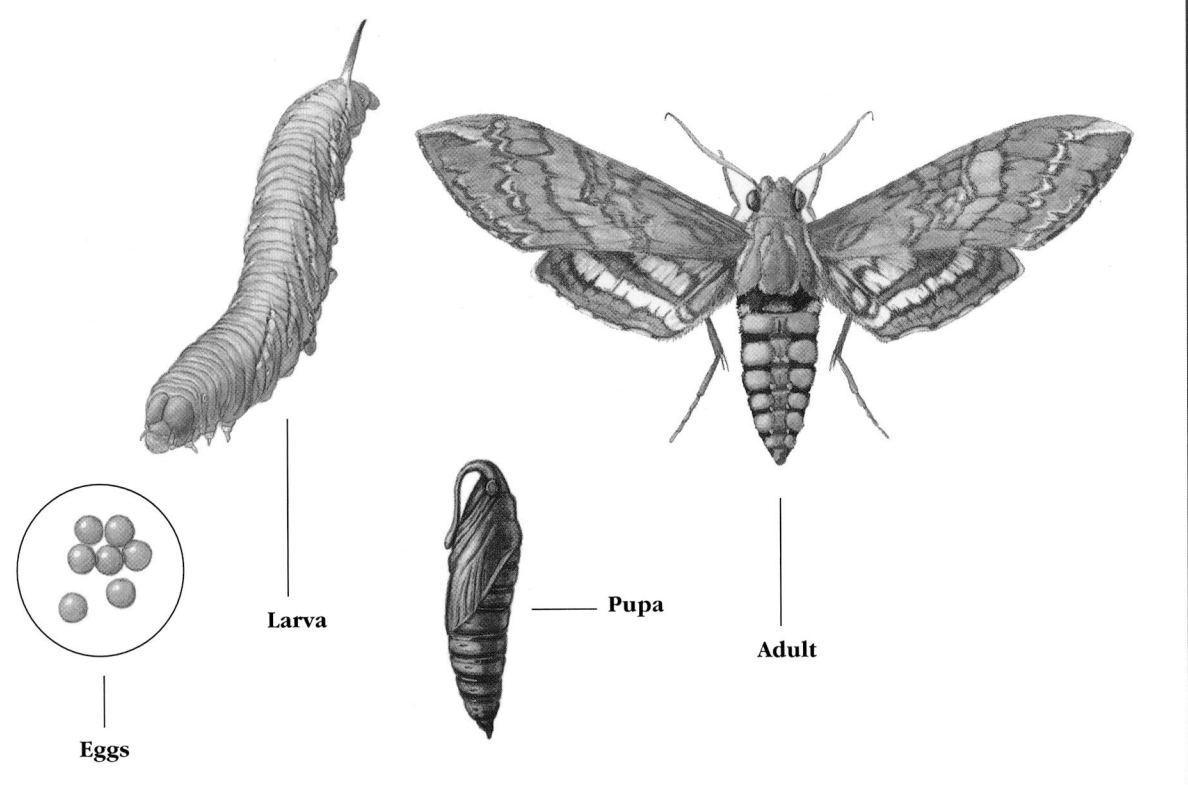

Larva

Pupa

Adult

Eggs

All butterflies and moths undergo what is called a complete metamorphosis to reach adulthood. First, eggs measuring no more than 1 millimeter attach themselves to the undersides of leaves, where they take about a week to hatch. Each emerging larva, or caterpillar, feeds voraciously for 2 to 4 weeks, shedding its skin several times, until it is fully grown. To advance to the next stage and become a pupa, the mature caterpillar attaches itself to a plant or other object and spins a cocoon around its body. Inside the cocoon, the pupa's body changes dramatically over the next 10 to 15 days into a winged, six-legged adult. The adult butterfly or moth breaks out of the cocoon and, by mating to produce eggs, perpetuates the life cycle.

Graceful Adult, Voracious Larva

Butterflies are among the most spectacular and colorful creatures in your garden. In their larval state, however, many of these elusive beauties can munch your plants down to nubs. By growing species that the larvae prefer *(below, left),* you can nourish these soon-to-be butterflies while minimizing the damage to your other plants.

To keep your garden attractive to the adult butterflies as they emerge from their cocoons, grow plants of various heights with colorful, nectar-bearing flowers from which butterflies can sip *(below, right).* Butterflies also need to bask in sunlight to keep their body temperatures up, so be sure to locate these plants in a sunny spot. Forgo pesticides; the chemicals will turn all butterflies away from your garden, no matter how many attractive plantings you provide.

Plants to Nourish Larvae

Anethum graveolens
(dill)
Artemisia spp.
(wormwood)
Barbarea
(winter cress)
Cirsium spp.
(thistle)
Daucus carota
(Queen Anne's lace)
Dicentra spp.
(bleeding heart)
Foeniculum vulgare
(sweet fennel)
Nasturtium
(nasturtium)
Pastinaca sativa
(parsnip)
Petroselinum crispum
(parsley)
Populus spp.
(poplar, aspen, cottonwood)
Ruta graveolens
(common rue)
Sedum spp.
(stonecrop)

Note: The abbreviation "spp." stands for the plural of "species"; where used in lists it means that many, but not all, of the species in a genus meet the criterion of the list.

Black Swallowtail Butterfly Larva

Black Swallowtail Butterfly

Plants to Attract Butterflies

Artemisia spp.
(wormwood)
Asclepias spp.
(milkweed)
Aster spp.
(aster)
Buddleia spp.
(butterfly bush)
Centaurea spp.
(knapweed)
Cephalanthus spp.
(buttonbush)
Coreopsis spp.
(tickseed)
Echinacea purpurea
(purple coneflower)
Lantana spp.
(lantana)
Lonicera spp.
(honeysuckle)
Mentha spp.
(mint)
Rudbeckia hirta
(black-eyed Susan)
Salix spp.
(willow)

Note: The abbreviation "spp." stands for the plural of "species"; where used in lists it means that many, but not all, of the species in a genus meet the criterion of the list.

Dealing with Pests on the Spot

For the gardener who wants to avoid overkill, a simple physical control is the first line of defense when a pest threatens to do serious damage. Most of these measures—barriers, traps, and the like—rely on common sense and traditional techniques of good gardening. However, discoveries in insect behavior and reproduction have provided several technological twists in the area of physical controls that have proven to be enormous boons.

As a rule, physical controls pose no environmental hazards and are inexpensive. Used singly or in combination, they offer you sensible options for managing pest problems.

Protecting Seedlings

An obvious way of heading off trouble is to erect a barrier that stops pests from getting to your plants. Seedlings are especially vulnerable to attack. Because of their small size, they can be chewed to the ground in no time and have little or nothing in the way of food reserves to help them replace shoots or leaves.

Plant collars and row covers are two easy ways of protecting seedlings until they are established. Collars, which are slipped around individual seedlings as shown in the illustration at far right, keep crawling pests like cutworms from reaching tender stems and foliage. Row covers, made of transparent fabric that allows sunlight to reach young plants, are most often used in the vegetable garden as barriers against birds and flying insects. The covers' edges are buried in the soil to keep crawling insects from wiggling underneath them.

Blocking Pests on Trees

Tree bands, a variation of the plant-collar idea, can be used to block gypsy moth caterpillars, webworms, root weevils, and other crawling pests that make their way up a tree trunk to feed on the foliage. Garden centers and mail-order catalogs carry bands, but it's easy and much less expensive to make them yourself. Using burlap or another sturdy fabric, cut a strip 8 to 12 inches wide and several inches longer than the tree trunk's circumference. Cut a piece of heavy string a foot or so

Barriers and Traps

The seedling above is shielded from crawling pests with a plant collar, here an inverted paper cup. You can also use sections of cardboard from a roll of paper towels. At left, burlap tied around the tree and folded down over the string stops gypsy moth larvae and other pests from climbing the trunk to feed on foliage. Sticky glue painted above the burlap catches any pests that elude the barrier.

Placed near plants that would otherwise be attacked, the sticky trap at right lures aphids and several other flying pests that share a strong attraction to yellow objects. Insects landing on the surface of the trap become mired in its adhesive coating and suffocate. White and blue traps are effective with other species of pests.

longer than the circumference. At a point several feet above the ground, wrap the strip of fabric around the trunk. Center the string on the fabric and tie it firmly in place. Then fold the top portion of the fabric down over the string to make a flap.

Some of the pests that wander into this dead end will find their way out and crawl back down the trunk. Others will remain trapped, and some, such as gypsy moths, may enjoy the shelter from sun and rain and pupate there. Check the bands about once a week, or more frequently in the case of heavy infestation. Wearing gloves, pick off any trapped pests and drop them into a bucket of soapy water to kill them.

Leaf-eating pests are especially hard on young trees, but established trees can also be vulnerable in years when a pest's population explodes. Install bands before the threatened trees produce new foliage in the spring.

Mulching for Pest Control

Among its many virtues, mulch helps combat pests in a variety of ways. A coarse organic mulch such as cocoa hulls discourages slugs and snails because their bodies are soft and scratch easily *(pages 362-363)*. A thick layer of shredded bark or other mulch

prevents overwintering pests like beetle grubs from finding food as they emerge from the soil. And black plastic, which is impenetrable as long as it isn't torn, disrupts the life cycles of thrips, leaf miners, and other pests that lay their eggs in soil or overwinter in a dormant stage. A newspaper mulch works much the same way but is effective for only one season, since it is biodegradable.

Aluminum to Foil Flying Pests

The light rays bouncing off a reflective mulch confuse aphids, thrips, and other flying pests and keep them from locating their target plants. You can buy aluminum-coated kraft paper insulation or aluminized plastic at home and garden centers, but ordinary aluminum foil works just as well. Given the utilitarian appearance of these materials, they are best reserved for the vegetable garden or a nursery bed tucked out of sight.

Lay strips of the reflective mulch under the leaf canopy, leaving spaces between the strips and near the plant's stem so that water can reach the soil. Since the aluminum reflects enough heat to scorch plants, especially tender seedlings, it should be removed before the weather becomes

Luring Pests with Sex Chemicals

During mating season, some insect pests release a pheromone—an airborne chemical signal that lets the opposite sex of the species know where to find them. Each species has its own unique pheromone, and its members have a remarkable ability to detect it, even at extremely low concentrations and over a distance of several miles. Insects are indifferent to alien pheromones.

The ability to produce synthetic versions of insect pheromones has resulted in a highly targeted technique of pest control. A trap impregnated with a pheromone catches males of one species only, eliminating them from the mating game and thus reducing the size of the next generation.

The traps come in a number of different shapes; the triangular or delta trap and the wing trap are shown at right. These two traps have sticky inner surfaces that hold insects fast. Other traps have a funnel-

shaped entrance that prevents escape.

In addition to serving as control devices, some pheromone traps are used for monitoring changes in a given pest population. If the number of pests captured begins to rise sharply, the gardener can take appropriate measures to short-circuit trouble, perhaps by using physical controls more diligently or by taking advantage of one of the biological controls described on pages 364-369.

Before you buy a pheromone trap, make certain the pest attacking your garden belongs to the species for which the trap was designed. Follow the directions for replacing the pheromone lure and cleaning the trap.

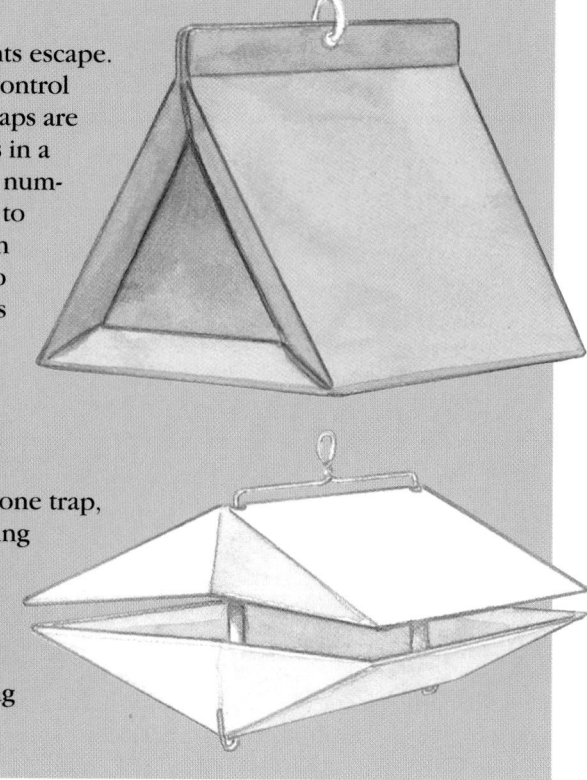

hot. A good practice is to remove the mulch as soon as young plants have become established.

Traps for Flying Pests

Along with barriers and mulches, traps are one of the most effective physical controls for the home garden. There are many types of traps on the market, almost all of which are designed to catch flying insects of a specific kind. Be sure to identify the pest you're targeting so that you'll select the right kind of trap. In addition to drawing pests away from your plants, the traps help you monitor changes in the size of a particular pest population. If the number of trapped pests begins to rise sharply, you can take defensive measures before a lot of plant damage is done.

Avoid using any type of electric-light trap. None of these traps discriminates between victims, killing all insects, pests and beneficials alike. Moreover, they are expensive.

Luring Pests with Scent

One popular type of trap uses a scented lure, which, in most cases, is designed to catch a particular insect. For apple maggot flies, for example, the traps contain fruit and floral scents. The traps that attract adult Japanese beetles use two different lures—a floral scent for the females and, for the males, a synthetic scent that mimics a sex pheromone females produce to attract a mate. (For more about pheromone traps, see the box on the opposite page.)

Unless it is used properly, a Japanese beetle trap can be counterproductive, actually attracting more insects to the plants you are trying to protect than would have appeared had you done nothing at all. Be sure to position the traps on nonhost plants such as pines, or on a structure like a fence post, at least 20 to 30 yards away and downwind from vulnerable plantings. If your area is suffering from an unusually large influx of Japanese beetles, it is probably better not to use the traps at all, or the pests might swarm to your garden from neighboring yards.

To protect a quarter-acre garden, set out at least one trap; a half-acre will need two or more. The smell of accumulated dead beetles keeps live ones from entering traps, so it's important to empty them at least twice a week. A trap that lets rainwater drain away quickly minimizes the odor. After a month or 6 weeks, if the influx of pests has not diminished, install a fresh lure.

A trap set amid cucumber plants is peppered with pests that were drawn to its color and became entangled in its coating. Yellow sticky traps snare numerous small insect pests, including aphids, whiteflies, and leafhoppers.

Luring Pests with Color

Some traps, like the one shown above, combine an alluring color with a sticky surface. Different insects are drawn to different colors. Aphids, leafhoppers, and whiteflies are partial to yellow, for instance, whereas tarnished plant bugs, flea beetles, and rose chafers prefer white, and most thrips flock to blue. When the pest lands on the trap's colored panel, it becomes entangled in the coating of glue covering the surface. Unlike Japanese beetle traps, these sticky traps, as they are called, should be placed near the plants you want to protect. Position the traps at about the same height as the plants.

Homemade Sticky Traps

Although sticky traps can be bought through many mail-order catalogs or at any well-stocked garden center, you can make one easily at home. Cut scrap wood into rectangles measuring about 6 by 6 inch-

Coping with Slugs and Snails

Snails and slugs are elusive pests, feeding at night and taking refuge during the day under rocks, boards, leaves, or dense ground cover, or in other moist, shaded spots. Their presence in the garden is betrayed by the silvery trails of mucus they leave behind and the large, ragged holes they chew in stems, bulbs, fruits, and leaves. Hostas, iris, and succulents are among their favorite plants, and in the vegetable garden, they nibble on tomatoes, lettuce, strawberries, and the pungent leaves of onions.

Gardeners have a number of effective options for fighting snails and slugs, including those illustrated at right—two kinds of traps and a barrier that exploits these pests' aversion to copper. Your level of squeamishness will influence which of the following methods you choose:

- Handpicking is most productive at night, when snails and slugs are actively feeding. Equip yourself with a flashlight and a pail of soapy water to dispose of the pests as you find them. Since their mucus is difficult to wash off, you may want to wear thin surgical gloves or use large tongs to pick the pests up.
- Salt sprinkled on slugs kills them by drawing fluid out of their bodies. However, repeated use of this technique carries the risk of making your soil salty enough to injure plants. This method is less successful with snails because their shells shield them from the salt.
- Place inverted flower pots or melon or grapefruit rinds in a shady spot to trap slugs or snails seeking daytime shelter.
- Sink a shallow can or pie tin to its rim in soil and fill with beer or other yeasty liquid. Empty every few days and replace the liquid.
- Spread a band of an abrasive material on the soil around plants as a deterrent; diatomaceous earth, sand, sawdust, and wood ashes are effective, but only when dry.

COPPER BARRIERS
The most reliable barriers against slugs and snails are made of copper, which is toxic to these mollusks. Thin sheets of copper, available at hardware stores, are easily cut in strips to use as barriers. For a raised bed, fasten strips at least 4 to 5 inches wide to each side (above). To edge a bed, cut strips 4 to 6 inches wide and install them with the top 2 inches above the soil line. As an extra deterrent, bend the strip's upper edge outward to form a lip.

es and paint them yellow, white, or blue, depending on the pest. You can buy a weather-resistant adhesive designed for coating traps or make the glue yourself. Simply combine equal parts of petroleum jelly or mineral oil and liquid dishwashing soap or laundry detergent and mix well. Spread the glue on the painted rectangles and hang them in the garden. In an exposed place, homemade glue should last about 2 weeks. When the trap is no longer sticky, remove the old glue and pest remnants with a paint scraper and apply a fresh coat of glue.

In addition to spreading it on traps, you can paint a stripe of glue around a tree trunk to catch crawling insects. If you've put a fabric trap on the tree *(page 359),* apply the sticky glue just above it.

Catching Pests in the Act

With traps, the need to actually handle pests is kept to a minimum. But if you're a gardener who doesn't mind the closer contact required, hand-

picking crawling creatures such as hornworms, cutworms, and Colorado potato beetles off leaves and stems is a very effective method of control. There are only a few plant pests that will cause you any discomfort if they come into contact with bare skin, and even then it is usually temporary. These include blister beetles, whose body fluids can irritate skin; caterpillars with stinging hairs; and black flies, which inflict bites like those of a mosquito. As a precaution, you should always wear garden gloves when handpicking pests. You can also use kitchen tongs instead of your fingers to grasp them. To kill handpicked pests, drop them into a container filled with soapy water. Dispose of them in the trash or your compost heap.

Techniques for Dislodging Pests

If you prefer to place a bit of distance between you and your garden pests, a stream of water from

BAITED TRAPS
Designed for use with bait, the plastic trap illustrated below has a removable lid and a small, lightweight door that swings inward only, preventing the snails and slugs that crawl in from escaping. If you use a poison bait, a trap with a tight-fitting lid like this one reduces the risk of harm to pets. The lid also makes it easy to dump out the dead snails and slugs and to clean the trap's interior. The trap is partially buried to make it easier for the pests to enter.

AN UNBAITED BOARD TRAP
Nail two strips of wood about an inch thick to one side of a board. Set the board strip-side down on the ground. After a night of feeding, snails and slugs will collect in the dark, moist space beneath the board to escape drying heat and sunlight. Check the trap early each morning. Pick or scrape off any slugs and snails you find, and dispose of them in a pail of soapy water.

a hose is often sufficient to remove invaders from plants. Be sure to spray the underside of the foliage, where aphids, whiteflies, mites, and other pests frequently feed, as well as the upper surfaces. If a plant's stems are fragile, hold them firmly with one hand as you wash the pests off. Make sure, however, not to turn the water on so high that the jet rips off leaves or damages new shoots.

If stems and branches are strong and resilient, vigorous shaking is enough to make many kinds of pests, including leaf-eating beetles and black vine weevils, fall to the ground. Place an old sheet or a tarpaulin around the base of the plant to collect the falling pests. When you are finished, shake the pests into a pail of soapy water.

Vacuuming pests off plants is another option, but only when it's done with a machine that has been made specifically for this purpose and has a gentle sucking action. Don't use a household vacuum, which is powerful enough to cause damage to the plant. Since the vacuum will pick up any insect in its path, it's important to distinguish pests from harmless or beneficial insects when using this technique.

Pruning Infested Plants

The best way to deal with some pests is to prune off the part of the plant that is afflicted. Fall webworm caterpillars, for example, hatch inside a gauzy-looking nest the female spins in susceptible trees. To rid the tree of the pests, crush the caterpillars or tear the bag open to expose the larvae to the elements. Then use sharp, well-made shears or a pruning saw and sever the infested stem or branch cleanly with a slanting cut about ¼ inch above a bud, as shown on page 394.

Insect-egg masses on foliage or stems can be pruned off; when you see leaf-miner trails on a susceptible plant, pinch off the infested leaves promptly. Add them to a hot compost pile—one that reaches at least 140° F—or put them in a tightly sealed plastic bag and place it in the trash.

Exploiting Natural Checks and Balances

In nature, the predator-prey system does a good job of keeping the size of pest populations within bounds. Even though a garden is an artificial environment, in which planting and cultivation practices can tip the balance in favor of pests, the checks and balances that operate in the wild can be adapted as a powerful and environmentally sound weapon against them.

The arsenal borrowed from nature includes predatory vertebrates, insects, insect relatives such as spiders and mites, beneficial nematodes, and bacteria that attack garden pests. Organisms that benefit the garden by feeding on pests are referred to as biological controls.

By encouraging the beneficial predators that already inhabit your garden and introducing others to augment its defenses, you can keep the pest population at a level that doesn't threaten the health or good looks of your plants. Moreover, this natural defensive system may become largely self-perpetuating, requiring little more of you than occasional tinkering. It is important to recognize, however, that biological controls are not over-night solutions to pest problems. Nor are they always complete solutions by themselves. An excellent way to apply them is in conjunction with many of the physical and cultural controls described on pages 348-352 and 359-363.

You must also recognize that biological controls function properly only if you minimize or even abandon the use of broad-spectrum pesticides. These products, which include most synthetic chemical pesticides as well as certain natural ones, such as pyrethrin and rotenone, kill many kinds of insects, including beneficials. At best, such pesticides provide you with a short-term solution to your pest problem.

Creating a Hospitable Environment

Just as there are conditions that make your garden attractive to pests, there are things you can do to attract and keep pest predators. A steady source of water such as a small pool is sure to draw benefi-

An insatiable predator, this convergent ladybird beetle eats its way along an aphid-infested plant stem. An adult beetle of this species can consume more than 30 of the insects a day; during its 3-week larval stage, the predator's intake can total 400 aphids. Other species of ladybird beetles, which are also known as ladybugs, feast on scale insects, mealybugs, white-flies, and mites.

How a Parasitoid Destroys a Pest

The body of an insect selected by a parasitoid is both a protective habitat and a food supply for developing offspring. The drawings below illustrate this sequence in the life of a typical parasitoid, the braconid wasp. At far left, the female wasp injects an egg into its victim through a tube called an ovipositor **(A)**. The egg-laying process usually paralyzes the host but does not kill it immediately.

The egg quickly develops into a larva **(B)**. By the end of this life stage, which lasts 8 to 10 days, the larva's feeding activity has killed the host aphid. The larva metamorphoses into a pupa **(C)**, which continues to develop within the aphid's dry shell. At the end of pupation, the braconid wasp has attained its adult form and cuts a neat escape hatch to emerge from the host's remains **(D)**.

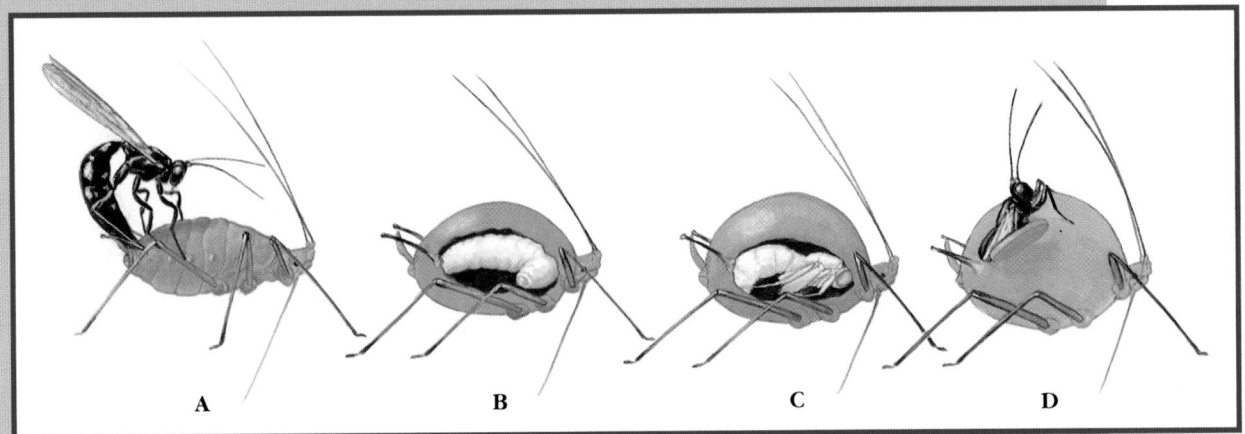

A   B   C   D

cial vertebrates, including frogs, toads, snakes, lizards, and birds. Toads also appreciate shelter in the garden—perhaps an overturned flower pot with a chipped rim for an opening. Fruiting shrubs and trees are magnets for birds, providing both shelter and food. The species that are mainly fruit or seed eaters in maturity catch prodigious numbers of insects to feed their young.

Insects, spiders, and other small predators can also be drawn to your garden by water and shelter; some types gravitate to shrubs, others to tall herbaceous plants or to a moist, cool layer of organic mulch. The more varied your landscape, the greater the chance that these creatures will find appropriate niches.

Spiders have an undeservedly bad reputation, for only a few species are dangerous to humans and none to plants. The wise gardener suppresses the impulse to kill spiders, since they are among the most efficient biological controls in the garden, consuming a wide variety of common garden pests. They are also present in great numbers in most areas. According to one study, for example, a typical 1-acre suburban plot has more than 60,000 spiders. Clearly, spiders play an important part in nature's system of checks and balances.

Purchasing Biological Controls

If the naturally occurring population of beneficials in your garden doesn't adequately contain pest outbreaks, it may be because they are too few in number or because they don't prey on the particular species of pest causing the trouble. In such cases, you can buy beneficials from a mail-order insectary for release in your garden. The information on the following pages will help you choose the beneficials you need to keep the pest populations at a manageable level.

Predatory Insects

Beneficial insects can be divided into two groups according to their feeding habits—predators and parasitoids. A predator's diet consists of other, usually smaller, insects. Green lacewings, ground beetles, ladybird beetles, rove beetles, and praying mantises are typical of these hunters. Some feed indiscriminately on a wide range of pests, including aphids, whiteflies, flea beetles, and spider

Predators for Sale

Many beneficial insects and other predators are available from mail-order insectaries. Before placing an order, identify your target pest. If you're uncertain of its type, send a specimen to your local Cooperative Extension Service. Or you may want to talk to a customer-service representative at a reputable insectary.

When your shipment of predators arrives, attend to it promptly. All predators need careful handling, and most must be released at a certain time. Read and follow all instructions. Three common mail-order predators are shown below in various life stages; since they'll be garden friends, you'll want to recognize them in all their various forms.

 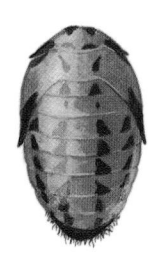 

The convergent ladybird beetle, shown as a larva above left and as a pupa at center, is sold in its adult form (above, right).

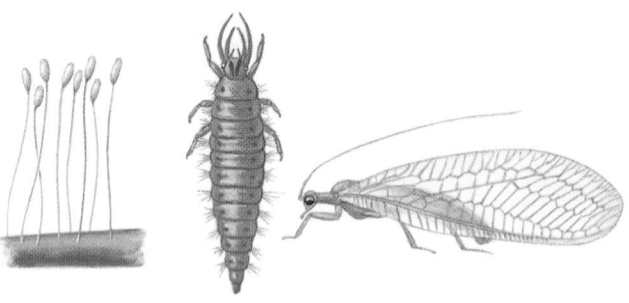

Green lacewings are typically sold as eggs (above, left). The larva is at center and the adult appears at right.

 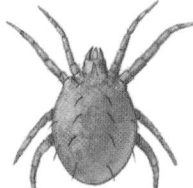

Predatory mites, which have eight legs like other arachnids, arrive as adults (near left). The egg stage appears at far left.

mites. Others are very specific about their food choices. Aphid midges, for example, feast on aphids and nothing else.

Most predators are voracious eaters. In its larval stage, for example, the green lacewing can devour 100 aphids in a day. But a shortcoming of predatory insects is that they also prey on other beneficials. Praying mantises, for instance, hunt down and devour their own kind.

Parasitoid Insects

Parasitoids, whose name means parasite-like, lay their eggs on or in a living insect host. After hatching, the larvae feed on the host, usually remaining attached to it until they have developed into adults *(diagram, page 365)*. Unlike a true para-

How to Release Beneficial Nematodes

Because of their ability to destroy more than 400 different soil-borne pests, beneficial nematodes are a popular biological control. The wormlike creatures are easy to handle and easy to apply to the soil. They arrive on sponges that usually measure about 5 by 7 inches, each of which has been saturated with a solution containing nearly 1 million nematodes—an amount sufficient to treat three or four large patio pots or window boxes. Before you can know how many nematodes to order, you'll need to determine the severity of your infestation and the size of the area to be treated. For a quarter-acre garden with a moderate infestation, you'll need around 25 to 30 million nematodes.

When the nematodes are delivered, immediately remove them from their packaging and inspect them *(Step 1, right)*. Apply them only during warm months, when temperatures range between 65° and 78°F. Wait until after sunset to release them into the garden; otherwise, ultraviolet rays from the sun can kill them. Nematodes work best in moist, loamy soil. If you are applying them to turf that has a thick mat of thatch, dethatch the lawn *(page 405)* so that the nematodes can easily penetrate the soil.

site, which feeds on its host but doesn't kill it, a parasitoid eventually kills the host.

Most parasitoid species target a particular type of pest and often only at one life-cycle stage. The trichogramma wasp, for instance, lays its eggs exclusively inside the eggs of specific butterfly and moth pests, thereby preventing the host eggs from hatching into troublesome caterpillars. Other pests controlled by parasitoids include aphids, whiteflies, and scale insects. Because the parasitoids are so selective, they are useful only when their chosen host infests your garden; without the host, the beneficial won't survive. This underscores the importance of learning to recognize garden pests, so that you'll be able to pick an appropriate control.

At least a dozen different parasitoids are widely available for purchase through the mail. Some species are shipped as adults, others in earlier stages of development. In the case of trichogramma wasps, the package you receive may contain a 1-inch-square card that holds up to 5,000 wasp eggs. Be sure to carefully read all instructions for unpacking, handling, and dispersing parasitoids. For further information and details on specific parasitoids available commercially, see the chart on page 369.

Predatory Mites

Like spiders, mites are arachnids rather than insects. The mite family includes several species of beneficials that prey on pests such as thrips and pest mites—for example, the spider mites and cyclamen mites that frequently cause serious dam-

1. Look over the sponges. They should feel damp and, to the naked eye, should appear to be coated with a cream-colored film. Using a magnifying glass, look to see if the nematodes are alive (they'll be wriggling). Proceed to Step 2, or reseal the sponges in their original plastic bag and store for no longer than 1 week in a refrigerator set at 40° to 50°F. (Caution: Because food refrigerators must be set lower than this to keep food from spoiling, do not store nematodes in them.)

2. Fill a bucket with 1 gallon of lukewarm distilled water or rainwater. Do not use chlorinated water, which can kill the nematodes. Wearing gloves, rinse the sponges in the water for a few minutes to release the nematodes into the water. Lightly squeeze the sponges, then dispose of them in the trash.

3. Pour the nematode solution into a watering can and apply evenly to the soil. Saturate the area but do not overwater; excess water can deplete the oxygen in the soil and kill the nematodes.

age to vegetables as well as many herbaceous ornamentals, trees, and shrubs.

Measuring less than $\frac{1}{50}$ inch in length, the predatory mite species are often smaller than their prey, which can include adult mites as well as mite eggs, larvae, and nymphs. Under optimal environmental conditions, the beneficials can go from egg hatching to egg laying in a week, outstripping the reproductive rate of the pests. Because their population can increase so rapidly, predatory mites are a particularly effective biological control. Unlike predatory insects, they do not attack beneficial insects or insect relatives. And because they are harmless to humans and so tiny as to be no annoyance at all, they can be used indoors safely and conveniently to control houseplant pests.

A Benevolent Snail

The decollate snail is a Mediterranean native that appeared in this country over a century ago and has since become widespread in the southern states and in California. A nocturnal hunter, this predator feeds voraciously on pest snails, eggs and adults alike. The decollate snail is useful for controlling the common brown garden snail, which chews holes in a wide variety of plants, especially those in warm, moist climates.

This benevolent creature does have its drawbacks, however. It feeds on the seedlings of a wide variety of plant species and can do serious damage to several succulents and other low-growing plants. You should also check local ordinances before ordering a supply of decollate snails. In some parts of California, buying these predators for release in the garden is illegal because they can pose a threat to benign native mollusk species.

Beneficial Nematodes

Barely large enough to be seen with the naked eye, beneficial nematodes are microscopic roundworms that live in the soil. Unlike pest nematodes *(page 386)*, which cause lesions and galls as they feed on plant stems and roots, beneficial nematodes destroy certain species of caterpillars, cutworms, borers, grubs, and beetle larvae. Like the parasitoids, beneficial nematodes are specialists: Certain species target certain pests. They do not damage plants, nor do they attack earthworms, which are natural aerators and essential to the health of the soil.

Applied to the soil *(pages 366-367)*, beneficial nematodes locate their prey by following the trail of carbon dioxide released by the pest as it moves through the ground. The nematodes then invade the pest's body. One species has a dorsal "tooth" that it uses to pierce the epidermis of a pest; the creatures can then enter the host through its vascular system. Once inside, nematodes release fast-multiplying bacteria that can kill the host within 24 to 48 hours. The nematodes feed on the host and also eat the lethal bacteria, then lay hundreds to thousands of eggs inside the host. When the food supply is exhausted, the new generation of nematodes begins searching for insect hosts on their own. As long as the soil remains moist and the temperature is somewhere between 65° and 78°F, the reproductive cycle continues uninterrupted; thus a single application of beneficial nematodes may be effective for up to one year. If soil-borne pests are a persistent problem in your area, however, you may need to replenish the nematodes once or twice a year. The nematodes will die out once the pests have been eradicated.

Beneficial Microbes

Microorganisms even smaller than nematodes are also being exploited as pesticides. The most popular of these are two bacteria strains that are extremely effective against particular target insects. Virtually nontoxic to other insects, animals, or humans, these controls are inexpensive, easy to mass-produce, and easy to apply.

The bacterium *Bacillus thuringiensis* (Bt) is lethal to leaf-eating caterpillars. There are 30 different strains of Bt, each of which infects only one host species. Other serious garden pests controlled by a strain of Bt include the elm leaf beetle and the larvae of the Colorado potato beetle. Given the specificity of Bt, correctly identifying the type of pest that is causing damage in your garden is essential. Bt can be purchased in a variety of forms—dusts, powders, liquids, and sprays—at most home and garden centers and from mail-order companies. As with all pest-control agents, read the instructions carefully before use.

The second bacterium widely used to control pests causes an infection called milky spore disease, which attacks Japanese beetle grubs, or pupae. Japanese beetles commonly lay their eggs just below the surface of a lawn. As the grubs develop there, they feed on the roots of the grass or on thatch, a matted accumulation of grass debris. When the bacterial spores are dusted onto the lawn, they attack the grubs and multiply inside their bodies. The grubs die, releasing the spores into the soil and continuing the cycle of infection.

BENEFICIAL INSECTS AND THEIR TARGETS

Beneficials	Target Pests	Comments
Braconid wasps	Aphids, beetle larvae, moth larvae	Overwinter as newly hatched larvae inside living hosts. Adults feed on nectar and pollen.
Flower flies, hover flies	Aphids, mealybugs, mites, thrips	Black-and-yellow-banded bodies resemble bees or hornets. Adults feed on nectar and pollen of daisylike flowers.
Green lacewings, brown lacewings	Aphids, thrips, mealybugs, scales, moth eggs, mites, small caterpillars, soft-bodied insects	Eggs overwinter on plants. Adults feed on nectar and pollen. To prevent cannibalism in larvae, distribute purchased eggs widely.
Lady beetles, ladybugs	Aphids, whiteflies, mealybugs, spider mites, scales	Adults overwinter in leaf litter. The migratory convergent ladybeetle overwinters in large groups.
Praying mantises	Aphids, beetles, bugs, caterpillars, flies, leafhoppers, wasps. Mantises also prey on butterflies, bees, and other desirable insects and on one another.	Eggs overwinter in a frothy gray case attached to stems or twigs. Mantises are highly territorial and feed mostly on large insects.
Predatory bugs: assassin bug, ambush bug, big-eyed bug, minute pirate bug, spined soldier bug	Aphids, beetle larvae, leafhopper nymphs, spider mites, thrips	Prefer permanent beds and garden litter for shelter.
Predatory mites	Citrus red mites, cyclamen mites, European red mites, rust mites, two-spotted spider mites, thrips	Found in soil, moss, humus, manure, and on plants. Thrive in high humidity; cannot survive at low humidity. Low temperature slows reproduction rate.
Rove beetles	Aphids, fly eggs, maggots, mites, nematodes, slugs, snails, springtails	Found in a wide variety of habitats. Prefer permanent beds for overwintering.
Soldier beetles	Aphids, beetle larvae, butterfly larvae, caterpillars, grasshopper eggs, moth larvae	Adults are nectar and pollen feeders; prefer goldenrod. Eggs laid in soil or ground cover. Both larvae and adults are predators.
Trichogramma wasps	Cabbage worms, cutworms, eggs of 200 moth species, leaf-roller caterpillars	Larvae parasitize and kill pest eggs. Adults feed on nectar; prefer the dais family and Queen Anne's lace and other members of the carrot family.

Earth-Friendly Pesticides

Buying Pesticides

Confronting the myriad bottles and containers in the pesticide aisle of the local garden center can be a bewildering experience for a gardener. Your first impulse may be to reach for the familiar package with the well-known manufacturer's name. But before you purchase your next pesticide, take a moment to consider the differences between an organic pesticide and a synthetic one.

Organic pesticides, as the name implies, are made from naturally occurring ingredients. They are effective against a wide range of pests and break down easily, with little effect on the environment. Although some organic pesticides have harmful effects on humans, bees, ladybird beetles, and other benign creatures, the danger is short-lived and can be minimized by proper handling. The chart on page 375 lists eight organic pesticides, the pests they target, and any precautions to follow in using the pesticide.

Synthetic pesticides are derived from both naturally occurring and manufactured materials. They are similar in chemistry to what are called persistent insecticides, which have been banned because of their damaging residual effects on the environment and all life forms. Synthetic pesticides can be highly toxic and tend to remain active for much longer periods of time than organics.

The product label will not tell you straight out whether the pesticide is organic or synthetic; you'll need to know the names of the botanical insecticides and the chemical names of the various synthetic products. Three groups of synthetics are widely available—organochlorines, organophosphates, and carbamates. Organochlorines contain carbon, chlorine, and hydrogen, in addition to pesticides such as chlordane and methoxychlor. Both chemicals are toxic to aquatic life if released into the water supply. Organophosphates, the most common of the synthetic pesticides, are derived from phosphoric acid and control a wide variety of garden pests. Although toxic to vertebrates, organophosphates break down quickly and have little residual effect. This group includes malathion, trichlorfon, and Diazinon. Carbamates are derived from carbamic acid; one of the best known is carbaryl, which is used to control lawn and garden pests as well as ticks and cockroaches. Carbaryl is highly toxic to natural predators, bees, and aquatic invertebrates, and moderately toxic to fish.

With both organic and synthetic pesticide products, it is imperative that you read the label and follow all instructions for applying the pesticide and disposing of it.

If you've given milder pest-control measures a fair trial and been disappointed with the results, you may decide to opt for a chemical control. As with other techniques, the prudent approach is always to use the pesticide least likely to harm humans, pets, or the environment. In practice, this means giving preference to pesticides derived from natural materials—principally minerals, plants, soaps, and oils—over the more toxic synthetics.

The reason that natural pesticides are relatively benign is that they generally target specific insects. These pesticides also break down into harmless substances shortly after they are applied; synthetic pesticides, on the other hand, may remain toxic far longer.

The fact that natural pesticides lose their potency quickly shouldn't mislead the gardener into underestimating their lethal capabilities. For instance, two of the most venerable botanicals—rotenone and pyrethrins—are powerful broad-spectrum poisons, killing a wide range of insects, including aphids, spider mites, and other serious pests, as well as some beneficials, such as honeybees, lacewings, spiders, and braconid wasps.

Higher animals, including humans, aren't immune to natural pesticides, either. Carelessly handled, these products can make a gardener very ill. And different creatures have peculiar sensitivities. While pyrethrins earn good marks for doing little harm to most mammals, cats are highly susceptible to pyrethrin poisoning.

Judging a Product's Safety

Many pesticides have not been fully tested, and being registered with the Environmental Protection Agency (EPA) does not necessarily mean they are safe. In fact, no pesticide on the market is designated "safe" on its label. Even the chemicals of low to moderate toxicity must be labeled with the word "caution" because they have the potential for doing serious harm to humans. Ingesting even a fraction of an ounce of one of the milder pesti-

terpret this information so you'll get full benefit from the pesticide with the least possible harm.

How Natural Pesticides Work

If you decide to use a pesticide, identify the pest first, then choose a chemical that targets your problem. There is no one cure-all; your natural arsenal will have a range of weapons. Some of them, including Bt, are stomach poisons and work only when an insect ingests a bit of a treated plant. Overall, chewing insects—beetles, caterpillars, and the like—are more vulnerable to stomach poisons than sucking insects. In fact, sucking insects may not be affected at all, since they pierce the leaf surface and suck out the sap rather than eat the pesticide-coated surface itself.

Contact poisons, as their name suggests, must make direct contact with the pest. They are best sprayed onto the pest—a technique that is easiest to carry out on eggs, pupae, slow-moving crawling insects, and insects such as scales, whiteflies, and aphids. Flying insects can be felled unintentionally by drifting spray, and creeping or crawling pests can pick up a poison on their feet or antennae as they make their way over the surface of a treated plant. When you apply a contact pesticide, don't neglect crevices and the undersides of stems or foliage *(page 373)*.

Using Soap Sprays

Insecticidal soap sprays are contact poisons that are absorbed through the cuticle covering the pest's body. Once inside, they make cell membranes leaky, causing severe dehydration. Most vulnerable to soap sprays are aphids, scales, mites, and other soft-cuticled pests. Beetles, grasshoppers, and other pests with hard cuticles are much less susceptible.

The soap sprays remain potent only as long as they are wet, so spray in the early morning or in the evening, when lower temperatures and higher humidity slow the rate of evaporation. To avoid killing beneficials, keep the pesticide aimed specifically at problem species. Also, test-spray a few leaves and inspect them for yellowing or other symptoms of injury before treating the entire plant.

Horticultural Oils

These pesticides are sprayed on infested plants, smothering pests in a fine film. Eggs are especially

vulnerable, as are soft-bodied mites and insects, including scales, mealybugs, and whiteflies. Beneficials coated by the spray may also be killed, but once the treated plant dries, beneficials aren't in danger. The oils are available as dormant oil, for use when plants are dormant, and as superior oil, for use during the growing season. Avoid using any oils when temperatures exceed 90°F, and spray in early morning or late evening when the sun is at its weakest. For details, see pages 372-373.

A Pesticide from Seeds

Neem is a remarkably versatile botanical insecticide extracted from the seeds of the neem tree and first registered by the EPA in the 1980s. It has been found to combat more than 200 species of pests, including gypsy moths, whiteflies, mealybugs, Japanese beetles, leaf miners, and the Colorado potato beetle. For some leaf-eating insects, the repellent is so powerful that they completely shun plants they would otherwise defoliate. Other leaf eaters may begin to feed but stop immediately. Neem can also halt a larva's metamorphosis at the pupal stage. Since fewer individuals mature and reproduce, the pest population declines.

Neem is available as a foliar spray and as a soil drench. When taken up by a plant's roots and transported throughout its tissues, neem protects the plant from voracious insects for as long as 2 months. Judged safe for use on vegetables and fruits by the EPA, neem has an extremely low toxicity rating for humans and other mammals. It does not harm butterflies, honeybees, or ladybird beetles, and it does not accumulate in soil or water.

A Variety of Pesticide Forms

Pesticides are available in a number of different forms—liquid, granular, or dust. Whatever a pesticide's formulation, use a delivery device that allows the maximum possible precision to protect yourself from exposure and the environment from contamination.

An aerosol can filled with a premixed pesticide is an easy-to-use, surefire applicator (and also the most expensive). More important, it eliminates the risk of accidental spills. Equally convenient and somewhat more economical are the small trigger sprayers that contain premixed pesticide. At a still lower cost, you can mix a small quantity of liquid concentrate or wettable powder with water in a small pail reserved for this specific purpose. Carefully pour the mixture into a small trigger sprayer for application.

When you have a large job to do—spraying a lawn, for instance, or a number of trees or shrubs—the best device for applying a liquid pesticide is a compressed-air sprayer (below). On a well-designed sprayer, the trigger that controls the spray is far enough from the nozzle that there is little danger of the pesticide dripping or spilling onto your hand.

That's not the case with hose-end sprayers, which are notorious drippers and splashers. Not only is it difficult to calibrate them to get the right proportion of pesticide to water, but if the sprayer lacks a backflow-prevention filter, the pesticide may flow backward into the hose—or even into the domestic water supply. For all of these reasons, you should avoid using hose-end sprayers to apply pesticides.

Soil infested with pests is commonly treated with granular pesticides, which can be applied with a drop spreader or sprinkled directly from the container onto the soil. However, birds can be killed by eating granules. A better dry pesticide choice is a dust, which can be safely spread with a bulb duster.

How to Use Horticultural Oils

Horticultural oils are safe and effective pesticides if you observe the following guidelines:

- Use either dormant oil or superior oil on plants that are in dormancy. In spring and summer, when plants are in active growth, use superior oil only.
- Choose the right strength. A 3-percent solution for dormant plants and a 2-percent solution in spring and summer are safe for the majority of plants. If the oil makes leaves burn or blister, try a 1-percent solution.
- Shake the sprayer occasionally to keep the oil and water solution well mixed.
- Apply horticultural oil early in the day in sunny, dry conditions so the oil will dry quickly.
- Spray each plant until every exposed surface—trunk, stems, branches, both sides of the leaves, and flowers—is wet.
- Allow at least 2 weeks between applications, and longer when plants are stressed by drought. Most species can be sprayed up to four times a year.

1. Before mixing or spraying horticultural oil, put on a face mask and goggles to prevent oil particles from getting into your lungs and eyes. Wearing rubber gloves, unscrew the top of a 1-gallon compression sprayer. Measure the amount of oil according to the strength of the solution needed and pour it into the sprayer. Recap the bottle of oil. Fill the sprayer with water.

Applying a Pesticide

A critical first step when working with a pesticide is to read the label thoroughly, even for a product that you have used before. Pay close attention to instructions for application, as well as any precautionary statements about the use of the chemical. Then, though it may be inconvenient, wait for a day when there is no wind to apply the pesticide. If it is imperative to go ahead with the job and no more than a slight breeze is stirring the air, proceed with caution, making sure that you keep your back squarely to the wind while you work; otherwise, you risk exposing yourself to the chemical.

In addition to being windless, the weather should be mild; low temperatures slow the breakdown process and pesticides remain toxic for a longer time. If the pesticide you are using is toxic to bees, apply it early in the morning or in the evening when they aren't active. Never apply a pesticide where it can run off into a drain, storm sewer, or stream. Treat only the plants or the parts of plants that are troubled by the pest, and use the lowest recommended dose. Because many natural pesticides are slow acting, you should give them several days to work before reapplying.

Spraying for Total Coverage

To ensure that a contact poison hits all target pests on a plant, begin spraying at its base and work up to the top, aiming the sprayer at the undersides of the leaves, as shown at left. Spray each surface, including stems and leaf axils, until the pesticide just begins to drip off. Next, spray the upper surfaces of the leaves, working from the top of the plant down.

2. Replace the top of the sprayer and screw it on tightly. Hold the container steady with one hand and pump the handle until you cannot pump it anymore (right). Shake the sprayer vigorously to make sure the oil and water are thoroughly mixed.

3. Spray an even coat of the oil solution on the entire plant (above). Shake the container occasionally to mix the oil and water. When you have finished, release the pressure valve on your sprayer, or carefully unscrew the sprayer's top. Dispose of any unused solution according to the pesticide label directions.

Dressing for the Job

The label of every pesticide describes any special protective equipment you will need, so read it carefully before you begin, and follow the directions scrupulously. With even the least toxic pesticide, you should always wear a long-sleeved, loose-fitting shirt; long pants; rubber work gloves (dishwashing gloves are not adequate); and non-porous shoes or boots (pesticides can soak into leather or fabric). As insurance against eye or lung irritation, you may also want to wear a mask and goggles. For more toxic chemicals, however, goggles and a respirator that has been specially designed for the chemical you are using are absolute necessities for ensuring your safety.

Once you begin handling a pesticide, do not smoke, drink, eat, or use the bathroom until the job is completed and you have washed your hands thoroughly. When you are preparing a mixture for spraying, measure out precisely the prescribed amount of pesticide. Be very careful not to splash the material on yourself, your clothes, or the surrounding area.

To avoid disposal or storage problems, mix only as much pesticide as you need for a single spraying. Should there be any left over at the end of the job, spray out the excess on other plants that can be treated, or follow the instructions on the label for proper disposal of unused material.

Cleaning Up

When you've finished applying the pesticide, wash the sprayer and mixing implements thoroughly with soap and water, rinse, and repeat. Store pesticides and any implements used with them in a cool, dry place, preferably a toolshed or garage rather than in the house. They should be out of a child's reach. Finally, wash your clothes separately from the rest of the laundry; dry them on high heat or outdoors in the sun.

Reading Pesticide Labels

The label on a pesticide container is your most complete source of information about a product. Although the words may be in microscopic type, it is important to read them before you buy. Each label has certain information required by law. It will inform you of the relative hazards of the material and how it may legally be used, along with any precautions you should take. Below are explanations for some of the most important components of a pesticide label:

- **Signal Word:** This is the most critical word—and the largest one—on the label. It reveals the relative acute toxicity of the pesticide, which is the measure of damage done if a product is ingested, inhaled, or absorbed through the skin. The least toxic materials are labeled with the word "Caution." The word "Warning" means the pesticide is moderately toxic. "Danger" or "Poison" on the label means the pesticide is highly toxic; this designation may also be accompanied by a skull-and-crossbones symbol. If there is no signal word on the package, the pesticide is relatively nontoxic. These signal words refer only to immediate damage sustained from one-time exposure to the pesticide; they reveal nothing about possible chronic effects.
- **Precautionary Statements:** These are the possible chronic effects, if any, including the chemical's ability to poison components of the nervous system (neurotoxici-ty), cause cancer (carcinogenicity), have adverse effects on the reproductive process, and create mutations in genetic structure (mutagenicity). Also under this heading are precautions that should be taken when applying the pesticide, such as protective clothing that must be worn. The amount of time that must pass before you harvest food crops that have been sprayed with the product, sometimes listed as "reentry times required," is also included here.
- **Active Ingredient:** The pesticide's chemical composition and the percentage of it contained in the mixture.
- **Inerts:** A general term for all fillers and inactive ingredients, listed by percentage.
- **Statement of Practical Treatment:** Emergency first-aid measures if you are exposed to the pesticide.
- **Environmental Hazards:** Includes effect on beneficial insects such as bees, waterfowl, and other wildlife.
- **Directions for Use:** How to mix the pesticide, and when and how to apply it. You are required by law to follow these directions to the letter.
- **Storage and Disposal:** States whether the material must be kept from heat or freezing, and how to dispose of packaging and unused material.
- **Crops and Insects Controlled:** Includes a list of plants this pesticide may be used on and pests for which it has been approved. By law, the product may not be used on any crop or against any pest not listed on the label.

CHOOSING A BOTANICAL PESTICIDE

Pesticide	Target Pests	Comments
Citrus oils	Spider mites, aphids	Relatively nontoxic to humans and other mammals. May cause an allergic reaction.
False hellebore	Beetles, caterpillars, grasshoppers, sawflies	Highly toxic if ingested.
Neem	Aphids, flea beetles, gypsy moths, leaf miners, thrips, whiteflies	Relatively nontoxic to humans and other mammals and to beneficial insects.
Pyrethrins	Aphids, leafhoppers, spider mites, thrips, whiteflies	Toxic to fish, aquatic insects, and ladybeetles. Moderately toxic to bees and mammals. Pest insects may appear dead but revive after metabolizing pyrethrin.
Quassia	Aphids, caterpillars, sawflies	One of the safest botanical insecticides. Nontoxic to ladybeetles and bees.
Rotenone	Aphids, flea beetles, leafhoppers, spider mites, whiteflies, and other sucking and chewing insects	Highly toxic to fish, aquatic insects, and birds. Moderately toxic to humans and other mammals. May cause an allergic reaction.
Ryania	Aphids, Japanese beetles, lepidopterous larvae including codling moths, painted lady butterflies, and sunflower moths	Low toxicity to humans and other mammals and to beneficial insects.
Sabadilla	Aphids, blister beetles, chinch bugs, citrus thrips, grasshoppers, harlequin bugs, tarnished plant bugs, webworms	Toxic to humans and other mammals and to bees. May cause an allergic reaction.

Nuisance Mammals

Wildlife in the garden can be a mixed blessing. Many gardeners enjoy having chipmunks and cottontail rabbits around; the animals are fun to watch, and the damage they do, although it can be annoying, is almost always minor. Moreover, fences and chemical repellents do a good job of minimizing their impact on the garden.

Then there are the animals that do so much harm to the garden even the kindliest of gardeners cannot tolerate their presence. Although it isn't easy, it is possible to rid a garden of such pests by depriving them of food and water and eliminating their access to shelter. Nuisance animals can also be captured in live traps or, more drastically, in lethal traps.

Several mammals are especially notorious for damaging American gardens. Moles dig underground burrows that disturb plant roots and disfigure lawns. Voles, pocket gophers, ground squirrels, and woodchucks also tunnel extensively, feeding underground on roots and bulbs, and making aboveground forays for leaves and stems. Jack rabbits, hares, rats, mice, and deer graze on shrubby ornamentals, fruit trees, and perennials. Skunks pockmark lawns in search of grubs and insects, and tree squirrels eat bulbs, fruits, and nuts.

Moles

Members of the shrew family, the seven species of moles found in the United States are torpedo-shaped creatures weighing about 4 ounces. Outfitted for digging with strong forepaws splayed outward, they can tunnel as far as 200 feet a day. Gardeners rarely see moles, which emerge from their network of burrows and feeding tunnels only to gather nesting materials. Active day and night year round, moles search constantly for the insects, slugs, and grubs that make up their diet; af-

The star-nosed mole pictured below has 22 fleshy pink appendages around its nostrils that it uses like fingers to explore the soil for grubs and insects. Like all moles, this species has large-toed, spade-shaped forepaws that are well adapted for efficient digging.

ter only a few hours without food they starve to death. They use their snouts, which have a highly developed sense of touch, to locate their prey.

Moles make their presence known by the small cones of loose soil—or molehills—around the openings to their burrows and by the telltale ridges made by shallow tunnels. The ridges are primarily an aesthetic problem, as are the molehills, although they can be high enough to damage a lawn mower.

Since moles devour soil pests such as cutworms and white grubs in large numbers and don't feed on plants at all, it makes sense to be as tolerant of their objectionable habits as possible. You can minimize the impact of their tunneling by tamping down raised strips of soil and watering them well to ensure that disturbed plant roots don't dry out.

Moles have hearing so acute that you may be able to get rid of them with a level of noise that is tolerable to human ears. A simple technique is to push the shaft of a plastic pinwheel down into a tunnel until you feel it touch the tunnel's floor. As it turns in the wind, the pinwheel may transmit vibrations strong enough to force the moles to abandon the tunnel. Partially buried bottles, which whistle and vibrate in the wind, may also help rid your garden of the pests.

Lethal traps are undoubtedly the most effective means of managing moles. Harpoon, scissor-jaw, or choker-loop traps should be set over frequently traveled tunnels in early spring or early fall. These devices kill quickly and are considered more humane than a live trap, since a mole could easily starve to death before the well-meaning gardener had a chance to check the trap.

Bury a dead mole where you trap it. Its remains will discourage other moles from reinfesting that part of your garden.

Voles and Pocket Gophers

Voles and pocket gophers are small rodents that deface lawns and beds with mounds of soil and feed on an entire range of plant materials. Voles, also called meadow or field mice, are found across the northern tier of the United States and as far south as northern Florida. About 6 inches long including their tails, they live in abandoned mole burrows, thick blankets of mulch, dense weeds, and grassy areas. They eat seeds, fruits, grasses, tender bark, and other soft plant materials, digging 1- to 2-inch-wide surface runways where they feed on roots. These runways crisscross a lawn like a brown maze. A vole eats twice its weight every

The meadow vole (left) feeds on strawberries and other fruits, seeds, and grasses, and in winter it strips bark from trees and shrubs. The lawn shown below has been ruined by the maze of runways made by voles.

377

A pocket gopher emerging from its tunnel (right) displays the sickle-shaped claws it uses for digging. On its aboveground forays, the pocket gopher fills its expandable cheek pouches with food and nesting materials.

Found in most parts of the United States, the striped skunk (above) digs holes and damages garden plants in its search for insects and grubs. When this pest is alarmed, the noxious, malodorous liquid it sprays to a distance of 10 feet or more can cause temporary blindness.

Adopting an erect posture meant to intimidate an enemy, the woodchuck at right may eat more than 1½ pounds of vegetation a day, including leaves, blossoms, and tougher fare such as woody stems. The woodchuck's sharp incisors grow at a rate of 14 inches a year to replace the portions worn away by incessant gnawing.

day but tends to destroy much more than it eats.

Reproducing at a rate of 10 litters of five offspring per year, voles tend to be so numerous that a gardener's options for control are few. A house cat that is a diligent mouser is a help, but traps scarcely make a dent in the population. Modifying the garden habitat by weeding, mowing the lawn often, and removing thick mulches deprives voles of favorite habitats. You can erase their runways by tilling the soil and replanting the area; you will likely kill some of the population in the process.

Pocket gophers, unlike voles, lead solitary lives. Named for the pocketlike cheek pouches in which they carry vegetation for food and nesting, pocket gophers are common throughout the West and Midwest. Like moles, they are active at all hours and in all seasons, and tunnel underground. You can easily distinguish the entrance of a pocket gopher's tunnel from the opening of a mole's burrow: Instead of a cone, the soil is arranged in a fan-shaped mound.

Pocket gophers feed both above ground and below. If you see a plant wiggle, then disappear beneath the soil's surface, a pocket gopher is at work. Besides destroying vegetation, these animals also chew through plastic irrigation lines.

Fumigating a pocket gopher's tunnel with smoke or gas cartridges, flooding it with water, dumping used kitty litter into it, or placing a few tablespoons of strychnine-laced bait in the tunnel are sometimes suggested as controls, but none of them is completely reliable. If you have a severe infestation, you may have to resort to a lethal trap. The best type for pocket gophers is the two-pronged pincher trap. Always wear gloves when checking traps, since pocket gophers are hosts to lice and external parasites. Stuffing a dead pocket gopher into the tunnel will discourage reinfestation.

Rats, Mice, and Squirrels

Together, these three groups of rodents account for nearly 40 percent of all mammalian species. They breed prolifically, can be found in all climates except the polar regions, and continuously compete with people for food and space.

Rats and mice dig up seeds and eat seedlings and fruits. Ground squirrels, which live in underground burrows, are omnivores. They eat seeds, fruits, grasses,

Commonly Used Controls

Prevention is the best way to control animal pests. Choose shrubs and perennials animals shun. To prevent pests from burrowing, lay down wire mesh before spreading topsoil and planting. Use fencing in your design. When damage occurs, identify the animal causing it. If possible, first make changes in the garden's habitats—remove brush piles, control weeds, fill in boggy areas, store firewood on pallets—to eliminate sources of food, water, and shelter. If this doesn't work, choose controls from the chart at right. The following controls help to exclude animals, manipulate their behavior, or reduce their population:

- Fences and protective guards: The height of a fence and whether it should extend underground depend on the ability of the pest to jump or burrow. Guards include metal flashing, wire mesh, and netting.
- Repellents: Chemical taste and odor repellents such as thiram, ammonium salts, and putrescent egg solids, sprayed directly on plants, can be effective if applied weekly.
- Scare tactics: Noise, the scent of natural predators (including people), and lifelike owl, snake, and cat decoys can ward off pests.
- Live and lethal traps: Live traps include baited cages and boxes. Spring-loaded snap, skewer, scissors, and choke traps kill the animal.

PESTS	CONTROLS					
	Habitat Alteration	Fences/Protective Guards	Repellents	Scare Tactics	Live Traps	Lethal Traps
Deer		✔	✔			
Ground Squirrels			✔	✔		✔
Jack Rabbits/Hares		✔	✔	✔	✔	
Meadow Voles	✔	✔				✔
Moles		✔	✔	✔		✔
Pocket Gophers	✔					✔
Rats/Mice	✔			✔		✔
Skunks	✔	✔	✔		✔	
Tree Squirrels		✔	✔		✔	
Woodchucks	✔	✔		✔	✔	

insects, and lizards, and raid birds' nests for both eggs and hatchlings. Tree squirrels, which have long, bushy tails and usually nest in trees, feed on buds, nuts, fruits, and the tender stems of woody plants. They strip bark from trees and gnaw through irrigation lines and telephone cables.

The yard cleanup recommended for discouraging voles may also work with rats and mice. Spread mothballs around the bases of shrubs and trees to repel both ground and tree squirrels. Two types of lethal traps—snap traps and jaw traps—are effective against ground squirrels, mice, and rats.

Using a Live Trap

You can also catch mice, rats, and squirrels in a live trap, either a box or a cage type. Special caution is called for, however, since these rodents can transmit viral diseases to humans. Decide beforehand where you will release any animal you catch, and

At home in rural, suburban, and urban areas, the highly adaptable American gray squirrel (left) eats buds, seeds, nuts, and fruits of ornamental plants; gnaws through the bark of trees to reach the edible inner layers; and chews holes in irrigation lines.

Deer-Resistant Plants

While only a handful of ornamentals are truly deer-proof, there are many that deer shun unless preferred food sources are scarce. Characteristics likely to make a plant deer resistant are thorns, tough or fuzzy leaves or stems, and strong flavors and aromas.

GROUND COVERS

Ajuga reptans
(carpet bugle)

Asperula odorata
(sweet woodruff)

Convallaria majalis
(lily of the valley)

Lamium 'Beacon Silver'
(dead nettle)

Pachysandra
(pachysandra)

Vinca minor
(periwinkle)

PERENNIALS

Achillea **spp.**
(yarrow)

Astilbe **spp.**
(false spirea)

Coreopsis **spp.**
(tickseed)

Dianthus **spp.**
(garden pink)

Echinacea **spp.**
(purple coneflower)

Eupatorium purpureum
(Joe-Pye weed)

Geranium **spp.**
(cranesbill)

Helleborus **spp.**
(hellebore)

Iberis **spp.**
(candytuft)

Liatris spicata
(spike gay-feather)

Linaria **spp.**
(toadflax)

Lychnis coronaria
(rose campion)

Perovskia atriplicifolia
(Russian sage)

Rudbeckia **spp.**
(coneflower)

Solidago **spp.**
(goldenrod)

Veronica officinalis
(speedwell)

VINES

Celastrus **spp.**
(bittersweet)

Clematis **spp.**
(clematis)

Hedera helix
(English ivy)

Lonicera **spp.**
(honeysuckle)

Wisteria **spp.**
(wisteria)

SHRUBS

Buddleia davidii
(butterfly bush)

Buxus sempervirens
(common boxwood)

Calycanthus occidentalis
(sweet shrub)

Ceanothus sanguineus
(wild lilac)

Cephalotaxus fortunei
(Chinese plum yew)

Cornus stolonifera
(red-osier dogwood)

Corylus americana
(American hazelnut)

Enkianthus campanulatus
(enkianthus)

Hibiscus syriacus
(rose of Sharon)

Ilex x meserveae
(blue holly)

Ilex glabra
(inkberry)

Leucothoe fontanesiana
(leucothoe)

Mahonia bealei

White-Tailed Deer Fawn

check the trap at least once a day. When you catch an animal, calm it by covering the trap with a tarpaulin or blanket before moving it; wear heavy gloves and keep children away from the trap. When you are ready to release the animal, back away from the trap as soon as you open it.

Skunks can also be controlled with live traps, but because of their offensive smell when they are alarmed, this is a job best left to a pest-control professional. Besides doing damage with their digging, skunks are undesirable because they can carry the rabies virus.

The Rabbit Family

Jack rabbits and snowshoe hares are far more destructive than cottontail rabbits because of their greater size and fecundity: The average female produces four litters of eight kits annually. These prolific pests consume up to 1 pound of vegetation each day, feasting on flowers, turf grass, foliage, shoots, stems, and the tender bark of young trees and shrubs.

Physical barriers and repellents are effective against jack rabbits and hares. These animals are stopped by a 3-foot-high fence of ¾-inch wire mesh, which need not extend underground, since these pests do not normally burrow. You can also protect a tree with a collar of sheet-metal flashing that extends 2 feet above the snow line. Commercial repellents containing thiram, ammonium soaps, putrescent egg solids, lime sulfur, copper carbonate, or asphalt must be reapplied to plants weekly or after a heavy rain.

Woodchucks

Although woodchucks (also known as groundhogs) are far less numerous per acre than the animals described so far, their size—as much as 20 pounds—and voracious appetite can create a serious problem for the gardener: These large rodents can devastate new plantings in a few hours. They dig burrows up to 50 feet long on two or

(leatherleaf mahonia)

***Philadelphus* spp.**
(mock orange)

***Spiraea* spp.**
(bridal wreath)

Syringa vulgaris
(common lilac)

Viburnum carlesii
(Koreanspice viburnum)

Viburnum opulus
(snowball bush)

Yucca filamentosa
(yucca)

TREES

Acer platanoides
(Norway maple)

Acer saccharinum
(silver maple)

Betula papyrifera
(white birch)

***Crataegus* spp.**
(hawthorn)

Cryptomeria japonica
(Japanese cedar)

Lithocarpus densiflorus
(tanbark oak)

Metasequoia glyptostroboides
(dawn redwood)

Parrotia persica
(Persian parrotia)

Picea abies
(Norway spruce)

Picea glauca
(white spruce)

Pinus sylvestris
(Scotch pine)

Pinus thunbergii
(black pine)

Tsuga canadensis
(Canadian hemlock)

Note: The abbreviation "spp." stands for the plural of "species"; where used in lists it means that many, but not all, of the species in a genus meet the criterion of the list.

Clematis (clematis)

Rudbeckia hirta (black-eyed Susan)

Syringa vulgaris (common lilac)

more levels. The apron of dirt at each of the two or three entrances serves as a sentry post and a safe spot for sunning and grooming. Slow-moving and easily frightened, woodchucks rarely venture far from their underground homes.

Because of their timidity, woodchucks prefer the protection of tall grass or undergrowth, so clearing away such vegetation may effectively discourage them. If this tactic fails, a sturdy fence that extends 3 feet above ground level and at least 2 feet below will keep a woodchuck out of a garden plot. You can also capture the animal in a baited box or cage trap. Release it more than 5 miles from its burrow; otherwise, it may find its way back home. A lethal trap can be used, of course, but you may not want to handle a dead mammal of this size.

Deer

Deer can pillage a garden even faster than woodchucks. The two species common to the United States—the white-tailed deer in the East and the mule deer in the West—strip shrubs and trees of foliage and devour perennials and vegetables in record time. While deer usually live at the edge of woodlands, they also roam suburban areas.

The same commercial repellents that succeed with jack rabbits and hares work with deer if plants are sprayed at the first sign of new growth in spring and at weekly intervals thereafter. Fences must be at least 7 feet high to prevent deer from leaping over them, and ideally they should slant outward from the protected area at a 45° angle. Another tactic is to fill your garden with plants that deer generally ignore; a list of these appears above. Keep in mind, though, that when the deer population in an area outstrips the available food supply, the hungry animals will eat virtually any kind of vegetation.

Betula papyrifera (white birch)

CHAPTER NINE

Preventing Plant Disease

At one time or another even the most conscientious gardener is likely to discover a plant with signs of disease. In the lovely spring garden at left, for example, blemished petals and leaves on the red tulips betray the presence of botrytis blight, a fungal disease. The outdoors is teeming with billions of microorganisms, and although most of them are beneficial, a few—called plant pathogens—feed on and damage living plants.

Instead of relying primarily on synthetic chemicals to prevent disease or restore plants to health, many gardeners have begun to adopt a more sophisticated, environmentally friendly strategy. It calls for selecting disease-resistant plants suitable for a garden's particular environment and keeping the soil in good condition. Cultural, physical, and biological means of preventing and controlling disease, many of which are described on the following pages, are the gardener's first choice. Chemical controls (pages 396-397) are reserved for use only when simpler, safer methods prove ineffective.

Identifying Diseases

It is impossible to predict when disease will strike the garden. A plant that grew vigorously one year may have wilting leaves or inferior blooms the next, for no apparent reason. With a little knowledge, however, the gardener can learn to detect signs of disease early on and may be able to prevent a small problem from turning into a large one.

An essential first step to knowing your garden is identifying your plants. Since different genera and species are vulnerable to different diseases, a plant's botanical name is an important diagnostic clue. Keep a list of your plants in a diary and update it with each acquisition. In addition, use the diary to note such events as the date you set out a new plant or transplanted an old one, and how a new disease-resistant cultivar is performing. Also note any periods of unusual weather and the application of fertilizers or other chemicals.

The more observant you are in the garden, the more likely you'll be to notice when your plants deviate from the norm. Make it a habit to stroll through the garden once a week to examine your plants, looking at the undersides of leaves and checking stems; a 10-power hand lens will help you inspect them more closely. Keep track of your observations, recording any unusual symptoms you may find. Some common symptoms of disease are illustrated on page 387. Typically, diseases are seasonal, so if there's an outbreak one year, your diary will remind you when to be on the alert in coming years for a recurrence.

If you have difficulty pinning down a plant's problem, ask the local Cooperative Extension Service or a reputable nursery for help. Your diary, along with a fresh specimen of the plant, will provide the expert with information needed to make an accurate diagnosis.

The Varieties of Diseases

Plant diseases are divided into two broad categories—infectious and noninfectious. Among the agents responsible for infectious diseases are a number of invasive, parasitic pathogens that include certain fungi, bacteria, viruses, and even a few plants. Noninfectious diseases, on the other hand, arise from environmental problems such as mineral deficiencies, severe weather, and overwatering. Understanding these causes should be the first line of defense for your garden.

Fungi

Approximately 80 percent of the infectious diseases you are likely to encounter in your garden are caused by various types of fungi. Most fungi are beneficial: They live off dead leaves and other organic matter, decomposing it in the process. Disease-causing fungi, by contrast, feed on living plants and release toxins as they spread over the plant's surface or invade its tissue. Some fungal infections, such as powdery mildew, are mainly a cosmetic problem, while others, such as root rot, can do serious damage and even kill the plant.

Fungi reproduce by releasing spores, which can be spread by water, wind, insects, birds, animals, or humans. Some spores can survive a trip of hundreds of miles, then germinate within minutes when deposited in a hospitable place. Spores need moisture to germinate, so dry weather will suppress fresh outbreaks of fungal disease.

Bacteria

As with fungi, most species of bacteria in the garden are valuable organisms, releasing nitrogen into the soil and breaking down dead plant and animal tissue. The species that cause plant diseases are most frequently transmitted by water, but can also be carried by foraging insects, or wind, or on gardening tools.

Some bacteria enter a plant by penetrating cells on its surface, while others invade through pores or other natural openings, or through wounds in stems or bark. An insect carrying a bacterium can inject it directly as it feeds. Once inside, bacteria may clog a plant's water-conducting system or drain nutrients from its cells. The symptoms of a bacterial disease often resemble those produced by a fungus, such as rotting tissue. If the rotted portion is slimy and smells foul, however, the cause can only be a bacterium; fungi don't produce either symptom.

Viruses

A plant that has stunted foliage, abnormal leaf curling, mosaic-like patterns on its foliage, or color changes such as yellow rings or lines may be in-

The owner of this lush Chapel Hill, North Carolina, garden shuns chemicals. She credits the garden's health to well-prepared soil and to disease-resistant shrubs, grasses, and perennials such as the Joe-Pye weed blooming at right.

fected with a virus. Most viruses travel among plants in the saliva of insects, but nematodes—microscopic, wormlike creatures—are also carriers. In addition, a gardener can transmit viruses via hands, shoes, or tools, especially those used for cutting. Thus pruning, grafting, dividing, and taking cuttings all carry a risk, however minimal, of exposing plants to viruses.

Viral diseases are the hardest to diagnose. A single virus may have a variety of symptoms, which often closely resemble those produced by a nutrient deficiency. The only sure way to diagnose a virus is to have the plant analyzed by experts in a laboratory. The simpler course is to maintain an adequate supply of nutrients in your soil; if the problem persists even after you have added nutrients to the soil, you can assume that a virus is the cause. Since there is no known cure of any kind for viral diseases, the prudent move is to destroy the infected plant.

Nematodes

Although most species of nematodes are harmless or even beneficial to plants *(page 368)*, some are destructive. Most parasitic nematodes feed on roots, stunting the plant and causing wilting and yellowing. A few species feed inside stems, while others damage leaves and sometimes blossoms. The damage done by nematodes, viruses, and cultural disorders can look very similar, but laboratory analysis of a soil sample or a plant can pinpoint the exact cause.

Cultural Problems

Mineral deficiencies, unsuitable light conditions, poor drainage, too much or too little water, air pollution, and injury can also be responsible for plant disorders. These can be hard to distinguish from infectious diseases, but one helpful clue is the way a problem is distributed in the garden. If all of the plants in one area share the same symptom, an environmental factor is likely to be at fault; infectious diseases, on the other hand, tend to be randomly distributed or to attack one plant at first, then spread to others. Again, noting the pattern of distribution in a garden diary can be an invaluable diagnostic tool.

Keeping an Eye on Trees

Many gardeners assume that trees can take care of themselves, especially if the plants have been around for a long time. In reality, the unnatural conditions of the garden, such as the lack of accumulated leaf litter, soil compaction, and inept pruning, are hazardous to trees. For this reason, the plants should be examined from time to time for signs of environmental stress or disease. This is especially important for a tree beyond the sapling stage. A tree slows its growth rate as it ages, but a slowdown that is too abrupt is a sign of declining health. A technique for tracking a tree's health from year to year is described at left.

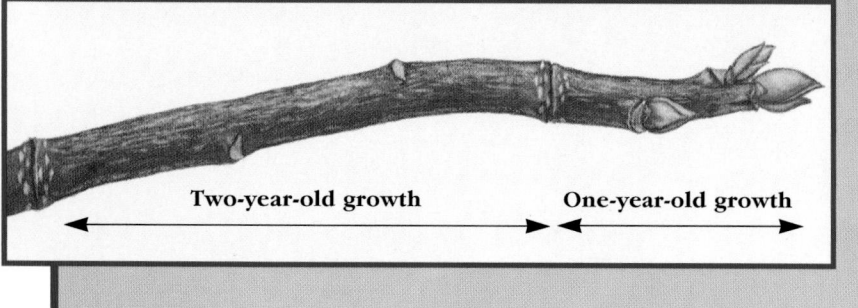

Disease Families and Their Symptoms

Plant diseases are commonly grouped by the kinds of symptoms they produce. Illustrated here are the eight symptoms that appear most frequently in home gardens, and the popular terms for the diseases involved. However, no single pathogen is responsible for each symptom. For instance, the wartlike swellings known as galls may be caused by a bacterium or by fungi.

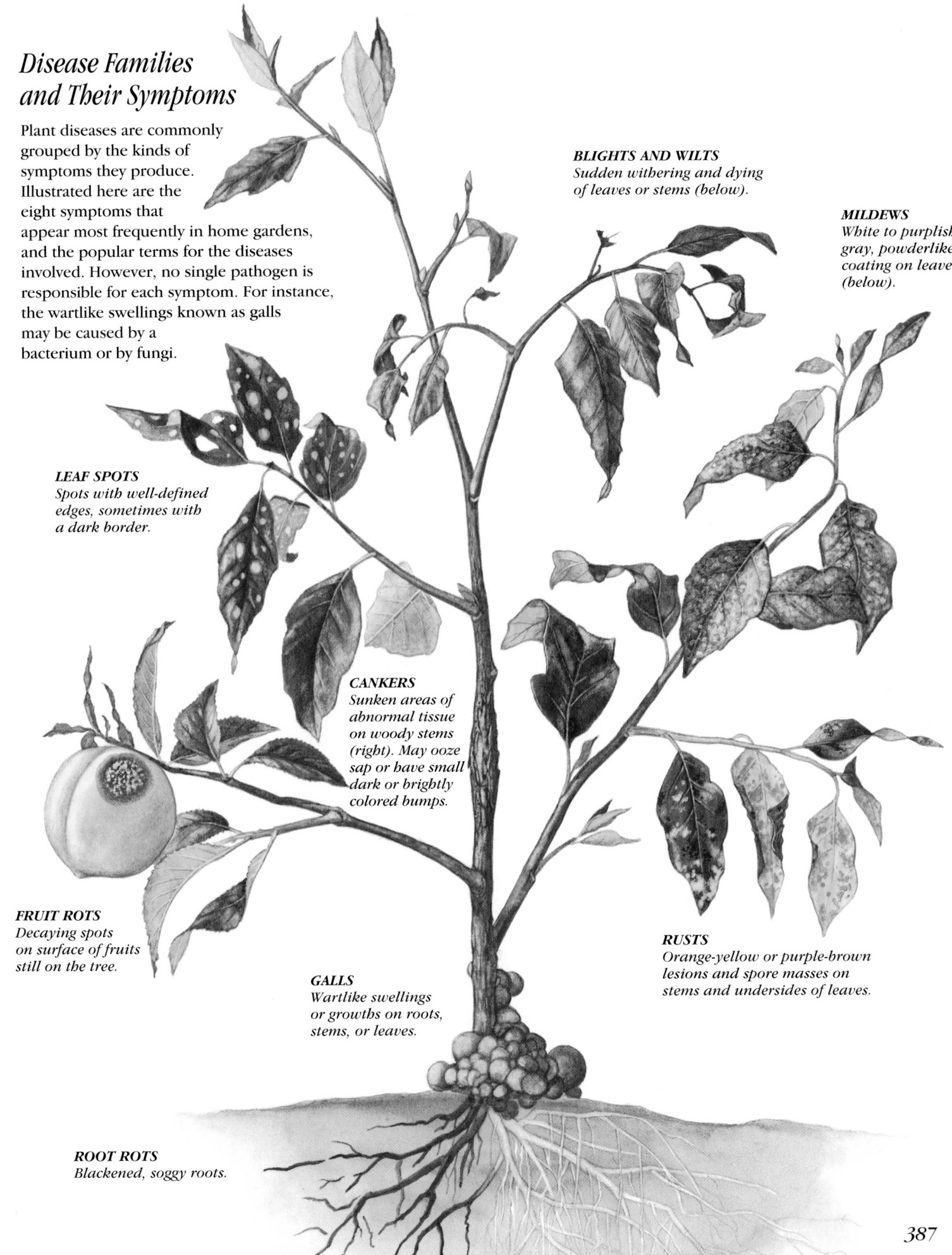

BLIGHTS AND WILTS
Sudden withering and dying of leaves or stems (below).

MILDEWS
White to purplish gray, powderlike coating on leaves (below).

LEAF SPOTS
Spots with well-defined edges, sometimes with a dark border.

CANKERS
Sunken areas of abnormal tissue on woody stems (right). May ooze sap or have small dark or brightly colored bumps.

FRUIT ROTS
Decaying spots on surface of fruits still on the tree.

GALLS
Wartlike swellings or growths on roots, stems, or leaves.

RUSTS
Orange-yellow or purple-brown lesions and spore masses on stems and undersides of leaves.

ROOT ROTS
Blackened, soggy roots.

387

Preventive Medicine for Plants

Every day, plant pathogens find their way into your garden, within striking distance of your favorite plants. But a well-planned garden—one that optimizes growing conditions for plants and discourages the presence of pathogens—has a much better chance of avoiding infection. Gardening defensively is a much more effective way of managing plant diseases than attempting to cure them. The techniques and approaches described here will help keep your garden disease free, and they can also prevent the recurrence of diseases that have been troublesome in the past.

The Right Plants

Plants have evolved to adapt to particular environments, and a gardener should strive to make a suitable match between the physical needs of plants and the physical conditions of the garden. Trying to fight the environment is a losing battle for gardener and plant alike, so before you buy a plant, make sure your garden will offer it what it needs to grow vigorously. If you are replacing a plant that has died, do not get an identical variety; chances are good that the same problem would beset the replacement plant, creating unnecessary work and expense for you.

Disease-Resistant Species and Cultivars of Popular Shrubs

The following shrubs are resistant to one or more diseases—listed after the plant's common name—that typically attack other members of the genus:

Chamaecyparis lawsoniana 'Ellwoodii' (false cypress)—armillaria

Cotoneaster adpressus, C. apiculatus, C. praecox (cotoneaster)—fire blight

Euonymus alata (winged euonymus)—crown gall, scale

Juniperus chinensis 'Femina', 'Keteleeri'; J. communis 'Aureo-spica', 'Depressa', 'Suecia'; J. conferta; J. sabina 'Broadmoor', 'Knap Hill', 'Skandia' (juniper)—phomopsis, cedar-apple rust

Pyracantha 'Apache', 'Fiery Cascade', 'Mohave', 'Navaho', 'Pueblo', 'Rutgers', 'Shawnee', 'Teton' (firethorn)—scab, fire blight

Rhododendron 'Copperman', 'Fashion', 'Pink Gumpo' (azalea)—phomopsis; *R. poukhanense, 'Corrine', 'Fakir', 'Formosa', 'Fred Cochran', 'Glacier', 'Hampton Beauty', 'Higasa', 'Merlin', 'Polar Seas'* (azalea)—phytophthora; *R. delavayi; R. occidentale; R. sanctum; R. simsii, 'Caroline', 'Martha Isaacson', 'Pink Trumpet', 'Red Head'* (rhododendron)—phytophthora; *R. 'Boursault', 'Cunningham's White', 'English Roseum', 'Le Bar's Red', 'Roseum 2'* (rhododendron)—botryosphaeria

Rosa 'All That Jazz', 'Carefree Wonder', 'Pascali', 'Peace', 'Queen Elizabeth', 'Sutter's Gold', 'The Fairy', 'Tropicana' (rose)—black spot

Thuja occidentalis 'Ellwangeriana', 'Lutescens' (arborvitae)—phomopsis, tip blight

Viburnum burkwoodii 'Mohawk'; V. carlcephalum 'Cayuga' (viburnum)—bacterial leaf spot, powdery mildew

Euonymus alata (winged euonymus)

Shopping for Disease-Resistant Plants

Some plants are naturally resistant to infection, possessing toxic compounds or physical features, such as a thick, impenetrable outer coating, to repel pathogens. Other resistant plants are the product of crossbreeding programs that seek to combine naturally occurring protective chemicals with outstanding ornamental features.

More and more attractive cultivars of virtually every kind of plant are being bred for disease resistance. Before you undertake a planting project, find out whether there are resistant varieties that would work well in your garden. On the opposite page and below are lists of some desirable species and cultivars of shrubs and trees that will outperform their unimproved relatives where the diseases indicated are a problem. Check with your Cooperative Extension Service agent for a list of diseases that commonly occur in your area.

When you are shopping at a nursery, read plant labels to see if they contain information about the plant's resistance to disease. This often takes the form of coded abbreviations—for example, "DMPM" means that the plant is resistant to downy mildew and powdery mildew. Also desirable, though their level of natural protection is somewhat less, are plants described as "tolerant" of a certain disease. This means that although the plant may become infected, it won't be significantly damaged by the disease.

Immunity vs. Resistance

A resistant plant is just that: It is unlikely to be infected by a pathogen, but it isn't totally immune. If a serious disease is widespread in your area, you

Disease-Resistant Species and Cultivars of Popular Trees

The following trees are resistant to one or more diseases—listed after the plant's common name—that typically attack other members of the genus:

Acer platanoides 'Jade Glen', 'Parkway' (maple)—verticillium wilt

Cornus kousa; C. florida x *kousa hybrids* (dogwood)—Discula anthracnose

Ficus carica 'Kadota', 'Mission' (fig)—armillaria

Fraxinus pennsylvanica (ash)—anthracnose; *F. velutina 'Modesto'*—armillaria

Ilex cornuta, 'Meserve', 'Blue Prince', 'China Boy', 'China Girl' (holly)—black root rot; *I. aquifolium*—armillaria

Lagerstroemia 'Acoma', 'Apalachee', 'Biloxi', 'Choctaw', 'Comanche', 'Hopi', 'Lipan', 'Miami', 'Natchez', 'Osage', 'Pecos', 'Sioux', 'Tonto', 'Tuskegee', *'Wichita', 'Zuma', 'Zuni'* (crape myrtle)—powdery mildew

Malus 'Beverly', 'Dolgo', 'Donald Wyman', 'Liset', 'Naragansett', 'Red Jewel', 'Snowdrift' (crab apple)—gymnosporangium rust, fire blight, frogeye leaf spot, rust, scab

Pinus nigra (Austrian pine)—armillaria; *P. palustris* (longleaf pine)—fusiform rust

Platanus 'Columbia', 'Liberty' (plane tree)—anthracnose

Populus 'Assiniboine' (poplar)—canker, rust

Quercus coccinea; Q. palustris; Q. rubra; Q. velutina (oak)—anthracnose

Malus 'Donald Wyman'
('Donald Wyman' crab apple)

may want to restrict yourself to plants that are never harmed by that particular pathogen. For instance, where flowering crab apples are plagued by apple scab (which defaces foliage and makes leaves and fruit drop prematurely), you might choose a redbud, Kousa dogwood, or serviceberry instead of a crab apple if you want a small ornamental tree that flowers in spring.

Choosing a Healthy Specimen

When you have decided what kind of plant to buy, select the individual specimen carefully. Use the guidelines on page 348 to examine a nursery plant for diseases and pests. If possible, check the root system by gently lifting the plant out of the pot. If the roots are dark, soggy, or malodorous, choose another plant. Also reject a plant that has a wound on it; nicked or torn bark or a broken branch provides an entry point for disease.

Some nurseries sell plants labeled "certified disease-free." These plants have been grown under carefully controlled conditions, protected from insects, and determined by a plant pathologist to be free of infection. Although such certification adds to the price of the plant, the expense may be well worth it in the long run.

Optimizing Growing Conditions

Relying heavily on resistant and tolerant cultivars is an essential tactic in creating a garden as free of disease as possible. Equally important is maintaining the health of your plants with proper cultural and physical practices: The more vigorous plants are, the less likely they'll succumb to disease.

Observing Good Planting Practices

Resist the temptation to crowd your plants together to achieve the effect of dense foliage and lush blooms. Instead, space them generously, following the recommended planting distances. This reduces competition for nutrients, water, and sunlight, and permits air to circulate freely around stems and leaves. Good air circulation is especially vital for preventing the humid conditions in which fungi thrive. The spores of botrytis blights and powdery mildews, for instance, are present in the air, the soil, or plant debris in most gardens, but they can't infect plants unless the environment is warm and moist.

Amending the Soil

Healthy soil leads to healthy plants that can fend off all but the most persistent diseases. If the soil has a proper balance of nutrients and a hospitable pH range, and is well drained, plants will develop good root systems and make efficient use of nutrients and water.

You will need to amend the soil in your garden every year to replenish nutrients consumed by growing plants. Compost is the most effective all-around amendment; you can make it yourself (pages 262-263) or buy it in bags. In the fall, spread a 2-inch layer over the soil and dig it in.

The Art of Watering

The following techniques will keep your plants well watered while making the garden less hospitable to disease organisms:

- When planning a garden, group plants according to their water needs.
- Most gardens need 1 to 1½ inches of water every 7 to 10 days. Install a rain gauge so you can measure how much rainfall your garden receives. If it is insufficient, make up the deficit with a single, slow soaking.
- Use soaker hoses or install an underground drip-irrigation system. Unlike sprinkling, these watering methods keep foliage dry and eliminate splashing, reducing the likelihood of fungal infections.
- If you do use a sprinkler, water early in the day so that the sun can quickly evaporate the moisture on the leaves. If your system is automated, be sure it does not automatically water when it's raining.
- After watering, use a trowel or a soil auger to check that the water has penetrated to a depth of 8 to 12 inches. If it hasn't, apply the water at a slower rate.
- Between waterings, dig down 6 to 8 inches with a spade or trowel to check the soil moisture. Don't water again until the top 1½ to 2 inches of soil begin to dry out.
- If the soil in one area is much slower to dry out, test the drainage (page 392) and, if necessary, take steps to improve it.

Overall soil fertility can also be enhanced with fertilizer. You can choose an inorganic, chemical-based fertilizer or one made from natural materials, such as dehydrated manure, cottonseed meal, dried blood, bone meal, or rock phosphate. Chemical fertilizers are often less expensive to use and may act more quickly, but they will burn a plant's roots if applied too heavily. An organic fertilizer, on the other hand, may take a little longer to work but has less chance of burning plant roots. Also, it won't harm the soil microbes that help control plant diseases.

If the soil has been well prepared, an application of fertilizer before the growing season begins will probably be sufficient for the year. Be moderate, though, especially when applying nitrogen; too much of this element can promote rapid leaf and stem growth, which is often soft and susceptible to pathogens.

Plants grown in a soil that lacks one or more nutrients will eventually show symptoms of deficiency—usually stunted growth and yellowing leaves. Four of the most frequently encountered deficiencies are iron, magnesium, nitrogen, and potassium, which are all essential elements for healthy vegetative growth and critical plant functions. If you suspect a nutrient imbalance, have your soil tested. Your local Cooperative Extension Service can recommend a kit you can use to administer the test yourself or, if you prefer, a laboratory where you can send a soil sample for analysis. Ask the laboratory to recommend the appropriate organic fertilizer and the rate at which it should be applied if there is a nutrient imbalance.

The Plant's Restorative: Manure Tea

Another environmentally safe way to give plants a mild dose of nutrients is by spraying them with manure tea. This homemade brew is easy to concoct: Just wrap 1 gallon of manure-based compost or well-rotted manure in burlap or some other coarse cloth and secure it at the top. Place the bag in a 5-gallon bucket and fill it with water. Leave the mixture in a warm place for at least 3 days, but preferably for a week. Then fill a spray applicator with the liquid and spray the plants well. Repeat every 3 to 4 days. You can also use manure tea for watering plants and to provide some protection against fungal diseases. For example, soaking seeds overnight in manure tea has been found to reduce the incidence of damping-off *(box, right)*.

Finding the Correct Soil pH

Most plants absorb nutrients and grow best in slightly acid soil, with a pH of around 6.5. There are a few exceptions to this rule—azaleas, for instance, prefer a more acidic soil—so you'll need to find out whether any of your plants have different pH requirements. Some soil-borne pathogens such as *Pythium*, a fungus that causes damping-off and root rot, are very sensitive to minor fluctuations in pH levels. These pathogens can be controlled simply by lowering the pH level with additions of lime or raising it with sulfur. If your plants have been infected by a soil-borne pathogen before, ask your Cooperative Extension Service agent if it would make sense to adjust the pH.

Rotating Annuals and Vegetables

Despite your best efforts at controlling soil-borne pathogens, they will thrive as long as a preferred food supply is present. In a fairly short time, they can multiply from negligible numbers to a population capable of launching a devastating attack. For instance, vinca is highly susceptible to root rot, which is caused by a fungus found in small numbers in most soils. If allowed to feed on vinca for several years in a row, however, the fungus will become rampant. To eliminate a pathogen that is partial to only one or a few species, try rotating your plants. This solution isn't practical for perennials and other plants in permanent locations, but it is easily accomplished with annuals and vegetables. Instead of planting them in the same spot year after year, skip at least 2 years before repeating an annual or vegetable in a site.

The Importance of Soil Drainage

Many fungi flourish in waterlogged soil, so it's wise to test how well your soil drains, especially if it is largely composed of clay. Dig a hole 10 inches deep and 12 inches in diameter and pour in 1 gallon of water. If any water remains in the hole after 10 minutes, the drainage needs to be improved. You may be able to correct the problem merely by digging in generous amounts of organic matter and coarse sand. Other solutions to try when simpler ones are inadequate include building a raised bed or installing drainage pipes.

Watering to Promote Garden Health

How and when one waters also plays an important role in whether disease takes hold in your garden. The powerful stream of a hose, for instance, can splash pathogens that are on or near the soil's surface onto leaves and stems. When humidity is high, overhead watering with a sprinkler can leave foliage wet for long periods, providing a favorable environment for fungi to germinate. The best method for discouraging disease is ground-level watering, whether through soaker hoses or through an underground system. For more tips on acquiring good watering habits, see the box on page 390.

Since pathogens spread most easily in moist environments, it is important to avoid working in the garden soon after a rainfall or a watering. You could inadvertently pick up the pathogens on your hands, shoes, clothing, or tools and transport them to other parts of the garden.

The Benefits of Mulching

Another way to keep soil-borne pathogens away from plant stems and leaves is to lay down a protective barrier of mulch. A 2- to 4-inch layer of compost, shredded bark, or other organic material not only blocks disease-causing pathogens, it also introduces into the soil various kinds of microorganisms that promote a healthy garden. Composted pine bark, for example, is particularly rich in beneficial nematodes and bacteria that prey on parasitic nematodes and other pathogens. Other microorganisms keep down the pathogen population by outcompeting them for food and habitat.

Mulch also helps keep plants in good health by conserving moisture and adding nutrients as it decays. And a circle of mulch at least 4 feet in diameter around the trunk of a tree will prevent the lawn mower from inflicting nicks and cuts that would expose the inner layers of living tissue to disease organisms. (When spreading the mulch, remember to keep it a few inches away from the trunk—it should surround the trunk but not touch it.) The tree will be even better protected if all of its roots that protrude above the soil are mulched.

Biological and Chemical Preventives

The microorganisms in decaying mulch are an example of biological disease control, which lets living organisms destroy harmful ones either by eating them or by appropriating their food and territory.

Besides the biological controls that are naturally present in a garden, there are also a handful of commercial fungicides and bactericides. If you have had trouble with a disease in the past, check with your local nursery to see if a biological fungicide or bactericide has been developed for home gardens. Apply the control to all susceptible plants to prevent a recurrence, following the instructions on the label.

Controlling Diseases

Once you've diagnosed a plant disease, there are often several ways to get rid of it or prevent a recurrence. Some of these methods, such as pruning, involve virtually no risk to your plants or to the environment. Earth-friendly sprays and dusts of low or no toxicity *(page 396)* offer another avenue of attack. For truly stubborn or serious diseases, you may decide to use one of the more toxic chemical controls *(pages 396-397)*.

But before you do anything, keep in mind that many diseases are merely cosmetic problems and will run their natural course without doing serious damage to the infected plant. If you feel you must take action in such instances, limit yourself to cultural or physical controls; these diseases don't warrant the use of toxic chemicals.

Destroying Pathogens with Sunlight

Solarization is a reliable, environmentally safe way to rid a garden plot of soil-borne diseases as well as weeds. Clear plastic is spread on the ground to trap the sun's heat, which raises the temperature of the top 3 to 5 inches of soil to 120°F or above, roasting microorganisms and weed seeds buried in it. The technique must be carried out in the

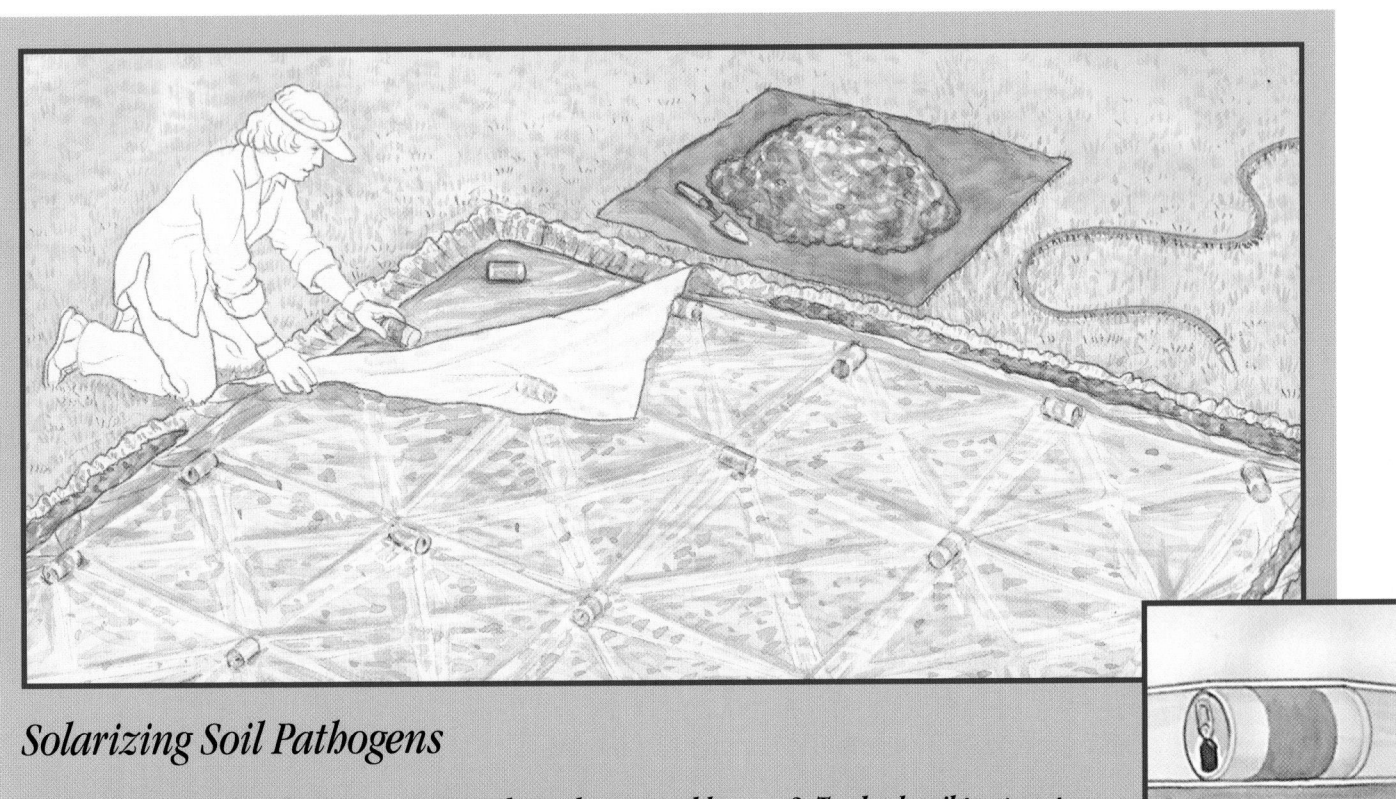

Solarizing Soil Pathogens

1. Clear a sunny plot of existing vegetation, rocks, and other debris, and dig in any soil amendments needed. Rake the soil smooth and dig a trench a few inches deep around the plot. Water the soil to a depth of at least 12 inches. Next, using clear plastic measuring 3 to 4 mils thick, cut two sheets large enough to cover the plot.

2. Spread one sheet smoothly on the soil. Lay empty soda cans about 2 feet apart on the sheet, then spread the second sheet over the cans (above and inset). Tuck the edges of the plastic sheets into the trench and pile soil on them to make a seal; this will trap heat and moisture in the air space between the sheets. After a rain, sweep off any water.

3. To check soil temperature, fold back a corner of the plastic and insert a soil thermometer; reseal the sheets afterward. Leave the sheets in place for several days after the temperature remains at 120°F or above; it may take 4 to 8 weeks for the bed to heat to this point.

Pruning Diseased Wood

Stems showing signs of disease should be pruned back promptly to healthy tissue to prevent further infection. (However, if the weather is rainy, wait for a dry day, since pathogens are easily transmitted by water.) To remove a stem completely, make the cut at its base, flush with the parent stem so there won't be a stub. If you are shortening a stem rather than removing it, prune back to a healthy bud. Cut the stem at a 45° angle in the same direction that the bud points, so that water will drain away from the bud.

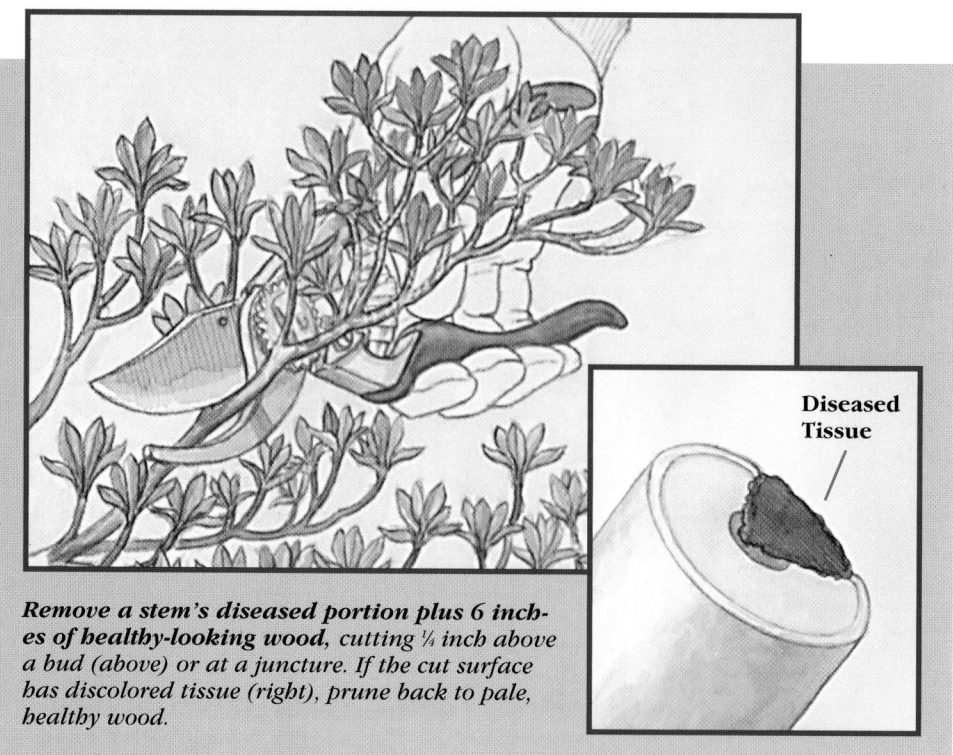

Remove a stem's diseased portion plus 6 inches of healthy-looking wood, cutting ¼ inch above a bud (above) or at a juncture. If the cut surface has discolored tissue (right), prune back to pale, healthy wood.

Diseased Tissue

Pruning Large Branches

The bulge at the base of a tree branch, called the branch collar, is a protective zone that helps heal the wound created when the branch is removed, whether naturally or by pruning. This specialized tissue produces a callus that seals the wound's surface, preventing wood-decay fungi from infecting the trunk.

When you prune, be very careful to leave the branch collar intact so that healing will take place. For the same reason, never cut into a callus, even to remove a rotted or diseased section of a trunk. The tree itself will seal off the dead tissue.

A single pruning cut made flush with the trunk (A) removes the branch's collar and tears bark, exposing wood to infection. Cutting too far from the trunk leaves a disease-prone stub (B). For good healing (C), use a series of three cuts (D). First, saw halfway through the branch from the underside, 8 to 12 inches from the collar (1). Then saw through the branch from above, a few inches beyond the first cut (2). Saw off the resulting stub just forward of the collar, following its natural angle (3).

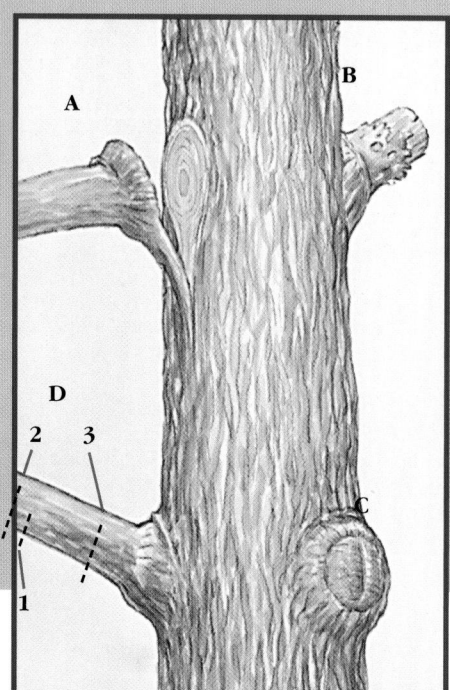

hottest, sunniest season and is suitable only for plots that are in direct sun for most of the day. Also, the soil must be bare—that is, unplanted.

How long the process takes depends on weather and climate. Solarization is complete in about 4 weeks when daytime temperatures average 90°F; it can take up to 8 weeks if temperatures average in the 70s. Fungi, nematodes, and weed seeds are killed when the soil temperature exceeds 120°F. At 160°F and above, some viruses and bacteria will also be destroyed. Unfortunately, solarization kills beneficial microbes as well, so be sure to dig a material rich in microbes, such as aged manure or compost, into the plot later to repopulate it. Earthworms survive the process by tunneling deeper into the soil.

After solarization, take care to cultivate the soil very shallowly; if you dig too deep, you may reinfest the plot with pathogens and seeds that survived in the cooler soil below.

Pruning

Some tree diseases, such as fire blight and twig canker, can be controlled by pruning out infected branches. You can also use pruning as a method of prevention. Thinning a plant—that is, removing some stems or branches from its center—discourages diseases that thrive in stagnant conditions, by improving air circulation and reducing humidity.

When pruning, take care not to inadvertently increase a shrub's or tree's vulnerability to disease with badly executed cuts *(opposite, below)*. Use a high-quality tool that is large enough to cleanly cut the wood you're working on. To keep from spreading disease as you work, some horticulturists recommend carrying along a pail containing a solution of 1 part household bleach to 9 parts water so that you can disinfect your clippers after each cut. Leave the clippers in the solution for 15 seconds. When you are finished pruning, sterilize them again, rinse in clean water, and dry, then coat the metal parts with a light oil to prevent rusting.

When to Prune a Tree

The timing of tree pruning is very important. Done in the wrong season, it can actually increase problems. Trees respond to pruning either by releasing sap or by quickly producing a burst of new growth, both of which attract pests and diseases. Most trees do best when pruned during their dormant stage, so you should postpone the job until then, if possible. Pruning diseased wood is an exception to this rule: It should be removed as soon as you notice it, unless the weather is wet, since pathogens spread easily in water.

Horticulturists now advise against using tree paint on pruning cuts. Not only does it have no known benefit, it may actually promote some wood rots by preventing the wound from drying, which is a natural protection against infection.

Removing Diseased Plants

For some diseases, there is no known cure. In these cases, the plant should be pulled up and disposed of as soon as possible. If the plant has a soil-borne disease such as nematodes or crown rot, dig it out, roots and all, being careful not to knock any soil off the rootball. Put everything in a plastic garbage bag and seal tightly. Replace the diseased plant with a resistant variety. Once the pathogens have lost their hosts, they will eventually die out.

Handling diseased plant material properly is crucial in preventing the further spread of pathogens. When you garden, keep a plastic bag with you for collecting clippings and other material. Fungus spores can spread in the garden as quickly as dandelion seeds in the breeze. Dispose of the bagged plant material with your household trash, or bury it in an out-of-the-way place. You can also compost it, but only if you are certain that your pile will heat up to a minimum of 140°F.

Although spot anthracnose can spoil the looks of a flowering dogwood's blossoms, as shown above, the tree suffers no serious or long-lasting effects. However, another fungal disease with similar symptoms, Discula anthracnose, is fatal to this species of dogwood.

A Safe, Simple Spray

Baking soda is a natural fungicide that is nontoxic to the environment. When sprayed on plants, it prevents fungal spores from penetrating plant tissue. In addition, it can halt the spread of an established infection. The box below gives directions for making and using baking soda spray.

Horticultural Oils

Spraying infected trees and shrubs with horticultural oils prevents the fungi responsible for rusts and mildews from germinating. These oils are even more widely used to control pests such as mites, plant bugs, and psyllids *(page 371)*. The sprays aren't toxic to mammals.

Horticultural oils are applied in two different concentrations depending on the season. The stronger of the two is applied in winter, while plants are dormant. For warmer weather, when plants are in active growth, a diluted solution is used to avoid damaging foliage *(pages 372-373)*.

Chemical Controls

When milder measures prove to be useless, the gardener must weigh the risks posed by a more potent method of control. If the disease's only effect on the plant is a less-than-perfect appearance, you may feel that a fungicide, which can kill beneficial microorganisms along with plant pathogens, is not warranted. Moreover, many fungicides harm wildlife, especially fish. Fortunately, the question of whether or not to spray rarely, if ever, arises with most ornamentals. For a handful, however, such as

Baking Soda Spray

1 tablespoon baking soda
1 gallon water
⅛ to ¼ teaspoon insecticidal soap

Dissolve the baking soda in the water, then add the soap, which helps the solution spread and stick to the foliage. Fill a spray can or bottle with the solution and spray all of the leaves on both sides. Repeat every 5 to 7 days until the symptoms disappear.

To prevent another outbreak the following year, begin spraying in spring and continue until the fall. This spray is effective against powdery mildews, leaf blights, and leaf spots.

hybrid tea roses, chemicals are essential for the plant to grow and bloom well. In such cases, you'll have to decide whether the plant is worth the risks, the expense, and the effort of spraying.

If disease symptoms are far advanced, it's probably too late for a spray to be effective, at least during the current season. If so, wait until the following year, then spray shortly before the season and the conditions—muggy, hot weather, for instance—are ripe for a renewed outbreak. In short, think in terms of prevention, and plan ahead.

Fungicides

Since fungi cause about 80 percent of the diseases that affect ornamental plants, most of the chemicals available for treating plant diseases are fungicides. Fungicides work in two ways. Most of them are surface protectants, which means they keep spores from germinating on or penetrating a plant. These fungicides prevent disease, but they cannot cure it. Apply these sprays when conditions favor infection. For example, in the case of garden phlox, which is susceptible to powdery mildew, spray shortly before the days turn warm and sunny but when nights are still cool.

The second group of fungicides are the systemics, which prevent disease and also cure it. A systemic penetrates a plant's tissue, where it interferes with the growth of the pathogen. Unlike most surface protectants, which prevent a wide range of diseases, systemics generally have a narrow spectrum, making accurate diagnosis especially important. Systemics are much less likely than surface protectants to injure plant tissues, and they seldom leave a visible residue.

The chart at right lists the most common fungicides available to home gardeners in ascending order of toxicity, with the safest one appearing first. Pick the least toxic product available for your disease problem. All of these fungicides are considered organic because they are active for only one day, unlike some other fungicides that persist in the environment.

Taking Precautions

Before you buy a fungicide, and again when you are preparing to use it, read the label carefully to make sure it is an appropriate chemical for the plant and the disease you are treating. Follow all instructions to the letter, and handle the fungicide with as much care as you would a pesticide or herbicide *(pages 290 and 370-375)*.

RECOMMENDED FUNGICIDES

Type	Diseases Controlled	Precautions and Hazards
Fungicidal soap. Surface protectant.	Black spot, brown canker, leaf spot, powdery mildews, and rust.	Before treating a plant, test a few leaves for browning or other symptoms of sensitivity.
Copper hydroxide, copper tanate. Surface protectants.	Many fungal and some bacterial leaf spots, botrytis, downy mildews, and powdery mildews.	Spray early on a dry, sunny day. Copper hydroxide is less expensive than copper tanate but may burn foliage in damp weather and leaves a visible residue. Both are eye irritants and toxic to wildlife.
Copper sulfate and hydrated lime (Bordeaux mixture). Surface protectant.	Many fungal and some bacterial diseases, including anthracnose, bacterial leaf spots, black rot, blights, fruit scab, septoria leaf spot, and wilts.	Spray on a windless evening, when no bees are active. Do not use in damp or humid weather if the temperature is below 50°F. Never use with other pesticides or fungicides.
Sulfur. Surface protectant.	Black spot, brown rot, powdery mildews, rusts, scabs, and other fungi. Also controls mites.	To avoid damaging foliage, do not apply when the temperature exceeds 85°F. Do not apply to open flowers, because bees will be harmed. Wait a month to use after applying horticultural oil.
Lime sulfur. Surface protectant.	Anthracnose, powdery mildews, rusts, and scabs.	Use only in cold weather on dormant plants. Lime sulfur is more caustic and thus more likely to damage plants than plain sulfur. Toxic to fish.
Horticultural oils. Surface protectant.	Powdery mildews, puccinia rust, and septoria leaf spot.	Do not use when temperatures exceed 90°F or when plants are water stressed. Do not use if a fungicide containing sulfur has been applied within the last month.
Captan. Surface protectant.	Damping-off fungi (used on seed).	Leaves visible residue. Causes spotting, yellowing, or defoliation if used in cool, moist weather on young leaves of roses and stone fruits. Eye irritant; wear goggles. Toxic to soil microorganisms.
Chlorothalonil. Surface protectant.	Blights, botrytis, leaf spots, and powdery mildews.	Eye irritant; wear goggles. Slightly toxic to wildlife and soil microorganisms.
Mancozeb. Surface protectant.	Blights, botrytis, downy mildews, and leaf spots.	Use sparingly on foliage only. Store in a cool, dry location in an airtight container; heat and moisture may decompose it. Toxic to soil microorganisms.
Propiconazole. Systemic.	Many diseases of ornamentals and turf grasses, including Discula anthracnose of dogwood, blights, leaf spots, powdery mildews, and rusts.	Severe eye irritant; always wear goggles and rubber gloves. Toxic to soil organisms.
Thiophanate-methyl. Systemic.	Many blights, black spot, Discula anthracnose of dogwood, and leaf and fruit spots.	Irritant to eyes, nose, and throat; always wear respirator, goggles, rubber gloves, and rubber boots.
Triadimefon. Systemic.	Powdery mildews, rusts, and a variety of leaf spots and blights.	Avoid contact with powder when mixing. Toxic to soil organisms.
Triforine. Systemic.	Powdery mildews and a variety of leaf spots and blights, including brown rot of stone fruit.	Resistance to this fungicide has appeared in some strains of fungi that cause black spot on roses. Toxic to soil organisms.

CHAPTER TEN

Growing a Healthy Lawn

The perfectly manicured lawn is an American institution. Nowhere else in the world do people devote so much effort to maintaining a large expanse of smooth green turf. In an effort to cultivate an unblemished carpet of grass, many homeowners put higher concentrations of chemicals on their lawns than American farmers apply to their crops. And yet, all that pampering doesn't necessarily improve the lawn's appearance. Large chemical doses can kill useful creatures such as earthworms and beneficial insects and microorganisms. Frequent fertilizing and watering make the grass grow faster, leading to more mowing, and close mowing encourages problems such as weeds, pests, and diseases.

The good news is that you can create a lawn that is both beautiful and undemanding, such as the lush, easy-care Baltimore lawn at left. On the following pages you'll learn how to choose the right grass for your site's conditions; how to care properly for your soil as well as your grass to keep it green and vigorous; and how to spot trouble and manage it in ways that are not only effective but also kind to the environment.

Lawn-Care Basics
and Preventive Measures

The most important component of a healthy lawn is the grass itself. Traditionally, American lawns have been made up of old varieties of grass that require considerable care to keep healthy. Recently, however, breeders have created improved grasses that need much less maintenance. A number are disease resistant, many are drought tolerant, and some even repel insects. Other varieties require less fertilizer and less frequent mowing.

Whether you are starting a new lawn, are overseeding an existing one, or simply want to make the most of what's now growing on your property, it helps to know something about the different types of grasses that are available, what their particular needs are, and which variety best suits your area.

What Is Turf Grass?

Unlike most other plants, which grow from the tips, turf grasses grow from the base—a feature that endows a lawn with the durability to survive heavy foot traffic and frequent mowing. Turf grasses are usually classified by the season and the part of the country in which they grow best, as indicated in the chart at right. Perennial ryegrass and Kentucky bluegrass, for example, are known as cool-season grasses; they are planted primarily in northern areas and grow most vigorously in spring and fall. Warm-season grasses—Bermuda and St. Augustine, for instance—grow actively in the hot summer temperatures of the South before going dormant in the fall and turning brown.

Turf grasses are also classified by their growth habits, which can be either creeping or bunching. Creeping varieties—also known as sod-forming—spread relatively quickly by sending out horizontal shoots, called stolons when above ground and rhizomes when underneath the soil *(box, page 402)*. Bunching grasses send up blades, called tillers, from a single crown, forming clumps and spreading slowly. If you live in the North, it's better to mix creeping and bunching grasses or two bunching varieties than to plant a single species. Combining cool-season species with different habits makes your lawn hardier and more resistant to stress. Warm-season grasses don't mix well, however, because they grow more aggressively; lawns

in the South are usually just a single species.

Different species of grass vary in their appearance by blade width and color. To Americans, the narrower the blade and the deeper the green, the more elegant the lawn. But the best lawns combine good looks with good growth characteristics. In

GRASSES		CHARACTERISTICS				
		Texture & Appearance	**Growth Habit**	**Drought Tolerance**	**Heat Tolerance**	
COOL SEASON	Bent grass	Very fine bladed; bright green	Bunching	Very low	Low	
	Kentucky bluegrass	Medium- to fine-bladed; medium to dark green	Creeping, rhizomes	Moderate	Moderate	
	Fine fescue	Very fine bladed; medium to deep green	Bunching or creeping, rhizomes	Moderate to high	Moderate	
	Tall fescue	Medium- to coarse-bladed; light to medium green	Bunching	High	High	
	Perennial ryegrass	Medium-bladed; shiny; medium to dark green	Bunching	Moderate to low	Moderate to low	
WARM SEASON	Bahia grass	Tough, coarse-bladed; light green	Creeping, rhizomes	High	High	
	Bermuda grass	Fine- to medium-bladed; medium to dark green	Creeping, rhizomes and stolons	High	High	
	Blue grama grass	Medium-bladed; grayish green	Bunching	Very high	High	
	Buffalo grass	Fine-bladed; light green to grayish green	Creeping, stolons	Very high	High	
	Centipede grass	Medium- to coarse-bladed; light green	Creeping, stolons	Moderate	High	
	St. Augustine grass	Coarse-bladed; bluish green to medium green	Creeping, stolons	Moderate	High	
	Zoysia	Coarse- to medium-bladed; medium green	Creeping, rhizomes and stolons	Moderate to high	High	

Know Your Turf Grass

The chart below describes 12 common lawn grasses—five cool-season varieties, which thrive in spring and fall, and seven warm-season grasses, which perform best in summer. The growing zones recommended for each grass appear on the map at right. At zone borders, you can grow both cool- and warm-season grasses.

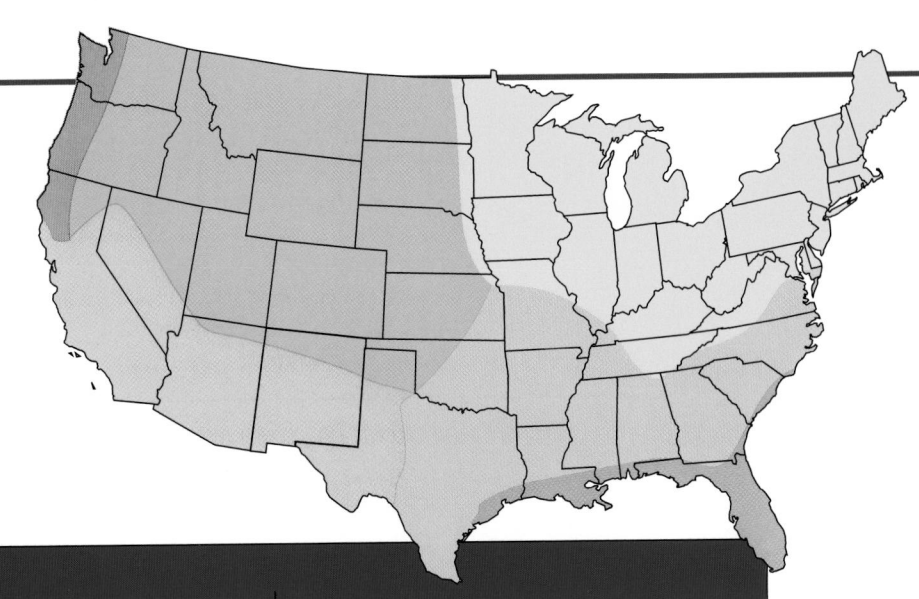

Cold Tolerance	Light Requirements	Propagation & Rate of Establishment	Lateral & Top Growth Rate	Soil Requirements	Fertilizer Needs	Wear Tolerance	Thatching Potential	Disease Susceptibility	Zones
Very high; thrives in cool, humid climates	Full sun; tolerates some light shade	Seed (germinates 5-12 days); moderate to slow	Fast; mow often to ¾ inch	Moist, fertile; compaction-intolerant; pH 4.5-6.7	High; 4-6 lbs. N per 1,000 sq. ft. per year	Moderate to low	High	Very high	A, northern parts of C
High	Full sun; some cultivars tolerate some shade	Seed (germinates 14-21 days), sod; moderate to slow	Moderate	Moist, fertile, well-drained; compaction-tolerant; pH 6-7	Moderate to high; 3-5 lbs. N per 1,000 sq. ft. per year	Moderate to high	Moderate to high	Moderate	A, B, C
High	Full sun to medium shade	Seed (germinates 10-14 days); moderate	Moderate	Silt, clay; tolerates sandy, infertile; compaction-intolerant; pH 5.5-6.5	Low; 0-2 lbs. N per 1,000 sq. ft. per year	Low	High	Moderate to high	A, B, C
Moderate	Full sun to medium shade	Seed (germinates 7-10 days) or sod; moderate	Very fast top growth	Silt, clay; tolerates sand, heavy clay, compaction; pH 4.7-8.5	Low to moderate; 2-4 lbs. N per 1,000 sq. ft. per year	Moderate	Low	Moderate	A, B, C, western parts of D
Moderate	Full sun to light shade	Seed (germinates 5-7 days); very fast	Fast	Fertile; tolerates moderate compaction; pH 6-7	High; 4-5 lbs. N per 1,000 sq. ft. per year	High	Low	High	Northern parts of D and E, southern parts of B and C
Low	Full sun to part shade	Seed (germinates 21-28 days); moderate to slow	Slow	Tolerates sand to clay, infertile, coastal areas; pH 6.5-7.5	Moderate; 2-4 lbs. N per 1,000 sq. ft. per year	Moderate to low	Low	Low	F, southern parts of E
Moderate to low	Full sun	Seed (germinates 10-14 days), sod, sprigs, plugs; all fast	Fast; invasive	Sand, silt; tolerates clay, compaction; pH 5.5-7.5	Moderate to high; 3-6 lbs. N per 1,000 sq. ft. per year	High	High	Moderate	D, E, F
High	Full sun	Seed (germinates 15-30 days); moderate to fast	Moderate	Tolerates all conditions but acidity and compaction; pH 7-8	Very low; 0-1 lb. N per 1,000 sq. ft. per year	Moderate to low	Low	Low	B, D, western parts of C and E
Moderate to high	Full sun; some hybrid cultivars tolerate light shade	Seed, sod, plugs; slow to moderate from seed, fast from plugs	Fast; invasive	Tolerates silt, clay, sand, alkalinity, compaction; pH 6-7.5	Low; 0-2 lbs. N per 1,000 sq. ft. per year	Moderate to low	Low	Moderate	B, D
Moderate to low	Full sun to part shade	Seed (germinates 14-20 days), sod, sprigs, plugs; slow to moderate	Slow	High tolerance; prefers infertile, acid; salt-intolerant	Low; 0-2 lbs. N per 1,000 sq. ft. per year; may need iron	Moderate to low	Moderate; avoid overfertilizing	Low	F, southern parts of E
Very low	Full sun to part shade	Sprigs, plugs, sod; all fast	Fast	Well-drained, fertile, sandy; tolerates salt, compaction; pH 6-7.5	Moderate to high; 3-5 lbs. N per 1,000 sq. ft. per year	Moderate to low	High	Moderate	D and F, southern parts of E
Moderate to high	Full sun to part shade	Sprigs, plugs, sod; slow	Slow lateral; moderate top	High tolerance; prefers well-drained, fine-textured; pH 5-7	Low; 0-3 lbs. N per 1,000 sq. ft. per year	Very high	Moderate; high if too much nitrogen	Low	D, E, F

the North, for example, Kentucky bluegrass makes a very attractive, cold-hardy lawn, but it needs full sun and much tending. Tall fescue is not as fine textured in appearance, but it requires much less fertilizer and resists weeds. A mixture of the two would provide the advantages of both. In a single-species southern lawn, zoysia may be the best choice for areas that experience frequent drought and other difficult weather conditions.

Soil: A Healthy Lawn's Foundation

Turf grass grows best in loamy soil that is well drained, slightly acidic, and rich in organic matter. A soil test will reveal your soil's pH level, the available nutrients, the presence of organic matter, and the soil's texture—determined by the proportions of sand, silt, and clay particles it contains. The chart opposite, which lists the characteristics of different soil types, will help you plan a maintenance strategy for your lawn.

Regardless of soil or turf-grass type, the ground under any established lawn becomes dense and hard over the years. As a result, air, water, and fertilizer cannot reach the plants' roots. Adding to the problem are excessive applications of chemicals. These can kill the beneficial microorganisms that break down the soil and produce humus and earthworms, which are natural soil aerators.

You can restore health to your lawn by aerating the soil yourself. This means removing small soil plugs—about ½ inch in diameter and 3 inches deep—at regularly spaced intervals. If your lawn is small, you can use an aerating fork—a manual tool with hollow tines that pulls up soil plugs. For larger areas, you may want to rent an aerating machine from your local garden center.

Aerate your lawn once a year, while the turf is actively growing, but not in hot weather. And be sure the soil is moist before you begin. Then, after you've removed the soil plugs, spread what is called a top dressing over the lawn and into the holes. The type of top dressing you use will vary according to your soil type. For a fast-draining sandy soil, spread ½ to 1 inch of finely screened shredded compost. This will not only help improve the soil's water-holding capacity over time, it will also replenish vital nutrients. For clay soils, which are often compacted and drain poorly, top-dress with sand or compost, or a mixture of both.

Most turf grasses grow best in soil with a slightly acid pH of 6 to 6.8. If your soil tests too acidic, you can correct it—or raise the pH—by adding lime. For an alkaline soil, you can lower the pH with elemental sulfur. Refer to the pH chart opposite to determine how to adjust your soil's pH.

Fertilizing the Lawn

Turf grass needs a slow and constant supply of nutrients, especially the major elements nitrogen, phosphorus, and potassium. Nitrogen is the most important for steady and vigorous growth of the grass. If plants receive too little, they will look light green or yellow and be vulnerable to pests and dis-

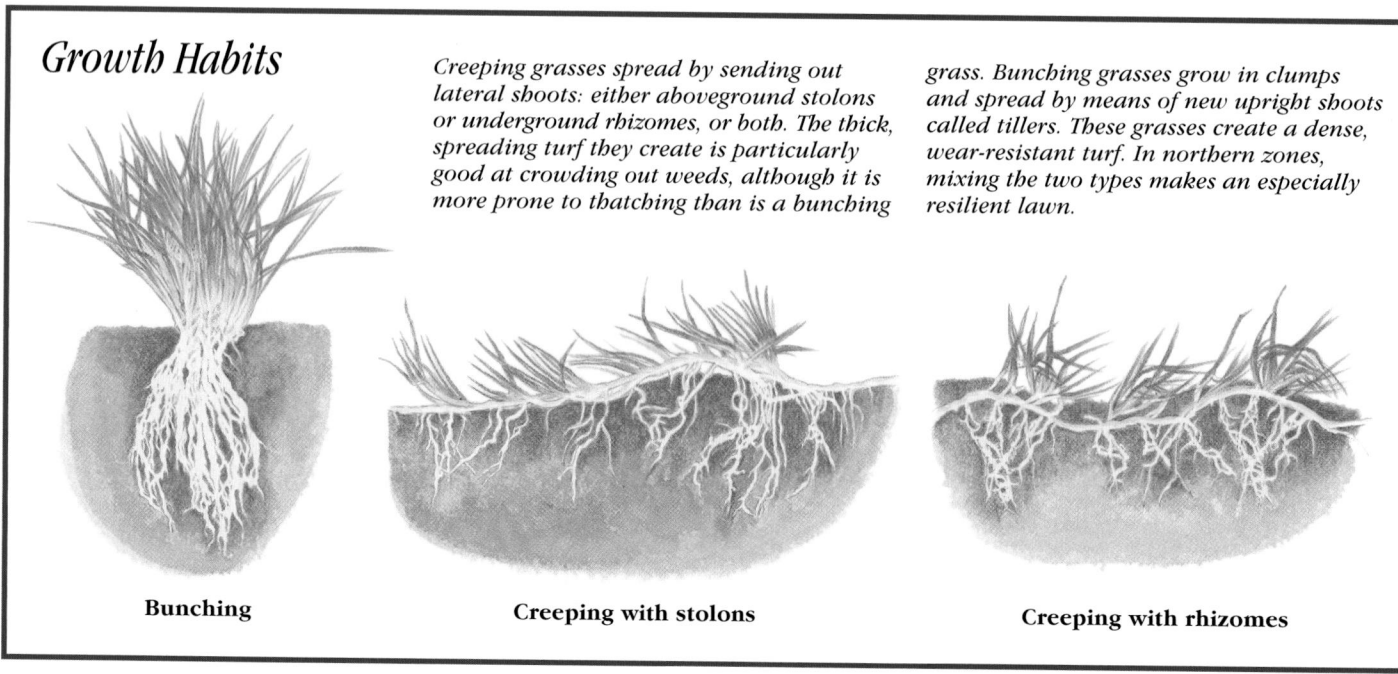

Growth Habits

Creeping grasses spread by sending out lateral shoots: either aboveground stolons or underground rhizomes, or both. The thick, spreading turf they create is particularly good at crowding out weeds, although it is more prone to thatching than is a bunching grass. Bunching grasses grow in clumps and spread by means of new upright shoots called tillers. These grasses create a dense, wear-resistant turf. In northern zones, mixing the two types makes an especially resilient lawn.

Bunching

Creeping with stolons

Creeping with rhizomes

eases. Too much nitrogen weakens the grass, which also invites trouble. Roots aren't forced to dig deep into the soil for nutrients, and the lawn then becomes dependent on regular doses of fertilizer. Also, because they are stimulated to grow quickly, overfertilized lawns need frequent mowing; this continually stresses the grass.

Lawn fertilizers are either synthetic or natural, or a combination of the two. Synthetics dissolve relatively quickly in the soil, especially the so-called fast-release types. As their name suggests, they work fast but disappear fast as well, subjecting the grass to stressful peaks and valleys of nutrient availability. They should be used only if your lawn needs an immediate dose of nutrients. Slow-release synthetics discharge their nutrients gradually, as do natural fertilizers. Although synthetics are cheaper, natural fertilizers have the additional benefit of adding bulk to the soil in the form of organic matter. There are many blended natural fertilizers on the market, which may contain combinations of dried poultry manure, blood meal, cottonseed meal, alfalfa meal, and seaweed. Commercial mixtures of organic and slow-release synthetic fertilizers also work well.

If you live in the northern regions of the United States, you need to fertilize only once in early fall and again 6 to 8 weeks later, before the grass goes dormant. Southern lawns require one to three applications a year, depending on the species of grass; they need fertilizing most in late spring and summer. The chart on pages 400-401 lists the needs for each turf species.

If you are applying dry or granular fertilizer to a

How Your Soil Affects Your Grass

Soil is the foundation of a lawn's health. The chart at right describes the characteristics of different soil types and will help you determine what amendments you need to incorporate into your soil as part of your lawn's regular maintenance program. If your soil is too acidic or too alkaline, the chart at lower right will guide you in correcting it.

Plant roots can absorb essential nutrients most easily from soil that is slightly acidic (pH 6 to 6.8); an improper pH not only impairs your lawn's capacity to extract nourishment, it also leaves it open to any number of problems. Don't make the recommended adjustments all at once, though; instead, gradually apply a fraction of the needed lime or elemental sulfur every 3 to 6 months, during any season and under any condition except on top of snow. Continue adjusting the soil—no more than 1 point in a year—until it has reached the right pH.

SOIL	CHARACTERISTICS						
	Texture	Drainage	Water Retention	Nutrient Retention	Organic Amendment Needs	Spring Warm-Up Rate	Compaction Potential
Clayey	Heavy, sticky when wet	Very slow	High	Very high	Compost, peat moss or humus, organic matter; sand for drainage	Slow	High
Silty	Silty or powdery	Slow	High	Moderate	Well-rotted compost or manure, peat humus	Moderate	High
Sandy	Light, dry, gritty	Fast	Low; needs frequent watering	Low; needs frequent fertilizing	Organic matter and fertilizer; peat humus and compost	Fast	Low
Loamy	Crumbly	Moderate	Moderate to high	Moderate to high	Compost, peat humus, any organic matter	Moderate	Moderate

ADJUSTING YOUR pH LEVEL

To Raise pH					To Lower pH				
Total lbs. of lime (calcium carbonate) needed per 1,000 sq. ft. to raise pH to 6.5					Total lbs. of elemental sulfur needed per 1,000 sq. ft. to lower pH to 6.5				
Soil pH	Clayey	Silty	Sandy	Loamy	Soil pH	Clayey	Silty	Sandy	Loamy
4.5	195	125	100	135	8.5	50	40	35	40
5.0	155	90	75	105	8.0	40	30	25	30
5.5	110	65	50	80	7.5	25	20	15	20
6.0	55	35	25	40					

large lawn, you can quickly cover a lot of ground with a broadcast spreader, which throws out the pellets in 6- to 8-foot swaths. Another device, the drop spreader—which drops the fertilizer in a 2-foot-wide path—can be calibrated to spread the amount recommended on the fertilizer bag. To ensure thorough coverage, first apply half of the recommended amount over the entire lawn, then make a pass in a perpendicular direction to spread the rest. Apply a liquid fertilizer with a hose-end sprayer or with a lawn sprinkler that has been out-fitted with a fertilizing siphon. This device will siphon fertilizer from a container and direct it to the sprinkler.

How and When to Mow

A lawn needs mowing to stay healthy, not just to keep it neat. Cutting off older growth at the top of the grass plant stimulates root growth and encourages new top growth that fills in bare spots and makes the lawn thicker and more cushiony. There is a right way and a wrong way to mow, however, and improper mowing can actually damage your lawn. Whenever the tips of the grass plants are cut, the roots are weakened to some degree, and if more than 40 percent of the blades' length is removed, root growth is drastically slowed. A rule of thumb is to never remove more than a third of the grass blade at any one time. If the grass gets too tall, don't try to cut it back to its proper height all at once. First, give it a light cut, then let it recover for a few days before cutting again. Continue to alternate cutting with periods of rest until the grass is the proper height. (See the chart opposite for correct mowing heights.)

Tailor your cutting schedule to conform to the growth of the lawn, mowing often when the grass

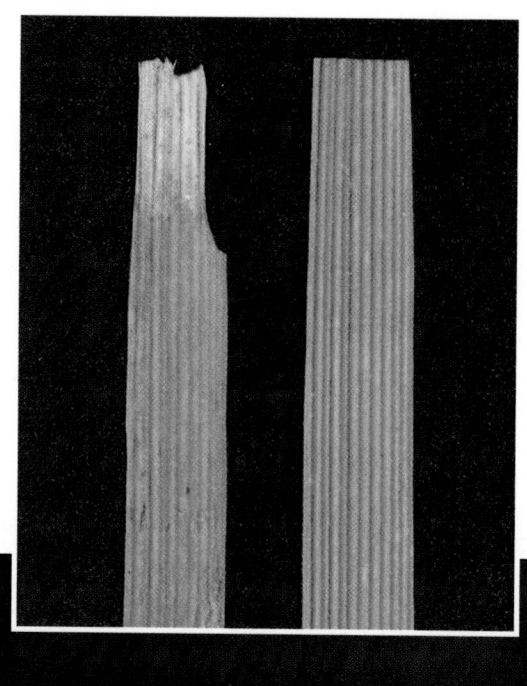

A lawn mower with dull blades can damage grass tips, causing yellowing and ragged edges (near right) that are entry points for disease. By contrast, a sharp mower blade makes a clean, straight cut that keeps grass healthy and gives the lawn a trim look (far right).

When grass is continually cut short, root growth slows and may stop entirely (near right). But when it is mowed at the higher end of its preferred range, the plant suffers less shock, allowing the roots to branch and grow deep to make a stronger plant (far right).

404

is growing most vigorously, and less frequently as growth slows. While you are cutting, make sure to overlap the previous swath by about one-third with each pass so as not to miss any grass blades. Grass blades tend to lean in the direction the mower travels, so vary your pattern every three or four times you mow; this helps the grass stand upright and also keeps ruts from forming in the lawn.

When it comes to lawn mowers, reel mowers—either manual or powered—make the cleanest cuts. However, they have been eclipsed over the years by the rotary power mower, which is faster and allows you to mow the grass higher. Mulching mowers offer the bonus of chopping up grass clippings and forcing them down to the soil line, thus returning nutrients to the soil. Clippings from any mower, however, will benefit the grass if left in place, although they won't break down quite as fast as those at soil level. Leaving the clippings also eliminates the task of raking and bagging the shorn grass. Be sure to remove the clippings from the first spring mowing and the last fall mowing, though, to discourage disease. And regardless of the type of mower you use, keep the blades sharp by taking the mower to a hardware store or other service shop at least once a season.

Watering the Right Way

During its active growing season, turf grass needs 1 to 2 inches of water a week. Much of that amount may come from rainfall, but in many parts of the country you'll have to provide the water yourself. When lawns are dry, they lose their resiliency: They wilt and are slow to spring back when you walk on them. Also, the blades may look dull and take on a blue tint.

Watering correctly is important. When a lawn is overwatered, the grass blades grow more rapidly than the roots, weakening the whole plant. Not only will you have to mow such a lawn more often, but a constantly moist turf encourages weeds and—worse—fungal diseases. On the other hand, watering too lightly results in shallow root growth. Without adequate root length and branching to anchor the plant and tap into stores of water and nutrients deeper in the soil, the grass has a hard time combating drought, disease, and pests.

The best way to water is slowly and deeply, allowing the fluid to penetrate 6 to 8 inches into the soil. In clay soil, it may take hours for an inch of water to percolate that deeply. If you have clay soil, it's a good idea to water in cycles of perhaps 10 minutes on and 50 minutes off to allow the soil time to take up the water.

GRASSES		MOWING HEIGHTS		
		Cool Weather	Hot Weather	Last Mow
COOL SEASON	Bent grass	½" - ¾"	¾" - 1"	½" - ¾"
	Kentucky bluegrass	2" - 2½"	3"	2"
	Fine fescue	1½" - 2"	2" - 2½"	1½" - 2"
	Tall fescue	2" - 2½"	2½" - 4"	2½"
	Perennial ryegrass	1½" - 2"	2" - 2½"	1½" - 2"
WARM SEASON	Bahia grass	2" - 3"	3" - 3½"	2½" - 3"
	Bermuda grass	½" - 1½"	¾" - 3"	¾" - 1"
	Blue grama grass	2" - 4"	3" - 4"	2" - 3"
	Buffalo grass	2" - 5"	2" - 5"	2" - 4"
	Centipede grass	1" - 2"	1½" - 2"	1½" - 2"
	St. Augustine grass	2" - 3"	3" - 3½"	2½"
	Zoysia	½" - 1½"	1" - 2"	1" - 1½"

Controlling Thatch

Even the best-maintained lawn eventually accumulates a layer of dead but undecomposed plant material, called thatch, on the soil surface. In a natural system, this material—fibrous roots, stolons, rhizomes, and clippings—is quickly broken down by soil microorganisms. Chemicals that are applied to the lawn slow that process. And some grasses are just naturally thatch builders. While a layer of thatch less than half an inch thick will do no harm, anything more not only blocks the flow of water, air, and nutrients into the soil but also provides a home for pests and diseases. Warm-season lawns should be dethatched once or twice a year, in spring or fall, and cool-season grasses once every 3 years in late spring or summer. If your lawn is small, you can use a metal thatch rake to scratch the matted plant material out. If you have a very large lawn, however, you may want to consider renting a gasoline-powered dethatcher. Minimizing your use of chemicals and aerating the lawn will help keep thatch under control.

Identifying and Solving Lawn Problems

Despite the best care and attention, any number of things can still go wrong with your lawn, especially if it hasn't been converted to a low-maintenance system. Before assuming that a pest or disease is causing a particular problem, consider whether environmental or cultural conditions might be responsible. Such problems can often be easily fixed, and doing so promptly may prevent the invasion of pests or diseases.

Recognizing Common Problems

Brown spots, though they can be a sign of possible infestation or infection, may also be a symptom of something less troublesome, such as chemical spills, dog-urine damage, or nutrient deficiency *(chart, below)*. Other problems have their own telltale signs. If the lawn appears yellow or grayish, for example, you've probably mowed it with a dull blade. Let it grow out, then mow lightly with a blade that is sharp. Compacted, moist, shady areas often provide the perfect environment for algae, which may appear as a green to black slimy scum on the soil and grass. Spray the area with copper sulfate, aerate the soil, and do what you can to improve drainage and increase the amount of light the site receives. A low pH level may exacerbate the problem; check to be sure your soil pH is in the 6 to 6.8 range.

Moss also settles on shady, infertile, acidic soils. Rake it up and, if necessary, apply iron sulfate at a dose of 3 tablespoons per 1 to 2 gallons of water to cover 1,000 square feet of turf. Afterward, correct your soil by raising the pH to the proper level and adding the right amount of organic fertilizer to make sure the moss doesn't return. Aerating and improving drainage will also help.

Controlling Weeds

A lawn doesn't have to be entirely weed free to be healthy and attractive, so it's up to you to decide how many uninvited guests you will tolerate. The stricter you are about weeds, the more time and money you will need to spend to thwart them—

Brown spots on the lawn (above) aren't always caused by pests or diseases. The chart at right lists five common environmental causes of such problems—including nutrient deficiencies and drought—and ways to recognize and treat them.

ENVIRONMENTAL CAUSES OF BROWN SPOTS AND HOW TO FIX THEM

Damage	Problem	Cause	Solution
Salt	Grass slowly turns brown and dies, especially in lowest areas; soil may have white or dark brown crust.	Salt buildup from natural level in soil, or residue from excess fertilizer. Possibly poor drainage.	If drainage is good, water heavily. Aerate soil, add sand. Fill in low spots. Fertilize in correct amounts.
Fertilizer Burn	Patches, stripes, or curves of dead grass that do not spread or enlarge; appear 2-5 days after fertilizing.	High level of nitrogen due to misuse of fast-release synthetic fertilizer, especially in warm weather.	Water thoroughly after fertilizing. Replace soil under spots that are bare after 3-4 weeks and replant.
Dog Urine	Circles of dead or brown grass, surrounded by healthy green grass; may appear as dark green patches.	Nitrogen and salts in dog urine burn or kill grass; especially damaging in hot, dry weather.	Water immediately. If grass dies, allow grass to fill in area, dig up and reseed, or patch with sod.
Drought/Heat	Grass wilts; becomes dull, bluish, or grayish green to brown. Footprints show. Areas thin out.	Symptoms appear first in hottest and driest areas: along sidewalks, driveways, sunny and sandy areas.	Mow cool-season grasses ½" higher. Water; check soil moisture. Overseed with drought-tolerant grass.
Nutrient Deficiencies	Lawn turns slightly yellow, purplish, or reddish brown; grows slowly; leaf tops wither, grass thins.	Lawn needs to be fertilized, or improper soil pH is keeping grass from taking up nutrients.	Have soil tested for nutrient levels; correct with recommended fertilizer. Adjust pH, if necessary.

and the more likely you'll be to resort to chemical herbicides to get rid of them.

You can rid your lawn of most weeds—and prevent them, too—using both cultural and mechanical methods. Turf that is growing vigorously and steadily will crowd out the lion's share of weeds. To that end, light fertilizing at the right time strengthens the grass and allows it to beat out the competition. And don't forget that weeds can be a sign that something else is wrong. Certain weeds thrive in compacted soil, for example, while others like wet conditions; the chart at right describes specific weeds and the environmental problems they may indicate.

Lawn weeds may be annual or perennial, broadleaf or grassy, and warm- or cool-season. Identifying them and understanding their habits can help to control them *(pages 586-589)*. For example, if you cut and remove annual weeds such as crab grass before they set seed, you'll go a long way toward eradicating them. However, perennial weeds, such as dandelion, must be removed roots and all to prevent them from spreading. Low-growing, spreading lawn weeds may be discouraged by continued high mowing of the grass.

Sometimes the best way to control lawn weeds is with plain old elbow grease. There are many effective weed knives, diggers, pullers, and poppers on the market. Taking them in hand for an hour or so every week will reduce your weed population dramatically. Pulling weeds can leave bare spots in your lawn, however, and new weeds will move in unless you take steps to foil them. After digging

Weeds in a lawn sometimes serve as warnings of underlying trouble. The perennial weed curly dock (top), for example, with its red-tinged leaves and seeds, can be a sign of excessive moisture. Annual bluegrass (bottom), an unwelcome Kentucky bluegrass relative, thrives in compacted, moist soils, especially when the turf is mowed too closely. Good weed control includes correcting those conditions to prevent recurrence.

WEEDS THAT SIGNAL TROUBLE	
Name of Weed	**Conditions Indicated**
Annual bluegrass	Compaction; high moisture; shade; infertile soil; low mowing
Black medic	Dry, infertile soil; drought
*Common chickweed	Compaction; thinning turf; excessive moisture; highly fertile or acid soil; moist shade
Clover	Thinning turf; low fertility; drought conditions; compaction
*Crab grass	Thinning turf; frequent, light, shallow watering; low mowing; compaction; low fertility; poor drainage; drought
Curly dock	Poor drainage; excess moisture; turf stressed by hot, dry weather
*Dandelion	Thinning grass; overwatering; low mowing; low fertility; drought; highly opportunistic
*Goose grass	Compaction; high moisture; poor drainage; low mowing; frequent or light watering; highly fertile soil
Ground ivy	Shade; moist soil; poor drainage; highly fertile soil
Henbit	Excessive moisture; highly fertile soil; thinning or new turf
Lespedeza	Dry, infertile, acid soil; drought
Plantain	Dense soil; excessive moisture; low fertility; low mowing
Prostrate knotweed	Compaction, especially in heavily traveled areas; drought; thinning turf
Red sorrel	Low pH (under 5); infertile soil; poor drainage
*Spurge	Sand or gravel soils; dry soil; drought stress; thin, undernourished, infertile turf; also found on well-maintained lawns subject to low mowing
Wild garlic	Thinning turf; tolerates almost any environment in cool seasons, including heavy, wet soil or sandy soil with low humus
Wild onion	Thinning turf; tolerates almost any environment in spring and fall
Wild violet	Shade with cool, moist soil; poor drainage
*Wood sorrel	Drought; highly opportunistic in many situations

*See also Guide to Common Garden Weeds, pages 586-589.

When Japanese beetle larvae feed underground on grass roots, the lawn develops brown patches as grass plants die (above). The turf eventually becomes loose and can be lifted from the soil. Mole crickets (left) tunnel about an inch below the surface of the ground, feeding on roots and leaving raised mounds of soil and wilted brown grass.

weeds up, fill in any spots with a bit of topsoil, put down some grass seed, and scratch the seeds into the soil with a rake.

If your lawn is more than 25 percent weeds, pulling and cutting won't do the trick. Such a large infestation results from faulty maintenance practices such as improper fertilizing, or an underlying problem such as the wrong kind of grass, too much shade, or poor soil. Start by overseeding your lawn with an improved grass variety, and consider what maintenance habits or environmental conditions might be allowing weeds to take hold.

As a last resort, you can try a selective herbicide, but be aware that while it may remove the weeds, it won't solve the problem that may be inviting them. In the worst cases, you might consider starting over entirely by removing the lawn, correcting the soil, and replanting with a better turf variety.

The Problem of Pests

Pests are less likely to attack a healthy lawn, but they may show up occasionally, especially when their natural enemies aren't present or when the grass is stressed by harsh weather. Like weeds, pests sometimes signal environmental problems, such as poor soil or improper mowing or fertilizing.

The damage often appears as discolored grass or brown and dying patches. You can usually get rid of the pest by using one of several natural insecticides, such as *Bacillus thuringiensis* (Bt). Check with your local Cooperative Extension Service for the right time to apply insecticides, and follow all package directions. Chemical pesticides should be used very carefully and only as a last resort.

Some of the pests most commonly found in lawns are the following:

- Armyworms are serious pests of warm-season grasses, especially Bermuda grass, although they can attack any species. The caterpillars are 1 to 2 inches long, striped, and yellow to brownish green; fall armyworms have an inverted Y on their heads. Active in the heat of summer, they chew grass blades to skeletons, leaving patches of ragged grass. Use Bt to control them.
- The white grubs of Japanese and other beetles attack the roots of many grasses, including Kentucky bluegrass, bent grass, and fescues. As the grubs feed, the turf loosens from the soil and turns brown. Unnoticed and untreated, an infestation of grubs can do irreversible damage and even kill an entire lawn. Many grubs can be controlled with neem,

parasitic wasps, tachinid flies, and beneficial nematodes. Milky spore disease will control Japanese beetle grubs.

- Adult billbugs are dark, snouted beetles that eat grass leaves and burrow in stems; root-eating grubs are legless and white with yellowish to reddish brown heads. They leave behind yellow or brown patches of turf that can be pulled up from the soil. Early-summer treatment with beneficial nematodes will control these pests.
- Chinch bugs feed on many grass varieties from early spring to late autumn, causing the turf to yellow and die in patches. Young nymphs—bright red with a white stripe—cause most of the damage. They prefer sunny lawns during hot, dry weather. Chinch bugs can be controlled with neem, pyrethrins, sabadilla, or soap sprays.
- Cutworms are minor pests unless their populations become large. The caterpillars are usually smooth and can be brownish, grayish white, or green tinged. They feed at night from spring through summer on grass stems and leaves. Control them with neem.
- Greenbugs are light green aphids that feed on grass blades—especially underwatered or overfertilized Kentucky bluegrass—in early summer and late fall, turning affected areas a rusty color. They can be controlled with insecticidal soap.
- Mites are minute spider relatives that usually attack Bermuda grass or Kentucky bluegrass, sucking the juice out of the blades and turning them yellow. Most active during hot, dry weather, mites can be controlled with insecticidal soap.
- Mole crickets—winged relatives of the grasshopper that are brown and 1½ inches long—cause problems in all types of southern lawns from April to October. They feed on grass roots as they tunnel beneath the lawn, causing the soil to dry out. Control them with *Nosema locustae* or beneficial nematodes.
- Sod webworms attack Kentucky bluegrass, bent grass, fescues, and zoysia. The light brown, spotted caterpillars feed at night in the thatch layer from late spring through summer, creating small brown patches in the lawn. Control these pests with beneficial nematodes or insecticidal soap.

A surface examination of your lawn may reveal adult or larval insects on the grass, but certain pests—such as sod webworms, cutworms, and chinch bugs—are hard to spot because they live in thatch or at the soil surface. You can force them

into the open by thoroughly drenching the soil with a solution containing 2 to 3 tablespoons of liquid dish detergent to every gallon of water.

Other pests, such as beetle grubs, live below the soil surface. If you can roll up the turf like a carpet, you will probably see grubs at work. If the turf doesn't roll but you suspect underground pests, check by digging up a few 1-foot-square, 2-inch-thick slabs of sod and searching the soil. Afterward, replace and thoroughly water the sod, and it will regrow.

If your lawn suffers from chronic problems, consider overseeding with an insect-resistant grass. Many new varieties of perennial ryegrass, tall fescue, and fine fescue resist damage from pests such as sod webworms, armyworms, cutworms, billbug larvae, chinch bugs, and greenbugs. Known as endophytic grasses, they host a beneficial fungus in their leaf and stem tissue that repels or kills these common lawn insects. See the box above for a list of recommended grass varieties that resist pests.

Pest-Resistant Grasses

These cultivated endophytic turf grasses resist attack from many common lawn pests. The percentages given indicate the proportion of the turf that will not be affected if a pest attempts to invade your lawn. Because endophytes are living organisms in the grass seed, the seed must be handled carefully. Be sure to buy fresh seed—the maximum shelf life is 2 years—and store it at 50° to 60°F.

Perennial Ryegrass

HIGH ENDOPHYTE LEVEL
(80-100%):
'Commander'
'Pennant'
'Pinnacle'
'Repell'
'Saturn'
'Saville'

MODERATELY HIGH
ENDOPHYTE LEVEL
(60-80%):
'Accolade'
'Citation II'
'Cowboy'
'Omega II'
'Stallion'

MODERATE ENDOPHYTE LEVEL
(30-60%):
'Caliente'
'Delray'
'Palmer'
'Premier'
'Vintage'

Tall Fescue

HIGH ENDOPHYTE LEVEL
(80-100%):
'Bonsai'
'Shenandoah'
'SR 8200'

MODERATE ENDOPHYTE LEVEL
(30-60%):
'Phoenix'
'Pixie'

Fine Fescue

HIGH ENDOPHYTE LEVEL
(80-100%):
'Aurora' with endophytes
'Discovery'
'Jamestown II'
'Reliant' with endophytes
'Shadow' with endophytes
'SR 5000'

Treating Turf Grass Diseases

Turf diseases are often a side effect of high-maintenance lawn programs. High temperatures and humidity, inadequate air circulation, poor soil, and too much shade also increase the chance that disease will strike your lawn, especially if your grass variety does not tolerate these conditions.

Most diseases are caused by fungi that live in the soil and the thatch layer. Many are choosy about climate and temperature and will appear only under the right circumstances. Also, some diseases are species specific, targeting only particular types of grass. When disease does strike, diagnosis can be difficult. General symptoms range from striped blades to brown patches of turf to a water-soaked appearance. The most reliable way to identify a disease is to send samples of your turf and soil to your local Cooperative Extension Service or a university's plant pathology lab.

To combat a disease, you'll need to assess and repair the cultural and environmental conditions that may be giving it a foothold. In almost all cases, dethatching and aerating will help, as will watering the lawn deeply and only in the morning. Top-dressing with compost can slow some diseases. You may need to use a light application of a fast-release synthetic fertilizer to get nutrients to ailing grass plants quickly. Also, consider overseeding with one of the newer grass varieties that are resistant to a specific disease.

Descriptions of 10 common lawn diseases and the conditions that trigger them are profiled here. When diagnosing a lawn problem, keep in mind that certain species of turf grass are also susceptible to diseases affecting other types of plants.

1. BROWN PATCH (Rhizoctonia solani)

This summertime disease strikes most turf grasses at some point. Leaves appear dark and water-soaked, then become dry and brown, creating irregular or circular patches as large as several feet across. It occurs primarily when temperatures and humidity are high; excessive nitrogen exacerbates the problem. Avoid heavy fertilizing, and don't overwater. Raise the mowing height, and apply the beneficial microorganism Trichoderma, neem, fungicidal soap, or garlic oil.

2. DOLLARSPOT (Sclerotinia homoeocarpa)

Most grass species are susceptible to this disease, which causes straw-colored spots that range from the size of a silver dollar to 6 inches across. Blades die from the tip down. Dollarspot is most common in late spring to early summer and again in early fall, in dry soil and high humidity. Control it with light, frequent applications of nitrogen fertilizer; water deeply, at most once a week; and use neem, fungicidal soap, or garlic oil.

3. FAIRY RINGS (Marasmius oreades)

This disease occurs most often in areas of high rainfall. Dark green circles or arcs of grass appear in spring; later, mushrooms may sprout. Deprived of water and nutrients, the grass within the ring dies. Fertilize with nitrogen, aerate the rings, keep the area watered, and mow frequently. There are no chemical controls. Complete eradication may mean replacing the turf and soil.

4. MELTING OUT (Drechslera poae)

This disease may attack Kentucky bluegrass during cool, moist spring and fall weather. Blades first develop tan spots with purplish brown borders. Later, lesions appear water-soaked, and the entire plant rots. Avoid synthetic nitrogen fertilizers, water deeply and infrequently, and mow high. Overseed the lawn with a resistant variety.

5. NECROTIC RING SPOT
(Leptosphaeria korrae)

Often found in Kentucky bluegrass, bent grass, and creeping red fescue, necrotic ring spot usually begins during cool, wet weather. The disease strikes plant roots. Circles of dead grass with living plants at the center, often greater than a foot in diameter, may appear; individual plants look purple. Avoid summer fertilizing, mow on schedule at the proper height, and overseed with perennial ryegrass or tall fescue.

6. PARASITIC NEMATODES

Of the thousands of nematode species, about 50 are turf grass parasites that feed on roots. Damage—yellowing, wilting, and thinning—is difficult to distinguish from environmental stress. Dig soil samples from several spots on the lawn where the damage borders healthy grass, keep the samples moist, and take them to a Cooperative Extension Service for treatment recommendations based on the species. Mow the grass high, water properly, and fertilize.

7. PYTHIUM BLIGHT
(Pythium species)

High humidity and warm nights, paired with excessive fertilizing and mowing and poor drainage, are ideal conditions for pythium blight. It appears first in shady areas as light brown or reddish brown patches, circles, or streaks. Leaf blades may look watery, and thin, cottony webbing may be evident early in the day. Good preventive maintenance is essential; once it strikes it is impossible to eradicate.

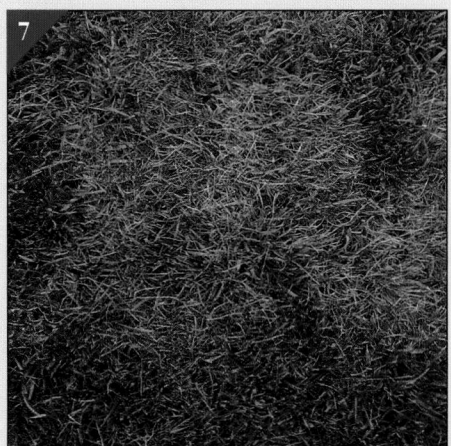

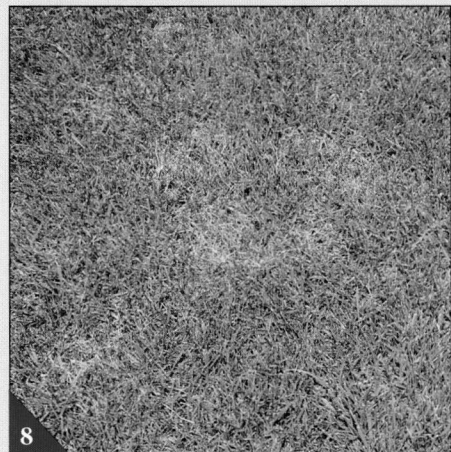

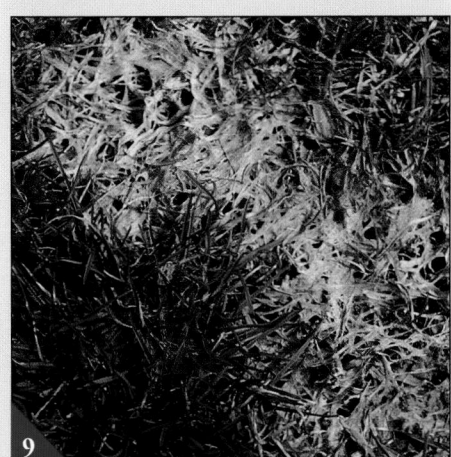

8. RED THREAD
(Laetisaria fuciformis)

This disease most commonly attacks fine fescue, perennial ryegrass, and Kentucky bluegrass during cool, wet, overcast weather. Infected blades in the final stage display reddish threads of cottony webbing; circular patches of infection may measure up to 2 feet across. Apply a synthetic fertilizer lightly and frequently; water deeply and regularly. Check soil pH. Plant a resistant variety.

9. SNOW MOLD (Microdochium nivale; Typhula species)

Snow mold can be active at temperatures just above freezing and most often strikes dormant grass. Moist soil, deep snow, and lush grass encourage the disease, which appears as 2- to 3-inch round patches that expand up to 2 feet. Inside the patch, the grass appears water-soaked; outside, there may be a pink or grayish ring around the patch. Monitor pH, improve drainage, and prune nearby trees and shrubs to increase air circulation.

10. STRIPE SMUT
(Ustilago striiformis)

A foe of Kentucky bluegrass, bent grass, and perennial ryegrass, stripe smut is most noticeable during spring and fall. Plants turn yellow or light green, grayish to black streaks appear on blades, and eventually blades shred and curl. The disease occurs most often when turf is treated with large doses of nitrogen. Mow high during summer, water deeply to avoid drought stress, and apply a balanced fertilizer in fall.

411

PART III

KITCHEN GARDENING

CHAPTER ELEVEN

Kitchen Gardening the Organic Way

Nothing tastes better than something you've grown in your own garden. And if your vegetables and herbs are raised organically, they are as healthful as they can be, free of contamination from synthetic pesticides and other possibly harmful substances.

Far from being an arcane or difficult science, organic gardening is a common-sense blend of traditional techniques and modern advances for building a fertile soil and creating a healthy garden environment. Like the owner of the New Jersey garden at left, who prepared the soil carefully, then planted crops in neat raised beds, you'll want to tackle organic kitchen gardening methodically. Assess your site, your climate, and your needs, and then concentrate on feeding the soil that will feed your plants. By following the techniques presented in this chapter for choosing and preparing the site and drawing up a plan for the plot, you'll not only protect your health and that of the environment, you'll also enjoy a robust, productive garden.

Siting a Successful Vegetable Garden

An orderly plot of dark, crumbly soil brimming with vigorous, carefully tended vegetables and fruits is a handsome expression of the gardener's art, as beautiful in its own way as an artfully composed perennial border. Before you begin the appetizing task of deciding which varieties to grow, however, you need to do some thoughtful planning so that the venture will be a productive one.

The first order of business is to choose the best site your property has to offer for this purpose. Although such matters as the size, convenience, and appearance of a vegetable garden are important factors to keep in mind, growing conditions should be at the top of your list of concerns as you compare the possibilities your yard offers.

Soil and Microclimates

The foundation of a successful organic garden is, literally, a fertile, well-drained soil teeming with microorganisms. If yours doesn't fill the bill in its present condition, this chapter details some reliable methods organic gardeners can use to turn inferior soil into a good growing medium *(pages 417-423)*. Climate, the other variable critical to garden success, is far less amenable to manipulation and control. In this instance, your goal is to find the microclimate on your property with the sunlight, temperature range, and air circulation your vegetables need to flourish.

The Primacy of Sunlight

Of the climatic variables, sunlight is the most important. Except for a handful of shade-tolerant crops—lettuce, for one—vegetables require at least 6 hours of direct sun per day for optimal growth; if you have a spot that is in full sun for 7 or 8 hours, so much the better.

If a survey of your property turns up several

A south-facing slope provides the Wisconsin garden below with the double benefit of long hours of sunshine and shelter from chilling northerly winds. In a sunny spot at the garden's center, a latticework trellis awaits the climbing tendrils of late-summer pole beans. Lettuce, which enjoys some protection from the sun, has been planted in the shade cast by trees at the east end of the garden.

places with ample sunlight, look for differences in their microclimates that can tip the balance in favor of one over the others. For gardeners in cold climates, an especially desirable location is a gentle, open slope that faces south and receives a full day of sun. Because the sunlight strikes the surface of the slope at an angle, the soil will warm up earlier in the spring and remain warm longer in the fall, making it more productive than it would be if the ground were level. A northern exposure has a very different set of conditions—fewer hours of direct sunlight, cooler soil temperatures, and, in many parts of North America, prevailing northwesterly winds that remove heat from the soil and shorten the growing season.

High Winds and Frost Pockets

From whatever direction they come, strong winds are harmful to the garden: They rob the soil of moisture, and they can also uproot plants and topple the supports that hold vining vegetables. As a rule, an exposed site at the top of a slope or hill is especially vulnerable to the cooling and drying effects of the wind, effects that are exacerbated in freezing weather or during a period of drought. If you have no alternative to such adverse conditions, you could plant a windbreak of two or three staggered rows of closely spaced evergreen trees or shrubs, then site your garden on the lee side and far enough away to avoid any root competition or shade from the windbreak.

Frost pockets can be equally destructive to tender plants. The result of cold, heavy air settling in low areas or on the uphill side of a building or a hedge running across a slope, frost pockets are colder in winter and prone to frost later in spring and earlier in fall, greatly shortening the growing season. If you have a dense, solid hedge that blocks air flow, you can alleviate the problem by removing a section of it to allow cold air to continue its downward movement.

Size, Looks, and Convenience

Next, you'll need to decide how much space you wish to devote to your garden plot or, if space is limited, how much you can spare for this purpose. If you are new to raising vegetables, it's prudent to keep the plot small the first year to avoid taking on more work than you bargained for. An area measuring no more than 10 feet square, for instance, can yield upwards of 60 pounds of vegetables a year and will give you a good idea of how much

time and effort tending your garden will require. After a season's trial run, you can always expand the size the following year. The chart on page 41 provides information on how much you can expect to harvest in a season from a 10-foot row of 30 different kinds of vegetables.

When it comes to how visible a vegetable patch should be, people differ in their opinions. Some may enjoy having a burgeoning plot in full view of the terrace, while others prefer to tuck theirs out of sight behind the garage or along one side of the house. But if you're a gardener for whom convenience outweighs aesthetics, a plot close to the kitchen has many advantages. For one, you'll be more likely to visit the garden every day, checking its progress, pulling weed seedlings, and harvesting vegetables at their peak. And you won't have to carry your prized produce more than a few short steps.

The vegetable garden should also have easy access to water. From planting time to harvest, watering is one chore that can't get short shrift. You'll also find it very handy to have the compost

In late summer, an edging of frilly green parsley and colorful marigolds decorates a raised bed that contains a mature clump of blooming basil, onions, and rows of romaine seedlings for fall salads (below). The clipped yews in the background protect the vegetables and herbs from the cold northeast winds that buffet this New Jersey garden.

Indigo-colored Lobelia erinus and mixed zinnias mingle with edible species—including pink-flowering garlic, a stand of yellow peppers, Phaseolus coccineus (scarlet runner bean) in full crimson bloom, and broad-leaved eggplant—rendering this California garden both practical and beautiful.

pile—an integral part of organic gardening—close to the vegetable plot and the kitchen, since both generate waste for composting.

A Tailor-Made Design

The classic layout for a vegetable garden is a rectangular plot, often fenced to keep animals out. The plot may be divided into a series of rows, but many gardeners prefer to divide it into two or more individual beds separated by paths of hardened earth, mulch, flagstone, or turf grass.

Dividing a plot into separate beds makes it easy to group vegetables that have similar soil, moisture, and nutritional requirements. Although the surface of a bed can be level with the surrounding soil, there are great advantages to mounding the soil so that the surface is elevated by 4 inches or more. Mounding not only ensures good drainage, it also allows the soil to warm up more quickly in the spring because more of it is exposed to the air; this lets you begin planting earlier than usual.

A raised bed is also the ideal space for applying intensive gardening techniques. Because the soil in the bed is tailored to meet the nutrient requirements of the vegetables you plant there, they can be placed very close to one another without suffering the adverse effects of competition. You will reap more produce from your initial planting and can also feel confident that a subsequent crop won't be shortchanged.

A plot with multiple beds is the most efficient way to grow vegetables. If space doesn't permit this layout, however, you can disperse beds around your property, fitting them in wherever there is room and the conditions are appropriate. Planting vegetables—especially dwarf varieties—in containers is another way to expand your growing area *(pages 476-477)*. And if you're still hungry for edible plants, consider making room among the perennials and annuals of an ornamental border for such attractive vegetable varieties as a ruffly bright chartreuse lettuce or purple broccoli *(pages 438-439)*. Like your vegetables, the flowering plants will thrive on an organic regimen.

Soil: Your Garden's Foundation

A vegetable garden imposes high demands on soil: It must nourish a succession of closely spaced plants with a variety of nutritional needs; produce a harvest within a few months; and, if the gardener wants to coax the highest yield possible from the plot, provide good growing conditions from very early spring until well after fall frosts arrive.

The raw material you have to work with may not seem promising. The typical city or suburban gardener in North America has inherited a soil that has been changed, seldom for the better, by activities such as farming, lumbering, and construction. The topsoil's natural fertility may have been depleted. Worse, the topsoil itself may have been bulldozed away, exposing the underlying, largely infertile, subsoil layer. With the right organic techniques, however, even the most discouraging plot can be made productive.

Testing Your Soil

To find out how your soil measures up in terms of pH, organic matter, and nutrients, you'll need to test it. To measure pH, you can use a hand-held electronic pH meter or litmus paper. For more detailed information on both pH and nutrient levels, analyze your soil with a ready-to-use testing kit. All of these devices are available at any large garden or home center.

To obtain a comprehensive professional analysis, submit a soil sample to your state Cooperative Extension Service or a commercial laboratory. The report you receive should state the type of soil you have and its pH level, organic matter content, and nutrient availability. It will also include recommendations for amendments and fertilizers you can use to improve the soil, so be sure to specify that you prefer organic products.

Organic Soil Enrichment

An amendment is a material that, when added to a soil, improves its structure by changing the way mineral particles adhere to one another. Sometimes it is necessary to add two or more amendments at the same time to get the desired effect. For example, you can work shredded leaves and a substance called greensand into a clay soil to help improve drainage. The greensand, a dark green, grainy mineral, loosens the clay particles, and the newly created open spaces allow air and water to move more freely through the soil. The shredded leaves nourish soil life and prevent the combination of clay and greensand from producing a soil so hard that roots and water can scarcely penetrate it.

Organic fertilizers supplement the soil's level of available nutrients, notably nitrogen, phosphorus, and potassium, and they also contribute to the soil's volume of organic matter. All of the fertilizers organic gardeners use are made of animal and plant materials such as blood, fish, and seaweed.

An organic fertilizer's nutrients are released into the soil slowly; most of them become available for use only after soil microorganisms, mainly bacteria, have broken the material down. Synthetic fertilizers, on the other hand, typically supply fast-acting shots of nutrients that stimulate rapid spurts of growth. With repeated use, synthetics eventually kill much of a soil's population of valuable organisms and can also acidify the soil. Commercial organic fertilizers are labeled to show the percentages by weight of nitrogen, phosphorus, and potassium, in that order. A labeling of 5-3-4, for example, means that the product contains 5 percent nitrogen, 3 percent phosphorus, and 4 percent potassium. See the chart on page 423 for detailed information on organic fertilizers and amendments.

All-Purpose Compost

Of the many soil amendments and fertilizers you can use, the best one for an organic garden is compost. Consisting mainly of partially decayed plant wastes, it is an excellent source of organic matter and a reservoir for many nutrients.

Compost can convert a sandy or clayey soil into loam, the ideal soil for growing vegetables. And because it has a nearly neutral pH value, it helps keep soil in the range vegetables prefer. In addition, compost that is made from a large variety of materials contains a healthy balance of nutrients.

To make compost properly, gardeners combine two kinds of plant materials—fibrous materials such as leaves, straw, and sawdust (often referred to collectively as "browns"), and succulent "greens" such as grass clippings and kitchen scraps. The browns are the source of the carbon

Starting a Vegetable Garden

A sunny patch of lawn is often the best place to site a new vegetable garden, and the best time to begin the work of creating it is the season prior to planting. Clearing and tilling the plot at that point, as described in the first two steps on this page, gives the soil time to fully incorporate any amendments and fertilizers you have added; the result is a more fertile medium for seeds and seedlings when planting season arrives. Several weeks in advance of planting, till the soil lightly with a garden fork or broadfork *(box, page 422)*. Then build the beds and mulch the paths, as described in Steps 3, 4, and 5. Shaping the prepared soil into raised beds is well worth the effort required; better drainage and more room for root growth mean more vigorous plants and a more bountiful harvest.

1. Mark the perimeter of your vegetable plot with stakes and string. *Using a sharp square-bladed spade and working just inside the string, slice down through the sod to the depth of the spade (above); do this all the way around the plot. Next, use the spade to cut the sod into sections small enough to lift easily. Pry each one loose with the spade or a garden fork and knock the topsoil off the roots. Remove the stakes and string.*

2. Till the plot with a rotary rear-tined tiller *(above) to the depth of one tiller blade—approximately 8 to 12 inches. Work your way up and down the length of the plot, then repeat the process across the plot. After you have tilled the soil, remove any large stones, roots, weeds, or bits of sod. Incorporate amendments or fertilizers as needed to correct soil deficiencies, working them into the top 6 to 8 inches of soil with a spading fork.*

3. Using stakes and string, measure and mark off the tilled plot *into individual beds and pathways (above). Make each bed 3 to 5 feet wide so the plants in the center will be within easy reach. For convenience in moving around the beds, make them no more than 15 to 20 feet long. Pathways 2 feet or more in width allow room to maneuver tools and equipment, such as a garden cart, between the beds.*

4. To mound up the soil for a raised bed, *first place a 1-by-4 board in the center of the bed: If you need to step into the bed, the board will distribute your weight, minimizing soil compaction. Standing on one side of the space you've staked out, use a raised-bed builder (below) or a flat rake to reach across the bed and rake tilled soil from the path area into the bed. Repeat from each side of the bed, sloping the sides a bit to minimize erosion. Then, with the back of the tool, smooth and level the surface of the bed (right). The bed should be 4 to 5 inches higher than the surrounding paths.*

5. Mulch the paths with straw, *as shown here, or another organic material to suppress weeds and conserve soil moisture. Spread straw, pine needles, and other loose, airy mulches 3 to 4 inches deep; for a denser mulch such as woodchips or ground bark, 1 to 2 inches is enough. By the end of the growing season, the mulch will have decomposed enough to be dug into the soil.*

The sandy soil of this Long Island vegetable garden is enriched with regular additions of compost and mulched with seaweed from nearby beaches. Before the seaweed is spread, it is washed to remove the salt; as it decomposes, it will add organic matter to the soil.

required for decomposition, while the greens furnish nitrogen. The greens and browns are assembled in a pile of alternating layers *(page 262)*.

When the pile is kept about as moist as a well-squeezed sponge and its layers are turned and mixed regularly to incorporate air, the decay microorganisms are very active. The energy released during decomposition raises the mound's internal temperature to as much as 160° F, which in turn stimulates chemical processes to break the material down even further. With this method, called "hot composting," the finished product will be ready in as little as a month; at the end of that time, the mass of material will have shrunk to approximately one-third of its original size.

Some gardeners prefer the "cold composting" method, which is less work: Once the pile is assembled, it is left undisturbed. However, the materials will decay slowly, and it may be 2 years before you have finished compost. Unless you have room for several piles in different stages of decomposition, this method probably won't provide enough compost for your vegetable garden.

Timing Soil Improvements

Enriching the soil is an ongoing chore for the vegetable gardener. When establishing a new plot *(pages 418-419),* dig in a 2- to 3-inch layer of com-

post to improve soil structure; at the same time, correct any deficiencies uncovered by soil testing.

In most parts of the country, applications of 1 to 2 inches of organic matter twice a year, in spring and fall, are sufficient to maintain good soil structure and to ensure a healthy population of soil organisms. In the Deep South, however, where summers are hot and humid and winters are short and mild, organic matter decomposes at a much faster rate, so gardeners need to replenish it at least three times a year.

Tilling the Garden

Tilling or cultivating the soil at least twice a year, in spring and in fall, is a task that can't be avoided. It is the time to work in fertilizers and amendments, and the simple act of turning the soil is itself beneficial in several ways: It restores lightness to compacted soil so plant roots get the water and air they

Closely spaced rows of lettuce grow to near perfection in the rich, well-drained soil of this Idaho garden. The raised bed has been double dug and planted with such varieties as 'Red Sails' (second from left) and the ruddy-leaved 'Red Salad Bowl' (far right). Purple-flowered Allium schoenoprasum (chives) edges the straw-covered path in the background.

A Tool for Easy Tilling

A bed that has been prepared and then left to rest for weeks or months will inevitably undergo some compaction because of rain, snow, and gravity. For loosening the soil at planting time, many organic gardeners prefer to use a broadfork (below), a tool that alleviates the work of lifting and turning the soil required by the more commonly used garden fork. The broadfork, also called a U-bar, has long handles and five or six tines attached to a horizontal crossbar. The tines vary in length from 10 to 18 inches; the long-tined models are designed for the deeply cultivated soil of double-dug beds, the short-tined ones for single-dug beds.

To use the broadfork, hold it upright and step up and onto the crossbar, using your weight to push the tines down into the soil. Step off and pull the broadfork's handles toward you until the tips of the tines lift out of the soil. Repeat this process at 6-inch intervals across the area to be planted, moving backward to avoid stepping on soil you have already cultivated.

need. The increased oxygen content also stimulates the activity of soil life. And in spring, the loosened soil warms up more quickly, giving the gardener a jump on the new growing season.

There are a variety of tools for tilling, including rotary tillers and hand tools such as spades, spading forks, and broadforks. A rotary tiller makes sense for large plots, and it makes the work of preparing a new garden or turning under a cover crop (pages 514-515) much easier. However, using this tool on the garden more than twice a year tends to compact the soil. For that reason, choose hand tools for tilling work during the growing season.

When you are ready to till, spread any amendment or fertilizer over the entire area to be cultivated (see chart at right for application rates). If you are using a spade or a spading fork, push the blade or the tines all the way into the soil, then lift the soil and turn it over. Use a broadfork as described in the box at left. If you can't avoid stepping in the area you are tilling, stand on a board to distribute your weight more evenly.

Beds versus Rows

A tilled plot is almost ready for planting. The last step is to subdivide the plot into either narrow rows or rectangular raised beds like those on page 418. Although row planting has its adherents, it has at least two major drawbacks. For one thing, an alternating pattern of rows and paths is an inefficient use of space because much less of the total area is actually devoted to crops. When you arrange your plants in beds, on the other hand, you greatly reduce the area occupied by paths. In addition, shrinking the area taken up by paths keeps the potential for soil compaction to a minimum.

Another advantage of raised beds is that their greater depth of topsoil provides better drainage and more space for the roots of vegetables to grow downward. The additional soil needed to raise the beds 4 or 5 inches is furnished by digging out the paths between the beds (page 419).

The center of each bed should be within easy reach so that there's no need to step into the bed when you are tending plants or harvesting vegetables. Beds with access from two sides should be no wider than 4 or 5 feet. If there is access from one side only, limit the width to 3 feet. The length of a bed is more flexible, but don't make it so long that you'll be tempted to take a shortcut across it instead of sticking to the paths surrounding it. Be sure to make the paths that run between the beds at least 2 feet wide so there will be enough room for a garden cart.

ORGANIC AMENDMENTS AND FERTILIZERS

Below is a selection of widely available organic amendments and fertilizers. In most cases, they can be worked into the soil during tilling in either fall or spring; fresh manures are best applied in the fall so they can partially decompose over the winter. Fertilizers can be applied once or twice during the growing season for crops needing a nutrient boost or for new plantings. Unless otherwise noted, amendments that change pH should be used as often as soil tests indicate.

Name	Function	Application Rate	Comments
Blood meal	Fertilizer. Provides nitrogen.	2 lbs./100 sq. ft.	Also called dried blood. When using as a side dressing, keep 2 to 3 inches away from plant stems.
Bone meal	Fertilizer. Provides phosphorus, calcium.	2 lbs./100 sq. ft.	Work into topsoil immediately after applying; otherwise, the pungent odor may attract rodents.
Chicken manure, rotted	Amendment/fertilizer. Adds organic matter. Provides nitrogen, phosphorus, potassium.	1-inch layer	Work into topsoil in fall or compost before using.
Compost	Amendment/fertilizer. Loosens clay soils, binds sandy soils, increases water-holding capacity. Adds organic matter. Provides nitrogen, phosphorus, potassium.	2- to 3-inch layer	Best all-purpose amendment.
Cottonseed meal	Fertilizer. Provides nitrogen, phosphorus, potassium.	2.5 lbs./100 sq. ft.	May be contaminated by pesticides.
Cow manure, rotted	Amendment/fertilizer. Adds organic matter. Provides nitrogen, phosphorus, potassium.	1- to 2-inch layer	Work into topsoil in fall or compost before using.
Fish emulsion	Fertilizer. Provides nitrogen.	¼ oz./100 sq. ft.	Sold as concentrated liquid that is diluted for use. Can also be applied as a foliar spray.
Fish meal	Fertilizer. Provides nitrogen, phosphorus.	2 lbs./100 sq. ft.	Also called fish scrap, fish tankage. Apply just before planting or as a side dressing during the growing season.
Greensand	Amendment/fertilizer. Retards soil compaction, loosens clay soils, increases water-holding capacity. Provides potassium, trace elements.	5 lbs./100 sq. ft.	Use in conjunction with organic matter to amend clay soil.
Gypsum	Amendment. Loosens clay soils, balances pH. Provides calcium, sulfur.	2 lbs./100 sq. ft.	Also called land plaster, sulfate of lime. Pellets easier to use than powder.
Horse manure, rotted	Amendment/fertilizer. Adds organic matter. Provides nitrogen, phosphorus, potassium, trace elements.	1- to 2-inch layer	Work into topsoil in fall or compost before using.
Leaf mold	Amendment/fertilizer. Builds up soil humus content quickly. Adds organic matter. Provides nitrogen, phosphorus, potassium.	2-inch layer	Also called woods-soil when sold commercially. Can also be used as a mulch; apply a 2- to 3-inch layer.
Limestone	Amendment. Raises pH. Provides calcium, magnesium.	6 lbs./100 sq. ft. for clay 4 lbs./100 sq. ft. for loam 2 lbs./100 sq. ft. for sandy	Also called ground limestone, dolomitic limestone. Avoid hydrated lime or quicklime—they dissolve too quickly in the soil and burn plant roots and kill soil life.
Peat moss	Amendment. Loosens clay soils, lowers pH, increases water-holding capacity. Adds organic matter.	1- to 2-inch layer	Also called sphagnum peat moss. Work into topsoil.
Rock phosphate	Amendment/fertilizer. Raises pH. Provides phosphorus, trace elements.	2.5 lbs./100 sq. ft.	Most effective if applied to acid soils.
Sawdust	Amendment. Adds organic matter. Provides nitrogen, potassium.	1-inch layer	Apply only well-rotted sawdust to soil. Best if added to the compost pile.
Seaweed meal	Fertilizer. Provides nitrogen, potassium, trace elements.	1 to 2 lbs./100 sq. ft.	Also called kelp meal. Apply in early spring and work into topsoil.
Straw	Amendment. Adds organic matter. Provides nitrogen, phosphorus, potassium.	2- to 3-inch layer	Buy straw labeled "weed free." Can also be applied as a mulch, then turned under when it decays.
Sulfur	Amendment. Loosens clay soils, improves water-holding capacity, lowers pH.	Up to 1 lb./100 sq. ft. applied every 8 weeks	Also called soil sulfur. After working into topsoil, water thoroughly.
Wood ashes (leached)	Amendment/fertilizer. Raises pH. Provides potassium, calcium.	2 lbs./100 sq. ft.	Keep stored wood ashes dry to prevent nutrients from leaching out. When using as a side dressing, keep 2 to 3 inches away from plant stems.

Siting a Successful Herb Garden

Both culinary herbs and ornamentals thrive in this formal Mobile, Alabama, garden. The growing conditions offered by the site support a variety of plants, including yellow-flowering dill and fennel in the four outer beds and low-growing hollies surrounding the sundial. White flowering tobacco blooms at the edge of the lawn.

As with vegetables, the first step in growing herbs successfully is to assess the growing conditions in your garden. Variations in soil, microclimate, and light exposure will produce several different habitats that are congenial to different kinds of herbs. Although some herbs are very choosy about their soil requirements, most will grow vigorously in an open, loamy, well-drained soil. If drainage is too slow—usually because the soil is clayey—the oxygen that is vital for normal growth will be replaced by water. Plants may suffocate or, in less extreme conditions, produce weak shoots that tend to wilt or die back at the tips.

Only a few herbs tolerate waterlogged soil. If you have a drainage problem in a spot where you want to plant a wide variety of herbs, you'll need to loosen the soil. Begin by laying out your bed in the fall and digging the soil to a depth of 12 to 18 inches. In early spring, work in a 1- to 2-inch layer of builder's sand or poultry grit and about 1 inch of organic matter such as compost or leaf mold. Let the bed settle for several weeks before planting. If amending the existing soil is too big a job, you may prefer to build a raised bed *(pages 456-457)*.

Some Like It Sandy

If your garden has a coarse, sandy soil, it will provide the fast drainage some herbs demand, no-

424

tably those that are native to the Mediterranean region. These include such favorites as rosemary, thyme, and oregano. To accommodate herbs that prefer moist, fertile soil, incorporate about 2 inches of organic matter; this will enhance the soil's ability to hold water and will prevent nutrients from draining away too quickly. Be diligent about watering, and replenish the supply of organic matter periodically.

Picky Eaters

Fast-growing annual herbs that are harvested repeatedly for their leaves and stems require high levels of nutrients to continue producing new growth. They should be fed with liquid fertilizer every 2 weeks. You can make your own fertilizer from the potassium-rich foliage of comfrey (*Symphytum officinale*), a perennial herb. Pour 4 cups of boiling water over a handful of fresh comfrey leaves. Steep them for at least 10 minutes, then strain the liquid through cheesecloth and let it cool before using. Along with potassium, this infusion will provide phosphorus, nitrogen, trace elements, and minerals. The leaves of a number of other herbs, such as tansy, goosefoot, nettle, yarrow, dill, and coltsfoot, can also be made into liquid fertilizer.

Restraint is called for when you fertilize perennial and woody herbs, which will respond to small doses of organic fertilizer with increased vigor and health. Bone meal, blood meal, fish emulsion, and kelp are all excellent choices. Working compost into the soil at the beginning of the growing season will also boost the level of nutrients.

Testing the Soil's pH

As with vegetables, before planting herbs it's prudent to determine the soil's pH, which is a measure of its acidity or alkalinity *(page 417)*. You can do it yourself with a kit bought at a garden center, or you can send a soil sample to your Cooperative Extension Service for testing. Most soils in the eastern half of the country are acidic because of high rainfall levels that leach alkaline elements from the soil. Conversely, alkaline soils are common in the drier West.

The majority of herbs grow well in soils ranging from 6, which is slightly acid, to 7.5, which is mildly alkaline. If the pH falls outside this range, nutrients in the soil may not be available to plants. To raise the pH level, dust the soil with dolomitic limestone at least 1 month before planting, fol-

lowing the directions on the package. An application of sulfur will lower the pH level if your soil is too alkaline. For gardeners in the eastern part of the country who want to grow any of the Mediterranean herbs, soil testing is essential. Although these plants will grow in slightly acid soil, their preference is for a pH range of 7 to 8.2.

Light and Climate

Most herbs are sun worshipers, requiring at least 6 hours of direct light each day. Ideally, then, an herb bed should have a southern exposure. When

This rustic dooryard garden in Texas provides the perfect spot for sun-loving herbs. Fennel and bay laurel grace the front of the bed, while silver artemisia and a border of lavender-flowered onion chives lead the eye toward the house. Mexican oregano, growing behind the fennel, is a native herb used in Southwest cuisine.

assessing how much light a site receives, be sure to factor in shade cast from structures such as sheds, trellises, and walls, as well as hedges, shrubs, and trees. Luckily for gardeners who lack full-sun sites, several culinary herbs—among them parsley, chives, chervil, and hot peppers—can be planted in partial shade (4 to 6 hours of sun a day).

The intensity of light is as important as the number of hours of sunshine. Herbs that prefer fewer than 6 hours of sun grow best with direct morning light and dappled light or shade during the afternoon. Bright afternoon sun may be filtered by planting herbs on the northeast side of a trellis covered with a quick-growing vine.

Climate is another factor to consider when growing herbs. Winter cold presents special challenges to gardeners who want to grow an herb that isn't reliably hardy in their zone. To greatly increase the prospects for winter survival:

• Locate your herb bed near a wall or an evergreen hedge for protection from winter winds.

• Avoid fertilizing or pruning borderline-hardy herbs late in the season; the new growth this stimulates will be more susceptible to winter injury than growth that has had time to mature.

• Mulch the bed with evergreen boughs after the ground has frozen.

• Pot up tender plants in the fall for overwintering indoors. Shrubby herbs like rosemary are good candidates for this treatment *(page 483)*.

Gardeners in the South have the advantage of a long growing season. There are, however, a few cultural practices that are critical for healthy herbs in the typically hot, steamy southern summers.

Improving air circulation is important for all herbs cultivated in high humidity, which favors fungal diseases such as powdery mildew. Allow plenty of growing space between plants, and thin them to keep the interior airy.

Herbs with gray or silver leaves are difficult to grow in muggy climates; the little hairs that give the leaves their grayish cast also slow evaporation. This trait is a boon in hot, dry climates but a drawback where the moisture level is high. Give these plants a sunny site and mulch them with a 2-inch layer of light-colored sand or gravel, which will reflect light and heat onto the plants.

Herbs that cannot tolerate the intense heat of midsummer can be planted in early spring and harvested as long as temperatures re-

Herbs for Hot, Humid Climates

Allium ampeloprasum
var. *ampeloprasum*
(elephant garlic)
Artemisia dracunculus
var. *sativa*
(French tarragon)
Cymbopogon citratus
(lemon grass)
Foeniculum vulgare
(fennel)
Ocimum spp.
(basil)
Rosmarinus officinalis
(rosemary)
Salvia elegans
(pineapple sage)

Salvia officinalis
'Berggarten'
(sage)
Tagetes lucida
(sweet marigold)
Thymus spp.
(thyme)

Note: The abbreviation
"spp." stands for the
plural of "species"; where
used in lists it means
that many, but not all,
of the species in a genus
meet the criterion of
the list.

Ocimum basilicum 'Dark Opal' (basil)

In the Texas herb garden below, a tall brick wall shelters plants from buffeting winds and creates a hospitable microclimate of reflected warmth for sun-loving herbs, including garlic chives and wormwood (lower left), rosemary and pink 'Fairy' roses (center), and Spanish lavender (lower right).

main moderate. After a midsummer break, a second planting can be made in early fall. Remember, too, that an herb that thrives in full sun in the North may perform well in the South only if it is sheltered from the blazing afternoon sun.

Finding a Home for Herbs

Herbs have traditionally occupied a separate and distinct place in the garden. In the monastery gardens of medieval Europe, for example, kitchen herbs were segregated from other plants and organized by type—say, leafy culinary herbs in one bed, and onions, garlic, and shallots in another. Similarly, herbs in dooryard gardens of Colonial America were grouped according to how they were used in the household.

Today, many gardeners continue this tradition by keeping valued culinary herbs close at hand. Foremost are flavorings and garnishes for the kitchen, including herbs for salads and soups, colorful and strong-flavored herbs to enliven bland dishes, and herbs that ease digestion, such as fennel, dill, and caraway. In addition, herbs for the teapot—chamomile, mint, hyssop, lovage, and lemon balm, to name just a few—are often only a few steps from the kitchen.

Culinary herbs needn't be relegated to a separate plot, however. In fact, many kitchen gardens contain both vegetables and herbs—and perhaps fruits as well. And like vegetables, many culinary herbs mix well with ornamental plants in beds and borders *(pages 438-439)*. If gardening space is limited, kitchen herbs are especially well suited to growing in containers, too *(pages 478-488)*.

In this New Jersey garden, kitchen herbs create a feast for the eyes as well as the palate. Curving blades of lemon grass arch over spiky rosemary, while broad-leaved borage elbows for space with neat mounds of lemon basil and orange mint. White-flowering cilantro brightens the scene.

Planning a Vegetable Garden

Planning is particularly important for the organic gardener. Providing the best environment for healthy and productive plants without using synthetic fertilizers requires preparation and forethought. Laying out your garden on paper, for example, allows you to use all of your available space to best advantage. Other techniques help you increase yield and improve the quality of your produce. Succession planting and interplanting, for instance, allow you to harvest two or more crops from the same space in one growing season, and crop rotation minimizes pests and diseases and slows the depletion of soil nutrients.

In this section, you'll learn specific techniques for planning and designing gardens consisting primarily of vegetables. For information on selecting culinary herbs and designing herb gardens, see pages 435-437.

Choosing Which Vegetables to Plant

To decide what crops to grow in your garden, begin with a list of the vegetables that you and your family most like to eat. You may also want the list to include vegetables that are picked by commercial growers before they reach maturity, such as tomatoes, or those that don't travel well and have lost some flavor by the time you purchase them in the grocery store. Or you may want to treat yourself to unusual vegetable varieties such as golden tomatoes, watermelon with bright yellow flesh, blue potatoes, and other exotic produce that is not widely available. Another addition to the list might be heirloom vegetables that were grown by our forebears and have been rescued from extinction by groups working to save and distribute the seed.

Go over your list and make sure your selections are ones that will grow well in your area. If some are questionable, check with other gardeners or your local Cooperative Extension Service. Keep in mind that by making minor adjustments in planting times, you can often expand the number of crops that will thrive in your garden. If you live in a very hot climate, for example, you can still grow crops such as lettuce and cabbage, which prefer cooler temperatures and a mix of sun and shade. You'll just need to plant them in spring and autumn, not in the middle of summer.

If you live in the part of the North where the

The pairing of 'Salad Bowl' and 'Red Sails' lettuce with onions in this garden not only makes a striking visual combination, it makes good sense as well. The dense growth of the lettuce plants keeps weeds at bay, and their shallow roots don't compete with the young onions for space. By the time the onions need more room, the lettuce will be finished.

growing season is no more than 90 days long, choose varieties that mature quickly so that you can harvest a ripe crop before cold weather arrives. In regions where a specific pest or disease is a problem, look for named varieties that are resistant to that particular affliction (box, page 465). For example, the cucumber 'Fanfare' is resistant to powdery and downy mildews, angular leaf spot, anthracnose, scab, and cucumber mosaic virus, making it an ideal vegetable for places with humid summers where fungal diseases are prevalent.

Deciding How Much of Each Crop to Plant

Given the delightfully varied selection of vegetables, it's easy to overbuy seeds and plants. Before you make any purchases, it pays to find out what you can expect to harvest from one mature plant. Although the yield will depend in part on your growing conditions, certain vegetables and specific varieties are known to be strong producers. For example, one plant of the spaghetti squash 'Tivoli' is expected to produce three to five squashes during the growing season, each weighing between 3 and 5 pounds. By contrast, one plant of the yellow scalloped squash 'Sunburst' can produce 35 squashes *each month* during the peak of the growing season. In either case, a family of four—depending on their taste for squash—could be

Low-growing, rambling pumpkin plants make excellent intercropping partners with tall-growing corn, which has been planted at 2-week intervals to extend the harvest season. Both vegetables are heavy feeders, however, so the soil should be amended with generous amounts of organic material.

HOW MUCH TO EXPECT FROM YOUR GARDEN

Vegetable	Length of Harvest	Average Yield per 10' Row	Average Harvest per Week
Asparagus	4-6 weeks	3 lbs.	0.6 lbs.
Bean, green (bush)	2 weeks	3 lbs.	1.5 lbs.
Bean, lima (bush)	3 weeks	2 lbs. with pod	0.7 lbs.
Bean, lima (pole)	4 weeks	4 lbs. with pod	1 lb.
Bean, pole	6 weeks	10 lbs.	1.7 lbs.
Beet	4 weeks	2.4 dozen	7 beets
Broccoli	4 weeks	4 lbs.	1 lb.
Cabbage	3-4 weeks	4 heads	1 head
Cantaloupe	3 weeks	9 melons	3 melons
Carrot	4 weeks	4 dozen	1 dozen
Chard	8 weeks	5 lbs.	0.6 lbs.
Corn, sweet	10 days	10 ears	1 ear/day
Cucumber	4 weeks	8 lbs.	2 lbs.
Kale	4-20 weeks	5 lbs.	0.5 lbs.
Lettuce, head	4 weeks	10 heads	2.5 heads
Lettuce, leaf	6 weeks	9 lbs.	1.5 lbs.
Okra	6 weeks	9 lbs.	1.5 lbs.
Onion	4-24 weeks	10 lbs.	0.8 lbs.
Parsnip	4 months	8 lbs.	2 lbs.
Pea, green	2 weeks	7 lbs. with pod	3.5 lbs.
Pepper, sweet	8 weeks	40 peppers	5 peppers
Potato	4 months	12 lbs.	0.8 lbs.
Potato, sweet	6 weeks	10 lbs.	1.7 lbs.
Pumpkin	1 month	10 lbs.	2.5 lbs.
Radish	2 weeks	7 dozen	3.5 dozen
Rhubarb	4-6 weeks	6 lbs.	1.2 lbs.
Spinach	4 weeks	5 lbs.	1.25 lbs.
Squash, summer	4 weeks	20 lbs.	5 lbs.
Tomato	8 weeks	30 lbs.	3.75 lbs.
Watermelon	3 weeks	4 melons	1.3 melons

A Three-Season Garden Plan

A vegetable garden that produces continuously from early spring to late fall by using succession planting would be most successful in Zones 5 to 7 and in the Pacific Coastal area. Each bed in the plan at right measures 2 feet by 4 feet, and the plants are drawn to scale.

To follow this three-season plan, plant bed No. 1 in the spring with a soil builder, such as rye. Till the rye under to make way for the summer pole beans. When the beans are spent, plant the bed with clover, the last crop of the growing season. Plant each of the other beds with the succession of crops shown in the three diagrams. To rotate the crops the next year, plant the soil builders in bed No. 2, and move each crop over by one bed. The plan schedules cabbage-family crops, which are vulnerable to the same soil-borne diseases, so that one member of the family does not follow another member either from season to season or from year to year.

Adaptations of this scheme are required in Zones 3 and 4, where the growing season is only 90 to 120 days long. There, two crops rather than three could be grown in the same space. Since northern summers tend to be shorter and cooler, spring vegetables will continue to bear through midsummer. After they are finished, replace them with a new crop of cool-season vegetables for fall, although it's wise to select frost-hardy ones such as kale, kohlrabi, and mustard greens. Start warm-season crops indoors so they can be harvested before the end of August, when early frosts may threaten. Leave space for them in the spring garden so you have somewhere to put them when it is safe to plant them outside.

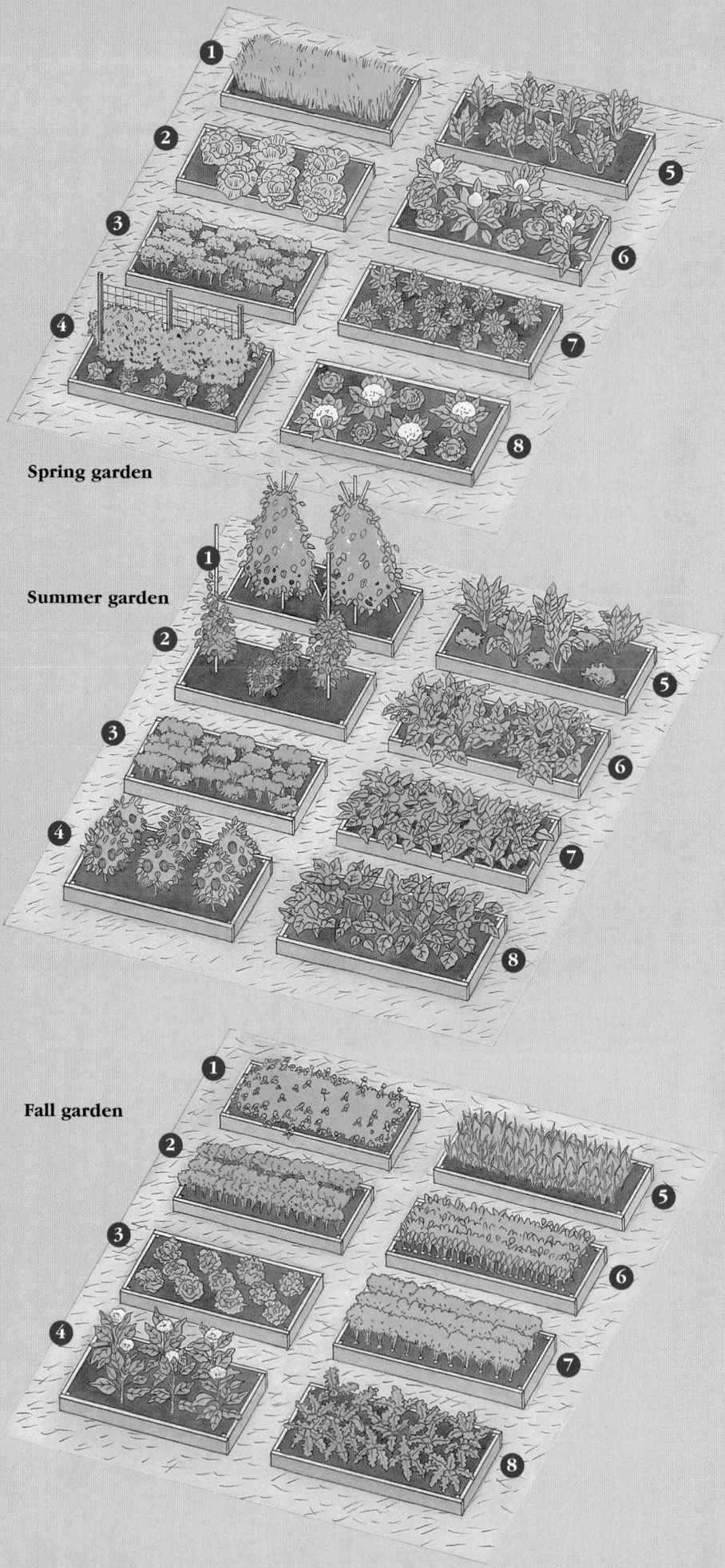

Spring garden

Summer garden

Fall garden

SPRING GARDEN
1. Annual rye
2. Cabbage
3. Carrots interplanted with spring radishes
4. Peas interplanted with salad greens
5. Swiss chard
6. Broccoli interplanted with lettuce
7. Spinach
8. Cauliflower interplanted with lettuce

SUMMER GARDEN
1. Pole beans
2. Tomatoes and eggplant
3. Carrots interplanted with radishes
4. Peppers
5. Swiss chard interplanted with parsley
6. Summer squash
7. Cucumbers
8. Winter squash

FALL GARDEN
1. Clover
2. Carrots
3. Head lettuce
4. Broccoli
5. Green onions
6. Turnips
7. Parsnips
8. Kale

430

satisfactorily fed by just one plant. To find out more about expected crop yields for particular plants, refer to the chart on the previous page.

If you plan to freeze, can, dry, or pickle some of your vegetables so that your family can enjoy the garden's bounty all year, you'll need to plant extra. Some varieties are better suited to preserving than others. The green bean 'Derby' is known to freeze well, as is the sweet corn 'Honey 'n' Pearl'. Cucumbers are divided into slicing and pickling types; choose varieties from both groups if you plan to preserve some of your crop.

If you have only a small plot for your vegetables, you may have to pare your list down to a number of plants that will fit comfortably. There are a few techniques that will help you get the most out of a small plot *(box, page 434),* but overcrowding a bed is not one of them. Cramped plants will yield less produce than those given ample room to grow, and are more susceptible to disease and infestation by insects.

Laying Out the Garden in Advance

Drawing a plan of your garden will give you the opportunity to think through important factors such as space requirements and nutrient needs before you put seeds or plants into the soil. Advance planning will also boost the results of using special techniques such as crop rotation, succession planting, and interplanting. You probably will need to work and rework the plan until you get it right, but it is much easier to erase a pencil line than to move a row of growing plants.

Artistic skills are not required for this task. Simply draw the outline of the plot to scale (using graph paper makes this easier), mark which direction is north, and then indicate plants and planting rows with circles and lines.

To begin, arrange tall plants to the north of the bed so they don't shade shorter plants, or use them to provide screening for crops that need the shade. Vining vegetables that like to sprawl across the ground, such as pumpkins, do well along the edges of a bed, where they can creep without encroaching on other plants. Group early-maturing plants together; once harvested, they will create space for another crop. Arrange perennial vegetables—those that come back year after year, such as asparagus and rhubarb—so that they aren't disturbed when the time comes for you to till the soil for the annual plantings. Cluster plants that demand especially large amounts of water so that you can water them all at once. And try to

keep vegetable families (cabbage and its relatives, legumes, squashes and melons, onions, and tomatoes and their relatives) together to simplify crop rotation.

Rotating Crops for Garden Health

Crop rotation has two enormous advantages for the organic gardener: It puts nutrients back into the soil, and it helps prevent attacks by pests and diseases. At its simplest, crop rotation means planting each crop in a different place in the garden each time you plant. (This technique applies only to annual vegetables; perennials should not be disturbed.)

Rotation is fairly easy to implement for crops that occupy the same bed for an entire growing season; simply move each crop over by one bed every time you plant it. Rotating vegetables that finish midseason and are succeeded by a different crop requires a little forethought. When laying out your garden, bear in mind whether plants are

A recent planting of cucumbers (center) has replaced a bed of harvested spring vegetables in this New Jersey garden. After the cucumbers are finished, a fall crop of turnips will follow in the same bed. Young fennel plants and red-ribbed Swiss chard flourish in the foreground.

431

WHAT VEGETABLES NEED TO GROW

	Vegetable	Soil Temp. to Germinate	Feeding Requirements	Primary Nutrient Needs
COOL SEASON	Beet	45 - 85	Heavy	Phosphorus (P), Potassium (K)
	Broccoli	45 - 85	Heavy	Nitrogen (N)
	Brussels sprouts	45 - 85	Heavy	Nitrogen (N)
	Cabbage	45 - 95	Heavy	Nitrogen (N)
	Carrot	45 - 95	Light	Potassium (K)
	Cauliflower	45 - 85	Heavy	Nitrogen (N)
	Celery	45 - 75	Heavy	Nitrogen (N), Potassium (K)
	Endive	45 - 75	Heavy	Nitrogen (N)
	Kale	40 - 90	Heavy	Potassium (K)
	Leek	50 - 95	Light	Potassium (K)
	Lettuce	40 - 75	Heavy	Nitrogen (N)
	Onion	50 - 95	Light	Potassium (K)
	Parsnip	45 - 85	Light	Potassium (K)
	Pea (soil builder)	45 - 85	Light	Potassium (K)
	Radish	45 - 95	Heavy	Potassium (K)
	Spinach	45 - 75	Heavy	Nitrogen (N)
	Swiss chard	45 - 95	Light	Nitrogen (N)
	Turnip	45 - 95	Light	Potassium (K)
WARM SEASON	Bean (soil builder)	60 - 90	Light	Potassium (K)
	Corn	55 - 105	Heavy	Nitrogen (N)
	Cucumber	60 - 105	Heavy	Nitrogen (N), Phosphorus (P)
	Eggplant	75 - 90	Heavy	Phosphorus (P)
	Melon	65 - 105	Heavy	Nitrogen (N), Potassium (K)
	Pepper	65 - 95	Light	Phosphorus (P)
	Pumpkin	65 - 105	Heavy	Phosphorus (P)
	Squash	65 -105	Heavy	Phosphorus (P)
	Tomato	60 - 85	Heavy	Phosphorus (P)

heavy or light feeders or are soil builders *(chart, left),* then arrange the crops according to their nutrient demands. For example, in one bed, first plant spring peas, which are light feeders that release nitrogen into the soil; after harvesting the peas, follow with summer squash, a heavy feeder that uses lots of nitrogen. Conversely, follow a heavy feeder such as summer squash or corn with a legume that releases nitrogen or with a cover crop that will be turned back into the soil to nourish it. Alfalfa, clover, and soybeans are examples of soil-building cover crops.

Varying where you plant your crops each season also minimizes problems caused by diseases that attack particular plants *(box, page 466).* These diseases settle into the bed where the plant is growing and overwinter in the soil, surviving to do their damage later on. Rotation of crops also discourages insect pests, even though they are more mobile than most diseases.

The Technique of Succession Planting

Succession planting, or planting one crop after another during the same season, maximizes your garden space and extends your harvest of certain crops. Instead of planting all your lettuce seeds at once, for example, and ending up with salad for a crowd, you can plant some of the seed, then wait 2 or 3 weeks and plant again. The different sections of the bed can then be harvested over a longer period of time. This technique works best with vegetables that do not produce continuously throughout the season, such as corn, carrots, radishes, bush green beans, cabbage, beets, spinach, and onions.

To use limited garden space most efficiently, you may want to try mixed crop succession. With this technique, you follow one season's harvest with a different crop in the same space. For example, in regions that have a long growing season, you can follow a cool-season crop such as lettuce with heat-loving summer squash. When you have harvested the squash in autumn, plant another cool-season vegetable, such as turnips. The Three-Season Garden Plan on page 430 offers additional examples of mixed crop succession practiced throughout the growing season.

'Winterbore' Kale

Interplanting: Making the Best Use of Space

Interplanting, or combining two plants in the same space, allows you to fit more vegetables into your allotted space. The practice, also called intercropping, can be mutually beneficial to the plants involved. A classic example of intercropping is the Native American custom of planting corn, squash, and pole beans together. This combination, called the Three Sisters of the Cornfield by the Indians, is ideal for nutrient exchange. As they grow, the beans release nitrogen into the soil for the squash and corn. In addition, the three crops use a minimum of space: Vining bean plants are supported by the tall cornstalks, while the squash spreads out along the ground.

Another way to exploit a small space is to combine fast-maturing, early crops with larger, slow-growing vegetables. For example, plant Brussels sprouts among spinach plants; by the time the slow-growing Brussels sprouts need more room, the spinach will have been harvested. To mark a row of seeds that are slow to germinate, such as parsnips, interplant radishes, the fast-sprouting wonder of the vegetable world. As an added bonus, when you pull the radishes, you are cultivating the soil for the nearby plants.

The practice of interplanting can also extend the growing season of spring vegetables if you combine them with taller warm-season plants. Sow spinach or lettuce on the east side of a row of trellised beans, a stand of sunflowers, or a bed of corn; the shade from the tall plants will protect the lettuce from going to seed or wilting in the hot afternoon sun. You can also extend your harvest by interplanting fast- and slow-maturing varieties of the same vegetable at the same time. The growing season will last longer, and you will have the opportunity to taste the different flavors of each vegetable type.

Sources for Seeds

Once your planning is done and you are ready to purchase seed, you should follow one basic rule: Do not make your choices based on price. Often,

As summer gives way to autumn, perennial crops such as the feathery asparagus at upper left have long since peaked. Newly planted crops such as Swiss chard and mizuna (center) take over the space vacated by harvested summer vegetables. Widely cultivated in China and Japan, mizuna's leafy tops make an excellent addition to soups or may be combined with other mild greens in salads.

In this intensively planted raised bed, cabbage, beans, lettuce, and carrots grow shoulder to shoulder; yarrow and daylilies nestle in the gaps; and vining tomatoes climb a simple trellis in back, using every available inch of ground.

retailers mark down seed because it is old and less likely to germinate. It makes no sense to put in hours of labor preparing your soil, planning your garden, and planting it, only to end up with weak plants—or no plants at all—because of faulty seed. Check the freshness date on seed packets and only buy seed that has been packaged to be sold in the year you are buying it.

Hardware stores, home and garden centers, and mail-order catalogs are the primary sources of vegetable seed for home gardeners. Local shops are often cheaper and more convenient, but catalogs offer a greater selection of plant varieties. Moreover, local or regional seed-catalog companies feature seed that is particularly suited to your area.

As you read descriptions of the various vegetables, look for the qualities that are most important to you. You may want early-maturing plants for a short growing season, compact plants for containers, or plants that are resistant to disease, heat tolerant, exceptionally flavorful, unusual looking, or a combination of these qualities. No doubt you will have to compromise on some features, but with the wealth of selections available, you should be able to find what you want. For good all-around performance, look for vegetable varieties listed as AAS, or All-America Selections, which have proved superior in gardens throughout the United States.

TIPS FROM THE PROS

Getting the Most from a Small Garden

Even the smallest of spaces can produce a lot of vegetables when you use intensive gardening methods. Your first consideration in a scaled-down garden must be to prepare and enrich the soil, since a large number of plants in a small area will compete for nutrients. See pages 417-423 for information on how to build healthy soil.

When planning your garden, emphasize vertical crops. Peas, pole beans, cucumbers, some melons, and some tomatoes are vining crops that actually perform better when they are kept off the ground. These can be grown on an attractive trellis, tied to stakes, or trained to follow twine that is anchored to the ground and an overhead frame.

Also, to reap as much harvest as possible from each plant, choose compact varieties or prolific producers. 'Tom Thumb', a "midget" head lettuce, requires comparatively little room, for example, and 'Jade Cross' Brussels sprouts yield an early, bountiful crop. As a rule, the smaller the fruit, the more the plants tend to produce, so make most of your selections from small varieties such as cherry tomatoes.

Avoid the temptation, though, to plant too many hugely prolific vegetables, such as zucchini. If you have extra plants, give or throw them away and save your space for other crops. When laying out the garden, make use of succession planting and intercropping to maximize your growing space.

Planning an Herb Garden

While many gardeners plant culinary herbs among vegetables and fruits, you may decide you'd like to devote a separate bed or two just to herbs. Most successful herb gardens use a combination of annuals, biennials, perennials, and woody subshrubs. Because perennials and subshrubs give an herb garden its structure, it's especially important to satisfy their cultural needs so that you can count on their long-term presence.

The short life span and rapid growth of annuals and biennials make them ideal subjects for sampling unfamiliar culinary herbs. Some annuals and biennials can be more or less permanent residents if they are allowed to sow themselves. But they don't necessarily stay put: Between the wind and birds scattering the seeds, sometimes the plants pop up in surprising places from year to year.

Making the Right Choices

It's best to start small when deciding how many culinary herbs to grow for the first time. One or two plants of any one kind are usually enough, though you'll want to make room for more if you develop a taste for a specialty such as pesto, which calls for large quantities of fresh basil.

Don't overbuy: Plants pinched for space are likely to grow tall and spindly, and the lack of air circulation may result in disease. Remember to factor in a particular variety's mature height and spread, growth rate, and any tendency toward invasiveness. For example, lovage, a perennial herb that takes its time reaching maturity, may surprise—or dismay—the unwary gardener when it eventually shoots up to a dizzying 6 or even 8 feet.

Herbs purchased at a local nursery or from a mail-order nursery in your region will often be better suited to your climate than plants raised farther afield. This is especially true for cultivars, which may not be quite as vigorous, hardy, or disease resistant as their parents. When purchasing container-grown herbs, look for plants that have brightly colored foliage, undamaged leaves, and bushy, full growth with no signs of insect infestation or disease. Check that no more than a few roots are growing out of the bottom of the pot; a root-bound plant is often weaker because it has depleted the nutrients in its container.

A few popular herbs for kitchen gardens are listed at right. For a more complete list, including plant size and cultural requirements, see the Encyclopedia of Plants on pages 608-953 at the back of this book.

Choosing a Style

If your taste leans toward the formal, consider planting a knot garden, composed of intertwined bands laid out like a bas-relief carpet in a mirroring symmetry. Achieved with careful planning *(page 436)*, it is beautiful even in winter, embossed with a blanket of snow. Herbs for each band of the knot garden should be of markedly different foliage colors to create a strong contrast between the intertwining areas of the design.

Choose plants that are roughly the same height at maturity—less than 24 inches tall and wide—and dense enough to create a seamless and solid design when pruned. Some naturally compact herbs are dwarf basil, curly chives, and burnet *(Poterium sanguisorba)*, as well as the more traditional knot-garden members like hyssop, lemon thyme, and dwarf sage. Fill in the ground between the bands with low-growing flowers or herbal ground covers such as creeping thyme, pennyroyal, or curly parsley, which makes an interesting ground cover when mass-planted. Or spread woodchip mulch, slate, crushed brick, tile, seashells, or colored sand.

If you prefer an informal herb garden, remember that it will still need careful planning. Although such gardens don't contain any strict geometric lines, they take on a satisfying sense of balance with sinuous lines of beds and paths that lead you to a focal point. Without this focal point, the garden will appear jumbled and formless. Consider adding a garden bench or an ornament to draw the eye and create atmosphere. Traditionally, a sundial, a

Herbs for Kitchen Gardens

Agastache foeniculum
(anise hyssop)

Allium schoenoprasum
(chives)

Allium tuberosum
(Chinese or garlic chives)

Aloysia triphylla
(lemon verbena)

Artemisia dracunculus
var. *sativa*
(French tarragon)

Cymbopogon citratus
(lemon grass)

Foeniculum vulgare
(fennel)

Foeniculum vulgare
'Purpurascens'
(copper fennel)

Levisticum officinale
(lovage)

Melissa officinalis
(lemon balm)

Mentha x piperita
(peppermint)

Mentha spicata
(spearmint)

Ocimum basilicum
(sweet basil)

Origanum majorana
(sweet marjoram)

Origanum onites
(Greek oregano)

Petroselinum crispum
(parsley)

Rosmarinus officinalis
(rosemary)

Rumex acetosa
(sorrel)

Salvia officinalis
(sage)

Satureja hortensis
(summer savory)

Thymus x citriodorus
(lemon thyme)

Thymus vulgaris
(thyme)

Tropaeolum majus
(nasturtium)

How to Construct and Plant a Knot Garden

The 10-by-10-foot closed knot garden described below consists of three bands of contrasting plants that make interlocking rectangles with a circle weaving through them. Site your knot garden in full sun on level ground; shade may cause the plants to grow unevenly.

To obtain true 90° square corners, lay out your bed using a process known as triangulation, as shown below. Materials you will need include wooden stakes and pegs; string; and sand, bone meal, or powdered lime to mark lines on the soil.

After marking the bed's perimeter, prepare the soil *(pages 424-425)*, and install a brick or wooden edging to keep the garden looking neat and trim.

Space the plants closely, and buy several extra plants in case you need replacements during the season. You will also need to mulch the ground between the bands with woodchips or gravel, or, alternatively, plant a low-growing ground-cover herb such as caraway thyme. Install a dwarf boxwood near each corner to finish the design.

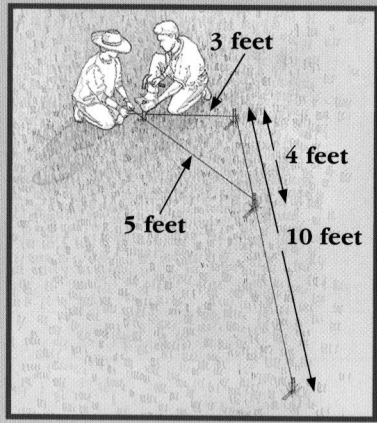

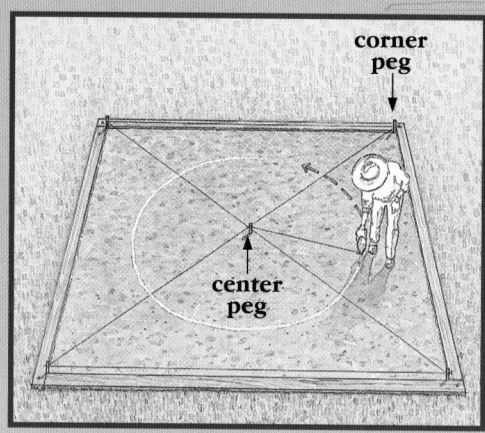

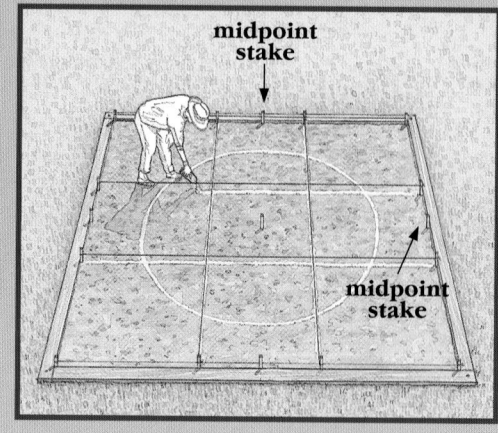

1. To create square corners, mark off one 10-foot side of the bed with stakes and string. Then, with a helper, set a peg 4 feet from the first stake and tie a string to it; mark the string at a point 5 feet from the peg. Tie a string to the first stake and mark it 3 feet from the stake. Cross the strings at the marks and set a new peg at that point. To stake off the next side, run a string from the first stake out to a length of 10 feet; repeat the squaring process. Repeat for remaining corners. Install edging along the string line and prepare the soil for planting.

2. Run string to link opposite corners; set a peg where the strings intersect at the center of the square. Next, to mark a circle at the garden's center, tie a string to a nail in the top of the center peg. Mark your string at a point that is half the distance from the center peg to a corner stake. Tie a sand- or lime-filled bottle to the string at the mark and, keeping the string pulled taut, walk around the peg with the bottle inverted so the sand pours out and marks a circle.

3. To outline the two interlocking rectangles, set stakes at the midpoint of each side of the bed. Then set two pegs on either side of each midpoint stake, 1½ feet away, so that the pegs are 3 feet apart. Run string between each of the opposite pegs to make two sets of parallel lines. Then mark the lines on the ground by dribbling sand or lime along the string lines. Remove the string, but keep the stakes and pegs in place.

4. Working outward from the center, space the plants 3 to 6 inches apart along the sand lines, adding a dose of slow-release fertilizer for each plant, following package directions. Plant a same-sized dwarf box at each corner, as shown in the diagram. In the spaces between the bands of plants, spread gravel or woodchips, or plant a ground cover. As the garden matures, trim the herbs every few weeks so that the bands appear to go under or over each other, like a lattice piecrust (inset).

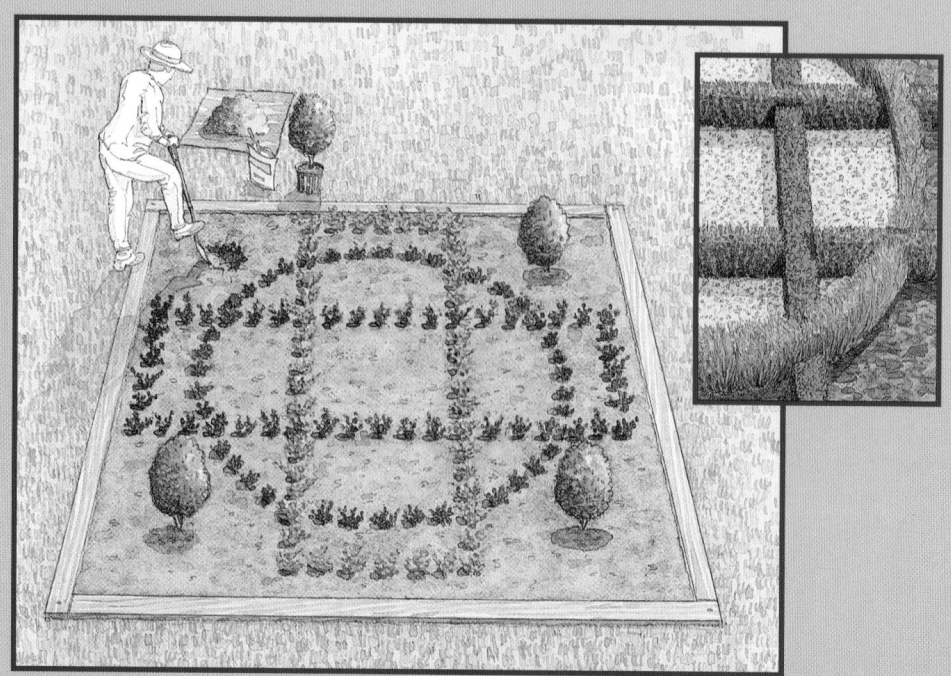

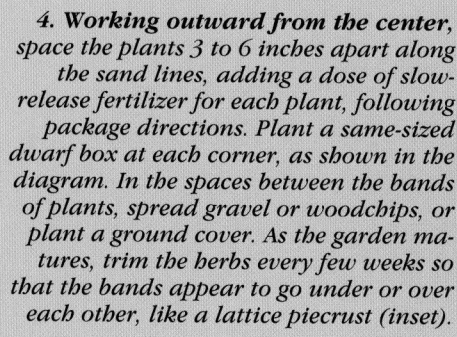

436

A small statue draws the eye and adds a decorative touch to the kitchen herb garden at left, which features a neat row of compact globe basil alongside green-and-purple sweet basil. Marjoram, tarragon, parsley, chives, and sage visually anchor the end of the bed.

A pot of sweet basil flanked by two sages—furry-leaved 'Berggarten' sage on the right and purple sage on the left—occupy a place of honor on the deck outside a Maryland gardener's kitchen door (below). Under the purple sage, lemon thyme cascades over its container, jockeying for space with silvery lavender and bright green sweet marjoram. A pot on the deck holds oregano, Italian parsley, and more purple sage.

stone or iron urn, or a small statue serves as a focal point, but a birdhouse or birdbath would also be effective, especially in an informal setting.

Once you have decided on the ideal place for your herb garden, you're ready to lay it out. Either plot your design on paper, or plan your garden at the site itself. Mark the outer corners of the garden with stakes, and tie string from one stake to the other to approximate the garden's perimeter. This will allow you to "see" the finished garden from all angles and to determine the best location for your plants. At the same time, mark features such as benches, ornaments, and pathways, keeping in mind that for two people to walk side by side—or to accommodate a wheelbarrow—your paths will need to be at least 4 feet wide.

Plan for a sheltering enclosure to keep out the wind and hold in the herbs' scents. Even one wall or hedge can make a difference. A trimmed boxwood hedge nicely complements formal architecture, while lattice or low walls of wattle—vines woven between stout branches driven into the earth—are especially well suited to informal or naturalistic settings.

Once you have planned the layout and the hard structures of your garden, go over your list of herbs, noting their heights so that you can assign their positions in the garden. Also take into account their bloom times; with a little planning, you can have flowers all season long. Finally, consider including evergreen herbs such as *Thymus vulgaris* (common thyme) and *Gaultheria procumbens* (wintergreen), which will maintain a presence all through the winter when the rest of the garden is bare.

Keep in mind that even a containerized garden like the one shown at right requires planning and forethought. For tips on designing container gardens with herbs, see pages 478-483.

437

Mixing Edibles and Ornamentals

Note: The abbreviation "spp." stands for the plural of "species"; where used in lists it means that many, but not all, of the species in a genus meet the criterion of the list.

This southern California garden produces a delightful array of cool-weather annuals that are ready to serve as either decoration or dinner. Displaying their varied forms and foliage as they cluster in harmony are marigolds, carrots, lettuce, rose-toned ornamental kale, organically grown pansies, and purplish stands of red mustard. Regular harvesting of leaves and flower heads ensures a long season of productivity.

More and more, gardeners are discovering that many garden vegetables and culinary herbs can be beautiful as well as delectable. Likewise, some plants that are usually grown as ornamentals, such as marigolds and pansies, are now appearing in the salad bowl. A bed that combines attractive vegetable plants, herbs with interesting or colorful foliage, and edible flowers can both dress up your property and enhance your meals.

Many edible plants rely on unusual coloration and texture for their visual appeal. Among these are ornamental cabbage and kale—varieties of *Brassica oleracea* that are indispensable in cool-season borders—and rhubarb chard, a variety of *Beta vulgaris* whose ruby red stems and glossy green foliage are spectacular in indoor arrangements as well as in the garden. Butterhead lettuce makes a charming early-spring edging at the front of a flower border, while taller edibles, such as burgundy-colored 'Rubine' Brussels sprouts, add interest in the midborder. For a range of color, plant ornamental peppers *(Capsicum annuum),* whose fruits ripen in shades of red, orange, purple, yellow, and green. At the back of the bed,
use annual sunflowers to vary the scale of your flowers; they can also screen an unwanted view and supply next winter's bird feeders to boot.

The sculptured foliage of *Cynara cardunculus* (cardoon) and its relative, the purple artichoke *(C. scolymus),* provide dramatically different accents. If you prefer fine detail, plant a minigarden of *Ocimum* (basil), including varieties with bright green tiny-leaved mounds of foliage and bushlike plants with leaves of rich purple.

When choosing any part of a plant for the dinner table, always be certain that it's safe to consume. Check seed packets, catalogs, and other literature, keeping in mind that some species in a genus are edible while others are not. Even some peppers are too fiery to eat—or even to handle.

Useful as well as beautiful, the backdoor garden at right combines ornamentals and culinary herbs in a tightly woven tapestry of contrasting colors and textures. Sage and rosemary mingle happily with irises, lamb's ears, pinks, and other perennials in neat raised beds. Handsome brick paths between the beds provide easy access for maintenance and harvesting.

CHAPTER TWELVE

Growing Vegetables and Herbs

There is no rule book or single set of instructions for putting in and caring for an organic kitchen garden. At first, the task can seem a bit daunting: You must decide whether you will purchase seedlings from a nursery, start plants indoors, or direct-sow seeds outdoors. Once you've started your garden, you'll need to make decisions about staking and supporting the plants, as well as mulching, watering, fertilizing, and other tasks. Garden maintenance also includes coping with pests and diseases that threaten your crops. And if you're growing herbs, you may want to consider increasing your stock of healthy plants by using various propagation methods (pages 459-461).

In the end, your garden will be unlike any other, reflecting your choices, your experiences, your land. The garden at left, for example, represents one gardener's approach to growing pole beans: Twine stretched vertically between wooden poles provides support for the clinging tendrils as the plants mature.

Planting Your Vegetables

After all the soil tilling, catalog perusing, and garden planning, at last the time has come to plant your seeds. Depending on the climate in your area and the type of vegetables you want to grow, you may decide to start plants indoors, buy seedlings from a nursery, or sow seeds directly into the ground.

Starting Seeds Indoors

In northern zones where the growing season is 90 days or less, starting seeds indoors is imperative, especially for warm-season crops such as tomatoes, melons, and peppers. Gardeners farther south can start seedlings to get a jump on the season. It is possible, however, to start seeds too early, and that can foil well-laid plans. For example, if you start tomato seeds indoors 10 weeks before the last frost date instead of the recommended 6 to 8 weeks, the plants will be ready to go outside too soon, and will become leggy and unhealthy while waiting for warmer weather.

You can start seeds indoors either by planting each seed in its own container, which will save you from having to repot them separately later on, or by planting many seeds together in a flat. If you're planting each seed separately, any sort of recycled container will do—waxed-cardboard milk cartons, yogurt cups, egg cartons, or cell packs saved from last year's purchases—as long as you poke drainage holes in the bottom. You can also buy peat pots and peat pellets. These containers are designed to be planted directly in the ground and work especially well for plants that do not like having their roots disturbed, such as cucumbers. One type of peat pellet is held together with netting. Although the netting disintegrates with time, many gardeners prefer to take it off to free the roots before putting the plant in the ground. Other pellets are held together with a built-in binder that disintegrates quickly once the container is planted.

Another excellent medium for starting seeds is a homemade soil block, created by compressing a peat-compost mixture into a cube using a blocking tool, available from mail-order catalogs. Larger vegetables, such as melons, cauliflower, broccoli, cabbage, eggplant, squash, peppers, and tomatoes, benefit from being started in peat pots, pellets, or soil blocks because the seedlings have plenty of room to develop their root systems and can be transplanted directly into the ground.

If you prefer to plant your seeds in a flat or are planting many seeds of smaller vegetables, splurge on plastic seed-starting trays. These handy trays have three components: a planting tray with holes for drainage, a liner to catch water that drains off, and a domed, clear plastic lid to maintain moisture while the seeds germinate.

Seed-Starting Soil

The ideal medium for starting seeds is fine grained and loosely packed so that a seedling can push through it without difficulty. It should also be as free as possible of weeds, harmful

Seedlings and seeds that have yet to sprout share a warm, sunny, south-facing window with pots of marigolds. Once the seeds have sprouted, turn the plants daily to give them even exposure to the light.

Making a Seed-Starting Mix

Many gardeners swear by a favorite seed-starting medium, each a little different, though the basic ingredients remain the same. Experiment to find the mix that works best for you.

RECIPE I

1 part sterilized compost

1 part sand, vermiculite, or perlite

1 part peat moss

RECIPE 2

4 quarts shredded sphagnum peat moss

4 quarts vermiculite

1 tablespoon superphosphate

2 tablespoons ground limestone

RECIPE 3

1 quart sphagnum peat moss

1 quart vermiculite

1 quart perlite

insects, and disease-causing contaminants such as fungi and other pathogens.

Seed-starting mixes usually consist of vermiculite and perlite for aeration and drainage, sphagnum moss or peat moss for bulk and moisture retention, and compost. You can make your own growing medium using any of the recipes given above or purchase it ready-mixed in bags from garden centers. If you do not wish to use peat moss, you can put together a satisfactory mix from 50 percent vermiculite or perlite and 50 percent screened compost. If you buy your mix, be sure to get the type formulated for seeds, rather than regular potting mix.

After Growth Begins: Seedling Care

Once your seeds are planted and covered with plastic *(right),* they'll need a warm spot in which to germinate. Most seeds sprout faster in warm conditions, and warm-season vegetables won't germinate at all until the soil reaches a temperature of 60° to 65° F. If the interior of your home in early spring tends to be cooler than this at

Starting and Transplanting Seeds

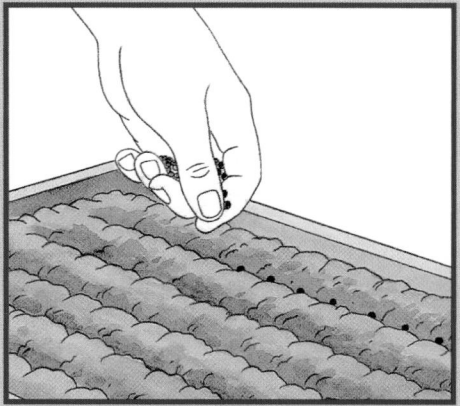

1. Fill each container to within ½ inch of the rim with moist seed-starting mix. *Gently press the soil to level it, but do not compact it. Make furrows in the soil to the appropriate depth for the seeds you are planting. Drop the seeds into the furrow, spacing them as recommended on the seed packet. Cover the seeds and gently tamp the soil along the furrow to make good contact between seed and soil.*

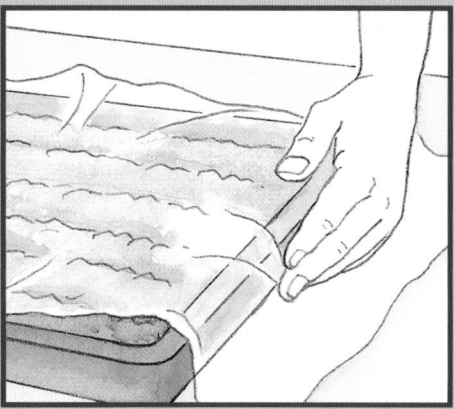

2. Mist the top layer of soil. *Cover the container to hold in moisture, using a plastic dome from a seed-starting kit, a grocery-store produce bag, or plastic wrap. Do not water again once the container is covered. Keep the seeds in a warm spot until they sprout. When the first sprouts appear, remove the cover and place the seedlings in a spot where they will get 12 hours of light a day.*

3. Repot crowded seedlings by scooping them out with a spoon. *Immediately replant the tiny seedlings into a large container filled with lightweight potting soil. Water carefully to make good contact between the roots and the soil, but avoid swamping the plants. Place the seedlings in a spot where they will get 12 hours of light a day.*

4. To remove a young plant from a cell pack or plastic container, *grasp the stem between your index and middle fingers and tip the container. Ease the plant out; do not pull on the stem. If the plant does not slide out easily, try tapping the bottom of the container gently on the ground or squeezing the sides of the container.*

443

Sheltering Plants from the Cold

Plant protectors such as cold frames, portable greenhouses, and cloches provide a sheltered setting for starting plants early, hardening off seedlings, and extending the growing season of autumn vegetables. They work by transmitting light and retaining heat.

A cold frame can be as simple as a bottomless box covered with clear glass or plastic, or as sophisticated as an elaborate high-tech creation with temperature sensors that automatically open and close the lid as needed. A cloche can be small enough to protect just one plant or large enough to cover an entire row of vegetables, and can be devised from overturned bushel baskets or 1-gallon plastic milk containers with the bottoms cut out.

The large portable greenhouse at right is made from clear plastic sheeting stretched over arched wire fencing. Versatile and inexpensive, the greenhouse protects young vegetables, like these lettuce plants, from cold weather.

Vegetable Seeds Best Sown Directly into the Ground

Beans, bush

Beans, pole

Beets

Carrots

Collards

Corn

Cucumbers
(except where season lasts less than 90-100 days)

Endive

Kale

Kohlrabi

Mustard greens

Parsnips

Peas

Potatoes

Radishes

Spinach

Swiss chard

Squash, summer
(except where season lasts less than 90-100 days)

Squash, winter
(except where season lasts less than 90-100 days)

Turnips

night, you must provide additional heat. A waterproof heating mat designed to go under pots and containers works well for this purpose. A less costly option is to place pots on top of a refrigerator or a clothes dryer.

When the seeds have sprouted, remove the plastic covering to allow air to circulate; otherwise, you may lose the seedlings to damping-off, a disease caused by several soil fungi. At this point, seedlings also need a lot of light—at least 12 hours a day. Lack of light creates thin, leggy plants and will affect a plant's vigor and productivity for the rest of the season.

For best results, place the plants in front of a south-facing window that gets direct sun most of the day. Be sure to rotate the containers every day so that the plants receive even exposure. If you must use artificial light instead, opt for fluorescent or "grow" lights rather than incandescent ones, which do not generate the ultraviolet light required by plants. Position fluorescent lights about 2 to 4 inches from the top of the plants. Hang the lights from chains for easy height adjustment as the plants grow.

To keep the soil moist without damaging fragile seedlings, mist plants daily or set the containers on top of several layers of wet newspaper; the water in the newspaper will be drawn up and absorbed through the drainage holes in the bottoms of the pots. Feed the seedlings with a weak mixture of liquid fertilizer every 2 weeks. Experienced gardeners regulate seedlings' rate of growth by the amount of food they provide. If the seedlings are coming along quickly and cold weather is lingering longer than expected, the plants' growth can be slowed by cutting back slightly on fertilizing. Conversely, if warm weather comes early, you can accelerate growth by feeding with a richer mixture of fertilizer.

Seedlings that have sprouted too closely together will need to be thinned. If you have more seedlings than you need, simply snip off the weaker specimens to give more growing space to the vigorous ones. If you want to use all of the seedlings, carefully lift the excess from the container and transplant them to pots filled with a seed-starting mixture. Before removing a seedling, poke a hole in the mixture with the eraser end of

Cloches of water-filled plastic tubes surround plants in this New Jersey garden. The water in the plastic cloches absorbs heat and radiates it to the plants, protecting them from killing frosts in fall and early spring, thus extending the growing season. For best results, use water cloches for single upright plants such as tomatoes, peppers, and eggplant.

a pencil. Either lift the seedling out with a spoon, as shown on page 443, or use the technique called pricking out. To do this, hold the top leaves of a seedling between your thumb and forefinger as you use the pencil or other narrow object to gently lift the seedling from the container. Ease it carefully into the planting hole and press the mixture around the plant.

Buying Healthy Plants from the Nursery

For those who don't have the time or the space to start their own seeds, buying seedlings from a nursery can be a satisfactory substitute. However, not all nursery transplants are healthy, so it's imperative to examine them carefully.

First, check the seedlings for insects or insect eggs. Favorite insect hiding places include under leaves, where the leaves meet the stem, and at the growing tip of the plant, where the young leaves are most tender. Also, don't forget to look underneath the container for night-feeding pests that like to congregate or hide in the crevices.

Choose young and vigorous plants. Avoid those that are oversized and too well established. If plants are already in flower or bearing fruit, don't be misled into thinking they will give you an earlier or more bountiful harvest. In fact, quite the opposite is true: The stress of transplanting is likely to reduce the main crop. Likewise, tall and leggy plants often fail to fill out and produce well. Instead, look for well-proportioned seedlings; plants that are ready to be transplanted will be about as wide as they are tall.

Reject plants that have roots growing several inches out of the bottom of their container; these plants have been in their pots too long and have become root-bound. In the case of cole crops such as kale, gently scrape away a little soil to check for swollen, distorted roots, which are an indication of a condition called clubroot. And any roots that are yellow, soft, or too woody also indicate an unhealthy plant.

445

Tricks for Easier Seed Sowing

- When sowing seeds outdoors, run a strip of white toilet tissue down the length of each furrow and lay the seeds on top. The whiteness of the paper will make it easier to see the seeds and to gauge their spacing and depth. The fine tissue will degrade quickly into the soil.
- To make it easier to distribute tiny seeds, such as those of carrots, mix them with sand and sprinkle the mixture over the ground using a clean salt shaker. For easier handling, carrot seeds are also sold on seed tape and in pellet form about the size of buckshot.
- Plant bean seeds with the scar side facing down; bean roots grow into the ground out of the scar point. Planting them all this way means they will surface at about the same time.
- To presprout seeds, space them on a double layer of damp paper towel, roll it up, and keep it moist in an open plastic bag. In 2 or 3 days the seeds will sprout. Then plant them in pots or put them into the ground, taking care not to break the fragile roots.

Hardening Off

Before transplanting any seedlings outside, you must prepare the young plants for the transition from a protected environment to the harsher conditions of the outdoors. This process is known as hardening off. A week or two before you plan to transplant the seedlings into your garden, take them outside and place them in a protected spot for about an hour. Repeat this process daily during the transition period, increasing the time by 1 hour each session.

Putting Transplants into the Ground

If you can, plant young seedlings on a cool, misty day; cooler temperatures are less likely to cause stress to new plants. If that isn't possible, transplant in the evening when the temperature begins to drop. The plants will have all night to settle in before they are exposed to the hot sun.

Three Ways of Supporting Plants

To construct a tripod plant support (below), push three poles measuring 6 to 8 feet long firmly into the ground to form a circle; tie them together at the top. Plant vining vegetables such as peas, pole beans, squash, and pumpkins at the base of each pole. Within the circle, grow lettuce and other crops that welcome shade.

For a support of crisscrossed poles, push 6- to 8-foot poles into the ground in two parallel rows about 12 inches apart as shown, and tie pairs together about 4 inches from the top. For stability, give the end units an extra leg to create a tripod, and tie a pole along the length of the support on top.

To create a simple trellis for vining vegetables such as peas, squash, pumpkins, pole beans, and cucumbers, choose sturdy poles that are 6 to 8 feet long and at least 1 inch square. Space them an equal distance apart and sink them about 12 inches into the ground. Staple wire fencing or nylon netting to the poles.

Once you have removed each plant from its pot or cell pack, examine the roots carefully. If they are crushed tightly against the edge of their container or curled in a circle around the bottom of the pot, gently massage the rootball in your hand to loosen the clump.

If your beds are bare or mulched with straw or any other loose, organic material, simply dig through the mulch and soil to create a planting hole. If the beds are covered with plastic mulch, use a penknife to cut through the sheeting. For each plant, cut an X in the plastic big enough to fit the rootball, then dig the hole and place the plant in it. To create the best possible contact between the soil and the roots, press the soil down firmly around each plant.

Space the plants far enough apart to allow ample growing room, but choose an arrangement that makes efficient use of the land. For example, you might place the plants in wide beds with staggered rows. A bed that is 30 inches wide could have three lettuce plants in the first row and two lettuce plants in the second row positioned between the plants in the first row. In the third row, there would be three lettuce plants parallel to the ones in the first row, and so on. Such a pattern will accommodate a few more plants without crowding. Once the seedlings are in the ground, be sure to water promptly and well, especially when using plastic mulch, which acts as a barrier to rainwater. (For more on using plastic mulch, see page 451.)

While the transplants are adjusting to their new environment, they may need shelter from strong sun. If the sun is particularly intense the first few days after planting, make a temporary shade structure with a beach umbrella, cloth anchored to cinder blocks or mounted on stakes, or even an overturned basket or box that allows some light to penetrate. During hot weather, be prepared to water your transplants daily until the roots are established and you see signs of growth.

Direct-Sowing Outdoors

Not all seed-grown vegetables are suited for early sowing indoors. The heading types of Chinese cabbage will go to seed from transplant stress, for instance, and carrots will die. Root disturbance to corn, peas, beans, and okra plants hinders their growth. These crops and others (list, page 444) are simply easier to start outdoors.

When sowing seed outdoors, keep in mind that the soil temperature must be within the range required by the plant type for germination to occur. Fortunately, surface soil temperature does not

fluctuate as radically as air temperature because of the thermal insulation provided by the earth. Once the soil is warm enough in spring to nurture the seeds, it's likely to stay that way until autumn. A soil and compost thermometer with an extended spike can help you determine when the soil is warm enough to begin planting. To use the thermometer, insert the spike into the soil to the planting depth of the crop to be sown there. Check each bed with the thermometer, as temperatures may vary significantly within a garden.

Before you plant, rake the soil's surface in one direction to make it smooth. Break up large clods and remove any stones, weeds, and grass roots. Then rake in the other direction to smooth and level the bed. To avoid compacting the soil, walk on the beds as little as possible. Mark each planting row with string stretched across the beds and

The clinging tendrils of pole beans spiral around these vertical support wires as the plants reach upward. A heavy cord stretched between two poles runs across the top of the structure and holds up the wires, which are also anchored to the ground with stakes. When the growing season is over, the gardener will take down the wire and string and store them for reuse.

Helpful Hints for Planting Tomatoes

To keep cutworms from feasting on a tomato stem, *cut a collar measuring 3 inches square from 3 layers of newspaper. Wrap the collar around the stem next to the rootball and position the tomato in the planting hole so that half of the collar is above ground (above, left). To plant a leggy tomato transplant, remove the lower leaves and lay the plant on its side in a trench. Gently bend the top of the stem upward and cover the roots and the horizontal section of stem with soil.*

To train a vining tomato plant, *pound a sturdy 8-foot-tall stake at least 1 foot into the ground, then plant the tomato at its base. Tie the plant to the stake with string or twine. To avoid damaging the stem, first loop the string around the stake and tie it tightly, then loop it around the vine and make a loose knot (inset). Continue to tie the tomato to the stake as the plant grows.*

tied at either end to stakes. Using the string as a guide, dig a shallow furrow in the earth with a trowel or hoe.

Sowing the Seeds

Sow seeds in rows according to the recommended spacing on the package; do not overcrowd them. Then cover the seed with soil. As a rule of thumb, you should bury seeds three times deeper than their width. Under certain conditions, though, you may have to adjust the planting depth slightly. Seeds require a little less covering when soil is very wet and heavy, and more when the soil is sandy or the weather is dry.

Hill planting is preferred for crops that need more warmth to germinate, such as corn, cucumbers, melons, pumpkins, and squash. To create a rich reservoir for them, dig a hole 12 inches deep and wide. Fill the hole with 8 inches of well-rotted compost or manure and top with 8 inches of soil. After watering, the hill should be about 3 inches high. Plant seeds at the appropriate distance and depth along the top and sides of the hill.

The technique called broadcasting, or scattering seed over a bed, works best for cover crops

such as clover and annual rye, and for large beds planted with the same crop. Prepare the bed as you would for row planting, but without furrows. On a windless day, broadcast the seed by shaking it out of your hand in a loose spray. Then rake the bed lightly with a fine rake or a spike-toothed rolling cultivator to settle the seed into the soil and cover it slightly.

Label each row, hill, or bed with the vegetable's complete name and the planting date. Do not use the paper seed packet as a label; rain will make it illegible, and besides, it will be far more useful in your garden-record notebook *(page 455).* Instead, purchase wooden tags at a garden center or nursery and write the information on them with a waterproof pen.

Once planted, seeds need to be kept continually moist in order to germinate. If you have planted rows of seeds in moist soil, it isn't necessary to water at planting time, but keep a watchful eye on the beds and sprinkle them daily, if necessary, to keep them moistened. For seed that has been broadcasted, water immediately after planting to ensure good contact between the seed and the soil, and sprinkle daily until the seeds have sprouted. Use only a gentle spray of water; a strong spray may dislodge the seeds and wash

Wire cages can support bush or vining tomatoes, but the cages for vining types need to be larger, about 24 inches across and 60 inches tall. Place a cage over the tomato when you plant it, and tie the cage to a tall stake so it will not topple under the weight of ripening fruit.

To encourage tomato vines to produce earlier and larger—but fewer—fruits, prune the side shoots. Once three leaves appear on the shoot, pinch off the top leaf (below), stopping the shoot's growth. Leave some foliage on the plant to protect ripening fruit from harsh sun.

Heavy with ripening red tomatoes, the 1984 All-America Selections tomato, 'Celebrity', is supported by a wire cage. This bush variety grows to maturity in 70 days, producing a generous crop of firm, flavorful fruits, each weighing 7 to 8 ounces. Known for its outstanding disease resistance, the cultivar adapts to most parts of the country.

them away completely or cause them to congregate in tight clumps.

Staking and Support Systems

Using stakes or other support systems to grow plants vertically does more than save space. When lifted off the ground, vining and trailing plants tend to be healthier and more productive. Supported in an upright position, they receive more sunlight and increased air circulation, which prevents fungus and rot. In addition, the produce stays cleaner and is easier to monitor and harvest. Cucumbers, melons, summer and winter squash, peas, pole beans, and tomatoes are all good candidates for training upward.

If you plan to stake plants, place the stake in the ground before you sow, or when you put transplanted seedlings into the ground. Do not wait until the plant grows larger, or you run the risk of damaging the roots when you insert the stake. Choose sturdy supports and bury them deep enough to bear the weight of the growing plant and its produce.

Vegetables that have twining tendrils, such as beans, will grip onto the support, but other vining plants, such as tomatoes and squash, need to be secured. Be careful not to tie the plant too tightly to the support, however, or you may damage the stem. Instead, first tie a tight loop around the support and then a looser one around the stem of the plant, as shown in the illustration opposite. Use string, cloth strips, or other biodegradable materials to tie the plants; when the season is over, both plants and ties can be thrown onto the compost pile.

Support systems for vegetables range from small and simple to large and fairly elaborate, depending on the gardener's preference and the space available. One common method for supporting vining vegetables such as pole beans, squash, and peas is the tripod plant support, consisting of three poles pushed into the ground to form a circle, with the ends tied together at the top. Another way to support vining vegetables is with a trellis, made of nylon netting or wire fencing stretched between poles sunk into the ground. For details on constructing these supports, see page 446.

449

Caring for Your Vegetables throughout the Season

A vegetable garden does not run on a set schedule. Although some tasks do need to be performed at certain times of the year, many maintenance chores will be in response to clues that your plants provide. Try to walk through your garden every day, preferably early in the morning or in the evening. Allow yourself time to enjoy the progress your crops are making and to watch for any problems. Carry a trowel and clippers so that you can perform the odd weeding or transplanting job on the spot. Your observations during these daily rounds will do much to keep your garden healthy.

Heading Off Problems with On-the-Spot Fixes

Early in the season, tend to crops that need thinning, since plants that are spaced an optimum distance apart will reward you with an abundant harvest. Conversely, if you come across a little extra room in a bed, tuck in a plant for some quick intercropping. Be on the lookout for weeds poking through the soil or mulch, and dig or pull them promptly. Likewise, nip insect problems in the bud before they become serious. (For more information on pests and diseases, see pages 462-473 or, for help with a specific problem, consult the Troubleshooting Guide on pages 576-583.)

If the weather has been dry, check the soil to make sure you've given your plants enough water. Probe the soil with your fingers to discover how deep the dry surface layer is; if it is dry down to the root mass of a crop, it's time to water. Remember that once plants show signs of water stress, the problem has gone too far.

Before long, your diligence in the garden will begin paying off in the form of plump, healthy produce. Take a basket or other container with you on your walks so you can collect vegetables at their peak. Keep a close eye on crops like zucchini, which can be harvested when they are only as big as your finger. These vegetables grow so fast that if you leave them an extra day or two, they'll be noticeably bigger and their taste and texture may have changed. (See Chapter 14 for information on how to tell when vegetables are ripe for harvesting and how to pick and store them to ensure maximum flavor.)

Routine Tasks

In addition to the chores you perform on your daily inspections of the garden, your vegetable plot will require such regular maintenance as mulching, watering, fertilizing, and weeding.

Your best ally in keeping your garden healthy and productive is a layer of mulch. It insulates the ground, keeping the soil warm in cool weather and cool when temperatures turn hot. It cuts down on the need for watering because it holds moisture, and it also discourages the growth of weeds. And organic mulches such as bark, grass clippings, and newspapers (black-and-white newsprint only) break down into the soil, adding nutrients and improving soil structure.

Applying Organic Mulch

For best results, apply a layer of mulch in the spring after the soil has warmed. A good rule of thumb is to wait until seedlings are up and growing, since putting down mulch too early may pre-

Cucumber plants with woodchip mulch (below)

450

Good Organic Mulches for Vegetables

Compost

Cottonseed hulls

Grass clippings

Ground corncobs

Hay and straw

Newspapers
(no colored inks)

Peanut hulls

Pine needles

Rotted manure

Shredded leaves

Black plastic mulch warming a melon patch

Winter squash 'Orangetti' on grass-clipping mulch

vent the ground from warming sufficiently for heat-loving plants. For effective weed control, apply organic mulch about 4 to 6 inches thick. Half that amount will suffice in shady areas where weeds struggle to grow. Take care not to pile the mulch against the stems of the plants, since this can promote rot. As the mulch thins and decays during the growing season, replenish it.

When you put the garden to bed for the winter, till the organic mulch into the ground; it will continue to break down during the cold months, improving the soil's nutrient value and structure. If your soil is nitrogen-poor, however, tilled-in mulch—especially one with a high carbon content like shredded bark—can further deplete the nitrogen level as it decomposes. To combat this problem, dig in nitrogen-rich cottonseed meal or blood meal in autumn, or plant a winter cover crop such as clover or annual rye.

Inorganic Mulch

Even the most devoted organic gardeners sometimes rely on an inorganic mulch like heavy black plastic sheeting because of its superior weed control and insulating properties. Weeds cannot penetrate it, and as a bonus, vegetables grown on or near the surface of the ground stay cleaner and are less prone to rot. In northern climates, cover beds with black plastic before you plant to hasten the warming of the soil. The dark color absorbs heat during the day and conducts it into the soil. After you have planted the beds, the dark plastic radiates warmth back to the plants at night. Obviously, this extra heat is a disadvantage in hot climates; there, the plastic should be covered with an organic mulch to keep the soil cool.

To use black plastic, lay the sheeting over a bed that has been watered, and weight the edges down with boards or large stones. The plastic will hold in the moisture, but little additional rainwater will get through. To water the beds, you'll need to install a drip-irrigation system or set up soaker hoses under the sheeting. When you're ready to plant, cut slits in the plastic and insert the seedlings. At the end of each season, if the plastic is still in good shape, remove it from the bed, wash it off, fold it when it has dried, and reuse it the following year.

Watering the Garden

You cannot always count on Mother Nature to water your vegetables. As a rule, a garden should receive 1 inch of water per week, including rainfall,

although more may be needed if you have fast-draining, sandy soil or if your area is experiencing extreme heat. To keep track of the amount of rain that falls, invest in an inexpensive rain gauge. Empty it after each rain and keep a tally of the measurements. Then supplement when necessary by hand watering, or with drip- or soaker-hose irrigation or sprinklers. Whenever possible, water early in the morning or in the evening to reduce the loss of moisture through evaporation.

Hand watering is time-consuming, but for a small garden it may be the most practical method. Aim the water at the plants' roots rather than at the foliage, and keep the flow of water light enough so that the water soaks in deeply and doesn't run off. A hand-held wand that attaches to a hose makes the job of directing the water easier; such wands come with a variety of spray nozzles, including one with a very fine mist for newly planted seeds.

Overhead sprinkling works well for germinating seeds because it keeps the surface of the ground continuously moist until the seeds sprout. Once the plants are well on their way, however, it is best to choose another method of irrigation.

Drip Irrigation/Soaker Hoses

Large vegetable gardens profit greatly from drip irrigation or soaker hoses. A drip system works best for plants that are spaced fairly far apart, like tomatoes. Soaker hoses are better for closely spaced crops like salad greens. Both systems operate with low water pressure, delivering water directly to the plants' roots at rates as slow as half a gallon per hour. The slow delivery of water to the areas that need it allows moisture to soak in deeply. As a result, plants tend to grow faster and more uniformly. And because the foliage doesn't get wet, there are fewer problems with fungal diseases, which are often spread by water.

Drip-irrigation and soaker systems can be installed by the home gardener and are easily modified throughout the season as the garden changes. Basic kits are available that include all the valves, feeder lines, and other attachments necessary to set up either type of system. In addition, new feeder lines may be added, old lines removed, and holes opened or plugged as the need arises. You may also purchase a timer that turns

The feeder lines of a drip-irrigation system snake through a recently planted bed in the garden above, but in a short time they will be completely covered by the growing vegetable plants (opposite). Such a setup can be designed to fulfill immediate watering needs and can also be adapted to meet new requirements simply by adding new feeder lines or removing old ones.

452

the water on and off automatically according to a programmed schedule.

If you use drip-irrigation lines in conjunction with black plastic mulch, lay the lines down under the plastic. Mark each drip emitter with a shovelful of compost to make a visible mound under the plastic sheeting, and plant accordingly.

Weed Control: Every Gardener's Problem

One of the great ironies of gardening is that while it takes a great deal of effort to produce a beautiful and productive garden, weeds flourish with virtually no attention at all. Although their persistence might tempt the gardener to give up the battle against them, they must be destroyed because they compete with crops for growing space, soil nutrients, and water, and often harbor damaging insect pests.

Weeds can be controlled effectively through mulching, which denies them the sunlight they need to grow. A few determined weeds will make their way through mulch, but the numbers will be drastically reduced. You can add to the effectiveness of any organic mulch by putting a thick layer of newspaper (with no colored ink) underneath it. Few weeds can penetrate that barrier, and eventually the newspaper will decompose, improving the soil's structure and nutrient value in the process.

Unfortunately, some mulches can actually increase your weed problem. For example, hay, compost made from seedy plants, or manure from animals grazing in seedy pastures can contain viable seed that has the potential to sprout among your vegetables. Opt for seed-free straw rather than hay, and be sure any compost or manure you use does not contain seedy materials.

Removing and Preventing Weeds

Early eradication is another weapon an organic gardener can use in the war against weeds. When weeds are young and their root systems are just developing, they are easier to pull or hoe, and if they are removed before they set seed, many more weeds will be prevented.

Digging with a hoe or other cultivating tool—the traditional way to weed a large vegetable garden—serves the dual purpose of uprooting weeds and aerating the soil. Be careful, though, not to disturb the roots of nearby vegetables. When hoeing around corn, squash, tomatoes, and potatoes, pile up a little extra soil around the base of the plants to protect their shallow roots.

If you do not use mulch, begin tilling the bed about 3 days after you sow your seeds. This preemptive strike will damage germinating weed seeds before they take root and become established. Continue tilling or hand pulling weeds as necessary throughout the season.

Pulling weeds by hand can be a backbreaking job, but it is a necessary one if weeds grow too large to be uprooted by the hoe. Take solace in knowing that each time you pull a weed you're aerating the soil, and remember that weeding does at least get your hands in the dirt. Throw pulled weeds into the compost pile if it reaches at least 140° F, or dispose of them in accordance with local ordinances for plant debris.

Another way to control weeds is by planting cover crops such as clover, annual rye, vetch, barley, and alfalfa. These crops, sometimes called green manure, thickly carpet the ground, choking out weeds as they grow. To minimize the possibility of wind-borne weed seeds taking hold in your soil, try planting hedges along the border of your vegetable plot.

Fertilizing the Garden Midseason

Weed-free, nutrient-rich soil can sustain many crops throughout the growing season without the addition of fertilizer. But some plants that produce fruits (as opposed to edible leaves, stems, or roots), such as tomatoes, eggplant, and peppers, benefit greatly from a boost in midseason, when the fruits are developing and maturing. And vegetables grown in containers require a steady diet of diluted nutrient supplements throughout the growing season (page 476).

If the soil is not rich enough to begin with, nutrients—especially nitrogen—can leach out with watering or can be depleted by plants that are heavy feeders. Nitrogen deficiency shows up in plants as yellowing leaves and stunted growth. Watch your plants closely; if you catch the problem early and apply a midseason fertilizer, you may be able to save your crop. Unfortunately, the warning signs sometimes become obvious only after it is too late to save the plants. When that happens, your only option is to prepare for the next growing season by amending your vegetable beds with plenty of nutrient-rich organic material such as compost and rotted manure.

When you go looking for fertilizers, you'll find two types—synthetic and organic. Synthetic fertilizers, which are produced by industrial processes, eventually decrease the organic matter in soil and change the biological activity. In addition, they contain mineral salts that acidify the soil and repel earthworms. By contrast, organic products, which are derived from animal or plant remains, or from mined rock minerals, actually build the soil as they feed the plants. Examples of these are dried blood, meat and fish meal, bone meal, com-

post, cottonseed meal, and well-rotted manure *(chart, page 423).*

Potassium-hungry crops, such as turnips, parsnips, beets, carrots, and cabbage, all benefit from an application of wood ashes during the growing season. Nitrogen feeders, including corn and tomatoes, are stimulated by a dose of rotted manure, fish emulsion, or manure tea. You can prepare your own fertilizer from compost or a combination of other ingredients, or you can purchase organic fertilizers that will provide the nutrient concentration you need.

Applying Supplemental Fertilizer

Fertilizers appropriate for established plants are sold in either solid or liquid form. Solid materials are best applied by top- or side-dressing, that is, by spreading the fertilizer around the base or beside the plants. Avoid getting solid fertilizer directly on plants, since it can burn tender shoots and stalks. Lightly rake or hoe the dressings into the soil, and water immediately to help them penetrate the soil.

Spray diluted liquid fertilizers, such as manure tea *(recipe, below)* or fish emulsion, directly onto the plant's leaves, which will absorb the nutrients quickly. Or pour the fertilizer onto the soil so that it soaks down to the plant's roots. Drip-irrigation systems have attachments that release measured amounts of liquid fertilizer while the system is running. The irrigation systems come with safety backflow preventers that stop water in the irrigation pipes from flowing back into the house drinking water.

Manure and Compost Teas

Fill a bucket two-thirds full of water. Add manure or compost to fill the container to the top, and steep for a day or two. Leaving the solid material at the bottom, pour off the liquid into another container and dilute it with more water to the color of weak tea. (To use the tea in small amounts, dip off what you need and dilute it.) Pour about 1 pint of tea around each vegetable plant that will benefit from extra nitrogen. Do not use on root vegetables, which require potassium for healthy growth.

Keeping Records of Your Garden

Keeping a complete record of your garden allows you to build on accumulated knowledge and experience so that you can repeat triumphs and avoid errors. Use a loose-leaf notebook for your garden journal; you can add pages when necessary and move them around if you choose. You'll need graph paper for garden plans, ruled paper for your notes, and heavy paper or photo-album refills for mounting photographs, invoices, and catalog descriptions. To get the most out of your record book, treat it as a combination journal and scrapbook. Collect and keep the following kinds of information:

- Your garden plan. This will help you keep track of crop rotations from year to year.
- Lists of the vegetables you planted. Save your invoices, receipts, and seed packets so you can go back to the seed vendor to reorder or seek help with problems. If you ordered from catalogs, paste in their cultivar descriptions. Over the course of the season, note the performance of each plant and how you liked it. Pictures of the vegetables, such as the eggplants above, will jog your memory.
- The number of plants you grew of each vegetable and the yield. This information will assist you in making future decisions about how many plants you want or need of any vegetable or variety.
- Temperature. A daily log of high and low temperatures will give you a good sense of the weather in your area. Also note soil temperatures during the planting season.
- Rainfall. Check your rain gauge weekly and record the results. This information, along with the temperature records, will give you a clear picture of weather trends.
- Dates, especially planting, harvest, and the last spring and first fall frost dates. Note if you seeded too early or too late.
- Pests and diseases. Record the date the problem began, what you did to treat it, and how successful you were.

Planting and Caring for Your Herbs

Herbs—adaptable, undemanding, and forgiving of mistakes—are perfectly suited to beginning and busy gardeners. Just be sure there's a good match between the herbs you choose and your garden's growing conditions, and that you get them off to a good start with proper planting. After that, you'll find them remarkably easy to care for.

Planting Primer

If your schedule and the weather give you a choice, a cool, cloudy day is ideal for planting herbs. And it's best to wait a few weeks after the last frost date to minimize the chance that an unusually late cold snap could damage the young plants. Before removing the herbs from their pots, arrange them in the bed according to your garden plan to see whether you want to make any last-minute adjustments. Once the herbs are placed to your satisfaction, you are ready to begin planting.

Dig each planting hole several inches wider and deeper than the container. Fill the hole with water, allow it to drain, then add a few inches of soil, tamping lightly to prevent excessive settling.

Gently ease your herbs from their containers. Using a garden knife or your fingers, loosen compacted soil around the roots of large container-grown herbs. Seedlings in large flats should be divided into fist-sized clumps with a trowel; leave as much soil around the roots as possible. If the seedlings were grown in peat pots, they can be planted, pot and all, directly in the garden. Just be sure to tear off the top half-inch or so of the peat pot, since any portion of the rim that is exposed above the surface of the soil will soak up water and nutrients, to the seedling's disadvantage.

Place each plant in the prepared hole and add

Building a Raised Bed of Stone

The raised bed described here can be planted from the side as well as the top, since a soil mixture fills the spaces between the stones. The stone walls rest on footings and are further stabilized by being stepped. Use large, flat stones 12 inches or more across for the footings; smaller or more rounded stones are fine for the rest of the structure. This bed stands 18 inches above ground level. For a higher bed, seek the advice of a mason.

2. Lay the second row of stones on top of the first, stepping their outer edges in slightly from the outer edge of the footing stones. Pack the gaps with soil. Continue laying stones in this manner until they are a maximum of 18 inches above ground level. Fill the gaps in the aboveground portion of the walls with a planting mix of equal parts of soil, leaf mold, and sand or poultry grit.

1. Mark off the outline of the bed with lime. Dig a trench about 15 inches deep and as wide as the footing stones. Next, put 10 inches of crushed stone into the trench. Lay the footing stones on this base so that they slope at a slight angle toward the bed's center; the ends of the stones should touch one another. Pack soil tightly into any spaces between and around the stones.

3. To plant in the wall pockets, remove each seedling or cutting from its container just before planting and wrap its tiny soil ball in damp sphagnum moss to protect the roots. Make a planting hole in the pocket with a widger—the spatula-shaped tool shown at left—or a tongue depressor. Lay the plant on the tool, ease it into place, and gently tamp soil mix around its roots.

enough soil to fill it. Firm the soil around the plant, and water thoroughly with a fine spray.

A number of popular herbs, including basil and chives, are very easy to grow from seed sown directly in the garden. And direct-sowing is the preferred method for herbs with fleshy, sparse roots or long taproots that make them difficult to transplant, such as coriander, chervil, dill, parsley, nasturtium, and summer savory.

Sow seeds according to the packet instructions for spacing and depth. If no instructions exist, a good rule of thumb is to plant in shallow trenches at a depth of twice the seed's diameter. Cover the seeds lightly with soil, and water well with a fine spray. To keep birds, insects, and other pests from feasting on your herbs-to-be, consider covering your seedbed with a floating row cover, which will let in rain, light, and air while protecting the seeds.

The soil must remain moist for the seeds to germinate, so check the seedbed frequently. When the seedlings emerge, thin them according to the directions on the seed packet. Don't allow the soil to dry out, and apply a water-soluble fertilizer every other week for approximately 6 weeks.

Thriving between a Rock and a Hard Place

Many herbs will flourish where other plants might not survive. For example, try tucking small thyme plants in gaps between stones (*photo, below*). Creeping thyme (*Thymus praecox* ssp. *arcticus*) and caraway-scented *T. herba-barona* are good low-growing varieties for crevice planting.

For most gardeners, steep inclines are troublesome areas to cultivate. You can turn hot, dry banks into an asset by planting them with drought-resistant herbs such as lavender, creeping savory (*Satureja spicigera*), or winter savory. Easy-care herbs with fibrous, spreading roots such as calamint (*Calamintha grandiflora*) and wild marjoram (*Origanum vulgare*) will clothe a bank with foliage and flowers as they slow erosion.

Herbs for Crevice Planting

Crocus sativus
(saffron)
Gaultheria procumbens
(wintergreen)
Origanum vulgare 'Aureum'
(golden oregano)
Rosmarinus offici-

nalis 'Prostratus'
(prostrate rosemary)
Thymus herba-barona
(caraway thyme)
Thymus praecox ssp. *arcticus*
(creeping thyme)
Thymus pulegioides
(broad-leaved thyme)

Below, a raised bed overflowing with catmint is home to creeping thyme rooted between stones (right, center). The yellow-tinted shrub is a dwarf false cypress.

4. To prepare the interior of the bed for herbs that prefer light, fast-draining soil, add garden soil to a depth of 6 to 8 inches. Then fill the bed to within 3 inches of the top with a mixture of 1 part each of gravel, loam, and sand or grit. After planting, mulch the herbs with a 2-inch layer of sand or pea-sized gravel to help keep their crowns dry, retain soil moisture, and thwart weeds.

Weeding and Mulching

When preparing your beds for planting, it's important to pull or dig out the roots of perennial weeds, since even small fragments will resprout if left behind. Bindweed, couch grass, and goutweed are particularly difficult to remove when they invade a planting of creeping herbs like chamomile or thyme. Be vigilant and pluck out weed seedlings as soon as you spot them.

To suppress weeds around tall herbs, spread a 2- to 4-inch layer of organic mulch around your plants. This will also help retain soil moisture and enrich the soil as it decays. Remember to keep the mulch an inch or two away from the crowns of the plants, however, to prevent rot. For plants that prefer a drier, leaner soil, use a mulch of sand, pea-sized gravel, or poultry grit.

In cold climates, an airy winter mulch of evergreen branches, straw, or salt hay will help plants survive low temperatures and drying winds. Remove the mulch in the spring to allow the soil to warm up and the sun to reach new sprouts. If you are growing alkaline-loving herbs, it is especially important to remove evergreen branches before they shed their needles because they will acidify the soil as they decay.

The Fine Art of Watering

Knowing when to water your plants is a skill acquired by carefully attending to the requirements of the particular herbs in your garden. Species adapted to dry conditions are likely to perform poorly in soil that is constantly moist, while others require even moisture and must be checked frequently during dry weather *(list, below)*. Wilting is usually considered a sign that a plant is short of water, but looks can be deceiving. On hot days, some thin-leaved herbs such as basil and hot peppers (*Capsicum* spp.) will wilt dramatically by early afternoon, even if the soil around their roots is moist. In the cool of the evening, the plants will perk up again. Always check the soil before watering herbs that wilt easily.

Although watering is largely a summertime chore, it may also be necessary in the winter. If there is no precipitation in your area for 3 or 4 weeks, give your beds a deep soaking to keep dormant herbs healthy. The following tips on when and how to water will help keep established herbs in good condition:

• For most herbs, allow the top inch or so of soil to become somewhat dry between waterings. To check whether it's time to water, dig down 3 to 4 inches with a trowel to see if the soil is still moist. If not, watering is in order.

• Drought-resistant herbs need no more than a half-inch of water per week. Other herbs should receive approximately 1 inch per week. Use a rain gauge to determine how much supplemental watering is needed.

• Give plants slow, deep soakings. Frequent light sprinklings encourage plants to produce shallow root systems, making them more vulnerable to drought.

Pointers on Pruning

Pruning, pinching, or deadheading your herbs at the right time will repay you with more attractive and productive plants. For example, periodically pruning away deadwood from shrubby herbs like sage and lavender encourages stronger, bushier growth. Remember, however, to stop pruning woody herbs approximately 4 weeks before the first expected frost in your area. Otherwise, the plants may waste their energy putting out new growth that could be damaged or killed by the cold.

Pinching back some herbs not only helps maintain a rounded, compact shape, it can also preserve flavor. Many culinary herbs valued for their foliage, such as basil, chervil, lemon balm, and oregano, will diminish in flavor if allowed to produce flowers. But if you promptly pinch off any new flower buds, the herbs will maintain their full flavor and aroma and continue to produce new foliage.

Unless you want to harvest seeds for cooking, you should remove spent flowers promptly. Deadheading prevents seeds from forming, so that the plants have more energy to spend on producing new flowers and foliage.

Herbs for Moist Soil

Angelica archangelica
(angelica)
Anthriscus cerefolium
(chervil)
Gaultheria procumbens
(wintergreen)
Laurus nobilis
(sweet bay)
Levisticum officinale
(lovage)

Lindera benzoin
(spicebush)
Melissa officinalis
(lemon balm)
Mentha x *piperita*
(peppermint)
Monarda didyma
(bee balm)
Myrrhis odorata
(sweet cicely)
Nepeta spp.
(catmint)
Ocimum basilicum
(sweet basil)

Panax quinquefolius
(American ginseng)
Polygonum odoratum
(Vietnamese coriander)
Viola odorata
(sweet violet)

Note: The abbreviation "spp." stands for the plural of "species"; where used in lists it means that many, but not all, of the species in a genus meet the criterion of the list.

Propagating Your Herbs

The fastest way to get an herb garden going is with nursery-grown plants, but don't overlook using your own mature plants to increase your stock. Dividing overcrowded clumps is simple, and growing new plants from cuttings is only a little more involved. If you need large numbers of plants for kitchen use or for a large knot garden, seeding is a low-cost alternative. Most annual herbs are easy to grow from seed, and starting the cold-sensitive types indoors will give you a head start on the growing season.

Good light is vital for growing healthy seedlings indoors. A very sunny window sill may suffice for winter sowings, but if the intensity of the sunlight is too low, the seedlings will be weak and leggy. If you plan to raise seedlings every year, it's smart to establish a propagation area in your basement or in a spare room. The setup can be as simple as a light fixture with two standard 4-foot-long fluorescent tubes suspended over a table or a sheet of plywood on sawhorse supports. Position the tubes so they will be about 4 inches above the seedlings. A timer set to 16 hours of light followed by 8 hours of darkness is a convenient way to ensure that the plants will get the light they need every day.

Planting the Seed

A soilless growing medium, which you can buy or mix yourself *(page 460, bottom),* is the best choice for starting seeds. For containers, you can purchase inexpensive seed-starting trays with domed plastic lids that let in light and retain warmth and moisture. Individual plastic pots or cell packs with a covering of clear plastic wrap work just as well and are a good choice when you will be sowing only a few seeds of a variety. To minimize the chances of transmitting a disease to your seedlings, sterilize previously used containers with a solution of a half-cup of bleach to a gallon of water.

When you are ready to plant, moisten the growing medium and fill the containers no more than 2½ inches deep. Plant the seeds according to the instructions on the packets. Herbs that have a low rate of germination, such as lavender and parsley, should be sown so thickly that the seeds touch one another. Make a label for each container with the name of the variety and the date of planting. Water thoroughly with a fine spray, then cover the container to keep the seedbed moist and warm.

When using plastic wrap, choose the thinnest you can find and drape it loosely over a support of sticks, pencils, or arched hoops so that it is several inches above the seedbed.

Care of Seedlings

Place the containers in a warm (70° to 80°F), bright room out of direct sunlight. After a week, begin checking for signs of germination. As soon as a few seeds have sprouted, place the containers in a sunny window or under fluorescent lights and remove the covering. Seedlings left under cover in moist, warm conditions may be stricken with damping-off, a fungal disease that can quickly destroy an entire flat of young seedlings. To help prevent damping-off, try misting seedlings with an infusion of German chamomile: Add a handful of fresh chamomile or 2 tablespoons of the dried herb to 4 cups of boiling water. Steep the mixture for 10 minutes, strain it through cheesecloth, and let it cool before using.

Be careful not to overwater the seedlings; soggy roots make them susceptible to root rot and foliage diseases. Water once each day in the morn-

Double Potting for Easy Watering

For an effective way to keep your herb cuttings constantly moist, first fill a 6-inch clay pot halfway with moistened soilless growing medium. Plug the drainage holes of a 3-inch clay pot and set it on top of the medium. Fill the space between the pots with more of the growing medium and tamp it lightly. Plant the cuttings in the larger pot, then fill the small pot with water; it will seep through the pot and water your herbs.

PROPAGATION METHODS FOR 23 POPULAR HERBS

Herb	Propagation Method
Allium schoenoprasum (chives)	seed, division
Aloysia triphylla (lemon verbena)	seed, cuttings
Anethum graveolens (dill)	seed
Angelica archangelica (angelica)	seed
Anthriscus cerefolium (chervil)	seed
Artemisia dracunculus var. *sativa* (French tarragon)	cuttings, division
Calendula officinalis (calendula)	seed
Chamaemelum nobile (Roman chamomile)	seed, cuttings, division, layering
Foeniculum vulgare (fennel)	seed
Laurus nobilis (bay laurel)	cuttings
Lavandula spp. (lavender)	seed, cuttings, layering
Melissa officinalis (lemon balm)	seed, cuttings, division
Mentha spp. (mint)	cuttings, division
Monarda didyma (bee balm)	cuttings, division
Myrrhis odorata (sweet cicely)	seed
Ocimum basilicum (sweet basil)	seed, cuttings
Pelargonium spp. (scented geranium)	seed, cuttings
Petroselinum crispum (parsley)	seed
Rosmarinus officinalis (rosemary)	cuttings, layering
Salvia spp. (sage)	seed, cuttings, layering
Satureja montana (winter savory)	seed, cuttings, layering
Thymus spp. (thyme)	seed, cuttings, division, layering
Tropaeolum majus (nasturtium)	seed

Note: The abbreviation "spp." stands for the plural of "species"; where used in lists it means that many, but not all, of the species in a genus meet the criterion of the list.

Making a Soilless Growing Medium for Herbs

A soilless growing medium gets seedlings and cuttings off to a healthy start. Air and water penetrate it easily to reach growing roots and, unlike garden loam or commercial potting soil, it is free of disease organisms and weed seeds. To make a good mix yourself, combine 3 parts each of vermiculite, composted pine bark, and sphagnum moss with 1 part leaf mold. To each gallon of the mix add a heaping tablespoon of ground limestone and a half-cup of a slow-release fertilizer such as 17-6-10. Store in dry, clean containers or plastic bags. Just before using, dampen the mix with warm water.

ing, then allow the growing medium to dry out until the following morning. Once a week, feed the seedlings with a water-soluble organic fertilizer, diluted as directed on the package.

Seedlings are ready for transplanting when they have two sets of leaves. Lift them carefully by their leaves, not by their fragile stems, and place them in 2- to 2½-inch plastic pots filled with dampened growing mix. After 3 to 6 weeks, the seedlings will be ready to be hardened off. Set them outdoors in a sheltered, sunny spot for the day and bring them back inside at night. In a week they will be ready for planting out in the garden.

New Plants from Cuttings and Division

If you have plants with long taproots that are hard to divide, you'll need to propagate them from stem cuttings. This method is also best for cultivars that don't come true from seed; the cuttings will yield offspring identical to the parent.

Spring is generally the best time to take cuttings, since fresh green growth roots quickly. First, prepare flats, trays, or shallow pots with dampened soilless growing medium. Using scissors or a sharp knife, make a clean cut just below a node or leaf 3 to 5 inches from the tip of the stem. If you will be taking cuttings for more than a few minutes, wrap each one as you go in dampened newspaper and place in a plastic bag to keep it moist and cool.

When you have enough cuttings, move to a shaded area to prepare them for potting. Strip all leaves from the lower half of the stem and pinch off all flowers or flower buds. To stimulate root formation, dip the base of the cuttings in rooting hormone, then plant the cuttings about an inch deep. Space them several inches apart to allow for air circulation. Water deeply and cover the container loosely with plastic wrap or a plastic bag held several inches above the cuttings by sticks or other supports. Keep the cuttings in a cool spot that gets plenty of bright, indirect light. Frequent misting—several times daily, if possible—will help maintain the high humidity needed to prevent wilting. Cuttings root most quickly when the air temperature is in the 60s and the root-zone temperature is around 75° F. For a steady source of bottom heat, set the container on an electric mat purchased at a garden center or through a garden supply catalog.

The appearance of new growth on a cutting signals that it has taken root and is ready to be transplanted to its own container and placed in a sunny window or under fluorescent lights. The new plant can be set out in the garden when a network of roots has developed on the surface of the rootball; this will take several weeks. To check its growth, gently slip the plant from its pot.

If you wish to propagate such herbs as basil, lemon verbena, mint, pineapple sage, and Vietnamese coriander, you can also root them in water. Fill a clear glass jar with enough water to submerge only the stripped portion of the cutting's stem. Place it in bright, indirect light and change the water daily to keep it free of the bacteria that cause rot. When a cutting has roots ¼ to ½ inch long, which generally takes about 2 weeks, pot it in a soilless growing medium and place it under fluorescent lights or in direct sunlight. In a few weeks, the cuttings can be planted in the garden.

Division is the easiest and quickest way to increase your stock of healthy established herbs many times over. In cold climates, spring is the best season to divide plants; in milder climates you can choose between spring or fall. Work on a cloudy day, if possible, and dig up the plant with a sharp spade. Using your hands, a trowel, or a knife, divide the plant, roots and all, into several clumps. As a rule, a large clump will be less stressed than a small one and will establish itself more quickly after planting. If a division has an ample root system and the weather is cool, it can be planted directly in the garden. Otherwise, plant the division in a container so that it can develop a larger root system before it is transplanted to a permanent place. Water well with a soluble organic fertilizer to reduce the stress of transplanting.

The Simplicity of Layering

Creeping herbs often put down roots on their own wherever stems or branches touch moist soil. This process, known as layering, can be helped along by a gardener who wants new plants. Choose a young, flexible stem and strip the growth from a 5- to 6-inch section growing close to the ground. With a sharp knife, nick the bare section, then bury it 2 to 3 inches deep; leave several inches of the stem's tip exposed above the soil. You may need to anchor the buried stem with a small stone or a U-shaped wire to keep it in place. Mulch the layered area and water deeply. In about a month, check for roots by gently tugging on the buried stem. If you meet with resistance, roots have probably formed. Sever the stem from the parent plant, lift it gently, and transplant it to a pot or directly to the garden.

A special version of layering is used to propagate herbs that have upright, woody stems. This process, which is called mound layering, is explained in the box at right.

Mound Layering Shrubby Herbs

The stems of a number of shrubby upright herbs with woody bases will take root when mounded with soil, yielding new plants for the garden. Lavender and other plants that are slow to root need to be cut back, as shown below in Step 1, then mounded with soil. You can skip this step with thyme, sage, rosemary, and other herbs that root easily, and proceed to Steps 2 and 3.

1. In early spring, cut the stems of the plant to be mound layered back to within 2 to 3 inches of the ground. Within several weeks after pruning, new shoots should appear.

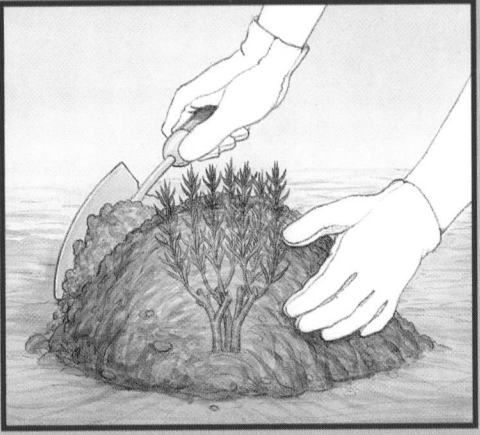

2. When the new shoots are about 5 inches long, mound a mixture of equal amounts of sand, peat moss, and soil over the plant's center, until only the tips of the new growth are showing. Keep the mound slightly moist. As the shoots continue to grow, add soil to the mound until it is 6 to 8 inches high. Be sure not to cover the tips of the shoots.

3. On an overcast day in late summer, gently wash away the mounded soil. Using hand pruners, cut each rooted stem at its base to separate it from the parent plant. Plant the rooted stems immediately in a well-prepared bed. The following year, you can mound layer the parent plant again or leave it to grow back into a healthy rejuvenated shrub.

Spotting Potential Problems

Managing pests and diseases organically depends on your ability to identify a threat to your garden so that you can take steps to prevent or eradicate it. You may already have successfully diagnosed attacks on your vegetables or herbs by pests or diseases. However, it's a good idea to contact your local Cooperative Extension Service for a list of the culprits common in your area; that way, you'll be forewarned of problems you haven't encountered personally. Such a list, along with the information on the following pages and in the Troubleshooting Guide on pages 576-583, will help you choose appropriate preventive measures.

A keen eye is crucial for heading off problems or solving them quickly. Make it a habit to examine your plants methodically every week, turning over their leaves and checking their stems—a 10-power hand lens will help you with this task. If you discover chewed or yellowing leaves or other signs of trouble, describe the damage and record the date in your garden diary *(page 455)*. Along with the other items in your diary, such as the date a vegetable was planted, rotation schedules, or unusual weather, this information will help you identify the cause of a problem. Good records will also help you anticipate seasonal outbreaks.

Pests and diseases can be hard to identify, even for a seasoned gardener, so consult your local Cooperative Extension Service agent if you are stumped. A plant specimen and your diary will help the agent make the correct diagnosis.

Chewing and Sucking Insects

Most of the insects that harm plants fall into two basic categories—chewing insects and sucking insects. Among the most voracious chewing pests are beetle larvae and caterpillars, which are the larvae of moths and butterflies. If chewing pests have invaded your garden, you'll see nibbled edges of leaves or holes chewed between leaf veins. Little piles of excrement, or drass, deposited on the leaves are another telltale sign.

In large enough numbers, chewing insects can defoliate a plant or completely devour a seedling, and they also open a plant's tissues to infection. There may be several generations of a particular pest in one season, so you have to be continuously on the alert for signs of chewing. If you find holes in foliage, look for eggs on the undersides of the leaves; remove any you find and drop them into a bucket of soapy water to keep them from hatching.

Sucking insects, such as aphids and leafhoppers, feed on juices in leaves, stems, or roots. Besides weakening a plant, a sucking insect can inject deadly pathogens as it feeds. Typical kinds of damage include wilting; stunted growth; yellowed, brown, or blotchy leaves; and misshapen leaves, shoots, or fruit. Aphids leave sticky trails of sugars and sap, known as honeydew, on the leaves.

Clinging to a wire support for peas, a raccoon on a nighttime raid surveys a garden's bounty. In the background is a stand of corn, a favorite food of this pest.

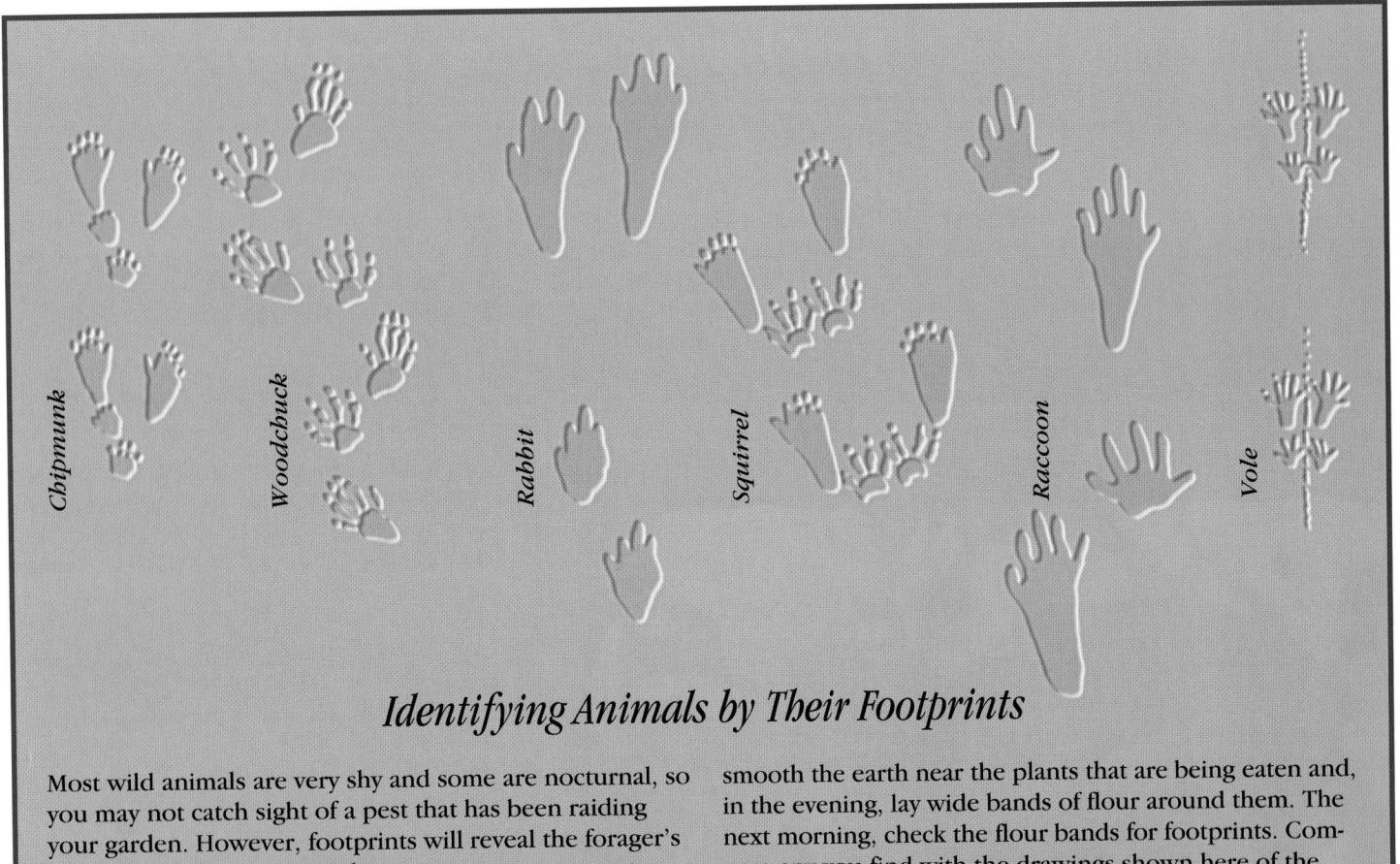

Identifying Animals by Their Footprints

Most wild animals are very shy and some are nocturnal, so you may not catch sight of a pest that has been raiding your garden. However, footprints will reveal the forager's identity and allow you to take steps to prevent repeat visits *(pages 467 and 469)*. To get a clear footprint, smooth the earth near the plants that are being eaten and, in the evening, lay wide bands of flour around them. The next morning, check the flour bands for footprints. Compare any you find with the drawings shown here of the prints of six common animal pests.

Chipmunk

Woodchuck

Rabbit

Squirrel

Raccoon

Vole

Diseases

Like other living creatures, plants occasionally fall victim to infectious diseases. Pathogens such as fungal spores, viruses, bacteria, and parasitic nematodes can be transported into your garden on the feet of insects or in their saliva, on infected plants bought at a nursery, or by way of wind or birds. Once in your garden, a disease organism may not manifest itself for years, remaining dormant until conditions become more favorable.

Your hands, shoes, and tools can also spread pathogens from place to place within the garden, and the simple act of accidentally nicking a stem when you are cultivating around a plant can provide an entryway for a disease organism. As a precaution, don't work in the garden when it is wet, since pathogens, especially fungal spores, are easily spread from plant to plant in drops of water.

Not all garden diseases are caused by pathogens. They also arise from environmental disorders such as mineral deficiencies or air pollution. The symptoms of noninfectious and infectious diseases can be confusingly similar, and close scrutiny is required to tell the difference. One way to distinguish the two is to examine how the symptoms are distributed. If most or all of the plants growing in the same area have the same symptoms, an environmental cause is likely. An infectious disease, by contrast, tends to attack one plant first and then spread in a random pattern to a few plants nearby. See the Troubleshooting Guide on pages 576-583 for help in diagnosis.

Animal Pests

The plants in a kitchen garden are just as appealing to a number of animals as they are to humans. Such common animals as raccoons, rabbits, and woodchucks, for example, are capable of devastating a crop in short order. As with insects or diseases, different species call for different control measures. If you suspect that an animal pest is slipping in and out of your garden unseen, the information in the box above may help you identify the elusive culprit.

An Ounce of Prevention

This 'Whopper Improved' green bell pepper plant is heavy with unblemished fruit and foliage. It is resistant to the tobacco mosaic virus, a common disease that can cause yellowing of leaves, stunting, and reduced yield.

One easy way to stop problems before they start is to fill your garden with plants that have been bred to resist one or more diseases without compromising flavor. Resistance is often indicated on plant labels or in catalogs by coded abbreviations of diseases. For instance, DMPM means that the plant is resistant to downy mildew and powdery mildew. In addition to the many disease-resistant cultivars, there are a smaller number that are resistant to attack by certain insects.

Not quite as trouble free but still very desirable are plants that are rated tolerant of a particular disease or pest. Although a tolerant variety may suffer infection or an infestation, the damage won't be bad enough to cut its production significantly.

Crops on the Move

Pests and pathogens that live in the soil will continue to multiply as long as their preferred food supply is present, so putting the same plants in the same bed year after year is asking for trouble. But if you shift crops from place to place every time you plant, an insect, bacterium, virus, or fungus that has established itself in your garden will be deprived of its food source and will die out.

A crop rotation scheme must be based on families of plants, since closely related species are likely to be attacked by the same pests and diseases. The chart on page 466 groups widely grown vegetables and herbs by family and will help you plot out a rotation scheme. Since the pathogens responsible for bean anthracnose, verticillium wilt, fusarium wilt, and other diseases can survive in the soil for up to 3 years, waiting at least that long before replanting a bed with the same family of crops will give you maximum protection.

It is also a good practice to work soil-building crops like clover and rye into your rotation plan to ensure a regular replenishment of nutrients and organic matter. The chart on page 515 provides information on six soil-building crops, including when to sow, seeding rate, and how each crop improves the soil.

Keeping the Garden Clean

Another way to interrupt the life cycle of pests and disease organisms is to develop good gardening habits. As soon as a plant reaches the end of its productive life, pull it up and add it to the compost pile; debris left in the garden can harbor insects or pathogens from one season to the next. After clearing away crop debris, till the soil to bring eggs and larvae to the surface, where birds, snakes, or other predators can find them. Turning the soil of an empty bed several times in late winter will expose insects such as corn ear worms and cutworms to freezing cold. Keeping weeds under control in and around the garden is also important. Besides competing with your plants for water, nutrients, and light, some weeds are hosts to harmful garden pests and disease organisms.

Encouraging Beneficials

All pests have natural predators. Known collectively as beneficials, these include toads, snakes, lizards, moles, songbirds, and a number of insects, such as parasitic wasps. You can buy certain insect predators, but it's also wise to make your garden attractive to native beneficials. For instance, including plants with pollen- and nectar-rich flowers, such as dill and yarrow, will draw the beneficial insects that depend on them for food. A constant water supply is also essential. A birdbath can do double duty if you make a little island of pebbles or float a piece of wood in the water for insects to alight on. See the chart on page 468 for other ways to encourage beneficials.

Barriers to Stymie Pests

A number of simple but effective barriers do a good job of keeping flying and crawling insects, slugs, raccoons, and other hungry pests away from vegetables and fruits. A sheet of black plastic or a thick layer of organic mulch will not only moderate soil temperatures and suppress weeds, it will also disrupt the life cycles of thrips, leaf miners, and other soil-borne pests. For example, 6 inches of straw mulch will deter Colorado potato beetles that have overwintered in the soil from emerging in time to feed on potato seedlings.

Plants covered by a lightweight, translucent fabric are shielded from a wide variety of flying and crawling insect pests, such as aphids, leafhoppers, and caterpillars. While these row covers offer no protection against soil-borne eggs, larvae, or adult pests that are already in the soil, they do prevent flying and crawling adults from laying a new generation of eggs in the soil. Another benefit of row covers is the protection they provide plants against bacteria and viruses transmitted by insects.

The most versatile materials for row covers are spunbonded polyester, polypropylene, and polyvinyl fabric. Because these fabrics are very lightweight, they can be draped directly over the plants—hence the name "floating row cover." They transmit to the plants about 85 percent of available sunlight, along with ample water and air. Floating row covers also slow the evaporation of soil moisture and shield plants from drying winds.

In this benign environment, plants grow as well—or better—than they would if they were fully exposed to the elements.

Some spunbonded row covers are designed to trap enough heat to protect plants from light frosts in spring and fall. There are also summer-weight row covers so airy that they can be left in place throughout the growing season without the risk of overheating your plants. These row covers are an especially good choice for protecting cool-

Pest- and Disease-Resistant Varieties of Vegetables

In addition to vegetables that resist particular diseases and pests, the list below includes several tolerant varieties, which can grow fairly well in spite of an infestation or infection.

CABBAGE
'Danish Ballhead', *'Early Jersey Wakefield'*—tolerate cabbage looper and imported cabbageworm; *'Golden Acre'*—tolerates fusarium yellows; *'Red Acre'*—tolerates cabbage looper and imported cabbageworm; *'Wisconsin All Seasons'*—fusarium yellows

CARROT
'Napoli'—tolerates alternaria blight

CHINESE CABBAGE
'Blues'—alternaria, black speck, downy mildew, soft rot

CORN
'Lancelot'—corn rust, Stewart's bacterial wilt; *'Miracle'*—corn rust; *'Silver Queen'*—northern corn leaf blight, southern corn leaf blight, Stewart's bacterial wilt; *'Tuxedo'*—corn rust, corn smut, Stewart's bacterial wilt

CUCUMBER
'Little Leaf'—angular leaf spot, anthracnose, cucumber mosaic, downy mildew, target leaf spot; *'Marketmore 76'*—scab; tolerates cucumber mosaic, downy mildew, powdery mildew; *'Salad Bush'*—cucumber mosaic, scab; *'Space Master'*—cucumber mosaic, scab; *'Sweet Slice'*—tolerates cucumber mosaic, powdery mildew, watermelon mosaic, zucchini yellows mosaic; *'Sweet Success'*—cucumber mosaic, scab, target leaf spot

GREEN BEANS AND POLE BEANS
'Kentucky Wonder'—rusts; *'Provider'*—bacterial blight, common bean mosaic, downy mildew, powdery mildew, white mold; *'Tendercrop'*—bacterial blight, downy mildew, powdery mildew, white mold

LETTUCE
'Ithaca'—brown rib, lettuce mosaic, tipburn; *'Paris Island Cos'*—lettuce mosaic, tipburn

ONIONS
'Early Yellow Globe'—onion smudge; *'Northern Oak'*—fusarium yellows, pink root; *'Texas Grano'*—pink root

PEPPERS
'Bell Boy'—tobacco mosaic; *'California Wonder'*—cercospora leaf spot; *'Gypsy'*—tobacco mosaic; *'Whopper Improved'*—tobacco mosaic; *'Yolo Wonder'*—tobacco mosaic

SQUASH
'Cocozelle'—aphids

TOMATOES
'Ace 55'—fusarium wilt, verticillium wilt; *'Beefmaster'*—alternaria, fusarium wilt, gray leaf spot, nematodes, verticillium wilt; *'Better Boy'*—alternaria, fusarium wilt, root knot nematodes, verticillium wilt; *'Celebrity'*—alternaria stem canker, fusarium 1-2, gray leaf spot, nematodes, tobacco mosaic, verticillium wilt; *'Early Cascade'*—alternaria stem canker, fusarium, gray leaf spot, verticillium wilt; *'Roma VF'*—alternaria, fusarium wilt, verticillium wilt; *'Sweet Million'*—fusarium wilt, nematodes, septoria leaf spot, tobacco mosaic

YELLOW BEANS
'Cherokee'—common bean mosaic, rust; *'Roc d'Or'*—anthracnose, common bean mosaic

weather greens like lettuce and spinach that tend to bolt when the temperature is too high.

Heavier row covers of polyethylene and polystyrene plastic are more efficient heat traps than any of the spunbonded fabrics. They are excellent for getting the garden started earlier in the year and keeping crops growing longer in the fall, but can easily overheat crops in milder weather. Also, these plastics need wire hoops or some other support to keep them from crushing the plants.

Before you drape a floating row cover over a planting, weed the area thoroughly and use the techniques described on pages 470-471 to get rid of as many insects as you can. Place the fabric over the row immediately after planting; if the day is breezy, the job will be easier to do if you have a helper. Leave plenty of slack in the cover so the plants will have growing room. Weight the edges down securely with soil, rocks, or boards, and check to be sure there are no gaps that insects could slip through.

For cucumbers, beans, tomatoes, and other fruiting vegetables that must be pollinated to develop, remove the row covers when the crops begin to bloom. Vegetables that don't need pollination can remain covered until harvest. When you need to remove a cover for weeding and thinning, replace it as soon as you have finished the chore.

Some young vegetable plants require special protection. For example, to defend members of the cabbage family against cabbage maggots that feed on their roots, you can make a barrier that prevents adults from laying eggs in the soil at the base of the plant. Use a piece of heavy cardboard, plastic, or tarpaper measuring 6 inches square. Make a slit from one edge to the center of the square and cut out a small circle at the inner end of the slit to make room for the stem. Slip the square around the stem of the seedling at planting time. For a barrier that discourages cutworms, which chew on the stems of young vegetables at soil level, place a collar around the seedling's stem at planting time. Use a small paper cup with the bottom removed, a toilet paper roll, or a square of newspaper rolled into a tube *(page 448)*. Bury the collar 1 to 1½ inches below ground level.

Slugs and snails are very destructive, chewing large, ragged holes in leaves and feeding on onion bulbs, strawberries, and tomatoes. Deter them by laying down a strip of abrasive material 2 inches wide and a quarter inch deep around a plant; when the animal crawls on the scratchy surface, its skin is damaged and it dies of dehydration. Particularly effective is diatomaceous earth, a commercial product derived from fossilized plankton. Wood ashes, talc, lime, and crushed eggshells also work well.

For a permanent barrier, surround a garden bed with a strip of copper sheet metal 4 inches wide. Bury the strip 1 to 2 inches below ground level and bend the top half-inch of the strip away from the bed. When a slug or snail touches the copper strip, a chemical reaction occurs that creates an electric current and gives the pest a shock.

A Family Plan for Crop Rotation

A reliable way to minimize or even eliminate soil-borne pest and disease problems is to plant a particular patch of ground with the same vegetable or its close relatives only once every 3 to 5 years. In the lean years, without their favored hosts to feed on, organisms that typically plague a certain vegetable family will decline in numbers. Use the family groups below to help you plot out a long-term rotation scheme for your garden.

BEET FAMILY

beets, chard, orach, spinach

CARROT FAMILY

carrots, celeriac, celery, fennel, parsley, parsnips

COMPOSITE FAMILY

cardoon, celtuce, chicory, endive, escarole, Jerusalem artichoke, lettuce, radicchio, salsify, sunflower

LEGUME FAMILY

beans, peas, peanuts, soybeans

MUSTARD FAMILY

arugula, broccoli, Brussels sprouts, cabbage, cauliflower, Chinese cabbage, collards, cress, kale, kohlrabi, mustard greens, radishes, rutabaga, turnips

ONION FAMILY

chives, garlic, leeks, onions, shallots

SQUASH FAMILY

chayote, cucumbers, melons, pumpkins, squash

TOMATO FAMILY

eggplant, peppers, potatoes, tomatillo, tomatoes

Mammals: Friends and Foes

A few mammals are actually more helpful than harmful in the garden, despite their reputation. For instance, skunks will eat berries and ears of corn that grow close to the ground, but they also catch insects, voles, mice, and rats. Moles ignore plants altogether; they dine on slugs, Japanese beetles, white grubs, and other pests in the soil. But some mammals, including rabbits and voles, are truly pests. Most organic gardeners prefer nonlethal methods, such as fences and repellent chemicals, to control them. Live traps are another option, but be careful you don't release an animal where it will become a headache for another gardener or where it cannot survive. Before using a trap, make sure your state does not have laws against transporting and releasing wild animals. The following is a list of a few mammals that can do damage in your garden, as well as some of the controls you can use to deter them:

Rabbits—A 3-foot-high fence of ¾-inch wire mesh will keep rabbits out of the garden. Dried blood meal, cow manure, or wood ashes sprinkled near plants will repel them; replenish after a rain.

Raccoons—To deter these animals, you can cover individual ears of corn or melon fruits with nylon stockings or net bags, but an electric fence—the only kind that works with raccoons—is easier. Two strands of electrified wire or cord around the garden are usually enough. Position the upper strand about a foot from the ground and the lower strand within 6 inches of the ground.

Woodchucks—Also called groundhogs, they eat almost anything succulent and rip up entire plants. The electric fence described above will discourage them, as will a wire-mesh fence that is at least 3 feet tall and extends 2 feet underground.

Squirrels—These animals relish tomatoes, sweet corn, and sunflower seeds. Try covering corn ears and sunflowers with nylon stockings or net bags, or spray the ears with a red pepper spray (the husks will shield the kernels from the spray).

Looming above its unwitting victim, a praying mantis prepares to strike a grasshopper, a pest that takes an especially heavy toll on seedlings. Though often helpful, praying mantises are indiscriminate predators, feeding on beneficial insects as well as destructive ones.

In search of a meal, a hungry green snake glides among bee balm blossoms ornamenting a vegetable garden. Nonpoisonous snakes like this one are a boon, hunting down insects and slugs as well as larger pests such as mice and voles.

467

BENEFICIALS THAT PREY ON VEGETABLE AND FRUIT PESTS

Beneficial	Pests Controlled	Comments
Aphid midges	More than 60 species of aphids	Attract with pollen- and nectar-producing plants. Buy six to 10 cocoons per plant and release half in early spring and the remainder 2 weeks later.
Assassin bugs	Flies, mosquitoes, beetles, caterpillars	Provide permanent beds in or near the garden for shelter. Purchase commercial attractant.
Braconid wasps	Aphids, moth and beetle larvae, flies, codling moth, cabbageworm, hornworm, corn borer, armyworm, other caterpillars	These wasps feed on the nectar of dill, parsley, mustard, white clover, yarrow, and other small-flowered plants. Also available by mail order.
Flower flies, syrphid flies	Aphids, mealybugs, mites, thrips	These predators are attracted by daisylike flowers that produce nectar and pollen.
Lacewings	Aphids, mealybugs, mites, moth eggs, scales, small caterpillars, soft-bodied insects, thrips	Attract with nectar- and pollen-producing plants such as goldenrod. Purchase eggs and distribute in the garden. Purchase commercial attractant.
Ladybugs, ladybeetles	Aphids, mealybugs, soft scales, spider mites, whiteflies	Plant pollen- and nectar-producing plants. Buy adults collected in spring only. Ladybugs collected at other times of year will migrate from your garden. Buy commercial attractant.
Nematodes, beneficial, type HH	Soil-borne insects, including armyworm, black vine weevil, cabbage root maggot, chafers, Colorado potato beetle, corn rootworm, cucumber beetle, cutworms, fungus gnat larvae, Japanese beetle grubs, mole cricket, root weevils, white grubs, and wireworms	Keep soil moist. Available by mail order.
Nematodes, beneficial, type NC	Soil-borne insects, including armyworm, cabbage root maggot, chafers, Colorado potato beetle, cutworm, earwig, Japanese beetle grubs, onion maggot, root weevils, seed corn maggot, sowbug, white grubs, and wireworms	Keep soil moist. Available by mail order.
Pirate bugs	Aphids, insect eggs, leafhoppers, rust mites, spider mites, small caterpillars, thrips	Attract with pollen-rich plants such as goldenrod, and provide a water source such as a birdbath.
Praying mantises	Aphids, beetles, bugs, caterpillars, flies, leafhoppers, and other insects	Available by mail order, but try other controls first because praying mantises eat beneficials.
Predatory mites	European red mites, rust mites, thrips, two-spotted spider mites	These mites prefer high humidity and rich soil and do not thrive in hot, dry areas.
Rove beetles	Aphids, fly eggs, maggots, mites, parasitic nematodes, slugs, snails, springtails	Provide organic mulch for shelter.
Soldier beetles	Aphids, beetle larvae, butterfly larvae, caterpillars, grasshopper eggs, moth larvae	Attract by growing goldenrod and other nectar- and pollen-producing plants.
Spiders	Most insects	Encourage by leaving webs intact.
Tachinid flies	Many kinds of caterpillars, including cutworms, codling moths, cabbage loopers, squash bugs, and grasshoppers	Attract by growing nectar-producing plants such as dill, parsley, sweet clover, and yarrow.
Trichogramma wasps	Eggs of many moths, including corn ear worm, cutworm, cabbage looper, corn borer, codling moth, tomato hornworm	Several species that prey on different pests are available by mail order; be sure you buy the appropriate one. Use pheromone traps to determine when the pest is at its peak, or release wasps every week for a month around the peak season.
Bats	Nocturnal flying insects	Install a bat house and provide water.
Birds	Many kinds of insects	Install birdhouses, provide water, and plant fruit-bearing shrubs and trees.
Snakes	Insects and small rodents	Provide shallow containers of water and shelter.
Toads, lizards, turtles	Slugs and most insects	Provide shallow containers of water and shelter.

Firmly weighted down by soil and logs, floating row covers shield young vegetables from pesky insects early in the growing season in the Maine garden above. The row covers also trap enough heat overnight to protect the plants against late, light frosts. Once all danger of insect infestation has passed, the covers can be removed.

Voles—Sprinkle household ammonia on the ground around plants to repel these rodents. Also try a small-mesh wire fence, bent horizontally so that it stands at least 18 inches high with 12 inches or more lying flat on the ground, to discourage voles from burrowing into the garden.

Deer—A fence is one option, though even a 7-foot fence may not keep the best jumpers out. (The top of the fence should slant outward at a 45° angle.) First, however, experiment with net bags filled with mothballs or hair (animal or human) hung every 20 feet throughout the garden; blood meal sprinkled around the perimeter; or sweaty clothes hung on stakes. You can also try laying chicken-wire fencing on the ground around the garden; the deer may become discouraged if their feet get tangled in the wire.

Birds—Songbirds are generally beneficials, eating hundreds of insects in a single day. Most other kinds of birds, however, eat vegetable seedlings, lettuce, berries, and other crops. Scare tactics such as inflatable owls and balloons on which you've

Rain, sunlight, and air pass easily through the translucent floating row cover protecting the cabbage plants at upper right. A sturdy wire cage that can be lifted for weeding and harvesting keeps the lettuce plants at right out of the reach of birds, rabbits, and other greens-loving animals.

drawn large eyes work fairly well; place them every 30 to 40 feet around the garden and change them often to keep the birds from getting used to them. A surer method is to cover vulnerable plants. Several weeks before the fruits ripen, drape berry plants with broad-mesh plastic netting with a ½- to ¾-inch grid. For seedlings and crops like lettuce that continue to attract birds as they mature, use spunbonded floating row covers.

Minimizing Damage in Your Garden

Sometimes even your best efforts to curb pests and diseases aren't enough. An outbreak occurs, and you may find your vegetables rotting, wilting, or chewed to shreds. Fortunately, there are ways to prevent a problem from getting out of hand without resorting to chemicals.

The first step is to physically remove as much of the problem as possible. If a plant is diseased, get rid of it, roots and all. Put it in a plastic bag and throw it out with your household trash. Do not compost diseased debris; pathogens may survive the decay process and reinfest the garden when you use the finished compost.

In the case of a plant with a soil-borne disease, dig it up with a garden fork, taking care not to knock the soil from the rootball. Put the plant and the soil clinging to its roots in a plastic bag for disposal. Replant with a resistant variety or a different vegetable that is immune to the disease.

After handling a diseased plant, clean your tools and gloves with a 10 percent bleach solution to avoid spreading the disease to other plants.

Coping with Pests

An infestation of pests usually doesn't call for total removal of the plant. If the intruders are confined to a stem or two, cut back to clean, uninfested tissue, put the plant parts in a plastic bag, and discard with the household trash. Large pests like caterpillars and snails can be picked off plants and dropped into a bucket of soapy water.

Some beetle pests, such as Japanese beetles or Colorado potato beetles, can be shaken out. For insects like aphids and spider mites that cling tightly to plants, you can injure or kill many of them with a stream of water from a hose.

Another fairly easy way to get rid of insect pests is to lure them away with traps. The best traps imitate certain sights or smells that insects associate with food or potential mates. These include pheromone traps, as well as homemade sticky traps painted yellow, blue, or white.

If slugs and snails have eluded the preventive barriers you have placed around vulnerable crops, you can also set traps for them. Garden centers and mail-order companies sell baited traps, or you can make your own.

Like other creatures, pests are susceptible to fatal infections, and the bacterium *Bacillus thuringiensis* (Bt) is an invaluable pesticide for the organic gardener. Among the common pests susceptible to infection are cabbage loopers, tomato hornworms, European corn borers, and beetle larvae that feed on leaves.

For more information on these and other methods of controlling pests, see pages 359-369.

Homemade Pesticides and Fungicides

If you have used the full arsenal of cultural, physical, and biological controls against a pest or disease without success, your remaining weapon is an organic pesticide or fungicide. The mildest and safest of these—and for that reason the ones to try first—are homemade preparations based on common, readily available ingredients. A spray made from baking soda, for instance, is effective against fungal diseases, especially powdery mildew, leaf blight, and leaf spot.

Recipes for baking soda fungicide and three other sprays are given below. The garlic and hot pepper sprays control insects. The soap-and-oil spray prevents fungal spores from germinating and is also an insecticide.

Before applying any of the preparations to an entire plant, spray it on a few leaves to test for sensitivity. After 2 days, examine the leaves to see whether there are any spots of discolored or dying tissue. If the leaves are damaged, dilute the spray with a little more water and test the plant again to see if it is safe to use.

When you spray a plant, be sure to cover the top and bottom of all of its leaves *(page 373)*. Repeat every 5 to 7 days until the pests are gone or the disease symptoms have disappeared. To prevent a repeat outbreak of a disease the following year, begin spraying in the spring and continue until the fall.

Baking soda spray—Dissolve 1 tablespoon of baking soda in 1 gallon of water and add ⅛ to ¼ teaspoon of insecticidal soap to help the solution spread and adhere to the foliage.

Soap-and-oil spray—Mix 1 teaspoon of liquid dishwashing soap with ⅓ cup of corn, soybean,

sunflower, safflower, or peanut oil. To apply, combine 1 to 2 teaspoons of this mixture with 1 cup of water in a hand sprayer.

Garlic spray—Combine 15 garlic cloves with 1 pint of water in a blender and purée. Alternatively, mince the garlic cloves and steep them in the water for 24 hours. Strain the liquid through cheesecloth and add a few drops of insecticidal soap.

Hot pepper spray—Purée ½ cup of hot peppers and 2 cups of water in a blender. Strain the liquid through cheesecloth. Wear gloves when handling the peppers and be careful not to get the liquid on your skin or in your eyes—it will sting and burn.

Commercial Chemicals

If a homemade preparation doesn't take care of a stubborn problem, you may decide that stronger measures are called for. Although the natural chemicals that organic gardeners use are derived from plants or minerals, they can have adverse effects and should be considered only as a last resort. Some are toxic not only to certain pests or diseases, but also to humans, mammals, birds, reptiles, fish, harmless insects, or soil microorganisms. Nevertheless, they are preferable to synthetic, or manufactured, chemicals because the natural substances break down quickly. In addition, they have no long-lasting detrimental effects on the environment. Synthetic chemicals, by contrast, may remain active for months or years and can be extremely harmful. The chart on pages 472-473 provides information on organic pesticides and fungicides that are safe to use on food crops. Whatever the pest or disease you are battling, always try the least toxic chemical first, apply it sparingly, and follow directions carefully. For information on handling chemicals safely, including what to wear for the job and how to clean up afterward, see pages 373-374.

A planting of African marigolds (above) can clear infested soil of root knot nematodes in one season. When the nematodes feed on the roots of these plants, they take in a chemical that keeps them from reproducing. At season's end, the marigolds can be turned under to improve the soil's texture.

A Guide to Commercial Organic Pesticides and Fungicides

The 13 organic products included in this chart are your last line of defense against pests and diseases in the garden. When using any of them, always read the label on the container, heed all warnings, and follow all directions. Before treating an entire plant, test the product on a small portion to see if it does any damage. Apply controls in the early morning or evening, and only when the air is still. Cover a plant thoroughly, including the undersides of leaves. If your local merchants don't stock a control you wish to buy, all those listed here can be ordered from mail-order nurseries or garden supply companies.

	Name	Type	Target Pests or Diseases	Form	Shelf Life	
PESTICIDES	*Bacillus thuringiensis* (Bt)	Biological insect control; infectious bacteria	Cabbage loopers, cabbageworms, tomato hornworms, and other leaf-eating caterpillars; Colorado potato beetle larvae	Dust; wettable powder; liquid concentrate	Dry form: 2-4 years; liquid concentrate: 2-3 years	
	Beneficial nematodes	Biological insect control; roundworms found naturally in soil	Soil-dwelling pests such as borers, cutworms, cucumber beetle larvae, root maggots, wireworms, white grubs	Sold in semidormant state on sponges, mixed with gel, or in granules. Products are mixed with water before applying.	Up to 2 months in refrigerator; dehydrated forms up to 6 months at room temperature, longer if refrigerated.	
	Diatomaceous earth (DE)	Abrasive, desiccating pesticide; finely ground fossilized marine algae	Most soft-bodied insects and pests such as aphids, caterpillars, cabbage root flies, corn borers, leafhoppers, mites, pill bugs, slugs, snails, sowbugs, thrips	Dust; can be mixed with water to make a spray.	Lasts indefinitely if kept dry.	
	Horticultural oil	Contact insecticide and miticide; ultrafine petroleum	Most pest eggs, larvae, and soft-bodied adults such as aphids, leafhoppers, leaf miners, mealybugs, mites, scales, thrips, whiteflies	Liquid concentrate	Indefinite	
	Insecticidal soap	Contact insecticide	Most effective against soft-bodied and sucking insects such as aphids, mites, leafhoppers, mealybugs, scales, spider mites, thrips, whiteflies	Liquid concentrate; ready-to-use spray	Up to 5 years. Keep tightly sealed.	
	Neem (azadirachtin)	Botanical broad-spectrum insecticide and repellent derived from neem tree	Aphids, beetles (cucumber, flea, Japanese, Mexican bean, potato), corn ear worms, leaf miners, loopers, mealybugs, spider mites, tomato hornworms, thrips, whiteflies. Kills juveniles; repels adults.	Liquid concentrate	Minimum of 18 months	
	Pyrethrum (pyrethrins)	Botanical contact insecticide containing pyrethrin compounds derived from the pyrethrum daisy	Aphids, beetles (asparagus, Colorado potato, cucumber, flea, Japanese, Mexican bean), caterpillars (cabbage loopers, corn ear worms, European corn borers, fall armyworms), leafhoppers, mites, stink bugs, tarnished plant bugs, thrips, whiteflies	Dust; liquid concentrate; ready-to-use spray	Dust: up to 1 year. Liquid concentrate and spray: 1-3 years	
	Repellents, garlic and hot pepper	Botanical insect and animal repellents	Aphids, cabbage loopers, leafhoppers, squash bugs, whiteflies; birds, cats, deer, dogs, rabbits	Both available as liquid concentrate	2 years	
	Rotenone	Botanical broad-spectrum contact and stomach-poison insecticide; derived from South American cube plant	Aphids, beetles (asparagus, Colorado potato, cucumber, flea, Japanese, Mexican bean), cabbage loopers, corn ear worms, European corn borers, leafhoppers, mites, spider mites, stink bugs, thrips, whiteflies	Dust; wettable powder; liquid concentrate, usually with pyrethrin	Dust: 2-3 years; liquid: 3 years or more	
	Sabadilla	Botanical broad-spectrum contact insecticide; derived from a South American lily	Aphids, armyworms, beetles (Colorado potato, cucumber, flea, Mexican bean), cabbage loopers, caterpillars, diamondback moth larvae, European corn borers, grasshoppers, leafhoppers, squash bugs, stink bugs, thrips	Dust; wettable powder	5 years or more	
FUNGICIDES	Copper	Mineral fungicide and surface protectant	Anthracnose, bacterial leaf spot, black rot, blights, downy mildews, leaf spot, powdery mildews, rusts, scabs	Dust; wettable powder; liquid concentrate	Up to 5 years	
	Lime sulfur	Mineral fungicide, insecticide	Anthracnose, brown rot, leaf spot, powdery mildews, rusts, scabs	Liquid concentrate	3-5 years. Keep from freezing.	
	Sulfur, elemental sulfur	Mineral fungicide, surface protectant, miticide	Black spot, botrytis molds, brown rot, leaf spot, powdery mildews, rusts, scabs	Dust; wettable powder; liquid concentrate; ready-to-use spray	Dust and powder: indefinite; concentrate and spray: 3 years	

472

Toxicity	When & How Often to Apply	How Soon Effective	Effective Period/ Biodegradability	Time Required Between Last Use & Harvest	Comments & Precautions
Low. Harmless to mammals, fish, and nontarget insects.	Spring and summer, when pest is actively feeding. Reapply every 10-14 days if necessary and after rain.	Feeding stops within 1 hour of ingesting; pest dies in 1-3 days.	Short. Ineffective if ingested more than 48 hours after application.	No restrictions	Different strains of Bt are effective against different pests, so read label carefully. Avoid inhaling when applying, because of possible allergic reaction.
Nontoxic	When soil is very moist and soil temperature is over 60°F. Single application may be effective up to 1 year.	Nematodes begin feeding on pests within 24-48 hours.	Feeding continues until food source is exhausted.	No restrictions	Follow storage and mixing directions very carefully. Spray or pour directly onto moist soil in the root zone of affected plants. Nematodes need constantly moist soil to survive.
Nontoxic to humans, mammals, birds, and earthworms; harmful to beneficial insects and bees.	When plants are still wet from dew, rain, or watering; reapply after every watering, rainfall, or heavy dew.	Within 48 hours	Works as long as it remains dry.	No restrictions	Eye and lung irritant; avoid breathing dust, and wear mask and goggles. Use only natural DE, not pool-filter grade, which is much more toxic.
Very low for mammals; beneficials in larval stage may be harmed.	Use weekly in spring and summer when pests or eggs are present and temperature is between 40° and 85°F.	Kills newly hatched insects within a day; smothers eggs to prevent hatching.	Continues working until it dries.	1 month	Use only the lighter-grade horticultural oils for vegetable crops and brambles. The heavier-grade dormant oils are for use on dormant plants only and will burn vegetable crops.
Virtually nontoxic to humans, mammals, and birds; larvae of beneficials may be affected, but not adults.	Every 7-10 days when pest is present. Spray three times at 2-day intervals for severe aphid or mealybug infestation.	Immediately on contact	Breaks down quickly; effective only while still moist.	No restrictions	Works only when wet spray contacts insect. Do not apply in direct sun or when the temperature is above 85°F. To avoid damage to plants, do not use at concentrations higher than recommended. Not effective if mixed with hard water.
Active ingredient very low, but stabilizers make it harmful if swallowed. May affect beneficials in juvenile stages.	Every 7-10 days when pest larvae are present, or as needed to repel adults.	Death occurs in 3-14 days.	Lasts up to 7 days; breaks down rapidly in sunlight.	No restrictions	Lung, skin, and eye irritant
Highly toxic to fish, aquatic insects, and some beneficials. Moderately toxic to mammals, birds, and bees.	When pest is present. Can be repeated at 3- to 4-day intervals.	Within 2 hours of direct contact	Broken down within 1 day by sunlight, air, moisture, and heat.	No restrictions	A pest is killed only when hit directly. If it receives an inadequate dose, it may appear dead at first, then revive. Do not confuse natural pyrethrins with the synthetic compounds called pyrethroids.
Garlic oil has low toxicity; hot pepper is an extreme eye and skin irritant.	Before pests begin feeding. Apply garlic twice each season. Reapply pepper spray after rain or overhead watering.	Immediate	Both break down rapidly.	Garlic: 1 day. Hot pepper: No interval needed, since spray should never be applied to edible portion of crops.	These sprays may kill some pests, but their main effect is to repel them and deter them from feeding. Protect eyes while mixing and using hot pepper spray.
Very toxic to fish, aquatic insects, birds, beneficial insects; moderately toxic to humans, mammals.	When pest populations cause unacceptable damage. Reapply in 7 days if necessary.	Pests quickly stop feeding and die within several hours to a few days.	Breaks down in 2-7 days.	5-7 days unless label recommends otherwise	Avoid using near ponds, streams, or wherever runoff may contaminate bodies of water. Avoid inhaling.
Moderately toxic to humans, mammals, bees.	When pest populations are excessive or as soon as eggs hatch, at 5- to 7-day intervals and after rain or overhead watering.	Pest may be killed immediately or be paralyzed for several days before dying.	Breaks down in 2 days when exposed to sunlight and air.	1 day	Sneezing is sign of overexposure to skin or lungs. Wear mask, goggles, and protective clothing. Sale and use not permitted in some states.
Moderately toxic to humans and mammals; little risk to insects.	Before disease appears; apply every 7-10 days.	Regular treatments needed to prevent disease or slow spread of existing disease.	Does not degrade; can build up in soil, causing toxicity to plants.	1 day	Liquid concentrate may settle; shake well. Spray early on dry, sunny day. Copper hydroxide will burn leaves in damp weather and may leave visible residue. Wash produce well before eating.
Very high to fish. Caustic and corrosive.	Once a year in early spring while plants are dormant is usually sufficient. If needed, reapply in fall as a preventive.	Immediate; lasts several weeks.	2 or more weeks	Not applicable; used before or after growing season.	Use only in cold weather on dormant raspberries, blackberries, and other bramble fruits. May burn some varieties. Wait 2-3 weeks after using oil spray to apply lime sulfur.
Low toxicity for humans, mammals. May be harmful to bees.	Early in spring and as needed for protection; when rain is forecast, to protect against waterborne disease spores.	Use as preventive or to slow spread of existing disease.	Does not break down; naturally present in soil and required by plants for normal growth.	1 day	Do not use on squash family. Repeated applications may acidify soil. Do not apply when temperature is over 85°F. Lung, eye, and skin irritant. Corrosive; wash metal sprayer after each use. Never use within a month of applying horticultural oil.

CHAPTER THIRTEEN

The Portable Kitchen Garden

Container-grown vegetables, fruits, and herbs can transform even the smallest space into a garden. You can locate the garden wherever the plants will thrive and look their best, and rearrange or move it as you wish. Potted herbs are especially versatile: Depending on the season, you can set them inside on a window sill or outside on a porch or patio.

With a bit of pampering, most herbs and many small vegetables and fruits adapt well to containers. And—in addition to providing food for the table—some offer delicious fragrances, while others display handsome foliage or colorful fruit or flowers. In the California patio garden shown at left, pots of pineapple mint, sage, and cilantro, backed by bright pink roses, are a feast for the eyes as well as the palate.

On the following pages, you will learn the basics of designing and caring for portable kitchen gardens, from choosing plants and containers to feeding, watering, and pruning the plants once they are established.

Vegetable Gardening in Containers

A colorful array of containers filled with red and green varieties of lettuce (foreground), silvery leaved sage, a large tomato plant with ripening fruit, and rich red peppers spills down the steps of a Los Altos, California, terrace. Many favorite vegetables are now available in dwarf varieties that grow well in containers.

If your only space or sunny spot is on a patio or deck, containers can serve as a garden for your vegetables. Many vegetables—especially dwarf varieties—will grow in boxes, tubs, or other planters, although they will require more attention than plants in the ground. Because the soil in containers dries out quickly, you'll need to water these plants regularly. The best watering setup is a drip-irrigation system with spaghetti lines to each pot and a timer to regulate the water flow. This system works especially well if you have lots of containers, if you plan to be away for several days at a stretch, or if you are growing vegetables that are extremely sensitive to moisture variation, such as cauliflower.

Every time you water container-grown plants, soil nutrients leach out, so plan to fertilize frequently. Start the plants off in a good-quality potting mix and supplement it on a weekly basis with fish emulsion, liquid seaweed, or other organic fertilizers.

The volume or depth of soil needed for the roots of a plant determines the size of the container required. For example, deep-rooted vegetables like leeks or beets need a container the size of a whiskey barrel to provide enough depth for healthy growth. By contrast, plants with shallow roots, such as peppers, green onions, and bok choy, do well in 8- to 12-inch pots. Window boxes make suitable containers for leafy vegetables, in-

cluding spinach, leaf lettuce, mustard greens, and arugula. You can plant a single plant type or a mixture of vegetables in one container, if you like; be sure to check the spacing and cultural requirements of the different plants you are considering using, and then plant your containers accordingly.

If you have a sunny spot on a porch, place a vining vegetable in a pot there. Tie one end of a string to the pot and the other to the roof or the eaves, and train the plant up the string. Pole beans, vining tomatoes, vining cucumbers, and cantaloupes are good choices for this treatment. 'Super Sweet 100' tomato plants, which bear bright red cherrylike fruit, and the 'Yellow Pear' variety, with its golden pear-shaped crop, are particularly decorative.

Minimum Container Sizes for Compact Gardening

Artichoke: whiskey barrel

Arugula: window box

Beets: whiskey barrel

Bok choy: 8" pot

Broccoli: 12"-18" pot

Brussels sprouts: whiskey barrel

Cabbage: 12"-18" pot
green-leaved: 'Early Jersey Wakefield', 'Stonehead'
red-leaved: 'Ruby Ball'

Carrots: 12"-18" pot 'Baby Spike', 'Babette', 'Little Finger', 'Minicor', 'Marmet', 'Planet', 'Thumbelina'

Cauliflower: 12"-18" pot

Chard: 12"-18" pot 'Charlotte', 'Perpetual Spinach'

Cucumber, bush: 12"-18" pot

vining: whiskey barrel, trained up string

Eggplant: 12"-18" pot

Endive/Escarole: 12"-18" pot

Garlic: 12"-18" pot

Kale: 12"-18" pot

Kohlrabi: 12"-18" pot

Leeks: whiskey barrel 'King Richard'

Lettuce, leaf: window box or 12"-18" pot

Melons: whiskey barrel *muskmelon:* 'Sweet Bush' *watermelon:* 'Bush Baby II' *cantaloupes:* trained up string

Mustard greens: window box

Onions, green: 8" pot

Peppers: 8"-12" pot

Radishes: 12" pot

Rhubarb: whiskey barrel

Shallots: 8"-12" pot

Spinach: window box

Squash, summer: whiskey barrel

Squash, winter: whiskey barrel *acorn:* 'Bush Table' *butternut:* 'Butterbush'

Strawberries, alpine: 8" pot

Tomatillo: 12" pot

Tomato, determinate varieties: 18" pot *indeterminate (vining)* varieties to train up string: 'Super Sweet 100', 'Yellow Pear', 'Gardener's Delight' 8"-12" pot: 'Florida Basket', 'Tiny Tim', 'Toy Boy'

Turnips: 12"-18" pot 'Tokyo Cross'

Container-grown tomatoes, peppers, parsley, and basil flourish among pots of flowering alyssum, lobelia, marigolds, and periwinkle on a backyard patio. Though overflowing, the small pots provide enough soil for these shallow-rooted plants to thrive.

477

Container Gardening with Herbs

Planting herbs in pots allows you to grow a garden wherever and whenever you choose. If your in-ground growing space is small, containers can expand it by incorporating surrounding areas—such as a walkway or a set of stairs—into your overall scheme. And if you have a roomy garden, you can still use container-grown herbs as accents and fillers or for indoor enjoyment.

Whether you allow them to develop their natural form or train them as espaliers or topiaries (*pages 489-491*), herbs in containers are excellent accents in a garden. A pair of large containers filled with tall herbs can add a dramatic touch at the entrance to a garden path, for example. And matching topiaries can be set up to march in a rhythmic geometric pattern across a bare wall or along a stockade fence.

A Portable Visual Feast

The simplest way to create a lovely display of container-grown herbs is to cluster together small pots holding different plants. A grouping of culinary herbs, for instance, can be situated right outside your kitchen door. A more ambitious design technique is to plant a large container with a variety of complementary herbs to form what is essentially a movable garden. You can take the container to any part of the property or, if it suits you, take it into your home or greenhouse. Using a dolly to transport your pots makes even heavy concrete containers portable.

Inside, the kitchen is a logical setting for a grouping of culinary herbs. In cold climates you can grow long-lived tender herbs such as sweet bay laurel and lemon grass outdoors in pots dur-

A winter garden provides a palette of fresh tastes for the Virginia cook who tends these herbs (right). At far left are slim-leaved garlic chives and thyme. Two kinds of oregano crown the strawberry pot at center, and a small variegated sage is tucked in its side pocket. A pot of catnip and a basket with curly parsley and dwarf basil complete the garden.

At the edge of a brick patio (below), culinary plantings of thyme, oregano, fennel, sage, tarragon, and mint share space with ornamental daisies, pinks, heliotrope, and alyssum in a trio of containers.

Culinary herbs are kept close at hand on a New Jersey deck (above) and outside a Washington State kitchen door (below). The rustic planter filled with thyme and the clay pots containing mint, oregano, and other herbs also create different design effects.

ing the summer months and move them indoors when temperatures drop and nights grow cold.

Containers also allow you to bring herbs that are at the peak of their season and are looking their best into prominent spots in the garden for viewing. For example, if you want to dress up a shady spot for a party, you can move containers planted with sun-loving herbs, display them there for the few hours they are needed, and then whisk them back to their original location.

Selecting Plants for Containers

Choosing different herbs to mix in a container can be as much of a creative challenge as designing a garden bed or border. Keep in mind the growth habits of the plants as well as which ones look good together. As a starting point, perennials are logical companions for other perennials, annuals for other annuals. For best results, combine plants with similar needs. Mediterranean herbs such as sage, lavender, and rosemary require well-drained soil and can tolerate a degree of drought. Don't mix them with plants like parsley, peppers, or ginger, which prefer rich, moist conditions.

Also consider the mature shape and size of each herb so the finished effect will show off all of the plants to best advantage. Be careful not to set a slow-growing or naturally small plant next to one that will quickly envelop its smaller companion in foliage. For example, marjoram, nasturtium, French tarragon, and parsley tend to get choked out by vigorous plants such as lemon verbena and lovage, which reach heights of 6 feet or more if allowed to grow unchecked.

Most herbs need a minimum of 6 hours of sunlight to flourish. When you plan your container garden, make sure sun-loving plants aren't shaded by taller neighbors. One likely trio for a sunny site would feature sweet basil, lemon basil, and sweet marjoram. Herbs that tolerate some shade include angelica, nasturtium, lovage, mint, and tarragon. Chervil, coriander, and parsley all enjoy a cool, moist environment.

Designing Plant Combinations

As you work out plant combinations based on similar growing requirements, use your imagination to create displays of herbs that are beautiful as well as functional.

Plant herbs with trailing habits on the edges of pots, where they can drape over the sides. Among your choices might be silver or golden lemon thyme, marjoram, and prostrate rosemary. To cover bare soil in a container planted with a tall plant or a standard, use low-growing herbs such as creeping thyme or Roman chamomile *(Chamaemelum nobile)*.

Pairings for Color and Texture

Consider planting a container with a color theme, combining, for example, the variegated pink, green, and cream foliage of tricolor sage with pink-flowering chives. Tricolor sage would also look stunning against the deep purple foliage of purple basil. For a golden motif, you might choose gold-leaved forms of sage (*Salvia officinalis* 'Icterina'), marjoram (*Origanum vulgare* 'Aureum'), and thyme (*Thymus* x *citriodorus* 'Aureus'). Herbs with gray or silver foliage include silver thyme and lamb's ears. For a large container, consider silver horehound *(Marrubium incanum)*, which can grow 2 feet or more in height.

To create a look that is subtle but no less striking, combine herbs that have contrasting leaf textures. For example, allow the large leaves of purple sage (*Salvia officinalis* 'Purpurea') to intermingle with delicate thyme foliage.

Perfuming the Air with Geraniums

If you're looking for kitchen herbs that are not only attractive but also highly aromatic, scented geraniums are the perfect choice.

Scented geraniums, tender perennials native to Africa's Cape of Good Hope, were introduced in England around 1795. Growers soon found that the plants would thrive indoors in winter if given ample light. The geraniums were an instant success because of their diverse, fascinating leaf forms—the herb mutates readily, and bee-crossed hybrids are common—and distinctive scents.

Today, although nursery catalogs may advertise scents as diverse as clove, apricot, and coconut, most experts agree that the possibilities are limited to variations of lemon, mixed citrus (combining lemon, lime, and orange), mint, rose, rose-lemon, apple, pepper, and a pungent odor—more or less pleasant, depending on the cultivar—that can only be described as spicy.

Fragrant geraniums boast leaf forms to satisfy just about any gardener. Size varies from the crinkly ½-inch-wide leaves of lemon-scented *Pelargonium crispum* 'Minor' to the pungent *P. hispidum*, with leaves that measure 4 to 5 inches across. Leaf shapes range from the ruffled, round foliage of apple geranium *(P. odoratissimum)* to the deeply indented leaves of rose geranium *(P. graveolens)*. Leaves come in many shades of green, some with a light brush of velvet, as well as variegated mixtures of green with cream, white, brown, and even maroon.

The most useful varieties of scented geranium for cooking are those with citrus-, rose-, or mint-scented foliage; use the fresh leaves in teas or as a flavoring for jam, baked goods, syrup, or vinegar. The resinous leaves of other varieties may be used to flavor pâté and sausage.

Pelargonium quercifolium 'Fair Ellen' (oak-leaved geranium)

Comely clay pots on a Virginia kitchen window sill keep dill (left), parsley, lemon balm, purple basil, sage, thyme, and rosemary (far right) convenient for flavoring a winter dinner. A sunny south-facing window is ideal for growing them; just remember to rotate the pots weekly so the herbs will grow evenly.

Herbs with Good Taste

If you'd like to make flavor your theme, create a lemon-scented garden in a large container. Plant lemon-scented gum *(Eucalyptus citriodora)* at the center, then surround it with a selection of edible herbs such as lemon grass *(Cymbopogon citratus),* golden lemon thyme *(Thymus x citriodorus* 'Aureus'), lemon basil *(Ocimum basilicum* 'Citriodorum'), and lemon-scented geraniums *(Pelargonium crispum* 'Prince Rupert' and *P. c.* 'Mabel Grey').

Many herbs are delicious brewed as tea, and some are said to have health-giving properties as well. To add to your pleasure, grow a tea garden in containers planted with bee balm, chamomile, mint (peppermint, apple mint, and orange mint have distinctive flavors), lemon balm, and lemon verbena.

Herbs to Start from Seed Indoors

Allium schoenoprasum
(chives)
Allium tuberosum
(Chinese or garlic chives)
Anthriscus cerefolium
(chervil)
Capsicum
(pepper)
Lavandula
(lavender)

Melissa officinalis
(lemon balm)
Nepeta cataria
(catnip)
Ocimum basilicum cultivars
(basil)
Origanum majorana
(sweet marjoram)

Melissa officinalis (lemon balm)

Enjoying Rosemary Year Round

Pine-scented rosemary lives for years if it is planted in gardens as temperate as those of its native Mediterranean. In summer, it will flourish in any sunny garden in well-drained soil if given a modicum of water. Though most rosemaries succumb to prolonged freezes, some varieties such as *Rosmarinus officinalis* 'Arp', 'Hill Hardy', 'Salem', 'Dutch Mill', and 'White Flowered' can survive winter temperatures as low as -10° F.

Indoors, potted rosemary does best in a cool, sunny spot. Dry indoor heat in winter will cause the plant to dry out and die. Rosemary plants are under the greatest stress in late January, when the stronger sun begins to draw moisture out of plants more quickly. But too much moisture in the air can promote powdery mildew.

To give your rosemary a fighting chance under such trying conditions, begin by potting the plant in a light growing medium of peat moss mixed with perlite and vermiculite. Then water your plant only when the mix is dried out—the pot will feel light, and the mix will have turned a pale brown; make sure to let all the excess water drain out. Brown leaves at the plant's base are a sign that your rosemary has been overwatered, whereas wilted terminal shoots indicate a thirsty plant.

As the plant grows, pinch off long shoots and branches to use in cooking and to promote bushiness. Flowers in lavender-blue, pink, or white will appear from winter through spring. Among the earliest bloomers are 'Beneden Blue' and 'Tuscan Blue', flowering in late winter; prostrate rosemary can bloom almost continually if it is given enough light.

Root-bound plants should be transplanted in spring to a slightly larger pot; too large a pot prevents the plant from using up the moisture in the soil and encourages rot. Fertilize your plant once every 2 weeks during the growing season with a balanced fertilizer. Stop fertilizing in autumn, a few weeks before you bring the plant indoors.

Annual Herbs in Winter

Many annuals that are valued for seasoning food germinate quickly from seed and are thus well suited for growing indoors *(list, opposite)*. Although the plants won't last as long as they would outdoors—about 6 weeks is the maximum life span, even under the best conditions—you will be able to harvest a steady supply of fresh herbs throughout the winter by making three or four successive sowings, spaced about 3 weeks apart. That way, new plants will be mature enough to use at about the time you're ready to throw the old ones away.

A top-quality, homemade soilless potting mix *(recipe, page 460)* should contain enough nutrients to satisfy the plants. If you want to supplement the mix, use an organic houseplant fertilizer, applying it at only half the recommended rate. A fertilizer with a low nutrient analysis of 3-6-4 or 5-5-5 will suffice; giving the plants more fertilizer than that may cause them to produce excess foliage and lose flavor.

Once the plants sprout, they will need the same light conditions as would any herb grown indoors. (For instructions on growing herbs from seed, see pages 459-460.)

Potting and Caring for Herbs

Once you have decided on which herbs to grow, your next step is to choose the containers in which to grow them. Almost any container will do as long as it is clean and has one or more holes in the bottom for ample drainage. However, there are some differences worth considering between the two main container types, plastic and clay.

Plastic pots hold moisture well, but plants in them must be monitored carefully—especially if they are in the shade—to make sure the soil doesn't stay too wet. By contrast, clay containers are porous, providing plants with good air circulation and drainage. For just these reasons, however, plants in clay pots need to be watered frequently, especially in hot weather, so that the soil doesn't dry out.

Cleaning and Reusing Clay Pots

Before using an old clay pot for a new plant, first check the pot for chips or cracks that might allow moisture to seep away. Then give the pot a good cleaning. To remove algae and fungi as well as any disease that may be lurking, scour the pot under cold running water with a nylon scrubbing pad, then soak it for several hours in a solution of 1 part bleach to 5 parts water. Rinse the pot thoroughly. If you won't be using the container right away, let it dry completely before storing it.

Even such a thorough cleaning may not remove the white salts—residue from alkaline water—that sometimes streak clay pots. Soak these pots in undiluted vinegar (buy it in gallon jugs to save money) for a day or two. Rinse them under cold water and scrub with a nylon pad. If salt streaks persist, repeat the process, using fresh vinegar. Gardeners with time to spare can set the salt-streaked containers outside; rain will leave them fresh and clean within a few months.

The square tiles used to line the inside of a chimney are imaginatively employed as containers—planted with parsley, purple basil, peppers, marigolds, and scented geraniums—in this Georgia garden. Other possibilities for unusual containers include decorative watering cans, discarded wheelbarrows, large shells such as those of giant clams or conchs, and weather-beaten, hollowed-out logs.

Ideal Potting Soil Mixtures

Soil collected directly from the garden should not be used in containers. In most cases it is too heavy, and it often harbors harmful insects and diseases. Soilless, commercially packed container mixes, on the other hand, tend to be so light that fast-growing roots soon make herbs potbound. These mixes also dry out very quickly.

To give a packaged potting mix more substance, blend it with sterilized compost (2 parts potting mix to 1 part compost).

Or, if you have access to top-quality loam soil from a mulch or landscape company, you can prepare a container mix by blending 1 part loam soil and 1 part soilless potting medium, such as a peat/perlite mix. Moisten with fish emulsion diluted at the rate of ¼ cup per gallon of water.

TIPS FROM THE PROS
Tricks to Retain Moisture in Containers

During the hot months of summer, container-grown plants dry out quickly and may need watering once—even twice—a day. Here are some ways to escape the tyranny of tending pots:

• Choose a container that retains moisture. The materials with the lowest evaporation rate are plastic, fiberglass, metal, and glazed ceramic, often called terra cotta. The most porous materials are clay (unglazed ceramic), wood, and concrete. Generally, plants in porous pots need watering three times more often than those in plastic or metal containers.

• Pick white containers, which tend to reflect heat, thus somewhat reducing the rate of evaporation. Dark-colored pots, on the other hand, absorb heat, causing the soil to dry out faster.

• Find a pot that is slightly larger than the plant requires. The extra soil will hold more moisture.

• Blend soil polymers—available at most garden centers—into your container mix to aid moisture retention.

• Place decorative bark or pebbles on top of the soil to slow surface evaporation. Or cover the soil with an organic mulch of compost or grass clippings and top with the bark or pebbles.

• Group containers together to shade and humidify each other. Place the small pots, which are likely to dry out first, in the center of the cluster.

• Shelter pots from the wind, which can dry out plants.

• Install an automatic irrigation system with a line running to each container. The initial effort may seem great, but so will the rewards.

The Well-Watered Strawberry Pot

To obtain even moisture throughout a large strawberry pot with six or more pockets, turn PVC (polyvinyl chloride) pipe into a watering tube. Choose pipe 2 to 4 inches in diameter and 4 inches less in length than the pot's height. Place the pipe upright in the pot and mark the location of each pocket on the pipe. This ensures that water will reach the roots of every plant directly. Drill ½-inch holes at those marks. Cover the bottom of the pipe with a square of plastic mesh and secure it by wrapping wire around the pipe. Fill the pipe with pebbles, tamping them as you go, then cap the top of the pipe with mesh. Next, put a mesh square over the pot's drainage hole, and center the pipe on the hole. Align the drilled holes with the pockets. Add soil to the pot to the level of the first pockets.

With a chopstick or screwdriver, gently push the first plant's rootball into the lowest pocket, roots pointed down. Keep the crown of the plant level with the lip of the pocket to allow for settling; add more soil to the level of the next pocket. Repeat until all the pockets are full and soil reaches to within 1 inch of the rim. Then center a plant over the pipe and fill in the rest of the pot with soil.

Set the container in a pan of water to soak up moisture. Then water the top and pockets with a fine spray.

Planting the Containers

Before you plant a new clay pot, soak it in water overnight. Then, for any type of container, cover the drainage hole with a piece of mesh screen, a large pebble, or a pottery shard. Fill the bottom of the container with potting medium and position the plant in the pot so that the soil level will be below the pot's rim. Then fill the pot with soil and tamp firmly to remove air pockets. Finally, water thoroughly.

If you are replanting a container of mixed herbs in the spring, first remove any perennials so you can work the soil without interference. Replenish the potting mix by adding a 1-inch layer of well-rotted chicken manure; mix it in thoroughly, aerating the soil at the same time. Replant the perennials and add new annual herbs.

Feeding Hungry Container-Grown Herbs

Herbs planted in the ground typically have a more intense flavor and a more pungent aroma if they are fertilized with a light hand. By contrast, those planted in containers require extra nourishment. Frequent watering leaches nutrients from the soil, and the problem is compounded when several plants are grown in one pot and they are all competing for food.

During the growing season, feed herbs in containers every 2 weeks with an organic fertilizer that is high in nitrogen; seaweed and fish emulsion are two good choices. Follow the directions on the package to measure out and dilute the fertilizer. At the end of summer, cut back on the feeding, and stop altogether in late fall.

Grooming Potted Herbs

Plants will grow bushier and be more attractive if stem tips are pinched off regularly to encourage more branching. In the case of container-grown herbs, this care is especially important to

Herbs for Strawberry Pots

ON TOP

Lavandula dentata
(French lavender)
Lavandula stoechas
(Spanish lavender)
Pelargonium graveolens
(rose geranium)
Petroselinum crispum
(parsley)
Salvia officinalis 'Nana'
(dwarf sage)
Tropaeolum minus
(dwarf nasturtium)

IN POCKETS

Allium schoenoprasum
(chives)
Mentha requienii
(Corsican mint)

Ocimum basilicum 'Minimum'
(bush basil)
Origanum majorana
(sweet marjoram)
Pelargonium odoratissimum
(apple geranium)
Petroselinum crispum
(parsley)
Thymus caespititius
(tufted thyme)
Thymus x citriodorus
(lemon thyme)
Thymus x citriodorus 'Silver Queen'
(silver lemon thyme)
Thymus herba-barona
(caraway thyme)
Thymus praecox ssp. ***arcticus***
(creeping thyme)
Viola tricolor
(Johnny-jump-up)

control plants like sage and lemon verbena that tend to grow large and sprawl. Even less vigorous herbs benefit from being trimmed when they share a container.

Make it a habit to carry clippers with you when you check on your container-grown herbs, and take a few moments to snip and shape the plants. Use the harvested pieces for the evening meal, for potpourri, or in flower arrangements.

Repotting Root-Bound Perennials

Over time, perennial herbs outgrow their containers. If roots protrude from the bottom of the pot, or if you notice that water doesn't soak through the soil properly, the plant has become rootbound and needs to be repotted. If possible, do the job in spring, when the plant is ready to begin a growth spurt. The least desirable time to repot is late autumn or winter, when the plant is dormant and will be slow to generate new roots.

Increase the container size gradually rather than in big jumps. Choose a pot 2 inches larger in diameter than the old one, and prepare it for planting by covering the drainage hole and spreading a layer of container mix in the bottom.

Remove your plant from its old pot and gently loosen the roots. Position it so it will sit at the same level in the pot as before. Fill in the gaps with soil, and water well.

Some herbs—tender perennials, trees, and shrubs such as myrtle or bay laurel—can live in a container for years. However, you'll need to refresh and replenish the soil annually. This can be as simple as carefully removing the top layer and replacing it with fresh potting mix enriched with a slow-release fertilizer. However, some experts recommend lifting the plant out of its pot and carefully scraping soil from the sides and bottom of the rootball as well, then replenishing with fresh soil mix as you replant the herb.

For a severely root-bound plant, lift the herb from the pot, slice off the outer layer of roots, and loosen the rootball before replacing the plant in its original container. Add fresh potting mix to fill the extra space, then trim back the foliage to compensate for the loss of roots.

Winter Care for Outdoor Containers

In the northern climate zones, even hardy herbs will need winter protection if they are grown

These long wooden planters take little space yet drape this Maryland deck with a lush curtain of herbs. The planters brim with (from left) lovage, redmint (Mentha x gracilis), madonna lily, nasturtium, lavender, lemon balm, Jerusalem sage, rose-lemon-scented geranium, lemon-scented geranium, and comfrey. Swags of wild yam (Dioscorea bulbifera) festoon the railing.

above ground. If you prefer to overwinter your hardy perennials outdoors, one option is to replant them in the ground in autumn or to bury the containers so that the roots are better insulated. Alternatively, you can cluster the pots together in a sheltered spot away from the wind and pile mulch around them. Otherwise, not only your plants but also your containers will be at the mercy of the vagaries of winter: Unglazed clay pots, for example, have a tendency to crack and flake when they freeze and thaw.

If you want to bring your container-grown herbs indoors, start getting them ready in early autumn. Cut back the plants by about half their new growth, trim back the roots if the plant is rootbound, and repot with fresh soil. Then move the plants to a sheltered area such as a patio or terrace to help them make the transition to their new environment. When the weather begins to turn cold, move the pots indoors.

You can also pot up tender perennials growing in the garden—rosemary, lemon verbena, lemon grass, and the like. If a plant is too large for the pot you want to use or the indoor space you have, trim the foliage back to a manageable size before you dig it up. Then, a few weeks before you put the plants into pots, trim the roots: Use a shovel to slice through the earth all around the rootball, cutting off the outer edge of the roots. This pruning will encourage the growth of new feeder roots that will help the plant cope with the transition indoors.

Overwintering Pots Indoors

Once indoors, your herbs will still need their 6 hours minimum of direct sunlight; a sunny, south-facing window is best. If you don't have a location with adequate natural light, purchase special "grow" lights or use ordinary fluorescents. (Incandescent lights give off too much heat.) Hang two to four light tubes 5 to 6 inches above the plants. If you mount the lights on chains, you can easily adjust the height as the plants grow. Ideally, the lights should be color-balanced to replicate natural light, but you can simulate the sun by pairing cool-white and warm-white tubes. Turn the lights on for 14 to 16 hours a day, which is the equivalent of 6 hours of sun.

The air inside your home during the winter is likely to be very dry and can take a toll on plants. Set each pot on top of pebbles in a water-filled tray or dish, making sure that the pot itself isn't sitting in the water; as the water evaporates, it will humidify the air. If the humidity level indoors drops below 40 percent, give the herbs a misting.

Because the plants are dormant during winter, you won't need to water as frequently as you would during the growing season. However, take care not to allow the soil to dry out completely.

Herbs for Hanging Baskets

Nepeta mussinii (catmint)	**Origanum majorana** (sweet marjoram)	(prostrate rosemary)
Ocimum basilicum 'Minimum' (bush basil)	**Origanum onites** (Greek oregano)	**Satureja spicigera** (creeping savory)
Ocimum basilicum 'Minimum Purpurascens' (purple bush basil)	**Petroselinum crispum var. crispum** (curly parsley)	**Thymus praecox** ssp. **arcticus** cultivars (creeping thyme)
	Rosmarinus officinalis 'Prostratus'	**Tropaeolum majus** (nasturtium)

Tropaeolum majus 'Double Gleam' (nasturtium)

Topiaries and Espaliers

Like trees and shrubs, dozens of sturdy herbs can be grown in marvelous shapes and forms using the techniques developed for producing topiaries and espaliers. The training process is creative and fun, and with fast-growing herbs you can enjoy the results of your efforts within months rather than several years.

There are many advantages to growing trained herbs in containers rather than in the ground. Since they are portable, you can move them to create special effects in different garden spots at different times, and any tender herbs can be taken indoors for the winter. In addition, most herbs have shorter lives than trees or shrubs. As older trained plants begin to decline, replacement plants can be trained behind the scenes and positioned in the garden when they are at their peak.

Tied Topiaries

Topiaries are simple to make; the process just involves bending supple new plant growth and tying it onto a wire frame. Shapes suitable for training plants include spirals, globes, hearts, teardrops, wreaths, and animals or birds with simple outlines. You can buy these wire forms or make your own using No. 8 or No. 9 gauge wire.

Tied topiaries make ideal tabletop decorations, but remember that most herbs require a lot of light (full sun for a minimum of 6 hours a day) and benefit from good air circulation. After use, carry them back outside as soon as possible.

Ornamental Standards

An easy topiary to create is the so-called standard, which doesn't require a wire frame. Resembling a stylized miniature tree, the simplest standard has one globe-like crown of foliage atop a single stem. The "poodle" variation has two or three balls of foliage growing on branches out of the straight, central stem at regular intervals.

Either type is easy to train *(pages 490-491)* and makes a striking garden accent. Put a pair of standards at the entrance to your home or garden for dramatic effect. If they are placed against a building, turn the pots regularly to ensure that all sides are exposed to the light. Or

consider featuring a standard topiary instead of a birdbath, statue, or sundial as the focal point in the center of a low-growing flower bed.

Standard topiaries tend to be top-heavy. You can provide a counterbalance by adding an attractive top dressing of pebbles to the soil in the container. (A top dressing will also help keep the soil moist.) Or try placing the pot inside a larger container and filling in the gap with pebbles. Just make sure the size of the outer container is in pleasing proportion to the plant.

Training a Tied Topiary

Using your topiary frame as a reference, plant one young herb for every leg of the frame. Place the frame in the pot with its legs next to the plants; remove any leaves that rub against the frame. Then gently bend the plants' stems to follow the wire. Taking care not to crush the leaves, tie the stems at about 1-inch intervals with ½-inch strips of nylon hose, cut horizontally. Continue to tie new growth until the frame is covered, and replace ties as they get too tight. When the plant becomes woody, it will keep its shape on its own and you can remove the ties. Prune regularly to accentuate the desired form, and pinch off the tip, or leader, of the central stem when it reaches the length you need.

Herbs Suitable for Training

AS STANDARDS

Aloysia triphylla
(lemon verbena)
Laurus nobilis
(bay laurel)
Lavandula dentata
(French lavender)
Lavandula* x *intermedia
(lavandin)
Lavandula stoechas
(Spanish lavender)
Myrtus communis
(myrtle)
Pelargonium crispum
(lemon geranium)
Pelargonium graveolens
(rose geranium)

***Rosmarinus officinalis* 'Arp', 'Tuscan Blue'**
(rosemary)
Salvia officinalis
(sage)
Thymus vulgaris
(upright form)
(thyme)

AS TIED TOPIARIES AND ESPALIERS

Myrtus communis
(myrtle)
Rosmarinus officinalis
(rosemary)

Rosmarinus officinalis (rosemary)

Decorative Espaliers

Because they are grown flat against a support, espaliered herbs make appealing decorations for a wall, fence, or trellis. Like a tied topiary, the plant is trained on a frame; the pattern can be casual and free-form or symmetrical and formal. Among the classic designs are the fan pattern known as palmette oblique, and the cordon, in which the plant is trained into several tiers of parallel horizontal rows. Other popular patterns include the candelabra, diamond, V-shape, U-shape, and triangle.

Pruning Trained Herbs

Some gardeners prune their trained herbal topiaries and standards every day—using nail scissors—to ensure absolutely perfect specimens with no leaf or branch out of place. Such commitment is hardly essential, although these plants do require frequent grooming. Anytime you notice branches growing long enough to distort the desired shape of the topiary, get out your scissors or clippers and do some trimming.

Don't shear plants, or you'll end up with ugly, blunt edges and maimed leaves. Instead, trim back each branchlet to a leaf node, cutting at a 45° angle just above a bud or node. Every time you cut back a branch to a bud, two new shoots will develop, eventually creating a beautiful, bushy plant.

In addition to maintaining a standard's shape, you must periodically clean out the inside of the foliage globe. Remove dead twigs and thin the crown so that light and air can penetrate.

New Pots for Topiary

To keep your topiary's root system from outgrowing its container, repot it annually—preferably in autumn or spring, when weather conditions are optimum for new root growth. Remove the plant from the container and gently loosen the rootball, shaking away the loose soil. Trim back any extra-long roots. If the rootball has grown very tight, cut off the outer edge of the roots, on the sides and the bottom, with scissors or a knife, reducing the rootball by about one-third. Use fresh soil to replant the herb in the same pot.

Water repotted herbs immediately. You can water from the top as usual, but you should also set the pot in a pan of water so it can draw up moisture from the bottom. That way, any loose soil around the roots will settle, preventing air pockets.

How to Train a Standard Topiary

Herbs amenable to training as standards have central stems that grow straight up until the plant reaches its full height. However, pinching off the tip, or leader, at any time encourages lateral buds along the stem to sprout branches and form a crown.

To create a standard, find a young plant with a stem that has never been pinched. Start in early spring so that the plant has a long season of favorable weather to grow tall and strong.

Before pinching the stem tip, consider how you want the topiary to look. The final height should be in proportion to the size of the pot as well as the crown.

1. Insert an 8- to 10-inch-long stake next to the plant in the pot. Remove side shoots along the plant's stem, but leave the primary leaves in place; remove any leaves that rub against the stake. Tie the stem to the stake at 1- to 1½-inch intervals, taking care not to damage the stem. As the plant grows, continue to tie the stem to the stake; when the plant outgrows the stake, replace it with a taller one. Also replace ties that have tightened as the stem has grown.

2. As the plant approaches the desired height, pinch off the tip of the central stem. Allow the side branches near the top of the plant to continue growing; when they are about 4 inches long, pinch each of these just above a node (right) to encourage vigorous growth. Continue pinching as needed to keep the head of the plant bushy and well branched.

*Two rosemary stand-
ards flank a tiered ivy
topiary in this formal
planting. Perfect as fo-
cal points or standing
sentry at the entrance
to a home or garden,
standards add a regal
air to a setting. The up-
right form of rosemary
is particularly suited to
growing as a standard,
and its narrow, needle-
like leaves give off a
strong fragrance remi-
niscent of pine.*

**3. Once the top
growth has filled in
and you are happy
with the way the topi-
ary looks,** *remove the
primary leaves grow-
ing along its central
stem. Repot the plant,
if necessary, in a con-
tainer appropriate for
its size. Pinch as need-
ed to maintain the
plant's shape. If you
like, you can under-
plant the topiary with
small herbs.*

491

CHAPTER FOURTEEN

Reaping the Harvest

Harvesting a bountiful crop is your reward for many months of hard work in the garden. After carefully preparing the soil and tending your plants, you can finally reap the benefits in the form of delicious, fresh-picked vegetables and fruits, and flavorful herbs still warm from the sun.

On the following pages, you will learn how to judge when various vegetables are ready to be picked and how to store them so that you can continue to enjoy homegrown produce—like the 'Red Leaf' garlic at left curing in the shade of a walnut tree—long after the growing season is over. This chapter also provides tips on picking, processing, and storing herbs to ensure optimal flavor. In addition, you'll find information on extending the growing season into late fall and even into winter, by planting the cold-tolerant varieties recommended here or by using protective devices for late-maturing plants as described on pages 509-512. The chapter closes with advice on mulching, leaf composting, and planting cover crops, which will help rebuild the soil and prepare the garden for the coming year.

Gathering and Storing Vegetables

Knowing when and how to pick vegetables helps safeguard their flavor, texture, and nutritional value. To be sure you pick at the optimal time, keep track of the expected dates of maturity for your crops and begin checking them for ripeness approximately 1 week earlier. Remember that ripening may be hastened or delayed by the weather, the condition of the soil, and the effects of pests and diseases.

Determining Ripeness

Fruiting vegetables tend to deepen in color and develop a gloss or sheen as they ripen; then, as the vegetables age, their skin becomes dull. Exceptions to this rule include most eggplant cultivars, which do not change color, and the rinds of water-melons, which look dull when ripe. Root crops such as carrots often protrude slightly from the soil when mature, and the foliage becomes somewhat dry and flattened. Leafy crops like lettuce can be harvested and eaten at any time, but will become bitter if they begin to bolt (produce flowers or seeds). In fact, many vegetables can be eaten before they are fully mature, with a marked difference in taste and texture. To decide what you like best, sample vegetables at different stages of growth.

Within these guidelines, a hands-on approach is the best way to determine ripeness. Gently press tomatoes to see if they are softening; feel along the shoulders of root vegetables to check their size; or pull a carrot to taste. In time, you will be able to tell when your crops are ripe and, perhaps more important, you will be able to harvest at the stage of maturity and flavor you prefer for each vegetable.

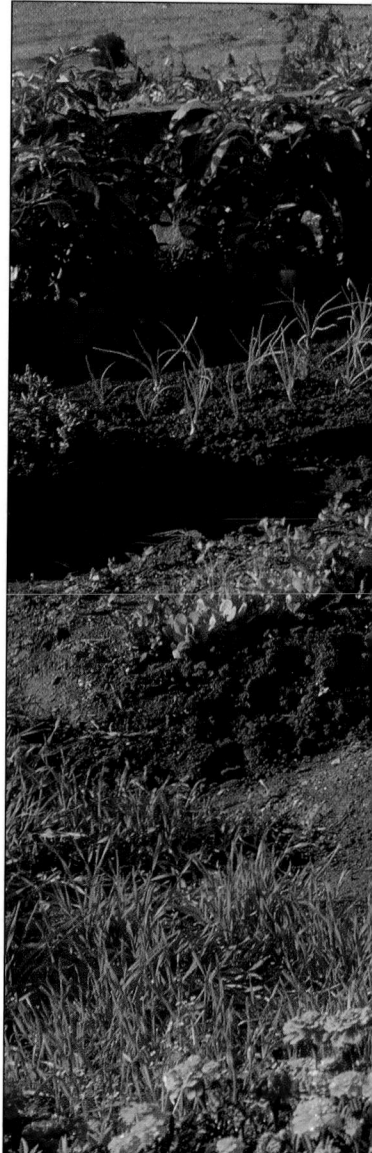

Carrots from a late planting in this garden have been pulled for fall eating. A mulch laid down later in the season will protect the remaining roots so that they can be harvested throughout the winter. Planted behind the carrots are Egyptian onions that overwinter in the ground and mature the following year.

Crop-by-Crop Harvesting Techniques

Asparagus—Begin harvesting after one season of growth. Choose firm, tightly closed spears 4 to 8 inches high. Snap spears off or cut with a dandelion digger slightly below ground level.

Beans—Harvest every 2 to 3 days to keep plants productive. Pick shell beans when the pod is plump and full, green beans when small and tender, and dry beans when they rattle in the pod.

Carrots—If root tops are above ground, harvest before a hard freeze. Loosen soil alongside the row with a garden fork and gently pull on the leaves just above the root. For easier pulling, water beforehand to soften soil.

Corn—Pick when the ears are plump and full and the corn silk is brown. To test for ripeness, make a small slit in the husk and press a kernel with your fingernail; the kernel will spurt milky fluid if ripe. To pick, hold the main stalk in one hand and pull down and twist the ear with the other hand.

Lettuce—Cut individual leaves of loose-leaved varieties as needed 1 inch above the ground. Cut butterhead and romaine lettuce when the heads are firm and full.

Onions—Harvest scallions when green leaves are 12 inches tall. Dig bulb onions when leaves turn brown and begin to fall over. To increase storage life, stop watering bulb onions a week before digging.

Peppers—Begin picking sweet peppers as soon as they are large enough to be usable. Cut stems 1 inch from the fruit with a sharp knife or pruning shears. Most sweet peppers become sweeter as they mature.

Potatoes—Dig new potatoes when vines begin to flower. For mature potatoes, dig when stems and leaves turn brown. Carefully loosen soil with a spading fork 2 feet from the plant's center. Work the fork toward the plant and slide it under the tubers so you can lift them without piercing them.

Squash—Harvest before the first frost. Most kinds of summer squash are ready to pick when fruits are 4 to 6 inches long and skins are still soft. Winter squash is ready when a fingernail cannot dent the rind and the stem is dry and woody. With a sharp knife or pruning shears, cut off winter squash at the juncture of the stem and vine. Leave the stem attached and handle carefully.

Tomatoes—Pick when evenly colored and firm. To ripen at room temperature, pick when the color is just beginning to develop. Twist fruit off gently; pulling may damage or uproot the plant.

Timely Harvest

Most crops respond to frequent picking by producing more vegetables. As a result, you get more vegetables onto the table, or into storage, while they are at their prime. As a rule of thumb, you cannot overpick a fruiting crop once it begins to bear mature vegetables. Root crops are usually once-only harvest plants, but you can enjoy a more sustained yield if you plant and thin a plot in stages. Leafy vegetables can be harvested as soon as the leaves form, but picking more than a third of a plant's leaves at one time can retard productivity.

Diligent and timely harvesting can be critical for many crops. For example, cucumbers, peas, beans, and summer squash plants will quit producing altogether if the vegetables are not picked

A Double Harvest from Cabbage and Broccoli

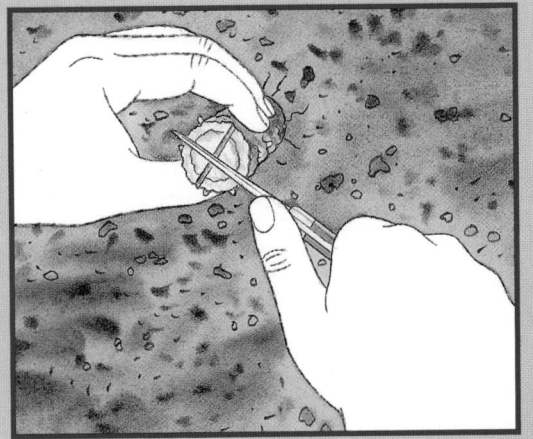

To encourage another crop from a cabbage plant that has a mature head ready for harvesting, cut off the head with a sharp knife at a point about an inch above the soil. To avoid disturbing the roots, hold the stem firmly as you cut, but do not tug on it. Then carve an X in the cut surface of the stub (left). Within a few weeks, the stub will sprout several small cabbage heads (left, below).

For a second harvest of broccoli, remove the first central head the plant produces by using a sharp knife to cut through the stem about 4 inches below the head (left); take care not to pull on the plant, or you might disturb the roots. Several small side shoots will subsequently develop around the stub at the plant's center (left, below). Continue cutting the side shoots as they mature to encourage production.

can avoid inadvertently spreading disease-causing fungi and bacteria, which travel in water particles, to other plants. When bad weather is predicted, harvest tender crops that might be damaged by hard rain, wind, or hail.

Tools and Containers

A gentle hand at harvest time will contribute greatly to the quality of your produce. Tearing vegetable stems and yanking fruits from vines can damage and uproot plants, decreasing or eliminating further yield from those plants. To handpick properly, support the plant with one hand and carefully take off the vegetables with the other.

As an alternative to handpicking, certain tools can make the process of separating vegetables from plants simpler, quicker, and less traumatic for both the plant and the produce. Utility knives help prevent damage to roots when you are gathering vegetables that form heads, such as cabbage and broccoli. Knives or pruning shears cut cleanly through the heavy stems of tomatoes, eggplants, bell peppers, pumpkins, squash, cucumbers, and okra. Scissors are useful for harvesting leafy crops like lettuce, whereas digging tools are essential for extricating root vegetables that are embedded in the ground or growing in soil that is hard and dry.

It's also a good idea to have on hand a variety of clean, dry containers for sorting and carrying vegetables. Place soft, fleshy vegetables that bruise easily in shallow containers with flat bottoms. Plastic buckets, crates, bushel baskets, and laundry baskets work well for firmer vegetables.

Washing the Vegetables

Cleaning the crop is important for prolonging storage life and for retaining flavor, texture, and nutritional value. And although you are unlikely to have exposed your organic garden to dangerous chemicals, even low-toxicity organic pesticides must be thoroughly washed away before you consume the food. Cleaning not only removes dirt and other unwanted substances, in some cases it also actually helps to preserve freshness. Greens, for instance, will quickly dry out unless they are rinsed in cool water, dried, and placed in an unsealed plastic bag before refrigeration. Be sure they are thoroughly dried before storage, since water droplets may harbor fungus spores that cause rot.

Vegetables grown on trellises or covered with floating row covers do not typically require much cleaning. Similarly, vegetables whose edible parts

These winter squash and pumpkins will sit in a sunny window for a week or so to toughen their skins and reduce their moisture content. After this period of sunning, they will keep all winter if stored in a dry, airy place at 50°F.

as soon as they ripen. Some vegetables, such as winter squash, pumpkins, and root crops, must be allowed to mature fully; otherwise, they will not keep well in storage.

Also, crops vary in their ability to retain flavor after ripening. Steady picking and prompt eating, drying, canning, or freezing are essential for tasty tomatoes, peas, beans, peppers, corn, cucumbers, and summer squash. Other vegetables, such as potatoes, carrots, onions, and winter squash, can be harvested in a more leisurely manner.

In general, harvesting is best done in the early morning because vegetables gathered before the sun warms them are less susceptible to spoilage and wilt. You should also try to harvest on clear, cool days when the foliage is dry. That way, you

are protected by thick skins, husks, or pods do not usually need to be washed if the exterior covering will be discarded. Vegetables to be stored, such as root crops, should simply be wiped off with a clean, dry cloth. Dip winter squash and pumpkins (including stems) in a solution of 1 part bleach to 10 parts water to kill surface bacteria and fungi.

Planning for Storage

Preparation for storage begins in the garden. Many of the cold-hardy plants, such as root vegetables, cabbage, onions, and winter squash, will last until spring if properly stored. When choosing varieties for your fall garden, look for traditional "good keepers" such as 'Long Season' beets, 'Yellow Globe' onions, and 'Kennebec' potatoes. To increase their storage life, do not fertilize vegetables for about a month before harvesting, since vegetables growing in nitrogen-rich soil late in the season tend to keep poorly. Likewise, withhold water for a month before harvesting; otherwise, the vegetables' tissues will be watery and more likely to spoil quickly.

All the produce you store should be free of blemishes. Even small breaks in a vegetable's skin can open the way to bacteria and fungi that cause rot.

Curing enhances the storage life of these vegetables. By drying and hardening the skin, shell, or rind, you protect the inner flesh from bacteria and fungi. Pumpkins and winter squash should be cured in a sunny room for 7 to 10 days. Most root vegetables need only a few days in a warm, sunny, well-ventilated room before storing. Potatoes, however, should be dried for 2 weeks in an area protected from the sun; in direct light, a toxin that turns the skins greenish often develops.

Storing Root Vegetables

Even though few homes today have root cellars, it is easy to adapt an area of your home for short-term storage. (For vegetables that prefer drier air and warmer temperatures, such as winter squash and pumpkins, an attic or spare room makes a good storage area.) Root vegetables such as beets, carrots, leeks, and turnips keep best at temperatures of 32° to 40° F and can be stored in sheds, garages, porches, or barns for up to a month after harvest. For longer storage, however, these vegetables need an area that mimics their underground growing environment—cool temperatures and high humidity. You can experiment with converting a corner of an unheated basement into

Storing Onions and Garlic

For onions and garlic that will keep all winter, select late-maturing types with thin necks and, if you plan to braid and hang them, long, strong stems. Gently dig the vegetables and brush off any soil. If the weather is dry, place the bulbs outdoors in a lightly shaded area; otherwise, choose an airy, dry shelter such as a carport. Spread the bulbs on wire mesh set on a support so that air can circulate on all sides. When the outer skins are dry and brittle and the stems have withered, the bulbs are ready to store. Either braid the stems together for hanging, or cut them off an inch above the bulbs and put the onions and garlic in mesh bags or other airy containers. For best results, store in a dry area at 36° F.

TECHNIQUES FOR A LONG STORAGE LIFE

Crop	Temperature/ Humidity	Storage Life	Comments
Beets	32° F; 95%	2-5 months	Clip tops to 1 inch and layer in boxes with saw-dust, sand, or peat moss in a basement or other cool, humid area. Can also be left in the ground and dug up as needed.
Cabbage	32° F; 90%	2-4 months	Store in separate area due to strong odor. Cut off damaged or rotten leaves. Wrap heads in paper or layer in straw and store in a basement or other cool, humid area.
Carrots	32° F; 95%	4-5 months	Cut off tops and layer in boxes with moist sand or sawdust and store in a basement or other cool, humid area. In mild climates carrots can be overwintered in the garden.
Potatoes	40° F; 90%	3-8 months	Harvest before the first hard freeze. Potatoes that have been frozen will rot in storage. After curing, pack loosely in well-ventilated boxes or mesh bags and store in a dark, cool, humid area such as a basement.
Winter squash	50° F; 60%	3-8 months	Choose unblemished high-quality fruits and store in a warm, dry area such as an attic or unheated spare room. Check often for signs of mold or spoilage and promptly remove damaged fruits.

a root cellar. Mount a humidity meter and ther-mometer in the area (see the chart above for the ideal temperatures and humidity levels). Place vegetables in well-ventilated containers such as mesh bags, baskets, or slatted wooden boxes, or hang them in braids and bunches. Open outside vents or windows periodically to let in cool air on fall nights. If your basement is dry, sprinkle water on the floor as needed. If you have trouble main-taining humidity levels, pack root vegetables in damp sand or sawdust to help them stay crisp.

Root vegetables can also be stored outdoors in a cold frame. To protect the frame from wind, place it adjacent to the foundation of your house or garage. Layer the produce in loose, clean straw or sawdust surrounded with rodent-proof wire mesh. For extra protection against cold, stack hay bales around the frame and cover the top with sev-eral layers of heavy canvas and a final layer of straw.

Even if you have stored only high-quality pro-duce, you'll still need to check regularly for signs of spoilage. Promptly remove any vegetable that has gone bad, along with the straw or sawdust immediately around it. As a precaution, wipe off adjacent vegetables with a dry cloth and, if neces-sary, add clean sawdust or straw.

Saving Seed

Gathering seed was a standard gardening task be-fore the proliferation of seed companies in the 19th century. Although the seeds of premium hy-brids may not reproduce or may revert to one of the parent types, collecting seed is a fairly simple process and is especially worthwhile if you are growing unusual varieties that may be difficult to obtain elsewhere.

Harvesting your own seeds also lets you devel-op varieties that are suited to your particular gar-den and tastes. When choosing plants for seed, look for specimens that are healthy and possess the variety's best features. Over time, you can have a hand in improving the quality of your vegetables by collecting seed from plants in your garden with exceptional yield, flavor, keeping quality, or resist-ance to pests and diseases.

Determining when to harvest vegetables for seed will depend on what type of crops you are us-ing for seed collection. In general, you will be gathering two types of seeds—wet and dry. Toma-toes, cucumbers, squash, and melons bear fleshy fruit and wet seeds. To collect seed from these plants, wait till the fruit is slightly overripe, then pick it and remove the seeds. Dry seeds are har-vested from crops such as beans, peas, and corn. These should be left to mature several weeks past their prime before picking for seed collection.

The next step in seed collection is cleaning. To clean fleshy fruits, scoop the seeds into a strainer, rinse with cool water, and dry on paper towels for a week or two. Seeds in pods can be shelled and spread to dry on a wire-mesh screen in a well-ventilated room.

Once they are thoroughly dry, the seeds of most vegetables can be stored in glass jars or in cans with tight-fitting plastic lids in a cool, dry area of your home. Do not use plastic bags and con-tainers, because they may be permeable to air and could expose the seeds to moisture, thus reducing their viability. Beans and peas, however, need dif-ferent handling because they are susceptible to fungus if stored in airtight containers. Keep them instead in small cloth bags or paper envelopes. As a preventive measure, you can give seeds a light sprinkling of silica gel. This desiccant, which is available at craft stores, hardware stores, and cam-era supply shops, will absorb moisture and help keep the seeds dry.

Harvesting Herbs

When harvested and handled with care, home-grown fresh and dried herbs are far superior to any you can buy. Knowing when to harvest them ensures intense flavor, scent, and color. And storing herbs to retain their just-picked savoriness doesn't have to be a long, involved process; it can be as simple as drying or freezing them.

Keep in mind that you don't necessarily need a large herb garden for a bountiful harvest. Even a few pots or a small bed near your back door can yield a plentiful supply of herbs for the kitchen. For example, just a few plants of parsley, chives, and mint can provide a wealth of flavor for soups, salads, and teas—and they will taste much better than their store-bought counterparts.

Most herbs—including basil, borage, parsley, angelica, chives, and sage—may be picked at any time. Harvesting a few leaves for immediate use is an efficient way to keep your plants well groomed. Cut back a stray branch of rosemary or snip off a few roving sprigs of wild marjoram and use the trimmings in your kitchen. To shape a plant and also make it fuller, remove only the growing tip of a stem, a method called pinching back. You can induce dense, bushy growth on a sprawling mat of thyme, for example, by removing a few inches from the tips of scraggly branches.

How to Gather Leaves

Harvest leaves early in the morning as soon as the dew has evaporated but before the sun gets bright and hot, ideally on a dry day following a day of good weather. Choose healthy, vigorous growth with leaves unblemished by pests and disease. Using sharp pruners, scissors, or a knife, cut only as much as you'll need for the day's meals or for processing immediately for storage. Handle the leaves as little as possible to avoid bruising them.

Because herbs change in appearance as they dry, gather leaves from one type of herb at a time, keeping each kind separate and labeling the batches. Spread the cut leaves in a thin layer on a screen or in a basket; piling up herbs generates heat that makes them wilt.

Culinary Classics

Both weekend cooks and professional chefs know from experience how quickly the flavor of many herbs starts to wane once they're harvested. Widely available curly parsley, for example, is often relegated to use as a garnish because it has languished in your grocer's produce bin. But gardeners who grow it and its stronger-tasting and longer-lasting cousin—flatleaf or Italian parsley—can enjoy them to the fullest extent: When minced with garlic and lemon peel, the herbs produce a tangy *gremolata*, adding a piquant finish to soups and stews. Fines herbes, a mixture of finely chopped chives, parsley or chervil, and more pungent herbs such as tarragon, thyme, and savory, is basic to French cook-

Culling Herbs from a Clump

To harvest the leafy growth of herbs that send up stems directly from the ground, such as the Italian parsley shown here, cut off individual stems at soil level from the outside edges of the plant. This will stimulate new growth at the center of the plant, keeping it compact and laden with leaves.

Clump-Forming Herbs

Allium schoenoprasum (chives)

Allium tuberosum (garlic chives)

Angelica archangelica (angelica)

Anthriscus cerefolium (chervil)

Cymbopogon citratus (lemon grass)

Petroselinum crispum var. *crispum* (curly parsley)

Petroselinum crispum var. *neopolitanum* (Italian parsley)

ing. The mixture can be bought dried, but the fresh version tastes far better.

Another indispensable component of French cooking is the bouquet garni, which is composed of three sprigs of parsley, a bay leaf, and a few sprigs of thyme tied into a bundle with string or wrapped in cheesecloth. After a bouquet has lent its blend of flavors to, say, a simmering pot of bean soup or a beef stew, it is removed before serving.

Unlike a bouquet garni, a chiffonade is made to be eaten. To make the delicate slivers that decorate and flavor a dish, gather clean, unblemished leaves of a large-leaved herb such as sorrel, washing them only if necessary and patting them dry. Roll the leaves into a cigar shape and slice the roll crosswise at one-quarter-inch intervals into fine strips. To make a visually striking salad or pep up a vegetable dish, use a mix of herbs with different leaf colors and compatible flavors, such as basil, perilla, and mint.

Adventurous cooks can make use of *Cymbopogon citratus* (lemon grass), an herb traditional to the cuisines of Southeast Asia, whose unique flavor blends the bite of lemon with the scent of roses. The young, tender shoots of lemon grass are delectable stir-fried with chicken, stuffed into the middle of a whole fish before baking, or added to soup. Or, for a delicate hint of lemon, put them in the water when you steam broccoli or other vegetables. Where winters are cold—USDA Zone

The Growth Rate of Different Herbs

SLOW GROWERS

Laurus nobilis
(bay)
Rosmarinus officinalis
(rosemary)
Satureja montana
(winter savory)

MODERATE GROWERS

Lavandula spp.
(lavender)
Origanum x *majoricum*
(hardy marjoram)
Salvia elegans
(pineapple sage)
Salvia officinalis
(common sage)
Thymus spp.
(thyme)

VIGOROUS GROWERS

Artemisia dracunculus var. *sativa*
(French tarragon)
Melissa officinalis
(lemon balm)
Mentha spp.
(mint)
Ocimum spp.
(basil)
Origanum vulgare
(oregano)
Satureja hortensis
(summer savory)

Note: The abbreviation "spp." stands for the plural of "species"; where used in lists it means that many, but not all, of the species in a genus meet the criterion of the list.

Slow-Growing Herbs

Woody herbs, including the potted bay laurel pictured here, *grow less rapidly than their herbaceous counterparts. Pick only a few leaves their first season. Wait until the plant is fully established in the fall of its second year before cutting one-quarter off the top. Cut back to a leaf node, preferably an outward-pointing one, to stimulate growth.*

7 and colder—pot up lemon grass and bring it inside to a sunny window; its slender, pale green leaves make it an attractive houseplant.

Herbs for Storage

Fresh herbs generally have more flavor than dried or frozen ones. One exception is bay leaves, which gain flavor when dried. In climates where even tender herbs grow year round, they can always be enjoyed fresh. But in colder areas, bay leaves must be preserved for winter use.

Preserving herbs need not be mystifying or labor-intensive, especially if you begin on a small scale. Simply pluck a few leafy stems of basil, tarragon, marjoram, or any culinary herb and place them in a single layer in a colander. Set the colander in a dry, airy place out of direct sunlight. When the leaves are dry enough to crumble,

break them into pieces, discarding the stems. Store the pieces in a tightly sealed jar and crush them just before using.

Gathering Herbs to Retain Quality

To preserve large quantities of herbs, you must know when to harvest them to capture their optimal flavor, fragrance, or color and how to retain those qualities through careful processing. The right time to harvest depends on which part of the plant is to be used. The maximum flow of essential oils, which furnish flavor and fragrance, generally occurs in leaves just before the plant's flowers open. But if you are harvesting blossoms, wait until they are newly opened; that's usually when a flower is richest in essential oils.

Because plants flower at different times, the

Robust Herbs

Moderately Fast Growers

Herbs that grow at a moderate pace, such as the thyme below, tolerate two light shearings per season. Cut off one-third of the new growth in early summer and another third in early fall. Time the last harvest to allow any new growth to harden off before heavy frost.

Some perennial herbs—such as the lemon verbena shown at right—as well as most annual herbs grow so vigorously that they tolerate two or more harvests a year. One-half of their lush new growth can be cut off once in late spring, a second time in summer, and again in early fall, when their essential oils are at their peak.

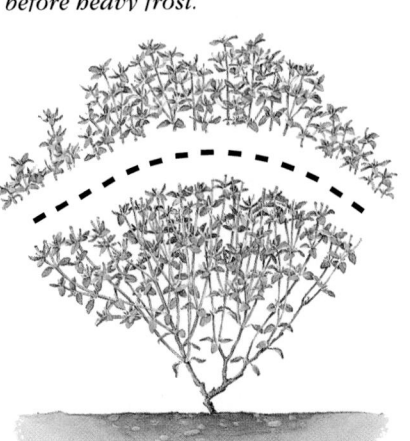

precise moment to harvest leaves varies from plant to plant and, of course, with a growing season's particular climate and weather conditions. In most areas, many herbs flower in midsummer. Keep an eye on your plants so you'll know when each one is ready to bloom.

When harvesting herbs, you may want to consider wearing gloves. Many people are allergic to the potent chemical compounds found in the plants. The hairy leaves of borage, for instance, can irritate sensitive skin, and angelica can cause dermatitis. Reactions are generally worse if contact occurs during the heat of the day.

Use a sharp knife or pruning shears to cut the herbs. Remove a branch or cut back part of one directly above a node, the place where the leaf grows from the stem; this will stimulate the plants to produce healthy new growth. For herbs that send up clumps of unbranched stems directly from the ground—parsley, chervil, and lemon grass, for example—cut the outer leaves at the base of the plant *(box, page 499)*. If you like, you can cut back all the stems of stalwart perennial herbs such as lovage and chives; they will promptly grow back.

Slow and Moderate Growers

How much you can safely cut from an herb at any one time depends on its vigor and growth habit. Some shrubby herbs—particularly bay, rosemary, and winter savory—grow slowly. Although you can pick a few leaves during their first year in the garden, wait until these plants are fully established before cutting them back. A few weeks before the first frost, take off one-quarter of the plants' growth. Pruning back to an outward-pointing bud encourages graceful branching *(box, page 500)*.

Herbs that grow slightly faster—lavender, marjoram, pineapple sage, common sage, and thyme, for instance—tolerate a somewhat sizable harvest once they are established. You can cut one-third off the top once, and sometimes twice, each year *(box, page 501)*. Just be sure to time your last pruning early enough in late summer or early fall so that new growth has a chance to harden off before winter.

Rambunctious growers like mint and lemon balm can withstand extensive shearing. Cut as much as one-half of the new growth off the top twice—or even three times—during the growing season *(box, page 501)*. Tarragon, while not as robust as mint and lemon balm, also tolerates severe pruning. Vigorous annuals like basil and summer savory can be cut back to 5 or 6 inches; be sure to

save the lower foliage, however, which is needed for further growth.

Picking Flowers

The flavor and color of blossoms generally peak when they have just bloomed. For example, golden yellow and orange calendula florets and showy red or pink-lavender bee balm petals—used to perk up salads or blended into soft cheese and butter for flavor and bright color—are best picked right after they have opened. (For a list of edible flowers, see page 438.)

The right time to harvest flowers for potpourri varies. Rose petals used to add scent to potpourri, for instance, should be picked when the blossoms are fresh and at the peak of fragrance. The best time to pick whole rosebuds, which combine nicely with crumbled flowers and flakes of petals, is when they are in tight bud. And lavender flowers used in potpourri should be harvested when the blossoms are fully formed and about to open. At this stage, the top of the bud will show faint color and be intensely fragrant.

Harvesting Seeds

An herb grown for its edible seeds must be watched carefully; once the plant flowers, its seedpods and seed heads will soon follow. Harvest the seed heads when the seeds start losing their green color and begin turning light brown and the plant's stems and pods—if it has any—begin to wither and look dry. After the seed heads are cut from the plant, the seeds will continue to ripen. The seeds of many herbs such as caraway, coriander, and fennel don't all ripen at the same time. With these herbs, harvest the seed heads when there are still immature seeds present. Above all, don't wait too long to gather seeds. Leaving seeds exposed to the vagaries of weather will turn them black, an indication that they have deteriorated. If you are planning to save some for spring planting, they will probably not germinate.

After a day of drying, seed heads should be checked carefully for insects. (Unwelcome pests such as tiny aphids will make their presence known by crawling away from seeds that have be-

The bright yellow and orange flowers of pot marigold mingle with the soft blue of borage in an edible planting. Pot marigold's petals and the blossoms of borage both make colorful additions to salads.

Herbs with Aromatic Seeds

Anethum graveolens
(dill)
Brassica juncea
(brown mustard)
Carum carvi
(caraway)
**Coriandrum
sativum**
(coriander)
Foeniculum vulgare
(fennel)
Nigella sativa
(black cumin)
Sesamum indicum
(sesame)

gun to lose moisture. If you see or suspect that there are insect eggs or larvae hidden in the seeds, pop them into the freezer for 48 hours.) Spread both immature and ripe seeds out on paper towels and leave them to cure in a warm, dry place. Then store the seeds in an airtight container, such as a screw-top glass jar, in a cool, dark place.

Seeds for Sowing

Seeds destined to start next year's herb garden should be allowed to ripen on the plant until no trace of green remains. This helps to ensure a higher rate of germination next spring. Some herbs—dill, German chamomile, and angelica, among others—will self-sow. Simply allow their ripe seeds to drop to the ground.

Make sure seeds to be held until spring are completely dry, then place them in an airtight glass jar with a package of commercial desiccant or an inch of powdered milk to keep the humidity low. Store the sealed jar in your refrigerator.

Saving Other Plant Parts

In addition to leaves, seeds, and flowers, the aromatic roots of herbs such as *Zingiber officinale* (ginger) and the fragrant and colorful stigmas of *Crocus sativus* (saffron crocus) are highly prized. To dry gingerroot, harvest the roots in fall, when their moisture content is low and the length of time it takes them to dry will be minimal.

Saffron, the world's most expensive spice, is the dried stigmas of the autumn-blooming saffron crocus. Labor alone accounts for its costliness, for it takes many thousands of the threadlike stigmas—which must be gathered by hand—to produce a single ounce. Fortunately, you need only a pinch to flavor cookies or rice. A few dozen bulbs grown in your garden will supply you with enough for a handful of uses. Pluck the bright orange stigmas when the flowers open over several weeks in the fall. Spread them out on a kitchen towel to dry, then store them in a tightly sealed glass container away from heat and light.

The Art of Preserving Herbs

Air-drying, the traditional way of preserving herbs, remains one of the best methods today. Speed is of the essence, because the faster an herb dries, the more flavor and color it will retain and the less likely it is to become contaminated or moldy. Conventional ovens, however, even at low temperatures, are too hot for drying herbs. Use them only in an emergency, when herbs are so wet that they are in danger of becoming moldy.

Two conditions important for drying herbs are good air circulation and a temperature that stays consistently between 80° and 85°F. Higher temperatures and sunlight dissipate an herb's essential oils. Another crucial factor in speedy drying is low humidity. For this reason, don't wash herbs unless it is absolutely necessary. Give dusty or mud-spattered herbs a shower with a garden hose a day or two before harvesting them.

The place you choose to dry your herbs will influence the finished product. In some climates, dry, breezy days in late summer render almost any room in the house ideal. In hot, muggy climates, however, you'll have to keep your herbs in an air-conditioned room or one equipped with a dehumidifier for them to dry properly. Avoid a basement that, while dry and cool, harbors stagnant air. And an attic, though airy and dry, may get too hot.

Hanging herbs in bunches tied with decorative knots of raffia and ribbon may be picturesque, but this method works well only for thyme and other tiny-leaved herbs that dry quickly. If you choose to hang-dry herbs, keep the bunches relatively small and tie them loosely; otherwise, the innermost leaves may mildew.

Most herbs, especially those with thick, fleshy leaves, should be dried in a single layer on a flat surface that allows for adequate air flow, like the shallow basket shown below. A large window screen that has been scrubbed and dried also makes an ideal drying tray. For smaller quantities, try cookie sheets or oven racks covered with kitchen towels, or hanging wicker baskets.

Freshly picked sage leaves line this flat-bottomed wicker basket, where they will dry. Their arrangement in a single layer and the coarse weave of the basket permit air to circulate around each leaf, promoting quick drying. The faster an herb dries, the more color and flavor it retains in storage.

Fleshy Leaves and Tender Tissues

Fleshy leaves such as those of scented geraniums contain a lot of moisture. To dry their thick tissues successfully, strip them from their stems to shorten the drying time and place them in a shallow basket or on a screen in one layer, with plenty of room surrounding each leaf.

Thin, tender leaves such as those of basil require great care in handling; they are easily bruised and crushed, which compromises their quality. Their fragility also makes them difficult to store without sacrificing flavor. Freezing is a good method of storage for the leaves of herbs with delicate tissues, such as basil, chervil, tarragon, lovage, and cilantro.

The leaves of feathery chervil, broad-leaved sorrel, and sage, with blue-violet flower spikes, all taste best fresh. To keep chervil, freeze leafy stems in plastic bags or make an herb butter. Freeze shredded sorrel leaves in oil or layer them in salt. Sage can be dried or frozen and makes a delicious flavored vinegar.

Helpful Appliances

Dehydrators, which force warm air through a series of screens, are excellent for drying herbs quickly. The fastest method, however, is drying with a microwave oven. Microwaves differ in power wattage, so you'll have to experiment if you choose this drying method, which works best for herbs with resinous leaves, such as rosemary, bay, and sage. Place the leaves between two sheets of paper towels and microwave on low for 20 seconds. Check the leaves for crispness; if they are still pliable, microwave them for several seconds more, then check them again. Avoid overdrying the leaves; they will be brittle and turn to powder when crumbled. You can also dry herbs between paper towels in a frost-free refrigerator. They should be dry and crisp in about 24 hours.

When your herbs are dry, remove the remaining stems, but take care to keep the leaves as intact as possible. The larger the pieces, the longer they retain their flavor in storage. Crumble them into smaller pieces right before you use them.

Herbal Teas

You don't need to be as careful when you prepare a harvest for making herbal tea, a beverage made from dried herbs steeped in hot water. Because the tea is strained before serving, whole leaves, stems, and flowers can go into it. You can make a tea of just one herb or several herbs. A particularly refreshing tea combines the dried leaves of lemon grass with other citrusy herbs such as lemon verbena and lemon balm.

Packaging and Storing Herbs

Because dried herbs can reabsorb moisture from the air, it's important to package them as soon as they are dry. Further exposure to air will cause them to lose essential oils, collect dust, and quite possibly become infested with insects. Use airtight glass or plastic containers for storage. Although clear containers let you see what's inside, opaque or colored ones are better because they keep out damaging light. Find a cool, dark place to store your herbs; heat from any source such as an oven or stove will sap their potency.

Freezing is a quick way to preserve herbs, especially hard-to-dry herbs such as chives, chervil, parsley, and fresh coriander, or cilantro *(Coriandrum sativum)*. The easiest way to freeze these herbs is simply to enclose them in a plastic bag labeled with the contents and the date. Wait to chop a frozen herb until you are ready to use it.

You can also try freezing herbs in oil. Start with clean, dry leaves that have been stripped from their stems. Chop them and mix with just enough oil to form a paste. Then pack into containers and label, date, and store them in the freezer. You'll be able to scrape out what you need with a spoon without thawing the whole containerful, because oil doesn't freeze as hard as water.

Culinary Treats

Herbs can also be preserved in oil, butter, salt, vinegar, or wine. Each of these preparations has a specific shelf life. For example, herb butter, a mixture of ½ pound of softened butter and 3 tablespoons of finely chopped herbs such as parsley or tarragon or a combination of herbs, must be kept refrigerated. It is best used within a week unless it is frozen, in which case it should be good for as long as 2 months.

Herbal oils must be used within 2 weeks. To infuse oil with herbal essence, combine ½ cup of oil and sprigs of an herb such as rosemary, thyme, or marjoram in a metal measuring cup or small metal bowl. Simmer in the lower third of a preheated 300° oven for 1 hour to flavor the oil and destroy any bacteria that cause botulism. Strain the oil, bottle it, and keep it refrigerated at all times. Herbal vinegars, made by steeping fresh herbs in vinegar or wine, last up to a year and don't require refrigeration.

You can also use salt to dry herbs. In an airtight canning jar that will keep the salt from caking, layer leaves of herbs such as basil or lovage over salt—the large crystals of kosher salt are best—covering each layer with more salt. In a week the herbs will be ready to use.

Sweetly scented geranium leaves and rose petals can be steeped in sugar, which will absorb their aromatic oils. Discard the leaves and petals after they are dry and use the flavored sugar to make cake icings, cookies, and candy.

Decorative glass bottles hold sparkling, unclouded vinegars infused with, from left, purple basil, salad burnet, rosemary, sage, and garlic chives. Make sure herbs are free of surface moisture before steeping them in vinegar, or the infusion may become murky. To retain their full flavor, store the vinegars in a cool, dark place.

Potpourri

An aromatic potpourri—a blend of dried flowers, spices, and leaves—lends the delectable scent of a summer garden to a room. Although there are many different recipes for potpourri, there are basically just two methods: the moist and the dry. The moist method is time-consuming and results in a highly fragrant but unattractive product. The dry method is far simpler and produces a potpourri that looks as pretty as it smells.

A few culinary herbs that can also be used in potpourri are listed on page 507. If you haven't made potpourri before, a good place to begin is with this classic recipe: Prepare a quart of bone-dry rose petals or a combination of petals and rosebuds from fragrant varieties such as the fruit-scented bourbon rose 'Madame Isaac Pereire'. In-

toxicatingly fragrant gallica and damask roses such as 'Camaieux' and 'Madame Hardy' are also perfect for potpourri.

Gently stir into the roses 1 pint of completely dry scented geranium leaves, a pint of dried lavender flowers, and 2 tablespoons each of cloves, cinnamon, and allspice. Blend in a fixative—an ingredient that extends the life of potpourri by absorbing aromatic oils and releasing them slowly. You can use 1 level tablespoon of orrisroot or gum benzoin for every cup of the potpourri mixture. Another excellent fixative is vetiver root, which also adds its own woodsy fragrance to the final product. Chop the dried root and crush it slightly, but do not pulverize it; using it powdered may make the potpourri look dusty. Mix the fixative with the flowers and spices and store the potpourri in a tightly sealed container for at least a month to allow the fragrances to meld.

Extending the Harvest

Extending your garden's growing season is challenging but well worth the effort. By either protecting plants to encourage their maturation early or late in the season or planting cold-tolerant vegetables for harvesting in fall and winter, you can grow crops during the months when cold weather would usually kill them. Since every garden is a unique combination of soil, climate, cultivars, and growing methods, you should experiment with various techniques for lengthening your garden's period of productivity.

Protecting Your Plants

Simple cold frames, row covers, and plant caps, or cloches, can help maintain a consistent microclimate, protecting crops from the damage inflicted by frost, wind chill, and sudden dips in temperature. By trapping solar energy, cold frames can extend your season a month or more at each end. Cloches and row covers aren't as efficient but can still add several weeks of growing time, allowing you to harvest warm-weather crops like tomatoes, peppers, and cucumbers even after the first frost.

You may need to try several kinds of protection—what works in your garden one year may not be as effective the next if the season is unusually cold or warm. When choosing the degree of protection you want, keep in mind that the more complicated the method, the more maintenance it will require—and even the simplest methods will need periodic monitoring. Some protective devices you can build yourself, or you can purchase readymade equipment through specialized mail-order catalogs.

Cozy Cloches

Cloches, small caps that protect a single plant or a few closely spaced small ones, can be either made or purchased to fit different crops. The very first cloches were bell-shaped glass jars used in 17th-

Polyethylene spread on a wire frame keeps a crop of greens warm on a frosty fall morning (foreground). When the day warms up, the plastic can be folded back lengthwise along the row to admit light and prevent overheating. In the background, a floating row cover of lightweight spunbonded fabric is draped directly over the plants.

century French market gardens. Today, you can choose from a variety of lightweight, portable cloches made of wax paper, plastic, glass, and polyethylene tubes filled with water *(page 445)*. You can also make cloches by recycling household articles such as gallon-sized plastic milk jugs with the bottoms cut out and the caps removed. To keep milk-jug cloches from blowing away, insert a slim stake beside the growing plant and set the jug over the plant so that the stake protruding from the jug's mouth.

Cone-shaped cloches can be constructed from sheets of fiberglass-reinforced plastic. Cut the material into a semicircle, pull the straight edges together, and staple them to form a cone. These cloches can be made in a wide range of sizes to fit your crops and will last for a number of years. The hole on top of the cone provides some ventilation, although on warmer days you may need to remove the cloche altogether.

A tomato cage can be easily adapted for use as a cloche. Set the tomato cage over the plant and wrap it with clear plastic, taping the overlap to hold it in place. On cold nights, drape a second piece of plastic over the top and secure it with tape.

Plants covered with a cloche should be monitored closely to avoid overheating and moisture buildup. You can cut slits in the cloche for ventilation, and you should periodically remove it, especially on warm days.

At right, corrugated fiberglass covers a row of greens, while plastic milk jugs with the bottoms removed keep single plants snug. A cylinder of reinforced plastic tied around a whiskey-barrel planter (below, left) blocks the wind and creates a warm environment for leaf lettuce; the house wall and the paving on which the planter is set absorb heat during the day and continue to radiate it after the sun goes down. In an autumn garden (below, right), a cold frame made of cinder blocks and old windows is open on a warm day to prevent the lettuce crop from overheating.

Hardworking Row Covers

Row covers are one of the most effective and practical season extenders. When frost threatens, you can quickly and easily install row covers over a single row or an entire section of your garden.

Floating row covers made of spunbonded polyester can be placed directly over plants without a supporting structure. These fabric covers allow water, air, and sunlight to reach the plants while offering frost protection to around 28° F. If winds

threaten, you can bury the edges of the covers in the soil or weight them down with rocks. Floating row covers come in rolls of various sizes and are sold at most garden supply stores or through specialty mail-order catalogs.

Another material commonly used for row covers is transparent polyethylene plastic. It is too heavy to lay directly on plants, however, and must be supported by wire, PVC pipes, or wood arches. A polyethylene row cover offers a greater degree of frost protection than a row cover of spunbonded fabric, but it needs more frequent monitoring than the fabric cover to prevent overheating and excessive humidity; on a sunny day, the temperature beneath a plastic row cover may be 20°F higher than the air outside. On warm days you'll need to fold half the polyethylene sheet back lengthwise to increase air circulation and moderate the temperature. You can also buy polyethylene with slits to allow for good air circulation, but it will provide less frost protection than a solid sheet.

Cold Frames, Warm Plants

With a cold frame set in your garden, you can overwinter ready-to-harvest frost-tolerant crops, as well as seedlings that will remain dormant during the cold months, then resume growth the following spring. You can either buy a cold frame or build it yourself out of lumber. For a makeshift cold frame, simply arrange concrete blocks or bales of hay in a rectangle around the plants and use a sheet of glass, an old window, or heavy clear plastic as a lid, slanting it slightly to prevent water from collecting. When cold nights threaten, you can cover the lid with thick canvas, old blankets, or several layers of hay.

Regulating the Cold Frame's Climate

Cold frames require daily monitoring. Early in the fall, steady sun can quickly dry out and damage plants grown under glass or plastic. Check your cold frame each day, watering as necessary to keep the soil slightly moist.

You must also be diligent about monitoring the temperature inside the cold frame. Sudden temperature changes can damage plants and cause wilting or retard growth. If daytime temperatures reach 60°F or more, raise the lid or remove it and replace it at night when the temperature falls. If the outside temperature is 40°F, the lid should be propped open only a few inches and closed again at night. The need to vent the cold frame will decrease as the season advances toward winter.

If you discover that manually opening and closing the cold frame is a chore you'd rather do with-

Cold-Hardy Cultivars

Arugula

Broccoli 'Waltham', 'Green Valiant'

Brussels sprouts 'Jade Cross'

Cabbage 'Danish Ballhead', 'Savoy Ace'

Carrot 'Napoli'

Cauliflower 'Violet Queen', 'Snow Crown'

Corn salad 'Vit', 'D'Etamps'

Endive 'Salad King', 'Tres Fin' ('Fine Curled')

Kale 'Dwarf Blue Curled Scotch Vates', 'Blue Siberian', 'Winterbor'

Leek 'Alaska', 'Blue Solaise'

Lettuce 'Black-Seeded Simpson', 'Four Seasons', 'Oakleaf', 'Salad Bowl', 'Rouge d'Hiver', 'Winter Density'

Onion 'Beltsville Bunching', Egyptian onion 'Ishikura'

Radicchio 'Augusto'

Radish 'Munich Bier', 'Round Black Spanish'

Arugula

511

Tips and Techniques for a Long Season

Beets—Sow outside about 10 weeks before the average first frost date. Pick mature beets before the first hard freeze. Harvest immature beets in autumn or mulch heavily to overwinter.

Broccoli—Sow seed directly by mid-July in colder climates and by August in milder ones. Protect with floating row covers. Some cultivars can withstand temperatures below freezing as long as the weather is evenly cool. Grow all winter where temperatures remain above 40° F.

Brussels sprouts—Sow in succession for harvesting from early fall to late spring. Cold-hardy cultivars survive temperatures as low as 14° F. Freezing temperatures enhance flavor.

Cabbage—Set out cold-hardy transplants no earlier than 10 to 12 weeks before the first frost.

Carrots—Mulch with 8 to 12 inches of hay before the ground freezes. Dig all winter.

Cauliflower—Plant in time for it to mature in cool weather, but before the first frost. Or, plant frost-tolerant cultivars like 'White Sails' and protect with floating row covers.

Celeriac—Mound soil around plants and mulch heavily to continue harvest into the winter. Grow as a winter crop in mild climates.

Chard—After the first frost, protect with floating row covers or mulch deeply to extend the harvest into winter. Plant as a winter crop in a cold frame.

Garlic—Plant 2 to 4 weeks before the first frost for harvest the following summer.

Leeks—Harvest cold-hardy cultivars such as 'Blue Solaise' all winter in areas where temperatures stay above 10° F. Pull the last of the leeks before seed stalks appear in the spring.

Lettuce—Sow leaf lettuce at least 7 weeks before the first frost and heading types 10 weeks before; mulch heavily to insulate soil. Cold-hardy cultivars can be overwintered in cold frames or under row covers in mild climates.

Onions—Some varieties, including Egyptian onions and 'Walla Walla', can be overwintered with a thick layer of mulch in mild climates or in a cold frame in severe climates. For an early-spring crop of shallots in cold climates, plant after the first frost. If planted earlier, they may send up top growth that would be damaged by winter cold.

Spinach—Plant hardy cultivars such as 'Winter Bloomsdale' about a month before the first frost. Sow in late winter in a cold frame for an early-spring crop.

Mulched Lettuce

out, you can buy a thermostatic device that automatically opens and closes the lid as needed. Many prefabricated cold frames come equipped with such a device.

Hardy Plants for Cold Weather

With planning and care, you can have a thriving cold-weather garden, one that will yield fresh vegetables long after the normal season has ended. Many crops that perform well in cool spring weather and are harvested in summer can be planted a second time for a fall harvest. In general, vegetables that grow best in cool weather are leafy greens and root crops. When choosing cultivars for harvesting in the cooler temperatures and shorter days of fall and winter, look for characteristics such as cold hardiness and quick maturity. Some good candidates for the late-season garden are listed on page 511.

Timing is critical in planning the autumn garden, and it may take a season or two of trial and error to determine the best time to begin your fall plantings. Keep in mind that your goal is to schedule plantings so that crops will be mature when winter arrives, a date that will vary with your particular climate. Shorter days and colder soil and air temperatures will increase the time required to reach maturity by 20 to 40 percent. You will be able to extend your harvest by continuing to plant at 1- to 2-week intervals until approximately 6 weeks before the first frost date for your region.

Some of the cultivation practices you use during other seasons will need to be modified to suit the fall garden's special conditions. The following are among the most important things to remember:

• Seedlings should be well thinned, and plants should be spaced slightly farther apart than in spring and summer gardens to allow greater exposure to the sun.

• You may need to shade fall seedlings from the late-summer sun. You can buy black shade cloth made of polyethylene mesh from a garden center or hardware store, or improvise your own sun protection from old window screens or open snow fencing supported on cement blocks.

• Newly planted crops will need to be watered frequently if your area typically receives little rain in late summer and early fall.

And finally, try using a diluted seaweed spray on your crops for a few weeks before the first frost date. This will raise mineral levels in the leaf tissue and help prevent freezing.

Putting the Garden to Bed

As the harvest season winds down and your garden turns from green to gold, there are still a few chores to be done. Putting the garden properly to bed can yield a substantial payoff in the form of earlier, healthier spring produce. Sowing cover crops such as alfalfa and winter rye will protect your beds from erosion and compaction of the soil and will provide nutrients when they are tilled under in the spring. A clean winter garden will be less likely to harbor pests and weeds, and soil that is cultivated, fertilized, and mulched will save you valuable time and labor when planting season comes.

Cleaning and Storing Tools and Equipment

Proper storage of garden equipment prolongs its life and can also help to protect next year's garden from disease. Tools, stakes, trellises, tags, and cages should be removed from the garden and cleaned. If any of the equipment has been used near diseased or infested plants, dip it in a disinfecting solution of 1 part bleach to 10 parts water. Wipe down the metal parts of tools with mineral oil to prevent rust, and sharpen dull blades. Drain and store hoses and irrigation systems.

Remove and store sheets of plastic mulch, or recycle them if they are damaged. Carefully check cold frames for cracks and make sure that the lids fit snugly; even a small leak can expose plants to damaging cold.

Dealing with Garden Debris

Garden debris is a favorite winter home for many harmful insects, which attach eggs, cocoons, or larvae to the stems and leaves of dried and faded plants. By cleaning out your garden beds now, you will help eliminate pest and disease problems next season.

Before the ground freezes in the fall, be sure to clear your garden of all vegetation except cover crops and overwintering or perennial plants such as asparagus, rhubarb, and rosemary; vegetables and other plants left to rot will encourage insect infestation. Weeding is especially critical at this time as well, since fall is when many perennial weeds establish deep root systems and prodigiously set seed. Be thorough in your weeding—

pull out all foliage, seed heads, stems, and roots. Any weeds left in the fall garden will return with renewed vigor the following spring.

Carefully dispose of all mature weed seed heads and any plants that show signs of disease or insect infestation. Put them in a tightly sealed bag and discard according to your local ordinances for plant debris.

If you notice signs of insects or diseases on your plants as you clear the garden, consult the Troubleshooting Guide on pages 576-583, a reputable nursery, or your local Cooperative Extension Service office for an analysis of the problem and possible solutions.

Fertilized, cultivated, and mulched in fall, these raised beds will be ready for spring planting weeks earlier than a slower-to-thaw plot at ground level would be. The two smaller beds at the rear are an ideal size for accommodating temporary cold frames that can shelter the new season's first hardy crops.

The shallots planted in this raised bed in the fall will grow until cold weather arrives. Dormant over the winter months, the plants will resume growing in the spring and produce an early harvest.

Looking Ahead to Spring

If you cultivate your beds in the fall, you can plant as soon as the soil warms up in the spring. Fall is a good time to apply fertilizers that require longer periods to break down. Ground phosphate rock, greensand, and granite dust will slowly release potassium, phosphorus, and other nutrients if lightly spaded into the soil and left over the winter. Fresh manure, applied directly to your beds at the rate of 2 to 3 bushels per 100 square feet, will rot by the time you plant the following spring.

Autumn's Gift to Spring

The scattered leaves of autumn can be a true windfall for a vegetable garden's soil. Decomposed leaves are rich in potassium and micronutrients, and they also increase the soil's capacity to retain moisture. Nature will compost the leaves for you if you simply pile them in an enclosure, but this method may take several years. To hasten the process, shred the leaves with a mulching mower or a leaf shredder and add them to your compost pile *(page 262)*. Or, if you have more leaves than the compost pile can handle, make a separate mound of shredded leaves. To prevent snow and rain from leaching nutrients, cover the mound with a sheet of black polyethylene weighted down with rocks or bricks. In the spring, you will have a supply of dark, crumbly leaf compost to use as mulch or as a soil amendment.

Winter Mulch and Cover Crops

Mulch applied to the fall garden is another way of adding organic matter to the soil. It also prevents soil erosion and protects your maturing cold-hardy vegetables. Even if you mulched heavily during the growing season, the parts of your garden that are not planted with a cover crop will benefit from a thick layer of mulch in the fall. Shredded leaves, alfalfa hay, peat, straw, and buckwheat hulls are all good choices. For perennial vegetables, berries, and herbs, apply several inches of loose, airy mulch such as straw or pine needles after the soil freezes. This will protect their roots from the damaging effects of alternate freezing and thawing.

In cool climates, crops like carrots, leeks, garlic, parsnips, salsify, and turnips can be left for winter harvest if they are covered with at least 6 inches of mulch in the fall. In areas with severe winters, cover the rows with bales of straw or at least a foot of mulch just before the first hard freeze. During winter thaws you can pull up the vegetables; just be sure to harvest all of them before the next planting season.

Growing a crop specifically to nourish and reinvigorate the soil can benefit even the smallest garden. Such cover crops, as they are known, prevent erosion, choke out weeds, and keep the soil aerated. And when tilled under, these plants act as green manure—a high-powered nutrient and a soil conditioner. Your choice of a cover crop will vary depending on the result desired for your specific garden. Deep-rooted plants such as alfalfa and clover bring up nutrients from deep in the ground to the topsoil; legumes add nitrogen to your garden; and winter rye protects against erosion and keeps down weeds.

To give your cover crop time to establish itself before winter, sow seeds directly among maturing fall vegetables or fill in bare spots. Clover, vetches, and winter peas lend themselves to interplanting with end-of-season crops. Quick-growing timothy or buckwheat can fill gaps between winter squash and pumpkin vines.

You can also reap the advantages of a cover crop throughout the growing season by planting one in the paths beside your raised beds. A low-growing variety such as Dutch white clover is especially suitable for this purpose. Clover will control weeds, lower soil temperature—which encourages root growth—and help to retain soil moisture.

Updating Your Journal

Finally, update your garden journal *(page 455)*. Make notes, record observations, and reflect on how well your garden served your needs. Were the beds spaced close enough for easy cultivation and harvesting? If not, you may want to redesign your garden plot. Did you have too many vegetables of one kind and not enough of another? Note which cultivars thrived in your garden, which didn't, and why. Record cultivation techniques and interplanting combinations that worked well. Indicate periods of unusual weather. If you spent hours watering by hand, consider installing a drip-irrigation system. If weeding overwhelmed you, next year you may want to try mulching with black plastic or solarizing the soil to kill weeds *(box, page 393)*. Record any pest or disease problems you may have had, how you solved them, and what steps need to be taken in the spring to avoid those problems. Floating row covers, beneficial insects, lures, traps, botanical insecticides, and disease- and pest-resistant cultivars can all be used as part of an organic approach to disease and pest management.

Reviewing the past growing season will give you a clearer sense of your own preferences as well as the particular needs of your garden. When you make next year's choices, you will have guidelines based on conditions prevailing in *your* plot—with its unique combination of soil, climate, cultivars, growing methods, and gardening style.

A cover crop of winter rye sown in the paths beside rows of cold-hardy cabbage in this New Jersey garden quickly covers the soil. Sown in early fall, the rye controls weeds, prevents erosion, and contributes nutrients to the soil when it is tilled under in the spring.

SOIL-IMPROVING COVER CROPS

Common Name	Seeding Rate (lbs./1,000 Sq. Ft.)	When to Sow	Comments
Austrian winter pea	2-4	Early spring or early fall	Winter-hardy, nitrogen building. Provides organic matter when tilled under in the spring.
Barley	2½	Early to midfall	Extensive root system prevents erosion. Winter-hardy; provides organic matter when tilled under in the spring.
Crimson clover	1	Early spring through early fall	Good for erosion control and nitrogen building. Winter-hardy and shade tolerant; can be sown under upright vegetables such as corn.
Hairy vetch	1	Late summer to early fall	Winter-hardy, nitrogen building. Provides large amounts of organic matter when tilled under.
Ryegrass	1	Early spring to late summer	Quick growing, cold tolerant. Extensive root system loosens compacted soil, protects against erosion. Dense growth chokes out weeds. Dies back during the winter in the North. Easy to till under.
Winter rye	2½	Fall	Winter-hardy, vigorous grower in a variety of soils. Extensive root system adds organic matter to the soil. Good source of straw for mulch.

Kitchen Garden Recipes

One of the greatest rewards of kitchen gardening is having fresh ingredients on hand for delicious home-cooked meals. While many people associate "homegrown produce" with tossed salads and zucchini bread, the myriad uses for fresh-picked vegetables, fruits, and herbs are limited only by your imagination.

Are you tired of slicing tomatoes for salads? Have you run out of ideas for using fresh mint? Are you wondering what to do with that rutabaga you just harvested? Do you have more blackberries than you know what to do with? On the following pages, you'll find ideas for using all of these, and more.

The 28 tasty, low-fat recipes are presented in the six sections: Appetizers, Soups, Salads, Main Dishes, Side Dishes, and Desserts. Each recipe provides nutritional information, as well as helpful hints and estimated preparation time. Interspersed throughout are illustrated tips on preparing vegetables for cooking and eating.

Bon appétit!

Artichokes with Garlic "Mayonnaise"

SERVES: 4
WORKING TIME: 20 MINUTES
TOTAL TIME: 45 MINUTES

1 all-purpose potato (6 ounces), peeled and thinly sliced

4 cloves garlic, peeled

¼ cup fresh lemon juice

3 tablespoons reduced-fat mayonnaise

3 tablespoons reduced-sodium chicken broth, defatted

¾ teaspoon dried rosemary

¾ teaspoon dried marjoram

½ teaspoon salt

4 large artichokes (12 ounces each)

3 tablespoons chopped fresh parsley

1. In a small pot of boiling water, cook the potato until tender, about 12 minutes. Add the garlic during the last 3 minutes of cooking. Drain. Transfer to a large bowl and mash until smooth. Add 2 tablespoons of the lemon juice, the mayonnaise, the broth, ¼ teaspoon of the rosemary, ¼ teaspoon of the marjoram, and the salt. Set aside.

2. In a large pot, combine 3½ cups of water, the remaining 2 tablespoons lemon juice, the remaining ½ teaspoon rosemary, and remaining ½ teaspoon marjoram. Bring to a boil over high heat.

3. Meanwhile, pull off the tough bottom leaves of the artichoke (see tip; top photo). With kitchen shears, snip the sharp, pointed ends from the remaining leaves (middle photo). With a paring knife, trim off the end of the stem (bottom photo). Add the artichokes to the boiling liquid, cover, and cook until the artichokes are tender, about 25 minutes. Stir the parsley into the garlic "mayonnaise" and serve with the artichokes.

Helpful hint: To eat an artichoke, pull off the outer leaves one at a time and scrape the fleshy base from each leaf by drawing it between your front teeth. When you've finished the leaves, remove the prickly "choke" from the artichoke bottom before eating it.

TIP

FAT: 3G/21%
CALORIES: 130
SATURATED FAT: 0.4G
CARBOHYDRATE: 25G
PROTEIN: 6G
CHOLESTEROL: 0MG
SODIUM: 525MG

Eggplant Dip

SERVES: 4
WORKING TIME: 15 MINUTES
TOTAL TIME: 40 MINUTES

*Similar to the Middle Eastern baba ghanouj, this smoky eggplant dip uses
just a few walnuts instead of the usual high-fat sesame paste.*

**4 slices firm-textured white
sandwich bread**

3 cloves garlic, peeled

**2 eggplants (about 1 pound each),
halved lengthwise**

**2 tablespoons coarsely chopped
walnuts**

2 tablespoons fresh lemon juice

**2 teaspoons olive oil, preferably
extra-virgin**

¾ teaspoon salt

¾ teaspoon dried oregano

¼ cup chopped fresh parsley

**2 carrots, quartered lengthwise
and cut into 2-inch-long strips**

**1 red bell pepper, cut into
2-inch-long strips**

**1 green bell pepper, cut into
2-inch-long strips**

1. Preheat the oven to 400°. Place the bread on a baking sheet and bake for 7 minutes, or until lightly golden and crisp. Set aside.

2. Meanwhile, in a small saucepan of boiling water, cook the garlic for 2 minutes to blanch. Drain and set aside.

3. Preheat the broiler. Place the eggplant halves, cut-sides down, on the broiler rack and broil 6 inches from the heat for 15 minutes, or until the skins are charred and the eggplants are tender. Set aside to cool slightly. When cool enough to handle, peel the eggplants, discarding the skin.

4. Transfer the eggplants to a food processor. Add the toasts, garlic, walnuts, lemon juice, oil, salt, and oregano, and purée until smooth. Stir in the parsley. Spoon the dip into a small serving bowl and serve with the carrots and bell pepper strips.

Helpful hints: Leftovers are delicious as a sandwich spread, particularly with cooked vegetables tucked into a pita pocket. Blanching the garlic subdues the raw taste—use this trick whenever a recipe calls for uncooked garlic.

FAT: 7G/29%
CALORIES: 216
SATURATED FAT: 0.9G
CARBOHYDRATE: 36G
PROTEIN: 6G
CHOLESTEROL: 0MG
SODIUM: 592MG

Red Pepper Dip

SERVES: 4
WORKING TIME: 20 MINUTES
TOTAL TIME: 50 MINUTES

Garlicky and piquant with a splash of balsamic vinegar, this dip will bring your taste buds to attention. Feel free to cut back on the garlic by one or two cloves, if you like. For added body, some toasted Italian bread is puréed with the red peppers. A yellow bell pepper makes a colorful serving container, but any color pepper will work just as well.

---

10 thin slices diagonally cut Italian or French bread

1 tablespoon olive oil

1 large onion, halved and thinly sliced

5 cloves garlic, minced

3 red bell peppers, thinly sliced

2 tablespoons no-salt-added tomato paste

2 tablespoons balsamic or red wine vinegar

½ teaspoon salt

1 yellow bell pepper

1 green bell pepper, cut into thin strips

¾ cup cherry tomatoes

1. Preheat the oven to 400°. Place the bread on a baking sheet and bake for 7 minutes, or until lightly golden and crisp. Set aside.

2. Meanwhile, in a large nonstick skillet, heat 2 teaspoons of the oil over medium heat until hot but not smoking. Add the onion and garlic and cook, stirring frequently, until the onion is tender and golden brown, about 10 minutes.

3. Add the red peppers, cover, and cook until the peppers are very tender, about 15 minutes. Stir in the tomato paste, vinegar, salt, and remaining 1 teaspoon oil until well combined. Transfer to a food processor, add 2 slices of the toasts, and purée until smooth.

4. Slice the top off the yellow pepper, then remove and discard the seeds and ribs. Spoon the pepper dip into the yellow pepper and place on a serving platter. Serve with the remaining toasts, the green pepper, and tomatoes.

Helpful hints: The dip will keep refrigerated for up to 2 days. It's also delicious as a sandwich spread with baked ham or sliced turkey or chicken breast, and it can enliven a pasta sauce or pizza topping.

FAT: 6G/20%
CALORIES: 286
SATURATED FAT: 1.1G
CARBOHYDRATE: 50G
PROTEIN: 8G
CHOLESTEROL: 0MG
SODIUM: 699MG

Greek Lemon Soup with Carrots, Leeks, and Dill

SERVES: 4

WORKING TIME: 20 MINUTES

TOTAL TIME: 45 MINUTES

This lovely starter, based on the Greek avgolemono (egg and lemon) soup, gets its body from rice instead of eggs.

3 cups reduced-sodium chicken broth, defatted, or reduced-sodium vegetable broth

1 teaspoon grated lemon zest

¼ cup fresh lemon juice

½ teaspoon salt

½ teaspoon ground ginger

½ teaspoon sugar

⅛ teaspoon ground nutmeg

¼ cup long-grain rice

2 carrots, halved lengthwise and cut into thin slices

1 leek (white and light green parts only), cut into fine julienne strips

½ cup snipped fresh dill

2 teaspoons cornstarch mixed with 1 tablespoon water

1. In a large saucepan, combine the broth, 2 cups of water, the lemon zest, lemon juice, salt, ginger, sugar, and nutmeg. Bring to a boil over medium heat and add the rice. Return to a boil, reduce to a simmer, cover, and cook until the rice is almost tender, about 15 minutes.

2. Stir in the carrots and leek, cover again, and simmer until the vegetables and rice are tender, about 5 minutes. Stir in the dill and cornstarch mixture, return to a boil, and cook, stirring constantly, until the soup is slightly thickened, about 1 minute longer. Ladle the soup into 4 bowls and serve.

Helpful hints: The delicate flavor of this soup is best savored as soon as it's made. If you buy dill (or any fresh herb), look for brightly colored, moist leaves or sprigs with no sign of wilting or decay. Wash the dill gently, shake off the excess water, wrap in paper towels, and refrigerate for up to 2 days.

FAT: 0G/0%

CALORIES: 110

SATURATED FAT: 0.1G

CARBOHYDRATE: 23G

PROTEIN: 5G

CHOLESTEROL: 0MG

SODIUM: 784MG

Cream of Broccoli Soup

SERVES: 4
WORKING TIME: 30 MINUTES
TOTAL TIME: 40 MINUTES

*With a few minor adjustments, this classic cheese-topped "cream" soup
has been transformed into healthy fare.*

2 teaspoons olive oil

1 onion, finely chopped

3 cloves garlic, minced

1¼ pounds broccoli

1 pound all-purpose potatoes, peeled and thinly sliced

2½ cups reduced-sodium vegetable broth

¾ teaspoon dried marjoram

½ teaspoon salt

¼ teaspoon freshly ground black pepper

1 cup evaporated skim milk

⅛ teaspoon cayenne pepper

2 tablespoons reduced-fat sour cream

2 teaspoons flour

½ cup shredded Cheddar cheese (2 ounces)

1. In a nonstick Dutch oven, heat the oil over medium heat until hot but not smoking. Add the onion and garlic and cook, stirring frequently, until the onion is softened, about 7 minutes.

2. Meanwhile, with a paring knife, separate the broccoli florets and stems; peel the stems and thinly slice them.

3. Add the potatoes to the pan, stirring well to combine. Add the broccoli stems and all but 1 cup of the broccoli florets, stirring to combine. Add the broth, 1 cup of water, the marjoram, salt, and pepper, and bring to a boil. Reduce to a simmer, cover, and cook until the potatoes and broccoli stems are tender, about 12 minutes. Meanwhile, in a small pot of boiling water, cook the reserved cup of broccoli florets for 2 minutes to blanch. Drain.

4. Transfer the vegetable mixture to a food processor and process to a smooth purée. Return the soup to the pan, stir in the evaporated milk and cayenne, and bring to a simmer. In a small bowl, stir together the sour cream and flour. Add the sour cream mixture and blanched broccoli florets to the pan and cook, stirring, until slightly thickened, about 1 minute. Divide the soup among 4 bowls, sprinkle the Cheddar on top, and serve.

Helpful hint: Adding flour to the sour cream helps keep it from curdling when added to the hot soup.

FAT: 9G/29%
CALORIES: 279
SATURATED FAT: 3.9G
CARBOHYDRATE: 37G
PROTEIN: 16G
CHOLESTEROL: 20MG
SODIUM: 636MG

Spiced Sweet Potato Soup

SERVES: 4
WORKING TIME: 30 MINUTES
TOTAL TIME: 50 MINUTES

*The confetti-like garnish that tops this puréed soup consists of bell peppers, tortilla strips,
and jack cheese. And despite the suave, velvety appearance of the soup itself, there's plenty
of spicy excitement going on beneath the surface: The potato-rice purée is laced with jalapeño,
chili sauce, and lime. Serve the soup with warmed tortillas or crisp breadsticks.*

1 tablespoon olive oil

Two 6-inch corn tortillas, cut into ½-inch-wide strips

1 green bell pepper, cut into thin strips

1 red bell pepper, cut into thin strips

6 scallions, thinly sliced

1 pickled jalapeño pepper, finely chopped

1¼ pounds sweet potatoes, peeled and thinly sliced

¼ cup long-grain rice

2 cups reduced-sodium vegetable broth

¼ cup chili sauce

½ teaspoon grated lime zest

¼ cup fresh lime juice

¼ teaspoon salt

1 cup evaporated low-fat milk

½ cup shredded Monterey jack cheese (2 ounces)

1. In a large saucepan, heat the oil over medium heat until hot but not smoking. Add the tortillas and cook, turning them, until lightly crisped, about 2 minutes. With a slotted spoon, transfer the tortilla strips to paper towels.

2. Set aside ¼ cup each of the green and red bell pepper strips. Add the remaining bell pepper strips, the scallions, and jalapeño pepper to the saucepan and cook, stirring frequently, until the peppers are tender, about 5 minutes. Add the sweet potatoes and rice, stirring to combine. Add the broth, 1 cup of water, the chili sauce, lime zest, 2 tablespoons of the lime juice, and the salt, and bring to a boil. Reduce to a simmer, cover, and cook until the potatoes and rice are tender, about 17 minutes. Meanwhile, in a small pot of boiling water, cook the reserved bell pepper strips for 1 minute to blanch. Drain. When cool enough to handle, dice the peppers.

3. Transfer the soup to a food processor and process to a smooth purée. Return the soup to the pan, stir in the evaporated milk, and bring to a simmer. Stir in the remaining 2 tablespoons lime juice. Divide the soup among 4 bowls. Sprinkle with the tortilla strips, diced bell peppers, and jack cheese, and serve.

Helpful hint: Instead of transferring the vegetables to a food processor, you can use a hand blender right in the pot. Run the blender in on/off pulses until the soup is a smooth purée.

FAT: 10G/25%
CALORIES: 364
SATURATED FAT: 3.1G
CARBOHYDRATE: 58G
PROTEIN: 13G
CHOLESTEROL: 25MG
SODIUM: 728MG

Cream of Tomato Soup

SERVES: 4
WORKING TIME: 25 MINUTES
TOTAL TIME: 40 MINUTES

1 teaspoon olive oil

4 scallions, thinly sliced

2 tablespoons flour

½ cup chopped fresh basil

¾ teaspoon salt

½ teaspoon dried oregano

½ teaspoon dried thyme

¼ teaspoon freshly ground
black pepper

1½ cups reduced-sodium chicken
broth, defatted, or reduced-
sodium vegetable broth

1 cup evaporated low-fat milk

1½ pounds tomatoes, peeled
and seeded (see tip), then finely
chopped

⅓ cup no-salt-added tomato paste

2 teaspoons firmly packed light
brown sugar

4 teaspoons reduced-fat
sour cream

1. In a large saucepan, heat the oil over medium heat until hot but not smoking. Add the scallions and cook, stirring frequently, until the scallions are tender, about 4 minutes. Add the flour and stir well to coat. Stir in the basil, salt, oregano, thyme, and pepper. Gradually stir in the broth and evaporated milk and cook, stirring constantly, until the mixture is smooth and slightly thickened, about 5 minutes.

2. Reduce the heat to low. Stir in the tomatoes, tomato paste, and brown sugar. Cover and simmer, stirring occasionally, until the flavors have developed and the soup is thickened, about 10 minutes longer. Ladle the soup into 4 bowls, spoon the sour cream on top, and serve.

Helpful hints: Tomatoes are best stored at room temperature rather than in the refrigerator, but keep them away from direct sunlight or they may become mushy. If you don't have fresh basil on hand or can't find good-quality fresh basil, substitute chopped mint for a refreshingly different flavor.

TIP

To peel tomatoes, drop them into boiling water just until the skins begin to wrinkle, 10 to 30 seconds. Remove with a slotted spoon and, when cool enough to handle, peel them with a paring knife. To seed tomatoes, cut each in half crosswise, and scoop out the seeds with a spoon.

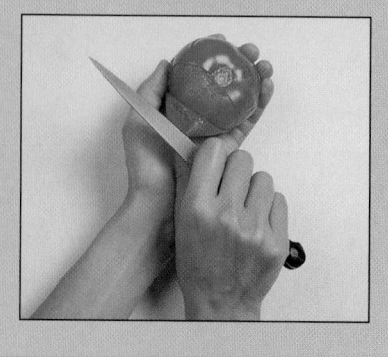

FAT: 4G/21%
CALORIES: 164
SATURATED FAT: 0.6G
CARBOHYDRATE: 26G
PROTEIN: 9G
CHOLESTEROL: 12MG
SODIUM: 754MG

Vegetable Soup with Pasta and Greens

SERVES: 4
WORKING TIME: 40 MINUTES
TOTAL TIME: 55 MINUTES

This garden-fresh soup is a welcome treat in any season, thanks to the year-round availability of quality produce. But keep the recipe in mind for the summer season, when basil is at peak freshness—the wonderful flavor of fresh basil makes the soup a real winner in summertime.

---

2 teaspoons olive oil

1 large onion, finely chopped

2 carrots, halved lengthwise and cut into thin slices

2 zucchini, halved lengthwise and cut into ¼-inch-thick slices

1 red bell pepper, diced

14½-ounce can no-salt-added stewed tomatoes, chopped with their juices

2 cups reduced-sodium chicken broth, defatted, or reduced-sodium vegetable broth

¼ cup chopped fresh basil

½ teaspoon salt

4 cups ¼-inch-wide shredded Swiss chard, spinach, or kale

½ cup ditalini pasta or small pasta shells

⅓ cup coarsely grated fresh Parmesan cheese

1. In a nonstick Dutch oven or large saucepan, heat the oil over medium heat until hot but not smoking. Add the onion and cook, stirring frequently, until the onion is softened, about 5 minutes. Add the carrots and cook, stirring frequently, until the carrots are softened, about 5 minutes.

2. Stir in the zucchini and bell pepper and cook, stirring frequently, until the pepper is tender, about 5 minutes. Add the tomatoes and their juices and cook, stirring frequently, until the liquid is slightly reduced, about 3 minutes.

3. Stir in the broth, 1½ cups of water, the basil, and salt, and bring to a boil. Stir in the Swiss chard and pasta, return to a boil, and cook until the pasta is just tender, about 10 minutes. Sprinkle the Parmesan on top and serve.

Helpful hints: For a change of pace, substitute orzo, the small rice-shaped pasta, for the ditalini. Leftovers of this soup are delicious; just add a little more broth or water when reheating, since the pasta will continue to absorb liquid as the soup sits.

FAT: 5G/24%
CALORIES: 194
SATURATED FAT: 1.7G
CARBOHYDRATE: 30G
PROTEIN: 10G
CHOLESTEROL: 6MG
SODIUM: 841MG

Three-Bean Salad with Walnuts

SERVES: 4
WORKING TIME: 15 MINUTES
TOTAL TIME: 20 MINUTES

This salad is usually served as a side dish, but since its main component is kidney beans (which are high in protein), it can make a substantial main dish, too. For variety's sake, you can mix and match the canned beans you use: One can of kidney beans and one of chickpeas, for instance, would also work well. Serve the salad with crusty rolls for a tasty meal.

2 cloves garlic, peeled

¾ pound green beans, cut into 2-inch pieces

¾ pound yellow wax beans, cut into 2-inch pieces

¾ cup plain nonfat yogurt

⅓ cup chopped fresh mint

2 tablespoons reduced-fat mayonnaise

¾ teaspoon salt

Two 16-ounce cans red kidney beans, rinsed and drained

1 cucumber, peeled, halved lengthwise, seeded, and cut into ¼-inch cubes

¼ cup chopped walnuts

16 leaves Boston, Bibb, or iceberg lettuce

1. In a large pot of boiling water, cook the garlic for 2 minutes to blanch. With a slotted spoon, remove the garlic and when cool enough to handle, chop finely.

2. Add the green beans and wax beans to the boiling water and cook until crisp-tender, about 5 minutes. Drain, rinse under cold water, and drain again.

3. In a large bowl, combine the chopped garlic, yogurt, mint, mayonnaise, and salt. Fold in the green beans, wax beans, kidney beans, cucumber, and walnuts. Divide the lettuce among 4 plates, top with the bean mixture, and serve at room temperature or chilled.

Helpful hints: The salad can be made up to 8 hours in advance; don't spoon it over the lettuce or add the walnuts until just before serving. If yellow wax beans are not available, you can substitute additional fresh green beans or frozen Italian green beans, if you like.

FAT: 8G/22%
CALORIES: 321
SATURATED FAT: 0.8G
CARBOHYDRATE: 47G
PROTEIN: 19G
CHOLESTEROL: 1MG
SODIUM: 803MG

Fresh Corn Confetti Salad with Jack Cheese

SERVES: 4
WORKING TIME: 20 MINUTES
TOTAL TIME: 20 MINUTES

Corn on the cob has an ineffable sweetness that is hard to duplicate. Here, raw kernels are sliced off the cob and tossed with colorful vegetables, cubes of jack cheese, and a tangy-sweet dressing fired up with jalapeño pepper. If you haven't discovered it already, you'll find the crunchy sweetness of raw corn to be one of the delicious pleasures of summertime.

⅓ cup balsamic vinegar

2 tablespoons honey

½ teaspoon salt

1 pickled jalapeño pepper, finely chopped

4 cups fresh corn kernels or 4 cups no-salt-added canned corn kernels, drained

2 cups cherry tomatoes, halved

2 ribs celery, thinly sliced

1 red bell pepper, cut into ½-inch squares

1 green bell pepper, cut into ½-inch cubes

1 red onion, finely chopped

¼ cup chopped fresh parsley

3 ounces Monterey jack cheese, cut into ¼-inch cubes

1. In a large bowl, combine the vinegar, honey, salt, and jalapeño pepper.

2. Add the corn, tomatoes, celery, bell peppers, onion, parsley, and cheese. Toss to combine, and serve at room temperature or chilled.

Helpful hints: Choose fresh ears of corn with moist green stalks and plump kernels. If you buy the corn, refrigerate it as soon as you get it home: Warmth hastens the conversion of its natural sugars to starch. Time also robs fresh corn of its sweetness, so use corn within a day or two of purchase or harvesting. If you use canned corn, be sure to get no-salt-added, which has a fresher taste and crunchier texture than regular canned corn.

FAT: 9G/28%
CALORIES: 290
SATURATED FAT: 4G
CARBOHYDRATE: 49G
PROTEIN: 12G
CHOLESTEROL: 23MG
SODIUM: 496MG

Red Cabbage Slaw

SERVES: 4
WORKING TIME: 20 MINUTES
TOTAL TIME: 20 MINUTES PLUS CHILLING TIME

⅔ cup plain nonfat yogurt

⅓ cup cider vinegar

3 tablespoons reduced-fat mayonnaise

1½ teaspoons sugar

¾ teaspoon salt

¼ teaspoon celery seed

6 cups shredded red cabbage (see tip)

4 carrots, shredded (see tip)

3 scallions, cut into 3-inch julienne strips

2 Granny Smith apples, cored, quartered, and cut into thin slices

¼ cup snipped fresh dill

1. In a large serving bowl, whisk together the yogurt, vinegar, mayonnaise, sugar, salt, and celery seed.

2. Add the cabbage, carrots, scallions, apples, and dill, and toss well to combine. Cover with plastic wrap and refrigerate until well chilled, about 1 hour.

Helpful hints: You can prepare this cole slaw up to 1 day ahead. Green cabbage will work just as well as the red, but with less vivid color. You will need about 1 pound of cabbage (1 medium head) to make the slaw.

TIP

You can use a food processor for shredding the vegetables, but it's often easier to use a hand grater—and there will be less to clean up. Quarter the cabbage, and then run each quarter across the coarse holes of the grater. Peel and then shred the carrots.

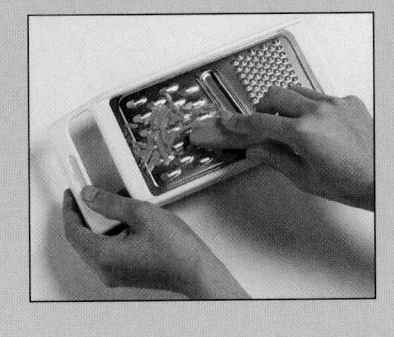

FAT: 3G/17%
CALORIES: 163
SATURATED FAT: 0.5G
CARBOHYDRATE: 33G
PROTEIN: 5G
CHOLESTEROL: 1MG
SODIUM: 571MG

Cucumber Salad

SERVES: 4

WORKING TIME: 30 MINUTES

TOTAL TIME: 30 MINUTES PLUS CHILLING TIME

This is a version of tzatziki, the yogurty cucumber salad that's a standard in Greece. Nonfat yogurt is used instead of the full-fat variety, and a little reduced-fat sour cream adds some richness while softening the flavor. Strongly accented with lime and mint, this salad can hold its own with spicy entrées of all sorts. It's also great served as a snack with crusty bread.

½ cup plain nonfat yogurt

2 tablespoons reduced-fat sour cream

½ teaspoon grated lime zest

1 tablespoon fresh lime juice

½ teaspoon salt

¼ teaspoon freshly ground black pepper

2½ pounds cucumbers (about 5), peeled and thinly sliced

½ cup julienne-cut radishes

½ cup thinly sliced scallions

3 tablespoons chopped fresh mint

1. In a large serving bowl, whisk together the yogurt, sour cream, lime zest, lime juice, salt, and pepper.

2. Add the cucumbers, radishes, scallions, and mint, and toss gently to combine. Cover with plastic wrap and refrigerate until well chilled, about 1 hour.

Helpful hints: This salad can be made and chilled up to 8 hours in advance, but no longer—further chilling may result in a watery mixture as the cucumbers release their moisture. If fresh mint is unavailable, substitute chopped fresh parsley—not the same flavor but refreshing nonetheless.

FAT: 1G/18%

CALORIES: 70

SATURATED FAT: 0.5G

CARBOHYDRATE: 12G

PROTEIN: 4G

CHOLESTEROL: 3MG

SODIUM: 319MG

Garden-Fresh Potato Salad

SERVES: 4
WORKING TIME: 25 MINUTES
TOTAL TIME: 40 MINUTES

*Lots of crunchy, sliced and diced vegetables show up in this version of an American favorite.
For healthful eating, the dressing has been lightened up: Nonfat yogurt and reduced-fat
mayonnaise add the expected creaminess but little extra fat. For a nice presentation,
line the serving bowl with crisp lettuce leaves and garnish with paprika.*

1½ pounds small red potatoes, quartered

2 carrots, halved lengthwise and cut into thin slices

¼ cup distilled white vinegar

1 tablespoon Dijon mustard

¾ teaspoon salt

½ teaspoon freshly ground black pepper

6 radishes, thinly sliced

4 scallions, thinly sliced

1 red bell pepper, diced

1 rib celery, thinly sliced

¾ cup plain nonfat yogurt

2 tablespoons reduced-fat mayonnaise

1. In a large pot of boiling water, cook the potatoes for 18 minutes. Add the carrots and cook until the potatoes and carrots are tender, about 2 minutes longer. Drain well.

2. Meanwhile, in a large serving bowl, whisk together the vinegar, mustard, salt, and black pepper. Add the warm potatoes and carrots, and toss well to coat.

3. Add the radishes, scallions, bell pepper, and celery, and toss to combine. Add the yogurt and mayonnaise, stir gently to combine, and serve.

Helpful hint: Dress the salad while the potatoes are still warm so they will absorb more of the flavor as they cool.

FAT: 2G/8%
CALORIES: 215
SATURATED FAT: 0.3G
CARBOHYDRATE: 43G
PROTEIN: 7G
CHOLESTEROL: 1MG
SODIUM: 633MG

Ratatouille Stir-Fry with Goat Cheese

SERVES: 4
WORKING TIME: 30 MINUTES
TOTAL TIME: 30 MINUTES

6 ounces orzo pasta

1 tablespoon olive oil

1 red onion, coarsely diced

4 cloves garlic, finely chopped

1 red bell pepper, cut into thin strips

1 zucchini, cut into 2 x ½-inch strips

1 yellow summer squash, cut into 2 x ½-inch strips

1 small eggplant, cut into 2 x ½-inch strips (see tip)

5½-ounce can low-sodium tomato-vegetable juice

1½ cups cherry tomatoes, halved

2 teaspoons capers, rinsed and drained

¾ teaspoon dried tarragon

¾ teaspoon salt

¼ cup chopped fresh basil

3 ounces goat cheese or feta cheese, crumbled

1. In a large pot of boiling water, cook the pasta until just tender. Drain well.

2. Meanwhile, in a large nonstick skillet or wok, heat the oil over medium heat until hot but not smoking. Add the onion and garlic, and stir-fry until the onion is slightly softened, about 2 minutes. Add the bell pepper, zucchini, and yellow squash, and stir-fry until crisp-tender, about 4 minutes.

3. Add the eggplant and stir-fry until lightly browned, about 4 minutes. Add the tomato-vegetable juice, tomatoes, capers, tarragon, and salt, and cook until the tomatoes are softened, about 4 minutes. Stir in the basil. Divide the orzo among 4 plates. Spoon the vegetables over the orzo, sprinkle the cheese on top, and serve.

Helpful hint: If you can't get low-sodium tomato-vegetable juice, use regular tomato-vegetable juice and reduce the salt in the recipe to ½ teaspoon.

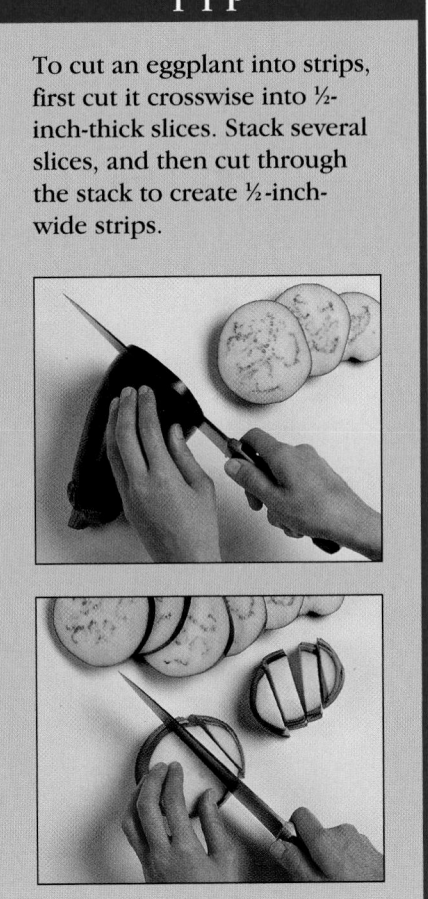

TIP

To cut an eggplant into strips, first cut it crosswise into ½-inch-thick slices. Stack several slices, and then cut through the stack to create ½-inch-wide strips.

FAT: 11G/29%
CALORIES: 347
SATURATED FAT: 5G
CARBOHYDRATE: 51G
PROTEIN: 14G
CHOLESTEROL: 17MG
SODIUM: 606MG

Zucchini and Potato Pancakes

SERVES: 4
WORKING TIME: 25 MINUTES
TOTAL TIME: 35 MINUTES

Impossible but true—these crispy potato pancakes can be savored without guilt. Egg whites are used instead of whole eggs; the pancakes are browned in just a little oil to keep the fat in check. The final fat-free baking in the oven ensures that the pancakes are cooked through. Offer with tomato or split pea soup and grilled mushrooms drizzled with balsamic vinegar.

1½ cups plain nonfat yogurt

2 tablespoons reduced-fat sour cream

¾ cup snipped fresh dill

¾ cup thinly sliced scallions

¾ teaspoon salt

2 zucchini, shredded and squeezed dry in paper towels

2 large baking potatoes (about 1 pound), peeled, shredded, and squeezed dry in paper towels

2 tablespoons flour

½ teaspoon baking powder

2 egg whites

4 teaspoons olive or vegetable oil

1. In a medium bowl, stir together the yogurt, sour cream, ¼ cup of the dill, ¼ cup of the scallions, and ¼ teaspoon of the salt. Cover with plastic wrap and refrigerate until serving time.

2. In a large bowl, stir together the zucchini, potatoes, flour, baking powder, egg whites, the remaining ½ cup dill, remaining ½ cup scallions, and remaining ½ teaspoon salt.

3. Preheat the oven to 400°. In a large nonstick skillet, heat 2 teaspoons of the oil over medium heat until hot but not smoking. Using a ½ cup measure, drop the potato mixture into the skillet to form 4 pancakes, then lightly flatten to a ½-inch thickness. Cook until the pancakes are golden brown, about 2 minutes per side. Transfer to a baking sheet. Repeat with the remaining 2 teaspoons oil and remaining potato mixture, cooking 4 more pancakes. Transfer to the baking sheet.

4. Place the pancakes in the oven and bake for 7 minutes, or until the pancakes are crisp and cooked through. Divide the pancakes among 4 plates and serve with the yogurt sauce.

Helpful hints: Squeeze the potatoes and zucchini very dry, or the pancakes will steam in the pan rather than brown. If desired, prepare and bake the pancakes up to 1 day ahead and reheat in a 350° oven. You can substitute yellow squash or butternut squash for a different taste.

FAT: 6G/25%
CALORIES: 215
SATURATED FAT: 1.3G
CARBOHYDRATE: 31G
PROTEIN: 11G
CHOLESTEROL: 4MG
SODIUM: 585MG

Stuffed Cabbage with Dill Sauce

SERVES: 4
WORKING TIME: 25 MINUTES
TOTAL TIME: 1 HOUR

1 small head cabbage (1 pound), cored

1 teaspoon olive oil

6 scallions, thinly sliced

2 carrots, quartered lengthwise and thinly sliced

1 zucchini, halved lengthwise and thinly sliced

¼ pound mushrooms, coarsely chopped

1 cup bulgur (cracked wheat)

2 tablespoons boiling water

½ teaspoon grated lemon zest

1 tablespoon fresh lemon juice

¾ cup snipped fresh dill

½ teaspoon salt

2 tablespoons chopped pecans (¾ ounce)

2 cups reduced-sodium vegetable broth

1¼ teaspoons cornstarch mixed with 1 tablespoon water

3 tablespoons reduced-fat sour cream

FAT: 7G/24%
CALORIES: 266
SATURATED FAT: 1.3G
CARBOHYDRATE: 46G
PROTEIN: 10G
CHOLESTEROL: 4MG
SODIUM: 454MG

1. Preheat the oven to 400°. In a large pot of boiling water, cook the whole head of cabbage until it is crisp-tender and the leaves are easily separated, about 5 minutes. Drain. When cool enough to handle, separate into leaves, selecting the 12 largest leaves for stuffing. (Save the remainder for another use.)

2. In a medium saucepan, heat the oil over medium heat until hot but not smoking. Add the scallions and cook until softened, about 1 minute. Add the carrots, zucchini, and mushrooms and cook, stirring frequently, until the carrots are softened, about 4 minutes. Add the bulgur, boiling water, lemon zest, lemon juice, ½ cup of the dill, and the salt. Let stand until the bulgur is slightly chewy, about 10 minutes. Remove from the heat; add the pecans.

3. Using a ½-cup measuring cup as a mold, stuff the 12 cabbage leaves with the bulgur mixture and place them, seam-side down, in a 13 x 9-inch baking dish (see tip). Pour the broth on top, cover with foil, and bake for about 25 minutes, or until the leaves are tender and the filling is heated through. Transfer the cabbage packets to 4 plates. Transfer the broth from the baking dish to a small saucepan and bring to a boil. Add the cornstarch mixture and cook, stirring constantly, until slightly thickened, about 1 minute. Stir in the remaining dill. Spoon the sauce over the cabbage packets, top with a dollop of sour cream, and serve.

TIP

Fit a cabbage leaf into a ½-cup measuring cup, then spoon in the filling and fold the leaf over it to form a round packet. Invert the cup to place the cabbage packet in the baking dish.

Three-Pepper Pizza

SERVES: 4
WORKING TIME: 10 MINUTES
TOTAL TIME: 45 MINUTES

Roasted peppers, a popular pizza topping, make for a striking pie when a mix of red, yellow, and green bell peppers is used. Char the peppers thoroughly under the broiler: That way, they'll not only be easier to peel, but they'll also have a more intensely smoky flavor. This pizza is a snap to fix because the pizza dough is store-bought.

---

4 bell peppers, mixed colors

1 tablespoon yellow cornmeal

1 cup chopped fresh basil

2 tablespoons grated Parmesan cheese

1 pound store-bought pizza dough

1 red onion, cut into thin rings

2 tomatoes, thickly sliced

1 cup shredded part-skim mozzarella cheese (4 ounces)

1. Preheat the broiler. Cut off the four sides of each bell pepper and remove the ribs. Broil the peppers, cut-sides down, for about 10 minutes, or until the skin is charred. When cool enough to handle, peel and cut into ½-inch-wide strips. Turn the oven to 450°.

2. Lightly dust a baking sheet with the cornmeal. Knead ½ cup of the basil and the Parmesan into the pizza dough and flatten the pizza dough into a circle. Place the dough on the cornmeal and press out to a 10-inch circle. Cover the dough with the onion and tomatoes and bake on the bottom rack of the oven for about 20 minutes, or until the crust is lightly browned.

3. Sprinkle with the mozzarella and the remaining ½ cup basil, top with the pepper strips, and bake for about 5 minutes, or until the cheese has melted and the peppers are piping hot.

Helpful hints: You can buy ready-to-use pizza dough from many pizzerias and Italian specialty stores; you may also find it in the dairy case in the supermarket. Or, you can use the refrigerated dough that comes in a roll. Either type of dough can be patted out into a rectangle rather than rolled into a circle, if you like.

FAT: 10G/20%
CALORIES: 444
SATURATED FAT: 4.2G
CARBOHYDRATE: 70G
PROTEIN: 20G
CHOLESTEROL: 18MG
SODIUM: 817MG

Baked Spaghetti Squash with Mushroom Sauce

SERVES: 4
WORKING TIME: 30 MINUTES
TOTAL TIME: 55 MINUTES

This enticing dish looks like pasta, but it's really spaghetti squash—just scrape out the cooked strands and there's your natural spaghetti.

1 spaghetti squash (about 5 pounds)

2 teaspoons olive oil

5 shallots, finely chopped

3 cloves garlic, minced

1 carrot, halved lengthwise and cut into thin slices

¾ pound mushrooms, thinly sliced

1 tablespoon flour

½ cup reduced-sodium chicken broth, defatted, or reduced-sodium vegetable broth

14½-ounce can no-salt-added stewed tomatoes, chopped with their juices

1 teaspoon salt

¾ teaspoon freshly ground black pepper

½ teaspoon dried rosemary

3 tablespoons coarsely grated fresh Parmesan cheese

1. Preheat the oven to 400°. Cut the squash in half lengthwise, scoop out and discard the seeds, and place the squash, cut-sides down, on a nonstick baking sheet. With a fork, prick the squash skin all over, cover with foil, and bake for 35 minutes, or until the squash is tender when pierced with a fork.

2. Meanwhile, in a large nonstick skillet, heat the oil over medium heat until hot but not smoking. Add the shallots and garlic and cook, stirring frequently, until the shallots are softened, about 3 minutes. Add the carrot and mushrooms and cook, stirring frequently, until the carrot and mushrooms are tender, about 7 minutes.

3. Stir in the flour and cook until the vegetables are well coated, about 1 minute. Add the broth and bring to a boil. Stir in the tomatoes and their juices, the salt, pepper, and rosemary, and cook until the mixture is slightly thickened, about 5 minutes.

4. Remove the squash from the oven and let it cool slightly. With a fork, scrape out the flesh (it will form spaghetti-like strands). Place the squash in a large bowl, add the sauce, and toss to coat. Divide the squash mixture among 4 plates, sprinkle the cheese on top, and serve.

Helpful hint: Choose a pale yellow spaghetti squash for the sweetest taste.

FAT: 6G/22%
CALORIES: 251
SATURATED FAT: 1.6G
CARBOHYDRATE: 46G
PROTEIN: 8G
CHOLESTEROL: 3MG
SODIUM: 801MG

Asparagus-Cheese Puff

SERVES: 4
WORKING TIME: 20 MINUTES
TOTAL TIME: 55 MINUTES

This puff is actually a luscious soufflé in disguise, made reasonably low-fat with more egg whites than yolks. To create the illusion of richness, mashed white kidney beans are stirred into the soufflé base. Using a strongly flavored full-fat cheese means you can use less of it— in this case, a little goat cheese or feta goes a long way.

¾ **pound asparagus, tough ends trimmed, cut into ½-inch pieces**

3 tablespoons flour

⅔ **cup low-fat (1%) milk**

¾ **cup canned white kidney beans (cannellini), rinsed, drained, and mashed**

2 egg yolks

1½ **ounces crumbled goat cheese or feta cheese**

½ **teaspoon dried tarragon**

½ **teaspoon salt**

⅛ **teaspoon cayenne pepper**

6 egg whites

⅛ **teaspoon cream of tartar**

1. Preheat the oven to 375°. In a medium saucepan of boiling water, cook the asparagus until barely tender, about 2 minutes. Drain well and blot dry on paper towels.

2. Place the flour in a large saucepan over medium heat, and gradually whisk in the milk until no lumps remain. Bring to a boil and cook, whisking frequently, until the mixture is slightly thickened, about 4 minutes. Remove from the heat and stir in the beans. Whisk in the egg yolks, cheese, tarragon, ¼ teaspoon of the salt, and the cayenne until well combined.

3. In a large bowl, with an electric mixer, beat the egg whites, remaining ¼ teaspoon salt, and the cream of tartar until stiff, but not dry, peaks form. Stir about 1 cup of the egg whites into the milk mixture, then gently fold in the remaining egg whites. Gently fold in the asparagus.

4. Spoon the mixture into an 8-cup soufflé mold and bake for 30 minutes, or until the soufflé is golden brown, puffed, and just set in the center. Serve immediately.

Helpful hints: For variety, replace the asparagus with cauliflower, green beans, or broccoli. Be sure to use the cream of tartar, since it helps stabilize the beaten egg whites and increases volume as well.

FAT: 5G/29%
CALORIES: 164
SATURATED FAT: 2.9G
CARBOHYDRATE: 15G
PROTEIN: 14G
CHOLESTEROL: 63MG
SODIUM: 499MG

Eggplant Parmesan

SERVES: 4
WORKING TIME: 25 MINUTES
TOTAL TIME: 1 HOUR

This Italian favorite has all the taste and visual appeal you're used to, but the dish has been altered slightly in order to lower the fat. Instead of frying fat-laden breaded slices of eggplant, you dip the slices into no-fat egg whites, then bread crumbs, and then oven-bake them. And, this recipe calls for less cheese than usual.

2 egg whites

⅔ cup plain dried bread crumbs

1 pound eggplant, peeled and cut into ¼-inch-thick slices

2 cups no-salt-added tomato sauce

14½-ounce can no-salt-added stewed tomatoes, chopped with their juices

¼ cup chopped fresh mint

½ teaspoon salt

½ teaspoon freshly ground black pepper

½ teaspoon dried oregano

¾ cup shredded part-skim mozzarella cheese (about 3 ounces)

2 tablespoons grated Parmesan cheese

2 teaspoons chopped fresh parsley

1. Preheat the oven to 400°. Line a baking sheet with foil. In a shallow dish, with a fork, beat the egg whites and 2 tablespoons of water until foamy. On a plate, spread the bread crumbs. Dip the eggplant into the egg whites, then into the bread crumbs, pressing the crumbs into the eggplant. Place the eggplant on the prepared baking sheet, spray the eggplant with nonstick cooking spray, and bake for 20 minutes. Turn the eggplant and bake for 10 minutes longer, or until the eggplant is crisp and golden brown.

2. Meanwhile, in a medium bowl, stir together the tomato sauce, tomatoes and their juices, the mint, salt, pepper, and oregano. In a 9-inch square baking dish, spread 3 tablespoons of the tomato mixture. Lay half of the eggplant on top, spoon half of the remaining tomato mixture over the eggplant, and sprinkle half of the mozzarella on top. Repeat with the remaining eggplant, tomato mixture, and mozzarella.

3. Sprinkle the Parmesan on top and bake for 20 minutes, or until the eggplant is piping hot and the sauce is bubbly. Sprinkle the parsley on top and serve.

Helpful hints: If good-quality fresh mint is not available, substitute fresh basil for a tasty variation. You can bake this up to 1 day ahead, and then reheat in a 350° oven, covered, for about 20 minutes. Leftovers would be great on a French roll for lunch.

FAT: 6G/22%
CALORIES: 238
SATURATED FAT: 2.9G
CARBOHYDRATE: 35G
PROTEIN: 14G
CHOLESTEROL: 14MG
SODIUM: 649MG

Roasted Potatoes with Parmesan and Herbs

SERVES: 4
WORKING TIME: 15 MINUTES
TOTAL TIME: 45 MINUTES

*When you cook potatoes in the pan along with a roast or bird, the result
is undeniably delicious but unfortunately loaded with fat. The potatoes absorb the fat
that runs off from the meat. But even with a spoonful of olive oil and a generous
sprinkling of Parmesan, these "al forno" (oven-cooked) potatoes are a healthier choice.
Try them with sage-rubbed roasted game hens.*

1½ pounds small red potatoes

1 tablespoon extra-virgin olive oil

3 cloves garlic, peeled and halved

¾ teaspoon dried rosemary

½ teaspoon dried sage

1½ teaspoons grated lemon zest

½ teaspoon salt

¼ cup grated Parmesan cheese

1. Preheat the oven to 400°. With a vegetable peeler, peel a thin band around the circumference of each potato. In a large pot of boiling water, cook the potatoes for 5 minutes. Drain.

2. In a large roasting pan, combine the oil, garlic, rosemary, and sage. Bake until the garlic is fragrant and the oil is hot, about 4 minutes. Add the potatoes, lemon zest, and salt and bake, turning occasionally, for 20 minutes, or until the potatoes are crisp, golden, and tender. Sprinkle the Parmesan over the potatoes and bake for 2 minutes, or just until the cheese is melted and golden brown.

Helpful hint: If you're in a hurry, you can skip the peeling step and roast the potatoes with all of their skins on.

FAT: 5G/23%
CALORIES: 193
SATURATED FAT: 1.4G
CARBOHYDRATE: 32G
PROTEIN: 6G
CHOLESTEROL: 4MG
SODIUM: 380MG

Succotash

SERVES: 4

WORKING TIME: 25 MINUTES

TOTAL TIME: 40 MINUTES

Sweet fresh corn stars in this New England classic. When scraping the kernels from the cob, be sure to include all the delicious "milk."

---

6 ears of corn

1 teaspoon olive oil

4 shallots, minced

10-ounce package frozen baby lima beans

1 pound tomatoes, seeded and coarsely chopped

¾ teaspoon dried tarragon

½ teaspoon salt

2 tablespoons chopped fresh parsley

2 teaspoons unsalted butter

1. Remove the husks and silk from the corn. With a sharp knife, working over a large bowl, cut the kernels off the cobs from the tips to the stems, making sure to catch the juices as well. Set aside.

2. In a large saucepan, heat the oil over medium heat until hot but not smoking. Add the shallots and cook, stirring frequently, until the shallots are softened, about 4 minutes. Add the lima beans and ¼ cup of water and bring to a boil. Stir in the tomatoes, tarragon, and salt and return to a boil. Reduce to a simmer, cover, and cook until the lima beans are almost tender, about 7 minutes.

3. Stir in the corn kernels and their juices, cover again, and cook until the corn and lima beans are tender, about 4 minutes. Stir in the parsley and butter and cook, uncovered, just until the butter is melted, about 1 minute longer.

Helpful hints: You can substitute frozen corn for the fresh to enjoy this dish all year round. Plan on using about 3 cups of corn kernels. If there are leftovers, stir in some reduced-sodium chicken broth, gently reheat, and you'll have a fine corn soup.

FAT: 5G/18%

CALORIES: 248

SATURATED FAT: 1.6G

CARBOHYDRATE: 46G

PROTEIN: 10G

CHOLESTEROL: 5MG

SODIUM: 339MG

Sautéed Spinach with Sun-Dried Tomatoes

SERVES: 4
WORKING TIME: 10 MINUTES
TOTAL TIME: 20 MINUTES

*Make a lovely meatless meal of a big baked potato and this garlicky spinach—
it's sautéed with bits of sweet sun-dried tomatoes.*

½ cup sun-dried (not oil-packed) tomato halves

1 cup boiling water

2 teaspoons olive oil

2 cloves garlic, minced

⅛ teaspoon red pepper flakes

2 pounds fresh spinach leaves

½ teaspoon salt

⅛ teaspoon sugar

¼ cup reduced-sodium chicken broth, defatted

1. In a small bowl, combine the sun-dried tomatoes and boiling water and let stand until the tomatoes have softened, about 15 minutes. Drain the tomatoes, reserving ¼ cup of the soaking liquid. Coarsely chop the tomatoes and set aside.

2. In a large nonstick skillet, heat the oil over medium heat until hot but not smoking. Add the garlic, red pepper flakes, spinach, salt, sugar, and broth, and cook just until the garlic is fragrant, about 3 minutes. Add the sun-dried tomatoes and the reserved soaking liquid. Cover and cook just until the spinach is wilted, about 4 minutes. Spoon onto 4 plates and serve.

Helpful hint: Sand and grit will rinse out of spinach more quickly if you rinse the leaves in lukewarm, rather than ice-cold, tap water.

FAT: 3G/28%
CALORIES: 98
SATURATED FAT: 0.4G
CARBOHYDRATE: 14G
PROTEIN: 8G
CHOLESTEROL: 0MG
SODIUM: 501MG

Creamy Mashed Rutabaga

MAKES: 5 CUPS
WORKING TIME: 20 MINUTES
TOTAL TIME: 45 MINUTES

The apple adds a tangy sweetness to the already subtly sweet rutabaga.
This is a natural with roast turkey or chicken.

1¾ **pounds rutabaga, peeled**
and thickly sliced

1 **Granny Smith apple, peeled,**
cored, and thickly sliced

3 **cloves garlic, slivered**

¾ **teaspoon dried marjoram**
or oregano

½ **teaspoon salt**

3 **tablespoons evaporated**
low-fat milk

2 **tablespoons grated Parmesan**
cheese

2 **teaspoons unsalted butter**

1. In a large saucepan, combine the rutabaga, apple, garlic, marjoram, and ¼ teaspoon of the salt. Add cold water to cover by 1 inch and bring to a boil. Reduce to a simmer, cover, and cook until the rutabaga is tender, about 25 minutes. Drain well and transfer the mixture to a large bowl.

2. Add the evaporated milk, Parmesan, butter, and remaining ¼ teaspoon salt, and mash until the mixture is well blended but still chunky. Spoon the rutabaga mixture onto a platter and serve.

Helpful hints: This recipe can be prepared 1 day ahead through Step 1 and refrigerated. To serve, gently reheat over low heat, stirring in the remaining ingredients. If you prefer a smooth vegetable purée, mash the mixture with a potato masher or an electric beater until no lumps remain.

VALUES ARE PER ½ CUP
FAT: 1G/24%
CALORIES: 48
SATURATED FAT: 0.7G
CARBOHYDRATE: 8G
PROTEIN: 2G
CHOLESTEROL: 4MG
SODIUM: 147MG

Cauliflower Milanese

SERVES: 4
WORKING TIME: 15 MINUTES
TOTAL TIME: 40 MINUTES

The bread crumbs and Parmesan that top the cauliflower are what make this "Milanese."
However, one traditional Milanese ingredient—butter—has been replaced by a touch
of olive oil for a more healthful dish.

5 cups cauliflower florets

½ cup reduced-sodium chicken broth, defatted

¾ teaspoon grated lemon zest

½ teaspoon salt

½ teaspoon dried marjoram

¼ teaspoon freshly ground black pepper

¼ cup plain dried bread crumbs

2 tablespoons grated Parmesan cheese

1 teaspoon olive oil

2 teaspoons fresh lemon juice

1. Preheat the oven to 400°. In a large pot of boiling water, cook the cauliflower for 4 minutes to blanch. Drain well.

2. Meanwhile, in a small bowl, combine the broth, lemon zest, salt, marjoram, and pepper. Set aside. In another small bowl, combine the bread crumbs and Parmesan. Set aside.

3. Spread the oil in a 13 x 9-inch baking dish and heat in the oven until hot, about 4 minutes. Add the cauliflower to the baking dish and bake, stirring occasionally, for 7 minutes, or until the cauliflower is golden. Pour the reserved broth mixture over the cauliflower and bake for 7 minutes, or until the cauliflower is tender. Sprinkle the bread crumb mixture over the cauliflower, drizzle with the lemon juice, and bake for 5 minutes, or until the topping is lightly crisped.

Helpful hint: Choose a firm cauliflower head that's creamy white with crisp, green leaves at the base. Pass up heads that have dark speckles or soft spots.

FAT: 3G/22%
CALORIES: 82
SATURATED FAT: 0.7G
CARBOHYDRATE: 12G
PROTEIN: 5G
CHOLESTEROL: 2MG
SODIUM: 478MG

Strawberry Cheesecake Mousse

SERVES: 4

WORKING TIME: 20 MINUTES

TOTAL TIME: 20 MINUTES PLUS CHILLING TIME

Compare this recipe to one for a baked cheesecake and you'll notice that both the ingredients list and the preparation time have been dramatically shortened. Of course, this isn't a cake— instead of baking the filling in a crust, you spoon it into dessert bowls. The "cheesecake" mixture has a touch of tartness, and the flavor of the strawberries is underscored with a swirl of strawberry spreadable fruit.

½ **teaspoon unflavored gelatin**

2 **pints fresh strawberries**

2 **tablespoons strawberry spreadable fruit**

8 **ounces nonfat cream cheese**

¼ **cup reduced-fat sour cream**

½ **cup sugar**

½ **cup evaporated milk, chilled**

1. Place ¼ cup of cold water in a small bowl, sprinkle the gelatin on top, and let stand until softened, about 4 minutes. Set the bowl over a small saucepan of simmering water and stir until the gelatin dissolves, about 3 minutes. Set aside to cool.

2. Meanwhile, reserving 4 whole berries for a garnish, halve the strawberries. In a medium bowl, combine the halved fresh strawberries and the spreadable fruit, tossing until well coated.

3. In a food processor, combine the cream cheese, 2 tablespoons of the sour cream, and ¼ cup of the sugar, and process until smooth. In a medium bowl, with an electric mixer, beat the evaporated milk with the remaining 2 tablespoons sour cream and remaining ¼ cup sugar until soft peaks form. Gradually beat in the cooled gelatin mixture.

4. Fold the cream cheese mixture into the evaporated milk mixture. Divide the strawberry mixture among 4 goblets or dessert bowls. Top with the "cheesecake" mixture and garnish with the reserved strawberries. Chill until set, about 1 hour, and serve.

Helpful hint: Spreadable fruit is like jam, but it is sweetened with fruit juice rather than sugar. It is used in this recipe because it is soft enough, even at room temperature, to coat the strawberries.

FAT: 5G/16%

CALORIES: 282

SATURATED FAT: 2.5G

CARBOHYDRATE: 49G

PROTEIN: 12G

CHOLESTEROL: 20MG

SODIUM: 314MG

Raspberry-Filled Chocolate Cupcakes

MAKES: 1 DOZEN
WORKING TIME: 30 MINUTES
TOTAL TIME: 50 MINUTES PLUS COOLING TIME

The cream-filled cupcakes of our childhood now have a grown-up counterpart: petite choco-late cakes with hearts of raspberry jam (which you can flavor with raspberry liqueur for a truly adult treat). The cupcakes are decorated with a swirl of semisweet chocolate and a few fresh berries. Red paper cups add a note of sophistication; look for them in kitchenware shops.

⅓ **cup raspberry spreadable fruit**

¾ **teaspoon raspberry-flavored liqueur (optional)**

1¼ **cups flour**

3 **tablespoons unsweetened cocoa powder**

½ **teaspoon baking soda**

⅛ **teaspoon salt**

¼ **cup unsalted butter, at room temperature**

½ **cup sugar**

1 **large egg**

⅔ **cup low-fat (1%) milk**

½ **ounce chocolate chips (about 1 tablespoon), melted**

1 **cup fresh raspberries**

1. Preheat the oven to 375°. Line twelve 2½-inch muffin-tin cups with paper liners or spray with nonstick cooking spray; set aside. In a small bowl, combine the raspberry spreadable fruit and the raspberry liqueur; set aside.

2. In a medium bowl, combine the flour, cocoa powder, baking soda, and salt. In a large bowl, with an electric mixer, beat the butter and sugar until light and fluffy. Add the egg and beat until well combined. Alternately beat in the flour mixture and the milk, beginning and ending with the flour mixture.

3. Spoon about 1 tablespoon of batter into each muffin cup. Make a small indentation in the batter. Dividing evenly, spoon the raspberry spreadable fruit mixture into each indentation (using about 1¼ teaspoons per cupcake). Spoon the remaining batter evenly over the raspberry mixture. Bake for 20 minutes, or until the tops of the cupcakes spring back when lightly touched. Turn the cupcakes out onto a wire rack to cool completely.

4. Spoon the melted chocolate into a small plastic bag, then snip off the very tip of one corner of the bag. Pipe the melted chocolate on top of each cupcake. Top with fresh raspberries before serving.

Helpful hint: If you like, cherry-flavored kirsch can be substituted for the raspberry-flavored liqueur.

VALUES ARE PER CUPCAKE
FAT: 5G/29%
CALORIES: 158
SATURATED FAT: 2.9G
CARBOHYDRATE: 26G
PROTEIN: 3G
CHOLESTEROL: 29MG
SODIUM: 89MG

Berry Cake

SERVES: 8
WORKING TIME: 15 MINUTES
TOTAL TIME: 50 MINUTES PLUS COOLING TIME

This irresistible buttermilk cake is a snap to make, and it comes with its own garnish to boot—fresh berries peeking out from a crispy, glossy top. It's perfect for a convivial morning coffee klatch, a gracious afternoon tea, or a casual dinner with friends. Try it in the summer, when berries are in season.

1½ cups assorted whole berries (such as blackberries, blueberries, and raspberries)

1 cup flour

¾ cup plus 1 tablespoon sugar

½ teaspoon baking soda

½ teaspoon ground ginger

¼ teaspoon salt

½ cup low-fat (1.5%) buttermilk

2 tablespoons vegetable oil

2 large eggs, lightly beaten

1. Preheat the oven to 375°. Spray an 8-inch round cake pan with nonstick cooking spray. In a small bowl, combine the berries; set aside.

2. In a medium bowl, combine the flour, ¾ cup of the sugar, the baking soda, ginger, and salt. Make a well in the center and pour in the buttermilk, oil, and eggs. Stir until no dry flour is visible.

3. Scrape the batter into the prepared pan. Spoon the berries on top and sprinkle with the remaining 1 tablespoon sugar. Bake for 35 to 40 minutes, or until a toothpick inserted in the center comes out clean. Cool in the pan on a wire rack. Remove from the pan, transfer to a plate, and serve.

Helpful hints: You can use any small berries for this recipe, except strawberries, which will add too much moisture. It's important to stir the dry ingredients thoroughly to mix them, and, conversely, to go easy on the mixing once you've added the liquid ingredients so that the cake turns out nice and tender.

FAT: 5G/22%
CALORIES: 207
SATURATED FAT: 1G
CARBOHYDRATE: 37G
PROTEIN: 4G
CHOLESTEROL: 54MG
SODIUM: 171MG

Answers to Common Questions

One side of our patio is quite open to view from several neighbors' yards, and we'd like more privacy. The patio is screened off with shrubs on the other open sides, but I was wondering if there are any annuals that could function as screening?

Annual vines such as *Humulus japonicus* (Japanese hopvine) and *Lagenaria siceraria* (calabash gourd) can be grown on 2-by-3-inch wood poles set in the ground and strung with durable twine or plastic fishline for plant supports. These plants, which can be grown in pots that are set on the edge of the patio, have dense enough foliage to block the view from outside.

One of my great joys is attracting wildlife to my garden. What are the most alluring annuals for butterflies and humming-birds? Do any annuals produce seed that birds can feed on over the winter?

Of the long list of annuals on the butterfly hit parade, the best are *Cosmos bipinnatus* (garden cosmos), *Gaillardia pulchella* (Indian blanket), *Helianthus* (sunflower), *Heliotropium arborescens* (cherry pie), *Hesperis matronalis* (dame's rocket), *Limonium sinuatum* (notchleaf statice), *Rudbeckia hirta* (black-eyed Susan), *Tithonia rotundifolia* (Mexican sunflower), *Verbena* (vervain), and *Zinnia elegans* (common zinnia). Hummingbirds will flock to *Alcea rosea* (hollyhock), *Antirrhinum majus* (common snapdragon), *Dianthus barbatus* (sweet William), *Digitalis purpurea* (common foxglove), *Ipomopsis aggregata* (scarlet gilia), and *Salvia* (sage). For seed heads that will feed a variety of birds during the cold months, plant *Amaranthus* (amaranth), *Coreopsis* (tickseed), *Cosmos, Gomphrena, Helianthus annuus* (common sunflower), *Rudbeckia hirta,* and *Verbena bonariensis* (Brazilian verbena).

We own a seaside cabin where we spend our summers, and I'd like to put several beds of annuals around it. What plants will do best in the conditions found at the beach?

Even in this trying environment of wind and salt-laden air, a fairly large variety of annuals will succeed. You can choose with confidence from among *Ageratum houstonianum* (flossflower), *Antirrhinum majus* (common snapdragon), *Calendula officinalis* (pot marigold), *Dimorphotheca* (Cape marigold), *Lavatera trimestris* (tree mallow), *Lobelia erinus* (edging lobelia), *Lobularia maritima* (sweet alyssum), *Pelargonium* (geranium), *Phlox drummondii* (annual phlox), *Portulaca grandiflora* (moss rose), *Salvia argentea* (silver sage), *Senecio cineraria* (dusty-miller), *Tagetes patula* (French marigold), and *Verbena* (vervain).

Because we can almost never find time to tend our garden except for a bit on week-ends, we're looking for flowers that can get along pretty well on their own. Are there any annuals that will bloom nicely from spring to frost without assistance?

Once you've gotten them off to a good start in well-prepared soil, you can expect self-sufficient performance from *Begonia* x *semperflorens-cultorum* (wax begonia), *Catharanthus roseus* (Madagascar periwinkle), *Heliotropium arborescens* (cherry pie), *Pentas lanceolata* (Egyptian star-cluster), *Petunia* x *hybrida* (common garden petunia), and *Salvia splendens* (scarlet sage).

There's a patch of ground out near my property line facing the road where the soil is rather infertile, dry, and sandy. I'd like to dress up the area a bit, but without putting in a lot of effort. Are there any annuals that would work in such soil?

Happily, a wide variety of annuals will do well in these unpromising conditions. You can choose from *Arctotis* (African daisy), *Calendula officinalis* (pot marigold), *Callistephus chinensis* (China aster), *Clarkia amoena* (farewell-to-spring), *Coreopsis tinctoria* (tickseed), *Dyssodia tenuiloba* (Dahlberg daisy), *Euphorbia marginata* (snow-on-the-mountain), *Gaillardia pulchella* (Indian blanket), *Kochia scoparia* (burning bush, summer cypress), *Lobularia maritima* (sweet alyssum), *Phlox drummondii* (annual phlox), *Portulaca grandiflora* (moss rose), *Tithonia rotundifolia* (Mexican sunflower), and *Verbena* x *hybrida* (vervain).

I have a little rill running through a corner of my property that I can see from my kitchen window, and I would like to brighten up its banks with annuals. Can you recommend some that will adapt to damp sites?

The versatile clan of annuals includes species that will be right at home in very boggy conditions, including *Limnanthes douglasii* (meadow foam), *Mimulus* x *hybridus* (monkey flower), and *Myosotis sylvatica* (forget-me-not). In soil that is not boggy but is generally moist, you can grow *Caladium* x *hortulanum* (fancy-leaved caladium), *Catharanthus roseus* (Madagascar periwinkle), *Cleome hasslerana* (spider flower), *Coleus* x *hybridus* (coleus), *Exacum affine* (Persian violet), *Impatiens*, *Torenia fournieri* (bluewings), and *Viola* x *wittrockiana* (garden pansy).

My favorite kind of foundation planting is an annual border, but I know from soil testing that the foundation of my house leaches limestone into the soil, keeping it on the alkaline side. What annuals are best for alkaline soil?

Within reasonable limits—say, a pH of no more than 8—you can confidently expect the following annuals to adapt comfortably to the soil around your foundation: *Calendula officinalis* (pot marigold), *Catharanthus roseus* (Madagascar periwinkle), *Dianthus barbatus* (sweet William), *Gaillardia pulchella* (Indian blanket), *Gypsophila elegans* (baby's-breath), *Iberis umbellata* (globe candytuft), *Lathyrus odoratus* (sweet pea), *Papaver rhoeas* (corn poppy), *Pelargonium* (geranium), *Phlox drummondii* (annual phlox), *Scabiosa atropurpurea* (pincushion flower), *Senecio cineraria* (dusty-miller), *Tropaeolum majus* (garden nasturtium), *Verbena* x *hybrida* (vervain), and *Zinnia elegans* (common zinnia).

I buy annuals at the home and garden center, and they look great, but when I plant them, they soon poop out. Am I doing something wrong?

To entice buyers, home and garden centers and roadside stands often display lushly blooming annuals—particularly tender annuals—several weeks before the ground is warm enough to accommodate them. Many of these plants have been forced into early bloom and may also have had extra applications of chemical fertilizers. Plants that have been raised like this are liable to suffer severe transplant shock when set out in the garden, especially if it's done too early in the season. To avoid this kind of frustration, buy plants that are not yet in full bloom and safeguard them under cover or in a cold frame until it is safe to set them out.

I would like to grow bulbs in partial shade, but I understand they don't do well under some trees. Which kinds of trees should I avoid?

Maples, beeches, and other trees with shallow, fibrous roots are the ones to avoid. Bulbs and most other kinds of plants have a hard time competing with them for nutrients, water, and growing space. Also avoid evergreens and other trees with low canopies that prevent at least a half-day of filtered light from getting through.

I have more bulbs than I need for this fall. Can I hold some to plant next fall?

Unlike some seeds, bulbs cannot be held from one year to the next, because the moisture in their tissues will dry out and they will die.

We have had a mild winter so far, and my daffodils and tulips are coming up too early. Now we are expecting some hard freezes. How do I protect my bulbs?

The surprisingly tough foliage of these plants can take temperatures down to around 15°F. Below that point, the leaves may be "burned"—dried out by the cold—unless you cover or surround the plants with a light mulch. Even if the foliage is damaged, however, it doesn't seem to greatly affect later bloom and overall plant performance.

I think my newly planted bulbs must have frozen, because we had a very cold winter and they didn't come up this spring. When I dug them, they were soft and mushy. How can I keep this from happening again?

You can do several things: Plant your bulbs early, and at a depth at least 3 times their height; water well after planting to initiate root growth, because well-rooted bulbs resist frost damage better; mulch after planting to keep the soil temperature stable while the bulbs are rooting; and make sure the area is well drained, because soil that holds too much moisture is more likely to freeze and to encourage rot.

My double daffodils send up nice big fat buds that never open. What is the problem?

Your plants are experiencing "blasting." Double daffodils are especially susceptible to blasting, which happens when the plump buds are subjected to sudden freezing, high temperatures, or insufficient moisture. Protect buds from temperature extremes and water well. Some new cultivars have been developed that are blast resistant.

My bulb foliage gets too long and flops over, leaving an unsightly mess in my garden. How can I keep my plants from getting so tall?

Plants grow too tall and leggy when they do not have enough light. Most bulbs that do not get at least a half-day of sun not only flop over but also have sparse blooms. Transplant the bulbs to a sunnier location; fertilize and water well; and thin out overhanging vegetation to let in more light. For future plantings on this site, choose cultivars that are more shade tolerant.

How can I figure out where to put down fertilizer for my bulbs in fall when there is no remaining foliage to guide me?

Plant *Muscari* (grape hyacinth) bulbs around the edges of your other bulbs; the foliage will emerge in the fall and show you where to fertilize. Or place markers such as vinyl plant labels or even golf tees around the edge of your planting in the spring; they will stay around to show you the way. Finally, you could take photographs of your plot in the spring and use them as a guide.

I use bone meal to fertilize my bulbs, as the old gardening books advise. But the bulbs just aren't blooming well. What's going wrong?

Bone meal is not a complete fertilizer; it supplies only phosphorus and calcium. Bulbs also need nitrogen, potash, and trace elements. If you wish to fully fertilize your bulbs using only organic nutrient sources, you must add blood meal or cottonseed meal for nitrogen and "New Jersey Greensand" or wood ashes for potash and trace elements. Or you can use a ready-formulated fertilizer made just for bulbs. A 9-9-6 slow-release formula is best for tulips and members of the lily family but can be used for all bulbs. A 5-10-20 slow-release formula with trace elements is best for daffodils and members of the amaryllis family.

Many of my bulbs have stopped blooming, and others aren't blooming as well as they used to. Do I need to dig them up and divide them?

That is one solution, but perhaps an easier and more efficient way would be to fertilize the clumps to resupply the nutrients the bulbs have used up as they multiplied over the years. Once they have enough nutrients, along with moisture and sunshine, most of those old clumps will bloom gloriously.

Something is eating my tulip and crocus bulbs underground. Could it be moles, and how do I deal with this problem?

Moles are carnivorous and do not eat plants. The underground bulb monster is more than likely a vole, also known as a field mouse. One way to protect your bulbs is to plant them a bit deeper than normal; voles work in the top 3 to 4 inches of soil. Another is to put a handful of sharp-edged, crushed gravel—pieces about the size of a fingernail—around each bulb; voles do not like to dig through or move around in gravelly soil.

PERENNIALS

I have a perennial border with lots of bold colors like red, orange, and yellow. These colors are compatible, but my garden seems to lack continuity. What can I do?

Tie your bold colors together by introducing perennials with blue flowers. Leadwort *(Ceratostigma)*, globe thistle *(Echinops)*, flax *(Linum)*, Siberian iris *(Iris sibirica)*, Russian sage *(Perovskia)*, false indigo *(Baptisia)*, and blue cultivars of moss phlox *(Phlox subulata)* are a few of the best. You may also want to try plants with silver or gray foliage, such as lavender *(Lavandula angustifolia)*, lamb's ears *(Stachys byzantina)*, or *Artemisia* 'Silver Mound'. For best results, repeat your selections along the length of the border, and remember to mass blue-flowered plants as much as possible because blue is a receding color.

I have tried unsuccessfully over the years to grow delphiniums in my garden. Plants that I purchase from nurseries will flourish for the summer and then fail to return the following year. Are delphiniums really perennials?

Most gardeners plant various forms of the Pacific Coast hybrids. Members of this strain do exceptionally well in climates where cold winters and cool summers prevail. But they do not do well in areas where winter temperatures fluctuate above and below freezing and where summer temperatures are hot. If you live in a less-than-perfect delphinium climate, you might try *Delphinium bellamosa, D. belladonna,* or *D. chinense* and their cultivars, which are more forgiving.

I'm having trouble establishing Oriental poppies despite planting them the recommended 2 inches deep and in ideal growing conditions. Any suggestions?

Most Oriental poppies prefer the colder regions (Zones 5-7). Where winter temperatures fluctuate, poppies may break dormancy during warm periods, only to be struck down a few days later by a frost. Winter mulching can sometimes protect them, but don't mulch during the rest of the year, or you'll invite crown rot. Also, poppies hate wet feet during their late-summer dormant period, so don't water them in late spring when their foliage begins to brown.

A lot of perennials in my garden need staking in late summer. This requires a good bit of work on my part, and the result looks rather artificial. Is there any way to avoid this tedious task?

First of all, if you know that a favorite plant is going to need support, put a protective hoop around it or make a frame of stakes and string as the plant is coming up; the developing foliage will soon hide the supports. Second, perennials require less staking if you select cultivars that are naturally more compact; if you space your plants far enough apart so that sunlight and circulating air reach all the foliage; and if you feed them a low-nitrogen organic fertilizer. Pinching back your unruly plants also helps.

How do I prepare soil in the different sections of my garden to accommodate various perennials I want to plant? It seems that some species like more acid soil and some like more alkaline soil.

Of the thousands of perennials to select from, only a few have pH requirements that fall outside the average range for most garden soils. Maintain a pH between 6 and 7, and almost any perennial will do well. For those plants that require more alkalinity, dig dolomitic limestone into the soil at the planting location; it won't leach out into the surrounding soil. In the case of acid-loving plants, try adding peat moss to the planting site.

My perennial bed gets 6 hours of morning sun. Will my plants thrive with this amount of light?

Plant requirements for sun are determined by the intensity and duration of sunlight. For sun-loving perennials, 6 hours of sun is adequate only when it occurs at midday or in the afternoon. In other words, when picking plants for a garden with morning sun and afternoon shade, you should opt for shade plants. If, on the other hand, your garden is shaded all morning but gets afternoon sun, pick plants that require full sun.

I'd like to grow perennials under a large Norway maple tree. What are some good choices?

Norway maples have a network of surface roots that can rob plants of moisture. Plants that can tolerate these dry shade conditions include violets *(Viola)*, woodland strawberries *(Fragaria)*, dead nettle *(Lamium)*, *Hosta, Epimedium,* and leadwort *(Ceratostigma)*.

One of my perennials has yellow, stunted foliage. When I dug it up, it had nodules all over the roots. What is the problem?

More than likely your plant has root knot nematodes. You can control this pest by using a nontoxic material made from ground crab shells that is available at better garden centers.

I have a bed of irises that is overrun with iris borer. What should I do?

First, establish a new iris bed in another location. Then dig up and divide irises from your infested bed in mid to late summer, selecting only healthy, young rhizomes. Throw away all the old rhizomes and plant debris. Dip the transplants in a solution of 1 part chlorine bleach to 9 parts water, and let them dry in the shade before planting. Keep the new bed clear of decaying foliage to discourage the adult moths from laying their eggs in the vicinity.

My peonies have petals that are brown all over, and they don't open properly. What is wrong and how can I correct it?

One of three things could be happening. First, your flower buds could be suffering from excessive heat—more than 85°F—at bloom time (called bullheading). Second, your peonies could have a fungal disease called botrytis blight. Third, the damage you describe could be caused by tiny sucking insects called thrips.

ROSES

We have a summer place right on the ocean in Massachusetts. Are there any roses that will grow in this setting?

Any of the rugosa species and most hybrid rugosas, such as 'Blanc Double de Coubert' or 'Belle Poitevine', will grow and bloom in your situation. Rugosas tolerate salt spray and will grow in sand dunes unattended. In fact, the Japanese native species has naturalized on beaches in the northeastern and northwestern United States.

My yard has a lot of shade. Are there any roses that will grow in it?

Roses need sun to perform well. The best ones to try under your conditions would be the modern hybrid musks, such as 'Ballerina', 'Belinda', 'Buff Beauty', or 'Prosperity'. If they don't grow and bloom there, no rose will.

I get black spot on my roses every year. I really don't want to use chemical fungicides, but I'm getting desperate. Is there any way I can keep the disease from ruining my plants without adding toxic chemicals to the garden?

Try this year-round preventive program that uses nonharmful products: Before the first frost, spray your roses with a commercial antidesiccant, according to label directions, to keep any fungus spores off the leaves during the winter. Then, while the plants are still dormant in the spring, spray them with wettable or liquid sulfur fungicide, followed by a thorough spray of dormant oil. Keep applying the sulfur periodically until frost—every week to 10 days at most. Don't spray sulfur, though, when the temperature is 85°F or higher, because it may burn the foliage, and keep it away from rugosa roses and their hybrids altogether; rugosas are damaged by sulfur—but they're immune to most fungi in the first place. This treatment will control not only black spot but also rust and powdery mildew, as well as infestations of aphids, thrips, and mites.

Are there any roses that deer do not eat?

Probably not. Try planting companions that deer dislike, such as rosemary or artemisia. Sometimes people put wire and fencing around their roses to keep deer from browsing, but this defeats the purpose of roses beautifying the garden. Instead, lay wire mesh on the ground near and in the rose bed, and plant ground covers such as ivy, phlox, or dianthus, making the mesh invisible. Deer will not step into these areas.

WILDFLOWERS

I have a traditional landscape that includes an evergreen foundation planting, a number of specimen shrubs, and a large lawn. Is there some way I can incorporate wildflowers into existing plantings, or will I need to tear them out and start from scratch?

You don't need to do anything drastic to incorporate wildflowers into your garden. Many of them are perfectly appropriate in a traditional garden that has a large proportion of nonnative plants. Your major concern will be to choose plants whose moisture, light, and soil requirements match the conditions of your site.

One of my gardening goals is to have color throughout the year. Is that possible with wildflowers?

With careful planning, year-round color is certainly possible. Just be sure to pick species with bloom periods that overlap each other; as one species completes its life cycle, another species will begin to bloom and will take its place. Also, be sure to plant a mix of perennials and annuals. The annuals will bloom for many weeks or even all season, providing continuous color and interest to fill any intervals between waves of perennial flowers. In fall and winter, foliage, fruits, and seed pods will offer a beauty unique to those seasons.

Four years ago I planted a small meadow of wildflowers and native grasses from a commercial seed mix. It's beautiful, but some of the plants that bloomed heavily the first season aren't as dominant anymore. Is it normal for a meadow to change like this from year to year?

Yes. A wildflower meadow is a complex, interactive plant community that evolves over time. Annuals are its main source of color until the slower-developing perennials mature. Also, the species that are best adapted to a particular site will eventually come to dominate. In time the balance of species will tend to stabilize, but there will always be differences from year to year because of weather conditions such as a mild winter or a wet summer.

My yard is rather small, and it's already so full of plants that I'm not sure I can fit in any wildflowers. Is it worth trying to grow some in pots or in window boxes?

Growing wildflowers in containers is a wonderful way to enjoy the benefits of native plants where space is at a premium, and they are just as appropriate as other annuals and perennials. They provide concentrated splashes of color and can be moved as light conditions change or retired to an unobtrusive spot when their blooming season ends. They are also a great way to introduce children to the pleasures of growing plants. Among the many attractive natives for container plantings are baby-blue-eyes, bitterroot, clarkia, common stonecrop and wild stonecrop, California poppy, Drummond's phlox, mealy blue sage, purple saxifrage, and Tahoka daisy. Water plants suited to container gardening include fragrant water lily and pickerelweed.

My family enjoys watching the birds that visit our garden, and we also value them as a natural means of pest control. We already have a number of trees and shrubs with fruits that attract birds and would like to plant some wildflowers that would increase the food supply. What are some especially good choices for this purpose?

You can attract a variety of birds with an array of different seed- or fruit-producing annuals, perennials, and grasses, such as asters, compass plant, fire pink, goat's-rue, goldenrod, jack-in-the-pulpit, mountain mint, partridgeberry, pickerelweed, purple coneflower, rudbeckia, Rocky Mountain bee plant, sideoats grama, spikenard, sunflowers, switch grass, tickseed, and wild geranium. Hummingbirds are attracted to nectar-producing flowers such as bee balm, cardinal flower, copper iris, columbine, lupine, monkshood, penstemon, fire pink, sage, spider lily, spigelia, verbena, wild four-o'clocks, wild hyssop, and yucca.

Are there any wildflowers that I could use as a ground cover to control soil erosion on a slope in my side yard?

New England aster, lanceleaf coreopsis, Indian blanket, and Rocky Mountain penstemon are all excellent choices for solving this problem.

Which wildflowers are suited to an exposed spot in a desert garden that is in full sun almost all day in summer?

Southwestern verbena, desert marigold, and desert mallow are just three of the many attractive wildflowers that will thrive in this hot, dry microhabitat.

Water drains from several neighboring properties into my backyard, so the soil is often damp and the lawn is growing poorly. Are wildflowers a sensible alternative to turf grass?

Although the majority of wildflowers would do no better than your lawn, some tolerate or even demand the soggy conditions you describe, including such fine ornamentals as sweet flag, swamp milkweed, rose mallow, blue flag, and cardinal flower.

How can I get my wildflowers to bloom for a longer period?

Deadheading—that is, removing blossoms that are past their prime—encourages wildflowers to bloom longer and more profusely, and it also keeps the plants looking fresh and tidy. However, this practice isn't appropriate if you want to collect seed from your wildflower garden for propagating, because it prevents seed production.

LAWN CARE

I am confused about which lawn-grass mixture I should buy for easy care. How can I decide among "playground mix," "park mix," or "estate mix" when those terms do not apply to my little yard?

The complex process of selecting the proper grass mix is not helped by the sales jargon you mention. There is no one lawn grass that can be planted throughout the United States. Like other perennials, grass species have unique requirements for moisture, light, temperature, and so on. The fine-bladed grasses that give the thick, luxurious lawns that most people prefer are bluegrass, Chewings and red fescues, and some of the new perennial ryegrasses. Find out what will grow in your area, and choose a grass mixture that includes those types. A combination of grasses in a mixture is best because some varieties will survive even if others have difficulty taking hold.

I love my lawn, but weed control is driving me crazy. What can I do to make things easier?

In temperate climates, cut your grass high. This promotes much deeper roots and a greener lawn, and the taller grass shades out many weeds such as crab grass. Also, keep the soil pH level between 6 and 6.8 to encourage grass growth and discourage weeds, and apply the appropriate amounts of fertilizer for your grass type. Leave lawn clippings in place to recycle into the ground.

One spot in my lawn stays wet, and I am always getting my riding lawn mower stuck in it. Is there anything I can do short of putting in a tile drain?

There are many trees that thrive in wet areas, where they take up lots of water, thus drying the area. Some members of the willow family—pussy willow *(Salix discolor),* weeping willow *(S. babylonica),* and the corkscrew willow *(S. matsudana* 'Tortuosa')—are good choices. Be sure, though, that there are no walkways, terraces, or drainfields close by; willow roots are extremely invasive and can damage them.

SHADE GARDENING

My outside sitting area is shaded by day, but I enjoy it the most at night during the hot summer months. How can I add horticultural interest for this very special time?

A few wonderful shade garden plants are perfect for these conditions. The pure white lilylike flowers of *Hosta plantaginea* open fully at night to release a honey-scented fragrance. Nicotianas are also fragrant at night. If you have a spot nearby that receives several hours of sun, be sure to put in the hauntingly fragrant *Ipomoea alba* (moonflower) vine, with its enormous white blossoms that open around sunset and glow in the moonlight. Look also for new *Hemerocallis* cultivars called nocturnal bloomers, which keep their blossoms open into evening, and extended bloomers, whose flowers stay open for up to 2 days.

I built a shaded flagstone terrace where the roots of a nearby maple restricted my gardening efforts. Now I spend too much time pulling weeds between the stones. Can I plant anything in these spaces to reduce maintenance and add interest?

Plant the narrowest crevices with *Sagina subulata* (Corsican pearlwort), a fine plant for paving areas with its creeping, mossy evergreen foliage and tiny white spring flowers. In wider spaces you can establish *Mentha requienii* (Corsican mint), with ground-hugging leaves that emit a delicious fragrance of peppermint when trod upon occasionally, and *Mazus reptans,* a creeper with purple-blue to white flowers. For extra interest, but not to be walked on, consider *Lysimachia nummularia* 'Aurea' (creeping Jenny), with rounded yellow leaves and yellow blossoms in summer, or one of the several cultivars of *Ajuga,* with colored or variegated foliage.

What can I plant to give me lots of fragrance in my shade garden?

You should rely upon a succession of plants through the seasons and avoid the many species that are fragrant only at close range. From late winter to early spring, cultivars of *Hamamelis mollis* and *H.* x *intermedia* waft their enticing fragrance over the awakening landscape. As spring progresses, *Viburnum carlesii* (Koreanspice viburnum) will add its own tangy scent. Few plants are more fragrant from midspring to early summer than azaleas. One of the best is *Rhododendron arborescens* (sweet azalea). In summer, mass plantings of night-fragrant *Hosta plantaginea* and annuals such as *Lobularia maritima* (sweet alyssum) and the night-fragrant nicotianas are very effective. Finish up in autumn with another native, *Hamamelis virginiana.*

What is the longest-blooming perennial I can plant in my shade garden?

In all but the hottest, driest parts of the country, the plant you seek is undoubtedly *Corydalis lutea*. It starts to bloom fairly early in spring and continues producing its small clusters of pendant, tubular yellow flowers until the onset of hard frost.

My shade garden really goes into the doldrums in summer. Although I plant drifts of impatiens and begonias, I miss the individuality and charm of blooming perennials and shrubs at this time. What can I plant to enliven the scene?

In addition to the unlimited potential of daylilies, here are a dozen stalwart perennials to bridge your early-to-late-summer flower gap: *Aconitum napellus*, *Astilbe* x *arendsii* cultivars, *Chelone lyonii* (pink turtlehead), *Chrysogonum virginianum*, *Cimicifuga racemosa* (black cohosh) and *C. americana* (American bugbane), *Dicentra eximia* cultivars and hybrids, hosta, *Ligularia dentata* 'Desdemona', *Lilium* (lily), *Physostegia virginiana* (false dragonhead) cultivars, *Stokesia laevis* (Stokes' aster), and *Thalictrum rochebrunianum* (lavender mist meadow rue). Two very hardy native shrubs for outstanding blossoms in July are *Aesculus parviflora* (bottlebrush buckeye) and *Rhododendron prunifolium* (plum-leaved azalea), a real beauty with blossoms of glowing orange-red.

I've had no luck luring hummingbirds to my shade garden. Most plants recommended for this purpose seem to be sun lovers, and others bloom only briefly. Do you have any suggestions?

One of the best plants for attracting hummingbirds is *Lonicera sempervirens* (trumpet or coral honeysuckle). It is also one of the most beautiful and longest-flowering vines you can bring into the garden. Train it up a trellis, where it will grow 10 to 15 feet high. The 2-inch-long blossoms are scarlet with orange throats and appear in great numbers from midspring to fall. The plant succeeds in partial shade, although it will blossom better in full sun. It is hardy to Zone 4.

The potted plants I grow on my shaded terrace never have that lush, overflowing look that I see in pictures in books and magazines. What am I doing wrong?

The secret is to be *very* generous initially with the number of plants used in each pot; regularly pinch back new buds on plants that require it to promote bushy growth; never let the soil dry out completely; and use a freely draining potting mix that contains a slow-release fertilizer. After 2 months, start applying a liquid fertilizer every 10 to 14 days. By early to midsummer your containers should be spilling over with lush growth.

I'm starting a woodland shade garden, but the site has lots of poison ivy. How should I get rid of it?

Use great caution when removing this plant; even people who have always been immune to it can develop a sensitivity. Avoid direct contact, contaminated clothing or pet fur, and even smoke from burning plants. With a long-handled hoe, uproot small plants as soon as you notice them. Spray larger plants with the herbicide glyphosate; repeat if necessary. If the poison ivy has ascended a tree, cut its stems near the base with a long-handled pole saw and treat the basal portions with herbicide. Wearing washable cloth gloves or a double layer of disposable latex gloves, dig a hole about 2 feet deep and bury all pruned and dead plant parts. If you are particularly sensitive or if the infestation is large, seek professional help to eradicate the plants.

Some of my rhododendrons have become overgrown. Can I cut them back? If so, when can I do this?

Rhododendrons usually need little or no pruning unless they get out of bounds, or if the growth becomes sparse, with long stretches of stem devoid of leaves. Then they will require drastic action. Cut back entire branches to within 2 feet of the ground, all at one time, just after the flowers have faded. You should see new sprouts from previously dormant buds on the old stems in about 4 to 8 weeks, but sometimes resprouting does not occur and the entire plant is lost. If this causes concern with a choice cultivar, you can take a more conservative approach by removing one-third of the branches at a time over a 3-year period.

How can I prevent red spider infestations on my astilbes? A miticide I used killed most of the foliage.

Moisture-retentive soil and an inch of water a week during drought are essential for astilbes, especially in warm climates. Dryness and sun are an open invitation to red spider infestations. If dull green leaves and characteristic webbing show that an infestation has occurred, spray the undersides of the leaves often with a forceful stream of water to knock off the pests.

GARDEN DESIGN

I have many garden ideas for different parts of my property, but I have a hard time visualizing how they might all fit together. How can I work them out?

Go out into the landscape and try them. Place tall stakes where you think you would like trees; use hose, string, or powdered lime to define lawn shapes, paths, and beds; string up lines to represent fencing; spread out sheets or blankets where you might like a small paved area. Set outdoor furniture in places where you might want seating. Then look at these elements from different angles and keep making adjustments until you feel satisfied.

I've recently bought an older home with a rather boring landscape. I can't afford to redo the entire property at once. How can I develop the garden gradually over a period of, say, 5 years? In what order should I proceed?

Spend the first year getting to know your garden. Keep a notebook to record such data as when the plants bloom and how the sun strikes different areas throughout the day and in different seasons. Test the soil, and begin correcting any deficiencies. Bring in an arborist to evaluate the trees. The autumn and winter of the first year is a good time for removing diseased or poorly placed trees and planting new ones. The second year, put your money into "hardscape" items—an irrigation system, if needed, and patios, walkways, retaining walls, and fences. Protect trees during the construction process by surrounding the root zone with temporary fencing. During the third year, concentrate on shrubbery—thinning, transplanting, and adding color and texture. Use the fourth year to establish herbaceous beds. By the fifth year you should be ready to add the finishing touches—a sundial, perhaps, or garden art to serve as focal points.

I have planted different gardens in our large suburban lot over the years, but now I don't have the time to keep up all the areas as well as I would like to. How can I revamp the gardens so they will look good with less maintenance?

Categorize the different garden areas according to the levels of maintenance needed to keep each looking good: intensive, moderate, or casual. Are the intensive areas too many, too scattered, and too far away to be noticed or enjoyed? If so, concentrate your efforts where they matter. Let the farther reaches revert to woodland. Turn a mixed border into a low-maintenance shrub border. Replace a struggling woodland garden with a hardy ground cover. Put your main effort into pruning a few key specimen trees and shrubs for shape and intensively maintaining a close-in flower border.

I loved a planting scheme I saw in a garden book, but when I tried to copy it in my garden it didn't look right. How can I tell what will work in my garden?

Apart from incompatible cultural requirements among plants, the most common cause for an unsuccessful duplication of a garden scheme in another location is the difference in scale, proportion, and conformation of the surrounding space. When you see a design that you like, check to determine whether the setting of the locale where you want to duplicate it is similar to that of the original. You're almost certain to be disappointed, for example, if you pick out an arrangement set against a fenced-in corner for reproduction at the edge of a lawn opening onto woods.

Many design books emphasize the importance of shape and mass in planting design, but I can't seem to get past the flower colors when I am making plant arrangements. How can I begin to see plants the way designers see them?

To see shape only, first try to look at your plant groupings as if they were all one color. Use a black-and-white photocopy of a garden view and trace an outline of trees, shrubs, and groups of smaller plants in the picture. Don't try to follow the outline shape in detail; generalize as much as possible, so that you end up with a diagram of circles, ovals, cones, horizontal lines, and so on. If the diagram turns out to be a series of boring circles, try adding vertical spikes or a taller cone shape to vary the composition. Once you have hit upon a pleasing combination of shapes, use this as the basis for working out a detailed planting plan that will include texture and color.

I need immediate screening from my neighbors. Should I put in a fence along my property line?

This only makes sense when you want to mark your property or keep out intruders and animals. A more effective way of screening unwanted views is to place a fence or screen where it gives you the greatest protection. On a sloping lot, for example, a screen placed at the edge of an elevated terrace will be more effective than one at the property line, where you may be able to see over the fence from where you sit. Also, fences and screens are expensive garden elements, and you should take full advantage of their architectural features by locating them where you gain the most from the definition they provide, such as near a terrace.

The back of my lot slopes down so steeply from my house that the soil is washing away. I want to terrace the land for planters, but I'm concerned because the area is large and I might be creating a monster in terms of maintenance. What do you suggest?

Why not terrace the upper portion closest to your house and clothe the lower part in shrubs and ground covers? Plants with dense root systems, such as cotoneaster, *Hypericum calycinum* (St.-John's-wort), or juniper, will help prevent erosion. You would be well advised to call a landscape architect to prepare a plan for the terraced portion. A professional can help you select the most cost-effective material for a retaining wall and can engineer the wall to stand up to the force of soil and water pushing against it.

What are some good trees to plant in front of a new two-story townhouse on a very small lot?

Choose deep-rooted species; avoid such trees as sweet gum and Norway maple, which have greedy, shallow roots that compete with nearby shrubbery and make it impossible to grow grass. In the past few years nurseries have introduced several narrow-crowned, upright selections of familiar shade trees suitable for use in small gardens and as street plantings. Trees with less than a 15-foot spread include *Pyrus calleryana* 'Chanticleer' (Callery pear), pyramidal *Carpinus betulus* 'Fastigiata' (European hornbeam), *Quercus robur* 'Fastigiata' (English oak), and one of the several red maples selected for upright form, such as *Acer rubrum* 'Armstrong'.

I have a tiny city garden that is walled in on all sides with almost no planting space around the patio. How can I make it a year-round garden that is full of plants that bloom in succession?

If you can't go outward go up: Plant the space thickly with climbers. Combine vines so that when one is finished, another will bloom—for example, a planting of *Clematis montana*, 'New Dawn' climbing roses, and *Clematis paniculata (C. maximowicziana)* to cover spring, summer, and fall. Use bold foliage plants like *Yucca filamentosa* and *Mahonia bealei* for accents. Make a dense evergreen background by planting ivies or *Clematis armandii*. On the patio, set pots of annuals and bulbs in groups, or arrange them on a baker's rack for even more planting space.

I've tried lots of plant combinations but am still not satisfied that I've hit on one with exquisite beauty. How do I get beyond pretty to truly beautiful?

The foremost quality of any beautiful plant combination is simplicity. You may be using too many different plants or arranging them in a way that makes them hard to read visually. Some of the best ways to achieve simplicity include limiting your palette to just two or three kinds of plants (although you may use several of each kind in a massed effect); limiting your flower colors to variations on a single color theme; and planting them so that there is open space around or between them, even when they grow to full, mature size. Simple, beautiful combinations possess restraint, yet enough contrast in form, foliage, and color to stir the viewer's interest.

I try to put together perennials and annuals with matched flower colors, but the effect is rather haphazard. What's the secret to making good-looking color combinations?

The problem you describe is usually caused by too few plants in the combination. Single plants tend to recede to mere points of color when viewed from even a short distance. Try using drifts rather than just one, two, or three plants. A drift is a group of five to nine plants, all of the same variety, usually arranged in a shape with tapered ends. Drifts will give you broad swaths of color that can be combined by weaving their tapered ends into one another. These generous areas of color will have much more impact than the spotty color afforded by single plants.

Most days I get to enjoy my garden only in the evening, after work, when the light is low and failing. Are there any plants that I can combine to add interest to the evening garden?

As daylight fails, the cones, or color-sensing cells in the eye, begin to stop functioning in favor of the rods, or light-sensing cells. Colors on the red end of the spectrum appear to darken first, and eventually red looks black. The violet- and lavender-sensing cones are the last to lose their function in the dimming light. Thus, planting lavender or violet flowers will give you a startlingly fluorescent display as this shift occurs in the eye. Among perennials, a combination of *Platycodon grandiflorus* 'Blue' (balloon flower), *Adenophora confusa* (ladybells), and *Linum perenne* (blue flax) is an excellent choice for an evening garden.

Along the foundation of my house I have combinations of evergreens, both needled and broadleaf, that tend to look like big lumps of green rather than a designed grouping. How can I create a more dramatic effect?

Select the most interesting evergreens as the basis for a revamped design—that is, the ones with the most distinct shape, foliage texture, or colors—and transplant to other areas the shrubs that have less character. If the open space is appealing, either keep it open and cover it with a mulch or plant it with a low ground cover whose color contrasts with the evergreens around it. If the open space calls for a plant, consider a deciduous one with twisting, sinuous trunks or branches, or one whose form or texture strongly contrasts with the plants around it.

I have a spot on a rise where the sun sets—a perfect place for backlighting plants with the late afternoon sun. What plants would look good with backlight?

The Japanese maple *Acer palmatum* with *Imperata cylindrica* 'Rubra' (Japanese blood grass) in front makes a great combination for backlighting, especially in fall, when the maple is turning color. Grapevines, black locust, and many other thin-leaved plants are also beautiful when the sun shines through them.

What designs would you advise for someone who has a limited budget as well as a limited amount of time?

After you decide which low-maintenance trees, shrubs, and evergreens you like, repeat them throughout your garden. The same holds true for herbaceous perennials: Limit the types of plants you choose, and plant more of them. However, you'll want to have a certain amount of plant diversity so that if disease strikes, you won't lose everything. Select and site your plants carefully to ensure against cultural, disease, or insect problems.

PLANTING AND MAINTENANCE

What's the easiest way to tackle the job of planting a steep bank?

Soil preparation is a must, since most banks have inadequate soil. For each plant, dig a deep hole and add amendments to the soil; stagger the placement of the holes to achieve a less linear effect. To control the growth of weeds on a slope, lay down landscape fabric and put the plants into the ground through slits cut in the fabric. Spread pine needles or shredded bark on top of the fabric; these materials tend to stay in place, whereas a chunky mulch like pine bark nuggets will slide off a steep slope. Terracing with landscape timbers or stone reduces potential erosion and increases moisture retention but requires a bigger investment of both labor and money.

Plant choices aside, are there certain garden designs that are more maintenance free than others?

Garden styles definitely affect maintenance requirements. In general, the more formal your design, the more upkeep the garden will need, because formality requires balance, symmetry, and exactness, which means more pruning and trimming of shrubs and trees. Informal designs, on the other hand, allow plants more freedom to follow natural growth patterns.

How can I prevent winter damage to my broadleaf evergreens—rhododendrons, azaleas, and hollies—and also to evergreen perennials such as bergenia and Christmas and Lenten roses?

Sun and wind are usually the culprits in winter injury to evergreen plants. Leaves are most susceptible to damage when the plant becomes dehydrated, and drought conditions can often exist in the winter garden. Even though your neighbors may think you're crazy, water your evergreen plants in winter to help prevent injury to leaves and tender twigs. If you know that a plant is susceptible to winter damage, select a sheltered site that will provide some protection from wind and afternoon sun, such as against the north wall of the house or on the shady side of a tall hedge.

What is the least time-consuming way to fertilize a garden?

Blended organic fertilizers are the backbone of any fertilizing program for low maintenance. They contain a great variety of mineral nutrients and organic molecules that are released slowly into the soil. Gardeners can also turn to timed-release fertilizer pellets; when applied in late winter, the pellets deliver nitrogen, phosphorus, and potassium evenly over an entire growing season.

Are there any shrubs that don't have to be pruned?

Unfortunately, no. You can start by buying shrub cultivars that have been selected specifically for their compact growth form and neat branching habits. But in any event, the conscientious gardener should follow the three Ds of pruning: Remove dead, diseased, and deformed branches at any time in a plant's life. To reduce the amount of pruning that you have to do, plant shrubs in a space large enough to allow them to achieve their mature dimensions without becoming obstacles. Also, try to remove no more than a third of the top growth at any time; this will limit the amount of suckering that occurs. Also, let shrubs assume their natural shape rather than pruning them into geometric globes and boxes.

I have tried to garden organically, and I compost all my plant debris—trimmings, old foliage, and weeds that I hoe from the garden—but it seems I have more weeds, disease, and insects every year. I thought organic gardening was going to be beneficial; what's wrong?

You are probably composting weeds that have seeds, giving them a fertile place to germinate before returning them to the garden to grow strong. Instead, put weeds that have gone to seed into the trash. Also, take care not to compost any diseased plant foliage. Many disease-causing organisms have resistant spores or go through resting stages that can survive the rigors of the composting process, particularly if your pile doesn't heat up sufficiently. Lacing your compost with 5-10-5 fertilizer or a compost activator, and turning it so that the outer, cooler portions are moved inward will help generate the heat necessary to kill insect larvae and disease organisms that may find their way into your compost pile.

I am continually mulching my garden to keep down weeds and conserve moisture. It not only costs a lot of money but is also very time-consuming. Do I have any alternatives?

One alternative is to switch from an organic mulch, which needs to be replenished periodically, to a stone mulch. Although stone doesn't have the soil-enhancing properties of an organic mulch, it is fairly permanent: One to 2 inches of uniform-size stones in earth colors provide a good-looking mulch that will last for decades. The best fertilizer to use for stone-mulched beds is one of the blended organics.

I would like to mulch all of my plants—trees, shrubs, and flower beds. When is the best time to do this?

Mulching after a recent rainfall would be ideal, and the best months are those during which the garden is dormant. Mulching later may bury and damage young bulb and perennial foliage. If you wait until the garden is actively growing to mulch, you'll spend a lot of extra time and effort working around your growing foliage so that you can apply the mulch evenly. The ground should be weed free before mulch is applied.

I'm a person who hates to weed. What can I do to keep weeding to a minimum?

It is much easier to remove a tiny weed seedling than a full-grown weed that has had time to develop long, tough roots. By weeding when the plants are young, you also remove them before they have a chance to go to seed, a situation that makes your weeding problems even worse.

How can I prepare a soil that will suit a wide number of plant varieties?

Every species of plant has its own range of tolerance for environmental factors such as pH, moisture, and nutrients, and it is impossible in a mixed planting to provide the ideal conditions for each one. Instead, try to achieve a happy medium by creating conditions that most plants can put up with. A pH of 5.8 to 6.5 will benefit the widest number of garden plants, and good drainage usually benefits all of them. Prepare a soil that is loose and crumbly and rich in nutrients; add organic matter in the form of compost and blended organic fertilizers.

My soil is a heavy clay. What amendments should I add to improve the structure of my soil?

Your first impulse might be to add sand, but while sand will loosen your heavy clay, it is not enough to transform it into a good garden soil. You will need to add lots of organic matter as well. Compost is an excellent choice; you can also use peat moss, leaf mold, bark chips or ground bark, sawdust, or well-rotted animal manure.

Do you recommend using traps to catch insects like Japanese beetles?

Insect traps today are quite improved over the ones on the market a few years ago. Be sure not to place them directly in the garden, however, because you will only attract insects from outside areas to the very plants you are trying to protect.

For insect problems in my garden, including aphids, thrips, and whiteflies, can you recommend a spray that will not harm the environment—or me?

All sprays can be harmful if not properly used, but one relatively safe kind is marketed under different brand names as insecticidal soap. Made up of various formulations of potassium salts of fatty acids, they kill by penetrating the shells of soft-bodied insects, causing dehydration and rapid death. They cannot penetrate eggs already laid, so a few repeat sprayings at 7- to 10-day intervals are necessary to kill emerging larvae and achieve complete control.

My father planted his vegetable garden in rows with good results, and I'm inclined to do the same thing. But nowadays everyone talks about raised beds. What are the advantages of raised beds?

The main advantages are that they are more productive and take less work than conventional row gardening. Because you prepare the soil intensively with organic matter and fertilizers *(pages 417-420)*, you can plant vegetables very closely, getting more crops from far less space than row gardening requires. As the leaves of the vegetables touch, they shade the soil and slow weed growth. Paths don't take up as much space in a raised-bed garden as they do when vegetables are planted in rows, so you don't have to spend as much time weeding and maintaining them.

I'm building a deck and have pressure-treated scrap wood left over. Can I use it as an edging material for raised beds, or would the chemicals used in the pressure treatment contaminate vegetables grown in the beds?

The chemicals used to pressure-treat wood are quite toxic and might very well contaminate your crops. For raised beds, use ordinary wood scrap or cheap grades of redwood, black locust, or other rot-resistant wood for longevity. You can also make raised beds without constructing edges *(pages 418-419)*. They really aren't needed except to improve appearance, although they may cut down on grasses creeping into the beds.

COMPOSTING AND SOIL CONDITIONING

Is there anything I shouldn't put into my compost pile?

Yes. Don't use domestic pet or human waste, since it may carry dangerous diseases or parasites. Don't use meat or meat scraps, which attract vermin and cause a stench as they decay. Don't compost diseased portions of plants that you've cut away; dispose of them with the household trash or by burning, if that is permitted in your area. Don't use coal ashes, as these contain toxic wastes; wood ashes in moderation are fine. Don't add any synthetic materials or chemicals or any plants that have been treated with herbicides or pesticides. And don't compost weeds that have set seed, or you'll spread them around the garden when you use the compost. Manures, vegetable and fruit kitchen waste, and nonseedy plant debris are all fine.

What is sheet composting?

It's a fancy name for covering the soil with the same kinds of organic matter used in a compost pile and letting them decay slowly, without turning or watering. Sheet composting has two advantages: It adds organic matter that conditions the soil as it decays, and it acts as a mulch to keep weed growth down and the soil moist. Make sure the material contains no weed seeds or other kinds of seeds; it won't be massive enough to heat up, so seeds will remain viable. On the downside, sheet-composted material may provide a breeding ground for slugs, pill bugs, earwigs, and other unwanted insects. It may also deplete the soil of nitrogen unless high-nitrogen materials such as farmyard manure are included.

Where's the best place to build my compost pile—in the shade or in the sun? And should I cover it with black plastic?

The best place for the pile is close to the garden so the hose reaches it and you don't have to carry the finished compost very far. A shady spot is probably best because the composting organic matter won't dry out as fast as it would in sun. Covering the pile with black plastic holds in moisture and keeps the temperature in the pile higher, so it decays faster. The plastic will also prevent hard rains from dissolving and leaching nutrients from the pile.

Whenever I put my kitchen waste into the compost pile, raccoons, opossums, dogs, and who-knows-what-else tear the pile apart to get at it. Is there a convenient way I can compost my kitchen waste without having this problem?

An easy solution is to keep special garbage-eating worms called red wigglers in a container that marauding animals can't get into, and let them turn your kitchen scraps into compost. A sturdy wood box with a lid and a hardware-cloth bottom will serve nicely, or you can buy a plastic worm bin from a mail-order garden supply company, along with red wigglers.

I've tried making compost, but it doesn't heat up, and it smells bad. What's the problem?

It probably doesn't heat up because the pile doesn't have enough nitrogen-rich material such as fresh farm-animal manure. A pile that's layered with 3 or 4 parts plant debris to 1 part fresh manure and that's kept moist but not sopping wet will heat up. Your compost smells bad because little or no air is getting into the pile, and anaerobic bacteria are decomposing it. Rebuild it, adding manure and layering in straw, pine needles, or other coarse materials to get air into the pile. Aerobic bacteria will continue to decompose the pile, but it will not smell bad.

My soil is very acid, and I need to raise its pH from 5 to at least 6.5. What's the organic way to do this?

Two substances that are especially good at raising a soil's pH are leached wood ashes and ground limestone. Wood ashes work faster, but ground limestone sweetens the soil over a longer period of time. Use 10 pounds of limestone or 2 pounds of wood ashes per 100 square feet, worked into the top 6 inches of soil, to raise the pH 1 point. Don't raise it more than 1 point per year. If you use 10 pounds per 100 square feet this year and 5 pounds next year, your soil pH should increase 1.5 points to reach your target level.

PLANTING AND CARE—VEGETABLES

Is rooting hormone—the kind you use to stimulate root formation on cuttings—organic?

Yes. Rooting hormones are naturally occurring plant substances and are perfectly safe to use in an organic garden. Cuttings from sweet potato vines should be dipped in rooting hormone before planting, and you can also dip root cuttings from small bush fruits such as currants to stimulate rooting. Gardeners in areas with long growing seasons can also use the hormone to root stem cuttings of their early eggplant, tomato, and pepper crops for subsequent plantings.

Is companion planting—for example, putting beans and onions side by side because they like each other—a valid organic technique or an old wives' tale?

Companion planting is a valid technique, but not because plants "like" each other. It works for one of several reasons: because the companions have different needs and thus don't compete with one another for nutrients; because their root zones are at different levels and their roots don't compete for space; or because one of the companions helps protect the other from predatory insects.

What is manure tea and how do I use it?

Manure tea is one of the secrets to success in an organic garden. Put 1 gallon of fresh, rotted, or dried farm-animal manure or manure-based compost in a burlap or muslin bag and close it securely (use poultry, goat, horse, or cow manure only). Put the bag in a 5-gallon bucket and fill it with water. Let the manure steep for 3 days to a week. Spray this manure tea onto growing plants every 3 to 4 days. It is especially helpful when they are growing rapidly or setting flowers or fruit. You'll be amazed at how well plants respond.

I know some organic gardeners who swear by foliar seaweed spray. Is there any value in this?

Yes. Foliar seaweed spray is an extract of seaweed containing many trace elements that are essential for vigorous growth in many plants. These nutrients can be absorbed through a plant's leaves as well as its roots, so regular applications of foliar seaweed spray are certainly beneficial.

Is one kind of mulch better than another?

Organic gardeners use all sorts of materials to cover bare soil—black plastic, cardboard, leaves, shredded bark, compost, grass clippings that are free of pesticides and herbicides, farm-animal bedding, and spoiled hay are just a few of the possibilities. Even stones can serve as mulch if they cover the surface of the soil completely. For most situations, it is best to use an organic mulch because it offers multiple benefits: suppressing weeds, conserving soil moisture, acting as a fertilizer, and decomposing into soil-conditioning humus.

HERBAL DESIGN AND LANDSCAPE USE

A cottage garden would fit in perfectly outside my kitchen door. How can I achieve the look of lush informality using herbs?

Herbs are particularly well suited to a cottage garden design. But don't let the seemingly random nature of a cottage garden fool you; it takes careful planning to achieve the casual effect. Begin by listing the plants and combinations you want to include. When you plant, place herbs, annuals, and perennials close together so that bare soil is covered quickly. If some plants die or simply don't look good together, remove them and experiment until the planting pleases you. Try arranging foliage and flowers in specific color combinations such as gray and red or blue and gold. Or plant freely and see what pairings of foliage, plant shape, and flower form and color arise.

I love to grow roses and wonder if I can plant my herbs with them.

Absolutely. Roses and herbs make ideal companions. Plant sun-loving herbs such as lavender, rosemary, thyme, and sage near roses to highlight their blooms. But be sure to space the plants generously to give roses good air circulation.

I've always wanted a knot garden, but I don't have a big yard. Any suggestions?

Create a miniature knot garden in a container. Select herbs that take well to container culture, such as basil, thyme, chamomile, and rosemary, and keep them neatly pruned. Devise a knot pattern that looks good when viewed from above—star shapes and figure eights are only two of the possibilities. If you can't overwinter the miniature knot garden, harvest the herbs at the end of the growing season and start over in the spring.

PLANTING AND CARE—HERBS

Which herbs are best grown from seed and which ones should I start from plants?

Sow fast-growing, short-lived annuals such as dill, coriander, and nasturtium directly in your garden. Many biennials, including angelica and clary sage, also take best to direct-sowing. Perennial herbs can be grown from seed, division, cuttings, or layering. The method will vary depending on the plant. For example, thyme, lavender, rosemary, and mint hybridize freely and are best grown from cuttings. Other perennials such as lovage are best propagated by division.

I would like to harvest seeds from my herbs, but I don't know when or how to harvest them.

Seeds are ripe when they have just turned brown. Cut the seed heads on a dry day and place them in a brown bag. Let the seeds dry for 1 to 2 weeks, and when they are completely dry, store them in airtight jars. For more information on harvesting seeds to start next year's herb garden, as well as a list of herbs with aromatic seeds, see page 504.

When I order new herb plants, how do I know if they are correctly labeled?

First check the plants in the herbs sections of the encyclopedia starting on page 608. If you believe a plant is labeled incorrectly but can't identify it yourself, cut a stem of the plant when it is in bloom and take both leaves and flowers to a nursery or garden center for identification. You can also press the specimen and have it identified at a later date. If there is a chance the herb in question is poisonous, be sure not to ingest it.

Are there any culinary herbs that will grow in a shady container?

Sweet cicely (*Myrrhis odorata*) and chervil (*Anthriscus cerefolium*) prefer shade; mint, angelica, and lovage grow well in light shade. Although you can grow sun-loving herbs in light shade, their flavor will be less intense and often they will not flower. In hot climates, some gardeners plant herbs in a location that gets midday shade to prevent them from being scorched by the summer sun.

Can I have a productive herb garden indoors?

Herbs generally grow best in the garden, where they can enjoy full sun, fresh air, and plenty of soil. If you want to cultivate herbs indoors, they will perform better under commercial plant lights. During warm seasons, the herbs will need more water, but take care not to overwater them in winter.

Is it true that herbs have better flavor if they are grown in poor soil?

No. Herbs have the fullest flavor when planted in moderately fertile soil that encourages healthy, strong growth. Soil that is too rich or too poor will result in herbs with compromised flavor and a greater susceptibility to disease.

Will the flavor of an herb decrease if I fertilize it? Should I limit the amount of compost applied to the soil?

Using moderate amounts of fertilizer will not diminish an herb's flavor. However, heavy fertilization will encourage weak and unhealthy growth, particularly in culinary herbs. Compost is a great soil amendment for herbs, but again, don't overdo it.

What is poultry grit? Why should I add it to the soil in which I grow herbs?

Poultry grit is finely crushed rock—usually granite—given to chickens and other poultry to aid their digestion. It is available in three sizes and can be purchased at a farm-supply store. Medium-sized poultry grit added to soil improves drainage best and increases aeration around plant roots. In heavy clay soils it works better than sand because its particles are larger than grains of sand. Since poultry grit is inorganic and does not break down over time, add it to the soil only once. Herb gardeners can also use poultry grit as a mulch, spreading a 3-inch layer over the soil surface.

Should I mulch my herbs? Which mulches do you recommend?

Like all plants, herbs should be mulched for weed control and in soils where moisture retention is a problem. But be sure to use a mulch that does not hold in too much moisture, and keep the mulch away from the crown of the plant to prevent rot. Mediterranean herbs such as rosemary, thyme, and oregano are especially prone to rotting if a heavy mulch is used. Gravel, sand, and poultry grit are good choices for herbs that like good drainage. Other options include cocoa hulls, fine pine chips, and pine needles, all of which add a handsome finish of color and texture to the garden.

When should I pinch back my herbs to make them bushier?

It varies with the life cycle of each herb. Rosemary, for example, benefits from an early, low pinching to encourage side branching. Most perennial herbs respond well to a midspring pinching back to stimulate dense growth. Annual herbs with a short life cycle, such as dill and coriander, do not require any pinching. When harvesting them, take the entire plant. Annual herbs whose leaves you plan to harvest throughout the growing season, such as basil and chervil, should be pinched back in early summer to encourage bushiness. Removing their flower buds whenever they appear will hasten the growth of new foliage.

I want to rejuvenate an established lavender plant that has grown leggy and produces few blooms. Will pruning it do the job?

Yes. Prune your lavender in early spring just as new growth emerges. To rejuvenate an old plant, cut it back close to the base instead of pruning it lightly. Although you may lose the plant completely if it has grown weak and feeble, more likely it will return stronger and healthier than before.

CULINARY TREATS

How do you make an herb tea?

Herb teas can be made with either fresh or dried herbs, but fresh herbs result in a more pungent brew. Place the shredded leaves, seeds, or chopped root or bark in a teapot, using about 3 teaspoons of fresh or 1 heaping teaspoon of dried ingredients per cup. Add boiling water, let the tea steep for 3 to 5 minutes, strain, and serve. If you like strong tea, use a larger quantity of herbs; brewing the tea more than 5 minutes may result in an off taste.

Which herbs should I grow for herb tea?

Delicious herb teas are made from pungent herbs such as lemon verbena, which has a tart, lemon flavor; chamomile, which is fragrant and relaxing; sage, which tastes best in the cold months because it has a warming quality; and anise seed, which possesses a warm and wonderful licorice flavor. Create blends to suit your own taste. For example, peppermint combined with spearmint makes a soothing tea.

Is there any trick to preparing herbal vinegars?

No, they are easy to make. To quickly extract herbal essences, warm up any type of vinegar—wine vinegar is a good choice—and pour it into a sterile bottle filled with your favorite culinary herbs. Avoid using metal utensils, which may react with the vinegar, producing an unpleasant taste. You can also make flavored vinegar by adding herbs to a bottle of vinegar and setting it in the sun for 2 weeks. Strain the vinegar and replace the herbs with attractive fresh ones if you plan to display the vinegar or give it as a gift. Choice herbs used to flavor vinegars include tarragon, lemon verbena, basil, garlic, and chili peppers.

Is there a fun way to teach children about the life cycle of plants from seed to harvest using herbs?

Try making a salad farm using edible herbs that grow easily from seed. As they tend the miniature farm, children will learn about seed germination, a seedling's growth cycle, plant care, and when and how to harvest. If you have seeds that were collected from the garden, show children how to separate the ripe seeds from the rest of the plant. Sow the seed in rows and label each row. Watch the plants grow, and harvest them for salads. Some of the best plants to grow from seed are coriander, corn salad, dill, lettuce, nasturtium, purple hyacinth bean, arugula, and sweet fennel.

PESTS AND DISEASES

How can I attract beneficial insects to my garden?

Reserve a portion of the garden for whatever weeds happen to appear there. Beneficial insects are adapted to the local flora, using it as a source of food, as hunting grounds for prey, and for shelter. Also, make sure you plant a number of umbelliferous plants—such as fennel, carrot, and dill—in your garden. These are nectar sources for several beneficials, including green lacewings. Finally, don't use pesticides. Beneficial insects are more susceptible to pesticides than pests and will be the first to be killed off.

573

I understand that rotenone, ryania, and sabadilla are all organically acceptable pesticides. Should I dust the garden routinely with them as a preventive?

No. Although these pesticides are derived from plants and are active for a comparatively short time, each of them kills a broad spectrum of insects and can do the same kind of ecological damage as chemical pesticides. The goal is not a garden free of pests—you simply want to keep their numbers to a manageable level. Try beneficial insects, the physical controls described in Chapter 12, and other, less toxic methods of organic insect control before reaching for these pesticides. They should be used only as a last resort.

I've heard that organic gardeners use homemade sprays containing hot chili peppers, garlic, or tobacco on their vegetables to ward off pests. Do they work?

Yes. Many insects won't go near a plant sprayed with these substances. But never use a tobacco spray on any vegetables of the nightshade family, which includes tomatoes, potatoes, and eggplant; tobacco is also a member of the nightshade family and harbors a mosaic virus that can be spread to these crops by spraying.

I carefully start my plants from seed, then set them in the garden. Many times I find them snipped off just above the soil line, as if they were felled like little trees, but I haven't seen any pests chewing on their stems. What's causing this?

Your problem is almost certainly cutworms, grayish brown wormlike grubs that eat through the stems of tender seedlings. The reason you haven't seen them is that they feed at night and hide in the soil, under mulch, or in other sheltered places during the day. The solution is to put protective paper collars around your seedlings at planting time. The illustration on page 448 shows how to make these barriers, which are very effective.

My beet leaves have little white trails twisting and turning on them. Eventually, the leaves turn yellow and die. What is this and how do I stop it?

The problem is leaf miners, little insect larvae that burrow through the soft tissue between the outer layers of the leaves. If there are nearby stands of lamb's-quarters, a common weed, pull them out, since they may harbor these pests. Also, cover your beets when young with a lightweight floating row cover that lets in air, water, and light; it will keep adults from laying their eggs in the beet leaves.

Most years my strawberry plants get powdery mildew on their leaves. How can I prevent this organically?

Thin your plants to increase the flow of air between them, and pick off and destroy infected foliage. You can apply lime sulfur, available at garden centers, as directed on the package, or spray plants with a solution of 1 tablespoon of baking soda in a gallon of water; adding ⅛ to ¼ teaspoon of insecticidal soap will help the spray stick to the leaves. Don't increase the proportion of baking soda, as a higher concentration can damage leaves.

Here in the West, gophers are an awful problem. They burrow through the soil, eating the roots off many plants, even pulling whole plants down into their burrows. What can I do to control them?

A king snake, black snake, or gopher snake is a great boon where gophers are a problem, and some cats are avid gopher hunters. But lacking these predators, you might try mechanical gopher traps.

I have tried growing broccoli several times, but something always eats tiny holes in the seedlings' leaves. What can I do about this?

Your problem is flea beetles, fast-moving little pests that eat holes in the leaves of many members of the cabbage family, including broccoli. Before setting out your seedlings, try planting early crops of radishes and mustard greens, which the flea beetles will attack. When these "trap crops" are full of beetles, pull the plants and destroy them. Next, place bright yellow commercial sticky traps or homemade traps *(pages 470-471)* every 10 feet in the space reserved for broccoli to attract and kill any remaining beetles. Then plant your seedlings.

The branches of my bay tree (Laurus nobilis) are often covered with a brown crust. What is the problem and what is the best way for me to get rid of it?

Piercing-sucking scale insects—shiny brown and shell-like in appearance—are a common problem on bay trees. Left untreated, scales will spread to the foliage of a bay tree and eventually kill it. To control a small infestation, try scrubbing them off with a cotton-tipped swab or soft toothbrush dipped in soapy water or a solution of 1 part each of rubbing alcohol and water. For a larger infestation, spray on a horticultural oil; once this is done, however, you must refrain from using the leaves for culinary purposes.

Some of my herbs die out in summer when the weather gets hot and humid. What is the problem and what can I do about it?

In regions of the country with extended periods of hot, humid weather, the branches of herbs may turn brown and die as a result of diseases caused by soil fungi. These disease organisms are activated when plants are stressed and the weather is humid. Removing all the diseased portions of the plant will help to revive it, but if the herb is severely infected, dispose of it entirely. Then try a new plant in a different location in soil that has been amended with poultry grit, which enhances air circulation at the root zone.

Are herbs used in companion planting? How do they benefit other plants nearby?

Yes, proponents of companion planting believe that some herbs make good neighbors. They can enhance a nearby plant's growth, repel or trap pests, or attract beneficial insects. Chamomile, for example, is sometimes referred to as a "physician plant" because it is said to revive nearby ailing plants. Herbs planted with some vegetables are said to amplify their flavor, such as basil with tomatoes, and summer savory with beans. French marigolds are said to repel nematodes, and catnip and nasturtiums are possibly effective against green peach aphids. Other herbs used to keep insects away include rue, southernwood, tansy, pennyroyal, and garlic.

What are beneficial insects and what herbs attract them?

Beneficial insects include predators that kill other insects, parasites that lay their eggs on other insects, and pollinators that carry pollen from male to female flowers. Creeping predators such as ground beetles like dense, low-growing herbs such as thyme and rosemary; flying predators such as hover flies prefer chamomile and mint. Parasitic wasps like dill, anise, and flowering members of the carrot family, such as Queen Anne's lace. Most predators and parasites are excellent pollinators, too.

Troubleshooting Guide

Even the best-tended gardens can fall prey to pests and diseases. It's always better to catch an infestation or infection at an early stage, so make it a habit to inspect your plants regularly for warning signs. Keep in mind that a lack of nutrients, improper pH levels, and other environmental conditions can cause symptoms resembling those of some infectious diseases. As a rule, if wilting or yellowing appears on neighboring plants, the cause is probably environmental; damage from pests and infectious diseases is usually more random.

This guide will help you identify a few common pest or disease problems you may encounter, along with some of the plants that are susceptible. In general, good drainage and air circulation will help prevent infection. Encourage or introduce beneficial insects that prey on pests, and use row covers, handpicking, and other nonchemical methods of control. If chemical treatment becomes necessary, treat only the affected plant or plants, use an organic insecticide or fungicide, and apply sparingly. Commercial products such as insecticidal soap and neem are the least disruptive to beneficial insects and will not destroy the soil balance that is at the foundation of a healthy garden.

PESTS

PROBLEM: Leaves curl, are distorted in shape, may turn yellow, and may be sticky and have a black, sooty appearance. Buds and flowers are deformed, new growth is stunted, and leaves and flowers may drop off.

CAUSE: Aphids are pear shaped, semitransparent, wingless sucking insects, about ⅛ inch long and ranging in color from green to red, pink, black, or gray. They suck plant sap and may spread viral disease. Infestations are worst in spring and early summer, when the pests cluster on tender new shoots, on the undersides of leaves, and around flower buds. Aphids secrete a sticky substance known as honeydew onto leaves, which fosters the growth of a black fungus called sooty mold.

SOLUTION: Spray plants frequently with a steady stream of water from a garden hose to knock aphids off plants and discourage them from returning. In severe cases, prune off heavily infested parts and spray with insecticidal soap, horticultural oil, or pyrethrins. Introduce beneficials such as ladybugs, green lacewings, gall midges, and syrphid flies into the garden. Do not apply excessive amounts of nitrogen fertilizer.
SUSCEPTIBLE PLANTS: MOST VEGETABLES; MANY ORNAMENTAL PLANTS.

PROBLEM: Holes appear in leaves, flowers, and fruits; stems may also be eaten.

CAUSE: Caterpillars, including armyworms, cabbage loopers, parsley worms, and tomato hornworms, come in varied shapes, sizes, and colors. They may be smooth, hairy, or spiny. These voracious pests are the larvae of moths and butterflies.

SOLUTION: Handpick to control small populations. The bacterial pesticide *Bacillus thuringiensis* (Bt) kills many types without harming plants. Identify the caterpillar species to determine the control options and timing of spray applications. Several species are susceptible to sprays of insecticidal soap. Introduce beneficials that prey on caterpillars, such as parasitic braconid wasps, tachinid flies, and beneficial nematodes. Destroy all visible cocoons and nests.
SUSCEPTIBLE PLANTS: MOST VEGETABLES, ESPECIALLY MEMBERS OF THE CABBAGE FAMILY; MANY HERBS, INCLUDING BEE BALM, CARAWAY, HOT PEPPER, MARIGOLD, MINT, NASTURTIUM, PARSLEY, AND PINKS; TENDER NEW SHOOTS OF ANNUALS AND PERENNIALS.

PROBLEM: Leaves and stems have ragged holes or are skeletonized and may be covered with black droppings. Young plants may die, and older plants may be defoliated.

CAUSE: Colorado potato beetles are ⅓-inch-long, oval-shaped chewing insects with yellow-and-black-striped wing covers. Emerging from the soil in spring, they feed and then lay bright orange eggs on the undersides of leaves; eggs hatch in 1 week. The plump ⅗-inch-long larvae are orange-red with black spots. They feed, enter the soil to pupate, and emerge as adults in 1 to 2 weeks. There are one to three generations a year.

SOLUTION: Handpick eggs, beetles, and larvae, and drop into soapy water. Use a thick layer of organic mulch to prevent adults from emerging from soil. Plant resistant varieties and rotate crops. Spray with Bt San Diego strain. Introduce ladybugs and spined soldier bugs. Cultivate soil in fall to kill overwintering adults. Spray plants with neem, pyrethrins, or rotenone.
SUSCEPTIBLE PLANTS: POTATOES, EGGPLANT, PEPPERS, TOMATOES.

PROBLEM: Holes appear in leaves, stalks, or husks and at the bottom of ears of corn, breaking the stems. Ears are disfigured, and kernels are eaten. Tomatoes are eaten away inside.

CAUSE: Corn ear worms are 1- to 2-inch-long yellow, green, or white caterpillars, and European corn borers are 1- to 2-inch-long beige caterpillars with brown spots and dark heads.

SOLUTION: Plant resistant varieties. Introduce tachinid flies and parasitic wasps. Spray with Bt, neem, or pyrethrins. Place 5 drops of mineral or vegetable oil in silk whorl just as silk starts to brown. Spade soil in fall to expose pupae.
SUSCEPTIBLE PLANTS: CORN EAR WORM— CORN AND TOMATOES; EUROPEAN CORN BORER—BEANS, BEETS, CELERY, CORN, PEPPERS, POTATOES, AND TOMATOES.

PROBLEM: Large oval holes appear in leaves and flowers, and new shoots may be eaten. Older plants are stunted and weakened and may fall over. Roots may be stunted. Plants may die.

CAUSE: Cucumber beetles are ¼ inch long and yellowish green with black spots or stripes. In spring, larvae hatch in 10 days to feed on plant roots and pupate in soil. Adults emerge to feed on leaves, flowers, and fruit. There are one to four generations a year. Adults and larvae carry cucumber mosaic and bacterial wilt, diseases that can kill plants.

SOLUTION: Handpick adults. Use row covers, but remove from plants that need insect pollination when flowering begins. Plant resistant varieties. Introduce beneficial nematodes, tachinid flies, and braconid wasps. Apply rotenone and sabadilla.
SUSCEPTIBLE PLANTS: CUCUMBERS, MELONS, PUMPKINS, SQUASH, AND OTHER MEMBERS OF THE CUCUMBER FAMILY. MAY ALSO ATTACK BEANS, CORN, EGGPLANT, PEAS, POTATOES, AND TOMATOES.

PROBLEM: Stems of emerging seedlings are cut off near the ground, and the plants topple over and die. Seedlings may be completely eaten. Leaves of older plants show ragged edges and holes.

CAUSE: Cutworms, the larvae of various moths, are fat, hairless, and a soft gray-brown in color. These 1- to 2-inch-long night feeders do most of their damage in the late spring. In the daytime, they curl up into a C-shape and are found under debris or below the soil surface next to the plant stem.

SOLUTION: Place cutworm collars around base of plants. Force cutworms to the soil surface by flooding the area, then handpick them. Introduce parasitic braconid wasps, tachinid flies, and beneficial nematodes. Use diatomaceous earth (DE), crushed eggshells, wood ashes, or oak-leaf mulch around plants to discourage cutworms. Cultivate the soil in late summer and fall and again in spring.
SUSCEPTIBLE PLANTS: YOUNG SEEDLINGS AND TRANSPLANTS.

PROBLEM: Numerous tiny round holes appear in leaves, making plant look as if it has been peppered with shot. Seedlings may weaken or die.

CAUSE: Flea beetles are 1/10-inch-long black, brown, bronze, or striped chewing insects that overwinter as adults and emerge in spring to feed. Eggs are laid in the soil near the plant; the larvae—3/4-inch-long white grubs with brown heads—pupate in the soil and emerge as adults, which jump when disturbed. Two to four generations are produced each year. These beetles spread several viral diseases.

SOLUTION: Use row covers and white or yellow sticky traps. Spread diatomaceous earth (DE) or wood ashes around plants. Cultivate soil often to expose eggs and larvae. Introduce beneficial nematodes, braconid wasps, and tachinid flies. Pyrethrins, rotenone, and sabadilla may be used.
SUSCEPTIBLE PLANTS: MEMBERS OF THE CABBAGE FAMILY, EGGPLANT, TOMATOES.

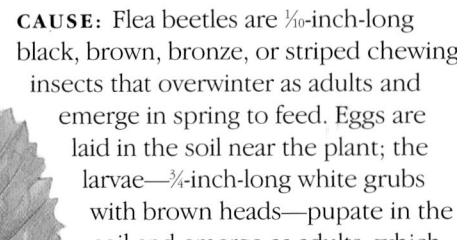

PROBLEM: Holes are chewed in leaves, which may be reduced to skeletons with only veins remaining. Eventually, plants may be stripped of all foliage.

CAUSE: Japanese beetles have shiny metallic blue or green bodies and copper-colored wings. Voracious in the summer, they prefer feeding in sunny locations. Eggs are laid in soil in grassy or weedy areas. The fat 3/4-inch-long grubs are grayish white with dark heads. They overwinter in the soil below the frostline, where they feed on the roots of grass. They pupate in late spring or early summer and emerge as adults in May, June, and July to feed and lay eggs. One generation is produced a year.

SOLUTION: Handpick small colonies, placing them in a can filled with soapy water. Use neem as a repellent. Spray with pyrethrins or rotenone. The larval stage can be controlled with milky spore disease or beneficial nematodes, both of which can be applied to the whole garden and nearby lawn areas. Introduce or encourage parasitic wasps and tachinid flies. Keep the garden well weeded.
SUSCEPTIBLE PLANTS: ASPARAGUS, BEANS, BLACKBERRIES, CORN, OKRA, POTATOES, RASPBERRIES, RHUBARB, STRAWBERRIES, TOMATOES; ASTILBE, AZALEA, CLEMATIS, FOXGLOVE, HOLLYHOCK, NEW YORK ASTER, PURPLE CONEFLOWER, ROSE, ROSE MALLOW.

PROBLEM: Leaves are skeletonized. Pods and stems may be eaten, and plants may die.

CAUSE: Mexican bean beetles are 1/4-inch-long, oval-shaped, yellowish brown to copper-colored insects. With 16 black dots forming three rows across the wing covers, they look very much like a lighter-colored version of the beneficial ladybug. The yellow to orange oval larvae have long black-tipped spines. Adults overwinter in debris and emerge in early summer to feed and lay yellow egg masses on the undersides of leaves. One to four generations are produced a year.

SOLUTION: Plant resistant cultivars. Handpick adults and larvae and remove leaves with orange egg masses; drop into a container of soapy water. Cover with floating row covers until well established. Encourage or introduce spined soldier bugs and parasitic wasps. Spray undersides of leaves thoroughly with pyrethrins, neem, sabadilla, or rotenone. In fall, remove infested plants, clean garden of debris, and cultivate soil to destroy overwintering adults.
SUSCEPTIBLE PLANTS: GREEN BEANS AND LIMA BEANS ARE ESPECIALLY SUSCEPTIBLE; BLACK-EYED PEAS, KALE, SOYBEANS.

PROBLEM: Leaves become stippled or flecked, then discolor, curl, and wither. Webbing may appear, particularly on undersides of leaves. Vegetables and fruits may be stunted.

CAUSE: Mites are pinhead-sized, spider-like sucking pests that may be reddish, pale green, yellow, or brown. They are a major problem in hot, dry weather, and several generations of mites may appear in a single season. Eggs and the adults of some species hibernate over the winter in sod and bark and on plants that retain foliage.

SOLUTION: Keep plants well watered and mulched, especially during hot, dry periods. To control nymphs and adults, spray the undersides of leaves regularly with a strong stream of water or a diluted insecticidal soap solution. Remove and destroy heavily infested leaves, stems, or entire plants. Introduce predators such as ladybugs and green lacewing larvae. In severe cases, apply horticultural oil, neem, or pyrethrins. *SUSCEPTIBLE PLANTS: ASPARAGUS, BEANS, CUCUMBERS, EGGPLANT, MELONS, SQUASH, STRAWBERRIES, SUGAR PEAS, TOMATOES; MANY HERBS, PERENNIALS, ANNUALS, SHRUBS, AND TREES.*

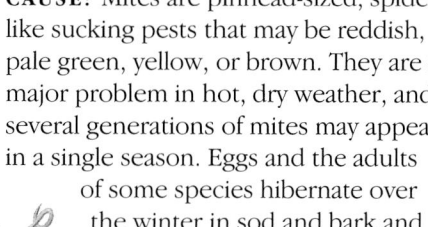

PROBLEM: Light-colored sunken brown spots appear on the upper surfaces of leaves, or tiny holes appear in leaves and stems (these are caused by stink bugs). Foliage may wilt, discolor, and fall from plants. Shoots and flower buds may be distorted or blackened, and plants may be stunted. Vegetables may be scarred or dimpled.

CAUSE: The plant bug family of sucking insects includes the ¼-inch-long oval tarnished plant bug, mottled brown and tan with a black-tipped yellow triangle on each forewing; the ⅝-inch-long squash bug, black or brown on top and yellow, yellowish brown, or grayish underneath; and the shield-shaped ½-inch-long stink bug, which is named for its unpleasant odor and is brown, tan, green, or mottled with five segmented antennae. Adults are active from late spring to late summer. Eggs are laid on the undersides of leaves. Up to five generations are produced a year.

SOLUTION: Handpick adults and larvae, remove leaves with egg masses, and drop into soapy water. Use row covers. Trap tarnished plant bugs with white sticky traps. Introduce or encourage beneficials including tachinid flies, big-eyed bugs, parasitic wasps, and damsel bugs. Spray plants with water, diluted soap solution, or insecticidal soap. Control adults and larvae with rotenone and sabadilla. *SUSCEPTIBLE PLANTS: TARNISHED PLANT BUG—MOST VEGETABLES; SQUASH BUG— ALL MEMBERS OF THE SQUASH FAMILY, ESPECIALLY PUMPKINS AND SQUASH; STINK BUG—BEANS, CABBAGE, CORN, OKRA, PEAS, SQUASH, TOMATOES.*

PROBLEM: Plants do not develop; young plants may wilt and die; older plants may be stunted. Roots and root crops have tunnels or are hollowed out, and eventually rot.

CAUSE: Root maggots are the larvae of various small flies, including cabbage, onion, and carrot rust flies. The legless, wormlike ⅓-inch-long larvae are white to yellowish white and enter the plant through roots or underground stems. Active from spring to midsummer, they thrive in cool, moist, highly organic soil. Eggs are laid at the bases of stems.

SOLUTION: Use floating row covers. Place diatomaceous earth or wood ashes around plants. Rotate crops. Do not fertilize with fresh manure. Apply beneficial nematodes to soil before planting. In fall, remove debris and infected plants. Cultivate soil in spring and fall. *SUSCEPTIBLE PLANTS: CABBAGE MAGGOT—CABBAGE FAMILY; ONION MAGGOT— ONION FAMILY; CARROT RUST MAGGOT—CARROT FAMILY.*

PROBLEM: Ragged holes appear in leaves, especially those near the ground. New shoots and seedlings may disappear entirely. Ripe fruits are destroyed. Tell-tale silver streaks appear on leaves and garden paths.

CAUSE: Slugs and snails hide during the day and feed on low-hanging leaves and fruits at night or on overcast or rainy days. They prefer damp soil in a shady location and are most damaging in summer, especially in wet regions or during rainy years.

SOLUTION: Keep garden clean to minimize hiding places. Handpick the pests or trap them by placing saucers of beer, sunk into the soil, near plants. Slugs and snails will also collect under a board laid on the ground or under inverted grapefruit halves or melon rinds. Salt kills the pests but may damage plants. Surround beds with copper-foil barriers or barrier strips of wood ashes, coarse sand, cinders, or diatomaceous earth (DE). Encourage rove beetles, and turn the soil in spring.
SUSCEPTIBLE PLANTS: MOST VEGETABLES, ESPECIALLY LEAFY VEGETABLES LIKE LETTUCE, AND THE FRUIT OF TOMATOES AND STRAWBERRIES; MANY PLANTS WITH TENDER FOLIAGE, INCLUDING BASIL, MARIGOLD, OREGANO, SAGE, VIOLET, AND HOSTA.

PROBLEM: Buds do not open, or flowers are tattered and deformed. Petals may be darkened or have brownish yellow or white streaks and small dark spots or bumps. Leaves and stems may be twisted, and plants may be stunted.

CAUSE: Thrips are quick-moving sucking insects barely visible to the naked eye; they look like tiny slivers of yellow, black, or brown wood. They emerge in early spring and are especially active in hot, dry weather. The larvae are wingless and feed on stems, leaves, and flower buds. Adults are weak fliers but are easily dispersed by wind and can therefore travel great distances.

SOLUTION: Controlling thrips is difficult, especially when they are migrating in early summer. Lacewings, minute pirate bugs, and several predaceous mites feed on them; late in the growing season, such predators often keep thrips populations under control. Remove and destroy damaged buds and foliage, and for severe cases, spray plants with an insecticidal soap.
SUSCEPTIBLE PLANTS: ARTEMISIA, MARIGOLD, MYRTLE, NASTURTIUM, ONION, POT MARIGOLD, AND ROSE.

PROBLEM: Leaves turn yellow and plants are stunted. When plants are shaken, a white cloud of insects appears.

CAUSE: Whiteflies, sucking insects 1/16 inch long that look like tiny white moths, generally collect on the undersides of young leaves. Found year round in warmer climates but only in summer in colder climates, they like warm, still air. Both adults and nymphs suck sap from stems and leaves, causing an infested plant to wilt. Whiteflies are often brought home with greenhouse-raised plants and can carry viruses and secrete honeydew, which promotes a fungus called sooty mold.

SOLUTION: Inspect plants before buying. Keep the garden weeded. Spray affected plants with a strong stream of water from a garden hose. Spray with insecticidal soap or horticultural oil. Use yellow sticky traps. Introduce lacewings and parasitic wasps. Pyrethrins or rotenone can be applied.
SUSCEPTIBLE PLANTS: MOST VEGETABLES, ESPECIALLY MEMBERS OF THE SQUASH AND TOMATO FAMILIES, AND MELONS; BASIL, HOT PEPPER, NASTURTIUM, POT MARIGOLD, ROSE, ROSEMARY, AND SAGE.

PROBLEM: Foliage develops irregular, yellow to purplish brown spots that darken with age. These spots also may expand and join to cover the leaves. Leaves turn brown and drop. Purplish lesions form along stems, and plant growth is often stunted.

CAUSE: Anthracnose is a fungus disease that is especially severe in wet weather.

SOLUTION: Grow resistant varieties. Thin stems and tops to improve air circulation, and water plants from below to keep the disease from spreading. Remove and destroy infected plants. For trees, prune deadwood and water sprouts. Water during dry spells and keep the root zone mulched to prevent drought stress. To keep a severe infection from spreading, spray plants with a fungicide according to directions while new leaves are growing in spring. *SUSCEPTIBLE PLANTS: PEONY, ROSE, AND SHRUBS, MANY TREES, INCLUDING ASH, BOX ELDER, DOGWOOD, ELM, MAPLE, AND OAK.*

PROBLEM: A brownish gray moldy growth appears on flowers and foliage. Stalks are weak and flowers and foliage droop. Buds may not open. Discolored blotches appear on leaves, stems, and flowers. Stem bases rot. Plant parts eventually turn brown and dry up. Flowering plants are most often affected.

CAUSE: Botrytis blight, known as gray mold, thrives in moist air and cool temperatures, survives winter in the soil or on dead plants, and spreads on wind or water.

SOLUTION: Limit watering to early in the day and avoid overhead watering. Place plants in well-drained soil, and thin to provide more light and air. Cut and destroy all infected plant parts. Spray plants with Bordeaux mixture. *SUSCEPTIBLE PLANTS: FLOWERING PLANTS ARE MOST AT RISK, INCLUDING RHODODEN-DRON, HELLEBORE, LILY, ROSE, AND TULIP.*

PROBLEM: Overnight, young seedlings suddenly topple over and die. Stems are rotted through at the soil line.

CAUSE: Damping-off, a disease caused by several soil fungi, infects seeds and the roots of seedlings. The problem often occurs in wet, poorly drained soil with a high nitrogen content.

SOLUTION: Add fresh compost to the planting medium to provide beneficial bacteria and fungi that will compete with the damping-off fungi. Top the medium with a thin layer of sand or perlite to keep seedlings dry at soil level. Provide well-drained soil and plenty of light, and avoid overcrowding. Plants started in containers are more susceptible than those sown outdoors. Do not overwater seed flats or seedbeds. *SUSCEPTIBLE PLANTS: VIRTUALLY ALL.*

PROBLEM: Leaves develop small yellow spots that gradually turn brown. Spots are frequently surrounded by a ring of yellow or brownish black tissue. Spots often join to produce large, irregular blotches. The entire leaf may turn yellow, wilt, and drop. Extensive defoliation can occur, weakening the plant. The problem usually starts on lower leaves and moves upward.

CAUSE: Leaf-spot diseases, caused by various fungi and bacteria, are spread by wind and splashing water. They are most prevalent from summer into fall, and thrive when humidity and rainfall are high.

SOLUTION: Destroy infected leaves as they appear; do not leave infected material in the garden over the winter. Water only in the mornings. Space and thin plants to increase air circulation. A baking-soda solution can protect healthy foliage but will not destroy fungi on infected leaves.
SUSCEPTIBLE PLANTS: ALL TYPES OF PLANTS, INCLUDING BEE BALM, CELERY, HORSE-RADISH, PARSLEY, POT MARIGOLD, AND PRIMROSE.

PROBLEM: Leaves become mottled with light green or yellow spots or streaks. New growth is spindly and misshapen, and plant is often stunted. Fruits and pods may be discolored or streaked.

CAUSE: Mosaic viruses can infect plants at any time during the growing season.

SOLUTION: Viral infections cannot be controlled. They spread by direct contact between plants and also by hands, tools, and insects. Plant resistant varieties. Remove and destroy infected plants. Introduce lacewings and ladybugs to control virus-transmitting aphids and leafhoppers. Don't plant susceptible crops where mosaic disease has occurred.
SUSCEPTIBLE PLANTS: BEANS, CUCUMBERS, PEPPERS, POTATOES, SQUASH, TOMATOES.

PROBLEM: White or pale gray powdery growth appears on upper surface of leaf, eventually spreading to cover entire leaf, followed by distortion, yellowing, withering, and leaf drop. The powdery growth may also be seen on stems, buds, and shoots. Plants are stunted.

CAUSE: Powdery mildew, a fungal disease, is especially noticeable in late summer and early fall when cool, humid nights follow warm days. Unlike most fungal diseases, powdery mildew does not occur readily in wet conditions. More unsightly than harmful, it rarely kills the plant.

SOLUTION: Grow mildew-resistant varieties. Allow adequate room between susceptible plants. Spray plants daily with water to kill spores. Remove and destroy badly infected plant parts or entire plant. Spray plants with a solution of baking soda. Apply a horticultural oil or sulfur.
SUSCEPTIBLE PLANTS: MANY PLANTS, ESPECIALLY BEANS, CUCUMBERS, MELONS, PUMPKINS, AND SQUASH; ARTEMISIA, BEE BALM, EUONYMUS, LILAC, POT MARIGOLD, ROSE, AND SAGE.

PROBLEM: Leaves turn yellow or brown or are stunted and wilted; the entire plant may wilt and die. Roots are dark brown or black, feel soft and wet to the touch, and emit a slightly foul odor.

CAUSE: Root rot, a common soil-borne disease, is caused by a variety of fungi found in moist soils.

SOLUTION: Remove and destroy affected plants and surrounding soil. Plant in well-drained soil; do not overwater; keep mulch away from base of plants. Avoid damaging roots when digging.
SUSCEPTIBLE PLANTS: VIRTUALLY ALL, PARTICULARLY LAVENDER, MARIGOLD, PINKS, POT MARIGOLD, AND ROSEMARY.

PROBLEM: Upper leaf surfaces have pale yellow or white spots, and undersides are covered with orange or yellow pustules. Leaves wilt or shrivel and hang down along the stem, but do not drop off. Pustules may become more numerous, destroying leaves and occasionally the entire plant. Plants may be stunted.

CAUSE: Rust, a fungus disease, is a problem in late summer and early fall and is most prevalent when nights are cool and humid. Rust spores are spread easily by wind and splashing water and overwinter on infected plant parts.

SOLUTION: Buy rust-resistant varieties whenever possible. Water early in the day and avoid wetting leaves. Remove and destroy infected plant parts in the fall and again in the spring. Do not compost. Spray with sulfur, lime sulfur, or Bordeaux mixture—a traditional antifungal treatment first used in vineyards. *SUSCEPTIBLE PLANTS: VIRTUALLY ALL.*

PROBLEM: Plants wilt on warm days or are stunted, abnormally yellowish in color, or low in yield. Roots may be swollen and have knotty growths. Individual stems may die back. Plants may die.

CAUSE: Soil nematodes, microscopic roundworms that live in the soil and feed on roots, inhibit a plant's uptake of nitrogen. Damage is worst in warm, moist, sandy soils in sunny locations. Nematodes overwinter in infected roots or soil, and are spread by soil and transplants, as well as tools.

SOLUTION: Since nematodes are microscopic, only a laboratory test will confirm their presence. Be suspicious if roots are swollen or stunted. Dispose of infected plants and the soil that surrounds them, or solarize the soil *(box, page 393)*. Plant resistant species or cultivars and rotate crops. Plant a cover crop of African marigolds *(page 471)*. Add nitrogen fertilizer, especially crab or fish meal. Add compost to soil and use organic mulch to encourage fungi that prey on soil nematodes. *SUSCEPTIBLE PLANTS: VIRTUALLY ALL.*

PROBLEM: One side or entire plant suddenly droops or wilts, with symptoms usually appearing first on lower and outer plant parts. Leaves may turn yellow before wilting. Plant fails to grow and eventually dies. Seedlings are stunted, wilt, and eventually die. A cut made across the stem near the base reveals dark streaks or other discoloration on the tissue inside or releases an oozing, sticky white substance.

CAUSE: Wilts, some caused by bacteria and others by fusarium or verticillium fungus, display similar symptoms. Bacterial wilt occurs in midsummer, fusarium wilt in hot weather, and verticillium wilt in cool weather. These microorganisms penetrate roots and stems and clog the water-conducting vessels. Both fungi and bacteria are long lived, remaining in the soil for years after the host plant has died.

SOLUTION: Plant resistant varieties. Fertilize and water regularly to promote vigorous growth. Immediately remove and destroy infected plants, including roots, and clear away garden debris in the fall. Wash hands and disinfect tools with a 10-percent bleach solution. Don't site susceptible plants in an area that has been infected previously. Solarize the soil *(box, page 393)*. *SUSCEPTIBLE PLANTS: CUCUMBERS, EGGPLANT, MELONS, PEPPERS, PUMPKINS, SQUASH, STRAWBERRIES, TOMATOES; BASIL, HOT PEPPER, MARIGOLD, MINT, NASTURTIUM, POPPY, AND SAGE.*

Zone and Frost Maps of the U.S.

To determine if a plant will flourish in your climate, first locate your zone on the map below and check it against the zone information given in the Plant Selection Guide that begins on page 590 or in the encyclopedia entries that begin on page 608. For annuals and biennials, planting dates depend on when frosts occur: Hardy annuals can be safely sown 6 weeks before the last spring frost, whereas tender annuals should be sown only after all danger of frost is past. Also, while cool-season annuals can withstand some frost, warm-season plants can be grown without protection only in the frost-free period between the last and first frosts. Used together, the zone map and the frost-date maps shown opposite will help you select plants suited to your area and determine when to plant them. Frost dates vary widely within each region, however, so check with your weather service or Cooperative Extension Service for more precise figures, and record the temperatures in your own garden from year to year.

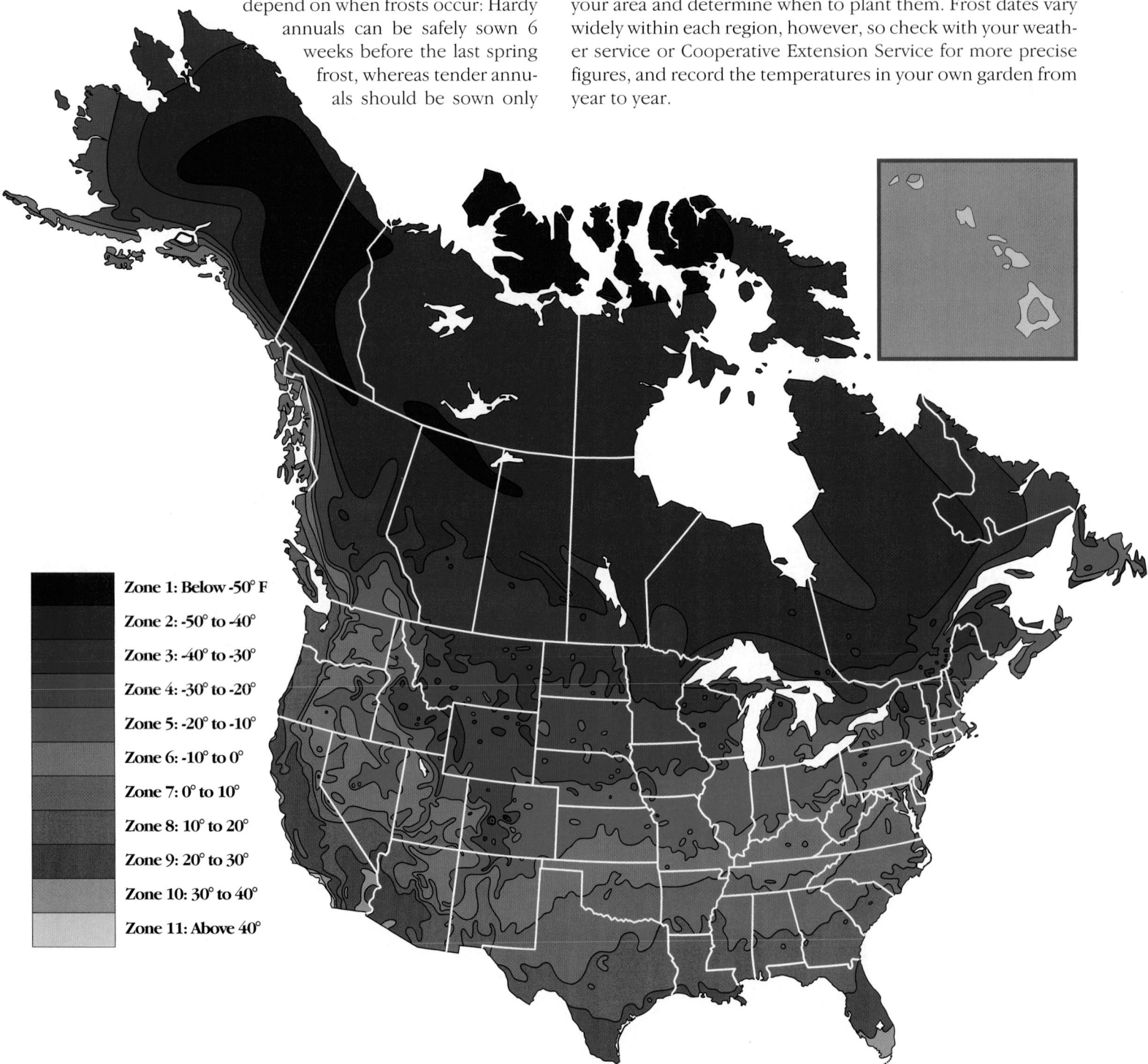

Zone 1: Below -50° F
Zone 2: -50° to -40°
Zone 3: -40° to -30°
Zone 4: -30° to -20°
Zone 5: -20° to -10°
Zone 6: -10° to 0°
Zone 7: 0° to 10°
Zone 8: 10° to 20°
Zone 9: 20° to 30°
Zone 10: 30° to 40°
Zone 11: Above 40°

AVERAGE DATES OF LAST SPRING FROST

	JUNE
	MAY
	APRIL
	MARCH
	FEBRUARY
	JANUARY

AVERAGE DATES OF FIRST FALL FROST

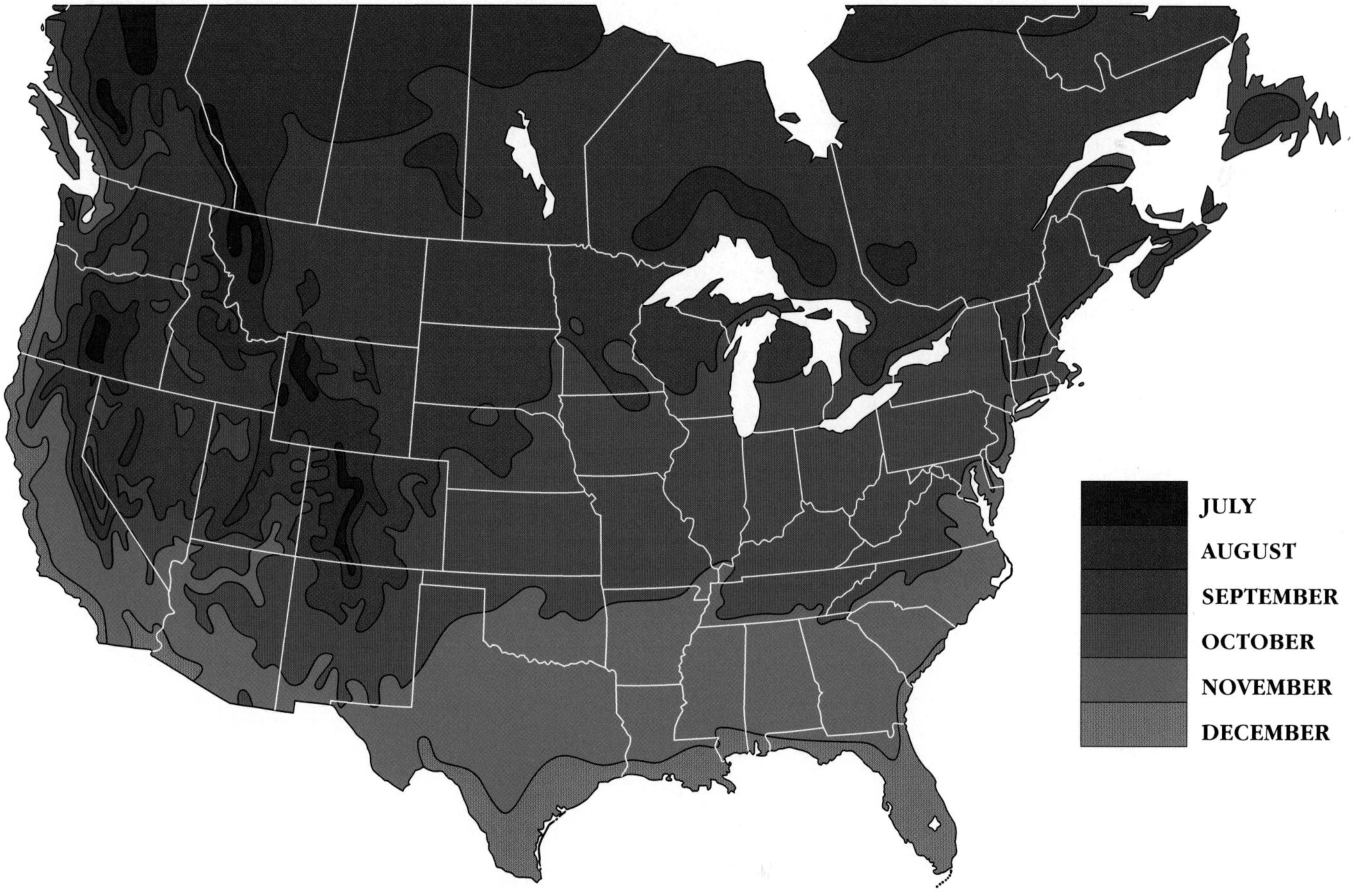

	JULY
	AUGUST
	SEPTEMBER
	OCTOBER
	NOVEMBER
	DECEMBER

585

Guide to Common Garden Weeds

1. AMARANTHUS RETROFLEXUS (Redroot Pigweed)

This annual produces as many as 200,000 seeds per plant. Some western pigweeds break loose from their roots and roll like tumbleweeds across the land, scattering their seeds as they go. Control pigweed by uprooting young plants or cutting the stems off at ground level.

2. AMBROSIA ARTEMISIIFOLIA (Common Ragweed)

Although the seed is a favorite food of birds, ragweed pollen is the bane of hay fever sufferers. The seeds need light for germination, so a layer of mulch is a good preventive. The shade cast by larger plants will also discourage growth. Mow or cut plants down before they go to seed.

3. BRASSICA KABER (Wild Mustard)

Introduced to the Americas as a seasoning, wild mustard has spread to become a pest species. Dig out or cut plants to the ground before they flower to prevent seeds from forming. The seeds are numerous and remain viable for years.

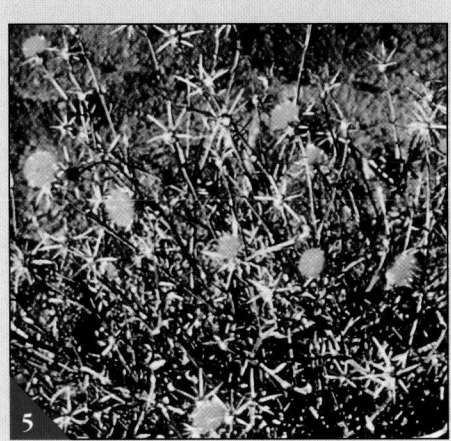

4. CENCHRUS SPECIES (Sandbur)

The spiny seeds of these annual or biennial grasses are painful for humans and animals alike and, if plentiful enough, can make a yard unusable. As the name implies, sandburs prefer sandy soils. When they invade a lawn, their blades are camouflaged and hard to see. Hand pull or dig, taking care not to touch the seeds.

5. CENTAUREA SOLSTITIALIS (Star Thistle)

Fast becoming a serious pest in California, Washington, and Oregon, star thistle usually grows as an annual but sometimes acts like a biennial. Cut it down before the flowers form; the bracts around the flowers bear sharp spines.

6. CERASTIUM ARVENSE (Field Chickweed)

This perennial weed grows in gardens throughout the United States. Destroy it with shallow cultivation before it can flower and go to seed. Gather up all the stems you've cut, since each one can form roots and develop into a new plant.

7. CHENOPODIUM ALBUM (Lamb's-Quarters)

An annual that appears early in the season, lamb's-quarters grows in gardens all over the United States. Mulch beds to discourage germination, and pull out or cut down any plants that appear before they flower.

10. CYPERUS ESCULENTUS (Nut Sedge, Nut Grass)

Nut sedge, a perennial, is usually found in moist or poorly drained soil. Its roots send up new shoots whenever the main stem is cut. Dig up the roots or cut off new growth as it appears; this will eventually kill the plants. Use landscape fabric, not woodchips or other organic mulches, to block the foliage.

8. CIRSIUM ARVENSE (Canada Thistle)

Despite its name, this perennial weed is a Eurasian native. A single plant can extend its root system over a large area, sending up numerous stems to create a massive stand. Cut stems down but don't hoe the plants, since root pieces start new plants. Treat persistent stands with a systemic herbicide.

11. DATURA STRAMONIUM (Jimson Weed)

All parts of this annual are poisonous, so remove it as soon as you see it. Most herbicides don't affect it; hoe it or hand pull it, wearing gloves to protect against the spines that form on the flower capsules. Because of its poisons, jimson weed should be disposed of according to local ordinances for plant debris.

9. CONVOLVULUS ARVENSIS (Field Bindweed)

This perennial has a huge root system that makes an established plant almost impossible to get rid of. Avoid tilling near the roots; severed pieces will produce new plants. Control with regular hoeing. Never allow plants to go to seed. Thick mulches help suppress germination.

12. DIGITARIA ISCHAEMUM, D. SANGUINALIS (Crab Grass)

Crab grass, an annual, is well known for its unsightly, sprawling presence in lawns, especially in places where the soil is compacted. Aerate the lawn and let turf grass grow taller than usual so it can shade out crab grass. In flower beds, dig it out before it sets seed; mulch to prevent seeds from sprouting.

13. ELEUSINE INDICA (Goose Grass)

Goose grass is an annual that commonly takes hold in a sparse lawn growing in compacted, nutrient-poor soil. Aerating the soil, fertilizing, and mowing the lawn higher all help to control the weed. Remove plants from the lawn by hand before they flower, and mulch beds to discourage seedlings.

14. EUPHORBIA MACULATA (Spotted Spurge)

This annual, which often takes root in pavement cracks, grows so low that the blades of a lawn mower pass above it, leaving the weed intact. Pull it out by the roots before it produces its tiny, pink-white flowers and thousands of seeds.

15. HORDEUM JUBATUM (Foxtail Barley, Wild Barley)

Foxtail barley grows to 2 feet and has sharp awns (bristles) on its seed heads that pose a danger to animals, since they can lodge in the ears, mouth, and eyes or be drawn into the lungs. Mow this perennial low or dig it out. Don't compost it; awns may not decompose completely.

16. OXALIS STRICTA (Wood Sorrel, Sourgrass)

This annual weed and its look-alike relative, the perennial O. corniculata, have seed capsules that explode and shoot seeds as far as 6 feet from the mother plant. Mulch to smother seeds or dig out the taproots.

17. PHYTOLACCA AMERICANA (Pokeweed)

Most pokeweed plants are seeded by birds, which relish pokeberries. If you can dig up this perennial's long taproot, do so. Otherwise, keep the stems cut to the ground; this will eventually starve out the plant.

18. POLYGONUM PERFOLIATUM (Mile-a-Minute)

A native of Asia, this fast-spreading vine thrives in many different habitats in the United States. If you discover no more than a plant or two in your garden, dig them out, taking care to avoid the sharp thorns. If the vines are more numerous, treat them with a systemic herbicide.

19. PORTULACA OLERACEA (Purslane)

Purslane lives on such a compressed schedule that there can be several generations of this drought-tolerant annual in a single growing season. Hoe regularly to destroy new plants, or pull them up by hand. Dispose of purslane promptly; left lying on the ground, it can go to seed or reroot weeks later.

20. RHUS DIVERSILOBA (Poison Oak)

This West Coast native produces an oil that causes a bad rash in most people. It may grow as a shrub or a vine. Dig out by the roots or use a systemic herbicide if the site allows, following the precautions recommended for poison ivy (right). Handle eastern poison oak (R. toxicodendron) in the same way.

21. RHUS RADICANS (Poison Ivy)

Another cause of nasty rashes, poison ivy varies in form but generally has leaves arranged in threes. Dig out the roots or use a systemic herbicide if the site allows. Wear protective clothing, and wash it and tools well afterward. Never compost or burn poison oak or poison ivy; inhaling the smoke is dangerous.

22. ROSA MULTIFLORA (Multiflora Rose)

Once sold as a decorative hedge plant, this tough perennial spreads by seeds and rooting stems, and takes hold tenaciously in uncultivated areas. Dig small plants up by the roots. Cut larger ones to the ground and treat the stubs with a systemic herbicide.

23. RUBUS SPECIES (Wild Bramble)

In time, the thorny canes of brambles such as raspberry, dewberry, and blackberry create impassable thickets. If you get at a plant when it is still young, however, digging out as much of the roots as you can and cutting new shoots to the ground, it will eventually die. This may take more than a year.

24. TARAXACUM OFFICINALE (Dandelion)

Dandelion's long taproots nourish it through many a beheading, so for effective removal, dig out the root. Try to get it all: New shoots spring from root pieces left in the ground.

Plant Selection Guide—General

Organized by plant type, this chart provides information needed to select species and varieties that will thrive in the particular conditions of your garden. For additional information on many of these plants, refer to the encyclopedia that begins on page 608.

	ZONES	SOIL		LIGHT			BLOOM SEASON				PLANT HEIGHT					NOTED FOR				
		Dry	Moist	Full sun	Partial shade	Shade	Spring	Summer	Fall	Winter	Under 3 ft.	3-6 ft.	6-10 ft.	10-20 ft.	Over 20 ft.	Form	Foliage	Flowers	Fruit/seeds	Bark/twigs
PERENNIALS AND GRASSES																				
Artemisia x 'Powis Castle'	5-8	✔		✔							✔						✔			
Bergenia cordifolia	3-8		✔	✔	✔		✔				✔						✔	✔		
Calamagrostis acutiflora 'Stricta'	6-9	✔	✔	✔				✔				✔				✔	✔	✔		
Cyrtomium falcatum	8-10		✔		✔	✔					✔						✔	✔		
Fargesia murielae	5-9	✔	✔		✔									✔		✔	✔			
Helleborus niger	4-8		✔		✔					✔	✔						✔	✔		
Hemerocallis 'Stella d'Oro'	4-9	✔	✔	✔	✔			✔	✔		✔							✔		
Heuchera micrantha 'Palace Purple'	4-8		✔	✔	✔			✔			✔						✔			
Hosta 'Krossa Regal'	3-9		✔		✔	✔		✔				✔				✔	✔			
Iris sibirica 'Caesar's Brother'	3-9		✔	✔	✔			✔				✔				✔	✔	✔		
Lavandula angustifolia	5-9	✔		✔				✔			✔						✔	✔		
Lavandula stoechas	8-10	✔		✔				✔			✔						✔	✔		
Miscanthus sinensis 'Zebrinus'	5-9		✔	✔					✔				✔			✔	✔	✔		
Pennisetum setaceum 'Rubrum'	8-10	✔	✔	✔				✔			✔					✔	✔	✔		
Potentilla nepalensis 'Miss Wilmott'	5-7	✔	✔	✔	✔			✔			✔						✔	✔		
Rudbeckia fulgida 'Goldsturm'	3-9		✔	✔	✔			✔	✔		✔							✔		
Sedum x 'Autumn Joy'	3-10	✔		✔	✔			✔	✔		✔					✔	✔	✔		
GROUND COVERS																				
Calluna vulgaris 'Mrs. Ronald Gray'	4-7		✔	✔	✔			✔			✔					✔	✔	✔		
Ceanothus griseus var. horizontalis	8-10	✔		✔			✔				✔							✔		
Cotoneaster dammeri 'Skogholm'	5-8	✔	✔	✔			✔				✔						✔	✔		
Cotoneaster salicifolius 'Autumn Fire'	6-8	✔	✔	✔	✔		✔				✔						✔	✔	✔	
Erica carnea 'Springwood Pink'	6-9		✔	✔	✔				✔	✔	✔							✔		
Euonymus fortunei 'Colorata'	4-9	✔	✔	✔	✔	✔					✔						✔			
Hypericum calycinum	5-9	✔		✔				✔	✔		✔							✔		
Juniperus horizontalis 'Wiltonii'	3-9	✔	✔	✔							✔						✔	✔		
Juniperus procumbens	3-9	✔	✔	✔							✔						✔			
Liriope muscari 'Variegata'	7-10	✔	✔	✔	✔	✔		✔			✔						✔	✔	✔	
Mahonia repens	5-10		✔	✔		✔	✔				✔						✔	✔	✔	

	Plant	ZONES	SOIL: Dry	Moist	LIGHT: Full sun	Partial shade	Shade	BLOOM: Spring	Summer	Fall	Winter	HEIGHT: Under 3 ft.	3-6 ft.	6-10 ft.	10-20 ft.	Over 20 ft.	NOTED FOR: Form	Foliage	Flowers	Fruit/seeds	Bark/twigs
VINES	*Clematis armandii*	7-9		✓	✓	✓		✓							✓			✓	✓		
	Clematis paniculata	5-8		✓	✓	✓				✓						✓			✓		
	Gelsemium sempervirens	6-9		✓	✓	✓		✓							✓				✓		
	Hydrangea anomala ssp. *petiolaris*	4-7		✓	✓	✓	✓	✓								✓		✓			✓
	Ipomoea alba	10		✓					✓	✓		✓							✓		
	Lonicera heckrottii	4-9	✓	✓	✓	✓						✓							✓		
	Rosa 'New Dawn'	3-10		✓	✓			✓				✓							✓		
	Wisteria floribunda	4-9	✓	✓	✓			✓								✓			✓		
DECIDUOUS SHRUBS	*Abelia* x 'Edward Goucher'	6-10		✓	✓	✓			✓	✓			✓					✓	✓		
	Acer palmatum 'Dissectum'	5-8		✓	✓	✓		✓						✓			✓	✓			✓
	Berberis thunbergii 'Crimson Pygmy'	4-8	✓	✓	✓			✓				✓						✓		✓	
	Chaenomeles speciosa 'Cameo'	4-8	✓	✓	✓			✓					✓					✓	✓		
	Cotinus coggygria 'Velvet Cloak'	5-8	✓	✓	✓				✓						✓			✓	✓	✓	
	Enkianthus campanulatus	4-7		✓	✓	✓		✓						✓				✓	✓		
	Euonymus alata 'Compacta'	5-8	✓	✓	✓	✓	✓	✓					✓					✓		✓	✓
	Forsythia x *intermedia* 'Spectabilis'	6-9	✓	✓	✓			✓						✓			✓	✓			
	Hamamelis x *intermedia* 'Arnold Promise'	5-8		✓	✓	✓					✓				✓			✓	✓		
	Hydrangea arborescens 'Annabelle'	3-9		✓	✓	✓	✓	✓				✓						✓			
	Jasminum nudiflorum	6-10	✓	✓	✓	✓					✓	✓					✓	✓	✓		
	Lagerstroemia indica 'Seminole'	7-10		✓					✓					✓				✓	✓		✓
	Ligustrum ovalifolium 'Aureum'	5-10	✓	✓	✓	✓		✓							✓			✓	✓	✓	
	Myrica pensylvanica	3-7	✓	✓	✓	✓	✓							✓				✓		✓	
	Potentilla fruticosa 'Klondike'	3-7	✓	✓	✓	✓			✓	✓	✓	✓						✓	✓		
	Punica granatum 'Legrellei'	8-10		✓	✓				✓					✓					✓	✓	
	Rhododendron mucronulatum	4-7		✓	✓						✓	✓	✓					✓	✓		
	Rhododendron schlippenbachii	4-7		✓		✓		✓					✓					✓	✓		
	Rosa rugosa 'Hansa'	3-7		✓	✓				✓				✓					✓	✓	✓	
	Spiraea x *bumalda* 'Gold Flame'	3-8		✓	✓	✓			✓			✓						✓	✓		
	Stewartia ovata	5-9		✓	✓	✓		✓							✓			✓	✓		✓
	Syringa patula 'Miss Kim'	3-8		✓	✓			✓					✓					✓	✓		
	Viburnum plicatum var. *tomentosum*	5-8		✓	✓	✓		✓						✓			✓	✓	✓	✓	
	Vitex agnus-castus 'Rosea'	7-9		✓	✓				✓	✓		✓	✓						✓		

	ZONES	SOIL		LIGHT			BLOOM SEASON				PLANT HEIGHT					NOTED FOR				
		Dry	Moist	Full sun	Partial shade	Shade	Spring	Summer	Fall	Winter	Under 3 ft.	3-6 ft.	6-10 ft.	10-20 ft.	Over 20 ft.	Form	Foliage	Flowers	Fruit/seeds	Bark/twigs
EVERGREEN SHRUBS																				
Aucuba japonica 'Variegata'	7-10		✔		✔	✔	✔						✔				✔		✔	
Berberis buxifolia var. *nana*	5-8		✔	✔	✔	✔	✔				✔						✔	✔	✔	
Berberis julianae	5-8			✔	✔	✔	✔					✔					✔	✔	✔	
Chamaecyparis obtusa 'Nana Gracilis'	4-8		✔	✔	✔						✔					✔	✔			
Cistus x *hybridus*	8-10	✔		✔			✔				✔						✔	✔		
Cistus x *purpureus*	8-10	✔		✔				✔			✔							✔		
Cotoneaster salicifolius	6-8		✔	✔	✔		✔						✔			✔			✔	
Eriobotrya japonica	8-10		✔	✔	✔				✔					✔	✔	✔			✔	
Escallonia x *langleyensis 'Apple Blossom'*	8-10	✔	✔	✔			✔	✔	✔		✔						✔	✔		
Euonymus fortunei 'Emerald Gaiety'	5-9	✔	✔	✔	✔	✔	✔				✔					✔	✔			
Fatsia japonica	8-10		✔			✔			✔		✔						✔	✔	✔	
Hebe 'Autumn Glory'	8-10	✔		✔				✔	✔		✔						✔	✔		
Ilex cornuta 'Berries Jubilee'	7-9			✔	✔		✔					✔					✔		✔	
Juniperus chinensis 'Mint Julep'	3-9	✔	✔	✔							✔					✔	✔			
Ligustrum japonicum	7-10	✔	✔	✔	✔	✔	✔						✔	✔			✔	✔	✔	
Mahonia bealei	7-10		✔		✔					✔		✔					✔	✔	✔	
Nandina domestica 'Harbour Dwarf'	6-9		✔	✔	✔	✔	✔		✔		✔					✔	✔		✔	
Picea abies 'Nidiformis'	3-7		✔	✔	✔						✔					✔	✔			
Pieris japonica 'Variegata'	5-8		✔	✔	✔	✔	✔					✔	✔			✔	✔	✔		
Pittosporum tobira	8-10	✔	✔	✔	✔	✔	✔						✔			✔			✔	
Prunus laurocerasus 'Otto Luyken'	6-10		✔	✔	✔		✔				✔					✔	✔			
Raphiolepis indica	9-10		✔	✔			✔				✔					✔	✔			
Rhododendron 'Scarlet Wonder'	6-8		✔		✔	✔	✔				✔					✔	✔			
Rosmarinus officinalis 'Lockwood de Forest'	7-10	✔	✔	✔	✔		✔		✔	✔	✔					✔	✔	✔		
Viburnum davidii	8-9		✔	✔	✔		✔				✔						✔	✔	✔	
DECIDUOUS TREES																				
Acer griseum	4-8		✔	✔	✔		✔							✔		✔				✔
Acer rubrum 'October Glory'	3-9		✔	✔	✔		✔							✔			✔			
Betula nigra	4-9		✔	✔	✔		✔									✔	✔			✔
Carpinus betulus 'Columnaris'	4-7	✔	✔	✔	✔		✔									✔	✔			✔
Chilopsis linearis	8-10	✔		✔			✔							✔	✔	✔	✔	✔		
Cladrastis kentukea	4-8	✔	✔	✔			✔							✔	✔	✔		✔		✔
Cornus alternifolia	3-7		✔	✔	✔		✔							✔	✔	✔		✔	✔	

	ZONES	SOIL		LIGHT			BLOOM SEASON				PLANT HEIGHT					NOTED FOR				
		Dry	Moist	Full sun	Partial shade	Shade	Spring	Summer	Fall	Winter	Under 3 ft.	3-6 ft.	6-10 ft.	10-20 ft.	Over 20 ft.	Form	Foliage	Flowers	Fruit/seeds	Bark/twigs
DECIDUOUS TREES																				
Cornus kousa var. chinensis	5-8		✔	✔	✔		✔	✔							✔	✔	✔	✔	✔	✔
Fagus sylvatica 'Aurea Pendula'	4-7		✔	✔	✔		✔								✔	✔	✔			✔
Fraxinus americana 'Champaign County'	3-9	✔	✔	✔			✔								✔		✔			
Gleditsia triacanthos var. inermis 'Imperial'	4-7	✔	✔	✔			✔								✔		✔			
Koelreuteria paniculata	5-9	✔	✔	✔	✔			✔							✔		✔	✔	✔	
Lagerstroemia indica 'Natchez'	7-10		✔	✔				✔	✔					✔			✔	✔		✔
Magnolia stellata 'Royal Star'	4-8		✔	✔	✔				✔					✔			✔	✔		
Magnolia virginiana	5-9		✔	✔	✔			✔						✔	✔		✔	✔	✔	
Malus 'Red Jade'	4-8		✔	✔			✔							✔			✔		✔	✔
Phellodendron amurense	3-8	✔	✔	✔			✔								✔					✔
Pistacia chinensis	6-9	✔	✔	✔			✔								✔		✔		✔	
Populus tremuloides	3-7	✔	✔	✔			✔								✔	✔	✔			✔
Prunus mume	6-9		✔	✔	✔				✔					✔					✔	✔
Pyrus calleryana 'Chanticleer'	5-8	✔	✔	✔			✔								✔	✔	✔	✔		
Quercus shumardii	5-9	✔	✔	✔			✔								✔	✔	✔			
Sapindus drummondii	6-9	✔		✔	✔		✔								✔		✔	✔	✔	✔
Stewartia pseudocamellia	5-7		✔	✔	✔			✔							✔		✔	✔		✔
Styrax japonicus	5-8		✔	✔	✔		✔								✔	✔		✔		✔
Syringa reticulata	3-7		✔	✔				✔							✔		✔			
Taxodium distichum	4-9		✔	✔			✔								✔	✔	✔			✔
Ulmus parvifolia	4-9		✔	✔				✔							✔		✔			✔
Zelkova serrata 'Green Vase'	5-8		✔	✔			✔								✔	✔	✔			✔
EVERGREEN TREES																				
Abies concolor	3-7	✔	✔	✔											✔	✔	✔			
Cedrus deodara	7-8	✔	✔	✔											✔	✔	✔			
x Cupressocyparis leylandii 'Silver Dust'	6-10	✔	✔	✔											✔	✔	✔			
Cupressus sempervirens	7-9	✔		✔											✔	✔				✔
Ilex opaca	5-9		✔	✔	✔		✔								✔		✔		✔	
Ilex vomitoria	7-10	✔	✔	✔	✔		✔							✔			✔		✔	✔
Picea glauca	3-6		✔	✔	✔										✔	✔	✔			
Pinus contorta var. contorta	7-10		✔	✔											✔		✔			
Pinus nigra	4-7	✔	✔	✔											✔	✔	✔			
Taxus x media 'Hicksii'	4-7	✔	✔	✔	✔									✔		✔	✔		✔	

Plant Selection Guide—Herbs

Organized by plant type, this chart provides information on culinary herbs as well as herbs used for ornamental and other purposes. For additional information on many of these plants, refer to the encyclopedia that begins on page 608.

	HARDINESS			HEIGHT				LIGHT			SOIL			BLOOM SEASON				PARTS USED				
ANNUALS AND BIENNIALS	HARDY	HALF-HARDY	TENDER	UNDER 1 FOOT	1 TO 3 FEET	3 TO 5 FEET	OVER 5 FEET	FULL SUN	LIGHT SHADE	SHADE	DRY	WELL-DRAINED	MOIST	SPRING	SUMMER	FALL	WINTER	LEAVES	FLOWERS	ROOT/BULB	SEEDS/FRUIT	STEMS/BARK
ALOE VERA			✓	✓				✓	✓			✓			✓			✓				
AMARANTHUS HYPOCHONDRIACUS			✓				✓	✓			✓	✓			✓			✓			✓	
ANETHUM GRAVEOLENS 'MAMMOTH'			✓		✓			✓				✓						✓			✓	
ANGELICA ARCHANGELICA*	✓						✓	✓	✓				✓		✓			✓			✓	
ANGELICA GIGAS*	✓						✓	✓	✓				✓		✓			✓			✓	
ANTHRISCUS CEREFOLIUM			✓	✓					✓	✓		✓			✓			✓	✓			
APIUM GRAVEOLENS*	✓			✓				✓	✓			✓	✓		✓						✓	
ARTEMISIA ANNUA	✓					✓		✓	✓			✓			✓			✓	✓			
ATRIPLEX HORTENSIS	✓						✓	✓				✓	✓		✓			✓				
BORAGO OFFICINALIS 'ALBA'	✓			✓				✓				✓	✓		✓			✓	✓			
BRASSICA JUNCEA	✓				✓			✓				✓			✓						✓	
CALENDULA OFFICINALIS	✓			✓				✓				✓		✓	✓	✓			✓			
CAPSICUM ANNUUM VAR. ANNUUM			✓	✓				✓				✓	✓	✓							✓	
CAPSICUM CHINENSE 'HABANERO'			✓	✓				✓				✓	✓	✓							✓	
CARTHAMUS TINCTORIUS			✓		✓			✓			✓	✓			✓				✓		✓	
CARUM CARVI*	✓			✓				✓	✓			✓			✓			✓		✓	✓	
CATHARANTHUS ROSEUS			✓	✓				✓	✓		✓	✓	✓	✓	✓				✓			
CENTAUREA CYANUS			✓		✓			✓				✓			✓	✓		✓	✓			
CHENOPODIUM AMBROSIOIDES	✓					✓		✓				✓			✓			✓			✓	
CHENOPODIUM BOTRYS	✓			✓				✓				✓			✓			✓				
COIX LACRYMA-JOBI			✓			✓	✓	✓				✓			✓			✓			✓	
CORIANDRUM SATIVUM			✓	✓				✓				✓			✓			✓			✓	✓
DIGITALIS LANATA*	✓				✓			✓	✓			✓			✓				✓			
DIGITALIS PURPUREA*	✓					✓		✓	✓			✓			✓				✓			
ERUCA VESICARIA SSP. SATIVA	✓			✓				✓	✓				✓	✓	✓			✓	✓			
FOENICULUM VULGARE 'PURPURASCENS'			✓			✓	✓	✓				✓		✓	✓			✓		✓	✓	✓
HEDEOMA PULEGIOIDES	✓			✓				✓	✓			✓			✓	✓						
HIBISCUS SABDARIFFA			✓			✓	✓	✓				✓			✓	✓		✓			✓	

*BIENNIAL

ANNUALS AND BIENNIALS

	HARDINESS			HEIGHT				LIGHT			SOIL			BLOOM SEASON				PARTS USED				
	Hardy	Half-Hardy	Tender	Under 1 Foot	1 to 3 Feet	3 to 5 Feet	Over 5 Feet	Full Sun	Light Shade	Shade	Dry	Well-Drained	Moist	Spring	Summer	Fall	Winter	Leaves	Flowers	Root/Bulb	Seeds/Fruit	Stems/Bark
ISATIS TINCTORIA*	✓				✓			✓				✓	✓	✓					✓			
MATRICARIA RECUTITA			✓	✓				✓				✓		✓	✓			✓	✓			
NICOTIANA RUSTICA			✓		✓	✓		✓				✓			✓	✓		✓	✓			
NIGELLA SATIVA			✓	✓				✓				✓		✓							✓	
OCIMUM 'AFRICAN BLUE'			✓	✓				✓				✓			✓	✓		✓	✓			
OCIMUM BASILICUM 'CINNAMON'			✓	✓				✓				✓			✓	✓		✓	✓			
OCIMUM BASILICUM 'DARK OPAL'			✓	✓				✓				✓			✓	✓		✓	✓			
OCIMUM BASILICUM 'MINIMUM'			✓	✓				✓				✓			✓	✓		✓	✓			
OCIMUM SANCTUM			✓	✓				✓				✓			✓	✓		✓	✓			
ORIGANUM DICTAMNUS		✓			✓				✓			✓			✓	✓		✓	✓			
ORIGANUM MAJORANA		✓			✓				✓				✓		✓	✓		✓	✓			
ORIGANUM X MAJORICUM		✓							✓				✓		✓	✓		✓	✓			
ORIGANUM ONITES		✓		✓					✓				✓		✓	✓		✓	✓			
PAPAVER RHOEAS			✓	✓				✓			✓	✓		✓	✓				✓	✓		
PELARGONIUM CAPITATUM			✓	✓				✓				✓			✓			✓	✓			
PELARGONIUM X FRAGRANS 'VARIEGATUM'			✓	✓				✓				✓			✓			✓	✓			
PELARGONIUM ODORATISSIMUM			✓	✓				✓	✓			✓			✓	✓		✓	✓			
PELARGONIUM QUERCIFOLIUM			✓		✓			✓				✓			✓	✓		✓	✓			
PELARGONIUM TOMENTOSUM			✓	✓				✓	✓			✓			✓			✓	✓			
PERILLA FRUTESCENS 'ATROPURPUREA'			✓	✓				✓	✓			✓			✓			✓			✓	
PETROSELINUM CRISPUM VAR. CRISPUM*	✓			✓				✓				✓			✓			✓				
PETROSELINUM CRISPUM VAR. NEAPOLITANUM*	✓			✓				✓				✓			✓			✓				
PLECTRANTHUS AMBOINICUS			✓	✓				✓	✓			✓			✓			✓				
RICINUS COMMUNIS 'CARMENCITA'			✓			✓	✓	✓				✓			✓							
SALVIA COCCINEA	✓				✓			✓			✓	✓			✓	✓		✓	✓			
SALVIA VIRIDIS*	✓				✓			✓			✓	✓			✓			✓	✓			
SATUREJA HORTENSIS	✓				✓			✓				✓			✓	✓		✓				
TAGETES LUCIDA			✓		✓			✓				✓			✓	✓		✓	✓			
TAGETES MINUTA			✓		✓			✓				✓			✓			✓				
TAGETES PATULA			✓	✓				✓				✓			✓	✓			✓			
TROPAEOLUM MAJUS			✓	✓	✓	✓		✓	✓			✓			✓	✓		✓	✓		✓	
VERBASCUM THAPSUS*	✓						✓	✓	✓			✓			✓	✓		✓	✓			

*BIENNIAL

PERENNIALS, FERNS, AND BULBS

	ZONES								HEIGHT				LIGHT			SOIL			BLOOM SEASON				PARTS USED				
	Zone 3	Zone 4	Zone 5	Zone 6	Zone 7	Zone 8	Zone 9	Zone 10	Under 1 Foot	1 to 3 Feet	3 to 5 Feet	Over 5 Feet	Full Sun	Light Shade	Shade	Dry	Well-Drained	Moist	Spring	Summer	Fall	Winter	Leaves	Flowers	Root/Bulb	Seeds/Fruit	Stems/Bark
ACHILLEA MILLEFOLIUM	✓	✓	✓	✓	✓	✓				✓			✓				✓			✓	✓		✓	✓			
ACORUS CALAMUS	✓	✓	✓	✓	✓	✓	✓					✓	✓	✓				✓		✓			✓		✓		
ADIANTUM CAPILLUS-VENERIS			✓	✓	✓	✓	✓			✓				✓	✓	✓	✓			✓			✓				
AGASTACHE FOENICULUM			✓	✓	✓	✓	✓			✓			✓	✓			✓	✓		✓			✓	✓			
ALCEA ROSEA	✓	✓	✓	✓	✓	✓						✓	✓	✓			✓			✓				✓			
ALCHEMILLA ALPINA	✓	✓	✓	✓	✓					✓			✓				✓			✓			✓				
ALLIUM AMPELOPRASUM VAR. AMPELOPRASUM		✓	✓	✓	✓	✓				✓			✓	✓			✓	✓		✓	✓		✓		✓		
ALLIUM SATIVUM		✓	✓	✓	✓	✓				✓			✓	✓				✓		✓	✓		✓	✓	✓	✓	
ALLIUM SCHOENOPRASUM	✓	✓	✓	✓	✓	✓	✓		✓				✓	✓			✓			✓			✓	✓			
ALLIUM TUBEROSUM	✓	✓	✓	✓	✓	✓				✓			✓	✓			✓			✓	✓		✓	✓	✓		
ALTHAEA OFFICINALIS	✓	✓	✓	✓	✓	✓						✓	✓					✓		✓			✓		✓	✓	
ANTHEMIS TINCTORIA	✓	✓	✓	✓	✓	✓	✓			✓			✓				✓	✓		✓	✓		✓	✓			
ARCTOSTAPHYLOS UVA-URSI	✓	✓	✓	✓	✓	✓			✓				✓				✓	✓	✓								✓
ARMORACIA RUSTICANA	✓	✓	✓	✓	✓	✓	✓				✓		✓	✓			✓	✓		✓			✓		✓		
ARNICA MONTANA			✓	✓	✓	✓				✓			✓				✓			✓				✓			
ARTEMISIA ABSINTHIUM 'LAMBROOK SILVER'	✓	✓	✓	✓	✓	✓				✓			✓			✓	✓			✓			✓				
ARTEMISIA ARBORESCENS				✓	✓					✓			✓			✓	✓			✓	✓		✓				
ARTEMISIA DRACUNCULUS VAR. SATIVA		✓	✓	✓	✓					✓			✓	✓		✓	✓			✓			✓				
ARTEMISIA LUDOVICIANA 'SILVER KING'		✓	✓	✓	✓	✓					✓		✓			✓	✓			✓			✓				
ASARUM CANADENSE	✓	✓	✓	✓	✓				✓					✓	✓	✓	✓	✓	✓				✓		✓		
ASCLEPIAS TUBEROSA	✓	✓	✓	✓	✓	✓				✓			✓			✓				✓				✓	✓		
CALAMINTHA GRANDIFLORA		✓	✓	✓	✓	✓	✓			✓			✓				✓			✓			✓				
CENTELLA ASIATICA					✓	✓	✓			✓			✓	✓				✓		✓			✓	✓			
CHAMAEMELUM NOBILE		✓	✓	✓	✓	✓			✓				✓	✓			✓		✓	✓	✓			✓			
CICHORIUM INTYBUS	✓	✓	✓	✓	✓	✓	✓				✓		✓				✓			✓	✓		✓	✓	✓		
CIMICIFUGA RACEMOSA	✓	✓	✓	✓	✓							✓	✓	✓	✓			✓		✓					✓		
COLCHICUM AUTUMNALE		✓	✓	✓					✓				✓	✓				✓			✓				✓		
CONVALLARIA MAJALIS	✓	✓	✓	✓	✓	✓	✓		✓					✓	✓		✓	✓	✓					✓			
CROCUS SATIVUS			✓	✓	✓				✓				✓	✓			✓				✓			✓			
CYMBOPOGON CITRATUS					✓	✓	✓			✓			✓	✓			✓			✓			✓				
DIANTHUS X ALLWOODII		✓	✓	✓	✓	✓				✓			✓	✓			✓		✓	✓	✓			✓			
DIANTHUS CARYOPHYLLUS			✓	✓	✓	✓	✓			✓			✓	✓			✓		✓	✓	✓			✓			

PERENNIALS, FERNS, AND BULBS

	ZONE 3	ZONE 4	ZONE 5	ZONE 6	ZONE 7	ZONE 8	ZONE 9	ZONE 10	UNDER 1 FOOT	1 TO 3 FEET	3 TO 5 FEET	OVER 5 FEET	FULL SUN	LIGHT SHADE	SHADE	DRY	WELL-DRAINED	MOIST	SPRING	SUMMER	FALL	WINTER	LEAVES	FLOWERS	ROOT/BULB	SEEDS/FRUIT	STEMS/BARK
DICTAMNUS ALBUS	✓	✓	✓	✓	✓	✓	✓		✓				✓	✓			✓	✓	✓					✓		✓	
EUPATORIUM PURPUREUM	✓	✓	✓	✓	✓	✓	✓	✓		✓			✓	✓				✓		✓	✓			✓			
FILIPENDULA ULMARIA	✓	✓	✓	✓	✓	✓	✓				✓	✓	✓	✓				✓		✓	✓		✓	✓			
GALIUM ODORATUM	✓	✓	✓	✓	✓	✓			✓				✓	✓	✓		✓	✓		✓			✓				
GERANIUM MACULATUM	✓	✓	✓	✓	✓	✓			✓				✓	✓			✓	✓		✓			✓				
GERANIUM ROBERTIANUM	✓	✓	✓	✓	✓				✓				✓	✓		✓		✓		✓	✓		✓				
GLYCYRRHIZA GLABRA				✓	✓	✓					✓		✓	✓			✓	✓		✓					✓		
HELICHRYSUM ANGUSTIFOLIUM				✓	✓	✓				✓			✓			✓	✓			✓			✓	✓			
HEUCHERA AMERICANA		✓	✓	✓	✓				✓					✓	✓	✓	✓	✓		✓				✓			
HIEROCHLOE ODORATA	✓	✓	✓	✓	✓	✓			✓				✓	✓			✓	✓	✓				✓				
HUMULUS LUPULUS	✓	✓	✓	✓	✓	✓					✓	✓	✓	✓			✓	✓		✓			✓	✓			
HYDRASTIS CANADENSIS		✓	✓	✓	✓	✓			✓						✓		✓	✓	✓				✓				
HYPERICUM PERFORATUM		✓	✓	✓	✓	✓			✓				✓	✓			✓			✓				✓			
HYSSOPUS OFFICINALIS	✓	✓	✓	✓	✓	✓			✓				✓	✓		✓	✓		✓	✓	✓		✓	✓			
INULA HELENIUM	✓	✓	✓	✓	✓	✓	✓				✓	✓	✓	✓			✓	✓		✓	✓			✓	✓		
IRIS VERSICOLOR	✓	✓	✓	✓	✓	✓			✓				✓					✓	✓					✓			
LAVANDULA ANGUSTIFOLIA		✓	✓	✓	✓				✓				✓				✓			✓			✓	✓			
LAVANDULA LANATA				✓	✓	✓				✓			✓				✓			✓			✓	✓			
LAVANDULA STOECHAS					✓	✓	✓		✓				✓				✓			✓			✓	✓			
LEVISTICUM OFFICINALE	✓	✓	✓	✓	✓	✓					✓	✓	✓				✓	✓	✓	✓			✓				✓
MARRUBIUM VULGARE		✓	✓	✓	✓	✓			✓				✓			✓	✓		✓	✓			✓				
MELISSA OFFICINALIS		✓	✓	✓	✓	✓	✓		✓				✓	✓			✓	✓		✓			✓				
MENTHA X PIPERITA		✓	✓	✓	✓	✓	✓		✓				✓	✓			✓	✓		✓			✓				
MENTHA REQUIENII				✓	✓	✓			✓					✓			✓			✓			✓				
MENTHA SPICATA	✓	✓	✓	✓	✓	✓	✓		✓				✓	✓			✓	✓		✓			✓				
MONARDA DIDYMA		✓	✓	✓	✓	✓	✓			✓			✓	✓			✓			✓	✓		✓	✓			
MONARDA FISTULOSA	✓	✓	✓	✓	✓	✓	✓			✓			✓	✓		✓				✓	✓		✓	✓			
MYRRHIS ODORATA	✓	✓	✓	✓	✓	✓			✓				✓				✓	✓	✓						✓	✓	
NEPETA CATARIA	✓	✓	✓	✓	✓	✓			✓				✓	✓			✓		✓	✓	✓		✓				
ORIGANUM ONITES					✓	✓	✓		✓				✓			✓	✓			✓	✓		✓	✓			
ORIGANUM VULGARE			✓	✓	✓	✓	✓		✓				✓				✓			✓			✓	✓			
PANAX PSEUDOGINSENG		✓	✓	✓	✓	✓			✓					✓	✓		✓	✓	✓						✓		

597

Table category: **PERENNIALS, FERNS, AND BULBS**

Plant	Zones								Height				Light			Soil			Bloom Season				Parts Used				
	Zone 3	Zone 4	Zone 5	Zone 6	Zone 7	Zone 8	Zone 9	Zone 10	Under 1 Foot	1 to 3 Feet	3 to 5 Feet	Over 5 Feet	Full Sun	Light Shade	Shade	Dry	Well-Drained	Moist	Spring	Summer	Fall	Winter	Leaves	Flowers	Root/Bulb	Seeds/Fruit	Stems/Bark
POGOSTEMON CABLIN							✓			✓			✓	✓				✓			✓		✓				
POLYGONUM ODORATUM					✓	✓				✓				✓				✓		✓			✓				
POTERIUM SANGUISORBA	✓	✓	✓	✓	✓	✓	✓			✓			✓				✓			✓			✓				
PRIMULA VERIS	✓	✓	✓	✓	✓	✓			✓				✓				✓	✓	✓				✓	✓			
PRIMULA VULGARIS	✓	✓	✓	✓	✓	✓			✓				✓				✓	✓	✓				✓	✓			
PRUNELLA VULGARIS		✓	✓	✓	✓	✓	✓			✓			✓	✓			✓			✓	✓		✓				
PULMONARIA SACCHARATA	✓	✓	✓	✓	✓	✓				✓				✓	✓		✓	✓	✓				✓				
PYCNANTHEMUM VIRGINIANUM		✓	✓	✓	✓	✓				✓			✓	✓			✓			✓			✓	✓			
ROSMARINUS OFFICINALIS					✓	✓	✓	✓				✓	✓				✓					✓	✓				
RUBIA TINCTORUM			✓	✓	✓	✓	✓			✓			✓				✓			✓	✓				✓		
RUMEX ACETOSA		✓	✓	✓	✓	✓				✓			✓	✓			✓			✓			✓				
RUMEX SCUTATUS		✓	✓	✓	✓	✓				✓			✓	✓			✓			✓			✓				
RUTA GRAVEOLENS		✓	✓	✓	✓	✓	✓			✓			✓				✓			✓			✓			✓	
SALVIA CLEVELANDII							✓	✓		✓			✓			✓	✓		✓	✓			✓	✓			
SALVIA DORISIANA								✓			✓		✓			✓	✓				✓	✓	✓	✓			
SALVIA LAVANDULIFOLIA				✓	✓	✓				✓			✓			✓	✓			✓			✓	✓			
SALVIA OFFICINALIS		✓	✓	✓	✓	✓	✓				✓		✓			✓	✓			✓			✓	✓			
SANGUINARIA CANADENSIS	✓	✓	✓	✓	✓	✓	✓		✓					✓	✓	✓	✓	✓					✓				
SANTOLINA CHAMAECYPARISSUS			✓	✓	✓					✓			✓				✓			✓			✓	✓			
SAPONARIA OFFICINALIS	✓	✓	✓	✓	✓	✓				✓			✓	✓			✓			✓			✓		✓		
SATUREJA MONTANA 'NANA'			✓	✓	✓				✓				✓				✓			✓	✓		✓				
SATUREJA THYMBRA					✓	✓				✓			✓				✓			✓	✓		✓				
SESAMUM INDICUM								✓	✓				✓				✓			✓						✓	
SOLIDAGO ODORA	✓	✓	✓	✓	✓	✓	✓				✓		✓			✓				✓	✓		✓	✓			
STACHYS OFFICINALIS		✓	✓	✓	✓	✓	✓			✓			✓	✓			✓	✓		✓			✓	✓			
SYMPHYTUM OFFICINALE	✓	✓	✓	✓	✓	✓	✓			✓			✓	✓			✓	✓	✓	✓			✓				
TANACETUM BALSAMITA		✓	✓	✓	✓	✓					✓		✓			✓	✓			✓			✓				
TANACETUM CINERARIIFOLIUM		✓	✓	✓	✓	✓	✓			✓			✓			✓	✓			✓	✓		✓	✓			
TANACETUM PARTHENIUM		✓	✓	✓	✓	✓	✓			✓			✓	✓			✓			✓	✓		✓	✓			
THYMUS CAPITATUS						✓			✓				✓			✓	✓			✓			✓	✓			
THYMUS X CITRIODORUS			✓	✓	✓	✓			✓				✓			✓	✓			✓			✓	✓			
THYMUS PRAECOX SSP. ARCTICUS		✓	✓	✓	✓	✓	✓		✓				✓			✓	✓			✓			✓	✓			

Category	Plant	Zone 3	Zone 4	Zone 5	Zone 6	Zone 7	Zone 8	Zone 9	Zone 10	Under 1 Foot	1 to 3 Feet	3 to 5 Feet	Over 5 Feet	Full Sun	Light Shade	Shade	Dry	Well-Drained	Moist	Spring	Summer	Fall	Winter	Leaves	Flowers	Root/Bulb	Seeds/Fruit	Stems/Bark
PERENNIALS, FERNS, AND BULBS	THYMUS SERPYLLUM		✓	✓	✓	✓	✓			✓				✓			✓	✓			✓			✓	✓			
	THYMUS VULGARIS		✓	✓	✓	✓	✓			✓				✓			✓	✓			✓			✓	✓			
	TULBAGHIA VIOLACEA							✓	✓		✓			✓	✓			✓	✓		✓			✓	✓			
	VALERIANA OFFICINALIS		✓	✓	✓	✓	✓	✓				✓		✓	✓			✓	✓		✓				✓	✓		
	VETIVERIA ZIZANIOIDES							✓	✓				✓	✓	✓			✓								✓		
	VIOLA ODORATA	✓	✓	✓	✓	✓	✓	✓	✓	✓				✓	✓			✓	✓	✓		✓	✓	✓	✓			
	VIOLA TRICOLOR	✓	✓	✓	✓	✓	✓	✓	✓	✓				✓	✓			✓	✓	✓	✓	✓		✓	✓			
	ZINGIBER OFFICINALE							✓	✓		✓			✓		✓		✓	✓		✓					✓		
SHRUBS AND TREES	ALOYSIA TRIPHYLLA							✓	✓				✓	✓	✓			✓			✓			✓	✓			
	ARTEMISIA ABROTANUM			✓	✓	✓	✓					✓		✓			✓	✓			✓			✓				
	CEDRONELLA CANARIENSIS								✓			✓		✓				✓			✓	✓		✓	✓			
	CINNAMOMUM CAMPHORA						✓	✓	✓				✓	✓	✓			✓	✓	✓	✓			✓				
	CINNAMOMUM ZEYLANICUM							✓	✓				✓	✓	✓			✓	✓		✓							✓
	CITRUS AURANTIUM							✓	✓				✓	✓	✓			✓	✓	✓				✓			✓	
	CITRUS LIMON							✓	✓				✓	✓	✓			✓	✓	✓				✓			✓	
	COMPTONIA PEREGRINA	✓	✓	✓	✓	✓					✓			✓	✓		✓	✓		✓				✓				
	EUCALYPTUS CITRIODORA							✓	✓				✓	✓	✓			✓				✓	✓	✓	✓			✓
	GAULTHERIA PROCUMBENS	✓	✓	✓	✓	✓	✓	✓	✓	✓					✓	✓	✓	✓	✓		✓			✓			✓	
	LAURUS NOBILIS 'AUREA'						✓	✓	✓				✓	✓	✓			✓		✓				✓				
	LINDERA BENZOIN		✓	✓	✓	✓	✓	✓					✓		✓	✓		✓	✓	✓				✓			✓	✓
	LIPPIA GRAVEOLENS							✓	✓				✓	✓	✓			✓	✓		✓			✓				
	MYRICA CERIFERA					✓	✓	✓					✓	✓			✓	✓	✓								✓	
	MYRICA GALE	✓	✓	✓	✓	✓	✓	✓			✓							✓	✓								✓	
	MYRTUS COMMUNIS 'FLORE PLENO'							✓	✓				✓	✓	✓	✓			✓		✓	✓		✓	✓		✓	
	PUNICA GRANATUM VAR. NANA				✓	✓	✓	✓		✓				✓				✓	✓		✓				✓		✓	
	ROSA CANINA	✓	✓	✓	✓	✓	✓	✓					✓	✓	✓			✓	✓		✓				✓		✓	
	ROSA DAMASCENA		✓	✓	✓	✓	✓						✓	✓	✓			✓			✓	✓			✓		✓	
	ROSA GALLICA 'OFFICINALIS'		✓	✓	✓	✓	✓				✓			✓				✓			✓	✓			✓		✓	
	ROSA GALLICA 'VERSICOLOR'		✓	✓	✓	✓	✓				✓			✓				✓			✓	✓			✓		✓	
	ROSA RUGOSA	✓	✓	✓	✓	✓	✓	✓					✓	✓	✓			✓			✓	✓			✓		✓	
	TEUCRIUM CHAMAEDRYS			✓	✓	✓	✓				✓			✓	✓			✓			✓	✓		✓				
	VITEX AGNUS-CASTUS					✓	✓	✓	✓				✓	✓	✓		✓	✓			✓	✓					✓	

Plant Selection Guide—Vegetables

This chart provides information on selected vegetables, plus a few fruits and herbs. "Days to maturity" applies to crops replanted yearly, either indoors or out, from seed, sets, roots, or tubers.

	HARDINESS				LIGHT		PLANTING DEPTH			PLANT SPACING			ROW SPACING			DAYS TO MATURITY				WAYS TO USE							
	cool-season annual	warm-season annual	hot-season annual	winter-hardy	sun	PARTIAL SHADE	<½ INCH	½ TO 2 INCHES	>2 INCHES	<1 FOOT	1 TO 2 FEET	>2 FEET	1 TO 2 FEET	2 TO 4 FEET	>4 FEET	70 DAYS	70 TO 100 DAYS	100 TO 130 DAYS	>130 DAYS	FRESH	FROZEN	CANNED	PICKLED	JAM/PRESERVES	DRIED	CONTAINERS	LANDSCAPING
ARTICHOKE 'GREEN GLOBE'		✔		✔	✔	✔	✔					✔		✔				✔		✔	✔	✔				✔	✔
ARUGULA	✔				✔	✔	✔			✔			✔			✔				✔							
ASPARAGUS 'JERSEY KNIGHT'			✔	✔				✔		✔			✔					✔		✔	✔						✔
BASIL 'SPICY GLOBE'		✔			✔		✔			✔			✔			✔				✔	✔				✔	✔	✔
BEAN, DRY 'BLACK TURTLE'		✔			✔			✔		✔				✔			✔			✔					✔		
BEAN, DRY 'FRENCH HORTICULTURAL'		✔			✔			✔		✔				✔			✔			✔	✔	✔					
BEAN, FAVA 'AQUADULCE'	✔				✔			✔		✔				✔			✔			✔					✔		
BEAN, FILET 'TAVERA'		✔			✔			✔		✔			✔			✔				✔							
BEAN, GREEN 'PROVIDER'		✔			✔			✔		✔			✔			✔											
BEAN, GREEN 'TENDERCROP'		✔			✔			✔		✔			✔			✔				✔	✔	✔					
BEAN, LIMA 'FORDHOOK 242'		✔			✔			✔		✔				✔			✔			✔	✔	✔			✔		
BEAN, POLE 'EMERITE'		✔			✔			✔	✔		✔		✔				✔			✔	✔						
BEAN, POLE 'TRIONFO VIOLETTO'		✔			✔			✔		✔				✔			✔			✔	✔						
BEAN, PURPLE 'ROYAL BURGUNDY'		✔			✔			✔		✔			✔			✔				✔							
BEAN, RUNNER 'SCARLET RUNNER'	✔				✔			✔	✔		✔			✔			✔			✔					✔		✔
BEAN, YARDLONG 'GREEN POD'		✔			✔			✔		✔				✔			✔			✔	✔						
BEAN, YELLOW 'DORABEL'		✔			✔			✔	✔				✔			✔				✔	✔						
BEET 'DETROIT DARK RED'	✔				✔			✔		✔			✔			✔				✔	✔	✔	✔				
BEET 'GOLDEN'	✔				✔			✔		✔			✔			✔				✔	✔	✔	✔				
BLACKBERRY 'RANGER'			✔	✔			✔			✔			✔					✔		✔	✔			✔			
BLACKBERRY 'THORNFREE'			✔	✔				✔			✔			✔				✔		✔	✔			✔			
BLACKBERRY 'YOUNG'			✔	✔				✔			✔		✔						✔	✔	✔			✔			
BLACK-EYED PEA 'MISSISSIPPI SILVER'		✔			✔			✔		✔			✔				✔			✔	✔	✔			✔		
BROCCOLI 'EMPEROR'		✔			✔	✔		✔			✔	✔						✔		✔	✔						
BROCCOLI RABE	✔				✔			✔			✔					✔				✔	✔						
BRUSSELS SPROUT 'PRINCE MARVEL'	✔				✔			✔			✔		✔					✔		✔	✔						
CABBAGE 'EARLY JERSEY WAKEFIELD'	✔				✔	✔		✔			✔		✔				✔			✔			✔				
CABBAGE 'WISCONSIN ALL SEASONS'	✔				✔	✔		✔			✔		✔					✔		✔			✔				

	HARDINESS				LIGHT		PLANTING DEPTH			PLANT SPACING			ROW SPACING			DAYS TO MATURITY				WAYS TO USE							
	cool-season ANNUAL	warm-season ANNUAL	hot-season ANNUAL	winter-hardy	SUN	PARTIAL SHADE	< ½ INCH	½ TO 2 INCHES	> 2 INCHES	< 1 FOOT	1 TO 2 FEET	> 2 feet	1 TO 2 FEET	2 TO 4 FEET	> 4 FEET	< 70 DAYS	70 TO 100 DAYS	100 TO 130 DAYS	> 130 DAYS	FRESH	FROZEN	CANNED	PICKLED	JAM/PRESERVES	DRIED	CONTAINERS	LANDSCAPING
CABBAGE, CHINESE 'TWO SEASONS HYBRID'		✓			✓			✓		✓			✓														
CARDOON			✓	✓	✓			✓			✓							✓	✓								
CARROT 'LITTLE FINGER'	✓				✓		✓			✓			✓				✓			✓	✓	✓	✓			✓	✓
CARROT 'NAPOLI'	✓				✓		✓			✓			✓			✓				✓	✓	✓				✓	✓
CARROT 'TENDERSWEET'	✓				✓		✓			✓			✓				✓			✓	✓	✓				✓	✓
CAULIFLOWER 'EARLY WHITE HYBRID'	✓				✓			✓			✓		✓			✓				✓	✓		✓				
CELERIAC 'BRILLIANT'		✓			✓	✓		✓			✓		✓					✓		✓							
CELERY 'UTAH 52-70R'		✓			✓			✓		✓			✓					✓		✓					✓		
CELTUCE	✓				✓	✓		✓			✓		✓				✓			✓							
CHARD 'RHUBARB CHARD'		✓			✓	✓		✓			✓		✓			✓				✓	✓					✓	✓
CHAYOTE			✓		✓	✓					✓							✓		✓							
CHICORY 'CERIOLO'	✓				✓	✓		✓			✓		✓				✓			✓							
COLLARD 'GEORGIA'	✓				✓			✓			✓		✓			✓				✓	✓						
CORN 'EARLIVEE'		✓			✓			✓			✓		✓	✓		✓				✓	✓	✓		✓			
CORN 'SENECA STARSHINE'		✓			✓			✓			✓		✓				✓			✓	✓	✓		✓			
CORN 'STARSTRUCK'		✓			✓			✓			✓		✓				✓			✓	✓	✓		✓			
CORN SALAD 'COQUILLE'			✓	✓	✓			✓		✓			✓				✓			✓							
CRESS 'WINTER CRESS'	✓				✓	✓	✓			✓			✓		✓					✓							
CUCUMBER 'BURPLESS'		✓			✓			✓			✓			✓	✓					✓			✓				
CUCUMBER 'SALADIN'		✓			✓			✓			✓				✓					✓			✓				✓
CUCUMBER 'SPACEMASTER'		✓			✓			✓			✓			✓	✓					✓			✓			✓	
EGGPLANT 'ICHIBAN'		✓			✓		✓				✓		✓			✓				✓							
ENDIVE 'TRES FIN'	✓				✓				✓		✓		✓				✓			✓							
FENNEL 'ZEFA FINO'	✓				✓		✓				✓		✓				✓			✓							
GARLIC 'ELEPHANT GARLIC'			✓	✓	✓		✓	✓			✓							✓	✓	✓	✓			✓			
GARLIC 'SPANISH ROJA GARLIC'			✓	✓	✓		✓	✓			✓							✓	✓	✓	✓			✓			
HORSERADISH 'MALINER KREN'			✓	✓	✓			✓		✓			✓					✓	✓	✓	✓						
JERUSALEM ARTICHOKE 'FRENCH MAMMOTH WHITE'			✓	✓	✓			✓		✓			✓					✓	✓	✓	✓						✓
JICAMA		✓			✓				✓		✓		✓					✓		✓	✓						
KALE 'WINTERBOR'	✓				✓	✓		✓		✓			✓			✓				✓	✓					✓	✓
KOHLRABI 'GRAND DUKE'	✓				✓	✓		✓		✓	✓		✓			✓				✓	✓						
LEEK 'BROAD LONDON'	✓				✓	✓	✓				✓		✓					✓	✓	✓	✓						

	HARDINESS				LIGHT		PLANTING DEPTH			PLANT SPACING				ROW SPACING			DAYS TO MATURITY				WAYS TO USE							
	cool-season ANNUAL	warm-season ANNUAL	hot-season ANNUAL	winter-hardy	SUN	PARTIAL SHADE	< ½ INCH	½ TO 2 INCHES	> 2 INCHES	< 1 FOOT	1 FOOT	1 TO 2 FEET	> 2 FEET	1 TO 2 FEET	2 TO 4 FEET	> 4 FEET	< 70 DAYS	70 TO 100 DAYS	100 TO 130 DAYS	> 130 DAYS	FRESH	FROZEN	CANNED	PICKLED	JAM/PRESERVES	DRIED	CONTAINERS	LANDSCAPING
LETTUCE 'LITTLE GEM'		✓			✓	✓	✓				✓			✓			✓				✓							
LETTUCE 'RUBY'		✓			✓	✓	✓				✓			✓			✓				✓						✓	
LETTUCE 'SUMMERTIME'		✓			✓	✓	✓				✓			✓			✓				✓							
LETTUCE 'TOM THUMB'		✓			✓	✓	✓				✓			✓			✓				✓							
MELON 'CASABLANCA'		✓			✓			✓				✓			✓			✓			✓	✓						
MELON 'PANCHA'		✓			✓			✓					✓			✓		✓			✓	✓						
MELON 'VENUS'		✓			✓			✓					✓			✓		✓			✓	✓						
MUSTARD GREENS 'SOUTHERN GIANT CURLED'	✓				✓		✓			✓		✓		✓			✓				✓							
NASTURTIUM 'TIP TOP MIX'	✓				✓	✓		✓		✓		✓		✓			✓				✓			✓			✓	✓
OKRA 'CLEMSON SPINELESS'			✓		✓				✓		✓	✓		✓	✓		✓				✓							
ONION 'ISHIKURA'	✓				✓			✓		✓				✓			✓				✓	✓						
ONION 'NORTHERN OAK'	✓			✓	✓			✓		✓									✓		✓	✓				✓		
ONION 'TEXAS GRANO 1015Y'	✓			✓	✓			✓		✓									✓		✓	✓				✓		
ORACH 'RED ORACH'	✓				✓			✓		✓		✓		✓			✓				✓							
PAK-CHOI 'MEI-QUING CHOI'	✓				✓			✓			✓		✓				✓				✓							
PARSLEY 'MOSS CURLED FOREST GREEN'	✓			✓	✓	✓		✓			✓			✓			✓				✓					✓	✓	
PARSNIP 'HOLLOW CROWN'	✓				✓			✓		✓		✓							✓		✓							
PEA, GARDEN 'LITTLE MARVEL'	✓				✓			✓				✓		✓			✓				✓	✓	✓					
PEA, SNOW 'OREGON SUGAR POD II'	✓				✓			✓				✓			✓		✓				✓	✓						
PEA, SUGAR SNAP 'SUGAR DADDY'	✓				✓			✓				✓		✓			✓				✓	✓						
PEANUT 'JUMBO VIRGINIA'			✓		✓			✓			✓		✓						✓		✓	✓						
PEPPER, CHILI 'LARGE HOT CHERRY'		✓			✓			✓			✓		✓						✓		✓			✓				
PEPPER, SWEET 'CALIFORNIA WONDER'		✓			✓			✓			✓		✓						✓		✓	✓						
PEPPER, SWEET 'GYPSY'		✓			✓			✓			✓		✓					✓			✓							✓
POTATO 'NORGOLD RUSSET'		✓			✓				✓		✓		✓	✓				✓			✓	✓					✓	
POTATO 'RED LA SODA'		✓			✓				✓		✓		✓		✓			✓			✓	✓				✓		
POTATO 'RUSSET BURBANK'		✓			✓				✓		✓		✓						✓		✓	✓					✓	
PUMPKIN 'CONNECTICUT FIELD'		✓			✓				✓		✓		✓			✓		✓			✓	✓						
PUMPKIN 'JACK BE LITTLE'		✓			✓				✓		✓		✓			✓		✓			✓	✓						
RADICCHIO 'CASTELFRANCO'		✓			✓			✓			✓	✓						✓			✓							
RADISH 'FRENCH BREAKFAST'	✓				✓		✓	✓		✓				✓			✓				✓							
RASPBERRY 'BLACK HAWK'				✓	✓	✓		✓			✓										✓	✓			✓			

	HARDINESS				LIGHT		PLANTING DEPTH			PLANT SPACING			ROW SPACING			DAYS TO MATURITY				WAYS TO USE							
	cool-season ANNUAL	warm-season ANNUAL	hot-season ANNUAL	winter-hardy	SUN	PARTIAL SHADE	< ½ INCH	½ TO 2 INCHES	> 2 INCHES	< 1 FOOT	1 TO 2 FEET	> 2 FEET	1 TO 2 FEET	2 TO 4 FEET	> 4 FEET	< 70 DAYS	70 TO 100 DAYS	100 TO 130 DAYS	> 130 DAYS	FRESH	FROZEN	CANNED	PICKLED	JAM/PRESERVES	DRIED	CONTAINERS	LANDSCAPING
RASPBERRY 'NEWBURGH'			✓	✓	✓			✓			✓			✓						✓	✓			✓			
RASPBERRY 'WINEBERRY'			✓	✓	✓	✓		✓			✓				✓					✓	✓			✓			✓
RHUBARB 'CHERRY RED'			✓	✓	✓			✓			✓	✓		✓						✓	✓			✓			
RUTABAGA 'IMPROVED PURPLE TOP YELLOW'	✓				✓		✓			✓			✓				✓			✓	✓						
SALSIFY 'MAMMOTH SANDWICH ISLAND'	✓				✓		✓			✓								✓		✓	✓						
SHALLOT 'SUCCESS'	✓			✓	✓			✓		✓							✓			✓							
SORREL				✓	✓	✓	✓			✓			✓				✓			✓	✓					✓	
SOYBEAN 'PRIZE'		✓			✓		✓			✓			✓				✓			✓	✓				✓		
SPINACH 'MELODY'	✓				✓	✓	✓		✓	✓			✓			✓				✓	✓						
SPINACH, MALABAR 'ALBA'		✓			✓			✓			✓		✓				✓			✓						✓	✓
SPINACH, NEW ZEALAND		✓	✓		✓			✓		✓			✓				✓			✓	✓					✓	
SQUASH, SUMMER 'PARK'S CREAMY HYBRID'		✓			✓			✓			✓			✓		✓				✓	✓						
SQUASH, SUMMER 'RAVEN'		✓			✓			✓			✓			✓		✓				✓	✓						
SQUASH, SUMMER 'SCALOPPINI'		✓			✓			✓			✓			✓		✓				✓	✓						
SQUASH, SUMMER 'SUNDANCE'		✓			✓			✓			✓			✓		✓				✓	✓						
SQUASH, WINTER 'BUTTERBUSH'		✓			✓			✓				✓		✓			✓			✓	✓						
SQUASH, WINTER 'CREAM OF THE CROP'		✓			✓			✓			✓	✓		✓				✓		✓	✓						
SQUASH, WINTER 'SWEET DUMPLING'		✓			✓			✓				✓		✓				✓		✓	✓						
SQUASH, WINTER 'TURK'S TURBAN'		✓			✓			✓			✓	✓					✓			✓	✓						
STRAWBERRY 'ALEXANDRIA'		✓	✓	✓			✓	✓		✓							✓			✓	✓			✓		✓	✓
STRAWBERRY 'PICNIC'		✓	✓	✓			✓	✓		✓							✓			✓	✓			✓		✓	
SUNFLOWER 'MAMMOTH'		✓			✓		✓				✓			✓			✓			✓							✓
SWEET POTATO 'CENTENNIAL'			✓		✓			✓		✓		✓		✓			✓			✓	✓						
TAMPALA		✓			✓	✓	✓		✓		✓		✓				✓			✓							
TOMATILLO 'TOMA VERDE'		✓			✓			✓			✓	✓		✓			✓			✓							
TOMATO 'BIG GIRL'		✓			✓	✓					✓	✓		✓			✓			✓		✓					
TOMATO 'EARLY CASCADE'		✓			✓	✓					✓	✓		✓		✓				✓		✓					
TOMATO 'HEINZ 1439'		✓			✓						✓	✓		✓			✓			✓				✓			
TOMATO 'SUGAR LUMP'		✓			✓						✓	✓		✓		✓				✓							
TOMATO 'VIVA ITALIA'		✓			✓	✓					✓	✓		✓			✓			✓		✓			✓		
TOMATO 'YELLOW CANARY'		✓			✓	✓					✓	✓		✓			✓			✓					✓		
TURNIP 'TOKYO CROSS'	✓				✓			✓		✓			✓			✓				✓	✓	✓					

Color Guide to Herbaceous Plants

Organized primarily by flower color, this chart provides information needed to select species and varieties that will thrive in the particular conditions of your garden. For more information on many of these plants, refer to the encyclopedia that begins on page 608.

	Zones	Dry	Well-drained	Moist	Full sun	Partial shade	Shade	Spring	Summer	Fall	Winter	Under 1 ft.	1-3 ft.	3-6 ft.	6-10 ft.	Over 10 ft.	Flowers	Foliage	Fruit/seeds	Fragrance
WHITE																				
Achillea ptarmica 'The Pearl'	4-9		✓		✓				✓				✓				✓	✓		
Ageratum houstonianum 'Summer Snow' [2]			✓	✓	✓				✓	✓		✓					✓	✓		
Anemone x hybrida 'Honorine Jobert'	4-9		✓	✓	✓	✓			✓	✓			✓	✓			✓	✓		
Aruncus dioicus	4-9			✓		✓			✓					✓			✓	✓		
Chrysanthemum parthenium	4-9		✓		✓				✓	✓			✓				✓	✓		✓
Crambe cordifolia	5-9		✓		✓			✓	✓					✓			✓	✓		✓
Datura metel 'Alba' [1]			✓	✓	✓	✓			✓					✓			✓	✓		✓
Dicentra spectabilis f. alba	4-8		✓			✓		✓					✓				✓	✓		
Galanthus nivalis	3-8		✓	✓		✓		✓				✓					✓			
Gaura lindheimeri	6-9		✓		✓				✓					✓			✓			
Helianthus annuus 'Italian White' [1]			✓	✓	✓				✓	✓				✓			✓			
Ipomoea alba [4]	9-10		✓		✓				✓	✓						✓	✓	✓		✓
Leucojum vernum	4-8			✓		✓		✓				✓					✓			
Lysimachia clethroides	4-8			✓	✓	✓			✓				✓				✓	✓		
Mandevilla laxa	8-10		✓	✓	✓				✓							✓	✓	✓		✓
Phlox stolonifera 'Bruce's White'	3-8			✓	✓	✓	✓	✓					✓				✓	✓		
Polygonatum commutatum	3-9			✓		✓	✓	✓							✓		✓	✓	✓	
Tiarella cordifolia	3-8		✓	✓		✓	✓	✓	✓				✓				✓	✓		
Yucca glauca	4-8	✓	✓		✓				✓				✓	✓			✓			
PINK																				
Acanthus spinosus	7-10	✓	✓		✓	✓			✓				✓	✓			✓			
Antirrhinum majus 'Pink Rocket' [4]	8-11		✓		✓	✓			✓				✓	✓			✓			
Bergenia 'Abendglut'	4-8		✓	✓		✓		✓					✓				✓	✓		
Chrysanthemum coccineum 'Helen'	3-7		✓		✓			✓	✓				✓				✓	✓		
Fuchsia x hybrida 'Pink Chiffon' [4]	9-11		✓	✓		✓			✓				✓				✓			
Geranium cinereum	4-9	✓	✓	✓	✓	✓			✓			✓					✓	✓		
Gypsophila paniculata 'Pink Fairy'	4-9		✓	✓	✓				✓				✓				✓			
Origanum vulgare	3-10	✓	✓		✓				✓	✓			✓				✓	✓		✓
Sedum sieboldii	5-9	✓	✓		✓					✓		✓					✓	✓		

[1] Tender annual   [2] Half-hardy annual   [3] Hardy annual   [4] Tender perennial grown as an annual in colder zones

Category	Plant	ZONES	SOIL			LIGHT			BLOOM SEASON				PLANT HEIGHT					NOTED FOR			
			Dry	Well-drained	Moist	Full sun	Partial shade	Shade	Spring	Summer	Fall	Winter	Under 1 ft	1-3 ft	3-6 ft	6-10 ft	Over 10 ft	Flowers	Foliage	Fruit/seeds	Fragrance
MIXED/MULTICOLORED	*Alcea rosea* 'Chater's Double'	3-9		✓		✓				✓						✓		✓			
	Anemone coronaria 'de Caen'	7-9		✓	✓	✓	✓		✓				✓					✓	✓		
	Antirrhinum majus 'Tahiti' [4]	8-11		✓		✓	✓			✓	✓		✓					✓	✓		
	Aristolochia macrophylla	4-8		✓	✓	✓				✓							✓	✓	✓		
	Cosmos bipinnatus 'Candy Stripe' [1]		✓	✓		✓	✓			✓	✓			✓				✓	✓		
	Impatiens wallerana 'Shady Lady' [4]	10		✓	✓		✓	✓		✓	✓			✓				✓	✓		
	Lathyrus odoratus 'Royal Family' [3]			✓	✓	✓			✓							✓		✓	✓		✓
	Nicotiana alata 'Domino Hybrids' [1]			✓	✓	✓				✓	✓			✓				✓	✓		
	Papaver rhoeas 'Fairy Wings' [3]		✓	✓		✓	✓		✓	✓				✓				✓			
	Tagetes patula [1]			✓		✓				✓	✓		✓					✓	✓		
YELLOW	*Achillea* 'Moonshine'	3-8	✓	✓		✓				✓	✓			✓				✓	✓		✓
	Alchemilla mollis	3-7		✓	✓	✓	✓		✓	✓				✓				✓	✓		
	Allium moly 'Jeannine'	3-9		✓	✓	✓	✓			✓			✓					✓	✓		
	Arum italicum	5-9		✓	✓		✓	✓	✓					✓				✓	✓	✓	
	Caltha palustris	3-8		✓	✓	✓	✓		✓					✓				✓			
	Digitalis grandiflora	3-9		✓	✓	✓	✓		✓	✓				✓				✓	✓		
	Doronicum 'Harper Crewe'	4-8		✓	✓	✓	✓		✓						✓			✓	✓		
	Helianthus angustifolius	6-9		✓	✓	✓				✓	✓				✓	✓		✓			
	Lysimachia punctata	4-8		✓	✓	✓	✓			✓				✓				✓	✓		
	Rudbeckia fulgida var. *sullivantii* 'Goldsturm'	4-9		✓		✓	✓			✓	✓			✓				✓			
	Rudbeckia nitida 'Herbstsonne'	4-9		✓		✓	✓			✓						✓		✓			
	Tanacetum vulgare	3-9		✓		✓	✓			✓				✓	✓			✓	✓		✓
	Tropaeolum peregrinum [1]		✓	✓		✓				✓						✓		✓	✓		
ORANGE	*Asclepias tuberosa*	4-9		✓		✓				✓				✓				✓			
	Calendula officinalis 'Geisha Girl' [3]			✓		✓			✓	✓	✓			✓				✓			
	Cosmos sulphureus 'Diablo' [1]		✓	✓		✓	✓			✓	✓			✓				✓			
	Euphorbia griffithii 'Fireglow'	4-9		✓		✓				✓				✓				✓			
	Helenium 'Moerheim Beauty'	4-8		✓		✓					✓			✓				✓			
	Hemerocallis fulva	3-9		✓	✓	✓	✓			✓				✓				✓	✓		
	Sphaeralcea ambigua	9-10		✓		✓				✓				✓				✓	✓		
	Thunbergia alata 'Aurantiaca' [4]	10-11		✓	✓	✓	✓			✓					✓			✓			
	Tithonia rotundifolia 'Torch' [1]			✓		✓				✓	✓			✓				✓			

[1] Tender annual   [2] Half-hardy annual   [3] Hardy annual   [4] Tender perennial grown as an annual in colder zones

	ZONES	SOIL			LIGHT			BLOOM SEASON				PLANT HEIGHT					NOTED FOR			
		Dry	Well-drained	Moist	Full sun	Partial shade	Shade	Spring	Summer	Fall	Winter	Under 1 ft.	1-3 ft.	3-6 ft.	6-10 ft.	Over 10 ft.	Flowers	Foliage	Fruit/seeds	Fragrance
RED																				
Achillea millefolium 'Red Beauty'	3-8	✔	✔		✔				✔	✔			✔				✔	✔		✔
Astilbe 'Fanal'	5-9			✔		✔			✔				✔				✔	✔		
Centranthus ruber	5-9		✔		✔			✔	✔	✔			✔				✔			
Dianthus deltoides 'Flashing Light'	4-7		✔	✔	✔	✔		✔				✔					✔	✔		
Hemerocallis 'Anzac'	3-9		✔	✔	✔	✔			✔				✔				✔	✔		
Knautia macedonica	5-9		✔		✔				✔				✔				✔			
Lobelia 'Queen Victoria'	3-8			✔	✔				✔	✔			✔				✔			
Lychnis chalcedonica	4-9		✔	✔	✔	✔		✔	✔				✔				✔			
Monarda didyma 'Cambridge Scarlet'	4-8		✔	✔	✔				✔				✔				✔			
Pelargonium x hortorum 'Ringo Scarlet' [4]	9-10		✔	✔	✔			✔	✔	✔		✔	✔				✔			
Penstemon 'Garnet'	4-9		✔		✔				✔	✔			✔				✔	✔		
Phaseolus coccineus [4]	9-10		✔	✔	✔			✔	✔	✔							✔			
Primula japonica 'Miller's Crimson'	6-8			✔		✔	✔	✔	✔				✔				✔			
Rheum palmatum 'Atrosanguineum'	5-9		✔	✔					✔						✔		✔	✔		
Salvia splendens [4]	10-11		✔		✔	✔			✔	✔		✔	✔				✔	✔		
Thymus praecox 'Coccineus'	4-9	✔	✔		✔			✔				✔					✔	✔		✔
PURPLE																				
Ageratum houstonianum 'North Sea' [2]			✔	✔	✔				✔	✔		✔					✔	✔		
Allium giganteum	5-8		✔	✔	✔				✔					✔			✔			
Campanula glomerata 'Superba'	3-8		✔	✔	✔	✔			✔				✔				✔			
Centaurea montana	3-8		✔		✔				✔				✔				✔	✔		
Cleome hasslerana 'Purple Queen' [1]			✔	✔	✔				✔	✔				✔			✔		✔	
Cynara cardunculus	9-10		✔		✔				✔						✔		✔	✔		
Lavandula dentata [4]	8-9		✔		✔				✔				✔				✔	✔		✔
Linaria triornithophora	6-9		✔		✔				✔				✔				✔	✔		
Liriope muscari	6-10	✔	✔	✔	✔	✔	✔		✔	✔			✔				✔	✔	✔	
Mentha spicata	4-9		✔	✔	✔				✔				✔				✔	✔		✔
Pelargonium peltatum 'Amethyst' [4]	9-10		✔	✔	✔			✔	✔	✔		✔					✔	✔		
Petunia x hybrida 'Heavenly Lavender' [1]			✔		✔				✔	✔		✔					✔			
Platycodon grandiflorus	4-9		✔		✔				✔				✔				✔	✔		
Salvia x superba 'East Friesland'	5-8		✔		✔	✔		✔	✔				✔				✔	✔		
Teucrium chamaedrys	5-10		✔		✔	✔			✔				✔				✔	✔		
Veronica longifolia 'Romiley Purple'	4-8		✔		✔				✔					✔			✔	✔		

[1] Tender annual [2] Half-hardy annual [3] Hardy annual [4] Tender perennial grown as an annual in colder zones

BLUE

Name	Zones	Dry	Well-drained	Moist	Full sun	Partial shade	Shade	Spring	Summer	Fall	Winter	Under 1 ft	1-3 ft	3-6 ft	6-10 ft	Over 10 ft	Flowers	Foliage	Fruit/seeds	Fragrance
Agapanthus africanus	8-10		✓	✓	✓				✓	✓			✓	✓			✓	✓		
Ajuga reptans 'Bronze Beauty'	3-9	✓	✓	✓	✓	✓		✓	✓			✓					✓	✓		
Allium azureum	4-10		✓		✓				✓				✓				✓			
Aquilegia flabellata	3-9		✓	✓	✓	✓		✓	✓			✓					✓	✓		
Borago officinalis [3]			✓		✓				✓	✓		✓					✓			
Campanula latifolia	4-8		✓	✓	✓	✓								✓			✓			
Cyananthus microphyllus	5-7		✓			✓						✓					✓	✓		
Echinops bannaticus	8-10		✓		✓				✓					✓			✓			
Gentiana sino-ornata	5-7			✓		✓				✓		✓					✓			
Geranium x 'Johnson's Blue'	5-8	✓	✓	✓	✓	✓		✓	✓				✓				✓			
Ixiolirion tataricum	7-10		✓		✓			✓	✓			✓					✓			
Lobelia erinus 'Crystal Palace' [3]			✓		✓				✓	✓		✓					✓	✓		
Meconopsis betonicifolia	8			✓		✓	✓	✓					✓				✓			
Mertensia virginica	3-8		✓	✓	✓	✓	✓	✓					✓				✓	✓		
Nepeta x faassenii	4-8		✓		✓			✓	✓				✓				✓	✓		✓
Perovskia atriplicifolia	5-9		✓		✓			✓	✓					✓			✓	✓		✓
Polygala calcarea	5-7		✓		✓			✓	✓			✓					✓			
Rosmarinus officinalis	7-10	✓	✓	✓	✓	✓		✓		✓	✓		✓	✓			✓	✓		✓
Scabiosa caucasica 'Fama'	4-9		✓		✓				✓				✓				✓			
Scilla siberica 'Atrocoerulea'	1-8		✓		✓			✓				✓					✓			
Sisyrinchium angustifolium	3-10			✓	✓	✓		✓					✓				✓			
Veronica longifolia	4-8		✓		✓	✓			✓	✓			✓	✓			✓	✓		
Vinca major [4]	7-9		✓	✓	✓	✓	✓	✓				✓					✓	✓		

GRASSES

Name	Zones	Dry	Well-drained	Moist	Full sun	Partial shade	Shade	Spring	Summer	Fall	Winter	Under 1 ft	1-3 ft	3-6 ft	6-10 ft	Over 10 ft	Flowers	Foliage	Fruit/seeds	Fragrance
Andropogon glomeratus	6-9			✓	✓					✓	✓			✓				✓	✓	
Bouteloua curtipendula	3-10	✓	✓		✓				✓	✓		✓						✓	✓	
Calamagrostis acutiflora 'Stricta'	6-9	✓		✓	✓				✓					✓				✓		
Imperata cylindrica rubra	5-9		✓	✓	✓				✓			✓						✓		
Miscanthus sinensis 'Morning Light'	5-9	✓	✓		✓				✓	✓	✓			✓				✓		
Muhlenbergia lindheimeri	6-10		✓		✓	✓				✓				✓				✓	✓	
Panicum virgatum 'Haense Herms'	5-9			✓	✓				✓	✓			✓					✓	✓	✓
Pennisetum alopecuroides	5-9		✓	✓	✓				✓	✓				✓				✓		
Schizachyrium scoparium	3-10	✓	✓		✓				✓	✓				✓				✓		

[1] Tender annual   [2] Half-hardy annual   [3] Hardy annual   [4] Tender perennial grown as an annual in colder zones

Encyclopedia of Plants

Picking the right plant depends on making a match between what a plant needs and what you and your garden can provide. No matter how appealing a plant may look displayed in a catalog or nursery, it will not grow well in your yard if you don't have the climate and gardening conditions it favors. Fortunately success and satisfaction are within reach for everyone who considers climate and conditions by using the seven principles of plant selection: Light, Type of Plant, Hardiness, Height, Soil and Moisture, Care, and Interest. Because your success starts with matching the light requirements of each plant to the conditions in your garden, the encyclopedia sections that follow are organized according to the plants' preferences for sun and shade. Each entry contains information about light requirements and the other six principles. And as you read, you will find yourself increasingly sure about what plants to grow to create a beautiful, flourishing garden wherever you live.

Plants for Places with Full Sun

Plants that flourish in full sun are by nature a tough lot. They spend each day beneath an unrelenting sun, and instead of being burned or desiccated these plants thrive. The hardy character of many sun-loving plants makes them generally an easy group to care for. Many have not only evolved ways to protect themselves from the sun's radiation, but have become drought tolerant as well. As self-reliant as these plants can be, most of them benefit from some little luxuries. These include being grown in soil that has been amended with compost, peat moss, or other type of organic matter; a periodic, thorough watering during dry periods; and having a layer of mulch spread around their bases to help conserve soil moisture through the long, hot days of summer.

AGERATUM
Ageratum

Light: full sun

Plant type: annual

Height: 6 inches to 2½ feet

Soil and Moisture: well-drained, moist

Interest: flowers, foliage

Care: easy

◀ Ageratum houstonianum 'Blue Horizon'

Ageratum has small, uniquely beautiful flowers composed of hundreds of threadlike petals that give the blossoms a fluffy, powder-puff appearance. The flowers come in a range of soft colors that accent the compact mounds of heart-shaped medium green leaves. Dwarf varieties are ideal for garden edgings. Taller forms combine well with other flowers in the middle or back of a border and add a perky touch to indoor arrangements.

Growing and care:
Sow seed indoors 6 to 8 weeks before the last spring frost. Space plants in well-worked soil 6 to 12 inches apart. Pinch early growth to promote more compact growth. Remove spent blooms to encourage continuous flower production all season long.

Selected species and varieties:
A. houstonianum bears small blue or bluish purple flowers in dense, fuzzy clusters from summer through fall; white- and pink-flowered varieties are available; 'Summer Snow' grows 6 to 8 inches tall with abundant pure white flowers from early spring to frost; 'Capri' is a heat-tolerant variety that grows to a uniform 1 foot tall, bearing bicolored flowers that are medium blue with white centers; 'Blue Horizon' grows to 2½ feet with deep blue flowers that are excellent for cutting.

AMARANTH
Amaranthus

Light: full sun

Plant type: annual

Height: 1½ to 6 feet

Soil and Moisture: well-drained, moist to dry

Interest: flowers, foliage

Care: easy

◀ Amaranthus caudatus

Amaranths are large, stately plants that add a bright, bold touch to borders and gardens. The strong plants bear long-lasting, tassel-shaped flowers in shades of red and purple that hang above the richly colored leaves. Tall types are effective as accents or massed as a colorful background. Shorter varieties are show-stoppers when used in beds or containers. Flowers of all varieties are excellent additions to both fresh and dried arrangements.

Growing and care:
Amaranth seed germinates best at room temperature and can be started indoors 4 to 6 weeks prior to the last frost. In warm areas sow seed directly in the garden once soil has warmed. Thin to allow 1 to 2 feet between plants. Water frequently during dry periods.

Selected species and varieties:
A. caudatus (love-lies-bleeding) grows 3 to 5 feet tall with green or red leaves and huge, drooping tassels of red flowers that may reach 2 feet in length; 'Viridis' grows 2 to 3½ feet with light green flower tassels. *A. cruentus* (purple amaranth, prince's-feather) produces huge 12-inch leaves along erect 6-foot stems, and drooping red or purple flower spikes. *A. tricolor* 'Joseph's-coat' grows from 1½ to 5 feet tall with upper leaves marked with red and gold and lower foliage green, yellow, and brownish red.

BABY'S-BREATH
Gypsophila

Light: full sun

Plant type: annual

Height: 8 inches to 2 feet

Soil and Moisture: well-drained, moist to dry

Interest: flowers

Care: easy

◀ Gypsophila elegans

Baby's-breath produces airy clouds of delicate, tiny white flowers in shades of pink and rose from mid-spring to early fall. It is beautiful when used as a filler in the border, where it softens the bright colors and coarse textures of other plants. Baby's-breath is an excellent cut flower and can be used in either fresh or dried arrangements.

Growing and care:
Sow seed directly in the garden in early spring when soil is cool and moist. Thin plants to 8 to 12 inches apart. For best results fertilize and water lightly. In regions with hot summers provide some afternoon shade. Supplement acid soils with limestone. Plants are short lived, even for annuals, so make successive sowings every 2 to 3 weeks for continuous bloom. Taller varieties may need staking.

Selected species and varieties:
G. elegans has a loose, mounded habit with thin, well-branched stems bearing pairs of narrow gray-green leaves and billowy clusters of white, pink, red, or purple flowers. Each flower is ¼ to ¾ inch across.

BELLS-OF-IRELAND
Moluccella

Light: full sun

Plant type: annual

Height: 2 to 3 feet

Soil and Moisture: well-drained, moist

Interest: flowers

Care: easy

◀ Moluccella laevis

This native to the eastern Mediterranean region provides a lovely vertical accent to beds, borders, and cottage gardens. The plants also provide a soft background for other, more boldly colored summer flowers. Bells-of-Ireland bloom from late summer to frost and make fine additions to both fresh and dried arrangements.

Growing and care:
Start seed indoors 8 to 10 weeks prior to the last frost or direct-sow in early spring. Do not cover seed, as it needs light to germinate. Space plants 9 to 12 inches apart. Once transplanted do not disturb the roots. Fertilize monthly and water regularly. Stake if plants appear floppy. Plants often self-seed.

Selected species and varieties:
M. laevis grows to 3 feet tall and 1½ feet wide with an erect habit and 1-inch rounded, slightly serrated leaves. The rather inconspicuous, fragrant pink or white flowers are borne on upright spikes surrounded by a large but subtle white-veined, pale green calyx that resembles a bell.

BLESSED THISTLE
Silybum

Light: full sun

Plant type: annual or biennial

Height: 3 to 4 feet

Soil and Moisture: well-drained, sandy, dry

Interest: flowers, foliage

Care: easy

◀ Silybum marianum

The rough, spiny leaves and flowers of blessed thistle add a primitive aspect to the garden few other plants can equal. In spring the 12- to 14-inch deeply lobed, green and white basal leaves are clustered into an attractive wide-spreading rosette. In late summer strong stems rise from the rosette and are adorned with delicate, reddish purple 2-inch thistlelike flowers, each guarded by a ring of spines. Blessed thistle provides coarse texture and contrast to borders and adds a distinctly wild element to naturalistic plantings.

Growing and care:
Sow seed indoors about 8 weeks before last frost or sow directly outdoors in early spring. Space plants 2 feet apart. Once established, plants often self-seed and may become weedy. Control slugs by setting slug traps or hand picking them from plants in the evening or early morning. *Silybum* will tolerate wet conditions but is most attractive when grown in poor, dry soils.

Selected species and varieties:
S. marianum grows to 4 feet with coarse, dark green leaves mottled with white, and solitary rose or purple flowers. The soft, thin flower petals are surrounded by a collar of curved, spiny bracts.

BLUE MILKWEED
Oxypetalum

Light: full sun

Plant type: tender perennial grown as annual

Height: 15 inches to 3 feet

Soil and Moisture: well-drained, fertile, moist to dry

Interest: flowers, foliage

Care: easy

◀ Oxypetalum caeruleum

This elegant tender perennial from South America produces exquisite star-shaped flowers borne in delicate, graceful sprays from summer to fall. The pink flower buds open to reveal flowers of clear baby blue, which mature to rich lilac-purple. Plant blue milkweed at the edge of a border or in a patio planter or hanging basket where its stunning, long-lasting flowers can be viewed up close.

Growing and care:
Start seed indoors 6 to 8 weeks prior to the last frost, and transplant to the garden after all danger of frost has passed. Seed may also be direct sown at time of last frost. Space plants 6 to 8 inches apart. Pinch back young plants to encourage branching. If plants become infested with whitefly, which is sometimes a problem, spray with insecticidal soap once a week.

Selected species and varieties:
O. caeruleum has a weakly twining, upright habit. When grown as an annual plants reach about 1½ feet tall. In Zone 10 it may grow into a 3-foot shrub. Leaves are heart shaped and covered with downy hairs. The ½- to 1-inch flowers are borne in open clusters from summer to early fall.

BURNING BUSH
Kochia

Light: full sun	
Plant type: annual	
Height: 2 to 4 feet	
Soil and Moisture: well-drained, medium to dry	
Interest: foliage	
Care: easy	

◀ Kochia scoparia
f. trichophylla

Burning bush is a fast-growing, heat-tolerant annual with lacelike, fine-textured green foliage that turns scarlet in fall. The plant's neat, symmetrical shrublike habit makes a beautiful hedge, screen, or background for flower borders. When grown in containers they are eye-catching conversation pieces.

Growing and care:

Start seed indoors in individual peat pots 6 to 8 weeks prior to the last frost or sow directly in the garden after all danger of frost has passed. Keep seed moist after planting but do not cover, as it needs light to germinate well. Plants often self-seed and may become invasive. Allow 1½ to 2 feet between plants. Plants can be sheared to maintain desired shape or size. Avoid overwatering. In windy locations, plants may require staking.

Selected species and varieties:

K. scoparia f. *trichophylla* (burning bush, summer cypress) has an erect, uniform habit with dense, feathery foliage that is light green in summer, turning bright red in fall; 'Acapulco Silver' produces variegated leaves marked with chrome-white tips.

CAPE MARIGOLD
Dimorphotheca

Light: full sun	
Plant type: annual	
Height: 12 to 16 inches	
Soil and Moisture: well-drained, fertile, dry	
Interest: flowers	
Care: easy	

◀ Dimorphotheca
sinuata

The gaily colored daisylike flowers of Cape marigold add a festive touch to the front of beds and borders and lend a wonderfully cheerful air to sunny rock gardens. The plants come in a wide range of bright colors and bloom over a very long season, from late spring to early fall. The flowers open in the morning and close at night.

Growing and care:

Start seed indoors 6 to 8 weeks prior to the last frost. From Zone 9 south sow directly in the garden in winter. Space plants 6 to 9 inches apart. Do not disturb after transplanting. In regions with hot summers provide some afternoon shade. Water plants early in the day and avoid wetting foliage.

Selected species and varieties:

D. pluvialis (weather prophet) grows to 16 inches with showy 2½-inch daisylike flowers with white petal-like ray flowers surrounding yellow and violet centers. *D. sinuata* (Cape marigold) grows 12 to 15 inches with a compact, mounded habit, producing 1½-inch flower heads composed of white, yellow, pink, or orange rays around golden centers.

CASTOR BEAN
Ricinus

Light: full sun

Plant type: tender perennial grown as annual

Height: 8 to 10 feet

Soil and Moisture: well-drained, moist to slightly dry

Interest: foliage

Care: easy

◀ Ricinus communis 'Carmencita'

The large, glossy foliage of castor bean is an attractive, textured addition to the annual garden. It makes an excellent screen or backdrop. The small pompom flowers are followed by prickly husks filled with beanlike brown, speckled, very poisonous seeds. Castor bean can be an interesting addition to the garden, but must be used cautiously.

Growing and care:

Soak seed in warm water for 24 hours before planting. Sow seed indoors in peat pots 6 to 8 weeks prior to the last frost. Fertilize and water regularly for best growth. Plants grow best in hot, humid climates and can become invasive in warm regions.

Selected species and varieties:

R. communis is a shrubby plant with branches up to 10 feet tall and spreading 3 to 4 feet wide; the 1- to 3-foot star-shaped leaves emerge tinged with red and turn glossy green as they expand; clusters of red or red and green flowers appear in summer followed by prickly seedpods; 'Carmencita' produces early-blooming bright red flowers and deep greenish brown leaves.

CORN COCKLE
Agrostemma

Light: full sun

Plant type: annual

Height: 1 to 3 feet

Soil and Moisture: well-drained, moist to dry

Interest: flowers, foliage

Care: easy

◀ Agrostemma githago

Corn cockles are trouble-free, vigorous plants from Europe that have become naturalized throughout much of eastern North America. They provide a long season of bright blooms for sunny borders and cottage gardens, where the old-fashioned appearance of the flowers is particularly effective. The dainty, trumpet-shaped blossoms come in shades of pink, lilac, cherry red, and magenta and are excellent for cutting.

Growing and care:

Corn cockle grows best in regions with long, cool summers. Sow seed in place in late fall or early spring. Thin when seedlings are about 2 inches tall to stand 6 to 12 inches apart. Corn cockle thrives in moist or dry conditions and needs fertilizing only in the poorest soils. The plants freely self-sow and can become invasive. Deadhead spent blossoms to prevent excessive self-seeding and encourage reblooming. Water during dry periods and support plants with stakes when needed.

Selected species and varieties:

A. githago has willowy stems up to 3 feet tall and narrow leaves covered with a silvery down; each flower has five petals that sport delicate stripes or spots that seem to radiate from the center; the black seeds are plentiful but poisonous if eaten.

CREEPING ZINNIA
Sanvitalia

Light: full sun

Plant type: annual

Height: 4 to 6 inches

Soil and Moisture: well-drained, sandy, medium to dry

Interest: flowers

Care: easy

◀ Sanvitalia procumbens

Creeping zinnia is a low-growing annual from Mexico that produces a profuse display of small, jaunty flowers from early summer to frost. The blossoms resemble miniature sunflowers, each one only ¾ inch across. The plants make a superb edging, a show-stopping ground cover for the sunny rock garden, or an attractive hanging basket.

Growing and care:

Start seed indoors in peat pots 4 to 6 weeks prior to the last frost, or sow directly outdoors in late spring. Transplant carefully being sure not to disturb roots. Allow 6 to 9 inches between plants. Once established do not disturb plants. Soak soil thoroughly when watering. Fertilize lightly during the growing season. *Sanvitalia* thrives in hot, humid weather and tolerates extended dry periods.

Selected species and varieties:

S. procumbens grows to a height of 6 inches, with trailing stems extending 1½ feet from the crown, with compact, oval ½- to 1-inch leaves. Flowers are composed of yellow or orange rays surrounding a dark purple center and may be single, semidouble, or double; 'Gold Braid' produces double yellow blooms; 'Mandarin Orange' bears semidouble orange flowers with prominent black centers.

DAHLBERG DAISY
Dyssodia

Light: full sun

Plant type: annual

Height: 4 to 12 inches

Soil and Moisture: well-drained, dry

Interest: flowers, foliage, fragrance

Care: easy

◀ Dyssodia tenuiloba

Dahlberg daisy blooms from summer to fall with petite yellow flowers at the tips of 3-inch-long branches. The highly dissected foliage has a pleasant fragrance reminiscent of thyme. The medium green leaves are short and finely divided into feathery segments. This native of southern Texas and Mexico is an exquisite plant for rock gardens, sunny borders, and containers, or as edging for pathways.

Growing and care:

Sow seed indoors in late winter and plant in the garden after danger of frost has passed. Or sow directly in the garden after the last frost, spacing plants 9 to 18 inches apart. Dahlberg daisy is heat and drought tolerant and may self-sow in dry, gravelly soil.

Selected species and varieties:

D. tenuiloba [also listed as *Thymophylla tenuiloba*] (Dahlberg daisy, golden-fleece) has ½-inch flower heads with bright yellow centers and stubby yellow, gold, orange, or red petals with lighter-shaded tips and feathery, aromatic 1-inch leaves covered with very fine hairs.

617

DEVIL'S-CLAW
Proboscidea

Light: full sun

Plant type: annual

Height: 1 to 2 feet

Soil and Moisture: well-drained, sandy, moist to dry

Interest: flowers, fruit

Care: easy

◀ Proboscidea louisianica

Devil's-claw is an unusual annual that bears tubular flowers followed by very interesting fruits: fleshy 4- to 6-inch pods that split into two clawlike, curved ends as they dry. While green the pods can be pickled and eaten. The dried pods are outstanding additions to dried arrangements.

Growing and care:
Start seed indoors 6 to 8 weeks before the last frost. In Zone 8 and warmer, seed can be sown directly in the garden in midspring. Devil's-claw may self-seed and become invasive in warm climates. Space plants 6 to 12 inches apart and at least 5 feet away from other plants so that the odor of the flowers does not overpower more delicate or appealing fragrances.

Selected species and varieties:
P. louisianica (unicorn flower) grows to 2 feet with a bushy, spreading habit. The 7- to 10-inch leaves have wavy margins and are covered with sticky hairs. The unpleasantly scented flowers are colored with blends of white, yellow, pink, or purple and commonly appear right after a rain. The unique fruits appear after the blooms have faded.

EUPHORBIA
Euphorbia

Light: full sun

Plant type: annual

Height: 1½ to 2 feet

Soil and Moisture: well-drained, medium to dry

Interest: flowers, foliage

Care: easy

◀ Euphorbia marginata

This hardy annual is native to the Great Plains and eastern Rockies and makes a wonderful addition to sunny wildflower gardens, annual beds, and perennial borders. The attractive variegated leaves and tiny white flowers of euphorbia add a beautiful, subtle touch to the garden from spring to fall. The soft stems support light green foliage generously decorated with clean white markings. The small flowers that appear above the leaves are surrounded by snow white bracts.

Growing and care:
Sow seed directly in the garden in late fall or early spring. Space plants 10 to 12 inches apart. Keep the seedbed moist from the time the seeds are sown until the plants are a few inches tall. As the plants grow they become increasingly drought tolerant. Euphorbia self-seeds so easily it may become invasive. Use gloves when handling stems to avoid contact with the sap, as it may be irritating to some people.

Selected species and varieties:
E. marginata (snow-on-the-mountain, ghostweed) has erect, stout, branched stems bearing gray-green oval leaves attractively striped and margined with white. The small late-summer flowers are surrounded by showy, pure white leaflike bracts.

EVERLASTING
Xeranthemum

Light: full sun

Plant type: annual

Height: 1½ to 2 feet

Soil and Moisture: well-drained, medium to dry

Interest: flowers

Care: easy

◀ Xeranthemum annuum

Everlasting is a longtime favorite for cutting and for dried arrangements. The daisylike purple, pink, or white flowers seem to float atop the long stems from summer to early fall, lending a cheerful air to the garden. The plants are easy to grow and do well even in poor, dry soils.

Growing and care:
In colder zones, start seed indoors in individual peat pots 6 to 8 weeks prior to the last frost. Be careful not to disturb the roots when transplanting. In warmer climates, sow seed directly in the garden in spring after all danger of frost has passed. Allow 6 to 9 inches between plants. To use in dried arrangements, cut flowers when they are fully open and hang them upside down in a dim, well-ventilated room until dry.

Selected species and varieties:
X. annuum (Immortelle) has tall, pliant stems with silvery-green leaves and crowned with bright, daisylike flowers. The delicate 1½-inch single or double blossoms are surrounded by papery bracts that are the same color as the true flowers.

GAZANIA
Gazania

Light: full sun

Plant type: tender perennial grown as annual

Height: 6 to 16 inches

Soil and Moisture: well-drained, dry

Interest: flowers, foliage

Care: easy

◀ Gazania rigens 'Fiesta Red'

This stunning tender perennial from South Africa produces large daisylike flowers from midsummer to frost. The blossoms open each morning when touched by the sun, and close at night and on overcast days. Gazanias provide brilliant color to borders and beds. They are especially suited for use in container gardens, where they brighten decks and patios all season long.

Growing and care:
Sow seed indoors in early spring to transplant to the garden after all danger of frost has passed. Space plants 1 foot apart. Do not overwater. They thrive in sunny, dry locations and tolerate wind and coastal conditions. Deadhead regularly to maintain a tidy appearance.

Selected species and varieties:
G. linearis grows to 16 inches with narrow leaves and 2¾-inch flower heads with golden rays surrounding orange-brown disks. *G. rigens* (treasure flower) grows 6 to 12 inches tall with 3-inch flower heads, borne on long stalks, in shades of orange, pink, or red; 'Chansonette' grows to 10 inches with a compact habit and flowers in a wide range of colors; 'Fiesta Red' bears flowers with burnt orange petals marked with a dark ring surrounding a yellow disk; 'Harlequin Hybrids' bear flowers in many shades with a brown zone around the central disk; 'Sunshine' has large, 4-inch-wide multicolored flowers on 8-inch stems.

GLOBE AMARANTH
Gomphrena

Light: full sun	
Plant type: annual	
Height: 8 inches to 2 feet	
Soil and Moisture: well-drained, medium to dry	
Interest: flowers	
Care: easy	

◀ Gomphrena globosa

The round, cloverlike flowers of globe amaranth add a unique look to gardens from summer to frost. A native of India, this half-hardy annual is easy to grow and imparts a cheerful, informal appearance to beds and borders as well as patio planters and window boxes. The flowers have a coarse, parchmentlike texture even when fresh, and are excellent for both fresh and dried arrangements.

Growing and care:
Start seed indoors 8 to 10 weeks before the last frost and transplant outdoors after all danger of frost has passed. Seed can also be sown directly outside in late spring after the soil has warmed. Allow 8 to 15 inches between plants. Globe amaranth grows slowly in spring but quickly once the weather warms. To use in dried arrangements, cut before the flowers are fully open and hang them upside down in an airy room until dry.

Selected species and varieties:
G. globosa produces strongly branched, erect stems and somewhat coarse, hairy leaves. The 1-inch-long globular flower heads may be pink, white, magenta, orange, or red and are borne atop the stems from summer to fall.

LATHYRUS
Lathyrus

Light: full sun	
Plant type: annual	
Height: 6 inches to 9 feet	
Soil and Moisture: well-drained, moist	
Interest: flowers, fragrance	
Care: easy	

◀ Lathyrus odoratus

Lathyrus is a hardy annual from southern Europe that has been grown in gardens for generations for its clusters of deliciously fragrant blossoms. The flowers come in many charming colors and appear over many weeks from spring to fall. Lathyrus makes an excellent trailing ground cover or an interesting hanging basket.

Growing and care:
Sow seed in 1-inch-deep drills in well-prepared soil in early spring. In the Deep South sow in fall for winter flowering. Nick seed coat or soak seed in warm water for 24 hours prior to planting for best germination. Provide climbing types with support. Mulch to keep soil cool, and provide abundant water. Remove faded blooms regularly to prolong flowering.

Selected species and varieties:
L. odoratus (sweet pea) produces fragrant spring or summer flowers up to 2 inches wide on compact 6-inch to 2½-foot-tall bushy, or 5- to 6-foot-tall twining vines. Flower colors include deep rose, blue, purple, scarlet, white, cream, salmon, pink, and bicolors; 'Bijou Mixed' is a bush type that grows to 1 foot with a full range of colors; 'Royal Family' is a vining type that comes in a wide range of colors, grows to 6 feet, and grows best in regions with hot summers.

LOVE-IN-A-MIST
Nigella

Light: full sun

Plant type: annual

Height: 1½ to 2 feet

Soil and Moisture: well-drained, moist

Interest: flowers, seed heads

Care: easy

◀ Nigella damascena

Love-in-a-mist adds a delicate, fine texture to any garden or flower arrangement. The solitary wide-petaled flowers seem to float atop a leafy mist of stems and foliage throughout the summer. The blossoms mature into interesting seed capsules that are attractive additions to dried flower arrangements. The plant is native to southern Europe and North Africa.

Growing and care:
Sow seed directly in the garden in spring when soil is cool and frost is still possible. Sow every 2 weeks to extend the flowering season. Once seedlings emerge do not transplant, and cultivate carefully so roots are not disturbed. Thin to allow 6 to 10 inches between plants. Water during dry periods and fertilize lightly every few weeks. Plants often self-seed.

Selected species and varieties:
N. damascena has an erect, branching habit with delicate, threadlike leaves. Flowers are 1 to 1½ inches across with blue, lavender, white, or pink notched petals. The papery 1-inch seed capsules are pale green with attractive reddish brown markings.

MENTZELIA
Mentzelia

Light: full sun

Plant type: annual or biennial

Height: 1 to 4 feet

Soil and Moisture: well-drained, moist to dry

Interest: flowers

Care: easy

◀ Mentzelia lindleyi

Mentzelias are bushy plants covered with an attractive display of star-shaped flowers from late spring until fall. The plants bear fragrant yellow or white flowers that often open in the evening and close on cloudy days. Mentzelia is used to add a soft, slightly wild look to beds and borders.

Growing and care:
North of Zone 8 sow seed directly in garden in spring after danger of frost has passed. From Zone 8 south, direct-sow in fall. Thin to allow 6 to 10 inches between plants. Keep seedlings moist, but once established keep plants on the dry side. When cultivating be careful not to disturb roots. Plants tolerate heat and drought but put on a much better floral show when regularly watered and fertilized.

Selected species and varieties:
M. decapetala (ten-petal mentzelia) is a biennial that grows 2 to 4 feet tall with 3- to 5-inch starburst-shaped flowers opening in the evening. *M. laevicaulis* (blazing-star) is a biennial that grows to 3½ feet with narrow leaves and pale yellow 4-inch flowers that also open in the evening. *M. lindleyi* [also known as *Bartonia aurea*] is an annual that grows 1 to 2½ feet tall with fragrant, bright yellow flowers displaying a colorful orange-red center with a prominent flush of yellow stamens.

MEXICAN SUNFLOWER
Tithonia

Light: full sun	
Plant type: annual	
Height: 2 to 6 feet	
Soil and Moisture: well-drained, medium to dry	
Interest: flowers	
Care: easy	

◀ Tithonia rotundifolia

Mexican sunflower is native to the hot, arid regions of Central America, where it has developed exceptional drought and heat tolerance. Its daisylike orange to red flowers and coarse-textured leaves stay perky even during the most torrid summer days. Plants are suitable for the background of borders and for cutting; they can also be used as a fast-growing summer screen.

Growing and care:
Start seed indoors 6 to 8 weeks prior to the last frost. Do not cover seed. Transplant after danger of frost has passed. Space plants 2 to 2½ feet apart. Stake plants in windy areas. Plants tolerate poor soil, heat, and drought, and usually do not need supplemental watering even during long dry periods. When cutting flowers for indoor arrangements, cut in the bud stage and sear the stem to preserve freshness.

Selected species and varieties:
T. rotundifolia has a vigorous, erect habit with large, broadly oval, velvety, serrated leaves. Flower heads consist of orange or scarlet sunflower-like petals surrounding a bright orange-yellow central disk; 'Goldfinger' grows 2 to 3 feet tall with 3-inch vivid orange blooms.

MOSS ROSE
Portulaca

Light: full sun	
Plant type: annual	
Height: 6 to 8 inches	
Soil and Moisture: well-drained, dry	
Interest: flowers, foliage	
Care: easy	

◀ Portulaca grandiflora 'Sundance'

Moss rose is a tough, hardworking plant that bears dozens of attractive, brightly colored flowers even in extreme summertime conditions. The creeping stems are covered with slender, succulent green leaves that serve as an excellent backdrop for the vivid flowers. *Portulaca* is a fine choice for the rock garden, an informal ground cover, or containers. The plants thrive in hot, dry sites where few other flowers would survive.

Growing and care:
Start seed indoors in peat pots 6 to 8 weeks prior to the last frost and transplant to the garden after the soil has warmed. Take care not to disturb roots. Seed can also be sown directly in the garden after danger of frost has passed. Do not cover seed. Space plants 6 to 8 inches apart. Moss rose flowers only in sunshine and blooms best in poor, dry soils and hot weather.

Selected species and varieties:
P. grandiflora produces sprawling succulent stems that bear fleshy, narrow leaves and showy bowl-shaped flowers resembling roses. Blooms come in many vivid colors including red, pink, white, yellow, orange, and magenta; 'Sundance' bears semidouble flowers in a mixture of red, orange, yellow, cream, and white.

NASTURTIUM
Tropaeolum

Light: full sun

Plant type: annual

Height: 6 inches to 8 feet

Soil and Moisture: well-drained, moist

Interest: flowers, foliage

Care: easy

◀ Tropaeolum majus

Nasturtium is an eye-catching annual with attractive, unusually shaped flowers and foliage. The white, yellow, orange, or red trumpet-shaped blossoms are decorated with long floral spurs. The unusual foliage has stems in the center of each shieldlike leaf. Blooms appear from summer through frost. Organically grown young flowers make a peppery addition to salads and are excellent for cutting.

Growing and care:
Nasturtiums do not transplant well and should be sown directly in the garden after the last frost. Space dwarf types 1 foot apart, climbers from 2 to 3 feet apart. Do not fertilize. Water during dry periods.

Selected species and varieties:
T. majus (common nasturtium) comes in dwarf, bushy forms, and vigorous, climbing ones; leaves are round, 2 to 7 inches across, with long stems and 2- to 3-inch showy flowers in red, yellow, white, or orange. *T. minus* (dwarf nasturtium) reaches 6 to 12 inches in height, with a bushy habit suitable for edging or massing; 'Alaska Mixed' grows 8 to 15 inches tall with variegated leaves and a wide range of flower colors. *T. peregrinum* (canary creeper, canarybird vine) is a climbing vine up to 8 feet long with pale yellow, fringed flowers and deeply lobed leaves that resemble those of a fig.

ORNAMENTAL CABBAGE
Brassica

Light: full sun

Plant type: biennial grown as annual

Height: 10 to 15 inches

Soil and Moisture: well-drained, moist

Interest: flowers, foliage

Care: easy

◀ Brassica oleracea

This decorative cousin of the familiar vegetable side dish is highly valued for the easy-care splash of color it provides to the fall and winter landscape. A biennial, it is grown as an annual for its brightly colored and intricately curled foliage, which grows in a flower-like rosette.

Growing and care:
For spring planting, start seed indoors 4 to 6 weeks prior to the last frost. For fall gardens, start seed 6 to 8 weeks prior to the first anticipated frost. Space plants 1½ to 2 feet apart. Plants tolerate light frost and will last all winter in Zones 8 to 10.

Selected species and varieties:
B. oleracea, Acephala Group, does not form heads but produces an open rosette of leaves that typically spreads 1 foot across. Foliage colors include lavender-blue, white, green, red, purple, pink, and assorted variegations. Color becomes brighter in cool weather; leaves of 'Cherry Sundae' are a blend of carmine and cream; 'Color Up' displays a center of red, pink, and white, surrounded by green margins; 'Peacock' series has feathery leaves in a variety of colors with notched and serrated edges.

ORNAMENTAL CORN
Zea mays

Light: full sun	
Plant type: annual	
Height: 2 to 15 feet	
Soil and Moisture: well-drained, moist, fertile	
Interest: seed heads	
Care: easy	

◀ Zea mays

Corn is most often associated with vegetable gardens, yet there are many varieties that can add interesting accents to almost any bed or border. Ornamental corn provides a strong vertical aspect to the garden from spring to fall. And the decorative ears full of colorful kernels make autumn holidays even more enjoyable.

Growing and care:
Corn is a heavy feeder and grows best in well-worked soil that has been amended with organic matter prior to planting. Sow seed directly in the garden after soil warms in spring. Avoid sowing seed in cool, wet weather when the plants are more susceptible to disease. Thin plants to stand 8 to 12 inches apart. For good pollination, plant in blocks at least four rows wide with rows spaced 1½ to 2½ feet apart. Fertilize and water regularly.

Selected species and varieties:
Z. mays grows from 2 to 15 feet tall with strong, upright stalks and large, graceful lance-shaped leaves up to 2 feet long. The spreading tassels that appear atop the stalks in summer are the male flowers, while the female flowers, or ears, are found in the leaf axils; var. *rugosa* bears small, rounded ears filled with red kernels that can be used as decorations or popcorn.

OWL'S CLOVER
Orthocarpus

Light: full sun	
Plant type: annual	
Height: 4 to 15 inches	
Soil and Moisture: well-drained, medium to dry	
Interest: flowers, foliage	
Care: easy	

◀ Orthocarpus purpurascens

Owl's clover is native to the southwestern United States, where it transforms desert hillsides into waves of rose, purple, and red. Individual flowers resemble snapdragons and are tipped with yellow or white on their lower lip and bracts of bright purple or crimson. These annuals are useful when massed in wildflower meadows and informal borders, where they provide a long season of color.

Growing and care:
Sow seed directly in the garden just beneath the surface as soon as the soil can be worked in early spring. Thin plants to stand 6 to 8 inches apart. Owl's clover does best in regions with long, warm summers. The plants are drought tolerant but benefit from extra water during dry periods.

Selected species and varieties:
O. purpurascens (escobita) grows from 4 to 15 inches tall with linear leaves often tinged with brown, either cut or smooth margins, and red-tipped bracts. The two-lipped rose-purple or crimson flowers are about 1 inch long and appear from early to midsummer.

PAINTED TONGUE
Salpiglossis

Light: full sun	
Plant type: annual	
Height: 2 to 3 feet	
Soil and Moisture: well-drained, moist, fertile	
Interest: flowers	
Care: easy	

◀ Salpiglossis sinuata 'Bolero'

The trumpet-shaped blossoms of painted tongue resemble petunias that have designs of gold etched onto the flowers. Painted tongue comes in an incredible range of colors, including red, pink, purple, blue, white, and yellow. Each blossom is marked with a contrasting inlay of rich color, most commonly gold. Plants add a cheerful, opulent accent to beds and borders, and are excellent cut flowers.

Growing and care:
Start seed indoors 6 to 8 weeks prior to the last frost or plant directly outdoors in late spring. Transplant to the garden after all danger of frost has passed. Space plants 10 to 12 inches apart. Loosen soil and amend with organic matter to increase fertility and aid drainage. Taller varieties may need staking. Water and fertilize regularly. Too much fertilizer will encourage leggy growth. Plants produce the best flower displays in areas with cool summers.

Selected species and varieties:
S. sinuata has an erect, bushy habit with narrow, 4-inch medium green leaves. Both foliage and stems are slightly hairy and sticky. Flowers are 2 to 2½ inches wide, have a soft, velvety texture, and appear in terminal clusters; 'Bolero' is 1½ to 2 feet tall with flower colors that include gold, rose, red, and blue.

PETUNIA
Petunia

Light: full sun	
Plant type: annual	
Height: 6 inches to 2 feet	
Soil and Moisture: well-drained, moist	
Interest: flowers	
Care: easy	

◀ Petunia x hybrida

Petunias, among the most popular of annuals, are renowned for producing a profusion of trumpet-shaped blooms in a wide variety of colors from summer to frost. The trailing or upright stems are slender, with small, pointed leaves covered with soft, sticky hairs. Dwarf varieties grow 6 to 12 inches tall, while bedding varieties can attain heights of 2 feet. Hybrid grandiflora varieties produce single ruffled or fringed flowers 4 to 6 inches across. Hybrid multiflora varieties produce smaller flowers, but in greater abundance. Petunias are effective as bedding plants, as borders, cascading over walls and banks, or as container plants.

Growing and care:
Sow seed indoors 8 to 10 weeks before the last frost or direct-sow in the garden after danger of frost has passed. Pinch back young plants to encourage a bushy form. Cut back plants if they become rangy. Remove withered flowers before they set seed to encourage further flowering. Keep soil moist and give extra water during dry periods. In areas with hot summers provide some afternoon shade.

Selected species and varieties:
P. x *hybrida* bears flowers with ruffled, fringed, or deeply veined petals in a wide range of colors; 'Blue Danube' is a double grandiflora with fringed blue petals; 'Flaming Velvet' has very deep red flowers; 'Purple Wave' has a low, trailing habit and violet-purple flowers.

PHACELIA
Phacelia

Light: full sun

Plant type: annual

Height: 6 inches to 3 feet

Soil and Moisture: well-drained, sandy, dry

Interest: flowers

Care: easy

◄ Phacelia campanularia

Phacelias are a diverse group of wildflowers with attractive blossoms in forms ranging from loose cymes of dainty bells to tightly packed spikes. Some are native to the southwestern United States, where they grow on dry, rocky desert slopes. The plants are beautiful additions to rock gardens and borders and make dynamic mass plantings.

Growing and care:

In most regions direct-sow in the garden in early spring when soil is cool. From Zone 9 south direct-sow in fall. Space plants 6 to 8 inches apart. Do not transplant. Phacelia prefers sandy, poor soils and grows well with California poppy, owl's clover, purple lupine, and golden yarrow.

Selected species and varieties:

P. campanularia (California bluebell) grows from 6 to 24 inches tall with 1-inch hairy, round or heart-shaped leaves and ¾- to 1-inch bright blue, mostly upright bell-shaped flowers borne in loose clusters. *P. tanacetifolia* (purple heliotrope) has erect, slightly hairy 1- to 3-foot-tall stems with feathery leaves and curled clusters of sweetly scented lavender flowers.

PINCUSHION FLOWER
Scabiosa

Light: full sun

Plant type: annual

Height: 1½ to 3 feet

Soil and Moisture: well-drained, moist, fertile

Interest: flowers

Care: easy

◄ Scabiosa atropurpurea

Pincushion flower is easy to grow, producing delightful dome-shaped blossoms from spring to fall. The long-lasting flowers are composed of a 1- to 2-inch mound of lacy petals beneath dozens of prominent stamens that resemble pins stuck in a pincushion. The flowers come in lavender, pink, purple, maroon, red, and white and are favorites for borders, massing, and both fresh and dried arrangements.

Growing and care:

Start seed indoors 4 to 6 weeks prior to the last frost and transplant to the garden after danger of frost has passed. Seed can also be direct sown in spring in the North, and in fall from Zone 8 south. Space plants 8 to 12 inches apart. Deadhead regularly to encourage blossoming. Supply extra water during dry periods.

Selected species and varieties:

S. atropurpurea grows 2 to 3 feet tall with slender, erect stems and showy, domed flower heads. *S. stellata* (paper moon) grows to 1½ to 2½ feet with pale blue flowers that feel papery when dry and are highly valued for dried arrangements; 'Drumstick' has pale blue flowers that fade to bronze; 'Ping-Pong' bears rounded white flowers the size of a Ping-Pong ball.

PLAINS COREOPSIS
Coreopsis

Light: full sun

Plant type: annual

Height: 2 to 3 feet

Soil and Moisture: well-drained, moist to dry

Interest: flowers

Care: easy

◀ Coreopsis tinctoria

This easy-to-grow, beautiful annual is native to the Great Plains and is a common component of wildflower mixtures. Coreopsis produces daisylike flowers that appear on supple, wiry stems throughout summer to early fall. Colors include yellow, orange, red, mahogany, and bicolors. Plant them in mixed borders and wildflower gardens, and use the fresh flowers to add a wild touch to indoor arrangements.

Growing and care:
Start seed indoors 6 to 8 weeks before the last frost or sow directly in the garden in early spring. Space plants 6 to 8 inches apart. Deadhead often to prolong flowering. Fertilize lightly for best flower production. Do not deadhead blossoms produced late in the season if self-seeding is desired.

Selected species and varieties:
C. tinctoria (calliopsis) produces pliant, many-branched stems draped with interesting lobed or dissected leaves. Flower heads may be solitary or appear in loose clusters. The blossoms have dark red or purple centers surrounded by notched and often banded ray flowers. Double-flowered and dwarf varieties are available.

PRICKLY POPPY
Argemone

Light: full sun

Plant type: annual or tender perennial grown as annual

Height: 2 to 4 feet

Soil and Moisture: well-drained, dry

Interest: flowers, foliage

Care: easy

◀ Argemone munita

The light blue-green, spiny foliage and large, showy flowers of prickly poppies make an attractive if bold statement in the garden. The sweetly fragrant white, yellow, or orange flowers have four to six crepe-paper petals surrounding a central mass of yellow stamens. The fruit of prickly poppies is composed of small, spiny capsules filled with tiny seeds. The plants are ideal for the backs of borders and beds.

Growing and care:
Prickly poppies are difficult to transplant, and grow best when sown directly in the garden after danger of frost has passed. Thin plants to 1 to 2 feet apart. Deadhead regularly to encourage blossoming. Plants grow best in poor, slightly dry soils. If spent flowers are not removed the plants often self-seed.

Selected species and varieties:
A. mexicana (Mexican poppy) is an annual with 1- to 2-foot spiny stems bearing 2- to 2½-inch yellow, golden, or orange flowers in summer above green leaves often spotted with white. *A. munita* (white prickly poppy), an annual or tender perennial, grows to 3 feet tall with many 2- to 5-inch showy white summer flowers surrounding yellow stamens and a purple stigma.

PURPLE BELL VINE
Rhodochiton

Light: full sun

Plant type: tender perennial grown as annual

Height: 5 to 15 feet

Soil and Moisture: well-drained, evenly moist, fertile

Interest: flowers, foliage

Care: easy

◀ Rhodochiton atrosanguineum

From summer to frost, purple bell vine bears pendent, tubular, deep violet flowers surrounded by a four-pointed calyx of bright fuchsia. Native to Mexico, where it is a perennial, the purple bell vine is grown as an annual north of Zone 9. This fast-growing vine climbs by twisting its long petioles around any nearby support. The vigorous plants are attractive when used as a seasonal cover for a fence or trellis, or when allowed to cascade from a hanging basket or patio container.

Growing and care:
Start seed indoors in individual peat pots 3 to 4 months prior to the last frost. Place several seeds in each pot, because germination may be erratic. Snip out all but the strongest seedling after plants show first true leaves. Transplant to the garden after soil has warmed, spacing plants 1 foot apart. Fertilize and water regularly. Purple bell vine grows best in hot weather.

Selected species and varieties:
R. atrosanguineum [also called *R. volubile*] grows to 15 feet in its native habitat but usually reaches 5 to 8 feet in temperate zones. Its thick-textured, heart-shaped green leaves are tipped with purple. Elongated bell-shaped flowers are about an inch in length and hang from slender stems.

SAGE
Salvia

Light: full sun

Plant type: annual or tender perennial

Height: 8 inches to 4 feet

Soil and Moisture: well-drained, dry to moist, sandy

Interest: flowers, foliage

Care: easy

◀ Salvia coccinea 'Lady in Red'

Hummingbirds and butterflies love a garden where sage is in bloom. There are many different types to choose from, each having soft, sometimes downy leaves, slender erect stems, and whorls of tiny hooded flowers from summer to fall. Sage is particularly effective when planted in large groups that multiply the impact of their flowers and encourage a steady stream of winged visitors.

Growing and care:
Start seed indoors in sterilized potting mix or vermiculite 6 to 8 weeks prior to the last frost. Space smaller types 1 to 1½ feet apart, larger types 2 to 3 feet apart. Pinch plants when about 6 inches high to encourage bushy growth. Sage is generally drought tolerant but needs extra watering during very dry periods. Remove faded flowers to extend bloom. Fertilize lightly during growing season.

Selected species and varieties:
S. coccinea (Texas sage) produces heart-shaped leaves on 1- to 2-foot branching stems; 'Lady in Red' has slender clusters of bright red flowers. *S. farinacea* (mealy-cup sage) grows 2 to 3 feet tall with gray-green leaves and spikes of small blue flowers; 'Silver White' grows 18 to 20 inches tall with silvery white flowers; 'Strata' reaches 16 to 24 inches with 6- to 10-inch spikes of bicolored flowers in blue and white that are useful in both fresh and dried arrangements; 'Victoria' grows to 1½ feet with

(continued)

a uniform habit and a 14-inch spread with violet-blue flowers. *S. greggii* (autumn sage) grows 2 to 4 feet tall with an erect, shrubby habit, medium green leaves, and red, pink, yellow, or white flowers that bloom from mid-summer through fall and attract hummingbirds. *S. leucantha* (Mexican bush sage) grows 2 to 4 feet with gracefully arching stems, gray-green leaves, and arching spikes of purple and white flowers in summer and fall. *S. splendens* (scarlet sage) grows to 8 to 30 inches with 2- to 4-inch bright green leaves and terminal clusters of red, pink, purple, lavender, or white flowers up to 1½ inches long; 'Blaze of Fire' grows to 12 to 14 inches with bright red blooms; 'Laser Purple' bears deep purple flowers that resist fading; 'Rodeo' grows to 10 inches with early red flowers. *S. viridis* (painted sage) grows to 1½ feet with white and blue flowers sporting showy pink to purple bracts throughout summer and fall, and is superb for fresh and dried arrangements.

SCOTCH THISTLE
Onopordum

Light: full sun	
Plant type: annual or biennial	
Height: 6 to 9 feet	
Soil and Moisture: well-drained, light, dry	
Interest: flowers, foliage	
Care: easy	

◀ Onopordum acanthium

Scotch thistle is a stately if well-armored plant bearing fuzzy, globular flower heads on tall, stiffly erect branching stems lined with spiny gray-green leaves. The foliage and unusual flowers, which look like upturned shaving brushes, add bold color and texture to the garden while supplying a strong vertical accent.

Growing and care:

Start seed indoors 6 to 8 weeks prior to the last frost, or sow directly in the garden after all danger of frost has passed. Space plants 3 feet apart. Once established they will self-seed and may become invasive. To prevent self-seeding remove entire plant from garden after flowering and toss in the compost pile. Plants can go weeks with little water or fertilizer and thrive in hot, dry locations.

Selected species and varieties:

O. acanthium (Scotch thistle, cotton thistle, silver thistle) produces stiff, downy leaves to 2 feet long, deeply lobed and scalloped into spiny segments on branching stems 6 to 9 feet tall. In late spring to summer, stems are tipped with round, prickly purple or white flowers that have flat, fuzzy tops up to 2 inches in diameter. The blossoms are often visited by butterflies.

STATICE
Limonium

Light: full sun

Plant type: annual or biennial

Height: 10 to 20 inches

Soil and Moisture: well-drained, sandy, dry

Interest: flowers

Care: easy

◀ Limonium sinuatum

Statice, also called sea lavender, is an essential part of any cutting garden. The plants bear clusters of brightly colored flowers surrounded by an attractive papery calyx that remains after the rest of the flower drops. This long-lasting display keeps beds, borders, and arrangements looking fresh for weeks. The flowers are easy to dry and retain their color well, making them popular additions to dried arrangements.

Growing and care:
Start seed indoors in individual peat pots 8 weeks prior to the last frost, or sow directly outdoors in midspring in warm climates. Allow 9 to 18 inches between plants. Statice thrives in drought and seaside conditions and prefers soil that is well drained and dry.

Selected species and varieties:
L. sinuatum (notchleaf statice) grows 16 to 18 inches tall with branched, winged flower stems. The papery blossoms are borne in short, one-sided clusters; colors include pink, blue, lavender, yellow, and white. *L. suworowii* [also known as *Psylliostachys suworowii*] (Russian statice) grows 10 to 20 inches tall with large basal leaves and spikes of lavender and bears green flowers from summer to frost.

STRAWFLOWER
Helichrysum

Light: full sun

Plant type: tender perennial grown as annual

Height: 12 to 28 inches

Soil and Moisture: well-drained, sandy, medium to dry

Interest: flowers

Care: easy

◀ Helichrysum bracteatum

This Australian native, also known as everlasting, bears attractive papery-textured flowers in shades of white, yellow, orange, salmon, red, and pink. What appear to be the flower's petals are actually colorful bracts; the true flowers arise from the center of the flower head. Dwarf types are excellent for adding color to rock gardens or the edge of the border. Taller varieties are prized as cut flowers, the brightly colored blossoms lending sparkle to dried arrangements.

Growing and care:
Start seed indoors 6 to 8 weeks prior to the last frost. In warm climates, seed can be sown directly in the garden. Space plants about 1 foot apart. Once established, plants thrive in dry soil and often self-seed. They do not perform well in areas with very high humidity. For winter arrangements, cut flowers when they are about half open and hang them upside down in an airy room to dry.

Selected species and varieties:
H. bracteatum produces narrow, coarsely toothed gray-green leaves on wiry, branching stems. Flower heads appear from midsummer to early fall and are 1 to 2½ inches across.

SUNFLOWER
Helianthus

Light: full sun

Plant type: annual

Height: 2 to 10 feet

Soil and Moisture: well-drained, moist

Interest: flowers

Care: easy

◀ Helianthus annuus 'Inca Jewels'

Few flowers add as much cheerfulness to the garden as sunflowers. Their large daisylike blooms appear from midsummer to frost atop strong, tall stalks. The flowers come in shades of yellow, cream, mahogany, and crimson and make a bold statement in mixed borders. A row of sunflowers makes a delightful summertime screen, and many varieties are also excellent cut flowers. In late summer and fall the ripe seeds attract many species of songbirds to the garden.

Growing and care:
Sow seed directly outdoors after the last frost. Thin seedlings to allow 1 to 2 feet between plants. Fertilize lightly every few weeks for best flower production. Plants thrive in hot, dry weather conditions but need extra water during droughts.

Selected species and varieties:
H. annuus (common sunflower) has an erect habit and pleasingly coarse texture, producing sturdy stems, broad leaves, and large flowers; 'Inca Jewels' has a branching habit with yellow-tipped orange rays; 'Italian White' has multiple stems to 4 feet and 4-inch cream-colored flowers with a brown center; 'Sunbeam' grows 5 feet tall with 5-inch pollenless flowers ideal for cutting; 'Teddy Bear' produces single and double yellow flowers on 2-foot plants.

SWAN RIVER DAISY
Brachycome

Light: full sun

Plant type: annual

Height: 9 to 14 inches

Soil and Moisture: well-drained, moist, fertile

Interest: flowers

Care: easy

◀ Brachycome iberidifolia

Swan River daisies produce tidy mounds of well-branched, feathery foliage smothered all season long with an abundance of small, dainty, daisylike flowers in enchanting shades of blue, lavender, and violet. They are excellent additions to beds and borders, where they add a soft, colorful accent, but are most popular when allowed to cascade over the edges of patio containers or hanging baskets.

Growing and care:
Start seed indoors 6 to 8 weeks before the last spring frost or sow directly in the garden after the soil has warmed. Thin seedlings to 6 to 12 inches apart. For continuous flowering do not allow soil to dry out. In areas with hot summers provide some afternoon shade. Fertilize lightly but regularly from spring to frost. In regions with cool summers sow every month for continuous bloom.

Selected species and varieties:
B. iberidifolia grows to 1 foot with a compact, mounding habit. The delicate, fernlike gray-green leaves are 3 inches long and are borne on slender stems. Flowers are asterlike and come in white, lavender, pink, rose, and blue.

TAHOKA DAISY
Machaeranthera

Light: full sun

Plant type: annual

Height: 6 to 12 inches

Soil and Moisture: well-drained, sandy, medium to dry

Interest: flowers

Care: moderate

◀ Machaeranthera tanacetifolia

Tahoka daisy is a free-flowering plant with abundant dainty, asterlike blossoms from late spring to frost. Native to the sunny, open spaces from southern Canada through the Great Plains, this low-spreading annual wildflower is a charming addition to borders and cutting gardens. The flowers are excellent for use in fresh floral arrangements.

Growing and care:
Start seed indoors 6 to 8 weeks before last frost or direct-sow in the garden in early spring when soil is still cool. Do not cover, as seeds need light to germinate. Space plants 9 to 12 inches apart. In areas with hot summers provide some afternoon shade. Tahoka daisy grows best in sandy soil where summers are cool.

Selected species and varieties:
M. tanacetifolia has clusters of 2-inch, thin-petaled lavender flowers with yellow centers, on 6- to 12-inch-tall stems densely covered with deeply cut, pointed foliage. Native to the Great Plains from Alberta south to northern Mexico. Plants readily self-seed.

TASSEL FLOWER
Emilia

Light: full sun

Plant type: annual

Height: 1 1/2 to 2 feet

Soil and Moisture: well-drained, light, dry

Interest: flowers

Care: easy

◀ Emilia javanica

Tassel flower is a lovely, informal plant with attractive, brilliantly colored flowers and a relaxed growth habit. The blossoms appear all season long and look like small brushes that have been dipped in red, orange, or yellow paint. Plant tassel flower among other annuals in a border or in a wildflower meadow. The flowers can be cut for both fresh and dried arrangements.

Growing and care:
Start seed indoors in peat pots 6 to 8 weeks prior to the last frost for earliest bloom. Do not disturb roots after transplanting. Sow outdoors 2 to 3 weeks before last frost. From Zone 8 south sow seed in fall. Space plants 6 to 9 inches apart. Plants often produce more flowers if slightly crowded. Tassel flower thrives in coastal conditions and prefers well-drained, dry soils.

Selected species and varieties:
E. javanica [also known as *E. coccinea* and *Cacalia coccinea*] develops a mounded, 6-inch-high clump of oblong leaves. Erect stems are topped with 1-inch clusters of dainty flowers in shades of red, orange, and yellow.

THORN APPLE
Datura

Light: full sun

Plant type: annual

Height: 2 to 6 feet

Soil and Moisture: well-drained, medium

Interest: flowers

Care: easy

◀ Datura inoxia

Thorn apple has thick, woody stems, large leaves, and huge trumpet-shaped flowers during summer. These fast-growing plants are excellent when grown in large containers for the deck or patio, or to add a tropical flavor to borders. The large leaves are pungently aromatic, while the night-blooming flowers are often pleasantly scented. Many species of *Datura* are poisonous and should be used in the garden with care. They should always be placed well away from children and pets.

Growing and care:
Start seed indoors 8 to 12 weeks prior to moving outdoors to warmed soil. From Zone 9 south, seed may be direct sown in the garden after danger of frost has passed. Space plants 1½ to 2 feet apart or grow a single plant in a large container. Provide shelter from wind. *D. inoxia* sometimes becomes a short-lived perennial in Zones 9 and 10. Elsewhere, it often self-sows.

Selected species and varieties:
D. inoxia (thorn apple, angel's-trumpet) commonly grows to 3 feet but may reach twice that height with 10-inch leaves and pendent pink, white, or lavender flowers 8 inches long and 5 inches wide. *D. metel* (Hindu datura) grows 3 to 6 feet tall with 8-inch leaves and 7-inch white, yellow-, or purple-tinged flowers.

TIDY-TIPS
Layia

Light: full sun

Plant type: annual

Height: 6 inches to 2 feet

Soil and Moisture: well-drained, moist, sandy

Interest: flowers

Care: easy

◀ Layia platyglossa

Tidy-tips is native to California, where it is a prized wildflower. The plants have slender, pliant stems and gray-green leaves decorated with abundant sun-yellow flowers. Its common name refers to the showy white-tipped ray petals that surround the brilliant golden disk. *Layia* is beautiful in borders, rock gardens, and wildflower meadows. The flowers are excellent for fresh arrangements.

Growing and care:
Start seed indoors 6 to 8 weeks prior to the last frost, or sow outdoors in early spring. In Zone 9 and warmer, seed can be sown in fall. Space plants 9 to 12 inches apart, and provide abundant moisture to seedlings. Once plants are established, they are quite drought tolerant. Remove flowers as they fade to prolong blooming period.

Selected species and varieties:
L. platyglossa has a neat habit and coarsely toothed gray-green leaves covered with dense hairs. The single, bright yellow daisylike flowers appear from spring to early summer. *Layia* is a popular ingredient in wildflower mixes.

TOADFLAX
Linaria

Light: full sun
Plant type: annual
Height: 10 to 18 inches
Soil and Moisture: well-drained, moist
Interest: flowers
Care: easy

◀ Linaria maroccana
'Fairy Bouquet'

This popular, hardy annual from Morocco has erect stems, slender lanced-shaped leaves, and stiff spikes of colorful flowers that resemble little snapdragons. Its dainty bicolored flowers come in a rainbow of colors and are at home in mixed borders and rock gardens. Cut flowers make nice additions to indoor arrangements.

Growing and care:
Sow seed directly in the garden 2 to 3 weeks before the last frost. Thin seedlings to stand 6 inches apart. Provide extra water during dry periods. Plants do best in regions with warm summer days and cool nights. In areas with hot summers provide afternoon shade and water frequently. Plants often reseed.

Selected species and varieties:
L. maroccana (Moroccan toadflax) has an erect, bushy habit with narrow, light green leaves and slender spikes of 1/2-inch flowers in shades of pink, purple, yellow, and white, usually with a contrasting throat; 'Fairy Bouquet' grows to 10 inches and bears flowers in shades of pink, rose, coppery orange, purple, white, and pale yellow, all with a deeper yellow throat. It is suitable for an edging or a window box.

TWINSPUR
Diascia

Light: full sun
Plant type: annual
Height: 8 to 12 inches
Soil and Moisture: well-drained, moist, fertile
Interest: flowers
Care: easy

◀ Diascia barberae
'Ruby Fields'

Twinspur is an elegant plant with slender, pliant stems bearing loose spikes of shell pink flowers from summer to fall. Each blossom has a pair of gently curving floral spurs at its back. The plants add a graceful touch to the front of beds or borders and are interesting additions to rock gardens. Twinspur also makes a charming container plant, suitable for window boxes and hanging baskets.

Growing and care:
Start seed indoors 6 to 8 weeks prior to the last frost. Transplant to the garden after the soil has warmed, spacing plants 8 inches apart. Plants can also be seeded directly in the garden in early spring. Pinch young plants to encourage bushiness. Cut back plants after flowering to encourage rebloom. In regions with hot summers provide some shade in midafternoon.

Selected species and varieties:
D. barberae has a mounding habit with slender stems bearing loose clusters of rosy pink flowers from early summer to early fall; 'Pink Queen' grows to 1 foot and bears 6-inch clusters of yellow-throated pastel pink flowers; 'Ruby Fields' produces deep-rose-colored flowers over an exceptionally long period.

VERBENA
Verbena

Light: full sun

Plant type: annual or tender perennial grown as annual

Height: 6 inches to 4 feet

Soil and Moisture: well-drained, moist, fertile

Interest: flowers

Care: easy

◀ Verbena bonariensis

Throughout the season verbena bears clusters of small, vividly colored flowers that are irresistible to butterflies. The plants make excellent annual ground covers or fillers for empty spots in the garden. Smaller forms look great in containers, while taller types add an airy touch to summer bouquets.

Growing and care:

Start seed indoors 8 to 10 weeks prior to the last frost and transplant outdoors after all danger of frost has passed. Allow 1 foot between plants of garden verbena and 2 feet between Brazilian verbenas. Pinch tips from young plants to encourage branching. Plants are drought tolerant but produce more abundant flowers when watered regularly.

Selected species and varieties:

V. bonariensis (Brazilian verbena) grows to 4 feet tall with slender, branching stems and fragrant, rosy violet flower clusters that seem to float above the wrinkled, toothed leaves. *V.* x *hybrida* (garden verbena) grows 6 to 12 inches tall and twice as wide, with wrinkled leaves and small pink, red, blue, purple, or white flowers arranged in rounded 2-inch heads; 'Peaches and Cream' bears flowers in shades of apricot, orange, yellow, and cream; 'Silver Ann' has bright pink blossoms that fade to watercolor shades of pink and white.

VIPER'S BUGLOSS
Echium

Light: full sun

Plant type: biennial grown as annual

Height: 1 to 10 feet

Soil and Moisture: well-drained, light, dry to moist

Interest: flowers, foliage

Care: easy

◀ Echium candicans

Viper's bugloss is a bold addition to borders or rock gardens. These tropical natives are particularly striking in flower, when large, bottlebrush-shaped spikes of blossoms loom high above the silvery gray foliage. The plants do especially well in sunny, dry locations where the soil is poor.

Growing and care:

Start seed indoors in peat pots 6 to 8 weeks before the last frost. Sow outdoors as soon as soil can be worked in spring. From Zone 9 south sow seed in fall. Space plants 1 to 1½ feet apart. Transplant carefully and do not disturb established plants. Viper's bugloss often self-seeds and can become invasive. It will grow in wet or dry soils but does best in dry locations.

Selected species and varieties:

E. candicans (pride-of-Madeira) grows 3 to 6 feet tall with narrow gray-green leaves covered with silvery hairs, and erect 20-inch clusters of white or purple ½-inch flowers held well above the leaves. *E. lycopsis* (viper's bugloss) grows 1 to 3 feet tall with a bushy habit; flowers are blue, lavender, purple, pink, or white and appear on dense 10-inch spikes. *E. wildpretii* (tower-of-jewels) grows to an eye-catching 10 feet, with pale red blooms.

WALLFLOWER
Cheiranthus

Light: full sun

Plant type: tender perennial grown as annual

Height: 6 to 24 inches

Soil and Moisture: well-drained, moist, fertile

Interest: flowers, fragrance

Care: easy

◀ Cheiranthus cheiri 'Bowles' Mauve'

Wallflowers are vigorous, bushy plants that bear abundant clusters of richly fragrant 1-inch flowers in a rainbow of colors including shades of yellow, orange, red, and purple. Dwarf varieties are perfect for rock gardens or filling in gaps of stone walls. Taller types are a must for informal borders and cottage gardens.

Growing and care:

Sow seed outdoors in spring or fall for bloom the following season. Early-flowering varieties can be started indoors in midwinter, hardened in a cold frame, and transplanted to the garden as soon as the soil can be worked in spring. Space plants about 1 foot apart. Pinch plants to encourage bushiness. Give extra water during dry periods. Wallflowers thrive in cool climates and do well in coastal and mountainous areas such as the Pacific Northwest.

Selected species and varieties:

C. cheiri [also listed as *Erysimum cheiri*] (English wallflower) has a low, erect habit; dwarf varieties grow to 6 to 9 inches, while tall varieties may reach 2 feet. Early-flowering strains often bloom their first year from seed if started early enough, but most varieties are treated as biennials; 'Bowles' Mauve' produces large clusters of deep pink flowers.

WALLFLOWER
Erysimum

Light: full sun

Plant type: biennial grown as annual

Height: 9 inches to 2 feet

Soil and Moisture: well-drained, light, dry

Interest: flowers, fragrance

Care: easy

◀ Erysimum x perofskianum

The sweet, spicy fragrance of wallflower is just as charming as the vivid flowers it comes from. From spring to early summer the plants are covered with open clusters of yellow or orange blossoms that perk up rock gardens, window boxes, or borders.

Growing and care:

In areas with mild winters, sow seed outdoors in fall; elsewhere, sow in early spring as soon as soil can be worked. Thin plants to stand 6 inches apart. Remove spent flowers regularly to encourage increased flowering. Plants often self-seed if old flowers are not removed. Grows well in dry, neutral soils.

Selected species and varieties:

E. x *perofskianum* (fairy wallflower) produces a rosette of narrow 3-inch leaves and erect 9- to 24-inch flower stems crowded with yellow, orange, or red-orange blossoms. Each flower is ½ inch long and is composed of four petals and four sepals. *E.* 'Blood Red' bears fragrant, magenta flowers; 'Cloth of Gold' has large, fragrant golden yellow blossoms; 'Eastern Queen' bears salmon-colored flowers.

YELLOW AGERATUM
Lonas

Light: full sun	
Plant type: annual	
Height: 10 to 18 inches	
Soil and Moisture: well-drained, light, moist	
Interest: flowers	
Care: easy	

◀ Lonas annua

This charming native of Italy and northwestern Africa has deep green, feathery leaves beneath showy clusters of yellow flowers that resemble miniature powder puffs. The everlasting blossoms appear all season long and are excellent for both fresh and dried arrangements. Yellow ageratum is a sure bet to add zip to sunny informal borders and cutting gardens.

Growing and care:
Start seed indoors 6 to 8 weeks prior to the last frost or sow directly in the garden when danger of frost has passed. Thin seedlings to 8 to 12 inches apart. Deadhead regularly to encourage flowering. Plants thrive in light, infertile soil and do well in seaside conditions. To use for winter arrangements, cut flowers when they reach full color, tie in bunches and hang them upside down in an airy room until dry.

Selected species and varieties:
L. annua (African daisy) is a vigorous grower with an open, rounded habit. It sports fine-textured, deeply divided leaves along erect, branched stems, and 1- to 2-inch clusters of tiny yellow flowers.

ZINNIA
Zinnia

Light: full sun	
Plant type: annual	
Height: 8 inches to 3 feet	
Soil and Moisture: well-drained, moist, fertile	
Interest: flowers	
Care: easy	

◀ Zinnia angustifolia

Zinnias brighten the border with vividly colored pompom or daisylike blooms composed of petal-like ray flowers surrounding a center of yellow or green. Colors range from riotous yellows, oranges, and reds to shades of pastel pink, rose, salmon, cream, maroon, and purple. Zinnias bloom from summer through frost and are best planted in large groups, used as edgings, or set in a mixed border. Low, spreading types are at home in window boxes and patio planters, while taller forms are excellent for fresh summer arrangements.

Growing and care:
Zinnias are among the easiest annuals to grow. Start seed indoors 6 weeks prior to the last frost, or sow directly outdoors after all danger of frost has passed. Keep soil moist but do not overwater young plants. Space seedlings 6 to 12 inches apart and pinch young plants to encourage bushiness. Remove spent blooms to keep plants attractive and to encourage flowering. Zinnias thrive in hot weather but benefit from regular watering.

Selected species and varieties:
Z. angustifolia (narrowleaf zinnia) has a compact, spreading habit, growing from 8 to 16 inches in height with narrow, pointed leaves and 1-inch-wide single orange flowers from summer to fall; 'White Star' bears abundant 2-inch flowers with snow white petals around orange-yellow centers.

AFRICAN DAISY
Osteospermum

Light: full sun

Plant type: perennial

Hardiness: Zones 9-10

Height: 6 to 12 inches

Soil and Moisture: well-drained, fertile, moist to dry

Interest: flowers

Care: moderate

◀ Osteospermum fruticosum

African daisy is a truly stunning flowering perennial for warm zones. The eye-catching flowers have round centers surrounded by long, graceful, nearly translucent white to pinkish petals. It has a trailing habit and spreads rapidly to create a dense mat. Flowers bloom most heavily in late winter and early spring, and intermittently throughout the rest of the year. It makes a lovely show in containers or behind stone walls, where it can spill over in graceful cascades.

Growing and care:
Sow seed directly in the garden in early spring or late fall. Plant thickly, for germination of seed is erratic. Because the stems root as they grow along the ground, African daisy spreads easily and quickly over large areas. It thrives in full sun and, once established, tolerates drought. Cut back old plants occasionally to encourage branching and to prevent stems from becoming straggly. Water early in the day so leaves can dry off. Cut back stems after flowering.

Selected species and varieties:
O. fruticosum grows 6 to 12 inches tall and 3 feet wide with oval, 1- to 2-inch-long leaves and 2-inch-wide flowers with lavender petals around a purple center; 'African Queen' bears very attractive deep purple flowers; 'Hybrid White' is more upright in habit with enchanting pure white flowers.

BABY'S-BREATH
Gypsophila

Light: full sun

Plant type: perennial

Hardiness: Zones 4-9

Height: 3 to 4 feet

Soil and Moisture: well-drained, slightly alkaline, moist

Interest: flowers, foliage

Care: easy

◀ Gypsophila repens 'Rosea'

Perennial baby's-breath resembles the annual types with the bonus that it comes back to the garden year after year. Baby's-breath bears airy clouds of tiny, single or multipetaled flowers on open-branched stems above fine-textured foliage. The plants are well suited for the middle of the border and are a must for the cutting garden. Dwarf forms make charming additions to rock gardens, especially when allowed to cascade over stone walls.

Growing and care:
Start seed indoors in peat pots 8 to 10 weeks before the last frost. Space dwarf forms 1 to 1½ feet apart and larger types 3 feet apart. Established plants are difficult to divide or transplant. Keep soil evenly moist while plants are actively growing. Use wire frames to support larger plants.

Selected species and varieties:
G. paniculata (perennial baby's-breath) has airy clusters of white flowers on stems to 4 feet tall; 'Bristol Fairy' has double white flowers; 'Perfecta' is similar to 'Bristol Fairy', with larger flowers; 'Pink Fairy' has pink double flowers on 1½-foot stems. *G. repens* (creeping baby's-breath) is a low-growing dwarf type with trailing stems 6 to 8 inches long; 'Rosea' has pale pink flowers.

BALSAMROOT
Balsamorhiza

Light: full sun

Plant type: perennial

Hardiness: Zones 4-10

Height: 2 to 2½ feet

Soil and Moisture: sandy, moderately dry

Interest: flowers

Care: easy

◀ Balsamorhiza sagittata

Aperennial native to the mountain grasslands and prairies of the American West, balsamroot has all the jaunty brightness of sunflowers on shorter, more compact stems. The vivid yellow blossoms appear in spring to early summer and look even more brilliant against the plant's broad, dark green leaves. Balsamroot is a novel and beautiful addition to borders or specialty gardens, or naturalized in upland wildflower meadows.

Growing and care:
Balsamroot thrives in full sun and deep, well-drained, sandy soil. The plants appreciate regular soakings and fertilizing but also do well if left on their own. Propagate from seed sown in fall where you want the plants to grow. Balsamroot generally requires 2 years of growth to reach flowering size. The plants produce a very long, woody taproot and transplanting should be avoided.

Selected species and varieties:
B. sagittata (balsamroot, Oregon sunflower) has a low clump of arrow- or heart-shaped, dark green leaves covered with silvery hairs and measuring up to 6 inches wide and 12 inches long; they may be undivided or deeply divided into fernlike segments; flower stems up to 32 inches tall bear a single 2½- to 4-inch flower with deep yellow petals surrounding a golden yellow center.

BASKET-OF-GOLD
Aurinia

Light: full sun

Plant type: perennial

Hardiness: Zones 3-10

Height: 6 to 12 inches

Soil and Moisture: well-drained, dry

Interest: flowers

Care: easy

◀ Aurinia saxatilis

Basket-of-gold bears masses of tiny golden yellow flowers in early to midspring atop thick, compact mats of silvery gray foliage. The plants are excellent for rock gardens and borders, or when allowed to cascade over rocks and walls. The flowers of this easy-to-grow plant look like golden versions of their close relative sweet alyssum *(Lobularia maritima),* but basket-of-gold has cleft leaves that are slightly long.

Growing and care:
Basket-of-gold has been a popular plant for generations, in part because it thrives in a wide variety of conditions. It spreads quickly and reliably produces a profusion of flowers every spring. After the flowers have faded, shear the top of the plant back by one-third to encourage rebloom. Old, woody plants bloom less abundantly and should be replaced. Propagate by division in early spring or sow seed (except double-flowered varieties) in summer for bloom the following year. Do not cover seed, as light is needed for germination. Space plants 9 to 12 inches apart.

Selected species and varieties:
A. saxatilis (also listed as *Alyssum saxatile*) has mounds of 10-inch stems bearing 3-inch lance-shaped leaves covered with smooth, silvery hairs and dense clusters of yellow flowers; 'Citrina' has pale yellow flowers; 'Plena' has deep yellow double flowers; Zones 3-7.

BLACKFOOT DAISY
Melampodium

Light: full sun

Plant type: perennial

Hardiness: Zones 4-9

Height: 6 to 12 inches

Soil and Moisture: well-drained, sandy, dry

Interest: flowers

Care: easy

◀ Melampodium leucanthum

Blackfoot daisy is an easy-to-grow, low-maintenance plant that is as beautiful as it is tough. The plant is native to the dry desert slopes, mesas, and high plains of the Southwest, where it has developed extreme tolerance to drought. Blackfoot daisy's deep taproot efficiently gleans moisture from the soil but also makes it difficult to transplant once established. This low-growing evergreen perennial naturally forms neat mounds that require no shaping, making it a good selection for rock gardens. It can also be massed on a sunny, sandy bank for attractive erosion control.

Growing and care:
Sow seed directly in the garden once soil has warmed. Thin plants to stand 12 to 16 inches apart. Keep soil moist until seedlings are about 4 inches tall. Fertilizing is not needed. Cut back plants in fall. Blackfoot daisy naturalizes quickly and often self-seeds.

Selected species and varieties:
M. leucanthum bears abundant solitary 1-inch white daisylike flowers with yellow centers borne on slender stalks throughout spring and summer. Gray-green leaves form a neat evergreen mound 6 to 12 inches tall and up to 16 inches wide.

BLANKET FLOWER
Gaillardia

Light: full sun

Plant type: perennial

Hardiness: Zones 3-8

Height: 1 to 3 feet

Soil and Moisture: well-drained, moist to dry

Interest: flowers

Care: easy

◀ Gaillardia x grandiflora 'Goblin'

Blanket flower is an easy-to-grow perennial with cheerful, very brightly colored, daisylike flowers from early summer to frost. The flowers that bloom provide vivid color to borders, rock gardens, and wildflower meadows. Blanket flower also makes an excellent cut flower.

Growing and care:
Start seed indoors 6 to 8 weeks before the last frost. Do not cover, as seed needs light to germinate. Transplant to the garden when soil has warmed. Space plants 1½ feet apart. Blanket flower tolerates hot, dry locations, poor soil, and seaside conditions, but puts on a more vibrant show when grown in bright sun. The plants are susceptible to root rot in wet soils and very well-drained conditions are required for best growth.

Selected species and varieties:
G. x grandiflora has 3-inch daisylike yellow ray flowers surrounding a yellow or purplish red central disk on stems up to 3 feet tall with large, hairy, gray-green leaves; 'Goblin' bears bright red flowers edged with yellow on stems to 1 foot; 'Monarch Strain' produces flowers in varying vivid combinations of red and yellow on 2½-foot stems.

BOLTONIA
Boltonia

Light: full sun

Plant type: perennial

Hardiness: Zones 4-8

Height: 3 to 5 feet

Soil and Moisture: well-drained, dry to moist

Interest: flowers

Care: easy

◀ Boltonia asteroides var. latisquama

Clouds of asterlike flowers atop the tall, branching stems of boltonia add an airy accent to island beds, borders, and meadows from midsummer through early fall. Boltonia's gray-green, willowlike, 5-inch leaves contrast nicely with the abundant white, pink, or lavender flowers. The plants are native to the eastern and midwestern United States, where they grow in gravelly, sandy soil along roadsides, stream banks, and waste places.

Growing and care:
Plant seed directly in the garden in spring when soil is cool. Space taller varieties 3 to 5 feet apart, and smaller varieties 1 to 2 feet apart. Propagate species by seed or division, and cultivars by division in early spring or late fall. Pinch tops in late spring to encourage bushy, compact growth. The tallest varieties may need staking. Plants often self-seed and can become invasive if not controlled.

Selected species and varieties:
B. asteroides (white boltonia) grows 3 to 5 feet tall with 1-inch daisylike flowers; var. *latisquama* (violet boltonia) has 1½-inch purple to pink flowers; 'Nana' bears white flowers on 1- to 2-foot stems; 'Pink Beauty' has pale pink blossoms in late summer on 4- to 5-foot stems, and delicate, dusky green, mildew-resistant foliage.

CALIFORNIA FUCHSIA
Zauschneria

Light: full sun

Plant type: perennial

Hardiness: Zones 9-10

Height: 6 inches to 2 feet

Soil and Moisture: well-drained, moist to dry

Interest: flowers, foliage

Care: easy

◀ Zauschneria californica

California fuchsias are shrubby perennials with lance-shaped dull green leaves and 2- to 3-inch-long tubular flowers of intense scarlet. They spread rapidly by rhizomes to form broad mats that make fine ground covers. The plants can be grown in borders or specialty gardens, where the brilliant flowers draw hummingbirds and butterflies from summer to fall.

Growing and care:
Sow seed directly in the garden in spring after soil warms. Do not cover seed, as light is necessary for germination. Thin seedlings to stand 14 to 18 inches apart. Pinch young plants to induce branching. California fuchsia prefers well-drained, dry, slightly alkaline soil. Propagate by seed, fall cuttings, or root divisions in early spring.

Selected species and varieties:
Z. californica is a broad shrubby perennial with much-branched stems 6 to 24 inches in height and woolly gray-green foliage; trumpet-shaped, brilliant scarlet flowers 2½ inches long bloom from late summer through fall; ssp. *latifolia* [also called *Epilobium canum* ssp. *latifolium*] (hummingbird trumpet) is a compact shrubby plant up to 2 feet tall with trumpet-shaped scarlet flowers from early summer through fall.

CALIFORNIA TREE POPPY
Romneya

Light: full sun

Plant type: perennial

Hardiness: Zones 7-10

Height: 4 to 8 feet

Soil and Moisture: well-drained, dry

Interest: flowers, fragrance

Care: difficult

◀ Romneya coulteri

California tree poppies are large, shrubby perennials that bear extraordinarily beautiful flowers in summer to early fall. The fragrant blossoms are 3 to 6 inches in diameter with a mounded center of pincushion stamens surrounded by wide, paper-thin, delicately ruffled white petals. Though short lived, the flowers are striking in fresh floral arrangements. To keep cut flowers fresh longer, sear the ends of the stems with a flame to seal in their milky sap.

Growing and care:
California poppies grow well only in regions with hot, dry summers followed by cool, moist winters. They are very difficult to grow in areas with pronounced humidity. Space California tree poppies 3 to 4 feet apart in sites where their wide-spreading, invasive roots will not present a problem. They grow best in Zones 8 and 9 but will survive in Zone 7 given a heavy winter mulch. Cut stems back to 6 inches in fall.

Selected species and varieties:
R. coulteri bears icy white flowers with nearly translucent, ruffled petals throughout summer on branching 8-foot stems with gray-green leaves in clumps 3 feet wide.

CANDYTUFT
Iberis

Light: full sun

Plant type: perennial

Hardiness: Zones 4-8

Height: 6 to 12 inches

Soil and Moisture: well-drained, fertile, moist

Interest: flowers, foliage

Care: easy

◀ Iberis sempervirens 'Snow Mantle'

The glossy, dark green leaves of candytuft provide a perfect background for the clusters of pure white flowers that cover the plant in spring. Candytuft is very effective when planted in the front of the perennial border, as an edging along a walkway, or allowed to cascade over a stone wall or sprawl across a rock garden.

Growing and care:
Plant candytuft in well-worked soil that has been generously amended with compost or peat moss. Space plants 12 to 15 inches apart. Keep soil evenly moist for best flowering. After blossoms have faded cut plants back 2 to 3 inches to encourage rebloom. Mulch around plants to keep soil moist and roots cool.

Selected species and varieties:
I. sempervirens produces 1-foot-tall mounds of linear, 1-inch-long evergreen leaves on semiwoody stems, and dense clusters of very showy white flowers; 'Snowflake' grows 10 inches high with 2- to 3-inch flower clusters; 'Snow Mantle' is 8 inches high with a dense, compact habit and pure white flowers.

CHICKWEED
Cerastium

Light: full sun

Plant type: perennial

Hardiness: Zones 3-7

Height: 6 to 12 inches

Soil and Moisture: well-drained, sandy, dry

Interest: flowers, foliage

Care: easy

◀ Cerastium tomentosum

Snow-in-summer is a robust creeping plant with small, usually silvery green leaves that nearly disappear beneath the mounds of starry white flowers. These vigorous plants make excellent ground covers for dry, sandy sites and can be used as accents near steps and walkways or in rock gardens, although they may crowd other plants. Snow-in-summer is often used to control erosion on sunny slopes where its masses of frosty white flowers lend coolness to the hottest summer day.

Growing and care:
Propagate by division in fall. Space divided clumps 1 to 1½ feet apart. Snow-in-summer grows well without regular watering or fertilizing. Once established, these plants often naturalize, becoming self-sustaining members of the garden. Divide them regularly to control their spread.

Selected species and varieties:
C. alpinum (alpine chickweed) has tight clusters of small, white, late-spring flowers atop spreading 6-inch mounds of tiny, oval gray leaves. *C. arvense* (starry grasswort) produces 1-inch oval leaves beneath 1-foot clusters of star-shaped, white, spring flowers; 'Compactum' has a spreading habit and pure white flowers nestled in a mat of 2- to 3-inch foliage. *C. tomentosum* (snow-in-summer) has 6- to 9-inch prostrate stems bearing narrow, 1-inch, lance-shaped woolly whitish green leaves and small spring to summer flowers; Zones 4-7.

CONEFLOWER
Rudbeckia

Light: full sun

Plant type: perennial

Hardiness: Zones 4-9

Height: 1 to 7 feet

Soil and Moisture: well-drained, moist to dry

Interest: flowers, foliage

Care: easy

◀ Rudbeckia hirta 'Goldilocks'

Coneflowers are prolific bloomers from early summer to frost and are the backbone of many perennial gardens. These natives of North American grasslands and meadows have daisylike flower heads with intense yellow rays that contrast to their centers of deep brown. Coneflowers have large, hairy leaves and stiff stems. They are excellent in sunny borders, mixed with clumps of ornamental grasses, or naturalized in meadows.

Growing and care:
Space plants 1½ to 2 feet apart. *R. hirta* grows as an annual, biennial, or short-lived perennial, and should be propagated by seed. Its flowering season can be prolonged by sowing seed at biweekly intervals. Other species of coneflowers can be propagated by seed or division in early spring.

Selected species and varieties:
R. fulgida (orange coneflower, black-eyed Susan) is a 1- to 3-foot perennial that produces 3- to 5-inch yellow-orange flowers with dark, domed centers from early summer through fall. *R. hirta* (black-eyed Susan) is a 1- to 3-foot short-lived perennial with 2-inch petals surrounding conical centers in late summer; 'Gloriosa Daisy' is yellow with a mahogany center; 'Goldilocks' has brilliant yellow semidouble flowers.

COREOPSIS
Coreopsis

Light: full sun

Plant type: perennial

Hardiness: Zones 4-9

Height: 6 inches to 3 feet

Soil and Moisture: well-drained, fertile, moist

Interest: flowers, foliage

Care: easy

◀ Coreopsis grandiflora

Coreopsis is easy to grow and famous for its reliable displays of intense, sunny yellow flowers and dainty, dark green foliage. The plants bloom for many weeks in summer and are eye-catching additions to borders, rock gardens, or naturalistic plantings. Coreopsis is excellent for cutting.

Growing and care:

Sow seed indoors 6 to 8 weeks before the last frost. In areas with mild winters direct-sow in the garden in fall. Space plants 6 to 12 inches apart. Water during dry periods and fertilize lightly in spring. Excessive fertilizer or dry soil can inhibit flowering. Remove spent flowers to extend bloom time. Grow coreopsis where it is sheltered from winds. Divide plants after flowering in northern areas, and in fall in southern regions.

Selected species and varieties:

C. grandiflora has yellow or orange single, semidouble, and double flowers 1 to 1½ inches across, blooming from early to late summer on 1- to 2-foot stems. *C. lanceolata* (lance coreopsis) 'Goldfink' is a 10- to 12-inch-tall dwarf with yellow flowers 1½ to 2½ inches across that blooms prolifically from summer to fall. *C. verticillata* (threadleaf coreopsis) bears golden yellow flowers from late spring to late summer; 'Zagreb' is 1½ feet tall with bright yellow flowers; 'Moonbeam' grows to 2 feet tall with abundant lemon yellow flowers.

COYOTE MINT
Monardella

Light: full sun

Plant type: perennial

Hardiness: Zones 6-10

Height: 4 to 24 inches

Soil and Moisture: well-drained, dry

Interest: flowers, foliage, fragrance

Care: easy

◀ Monardella odoratissima

Coyote mints have round, ragged clusters of thin-petaled flowers that resemble more casual versions of bee balm. These informal plants have strong, flexible stems and aromatic, minty blue-green leaves. Coyote mints are often used in sunny, dry rock gardens, especially in the American Southwest, where they are native. Like those of their bee balm cousins, the blossoms of coyote mints are very attractive to butterflies and hummingbirds.

Growing and care:

Sow seed directly in the garden in spring after soil has warmed, or start indoors 6 to 8 weeks before the last frost. Space plants 10 to 12 inches apart. Water regularly until seedlings are a few inches high. Once established the plants are very drought tolerant and need supplemental water only during extended dry periods. Overwatering leads to weak growth and less aromatic foliage. Divide plants after they go dormant in fall.

Selected species and varieties:

M. macrantha (hummingbird mint, scarlet coyote mint) grows 4 to 12 inches tall with glossy green foliage and tubular bright red flowers in showy, round terminal clusters in summer; Zones 8-10. *M. odoratissima* (coyote mint, mountain mint) bears flowers ranging from nearly white to bright blue-purple in 2-inch clusters; the stems form large mats about 1 foot tall with fragrant leaves.

CRAMBE
Crambe

Light: full sun

Plant type: perennial

Hardiness: Zones 5-9

Height: 2 to 6 feet

Soil and Moisture: well-drained, fertile, slightly alkaline

Interest: flowers, foliage, fragrance

Care: moderate

◀ Crambe cordifolia

Crambe is a very large shrubby perennial with huge, billowy clouds of tiny white blossoms in late spring to early summer. In form these airy plants resemble baby's-breath but are much larger. Mingled among the fragrant gossamer flowers are masses of wrinkled gray-green leaves. Crambe is a good choice for the back of the border or as a filler in large specialty gardens. When grown in wildflower meadows the plants nicely complement daisies, asters, and boltonias.

Growing and care:
Crambe does not transplant well and seed should be sown directly in the garden in early spring or in fall soon after ripening. Thin plants to stand 2 to 3 feet apart. Plants grown from seed usually require about 3 growing seasons to reach flowering size. Crambe is attractive to a number of insect pests and should receive regular sprayings of insecticidal soap. Stake plants if they seem floppy, and prune to ground level in fall.

Selected species and varieties:
C. cordifolia (colewort) produces broad leafy mounds up to 4 feet across crowned by an equally wide froth of icy white flowers on stalks to 6 feet tall. *C. maritima* (sea kale) produces 2-foot-wide mounds of attractive blue-green leaves with a powdery coating topped by a billow of tiny white flowers on stalks up to 3 feet tall.

DELPHINIUM
Delphinium

Light: full sun

Plant type: perennial

Hardiness: Zones 3-7

Height: 2 to 8 feet

Soil and Moisture: well-drained, fertile, moist

Interest: flowers

Care: moderate

◀ Delphinium 'Blue Fountains'

Delphiniums are stately, majestic plants that give any perennial border or specialty garden a touch of class. The plants bear enormous showy spikes packed with scores of 2-inch flowers on upright stalks above clumps of finely cut, lobed leaves. The various colors of the spurred flowers are stunning shades of royal blue, lavender, rose, and white. Many of the flowers also have a ruffled, contrastingly colored center called a bee.

Growing and care:
Start seed indoors 8 to 10 weeks before planting out or sow directly in the garden in early spring or fall. The plants do best in areas with cool summers and are grown as annuals where summers are hot. Space plants 1 to 2 feet apart in soil enriched with organic mater. Water and fertilize regularly throughout the growing season. Cut back flower stalks after flowering to encourage rebloom in late summer. Tall varieties should be staked.

Selected species and varieties:
D. x *belladonna* (belladonna delphinium) produces porcelain blue or white flowers on delicate, branching 3- to 4-foot-tall stems. *D.* 'Blue Fountains' is a dwarf delphinium 2½ to 3 feet tall with flowers in enchanting shades of blue. *D. elatum* 'Pacific Hybrids' has spires of intensely colored blue, violet, lavender, pink, or white mostly double flowers on stalks 4 to 6 feet tall.

FALSE SUNFLOWER
Heliopsis

Light: full sun	
Plant type: perennial	
Hardiness: Zones 4-9	
Height: 3 to 5 feet	
Soil and Moisture: well-drained, fertile, moist	
Interest: flowers	
Care: easy	

◄ Heliopsis
helianthoides

False sunflower bears bright flowers in shades of yellow and gold, each blossom with single or double rows of petals surrounding prominent centers. The tall, strongly upright stems and perky flowers are good for adding colorful accents to the back of the border but are best when allowed to naturalize and spread in wildflower meadows. False sunflowers make excellent cut flowers.

Growing and care:

Start seed indoors 8 to 10 weeks before the last spring frost or sow directly in the garden in early spring or fall. Space plants 2 feet apart and stake taller forms. Water plants during extended dry periods. Divide clumps every 3 to 4 years in spring.

Selected species and varieties:

H. helianthoides var. *scabra* bears single, semidouble, or double flowers 2 to 3 inches across on plants 3 to 5 feet tall; 'Golden Plume' grows double yellow flowers; 'Incomparabilis', semidouble yellow flowers with dark centers; 'Karat', large single yellow flowers; 'Summer Sun', semidouble golden yellow flowers.

FIREWEED
Epilobium

Light: full sun	
Plant type: perennial	
Hardiness: Zones 2-9	
Height: 4 inches to 7 feet	
Soil and Moisture: well-drained, moist	
Interest: flowers	
Care: easy	

◄ Epilobium
angustifolium

Fireweeds are vigorous, strongly upright plants with strong, pliant stems, coarse medium green leaves, and bright conical spikes of lilac, ruby, pink, or white flowers in summer. The plants are easy to grow and are good choices for informal borders, clearings, meadows, open slopes, or the wet areas along streams, ponds, and marshes. Fireweeds are so vigorous that they can quickly colonize wide areas, a trait that should be considered before planting.

Growing and care:

Fireweed does not transplant well and seed should be sown directly in the garden in fall. Small seedlings can be transplanted for a few weeks following germination. Space plants 1 to 2 feet apart. Fireweed grows best where summers are cool.

Selected species and varieties:

E. angustifolium (fireweed, willow herb) produces clumps of reddish stems 3 to 7 feet tall with elongated, willowlike leaves 3 to 8 inches long. Spikes of lilac-purple, rose, or occasionally white flowers appear atop the stems throughout summer over much of Canada and the United States. *E. latifolium* (dwarf fireweed), found from Alaska south through the mountain states, grows 4 to 16 inches tall with clusters of large magenta-pink flowers and bluish green leaves.

FLAX LILY
Phormium

Light: full sun	
Plant type: perennial	
Hardiness: Zones 9-10	
Height: 7 to 15 feet	
Soil and Moisture: well-drained, moist	
Interest: flowers, foliage	
Care: easy	

◀ Phormium tenax

Flax lily bears dramatic fans of very long spear-shaped evergreen leaves, sometimes split at their ends or edged with red. The sharp appearance of the leaves coupled with their vibrant color makes the plant perfect for adding a bold statement to the landscape. In summer an impressively tall stem emerges from the foliage, bearing dull red 2-inch flowers. Use flax lily like yucca—as a specimen, at the back of informal borders, or as a screen.

Growing and care:

Flax lily thrives in evenly moist soil enriched with rotted manure or compost. Space plants from 1 foot apart for small types to 3 feet apart for large varieties. Provide extra water during hot, dry periods. Flax lily can be propagated from seed, but division in spring is preferred. Plants tolerate seaside conditions and pollution.

Selected species and varieties:

P. tenax (New Zealand flax) has large swordlike leathery leaves 3 to 10 feet tall with flower stalks to 10 feet; 'Atropurpureum' produces large leaves of rich purple; 'Bronze' has long, deep red-brown leaves; 'Maori Sunrise' bears large bronze leaves striped with pink and cream; 'Tiny Tim' is a semidwarf cultivar with yellow-striped bronze leaves; 'Variegatum' has creamy white striping on long green leaves.

GAURA
Gaura

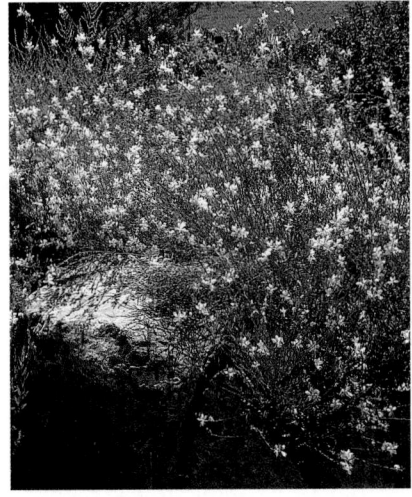

Light: full sun	
Plant type: perennial	
Hardiness: Zones 5-9	
Height: 2 to 5 feet	
Soil and Moisture: well-drained, sandy, medium to dry	
Interest: flowers	
Care: easy	

◀ Gaura lindheimeri

Gauras were once rarely seen in gardens but in recent years have become very popular. The plants produce abundant pale pink tubular flowers from summer to fall above neat, airy mounds of lance-shaped leaves. The unique blossoms, which have four spatula-shaped white petals and long red stamens, are beautiful when viewed close up. In addition to their beauty gauras are also tough plants well suited for use in coastal gardens, natural meadows, or informal borders.

Growing and care:

Sow seed indoors in late winter for planting out after danger of frost has passed, or direct-sow in the garden in spring when soil is still cool. Space plants 2 to 4 feet apart. Fertilize lightly and provide extra water only during hot, dry periods to prevent plants from going dormant before flowering. Seedlings will grow to flowering-size plants the first season. Gaura can also be propagated from softwood cuttings in summer or by dividing plants in fall.

Selected species and varieties:

G. lindheimeri (white gaura) has loose panicles of white tubular flowers touched with pale pink and fading to coral, in late summer to fall, on lanky 2- to 5-foot stems with lance-shaped 3½-inch leaves and spreading clumps of carrotlike taproots; 'Corre's Gold' has white flowers on 2-foot stems and green leaves edged with gold; 'Siskiyou Pink' has maroon buds and pink blossoms.

GLOBE MALLOW
Sphaeralcea

Light: full sun

Plant type: perennial

Hardiness: Zones 3-10

Height: 2 to 3 feet

Soil and Moisture: well-drained, sandy, dry

Interest: flowers

Care: easy

◄ Sphaeralcea coccinea

Globe mallows are easy-to-grow, drought-resistant perennials that thrive in regions with dry, sandy soils and hot summers. They bear brightly colored cupped flowers in shades of apricot, orange, red, and violet that resemble hollyhocks. Globe mallows are an excellent choice for sunny, dry rock gardens or informal borders.

Growing and care:

Globe mallows do not transplant well and seed should be planted directly in the garden in fall as soon as seed is ripe. Thin plants to stand 1½ to 2 feet apart. Once established do not disturb. Globe mallows are very drought tolerant but, when supplied with even moisture, grow quite large with more abundant flowers. Allow plants to self-seed for years of attractive blooms.

Selected species and varieties:

S. ambigua (desert mallow) has 3-foot stems bearing wandlike clusters of apricot-orange flowers up to 2 inches across in spring; Zones 6-10. *S. coccinea* (scarlet globe mallow) grows to 3 feet tall with orange-pink flowers surrounded by red bracts in spring, summer, or fall, and hairy gray-green leaves. *S. munroana* (Munro's globe mallow) produces 2- to 3-foot-tall spikes of numerous bright pink to deep apricot flowers and gray-green foliage. *S. parvifolia* is 2 to 3 feet tall with clusters of orange-red flowers and whitish gray leaves from spring to summer.

GLOBE THISTLE
Echinops

Light: full sun

Plant type: perennial

Hardiness: Zones 3-8

Height: 6 inches to 8 feet

Soil and Moisture: well-drained, moist to dry

Interest: flowers, foliage

Care: easy

◄ Echinops ritro 'Veitch's Blue'

Globe thistles have bold, slightly wild-looking foliage that contrasts nicely to the refined look of their ornate, spherical, summer-blooming flowers. The stiff, upright stalks are lined with thick, hairy, deeply lobed leaves bearing attractive if intimidating metallic blue spines at their tips, and topped with soft blue to white flowers that bloom for 2 months. Globe thistles are excellent for attracting butterflies and honeybees to the garden, and make beautiful and unusual additions to dried flower arrangements. Use globe thistle in borders as an informal accent or as a background to rock gardens.

Growing and care:

Globe thistles thrive in heat and drought, but in hot regions they produce more intensely colored flowers when given some afternoon shade. Space plants 1½ to 2 feet apart. Propagate by division in early spring. Globe thistle can be propagated from seed but plants produced in this way are often inferior to their parents in form and flower color. Wear leather gloves when handling these plants to protect hands from the spiny leaves.

Selected species and varieties:

E. ritro (small globe thistle) has blue-violet or deep blue flowers, rarely white, in 2-inch spheres on 2- to 5-foot white, woolly stems, and 8-inch glossy, dark green leaves with white undersides; 'Veitch's Blue' has lapis blue flowers on strong 3- to 4-foot stems.

GOAT'S RUE
Tephrosia

Light: full sun	
Plant type: perennial	
Hardiness: Zones 5-10	
Height: 1 to 2 feet	
Soil and Moisture: well-drained, sandy, dry	
Interest: flowers, foliage	
Care: easy to moderate	

◀ Tephrosia virginiana

Goat's rue is a perennial wildflower with complex pealike blossoms in vivid, contrasting bicolors of red and white or yellow and purple. The plants are easy to grow and quite tolerant of dry, hot conditions. When goat's rue is not in flower the delicate, finely cut compound leaves and 1- to 2-inch silky seedpods give the plants a soft textured appearance. Goat's rue is excellent for specialty gardens, wildflower meadows, or informal borders. The seeds attract ground birds such as quail and grouse.

Growing and care:
Plant goat's rue seed directly in the garden in fall or spring after the soil has warmed. Thin plants to stand 1 foot apart. Water regularly until seedlings are about 4 inches tall. For best growth inoculate soil with the appropriate nitrogen-fixing bacteria. Plants can be allowed to self-sow or can be divided in fall.

Selected species and varieties:
T. virginiana grows 1 to 2 feet tall with compact clusters of ¾-inch flowers composed of yellowish to white upper petals and purple to pinkish red lower petals from late spring to early summer. The foliage forms a mound of attractive, silvery, pinnately compound leaves with eight to 15 pairs of small leaflets covered with silky white hairs. In late summer to fall small, silky seedpods decorate the plant.

GOLDEN ASTER
Chrysopsis

Light: full sun	
Plant type: perennial	
Hardiness: Zones 4-10	
Height: 6 inches to 5 feet	
Soil and Moisture: well-drained, sandy, medium to dry	
Interest: flowers	
Care: easy	

◀ Chrysopsis mariana

The perennial golden asters are tough, vigorous plants that punctuate the landscape with long-lasting clusters of bright, daisylike blossoms. They are especially useful at the back of informal borders or naturalized in wet areas along ponds and streams or on dry hillsides and fields. They do best if planted with care and then left to their own devices.

Growing and care:
Grass-leaved and golden aster are easy to grow on sunny, dry sites but may do poorly in rich, fertile soil. Propagate by seed sown in fall or early spring while soil is cool. Thin plants to stand 2 to 3 feet apart. Plants may be divided every 3 to 4 years in spring.

Selected species and varieties:
C. graminifolia [also called *Pityopsis graminifolia*] (grass-leaved golden aster) has 1-foot grasslike leaves and clusters of bright yellow flowers on 2½-foot stems, and makes a good evergreen ground cover; Zones 5-10. *C. mariana* (Maryland golden aster) grows 1½ to 2½ feet tall with showy clusters of flowers on sturdy stems; Zones 4-9. *C. villosa* can grow from as little as 6 inches to as much as 5 feet in height, with flowers near the tips of stems that may be upright or trailing; Zones 4-9.

HENS AND CHICKS
Echeveria

Light: full sun	
Plant type: perennial	
Hardiness: Zones 9-10	
Height: 3 inches to 3 feet	
Soil and Moisture: well-drained, dry	
Interest: flowers, foliage	
Care: easy	

◄ Echeveria agavoides

Hens and chicks are easy-to-grow perennials that provide a wonderfully interesting and attractive accent to rock gardens. The plants are known for their colorful, succulent leaves that grow in compact rosettes. Bell-shaped, nodding flowers develop on slender stems in summer that rise well above the foliage. Hens and chicks thrive in warm, hot climates, where they spread reliably with very little care.

Growing and care:
Plant hens and chicks in dry, sandy soil. Water regularly for a few weeks until the plants have become established. Hens and chicks thrive in warm locations and are quite tolerant of drought and coastal conditions. Propagate from offsets anytime by cutting the "chick" from the mother plant and setting it directly in the garden, or potting it in a container to grow as a houseplant.

Selected species and varieties:
E. agavoides has 6- to 8-inch rosettes of bright green leaves with reddish margins, topped in summer by red and yellow flowers. *E. crenulata* bears loose rosettes of pale green leaves with wavy margins growing up to 1 foot long and covered with white powder, and red to orange flowers on stems up to 3 feet tall. *E.* x *imbricata* has 4- to 6-inch rosettes of gray-green leaves and delicate stems of orange, red, and yellow flowers, and develops many offsets around the base.

HOLLYHOCK
Alcea

Light: full sun	
Plant type: perennial or biennial	
Hardiness: Zones 2-9	
Height: 2 to 9 feet	
Soil and Moisture: well-drained, fertile	
Interest: flowers	
Care: moderate	

◄ Alcea rosea

The eye-catching, bell-shaped flowers of hollyhock are borne on sturdy, erect, wandlike stems. The lower flowers open first, and new blossoms appear from midsummer to early fall, with approximately 1½ to 2 feet of the stem covered with blooms throughout the season. This old-fashioned favorite provides both height and a long season of color for the back of a mixed border. It is also a good choice for growing along a fence or wall. While technically a biennial, hollyhock will last for several years under favorable conditions in cooler areas.

Growing and care:
Plant seed indoors in winter for spring transplanting. Some varieties will bloom their first summer. Seed sown outdoors in late summer will bloom the following year. Space plants 1 to 1½ feet apart in neutral to slightly alkaline soil. In windy locations they may require staking. When blossoms fade, remove the entire flower stalk to encourage the plant to behave as a perennial. Once established, hollyhocks will self-sow.

Selected species and varieties:
A. rosea has 5- to 9-foot-tall stems bearing 2- to 4-inch single or double flowers in colors that include white, pink, red, and yellow above a clump of hairy, coarse leaves 6 to 8 inches long; 'Chater's Double' grows 6 to 8 feet tall, producing peony-shaped flowers in shades of white, scarlet, pink, and yellow from early to midsummer.

KNAUTIA
Knautia

Light: full sun

Plant type: perennial

Hardiness: Zones 6-10

Height: 2 to 4 feet

Soil and Moisture: well-drained, sandy, dry to moist

Interest: flowers

Care: easy

◀ Knautia macedonica

Knautias are less common than their relatives the pincushion flowers, but are just as attractive. The lilac or deep red blossoms accented with white pinlike stamens are neatly arranged in rounded, dome-shaped clusters that appear from late spring to fall. The informal flowers are held on long, wiry stems and seem to float in the air. Knautias are good as fillers at the backs of borders, or for interplanting with ornamental grasses in naturalized gardens.

Growing and care:

Knautia arvensis performs best in slightly alkaline, gravelly soil, while *K. macedonica* prefers sandy loams. Mulch plants in Zones 6 and 7 in fall. Propagate knautias by seed in spring, or by division or transplanting of self-sown seedlings in fall.

Selected species and varieties:

K. arvensis (blue-buttons, field scabious) has 2- to 4-foot stems with pairs of narrowly oval, highly dissected leaves and nearly globular 1-inch lilac or white flowers with pink anthers from midsummer to frost. *K. macedonica* [also listed as *Scabiosa macedonica* or *Scabiosa rumelica*] grows 1½ to 2½ feet tall with slender, curved stems, lyre-shaped pale green leaves, and 1¼-inch rounded, dark purple, red, or maroon summer flowers. *K. tatarica* is a biennial that grows to 6 feet tall with 10-inch toothed, oblong-elliptic leaves and 1½-inch bright yellow flowers.

LAMB'S EARS
Stachys

Light: full sun

Plant type: perennial

Hardiness: Zones 4-8

Height: 8 to 18 inches

Soil and Moisture: well-drained, fertile, moist to dry

Interest: flowers, foliage

Care: easy

◀ Stachys byzantina 'Silver Carpet'

There are few plants that people love to touch more than lamb's ears. The plant produces thick mats of woolly, wonderfully velvety leaves that are so soft they were used as bandages during colonial times. In summer slender stems bearing loose spikes of pinkish flowers rise from the clumps of low-growing foliage. Lamb's ears make wonderful additions to specialty gardens, edges, or the front of borders.

Growing and care:

Plant lamb's ears in soil that is sandy and amended with organic matter. Sow seed indoors 8 to 10 weeks before last frost. Space plants 1 to 1½ feet apart. Remove dead leaves in late fall or early spring before new growth begins. Lamb's ears often self-sow, and volunteer seedlings can be transplanted easily in early spring. Divide established plants every 3 to 4 years.

Selected species and varieties:

S. byzantina (lamb's ears, woolly betony) forms dense 8-inch-high mats of soft, 6-inch-long velvety gray-green leaves and woolly, pinkish flower spikes up to 1½ feet tall in summer; 'Silver Carpet' is a flowerless cultivar with beautiful chrome-gray, furry leaves. *S. macrantha* (big betony) has stems to 1½ feet, tipped with whorls of purple summer flowers above heart-shaped, rippled green leaves.

LAVENDER COTTON
Santolina

Light: full sun

Plant type: perennial

Hardiness: Zones 6-8

Height: 1½ to 2 feet

Soil and Moisture: well-drained, medium to dry

Interest: flowers, foliage

Care: easy

◀ Santolina chamaecyparissus

Lavender cotton forms an attractive, spreading clump of pewter gray aromatic leaves, with slender stems topped by tiny yellow flowers that resemble miniature buttons. Lavender cotton is a hardworking, tough plant that not only thrives in dry, hot locations but even grows well near the ocean, where it is daily doused with salt spray. The foliage makes an attractive edging for a bed or walkway, or can be used as an accent in rock gardens. It also makes a beautiful, low hedge around herb or kitchen gardens.

Growing and care:
Space plants 1½ to 2 feet apart. Prune after flowering to promote dense growth, or shear anytime for a formal, low hedge. Lavender cotton prefers dry soils of low fertility and becomes unattractive and straggly in moist, fertile soils. Avoid excess moisture, especially in winter. Propagate from seed or from stem cuttings taken in early summer.

Selected species and varieties:
S. chamaecyparissus produces cushionlike mounds of evergreen foliage up to 2 feet tall with equal or greater spread. Leaves are silvery gray-green, ½ to 1½ inches long. In summer yellow flowers are held above the leaves. *S. virens* has green, tooth-edged leaves in dense 1½-foot clumps bearing solitary yellow flowers in summer.

LEOPARD'S-BANE
Doronicum

Light: full sun

Plant type: perennial

Hardiness: Zones 4-8

Height: 1 to 2 feet

Soil and Moisture: well-drained, fertile, moist

Interest: flowers, foliage

Care: moderate

◀ Doronicum cordatum

Leopard's-bane is a sophisticated spring-blooming perennial, native to the steppes of Asia, with clear yellow, daisylike flowers and dark green heart-shaped leaves. These short-lived perennials grow best in cool, evenly moist soils and are bright additions to borders and fresh floral arrangements.

Growing and care:
Start seed indoors 8 to 10 weeks before planting out in spring. Do not cover, as seed needs light to germinate. Space plants 1 to 2 feet apart. In areas with cool summers plant in full sun. In regions with warmer summers provide plants with partial shade. Foliage dies back and plants go dormant after flowers bloom in spring. Mulch to keep roots and soil cool. Propagate from seed or by division every 2 to 3 years.

Selected species and varieties:
D. cordatum produces lemon yellow flowers 2 to 3 inches across on 1- to 2-foot stems above mounds of deep green leaves; 'Miss Mason' has a compact, mounding habit with long-lasting foliage; 'Spring Beauty' bears double-petaled yellow flowers.

MACLEAYA
Macleaya

Light: full sun

Plant type: perennial

Hardiness: Zones 3-8

Height: 6 to 10 feet

Soil and Moisture: well-drained, moist, fertile

Interest: flowers, foliage

Care: easy

◀ Macleaya cordata

Macleaya is a very large perennial with massive, irregularly rounded clumps of wavy, deeply lobed leaves. The small pink or white flowers are displayed in misty sprays atop very tall, upright stems in summer. The plants make a wonderful substitute for shrubs, and can be used at the back of a border, as a temporary screen, or beneath eaves where falling winter ice would damage woody shrubs.

Growing and care:
Macleaya grows best in moist soil well amended with rotted manure or compost. Plant volunteer seedlings, divisions, or container-grown plants in the garden in spring after soil has warmed, spacing plants 3 to 4 feet apart. Provide extra water during dry periods. If soil dries out the plants may go dormant earlier than normal. Propagate by division in spring, or by transplanting plantlets that develop along the roots.

Selected species and varieties:
M. cordata (plume poppy) bears creamy or pink ½-inch flowers on 6- to 10-foot-tall stems above 8- to 10-inch-wide, wavy-edged gray-green leaves. The plant is very vigorous and can spread rapidly.

MILKWEED
Asclepias

Light: full sun

Plant type: perennial

Hardiness: Zones 3-9

Height: 1 to 3 feet

Soil and Moisture: well-drained, sandy, moist to dry

Interest: flowers

Care: easy

◀ Asclepias tuberosa

In summer, milkweed's thick, stiff stems lined with willowy deep green leaves are tipped with broad, domed clusters of tiny nectar-rich flowers attractive to bees and butterflies. The flowers are long lasting in arrangements. The boat-shaped pods produced by some species burst open in fall to release tiny seeds that float through the air on downy tufts of silky hair. Milkweed's stems and leaves are thought to be poisonous to animals. The dried roots have been used in herbal medicines.

Growing and care:
Propagate milkweeds from seed or root cuttings in spring or fall, spacing plants 1 foot apart. Because of their long taproots, milkweeds are not easily propagated by division and should not be transplanted once established. Mature plants often self-sow. For long-lasting arrangements of milkweed cut for fresh use, sear the stems. To dry pods, cut before the seeds are released and hang until dry.

Selected species and varieties:
A. tuberosa (butterfly weed) has deep orange flower clusters throughout summer on thick stems filled with milky sap and lined with narrow, 4-inch-long leaves. *A. syriaca* (common milkweed) bears round clusters of richly fragrant, pinkish maroon flowers and interesting greenish seedpods that turn silvery brown when dried.

653

MULLEIN
Verbascum

Light: full sun

Plant type: biennial, perennial

Hardiness: Zones 4-9

Height: 3 to 6 feet

Soil and Moisture: well-drained, dry

Interest: flowers, foliage

Care: easy

◀ Verbascum chaixii 'Album'

Mulleins are sturdy, stately plants with rosettes of coarse, sometimes velvety leaves and tall, sturdy spikes of beautiful, long-lasting summer flowers. These versatile plants are easy to grow and add a strong vertical element to the rear of a border, specialty gardens, or when naturalized in wildflower meadows.

Growing and care:
Start seed indoors 6 to 8 weeks before last frost or direct-sow in the garden in early spring when soil is cool. Space mulleins 1 to 2 feet apart. Plants tolerate and even thrive in dry conditions. Do not disturb established plantings. Cut back flower stalks in late summer or early fall.

Selected species and varieties:
V. bombyciferum (silver mullein), a biennial, bears attractive rosettes of oval leaves covered with silvery, silky hairs and 4- to 6-foot spikes of sulfur yellow flowers in summer; Zones 5-9. *V. chaixii* (Chaix mullein) produces ½- to 1-inch-wide yellow flowers with fuzzy purple stamens creating a prominent eye; 'Album' has white flowers and gray foliage. *V.* x 'Cotswold Queen' grows to 4 feet tall and 1 to 2 feet wide with apricot flowers; 'Pink Domino' grows 3 to 4 feet tall with deep pink flowers.

PHLOX
Phlox

Light: full sun

Plant type: perennial

Hardiness: Zones 3-9

Height: ½ to 4 feet

Soil and Moisture: well-drained, moist

Interest: flowers, foliage, fragrance

Care: moderate

◀ Phlox paniculata 'Starfire'

Phlox produces clusters of dainty, brightly colored five-petaled flowers in spring, summer, or fall. The flowers often sport a conspicuous eye that adds to their attractiveness. Species of phlox vary widely in their heights, habits, uses, and cultural requirements but they all produce exquisite flowers.

Growing and care:
Plant low-growing phlox 1 to 1½ feet apart, tall species 2 feet apart. Phlox prefers full sun with ample moisture and regular fertilization. Allow space between plants for good air circulation to discourage mildew. Set phlox in a sheltered location away from strong breezes. Promote dense growth and prolong the flowering season by cutting plants back after flowering. Propagate by division or from cuttings.

Selected species and varieties:
P. maculata (wild sweet William) grows to 3 feet with fragrant, conical, summer to fall flower clusters; 'Alpha' has rosy pink flowers with darker centers. *P. paniculata* (garden phlox) has 4-foot stems tipped with very fragrant flower clusters to 8 inches wide in summer and fall; 'David' is a mildew-resistant selection that bears huge white flower clusters on 3- to 4-foot stems; 'Starfire' has large clusters of brilliant cherry red flowers in late summer; Zones 3-8.

PINCUSHION FLOWER
Scabiosa

Light: full sun	
Plant type: perennial	
Hardiness: Zones 4-9	
Height: 1½ to 2 feet	
Soil and Moisture: well-drained, fertile, moist	
Interest: flowers	
Care: easy	

◀ Scabiosa caucasica 'Clive Greaves'

Pincushion flowers are some of the workhorses of the garden, providing beautiful, long-lasting summertime flowers with very little care. The plants produce abundant lilac, blue-violet, or white blooms up to 3 inches across with prominent stamens resembling a dome of pinheads surrounded by a ruffle of petals. Pincushion flower is excellent for the middle of the border or for cutting gardens. The blossoms make stunning fresh arrangements.

Growing and care:
Start seed indoors 8 to 10 weeks before last frost or direct-sow in the garden in early spring. Space pincushion flowers 1½ to 2 feet apart. Remove faded flowers for continuous bloom. Cut plants back to ground level after flowering is completed. Divide clumps every 2 to 4 years to rejuvenate plants.

Selected species and varieties:
S. caucasica (pincushion flower, Caucasian scabiosa) has pinkish blue 3-inch flowers on long, pliant stems from summer to fall; 'Clive Greaves' has lavender-blue flowers touched with white in the center; 'Fama' bears deep blue petals encircling silver centers on 1½-foot stems. *S. columbaria* 'Butterfly Blue' is a prolific compact form with small, beautiful flowers that resemble butterflies on 15-inch slender stems.

POPPY MALLOW
Callirhoe

Light: full sun	
Plant type: perennial	
Hardiness: Zones 3-10	
Height: 6 inches to 3 feet	
Soil and Moisture: well-drained, sandy, dry	
Interest: flowers	
Care: easy	

◀ Callirhoe involucrata

Poppy mallow is a care-free flower for the wild meadow, field, rock garden, or other naturalistic planting. These long-blooming, drought-tolerant perennials are native to the open woods and dry plains over much of the central United States. In spring to summer the showy, ruby-colored cup-shaped flowers appear on very slender, nearly invisible stems.

Growing and care:
Before sowing seed scarify seed coat by scratching it with a nail file. Sow seed in flats in early spring. After the plants have gone dormant at the end of the first growing season transplant to the garden, spacing plants 1½ to 2 feet apart. Poppy mallows develop a thick taproot and should not be transplanted once established. Extend flower season by deadheading spent flowers.

Selected species and varieties:
C. involucrata (purple poppy mallow, winecups) is a trailing plant that grows 6 to 12 inches tall and 2 to 3 feet wide with attractive, deeply lobed hairy leaves, and 2-inch magenta flowers with a white spot at the base of the petals in spring and summer, opening during the day and closing in the evening; Zones 4-8. *C. papaver* (poppy mallow) has prostrate stems as much as 10 feet in length and solitary 2- to 3-inch magenta flowers; Zones 5-8.

PURPLE CONEFLOWER
Echinacea

Light: full sun

Plant type: perennial

Hardiness: Zones 3-8

Height: 2 to 4 feet

Soil and Moisture: well-drained, moist to dry, fertile

Interest: flowers

Care: easy

◄ Echinacea purpurea

Purple coneflowers are robust natives of the prairies and open spaces of the eastern United States. These hardy perennials combine beauty with tough character, making them invaluable additions to borders, massed in beds or herb gardens, or naturalized in wildflower meadows. Their very large, daisylike flowers have softly drooping pink to purple petals surrounding spiny, conical centers that glow purple, orange, or bronze depending on how the sunlight strikes them. Coneflowers blossom from early summer to fall, and make excellent cut flowers.

Growing and care:
Purple coneflowers grow best in full sun, but in hot climates the flower color is more intense if the plants are grown in light shade. Propagate in spring by division or by transplanting self-sown seedlings. Seed can also be sown directly in the garden in spring while soil is still cool. Space plants 2 feet apart. Wear gloves if collecting the prickly seeds, and gently tap the seed heads with a hammer to extract them.

Selected species and varieties:
E. purpurea has pink, purple, or white flowers 2 to 4 inches across in summer and fall on strong 2- to 4-foot stems, and broad, pointed, tooth-edged leaves; 'Magnus' has brilliant rosy pink flowers; 'White Swan' has snow white flowers; Zones 5-8.

PUSSY-TOES
Antennaria

Light: full sun

Plant type: perennial

Hardiness: Zones 3-8

Height: 2 to 16 inches

Soil and Moisture: well-drained, dry to moist

Interest: flowers, foliage

Care: easy

◄ Antennaria rosea

Pussy-toes are easy-to-grow perennial wildflowers that form velvety soft carpets of fuzzy, gray-green leaves generously sprinkled with delicate tubular flowers from spring to summer. The tidy flowers can be red, pink, or white and are held on silvery stems. Pussy-toes are excellent as ground covers in open, sunny places, for rock gardens, or when used to frame steppingstones and garden paths. The vigorous plants naturalize quickly and can also be used for erosion control in dry areas where few other plants would thrive.

Growing and care:
Sow seed indoors in late winter or early spring or direct-sow in the garden in spring while soil is still cool. Space plants 12 inches apart. Fertilize lightly and water regularly until plants are established. Alpine everlasting prefers moist, well-drained soil; the other two species grow best in dry conditions. Under ideal conditions *Antennaria* may become invasive. Divide plants every 2 to 3 years in late summer or fall.

Selected species and varieties:
A. alpina (alpine everlasting) is native to the western mountains and has hairy leaves and white summer flowers on 4-inch stems; Zones 4-8. *A. rosea*, native to western states, has soft gray leaves that form a 2- to 3-inch mat and bears clusters of six to 10 small, light pink flowers on 10-inch stalks in spring; Zones 3-7.

RED-HOT POKER
Kniphofia

Light: full sun	
Plant type: perennial	
Hardiness: Zones 5-9	
Height: 2 to 4 feet	
Soil and Moisture: well-drained, moist	
Interest: flowers, foliage	
Care: easy	

◀ Kniphofia uvaria

Red-hot pokers are some of the most brilliantly colored perennials available. The plants produce long, cylindrical flower clusters in bold shades of orange or yellow on thick stems that gracefully arc over clumps of narrow, sword-shaped leaves. Red-hot pokers produce a succession of flower spikes from summer to early fall. Spectacular as specimens, they add unique color and texture to beds and borders.

Growing and care:
Plant red-hot pokers 1½ to 2 feet apart in sunny locations sheltered from the wind. Remove flower stalks after blossoms have faded. In late fall cut back foliage and cover with salt hay or other light mulch. Propagate by seed or division in early spring. Seedlings and offsets may require several years to reach flowering size.

Selected species and varieties:
K. uvaria has narrow, rough-textured leaves, and produces many 1- to 2-inch individual blossoms forming a 6- to 10-inch bottlebrush-shaped flower cluster atop 2- to 4-foot stems. *K.* 'Little Maid' has pastel yellow flowers that fade to antique white; 'Primrose Beauty' produces light yellow flowers; 'White Fairy' is a dwarf with creamy white flowers in midsummer.

ROCK CRESS
Arabis

Light: full sun	
Plant type: perennial	
Hardiness: Zones 3-7	
Height: 6 to 12 inches	
Soil and Moisture: well-drained, moist to dry	
Interest: flowers, foliage, fragrance	
Care: easy	

◀ Arabis caucasica

Rock cress is a durable, low-growing plant that produces carpets of snow white, fragrant flowers in spring. When not in bloom the small, attractive green leaves fill in the spaces in rock gardens or low borders.

Growing and care:
Rock cress is easily grown, but humid weather and standing water will cause rot. Prune after flowering to keep the plants compact. In regions with hot summers set plants where they will receive some afternoon shade. Propagate from seed sown in spring or divide clumps every 3 to 4 years in fall. Do not disturb established plantings.

Selected species and varieties:
A. alpina 'Flore Pleno' has small, white, fragrant double-petaled flowers in spring. *A. caucasica* 'Rosabella' is a low-growing, compact, 5-inch-tall plant with rosy pink flowers; 'Snow Cap' is a creeping form with plentiful pure white single flowers. *A. procurrens* is a low-growing plant with a spreading habit bearing sprays of white flowers above mats of glossy evergreen leaves.

RUSSIAN SAGE
Perovskia

Light: full sun

Plant type: perennial

Hardiness: Zones 5-8

Height: 2 to 3 feet

Soil and Moisture: well-drained, dry to moist

Interest: flowers, foliage, fragrance

Care: easy

◀ Perovskia atriplicifolia

Russian sage is a low, shrubby perennial bearing long clusters of small, soft, slightly hairy blue-violet flowers from late summer to early fall. It forms somewhat woody clumps with fine-textured, aromatic, gray-green foliage. The leaves have a warm, sagelike fragrance when bruised. Russian sage is a hardworking, easy-care perennial that is most effective when massed in mixed borders with ornamental grasses.

Growing and care:
Plant Russian sages 2 to 3 feet apart and lightly fertilize in spring. To promote bushy form and promote better flowering, cut woody stems back in spring before new growth begins. Propagate by cuttings taken in spring or summer.

Selected species and varieties:
P. atriplicifolia (Russian sage, azure sage) has tiny, lavender-blue, two-lipped summer to fall flowers on 1-foot spikes, and 1½-inch downy, toothed, finely divided gray leaves on woody stems; 'Blue Mist' has pale blue flowers in summer; 'Filagran' has fine-textured foliage and blue flowers from summer to fall; 'Longin' has erect 3-foot stems and blue flowers. *P. scrophulariifolia* produces 2- to 3-foot stems with oval leaves and sprays of light blue flowers from late spring to early summer.

SAGE
Salvia

Light: full sun

Plant type: perennial

Hardiness: Zones 4-10

Height: 1 to 8 feet

Soil and Moisture: well-drained, moist to dry

Interest: flowers, foliage, fragrance

Care: easy

◀ Salvia leucantha

Sages are classic garden plants that have spikes or whorls of hooded, two-lipped flowers at the tips of their branched stems, and pairs of aromatic leaves that clasp or are attached by petioles to their square stems, while the larger shrubby species are well suited to shrub borders and filling spaces in gardens south of Zone 7.

Growing and care:
Sages tolerate drought well but grow poorly in sites that are wet in winter. Space smaller varieties 1½ feet apart, larger ones 2 to 3 feet apart. Deadheading stimulates rebloom. Prune old stems in fall or early winter. Provide tender perennials with mulch over winter in regions colder than Zone 8. Propagate by division in spring or fall, or by softwood cuttings in summer.

Selected species and varieties:
S. leucantha (Mexican bush sage, white sage) is a 3- to 4-foot, very drought-resistant shrubby perennial with white, woolly leaves and long, open clusters of pink flowers, and is excellent for xeriscaping; Zones 7-10. *S.* x *superba* (violet sage) is a 1½- to 3-foot perennial with dense whorls of violet to dark blue-violet flowers above narrow, medium green leaves from late spring to early summer; Zones 5-8.

SEA HOLLY
Eryngium

Light: full sun

Plant type: perennial

Hardiness: Zones 4-9

Height: 1 to 6 feet

Soil and Moisture: well-drained, sandy, dry

Interest: flowers, foliage

Care: easy

◀ Eryngium bourgatii

Sea holly is an intriguingly interesting-looking plant with spiny collars of pewter-purple bracts surrounding the conical, bluish white flower heads. The long-lasting summer-blooming flowers rise on stiff stalks above crisp, leathery, often wavy leaves with deeply cut, spiny margins. Sea holly adds an unusual, coarse texture to specialty gardens or the back of borders.

Growing and care:
Sow seed on soil surface in flats in spring. Cover with plastic and refrigerate for 3 weeks. Place flats outdoors in a shady place until seedlings appear. Transplant to the garden, spacing plants 1 to 1½ feet apart. Water during extended periods of dry, hot weather. Sea holly requires little care once established and self-seeds readily.

Selected species and varieties:
E. alpinum (bluetop sea holly) bears frilled bracts and rounded flower heads on 1- to 2-foot-tall plants. *E. bourgatii* (Mediterranean sea holly) has narrow, pointed bracts and wavy, gray-green leaves with prominent white veins on plants to 2 feet. *E. giganteum* (stout sea holly) produces wide bracts similar in size to silvery holly leaves on plants 4 to 6 feet tall. *E. planum* (flat-leaved eryngium) has steel blue flower heads with blue-green bracts on plants to 3 feet. *E. yuccifolium* (rattlesnake master) is covered with narrow, drooping gray-green leaves with spiny edges on 4-foot stalks.

SEA LAVENDER
Limonium

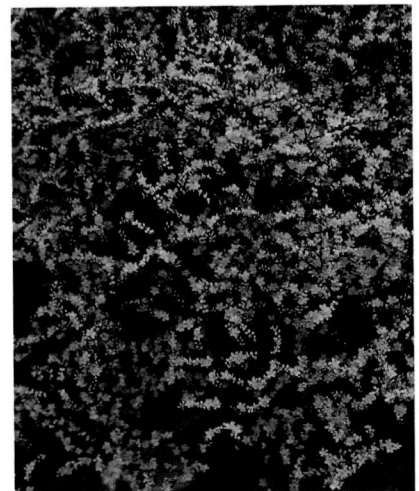

Light: full sun

Plant type: perennial

Hardiness: Zones 4-9

Height: 18 to 30 inches

Soil and Moisture: well-drained, sandy, dry

Interest: flowers

Care: easy

◀ Limonium latifolium

Sea lavender is prized for the abundant sprays of small, lacy flowers that seem to smother the pliant stems from spring to fall. Beneath the flowers are dense clumps of glossy, forest green leaves that are handsome all by themselves. Sea lavender's casual form adds informal beauty to borders and cutting gardens and is a must for fresh and dried arrangements.

Growing and care:
Start seed indoors 6 to 8 weeks before last frost or direct-sow in the garden in early spring when the soil is still cool. Space plants 1½ feet apart. Sea lavender thrives in dry conditions and does very well in coastal gardens. Extremely fertile soils produce weak branches that require staking. Do not disturb established plantings. Cut plants back to the ground in fall after flowering is completed.

Selected species and varieties:
L. latifolium has branching flower stems that carry panicles of airy, rounded lavender-blue blossoms above a tuft of leathery, oblong evergreen leaves; 'Blue Cloud' produces soft, light blue flowers; 'Violetta' bears enchanting sprays of deep violet blossoms.

659

SENNA
Chamaecrista

Light: full sun

Plant type: perennial

Hardiness: Zones 4-10

Height: 1 to 4 feet

Soil and Moisture: well-drained, sandy, wet to dry

Interest: flowers

Care: easy

◀ Chamaecrista fasciculata

Senna is an unusual perennial with a shrubby habit that makes it look like a miniature tree. The branching stems are upright, stiff, and covered with ferny compound leaves. In summer the plants bear small, bright yellow pealike flowers. This native wildflower doesn't appeal to everyone, but those who like it, love it. Senna is excellent in naturalized plantings, where it adds color when most other flowers have gone by. It is also an excellent choice for difficult sites where the soil is too wet or dry for other plants.

Growing and care:
Before sowing scratch seed with a file and soak in warm water for 24 hours. Plant indoors 2 months before planting out or sow directly in the garden in fall or spring. Space plants 2 to 3 feet apart. For best growth inoculate soil with nitrogen-fixing bacteria and water, and fertilize regularly until plants are established. Plants can be divided every 3 to 4 years in spring.

Selected species and varieties:
C. marilandica [also classified as *Senna marilandica* and *Cassia marilandica*] (wild senna) is a semiwoody perennial with branching stems to 4 feet, bold yellow flower clusters, and finely divided leaves.

SMARTWEED
Polygonum

Light: full sun

Plant type: perennial

Hardiness: Zones 3-9

Height: ½ to 3 feet

Soil and Moisture: well-drained, fertile, moist to wet

Interest: flowers, foliage

Care: easy

◀ Polygonum bistorta 'Superbum'

The genus *Polygonum* contains many hardy perennials, some with large, primroselike dark green leaves and cylindrical clusters of rose or pink flowers borne high above the foliage on strong stems. These versatile plants add color to bog and wildflower gardens as well as along garden paths or the front of the border.

Growing and care:
Space plants 1 foot apart. In areas with cool summers plant in full sun. In regions with hot summers provide some afternoon shade. Water well during dry periods. Propagate by division in spring. Cut back plants to about ground level in fall.

Selected species and varieties:
P. affine (Himalayan fleeceflower) produces spikes of rose pink flowers 6 to 9 inches tall above dark green leaves turning bronze in fall; 'Superbum' produces crimson flowers; Zones 4-9. *P. bistorta* (snakeweed) bears pink flowers like bottlebrushes on 2-foot stems above striking clumps of 4- to 6-inch-long wavy green leaves with a white midrib; 'Superbum' grows to 3 feet with dense spikes of rose pink flowers.

SNEEZEWEED
Helenium

Light: full sun

Plant type: perennial

Hardiness: Zones 3-10

Height: 2 to 6 feet

Soil and Moisture: well-drained, moist to wet

Interest: flowers, foliage

Care: easy

◀ Helenium autumnale 'Brilliant'

Free-flowering sneezeweeds provide masses of vividly colored daisylike flowers from late spring through early fall, when most perennials have long since stopped flowering. The fiery yellow, orange, or red fan-shaped petals surround a prominent, burnt red center, and sit atop the 2- to 6-foot-tall stems and above the attractive, willowy foliage. Sneezeweeds are native to streamsides and wet meadows in much of the United States, and are stunning when naturalized in wildflower gardens or planted in large groups in borders.

Growing and care:
Sneezeweeds are virtually pest-free as well as being heat and drought tolerant, making them low maintenance as well as attractive. Plant in either spring or fall, spacing plants 1½ to 2 feet apart. Pinch stems in spring to promote bushy growth and more flowers, and fertilize lightly. For best flower production keep soil moist during growing season. Cut back plants in fall. Propagate by division of clumps every 3 to 4 years.

Selected species and varieties:
H. autumnale (yellow star) has 2-inch flaring, slightly reflexed yellow petals surrounding a raised yellow disk on branched stems up to 6 feet; 'Brilliant' has bright red-orange flowers that fade to lighter watercolor shades on 3-foot stems; 'Butterpat' produces light yellow petals surrounding a bronze disk.

SPURGE
Euphorbia

Light: full sun

Plant type: perennial

Hardiness: Zones 3-10

Height: 6 inches to 3 feet

Soil and Moisture: well-drained, dry

Interest: flowers, foliage

Care: easy

◀ Euphorbia griffithii 'Fireglow'

Spurge is a diverse group of easy-to-grow plants bearing small clusters of flowers surrounded by colorful bracts. The foliage of many species turns from medium green in summer to intense shades of red in fall. The plants make wonderful additions to borders or specialty gardens.

Growing and care:
Sow seed in peat pots 6 to 8 weeks before the last frost. Space plants 1 to 2 feet apart. Once established do not transplant. Spurge thrives in soils that are infertile and dry. If grown in moist, fertile locations growth may become rangy and unattractive. Use gloves when handling plants, as they exude a milky sap that can cause skin irritation in some people.

Selected species and varieties:
E. corollata (flowering spurge) grows 1 to 3 feet tall, with slender green leaves that turn red in fall. In mid- to late summer it bears clusters of flowers resembling baby's-breath. *E. epithymoides* (cushion spurge) forms a neat, symmetrical, 1- to 1½-foot mound of green leaves that turn dark red in fall. In spring it produces small green flowers surrounded by showy, chartreuse-yellow bracts; Zones 4-8. *E. griffithii* 'Fireglow' has well-branched, 3-foot upright stems topped with umbels of fiery red flowers; Zones 4-9.

STOKES' ASTER
Stokesia

Light: full sun

Plant type: perennial

Hardiness: Zones 5-9

Height: 1 to 1½ feet

Soil and Moisture: well-drained, moist, fertile

Interest: flowers

Care: easy

◀ Stokesia laevis
'Blue Danube'

The large, very showy, fringed flowers of Stokes' aster are held on strong stalks rising from neat rosettes of glossy green, straplike, leathery leaves. The flowers, which come in soft pastel shades of purple, blue, lilac, pink, and white, contrast nicely to the shiny dark green leaves. Stokes' aster is an excellent choice for the perennial border and adds a refined touch to fresh summertime bouquets.

Growing and care:
Space Stokes' asters 1½ feet apart. Mulch with straw to protect plants over winter in colder climates. Plants are prone to disease when grown in wet soils. The species may be propagated from seed or by division in spring. Propagate cultivars by division in spring. Cut plants back after flowering is complete.

Selected species and varieties:
S. laevis bears solitary flower heads 2 to 5 inches across, blooming over a 4-week season in summer; 'Blue Danube' has 5-inch clear blue flowers; 'Blue Moon' bears lilac flowers; 'Klaus Jelitto' has 4-inch deep blue blossoms; 'Silver Moon' blooms white.

STONECROP
Sedum

Light: full sun

Plant type: perennial

Hardiness: Zones 3-10

Height: 1 to 2 feet

Soil and Moisture: well-drained, dry to moist

Interest: flowers, foliage

Care: easy

◀ Sedum spectabile

Stonecrops have thick, succulent stems topped by dense clusters of five-petaled star-shaped flowers. The plants add color and texture in perennial borders and rock gardens, and the leaves often are covered with a white, waxy bloom or tinged with copper or bronze. *Sedums* can be massed as a succulent ground cover that attracts numerous species of butterflies to its summer and fall flowers.

Growing and care:
Sedums are heat and drought tolerant, and spread slowly. Space plants 1½ to 2 feet apart. Propagate species by seed or division in spring, and all cultivars by division in early spring or by stem cuttings in late spring through summer. Fertilize lightly in spring. Wet conditions can lead to fungal and bacterial diseases. Cut back plants in fall once flowering is completed.

Selected species and varieties:
S. spectabile (showy stonecrop) produces round clumps of 1½- to 2-foot stems lined with 3-inch fleshy, rounded blue-green leaves and topped by flat clusters of white or pink flowers from summer to frost; 'Brilliant' has deep rose red flowers. *S. telephium* (orpine, live-forever) grows 1 to 2 feet tall with oblong, toothed leaves and rounded clusters of pink, red, or sometimes white flowers in late summer; *S.* x 'Vera Jameson' has coppery purple leaves and dusty pink or magenta flowers in early fall.

SUNDROPS
Oenothera

Light: full sun

Plant type: perennial

Hardiness: Zones 4-8

Height: 6 inches to 2 feet

Soil and Moisture: well-drained, fertile, moist

Interest: flowers

Care: easy

◀ Oenothera fruticosa

Sundrops produce perhaps the most intensely yellow flowers of any perennial. The showy, four-petaled, saucer-shaped blossoms open atop gracefully pliant stems and are stunning when planted in masses or as bright focal points in the middle of borders.

Growing and care:
Plant sundrops in well-worked soil that has been amended with compost or rotted manure. Space small species 8 inches apart and large ones 18 inches apart. Provide extra water during dry periods. Cut back plants 2 to 3 inches after flowering. From Zone 6 north divide plants in spring. From Zone 7 south divide in fall.

Selected species and varieties:
O. fruticosa (sundrops) is a prolific bearer of 1- to 2-inch bright yellow flower clusters atop 1½- to 2-foot stems. *O. macrocarpa* [also classified as *O. missouriensis*] (Ozark sundrops) has large 5-inch yellow flowers on 6- to 12-inch plants. *O. speciosa* (evening primrose) bears showy white or pink blossoms on spreading, 6- to 18-inch-tall stems. *O. tetragona* [also called *O. fruticosa* ssp. *glauca*] produces abundant red-tinged buds that open to bright yellow flowers.

SUNFLOWER
Helianthus

Light: full sun

Plant type: perennial

Hardiness: Zones 4-9

Height: 3 to 7 feet

Soil and Moisture: well-drained, fertile, moist

Interest: flowers

Care: easy

◀ Helianthus x multiflorus 'Flore Pleno'

The large, cheerful yellow blossoms of sunflowers brighten the garden even on gloomy days. Sunflowers bear large, yellow, single or double blossoms from summer to fall on strong, erect stems lined with medium green, coarse-textured leaves. They add zip to the back of the border or when naturalized in wildflower meadows. Sunflowers are excellent for cutting. The ripe seeds attract many species of songbirds to the garden in fall.

Growing and care:
Sow seed directly in the garden after danger of frost has passed. Thin plants to stand 1 foot apart for dwarf forms and 3 feet apart for larger types. Pinch young plants to encourage branching and increased flowering. Water regularly during the growing season and fertilize lightly once a month.

Selected species and varieties:
H. angustifolius (swamp sunflower) bears flowers 2 to 3 inches across with dark brown to purple centers on stems to 7 feet tall. *H. x multiflorus* (many-flowered sunflower) grows blooms 3 to 5 inches wide, often with overlapping petals; 'Flore Pleno' has double flowers on 4-foot stems; 'Lodden Gold' bears deep yellow double flowers on 5-foot stems; 'Morning Sun' has golden yellow flowers on 5- to 6-foot stems.

THRIFT
Armeria

Light: full sun

Plant type: perennial

Hardiness: Zones 3-8

Height: 6 inches to 2 feet

Soil and Moisture: well-drained, moist to dry

Interest: flowers, foliage

Care: moderate

◀ Armeria maritima 'Laucheana'

Thrifts have adorable round clusters of small, brightly colored flowers held high above tufted mounds of narrow, needle-shaped leaves. The plants make excellent additions to rock gardens, serve as edging around borders, or can be massed in formal gardens. They do not do well in hot, humid areas but are extremely tolerant of seaside locations.

Growing and care:
Soak seed in warm water for 8 to 10 hours before planting. Direct-sow in the garden in early spring when soil is cool. Space plants 6 to 12 inches apart. Replace clumps when center begins to die back. Provide extra water during dry periods and mulch with straw or pine needles in winter.

Selected species and varieties:
A. alliacea [also called *A. plantaginea*] (plantain thrift) has 1¾-inch rosy pink or white flower clusters on 2-foot stems; 'Bee's Ruby' bears intense ruby red flower clusters. *A. maritima* (common thrift) has white to deep carmine pink flowers on 1-foot stems; 'Alba' is a dwarf with white flowers on 5-inch stems; 'Bloodstone' has brilliant, bright red flowers on 9-inch stems; 'Laucheana' has dark green foliage and bright pink flowers.

VERBENA
Verbena

Light: full sun

Plant type: perennial

Hardiness: Zones 8-10

Height: ½ to 4 feet

Soil and Moisture: well-drained, fertile, dry to moist

Interest: flowers, foliage, fragrance

Care: easy

◀ Verbena rigida

Verbenas are rugged plants that provide week after week of flowers in vivid whites, reds, purples, and blues. Their small, five-petaled, tubular flowers are often highly fragrant and borne in rounded or domed clusters on wiry stems. Butterflies and hummingbirds are drawn to the blossoms. Verbenas are versatile plants that fit well into many areas of the garden. They add color and form to mixed beds and borders, and accent rock gardens.

Growing and care:
Once established, these plants thrive in hot, dry sites, are low maintenance, and are excellent in naturalistic plantings. They grow more vigorously and produce more flowers if given additional water during dry spells. Pinch young plants to encourage branching and increase flowering. Propagate by seed sown in spring, spacing plants 1 foot apart, or take cuttings in late summer, root them, and overwinter indoors for planting the following spring. Verbenas are short-lived perennials that will self-sow in warm climates, and are grown as annuals in northern regions.

Selected species and varieties:
V. rigida [also listed as *V. venosa*] grows 1 to 2 feet tall and 2 feet wide with erect, branching stems and dense clusters of deep purple flowers from summer through fall, and narrow, medium green 2- to 3-inch leaves mostly at the bases of the stems; Zones 8-10.

WILD BUCKWHEAT
Eriogonum

Light: full sun

Plant type: perennial

Hardiness: Zones 3-10

Height: 3 inches to 3 feet

Soil and Moisture: well-drained, gravelly, dry

Interest: flowers

Care: moderate

◀ Eriogonum compositum

Wild buckwheat is an informal, rather wild-looking plant with tall, sturdy stems capped with white, red, or sulfur yellow blossoms in spring, summer, or fall. The plants grow best in hot, dry conditions and are most popular in California and other areas of the far West. Wild buckwheat is exceptionally attractive to bees and is often planted near vegetable gardens or orchards to aid pollination.

Growing and care:
Sow wild buckwheat in gravelly soils in spring. Water well until seed germinates. The plants often self-sow and naturalize freely. The low-growing sulfur buckwheat is the easiest species to grow, as it does not need gravelly soil to do well.

Selected species and varieties:
E. compositum (northern buckwheat) bears 1- to 4-inch clusters of white or yellow flowers on 8- to 18-inch stalks in late spring to summer, and forms a cushiony mat of oval to heart-shaped leaves that are green above and white and fuzzy below; Zones 4-7. *E. umbellatum* var. *subalpinum* (sulfur buckwheat) has 2- to 4-inch rounded clusters of creamy yellow summer flowers on 3-inch stems; Zones 3-8. *E. wrightii* (Wright buckwheat) is shrubby, growing 2 to 3 feet tall with gray leaves, and clusters of white flowers in summer and fall that turn reddish orange in cool weather; Zones 6-10.

WILD INDIGO
Baptisia

Light: full sun

Plant type: perennial

Hardiness: Zones 3-9

Height: 3 to 4 feet

Soil and Moisture: well-drained, dry, sandy

Interest: flowers

Care: moderate to easy

◀ Baptisia australis

Wild indigo is often considered a workhorse of the perennial garden with a tough, hardy character ably balanced by delicate compound leaves and porcelain blue or ice white pealike flowers from midspring to early summer. The tall stems and blue-green leaves provide an excellent background to borders or when massed in wildflower meadows. The flowers are followed by attractive, dark-colored seedpods that are often dried and used in arrangements.

Growing and care:
Soak seed in warm water for 24 hours before planting. Direct-sow in the garden in fall or in spring after danger of frost has passed. Space plants 2 to 3 feet apart. Wild indigo takes 1 to 2 years to become fully established. Cultivate carefully so roots are not disturbed. Do not transplant. Tall selections may require staking.

Selected species and varieties:
B. alba grows to 3 feet tall with upright clusters of white flowers sometimes tinged with purple; Zones 5-8. *B. australis* has erect stems reaching 4 feet tall with attractive compound leaves and pealike indigo blue flowers in long, terminal racemes, good for cutting.

WORMWOOD
Artemisia

Light: full sun

Plant type: perennial

Hardiness: Zones 5-8

Height: 3 feet

Soil and Moisture: well-drained, dry

Interest: foliage, fragrance

Care: easy

◀ Artemisia x 'Powis Castle'

Wormwood is wonderfully easy to grow, with distinctive silvery gray foliage that is strongly aromatic. Forms range from woody evergreen perennials 4 to 5 feet high to soft, feathery mounds scarcely 6 inches tall. The larger types are perfect for the back of the border, while the smaller forms shine in rock gardens or as edgings. The pewter-gray color of the leaves allows *Artemisia* to blend especially well with blue, lavender, and pink flowers, and softens plants with coarse textures.

Growing and care:
Start seed indoors 10 to 12 weeks before the last frost or direct-sow in the garden in fall. Space smaller forms including 'Silver Mound' 1 foot apart and larger types, such as 'Powis Castle', 2 to 3 feet apart. *Artemisia* grows best in sunny, warm, dry sites with excellent air circulation. In humid locations some types are prone to fungal diseases. Cut back in late fall or early spring to keep plants shapely and reduce chance of disease.

Selected species and varieties:
A. x 'Powis Castle' forms an airy, 4-foot-wide mound of lacy, finely divided, steel gray to silvery leaves up to 4 inches long on woolly stems; Zones 6-8. *A. schmidtiana* 'Silver Mound' produces a low, 8-inch-high mound of very airy, fernlike, chrome-gray foliage; Zones 3-7. *A. stellerana* forms a compact carpet of deeply lobed, bluish silver leaves on 1-foot stems; Zones 3-7.

YARROW
Achillea

Light: full sun

Plant type: perennial

Hardiness: Zones 4-8

Height: 6 inches to 4 feet

Soil and Moisture: well-drained, dry

Interest: flowers

Care: easy

◀ Achillea 'Coronation Gold'

Yarrow bears large, vividly colored, flat-topped flower clusters atop strong stems covered with lacy gray-green leaves. The plants provide exquisite form and color to borders and rock gardens and may flower from early to late summer, depending on the variety. The plants are also excellent for fresh and dried arrangements.

Growing and care:
Sow seed indoors 8 to 10 weeks before last frost. Do not cover seed. Space plants 1 to 2 feet apart. Once plants are established, propagate by dividing clumps in spring or fall every 3 to 4 years. Cut plants back to ground level after first few frosts in fall. Some tall forms may need support. Provide extra water during dry periods.

Selected species and varieties:
A. 'Coronation Gold' is a hybrid with 3-inch, deep yellow flower clusters on 3-foot stems. *A. filipendulina* (fernleaf yarrow) bears bright yellow flower clusters up to 5 inches across; 'Gold Plate' has 6-inch yellow flower heads on 4-foot stems. *A.* x *lewisii* 'King Edward' has small yellow flowers on 4-inch stalks. *A. millefolium* (common yarrow) bears 2-inch white flowers, with cultivars blooming in shades from pink to red.

AMARYLLIS
Hippeastrum

Light: full sun	
Plant type: bulb	
Hardiness: Zones 9-10	
Height: 1 to 2 feet	
Soil and Moisture: well-drained, moist, sandy	
Interest: flowers	
Care: easy to moderate	

◀ Hippeastrum
'Bold Leader'

The only word fit to describe an amaryllis in flower is "spectacular." Amaryllis bears enormous, vividly colored flowers up to 8 inches across atop stout, very sturdy stems. In warm regions the flowers brighten sunny borders. In northern areas the plants are potted in containers and forced into flower during the winter months.

Growing and care:

Outdoors in Zone 10, plant in fall or spring, setting bulbs 6 inches deep and 1 foot apart in well-worked soil rich in rotted manure or compost. Indoors, plant the bulb with its top third exposed in a pot 2 inches wider than the width of the bulb anytime from late fall through winter. Keep soil around bulb barely moist until growth starts. After flowering, remove flower stalk and provide regular watering and fertilizing until foliage dies back in late summer or fall. Allow soil to dry out and repot bulb into fresh potting soil with a high organic matter content. Propagate by separating offsets while plant is dormant.

Selected species and varieties:

H. 'Apple Blossom' is cherry pink flushed white; 'Bold Leader' is signal red; 'Double Record' has double white flowers veined and tipped red; 'Lady Jane', deep salmon-orange double flowers; 'Picotee', white petals rimmed red; 'Red Lion', velvety red flowers.

AUTUMN DAFFODIL
Sternbergia

Light: full sun	
Plant type: bulb	
Hardiness: Zones 6-10	
Height: 6 to 12 inches	
Soil and Moisture: well-drained, sandy, dry	
Interest: flowers, foliage	
Care: easy	

◀ Sternbergia lutea

Autumn daffodil is a bright, charming addition to any fall garden. The small, egg-shaped flower buds open to reveal clear yellow, shimmering, waxy flowers reminiscent of crocuses. The blossoms appear on slender stems shorter than the grassy foliage. Use autumn daffodils in sunny, dry rock gardens, or any hot, dry location. The plants can also be forced indoors to provide color during dreary winter months.

Growing and care:

Plant autumn daffodils in summer, setting bulbs 4 inches deep and 4 to 6 inches apart. In Zone 6 mulch with straw or pine needles to provide winter protection. North of Zone 6, grow as annuals or in bulb pans, placing five or six bulbs 2 inches deep in each 6-inch pan. Autumn daffodils can be propagated by removing the small bulb offsets from larger clumps after plants have finished flowering.

Selected species and varieties:

S. lutea bears 1½- to 2-inch cup-shaped golden yellow blossoms on sturdy 4-inch stems above upright clusters of thin, glossy green, 6- to 12-inch leaves.

667

AZTEC LILY
Sprekelia

Light: full sun

Plant type: bulb

Hardiness: Zones 9-10

Height: 1 foot

Soil and Moisture: well-drained, fertile, dry to moist

Interest: flowers, foliage

Care: moderate

◀ Sprekelia formosissima

Aztec lily produces spectacular orchidlike flowers with six long, velvety petals. The three upper petals curve gracefully, like a bird in flight, while the lower ones form a colorful trumpet accented by the long, yellow-tipped stamens. The solitary flowers are borne on leafless stems before narrow, straplike leaves appear. In warm zones, Aztec lily can be grown in the border. Elsewhere, it is grown as an annual or container plant.

Growing and care:
From Zone 9 south, plant Aztec lilies in any season, setting bulbs 3 to 4 inches deep and 8 to 12 inches apart. The bulbs sprout quickly and will bloom in about 6 weeks. From Zone 8 north, plant the bulbs outdoors in spring and lift in fall, drying and storing the bulbs like gladiolus. Indoors, plant with half the bulb above the soil surface, allowing one bulb per 4-inch pot or three bulbs per 6-inch pot. Propagate by removing bulblets that develop around the base of mature bulbs.

Selected species and varieties:
S. formosissima (Aztec lily, Jacobean lily, St. James's lily, orchid amaryllis) has 1-foot-long, lance-shaped green leaves and very showy, 4- to 6-inch, deep red-orange or deep crimson flowers with long, graceful petals and bright yellow stamens.

BELLADONNA LILY
Amaryllis

Light: full sun

Plant type: bulb

Hardiness: Zones 9-10

Height: 1 to 2 feet

Soil and Moisture: well-drained, moist

Interest: flowers

Care: moderate

◀ Amaryllis belladonna

In late summer the splendid blossoms of belladonna lily provide a pleasant surprise when they rise from what seems like barren ground. The straplike foliage, which appears in early to late spring, disappears in summer a few weeks before the bold clusters of six to 12 sweetly scented, flowery trumpets seem to appear from nowhere. Force belladonna lilies indoors as houseplants or use as border plantings in Zones 9 and 10.

Growing and care:
Pot in containers in late winter with the neck of the bulb at the soil surface, or set bulbs outdoors 4 to 6 inches deep and 1 foot apart in spring when soil has warmed. Water well from the time foliage appears until the leaves turn brown and disappear. When the flower stalk emerges resume watering and fertilize regularly until all flowers have faded. If planted in sheltered, warm spots and mulched heavily, belladonna lilies have survived as far north as Zone 5. Propagate from seed, planting the fleshy seeds as soon as they appear after flowers fade, or by removing bulblets from parent bulbs. Caution: Belladonna lily bulbs are poisonous and must be kept out of the reach of children.

Selected species and varieties:
A. belladonna has 3-inch white, pale pink, or rose blossoms on 1- to 2-foot-tall stems in late summer; 'Cape Town' has deep rose red flowers.

BELLEVALIA
Bellevalia

Light: full sun	
Plant type: bulb	
Hardiness: Zones 6-10	
Height: 6 to 18 inches	
Soil and Moisture: well-drained, fertile, moist	
Interest: flowers	
Care: easy	

◀ Bellevalia pycnantha

Bellevalia at first glance looks like grape hyacinth that has had too much fertilizer. The conical flower clusters hold 20 to 30 small flower bells that open from bottom to top. The single, fleshy stalk rises from a clump of thick, glossy green, straplike leaves. After the flowers fade they are replaced by blue-black seeds in fall. Use bellevalia anywhere hyacinth would be at home—in borders, rock gardens, or where it may naturalize.

Growing and care:
Plant bellevalias in fall, setting bulbs 3 inches deep and 3 inches apart. Bulbs tolerate both wet spring conditions and summer drought. Propagate by removing and replanting the small bulblets that develop at the base of parent bulbs in fall. For container growing, plant three to five bulbs in a 6-inch pot filled with potting soil. Moisten well and place pot in a cool, shaded place while roots develop. When leaves and shoots emerge place on a sunny window sill in a warm room.

Selected species and varieties:
B. pycnantha has downward-facing clusters of flat, blue-black flowers with yellow edges that slowly unfold in spring on 1-foot-tall stalks above 12-inch-long, semisucculent leaves. *B. romana* [also called *Hyacinthus romanus*] has grayish blue clustered flower buds that open into dull white, 1/4-inch flowers sometimes tinged with violet, brown, or green on 6- to 18-inch stalks in spring.

BLAZING STAR
Tritonia

Light: full sun	
Plant type: bulb	
Hardiness: Zones 7-10	
Height: 1 1/2 feet	
Soil and Moisture: well-drained, moist	
Interest: flowers	
Care: moderate	

◀ Tritonia crocata

Blazing star is often confused with montbretia, but is actually more closely related to freesia. The very attractive flowers are arranged along one side of an arching flower spike and shaped like small bowls of pointed petals. The flower stems rise from small fans of narrow, pointed leaves. Blazing star provides stunning color in beds, borders, or rock gardens, and is a long-lasting cut flower.

Growing and care:
From Zone 7 south, plant bulbs in fall, setting corms 3 to 4 inches deep and 6 inches apart. From Zone 6 north, plant bulbs in spring. Fertilize in spring and keep soil evenly moist during growing season. As leaves begin to yellow allow soil to dry out. In northern areas lift corms in fall and dry in a cool, dark place for a few days. Cut off foliage and store in a cool, dry place over winter. Propagate from seed or by removing the small cormels growing around mature corms.

Selected species and varieties:
T. crocata has long, sword-shaped leaves and 2-inch-wide flowers on 1 1/2-foot-tall stems in a wide range of colors including salmon, white, pink, and red.

BUGLE LILY
Watsonia

Light: full sun	
Plant type: bulb	
Hardiness: Zones 8-10	
Height: 1½ to 4 feet	
Soil and Moisture: well-drained, moist	
Interest: flowers, foliage	
Care: moderate	

◀ Watsonia 'Pink Opal'

Bugle lily's simple, funnel-shaped flowers appear at the tips of the tall, slightly arching stems. The soft texture of the blossoms contrasts to the sharp-looking clumps of narrow, sword-shaped leaves. The spikes of blossoms, which open from bottom to top, are similar to those of the gladiolus but are daintier and less formal. Bugle lilies will slowly form clumps in gardens in warm climates. Elsewhere, they can be grown as annuals or lifted in fall and stored like gladiolus. They make very attractive, long-lasting cut flowers.

Growing and care:
From Zone 8 south, plant bugle lily corms directly in the garden 3 inches deep and 6 to 9 inches apart in fall for spring flowering. From Zone 7 north, plant in the garden in spring for summer blooms, then lift in fall after foliage withers. Dry bulbs in a cool, dark place for a few days, then trim off leaves a few inches above top of bulb. Store over winter in a cool, dry basement or shed. Propagate from seed, although seedlings can be difficult to transplant, or by removing cormels.

Selected species and varieties:
W. hybrids bear 2- to 3-inch flowers in pastel shades; 'Bright Eyes' is powder pink; 'Dazzle', soft orange with a purple throat; 'Humilis' has pink flowers on 1½-foot dwarf stems; 'Mrs. Bullard's White' is pure white; 'Pink Opal', bright pink; 'Rubra', dusty reddish purple.

BUTTERCUP
Ranunculus

Light: full sun	
Plant type: bulb	
Hardiness: Zones 9-10	
Height: 10 to 18 inches	
Soil and Moisture: well-drained, sandy, moist	
Interest: flowers	
Care: moderate	

◀ Ranunculus asiaticus

These are not the little buttercups of fields and pastures but spectacular relatives. Buttercups produce very formal flowers in a wide range of colors composed of dozens of richly colored petals arranged in roselike swirls. Each tuber may produce five or six dozen flowers up to four at a time throughout the season on stems lined with lacy green leaflets. Buttercups can be used in borders and rock gardens where the weather is warm, or grown indoors in containers for early-spring flowering.

Growing and care:
Plant Persian buttercups in fall, soaking the tubers overnight then setting them in the soil with the claws down and the tops 1½ inches deep. Space tubers 8 inches apart. For plants set outdoors good drainage is essential to avoid rotting of the tubers. As tubers go dormant in summer, stop watering and allow soil to dry out. North of Zone 9, treat plants as annuals, setting them out in spring and lifting them in fall for winter storage. Propagate from seed or by dividing tubers.

Selected species and varieties:
R. asiaticus 'Tecolote Giants' (Persian buttercup) produces gorgeous flowers up to 5 inches across in pastel shades of pink, rose, yellow, tangerine, and white, with bi- and tricolors.

CALLA LILY
Zantedeschia

Light: full sun

Plant type: bulb

Hardiness: Zones 9-10

Height: 2 to 3 feet

Soil and Moisture: well-drained, moist to wet

Interest: flowers, foliage

Care: moderate

◀ Zantedeschia
aethiopica

Calla lily's gracefully curved and sculpted flowers have a cool, formal elegance few other blooms can match. Petal-like spathes curl into elongated trumpets with a flared lip pulled to a point. The waxy spathe folds around a colorful, sometimes fragrant, fingerlike spadix bearing the true flowers, which are tiny and inconspicuous. Up to 12 or more blossoms open at the same time amid broad, stalked, arrow-shaped, wavy-edged leaves that are often attractively flecked and spotted with white. In warm zones, calla lilies are eye-catching specimens for beds or borders and will naturalize where conditions suit them. Elsewhere they are grown as annuals or as potted plants for patio or indoor use. Callas are prized as cut flowers.

Growing and care:
Outdoors in Zones 9 and 10, plant calla lilies in spring or fall, setting rhizomes 1 to 4 inches deep and spacing them 1 to 2 feet apart. Calla lilies tolerate boggy conditions and can be grown with their roots in water at the edges of ponds. North of Zone 9, start them indoors in early spring and transplant them outside after all danger of frost has passed for blooming in summer. Lift rhizomes in fall after foliage withers and store for winter. For pot culture, set growing tips of rhizomes at soil level and allow one root per 6-inch pot. Callas bloom about 2 months after planting. Golden calla lily can be propa-gated from seed. Propagate all calla lilies by dividing their rhizomes in spring or fall.

Selected species and varieties:
Z. aethiopica (common calla, giant white calla, arum lily, trumpet lily) bears fragrant, snowy white flowers 10 inches long on 2-foot plants; 'Perle Von Stuttgart' is somewhat smaller than the species, with abundant blossoms. *Z. albomaculata* (spotted calla, black-throated calla) has 5-inch white flowers with purple throats on 2-foot plants. *Z. elliottiana* (golden calla, yellow calla) produces 6-inch golden yellow flowers, tinged greenish yellow on the outside, on 2½-foot plants. *Z. rehmannii* (red calla, pink calla) has 3-inch pink flowers on 1½- to 2-foot plants. *Z.* 'Black-Eyed Beauty' produces creamy white blossoms veined green, with a black throat or eye rimming the spadix; 'Black Magic' is yellow with a black eye; 'Cameo', salmon; 'Harvest Moon' is yellow with a red eye; 'Pink Persuasion', purple-pink; 'Solfatare' is a creamy pale yellow with a black eye.

CANNA
Canna

Light: full sun

Plant type: bulb

Hardiness: Zones 8-10

Height: 2 to 10 feet

Soil and Moisture: well-drained, fertile, moist to wet

Interest: flowers, foliage

Care: moderate

◀ Canna x generalis 'The President'

Cannas have stately spikes of flashy, colorful flowers and bold foliage that add a carnival atmosphere to any garden. Underground rhizomes produce clumps of 8- to 24-inch-long, glossy deep green leaves on fleshy stems. The impressive 4- to 5-inch flowers have three true petals and several petal-like stamens, and are borne on stiff stems above the foliage. These tropical plants are used as lush summer to fall bedding plants and are stunning when massed in large groups.

Growing and care:
Plant after all danger of frost has passed in thoroughly warmed soil rich in organic matter. North of Zone 8, cut back tops to 6 inches after flowering is completed. In fall lift rhizomes after first killing frost, and store them in a cool place in barely moist peat moss. Leave rhizomes in the ground over winter in Zones 8 to 10, but provide them with a protective mulch of straw or pine needles. Propagate by dividing rhizomes in spring.

Selected species and varieties:
C. x *generalis* [also listed as *C.* x *hybrida*] comes in 4- to 6-foot standard varieties, 2- to 3-foot dwarfs, and 7- to 10-foot giants; 'Mohawk' has orange blossoms; 'Panache' is ivory and rose; 'Pfitzer's Primrose Black Knight' has deep blood-red flowers; 'The President' has deep green leaves and bright red flowers.

CAPE COWSLIP
Lachenalia

Light: full sun

Plant type: bulb

Hardiness: Zones 9-10

Height: 6 to 12 inches

Soil and Moisture: well-drained, sandy, moist

Interest: flowers

Care: moderate

◀ Lachenalia aloides

Cape cowslips bear long spikes of drooping, uniquely shaped tubular flowers that look like brightly colored peanuts. The waxy, inch-long blossoms are often tinged and tipped in multiple colors, and contrast nicely with the fleshy purple and green leaves. Cape cowslips are eye-catching plants in rock gardens where winters are warm, and are grown as container specimens elsewhere. They make long-lasting cut flowers.

Growing and care:
In Zones 9 and 10, plant Cape cowslips outdoors in fall, setting bulbs 1 inch deep and 2 inches apart in sandy soil amended with some organic matter. Indoors, set five or six bulbs 1 inch deep in a 6-inch pot. Propagate by removing the bulblets that grow alongside mature bulbs or, for *L. bulbiferum,* potting the small bulbils that develop in the leaf joints of the plant.

Selected species and varieties:
L. aloides (tricolored Cape cowslip) bears flowers with yellow petals tinged green and touched with red; 'Aurea' blooms bright yellow-orange; 'Pearsonii' has golden yellow blossoms with maroon tips. *L. bulbiferum* (nodding Cape cowslip) has coral pink to red flowers, tipped with green and purple.

CORN LILY
Ixia

Light: full sun

Plant type: bulb

Hardiness: Zones 8-10

Height: 1 1/2 to 2 feet

Soil and Moisture: well-drained, sandy, fertile, moist

Interest: flowers

Care: moderate

◄ Ixia viridiflora

Corn lilies are reliable warm-weather bulbs that produce clusters of cup- or star-shaped, gaily colored flowers at the tips of wandlike stems rising from clumps of sparse, grassy leaves. In warm, dry climates, their multicolored blossoms can be used to decorate beds or borders. Elsewhere, grow them in containers for winter or spring indoor color.

Growing and care:
In Zones 8 to 10, plant outdoors in late fall, setting corms 3 inches deep and 6 inches apart. North of Zone 8, plant them in late spring or early summer after the soil has warmed. After plants have finished flowering allow soil to stay dry over summer. Lift corms in fall and store over winter. Indoors, plant five or six corms 1 inch deep in 6-inch pots in fall for winter to spring bloom. Propagate by removing cormels growing around mature bulbs.

Selected species and varieties:
I. hybrids produce flower bells in shades of white, yellow, orange, pink, red, or blue; 'Bluebird' has violet petals streaked purple outside and white inside and a black throat; 'Marquette' has purple-tipped yellow blossoms. *I. maculata* has foot-long, narrow, slightly ribbed leaves and softly colored yellow, orange, or white flowers accented with a gold or orange throat; Zones 9-10. *I. viridiflora* (green ixia) has 1-inch pale green flowers with black throats and black anthers at the tips of their stamens.

CRIMSON FLAG
Schizostylis

Light: full sun

Plant type: bulb

Hardiness: Zones 6-10

Height: 1 to 2 feet

Soil and Moisture: moist to wet, fertile

Interest: flowers, foliage

Care: moderate

◄ Schizostylis coccinea 'Mrs. Hegarty'

Crimson flag is a beautiful flower, with satiny, pointed petals embracing a cluster of curled stamens. The multiple blossoms are borne on a slender stem above a clump of narrow, sometimes evergreen, leaves. In warm climates, crimson flag may produce sparse flowers in spring and summer and a full burst of fall bloom. Crimson flag thrives in bog gardens or along streams and ponds. In colder areas, grow crimson flag indoors in containers. It produces excellent cut flowers.

Growing and care:
Plant crimson flag outdoors in spring or fall, setting roots 2 inches deep and 9 to 12 inches apart. For containers, set plants outdoors in spring after the threat of frost has passed, then pot them to bring indoors for fall to winter bloom. The plants can then be stored and planted again the following spring. Propagate by division in spring or fall, although disturbed roots may take a year or more to resume flowering.

Selected species and varieties:
S. coccinea (river lily) produces 1- to 2-inch-wide crimson flowers on slender stems above green, grasslike leaves; 'Major' has flowers slightly larger than the species; 'Mrs. Hegarty' produces blossoms colored a pale rose pink.

DAHLIA
Dahlia

Light:	full sun
Plant type:	bulb
Hardiness:	Zones 9-10
Height:	1 to 8 feet
Soil and Moisture:	well-drained, moist, fertile
Interest:	flowers
Care:	moderate

◀ Dahlia tamjoh

Dahlias reliably brighten the flower border over a long season of bloom with highly diverse blossoms varying from flat-faced, single-petaled types to those with round, dense mounds of petals. Dahlia sizes are as variable as petal forms, with some flowers only a few inches across and others the diameter of a dinner plate. The centers of dahlia blossoms are composed of small, tightly packed disk flowers surrounded by one or more rows of broad, petal-like ray flowers. Colors vary widely, and some dahlias are bicolored or variegated, with petals tipped, streaked, or backed with contrasting color. The types with smaller flowers are easier to work into a bed or border design. Regardless of their size, all dahlias make long-lasting cut flowers.

Growing and care:
Plant dahlia tubers in spring, in well-worked soil amended with compost or other organic matter. Place taller cultivars in a hole 6 to 8 inches deep and cover with 2 to 3 inches of soil. Space the holes 3 to 4 feet apart. Plant tubers of shorter cultivars 2 to 3 inches deep and 1 to 2 feet apart. When transplanting potted seedlings, position them 2 inches deeper than the depth of their pot. Stake all but dwarfs, pompoms, and miniatures. For long-lasting cut flowers, pick dahlias when outdoor temperatures are cool, and stand cut stems in hot water (100° to 160°F) in a cool, shaded location for several hours before arranging. Propagate dahlias from seed started indoors in very early spring to flower that season, from stem cuttings, or by dividing tubers in spring.

Selected species and varieties:
Single dahlias have one or two rows of flat petals surrounding a flat central disk; 'Bambino White' is a dwarf cultivar with 1-inch flowers on 14-inch bushes. *Anemone-flowered dahlias* have a central disk obscured by a fluffy ball of short, tubular petals and rimmed by one or more rows of longer flat petals; 'Siemen Doorenbosch' has flat lavender petals surrounding a creamy central pincushion on 20-inch plants. *Collarette dahlias* have central disks surrounded by a collar of short, often ruffled or cupped petals, backed by a second collar of broader, flat petals; 'Jack O'Lantern' has an inner collar streaked yellow and orange, and deep orange outer petals on 4-foot plants; 'Mickey' has a yellow inner collar backed by deep red outer ray flowers on 3-foot bushes. *Ball dahlias* have cupped, double petals crowded into round domes; 'Nijinsky' has purple flowers on 4-foot stems; 'Rothsay Superb' has red blooms on 3-foot plants. *Pompom dahlias* produce small, round balls of tightly curled petals; 'Amber Queen' has golden to bronze flowers on 4-foot stems; 'Chick-a-dee' has wine red blossoms touched with pink. *Cactus dahlias* have straight or twisted petals rolled like quills; 'Brookside Cheri' has salmon pink petals tinged with gold on 4-foot plants; 'Juanita' bears ruby red flowers on 4-foot stems. *Semi-cactus dahlias* have flat, slightly curling petals with less than half their length rolled into tubes; 'Amanda Jarvis' has rose colored flowers on 3-foot plants; 'Bella Bimba' bears apricot pink flowers on 4-foot plants. *Chrysanthemum dahlias* have double rows of petals all curving inward and hiding the flower's central disk. *Waterlily dahlias* bear short petals clasped tightly over the central disk surounded by several rows of broad, flat petals; 'Lauren Michelle' has rosy-lavender petals with purple underneath on 4-foot plants; 'Gerry Hoek' bears shell pink flowers.

DELICATE LILY
Chlidanthus

Light: full sun

Plant type: bulb

Hardiness: Zones 9-10

Height: 8 to 10 inches

Soil and Moisture: well-drained, sandy, moist

Interest: flowers, foliage

Care: moderate

◄ Chlidanthus fragrans

Everyone should grow delicate lily at least once. This summer-blooming native of tropical South America bears large, daffodil yellow flowers sweetly scented with a lemony perfume. The funnel-shaped flowers appear in clusters, each having six pointed petals layered like overlapping triangles at the tips of the slender stalks. Narrow gray-green leaves appear after the flowers. Delicate lilies slowly naturalize in Zones 9 and 10, where they lend a graceful element to beds and borders or cutting and specialty gardens. North of Zone 9, delicate lilies are grown as indoor container plants.

Growing and care:
In Zones 9 and 10, plant outdoors in spring, setting bulbs 2 inches deep and 6 to 8 inches apart in loose soil amended with organic matter. North of Zone 8, plant bulbs in spring and lift in fall before the first frost. Store in a cool, dry place over winter. In containers, allow one bulb per 6-inch pot, setting bulb tops at the soil line. Remove bulbs in fall, dry and store. In spring repot in fresh potting soil. Propagate by removing and replanting small bulblets from the base of larger bulbs.

Selected species and varieties:
C. fragrans (perfumed fairy lily) is native to the Andes Mountains and bears loose clusters of three or four yellow blossoms up to 3 inches across and clumps of green, daffodil-like leaves in summer.

DICHELOSTEMMA
Dichelostemma

Light: full sun

Plant type: bulb

Hardiness: Zones 5-7

Height: 1½ to 3 feet

Soil and Moisture: well-drained, sandy, moist to dry

Interest: flowers

Care: moderate

◄ Dichelostemma
congestum

Dichelostemma grows wild across far western North America from central Washington to southern California. The attractive, bluish purple 1-inch-wide flowers are borne in loose clusters atop slender stems and above the sparse, grassy green leaves. The plants thrive in dry grasslands and chaparral, where they blossom each spring. In the garden, dichelostemmas prefer long periods of dry weather interspersed with soaking rains. They are excellent planted in large groups or naturalized in wildflower meadows. The flowers are also useful in fresh floral arrangements.

Growing and care:
Plant dichelostemma corms in fall, setting them 3½ to 5 inches deep and 3 inches apart. The plants thrive in hot, dry weather, especially in summer after they have flowered. In areas with wet summers, dig corms after foliage fades and replant in fall. Protect bulbs in northern zones with a layer of mulch applied in fall. In pots, plant four or five bulbs per 6-inch container. Propagate by removing the small cormels that develop alongside mature bulbs for planting in fall.

Selected species and varieties:
D. congestum bears clusters of trumpet-shaped, pale blue-violet flowers decorated with long, split stamens on 1- to 3-foot stems. *D. pulchellum* has 2-foot stems topped with clusters of purple or white flowers in spring.

675

FRITILLARY
Fritillaria

Light: full sun	
Plant type: bulb	
Hardiness: Zones 3-8	
Height: 6 inches to 2½ feet	
Soil and Moisture: well-drained, sandy, moist	
Interest: flowers, foliage	
Care: moderate	

◀ Fritillaria imperialis

Fritillaries are a wonderfully diverse group of plants that range from the bold, imposing crown-imperial with a garland of garish blossoms on stout stalks, to the small, dainty woodland species with single, modest flowers on slender stems. Fritillaries produce nodding flower bells in unusual colors and patterns in a variety of forms, providing a variety of ways for gardeners to accent their spring gardens. The flowers have prominent, colorful stamens and are often striped, speckled, or checkered in a wide range of watercolor hues. Touching the petals sometimes produces a small "tear" from reservoirs of nectar at the base of each petal. The often glossy leaves are highly variable, sometimes appearing in whorls extending halfway up the flower stalk, sometimes alternating from one side of the stem to the other along its length, and occasionally growing in a tuft at the base of the stem. Mass fritillaries in wildflower gardens, rock gardens, or perennial borders where other plants will fill in when their foliage dies down in early summer.

Growing and care:

Plant fritillaries in late summer or fall, setting large bulbs 4 inches deep and 1 foot apart and smaller bulbs 2 inches deep and 8 inches apart. Bulbs may take a year to become established in new locations before they flower. Most fritillaries like full sun and very well-drained soil, but *F. meleagris* and *F. pallidiflora* prefer some light shade

and moist soil. For all fritillaries, avoid sites with cold, wet soils, and reduce watering once foliage dies back. Both *F. imperialis* 'Rubra Maxima' and *F. persica* are endangered in the wild and should be purchased only from reputable growers selling stock propagated by themselves or other growers. The musky, faintly skunklike odor of crown-imperial is said to repel rodents. Propagate by removing and replanting bulb offsets in late summer or early fall. Plants started from offsets will reach flowering size in 3 to 4 years.

Selected species and varieties:

F. imperialis (crown-imperial) has bold 2½-foot stalks, the lower half lined with whorls of glossy, pointed leaves, the tip crowned by a tuft of shorter leaves with a ring of large 2-inch flower bells with dangling yellow stamens below it; 'Maxima Lutea' is lemon yellow; 'Rubra Maxima', dark red; Zones 4-7. *F. meleagris* (snake's-head fritillary, checkered lily, guinea-hen tulip, leper lily) bears 1½-inch flower bells checkered dark maroon and white on 8- to 10-inch stems; 'Alba' is pure white. *F. michailovskyi* produces up to five deep purplish red and yellow flower bells with their tips flipped daintily outward on 4- to 8-inch stems; Zones 5-8. *F. pallidiflora* has up to a dozen 1- to 1½-inch pale yellow and green flower bells flecked with brown and red, borne in the upper leaf joints along arching 1½-foot stems. *F. persica* has up to 30 velvety purple blossoms lining 2½-foot stems; 'Adiyaman' yields inch-wide plum flowers; Zones 4-8. *F. pudica* (yellow fritillary, yellow bell) bears ¾-inch yellow-orange flowers tinged purple in clusters of three on 9-inch stems; Zones 4-8. *F. purdyi* 'Tinkerbell' has six or seven dainty white flower bells striped rusty brown on the outside and spotted red inside on 6-inch stems above a low rosette of 6-inch leaves; Zones 5-8. *F. uva-vulpis* produces solitary purplish gray flower bells edged in yellow on 1- to 1½-foot stems. *F. verticillata* has 1¼-inch cup-shaped pale yellow blossoms flecked with green outside and spotted purple inside lining 2-foot stems, the tips of the upper leaves elongating into tendrils; Zones 6-8.

GLADIOLUS
Gladiolus

Light: full sun	
Plant type: bulb	
Hardiness: Zones 7-10	
Height: 1 to 7 feet	
Soil and Moisture: well-drained, fertile, moist	
Interest: flowers	
Care: moderate	

◄ Gladiolus communis ssp. byzantinus

Gladiolus is one of the most beautiful of garden flowers, producing very showy spikes of 1½- to 5½-inch flowers above ornamental fans of stiff, sword-shaped leaves. The closely spaced flowers open from bottom to top on alternate sides of the upright flower stems. The abundant, sometimes fragrant flowers open one at a time to provide a long-lasting display that looks fresh for up to several weeks. Tall gladiolus are striking when massed in large groups or planted at the back of a border. Shorter species liven up rock gardens or mixed borders and look charming planted alongside late-blooming daffodils. Gladiolus are long-lasting cut flowers and turn ho-hum floral arrangements into flamboyant bouquets.

Growing and care:
Work well-rotted manure or other organic matter deeply into the soil a year before planting. North of Zone 8, plant hardy gladiolus in fall, tender ones in spring. Set large corms 4 to 6 inches deep and 6 to 9 inches apart, smaller ones 3 to 4 inches deep and 4 to 6 inches apart. Provide ample water while growing and blooming. North of Zone 8, tender gladiolus should be dug in fall for replanting in spring. Early-blooming hybrids flower 90 days after planting, midseason varieties in 110 days, and late-midseason ones in 120 days. To avoid fungus problems, do not plant gladiolus in the same location from year to year. Pick for cut flowers as the first bloom begins to open, leaving four or five leaves in place to feed the corm. Propagate by removing the cormels that develop around mature mother corms in fall.

Selected species and varieties:
G. callianthus [formerly classified as *Acidanthera bicolor*] 'Murielae' yields fragrant, 2- to 3-inch white flowers with purple throats on 2-foot stems in summer. *G. carneus* (painted lady) produces white, cream, mauve, or pink blossoms flecked purple on 2-foot stems, blooming spring to summer; Zones 9-10. *G.* x *colvillei* (Coronado hybrid) has 2-inch scarlet flowers blotched yellow on branching 2-foot stems in spring. *G. communis* ssp. *byzantinus* (Byzantine gladiolus) has white-streaked burgundy flowers on 2-foot stems in spring to summer; Zones 5-10. *G.* hybrids have ruffled, waved, crimped, or frilled flowers in shades of white, yellow, red, purple, blue, or green, sometimes bicolored or multicolored, on stems to 7 feet in summer through fall; 'Nova Lux' is pure velvety yellow; 'Red Bird', flaming red; 'Priscilla', white-feathered pink with a yellow throat; 'Royal Blush' has deep rose red petals edged in white; 'White Knight' is pure white; tender. *G. nanus* [also classified as *Babiana nana*] is a spring- to summer-blooming dwarf plant 1 to 2 feet tall; 'Amanda Mahy' is salmon with violet splotches; 'Desire', cream; 'Guernsey Glory' has pink to purple petals with red edges and cream blotches; 'Impressive' is pinkish white splotched deep rose; 'Prins Claus', ivory with purple spotting.

GLORY-OF-THE-SUN
Leucocoryne

Light: full sun

Plant type: bulb

Hardiness: Zones 9-10

Height: 10 to 12 inches

Soil and Moisture: well-drained, moist to dry

Interest: flowers, fragrance

Care: moderate

◄ Leucocoryne ixioides

Glory-of-the-sun is an uncommon plant that bears small clusters of fragrant, uncommonly attractive star-shaped flowers. The pure white or lapis blue flowers are sparingly produced on slender stems above clumps of foot-long grassy leaves. Glory-of-the-sun thrives in warm, seasonally dry climates such as southern California's, where it adds a dainty accent to rock gardens or borders. Elsewhere the plants are grown in containers and appreciated indoors. Glory-of-the-sun makes an excellent, long-lasting cut flower.

Growing and care:
Outdoors, plant glory-of-the-sun in early to midfall, setting bulbs 4 to 6 inches deep and 6 to 8 inches apart. Water well while plants are actively growing but keep bulbs dry after foliage withers in early summer. Indoors, set bulbs in pots 1 inch deep, allowing two or three bulbs per 6-inch pot. Propagate from seed or from offsets that develop at the base of mature bulbs.

Selected species and varieties:
L. ixioides has up to a half-dozen white to sky blue blossoms ½ inch long and ¾ inch across on stems up to 1 foot tall, and narrow, 10- to 12-inch leaves.

HABRANTHUS
Habranthus

Light: full sun

Plant type: bulb

Hardiness: Zones 9-10

Height: 9 to 12 inches

Soil and Moisture: well-drained, moist

Interest: flowers, foliage

Care: moderate

◄ Habranthus robustus

Habranthus are relatives of amaryllis, and add a soft, lilylike accent to warm-climate rock gardens and flower beds. Each plant produces a single, slender, 12-inch stem bearing two or three blossoms composed of six pointed, delicately recurved petals surrounding a group of prominent stamens. The attractive tuft of dark, glossy green foliage seems to cradle the flower stem. The upright or slightly pendent blossoms of habranthus are beautiful but do not last long. In northern regions the plants are frequently grown indoors in containers.

Growing and care:
From Zone 9 south, plant habranthus outdoors anytime, setting bulbs 4 to 5 inches deep and 6 inches apart in well-worked, evenly moist soil. Water and fertilize regularly while plant is actively growing. Indoors, plant bulbs singly in 6-inch pots in spring for summer blooms. Propagate from seed or from the small bulblets that develop at the base of mature bulbs.

Selected species and varieties:
H. brachyandrus [formerly *Hippeastrum brachyandrum*] has 3-inch flowers edged in light pink with deep burgundy throats on 1-foot stems. *H. robustus* bears slightly pendent, 1-inch rosy pink to red flowers with lime green throats on 9- to 12-inch stems.

HARDY GLOXINIA
Incarvillea

Light: full sun	
Plant type: bulb	
Hardiness: Zones 5-7	
Height: 1 to 2 feet	
Soil and Moisture: well-drained, moist	
Interest: flowers, foliage	
Care: moderate	

◀ Incarvillea delavayi

Hardy gloxinias bear ornate, funnel-shaped flowers with fused, flaring petals in complex shades of pink, rose, and cream. The blossoms line the tips of leafless stems that rise above a graceful clump of ferny foliage. Hardy gloxinias are great for adding splashes of color to rock gardens or sunny borders.

Growing and care:

Plant hardy gloxinias in spring, setting tubers 3 to 4 inches deep and 15 inches apart. Keep soil moist throughout the growing season and fertilize regularly. In northern areas mulch plants in fall with straw or pine needles. Plants grown from seed will reach blooming size in 3 years. Hardy gloxinia can also be propagated by division but plants will produce more flower buds if left undisturbed.

Selected species and varieties:

I. compacta has abundant purple flowers 2½ inches long and 1½ inches across on 1-foot stems above 8-inch dark green leaves; 'Bee's Pink' has white to pink flowers. *I. delavayi* bears 3-inch purplish pink flower trumpets with yellow throats on 2-foot stems above 10-inch leaves.

HERMODACTYLUS
Hermodactylus

Light: full sun	
Plant type: bulb	
Hardiness: Zones 6-9	
Height: 1½ feet	
Soil and Moisture: well-drained, fertile, moist	
Interest: flowers, foliage	
Care: moderate	

◀ Hermodactylus tuberosus

The very unusual flowers of hermodactylus look like a cross between a daylily and an iris. The solitary blossoms are richly colored with contrasting shades of green, yellow, and purple and emit a subtle, rosy fragrance. Beneath the flowers are square, blue-green leaves shaped like upright swords. Hermodactylus are very showy in rock gardens or sunny borders, where they will slowly grow into large colonies. They can also be grown in containers. The plant is still uncommon in the United States but has been popular in Europe for many years.

Growing and care:

Plant tubers 3 inches deep and 6 to 8 inches apart in well-worked, neutral to slightly alkaline soil in late summer or fall. After flowering, the main tuber produces fingerlike offsets before dying. The offsets then bloom the following year. In regions with mild winters hermodactylus will naturalize. Repot container-grown specimens annually after plants go dormant in late summer or fall. Separate offsets from old tubers and replant in fresh potting mix.

Selected species and varieties:

H. tuberosus (snake's-head iris, widow iris) has 2-inch vase-shaped flowers with delicate, lime green, ruffled inner petals enclosed in broad, yellow-green outer petals tipped with dark purple, rising from 1½-foot-tall squared, leafy stems.

HYACINTH
Hyacinthus

Light: full sun

Plant type: bulb

Hardiness: Zones 3-7

Height: 4 to 12 inches

Soil and Moisture: well-drained, fertile, moist

Interest: flowers

Care: easy

◀ Hyacinthus orientalis 'Blue Jacket'

With their heady fragrance and richly colored blossoms, hyacinths have long been regarded as a classic plant for the spring border. The plants have stiff, narrow, slightly glossy leaves and short, stout stems packed with star-shaped flowers from mid- to late spring. The tips of the petals curve backward gracefully, giving the dense clusters a frilly appearance, an effect that is heightened when flowers are shaded in two tones of the same color. Hyacinths come in many different types, ranging from double-flowered cultivars with whorls of petals to multiflora varieties that produce several flower stems decorated with loose, open flower clusters. Hyacinths make excellent companions to other spring-flowering bulbs in sunny beds and borders. When forced indoors in containers the flowers emit a floral fragrance that can perfume an entire room for weeks.

Growing and care:
Outdoors, plant bulbs in fall, setting them 4 to 6 inches deep and 6 to 8 inches apart in rich soil well amended with compost or well-rotted manure. Indoors, allow four or five bulbs per 6-inch pot. Plant indoor bulbs in fall as well. Prechilled bulbs will bloom earlier than ordinary bulbs. Keep newly potted, previously unchilled bulbs in a dark location below 50°F for about 12 weeks or until roots fill the pot and bulbs show 2 inches of leaf growth.

Then move the pots into filtered sunlight at a temperature no higher than 65°F. If using special hyacinth vases, suspend the bulb above (but not touching) the water and treat the same as potted bulbs. 'Anne Marie' and 'Blue Jacket' are particularly good cultivars for forcing, providing more reliable flowering than other types. Hyacinths are difficult to propagate but sometimes form offsets alongside mature bulbs. Plants propagated from offsets can reach blooming size in about 6 years.

Selected species and varieties:
H. orientalis (Dutch hyacinth, common hyacinth, garden hyacinth) has clusters of star-shaped blossoms in an array of colors above foot-long leaves; 'Anne Marie' is pastel pink aging to salmon; 'Blue Giant' has large, pastel blue clusters; 'Blue Jacket' is deep purple with paler petal edges; 'Blue Magic', purple-blue with a white throat; 'Carnegie', elegant pure white; 'City of Harlem', pastel lemon yellow; 'Delft Blue', porcelain blue with paler edges; 'French Roman Blue' is a multiflora cultivar with blue blooms; 'Gipsy Queen', yellow-tinged clear orange; 'Hollyhock' has flowers with double red petals on 4-inch stalks; 'Jan Bos' is clear candy-apple red on slender spikes; 'Lady Derby', rosy pink; 'Lord Balfour' has loose clusters of rose-purple blossoms; 'Oranje Boven' is salmon; 'Peter Stuyvesant', deep purple-blue; 'Pink Pearl', deep luminescent pink; 'Snow White' is a white multiflora variety; 'Violet Pearl' is lilac-rose aging to silver.

IRIS
Iris

Light:	full sun
Plant type:	bulb
Hardiness:	Zones 5-9
Height:	4 inches to 5 feet
Soil and Moisture:	well-drained, moist to dry
Interest:	flowers, foliage
Care:	moderate

◀ Iris ensata

Irises blossom in a rainbow of colors in spring and summer on zigzag stems rising above clumps of flat, sword-shaped foliage that remains attractive long after the flowers fade. Each flower is composed of three drop-ping petal-like sepals called falls, three erect petals called standards, and three narrow, petal-like styles. Some spread from rhizomes, while others grow from bulbs. Irises can be used in borders or rock gardens, or natural-ized in woodland settings. Many irises are quite fragrant, and those with long stalks make good cut flowers. With more than 200 species and countless varieties, there is a type of iris to fit any garden anywhere.

Growing and care:
Plant irises in summer in the North and in fall in the South, spacing smaller types 1 foot apart and taller vari-eties 1½ feet apart. Dig a hole and refill until the top of the mound of soil is at ground level. Place rhizomes on mound and spread roots. Finish filling the hole and gen-tly tamp the soil. Bearded iris should have the top half of the rhizomes above soil level while Siberian iris should have the rhizome completely buried beneath the soil sur-face. *I. pseudacorus* prefers wet meadows or the shallow edges of ponds. Siberian, Louisiana, and Japanese irises need constant moisture and thrive in soil high in organic matter. Propagate rhizomatous irises after flowering by first trimming foliage to a 6-inch fan with a sharp, clean knife. Cut the rhizome cleanly into sections, being sure each piece has several buds and a quantity of healthy roots.

Selected species and varieties:
I. bearded hybrids bear 3- to 5-inch white to purple flow-ers with yellow beards on 2- to 3-foot stems, and clumps of light green leaves in summer; 'Austrian Sky' has sky blue flowers with navy blue falls; 'Broadway' has golden standards and white falls; 'Vanity' has light pink flowers splashed with white. *I. cristata* (crested iris, dwarf crested iris) grows from small, spreading rhizomes that produce grassy 6-inch leaves and 2-inch white or blue-violet flow-ers crested in yellow or white in midspring on 4-inch stems; 'Shenandoah Sky' has pale blue flowers; 'Summer Storm' has dark blue blossoms. *I. ensata* [also listed as *I. kaempferi*] (Japanese iris) has graceful, stiff 2-foot leaves with beardless 3- to 6-inch flowers in many differ-ent colors on 4-foot stalks in summer; 'August Emperor' has giant, deep red flowers in late summer; 'Pink Tri-umph' bears 8-inch deep pink, double-petaled flowers. *I. pallida* 'Variegata' grows 3 feet tall with fragrant laven-der-blue flowers in early spring and lovely foliage all summer. *I. pseudacorus* (yellow flag, yellow iris) has 2-inch bright yellow, beardless flowers from late spring to early summer on 4- to 5-foot stems, spreading vigorous-ly from rhizomes. *I. reticulata* (reticulated iris) has 8- to 10-inch-tall stems rising from bulbs in late winter bear-ing blue to red-purple flowers in early spring; 'Harmony' has 6-inch brilliant blue flowers. *I. sibirica* (Siberian iris) produces 2- to 4-foot clumps of leaves with 3- to 5-inch beardless, late-spring flowers in many colors including violet, blue, white, and red, on 3-foot stems, growing from rhizomes; 'Eric the Red' has dark red flowers; 'Peri-winkle' has powder blue flowers; 'Super Ego' has robust 3-foot stems and striking 5-inch pale blue petals boldly etched with navy blue. *I. versicolor* (blue flag) has 2- to 3-foot-tall clumps of graceful, lance-shaped leaves and strong stalks bearing several showy violet-blue flowers in summer; 'Rosea' has pink flowers; Zones 3-6.

MARIPOSA LILY
Calochortus

Light: full sun

Plant type: bulb

Hardiness: Zones 6-10

Height: 8 inches to 2 feet

Soil and Moisture: well-drained, sandy, moist to dry

Interest: flowers

Care: moderate

◀ Calochortus venustus

These eye-catching native wildflowers of the American West are stunning additions to naturalistic plantings, rock gardens, and fresh floral arrangements. The teacup-shaped flowers come in many colors depending on the species, including white, pink, yellow, lilac, and purple. The blossoms appear from the leaf axils or atop the erect stems that rise from a small clump of shiny, fleshy, narrow leaves, and are usually stained with darker tones along the flower's throat.

Growing and care:
Purchase only nursery-grown bulbs. Plant mariposa lilies in fall, setting the bulbs 2 to 4 inches deep and 8 to 10 inches apart. Keep soil dry while bulbs are dormant from late summer to winter, and evenly moist while plants are actively growing from late winter to summer. In areas with wet summer and fall seasons, lift bulbs in late summer, store in a cool, dry place, and replant in fall. Propagate from seed or by removing and replanting bulblets growing alongside mature bulbs in summer after plants are dormant.

Selected species and varieties:
C. clavatus has charming yellow blossoms borne on 2-foot-tall stems in summer. *C. venustus* (white mariposa) bears 2-inch white, yellow, purple, or red flowers with throats splotched in darker shades or contrasting colors on 8-inch to 2-foot stems.

MONTBRETIA
Crocosmia

Light: full sun

Plant type: bulb

Hardiness: Zones 5-9

Height: 2 to 4 feet

Soil and Moisture: well-drained, moist

Interest: flowers, foliage

Care: moderate

◀ Crocosmia 'Lucifer'

Montbretias produce dozens of small, vibrantly colored flowers in summer that seem to float above masses of long, sword-shaped leaves. They make excellent container plants in northern regions, and naturalize where winters are mild, forming thick beds that are striking when in bloom. Montbretias are excellent plants for sunny borders and for moist areas near streams, ponds, or lakes.

Growing and care:
Plant montbretia corms in spring, setting them 3 to 5 inches deep and 6 to 8 inches apart. Fertilize in spring with a well-balanced fertilizer. Protect from frost with mulch applied in early winter, or lift corms in fall and store at 50°F for spring planting. Propagate montbretias by replanting small cormels that develop at the base of mature corms, or from seed sown as soon as it ripens in fall.

Selected species and varieties:
C. x *crocosmiiflora* produces horizontal sprays 2 to 4 feet long in red, orange, yellow, maroon, or bicolors, with large-flowered types bearing 1½- to 3-inch blossoms and leaves ½ to 1 inch wide and 2 to 3 feet long; 'Aurantiaca' has deep orange flowers; 'Venus' has peach-yellow flowers; Zones 6-9. *C.* 'Citronella' has yellow flowers with maroon markings in the center; 'Lucifer' bears fiery red blossoms on 3-foot stems.

NECTAROSCORDUM
Nectaroscordum

Light: full sun

Plant type: bulb

Hardiness: Zones 6-10

Height: 4 feet

Soil and Moisture: well-drained, moist

Interest: flowers

Care: easy

◀ Nectaroscordum siculum

Nectaroscordum is one of the most attractive members of the onion family. The plants bear large, loose clusters of pendent, flowery bells atop 4-foot stems. While in flower the blossoms are pendulous but become more erect as the seedpods form. The long, straplike leaves are bright green and emit an oniony odor when bruised. Nectaroscordum adds a strong upright presence to borders or sunny wildflower gardens, where it slowly spreads into larger clumps. The dried seedpods are very attractive in arrangements.

Growing and care:
Plant nectaroscordum in fall, setting bulbs 2 inches deep and 1½ feet apart. They bloom best when clumps are undisturbed, and they often freely self-sow. Keep soil moist while plants are actively growing. Fertilize lightly in spring. Plants grown from seed will reach flowering size in 2 years. Clumps can also be divided in fall after leaves wither.

Selected species and varieties:
N. siculum (Sicilian honey garlic) has clusters of ½-inch-wide flowers composed of six rounded petals, overlapping at their bases and flared open at their tips, each dull buff petal tinged green to purple-green with a darker purple stripe down its center.

NERINE
Nerine

Light: full sun

Plant type: bulb

Hardiness: Zones 9-10

Height: 8 inches to 2 feet

Soil and Moisture: well-drained, sandy, dry to moist

Interest: flowers, foliage

Care: moderate

◀ Nerine bowdenii

Nerines bear large clusters of star-shaped flowers with prominent stamens that resemble giant honeysuckle blossoms. The flowers appear on leafless stems in fall, followed by narrow, strap-shaped, glossy leaves from late winter to early spring. In warmer zones nerines make bold additions to beds or borders. Elsewhere they make excellent container plants for portable autumn color. Nerine is good for cutting and adds an unforgettable, exotic touch to arrangements.

Growing and care:
Plant nerine bulbs in late summer, setting them 8 inches apart with the upper half of the bulb above the soil surface. In northern areas, grow in containers and bring plants indoors after they flower in fall. When the foliage turns brown in spring, stop watering and keep bulbs dry until late summer. Propagate from seed or by removing bulb offsets.

Selected species and varieties:
N. bowdenii has 9-inch open clusters of lively, rose pink flowers on 2-foot-tall stems that appear with the leaves; 'Pink Triumph' produces blossoms of shockingly iridescent pink. *N. sarniensis* (Guernsey lily) bears 10-inch clusters of icy white to dark scarlet flowers on 1½-foot stems; 'Cherry Ripe' has rosy red blossoms; 'Early Snow' produces flowers of pure white; 'Radiant Queen' has rosy pink flowers; 'Salmon Supreme' bears light pink blossoms.

PANCRATIUM
Pancratium

Light: full sun	
Plant type: bulb	
Hardiness: Zones 9-10	
Height: 1 to 2 feet	
Soil and Moisture: well-drained, sandy, dry	
Interest: flowers, fragrance	
Care: moderate	

◀ Pancratium maritimum

Pancratium produces clusters of clear white, extremely fragrant, exotic flowers reminiscent of frilled daffodils. The blossoms are borne on sturdy stems above a nest of gray-green sword-shaped leaves. Where climates are reliably frost-free they are a sophisticated addition to borders and rock gardens. North of Zone 9, plant them in containers for patio display or indoor use.

Growing and care:
Plant pancratium bulbs where they can remain undisturbed for several years, setting them 3 inches deep and 10 to 12 inches apart. Set one large bulb per 1-foot pot to allow room for bulb offsets to develop. Plant so the tip of the bulb is level with the soil surface. Repotting or division may reduce flowering the following season. Propagate by carefully removing the offsets from around the fragile, mature bulbs.

Selected species and varieties:
P. maritimum (sea daffodil, sea lily) has 3-inch flaring, snow white flowers with a deeply toothed, trumpet-shaped corona surrounded by six narrow, pointed petals in clusters at the tip of each stem.

PEACOCK FLOWER
Tigridia

Light: full sun	
Plant type: bulb	
Hardiness: Zones 7-10	
Height: 1 to 2 feet	
Soil and Moisture: well-drained, fertile, moist	
Interest: flowers, foliage	
Care: moderate	

◀ Tigridia pavonia

Peacock flower's unique blossoms are composed of three large outer petals forming a broad triangle enfolding three gaily spotted inner petals united to form a deep cup. The blossoms appear singly on erect stems rising from stiff fans of swordlike leaves. Each flower lasts only a day, but the corms produce a succession of blossoms over 6 to 8 weeks. The vivid tones of peacock flowers are stunning when massed in borders and beds. In southern regions the plants often naturalize.

Growing and care:
Plant peacock flowers in spring, setting corms 3 to 4 inches deep and 6 to 9 inches apart. Provide a protective winter mulch in Zone 7. North of Zone 7, plant bulbs in spring and lift in fall. Allow plants to dry for a few days and snip off foliage 2 to 3 inches above the bulb. Store over winter in a cool, dark place. Plants grown from seed will bloom the first year. Peacock flower can also be propagated from the small cormels that develop at the base of mature corms.

Selected species and varieties:
T. pavonia (peacock flower, tiger flower) bears 3- to 6-inch white, yellow, orange, purple, or pink flowers with conspicuously spotted and mottled centers; 'Alba' has white outer petals; 'Aurea' is yellow; 'Rosea', rosy pink.

POLIANTHES
Polianthes

Light: full sun

Plant type: bulb

Hardiness: Zones 9-10

Height: 2 to 4 feet

Soil and Moisture: well-drained, moist

Interest: flowers, foliage, fragrance

Care: moderate

◀ Polianthes tuberosa 'The Pearl'

Polianthes is one of the most intensely fragrant flowers around. The long, curving buds open above grassy, gray-green leaves into clusters of waxy flowers with a rich, sweet, jasminelike fragrance. Each bud forms a narrow trumpet whose petal ends depict a tiny, succulent star. In warm regions use polianthes outdoors in beds and borders. In cooler regions use containers indoors; a single blossom can perfume an entire room. As cut flowers, they last as long as 2 weeks.

Growing and care:

Plant outdoors in spring, setting the tubers 3 inches deep and 6 inches apart. Mature tubers bloom then die, leaving behind many small offsets that reach blooming size in 1 or 2 years. North of Zone 9, start tubers indoors 4 to 6 weeks before night temperatures reach 60°F, and lift for winter storage. For potted plants, allow one tuber per 6-inch pot, setting bulbs 1 inch deep. Propagate by removing offsets that develop around mature tubers.

Selected species and varieties:

P. tuberosa (tuberose) bears very fragrant 2½-inch-long white flowers above 1- to 1½-inch rich green leaves; 'The Pearl' has double-petaled, richly fragrant blossoms on 2-foot stems; 'Single Mexican' produces single flowers on 3- to 4-foot stems.

RED-HOT POKER
Veltheimia

Light: full sun

Plant type: bulb

Hardiness: Zone 10

Height: 15 to 20 inches

Soil and Moisture: well-drained, sandy, moist to dry

Interest: flowers

Care: moderate

◀ Veltheimia bracteata

Red-hot poker bears oval clusters of up to 50 pink or white blossoms. The attractive flower spikes open from bottom to top into long, drooping funnels with curled lips. Clusters are carried on sturdy stems above attractive rosettes of glossy green leaves with wavy edges. Both leaves and stems are attractively mottled. Use red-hot poker outdoors in warm climates, and as a container plant for the patio or deck in cooler regions.

Growing and care:

Outdoors in Zone 10 plant red-hot poker bulbs 1 inch deep and 6 to 10 inches apart in fall. In pots, group several of the 6-inch bulbs together in large bulb pans for best effect. Plant them 4 to 6 inches apart with the top third of the bulb exposed, and allow bulbs to dry off during summer dormancy. Propagate by removing bulb offsets after foliage withers.

Selected species and varieties:

V. bracteata has 2-inch pink-red or pink-purple blossoms with green- and white-flecked lips above foliage and stems marbled green and purple. *V. capensis* has long, lance-shaped leaves and 1-foot-tall stems topped with pale pink flowers; 'Rosalba' has white flowers lightly spotted with pink.

RHODOHYPOXIS
Rhodohypoxis

Light: full sun	
Plant type: bulb	
Hardiness: Zones 6-10	
Height: 3 to 4 inches	
Soil and Moisture: well-drained, sandy, dry	
Interest: flowers	
Care: moderate	

◀ Rhodohypoxis baurii

Rhodohypoxis are perky summertime plants with tufts of 3-inch, stiff, grassy leaves covered with downy hairs in spring, followed by dainty, flat-faced blossoms that appear throughout the season. Each blossom sits atop a slender stem, with each plant producing several stems at a time. Rhodohypoxis are excellent planted among paving stones and will naturalize in rock gardens or borders. They can also be grown as container specimens.

Growing and care:
Plant rhodohypoxis in fall, setting rhizomes 1 to 2 inches deep and 2 to 3 inches apart. Protect plants with mulch in winter in Zones 5 and 6. North of Zone 5, plant rhodohypoxis in spring and lift in fall after foliage has turned brown. Dry and store like gladiolus. To grow as a container plant, set four or five rhizomes in a 6-inch bulb pan. Propagate by division of roots in spring before the leaves appear.

Selected species and varieties:
R. baurii (red star) has low-growing, 3- to 4-inch-high stems bearing 1- to 1½-inch white, pink, rose, or red flowers with petals crowded closely together at the center, obscuring the stamens and dainty clusters of grasslike green leaves.

SANDERSONIA
Sandersonia

Light: full sun	
Plant type: bulb	
Hardiness: Zones 9-10	
Height: 2 to 3 feet	
Soil and Moisture: well-drained, sandy, dry	
Interest: flowers	
Care: moderate	

◀ Sandersonia
aurantiaca

Children love the chubby little lantern-shaped blossoms of sandersonia. The petals fuse into tiny, balloon-shaped flowers that dangle from thin stalks growing in the upper leaf joints along semierect, climbing stems. Soft green, narrow, pointed leaves line the stems, sometimes tapering into threadlike tendrils. Sandersonia not only is enchanting to children but will impress adults as well when planted along fences or walls, or grown in containers as patio specimens. Sandersonia also makes an excellent cut flower.

Growing and care:
Plant sandersonia in spring, after danger of frost has passed, carefully setting the brittle tubers 4 inches deep and 8 to 12 inches apart. North of Zone 9, lift tubers in fall and store over winter in a cool, dry place. The plants can also be grown outdoors in containers during summer and brought indoors during the colder months. Plants propagated from seed will bloom in about 2 years. Established plantings can be divided in spring.

Selected species and varieties:
S. aurantiaca (Chinese-lantern lily, Christmas-bells) has 1-inch lantern-shaped golden orange blossoms hanging from 2- to 3-foot-tall stems covered with narrow green leaves.

SAUROMATUM
Sauromatum

Light: full sun	
Plant type: bulb	
Hardiness: Zone 10	
Height: 1 to 2 feet	
Soil and Moisture: well-drained, moist to wet	
Interest: flowers, foliage	
Care: moderate	

◄ Sauromatum venosum

Sauromatum is a plant for wet places, where the colorful spathe and feathery foliage add a distinctive, tropical touch to water gardens. The tiny, inconspicuous true flowers are carried on a pencil-shaped spadix that emerges from an exotically shaped and colored hood or spathe. The pointed, curled spathe rises from the thick, bottle-shaped stem. The blossoms look pretty but smell awful. After the spathe withers, a finely divided leaf resembling a miniature palm tree appears. Sauromatums are great for warm-climate bog gardens or in containers as specimen plants.

Growing and care:
In Zone 10 where the air is humid and temperatures remain above 68°F, the tubers can be set in a saucer of water on a sunny window sill, where they will grow without soil. For a more conventional garden, plant them outdoors, setting tubers 4 to 6 inches deep and 1 foot apart. North of Zone 10, grow them as container plants, with the tubers set 2 inches deep in pots.

Selected species and varieties:
S. venosum [formerly *S. guttatum*] (voodoo lily, monarch-of-the-East, red calla) produces a 12- to 20-inch-tall spathe mottled and flecked purple, brown, green, and yellow, followed by 20- to 24-inch palmlike foliage.

SCARBOROUGH LILY
Vallota

Light: full sun	
Plant type: bulb	
Hardiness: Zone 10	
Height: 3 feet	
Soil and Moisture: well-drained, sandy, fertile, dry to moist	
Interest: flowers, foliage	
Care: moderate	

◄ Vallota speciosa

Scarborough lily (also called *Cyrtanthus*) bears whorls of vividly colored amaryllis-like blossoms with star-like pointed petals forming deep trumpets around long, prominent stamens. Clusters of up to 10 flowers are borne atop sturdy stems above clumps of straplike evergreen leaves. *Vallota* can be used in beds and borders in very warm regions. In cooler climates it makes an excellent container plant.

Growing and care:
In frost-free climates plant outdoors in early spring, setting bulb tips at the soil line and spacing them 15 to 18 inches apart. For pot culture, plant one bulb in a 6-inch pot, leaving the top half of the bulb above the soil line. Bulbs potted in spring will bloom in fall. Keep soil moist during winter dormancy. Repot bulbs every 5 to 6 years. Propagate at repotting time by removing the small bulblets that grow around the base of mature bulbs.

Selected species and varieties:
V. speciosa [also called *Cyrtanthus elatus*] bears 3-inch-wide deep scarlet, sometimes pink or white, flower funnels above attractive, deep green, glossy leaves.

SEA ONION
Urginea

Light: full sun	
Plant type: bulb	
Hardiness: Zones 8-10	
Height: 3 to 5 feet	
Soil and Moisture: well-drained, sandy, dry	
Interest: flowers	
Care: easy	

◀ Urginea maritima

Sea onion is an interesting addition to warm-climate gardens and has long been a favorite houseplant in northern regions. The plants produce long spikes of up to 100 tiny flowers at the tips of erect, tall stems that are often bent or twisted by the weight of the blossoms. The flower stalks appear in advance of a rosette of shiny, fleshy, narrow green leaves. In warm, dry areas of the Southwest these plants are perfect for the backs of beds and borders. Elsewhere, enjoy them as indoor potted specimens.

Growing and care:
Plant sea onions in summer with the upper portion of the bulb out of the soil, spacing bulbs 1 to 1½ feet apart. The bulb juice is irritating, and all parts of the plant are poisonous. In cool regions pot bulbs in containers in summer. Grow outdoors until a week or so before the first frost, when they should be brought indoors for winter. Propagate by removing bulb offsets in summer.

Selected species and varieties:
U. maritima has 1½-foot spikes of ½-inch white, yellow, or pink blossoms that open from bottom to top on 3- to 5-foot-tall upright stems. After flowering, 10 to 20 dark green, straplike leaves emerge from the top of the bulb.

SIBERIAN LILY
Ixiolirion

Light: full sun	
Plant type: bulb	
Hardiness: Zones 7-10	
Height: 1 foot	
Soil and Moisture: well-drained, moist to dry	
Interest: flowers	
Care: moderate	

◀ Ixiolirion tataricum

Siberian lilies are small plants that put on a dynamic floral display, each tiny bulb producing a large cluster of lilylike flowers with gracefully curved petals and prominent yellow stamens. The flowers cluster atop slender, pliant stems lined with narrow, grassy leaves. They will slowly naturalize in rock gardens where summers are hot and dry, and can be grown as annuals or container plants in northern zones. Siberian lilies make excellent cut flowers.

Growing and care:
In Zones 7 to 9, plant Siberian lilies outdoors in fall, and from Zone 6 north, in spring after danger of frost has passed. Set bulbs 3 to 4 inches deep and 2 to 6 inches apart in well-worked, moist soil. In Zone 7 provide winter mulch; in more northern areas lift bulbs in fall and store over winter. For container growing, plant five or six bulbs in a 6-inch pot in spring. Keep soil moist and cool for several weeks while roots develop, then grow in full sun until blossoming is completed.

Selected species and varieties:
I. tataricum bears up to 15 clear blue to lilac, slightly fragrant 2-inch flowers with narrow petals on 1-foot stems in spring.

TRITELEIA
Triteleia

Light: full sun	
Plant type: bulb	
Hardiness: Zones 7-10	
Height: 1½ to 2½ feet	
Soil and Moisture: well-drained, sandy, dry	
Interest: flowers, foliage	
Care: moderate	

◀ Triteleia laxa

Triteleias are good looking if uncommon plants that produce loose clusters of dainty, starlike flowers on tall stems above sparse clumps of glossy green leaves. They make good cut flowers and are charming when naturalized in sunny beds, borders, or rock gardens.

Growing and care:
Plant triteleias in fall, setting corms 3 inches deep and 2 to 3 inches apart. They grow best where summers are completely dry, as in the western portions of Zones 8 to 10. Elsewhere, lift corms after foliage withers to dry for summer, and replant in fall. Provide a protective winter mulch in Zone 7. Propagate from seed to bloom in 2 years or by removing and replanting small cormels that develop around mature bulbs.

Selected species and varieties:
T. hyacinthina (wild hyacinth) has 1- to 2-foot-tall stems of flat-topped clusters of up to 30 ½-inch white, blue, or lilac star-shaped flowers in late spring to summer. *T. laxa* (grass nut, triplet lily) bears loose, open spheres of 1¾-inch blue to violet, sometimes white, flowers on 2½-foot stems in spring; 'Queen Fabiola' has dense spheres of pale blue blossoms.

TULIP
Tulipa

Light: full sun	
Plant type: bulb	
Hardiness: Zones 3-8	
Height: 8 inches to 1½ feet	
Soil and Moisture: well-drained, fertile, moist	
Interest: flowers	
Care: moderate	

◀ Tulipa 'Easter Fire'

Tulips are available in almost every color but blue, and often are splashed with a second hue. They spring forth as single flowers or in clusters from clumps of fleshy, wavy-edged leaves, providing accents in borders and rock gardens, or naturalized in meadows. They come in many forms, including Darwins, with softly curved, cup-shaped petals; peony-flowered, with blossoms crowded with wavy petals; and species types, with open, starry flowers.

Growing and care:
Plant tulip bulbs in late fall in a warm, sunny location at a depth equal to three times their diameter. They can withstand crowding with no ill effects—even five bulbs per square foot. Species tulips can provide years of beautiful blossoms, but the flower production of even well-tended hybrids declines after the second or third year.

Selected species and varieties:
T. fosteriana grows 1½ feet tall with very large spring flowers and leaves often streaked or mottled with darker colors; 'Red Emperor' is an old favorite with brilliant red flowers edged with yellow. *T.* hybrids comprise 15 divisions, including single early, double early, Darwins, single late, lily-flowered, fringed, multiflowering, parrot, and double late, flowering from early spring to early summer.

ALOE
Aloe

Light: full sun

Plant type: tender perennial

Hardiness: Zone 10

Height: 2 to 3 feet

Soil and Moisture: well-drained, sandy, moist to dry

Interest: foliage

Care: easy

◀ Aloe vera

Aloes are easy-to-grow succulent plants, some of which have a well-deserved reputation for soothing burns and skin irritations. The plants produce rosettes of fleshy, pointed, medium green leaves mottled with splashes of pale white. Where aloe can be grown outdoors, plants produce a slender flower stalk in summer, but those grown as houseplants seldom bloom. Studies have proved that when applied to the skin, the thick, clear sap relieves the pain of burns and scrapes.

Growing and care:
Grow aloes from the small offsets produced by mature plants, removing 1-inch offsets for potted plants or 6- to 8-inch offsets for outdoor specimens. Allow offsets to harden 2 days before replanting outdoors or potting in a 50:50 mixture of compost and sand. Water aloes infrequently. To use the gel-like sap, split leaves lengthwise and rub the cut surface on the skin; fresh sap is best, as stored sap loses its healing properties.

Selected species and varieties:
A. vera [also classified as *A. barbadensis*] (medicinal aloe, Barbados aloe, unguentine cactus) has mottled gray-green leaves up to 3 feet long and 3- to 4-foot-tall flower stalks with dense clusters of 1-inch yellow to orange or red flowers.

ARNICA
Arnica

Light: full sun

Plant type: perennial

Hardiness: Zones 6-9

Height: 6 inches to 2 feet

Soil and Moisture: well-drained, sandy, moist

Interest: flowers, foliage

Care: easy

◀ Arnica montana

The small, golden, asterlike summer flowers of arnica have a casual, dainty appearance and are held above rosettes of narrow, aromatic leaves. Arnica once figured prominently in herbal medicine but is now regarded as toxic when taken internally and is legally restricted in some countries. Arnica preparations for external use, however, are important homeopathic remedies, and ointments made from its flowers are used in Europe for sprains and bruises, though they may cause dermatitis in some.

Growing and care:
Sow arnica seeds in fall or divide mature plants in spring, setting divisions 6 to 8 inches apart. Arnica does not do well in hot, humid sites or where winters are wet. Flower stems become leggy and floppy in rich soils. For an aromatic muscle liniment, pick flowers when fully open, heat equal parts of flowers and oil or lard, then strain and cool.

Selected species and varieties:
A. montana (leopard's-bane) bears tufts of 2- to 5-inch-long blunt-tipped, finely toothed leaves and golden yellow 3-inch flowers composed of narrow petals surrounding a buttonlike center.

BALM-OF-GILEAD
Cedronella

Light: full sun

Plant type: tender perennial grown as annual

Hardiness: Zone 10

Height: 3 to 5 feet

Soil and Moisture: well-drained, fertile, moist

Interest: flowers, foliage

Care: moderate

◀ Cedronella canariensis

Balm-of-Gilead's aromatic leaves lend an earthy air to the garden and impart a warm, woodsy smell with a hint of citrus to potpourri. The pointed, oval leaves line square stems tipped with tufts of small tubular flowers from summer through fall. In frost-free gardens, train it against trellises or walls or grow it in patio containers where its fragrance can be enjoyed. Elsewhere, it grows well as a houseplant. The fresh leaves make a delightful tea when blended with other herbs. The dried leaves and flower buds are wonderful in sachets and potpourris.

Growing and care:
Sow balm-of-Gilead seed or plant divisions of mature plants in spring, spacing transplants or thinning seedlings to stand 1½ feet apart. Prune in early spring and again in fall after flowering to encourage branching and bushiness. Pick leaves just before flowers open, or use leaves from pruned branches. Dry the leaves and buds in a single layer in a shady, well-ventilated area.

Selected species and varieties:
C. canariensis (balm-of-Gilead, canary balm) has toothed leaves up to 4 inches long and dense spikes of pink to lilac flowers on upright, square stems.

BASIL
Ocimum

Light: full sun

Plant type: annual

Height: 6 inches to 3 feet

Soil and Moisture: well-drained, fertile, moist

Interest: foliage

Care: easy

◀ Ocimum 'African Blue'

Basil is one of the most valued culinary herbs, with pointed, oval, slightly up-curved leaves richly fragrant with the aromas of cinnamon, clove, anise, lemon, rose, orange, thyme, mint, or camphor. The plants not only add a classic touch to hundreds of recipes, but contribute spicy fragrance to the garden as well. All species do well in containers, and most are ideal for window sill gardens throughout winter. Whorls of tiny flowers grow in spikes at the tips of stems from summer through fall. Add fresh or dried basil leaves to salads, sauces, soups, and vegetable dishes or steep them for tea. Use flowers as an edible garnish or in herbal bouquets. Add dried basil to herbal potpourri.

Growing and care:
Sow basil indoors 8 to 12 weeks before the last frost or outdoors where it is to grow, spacing or thinning plants to 1 to 2 feet apart. Basil can be sown in pots for indoor culture year round. It can also be propagated from cuttings, which remain true to type. Basil needs soils 50°F or warmer to thrive. Provide mulch to keep roots from drying out and to keep leaves clean. Leaves are best picked before flowers appear; to delay flowering and encourage bushiness, pinch stems back to four sets of leaves as flower buds form. Avoid wetting the leaves of basil, as mold forms quickly on damp leaves. Preserve by blending fresh leaves into olive oil and refrigerating the

BASIL
(continued)

oil or freezing it in small batches. Whole leaves can be layered in olive oil to preserve them, frozen flat on trays after first brushing both sides with olive oil, or layered in white vinegar; the leaves of purple bush basil give vinegar a burgundy tint. Basil can be difficult to dry successfully; lay the leaves in a single layer on trays between layers of paper towels to keep them from turning black.

Selected species and varieties:

O. 'African Blue' has resinous leaves tinged with purple-green on 3-foot stems tipped with purple flower spikes, and is valued as a border specimen and for fresh flowers. *O. basilicum* (common basil, sweet basil) produces bushy, 8- to 24-inch plants prized by cooks and ideal for garden edging, with fragrant 2- to 3-inch leaves lining stems tipped with white flowers; 'Anise' has purple-tinged licorice-scented leaves and pink flowers; 'Cinnamon' has cinnamon-scented leaves especially good in tea; 'Dark Opal' has deep purple leaves and pink flowers; 'Minimum' (bush basil, Greek basil) is a 6- to 12-inch dwarf with 1/2-inch leaves that is ideal indoors; 'Minimum Purpurascens' (purple bush basil) has small purple leaves on 1-foot plants; 'Purple Ruffles' has purple-black leaves whose edges are curled and frilled and is excellent in pots. *O. sanctum* [also classified as *O. tenuiflorum*] (holy basil, clove basil, sri tulsi) bears clove-scented 1 1/2-inch leaves and branching spikes of tiny white flowers on stems 1 1/2 to 2 feet tall, primarily used in landscaping.

CALAMINT
Calamintha

Light: full sun

Plant type: perennial

Hardiness: Zones 5-9

Height: 1 to 2 feet

Soil and Moisture: well-drained, moist to dry

Interest: flowers, foliage, fragrance

Care: easy

◀ *Calamintha nepeta*

Calamints are members of the mint family with attractive, aromatic leaves and decorative flowers. The vigorous, upright plants often are used to add an airy touch to walkway edges, where their fragrant foliage emits a pungent, minty aroma when brushed by passersby. In summer the plants are sprinkled with clusters of white, pink, or violet flowers that last until fall.

Growing and care:

Calamints are heat and drought tolerant. Plant them in spring, spacing them about 1 foot apart, and mulch. Calamints spread rapidly by underground stolons or self-sown seed. Cut back the foliage after plants have finished flowering in fall, and mulch with pine boughs in areas north of Zone 6.

Selected species and varieties:

C. grandiflora [formerly listed as *Satureja grandiflora*] (greater calamint) grows 1 to 1 1/2 feet tall with 2-inch coarsely toothed, oval leaves, and small clusters of 1-inch pink flowers in summer; 'Variegata' has the same bright pink flowers as the species but has attractive light green foliage mottled with golden splotches. *C. nepeta* [formerly listed as *Satureja calamintha,* and sometimes listed as *C. nepetoides*] grows 1 to 2 feet tall with hairy, finely toothed leaves and 1/2-inch white or lilac flowers.

CHAMOMILE
Anthemis

Light:	full sun
Plant type:	perennial
Hardiness:	Zones 3-8
Height:	2 to 3 feet
Soil and Moisture:	well-drained, dry
Interest:	flowers, foliage
Care:	easy

◀ Anthemis tinctoria

Chamomile has daisylike blossoms resembling yellow buttons 2 to 3 inches across and scattered over mounds of sweetly scented, silvery green foliage. The blossoms appear from early summer through fall and range from a clear, sunny yellow to pale sunset orange. The plants are excellent choices for low borders, specialty gardens, or when grown beside stone walls or fences.

Growing and care:

Start seed indoors 8 to 10 weeks before last frost or direct-sow in early spring when soil is still cool. Do not cover, as seeds need light to germinate. Space plants 10 to 18 inches apart. Remove spent flowers for continuous bloom over several months. Propagate by division every 2 years, from seed, or from stem cuttings in spring. *Anthemis* can become infested with powdery mildew during hot, humid weather and should be grown in a breezy, open location.

Selected species and varieties:

A. sancti-johannis (St. John's chamomile) bears 2-inch bright orange flowers on evergreen shrubs; Zones 5-8. *A. tinctoria* (golden marguerite) has 2-inch upturned, gold-yellow flowers above finely cut, aromatic foliage; 'Kelwayi' has bright yellow flowers; 'Moonlight', pale yellow; 'E. C. Buxton', creamy white.

CHICORY
Cichorium

Light:	full sun
Plant type:	perennial
Hardiness:	Zones 3-10
Height:	1 to 5 feet
Soil and Moisture:	well-drained, moist to dry
Interest:	flowers
Care:	easy

◀ Cichorium intybus

Chicory is an informal, charming plant with loose mounds of coarsely toothed leaves and plentiful azure blue, sometimes pink or white flowers from summer to fall. Common chicory forms conical heads of young leaves called chicons. While it can be grown for ornament in a wildflower garden, chicory is most useful in the kitchen. Steam or braise young seedlings and roots. Toss bitter young leaves into salads. Roast and grind the young caramel-flavored roots to blend with coffee. Cultivars can be forced to produce blanched chicons ideal for salads or braising. Dried flowers add color to potpourri.

Growing and care:

Sow chicory seed in spring and thin to 1½ feet. Chicory self-sows freely. The flowers open in the morning and close in the late afternoon and on cloudy days. To roast, lift year-old roots in spring, slice and dry at 350°F. For blanched chicons, lift roots their first fall, cut back all but 1 inch of foliage, and shorten root 1 inch; bury in moist, sandy compost and keep in total darkness at 50°F for 4 weeks.

Selected species and varieties:

C. intybus (common chicory, witloof, barbe-de-capuchin, succory) bears beautiful, daisylike, 1- to 1½-inch sky blue, white, or pink flowers in summer to fall on freely branched, open stems with dark green leaves.

CINNAMON
Cinnamomum

Light:	full sun
Plant type:	tree
Hardiness:	Zone 10
Height:	30 to 50 feet
Soil and Moisture:	well-drained, fertile, moist
Interest:	foliage, bark
Care:	moderate

◀ Cinnamomum zeylanicum

Cinnamon and camphor are best known for their fragrant bark and aromatic leaves but the plants make beautiful specimens as well. Both trees have very attractive, glossy evergreen leaves that are tinged with red, pink, or bronze when young. Use either species as a specimen tree, as their vigorous roots crowd out other plants. Alternately, pot them for indoor enjoyment. Use camphor tree's foliage in potpourri or moth-repellent sachets. When cut and dried, the inner bark of cinnamon curls into sticks or quills, which can be used whole or powdered to flavor teas, baked goods, and fruit dishes, and to scent potpourri.

Growing and care:
Sow camphor tree or cinnamon seed in spring, or root softwood cuttings in spring or summer. Plants are susceptible to root diseases if planted in heavy, wet locations. Pinch and prune potted specimens to maintain a height of 6 to 8 feet.

Selected species and varieties:
C. camphora (camphor tree) grows slowly to 50 feet and half as wide or wider with 3- to 6-inch, pungently aromatic oval leaves and yellow-green spring to summer flowers. *C. zeylanicum* (cinnamon, Ceylon cinnamon) grows to 30 feet and half as wide with russet brown, papery outer bark, leathery 7-inch leaves, and clusters of yellowish white summer flowers.

DILL
Anethum

Light:	full sun
Plant type:	annual
Height:	3 to 4 feet
Soil and Moisture:	well-drained, fertile, moist
Interest:	foliage, seeds
Care:	moderate

◀ Anethum graveolens

The tall, softly scented stems and leaves of dill have been part of the herb garden for centuries. The aromatic, feathery leaves and flat, open clusters of yellow summer flowers add delicate texture to garden beds and kitchen and herb gardens. In winter, dill makes a fine addition to window sill gardens. The ferny, delicate leaves of this very versatile herb are used to flavor fish, egg, meat, and vegetable dishes. The immature flower heads add tang to cucumber pickles, and the flat, ribbed seeds add a warm flavor to breads and sauces.

Growing and care:
Sow dill seed in the garden every 2 to 3 weeks from early spring to summer. Thin seedlings to stand 8 to 10 inches apart. Plants often need staking and should not be planted in breezy locations. Do not plant near fennel. Snip leaves and immature flower heads as needed. Harvest seed heads just before they turn brown, and place in paper bags until seeds loosen and fall. For best flavor preserve leaves by freezing whole stems or drying in a microwave oven or refrigerator; air-dried dill has weak flavor.

Selected species and varieties:
A. graveolens has soft 3- to 4-foot stems lined with fine, aromatic, threadlike foliage; 'Bouquet' is a compact cultivar producing abundant crops of leaves and few flowers; 'Mammoth' is fast growing with large blue-green leaves.

EUCALYPTUS
Eucalyptus

Light: full sun

Plant type: tree

Hardiness: Zones 9-10

Height: 60 to 100 feet

Soil and Moisture: well-drained, fertile, moist

Interest: foliage, bark

Care: moderate

◄ Eucalyptus citriodora

Eucalyptus is best known for its penetratingly aromatic lemon-camphor-scented evergreen leaves, but the smooth bark on the bare, branching trunks is stunningly beautiful in the landscape. The tree grows rapidly outdoors, quickly draping the yard in shade. The plants can also be grown as container specimens for patios and city gardens. Use dried leaves in potpourri, and the dried branches or seed capsules in arrangements. The oil derived from the leaves, roots, and bark is often used as a respiratory aid.

Growing and care:
Sow eucalyptus seed in spring or fall in soil generously amended with compost or rotted manure. Choose planting sites carefully, as roots secrete toxins that inhibit the growth of nearby plants. Once established, trees grow 10 to 15 feet per year. Prune in spring to contain size and develop sturdier trunks.

Selected species and varieties:
E. citriodora (lemon-scented gum) has white, sometimes pink to red bark on trees up to 160 feet tall and spreading half as wide, with 3- to 7-inch golden green, narrow leaves and clusters of tiny white winter blooms followed by ⅜-inch seed capsules.

FENNEL
Foeniculum

Light: full sun

Plant type: tender perennial

Hardiness: Zones 9-10

Height: 4 to 6 feet

Soil and Moisture: well-drained, fertile, moist

Interest: foliage, seeds

Care: easy

◄ Foeniculum vulgare

Fennel is a tall, boldly graceful herb with erect, succulent stems and abundant feathery, aromatic foliage. From summer to fall, pale yellow flowers form atop the stems, followed by seed heads in late summer and fall. The stems, leaves, and seeds all taste of anise. Leaves complement seafood or garnish salads. Add seeds to baked goods, chew to freshen breath, or sprout for use in salads.

Growing and care:
Fennel, though a tender perennial, is usually grown as an annual. Sow seeds successively from spring through summer for a continuous supply of leaves and stems. Left to form seed, fennel readily self-sows in fall for a spring harvest. Snip leaves anytime and use them fresh or frozen; they lose flavor when dried. Collect seed heads as they turn from yellow-green to brown, and store in a paper bag until the seeds drop. Store in airtight containers.

Selected species and varieties:
F. vulgare (fennel, sweet anise) has upright, branching stems to 6 feet with soft, needlelike foliage and pale yellow flowers in summer; 'Purpurascens' (copper fennel) has pink, copper, or bronze young foliage.

GERMAN CHAMOMILE
Matricaria

Light: full sun	
Plant type: annual	
Height: 2 to 3 feet	
Soil and Moisture: well-drained, moist to dry	
Interest: flowers, foliage	
Care: easy	

◀ Matricaria recutita

German chamomile is a delightfully pleasant herb with ferny green foliage and daisylike, honey-scented flowers from late spring to early summer. The soft foliage is excellent as a filler in the herb garden. The flowers can be brewed alone or with other herbs to make a soothing, relaxing tea with a fruity, floral aroma.

Growing and care:
Sow German chamomile in early spring while the soil is cool. Do not cover, as the seed needs light to germinate. Thin or transplant seedlings to stand 8 to 10 inches apart. Fertilize when plants are coming into flower and keep soil evenly moist. Pinch back young plants to encourage bushier growth. Harvest flowers on a dry, sunny day that is not overly warm. Dry flowers in the microwave oven or the refrigerator. Store in an airtight container.

Selected species and varieties:
M. recutita (German chamomile, sweet false chamomile, wild chamomile) produces airy clumps of fine-textured, ferny leaves and inch-wide daisylike flowers with yellow centers fringed with small, slightly drooping white petals.

GOOSEFOOT
Chenopodium

Light: full sun	
Plant type: annual	
Height: 2 to 5 feet	
Soil and Moisture: well-drained, fertile, moist	
Interest: foliage	
Care: easy	

◀ Chenopodium ambrosioides

Goosefoot can be planted in two varieties—epazote and ambrosia—that add beauty to the garden and zest to the house. Epazote's leaves are prized for flavoring beans, corn, and fish in Central American cuisines. They should be used sparingly, however, as the plant's oils are a potent, sometimes toxic vermifuge and insecticide. Ambrosia's fragrant foliage and plumy flower spikes are valued in both fresh and dried arrangements; leaves and seeds can be used to spice up potpourri.

Growing and care:
Sow seed in spring or fall, and thin seedlings to stand 1 foot apart. Pinch plants to keep them bushy. Both epazote and ambrosia self-sow freely and can become invasive weeds. Use epazote leaves either fresh or dried for cooking. For dried arrangements, hang ambrosia in a shady, well-ventilated area or stand stems in vases without water.

Selected species and varieties:
C. ambrosioides (epazote) has spreading clumps of woody stems to 5 feet tall, lined with broad, toothed, oval leaves and with finely lacy leaves. *C. botrys* (ambrosia) has lobed 1/2- to 4-inch leaves that are deep green above and red below, and airy sprays of tiny yellow-green summer flowers without petals along arching 2-foot stems.

HOREHOUND
Marrubium

Light: full sun	
Plant type: perennial	
Hardiness: Zones 4-9	
Height: 1½ to 2 feet	
Soil and Moisture: well-drained, dry	
Interest: flowers, foliage	
Care: moderate	

◀ Marrubium vulgare

There is no middle ground with horehound: Either you like the distinctive, aromatic flavor of the leaves, or you don't. Horehound's deeply puckered, woolly, very fragrant gray-green leaves add texture and soft color to the edges of herb gardens or the middle of borders. The small white flowers attract bees. Use the branching foliage as a filler in fresh or dried bouquets. Steep the fresh or dried leaves, which taste slightly of thyme and menthol, for a soothing tea, or add seeds to cool drinks for flavor. Horehound is a staple for cough remedies in herbal medicine.

Growing and care:
Sow horehound seed in spring in light, sandy soil, thinning seedlings to stand 1 foot apart. Horehound can also be grown from divisions in spring and from stem cuttings taken in summer. If allowed to go to seed, horehound self-sows freely. Prune before or after flowering to keep edgings or container plants compact. Dry the leaves in a single layer and store in airtight containers.

Selected species and varieties:
M. vulgare (common horehound, white horehound) has pairs of 2-inch heart-shaped leaves with deeply scalloped edges along square stems, and whorls of tiny white spring to summer flowers.

LAVENDER
Lavandula

Light: full sun	
Plant type: perennial	
Hardiness: Zones 5-10	
Height: 1 to 3 feet	
Soil and Moisture: well-drained, moist	
Interest: flowers, foliage, fragrance	
Care: moderate	

◀ Lavandula dentata

Lavender's clean, invigorating fragrance and beautiful form have made it one of the best loved of all herbs. The fragrant purple flowers blossom in late spring to summer above pairs of metallic gray-green leaves that line erect, square stems. Plants form shrubby cushions of soft foliage that can be clipped into a low hedge. They can also add an informal accent to edgings, borders, and rock or herb gardens.

Growing and care:
Plant lavenders in spring, spacing them 1 to 1½ feet apart in well-worked soil. Cut back to 8 inches to encourage a bushy form. Lavenders can be propagated from cuttings made in late spring or early fall, or by divisions made in early spring.

Selected species and varieties:
L. angustifolia ssp. *angustifolia* [also listed as *L. officinalis*] (English lavender, true lavender) produces 3- to 4-inch whorls of ¼-inch flowers atop 2- to 3-foot stems with 1- to 2-inch aromatic leaves; 'Fragrance' has particularly pungent flowers; 'Hidcote' is a tightly compact dwarf with deep purple flowers and silvery foliage on 20-inch stems; 'Munstead Dwarf' is more spreading and only 1 foot tall. *L. dentata* (French lavender) has dense, woolly gray foliage at the base of 1- to 3-foot shrubby stems, topped by 1½-inch clusters of slightly fragrant lavender-blue flowers; Zones 8-9.

LEMON, ORANGE
Citrus

Light: full sun

Plant type: shrub, tree

Hardiness: Zones 9-10

Height: 8 to 30 feet

Soil and Moisture: well-drained, fertile, moist to dry

Interest: flowers, foliage, fruit

Care: moderate

◀ Citrus aurantium

Few plants combine beauty and utility as well as citrus. The trees have a lovely, formal appearance with dense, glossy, evergreen foliage plentifully sprinkled with pure white, intensely fragrant flowers, and colorful, juicy fruits. Citruses can be massed into barrier hedges, grown as specimen trees, or planted in containers for patio and deck gardens. Use Seville oranges for piquant marmalade or dry their peels for potpourri. Add lemon slices to tea, or squeeze the juice for cool drinks. Grate lemon or orange peels for flavoring, or dry them for potpourri.

Growing and care:

Sow lemon seed in spring or propagate from softwood cuttings in summer. Choose sites protected from wind and frost. Plants thrive in well-drained soil that has been amended with sand as well as organic matter. Provide mulch around base of plant to conserve soil moisture. Grow potted citruses in containers 1½ feet in diameter or larger. Prune branches as needed to keep plant in shape, and prune roots whenever tree is repotted.

Selected species and varieties:

C. aurantium (bitter orange) reaches up to 30 feet tall and 30 feet wide with bright orange fruits. *C. limon* (lemon) 'Eureka' is a nearly thornless spreading tree that grows to 20 feet tall; 'Meyer' is a cold-resistant 8- to 12-foot-tall dwarf with sweet yellow fruits; 'Ponderosa' has large, grapefruit-size yellow fruits.

LEMON VERBENA
Aloysia

Light: full sun

Plant type: tender perennial

Hardiness: Zones 9-10

Height: 2 to 8 feet

Soil and Moisture: well-drained, moist to dry

Interest: flowers, foliage, fragrance

Care: easy

◀ Aloysia triphylla

Lemon verbena has an uncommonly sweet fragrance. The aromatic citrus scent of the long, lance-shaped leaves, perfumes the garden from spring through fall. In summer slender spikes of lilac or white flowers add a gentle accent. Where lemon verbena can be grown outdoors, it is often pinched and pruned as an espalier or standard to give it special shape. The young, fresh leaves are used to add a fruity zip to cold drinks, salads, and fish or poultry dishes. Steep fresh or dried leaves for tea. Dried leaves retain their fragrance for several years in potpourri.

Growing and care:

Sow lemon verbena seed directly in the garden 3 feet apart in spring after danger of frost has passed. In Zones 9 and 10, cut stems to 6 to 12 inches in fall and provide protective winter mulch. Potted plants drop their leaves in winter and do best if moved outdoors during warmer months. Propagate lemon verbena from seed or from cuttings taken in summer.

Selected species and varieties:

A. triphylla (lemon verbena, cidron, limonetto) has whorls of lance-shaped, strongly lemon-scented leaves along open, sprawling branches growing 6 to 8 feet tall in warm climates and 2 to 4 feet tall as an indoor potted plant. Loose clusters of tiny white to lilac flowers appear on thin, upright stems in late summer.

MADDER
Rubia

Light: full sun	
Plant type: perennial	
Hardiness: Zones 6-10	
Height: 10 inches to 3 feet	
Soil and Moisture: well-drained, fertile, moist	
Interest: roots	
Care: moderate	

◀ Rubia tinctorum

Madder's jointed, prickly stems ramble along the ground or climb weakly over other plants. Leathery leaves grow in whorls at each joint, and in summer and fall a light froth of tiny, pale flowers blooms among the foliage. Madder forms mats of pencil-thick, red-fleshed roots up to 3 feet long, which yield red dye valued by textile craftspeople or, with various mordants, shades of pink, lilac, brown, orange, or black.

Growing and care:
Sow seed while ripe in fall, divide plants anytime between spring and fall, or start new plants from cuttings. Plants root wherever joints touch the ground. Provide supports to control madder's spread and give plants structure. Dig roots of plants that are at least 3 years old in fall.

Selected species and varieties:
R. tinctorum has 2-inch oblong, pointed leaves in whorls of four to eight and $\frac{1}{10}$-inch pale yellow or white open flower bells in airy clusters on plants 3 years old or older, followed by $\frac{1}{8}$-inch reddish brown fruits, which turn black.

MARJORAM
Origanum

Light: full sun	
Plant type: perennial	
Hardiness: Zones 5-10	
Height: 6 inches to 2 feet	
Soil and Moisture: well-drained, fertile, moist to dry	
Interest: flowers, foliage	
Care: easy	

◀ Origanum majorana

Mounds of small, fragrantly spicy oval leaves and branching clusters of tiny, appealing flowers are the hallmarks of this classic culinary herb. The plants can be used as border edgings or ground covers and are essential to the well-stocked herb or kitchen garden. The aromatic leaves can be snipped and added to flavor meat, vegetable, cheese, and fish dishes. The dried leaves and flowers are used in herbal teas or added to potpourri. Tender perennial species are grown as annuals in cooler climates or potted in containers and enjoyed both indoors and out.

Growing and care:
Sow marjoram seed or plant divisions in spring or fall, spacing or thinning plants to 1 to $1\frac{1}{2}$ feet apart. Give golden-leaved cultivars light afternoon shade to prevent leaf scorch. Pinch stems to promote bushiness and delay flowering. Cut perennial marjorams back to two-thirds of their height before winter to promote bushier growth the following season. *O. vulgare* can be invasive. Indoors, pot up divisions or sow seed in pots. Propagate marjorams from seed, from early-summer stem cuttings, or by division in spring or fall. For best flavor, harvest leaves just as flower buds begin to open. Mash leaves in oil to preserve them, layer with vinegar, or freeze. Dry leaves or flowers in the microwave or refrigerator, or in an airy, well-ventilated area.

MARJORAM
(continued)

Selected species and varieties:

O. dictamnus (dittany-of-Crete) has tiny, woolly white leaves and loose, nodding clusters of tiny pink summer to fall flowers on sprawling 1-foot-high plants that are ideal in rock gardens or hanging baskets; Zones 8-9. *O. majorana* (sweet marjoram) has spicy 1¼-inch leaves, an essential seasoning in Greek cuisine and more intensely flavored than those of *O. vulgare,* along 2-foot stems tipped with white to pink flowers; Zones 9-10. *O. x majoricum* (hardy marjoram, Italian oregano) is a hybrid similar to sweet marjoram but slightly hardier; Zones 7-10. *O. onites* (Greek oregano, pot marjoram) bears very mildly thyme-flavored medium-green leaves used in bouquets garnis or laid across charcoal to flavor grilled foods, and mauve to white flowers from summer to fall on 2-foot plants; Zones 8-10. *O. vulgare* (oregano, pot marjoram, wild marjoram, organy) has mildly pepper-thyme-flavored green leaves on sprawling 2-foot stems. It is not the same plant used in commercial dried oregano, but is used for flavoring and valued in landscaping for its branching clusters of white to red-purple summer flowers; Zones 5-9; 'Aureum' has golden leaves; Zones 6-9; 'Aureum Crispum' has round, wrinkled, ½-inch golden leaves on 1-foot plants; Zones 7-9; 'Nanum' is an 8-inch dwarf with purple flowers; Zones 6-9; 'White Anniversary' has green leaves edged in white on 6- to 10-inch plants ideal for edging or containers; Zones 8-9.

MARSH MALLOW
Althaea

◄ Althaea officinalis

Light: full sun	
Plant type: perennial	
Hardiness: Zones 3-9	
Height: 4 to 5 feet	
Soil and Moisture: well-drained, fertile, moist	
Interest: flowers, foliage	
Care: easy	

Marsh mallows are old-fashioned plants with tall, upright spikes of showy flowers that give any planting the ambiance of an English cottage garden. The plants create colorful border backdrops and temporary screens in marshy, wet garden sites or moist upland soils. The tender young leaves and the cup-shaped flowers growing from the leaf axils can be tossed in salads, as can the nutlike seeds contained in the plant's ring-shaped fruits, called cheeses. Steam leaves or fry roots after softening by boiling and serve as a side dish. Roots release a thick mucilage after long soaking, which was once an essential ingredient in the original marshmallow confection and is sometimes used in herbal medicine.

Growing and care:

Sow seed in spring or divide in spring or fall, setting plants 2 feet apart. Keep marsh mallow's woody taproot constantly moist. Pick leaves and flowers just as the blossoms reach their peak. Dig roots of mature 2-year-old plants in fall, remove rootlets, peel bark, and dry whole or in slices.

Selected species and varieties:

A. officinalis (marsh mallow, white mallow) has clumps of stiffly erect 4- to 5-foot-tall stems lined with velvety triangular leaves and showy pink or white summer flowers.

MEXICAN OREGANO
Lippia

Light: full sun

Plant type: shrub

Hardiness: Zones 9-10

Height: 3 to 6 feet

Soil and Moisture: well-drained, fertile, moist to dry

Interest: flowers, foliage

Care: moderate

◀ Lippia graveolens

Mexican oregano has spicy, wrinkled leaves that add a bold accent to tomato and other vegetable dishes as well as seafood, cheese dishes, and chili. Add them to salads and dressings, or steep them with other herbs for teas. In frost-free areas, Mexican oregano can be grown as a specimen plant or pruned into a hedge. Elsewhere, grow it as a container plant to move indoors for the winter.

Growing and care:

Sow Mexican oregano seed anytime, or start new plants from softwood cuttings taken anytime. Keep soil moist until seedlings are a few inches high, then allow to grow in moderately dry conditions. Remove deadwood in spring and prune severely to keep the vigorous shrubs from becoming gangly. Pinch to promote branching and bushiness. Container-grown plants should be pruned annually and root pruned when repotted. Pick leaves anytime for fresh use, or dry and store in an airtight container.

Selected species and varieties:

L. graveolens [also called *Poliomintha longiflora*] produces pointed, oval, 1- to 2½-inch downy leaves and tiny yellow to white winter to spring flowers growing where leaves meet stems on vigorous, spreading branches.

MULLEIN
Verbascum

Light: full sun

Plant type: biennial

Hardiness: Zones 3-10

Height: 4 to 6 feet

Soil and Moisture: well-drained, sandy, dry

Interest: flowers, foliage

Care: easy

◀ Verbascum thapsus

Mullein is an easy-to-grow perennial with two very different personalities. From afar the plant is bold and imposing with strong, starkly upright stems and large leaves. Viewed more closely mullein reveals its velvety soft foliage and delicate, pastel yellow blossoms. Mullein is a biennial that forms a broad rosette of gray-green velvety leaves its first year, followed by dramatic, tall flower spikes the second. Woolly leaves clasp each thick stalk, crowded at its tip with large green buds that open into small flowers with prominent stamens. Yellow spiders or moths commonly seek out the blossoms as camouflaged refuges. Great mullein is one of the few gray-leaved plants that tolerate heat and humidity, making it a back-of-the-border specimen. Dry the honey-scented flowers for potpourri.

Growing and care:

Sow great mullein seed in fall or spring and space seedlings 2 to 2½ feet apart. Plants die after flowering but reseed themselves freely if flowers remain on plants. Once established the plants are very drought and heat tolerant and need no fertilizing.

Selected species and varieties:

V. thapsus (great mullein, common mullein, flannel plant, Aaron's rod) has thick, woolly leaves 6 to 18 inches long and spreading 3 feet wide, and ¾- to 1-inch-wide yellow flowers with orange stamens.

MUSTARD
Brassica

Light: full sun

Plant type: annual

Height: 3 to 4 feet

Soil and Moisture: well-drained, moist to dry

Interest: flowers, foliage, seeds

Care: easy

◀ Brassica juncea

Mustard is a prolific herb that produces peppery foliage that adds zest to salads. The medium green oval leaves can also be boiled or sautéed as a side dish. The four-petaled yellow summer flowers are followed by small pods filled with tiny round seeds that give pickles and curries a zippy flavor. They can also be ground and mixed with vinegar for a tasty condiment. Mustard can be grown in pots indoors for a continuous supply of young salad greens in winter.

Growing and care:
Sow mustard seed ¼ inch deep in spring in rows 1½ feet apart and thin plants to stand 8 inches apart. Use the thinnings in salads; young leaves are ready for salad picking in 8 to 10 days. Mustard self-sows freely for future crops. Harvest pods as they begin to brown, and finish drying them in paper bags to collect the ripening seed. Brown mustard develops its hottest flavor when ground seeds are mixed with cold, water-based liquids.

Selected species and varieties:
B. juncea (brown mustard, Chinese mustard, Indian mustard, mustard cabbage, mustard greens) has leaves 6 to 12 inches long with open, branching clusters of pale yellow flowers followed by 1½-inch beaked pods filled with dark reddish brown seeds.

ORACH
Atriplex

Light: full sun

Plant type: annual

Height: 2 to 6 feet

Soil and Moisture: well-drained, moist to dry

Interest: foliage

Care: moderate

◀ Atriplex hortensis 'Rubra'

Garden orach is a large, upright plant with huge, imposing, arrowhead-shaped leaves that have a unique, rough beauty. The plants are best used planted close together to make a seasonal screen or background. The greenish burgundy leaves add color and a slightly salty tang to salads. Leaves and young shoots can be boiled like spinach. Use the colorful foliage as a filler in fresh arrangements.

Growing and care:
Sow orach seed indoors 6 weeks before planting out or direct-sow in early spring. Thin plants to stand 8 to 12 inches apart. If started indoors transplant seedlings when small. Do not disturb plants once established. Orach will tolerate both saline soils and dry conditions but produces the most succulent leaves when kept constantly moist. Successive sowings every 2 weeks ensure a continuous supply of young salad leaves. Pinch out flower heads to encourage greater leaf production. Orach self-sows freely and can become invasive. Dip stem ends in boiling water to seal them before using in arrangements.

Selected species and varieties:
A. hortensis (orach, mountain spinach) has smooth, deep green leaves with a port wine tinge and branching clusters of tiny yellow-green flowers tinged red in summer on stems to 6 feet; 'Rubra' (purple orach) has deep burgundy red leaves and stems.

PEPPER
Capsicum

Light: full sun

Plant type: annual

Height: 1 to 3 feet

Soil and Moisture: well-drained, fertile, moist

Interest: fruit

Care: moderate

◀ Capsicum frutescens 'Tabasco'

Peppers are much more versatile than many people imagine and are used in herbal remedies and as ornamental plants, as well as being a tasty vegetable. Some varieties produce hundreds of small, colorful fruits from summer through fall, held above low clumps of narrow, dark green oval leaves. Use them as border edgings, massed in beds, or in patio containers as well as in kitchen and herb gardens. Chop the fiery fruits into salsas, chutneys, marinades, vinegars, salad dressings, and baked goods. The peppers become spicier when dried.

Growing and care:
Start peppers indoors 8 to 10 weeks before the last frost and transplant to the garden when soil temperature reaches 65°F or more. Set plants 1½ feet apart and mulch from midsummer on to prevent drying out. Peppers thrive in hot conditions. Harvest by cutting stems above the fruit. To dry, string on a line or pull entire plants and hang in a cool, dark place.

Selected species and varieties:
C. annuum var. *annuum* 'Jalapeno' (chili pepper) bears narrow, conical 2½- to 4-inch-long fruits ripening from green to red. *C. chinense* 'Habañero' (papaya chili) bears extremely hot, bell-shaped 1- to 2-inch fruits ripening from green to yellow-orange. *C. frutescens* 'Tabasco' (tabasco pepper) has small, upright green fruits ripening to red with a zesty, slightly smoky flavor.

POT MARIGOLD
Calendula

Light: full sun

Plant type: annual

Height: 1 to 2 feet

Soil and Moisture: well-drained, moist to dry

Interest: flowers

Care: easy

◀ Calendula officinalis

Pot marigold got its common name from its marigold-like flowers that were routinely tossed into cooking pots to add saffron color to recipes. The long-lasting blooms are flattened, with broad ray petals in shades of orange, yellow, or cream from spring to frost. Their bright colors and long season of bloom make them valuable for use in borders, mixed beds, herb gardens, and containers. Use the fresh, slightly salty-tasting flower petals in salads, soups, sandwiches, and pâtés. Dried and ground, the petals add saffron color to puddings and rice dishes.

Growing and care:
Start seed indoors 6 to 8 weeks prior to the last frost. Transplant into loosened soil amended with some organic matter once soil has warmed. In areas with mild winters it can be sown directly outdoors in fall or early spring. Space plants 1 to 1½ feet apart. Deadhead to increase flowering. Calendulas thrive in cool conditions and tolerate poor soils if they have adequate water.

Selected species and varieties:
C. officinalis has a neat, mounding habit and grows 1 to 2 feet tall with a similar spread. Leaves are 2 to 6 inches long, blue-green, and aromatic. The solitary 2½- to 4½-inch flower heads close at night; 'Bon-Bon' grows 1 feet tall with a compact, early-blooming habit and a mixture of flower colors.

703

ROCKET
Eruca

Light:	full sun
Plant type:	annual
Height:	2 to 3 feet
Soil and Moisture:	well-drained, fertile, moist
Interest:	flowers, foliage
Care:	easy

◀ Eruca vesicaria ssp. sativa

Rocket's tangy young leaves add biting zest to mixed green salads. This easy-to-grow plant is an essential ingredient in mesclun blends of salad greens, and can also be chopped and added to sauces or steamed as a spicy side dish. The whitish pink, violet-veined flowers have a slightly milder flavor than the leaves and are added to late-summer salads.

Growing and care:

Sow rocket directly in the garden in early spring while the soil is still cool. Make successive sowings every 2 weeks through early summer. Thin plants to stand 6 to 8 inches apart. Leaves are ready to pick 6 to 8 weeks after sowing. Plants develop their best flavor when they grow quickly in cool, evenly moist soil. Older leaves or those grown in dry ground during hot weather become strong and bitter.

Selected species and varieties:

E. vesicaria ssp. *sativa* (arugula, rocket, Italian cress, roquette) bears rounded or arrowhead-shaped mustard-like leaves, coarsely toothed along their midrib, with delicate, purple-veined, creamy late-summer to fall flowers followed by slender, upright seedpods.

ROMAN CHAMOMILE
Chamaemelum

Light:	full sun
Plant type:	perennial
Hardiness:	Zones 4-8
Height:	1 to 6 inches
Soil and Moisture:	well-drained, moist to dry
Interest:	flowers, foliage
Care:	easy

◀ Chamaemelum nobile

Roman chamomile is one of the most popular herbs grown, with feathery, intensely aromatic leaves that release a soothing, fruity scent when crushed. The plants spread quickly into dense mats ideal as informal ground covers or as fillers among walkway stones and rock gardens. Dry the leaves for potpourri. The flowers that bloom from late spring through early fall can be dried and steeped for a relaxing tea.

Growing and care:

Sow Roman chamomile seed in spring or fall or plant divisions in spring. The species self-seeds freely, but cultivars only come true from division. To make a chamomile lawn, space plants 4 to 6 inches apart and allow to spread before mowing. Harvest flowers as petals begin to fade, and dry on screens in a shady, well-ventilated area. Store in a sealed container away from bright light.

Selected species and varieties:

C. nobile [formerly classified as *Anthemis nobilis*] (Roman chamomile, garden chamomile) produces very attractive, lacy, bright green leaves and dainty 1-inch white daisylike flowers with golden yellow centers; 'Flore Pleno' has double-petaled cream flowers on plants 6 inches high spreading 1½ feet wide; 'Treneague' is a nonflowering cultivar that grows 1 to 2 inches tall and 1½ feet wide.

ROSE
Rosa

Light: full sun

Plant type: shrub

Hardiness: Zones 3-10

Height: 10 feet

Soil and Moisture: well-drained, moist

Interest: flowers, fruit

Care: easy to moderate

◀ Rosa canina

Besides using roses in arrangements, try adding the petals to salads or crystallizing them as a garnish. Dry the buds and petals for potpourri. Use the fruit, or hips, for tea or jam. Herbs for the teapot make soothing beverages, and the steeped hips of *Rosa canina* provide a healthy dose of vitamin C.

Growing and care:
Sow fresh rose seed, root hardwood cuttings, or plant commercial rootstock in fall. Mulch to conserve moisture. Prune dead or damaged wood in late winter, avoiding the previous season's growth, on which this season's flowers grow.

Selected species and varieties:
R. canina (dog rose, brier rose) has 10-foot canes with white or pink 2-inch blooms and ¾-inch hips; Zones 4-9. *R. damascena* (damask rose) bears very fragrant 3-inch blooms on 6-foot canes; 'Autumn Damask' is a double pink; 'Madame Hardy', a double white; Zones 5-9. *R. gallica* (French rose) has 2- to 3-inch blooms on 3- to 4-foot plants; 'Officinalis' (apothecary rose) is a semidouble deep pink; 'Versicolor' (rosa mundi) is a semidouble pink- or red-striped white, red, or pink; Zones 4-10. *R. rugosa* (Japanese rose) produces crimson 3½-inch blossoms and 1-inch hips; 'Alba' is white; 'Rubra', burgundy red; Zones 3-8.

RUE
Ruta

Light: full sun

Plant type: perennial

Hardiness: Zones 5-9

Height: 1 to 3 feet

Soil and Moisture: well-drained, moist

Interest: flowers, foliage

Care: easy

◀ Ruta graveolens

Common rue forms delicate clumps of lacy, aromatic blue-green foliage that adds a soft, surreal quality to beds and borders. For several weeks in summer, frilly, spidery flowers bloom from pliant stems held high above the foliage. The inflated lobed seed capsules that appear in late summer and fall can be gathered and dried for use in dried arrangements. Once used in herbal medicine, rue is now considered poisonous. Sensitive individuals develop a blistering dermatitis after touching the leaves. Wear gloves when handling the plants.

Growing and care:
Start rue seed indoors 8 to 10 weeks before the last frost; sow outdoors once soil has warmed. Divide mature plants in spring or fall. *R. graveolens* 'Variegata' comes true from seed, but 'Jackman's Blue' must be grown from cuttings or divisions. Wearing gloves, prune back hard to force new growth and to keep plants compact.

Selected species and varieties:
R. graveolens (common rue) has upright stems lined with oblong leaflets and ½-inch yellow flowers in loose, open clusters; 'Jackman's Blue' is a compact, nonflowering cultivar with waxy blue foliage; 'Variegata' has leaves splashed with cream.

SAFFLOWER
Carthamus

Light: full sun

Plant type: annual

Height: 1 to 3 feet

Soil and Moisture: well-drained, moist to dry

Interest: flowers

Care: moderate

◀ Carthamus tinctorius

Safflower bears attractive yellow flowers in summer that add color to annual gardens and also are a wonderfully economical substitute for saffron. The plants produce stiff, upright stems lined with spiny leaves and thistlelike summer flowers surrounded by a cuff of spiny bracts. The blossoms make excellent cut flowers. When in full bloom the blossoms are gathered and dried, the petals ground and used to season sauces, soups, and other dishes calling for saffron.

Growing and care:
Sow safflower seed in spring and thin seedlings to stand 6 inches apart. Safflower does not transplant well. Young plants should be protected from rabbits, which find them a tasty nibble. Safflowers grow best under dry conditions and are subject to disease in rainy or humid areas. Cut and dry the mature flowers, storing in airtight containers until ready to use.

Selected species and varieties:
C. tinctorius (safflower, saffron thistle, false saffron, bastard saffron) bears yellow to yellow-orange tousled flowers nestled in a collar of thistlelike bracts up to 1 inch across followed by white seeds.

SAGE
Salvia

Light: full sun

Plant type: annual, biennial, perennial, shrub

Hardiness: Zones 4-10

Height: 1 to 8 feet

Soil and Moisture: well-drained, moist to dry

Interest: flowers, foliage

Care: easy

◀ Salvia officinalis 'Purpurea'

Sages are some of the most important garden herbs, with distinct gray-green leaves and pronounced veins. Sage brings both interesting texture and an aroma reminiscent of pine or rosemary to the border or kitchen garden. The leaves vary in different species from rounded, lance-shaped forms to oval types with pointed tips. In addition to the fragrant, spicy foliage, sage produces long flower spikes covered with white, lilac, pink, red, or purple blossoms. Sages are useful as edgings or when mixed throughout the border. Many are indispensable ingredients of herb and kitchen gardens and can be grown as container plants to perk up a winter window sill. Those suitable only for mild winter climates are often grown as half-hardy annuals in cooler zones.

Growing and care:
Sow sage seed in spring or set divisions out in spring or fall, spacing them 1½ to 2 feet apart. Avoid hot, humid locations or those with too rich soils. Provide a protective winter mulch in cooler climates. Prune sage heavily in spring to remove winter-killed stems and encourage bushy growth. Prune lightly after plants have finished flowering. Perennial sages are short lived as perennials go and should be replaced every 4 or 5 years. Propagate by division or by rooting 4-inch stem cuttings taken in summer to plant in fall. Seedlings or rooted cuttings take 2 years to reach maturity for picking. Fresh leaves can be

(continued)

harvested anytime but are most flavorful when grown in moist soil in full sun and gathered just as the flower blossoms begin to open. Dry leaves slowly to prevent a musty odor, laying them in a single layer on a screen or cloth; refrigerate or freeze the dried leaves, as the aromatic oils dissipate easily. To make an infusion for an aftershave or a hair rinse, steep leaves in boiling water, cool to room temperature, strain, and bottle. Refrigerate unused portion.

Selected species and varieties:

S. clevelandii (blue sage) is an evergreen shrub with wrinkled 1-inch leaves on downy stems 2 to 3 feet tall tipped with violet or white spring to summer flowers; Zones 9-10. *S. coccinea* (Texas sage, scarlet sage) is a perennial or subshrub grown as an annual, with 2-inch heart-shaped leaves having wavy, indented edges on 3-foot stems tipped with branched spikes of red or white summer flowers that are valued in landscaping. *S. dorisiana* (fruit-scented sage) is an evergreen perennial with sweetly scented, velvety oval leaves 4 inches wide and up to 7 inches long on stems to 4 feet tall tipped with 6-inch spikes of 2-inch magenta to pink flowers in fall and winter; Zones 10-11. *S. elegans* (pineapple sage) is an evergreen perennial with fruit-scented, red-edged 3½-inch oval leaves lining 3- to 4-foot red stems tipped with red to pink 8-inch late-summer flower spikes used in cold drinks and fruit salads; Zones 8-10. *S. fruticosa* (Greek sage) is an evergreen shrub to 4½ feet with lavender-scented leaves and loose, 8-inch clusters of mauve to pink spring to summer flowers; Zones 8-9. *S. lavandulifolia* (Spanish sage, narrow-leaved sage) is a spreading evergreen shrub 12 to 20 inches tall with 1-inch white woolly leaves having a piny lavender aroma and red-violet summer flowers; Zones 7-9. *S. officinalis* (common sage, garden sage) is an evergreen shrub in mild climates, with 2-inch velvety leaves on branching 2- to 3-foot stems tipped with edible violet to purple flower spikes in summer; 'Purpurea' has aromatic purple leaves.

SALAD BURNET
Poterium

◀ Poterium sanguisorba

Light: full sun	
Plant type: perennial	
Hardiness: Zones 3-9	
Height: 1 to 3 feet	
Soil and Moisture: well-drained, moist	
Interest: flowers, foliage	
Care: easy	

Salad burnet is a tasty addition to perennial borders or kitchen and herb gardens, with mounds of delicate blue-green foliage and tall stalks of thimble-shaped clusters of tiny summer flowers. The young leaves have a distinct, slightly nutty, cucumber flavor and add an unusual accent to salads, coleslaw, soups, and vegetables and brighten up cool summer drinks. Preserve the leaves in vinegar as a base for flavorful salad dressings.

Growing and care:

Sow burnet seed in spring or fall or divide young plants before taproots become well established. Space plants 8 to 12 inches apart. Established plants self-sow freely. Burnet is evergreen in milder climates; elsewhere, shear old foliage to the ground in late fall or early spring. Leaves are most flavorful when picked in early spring or late fall and when plants are grown in soil amended with well-rotted manure or compost.

Selected species and varieties:

P. sanguisorba [also classified as *Sanguisorba minor*] (burnet, garden burnet, salad burnet) produces ¾-inch oval leaflets with deeply scalloped edges paired along the flexible leafstalks that grow to 1 foot, and dense ½-inch heads of minute greenish flowers tinged pink on stems to 3 feet.

707

SAVORY
Satureja

Light: full sun

Plant type: annual, perennial

Hardiness: Zones 4-10

Height: 2 to 18 inches

Soil and Moisture: well-drained, dry

Interest: flowers, foliage, fragrance

Care: easy

◄ Satureja montana

While most familiar in the herb garden, savories have distinctive gray-green foliage and masses of delicate, subtle-hued flowers that make them deserving of use in rock gardens and borders or as edging. The leaves are highly aromatic and frequently used as a culinary herb for their peppery flavor. Members of the mint family, they have square stems that bear clusters of two-lipped flowers that are highly attractive to bees.

Growing and care:
Savories can be grown in ordinary garden conditions as long as the soil is not soggy. Propagate by seed sown indoors in early spring. Do not cover seed, as light is needed for germination.

Selected species and varieties:
S. hortensis (summer savory) is a 1- to 1½-foot shrubby, branching annual with narrow, 1-inch-long, finely hairy leaves and ¼- to ⅓-inch lavender, pink, or white two-lipped flowers in small clusters at the base of the top pairs of leaves from midsummer to frost. *S. montana* (winter savory) is a 9- to 15-inch woody species with narrow, ¾-inch shiny evergreen leaves and tiny lavender or white flowers dotted with purple spots in spikes at the end of branch tips from summer to early fall; 'Prostrate White' has white flowers atop a 3- to 6-inch-tall creeping mat of glossy leaves.

SESAME
Sesamum

Light: full sun

Plant type: tender perennial

Hardiness: Zone 10

Height: 1½ to 3 feet

Soil and Moisture: well-drained, moist

Interest: flowers, seeds

Care: moderate

◄ Sesamum indicum

Sesame is an exotic herb originally from Asia and Africa with delicate, lightly colored bell-shaped flowers and distinctive, very tasty seeds. The plants are naturalized along the Gulf Coast, where each summer and fall the upright, pointed, oval capsules yield small tan seeds prized for their oil and nutty flavor. The seeds are used whole in candies and baked goods, such as hamburger buns and bagels, and to add a unique taste to vegetable dishes and salads. They can also be ground into dips, spreads, and sauces or pressed for cooking oil.

Growing and care:
Sow sesame seed directly in the garden ¼ inch deep once nighttime low temperatures climb to 60° F, or start indoors 6 to 8 weeks before last frost. Space plants 6 to 8 inches apart. Plants need at least 120 days of hot weather to set seed. Harvest just as oldest pods begin to dry, cutting stems off at ground level. Hang plants upside down within a paper bag until pods dry and release the seeds. Each plant produces approximately 1 tablespoon of dried seeds.

Selected species and varieties:
S. indicum (sesame, benne) has square, sticky stems lined with oval, pointed 3- to 5-inch leaves and 1-inch white flowers lightly tinged with pink, yellow, or red accents.

THYME
Thymus

Light: full sun

Plant type: perennial

Hardiness: Zones 4-9

Height: 1 to 1 1/2 feet

Soil and Moisture: well-drained, moist to dry

Interest: flowers, foliage

Care: easy

◀ Thymus x citriodorus
'Aureus'

Thyme is another classic herb with very slender stems, densely packed small green leaves bursting with a warm, spicy aroma, and countless tiny bundles of gaily colored summer blossoms. The many varieties range from ground-hugging types to mounding perennials to billowy low-growing shrubs. They are excellent for adding fine texture and soft color to borders, rock gardens, and garden paths. Shrubby species can be grown as specimens or low hedges while creeping types quickly fill niches among rocks or between paving stones. Thyme is also easy to grow in containers on window sills. The plentiful white, pink, or rose red blossoms are attractive to bees. Fresh or dried, the tiny 1/4- to 1/2-inch, narrow, green to gray-green, sometimes variegated leaves are used as a basic ingredient in bouquets garnis and fines herbes and are used to make tea. Both leaves and flowers are used in potpourris and toiletries. Herbalists use thyme as an insect repellent, medicinal plant, household disinfectant, and preservative.

Growing and care:
Start seed indoors by sowing thickly in pots 6 to 8 weeks before the last frost, then set 4- to 6-inch seedlings out in clumps. Space transplants 1 to 2 feet apart in well-worked, sandy soil with some organic matter and bone meal blended in. Start thyme for a window sill garden from seed, or pot divisions in late summer to bring in-doors in late fall. To shape plants and encourage branching, prune hard in early spring before flowering or lightly after blooms appear. Remove shoots with solid green leaves from variegated cultivars. Leaves are most fragrant when picked from plants grown in full sun and in bloom. Add leaves to meat dishes, stuffings, pâtés, salad dressings, vegetable dishes, herb butter, vinegars, and mayonnaise. To dry, hang bundles of branches upside down in a shady, warm, well-ventilated location for a few days, then crumble or strip fresh leaves from stems and dry on screens; store in airtight containers for use in cooking or sachets. An infusion of thyme made by boiling fresh leaves and flowers in water, then straining the liquid, creates a soothing facial rinse; add rosemary to the infusion for a hair rinse. To propagate thyme, root softwood cuttings taken in late spring or early summer or divide mature plants in early spring or late summer.

Selected species and varieties:
T. caespititius [formerly classified as *T. azoricus*] (tufted thyme, Azores thyme) is a subshrub forming 6-inch-high mats of twiggy branches lined with sticky, resinous leaves and tipped with white, pink, or lilac flowers; 'Aureus' has deep yellow-green leaves and pink flowers; Zones 8-9. *T. capitatus* (conehead thyme) produces upright, bushy plants 10 inches tall and as wide with gray leaves and pink flowers crowded into cone-shaped tufts at the tips of branches; Zone 9. *T. cilicicus* (Cilician thyme) has deep green lemon-scented leaves and clusters of pale mauve to lilac blossoms on 6-inch stems; Zones 6-8. *T.* x *citriodorus* (lemon thyme) forms a shrubby carpet up to 2 feet wide of foot-tall branches with tiny lemon-scented leaves; 'Aureus' (golden lemon thyme) has gold-edged leaves; 'Silver Queen' has leaves marbled cream and silvery gray; Zones 5-9. *T. herba-barona* (caraway thyme) is a fast-growing subshrub forming mats 4 inches tall and 2 feet across with leaf flavors reminiscent of caraway, nutmeg, or lemon, and loose clusters of rose flowers; Zones 4-8.

TOBACCO
Nicotiana

Light: full sun	
Plant type: annual	
Height: 2 to 4 feet	
Soil and Moisture: well-drained, fertile, moist	
Interest: flowers, foliage	
Care: easy	

◀ Nicotiana rustica

Indian tobacco's bold leaves, sturdy stems, and hundreds of summer to fall flowers create a dramatic background for beds and borders. Plants contain nicotine, a natural insecticide that is poisonous if taken internally or absorbed through the skin. Dry and powder the leaves for an insecticidal dust effective against both root- and leaf-chewing insects.

Growing and care:
Sow Indian tobacco seed outdoors in warm soil or start indoors 6 to 8 weeks before the last frost. Do not cover, as seeds need light to germinate. Space seedlings 1½ to 2 feet apart. Harvest wearing protective rubber gloves, picking leaves individually as they begin to yellow. Hang to dry, then crumble, remove stems, and store in airtight containers. Wearing protective clothing and equipment, grind the dried leaves to a powder and dust on plants at least 1 month before harvest.

Selected species and varieties:
N. rustica (wild tobacco) has large, pointed oval leaves 4 to 8 inches long and half as wide, covered with sticky hairs and hundreds of ½-inch yellow-green flowers atop sturdy 2- to 4-foot-tall stems.

WOAD
Isatis

Light: full sun	
Plant type: perennial	
Hardiness: Zones 4-8	
Height: 2 to 4 feet	
Soil and Moisture: well-drained, fertile, moist	
Interest: flowers, foliage	
Care: easy	

◀ Isatis tinctoria

Before the discovery of indigo, weavers used fermented leaves of dyer's woad to produce blue hues. Now dyer's woad is enjoyed as a specimen or border backdrop, where the clouds of tiny yellow spring flowers produced on 2-year-old plants contrast attractively to the blue-green foliage. Dangling fiddle-shaped black seeds decorate the plants in fall. Dry the flowers to add color to potpourri.

Growing and care:
Sow dyer's woad in late summer for flowering the following year. Space plants 6 inches apart in deep, loosened soil, well amended with compost or rotted manure, to accommodate the plant's long taproots. Pick flowers just after opening and dry on screens in a well-ventilated area. Woad self-sows freely and looks charming naturalized in a wildflower meadow.

Selected species and varieties:
I. tinctoria (dyer's woad, asp-of-Jerusalem) produces rosettes of oval leaves the first year, followed the second year by tall flowering stalks tipped with large, airy clusters of ¼-inch four-petaled yellow flowers on sprawling to erect stems lined with narrow leaves.

BUGLEWEED
Ajuga

Light: full sun	
Plant type: perennial	
Hardiness: Zones 3-9	
Height: 3 to 9 inches	
Soil and Moisture: well-drained, moist to dry, fertile, acidic	
Interest: foliage, flowers	
Care: easy	

◀ Ajuga reptans 'Burgundy Glow'

Bugleweed is a vigorous and reliable ground cover in sun or bright shade and is very useful under trees where grass is difficult to grow. Its colorful foliage is effective year round, and is available in shades of green, purple, and bronze, as well as variegated hues. It makes an excellent choice for the foreground of a shrub border or rock garden. The tiny, two-lipped blue, white, pink or purple flowers appear along short, erect spikes from spring to early summer. The leaves produce their best color in full sun.

Growing and care:
Carpet bugle thrives in poor soil. Space plants 6 inches apart for best growth. This species spreads rapidly by stolons and chokes out weeds; however, it may become invasive in the garden. If planted near a lawn, carpet bugle will encroach upon the grass, but it does not withstand heavy foot traffic. Propagate by division. Plants should be divided in spring or fall when they become crowded, to promote air circulation and prevent crown rot.

Selected species and varieties:
A. reptans (carpet bugle) grows to 9 inches tall with oblong leaves that form a basal clump, and violet-blue flowers appearing on an erect spike in spring; 'Alba' bears white blooms; 'Bronze Beauty' produces waxy bronze-purple leaves and blue flowers; 'Burgundy Glow' has white, green, and dark pink variegated leaves and blue flowers.

CALABASH GOURD
Lagenaria

Light: full sun	
Plant type: annual	
Height: 10 to 30 feet	
Soil and Moisture: well-drained, fertile, moist	
Interest: fruit, flowers, fragrance	
Care: easy	

◀ Lagenaria siceraria

The large, fragrant white flowers and strange-shaped fruit of calabash gourd make these very vigorous vines the conversation piece of any garden. The strong stems can grow up to 30 feet in one season, making them ideal as a temporary ground cover or screen. In the fall the fruit can be harvested and, depending upon its shape, be used for containers, bird feeders, or autumn decorations.

Growing and care:
Start seed indoors in peat pots 6 to 8 weeks prior to the last frost. In areas with long growing seasons, seed can be planted directly in the garden after the last frost and when soil is warm. Space plants 2 feet apart, and provide a sturdy support for climbing. Harvest fruits before the first hard frost, and dry in an airy room.

Selected species and varieties:
L. siceraria produces a hairy stem with branched tendrils and broad 6- to 12-inch leaves. The 5-inch white flowers open in the evening or on overcast days, and are sweetly fragrant. The fruit ranges from 3 to 36 inches in length and may be rounded or flattened, coiled, bottle shaped, or dumbbell shaped.

CROSS VINE
Bignonia

Light: full sun

Plant type: woody vine

Hardiness: Zones 6-9

Height: 30 to 50 feet

Soil and Moisture: well-drained, moist

Interest: flowers, foliage

Care: easy

◀ Bignonia capreolata

A vigorous, rapidly growing plant, cross vine is graced in spring with clusters of large, trumpet-shaped flowers that are dark orange on the outside and yellow-orange on the inside. In summer slender, 4- to 6-inch flattened fruit appears that turns from green to brown. Cross vine's attractive, 2- to 6-inch dark green compound leaves are borne in pairs along with clasping tendrils by which the vine attaches itself to supports. Where winters are mild, the foliage turns reddish purple in fall. Cross vine is a wonderful addition to naturalistic plantings, where their blossoms attract hummingbirds in summer.

Growing and care:
Cross vine is easy to grow and thrives in all soils excluding those that are excessively wet or dry. In Zone 6 cross vine dies back to the ground each winter, but sends up vigorous new shoots in spring. In warmer regions prune to help restrain growth and keep tidy. Propagate by seed or cuttings.

Selected species and varieties:
B. capreolata (cross vine, trumpet flower) grows 30 to 50 feet with lustrous, thinly spaced, dark green, semievergreen to evergreen leaves and orange-red, mocha-scented flowers in clusters of two to five; 'Atrosanguinea' has narrower, dark purple-red flowers tinted with brown or sometimes orange-red, and long, narrow leaves.

CUP-AND-SAUCER VINE
Cobaea

Light: full sun

Plant type: tender perennial grown as annual

Hardiness: Zones 9-10

Height: 10 to 25 feet

Soil and Moisture: well-drained, moist to dry

Interest: flowers

Care: easy

◀ Cobaea scandens

This extremely vigorous, sturdy vine from Mexico has showy, velvet blue, cup-shaped flowers with masses of tendril-like stamens surrounded by an attractive green saucer-shaped calyx. This tender perennial is usually grown as an annual and can reach 25 feet in a single season. In Zones 9 and 10, where the plants are perennial, they can reach up to 40 feet. Cup-and-saucer vine is very useful for providing quick cover for a fence, a wall, an arbor, or a trellis.

Growing and care:
Start seed indoors in individual peat pots 6 weeks prior to the last frost, first nicking the hard seed coat, and barely covering the seed. Transplant outdoors in late spring to a warm, sunny site in soil well amended with organic matter. Space plants 1 to 2 feet apart, and provide abundant water. Pinch tips from young plants to encourage branching. Provide a trellis or staking for support as the plant grows.

Selected species and varieties:
C. scandens climbs easily on any support, using tendrils to cling to its anchor itself. Each leaf is divided into two or three pairs of oblong leaflets. Flowers are green at first, turning deep violet or rose-purple as they mature; 'Alba' bears flowers in a pale shade of greenish white.

GOURD
Cucurbita

Light: full sun

Plant type: annual, tender perennial

Hardiness: Zones 9-10

Height: 5 to 12 feet

Soil and Moisture: well-drained, sandy, moist to dry

Interest: flowers

Care: easy

◀ Cucurbita pepo var. ovifera

Plant these tropical squash and pumpkin vines on a trellis, a fence, or an arbor, and watch how quickly they will cover it with their lush foliage. In late summer and fall the brightly colored ornamental fruit can be harvested and used for fall holiday decorations.

Growing and care:

Sow seed directly in the garden after the last frost, allowing 9 to 12 inches between plants. Or start indoors in individual peat pots 4 weeks before the last frost. Plants thrive in warm weather and grow best when given some support for climbing. Water regularly from sowing until fruit set.

Selected species and varieties:

C. ficifolia (Malabar gourd, fig-leaf gourd) is a perennial in Zones 9 to 10 and is grown as an annual elsewhere. It climbs to 12 feet, producing smooth, rounded, white-striped green fruit up to 1 foot long. *C. maxima* (Hubbard squash) is an 8-foot annual vine bearing edible rounded or oblong furrowed fruit; the variety 'Turbaniformis' (Turk's-cap squash, Turban squash) produces 6- to 7-inch orange, white, and green fruit that looks as if it is made of two separate parts. Annual *C. pepo* var. *ovifera* (pumpkin gourd) grows to 5 to 12 feet and produces small fruit in a wide range of shapes and colors.

HEATH
Erica

Light: full sun

Plant type: shrub

Hardiness: Zones 6-9

Height: to 16 inches

Soil and Moisture: well-drained, sandy, rich, acidic, moist

Interest: flowers, foliage

Care: moderate

◀ Erica carnea 'Winter Beauty'

Spring heath produces a mass of colorful flower spikes from winter to spring above an airy, spreading evergreen carpet of bright green needlelike foliage. The plants create a festive, holiday mood and are excellent in rock gardens and flower beds, or when planted in masses to cover a sunny slope or as an edging along a path.

Growing and care:

Plant in very well-drained sandy loam amended with peat moss or acidic leaf mold. Heath does not grow well in heavy clay. Mulch to conserve moisture for the shallow roots, and water during dry periods. Spring heath needs acid soil. Prune after flowering to encourage compactness. Heaths are slightly more difficult to grow than heathers, and thrive in areas with long, cool summers, mild winters, and plentiful, frequent rains.

Selected species and varieties:

E. carnea (spring heath, snow heather) has slender, prostrate branches up to 16 inches high and spreading 2 to 6 feet wide bearing bell-shaped flowers of white, pink, rose, red, or purple in nodding clusters; 'Springwood Pink' grows 6 to 8 inches high with clear pink flowers; 'Springwood White', 6 to 8 inches high with pure white flowers and bronze new growth; 'Winter Beauty', to 5 inches high with a profusion of dark pink flowers.

HEATHER
Calluna

Light: full sun	
Plant type: shrub	
Hardiness: Zones 4-7	
Height: 2 feet	
Soil and Moisture: well-drained, moist, acidic, rich	
Interest: flowers, foliage	
Care: moderate	

◀ Calluna vulgaris 'Corbett's Red'

Scotch heather produces a wavy sea of deep green, scalelike evergreen leaves that are smothered with hundreds of tiny pink or white flowers in midsummer. These beautiful plants make stunning ground covers and add an artistic dimension to rock gardens.

Growing and care:

Scotch heather must be grown in a slightly acid, sandy soil rich in organic matter. Good drainage is critical to its proper growth. Plant in full sun for best flowering and protect from drying winds. Mulch to conserve moisture, and water during dry spells. Prune faded flowers and stem tips to reduce legginess.

Selected species and varieties:

C. vulgaris (Scotch heather) grows up to 2 feet, spreading 2 feet or more, and bearing purplish pink flower clusters up to 1 foot long until fall; 'County Wicklow' is one of the best double-flowered varieties, with dark green foliage and pink, fully double flowers in summer; 'Else Frye' has double white summer flowers and reaches 1½ feet; 'H. E. Beale' grows 2 feet high with silvery pink flowers in late summer to fall; 'Mrs. Ronald Gray' is 4 inches high with reddish flowers in summer; 'Robert Chapman' has pale green foliage turning shades of orange and red in fall and winter, with rose-purple flowers in late summer.

HYACINTH BEAN
Dolichos

Light: full sun	
Plant type: annual	
Height: 10 to 20 feet	
Soil and Moisture: well-drained, moist, fertile	
Interest: flowers, foliage, fruit	
Care: easy	

◀ Dolichos lablab

This lush, tropical twining vine produces abundant pink, purple, or white pealike flowers in loose spikes from late spring to fall. The flowers are followed by vivid red to purple seedpods. The attractive, dark green compound leaves are veined in deep purple and rise from rose-violet-colored stems. The seeds are edible and are an important food source in many parts of the world. As an ornamental, hyacinth bean is one of the more beautiful annual vines and provides a colorful screen or covering for a fence, an arbor, or a trellis.

Growing and care:

Start seed indoors in peat pots 4 to 6 weeks prior to the last frost, or sow directly in the garden after the soil has warmed. Soak seed in warm water for 24 hours before planting. Space plants 1 to 2 feet apart and provide support for climbing. Hyacinth bean thrives in warm weather.

Selected species and varieties:

D. lablab climbs to 20 feet in one season by twining stems. Leaves are composed of three heart-shaped leaflets, each 3 to 6 inches long. The loosely clustered flowers stand out against the deeply colored leaves. Colorful pods are 1 to 3 inches long.

JASMINE
Jasminum

Light: full sun	
Plant type: perennial, shrub	
Hardiness: Zones 6-10	
Height: 3 to 15 feet	
Soil and Moisture: well-drained, moist to dry	
Interest: flowers, foliage, fragrance	
Care: moderate	

◀ Jasminum mesnyi

A perfect solution for sunny slopes with poor soil, jasmine forms a wide-spreading mound of arching stems that bear bright yellow trumpetlike flowers and triplets of dark green leaflets. Branches root wherever they contact the soil and can soon cover a large area. Jasmine can also be trained to climb a support, where it may reach 15 feet. In winter, the naked green stems are effective, especially when allowed to trail over a wall.

Growing and care:

Jasmine is easy to transplant and spreads quickly. Water regularly until plantings are established and during extended dry periods. Cut back almost to the ground every 3 to 5 years to restore vigor. Propagate by cuttings taken in summer.

Selected species and varieties:

J. mesnyi (primrose jasmine, Japanese jasmine, yellow jasmine) is an evergreen shrub reaching 5 to 6 feet high with yellow flowers up to 1¾ inches wide, often semi-double to double, from early spring sporadically to midsummer, and leaflets 1 to 3 inches long; Zones 8-9. *J. nudiflorum* (winter jasmine) bears 1-inch-wide single yellow flowers that bloom erratically on warm days in winter before 1-inch leaflets appear, the thicket of arching vines reaching 3 to 4 feet high and 4 to 7 feet wide or up to 15 feet if trained to a support; 'Aureum' has dark green leaves marked with irregular patches of yellow.

JUNIPER
Juniperus

Light: full sun	
Plant type: shrub	
Hardiness: Zones 2-9	
Height: 6 inches to 60 feet	
Soil and Moisture: well-drained, moist to dry	
Interest: foliage	
Care: easy	

◀ Juniperus conferta

Junipers are a very diverse group of woody shrubs that include some of the best ground covers available. Their scalelike evergreen foliage ranges in color from green to silvery blue to yellow. The cold temperatures and winds in winter often turn the foliage from green to shades of greenish purple. Female plants produce small blue berries that are strongly aromatic when crushed.

Growing and care:

Junipers are easy-to-grow shrubs that require no fertilizer and little supplemental watering under normal conditions. Most junipers tolerate drought and pollution. Shore junipers grow well in seaside gardens. Savin and Chinese junipers accept limestone soils. Plant container-grown or balled-and-burlapped specimens in spring, summer, or fall, watering regularly until plants become established. Prune winter damage in spring.

Selected species and varieties:

J. chinensis (Chinese juniper) comes in many forms, from narrow, conical trees 50 to 60 feet high with green to bluish to gray-green foliage, to thick ground covers; Zones 3-9; 'Arctic' is a hardy, spreading variety with blue-green needles, and stems reaching 1½ feet in height and 6 feet across; 'Blue Cloud' is a large, spreading ground cover type with attractive, steel blue-green foliage; 'Pfitzeriana Glauca' has bluish foliage becoming purplish blue in winter, normally 5 feet high by 10 feet

JUNIPER
(continued)

wide but often larger; 'San Jose' is a creeping variety that reaches just over a foot tall and spreads up to 8 feet wide; 'Sea Spray' has blue-green foliage and a vigorous, spreading habit reaching 1 foot tall and 6 feet wide. *J. conferta* (shore juniper) is a shrub spreading 6 to 9 feet and 1 to 1½ feet high with soft, needlelike bluish green foliage in summer turning bronzy or yellow-green in winter; Zones 6-9; 'Boulevard' has a very low-growing habit and deep green foliage. *J. horizontalis* (creeping juniper, creeping savin) grows 1 to 2 feet high by 4 to 8 feet wide, with trailing branches bearing glaucous green, blue-green, or blue plumelike foliage turning plum purple in winter; Zones 3-9; 'Bar Harbor', discovered along the coast of Maine, has a creeping habit, reaching less than 1 foot high with a spread of 8 feet, and is very tolerant of coastal conditions; 'Wiltonii' (blue rug juniper) forms a flat mat less than 6 inches high, spreading up to 8 feet, with grayish blue foliage. *J. procumbens* [sometimes classified as *J. chinensis* var. *procumbens*] (Japanese garden juniper) grows 1 to 2 feet high and 10 to 15 feet wide, with bluish green to gray-green foliage; 'Nana', a dwarf of the species, forms a low, rounded, compact mat 6 to 12 inches high and spreading up to 12 feet, with overlapping branches of bluish green foliage turning purplish in winter. *J. sabina* (savin) is a vase-shaped shrub 4 to 6 feet high by 5 to 10 feet wide, with dark green foliage turning a drab green tinged with yellow in winter; 'Broadmoor' grows 2 to 3 feet high with a 10-foot spread, bearing soft gray-green foliage in short, upright sprays; Zones 4-9.

MOONFLOWER
Ipomoea

Light: full sun

Plant type: tender perennial

Hardiness: Zone 10

Height: 15 to 20 feet

Soil and Moisture: well-drained, sandy, moist

Interest: flowers, fragrance

Care: easy

◀ Ipomoea alba

Moonflowers are night-blooming vines with large, fragrant, pure white blossoms in mesmerizing hues of moonlight white. The strong, easy-to-grow plants can reach to 20 feet in a season and quickly cover fences, trellises, and arbors with large, heart-shaped leaves and showy blossoms. Moonflowers are excellent for hanging baskets and are popular in summer moon gardens.

Growing and care:
Amend heavy soils with sand, and add only a modest amount of organic matter; too rich soil will produce lush foliage but few flowers. Plant seed 1 to 1½ feet apart in a sunny location after all danger of frost has passed, or start indoors in individual pots 4 to 6 weeks before the last frost date. Germination takes 5 to 7 days but can occur more quickly if the seeds are nicked with a nail file or soaked in water for 2 days before planting. Transplant gently, being careful not to disturb the roots. Pinch plants once when they begin to climb.

Selected species and varieties:
I. alba [also listed as *Calonyction aculeatum*] is a semi-woody tender perennial vine that quickly climbs to 20 feet, with shiny, bright green leaves up to 8 inches long and white, trumpet-shaped, very fragrant flowers up to 6 inches long and wide, opening after sundown and closing before noon the next day, blooming from midsummer to frost.

PASSIONFLOWER
Passiflora

Light: full sun

Plant type: perennial vine

Hardiness: Zones 6-10

Height: 15 to 25 feet

Soil and Moisture: well-drained, moist

Interest: flowers, foliage, fruit

Care: easy

◀ Passiflora incarnata

Passionflowers bear complex, spectacular blossoms in shades of blue, white, and greenish yellow along trailing vines covered with dark green, sometimes evergreen leaves. These vigorous plants are perfect for seaside plantings, or when allowed to freely ramble over fences and trellises. Passionflower also grows well in containers, where the plants add class to patio gardens in summer and elegance indoors in winter.

Growing and care:
Grow passionflowers in well-drained soil that has been well amended with rotted manure or compost. Their vigorous growth requires the sturdy support of a wall or trellis. Pinch vines regularly to increase bushiness. Propagate by seed or cuttings, or separate suckers from the base of established plants.

Selected species and varieties:
P. incarnata (passionflower, maypop) reaches to 25 feet with white to lavender flowers 2 to 3 inches across followed by large apricot-colored fruit. The 4- to 6-inch leaves have three lobes and are dark green above and whitish below. *P. lutea* grows to 15 feet with greenish yellow flowers and purple-black fruit. Its leaves turn yellow in fall.

SCARLET RUNNER BEAN
Phaseolus

Light: full sun

Plant type: tender perennial grown as annual

Hardiness: Zone 10

Height: 6 to 10 feet

Soil and Moisture: well-drained, moist, fertile

Interest: flowers, fruit

Care: easy

◀ Phaseolus coccineus

Scarlet runner bean is a fast-growing, low-maintenance plant that adds color to the garden and food to the table. This twining tender perennial is grown as an annual and produces abundant dark green leaves that are a perfect foil for its brilliant scarlet flowers. The vine quickly covers trellises, fences, and outdoor railings, creating a dense and dramatic backdrop. Use scarlet runner bean in the back of the border, in specialty gardens, or to add color to the vegetable patch, where the brilliant flowers will attract hummingbirds all season long.

Growing and care:
Start seed indoors 4 weeks before planting out or sow directly in the garden after the last frost. Set seed in 1-inch-deep drills with eye facing down. Inoculate soil with nitrogen-fixing bacteria for best growth. Water regularly until seedlings are a few inches high. Thin to allow 2 to 4 inches between plants. Provide support for climbing.

Selected species and varieties:
P. coccineus produces twining stems with 5-inch dark green leaves composed of three leaflets. Bright red, pealike flowers appear in large clusters from early to midsummer, followed by flat 4- to 12-inch pods filled with black-and-red-mottled seeds. Both flowers and beans are edible.

SUN ROSE
Helianthemum

Light: full sun

Plant type: shrubby perennial

Hardiness: Zones 5-7

Height: 6 to 12 inches

Soil and Moisture: well-drained, alkaline, dry

Interest: flowers

Care: difficult

◀ Helianthemum nummularium

Sun roses provide a colorful, cheerful cover for dry, sunny slopes and brighten rock gardens with their beautiful flowers from late spring to early summer. The blossoms resemble wild roses with crepe-paper petals and are freely sprinkled atop the low-growing evergreen foliage. Varieties come in yellow, orange, red, rose, pink, apricot, salmon, peach, white, and bicolors, and in double-flowered forms.

Growing and care:
Sun roses prefer dry, poor, gravelly or sandy soils and do not grow well in fertile soils. Good drainage is essential, as plants will not tolerate wet conditions, especially in winter. Prune in early spring to encourage dense growth, and prune again after flowering to get a flush of bloom in late summer. Protect with mulch over winter. Propagate by division in spring or by soft stem cuttings.

Selected species and varieties:
H. nummularium (yellow sun rose) forms a sprawling mound, 1 to 2 feet wide, with trailing stems that bear grayish green leaves 1 to 2 inches long with silvery undersides and 1-inch-wide flowers with broad petals and prominent stamens.

WISTERIA
Wisteria

Light: full sun

Plant type: woody vine

Hardiness: Zones 4-9

Height: 10 to 30 feet

Soil and Moisture: well-drained, moist

Interest: flowers, foliage

Care: moderate

◀ Wisteria sinensis

Wisteria is one of the most popular garden vines, with long panicles of lavender, white, or pinkish lilac, softly fragrant flowers. These elegant plants are sure to stir images of romantic springtime places or nostalgic memories of Grandma's. The lovely, twining vines are picturesque additions to patios, porches, or sturdy arbors, where the bright green foliage provides dense summertime shade.

Growing and care:
Amend soil with organic matter and add lime if soil is very acid. Prune roots before planting. Water regularly during dry periods and fertilize with a high-phosphorus, high-potassium, low-nitrogen fertilizer to promote flowering. Only grow wisteria on very strong supports.

Selected species and varieties:
W. floribunda (Japanese wisteria) twines clockwise, bearing small, slightly fragrant, violet, white, or violet-blue flowers in clusters 9 to 20 inches long in early to mid-spring just before the leaves emerge; 'Alba' bears snow white flowers in 11-inch-long, fragrant clusters; 'Rosea' produces long 1½-foot panicles of very fragrant lilac-rose flowers in spring. *W. sinensis* (Chinese wisteria) twines counterclockwise and produces blue-violet flowers, not as fragrant as those of Japanese wisteria, borne in dense, 6- to 12-inch-long clusters in mid- to late spring; cultivars include white, dark purple, double varieties; Zones 5-8.

BLUESTEM
Andropogon

Light: full sun

Plant type: ornamental grass

Hardiness: Zones 4-9

Height: 2 to 8 feet

Soil and Moisture: well-drained, moist to dry

Interest: foliage

Care: easy

◀ Andropogon gerardii

Bluestems are perennial bunch grasses native to the prairies, open woods, fields, and lowlands over much of the United States. Unlike many other ornamental grasses that produce large displays, bluestem's small clumps add a subtle touch to rock gardens and wildflower meadows. The narrow leaves are blue-green in spring and summer and turn tan-copper or maroon in fall.

Growing and care:
Big bluestem grows best in a sandy loam and withstands periodic flooding and clay soil. Bushy bluestem prefers a site that stays evenly moist. Cut bunches nearly to ground level in late winter or early spring before new growth begins. Propagate by seed sown directly in the garden in spring or by division in spring or fall.

Selected species and varieties:
A. gerardii (big bluestem, turkeyfoot) produces upright clumps 4 to 8 feet tall with purplish late-summer flowers in branched clusters resembling a turkey's foot, and leaves that are blue-green in summer and maroon to tan in fall. *A. glomeratus* (bushy bluestem) has clumps 2 to 5 feet tall with silvery green to pinkish flowers in bold, feathery racemes surrounded by salmon sheaths in fall followed by fluffy white seed heads. Leaves and stems turn a coppery bronze after frost and remain attractive through winter; Zones 6-9.

DROPSEED
Sporobolus

Light: full sun

Plant type: ornamental grass

Hardiness: Zones 3-8

Height: 2 feet

Soil and Moisture: well-drained, sandy, dry

Interest: flowers, foliage

Care: easy

◀ Sporobolus heterolepis

Dropseed is a truly charming ornamental grass with fountainlike sprays of fine-textured, gracefully arching stems and leaves. Native to the prairies of the central United States and Canada, this perennial grass is ideal for small and large meadow gardens, herbaceous borders, and as a ground cover for dry, sunny sites. In autumn the leaves and seed heads turn a metallic tan color that persists through winter, making this plant valuable every season of the year.

Growing and care:
Northern prairie dropseed grows best in dry, sandy soil and full sun, but in areas with very hot, dry summers the plants benefit from a little afternoon shade. Sow seed directly in the garden in either fall or spring. Plants require about 3 years to reach their mature size. Divide every 2 to 3 years, though the thick roots make this task more difficult than it looks.

Selected species and varieties:
S. heterolepis (northern prairie dropseed) has narrow, rich green leaves 20 inches long in a clump 2 feet tall and 3 feet wide, and loose clusters of dark green flowers that bloom in summer and fall. The entire plant, including the seed heads, turns an attractive tan-bronze in fall.

EULALIA
Miscanthus

Light: full sun

Plant type: ornamental grass

Hardiness: Zones 5-9

Height: 5 to 8 feet

Soil and Moisture: well-drained, moist

Interest: flowers, foliage

Care: easy

◀ Miscanthus sinensis 'Zebrinus'

These tall, fine-textured grasses with their long, narrow, arching leaves and feathery fan-shaped plumes of fall flowers make striking specimens or screens and are some of the most popular ornamental garden grasses. They are easy to grow and add multiseason interest to borders and mass plantings.

Growing and care:
Eulalia grows well in any ordinary garden soil with adequate moisture and grows best with little or no fertilizing. Excessive nitrogen in the soil produces weak stems that flop over. Cut clumps to within 2 to 6 inches of the ground in late winter. Propagate by division in spring.

Selected species and varieties:
M. sinensis (Japanese silver grass, Chinese silver grass) has upright clumps 6 to 8 feet tall and 3 feet wide or more, consisting of leaves 3 to 4 feet long and 3/8 inch wide, with pale pink to reddish flower clusters 8 inches long blooming in fall and lasting nearly all winter; 'Gracillimus' (maiden grass) has 5- to 8-foot-tall clumps and narrower leaves than the species, with a prominent white midvein; 'Morning Light' has light green leaves with silvery white margins and midrib; 'Zebrinus' (zebra grass) has distinctive yellow bands across the leaves, and pinkish brown flower clusters.

FOUNTAIN GRASS
Pennisetum

Light: full sun

Plant type: ornamental grass

Hardiness: Zones 5-10

Height: 2 to 4 feet

Soil and Moisture: well-drained, fertile, moist

Interest: flowers, foliage

Care: easy

◀ P. alopecuroides 'Hameln'

Fountain grass produces stunning clumps of arching leaves and sweeping sprays of bottlebrush flower heads borne on thin, arching stems in summer and fall. The plants are extremely versatile with a fluid, sinuous form that complements rock gardens, mixed borders, and water gardens, and are spectacular massed in large plantings in meadows or wildflower gardens.

Growing and care:
Set plants 2 feet apart. In spring, cut to within 6 inches of the ground before new growth begins. Divide every 5 to 10 years to prevent the center from falling open. *P. setaceum* self-sows readily and is often grown as an annual in regions north of Zone 5.

Selected species and varieties:
P. alopecuroides (Chinese fountain grass, swamp foxtail grass) has clumps of light green foliage 3 to 4 feet high, with nodding, reddish brown flowers 6 inches long; 'Hameln' is a semidwarf form growing to 2 feet; 'National Arboretum' grows to 2 feet with a dark brown inflorescence; Zones 7-9. *P. setaceum* grows 2 to 3 feet tall, with narrow leaves and pinkish spikes 1 foot long; Zones 8-10; 'Rubrum' (purple-leaved fountain grass) has rose-colored foliage and rosy to dark red spikes.

GRAMA
Bouteloua

Light: full sun

Plant type: ornamental grass

Hardiness: Zones 3-10

Height: 1 to 2 feet

Soil and Moisture: well-drained, moist to dry

Interest: flowers, foliage

Care: easy

◀ Bouteloua curtipendula

These clump-forming drought-tolerant grasses are found in prairies, open woodlands, and on rocky slopes throughout much of the United States. Their tough, hardy nature makes them very useful in wild-flower meadows or used as accents in specialty gardens where the tall, slender flower spikes add an informal, wild look. When planted in mass and mowed, the plants produce a good grassy cover for dry areas.

Growing and care:
For best growth grama grasses require full sun and a well-drained, moist soil, but do very well in dry conditions. The plants require almost no care and are well suited for low-maintenance gardens. To propagate, collect seed in fall and sow immediately in well-worked soil. Seed can also be stratified over winter and sown in spring. Divide clumps every 4 years in early spring or fall when plants are dormant.

Selected species and varieties:
B. curtipendula (sideoats grama, mesquite grass) has wiry clumps 1 to 2 feet tall and small flowers arranged in numerous spikelets with downward-pointing tips along one side of each flower stem in summer; in fall the seed heads bleach to a tan color and foliage often turns red or purple. *B. gracilis* (blue grama) grows 1 to 1½ feet tall with narrow, fine-textured foliage forming a dense sod when mowed.

LITTLE BLUESTEM
Schizachyrium

Light: full sun

Plant type: ornamental grass

Hardiness: Zones 3-10

Height: 2 to 3 feet

Soil and Moisture: well-drained, moist to dry

Interest: foliage, seed heads

Care: easy

◀ S. scoparium

Little bluestem is a cute, casual ornamental grass native to the prairies, rocky slopes, open woodlands, and fields from eastern Canada to the Gulf of Mexico and west to Idaho. In spring and summer the plants have upright, pliant blue-green stems and leaves that turn soft shades of tan to mahogany in fall through winter. Little bluestem is lovely massed as a ground cover, used in a meadow garden, or planted singly in a perennial border. Its flowers and seed heads are attractive in arrangements.

Growing and care:
Little bluestem is adaptable and easy to grow, thriving in most soils, moist or dry, including those of low fertility. It does not, however, tolerate wet conditions. Cut plants nearly to the ground in early spring before new growth begins. Propagate by seed or by dividing plants in spring or fall before new growth begins.

Selected species and varieties:
S. scoparium (little bluestem, prairie beard grass) has narrow blue-green foliage in an upright clump, most often about 3 feet tall and to 8 inches in diameter. In fall the foliage turns shades of khaki to burgundy brown. Loose clusters of tiny flowers on 2½-inch spikes open from late summer to fall and are followed by soft, shiny white seed heads.

PANIC GRASS
Panicum

Light: full sun

Plant type: ornamental grass

Hardiness: Zones 5-9

Height: 3 to 6 feet

Soil and Moisture: well-drained, moist

Interest: flowers, foliage

Care: easy

◀ Panicum virgatum 'Heavy Metal'

Panic grass is a large, erect grass that is attractive nearly all year round and is easy to care for as well. The plants produce tall, branching stalks up to 6 feet high topped with airy feathers of tiny buff-colored flowers above 3-foot-high clumps of arching, colored leaves in fall. The distinctive seed heads that follow remain attractive through winter. *Panicum* is widely used as a specimen or filler for large borders. It is very effective when interplanted with other ornamental grasses in mass displays. Brooms have long been made from the stiff, dried stalks.

Growing and care:
Switch grass grows most vigorously in evenly moist soil but will tolerate much drier conditions, even drought, and doesn't mind the sea spray of coastal locations. Cut it back nearly to ground level in early spring, before new growth begins. Propagate by division every 2 to 3 years in spring in the North and in fall in southern regions. Sow seed directly in the garden in spring after last frost.

Selected species and varieties:
P. virgatum (switch grass) has loose, open flower clusters above green leaves that turn yellow and red in fall and fade to brown in winter; 'Haense Herms' has red foliage from summer to fall and grayish seed heads on 3- to 3½-foot stalks; 'Heavy Metal' bears 3- to 4-foot flower stalks above stiff, deep blue leaves that turn yellow in fall.

RABBIT-TAIL GRASS
Lagurus

Light: full sun

Plant type: annual

Height: 6 to 18 inches

Soil and Moisture: well-drained, light, moist to dry

Interest: foliage, seed heads

Care: easy

◀ Lagurus ovatus

The long, furry seed heads of rabbit-tail grass resemble the cottony puff of a rabbit's tail. This neat, good-looking ornamental grass produces a low mound of slender leaves and pliant stalks topped with creamy white, silky seed heads that add soft texture to the late-summer and autumn garden and are very attractive in dried arrangements. Rabbit-tail grass is good for borders, specialty gardens, or when planted in drifts in wildflower meadows. The dwarf varieties are great for rock gardens.

Growing and care:
Start seed indoors 8 weeks prior to the last frost or sow directly outdoors as soon as the soil can be worked. Allow 6 to 12 inches between plants. Water well while seedlings establish themselves and during dry periods. Rabbit-tail grass tolerates heat very well and freely self-seeds, especially in areas of the western states.

Selected species and varieties:
L. ovatus produces narrow, hairy leaves and distinctive seed heads that are fuzzy and light green, turning creamy white as they mature. At 1½ to 2½ inches long, they resemble a rabbit's tail, hence the common name; 'Nanus' is a dwarf variety that grows to 6 inches.

REED GRASS
Calamagrostis

Light: full sun

Plant type: ornamental grass

Hardiness: Zones 5-9

Height: 5 to 7 feet

Soil and Moisture: well-drained to heavy, wet to dry

Interest: flowers, foliage

Care: easy

◄ C. acutiflora 'Stricta'

One of the most adaptable of ornamental grasses, reed grass produces dense, picturesque clumps of narrow, arching leaves and feathery flower plumes on tall, upright stems. One of the first ornamental grasses to bloom, reed grass is a fine multiseason specimen, singly or in groups, for perennial beds, borders, or streamside plantings. It also blends well with rocks and walls and provides interesting wintertime contrast to dark green, broad-leaved evergreens.

Growing and care:

Plant container-grown plants 3 feet apart in spring or fall. Reed grass is remarkable for being able to thrive just about anywhere and grows equally well in heavy, wet soils and in poor, dry ones. Little attention is required. Cut the clump to within 6 inches of the ground before new growth begins in spring. Propagate by division in spring.

Selected species and varieties:

C. acutiflora 'Stricta' has attractive 2-foot-wide clumps of matte green leaves ½ inch wide that arch below 4-foot shafts bearing 15-inch-long flower panicles in early summer. The pinkish green summer foliage turns tan in summer, and golden brown throughout winter.

VETIVER
Vetiveria

Light: full sun

Plant type: ornamental grass

Hardiness: Zones 9-10

Height: 6 to 9 feet

Soil and Moisture: well-drained, moist to wet

Interest: flowers, foliage

Care: easy

◄ Vetiveria zizanioides

Vetiver forms fountains of narrow, rough-edged leaves with blades that are bent to look as if they are blowing in the breeze. Its deep, fibrous roots hold soil very well, making it useful for erosion control of sunny slopes and stream banks. Flowers are flat, plumed spikes on tall stems above the leaf clumps. The fragrant roots have a woodsy, resinous scent with violet overtones and can be dried to scent sachets. In the Far East, roots are woven into mats, screens, and baskets whose fragrance is renewed by dampening to scent rooms. Vetiver also yields an oil prized in expensive perfumes, soaps, and cosmetics.

Growing and care:

Vetiver grows best from divisions. Space plants 2 to 3 feet apart. The complex roots form dense sods that choke out weeds. Harvest roots and renew plants by lifting and dividing every 3 to 4 years. Scrub the roots and spread on racks or screens to dry slowly. Use dried roots as weaving material or crumble for potpourri and sachets.

Selected species and varieties:

V. zizanioides (vetiver, khus-khus) produces leaves ⅓ inch wide and up to 3 feet long with foot-long flowering spikes on stalks to 9 feet.

ACACIA
Acacia

Light: full sun

Plant type: tree

Hardiness: Zones 9-10

Height: 20 to 60 feet

Soil and Moisture: well-drained, moist to dry, acidic

Interest: flowers, foliage

Care: moderate

◀ Acacia dealbata

Acacias thrive in dry, tropical climate. In the United States they are grown in southern California and Arizona, where they provide some of the earliest flowers of the season. Typically, each flower is composed of a mass of stamens that form a dense cluster. Though not long lived, these trees are remarkably fast growers and may reach 30 feet in only 5 years.

Growing and care:

Acacias require warm climates and, once established, tolerate both drought and seaside conditions. They are easy to care for and are virtually pest- and disease-free. Their rapid growth, however, results in weak wood that is subject to wind damage. Plant container-grown specimens and stake them until roots are well established. Prune young plants to desired shape at anytime. Propagate by seed or cuttings.

Selected species and varieties:

A. baileyana (cootamundra wattle) grows 20 to 40 feet tall with a wide canopy of fernlike leaves, and tiny yellow flowers in winter; Zone 10; 'Purpurea' (purple-leaf acacia) has young foliage tinged with burgundy. *A. dealbata* (silver wattle) grows 30 to 60 feet tall with silvery green, doubly pinnate leaves, silvery bark, and extremely fragrant yellow flowers, and is less drought tolerant than cootamundra wattle.

'AMERICAN PILLAR' ROSE
Rosa

Light: full sun

Plant type: shrub

Hardiness: Zones 5-9

Height: 10 to 20 feet

Soil and Moisture: well-drained, fertile, moist

Interest: flowers, fruit

Care: easy to moderate

◀ Rosa
'American Pillar'

The climbing rose 'American Pillar' has been one of the most beautiful garden roses for nearly a century. The plants bear huge clusters of bright, carmine red flowers accented with a white eye. This vigorous plant reaches 15 to 20 feet tall with dark green, leathery leaves on thorny canes and is virtually disease- and pest-free. Use 'American Pillar' on trellises or train it into trees for an unforgettable effect.

Growing and care:

Plant 'American Pillar' in well-worked, fertile soil that has been amended with some organic matter. The plant prefers full sun but will tolerate some very light shade. Fertilize in early spring and again after flowering. Prune trained specimens to shape in summer. Remove older canes in fall. Mulch around plants with compost in spring and fall.

Selected species and varieties:

R. setigera (prairie rose) is another 'American Pillar' parent with thorny, reddish canes with rough-textured green leaves and single, pink flowers with a pale white eye on canes reaching 10 to 15 feet; Zones 4-9. *R. wichuraiana* (memorial rose) is a parent of 'American Pillar' and a vigorous grower with dark green foliage on canes reaching 15 feet and clusters of pure white flowers.

BALD CYPRESS
Taxodium

Light: full sun

Plant type: tree

Hardiness: Zones 4-9

Height: 50 to 70 feet or more

Soil and Moisture: moderately well-drained to heavy, wet to moist

Interest: foliage, bark

Care: easy

◄ Taxodium distichum

Bald cypresses are strong, dramatic-looking trees that are most often envisioned draped with Spanish moss in a southern swamp. While these stately trees grow well in wet sites, they also thrive in deep, moist upland soils as far north as New England. Bald cypress has soft, sage green needlelike foliage that turns burnt orange in fall. In wet areas the shaggy, reddish brown main trunk is flanked by narrow root projections called knees that absorb oxygen for the tree. In fall the graceful branches hold 1-inch-round, greenish purple, fragrant cones. Use bald cypress as a dramatic, fine-textured vertical accent in the garden, or plant in groups along the edge of a pond.

Growing and care:
Plant in deep, well-worked soil amended with generous amounts of compost or rotted manure. The plants are very strong and resist strong winds and winter storm damage. Once established they are care-free with no pest or disease problems.

Selected species and varieties:
T. distichum (common bald cypress) produces new foliage that opens bright yellow-green in graceful sprays amid short, ascending branches on a slender pyramid 50 to more than 70 feet high by 20 to 30 feet wide; 'Shawnee Brave' has a narrow, almost conical habit reaching 75 feet tall and nearly 20 feet in width.

BANKSIAE (LADY BANKS ROSE)
Rosa

Light: full sun

Plant type: shrub

Hardiness: Zones 8-10

Height: 12 to 25 feet

Soil and Moisture: well-drained, moist

Interest: flowers, fragrance

Care: easy

◄ Rosa banksiae 'Lady Banks'

Lady Banks rose is a free-flowering, vigorous grower bearing abundant double white flowers for up to 6 weeks in spring. While in bloom the plant seems smothered in sweetly fragrant blossoms. Each flower is less than 1 inch across, pure white, and extremely fragrant with the scent of violets. Leaves are long, light green, and shiny, and the canes are nearly thornless. Lady Banks rose looks beautiful scrambling up a tree, wall, or trellis.

Growing and care:
Plant Lady Banks rose in loosened soil amended with a little organic matter. Provide support for the fast-growing canes. Once established the plants need little care and are not troubled by insects or disease. Prune as needed to control growth or shape plant.

Selected species and varieties:
R. banksiae var. *lutea* (yellow Lady Banks rose) bears small, fully double yellow flowers with no fragrance along vigorous, 20-foot-tall canes in spring; 'Fortuniana' produces fragrant, double, large white blossoms on 20-foot-tall canes covered with abundant, glossy green foliage.

BARBERRY
Berberis

Light: full sun

Plant type: shrub

Hardiness: Zones 4-8

Height: 1½ to 8 feet

Soil and Moisture: well-drained, moist to dry

Interest: foliage, fruit

Care: easy

◄ Berberis x gladwynensis 'William Penn'

Barberries are neat, tidy shrubs with dense foliage and brightly colored fruit. All are more or less thorny, making them perfect for barrier hedges. Deciduous forms exhibit bright fall foliage and colorful berries that persist through winter. Barberries are useful as hedges, barriers, foundation plants, or specimens. Varieties with red or yellow leaves provide dramatic contrast in green landscapes and work especially well in combination with low-growing junipers.

Growing and care:

Barberries are easy to grow and require very little care. Plant container-grown specimens anytime in spring, summer, or fall. Water well until plants are established. Evergreen barberries grow best in moist, slightly acid soil in sites that are protected from drying winds and strong sun. Deciduous barberries adapt to almost any soil and are tolerant of drought and urban pollution. They show their best fall color in full sun. The red and yellow forms revert to green in shade. Pruning is usually not necessary.

Selected species and varieties:

B. buxifolia var. *nana* (dwarf Magellan barberry) has spiny leaves up to 1 inch long on an evergreen shrub 1½ feet tall and 2 feet wide, usually bearing orange-yellow flowers and purple berries; hardy to Zone 5. *B.* x *gladwynensis* 'William Penn' is a mounded evergreen 4 feet high and wide, with showy flowers and lustrous dark green foliage that turns bronze in winter; hardy to Zone 6, but deciduous north of Zone 8. *B. julianae* (wintergreen barberry) is an evergreen mound with an upright habit, 6 to 8 feet high and wide, with often light-colored stems bearing spines up to 1 inch long and narrow, spiny leaves 2 to 3 inches long that may turn bronze or dark reddish in color in winter, profuse bloom in spring, and ⅓-inch bluish black berries that may linger into fall; hardy to Zone 5. *B. thunbergii* (Japanese barberry) is a multibranched deciduous shrub, 3 to 6 feet tall and 4 to 7 feet wide, producing bright green leaves that appear early to hide small flower clusters and turn orange, red, and reddish purple in fall as ⅓-inch bright red berries form; 'Aurea' grows 3 to 4 feet tall, with vivid yellow leaves in the growing season but relatively few flowers and fruit; var. *atropurpurea* 'Crimson Pygmy' (sometimes referred to as 'Little Gem', 'Little Beauty', 'Little Favorite', or 'Atropurpurea Nana') has maroon to purplish red summer foliage and grows to 2 feet tall and 3 feet wide; 'Rose Glow' reaches 5 to 6 feet tall and produces foliage opening rosy pink with splotches of darker red-purple changing later to solid red-purple; 'Kobold' is 2 feet tall with very rich, dark green boxwoodlike leaves and a formal, round habit that needs no pruning; 'Vermillion' grows to 3 feet with dense green leaves turning brilliant red in fall.

'BLANC DOUBLE DE COUBERT'
Rosa

Light: full sun

Plant type: shrub

Hardiness: Zones 3-10

Height: 4 to 6 feet

Soil and Moisture: well-drained, moist

Interest: flowers, fragrance

Care: easy

◀ Rosa 'Blanc double de Coubert'

The rose 'Blanc double de Coubert' is very hardy and easy to grow, with beautiful, intensely fragrant, linen white double flowers in spring with rebloom in fall. The plant belongs to the hybrid rugosa group and has long, gracefully arching canes forming a mounded shrub 3 to 4 feet high. The leaves are deep forest green in summer turning russet yellow in fall. When the foliage drops the canes are covered with large, orange-red hips that persist into winter. 'Blanc double de Coubert' is one of the best specimen roses but also blends nicely into mixed borders and herb gardens. The petals can be dried and used in potpourri.

Growing and care:
Plant in loosened soil, spacing plants 3 to 4 feet apart. Prune like rugosa roses, removing about one-third of the cane in late winter to shape plant. 'Blanc double de Coubert' can be used almost everywhere: in seaside gardens, as city plantings, or on dry, sandy hillsides. The plants are virtually pest- and disease-free, although Japanese beetles sometimes are attracted to the flowers.

Selected species and varieties:
'Frau Dagmar Hartopp' is a hybrid rugosa type with a dense, compact form reaching 3 feet tall and 3 feet wide with nearly everblooming blush pink single blossoms and misty yellow stamens, dark green leaves, and bright red hips in fall.

BLUEBERRY
Vaccinium

Light: full sun

Plant type: shrub

Hardiness: Zones 2-8

Height: $1/2$ to 12 feet

Soil and Moisture: well-drained, moist, acidic

Interest: flowers, foliage, fruit

Care: moderate

◀ Vaccinium corymbosum

Blueberries are well known as providers of some of the tastiest fruit around, yet they also add delicate white flowers in spring and vibrant, intensely colored foliage in fall. Blueberries are available in a range of heights, from ground cover types to upright shrubs, and grow well in poor soils as well as rich ones. They are useful mixed into perennial borders or naturalized in sunny wildflower meadows.

Growing and care:
Plant blueberries in moist, well-drained soil with a pH of 4.5 to 5.5. Add generous amounts of organic matter prior to planting. Mulch to preserve moisture around highbush types. Lowbush forms are drought tolerant once established. Prune after fruiting to encourage better fruit set.

Selected species and varieties:
V. angustifolium (lowbush blueberry) grows 6 to 24 inches tall with a low, spreading habit. Leaves are small, blue-green in summer, turning bright red in fall; flowers are white with reddish tinge. Fruit is delicious, pale blue to blue-black with tart, wild taste; Zones 2-6. *V. corymbosum* (highbush blueberry) reaches 6 to 12 feet tall with multiple stems and a rounded, upright habit. Leaves are blue-green in summer, turning red, orange, yellow, and bronze in fall. Flowers are white, urn shaped, $1/2$ inch long; fruit is a sweet, blue-black berry; Zones 3-8.

727

BROOM
Cytisus

Light: full sun	
Plant type: shrub	
Hardiness: Zones 5-10	
Height: 6 inches to 5 feet	
Soil and Moisture: well-drained, moist to dry	
Interest: flowers, foliage, fragrance	
Care: moderate	

◀ Cytisus x kewensis

Broom is a fast-growing, reliable shrub that brightens the spring border with its masses of pealike, often fragrant flowers. Small simple or trifoliate leaves line arching stems that remain green all year, providing welcome interest during winter months. Broom's spreading habit and minimal requirements make it ideal for stabilizing the soil of a sunny hillside or dry bank. Low-growing types are useful in rock gardens or borders.

Growing and care:
Plant in early spring in well-worked soil. Broom is adaptable to seaside conditions, but does poorly in damp locations. Prune flowering stems by two-thirds immediately after flowering. Do not cut back stems more than a year old, because they will not resprout. Propagate by cuttings or by layering in spring.

Selected species and varieties:
C. x *kewensis* (Kew broom) grows 6 inches tall, spreading to form a mat of green stems up to 6 feet across, with pale yellow spring flowers and small, hairy leaves; excellent for the rock garden; Zones 6-10. *C.* x *praecox* (Warminster broom) grows 3 to 6 feet tall with a similar spread and graceful, slender, cascading stems that produce lemon yellow blooms in early spring; 'Albus' is a slightly smaller shrub with white flowers; 'Luteus' is a dwarf variety with darker yellow blooms.

BUSH CLOVER
Lespedeza

Light: full sun	
Plant type: shrub	
Hardiness: Zones 4-8	
Height: 3 to 10 feet	
Soil and Moisture: well-drained, sandy, dry	
Interest: flowers	
Care: easy	

◀ Lespedeza thunbergii 'White Fountain'

Bush clovers are vigorous deciduous shrubs valued for their late-season flowers that appear from midsummer to fall. The small rose-purple blossoms are borne on 5- to 6-inch-long clusters that hang from the thin, pendulous branches. These easy-care plants are not troubled by pests or disease, making them good for borders or interplanted with spring-flowering shrubs.

Growing and care:
Well-drained soils are essential. Avoid fertilizers. Prune stems to the ground in early spring before growth begins. New stems will reach 3 to 4 feet by flowering time. Propagate by seed or stem cuttings.

Selected species and varieties:
L. bicolor (shrub bush clover) reaches 6 to 10 feet, with trifoliate leaves along arching stems, and rosy purple flowers in 2- to 5-inch-long clusters arising from the current season's growth from mid- to late summer. *L. thunbergii* [also listed as *L. sieboldii*] (purple bush clover) grows to 6 feet tall and 10 feet wide with slender arching stems that become weighted down by the 8-inch-long dark purple flower clusters from late summer to early fall; 'White Fountain' has white flowers; Zones 5-8.

BUTTERFLY BUSH
Buddleia

Light: full sun

Plant type: shrub

Hardiness: Zones 5-9

Height: 4 to 20 feet

Soil and Moisture: well-drained, moist, fertile

Interest: flowers, fragrance

Care: easy

◀ Buddleia alternifolia

Butterfly bushes have long, arching stems covered with long, conical clusters of tiny, exceptionally fragrant summer flowers in shades of white, red, pink, lavender, or purple. Butterflies find the blossoms irresistible, sometimes completely covering the flower heads with their slowly beating wings on warm days. The willow-shaped leaves are dark green above and slightly hairy beneath. These shrubs are superb as specimens or massed as background in a shrub border.

Growing and care:
Butterfly bushes are vigorous, pest-free plants. Prune flower heads after blossoms fade to prolong the flowering season. Prune *B. davidii* in early spring before growth begins. In regions north of Zone 6 it dies back to the ground and resprouts in the spring. Prune *B. alternifolia* immediately after flowering in summer.

Selected species and varieties:
B. alternifolia (fountain butterfly bush) reaches 8 to 15 feet with 4-inch dull, dark green leaves that are gray on the underside, and long, drooping clusters of soft purple flowers. *B. davidii* (summer lilac, orange-eye butterfly bush) grows to 10 feet with 10-inch leaves that are white underneath, and 8- to 18-inch clusters of orange-throated flowers in a wide array of colors; var. *magnifica* has dark blue-purple blossoms with a bright orange eye; 'Peace' has ivory flowers.

CAPE FUCHSIA
Phygelius

Light: full sun

Plant type: shrub

Hardiness: Zones 7-10

Height: 2 to 6 feet

Soil and Moisture: well-drained, moist

Interest: flowers

Care: easy

◀ Phygelius aequalis 'Yellow Trumpet'

Cape fuchsias have dramatic clusters of dangling, colorful, five-lobed tubular flowers and pairs of dark green, triangular to lance-shaped leaves that are most dense toward the base of the stems. These woody-based perennials will grow as small shrubs where winters are mild. In colder regions the plants die back to the ground in winter and resprout in spring. Cape fuchsias are excellent container plants that add summer color to patio and deck gardens. The plants also attract hummingbirds.

Growing and care:
The long flower clusters of cape fuchsias need to be sheltered from strong breezes. In Zones 7 and 8 the entire plant should be protected from cold winter winds as well. They benefit from additional water and fertilizer. Prune old stems and winter-damaged shoots in very early spring. Propagate by seed or softwood cuttings made in late autumn or spring.

Selected species and varieties:
P. aequalis grows 3 to 4 feet tall with dense, cylindrical clusters of 2-inch brown, red, or dusky pink late-summer flowers; 'Yellow Trumpet' has a dense, bushy habit and creamy yellow flowers. *P.* x *rectus* grows 3 to 4 feet tall with pendulous clusters of light red summer to fall flowers and lance-shaped, slightly toothed leaves; 'Devil's Tears' has deep red flowers with a yellow throat.

'CÉCILE BRUNNER' ROSE
Rosa

Light: full sun

Plant type: shrub

Hardiness: Zones 4-9

Height: 1 to 3 feet

Soil and Moisture: well-drained, fertile, moist

Interest: flowers, fragrance

Care: moderate

◄ Rosa 'Cécile Brunner'

One of the most popular polyantha roses, 'Cécile Brunner' has abundant clusters of richly scented double flowers from late spring to fall. The plants are small, reaching from 2 to 3 feet tall with dainty spiraled buds and small, rich pink flowers. The slender canes have few thorns and are lightly covered with glossy, dark green leaves. 'Cécile Brunner' is well suited for mixed borders and is an excellent source of cut flowers.

Growing and care:
Plant in a bright, sunny place in soil that has been well amended with compost or rotted manure. Top-dress annually with compost. Prune in spring as buds are breaking, removing the top one-third of the canes. Fertilize after pruning and again after first flush of blooms has faded.

Selected species and varieties:
R. 'Climbing Cécile Brunner' is a very vigorous, rambling rose reaching to 20 feet with light pink, fragrant flowers in late spring; 'Baby Cécile Brunner' is a miniature rose with small 1-foot-tall stems and light pink blossoms; 'Baby Betsy McCall' grows 6 to 10 inches high with dark green, leathery foliage and very small, double, fragrant pink blossoms; 'Perle d'Or' grows 3 feet tall with clusters of fragrant, yellow-pink double blossoms.

'CHICAGO PEACE' ROSE
Rosa

Light: full sun

Plant type: shrub

Hardiness: Zones 5-9

Height: 4 to 5 feet

Soil and Moisture: well-drained, fertile, moist

Interest: flowers, fragrance

Care: moderate

◄ Rosa 'Chicago Peace'

The hybrid tea rose 'Chicago Peace' has been a favorite of gardeners since the early 1960s. It is related to the famous 'Peace' rose and bears stunning, fragrant double blossoms, each with slightly curved petals colored rose pink at the edges and blending to golden yellow at the base. The plants are upright and vigorous with good disease resistance. Plant 'Chicago Peace' as a specimen or mingled with other roses and shrubs in an informal border. The flowers are excellent for cutting.

Growing and care:
Plant 'Chicago Peace' in a sunny location in well-worked soil generously amended with compost or other organic matter. Prune bushes lightly in spring, removing only dead or damaged branches. Do not cut back healthy canes. Fertilize in spring as buds begin to swell and again when flowering begins. Mulch in fall in Zones 5 and 6.

Selected species and varieties:
R. 'Climbing Peace' bears abundant, golden double blossoms in spring and fall on vigorous, 10-foot-tall canes. *R.* 'Peace' grows from 3 to 4 feet tall with moderately vigorous upright canes, dark, glossy green foliage, and classic golden yellow, fragrant double blossoms. The plants are susceptible to black spot and mildew in warm, humid regions.

CORK TREE
Phellodendron

Light: full sun

Plant type: tree

Hardiness: Zones 3-8

Height: 30 to 45 feet

Soil and Moisture: well-drained, moist to dry

Interest: bark

Care: easy

◀ Phellodendron amurense

Cork tree is valued for its very ornamental, deeply ridged and furrowed gray-brown corky bark, which cloaks the wide-spreading horizontal main branches of mature trees. Lustrous green compound leaves, like those of black walnut, cast a light shade and sometimes turn yellow in autumn before dropping. Small yellowish green flowers bloom in late spring, followed by small clusters of black berries in late fall on female trees. Both flowers and fruit have a turpentine-like odor when they are bruised.

Growing and care:
Cork tree is easy to transplant and has moderate tolerance for drought and pollution. In hot conditions it can defoliate, sometimes completely. For best growth plant in soil freely amended with compost or rotted manure and water regularly. Mulch around root zone to keep soil cool and moist.

Selected species and varieties:
P. amurense (Amur cork tree) reaches 30 to 45 feet with an equal or greater spread, with orange-yellow stems bearing glossy dark green leaflets to 4 inches long, and corky bark developing in old age. *P. chinense* (Chinese cork tree) grows 30 feet tall, with dark yellow-green leaflets to 5 inches long on red-brown stems; hardy to Zone 5.

CRAB APPLE
Malus

Light: full sun

Plant type: shrub, tree

Hardiness: Zones 2-8

Height: 6 to 50 feet

Soil and Moisture: well-drained, moist, acidic

Interest: flowers, fruit, fragrance

Care: moderate

◀ Malus floribunda

Crab apples are very popular ornamental shrubs and trees that bear clusters of white to red, usually fragrant spring blossoms before the leaves appear. Small green, yellow, or red applelike fruit is produced in summer and often persists into fall. Crab apples are excellent specimen trees and make good additions to shrub borders. The flowers attract bees in spring and the fruit brings songbirds to the garden in fall.

Growing and care:
Plant in spring or fall in well-worked soil amended with compost or rotted manure. Water regularly during the first growing season. Prune crab apples each year immediately after flowering to maintain shape, and remove suckers. Feed in spring with a balanced fertilizer, and mulch with compost.

Selected species and varieties:
M. floribunda (Japanese flowering crab apple) is a rounded, 15- to 25-foot tree with pink to red buds opening to white or pink fragrant flowers, followed by red or yellow fruit; Zones 5-8. *M. sargentii* (Sargent crab apple) is a spreading, densely branched, 6- to 8-foot-tall shrub with clusters of red buds opening to ½-inch to 1-inch highly fragrant white flowers, and bright red ¼-inch fruit; 'Callaway' grows 15 to 20 feet tall with a rounded canopy and abundant snow white flowers in spring.

CRAPE MYRTLE
Lagerstroemia

Light: full sun

Plant type: shrub, tree

Hardiness: Zones 7-9

Height: 7 to 25 feet

Soil and Moisture: well-drained, moist

Interest: flowers, bark

Care: easy

◀ Lagerstroemia indica 'Seminole'

Crape myrtle is a reliable, easy-to-grow plant that also looks fantastic in flower. The large clusters of crinkly pink, white, rose, or purple flowers blossom in late summer at a time when little else may be in bloom. In fall, the summer's dark green leaves turn into a painter's palette of red, orange, and yellow. The light gray bark exfoliates as it ages, revealing shades of gray and brown. Crape myrtle is often grown as a specimen or grouped into large screens.

Growing and care:
Plant into well-worked soil generously amended with compost or rotted manure. Prune hard in fall to encourage increased flowering and restrain the plant's vigorous growth. In northern areas crape myrtle is grown as an herbaceous perennial that dies to the ground each winter. Mulch around plant to keep soil moist and reduce heaving.

Selected species and varieties:
L. indica (common crape myrtle) is a fast-growing multistemmed shrub or tree 15 to 25 feet tall, with flower clusters 6 to 8 inches long; 'Natchez' reaches 20 feet tall and wide, with cinnamon brown exfoliating bark and white flower clusters 6 to 12 inches long from early summer to fall, when glossy dark green leaves turn orange and red; 'Seminole' bears medium pink flowers for 6 to 8 weeks beginning in midsummer on a 7- to 8-foot shrub.

CYPRESS
Cupressus

Light: full sun

Plant type: tree

Hardiness: Zones 7-9

Height: 30 to 40 feet

Soil and Moisture: well-drained, moist to dry

Interest: foliage

Care: easy

◀ Cupressus sempervirens

These graceful, fine-textured trees make handsome specimens, screens, or windbreaks, and add a stately elegance to their surroundings. Their aromatic foliage consists of scalelike leaves closely pressed on braided-cord stems. Reddish brown exfoliating bark becomes dark brown and furrowed with age. Attractive cones with shieldlike scales are 1 inch across.

Growing and care:
Best suited to the West and the Southwest, cypress enjoys mild to hot, dry climates and needs no supplemental water once established. Soil must be perfectly drained, as the trees do poorly in wet soils. Cypress transplants best from container-grown plants, and is generally insect- and disease-free.

Selected species and varieties:
C. glabra [sometimes labeled by nurseries as *C. arizonica,* which is actually a separate species] (smooth-barked Arizona cypress) grows to a dense, bushy pyramid 30 to 40 feet tall and 15 to 20 feet wide with soft green, gray-green, or blue-green foliage. *C. sempervirens* (Italian cypress, Mediterranean cypress) produces a slender column 30 or more feet tall, with horizontal branches and dark green foliage; cultivars include bright green, gold, and blue forms.

DESERT WILLOW
Chilopsis

Light: full sun	
Plant type: shrub, tree	
Hardiness: Zones 8-10	
Height: 10 to 25 feet	
Soil and Moisture: well-drained, sandy, dry	
Interest: flowers, foliage	
Care: easy	

◀ Chilopsis linearis

Desert willow is a great ornamental shrub or tree for hot, arid areas. The showy, trumpet-shaped, fragrant spring flowers resembling snapdragons bloom in clusters at the tips of desert willow's branches in spring and often sporadically until fall. Its open, branching, and willowlike leaves, evergreen in milder climates, lend an airy appearance. A heavy crop of thin, foot-long pods persists through winter. Desert willow can be trained into a graceful specimen for dry gardens.

Growing and care:
Native to arid lands of the Southwest, desert willow enjoys light soil that is very well drained. Prune to develop a tree form or to eliminate shagginess. Transplant container-grown plants in spring or late fall and water until the roots establish themselves.

Selected species and varieties:
C. linearis (desert catalpa, flowering willow) is a shrubby tree 10 to 25 feet tall and 10 to 15 feet wide, with interestingly twisted branches bearing narrow 6- to 12-inch-long leaves and fragrant lilac, rosy pink, purple, or white flowers with curled lobes and white or yellow markings.

'DORTMUND' ROSE
Rosa

Light: full sun	
Plant type: shrub	
Hardiness: Zones 4-10	
Height: 7 to 15 feet	
Soil and Moisture: well-drained, moist	
Interest: flowers, fruit	
Care: easy	

◀ Rosa kordesii 'Dortmund'

The variety 'Dortmund' is a spectacular climbing rose with rafts of vivid scarlet single blossoms in spring. This *kordesii* hybrid is a very hardy, easy-to-care-for plant with vigorous, thorny canes reaching to 15 feet and attractive glossy green foliage. Each blossom has broad red petals surrounding a white center marked with a tuft of yellow stamens and has a light fragrance. Use 'Dortmund' against a wall or fence for a show-stopping spring display or plant in a rock garden and allow the canes to cascade.

Growing and care:
Plant in well-worked soil that has been lightly amended with organic matter. Fertilize in early spring and again after flowers fade in spring. With vigorous deadheading, blooming continues throughout the growing season. If spent blooms are allowed to remain, flowering ceases and bright orange hips develop.

Selected species and varieties:
R. 'Hamburger Phoenix' is similar in habit to 'Dortmund' but has fragrant, double, bright red flowers in large clusters followed by orange-red hips in late summer and fall; 'Raymond Chenault' has strong 12-foot-tall canes and stunning single red flowers in huge clusters in spring and again in late summer.

ESCALLONIA
Escallonia

Light: full sun

Plant type: shrub

Hardiness: Zones 8-10

Height: 3 to 5 feet

Soil and Moisture: well-drained, dry to moist

Interest: flowers, foliage, fragrance

Care: easy

◄ E. x langleyensis 'Apple Blossom'

Escallonia is a very attractive, warm-climate shrub that forms an informal mound of glossy, often fragrant evergreen foliage. The pink, white, or red funnel-shaped flowers are arranged in small clusters and bloom profusely over a long season. Escallonia thrives in coastal locations and needs little pruning. It is a good choice for informal hedges or screens.

Growing and care:

Plant escallonia in a loose, well-drained soil that has been amended with some compost or other organic matter. It is tolerant of soils with some salts but does not like high alkalinity. Water well when transplanting. Once established the plants are moderately drought tolerant but should be given extra water during extended dry periods. Do not locate plantings in windy areas.

Selected species and varieties:

E. x *langleyensis* 'Apple Blossom' is a dense, sprawling shrub 3 to 5 feet high, with arching branches bearing large leaves and pink buds opening to pinkish white flowers throughout the warm months. *E.* 'Pride of Donard' has a dense, broad-spreading habit with rosy pink flowers throughout the year in mild climates. *E. rubra* 'C. F. Ball' (red escallonia) is one of the best varieties, with a compact, upright habit reaching 5 feet high. Excellent for hedging, the plant bears very glossy leaves and bright red flowers.

FALSE CYPRESS
Chamaecyparis

Light: full sun

Plant type: shrub, tree

Hardiness: Zones 4-8

Height: 4 to 75 feet

Soil and Moisture: well-drained, fertile, moist

Interest: foliage

Care: easy

◄ Chamaecyparis obtusa

False cypresses are a diverse group of evergreens that contain some of the most ornamental conifers in the world. The plants range from slow-growing dwarf forms that resemble bonsai to tall, graceful, soft-textured trees. False cypresses have fan-shaped sprays of dark green to golden yellow foliage and beautiful shapes that accent formal gardens, wildflower meadows, and all styles of plantings in between.

Growing and care:

Plant in loosened soil generously amended with organic matter. Transplant container-grown specimens in spring or fall and water well until established. Mulch around base of tree with pine needles or bark chips to retain moisture and keep soil cool. False cypress grows well in many regions and thrives in areas with moist, cool summers and mild winters. Locations with hot, humid summers or heavy soils are not appropriate. The plants should not be placed in windy locations.

Selected species and varieties:

C. obtusa (hinoki false cypress, hinoki cypress) produces a dark green, slender pyramid growing 50 to 75 feet tall; 'Crippsii' forms a broad pyramid with drooping golden yellow branch tips; 'Gracilis' grows 6 to 10 feet tall with a narrow conical form; 'Nana Gracilis' is 4 to 6 feet tall and 3 to 4 feet wide with very dark green foliage arranged in slightly curved sprays.

FIR
Abies

Light: full sun	
Plant type: tree	
Hardiness: Zones 3-7	
Height: 30 to 50 feet	
Soil and Moisture: well-drained, moist	
Interest: foliage	
Care: easy	

◄ Abies concolor

White fir is a majestic tree of mountains and northern forests with soft, gray-green evergreen needles, maroon-purple cones, and a stately pyramidal form. The upper branches are upright in habit; the middle and lower are horizontal to descending. The trees bear flat, wonderfully aromatic needles that yield a homey, slightly resinous fragrance. Greenish or purplish upright cones, up to 6 inches long, mature to a brown hue and fall apart when ripe. White fir is excellent as a specimen plant, or used as a thick, soft-textured screen.

Growing and care:
Plant white fir in deep, sandy or gravelly loams, well amended with organic matter. The plants need little attention and withstand drought, heat, and cold well. Mulch well with shredded bark, woodchips, or leaves.

Selected species and varieties:
A. concolor (white fir, Colorado fir) grows 30 to 50 feet high (but reaches 100 feet under ideal conditions) by 15 to 30 feet wide, with a central trunk and whorled branches, and produces bluish green, grayish green, or silvery blue needles up to 2½ inches long; 'Compacta' is a densely branched dwarf usually 3 feet high, with 1½-inch blue needles, acquiring an attractively irregular form as it matures; 'Violacea' has silvery blue-green needles resembling blue spruce.

FIRETHORN
Pyracantha

Light: full sun	
Plant type: shrub	
Hardiness: Zones 6-9	
Height: 2 to 16 feet	
Soil and Moisture: well-drained, moist	
Interest: flowers, foliage, fruit	
Care: moderate	

◄ Pyracantha coccinea 'Mohave'

Firethorn is as vibrant as its name, with shiny, dark brown branches, plentiful ½-inch thorns, and dark, glossy evergreen or semievergreen leaves. In spring clusters of tiny white flowers are followed by bright, fire red or orange berries that persist through fall. Firethorn adds sparkle to informal hedges, and dresses up walls and trellises when trained into espaliers.

Growing and care:
Plant container-grown specimens in spring or fall in well-worked soil amended with compost or rotted manure. Firethorn grows best in evenly moist soil but is tolerant of dry, summer conditions. Once established, plants should not be moved.

Selected species and varieties:
P. coccinea (scarlet firethorn) has 1- to 1½-inch oval leaves and red-orange fall berries; 'Apache' bears bright red berries on compact, evergreen shrubs to 5 feet tall and 5 feet wide; 'Mohave' is a cold-hardy, disease-resistant, evergreen shrub with heavy crops of berries growing to 12 feet tall and as wide; 'Navajo' has red-orange fruit on dense, 6-foot-round mounds of branches; 'Teton' grows narrow columns of branches 16 feet tall and half as wide with yellow-orange berries.

FLOWERING QUINCE
Chaenomeles

Light: full sun	
Plant type: shrub	
Hardiness: Zones 4-8	
Height: 3 to 10 feet	
Soil and Moisture: well-drained, moist to dry, acidic	
Interest: flowers, fruit	
Care: moderate	

◀ Chaenomeles speciosa 'Texas Scarlet'

Flowering quince is an old-fashioned plant that has never lost its popularity. A thorny, rounded, spreading shrub, flowering quince puts on a sparkling spring show when a profusion of showy flowers in a wide range of colors appears before the leaves. The small, yellowish green quincelike fruits that ripen in fall make unforgettable jams and jellies. Budded stems can be used for late-winter arrangements.

Growing and care:
Plant container-grown flowering quince in well-worked soil amended with some organic matter in spring or fall. Prune each spring to remove dead or broken branches and restore shape. Some leaves usually drop in the summer but long periods of wet weather can exaggerate this tendency.

Selected species and varieties:
C. speciosa (common flowering quince, Japanese quince) reaches 6 to 10 feet tall with equal or greater width, usually with red or scarlet but sometimes pink or white flowers and lustrous dark green leaves that open bronzy red; 'Cameo' produces peachy pink double flowers in early spring; 'Jet Trail' has contrail white flowers; 'Nivalis' bears pure white flowers; 'Texas Scarlet' produces profuse tomato red flowers on an attractive, spreading 3- to 5-foot plant.

FORSYTHIA
Forsythia

Light: full sun	
Plant type: shrub	
Hardiness: Zones 4-9	
Height: 4 to 10 feet	
Soil and Moisture: well-drained, moist	
Interest: flowers	
Care: moderate	

◀ Forsythia x intermedia

Forsythia is the traditional harbinger of spring, gracing gardens with vibrant yellow flowers about the time the crocus blossoms open. The plants are a standard in shrub borders, masses, and banks, where the fountain-like sprays of yellow blooms are a welcome relief from winter gloom. The budded twigs can be snipped in late winter and easily forced indoors for early floral bouquets.

Growing and care:
Forsythia is easy to transplant from containers, balled and burlapped, or even bareroot, in early spring. Plant in well-worked soil generously amended with organic matter. Water during dry periods. The plants are often hardy into Zone 3 but the flower buds often hardy only to Zone 5.

Selected species and varieties:
F. x *intermedia* (border forsythia) grows 12 feet wide with upright, arching canes that bear 1- to 1½-inch pale to deep yellow flowers and dark green leaves 3 to 5 inches long turning dull olive purple in fall; 'Spectabilis' bears a profusion of richly hued, bright yellow flowers at the stem axils and is easily the showiest-blooming cultivar. *F. suspensa* var. *sieboldii* (weeping forsythia) has an arching habit with long, trailing branches with fewer flowers than border forsythia; 'Northern Sun' is a hardy variety that reliably flowers as far north as Zone 4 with bright, sunny yellow flowers on stems reaching 10 feet.

GOLDEN-RAIN TREE
Koelreuteria

Light: full sun

Plant type: tree

Hardiness: Zones 5-9

Height: 30 to 40 feet

Soil and Moisture: well-drained, moist

Interest: flowers, foliage

Care: easy

◀ K. paniculata 'September'

Adelightful small tree to shade a garden bench, walkway, or patio, golden-rain tree produces arching, wide-spreading branches and airy sprays of yellow flowers in early to midsummer. The dense canopy consists of abundant, large compound leaves that are medium bright green, changing to yellow before dropping in fall. Golden-rain tree adds a tasteful touch to any garden and is useful as a specimen or planted to shade a gazebo or quiet retreat.

Growing and care:

Golden-rain tree is easy to care for and tolerates a wide variety of conditions, including drought. It grows best— about 1½ feet per year—in soil well amended with compost or rotted manure. Provide shelter from wind and prune broken or dead branches in spring.

Selected species and varieties:

K. paniculata (golden-rain tree, varnish tree) has a rounded crown with a spread equal to or greater than its height, bearing 6- to 18-inch-long leaves composed of seven to 15 toothed and lobed leaflets 1 to 3 inches long, purplish red when opening, and flower clusters 12 to 15 inches long and wide; 'September' flowers in late summer and is less hardy than the species; Zones 6-9.

HAWTHORN
Crataegus

Light: full sun

Plant type: shrub, tree

Hardiness: Zones 4-7

Height: 20 to 35 feet

Soil and Moisture: well-drained, moist

Interest: flowers, fruit

Care: moderate

◀ Crataegus viridis 'Winter King'

Hawthorns are neat, small trees or large shrubs that produce flowers in spring, beautifully colored leaves in fall, and attractive fruit through winter. The plants have round crowns of finely toothed leaves and a delicate texture, making them very useful as specimen trees or in a shrub border. The green foliage turns reddish purple in fall. The dainty clusters of small white flowers yield to bright red berries in late summer that persist through winter, if the birds don't get them first. The plants are tolerant of urban conditions and their long thorns make them great for barrier hedges.

Growing and care:

Plant hawthorns in loose, well-worked soil amended with organic matter. The thorns make pruning or shearing difficult, so allow room for the tree or shrub's mature spread. Remove broken or dead branches in spring and prune lightly to shape if desired. Water during dry periods and fertilize in spring just before flowering.

Selected species and varieties:

C. phaenopyrum (Washington hawthorn) is a multiple-stemmed shrub or tree growing to 30 feet with foliage that turns scarlet in fall, and clusters of white flowers in spring. *C. viridis* 'Winter King' (green hawthorn) is a round to vase-shaped tree reaching to 35 feet with lustrous green foliage turning purple or red in fall, and 1-inch bright red fruit from fall through winter.

HONEY LOCUST
Gleditsia

Light: full sun	
Plant type: tree	
Hardiness: Zones 3-9	
Height: 30 to 70 feet	
Soil and Moisture: well-drained, moist to dry	
Interest: foliage	
Care: easy	

◄ Gleditsia triacanthos var. inermis

Honey locust has become one of the most popular shade trees chiefly because it combines beauty with unmatched versatility. The trees develop a wide-spreading canopy of arching branches and bright green ferny foliage, creating light to dappled shade beneath. Small fragrant flowers in late spring are followed by 12- to 18-inch reddish brown to brown strap-shaped pods, usually viewed as a nuisance. In fall the leaves turn golden yellow before falling.

Growing and care:
Honey locusts grow best in moist, rich loam but tolerate acid and alkaline soils, drought, and salt. The trees transplant well and should be set in loosened soil amended with some organic matter. Under average conditions the trees are very vigorous, growing up to 2 feet per year. Recently some serious insect and disease problems have been noted.

Selected species and varieties:
G. triacanthos var. *inermis* (thornless honey locust, sweet locust) is highly variable in size, from 30 to 70 feet tall and equally wide ranging in spread, with a short trunk and an open crown bearing doubly compound leaves with oblong leaflets ⅓ to 1½ inches long and greenish yellow flowers; 'Imperial' [also called 'Impcole'] is a seedless version that grows to 35 feet high; Zones 4-7.

INDIAN HAWTHORN
Raphiolepis

Light: full sun	
Plant type: shrub	
Hardiness: Zones 9-10	
Height: 3 to 5 feet	
Soil and Moisture: well-drained, moist	
Interest: flowers, foliage, fragrance	
Care: moderate	

◄ Raphiolepis indica

Indian hawthorn is a dense, glossy-leaved evergreen shrub generously decorated with loose, showy clusters of apple-blossom-like fragrant flowers in early spring. The pink or white flowers yield to purplish to blue-black berries that ripen in fall and linger though winter. This slow-growing, sturdy shrub is often used in low hedges and borders or as background for a flower bed. It also makes a good container plant for the patio or deck.

Growing and care:
Pinch the tips of growing branches to encourage a bushy habit and prune to shape if plant becomes leggy. Water regularly and provide extra moisture during dry periods. Once established, Indian hawthorn withstands drought and is tolerant of salt and seaside conditions.

Selected species and varieties:
R. indica forms a 3- to 5-foot-wide dense mound of 2- to 3-inch-long dark green lance-shaped leaves with toothy margins clustered at the ends of the branches, sometimes turning a dull purplish green in winter, and ½-inch-wide fragrant white flowers blushed with pink toward the center with red stamens; 'White Enchantress' is a dwarf form with single white flowers.

'JOHN CABOT' ROSE
Rosa

Light: full sun

Plant type: shrub

Hardiness: Zones 3-10

Height: 4 to 10 feet

Soil and Moisture: well-drained, fertile, moist

Interest: flowers, fragrance

Care: easy

◀ Rosa kordesii 'John Cabot'

This beautiful, versatile, easy-to-care-for rose is just about perfect. 'John Cabot' is one of the Canadian Explorer series and bears satin red, nicely fragrant double flowers on strong, gently arching 6-foot canes covered with dark green glossy foliage. The plants are disease-free and will grow just about anywhere. 'John Cabot' looks beautiful when trained along a fence or over a trellis and is outstanding when planted near plants with blue flowers or gray foliage.

Growing and care:
Plant 'John Cabot' in well-worked soil that has been amended with organic matter. The plants are slow to establish and should be regularly watered for the first 2 growing seasons. Prune out dead or damaged canes in late winter or early spring. Deadhead faded flowers as they occur. 'John Cabot' is not troubled by disease or insects and is virtually trouble-free.

Selected species and varieties:
R. kordesii 'Henry Kelsey' resembles 'Don Juan' but is much hardier, with dark, velvet red double blossoms marked with yellow stamens on strong 8-foot canes; 'William Baffin' is nearly as perfect a plant as 'John Cabot', with abundant sprays of strawberry pink blossoms from spring to fall on arching 8- to 10-foot canes.

LANTANA
Lantana

Light: full sun

Plant type: shrub

Hardiness: Zones 9-10

Height: 1 to 6 feet

Soil and Moisture: well-drained, moist

Interest: flowers, foliage, fragrance

Care: moderate

◀ Lantana montevidensis

The abundant flowers of lantana are arranged in perky little bouquets that can't help but brighten the garden. The blossoms appear from spring through summer in pastel shades of white, pink, yellow, and lavender at the tips of somewhat stiff stems lined with cool green, pungently aromatic foliage. Lantanas are beautiful accents for rock gardens or when allowed to flow over stone walls. In the North they are often planted in containers, used in patio or deck displays, and brought indoors for the winter. The flowers are very attractive to hummingbirds and butterflies.

Growing and care:
Start seed 6 to 8 weeks before planting out. Space plants 1½ feet apart. They can be trained to standards, and are easily dug and potted in fall for indoor winter flowering. Pinch young plants to encourage branching. The plants sometimes suffer from infestations of whitefly or spider mites.

Selected species and varieties:
L. camara (yellow sage) is a 2- to 6-foot shrub with dark, hairy leaves and flat-topped clusters of tiny flowers that start yellow and turn orange-red; 'Confetti' bears white, pink, and red flowers all on the same plant. *L. montevidensis* [also listed as *L. sellowiana*] (weeping lantana) grows to 2½ feet with a mounding habit, dark green leaves, and flat-topped clusters of tiny yellow flowers.

LEYLAND CYPRESS
x Cupressocyparis

Light: full sun

Plant type: tree

Hardiness: Zones 6-10

Height: 60 to 70 feet

Soil and Moisture: well-drained, moist to dry

Interest: foliage

Care: easy

◄ x Cupressocyparis leylandii 'Silver Dust'

A dense, towering, very vigorous columnar or pyramidal tree, Leyland cypress is a hybrid of *Cupressus* and *Chamaecyparis*. It produces some of the fastest-growing and finest-textured screen or hedge plants available. The fanlike arrangement of bluish green scalelike needles appears soft and feathery. In addition to its versatile use in the landscape, Leyland cypress is also a very popular Christmas tree in the South.

Growing and care:
Leyland cypress grows best in moist, well-drained, moderately fertile loams but grows very well in almost any soil. Provide protection from drying winter winds. It is best transplanted from container-grown plants. Leyland cypress is virtually pest- and disease-free and is resistant to salt spray and cold damage.

Selected species and varieties:
x *C. leylandii* (Leyland cypress) is a cross between *Cupressus macrocarpa* (Monterey cypress) and *Chamaecyparis nootkatensis* (Alaska cedar) that grows 3 feet a year or more to 70 feet tall and usually 10 to 18 feet wide, with reddish brown scaly bark; cultivars include silvery green, variegated, and golden yellow forms; 'Silver Dust' has creamy white markings on green foliage.

LILAC
Syringa

Light: full sun

Plant type: shrub, tree

Hardiness: Zones 3-8

Height: 4 to 15 feet

Soil and Moisture: well-drained, moist

Interest: flowers, foliage, fragrance

Care: moderate

◄ Syringa vulgaris 'Sarah Sands'

L ilacs are sturdy, elegantly old-fashioned favorites with dense, grapelike clusters of fragrant single or double flowers in shades of white, lavender, and red in late spring. The pairs of pointed, oval dark green leaves add medium foliage texture to the garden after the flowers have faded. Lilacs make attractive specimens or informal hedges, and add a nostalgic ambiance to mixed-shrub borders.

Growing and care:
Lilacs grow best in loamy soil, and benefit from annual additions of compost and extra moisture during dry spells. Prune older stems with reduced flower production immediately after flowering, and deadhead faded flowers as well. Lilacs often suffer from powdery mildew on their leaves during summer, so plant them where they will receive good air circulation.

Selected species and varieties:
S. vulgaris is an erect, spreading, 8- to 15-foot shrub with 2- to 5-inch leaves concentrated near the top of the crown, and 4- to 8-inch clusters of extremely fragrant flowers in colors ranging from classic lilac to white and shades of blue, purple, or red; 'Albert F. Holden' is bicolored; 'Blue Boy' is heat tolerant and has blue flowers; 'Edith Cavell' has double white flowers; 'Sarah Sands' has purple flowers; Zones 3-7.

LOQUAT
Eriobotrya

Light: full sun	
Plant type: shrub, tree	
Hardiness: Zones 8-10	
Height: 15 to 25 feet	
Soil and Moisture: well-drained, moist	
Interest: foliage, fruit, fragrance	
Care: easy	

◀ Eriobotrya japonica

Loquat is a gorgeous shrub or tree with lustrous, large evergreen leaves and deliciously fragrant wintertime flowers. In very warm regions the plants bear quantities of tasty yellow fruit. Loquats are often used as street trees or specimens, or are trained as espalier and grown as container plants for more northern patio gardens. Tucked among the coarsely textured leaves are stiff panicles of fragrant, but not showy, woolly flowers in fall or winter, and by late spring edible yellow-orange fruits decorate the plant.

Growing and care:

Loquat is easy to grow. Plant in well-worked soil amended with organic matter, and water well until established. Loquats will adapt to slightly alkaline soil and weather droughts reliably once established. Provide protection from wind. Feed only lightly. Rampant new growth is subject to fire blight.

Selected species and varieties:

E. japonica (Chinese loquat, Japanese plum, Japanese medlar) is a tree or rounded multistemmed shrub 15 to 25 feet tall and wide, with supple branches bearing heavily veined 6- to 12-inch-long toothy leaves that are deep green above and a rust color on the undersides, with five-petaled, dull white 1/2-inch-wide flowers borne in 6-inch clusters and covered with brown fuzz. In the southern half of its range, it bears 2-inch pear-shaped fruit.

'LOUISE ODIER' ROSE
Rosa

Light: full sun	
Plant type: shrub rose	
Hardiness: Zones 5-9	
Height: 4 1/2 to 6 feet	
Soil and Moisture: well-drained, fertile, moist	
Interest: flowers, fragrance	
Care: moderate	

◀ Rosa 'Louise Odier'

The very large, richly fragrant blossoms of 'Louise Odier' roses are wonderful additions to the flower garden. The plants are vigorous growers with strongly upright canes reaching 5 feet tall. In midseason and again in fall the bushes bear large, 3- to 4-inch-wide, very double rose pink blossoms that are enchantingly fragrant. 'Louise Odier' is excellent for the shrub or rose border and makes a good companion for perennial flowers.

Growing and care:

Plant 'Louise Odier' in well-worked soil generously amended with compost or other organic matter. Prune in late winter or early spring, cutting canes back by one-third and removing any dead or damaged stems. Fertilize lightly in spring and again as flower buds begin to open. The plants are susceptible to black spot.

Selected species and varieties:

R. 'Madame Isaac Pereire' is a bourbon rose with vigorous 6-foot very thorny canes and glossy green leaves. In midseason the bushes are covered with large, fully double, intensely fragrant deep pink flowers.

'NEARLY WILD' ROSE
Rosa

Light: full sun	
Plant type: shrub	
Hardiness: Zones 4-10	
Height: 2 to 4 feet	
Soil and Moisture: well-drained, fertile, moist	
Interest: flowers, fragrance	
Care: moderate	

◄ Rosa 'Nearly Wild'

The small, tapered buds of 'Nearly Wild' open to rose pink blooms that have five petals and are very fragrant. The flowers occur prolifically along the length of each stem. The main flowering season is spring, but some blooms appear through summer. Plants are very hardy, compact, and bushy, often wider than tall. This rose is very effective when planted in masses on sunny banks. Placed in front of taller shrubs, it provides good foreground color, and it makes a fine container specimen.

Growing and care:
Space plants 2½ to 3 feet apart in soil that has been amended with organic matter. Prune hard in late fall and remove all fallen leaves and twigs from around base of plant. Fertilize after blooming in spring and water regularly. Mulch with bark chips in spring and fall. 'Nearly Wild' tolerates slightly alkaline soil and is very hardy.

Selected species and varieties:
R. 'Dr. W. van Fleet' is a parent of 'Nearly Wild' and bears pointed buds opening to reveal large, double pink, very fragrant flowers. Foliage is glossy dark green with long canes easily trained to trellises or fences; 'Leuchtstern', the other parent of 'Nearly Wild', produces single, deep rose pink blossoms in small clusters atop 8- to 10-foot-tall canes.

OLEASTER
Elaeagnus

Light: full sun	
Plant type: tree	
Hardiness: Zones 2-9	
Height: 10 to 20 feet	
Soil and Moisture: well-drained, moist to dry	
Interest: flowers, foliage, fragrance	
Care: easy	

◄ Elaeagnus angustifolia

Oleasters are valued as landscape plants for difficult sites because they are extremely adaptable. Their silvery gray foliage contrasts well with that of green-leaved plants. The small but very fragrant flowers attract bees and butterflies in late spring to early summer, and the fall fruit brings a wide variety of birds to the garden. Oleasters are excellent as a windbreak, hedge, or accent in a shrub border, or naturalized in a wildflower meadow. They are frequently planted along roadsides to provide food and shelter for wildlife.

Growing and care:
Oleasters adapt to a wide range of soil types but perform best in a light, sandy loam. They tolerate wind, drought, alkaline soil, and seaside conditions. They transplant easily, grow rapidly, and, although pruning is not necessarily required, they respond well to shearing. For use as a hedge, plant shrubs 3 to 5 feet apart.

Selected species and varieties:
E. angustifolia (Russian olive) is usually a 12- to 15-foot-tall shrub with equal or greater spread, but may grow to 20 feet as a single-trunk tree. Its inconspicuous but very fragrant flowers are followed in late summer and fall by ½-inch yellow fruit coated with silvery scales, and 1½- to 3-inch gray to silvery green leaves that provide dramatic color contrast in the garden.

PEAR
Pyrus

Light: full sun

Plant type: tree

Hardiness: Zones 5-8

Height: 30 to 40 feet

Soil and Moisture: well-drained, moist to dry

Interest: flowers, foliage

Care: moderate

◀ Pyrus calleryana 'Chanticleer'

Callery pears are picturesque, very showy trees that burst with abundant white flowers in early spring. Their lustrous dark green leaves form a dense, symmetrical canopy until midfall, when they turn shades of sunset red and wine purple. The small rounded fruit persists for many weeks and is enjoyed by many species of birds. Use callery pears as an accent in gardens, planted in masses as screens, or as an easy-care shade tree.

Growing and care:
Callery pears adapt to almost any well-drained soil and tolerate drought and pollution better than most flowering trees. If pruning is needed it should be done in late winter while tree is still dormant. They tend to lose their tight form after 20 years or so, due to many branches arising close together on the trunk. 'Chanticleer' has stronger crotches than other cultivars, is less subject to snow and ice damage, and shows good resistance to fire blight. Transplant in spring or fall when plants are not leafed out.

Selected species and varieties:
P. calleryana 'Chanticleer' (callery pear) grows 35 feet high to 16 feet wide in 15 years, with a pyramidal crown narrower than some other cultivars in this species, bearing ⅓-inch-wide flowers in profuse 3-inch clusters and rounded oval leaves to 3½ inches long.

PERSIAN PARROTIA
Parrotia

Light: full sun

Plant type: small tree

Hardiness: Zones 4-8

Height: 20 to 40 feet

Soil and Moisture: well-drained, moist

Interest: foliage, bark

Care: easy

◀ Parrotia persica

Parrotia is one of the best small trees for the yard and garden. The trunk and branches grow in a distinctive, very attractive form with brownish bark that exfoliates as it ages, revealing underbark in shades of green, gray, and brown. Tiny, inconspicuous flowers with red stamens blossom along the younger branches before the leaves emerge in spring. The oval leaves have a red tint when unfolding that cools into green, then brightens into yellows, reds, and oranges in fall. It is virtually pest-free and tolerates even city conditions. As a specimen tree, few can compare.

Growing and care:
Plant Persian parrotia in well-worked, slightly acidic soil that has been generously amended with organic matter. Leave space for its mature spread, as these trees grow best if left undisturbed once established. Plants are drought tolerant but should receive extra water during long periods of dry weather.

Selected species and varieties:
P. persica grows to 30 feet tall with a spread as wide or wider and with 3- to 4-inch-long lustrous green leaves in brilliant shades of yellow and orange, turning rosy pink and scarlet in fall.

PINE
Pinus

Light: full sun	
Plant type: tree	
Hardiness: Zones 2-10	
Height: 6 to 100 feet or more	
Soil and Moisture: well-drained to heavy, wet to dry	
Interest: foliage, fruit	
Care: easy	

◀ Pinus strobus

Simply stated, there is a pine for nearly every garden or yard. This diverse genus of needle-leaved evergreens includes picturesque and stately trees, low-growing, spreading forms, and unique dwarf specimens.

Growing and care:
Pines often develop a deep taproot and should be transplanted only when young. The area around the root zone should be mulched with pine needles yearly to retain soil acidity. Bristlecone pine does well in poor, dry soils but suffers in drying winds or pollution. Shore pine grows naturally in boggy areas. Japanese red pine prefers well-drained, slightly acid soil. Afghanistan pine and pinyon thrive in desert conditions; the former also tolerates salt spray. Mountain pine needs moist, deep loam. Austrian pine tolerates alkaline soils, moderate drought, salt, and urban pollution but grows best where moisture is assured. White pine grows best in moist loams but is also found in dry, shallow soils and wet bogs; it is intolerant of air pollutants, salt, and highly alkaline soil. Japanese black pine thrives in moist loams but is tolerant of sand and salt.

Selected species and varieties:
P. aristata (bristlecone pine) is a very slow grower, some examples of which are, at more than 4,000 years old, the oldest living things on earth. It grows 8 to 20 feet tall with bluish white to dark green needles; Zones 4-7.

P. contorta var. *contorta* (shore pine) is a 25- to 30-foot-tall tree with twisted trunk and branches; hardy to Zone 7. *P. densiflora* 'Umbraculifera' (Japanese red pine) has an upright, spreading habit, with an umbrella-like crown. It grows to 9 feet tall or more, with exfoliating orange bark and bright to dark green needles; Zones 3-7. *P. edulis* [also classified as *P. cembroides* var. *edulis*] (pinyon, nut pine) is slow growing, 10 to 20 feet tall, with horizontal branches, an often flat crown, and dark green needles; hardy to Zone 5. *P. eldarica* (Afghanistan pine) is fast growing, 30 to 80 feet tall, with dark green needles to 6 inches long; hardy to Zone 7. *P. mugo* (mountain pine, mugo pine) forms a broad pyramid to 20 feet tall or a low, broad, bushy shrub, with usually medium green foliage; Zones 2-7. *P. nigra* (Austrian pine) has a pyramidal shape broadening over time to a flat top with heavy, spreading branches, 50 to 60 feet tall by 20 to 40 feet wide, with dark green needles; Zones 4-7. *P. palustris* (longleaf pine, southern yellow pine, pitch pine) is a sparsely branched tree, 55 to 90 feet tall, bearing needles to 9 inches long on mature trees, and 10-inch cones; Zones 7-10. *P. strobus* (white pine) is a low-branched tree growing 50 to more than 100 feet tall and half as wide. It is pyramidal when young but becomes broad crowned with age, producing a dense growth of bluish green needles; 'Pendula' is a weeping form with long, drooping branches; 'UConn' grows to 20 feet with a thick-branching, heavily needled conical form that stays dense with no pruning; Zones 3-8. *P. thunbergiana* (Japanese black pine) forms an irregular pyramid usually 20 to 40 feet tall, with sometimes drooping, wide-spreading branches bearing dark green, crowded, twisted needles 2½ to 7 inches long, and 1½- to 2½-inch cones; Zones 5-7.

PISTACHIO
Pistacia

Light: full sun	
Plant type: tree	
Hardiness: Zones 6-9	
Height: 30 to 35 feet	
Soil and Moisture: well-drained, moist to dry	
Interest: foliage, fruit	
Care: easy	

◀ Pistacia chinensis

One of the best deciduous trees for fall foliage in the South, Chinese pistache has lustrous dark green compound leaves that turn a brilliant orange to orange-red even in hot, arid conditions. Tiny clusters of inedible fruits turn from red and to robin's-egg blue when mature. Use Chinese pistache for shade, or along sidewalks and garden paths.

Growing and care:
Chinese pistache grows best in moist, well-drained soil, where it may achieve 2 to 3 feet per year, but it tolerates other soil types and drought. Young trees sometimes go through a gangly stage and should be pruned to a single leader. Once corrective pruning is done, Chinese pistache usually needs little other special attention and is disease- and insect-free.

Selected species and varieties:
P. chinensis (Chinese pistache) grows 30 to 35 feet high with an equal spread. It is rather awkward in youth but eventually oval to rounded, bearing 10 to 12 leaflets, 2 to 4 inches long per leaf, and inconspicuous male and female flowers on separate trees.

ROCK ROSE
Cistus

Light: full sun	
Plant type: shrub	
Hardiness: Zones 8-10	
Height: 3 to 5 feet	
Soil and Moisture: well-drained, dry	
Interest: flowers, foliage	
Care: easy	

◀ Cistus x purpureus

Rock roses have an eye-catching beauty that provides a memorable accent to the garden. The flowers are stunning, with roselike petals colored in warm shades of red, pink, and white usually marked with darker spots near the golden centers. In addition to their beauty, rock roses are versatile, tough shrubs that grow equally well in coastal gardens and desert plantings. They are useful in rock gardens or mixed borders, massed, or as a ground cover on banks. The leaves of rock rose are nicely fragrant and resist burning, making the plant a top choice for landscapes near areas prone to fire.

Growing and care:
Rock roses grow well in poor, dry soil and accept heat, ocean spray, and alkaline or even slightly acid soils. They are most often grown along the West Coast. Transplant container-grown plants in spring or late fall. Water until established.

Selected species and varieties:
C. x hybridus (white rock rose) bears 1½-inch-wide white flowers with yellow centers in late spring and crinkly gray-green leaves to 2 inches long on a shrub 3 to 5 feet high and wide, sometimes spreading 6 to 8 feet. *C. x purpureus* (orchid rock rose) is a compact shrub 4 feet tall and wide, with wrinkled dark green leaves 1 to 2 inches long, and 3-inch-wide reddish purple flowers in early to midsummer, each petal with a red blotch at its base.

RUGOSA ROSE
Rosa

Light: full sun

Plant type: shrub

Hardiness: Zones 3-8

Height: 4 to 6 feet

Soil and Moisture: well-drained, moist to dry

Interest: flowers, fragrance

Care: easy

◀ Rosa rugosa 'Alba'

Rugosa roses are very reliable, easy-to-grow roses that are as hardy as they are beautiful. The plants bear large, single, softly fragrant rose pink blossoms nearly continually from late spring to fall. Rugosa roses have an informal, mounding habit with gently arching, prickly canes and dark green, slightly wrinkled leaves that turn bronze in autumn. The plants are well known for producing very large, scarlet-colored hips that persist into winter. Rugosa roses naturalize readily and are excellent for wildflower meadows, seaside plantings, or city environments.

Growing and care:
Plant rugosa roses in a bright, sunny spot in loosened well-drained soil. The plants thrive in hot, dry locations and need little care once established. They do poorly in wet sites or heavy soil. Prune canes back by one-third in winter. Rugosa roses are virtually pest- and disease-free.

Selected species and varieties:
R. rugosa 'Alba' bears beautiful, pure white single flowers from spring to fall on spreading 4-foot canes. The dark green leaves yellow in fall; 'Rubra' bears magenta-purple flowers continuously from spring to fall and red hips in autumn.

'SEA FOAM' ROSE
Rosa

Light: full sun

Plant type: shrub

Hardiness: Zones 4-9

Height: 2 to 3 feet

Soil and Moisture: well-drained, moist to moderately dry

Interest: flowers

Care: easy

◀ Rosa 'Sea Foam'

Easy to care for, 'Sea Foam' splashes forth a seemingly endless supply of double, snow white flowers from summer to fall. The vigorous canes have a low-growing, spreading habit, reaching about 3 feet high and twice as wide with small, dark, glossy leaves. 'Sea Foam' is stunning when planted in masses over slopes or in wildflower meadows, and is well suited for use as a low hedge or specimen plant. The blossoms make good cut flowers for summer floral arrangements.

Growing and care:
Plant 'Sea Foam' in well-worked soil that has been amended with some organic matter. For mass plantings or hedges set plants 3 to 4 feet apart. Fertilize in early spring and again after first flush of flowers have faded. Provide extra water during dry periods. Prune old or crowded canes every 2 to 3 years.

Selected species and varieties:
R. 'Fiona' has a low, mounding habit with double, nearly ever-blooming rich red flowers; 'Two Sisters' forms dense thickets of glossy green leaves and arching canes reaching to 4 feet high and 6 feet wide with double pink flowers that fade to antique white.

SERVICEBERRY
Amelanchier

Light: full sun

Plant type: shrub, tree

Hardiness: Zones 4-9

Height: 2 to 40 feet

Soil and Moisture: well-drained, moist to dry

Interest: flowers, foliage, fruit

Care: easy

◄ *Amelanchier alnifolia*

Serviceberries have billowy clusters of dainty five-petaled small white blooms in early spring followed in summer by small red to black tasty fruit. The oval leaves emerge purplish green in spring, turn green in summer, and finally change to dramatic shades of yellow, apricot, and red in fall. The plant's delicate form and light gray bark add interest to the winter garden. Serviceberries can be grown as specimen trees or used to great effect in sunny wildflower meadows.

Growing and care:

Serviceberries are easy-to-grow plants that thrive everywhere from stream banks to open woodlands and along rocky mountain cliffs. In the garden they tolerate a wide range of moisture conditions, although a well-drained, evenly moist soil is best. Propagate serviceberries by seed. Stoloniferous types can also be propagated by root cuttings or by separating offshoots.

Selected species and varieties:

A. alnifolia is a 3- to 6-foot-tall shrub that spreads by stolons to form colonies, with white midspring flowers and small black fruit; Zones 5-8. *A. arborea* (downy serviceberry) is 20 to 30 feet tall with pendulous 2- to 4-inch flower clusters in midspring, small red fruit that turns dark purple, and gray-green leaves that turn orange to deep red in fall.

SWEETBRIAR ROSE
Rosa

Light: full sun

Plant type: shrub

Hardiness: Zones 4-8

Height: 4 to 14 feet

Soil and Moisture: well-drained, moist

Interest: flowers, fragrance, fruit

Care: easy

◄ *Rosa eglanteria*

Sweetbriar is a very popular species rose that has been grown in gardens for more than 400 years. The single blush pink flowers are sweetly fragrant while the dark, glossy green leaves have an aroma all their own, filling the garden with a fruity aroma when bruised. In fall the long canes are decorated with bright red hips. This large, vigorous rose has a rambling, shrubby habit and looks beautiful when naturalized in wildflower meadows or planted as an informal barrier hedge.

Growing and care:

Plant sweetbriar in loosened soil in either spring or fall. For hedges set plants about 4 feet apart. Prune to control growth or to shape plants. Every 2 to 4 years remove older canes at ground level to invigorate plants. Sweetbriar is rarely troubled by insects or diseases.

Selected species and varieties:

R. eglanteria 'Amy Robsart' bears deep pink, fragrant semidouble blossoms in spring and bright red hips in late summer to fall; 'Greenmantle' has stunning vivid scarlet single flowers in spring; 'Manning's Blush' produces abundant whitish pink, fragrant double flowers in spring on compact 4-foot-tall plants with apple-scented dark green leaves.

SWEET GUM
Liquidambar

Light: full sun	
Plant type: tree	
Hardiness: Zones 5-9	
Height: 60 to 120 feet	
Soil and Moisture: well-drained, moist to wet	
Interest: foliage	
Care: easy	

◀ Liquidambar styraciflua

The sweet gum is a neatly conical, very stately tree with star-shaped medium green leaves that turn lovely shades of yellow, purple, and scarlet and linger late into fall. The bark is deeply furrowed and resembles cork. The small, spiny globe-shaped fruits drop in late fall to early spring, which adds adventure to late-season walks in the grass. Its name is derived from its fragrant, gummy sap, used in making perfume.

Growing and care:

Sweet gum is native to rich, moist bottom lands but grows well in a wide variety of soil types. The roots need plenty of room to develop and the tree can get quite large. Plant in spring in soil amended with peat moss or leaf mold. Sweet gum usually takes 2 to 5 years to become established, during which time it should be watered regularly.

Selected species and varieties:

L. styraciflua (American sweet gum, red gum, bilsted) has a narrow pyramidal habit when young, maturing into a semirounded crown with a spread two-thirds that height. The branches are edged with corky wings and bear glossy, rich, medium green leaves 4 to 7½ inches long and wide, with five to seven finely serrated, pointed lobes; 'Aurora' has leaves marked with golden yellow variegation in summer, turning vivid orange and red in fall.

'TOUCH OF CLASS' ROSE
Rosa

Light: full sun	
Plant type: shrub rose	
Hardiness: Zones 5-9	
Height: 4 to 5 feet	
Soil and Moisture: well-drained, moist, fertile	
Interest: flowers	
Care: moderate	

◀ Rosa 'Touch of Class'

This hybrid tea rose produces spiraled orange buds that take on a coral and cream shading as they open, eventually evolving to pink. Flowers are 4½ to 5½ inches across and double, but have little or no fragrance. They are borne singly on long stems, making them good candidates for long-lasting indoor arrangements. The dark green, semiglossy foliage provides an attractive contrast to the showy blooms, although the leaves are prone to mildew. Tall and upright, the 'Touch of Class' is well suited to beds and borders, and flowers over a lengthy season.

Growing and care:

Plant 'Touch of Class' in sunny, well-drained sites. Work in organic matter and fertilize after pruning and again after first bloom. Prune in late winter or early spring to remove damaged canes and disease spores. Add a layer of compost each year. Deadhead spent blooms to encourage more blooming. Mulch to suppress weeds and, in Zone 5, to protect roots in winter.

Selected species and varieties:

R. 'Queen Elizabeth' is an ever-blooming rose with large, clear pink double flowers in attractive sprays on upright 6-foot-tall canes.

TREE PEONY
Paeonia

Light: full sun

Plant type: shrub

Hardiness: Zones 3-8

Height: 4 to 5 feet

Soil and Moisture: well-drained, fertile, moist

Interest: flowers, fragrance

Care: difficult

◄ Paeonia suffruticosa

In the world of gardening the tree peony is in a class by itself. Native to eastern Asia, these regal, mounded, multibranched shrubs bear huge 6-inch-wide flowers of incredible beauty. The showy springtime blossoms may be single, semidouble, or double, and they come in shades of white, pink, red, or yellow. Tree peonies are not easy to grow and require patience and careful tending.

Growing and care:
Plant tree peonies in midfall in well-worked, near neutral soil generously amended with compost. Provide afternoon shade in the South. Water regularly, especially during dry periods. Prune out old and diseased wood, being careful to disinfect the pruning shears to avoid transmission of diseases. Fertilize in spring before and after flowering with a well-balanced fertilizer. Avoid using animal manures on tree peonies. Mulch around base of plant to keep roots cool and retain soil moisture. Stake blossoming branches to avoid breakage.

Selected species and varieties:
P. suffruticosa bears 6- to 10-inch-wide midspring flowers from white to pink to deep red and yellow with crinkled, satiny petals often bearing a red blotch at their bases. Large, deeply lobed medium green leaves turn yellowish green in fall on 4- to 5-foot woody stems; 'Souvenir de Maxine' bears very large, fully double golden yellow blossoms marked with red in spring.

TULIP TREE
Liriodendron

Light: full sun

Plant type: tree

Hardiness: Zones 4-9

Height: 70 to 100 feet

Soil and Moisture: well-drained to heavy, moist

Interest: flowers, foliage

Care: easy

◄ Liriodendron tulipifera

Tulip trees are very attractive, vigorous trees that grow into towering giants up to 100 feet tall. The plants have a neat columnar to oval shape with distinctive, hand-shaped, bright green foliage that turns golden yellow in fall. In mid- to late spring, tuliplike greenish white flowers with a deep orange blotch at the base of the petals appear high on the tree after the foliage unfurls. Conelike clusters of winged fruit persist into winter.

Growing and care:
Plant tulip trees in moist, deep loam with plenty of room to grow. They prefer slightly acid soils but will tolerate neutral to slightly alkaline ones. In some regions the trees are prone to damage from ice and snow. In ideal conditions tulip trees may grow 2½ to 3 feet per year.

Selected species and varieties:
L. tulipifera (yellow poplar, tulip magnolia, tulip poplar, whitewood) is fast growing with a spread of 35 to 50 feet and the potential of topping 100 feet tall. It is pyramidal when young, bearing lobed leaves up to 8 inches wide and long that open early in spring, and cup-shaped yellow-green, white, and orange flowers 2½ inches wide with six petals, borne singly at or near branch tips.

'TUSCANY' ROSE
Rosa

Light: full sun	
Plant type: shrub	
Hardiness: Zones 4-10	
Height: 3 to 4 feet	
Soil and Moisture: well-drained, fertile, moist	
Interest: flowers, fragrance	
Care: easy	

◀ Rosa 'Tuscany'

A high-quality rose, 'Tuscany' is recognizable for its velvet red, richly fragrant semidouble petals surrounding a golden yellow splash of stamens in the center. The vigorous plants have a tidy, rounded form with slightly arching 2- to 3-foot canes covered with dark green leaves. The blossoms are produced abundantly for a few weeks in spring with no repeat in fall. 'Tuscany' is ideal for small borders or when used in kitchen or herb gardens.

Growing and care:
Plant in loosened soil that has been well amended with compost or rotted manure. Fertilize in early spring when growth begins and again after flowering season has passed. Prune to shape while plant is dormant, and remove older canes every other year. Black spot sometimes occurs on the leaves in humid weather but is seldom a serious problem.

Selected species and varieties:
R. 'Superb Tuscan' [also called 'Tuscany Superb'] produces large, well-formed, loosely double burgundy red flowers with yellow centers in late spring on vigorous canes reaching 3 to 4 feet high.

VIRGINIA ROSE
Rosa

Light: full sun	
Plant type: shrub	
Hardiness: Zones 3-7	
Height: 3 to 5 feet	
Soil and Moisture: well-drained, moist	
Interest: flowers, foliage, fruit	
Care: moderate	

◀ Rosa virginiana

Virginia rose is a graceful, hardy rose that is easy to care for, providing the garden with beautiful flowers, bright fall foliage, and colorful, tasty fruit. The plants burst into bloom in late spring to early summer, the long, arching canes sprinkled with single, rose pink flowers. In fall the leaves turn a brilliant scarlet-orange and the stems carry the plump, red rose hips well into winter. Virginia rose is excellent in wildflower meadows or when combined with perennials in beds and borders.

Growing and care:
Plant Virginia rose in well-drained soil generously amended with compost or rotted manure. Allow plants to develop long, arching canes in open areas, or prune canes to fit in smaller spaces. Cut back older plants to the ground to encourage new growth. Virginia rose tolerates salt spray and sandy soils.

Selected species and varieties:
R. carolina (pasture rose) is similar to Virginia rose, with vigorous 6-foot-tall canes, medium green leaves, and single pink flowers in late spring or early summer followed by red fruits; var. *alba* bears white flowers; var. *plena* has double pink blossoms; Zones 4-9.

YELLOWWOOD
Cladrastis

Light: full sun	
Plant type: tree	
Hardiness: Zones 4-8	
Height: 30 to 50 feet	
Soil and Moisture: well-drained, moist	
Interest: flowers, foliage, bark	
Care: moderate	

◄ Cladrastis kentukea

An excellent deciduous shade tree for small landscapes, yellowwood produces long, hanging panicles of fragrant white flowers in mid- to late spring and a broad canopy of bright green foliage that turns a warm yellow in fall. The open, delicate branches grow in a zigzag pattern, creating a light, airy form. In winter the smooth gray bark contrasts well to the white snow. The color of the interior wood, which is a rich yellow, gives the tree its name.

Growing and care:
Although it occurs naturally in rich, limestone soils, American yellowwood adapts to a wide range of soil types, from acid to alkaline, and is remarkably pest-free. Once established, it is drought tolerant. Prune only in summer, to prevent heavy sap bleeding. Cable branches that develop weak crotches.

Selected species and varieties:
C. kentukea [formerly called *C. lutea*] (American yellowwood, Kentucky yellowwood, virgilia) has a low-branching habit with a rounded crown 40 to 55 feet wide, producing 3- to 4-inch-long compound leaves opening bright yellowish green before darkening slightly later, with flower clusters up to 14 inches long, and thin brown seedpods 4 to 5 inches long in fall.

ZELKOVA
Zelkova

Light: full sun	
Plant type: tree	
Hardiness: Zones 5-8	
Height: 50 to 80 feet	
Soil and Moisture: well-drained, moist	
Interest: foliage	
Care: easy	

◄ Zelkova serrata

Japanese zelkova is an elegant tree with a symmetrical, vase-shaped habit similar to that of an elm, but with no disease problems. This easy-care plant has smooth gray bark on young trees that exfoliates in mature specimens. The rough-textured, toothed dark green leaves turn a warm russet yellow in fall. This tree, with its noble form, is perfect as a shade or specimen tree and even looks great in winter when the garden is full of snow.

Growing and care:
Japanese zelkova grows best in deep, moist, fertile soil. Plant in spring or fall and water regularly during the first growing season. Mulch to conserve soil moisture, and provide extra water during extended dry periods. Once established, the tree tolerates wind, drought, and pollution and is resistant to storm damage.

Selected species and varieties:
Z. serrata (Japanese zelkova, saw-leaf zelkova) reaches 50 to 80 feet high and wide, with ascending branches bearing 2- to 5-inch-long pointed oval leaves that are somewhat rough with prominent veins, and bark that is smooth, gray, and beechlike in youth, eventually flaking to expose patches of orange; 'Green Vase' is a vigorous, extremely fast-growing tree 60 to 70 feet tall with arching branches bearing orange-brown to bronze-red fall foliage.

Plants for Mostly Sunny Places

Plants that prefer mostly sunny places are sunbathers that like a brief, shady break sometime during the day. Usually this respite is best for the plants if it comes in the early afternoon, when the sun is most intense and the air is at its hottest. An hour or two of shade at this time gives the plants an opportunity to cool down and begin to replenish some of the moisture lost to the atmosphere during the first part of the day. A light watering just as the plants enter the shade is helpful, as is a layer of mulch spread over the soil surface to keep the roots cool throughout the hot summer months. The bright sun not only steals precious moisture from leaves but often fades the vivid colors of many flowers, turning sharp, bold colors to watercolor pastels. A shady siesta can often help keep the flower border more colorful for longer periods of time. Look for mostly sunny places on the southeast and southwest corners of structures or shrub borders.

BABY-BLUE-EYES
Nemophila

Light: mostly sun

Plant type: annual

Height: 6 to 10 inches

Soil and Moisture: well-drained, moist

Interest: flowers

Care: moderate

◄ Nemophila menziesii

Baby-blue-eyes are dainty, cool-weather plants with tidy mounds of dark green leaves dotted with 1-inch-wide lapis blue flowers with white centers. These beautiful wildflowers make good edgings, rock garden specimens, and companions for spring-flowering bulbs. They are also attractive when planted so that their trailing stems spill over the edge of a wall.

Growing and care:
Sow seed directly in the garden in early spring, thinning the seedlings to stand 6 inches apart. Enrich the soil with organic matter and provide abundant moisture. Mulch around plants to keep soil cool. Plants thrive in areas with cool summers and will self-seed under favorable conditions. Baby-blue-eyes can die during periods of hot, humid weather.

Selected species and varieties:
N. menziesii produces trailing stems to form a mounding plant, usually about 6 inches tall and 12 inches across, with deeply cut light green leaves. Flowers are tubular, 1 to 1½ inches across, and sky blue in color with white centers; 'Pennie Black' has deep purple ¾-inch blooms edged with silvery white.

BISHOP'S FLOWER
Ammi

Light: mostly sun

Plant type: annual

Height: 2 to 3 feet

Soil and Moisture: well-drained, fertile, moist

Interest: flowers

Care: easy

◄ Ammi majus

The delicate flower heads of bishop's flower resemble Queen-Anne's-lace in appearance, but the plant is far more manageable in the garden. Originally from Eurasia, it has naturalized in many parts of North America. It is well suited to flower borders, where it provides fine-textured contrast with coarser and more colorful plants. It can be sprinkled among annuals and perennials or planted in drifts. The flowers are highly valued for indoor arrangements; wear gloves when cutting as sap can irritate skin.

Growing and care:
Start seed about 6 weeks indoors—or 2 weeks outdoors—before the last frost. Thin or transplant to allow 6 to 12 inches between plants. Plants transplant easily at nearly any stage and, once established, are free flowering. They thrive in cooler regions but may be stressed by high temperatures and humidity.

Selected species and varieties:
A. majus develops thin, well-branched stems up to 3 feet tall with sharply serrated leaves. In summer, stems are topped with 5- to 6-inch umbels, each containing numerous delicate white flowers that tremble with the slightest wind or touch.

BUTTERFLY FLOWER
Schizanthus

Light: mostly sun

Plant type: annual

Height: 1 to 4 feet

Soil and Moisture: well-drained, moist, fertile

Interest: flowers

Care: difficult

◄ Schizanthus pinnatus

Butterfly flower is a truly beautiful plant, with exotic flowers resembling orchids. Borne in loose clusters, the two-tone flowers, which come in many colors, are pleasantly displayed against fernlike foliage. They are useful in beds or containers and are excellent for cutting.

Growing and care:
Start seed indoors 8 weeks before the last frost. In Zones 9 and 10 seed may be sown outdoors in spring. Space plants 1 to 1½ feet apart. Pinch plants when about 3 inches tall and again when 6 inches high to encourage branching. Water regularly, keeping leaves and flowers dry. Set stakes for tall varieties in the ground while plants are small. Dwarf forms make excellent edging plants.

Selected species and varieties:
S. pinnatus grows to 4 feet with light green, finely cut leaves and 1½-inch flowers produced in open clusters from early summer to early fall. Flowers have a tropical appearance, and colors include pink, rose, salmon, vivid red, lavender, violet, and cream. Each displays contrasting markings on the throat.

CALIFORNIA POPPY
Eschscholzia

Light: mostly sun

Plant type: annual, tender perennial

Height: 4 inches to 2 feet

Soil and Moisture: well-drained, dry

Interest: flowers

Care: easy

◄ Eschscholzia californica

California poppies are popular garden plants with gaily colored, broad-petaled flowers on long, graceful stalks. The brilliant flowers open during the day and close at night and in cloudy weather. California poppies are effective for massing in beds and borders, and thrive in wildflower meadows.

Growing and care:
California poppies are difficult to transplant. Sow seed directly in the garden in early spring. Thin plants to stand 6 inches apart. Plants do well in sunny or mostly sunny conditions and in dry soil but flower best when watered regularly. Once established, plants self-seed freely. Though they tolerate most soil, they prefer a poor, sandy one.

Selected species and varieties:
E. caespitosa (tufted California poppy, pastel poppy) is an annual with pale yellow flowers on 4- to 12-inch stalks above finely cut basal foliage. *E. californica* is a 1- to 2-foot tender perennial from Zone 8 south but is grown as an annual elsewhere, with 1- to 3-inch yellow or orange flowers from spring to fall and feathery blue-green foliage; 'Aurantiaca' is an old variety with rich orange single blooms; 'Monarch Mixed' bears single and semidouble flowers in yellow, orange, red, and pink; 'Orange King' bears translucent orange flowers.

CAMPION
Silene

Light: mostly sun

Plant type: annual, biennial

Height: 6 inches to 2 feet

Soil and Moisture: well-drained, moist to dry

Interest: flowers

Care: easy

◀ Silene coeli-rosa

Robust and easy to grow, campion provides an abundance of cheerful summer flowers for borders and beds. Low-growing types are well suited to rock gardens or for use as edgings, and taller types are attractive when cut for fresh arrangements. The blossoms are white, pink, lavender, or violet with a deep-colored contrasting eye in the center and notched petals.

Growing and care:
Sow seed directly outdoors in early spring as soon as the soil can be worked. Established plants often self-seed. Allow 8 inches between plants. They perform best in well-drained, sunny locations but will tolerate light shade.

Selected species and varieties:
S. armeria (sweet William catchfly) grows 1 to 1½ feet tall with blue-gray leaves and 3-inch clusters of pink or red flowers. It is often included in wildflower mixes and is suitable for naturalizing. *S. coeli-rosa* [also known as *Lychnis coeli-rosa* and *Viscaria coeli-rosa*] usually grows to about 1 foot with narrow, pointed leaves and blue, lavender, pink, or white flowers that often sport a contrasting eye; each single, saucer-shaped flower is 1 inch across. *S. pendula* (drooping catchfly) grows 6 to 16 inches tall with a compact habit, hairy medium green leaves, and loose clusters of pale pink flowers.

CANDYTUFT
Iberis

Light: mostly sun

Plant type: annual

Height: 6 inches to 1½ feet

Soil and Moisture: well-drained, moist

Interest: flowers, fragrance

Care: easy

◀ Iberis umbellata

These European wildflowers are easy to grow and free flowering with abundant clusters of tiny four-petaled flowers above dark green leaves. Candytuft flowers throughout the summer and is very effective in rock gardens and borders, as an edging, or in a planter. Set the plants where their fragrance can be appreciated.

Growing and care:
Sow seed in the garden in fall or as soon as soil can be worked in the spring, thinning to allow 6 to 9 inches between seedlings. Make successive sowings to extend the flowering season. Cut back lightly after bloom if flowering stops in summer. Plants thrive in city conditions.

Selected species and varieties:
I. amara (rocket candytuft) grows 1 to 1½ feet tall with fragrant white flowers in cone-shaped spikes that can be cut for fresh arrangements. *I. odorata* (fragrant candytuft) grows 6 to 12 inches with flat clusters of white flowers. *I. umbellata* (globe candytuft) grows 8 to 16 inches with clusters of pink, red, lilac, or violet flowers that are not fragrant.

CELOSIA
Celosia

Light: mostly sun

Plant type: annual

Height: 6 inches to 2 feet

Soil and Moisture: well-drained, moist to dry

Interest: flowers, foliage

Care: easy

◀ Celosia cristata 'Pink Tassels'

These vibrant annuals sport bold, crested or plumed flowers that are extremely long lasting, making them ideal for bedding and cutting for both fresh and dried arrangements. They are easy to grow and are perfect for filling empty places in perennial borders.

Growing and care:
Start seed indoors 4 to 6 weeks before transplanting to the garden after all danger of frost has passed. In warm areas, sow directly outside once soil has warmed. Space plants 6 to 18 inches apart. Celosias thrive in warm weather and some afternoon shade. For use in winter arrangements, cut flowers at their peak and hang them upside down to dry.

Selected species and varieties:
C. cristata displays a range of heights and flower types. Leaves may be green, purple, or variegated. Flowers appear from midsummer to fall and are usually deep shades of red, orange, yellow, or gold. The species is divided according to flower type: Childsii group (crested cockscomb) produces crested or convoluted flower heads that resemble lumps of coral. Plumosa group (feather amaranth) bears feathery 6- to 12-inch flower heads. Spicata group bears flowers in slender spikes; 'Pink Tassels' bears long, pale pink spikes with bright pink tips.

CHRYSANTHEMUM
Chrysanthemum

Light: mostly sun

Plant type: annual

Height: 1 to 3 feet

Soil and Moisture: well-drained, moist

Interest: flowers

Care: moderate

◀ Chrysanthemum coronarium 'Primrose Gem'

Annual chrysanthemums are vigorous plants with dark green, deeply lobed foliage and an abundant supply of summer and fall daisylike flowers. Chrysanthemums are perfect as edging plants or tucked into beds and borders. They are also cheerful and dependable cut flowers.

Growing and care:
These plants are easily grown from seed planted directly in the garden as soon as soil can be worked in spring. Thin plants to stand 1 to 1½ feet apart. Pinch seedlings to encourage bushy growth. Once established they will self-seed.

Selected species and varieties:
C. carinatum (tricolor chrysanthemum) grows 2 to 3 feet tall with dark green toothed leaves. It derives its common name from its 2½-inch flower heads that are white with a yellow band surrounding a purple or chocolate brown central disk; 'Court Jesters' produces red, pink, orange, yellow, maroon, and white flowers with red or orange bands. *C. coronarium* (crown daisy, garland chrysanthemum) grows 1 to 2½ feet tall with coarsely cut leaves and yellow and white flowers, 1 to 2 inches across, which may be single, semidouble, or double; 'Primrose Gem' bears semidouble soft yellow blooms with darker yellow centers.

CIGAR PLANT
Cuphea

Light: mostly sun

Plant type: tender perennial grown as annual

Height: 8 inches to 3 feet

Soil and Moisture: well-drained, moist

Interest: flowers, foliage

Care: easy

◀ Cuphea ignea

These eye-catching plants bear abundant, shiny green foliage richly decorated with brilliant scarlet flowers from summer to frost. Cigar plant's mounded habit is excellent for rock gardens or mixed with perennials in beds and borders. From Zone 9 south, the plants are winter hardy and can reach 3 feet tall in a few seasons. In cooler areas grow cigar plant as an annual or plant in containers for summer use on patios and overwinter indoors as a houseplant.

Growing and care:
Start seed indoors in midwinter. Do not cover seed, as it needs light to germinate properly. Transplant to the garden after soil has warmed. Allow 1 to 1½ feet between plants. They adapt to any well-drained soil and thrive in warm weather.

Selected species and varieties:
C. ignea (Mexican cigar plant, firecracker plant) grows to 1 foot with an equal spread and narrow dark green leaves. Its scarlet tubular flowers are 1 inch long with a black and white tip. *C. llavea* 'Bunny Ears Mixed' grows to 1½ feet with a neat, uniform habit and bright red flowers with two protruding stamens bearded with violet hairs. *C.* x *purpurea* grows to 1½ feet with hairy 3-inch leaves. Its bright rose red flowers are tinged with purple and borne in terminal clusters.

COSMOS
Cosmos

Light: mostly sun

Plant type: annual

Height: 3 to 6 feet

Soil and Moisture: well-drained, moist to dry

Interest: flowers

Care: easy

◀ Cosmos bipinnatus 'Sonata'

Cosmos enlivens the summer and fall garden with long-lasting displays of brightly colored daisylike flowers on loose clumps of slender, pliant stems. The cheerful flowers accent graceful masses of feathery-textured foliage. The smaller varieties can be used as edging plants or fillers in borders; taller ones are effective as backdrops or transition plants.

Growing and care:
Cosmos produces abundant flowers in poor soil. Taller varieties may need staking, and should be planted in sites protected from summer winds. They are easily propagated from seed sown ¼ inch deep after all danger of frost has passed. Plant seedlings 1 to 1½ feet apart.

Selected species and varieties:
C. bipinnatus is an annual with 4- to 6-foot stems bearing 3- to 4-inch pink, white, or red flowers from summer to frost with yellow centers; 'Daydream' has bright pink flowers with dark red centers; 'Sonata' has pink, white, or red blossoms on 2-foot stems. *C. sulphureus* (yellow cosmos) is an annual bearing 2- to 3-inch yellow, orange, gold, or red flowers in early summer on 3- to 6-foot stems; 'Goldcrest' has a sturdy, compact form with bright golden flowers, and is more robust and wind resistant than other species.

DUSTY-MILLER
Senecio

Light: mostly sun

Plant type: tender perennial grown as annual

Height: 6 inches to 2 ½ feet

Soil and Moisture: well-drained, medium to dry

Interest: foliage

Care: easy to moderate

◀ Senecio cineraria

Dusty-miller has soft, woolly white to silvery gray leaves that combine well with brightly colored flowers in borders and beds. Native to the Mediterranean region, dusty-miller is perennial from Zone 9 south but is grown as an annual elsewhere. It makes an attractive edging, rock garden specimen, or container plant, and is stunning when interplanted with salmon-flowered begonias.

Growing and care:
Start seed indoors 8 to 10 weeks prior to the last frost. Do not cover the seed, as light is necessary for germination. Transplant outdoors when all danger of frost has passed, spacing plants 10 inches apart. Avoid soils that are too fertile. Overwatering will result in weak growth and susceptibility to disease. Plants tolerate drought.

Selected species and varieties:
S. cineraria (dusty-miller, silver groundsel) has a rounded, branched habit. Leaves are thick, up to 8 inches long, and deeply cut into rounded lobes; they are covered with dense woolly hairs, giving the foliage a felt-like texture. Flowers are yellow or cream, appearing in small terminal clusters in late summer, but are best removed to encourage foliage growth.

EDGING LOBELIA
Lobelia

Light: mostly sun

Plant type: tender perennial grown as annual

Height: 4 to 8 inches

Soil and Moisture: well-drained, moist, fertile

Interest: flowers

Care: easy

◀ Lobelia erinus

Edging lobelia is an easy-to-grow plant with abundant clusters of intensely colored flowers from spring to fall. The plants produce very neat, tidy mounds of dark green foliage that are perfect for edging walkways, beds, or borders. The bright flowers range from an intense sapphire blue to softer shades of violet and white. Edging lobelia is also excellent for container growing, including window boxes and hanging baskets.

Growing and care:
Plant edging lobelias in spring, spacing plants 4 inches apart. The plants respond well to periodic additions of organic mulch and compost. The best flower colors result when they are grown in a mostly sunny place with shade during the hottest time of the day. Cut back *L. erinus* after its first flowering to encourage reblooming.

Selected species and varieties:
L. erinus (edging lobelia, trailing lobelia) is a tender perennial producing mounds of 4- to 8-inch stems with blue or white ½-inch flowers from summer to frost and thin, ½-inch leaves; 'Cambridge Blue' has light green foliage and light blue flowers; 'Crystal Palace' has dark blue flowers.

759

EVENING PRIMROSE
Oenothera

Light: mostly sun

Plant type: biennial

Height: 2 to 8 feet

Soil and Moisture: well-drained, moist to dry

Interest: flowers

Care: easy

◀ Oenothera biennis

Among this genus of mostly perennial plants are a few hardy biennials that are often grown as annuals. Evening primrose sports vivid to pastel yellow blooms from early summer to midfall, opening in the evening atop tall, erect stems. The plants are easy to grow and are well suited for massing at the rear of a border or for use in a wildflower garden.

Growing and care:

Start seed indoors 8 to 12 weeks prior to the last frost, or outdoors in early spring. Where winters are mild, seed can be sown outdoors in fall. Space plants 1 foot apart. Once established, plants will often self-seed, and may become invasive if not confined. They thrive in warm weather and tolerate poor soil.

Selected species and varieties:

O. biennis produces a clump of coarse basal leaves from which a stout, erect flower stem rises. Stems may reach 6 feet and bear 1- to 2-inch flowers that open pale yellow and turn gold. *O. erythrosepala* [also called *O. glaziovinia*] grows 2 to 8 feet tall with yellow flowers that turn orange or red; 'Tina James' grows 3 to 4 feet with showy yellow flowers that burst open in 1 to 2 minutes and are pleasantly fragrant.

FLOWERING TOBACCO
Nicotiana

Light: mostly sun

Plant type: annual, tender perennial grown as annual

Height: 1 to 6 feet

Soil and Moisture: well-drained, moist, fertile

Interest: flowers, fragrance

Care: easy

◀ Nicotiana alata

The blossoms of many flowering tobaccos open in late afternoon and fill the evening with a heavy, sweet perfume. Erect stems arise from coarse clumps of large, sticky leaves and are topped by loose clusters of long, tubular flowers that are pollinated by honeybees, hummingbirds, and nocturnal moths. Flowering tobacco makes an excellent border filler or specimen for the back of beds.

Growing and care:

Propagate flowering tobaccos by seed, sowing seed indoors 6 to 8 weeks before the last frost. Seed needs light to germinate, so sprinkle on top of the soil, moisten, and cover the container with plastic wrap. Space transplants 1 foot apart. Remove dead flowers before they set seed to encourage further blooming.

Selected species and varieties:

N. alata (jasmine tobacco, flowering tobacco) produces 1- to 4-foot clumps bearing 2- to 4-inch flowers from spring to fall above 4- to 10-inch leaves; 'Daylight Sensation' has flowers in shades of lilac, white, purple, and rose that open at dawn; 'Fragrant Cloud' has heavily scented snow white blossoms that open in the evening; 'Lime Green' has bright yellow-green flowers from summer to fall on 1½-foot stems; 'Nikki' series produces bushy, 1½- to 2-foot plants with flowers in a range of colors that includes shades of pink, red, white, and yellow.

GERANIUM
Pelargonium

Light: mostly sun
Plant type: tender perennial grown as annual
Height: 10 inches to 6 feet
Soil and Moisture: well-drained, moist
Interest: flowers, foliage
Care: easy

◀ Pelargonium x hortorum

These easy-to-grow tender perennials are some of the most popular bedding plants grown. They have a shrubby habit with showy, often heavily zoned leaves and clusters of vividly colored flowers from spring to frost. Geraniums will bloom their first year when grown from seed. Their reliable and long-lasting flowers are useful in beds and borders and are especially suited to container growing, providing nonstop color for hanging baskets and window boxes.

Growing and care:
Start seed indoors 10 to 12 weeks prior to the last frost. Geraniums can also be started indoors from cuttings taken from overwintered plants. Transplant outdoors after danger of frost has passed, spacing plants 8 to 15 inches apart. Geraniums prefer cool climates and may die out during the heat of the summer in southern zones. Water during dry periods. Remove faded flowers to encourage continuous flowering. Geraniums can be dug up and potted in fall for growing indoors during winter.

Selected species and varieties:
P. x *hortorum* (zonal geranium) has a rounded habit and grows from 10 inches to 6 feet tall. It produces rounded, pale to medium green leaves with scalloped edges, usually marked with a brown or maroon horseshoe-shaped zone, and single, semidouble, or double flowers in dense, long-stemmed, 5-inch clusters in many colors.

GODETIA
Clarkia

Light: mostly sun
Plant type: annual
Height: 1 to 3 feet
Soil and Moisture: well-drained, dry
Interest: flowers
Care: easy

◀Clarkia amoena

Godetias are free-flowering wildflowers from the coastal ranges of the western United States. The flowers resemble a wild rose with broad, richly colored petals surrounding a light-colored center. They are named after the explorer William Clark, who collected their seed during the Lewis and Clark expedition. *C. amoena* and *C. purpurea* are also listed under the genus *Godetia*.

Growing and care:
Sow seed outdoors in fall where winters are mild, and elsewhere in spring as soon as the soil can be worked. Sow fairly heavily, since crowding will encourage flowering. Plants perform best where nights are cool.

Selected species and varieties:
C. amoena (farewell-to-spring, satin flower) grows 1 to 3 feet tall. Throughout summer, 2- to 4-inch cup-shaped flowers appear in the axils of the upper leaves. Its four petals are pink to lavender with a bright red or pink splash at the base; the four sepals are red. *C. concinna* (red-ribbons) grows 1 to 2 feet tall and bears rose-purple flowers with deeply cut fan-shaped petals in late spring and early summer. *C. purpurea* grows to 3 feet tall with 1-inch flowers in shades of purple, lavender, red, and pink, often with a dark eye.

HELIOTROPE
Heliotropium

Light: mostly sun

Plant type: tender perennial grown as annual

Height: 1 to 3 feet

Soil and Moisture: well-drained, moist, fertile

Interest: flowers, fragrance

Care: moderate

◀ Heliotropium arborescens 'Marine'

Heliotrope is an old-fashioned plant with sprays of small white, lilac, or burgundy-violet flowers that emit an enchantingly rich vanilla fragrance. The plants have dark green leaves and a bushy habit that make them welcome additions to mixed borders. They are ideal container plants, and flowers can be cut for fresh arrangements. Heliotropes can also be trained into standards for a more formal Victorian look.

Growing and care:
Start seed indoors 10 to 12 weeks prior to the last frost, or buy young plants in spring. Plants can also be started from cuttings. Do not transplant to the garden until soil has warmed, as plants are very frost sensitive. Allow 1 foot between plants and keep them well watered.

Selected species and varieties:
H. arborescens (cherry pie) grows 1 to 3 feet in the garden, though plants grown in a greenhouse or in their native range may reach 6 feet. Foliage is dark green and wrinkled. Five-petaled flowers are 1/4 inch across, occurring in clusters as large as a foot across; 'Marine', a compact variety reaching 2 feet, has large, deep purple flowers and is excellent for bedding, although it lacks intense fragrance.

HONESTY
Lunaria

Light: mostly sun to part shade

Plant type: biennial

Height: 2 to 3 feet

Soil and Moisture: well-drained, moist to dry

Interest: fruit

Care: easy

◀ Lunaria annua

This old-fashioned biennial is native to southern Europe. It is grown primarily for its fruit, a flat, oval, silvery seedpod. Plants are best suited to the cutting garden, an informal border, or a wildflower meadow. Their papery seedpods are highly valued for dried arrangements.

Growing and care:
Lunaria can be grown as an annual or a biennial. For flowers and seedpods the first year, sow seed outdoors in very early spring, or plant in midsummer to early fall for flowers and seedpods the following year. Once established plants will reseed through Zone 4. Space plants 8 to 12 inches apart. They tolerate wet and dry conditions and are not fussy about soil quality, as long as they are well drained. They grow well in mostly sun or partial shade.

Selected species and varieties:
L. annua (silver-dollar, bolbonac) has an erect habit with broad, coarsely toothed leaves and fragrant pink or purple flowers, each with four petals, borne in terminal clusters in late spring. Flowers are followed by the seedpods, which fall apart, revealing a thin, silvery white disk, 1 to 2 inches across, to which the seeds cling; 'Alba' produces white flowers well displayed when grown against a dark background.

HOUND'S TONGUE
Cynoglossum

Light: mostly sun

Plant type: biennial

Height: 1½ to 2 feet

Soil and Moisture: well-drained, moist to dry

Interest: flowers

Care: easy

◄ Cynoglossum amabile

Hound's tongue has an open, casual habit with slender, slightly droopy stems and clusters of tiny clear blue flowers throughout summer and into fall. The blossoms are reminiscent of forget-me-nots, and put on a fine show in borders or beds. Hound's tongue is excellent for massing and fresh flower arrangements.

Growing and care:
Though biennial, *C. amabile* usually flowers the first year from seed, especially if started indoors in late winter or early spring. Plant seedlings in garden after last frost, spacing plants 9 to 12 inches apart. It thrives in a wide range of soils and will often self-seed. When cutting for arrangements, immediately submerge the stems three-quarters of their length in water to prevent flowers from collapsing.

Selected species and varieties:
C. amabile (Chinese forget-me-not) has an irregular to rounded habit with a clump of erect stems with somewhat coarse leaves. Each stem is topped with an arching cluster of light blue blossoms. Individual flowers are ¼ inch across and have five petals. Pink- and white-flowered forms are also available.

LARKSPUR
Consolida

Light: mostly sun to part shade

Plant type: annual

Height: 1 to 4 feet

Soil and Moisture: well-drained, fertile, moist

Interest: flowers

Care: easy

◄ Consolida ambigua

This native of southern Europe produces tall, pliant spikes of stately blue, lilac, pink, red, white, and violet flowers that accent the garden for weeks in summer. The soft-textured, lacy foliage provides an excellent foil for the pastel flowers, which are a graceful accent to the back of the border. Larkspur is regarded as a fine cut flower for fresh floral arrangements.

Growing and care:
Start seed indoors in peat pots 6 to 8 weeks prior to the last frost. Seed can be sown directly outdoors in fall from Zone 7 south, and in early spring elsewhere. Space plants to stand 8 to 15 inches apart. Tall varieties often require staking. Plants thrive in cool conditions and light shade. Keep soil evenly moist throughout the growing season.

Selected species and varieties:
C. ambigua (rocket larkspur) produces lacy, deeply cut leaves. Spurred flowers in many pastel shades are borne in dense, graceful spikes throughout the summer; 'Imperial Blue Bell' grows to 4 feet with double blue flowers; 'Imperial White King' is similar with double white flowers.

MARIGOLD
Tagetes

Light: mostly sun

Plant type: annual, tender perennial grown as annual

Height: 6 inches to 3 feet

Soil and Moisture: well-drained, moist

Interest: flowers, foliage

Care: easy

◀ Tagetes erecta 'Primrose Lady'

Marigolds are among the most popular bedding plants in the United States. They are easy to grow, provide a reliable display, and are available in a wide range of heights. Their flowers typically range from pale yellow to bright orange and burgundy and are produced nonstop from early summer to frost in many varieties. Some species are grown for their fernlike foliage, which is often quite aromatic. Marigolds are suited to many uses, depending on their size: They can be placed in the background of a border, used as an edging, or massed in a bed. They are suitable for cutting for fresh arrangements and can be effectively grown in patio planters and window boxes. Despite some of their common names, marigolds are native to Mexico and Central and South America.

Growing and care:

Start seed indoors 6 to 8 weeks prior to the last frost, or sow directly outdoors 2 weeks before that date. Space plants 6 to 18 inches apart, depending on the variety, and pinch the seedlings to promote bushiness. Marigolds thrive in a moist, well-drained soil but tolerate dry conditions. Remove dead blossoms to encourage continuous flowering. Avoid overwatering.

Selected species and varieties:

T. erecta (American marigold, African marigold, Aztec marigold) has an erect to rounded habit and a wide range of heights, categorized as dwarf (10 to 14 inches), medium (15 to 20 inches), or tall (to 3 feet). Flower heads are solitary, single to double, and 2 to 5 inches across; 'Primrose Lady' is 15 to 18 inches with a compact habit and double yellow carnation-like flowers. *T. filifolia* (Irish lace), grown primarily for its finely divided fernlike foliage, is 6 to 12 inches tall and wide and produces small white blooms in late summer. *T. lucida* (Mexican tarragon, sweet-scented marigold) grows 2 to 2½ feet tall with dark green tarragon-scented leaves and small, single yellow flowers in clusters. It may be perennial in warm climates. *T. patula* (French marigold, sweet mace) grows 6 to 18 inches tall with a neat, rounded habit and deeply serrated bright green leaves. Flower heads are solitary, up to 2½ inches across, and may be single or double; double flowers often display a crest of raised petals at their center. Colors include yellow, orange, maroon, and bicolors. *T. tenuifolia* (dwarf marigold, signet marigold) grows 6 to 12 inches tall with compact mounds of fernlike foliage and single yellow or orange 1-inch flowers that are so profuse they almost completely cover the leaves. It is excellent for edgings and window boxes.

MIGNONETTE
Reseda

Light: mostly sun

Plant type: annual

Height: 6 inches to 1½ feet

Soil and Moisture: well-drained, moist to dry, fertile

Interest: flowers

Care: moderate

◀ Reseda odorata

Mignonette is a casual, open-growing annual with veils of soft-textured, grassy green foliage and conical clusters of wonderfully fragrant white or yellow summer to fall flowers. The star-shaped flowers are creamy white to greenish yellow with bright orange stamens and are excellent planted at the edge of a border or in a patio planter or window box, where their free-flowing fragrance can be most appreciated. Flowers are long lasting and excellent for cutting.

Growing and care:
Plants are difficult to transplant, so sow seed directly in the garden in early spring. Do not cover seed, as it requires light to germinate. A second sowing a month later will extend the flowering season. In Zones 9 and 10 seed can be planted in fall for flowering in late winter or spring. Thin seedlings to stand 6 to 12 inches apart. Water and mulch to keep soil evenly moist and cool.

Selected species and varieties:
R. odorata develops thick stems and small oval leaves. Flowers are ⅓ inch across with four to seven fringed petals. Although not extremely showy, the flowers are so fragrant as to be well worth growing.

NAVELWORT
Omphalodes

Light: mostly sun

Plant type: annual

Height: 6 to 12 inches

Soil and Moisture: well-drained, moist

Interest: flowers, foliage

Care: easy

◀ Omphalodes linifolia

This dainty little annual from Spain and Portugal produces loose one-sided spikes of white flowers sprinkled among rafts of compact silvery gray leaves. Appearing from summer to fall, the flowers are slightly fragrant and well suited for use in fresh floral arrangements. Plants are effectively used in rock gardens and are quite decorative when planted along a stone wall.

Growing and care:
Start seed indoors 4 to 6 weeks prior to the last frost, or sow directly outdoors in midspring. Allow 4 to 6 inches between plants. They prefer a somewhat acid soil rich in organic matter. Water plants during dry periods. Mulch with peat moss or pine needles after planting to keep roots cool. Navelwort often self-seeds. Cut back plants after flowering to encourage rebloom.

Selected species and varieties:
O. linifolia produces narrow gray-green lance-shaped leaves and sprays of ½-inch-wide five-petaled flowers. Each petal displays a prominent vein running from its tip to its base, giving it a starlike appearance. Seeds resemble navels.

NEMESIA
Nemesia

Light: mostly sun

Plant type: annual

Height: 9 inches to 2 feet

Soil and Moisture: well-drained, moist

Interest: flowers

Care: easy

◀ Nemesia strumosa 'Carnival Mixed'

These brightly colored annuals from South Africa bear pouched, orchidlike flowers from early summer to fall, and are perfect for massing in beds and borders or for growing in containers in areas where summers are cool. They also make effective edgings and provide an attractive cover for the yellowing foliage of spring bulbs.

Growing and care:

Start seed indoors 4 to 6 weeks prior to the last frost in a sterilized medium such as vermiculite. Transplant to the garden after danger of frost has passed in soil well amended with organic matter. Allow 6 inches between plants. Plants require a long, cool growing season to perform well and benefit from some afternoon shade. Pinch young plants to encourage bushiness, and provide water during dry periods.

Selected species and varieties:

N. strumosa has an attractive, bushy, mounded habit with narrow, bright green toothed leaves and spurred five-lobed flowers in clusters 4 inches long. Flower colors include yellow, white, red, purple, orange, pink, and bicolors; 'Carnival Mixed' is a dwarf variety that grows to 9 inches with brightly colored flowers.

PERIWINKLE
Catharanthus

Light: mostly sun

Plant type: tender perennial grown as annual

Height: 3 inches to 1½ feet

Soil and Moisture: well-drained, moist

Interest: flowers, foliage

Care: easy

◀ Catharanthus roseus

Periwinkle provides charming, star-shaped flowers in a range of pastel shades from summer to fall. The flowers resemble those of *Vinca*. Available in both creeping and upright varieties, periwinkle can be used as a summer ground cover or in mass plantings, annual borders, or containers. It is stunning when grown in hanging baskets.

Growing and care:

Start seed indoors 10 to 12 weeks prior to the last frost for late-spring transplanting to the garden. Set plants 1 to 2 feet apart. Plants can also be started from cuttings. They thrive in warm, humid conditions and are perennial in Zones 9 and 10.

Selected species and varieties:

C. roseus [sometimes listed as *Vinca rosea*] (Madagascar periwinkle) produces glossy oblong leaves 1 to 3 inches long. Creeping varieties grow 3 inches tall, spreading 1½ to 2 feet across. Erect strains grow 8 to 18 inches tall. Flowers are 1½ inches wide and cover the plant throughout the summer; colors range from shades of pink or mauve to white; 'Parasol' produces large 1½- to 2-inch white flowers with pink eyes on 1- to 1½-foot plants; 'Tropicana' grows to 1 foot and produces flowers in several shades of pink, from pale blush to deep rose, with contrasting eyes.

PHLOX
Phlox

Light: mostly sun

Plant type: annual

Height: 6 to 20 inches

Soil and Moisture: well-drained, moist to dry

Interest: flowers

Care: moderate

◀ Phlox drummondii 'Palona Rose with Eye'

This native Texas wildflower bears profuse blossoms of white, pink, red, purple, yellow, and bicolors over a long season on low, spreading plants. Annual phlox are versatile—useful as edgings, in rock gardens, massed in beds, and in containers. Flowers are also good for cutting.

Growing and care:
Start seed indoors 8 weeks prior to the last frost. In Zone 8 and warmer, seed should be sown in fall. Space plants 6 to 12 inches apart. Remove spent flowers to extend bloom, and provide water when dry. If flowering declines in midsummer cut back plants to encourage new bud set. The plants are ideal for sandy soil.

Selected species and varieties:
P. drummondii (annual phlox, Drummond phlox) grows to 20 inches with a spreading, mounded habit, hairy leaves and stems, and five-lobed flowers that are 1 inch across; 'Palona Rose with Eye' is compact, 6 to 8 inches tall, and has rose flowers with contrasting white eyes; 'Petticoat' series are compact 6-inch plants that come in a mix of colors with good drought and heat tolerance; 'Twinkle' series are 8 inches tall with small, early star-shaped flowers in mixed colors.

PINK
Dianthus

Light: mostly to full sun

Plant type: annual, biennial, tender perennial

Height: 4 inches to 2 1/2 feet

Soil and Moisture: well-drained, moist

Interest: flowers, foliage

Care: easy

◀ Dianthus chinensis 'Telestar Picotee'

Pinks are perky flowers with a tidy habit, forming mats of grassy foliage with white, pink, red, and bicolored flowers with fringed or "pinked" petals. Low-growing types make delightful edgings or rock garden or container specimens, while taller selections are useful in the foreground or middle of a border, and as cut flowers.

Growing and care:
Sow sweet William seed outdoors in late spring for flowers the following year. Start seed of China pink indoors 6 to 8 weeks prior to the last frost for transplanting to the garden in midspring. Space plants 8 to 18 inches apart. Sweet William grows best in mostly sunny locations but will tolerate some shade. China pink prefers mostly sun but does well in full sun also.

Selected species and varieties:
D. barbatus (sweet William) is a biennial that self-seeds freely. Dwarf varieties grow 4 to 10 inches tall, while tall varieties may reach 2 feet. Flowers are borne in dense, flat-topped clusters from late spring to early summer. *D. chinensis* (China pink, rainbow pink) is an annual, biennial, or short-lived perennial that grows 6 to 30 inches tall with a dense, mounded habit; 1- to 2-inch flowers, often fragrant, are borne singly or in loose clusters from early summer to fall; 'Telestar Picotee' has a compact habit with deep pink flowers fringed with white.

POPPY
Papaver

Light: mostly sun	
Plant type: annual, tender perennial grown as annual	
Height: 1 to 4 feet	
Soil and Moisture: well-drained, moist to dry	
Interest: flowers	
Care: easy	

◀ Papaver nudicaule

Poppy's broad, showy petals surround prominent centers above clumps of coarse, hairy, deeply lobed leaves in spring. The brightly colored flowers are extremely delicate in appearance, with a transluscent, tissuelike quality. Flowers may be single, with four overlapping petals, or double, with many petals forming a rounded bloom. They are borne on solitary stems, and are suitable for mixed borders and good for cutting.

Growing and care:
Annual species are so difficult to transplant that they are best sown in place. *Papaver* seed is very small and can be mixed with sand for easier handling. *P. rhoeas* does best in full shade to mostly sun. Thin plants to stand about 1 foot apart. *P. somniferum* likes mostly sun and can be thinned to stand 4 to 8 inches apart. Double-flowered varieties of *P. somniferum* often require staking. Poppies will often self-seed. Deadhead plants to prolong flowering season. For use in indoor arrangements, cut the flowers as the buds straighten on their nodding stems but before the flowers actually open.

Selected species and varieties:
P. nudicaule (Iceland poppy, Arctic poppy) produces a fernlike clump of 6-inch lobed gray-green leaves from which 18-inch leafless flower stems rise from spring to early summer. Flowers are fragrant, 2 to 4 inches across, and saucer shaped in a range of colors including white yellow, orange, salmon, and scarlet. *P. rhoeas* (corn poppy, Flanders poppy, Shirley poppy, field poppy) grows to 3 feet with wiry, branching stems and pale green deeply lobed leaves. Flowers may be single or double, and are borne from late spring to early summer in colors of red, purple, pink, and white; 'Fairy Wings' produces flowers in soft shades of blue, lilac, dusty pink, and white with faint blue margins; 'Mother of Pearl' bears flowers in shades of blue, lavender, pink, gray, white, and peach, and the flowers may be solid or speckled. *P. somniferum* (opium poppy) grows 3 to 4 feet tall with large white, red, pink, or mauve flowers that appear throughout summer and are often double or fringed; 'Alba' bears white blooms; 'Pink Chiffon' produces double bright pink flowers; 'White Cloud' bears large, double white blooms on sturdy stems.

QUEEN-ANNE'S-LACE
Daucus

Light: mostly sun

Plant type: biennial

Height: 3 to 4 feet

Soil and Moisture: well-drained, moist to dry

Interest: flowers

Care: easy

◀ Daucus carota
var. carota

Queen-Anne's-lace is a weedy plant to the unimaginative, and a hardy, very graceful addition to the garden to others. The plant produces large, flat umbels of intricate, lacy white flowers atop strong, pliant stems from summer to fall. The plant's beautiful flowers and ferny foliage make it a nice filler in a sunny border. It naturalizes easily in wildflower meadows, attracting butterflies and bees. Flowers are valued for both fresh and dried arrangements.

Growing and care:
Sow seed outdoors in late spring for flowers the following year. Once established, plants will vigorously self-seed. To prevent unwanted plants, remove flowers before seeds mature. Plants are easy to grow and thrive in nearly any well-drained soil.

Selected species and varieties:
D. carota var. *carota* (Queen-Anne's-lace, Queen's-lace, wild carrot) produces a prominent rosette of fernlike leaves in early spring, from which grows a 3- to 4-foot branched flowering stem. Each branch is topped by a 3- to 4-inch umbel of tiny white flowers.

ROSE MALLOW
Hibiscus

Light: mostly sun

Plant type: tender perennial

Height: 1 1/2 to 8 feet

Soil and Moisture: well-drained, moist

Interest: flowers, foliage

Care: easy to moderate

◀ Hibiscus acetosella

Rose mallows are a diverse group of tender perennials with distinctive ornamental foliage and showy, funnel-shaped exotic flowers. The plants lend a tropical ambiance to beds, borders, and specialty gardens. Plant rose mallows individually as specimens or in groups for a fast-growing, informal summer hedge. Tall types are effective as a background for mixed borders or as the centerpiece of an island bed. Shorter forms are useful for fronting shrub borders or planting in the foreground of annual beds. Both large and small types are excellent choices for patio containers.

Growing and care:
Start seed of *H. acetosella* indoors about 8 weeks prior to the last frost and transplant outdoors after all danger of frost has passed. Space *H. acetosella* 12 to 14 inches apart. Because *H. trionum* is difficult to transplant, seed should be sown directly in the garden after all danger of frost has passed, allowing 1 foot between plants. Plants tolerate heat as long as abundant moisture is supplied.

Selected species and varieties:
H. acetosella hails from Africa and is grown primarily for its attractive foliage. Purple flowers form so late in the season in most areas that they fail to open before frost. The plant grows to 5 feet tall, with glossy red leaves and stems. Leaves may be either smooth in outline or deeply lobed. This plant makes a bold accent mixed with other

769

ROSE MALLOW
(continued)

annuals, or a stunning summer hedge; the variety 'Red Shield' produces burgundy leaves with a metallic sheen that resemble maple leaves in shape. *H. moscheutos* (common rose mallow, swamp rose mallow, wild cotton) grows 3 to 8 feet tall with a shrubby habit. It is native to marshlands of the eastern United States and can be grown as a perennial in Zone 7 and south but is often grown as a half-hardy annual. The large gray-green leaves provide a soft foil for the huge white, pink, rose, or red summer flowers that are often 8 inches across; *'Southern Belle'* grows 4 to 6 feet tall with red, pink, or white flowers with a distinct red eye, up to 10 inches across. *H. trionum* (flower-of-an-hour) grows 1½ to 3 feet with a bushy habit and dark green three- to five-lobed leaves. Flowers are 2 inches across and are creamy yellow with a deep maroon throat. Though flowers are short lived, they appear in abundance from midsummer to late fall.

SNAPDRAGON
Antirrhinum

◀ Antirrhinum majus

Light: mostly sun	
Plant type: tender perennial grown as annual	
Height: 6 inches to 4 feet	
Soil and Moisture: well-drained, moist, fertile	
Interest: flowers	
Care: easy	

Snapdragons are easy-to-grow plants with distinctive, brightly colored flowers that have been grown since ancient times. Their lasting popularity is easy to understand given their wide range of heights and flower colors and their long season of bloom. Short varieties add color to rock gardens and edgings, while taller types are well suited to the middle and rear of mixed borders. They are outstanding flowers for fresh arrangements.

Growing and care:
Though snapdragons are technically tender perennials, they are commonly grown as annuals except in the Deep South. Sow seed indoors 8 to 10 weeks prior to the last frost. Do not cover seed, which needs light to germinate. Space smaller varieties 6 inches apart, taller types 1½ feet apart in soil amended with compost. Pinch young plants to promote bushiness, and deadhead to encourage continuous flowering. Taller types may need staking.

Selected species and varieties:
A. majus bears terminal clusters of flowers, each with five lobes, divided into an upper and lower lip; varieties are classified by height: dwarf, 6 to 9 inches; intermediate, 1 to 2 feet; and tall, 2 to 4 feet; 'Madame Butterfly' grows to 3 feet with wide flaring blossoms in a range of colors; 'Pink Rocket' grows 2 to 3 feet tall with pink blooms; 'White Sonnet' reaches 22 inches and has white flowers.

SPIDER FLOWER
Cleome

Light: mostly sun

Plant type: annual

Height: 3 to 4 feet

Soil and Moisture: well-drained, moist

Interest: flowers, seedpods

Care: easy

◀ Cleome hasslerana 'Helen Campbell'

Spider flowers bear enormous clusters of 1-inch flowers atop tall, graceful stems continuously from summer until frost. Pink, lavender, or white flower petals surround 2- to 3-inch-long stamens that protrude from the center, creating a spiderlike effect further enhanced by the slender, conspicuous seedpods that follow the flowers. *Cleome* makes a graceful summer hedge, accent, or border plant.

Growing and care:
Start seed indoors 4 to 6 weeks prior to the last frost, or plant directly in the garden in early spring. Plants often self-seed. Space plants about 2 feet apart. Spider flower thrives in warm weather and responds well to abundant moisture.

Selected species and varieties:
C. hasslerana [also known as *C. spinosa*] has an erect habit with dark green palmately compound leaves and airy, ball-shaped flower heads. Although flowers are short lived, new ones are produced continuously at the top of the stem; 'Cherry Queen' bears rose red flowers; 'Helen Campbell' has white blooms; 'Pink Queen' bears clear pink blossoms; the flowers of 'Violet Queen' are purple, and leaves display a purple tint at their edges.

STOCK
Matthiola

Light: mostly sun

Plant type: annual, biennial

Height: 1 to 2 1/2 feet

Soil and Moisture: well-drained, moist, fertile

Interest: flowers

Care: moderate

◀ Matthiola incana

The abundant blossoms of stock perfume a garden throughout summer. Plant them in beds, window boxes, or patio containers where their fragrance can be appreciated. Flowers add a dainty appearance and sweet scent to fresh indoor arrangements.

Growing and care:
Start seed indoors 6 to 8 weeks prior to the last frost, or sow directly in the garden in early spring. Space plants to stand 6 to 12 inches apart; they tolerate crowding. Plants thrive in cool weather and may stop flowering when temperatures rise. *M. bicornis* will tolerate poorer soil and drier conditions than will *M. incana.*

Selected species and varieties:
M. bicornis [also known as *M. longipetala* ssp. *bicornis*] (night-scented stock, evening stock, perfume plant) has a bushy habit and grows 1 to 1½ feet tall. It bears single ¾-inch flowers in shades of lilac and pink that open at night from mid- to late summer and are extremely fragrant. *M. incana* (common stock, gillyflower) grows 1 to 2½ feet with gray-green oblong leaves and terminal clusters of 1-inch-long flowers that may be single or double and bear a spicy fragrance; colors include pink, purple, white, and blue.

SWEET ALYSSUM
Lobularia

Light: mostly sun

Plant type: tender perennial grown as annual

Height: 3 to 6 inches

Soil and Moisture: well-drained, moist

Interest: flowers, fragrance

Care: easy

◀ Lobularia maritima

Sweet alyssum produces robust mounds of narrow, lance-shaped gray-green leaves that are usually hidden beneath masses of petite, fragrant four-petaled flowers from spring to frost. Long a favorite for beds, borders, rock gardens, and containers and as a cover for the withering foliage of spring bulbs, it is usually grown as an annual except in warmer climates.

Growing and care:
Propagate from seed sown indoors 6 to 8 weeks before the last frost, or outdoors after danger of frost has passed. Thin seedlings to 6 inches apart. Young plants will spread quickly and flower rapidly if kept moist and cool with light afternoon shade. Periodic shearing of old blossoms during summer will stimulate further flowering. In warm climates they will self-sow.

Selected species and varieties:
L. maritima [also listed as *Alyssum maritimum*] grows 3 to 6 inches tall with white, pink, or violet flowers; 'Little Dorrit' has a greater abundance of more densely packed clusters of white flowers and a more compact form than many other sweet alyssums; 'Pastel Carpet' has flowers with a variety of pastel shades and white centers; 'Royal Carpet' has violet-purple flowers; 'Tiny Tim' is 3 inches tall with white flowers.

THISTLE
Cirsium

Light: mostly sun

Plant type: biennial

Height: 1 1/2 to 2 1/2 feet

Soil and Moisture: well-drained, moist to dry

Interest: flowers, foliage

Care: easy

◀ Cirsium japonicum

Thistle is a coarse-textured plant with bold, dark green spiny leaves and solitary rose or magenta flowers that are as soft as velvet. The abundant leaves and upright stems provide a dramatic foil for the intensely colored flowers. Thistle adds a dynamic element to the mixed border or wildflower meadow. The blossoms attract butterflies, and are also beautiful in floral arrangements.

Growing and care:
Sow seed directly in the garden as soon as soil can be worked in spring for late-summer flowers. Once established, plants will self-seed. Space plants 1 to 2 feet apart. They are adaptable to a wide range of soils as long as drainage is good.

Selected species and varieties:
C. japonicum (rose thistle) produces an erect, branched stem with deeply lobed 4-inch leaves. The leaves are deep green with spiny edges and often display silvery veins. Flower heads top each stem in summer. The buds are covered with silvery overlapping scales, and the opened flower heads are 1 to 2 inches across. Each head consists of a mass of tiny tubular flowers.

TREE MALLOW
Lavatera

Light: mostly sun

Plant type: annual

Height: 2 to 6 feet

Soil and Moisture: well-drained, moist

Interest: flowers

Care: easy

◀ Lavatera trimestris

Native to the Mediterranean region, tree mallow is a hardy annual with a bushy habit and cup-shaped summer flowers that resemble hollyhocks. Their long blooming season makes these plants a good choice for the mixed border. They are also useful as a summer hedge, and flowers can be cut for fresh arrangements.

Growing and care:
Sow seed outdoors in midspring, thinning to allow plants to stand 1½ to 2 feet apart. Young plants require abundant water and should be mulched. Once established, plants are drought resistant. Deadhead to prolong flowering.

Selected species and varieties:
L. trimestris produces pale green rounded leaves on branched stems that may reach 6 feet, although most varieties are between 2 and 3 feet; both leaves and stems are hairy. Solitary 2½- to 4-inch flowers, each with five wide petals, are borne in great numbers throughout the summer. Colors include shades of pink, red, and white; 'Mont Blanc' grows only 2 feet tall and bears pure white flowers; 'Silver Cup' also grows to 2 feet, bearing salmon-pink flowers with darker veins.

TULIP GENTIAN
Eustoma

Light: mostly sun

Plant type: biennial

Height: 2 to 3 feet

Soil and Moisture: well-drained, moist

Interest: flowers, foliage

Care: difficult

◀ Eustoma grandiflorum 'Lion Mixed'

This native American Great Plains wildflower produces waxy blue-green leaves on a thick stem with intricate, very beautiful upturned flowers. Though exacting in their requirements, the grace these plants lend to the garden make the effort well worthwhile. When grown properly they are exquisite border or container plants and make superb cut flowers, lasting up to 2 weeks.

Growing and care:
Start seed indoors in peat pots about 3 months prior to the last frost. Do not cover seed, as light is needed for proper germination. Keep soil moist and temperatures about 70°F. Transplant to the garden when about 6 inches tall, planting seedlings very carefully. Space plants 6 to 10 inches apart. Water only enough to keep soil evenly moist but not too wet. Do not allow blossoms to get wet. Gentians are slow growers and need a long growing season to perform well.

Selected species and varieties:
E. grandiflorum [also known as *Lisianthus russellianus*] (prairie gentian) has an erect habit with sturdy stems and 3-inch oblong leaves. Flowers may be single or double; they are 2 inches wide and usually purple, although pink, blue, and white varieties are available; 'Lion Mixed' is a double-flowered strain with colors from white to deep purple.

AEONIUM
Aeonium

Light: mostly sun

Plant type: perennial

Hardiness: Zones 9-10

Height: 1 to 3 feet

Soil and Moisture: well-drained, moist to dry

Interest: flowers, foliage

Care: moderate

◀ Aeonium arboreum 'Schwartzkopf'

Aeoniums bear colorful fleshy leaves in attractive rosettes on succulent stems that provide a desertlike ambiance to borders, containers, and rock gardens. The flowers develop in terminal pyramidal clusters in striking shades of yellow. The plants are prized in areas of the Southwest, where the warm, dry climate allows these decorative perennials to thrive.

Growing and care:
Aeoniums thrive in California coastal conditions, where their soil and light needs are best met. Site the plants where they will receive a little afternoon shade during the hottest portion of the day. Aeoniums make good container plants for patio gardens but should be brought indoors before frost.

Selected species and varieties:
A. arboreum 'Schwartzkopf' grows 2 to 3 feet tall with an upright shrubby habit and golden yellow flowers with dark, shiny purple-black leaves appearing in 6- to 8-inch rosettes on branched stems. *A. tabuliforme* reaches 1 foot tall with pale yellow flowers and succulent leaves forming saucer-shaped stemless rosettes 3 to 10 inches across.

ALUMROOT
Heuchera

Light: mostly sun

Plant type: perennial

Hardiness: Zones 3-8

Height: 1 to 2 ½ feet

Soil and Moisture: well-drained, moist, fertile

Interest: flowers, foliage

Care: easy to moderate

◀ Heuchera micrantha 'Palace Purple'

Alumroot produces handsome mounds of deeply colored lobed leaves and delicate, gracefully arching stems of small flowers. The spring and summer bell-shaped blossoms are gentle shades of white or pink, or bold hues of red. Some types sport rich ruby red leaves that accent rock gardens, edgings, and perennial beds.

Growing and care:
Plant alumroot in well-worked soil generously amended with rotted manure or compost. Water well at planting and regularly over the growing season. Mulch in areas with hot summers. As stems become woody, the plant falls open in the center. Divide every 3 to 4 years after flowering or in fall.

Selected species and varieties:
H. x *brizoides* bears red, pink, or white blooms on 1- to 2½-inch stems and dark green leaves; 'Pluie de Feu' ('Rain of Fire') grows to 1½ feet tall with red flowers. *H. micrantha* 'Palace Purple' (small-flowered alumroot) bears 15- to 18-inch-high mounds of wrinkled leaves that are deep purple-red in spring and fall, fading to purplish bronze-green in hot weather, bearing pinkish white flowers; it is grown primarily for its foliage. *H. sanguinea* (coral bells) grows 1 to 1½ feet tall with dark green leaves and pink, white, or red flowers among the hybrids; Bressingham Hybrids have rose-colored flowers.

ANEMONE
Anemone

Light:	mostly sun
Plant Type:	perennial
Hardiness:	Zones 2-9
Height:	6 inches to 4 feet
Soil and Moisture:	well-drained, dry
Interest:	flowers
Care:	easy

◀ Anemone pulsatilla

This diverse genus carries sprightly 1- to 3-inch-wide flowers with single or double rows of petals shaped like shallow cups surrounding prominent stamens and pistils. The flowers are held on branched stems above mounds of handsome deeply cut foliage. Many species brighten the garden during periods when few other plants with similar flowers are in bloom. Native to North America, anemone species can be found in moist woodlands, meadows, and dry prairies.

Growing and care:

Plant small anemones 1 foot apart, taller varieties 2 feet apart. The latter may require staking. Meadow anemone prefers a moist, sandy soil and needs frequent division to prevent overcrowding. Pasqueflowers need full sun and a neutral to alkaline soil in a cool location. Snowdrops windflowers prefer moist soil; grapeleaf anemones tolerate dry conditions. Protect all anemones from afternoon sun and do not allow to dry out completely. Propagate cultivars of Japanese anemone by root cuttings or division, others from seed. Divide Japanese and grapeleaf anemones in spring every 3 years to maintain robustness. Other species grow slowly and division is rarely needed.

Selected species and varieties:

A. canadensis (meadow anemone) grows 1 to 2 feet tall with deeply lobed basal leaves and 1½-inch white flowers with golden centers on leafy flower stems in late spring; Zones 2-6. *A. caroliniana* (Carolina anemone) grows 6 to 12 inches tall with numerous 1½-inch white flowers with yellow centers in spring; Zones 6-8. *A. x hybrida* (Japanese anemone) bears white or pink flowers with a silky sheen on their undersides above dark green foliage from late summer to midfall; Zones 6-8; 'Alba' grows 2 to 3 feet tall with large clear white flowers; 'Honorine Jobert' has white flowers with yellow centers on 3-foot stems; 'Prince Henry' has deep rose flowers on 3-foot stems; 'Queen Charlotte' has full, semidouble pink flowers; 'September Charm' has single-petaled silvery pink flowers; 'September Sprite' has single pink flowers on 15-inch stems. *A. magellanica* bears cream-colored flowers from late spring through summer atop 1½-foot stems; Zones 2-8. *A. multifida* (early thimbleweed) produces loose clumps of silky-haired stems up to 20 inches tall with deeply divided leaves on long stalks; sepals of the ⅜-inch flowers that appear from late spring to summer are usually yellowish white but occasionally bright red; Zones 3-9. *A. pulsatilla* [also classified as *Pulsatilla vulgaris*] (pasqueflower) is known by its 2-inch-wide blue or purple bell-shaped spring flowers on 1-foot stems above hairy leaves; Zones 5-8. *A. sylvestris* 'Snowdrops' (snowdrops windflower) stands 1 to 1½ feet tall with light green foliage topped by dainty, fragrant 2-inch spring flowers. *A. vitifolia* 'Robustissima' (grapeleaf anemone) features branching clusters of pink flowers from late summer to fall on 1- to 3-foot stalks; it is an invasive variety good for naturalizing; Zones 3-8.

ASTER
Aster

Light: mostly sun

Plant type: perennial

Hardiness: Zones 3-9

Height: 6 inches to 8 feet

Soil and Moisture: well-drained, dry, fertile

Interest: flowers

Care: easy

◀ Aster novae-angliae 'Harrington's Pink'

Asters are a large group of versatile, hardy plants prized for their large, showy, daisylike flowers that appear over weeks and even months. The blossoms are distinctive and delicate with very slender ray flowers surrounding a small button-shaped disk. Asters brighten the late summer and fall garden with a rainbow of whites, light blues, pinks, purples, and lavender. The plants are perfect for beds, borders, and rock gardens or planted in large groups in meadows and fields.

Growing and care:

Plant asters in an open, airy location with good air circulation to lessen the risk of powdery mildew. Water plants in the early morning when possible and avoid wetting leaves. Space dwarf asters 1 foot apart, taller ones 2 to 3 feet apart, and thin out young plants to improve air circulation. Taller varieties may require staking. Prompt deadheading encourages a second flowering in early-summer bloomers. *A.* x *frikartii* grown in Zone 5 or colder must be mulched over the winter and should not be cut back or divided in fall; otherwise, divide asters in early spring or fall every 2 years or so when a plant's center begins to die out. Asters can also be propagated by stem cuttings in spring and early summer. Cultivars seldom grow true from seed.

Selected species and varieties:

A. alpinus is a low-growing species forming 6- to 12-inch-high clumps topped by violet-blue 1- to 3-inch flowers with yellow centers; 'Dark Beauty' produces deep blue flowers; 'Goliath' grows a few inches taller than the species, with pale blue flowers; 'Happy End' has semidouble lavender flowers. *A.* x *frikartii* (Frikart's aster) produces 2- to 3-foot-tall plants topped by fragrant 2½-inch lavender-blue flowers with yellow centers blooming in summer and lasting 2 months or longer; 'Monch' has profuse blue-mauve flowers and is resistant to mildew. *A. novae-angliae* (New England aster) grows 2 to 5 feet tall with 4- to 5-inch leaves and 2-inch violet-purple flowers with bright golden disks; it is less important than its many cultivars, most of which are quite tall and require staking; 'Alma Potschke' has vivid rose-colored blossoms from late summer to fall; 'Harrington's Pink' grows to 4 feet tall with large salmon-pink flowers in fall; 'Purple Dome' is a dwarf variety growing 1½ feet tall and spreading 3 feet wide, with profuse deep purple fall flowers. *A. novi-belgii* (New York aster, Michaelmas daisy) cultivars range from 10 to 48 inches tall and bloom in white, pink, red, blue, and purple-violet from late summer through fall; 'Eventide' has violet-blue semidouble flowers on 3-foot stems; 'Professor Kippenburg' is compact and bushy, 12 to 15 inches tall with lavender-blue flowers; 'Royal Ruby' is a compact cultivar with large crimson fall flowers; 'Winston S. Churchill' grows violet-red flowers on 2-foot stems.

BALLOON FLOWER
Platycodon

Light: mostly sun	
Plant type: perennial	
Hardiness: Zones 4-9	
Height: 1 to 3 feet	
Soil and Moisture: well-drained, moist	
Interest: flowers	
Care: easy	

◀ Platycodon grandiflorus

Balloon flowers have inflated buds that form 2- to 3-inch-wide cup-shaped blossoms with pointed translucent petals that add a uniquely beautiful touch to summer gardens. Flowers are usually blue, but cultivars with white or pink blossoms are also available. The branched 2- to 3-foot-tall shoots have 3-inch toothed oval leaves. Taller varieties may need staking. Balloon flowers are excellent for massing and borders, while dwarf cultivars can be used in rock gardens. Taller varieties make good cut flowers.

Growing and care:
Balloon flowers grow well in mostly sun, where they get enough light to thrive and enough shade to preserve the soft flower color. Propagate by seed or division in early spring or late autumn. Since shoots are late to emerge in spring, mark the locations of plants during the summer so plants are not damaged when soil is cultivated the following spring. Space plants 1½ feet apart. It usually takes 2 years for seedlings to reach flowering size.

Selected species and varieties:
P. grandiflorus (balloon flower, Japanese bellflower) sprouts deep blue flowers on slender 2- to 3-foot stems above neat clumps of blue-green leaves from mid- to late summer; 'Album' has white flowers; 'Shell Pink' and 'Mother-of-Pearl' have pale pink flowers; 'Sentimental Blue' has bright blue flowers on 15-inch stems.

BEAR'S-BREECH
Acanthus

Light: mostly sun	
Plant type: perennial	
Hardiness: Zones 7-10	
Height: 3 to 4 feet	
Soil and Moisture: well-drained, moist	
Interest: flowers, foliage	
Care: easy to moderate	

◀ Acanthus spinosissimus

Bear's-breech is valued for its bold sculptural effects, with spreading clumps of broad, deeply lobed shiny leaves up to 2 feet long and stiff spikes of tubular flowers borne well above the foliage in summer. The plants provide a strong vertical accent to the back of the border and look very appealing in natural plantings. The flowers and seed heads are effective in arrangements.

Growing and care:
Bear's-breech thrives in sunny places where a little afternoon shade tempers the heat of summer days. Plant 3 feet apart, and propagate by seed or by division in early spring or fall after the plant has bloomed at least 3 years. Tolerant of moderate drought, bear's-breech abhors wet winter soil. Once established, this plant is difficult to remove from a site, as bits of fleshy roots inadvertently left behind easily grow into new plants.

Selected species and varieties:
A. spinosissimus (spiny bear's-breech) produces dense flower spikes, usually mauve but sometimes white, on 3- to 4-foot stalks overarching, deeply cut thistlelike leaves.

BEE BALM
Monarda

Light: mostly sun

Plant type: perennial

Hardiness: Zones 4-9

Height: 3 feet

Soil and Moisture: well-drained, moist

Interest: flowers, foliage, fragrance

Care: easy to moderate

◀ Monarda didyma 'Cambridge Scarlet'

Bee balms have round clusters of purple, lilac, red, pink, or white two-lipped tubular flowers arranged in moplike tufts at the tops of tall leafy stems. Their lance-shaped leaves are aromatic when crushed, and are used to make refreshing teas. Bee balms are members of the mint family and are excellent for planting in beds and borders or naturalizing in woodland plantings.

Growing and care:
Plant in spring or fall. Space plants 1½ to 2 feet apart. Prune withering flower heads to prolong the flowering season. Propagate by seed or division every few years in early spring, or from early-summer cuttings. Bee balms need good air circulation so they do not get mildew. Water during hot, dry periods.

Selected species and varieties:
M. didyma (bee balm, Oswego tea) bears 1- to 2-inch scarlet flowers in rounded 2- to 3-inch-wide clusters from late spring to late summer on 3- to 4-foot stems; 'Cambridge Scarlet' is wine red; 'Croftway Pink' is rosy pink; 'Granite Pink' is a dwarf with pink flowers; 'Mahogany' has dark red flowers; 'Marshall's Delight' is mildew resistant and bears large pink flowers over a longer season; 'Salmonea' has salmon-pink flowers; 'Snow Queen' has icy white blossoms. *M. fistulosa* (wild bergamot) produces 2- to 4-inch pompom-like clusters of lilac to pink flowers from mid- to late summer.

BLUE-EYED GRASS
Sisyrinchium

Light: mostly sun

Plant type: perennial

Hardiness: Zones 3-10

Height: 3 inches to 1½ feet

Soil and Moisture: well-drained, moist to dry

Interest: flowers, foliage

Care: moderate

◀ Sisyrinchium bellum

Dainty-looking blue-eyed grass bears starry six-petaled flowers and clumps of narrow leaves that add subtle beauty to the garden. It is a member of the iris family, and its flowers, which appear in spring and early summer, may be blue, reddish purple, or white. Its grasslike foliage is attractive in spring even when the plant is not in bloom. Blue-eyed grass looks especially good planted in drifts in the dappled shade of deciduous trees, among other wildflowers in a meadow garden, or with alpine plants in rock gardens.

Growing and care:
S. angustifolium needs poor to average, evenly moist soil; it tends to be short lived if allowed to dry out. *S. bellum* needs soil that is moist in spring and dry in summer. Grow blue-eyed grass from seed; plants also often self-sow. Plant in late winter or early spring about 6 to 12 inches apart, setting crowns about ½ inch deep. Divide every other year in spring or fall.

Selected species and varieties:
S. angustifolium (narrow-leaved blue-eyed grass) bears ½-inch-wide light blue flowers with a star-shaped yellow eye on twisted stalks that rise above the 1- to 1½-foot foliage clump from spring to summer. *S. bellum* (California blue-eyed grass) grows 3 to 18 inches high with large numbers of blue, violet, or white spring flowers that have yellow centers and 4- to 20-inch-long leaves.

BRUNNERA
Brunnera

Light: mostly sun to mostly shade

Plant type: perennial

Hardiness: Zones 4-8

Height: 1 to 2 feet

Soil and Moisture: well-drained, moist

Interest: flowers, foliage

Care: easy

◀ Brunnera macrophylla

Brunnera is native to the Caucasus, where its mounds of lightly wrinkled heart-shaped leaves grow beneath groves of spruce and on grassy hillsides. In early spring the plants produce masses of showy, small blue flowers that resemble forget-me-nots. The foliage enlarges after the plants flower, and remains attractive throughout fall. These are excellent plants for borders or rock gardens, and put on an unforgettable springtime show when naturalized with forget-me-nots and daffodils in woodland gardens or meadows.

Growing and care:
Space plants 1 foot apart and mulch to keep roots cool and soil moist. Fertilize lightly after flowers have faded. Propagate by division in spring or fall, or by transplanting self-sown seedlings. This also rejuvenates older clumps. Brunnera does best in mostly sun and also does well in partial shade.

Selected species and varieties:
B. macrophylla [also listed as *Anchusa myosotidiflora*] (Siberian bugloss) bears loosely branched flower clusters on 1- to 1½-foot stems above rough-textured clumps of heart-shaped leaves with fuzzy petioles; 'Hadspen Cream' has sky blue flowers and light green leaves edged with white.

BUGLOSS
Anchusa

Light: mostly sun

Plant type: perennial

Hardiness: Zones 3-8

Height: 3 to 5 feet

Soil and Moisture: well-drained, moist

Interest: flowers

Care: easy

◀ Anchusa azurea

Bugloss has a loose habit with clusters of small, lapis blue trumpetlike flowers above hairy, tongue-shaped leaves. The eye-catching blossoms persist a month or more and add an airy, vibrant splash to beds, borders, and wildflower gardens.

Growing and care:
Plant 1½ to 3 feet apart in spring or fall. Water plants regularly and fertilize in spring as plants begin active growth. Tall varieties may require staking, especially in breezy locations. Cutting plants to the ground after flowers fade forces a second show of blossoms in late summer or fall and prevents foliage from becoming lank. Provide good drainage, as standing moisture will rot roots in winter. Propagate by division every 2 to 3 years or from root cuttings.

Selected species and varieties:
A. azurea (Italian bugloss) has bright blue ¾-inch flowers that bloom abundantly on 3- to 5-foot stems; 'Little John' is a dwarf cultivar growing to 1½ feet with deep blue flowers and hairy dark green leaves; 'Loddon Royalist' grows 3 feet tall with royal blue flowers and an open habit.

BURNET
Sanguisorba

Light:	mostly sun
Plant type:	perennial
Hardiness:	Zones 3-8
Height:	2½ to 6 feet
Soil and Moisture:	well-drained, moist
Interest:	flowers, foliage
Care:	easy

◀ Sanguisorba
canadensis

Burnets have spikes of white flowers resembling a bottlebrush on wandlike stems that add a coarse, bold aspect to gardens. The buds at the base of the flower spike open first, forming a wave of white moving upward from summer to midfall. The tall stems rise above the very attractive, toothed compound leaves. Native to low meadows and bogs in eastern North America, burnets are an excellent choice for perennial beds, natural gardens, and waterside plantings. They form spreading clumps over time.

Growing and care:
Burnets adapt to most conditions as long as the soil does not dry out completely. Taller varieties may need staking, so avoid adding extra fertilizer or plants may become even lankier than under ordinary conditions. Space plants 1½ to 2 feet apart. Propagate by division in early spring, or by seed sown in damp soil in fall or spring.

Selected species and varieties:
S. canadensis (Canadian burnet, American burnet) grows 3 to 6 feet tall with upright leafy-stemmed clumps and 6- to 8-inch-long flower spikes in summer made up of individual flowers, each having a four-lobed petal-like calyx and long white stamens but no petals. Its attractive compound leaves have seven to 15 oblong leaflets with sharply toothed edges.

CAMPION
Lychnis

Light:	mostly sun
Plant type:	perennial
Hardiness:	Zones 4-9
Height:	1 to 3 feet
Soil and Moisture:	well-drained, moist
Interest:	flowers, foliage
Care:	easy

◀ Lychnis chalcedonica

Catchfly produces distinctive cross-shaped flowers of intense fiery scarlet. The brilliantly colored spring or summer blooms are set off by handsome dark green foliage. Catchfly is most impressive when planted in small groupings, where it provides a splash of intense color in a perennial border or bed. It is also effective massed as an accent in natural plantings such as wildflower meadows. The flowers of taller varieties are excellent for indoor arrangements.

Growing and care:
Catchfly thrives in mostly sunny places with a few hours of bright shade during hot summer days. Poorly drained soil results in short-lived plants; otherwise, the genus has very few pest or disease problems. Space plants 1 to 1½ feet apart. Propagate by seed in spring or by division in spring or fall.

Selected species and varieties:
L. x *arkwrightii* (Arkwright campion) is a bushy plant 12 to 15 inches tall with dark bronze foliage and bright orange-red summer flowers. *L. chalcedonica* (Maltese cross) produces 2- to 3-foot erect stems bearing pointed, clasping leaves and dense 3- to 4-inch terminal clusters of scarlet flowers, each blossom shaped like a small cross. *L. coronaria* (mullein pink, rose campion) has a spreading habit, woolly silvery white leaves, and 1-inch-wide magenta-pink flowers in late spring; Zones 5-9.

CATMINT
Nepeta

Light: mostly sun

Plant type: perennial

Hardiness: Zones 3-9

Height: 1 to 3 feet

Soil and Moisture: well-drained, moist

Interest: flowers, foliage, fragrance

Care: easy

◀ Nepeta x faassenii

Catmints have fragrant, soft, dusty green heart-shaped leaves and square stems topped by spikes of tiny white or blue flowers. The plants are easy to grow and very durable, with flower spikes appearing nearly all summer long. Catmints are excellent as ground covers, in rock or herb gardens, or as edgings in informal plantings.

Growing and care:
Plant catmints in spring, spacing them 1 to 1½ feet apart. Shear plants after flowering to encourage rebloom. Fertilize lightly in spring when growth begins. To propagate, take softwood cuttings in summer from non-flowering shoots and stick directly in moist sand away from direct sunlight.

Selected species and varieties:
N. cataria (catnip) spreads in 2-foot clumps on pliant stems covered with gray-green leaves and topped with spikes of white and violet flowers; 'Citriodora' has tart lemon-scented leaves. *N. x faassenii* (blue catmint) produces 1½- to 2-foot mounds of silvery gray leaves and lavender-blue sterile flowers from spring to summer; 'Dropmore' has upright stems with lavender flowers; 'Six Hills Giant' is robust, very hardy, and grows to 3 feet tall with large sprays of deep blue flowers; 'Superba' has spreading branches covered with gray-green leaves and abundant dark blue flowers; Zones 4-9.

CHECKERMALLOW
Sidalcea

Light: mostly sun

Plant type: perennial

Hardiness: Zones 4-10

Height: 2 to 4 feet

Soil and Moisture: well-drained, wet to dry

Interest: flowers

Care: moderate

◀ Sidalcea malviflora

Checkermallows are perky, hardworking wildflowers from the western United States. The plants bear showy pink or purple flowers resembling small hollyhocks and provide a colorful vertical accent in mixed herbaceous borders or meadow plantings.

Growing and care:
S. malviflora prefers soil that is moist in winter and well drained to dry in summer. It is an ideal choice for coastal gardens. *S. neomexicana* grows best in moist, well-drained to wet soils. Remove faded flowers or cut back spent flower stems to prolong blooming. Cut stems to ground in fall. Tall varieties may need staking, especially in breezy locations. Propagate by seed sown directly in the garden after last frost, or by division in fall.

Selected species and varieties:
S. malviflora (checkermallow, checkerbloom) grows up to 4 feet tall with pink or purple flowers on erect stems in spring and summer and dark green lobed leaves; the flowers open in the morning and close up in the evening; Zones 5-10. *S. neomexicana* (prairie mallow) grows up to 3 feet tall with mauve flowers in spring and early summer on pliant stems with dark green leaves; Zones 4-10.

781

CHRYSANTHEMUM
Chrysanthemum

Light: mostly sun

Plant type: perennial

Hardiness: Zones 3-9

Height: 6 inches to 3 feet

Soil and Moisture: well-drained, moist, fertile

Interest: flowers, foliage

Care: easy to moderate

◀ Chrysanthemum parthenium

Chrysanthemums are the backbone of many fall gardens, with the varied forms reliably providing a long-lasting display both in the garden and cut for fresh arrangements. These hardworking plants bloom throughout summer and into fall. Their mounds of attractively lobed foliage blend well with other border plantings, or they can be massed for effect.

Growing and care:
Space chrysanthemums 1 to 2 feet apart in soil enriched with organic matter. Water plants during dry periods of the growing season but do not allow them to stay wet over winter or to become overcrowded. Provide a winter mulch. Divide in spring.

Selected species and varieties:
C. coccineum [also listed as *Tanacetum coccineum*] (painted daisy) has wiry 2- to 3-foot stems lined with fine-textured ferny leaves supporting 2- to 3-inch, usually single, red, pink, or white flowers with yellow centers from late spring to early summer; 'Helen' has pink double blooms; Zones 3-7. *C. parthenium* (feverfew) grows 1 to 3 feet tall, producing prolific white flower buttons with yellow centers in clusters from midsummer to fall above aromatic fernlike foliage; Zones 4-9. *C.* x *superbum* (Shasta daisy) bears white flowers with yellow centers 3 to 6 inches across on 2½-foot stems; 'Alaska' bears large, single white flowers on 2-foot stems.

CINQUEFOIL
Potentilla

Light: mostly sun

Plant type: perennial

Hardiness: Zones 2-7

Height: 1 to 4 feet

Soil and Moisture: well-drained, moist to dry

Interest: flowers, foliage

Care: easy

◀ Potentilla nepalensis 'Miss Wilmott'

Cinquefoils are very hardy, easy-to-grow perennials with cheerful yellow, white, or rose flowers and attractive silvery green compound leaves. The plants range from ground-hugging dwarf types that resemble yellow-flowered strawberries to loosely branched, more upright forms with an open, airy appearance. Cinquefoil is a tasteful addition to the mixed border and rock garden, and offers special charm when naturalized in wildflower gardens and meadows.

Growing and care:
Cinquefoils grow almost anywhere but perform best in moist, well-drained soil that has some organic matter. Provide extra water during dry times. Mulch lightly in spring and fall with compost. Propagate by dividing established plants in spring every 3 to 4 years or by sowing seed in spring while soil is still cool.

Selected species and varieties:
P. nepalensis (Nepal cinquefoil) is a sprawling perennial 1½ feet tall with weak stems bearing serrated leaves in a star-shaped pattern and 1-inch-wide cup-shaped flowers in a range of colors from late spring to summer, hardy to Zone 5; 'Miss Wilmott' grows to 1 foot high and has cherry pink flowers. *P. tridentata* is a low-growing sub-alpine plant with three-part compound leaves that turn red in fall, and small white flowers in summer.

CULVER'S ROOT
Veronicastrum

Light: mostly sun to mostly shade

Plant type: perennial

Hardiness: Zones 3-8

Height: 2 to 6 feet

Soil and Moisture: well-drained, fertile, moist

Interest: flowers, foliage

Care: easy to moderate

◄ Veronicastrum virginicum

Culver's root is a perennial found on stream banks and moist prairies of the eastern United States. It produces showy erect clusters of narrow flower spikes atop tall stems from mid- to late summer, making it a valuable performer at the back of a herbaceous border.

Growing and care:

V. virginicum is easy to grow in full sun or light shade in moist, well-drained soil. Plants also do well in shady places. Plant in well-worked soil generously amended with compost or rotted manure. The upright, strong stems require no staking. Propagate by seed, cuttings, or root division.

Selected species and varieties:

V. virginicum [also listed as *Veronica virginica*] (Culver's root, bowman's-root) has strong unbranched stems up to 6 feet tall with white or pale blue flowers in spikes up to 9 inches long arranged in candelabra-like clusters at the tops of stems. The sharply toothed 6-inch leaves fan out horizontally from the stem in symmetrical whorls; the cultivar 'Roseum' has pale pink blossoms.

DAYLILY
Hemerocallis

Light: mostly sun

Plant type: perennial

Hardiness: Zones 3-10

Height: 1 to 6 feet

Soil and Moisture: well-drained, moist

Interest: flowers, foliage, fragrance

Care: easy

◄ Hemerocallis 'Stella d'Oro'

Daylilies are old-fashioned favorites that are easy to care for. The original 15 species have yielded more than 26,000 varieties with flowers in every color except blue. So many cultivars and hybrids allow you to create beds and borders graced with daylily flowers from late spring to fall. The flowers are borne on stems that often are twice as tall as the mounds of foliage. Each flower lasts from 1 to 2 days, but the numerous buds keep daylilies blooming for many weeks.

Growing and care:

Plant daylily crowns 1 inch below the soil surface, 1½ to 2 feet apart for smaller types and 2 to 3 feet apart for taller ones, in spring, summer, or fall. Provide organic mulch to conserve water and prevent frost heaving where winters are cold, and afternoon shade where summers are hot and dry. A light application of fertilizer in spring is helpful. Rejuvenate established plants by dividing clumps every 3 to 6 years in early spring, or after flowering in late summer or fall.

Selected species and varieties:

H. fulva 'Europa' (orange daylily, tawny daylily) is a vigorous, growing 4-foot-tall cultivar with clusters of six to 12 tawny orange 4- to 5-inch flowers in midsummer. *H.* 'Stella d'Oro' is a nearly ever-blooming miniature hybrid with slightly ruffled 2½-inch orange-throated canary yellow flowers.

EVERLASTING
Anaphalis

Light: mostly sun	
Plant type: perennial	
Hardiness: Zones 3-9	
Height: 1 to 3 feet	
Soil and Moisture: well-drained, moist to medium	
Interest: flowers, foliage	
Care: easy	

◄ Anaphalis margaritacea

Everlastings are vigorous, woolly plants that add contrast to borders and rock gardens from summer through fall. Narrow, elongated white leaves clasp the stems. The small, tight, globular summer flowers often are cut before they are fully open, to be dried and used in flower arrangements. In addition to their ornamental qualities, everlastings repel some insects harmful to garden plants and also attract butterflies.

Growing and care:
Everlastings do well in nutrient-poor sandy soil. They need no additional fertilizers and, once established, are quite drought resistant. They spread freely by underground stems called rhizomes, and form large clumps in just a few years. Separate rhizomes in early spring and plant ½ inch deep; or propagate from fresh seed sown in the fall, planting ⅛ inch deep; or start in flats and transplant seedlings 1½ feet apart.

Selected species and varieties:
A. margaritacea (pearly everlasting, silverleaf) is native to the North Temperate Region, including North America. Its ¼- to ½-inch pearly white flower heads with burnt yellow centers that appear in late summer on 8- to 24-inch stems, and narrow 4- to 8-inch green leaves often so densely covered with hairs that they appear to have a silvery cast.

FALSE LUPINE
Thermopsis

Light: mostly sun	
Plant type: perennial	
Hardiness: Zones 3-9	
Height: 1½ to 5 feet	
Soil and Moisture: well-drained, moist to dry, fertile	
Interest: flowers, foliage	
Care: easy to moderate	

◄ Thermopsis montana

False lupines are strong, handsome plants with stout stems and spikes of vivid yellow flowers from spring to summer. These hardy perennials are native to open woodlands, meadows, and stony flats, where they have evolved a tolerance to heat and drought. False lupines combine well with ornamental grasses in a mixed perennial border and are excellent when naturalized in a meadow.

Growing and care:
Grow *T. montana* in a well-drained sandy soil and *T. villosa* in a humus-rich soil. The plants flower best with extra water during dry periods. Propagate *T. montana* by seed and *T. villosa* by seed or division.

Selected species and varieties:
T. montana (golden pea) is a western native with slender branched stems to 32 inches tall bearing dense 4- to 12-inch clusters of bright yellow flowers in spring, followed by velvety pods; Zones 3-8. *T. villosa* (bush pea) is native to the Appalachian Mountains and grows 3 to 5 feet tall with dark green foliage and deep yellow flowers in dense clusters up to a foot long from spring to summer, followed by hairy pods; Zones 4-9.

FLAX
Linum

Light: mostly sun	
Plant type: perennial	
Hardiness: Zones 5-9	
Height: 1 to 2 feet	
Soil and Moisture: well-drained, sandy, moist to dry	
Interest: flowers	
Care: easy	

◀ Linum perenne

The delicate, softly colored blossoms of flax decorate the open, branching stems with abundant porcelain blue, golden yellow, or linen white flowers from spring to summer. The fine-textured, deep green foliage provides a light aspect to borders and rock gardens. Though blossoms last only a day, new buds open continuously for 6 weeks or more.

Growing and care:
Direct-sow in the garden in spring in northern regions and in fall from Zone 8 south. Thin plants to stand 6 inches apart for smaller types and to 1½ feet apart for larger forms. Cut the stems back in spring to encourage branching, and snip stems to ground level in fall. Do not transplant, as flax does not like being disturbed. The plants are short lived and best propagated by seed.

Selected species and varieties:
L. flavum (golden flax) bears bright yellow flowers on stems 1 to 1½ feet tall. *L. perenne* (perennial flax) has abundant sky blue, saucer-shaped flowers on stems up to 2 feet tall; 'Diamant White' has abundant white blossoms on 1- to 1½-foot stems.

FLEABANE
Erigeron

Light: mostly sun	
Plant type: perennial	
Hardiness: Zones 3-8	
Height: 6 inches to 2 feet	
Soil and Moisture: well-drained, moist to dry	
Interest: flowers	
Care: easy	

◀ Erigeron speciosus 'Pink Jewel'

Fleabane's asterlike blossoms grow singly or in branched clusters with a fringe of slender ray flowers surrounding a yellow center. Flowers sit atop graceful leafy stems that rise from basal rosettes of fuzzy swordlike or oval leaves. Fleabane is an easy-to-grow, vigorous plant that brings the distinctiveness of asters to the spring and early-summer garden. The plants are excellent in borders or displayed in natural plantings.

Growing and care:
Plant fleabane 1½ feet apart in soil amended with some organic matter. Water during dry, hot periods to extend flowering season. Propagate by transplanting self-sown seedlings or by division in spring.

Selected species and varieties:
E. pulchellus (poor Robin's plantain) bears pink, lavender, or white flowers 1½ inches across on plants up to 2 feet tall. *E. speciosus* (Oregon fleabane), the most popular species in the genus, bears purple flowers 1 to 2 inches across on stems to 2½ feet; 'Azure Fairy' has semidouble lavender flowers; 'Double Beauty', double blue-violet flowers; 'Foerster's Liebling', deep pink semidouble flowers; 'Pink Jewel', single lavender-pink flowers; 'Sincerity', single lavender flowers.

FOUR-O'CLOCK
Mirabilis

Light: mostly sun	
Plant type: perennial	
Hardiness: Zones 5-10	
Height: 1½ to 3 feet	
Soil and Moisture: well-drained, dry	
Interest: flowers	
Care: easy	

◄ Mirabilis multiflora

Among the many types of four-o'clocks are several wildflowers native to dry areas of the western United States. These hardy perennials are easy to grow and quickly spread over slopes and rocky areas, stabilizing the soil and reducing erosion. The brightly colored tubular flowers open in the afternoon and close the following morning. Wild four-o'clocks are lovely massed as a ground cover or trailing over a wall.

Growing and care:
Four-o'clocks are low-maintenance plants that are also long lived and very drought tolerant. Supplemental watering during dry periods will extend the season of bloom. Propagate by seed or by dividing roots in fall.

Selected species and varieties:
M. froebelii (wild four-o'clock, wishbone plant) bears numerous clusters of 1½- to 2¼-inch-long deep rose pink to reddish purple flowers at the ends of multi-branched stems up to 3 feet; Zones 7-10. *M. multiflora* (wild four-o'clock) grows up to 1½ feet with magenta tubular flowers about 2 inches long and dark green leaves.

GAS PLANT
Dictamnus

Light: mostly sun	
Plant type: perennial	
Hardiness: Zones 3-9	
Height: 2 to 3 feet	
Soil and Moisture: well-drained, moist	
Interest: flowers, foliage, fragrance	
Care: moderate	

◄ Dictamnus albus 'Purpureus'

Gas plant offers open, decorative mounds of lemon-scented glossy foliage crowned in late spring to early summer with tall flower spikes of white, pink, rose or purple blossoms. The flowers are excellent in fresh bouquets. In late summer star-shaped seed capsules appear that add interest to dried arrangements. Gas plant is a nice addition to borders and informal plantings.

Growing and care:
Sow gas plant seed outdoors in spring or fall in soil generously amended with organic matter. Thin plants to stand 2 to 3 feet apart. Do not disturb or transplant. Mulch in spring and fall. Cut back stems to ground level in fall, especially in warm regions. Propagate from seed, as dividing plants is rarely successful.

Selected species and varieties:
D. albus (gas plant, fraxinella, white dittany) features leathery oval leaflets with finely toothed edges in mounds to 3 feet high and as wide with spikes of 1-inch white flowers on erect stems; 'Purpureus' has mauve-purple blossoms veined deeper purple; 'Ruber' bears rose pink flowers.

GEUM
Geum

Light: mostly sun

Plant type: perennial

Hardiness: Zones 5-8

Height: 6 inches to 2½ feet

Soil and Moisture: well-drained, moist, fertile

Interest: flowers, foliage

Care: moderate

◀ Geum x borisii

Geums produce open, attractive flowers in single or double blooms. The flowers, which resemble wild roses in some types and buttercups in others, have satiny or ruffled petals surrounding frilly centers that grow singly on slender stems; they make excellent cut flowers. The bright green hairy leaves, which are lobed and frilled at their edges, form attractive mounds of foliage ideal for the front of a border or for the rock garden.

Growing and care:
Space geums 1 to 1½ feet apart in soil enriched with organic matter. They grow best in moist but well-drained sites in cooler climates and will not survive wet winter soil. Mulch around plants to keep soil moist and cool. Site geums in locations that receive some shade during the hottest portion of the day. Water regularly during hot, dry periods. Mulch in fall north of Zone 7. Keep geums robust by dividing every 3 to 4 years in late summer. Direct-sow seed in early spring while soil is still cool.

Selected species and varieties:
G. x *borisii* produces orange-scarlet flowers on 1-foot plants. *G. coccineum* (scarlet avens) bears early-summer-blooming ½-inch bright orange flowers that ride above bright green, toothed leaves on 1-foot-tall stems; 'Red Wings' has semidouble scarlet flowers atop 2-foot stems. *G.* 'Georgenberg' bears drooping orange flowers on 10- to 12-inch stems.

GLOBEFLOWER
Trollius

Light: mostly sun

Plant type: perennial

Hardiness: Zones 4-10

Height: 1½ to 5 feet

Soil and Moisture: well-drained, moist

Interest: flowers, foliage

Care: easy

◀ Trollius ledebourii 'Golden Queen'

Globeflower is a bright addition to any garden, with vivid 2- to 4-inch golden yellow blossoms on graceful stems. The flowers consist of waxy, curved petals forming dense balls that provide a long-lasting display in perennial borders, rock gardens, or wildflower meadows.

Growing and care:
Space globeflowers 1½ feet apart in soil containing generous amounts of organic matter. Mulch around base of plants during warm, dry periods and water regularly. Propagate from seed or by division in fall every 4 years. Globeflower is long lived but does not like to be disturbed once established.

Selected species and varieties:
T. x *cultorum* (hybrid globeflower) bears yellow to orange flowers. *T. europaeus* (common globeflower) has lemon yellow flowers on stems up to 2 feet tall with dark green lobed leaves; 'Superbus' has light yellow flowers in spring and often again in late summer or fall. *T. ledebourii* (Ledebour globeflower) has bright orange flowers on graceful 3-foot stems; 'Golden Queen' has golden orange blossoms.

GOAT'S RUE
Galega

Light: mostly sun	
Plant type: perennial	
Hardiness: Zones 4-10	
Height: 1½ to 5 feet	
Soil and Moisture: well-drained, moist	
Interest: flowers, foliage	
Care: easy	

◀ Galega officinalis

Goat's rues are rambling members of the bean family with upright clusters of white, lavender, or violet-blue pealike flowers in summer on erect stems. Their bold, featherlike compound leaves have oval leaflets and form dense mounds that completely cover the ground. A robust growth habit makes them useful at the back of borders or naturalized in wildflower gardens. Goat's rues make good cut flowers.

Growing and care:
Goat's rues thrive in locations with plentiful afternoon shade, especially in regions with hot summers. Plant in spring or fall 2 inches deep and 1 to 2 feet apart, and mulch lightly. Propagate in early spring from seed sown where plants are desired, or by dividing root crowns.

Selected species and varieties:
G. officinalis bears sprays of white, lilac, pink, or lavender flowers on 2- to 5-foot stems from summer to early fall, and five to eight narrow, blue-green leaflets with pointed tips; 'Carnea' has rosy pink flowers that contrast beautifully with its blue-green leaves; 'Lady Wilson' has fine, slender spikes of lilac-blue flowers. *G. orientalis* is a more compact species with 1½-foot stems spreading to 2 feet, and violet flowers tinged with blue in early summer; Zones 6-10.

GROUNDSEL
Senecio

Light: mostly sun	
Plant type: perennial	
Hardiness: Zones 4-10	
Height: 1 to 5 feet	
Soil and Moisture: well-drained, moist to dry	
Interest: flowers	
Care: moderate	

◀ Senecio aureus

Groundsels are vigorous perennials that quickly ramble over meadows and open woodlands, creating masses of bright golden yellow flowers from mid-spring to fall. The plants are easy to grow and maintain, and the daisylike flowers are cheerful additions to natural plantings and informal gardens.

Growing and care:
Plant groundsel in spring or fall in loose, sandy soil amended with some organic matter. Water regularly for a few weeks after planting. Propagate by seed, division, or cuttings.

Selected species and varieties:
S. aureus (golden groundsel, golden ragwort) grows 1 to 3 feet tall with clusters of deep golden yellow flowers in late spring and summer above the heart-shaped dark green basal foliage. It spreads rapidly by horizontal offshoots to form attractive colonies; native to eastern North America; Zones 4-8. *S. douglasii* (shrubby senecio) is a shrubby perennial up to 5 feet tall with bright yellow flowers in summer and fall and fuzzy greenish white foliage; native to California; Zones 6-10.

INULA
Inula

Light: mostly sun	
Plant type: perennial	
Hardiness: Zones 4-9	
Height: 6 to 12 inches	
Soil and Moisture: well-drained, moist	
Interest: flowers	
Care: easy	

◀ Inula ensifolia

Inula produces cheerful, bright yellow daisylike flowers that enliven summer gardens. The blossoms have slender ray petals surrounding a yellow center, making each flower look like a child's drawing of the sun. Inula is excellent in mixed borders and sprinkled through wildflower gardens and meadows.

Growing and care:
Sow seed indoors 6 to 8 weeks before last frost, or direct-sow in garden in early spring while soil is cool. Plant seedlings 1 foot apart for smaller types and 1½ to 2 feet apart for larger forms. Water regularly during growing season; mulch in spring and again in fall. Cut plants back in fall. Divide every 3 years.

Selected species and varieties:
I. acaulis (stemless inula) has single yellow flowers borne on 6-inch stems in midsummer, over tufts of spatulate leaves. *I. ensifolia* (swordleaf inula) forms dense, rounded clumps 1 foot tall and wide of wiry erect stems lined with narrow 4-inch pointed leaves and tipped with 1- to 2-inch yellow flowers. The blooms last 2 to 3 weeks in warmer zones, up to 6 weeks in cooler areas.

IRONWEED
Vernonia

Light: mostly sun	
Plant type: perennial	
Hardiness: Zones 4-9	
Height: 4 to 8 feet	
Soil and Moisture: well-drained, moist to wet	
Interest: flowers	
Care: easy	

◀ Vernonia
noveboracensis

Ironweeds are tall, vigorous perennials native to moist meadows and prairies in the eastern half of the United States. Their loosely branched terminal clusters of purple flowers are effective in the back of a wildflower border or in a meadow garden.

Growing and care:
Ironweeds thrive in rich to average moist soil. *V. altissima* grows equally well in marshes and other wet sites. *V. noveboracensis* will tolerate wet soil. Ironweeds have sturdy stems that rarely require staking. Propagate by seed, cuttings, or division.

Selected species and varieties:
V. altissima (tall ironweed) grows 5 to 8 feet tall with ½-inch reddish purple flower heads in clusters of 30 to 40 from late summer through midautumn. The lance-shaped dark green leaves are up to 1 foot long; native from New York south to Louisiana and west to Nebraska. *V. noveboracensis* (New York ironweed) grows 4 to 6 feet tall with clusters of as many as 50 frilly purple flower heads in late summer; native to southern New England, the mid-Atlantic states, and the Southeast; Zones 5-8.

JACOB'S-LADDER
Polemonium

Light: mostly sun

Plant type: perennial

Hardiness: Zones 2-9

Height: 4 inches to 3 feet

Soil and Moisture: well-drained, moist, fertile

Interest: flowers, foliage

Care: easy

◀ Polemonium viscosum

Jacob's-ladder is native to meadows, open woodlands, and stream banks. Its dark green compound leaves provide an attractive foil for its upward-facing cup-shaped flowers.

Growing and care:

P. viscosum grows in full sun and well-drained rocky soil. The other species prefer partial shade and moist soil; for P. reptans, provide ample organic matter. Propagate by seed or division in spring.

Selected species and varieties:

P. carneum (royal polemonium) grows 1 to 2 feet tall with clusters of purple, pink, or salmon flowers 1½ inches across from spring through summer; California and Oregon; Zones 7-9. P. occidentale [also called P. caeruleum ssp. amygdalinum] (western polemonium) grows to 3 feet with clusters of pale blue summer flowers; Alaska to Colorado; Zones 3-9. P. reptans (creeping polemonium) reaches to 2 feet with large clusters of blue or pink flowers from spring to summer; eastern United States. P. viscosum (sky pilot) grows 4 to 20 inches tall with light blue or white flower clusters in spring and summer; western mountains; Zones 3-7.

JUPITER'S-BEARD
Centranthus

Light: mostly sun

Plant type: perennial

Hardiness: Zones 4-9

Height: 1 to 3 feet

Soil and Moisture: well-drained, fertile, moist

Interest: flowers

Care: easy

◀ Centranthus ruber

Jupiter's-beard is a robust, vigorous plant with strong upright stems amid dense, round flower clusters in summer. The lance-shaped bluish green leaves accent the handsome wine red flowers. Jupiter's-beard is a good choice for the back of the border or planted in masses in woodland gardens. The plants are also popular cut flowers in fresh floral arrangements.

Growing and care:

Plant Jupiter's-beard in well-worked soil with plentiful organic matter and a pH near neutral. Space plants 1 to 1½ feet apart. Fertile soil results in larger growth. Cut back stems after flowering is completed to encourage rebloom. Trim to ground level in fall. Propagate by transplanting self-sown seedlings. Established plantings do not transplant well and should not be disturbed.

Selected species and varieties:

C. ruber forms bushy plants to 3 feet tall with fragrant ½-inch spurred flowers in rounded terminal clusters above paired blue-green leaves; 'Albus' has white flowers; 'Atrococcineus', deep red flowers; 'Coccineus', scarlet flowers.

LILY-OF-THE-NILE
Agapanthus

Light: mostly sun

Plant type: perennial

Hardiness: Zones 8-10

Height: 3 to 5 feet

Soil and Moisture: well-drained, moist

Interest: flowers, foliage

Care: easy

◀ Agapanthus africanus

Lily-of-the-Nile is an easy-to-grow plant with long, narrow, glossy green leaves and stout stems bearing open clusters of lilac-blue blossoms in summer. The plants are gorgeous when planted in masses or in borders in warm regions. In colder areas lily-of-the-Nile is a reliable container plant that graces the deck or patio in summer and the living room in winter.

Growing and care:
Plant *Agapanthus* 2 feet apart and water well during the growing season. In containers set plants in rich soil well amended with organic matter. Plants tolerate dryness while dormant in winter. Do not repot too often, as plants bloom best when slightly potbound. Cut stems back after flowering. Propagate by dividing every 4 to 5 years in spring.

Selected species and varieties:
A. africanus bears up to 30 eye-catching deep blue blossoms on 3-foot stems; leaves are 4 to 10 inches long. *A. orientalis* grows 5 feet tall with up to 100 blue flowers in each cluster; 'Albidus' has white flowers; the leaves of 'Variegatus' are striped white.

LOOSESTRIFE
Lysimachia

Light: mostly sun

Plant type: perennial

Hardiness: Zones 4-8

Height: 2 inches to 3 feet

Soil and Moisture: well-drained, fertile, moist

Interest: flowers, foliage

Care: easy

◀ L. nummularia 'Buttercup'

Loosestrifes have neat, very attractive blossoms that add a warm, pleasant touch to gardens. Flowers bloom singly or in small spikes amid attractive foliage. Loosestrife is native to moist prairies and stream banks, and can be planted near a garden pond or at the edge of a moist woodland, where its flowers present a fine summer display. However, in moist soil it may spread too rapidly and take over the garden. Gooseneck loosestrife flowers are excellent for fresh arrangements.

Growing and care:
Space plants 1 to 2 feet apart in well-worked soil amended with some organic matter. Loosestrife will need frequent division in spring or fall to contain its growth if planted in a border. Propagate by seed or division in spring.

Selected species and varieties:
L. clethroides (gooseneck loosestrife) grows to 3 feet tall with an erect habit, rich green leaves that turn bronze to yellow in fall, and 3- to 6-inch-long gracefully arching white flower spikes from mid- to late summer that resemble a goose's neck. *L. nummularia* (creeping Jenny) is a 2- to 4-inch creeper with yellow flowers in late spring; 'Buttercup' has intense sunny yellow flowers atop dark green leaves. *L. punctata* (yellow loosestrife) grows 1½ to 2½ feet tall with lemon yellow summer blooms.

791

LUPINE
Lupinus

Light: mostly sun	
Plant type: perennial	
Hardiness: Zones 4-6	
Height: 1½ to 4 feet	
Soil and Moisture: well-drained, moist	
Interest: flowers, foliage	
Care: moderate	

◀ Lupinus
'Russell Hybrids'

Lupines bear stout, elongated spikes of small, densely packed butterfly-shaped flowers in a wide array of bright colors. The long-lasting blossoms cover the tips of stiff stalks lined with whorls of narrow leaves that dramatically embellish the flower border. Lupines are most effective massed into large groups in meadows or wildflower gardens, or mixed into the perennial border.

Growing and care:

Plant lupines in acidic soil enriched with rotted manure or compost. Space plants 1½ to 2 feet apart. Provide a little afternoon shade and water regularly. Mulch plants in spring to keep roots cool. Plants may require staking. Propagate from seed or from root cuttings taken with a small piece of crown in early spring.

Selected species and varieties:

L. 'Russell Hybrids' is a large group of plants to 4 feet tall with showy 1½- to 2-foot-long summer-blooming flower spires that open from the bottom up in a multitude of colors and combinations; dwarf strains 1½ feet tall include 'Little Lulu' and 'Minarette'.

MALLOW
Hibiscus

Light: mostly sun	
Plant type: perennial	
Hardiness: Zones 5-9	
Height: 3 to 8 feet	
Soil and Moisture: well-drained, moist to wet	
Interest: flowers	
Care: easy	

◀ Hibiscus coccineus

Mallows thrive in wet meadows and along the banks of streams and ponds, lending color and form to these moist areas. The plants bear white, pink, rose, or purple bell-shaped flowers in summer on tall, pliant stems reaching to 8 feet high. Mallows grow well in the moist soils of perennial beds as well as accenting natural plantings near water.

Growing and care:

Plant mallows in a moist spot where they will receive some high-afternoon shade. Allow plenty of room between plants, which may spread to 5 feet in width. The plants are vigorous, and once established need little attention. Propagate by seed or early-summer cuttings.

Selected species and varieties:

H. coccineus (wild red mallow) grows 4 to 7 feet tall with blue-green leaves and scarlet flowers 6 inches across; Zones 7-9. *H. grandiflorus* (great rose mallow) grows up to 6 feet tall and bears pale pink to purplish rose flowers, sometimes with crimson centers. *H. lasiocarpus* (woolly mallow) grows 3 to 5 feet tall with terminal clusters of 5- to 8-inch pink or white flowers that sometimes have purple centers. *H. moscheutos* (swamp rose mallow, wild cotton) grows 3 to 8 feet tall with a shrubby habit gray-green leaves, and white, pink, or rose flowers 8 inches across, often with red or purple centers; Zones 6-9.

MARSHALLIA
Marshallia

Light: mostly sun

Plant type: perennial

Hardiness: Zones 5-9

Height: 8 inches to 2 feet

Soil and Moisture: well-drained, moist to dry, sandy

Interest: flowers

Care: easy

◀ Marshallia grandiflora

Marshallia is a clump-forming perennial with buttonlike flowers and a tidy form, making them suitable for planting at the front of a mixed border, along a garden walk, or among stones in a rock garden, terrace, or in a moist meadow. These beautiful wildflowers bear rounded clusters of small rose pink flowers from spring to summer on graceful, slender 1- to 2-foot stems.

Growing and care:
Marshallias grow well in either moist or dry soils as long as drainage is excellent. Plant in spring or fall in soil well amended with rotted manure or compost. In areas that stay wet, dig the planting hole twice as deep as needed and fill halfway with peastone. Propagate by seed or division.

Selected species and varieties:
M. caespitosa (Barbara's buttons) bears ball-shaped clusters of dainty, fragrant white flowers on leafless stalks 8 to 18 inches tall above a rosette of narrow leaves. *M. grandiflora* (large-flowered marshallia) has large, densely packed balls of rose pink flowers with purple stamens on 1- to 2-foot stalks above a dense rosette of glossy dark green oval leaves.

MEADOW BEAUTY
Rhexia

Light: mostly sun

Plant type: perennial

Hardiness: Zones 4-9

Height: 1 to 2 feet

Soil and Moisture: well-drained to heavy, wet to moist

Interest: flowers

Care: easy

◀ Rhexia mariana

Meadow beauties are dainty perennials that bear small, distinctive pinkish flowers from early to late summer. The plants thrive in boggy soils and are native to wetlands and moist meadows in the eastern United States. The individual blossoms are uniquely shaped with pink to white slightly reflexed petals highlighted by slender central filaments that look like the protruding legs of a wayward insect. Meadow beauties are excellent for wet sites and water gardens.

Growing and care:
Meadow beauties thrive in boggy soil or in rich, sandy garden soil as long as moisture is abundant. They prefer full sun but tolerate light shade. *Rhexia* spreads by rhizomes to form colonies. Propagate by seed or by dividing the rhizomes.

Selected species and varieties:
R. mariana (Maryland meadow beauty) grows to 2 feet with loose clusters of white, pink, or pale rose flowers 2 inches across with bright yellow stamens. *R. virginica* (Virginia meadow beauty) grows 1 to 2 feet in height with deep magenta petaled flowers 1½ inches across with golden yellow stamens and bright green foliage; Zones 5-9.

MEADOWSWEET
Filipendula

Light: mostly sun

Plant type: perennial

Hardiness: Zones 3-8

Height: 1 to 8 feet

Soil and Moisture: well-drained, moist

Interest: flowers, foliage

Care: easy to moderate

◀ Filipendula rubra 'Venusta'

Meadowsweets have long-lasting feathery plumes of midsummer flowers that rise above thick clumps of reddish green compound leaves. These tall, stately plants are especially striking when massed at the back of borders, or naturalized in meadows or fields.

Growing and care:

Meadowsweets benefit from additions of compost and organic mulch in spring. Plant in spring or fall, spacing plants 1 to 2 feet apart. Add a thin layer of mulch again in fall. Divide clumps every 3 to 4 years in spring by cutting the rhizome that connects the main clump to the new shoots. Plant the divisions about 2 inches deep. Cut foliage to the ground in late summer or early fall when the leaves begin to turn brown.

Selected species and varieties:

F. palmata bears large clusters of small pink flowers fading to snowy white on 2- to 3-foot stems with dark green leaves with pale undersides; 'Rubra' has dark red flowers. *F. rubra* (queen-of-the-prairie) has clusters of very ornamental pink flowers on sturdy 4- to 8-foot stems; 'Venusta' has plumes of rosy pink flowers on 6-foot stems. *F. ulmaria* (queen-of-the-meadow) bears creamy white flower clusters in summer on 3- to 6-foot stems bearing large compound leaves; 'Variegata' has leaves marked with a prominent yellow stripe.

PEONY
Paeonia

Light: mostly sun

Plant type: perennial

Hardiness: Zones 3-8

Height: 1½ to 3 feet

Soil and Moisture: well-drained, moist, fertile

Interest: flowers

Care: easy to moderate

◀ Paeonia lactiflora

Peonies are classic garden plants renowned for their large, regal blossoms and attractive mounds of deeply cut foliage. Stately and dramatic in the garden, peonies are also stunning in bouquets. This large, diverse group of plants is classified by form. Single-flowered peonies have a single row of five or more petals surrounding a center of bright yellow stamens. Japanese and anemone peonies have a single row of petals surrounding modified stamens that resemble finely cut petals. Semidouble peonies have several rows of petals surrounding conspicuous stamens. Double-flowered peonies have multiple rows of petals crowded into ruffly hemispheres. Peonies add a touch of class to borders and specialty gardens and make exceptional displays when planted as a low hedge or edging or grouped in a mass display.

Growing and care:

Plant peonies 3 feet apart in soil containing some organic matter other than manure. Set the buds (eyes) 2 inches below the soil surface; setting them deeper delays flowering and reduces vigor. Fertilize lightly in spring as leaves are emerging and again after blossoms have faded. Cut back stems to ground level in fall. Propagate by dividing clumps into sections containing three to five eyes each in late summer or early fall every 10 years.

(continued)

Selected species and varieties:

P. lactiflora (garden or Chinese peony) bears white, pink, or red flowers on 3-foot stems. *P. mlokosewitschii* (Caucasian peony) has very early-blooming, 2-inch single lemon yellow flowers on 2-foot-tall stems with soft gray-green foliage. *P. officinalis* (common peony) comes in hundreds of varieties with 3- to 6-inch blooms in various forms and colors ranging from red to light pink to white on 2-foot stems. *P. tenuifolia* (fern-leaf peony) bears single deep red flowers and finely divided fernlike leaves on 1½- to 2-foot stems; 'Flore Pleno' has double flowers. Hundreds of peony hybrids are available: 'Lobata' (red-pink), 'Krinkled White' and 'Lotus Bloom' (pink) are outstanding singles; 'Isani-Gidui' (white) and 'Nippon Beauty' (dark red) are lovely Japanese types; 'Gay Paree' (pink with white-blush center) grows anemone-type blossoms; semidouble varieties include 'Lowell Thomas' (deep red) and 'Ludovica' (salmon-pink); among the double-flowered varieties 'Festiva Maxima' (white with red marking), 'Karl Rosenfeld' (deep red), 'Mons. Jules Elie' (early pink), 'Nick Shaylor' (blush pink), and 'Red Charm' (deep true red, early blooming) are all exceptional.

PICKERELWEED
Pontederia

◄ *Pontederia cordata*

Light: mostly sun	
Plant type: perennial	
Hardiness: Zones 4-9	
Height: 1 to 4 feet	
Soil and Moisture: wet to water-covered	
Interest: flowers, foliage	
Care: easy	

Pickerelweed is an aquatic perennial that grows wild in shallow freshwater ponds, streams, and marshes in the eastern half of the United States. Its vivid lavender flowers, long blooming season, and attractive dark green foliage make it a good choice for bog and water gardens or naturalized along the banks of ponds, lakes, or slow-moving streams.

Growing and care:

Pickerelweed will grow in wet boggy soil, but it performs best when its roots are completely covered by several inches of water. When setting out new plants, use stones or pebbles to hold them in place until their roots are established. In the case of a small garden pool, plant pickerelweed in a large pot or shallow wooden flat. Propagate by division in summer.

Selected species and varieties:

P. cordata has spikes of pastel blue-purple funnel-shaped flowers held 1 to 2 feet above the water's surface on sturdy stems from early summer through fall. Dark green heart-shaped leaves up to 10 inches long and 6 inches wide rise 2 to 4 feet above the surface on long stems.

PITCHER PLANT
Sarracenia

Light: mostly sun

Plant type: perennial

Hardiness: Zones 2-10

Height: 8 inches to 4 feet

Soil and Moisture: organic, wet

Interest: flowers, foliage

Care: moderate

◀ Sarracenia leucophylla

Excellent for bog gardens, pitcher plants are valued for their striking upright trumpets of tightly furled leaves as well as for their handsome umbrella-shaped chocolate-colored flowers borne on tall leafless stems. Insects trapped in the water-filled trumpets are slowly dissolved by acids released by the plants, and the freed nutrients are then absorbed by the plants—a little gruesome, but effective. Pitcher plants thrive in peaty wet soils.

Growing and care:
Pitcher plants thrive in wet sandy soil or peat bogs and require constant moisture. Propagate by seed sown immediately after collection or by division.

Selected species and varieties:
S. flava (yellow pitcher plant, trumpet pitcher plant) bears a trumpets of yellowish green red-veined leaves up to 4 feet tall and drooping yellow flowers up to 4 inches across; Zones 6-7. *S. leucophylla* (crimson pitcher plant) bears a red-veined trumpets 2 to 4 feet tall and dark red flowers 3 to 4 inches across; Zones 8-10. *S. purpurea* (northern pitcher plant) has a bronze-green trumpets 8 to 18 inches tall and solitary 2-inch maroon-purple flowers.

PLUMBAGO
Ceratostigma

Light: mostly sun

Plant type: perennial

Hardiness: Zones 5-10

Height: 8 to 12 inches

Soil and Moisture: well-drained, moist

Interest: flowers, foliage

Care: easy

◀ Ceratostigma plumbaginoides

Plumbago's brilliant blue 1-inch-long slightly flattened flowers are borne in profusion on reddish stems from late summer to frost. The plant makes an effective, fast-spreading semievergreen ground cover or low shrubby perennial. Its glossy green oval leaves turn bronzy red in fall.

Growing and care:
Divide plants every 4 years in spring, spacing them 1 to 2 feet apart in soil amended with peat moss and compost. Mulch young plants in late spring, and water regularly. In Zones 5 and 6, cover with pine boughs in winter. Plumbago benefits from yearly additions of compost and light fertilizing in spring.

Selected species and varieties:
C. plumbaginoides (dwarf plumbago) has intensely blue, five-lobed tubular 1/2-inch flowers in dense clusters above tufts of 3-inch-long glossy semievergreen leaves on 8- to 12-inch zigzag stems that turn bronzy red in winter in cold regions. *C. willmottianum* (Chinese plumbago) bears 4-foot multibranched woody stems with vibrant blue flowers from late summer to fall, and bright green leaves that turn red in late fall; Zones 8-10.

POPPY
Papaver

Light: mostly to full sun

Plant type: perennial

Hardiness: Zones 3-9

Height: 1 to 4 feet

Soil and Moisture: well-drained, moist

Interest: flowers

Care: moderate to difficult

◀ Papaver orientale

Stately plants, poppies have large, brilliantly colored silky-textured blossoms that are mesmerizing in the garden. The flowers are held at the ends of strong wiry stems above finely cut hairy leaves. Poppies add vivid accents to borders and specialty gardens, where their bold presence is impossible to overlook.

Growing and care:
Poppies grow well in mostly sun or full sun as long as the soil is kept moist. Space poppies 1½ feet apart. Water regularly during the growing season but do not fertilize. Once established the plants should not be disturbed. If plants must be moved, transplant carefully when fully dormant. Propagate Oriental poppies, which are tough, long-lived plants, from seed or from root cuttings. Grow Iceland poppies from seed to flower in their first year; sow in late summer in the North and in fall in southern climates.

Selected species and varieties:
P. nudicaule (Iceland poppy) bears fragrant flowers up to 3 inches across on 1- to 2-foot stems. *P. orientale* (Oriental poppy) has blossoms up to 8 inches across composed of tissue-thin petals on wiry stems rising from mounds of coarse, hairy leaves; 'Beauty of Livermore' has deep red petals spotted black at the base; 'Glowing Embers' has orange-red ruffled petals; 'Mrs. Perry', clear pink flowers; 'Princess Victoria Louise', bright salmon-pink flowers.

PRAIRIE CONEFLOWER
Ratibida

Light: mostly to full sun

Plant type: perennial

Hardiness: Zones 3-9

Height: 2 to 5 feet

Soil and Moisture: well-drained, moist to dry

Interest: flowers

Care: easy

◀ Ratibida columnifera

Prairie coneflowers are sturdy, tough perennials with brightly colored daisylike summer flowers in shades of yellow and red that add a civilized yet wild touch to gardens and landscapes. The tall, pliant stems rise from a rosette of hairy green leaves and sport long-lasting flowers that look as good in a vase on the dining room table as in a perennial border.

Growing and care:
Coneflowers thrive in well-drained soil that has some organic matter. They do well in sun or mostly sun, and once established the plants are very drought tolerant and flower well even during hot, dry summers. Coneflowers often self-sow freely; they should be controlled in beds and borders, but allowed to spread in natural plantings. Propagate by seed.

Selected species and varieties:
R. columnifera (Mexican hat) has branching stems 1½ to 3 feet tall bearing daisylike flowers with drooping yellow, red, or bicolored notched petals surrounding an elongated purplish brown cylindrical cone that rises as much as 2 inches above the petals; it is native to prairies and waste areas from the central United States to British Columbia. *R. pinnata* (gray-headed coneflower) grows 3 to 5 feet tall with long-stalked flowers composed of yellow petals surrounding a grayish brown cone; Zones 3-8.

ROSINWEED
Silphium

Light: mostly to full sun

Plant type: perennial

Hardiness: Zones 3-9

Height: 2 to 12 feet

Soil and Moisture: well-drained, moist

Interest: flowers, foliage

Care: easy

◀ Silphium perfoliatum

Rosinweeds are handsome plants native to prairies and woodland openings of eastern and central North America, with small, pure yellow sunflower-like heads from summer to fall held far above clumps of interesting foliage. Their bold foliage accents the backs of borders. Interplant with ornamental grasses, or naturalize in meadows. The lower leaves of *S. laciniatum* point north and south to avoid the heat of the noonday sun, giving the plant its common name of compass plant.

Growing and care:
Rosinweeds require a lot of space to grow, so plant them 1 to 2 feet apart in sites where they will not dwarf other plants. Propagate by seed, since the roots of these plants can be massive. Seeds require several months of chilling at 40°F before germinating, and benefit from having their hard coats nicked with a sharp knife before being planted ⅓ to ½ inch deep. It takes 2 to 3 years for seedlings to reach flowering size. Plants do well in sun or mostly sun.

Selected species and varieties:
S. laciniatum (compass plant) has 3- to 12-foot rough stems with 1- to 2-foot deeply pointed leaves and showy clusters of 5-inch flower heads. *S. perfoliatum* (cup plant) has 3- to 8-foot hairy stems clasping pairs of 6- to 12-inch leaves joined at the base to form a cup, and small clusters of 3-inch flowers.

SANDWORT
Arenaria

Light: mostly to full sun

Plant type: perennial

Hardiness: Zones 5-9

Height: 2 inches to 1½ feet

Soil and Moisture: well-drained, moist to dry

Interest: flowers, foliage

Care: easy

◀ Arenaria montana

Sandwort is one of the easiest perennials to grow, quickly forming mats of small, feathery evergreen foliage liberally sprinkled with tiny white flowers in spring. This low, spreading perennial is ideal for growing in wall crevices and between pavers. Sandwort is so vigorous it can easily become a weed in beds and borders if not confined.

Growing and care:
Sow seed indoors 6 to 8 weeks before last frost or directly in the garden in early spring when soil is workable but cool. Do not cover seed, as light is needed for germination. Plant sandworts 6 to 12 inches apart. Water well during dry spells in the growing season and fertilize lightly for fastest growth and abundant flowering. Sandwort does well in sun or mostly sun. Propagate by division in late summer or early fall.

Selected species and varieties:
A. montana has trailing stems up to 1 foot long topped by 1-inch white flowers with yellow centers. *A. verna* (Irish moss) has narrow mosslike leaves and very small star-shaped white flowers in dainty 2-inch clumps that withstand heavy foot traffic.

SPEEDWELL
Veronica

Light: mostly to full sun

Plant type: perennial

Hardiness: Zones 4-8

Height: 1 to 2 feet

Soil and Moisture: well-drained, moist

Interest: flowers, foliage

Care: easy

◄ Veronica spicata 'Rosea'

Speedwells form bold upright clumps of spreading stems lined with narrow soft-textured leaves and tipped with spikes of tiny flowers densely packed into tapered conical spires from spring to summer. They fit well into rock gardens and are a good choice for edging, as a filler, or for naturalizing in shady informal gardens.

Growing and care:
Space plants 1 to 2 feet apart. Speedwells will flower best in full sun where moisture is abundant. Deadhead withering flower spikes to encourage an extended season of bloom. Propagate by seed, cuttings, or by division in spring or fall. Taller types may need support. Plants do well in mostly sun to full sun.

Selected species and varieties:
V. austriaca ssp. *teucrium* (Austrian speedwell) grows to 2 feet tall with ½-inch deep blue flowers from late spring to early summer and deeply cut leaves; 'Crater Lake Blue' has many flower spikes crowded in early summer with large, brilliant blue blossoms above compact mounds of dark green foliage. *V. incana* (silver speedwell, woolly speedwell) grows 1 foot tall with pale lilac-blue flowers in early summer and 6-inch-tall mats of woolly, silvery gray foliage. *V. spicata* (spike speedwell) is 1½ feet tall with lavender-blue to pink flowers from late spring to midsummer; 'Rosea' has tall spikes of rose red flowers.

TANSY
Tanacetum

Light: mostly to full sun

Plant type: perennial

Hardiness: Zones 3-9

Height: 2 to 5 feet

Soil and Moisture: well-drained, moist to dry

Interest: flowers, foliage

Care: easy

◄ Tanacetum vulgare

Tansy has been grown in American gardens since colonial times, when it was planted near the entrances of homes to repel insects. Its aromatic fernlike foliage provides lush contrast to colorful flowering plants grown nearby. Clusters of golden yellow button-shaped flowers appear in late summer and brighten the backs of borders. Tansy leaves can be used in fresh or dried arrangements, and frequently are used in potpourris.

Growing and care:
Tansy grows particularly well in a moist loamy soil. Because it is aggressive and somewhat invasive, poorer soil may be desirable; otherwise, its growth may need to be restricted by planting it in a bottomless container. Plants may require staking, especially in windy locations. Tansy also self-sows, but this can be avoided by removing flowers as they develop. Space plants 1 to 2 feet apart. Tansy grows well in mostly sun or full sun.

Selected species and varieties:
T. vulgare has 2- to 5-foot-tall stems with pungently scented, deeply cut 4-inch-wide lacy leaves each and clusters of ¼-inch petal-less flowers appearing from mid- to late summer, followed by flat-topped seed heads that persist throughout winter; var. *crispum* (fernleaf tansy) grows 2 to 3 feet tall, produces lush, wavy, rich green leaves that are more finely dissected than the species, and is valued for indoor arrangements.

TRANSVAAL DAISY
Gerbera

Light: mostly sun

Plant type: perennial

Hardiness: Zones 8-10

Height: 1 to 1½ feet

Soil and Moisture: well-drained, moderately moist

Interest: flowers

Care: moderate to difficult

◀ Gerbera jamesonii

Transvaal daisies produce spectacular 4-inch daisylike flowers on stout, sturdy stems, providing a fine display in the garden, in containers, or as cut flowers for indoor arrangements. Although they are hardy only to Zone 8, in cooler areas they can be planted as annuals or dug up in fall and planted in containers to grow indoors as houseplants. The blossoms come in a wide range of clear pastel shades that complement most other colors.

Growing and care:

Plant Transvaal daisies in soil that has been amended with organic matter. The plants are very susceptible to disease in soil that is kept too moist, but are not tolerant of dry conditions, either. Water deeply, allowing soil to dry before watering again. For massing, space plants 2 feet apart. Protect plants over winter in Zone 8 with a nonmatting mulch.

Selected species and varieties:

G. jamesonii has deeply lobed gray-green leaves 5 to 10 inches long growing in the form of a basal rosette, erect flower stems 1 to 1½ feet tall, and flowers 2 to 4 inches across with strap-shaped petals in yellow, salmon, cream, pink, rose, or red.

VERBENA
Verbena

Light: mostly sun

Plant type: perennial

Hardiness: Zones 3-10

Height: 8 inches to 5 feet

Soil and Moisture: well-drained, fertile, moist to dry

Interest: flowers, foliage

Care: easy

◀ Verbena stricta

The perennial verbenas are native to meadows, prairies, and open woods. They feature small brightly colored flowers arranged in terminal spiked clusters of white, lavender, rose, or purple. The leaves of *Verbena stricta* have a soft gray-green appearance underneath the plant's downy cover. The flowers of this species grow in 6-inch-long slender purple spikes that bloom from June to September.

Growing and care:

Plant verbena in spring in well-worked soil that has some organic matter. Once established the plants are drought tolerant and thrive in sunny locations. Fertilize in spring and prune lightly after flowering. Propagate by seed.

Selected species and varieties:

V. canadensis (rose verbena) produces fragrant ¾-inch pink flowers in rounded clusters in summer and fall on a mat of creeping stems 8 to 12 inches tall and 3 feet across; native from the Southeast to Colorado; Zones 6-10. *V. hastata* (blue verbena) reaches heights of 2 to 5 feet with spikes of blue-purple flowers in late spring and summer; widely found in moist sites in the United States and Canada; Zones 4-10. *V. stricta* (woolly verbena, hoary vervain) matures at 1 to 4 feet tall with dense 1-foot spikes of blue to violet flowers in summer and fall and large woolly leaves; it is found from Ontario south to Texas and west to Idaho.

WATER LILY
Nymphaea

Light: mostly to full sun

Plant type: perennial

Hardiness: Zones 2-10

Height: 2 to 4 inches above water

Soil and Moisture: shallow water

Interest: flowers, foliage

Care: moderate

◀ Nymphaea odorata

The sweetly scented, sophisticated flowers of these hardy aquatic perennials grace ponds, lakes, and slow-moving streams over much of the eastern and central United States. The blossoms, each of which lasts for about 3 days, float upright on the surface of the water, surrounded by a sea of dark green lily pads. The lotus-shaped flowers close at night and on cloudy days.

Growing and care:

Plant water lily rhizomes 3 to 4 inches deep in pots or shallow wooden flats containing clayey soil and cover the soil surface with 2 inches of fine gravel. Submerge the containers in up to 4 feet of water. In far northern regions remove the containers from the water in fall and store indoors in a cool location over winter. Propagate by dividing the rhizomes. Grows well in mostly sun or full sun.

Selected species and varieties:

N. odorata (water lily, pond lily) bears white or pink flowers 3 to 5 inches across with numerous gold stamens from mid- to late summer. Flat 4- to 12-inch leaves are glossy green on the upper surface, reddish below, and float on the surface of the water.

ZINNIA
Zinnia

Light: mostly to full sun

Plant type: perennial

Hardiness: Zones 4-10

Height: 6 to 8 inches

Soil and Moisture: well-drained, medium to dry

Interest: flowers

Care: easy

◀ Zinnia grandiflora

Most gardeners are familiar only with annual zinnias. The two perennial species described here are native to the central and southwestern United States, where they are commonly found along roadsides and on dry slopes. Both of these wildflowers bloom profusely for months and are attractive in rock gardens and on dry banks, where they help control erosion.

Growing and care:

Perennial zinnias require average, well-drained, medium to dry soil and are very tolerant of drought and heat. Zinnias grow well in mostly sun to full sun. Fertilize lightly just before flower buds appear. Sow seed directly in the garden after danger of frost has passed, or in fall. Young plants can also be divided in spring.

Selected species and varieties:

Z. acerosa (dwarf white zinnia) is a multibranched, shrubby plant 6 inches tall with ¾-inch white flowers with yellow centers and narrow, silvery leaves less than an inch long; Zones 8-10. *Z. grandiflora* (little golden zinnia, prairie zinnia, Rocky Mountain zinnia) has 1½-inch yellow flowers with red or green centers on an 8-inch mound of needlelike, nearly evergreen foliage.

ALPINE HYACINTH
Brimeura

Light: mostly sun

Plant type: bulb

Hardiness: Zones 4-10

Height: 6 to 12 inches

Soil and Moisture: well-drained, moist

Interest: flowers

Care: easy

◀ Brimeura amethystina

Alpine hyacinths are easy-to-grow spring flowers with glossy clumps of narrow leaves and showy spikes of nodding blue flower bells. The plants resemble *Hyacinthus* in shape and form but bloom later in spring. These dainty plants easily naturalize in most soils and climates, making great additions to borders, rock gardens, or wildflower meadows. The bulbs can also be planted in containers and forced indoors to brighten up late-winter days.

Growing and care:
Plant alpine hyacinths in fall, setting bulbs 1 to 2 inches deep and 4 to 5 inches apart. Fertilize at planting time with an organic fertilizer and again as flower shoots are emerging. These small bulbs make the best show when planted close together and left to multiply on their own. Save bulbs forced as potted plants to set out in the garden in fall. Propagate by removing and replanting the small bulblets that form alongside parent bulbs.

Selected species and varieties:
B. amethystina [formerly *Hyacinthus amethystinus* and *Scilla amethystina*] bears up to 15 tiny ½-inch blue bells lining one side of the stalks in spring; 'Alba' yields pure white flower bells.

AUTUMN CROCUS
Colchicum

Light: mostly sun

Plant type: bulb

Hardiness: Zones 4-9

Height: 8 to 12 inches

Soil and Moisture: well-drained, fertile, moist

Interest: flowers

Care: easy

◀ Colchicum speciosum

Autumn crocus is a lovely fall plant with several leaf-less stems topped with showy pink, purple, or red flowers. The strap-shaped foliage appears in late winter or early spring, and disappears in late summer a few weeks before the cupped, star-shaped flowers appear. Autumn crocus is excellent for naturalizing in meadows or as an addition to borders or rock gardens. The bulbs can also be planted in containers and forced indoors.

Growing and care:
Plant in summer, setting corms 3 to 4 inches deep and 6 to 9 inches apart in loose soil. *C. autumnale* thrives in mostly sunny spots with evenly moist soil. Propagate from cormlets that form at the base of mature corms. If the plant is naturalized in a meadow or field, be careful not to mow while foliage or flowers remain above ground.

Selected species and varieties:
C. autumnale bears 4-inch white, pink, or purple flowers on 8-inch stems; 'Alboplenum' has pure white double flowers; 'Plenum' has lilac-pink double flowers. *C. speciosum* (showy autumn crocus) has 4- to 8-inch rose to purple flowers with white throats on 8- to 12-inch stems; 'Atrorubens' has dark red flowers; 'Waterlily' has large, bright pink double-petaled flowers on 10-inch stems, and makes an excellent cut flower.

BLACKBERRY LILY
Belamcanda

Light: mostly sun	
Plant type: bulb	
Hardiness: Zones 5-10	
Height: 1 to 4 feet	
Soil and Moisture: well-drained, moist	
Interest: flowers, fruit	
Care: easy	

◀ Belamcanda chinensis

Blackberry lilies carry cheerful sprays of flat, star-shaped flowers with narrow, pointed petals on zigzag-branching flower stalks above fans of swordlike leaves. Each flower lasts only a day, but new blossoms open over several weeks. Flowers are followed by attractive seedpods that burst open to reveal shiny, black, berrylike seeds. Use blackberry lilies in the midground of a sunny border or as cut flowers. Dried seedpods decorate the winter garden and can be used in dried arrangements.

Growing and care:
Plant blackberry lilies in spring or fall, setting rhizomes 1 inch deep and 6 to 8 inches apart. They grow best in moist, fertile soil well amended with organic matter. Plants grown in dry soil are shorter with slightly smaller flowers. Propagate by division in spring or fall. Blackberry lilies often self-sow, producing flowers in 2 years.

Selected species and varieties:
B. chinensis has 2-inch orange flowers with pointed, curving petals spotted with red on 2- to 4-foot stalks. *B. flabellata* bears light yellow flowers.

BLOOD LILY
Haemanthus

Light: mostly sun	
Plant type: bulb	
Hardiness: Zones 9-10	
Height: 1 to 1½ feet	
Soil and Moisture: well-drained, moist	
Interest: flowers, fragrance	
Care: moderate	

◀ Haemanthus katherinae

Blood lilies give the garden an infusion of summer color with starburst blossoms collected into airy clumps. The clusters of tubular flowers are decorated with colorful protruding stamens cradled within broad, petal-like bracts atop stout, leafless stems. In warm regions the plants add an interesting accent to borders. In cooler areas blood lilies are excellent container plants that brighten patios and decks.

Growing and care:
Plant blood lilies 6 to 8 inches apart outdoors or in pots, with the tip of the bulb at the soil surface. Start potted lilies in spring, then lift and dry the bulbs before storing over winter. Propagate from seed or from bulb offsets.

Selected species and varieties:
H. albiflos 'White Paintbrush' has 2-inch flower clusters with yellow-orange stamens within greenish white bracts on 1- to 1½-inch stems. *H. coccineus* (Cape tulip) has 3-inch clusters of 1-inch flowers with golden stamens within red bracts on 1-foot stems. *H. katherinae* [also known as *Scadoxus multiflorus* ssp. *katherinae*] (Catherine-wheel) produces more than 200 small 2½-inch pink-red flowers in 9-inch globes on 1½-foot stems. *H. multiflorus* (salmon blood lily) bears up to 200 inch-long coral red flowers with spiky stamens in 3- to 6-inch spheres on 1½-foot stems.

BULBOCODIUM
Bulbocodium

Light: mostly sun	
Plant type: bulb	
Hardiness: Zones 3-10	
Height: 4 inches	
Soil and Moisture: well-drained, sandy, moist	
Interest: flowers	
Care: easy	

◄ Bulbocodium vernum

One of the earliest flowers to brighten the spring garden, bulbocodium sends up delicate sprays of rose-violet blossoms that open into upright trumpets of narrow, ribbonlike petals. The narrow, grassy leaves appear after the flowers bloom. The plant will naturalize in a border, rock garden, or wildflower meadow, providing years of care-free beauty.

Growing and care:
Plant in late summer or fall, spacing corms 3 to 4 inches apart and setting them 3 inches deep in well-worked soil amended with organic matter. Locations that provide moisture in spring when bulbs are blooming and foliage is maturing but are slightly dry in summer are ideal. Propagate after the grassy leaves die back in early summer by removing and replanting the small cormels that grow at the base of each corm every 3 to 4 years.

Selected species and varieties:
B. vernum (spring meadow saffron) bears one to three 2- to 3-inch-wide rose-violet flower trumpets on short stalks in early spring before grasslike glossy leaves appear.

CAMASS
Camassia

Light: mostly sun	
Plant type: bulb	
Hardiness: Zones 5-8	
Height: 1 to 3 feet	
Soil and Moisture: well-drained, moist	
Interest: flowers, fragrance	
Care: moderate	

◄ Camassia quamash

Camass is a striking wildflower of open woods, wet meadows, and prairies, with fragrant velvet purple, white, or lilac flowers from spring to early summer. The plants produce loose clusters of star-shaped flowers on upright stalks beneath clumps of erect lance-shaped leaves. Camass is especially handsome planted in drifts in a woodland border or meadow.

Growing and care:
Grow camass in a moist, well-drained soil that has had some organic matter added to it. Fertilize established plantings in spring as growth begins. Water regularly while plants are actively growing but allow soil to dry out after plants go dormant. Propagate from seed or offsets.

Selected species and varieties:
C. quamash (common camass, quamash) is a western species with bright green grasslike leaves and 1- to 3-foot flower stalks bearing dozens of star-shaped flowers in white and shades from light blue to deep blue or lavender-blue. *C. scilloides* (wild hyacinth, eastern camass), native to the central and southern United States, produces a clump of leaves up to 16 inches long, and the leafless 6- to 24-inch stems bearing loose clusters of fragrant white, blue, or lavender-blue flowers.

CRINODONNA
x Crinodonna

Light: mostly sun

Plant type: bulb

Hardiness: Zones 9-10

Height: 2 to 3 feet

Soil and Moisture: well-drained, moist

Interest: flowers, fragrance

Care: moderate

◀ x Crinodonna corsii

Crinodonna bears enchanting pastel pink and white flowers that perfume the garden with a rich fragrance in late summer and fall. The dense heads of oval, pointed flower buds open into large funnels with gracefully curving stamens and prominent anthers to add color and interest. The fragrant flowers unfold at the tips of sturdy, erect flower stalks. Each stalk rises from a clump of arching, narrow evergreen leaves that remain attractive year round. Crinodonnas can be grown as border specimens in frost-free areas but bloom best as root-bound container plants.

Growing and care:
Outdoors, plant crinodonna bulbs at the soil line in well-worked soil, spacing them 8 to 12 inches apart. Indoors, plant one 4-inch bulb per 6- to 8-inch pot. Bulbs should be left undisturbed for several years, as they bloom best when roots are crowded. Propagate by removing offsets, which grow at the base of larger bulbs.

Selected species and varieties:
x *C. corsii* [also called x *Amarcrinum memoria-corsii*] bears 4- to 5-inch-wide pink flowers accented with blush white edges on graceful 3-foot-tall stalks in late summer and early fall.

CROCUS
Crocus

Light: mostly sun

Plant type: bulb

Hardiness: Zones 3-8

Height: 2 to 8 inches

Soil and Moisture: well-drained, moist

Interest: flowers, fragrance

Care: easy

◀ Crocus chrysanthus 'Cream Beauty'

Crocuses are one of the best-loved spring bulbs, with abundant, cheerful flowers in a rainbow of perky colors. Crocus flowers hug the ground on short stems from late winter through midspring. There are also fall-blooming species, not to be confused with the flowers commonly known as autumn crocus, which are actually *Colchicum*. Narrow, grassy crocus leaves are sometimes attractively banded down their centers in gray-green or white and may appear before, at the same time as, or after several flowers rise from each small corm. They last several weeks before dying back. Some are fragrant. Each flower has six wide petals that open into a deep, oval cup shape, then relax into a round, open bowl. Crocuses are available in a broad range of hues, and are often striped, streaked, or tinged with more than one color. Prominent yellow or orange stigmas decorate the center of each blossom. Mass crocuses for best effect in beds, borders, and rock gardens. They naturalize easily and are often planted as edgings and allowed to ramble in lawns. Force them for indoor winter display.

Growing and care:
Plant corms 3 to 4 inches deep and 4 to 5 inches apart in groups. They are not fussy about soil, but good drainage is essential. Space more closely in pots for forcing, allowing six to eight corms per 6-inch pot or shallow bulb pan, and setting the corms 1 inch deep. Hold potted

CROCUS
(continued)

corms at 40°F until roots form, then bring indoors at 65°F for flowering. After forcing, allow foliage to die back, then plant corms out in the garden for reflowering the following spring. To plant crocuses in lawns, cut and lift small patches of grass, place the corms, then replace the sod. Plant spring-flowering varieties from September to November, fall-flowering ones no later than August. Where crocuses have established themselves in lawns, avoid mowing in spring until the foliage of spring-flowering crocuses dies back; in fall, postpone mowing once the buds of fall-blooming species have broken through the ground until their flowers fade and foliage withers. Propagate by lifting and dividing crowded clumps after foliage dies back, or by removing and replanting the smaller cormels that develop alongside mature corms.

Selected species and varieties:

C. chrysanthus (snow crocus) bears late-winter flowers on 4-inch stems before the 1-foot leaves appear; 'Blue Bird' has blooms that are blue-violet outside, creamy inside; 'Blue Pearl', petals that are lavender outside touched with bronze at their base, white inside blending to a yellow throat; 'Cream Beauty' has long-lasting creamy yellow flowers; 'Snow Bunting' has white flowers with lilac streaking and yellow throats; Zones 4-8. *C. speciosus* produces light blue fall flowers with darker blue veining and prominent orange stigmas on 3- to 6-inch stems; 'Artabir' grows fragrant light blue flowers with conspicuous veining; 'Cassiope', lavender-blue blooms with creamy yellow throats; 'Conqueror', clear blue flowers; var. *aitchisonii* has pale lilac flowers veined with deeper lilac, the largest of all crocus blossoms; Zones 5-8. *C. vernus* (Dutch crocus, common crocus) bears large flowers on stems to 8 inches tall, appearing at the same time as leaves in late winter to spring; 'Flower Record' is deep purple; 'Jeanne d'Arc', white; 'Paulus Potter', shiny reddish purple; 'Remembrance', bluish purple.

FREESIA
Freesia

Light: mostly sun	
Plant type: bulb	
Hardiness: Zones 9-10	
Height: 1 to 2 feet	
Soil and Moisture: well-drained, sandy, moist	
Interest: flowers, fragrance	
Care: moderate	

◀ Freesia 'Ballerina'

Of all the alluring fragrances in the world, none is quite like the perfume of freesias. These lovely flowers have a unique, ethereal aroma that is faint and intense at the same time. Freesias have crowded fans of flaring tubular flowers held at right angles to branched, arching stems that rise from clumps of 6-inch sword-shaped leaves, which persist after flowers fade. The flowers open in sequence along each upright cluster for a long period of bloom. In warm zones, grow freesias in borders or rock gardens. Elsewhere, pot them for houseplants or greenhouse specimens.

Growing and care:

Plant freesias outdoors in fall or winter in Zones 9 and 10, setting corms 2 inches deep and 2 to 4 inches apart. Provide support for their weak stems. Indoors, pot six to eight corms per 6-inch bulb pan or 10 to 12 per 8-inch pan, setting corms barely below the surface. Water and feed freesias while growing and blooming, then withhold water after foliage fades to induce dormancy. Remove corms from pots and store in a cool, dark place.

Selected species and varieties:

F. x *hybrids* produces 2-inch flowers on stems 1½ to 2 feet tall; 'Ballerina' produces large white flowers touched with yellow at the throat; 'Diana', double white flowers; 'Fantasy', cream-colored double petals; 'Riande' is yellow-gold; 'Royal Gold', golden yellow.

GLORIOSA LILY
Gloriosa

Light: mostly sun	
Plant type: bulb	
Hardiness: Zone 10	
Height: 6 to 12 feet	
Soil and Moisture: well-drained, fertile, moist	
Interest: flowers	
Care: moderate	

◀ Gloriosa superba 'Rothschildiana'

Gloriosa lilies produce wonderfully exotic flowers that add a tropical ambiance wherever they blossom. The flowers have narrow, strongly reflexed, fiery petals with wavy or crimped edges that expose a spray of prominent stamens. The tips of the slender 4- to 6-inch-long leaves elongate into clasping tendrils to enable the plant to cling to fences or trellises at the back of a border. In northern zones, plant gloriosa lilies outdoors as annuals or grow them indoors as container plants. They make excellent cut flowers.

Growing and care:

In Zone 10, plant gloriosa lilies anytime, laying tubers on their sides 4 inches deep and 8 to 12 inches apart. North of Zone 10, plant in spring and lift in fall for winter storage. Indoors, pot tubers 1 to 2 inches deep in midwinter for blooms from late summer through fall. Propagate from seed or by dividing tubers.

Selected species and varieties:

G. superba (Malabar gloriosa lily, crisped glory lily) has twisted yellow petals tipped with red, aging to dark red; 'Africana' has orange petals edged in yellow; 'Rothschildiana', wavy reddish purple petals edged in yellow.

GLORY-OF-THE-SNOW
Chionodoxa

Light: mostly sun	
Plant type: bulb	
Hardiness: Zones 4-9	
Height: 4 to 10 inches	
Soil and Moisture: well-drained, moist	
Interest: flowers	
Care: easy	

◀ Chionodoxa luciliae 'Pink Giant'

Glory-of-the-snow is one of the hardiest bulbs and, as a bonus, is one of the earliest flowers to appear in spring, often before snows have completely melted. The small clusters of white to pink flowery stars with narrow, gracefully curved petals are held above the grassy leaves on short stems. Glory-of-the-snow naturalizes easily in rock or wildflower gardens to create carpets of color beneath taller spring bulbs or deciduous shrubs. Once established the plants are pest- and disease-free and provide years of beauty with little effort. Glory-of-the-snow can also be planted in containers and forced for indoor winter bloom.

Growing and care:

Plant glory-of-the-snow in masses for best effect, setting bulbs 3 inches deep and 3 inches apart. For forcing, allow 12 to 18 bulbs per 8-inch bulb pan. Propagate from seed or by removing and replanting bulblets growing alongside older bulbs.

Selected species and varieties:

C. luciliae has clusters of three or more 1-inch blue flowers with centers suffused with white on 4-inch stems; 'Alba' grows pure white; 'Pink Giant' produces bright pink flowers on 3- to 6-inch stems; 'Rosea' is pink. *C. sardensis* bears deep blue flowers on stems to 6 inches.

IPHEION
Ipheion

Light: mostly sun

Plant type: bulb

Hardiness: Zones 5-10

Height: 1 to 1 1/2 feet

Soil and Moisture: well-drained, moist

Interest: flowers, fragrance

Care: moderate

◀ Ipheion uniflorum

Ipheion bears subtle, softly colored flowers from a maze of grasslike leaves in spring. The flowers have tiny, triangle-shaped pointed petals surrounding a cluster of bright orange stamens. The blossoms have a faint mint scent, while the foliage gives off an onion odor when bruised. The leaves appear in fall, and persist through winter and spring until the bulbs go dormant in summer. Plant ipheion in woodland or rock gardens, in meadows, or among paving stones, where it will rapidly naturalize. It can also be forced indoors for midwinter bloom.

Growing and care:
Plant ipheion in late summer or fall, setting bulbs 3 inches deep and 3 to 6 inches apart in well-worked soil. Provide winter mulch in Zones 5 and 6. Pot bulbs 1 inch deep for forcing. Propagate by dividing clumps of bulb offsets.

Selected species and varieties:
I. uniflorum [formerly *Brodiaea uniflora* and *Triteleia uniflora*] (spring starflower) has 1-inch white flowers tinged with blue; 'Rolf Fiedler' has deep electric blue blossoms; 'Wisley Blue' bears light blue flowers with a white center.

LILY
Lilium

Light: mostly sun

Plant type: bulb

Hardiness: Zones 4-8

Height: 2 to 8 feet

Soil and Moisture: well-drained, fertile, moist

Interest: flowers, fragrance

Care: easy to moderate

◀ Lilium columbianum

Few garden flowers can compare with the majesty of lilies. These aristocratic plants have been prized for centuries for their beauty, form, and fragrance. There are many diverse types of lilies to choose from, yet each maintains a stately presence that is enchanting. Lilies offer a wide range of colors and color combinations. They bloom either singly or in clusters, at the tips of stiff, erect stems lined with short, grassy leaves. Up to 50 often highly fragrant flowers may appear on a single stem. The wide range of choices allows fanciers to plant lilies for continuous bloom throughout the summer. Lilies are excellent for borders. Many types naturalize quickly and look stunning in meadows or large rock gardens. Lilies can also be grown in patio containers, forced for indoor bloom, or used as long-lasting cut flowers.

Growing and care:
Plant lilies in spring or fall in well-worked, well-drained soil that has some organic matter. If grown in beds and borders the soil around the bulbs should be mulched to keep it cool. The plants also thrive when set among suntolerant ferns and ground covers. Space bulbs 4 to 6 inches apart. Fertilize plants in spring as plants emerge from the soil. Keep soil moist but not wet during dry periods. Propagate lilies by removing and replanting the small bulblets that grow along the underground stem.

(continued)

Selected species and varieties:

Asiatic hybrids: Early summer flowering compact lilies usually 2 to 4 feet tall with 4- to 6-inch flowers, borne singly or in clusters; Zones 4-8; 'Connecticut King' bears abundant sunny yellow flowers on 30-inch stems; 'Dreamland' has upright deep golden yellow flowers on strong 30-inch stems; 'Marseille' bears elegant satin white flowers touched with a brush of rose near the base of the petals; 'Scarlet Emperor' has rich red, upward-facing flowers on 30-inch stems; 'Sorbet' has white blossoms edged with burgundy-pink on 40-inch stems. *Oriental hybrids:* Mid- to late-summer-blooming garden favorites from 2 to 8 feet tall bearing trumpet-shaped, flat-faced, or bowl-shaped flowers up to 12 inches across or trusses of smaller turban-shaped flowers; Zones 4-8; 'Arena' bears upward-facing white flowers with a solid yellow streak along the center of each petal on 3-foot stems; 'Belle Epoque' has large, outward-facing blossoms of the softest blush pink on 4-foot stems; 'Gold Band' has very large, fragrant white flowers freckled with red on 3-foot stems; 'Muscadet' bears stunning flat-faced flowers of linen white, freckled and streaked with blush pink on 30-inch stems; 'Tompouce' has rose-pink petals with a center stripe of lemon-yellow on 30-inch stems. Species lilies: *L. canadense* (Canada lily) has down-facing yellow to reddish orange blossoms in summer on 4-foot-tall stems; Zones 4-8 *L. columbianum* (Columbia lily, Oregon lily) has nodding yellow to reddish flowers with maroon spots and gently recurved petals; Zones 6-8. *L. martagon* (Martagon lily) bears abundant rose-purple flowers spotted with dark violet in summer on 6-foot stems; Zones 4-8. *L. pumilum* (coral lily) has abundant vivid red, nodding flowers with sharply recurved petals in summer on 2-foot stems; Zones 4-8. *Trumpet Hybrids* have trumpet, star-burst, or bowl-shaped flowers in summer atop strong 3- to 6-foot stems; Zones 4-8; 'Bright Star' has white flowers marked with a golden yellow, star-shaped eye.

ONION
Allium

Light: mostly sun

Plant type: bulb

Hardiness: Zones 3-9

Height: 9 inches to 5 feet

Soil and Moisture: well-drained, sandy, moist

Interest: flowers, foliage, fragrance

Care: easy

◀ Allium giganteum

Though *Allium* are related to edible onions, these spectacular plants bear little resemblance to their culinary cousins. Their showy 2- to 12-inch-wide flower clusters are dynamite in the garden. The dense, spherical flower heads are composed of hundreds of tiny blooms packed tightly together. Most species flower in late spring and early summer. Many species smell faintly like onion or garlic when the leaves or stems are cut or bruised, but a few bear sweetly fragrant flowers. Mass small or medium *Allium* for striking displays and site larger ones as stately accents. *Allium* are durable, very attractive cut flowers. Rodents that like to dine on other flowering bulbs usually find *Allium* bulbs unappealing.

Growing and care:

Plant ornamental onions in the fall in northern zones, in spring or fall in warmer areas. They grow rapidly in spring, produce blooms, and then die back to the ground. Because their foliage must be allowed to wither naturally, site *Alliums* where other plants will hide the dying leaves. Even those species that tolerate partial shade need full sun for part of the day. *A. cernuum* prefers humus-rich soil and thrives in dry or moist conditions in full sun or partial shade; divide clumps about every 3 years. *A. aflatunense, A. christophii,* and *A. giganteum* require full sun. Since its flower stalk is so tall, *A. giganteum* should not be planted in windy sites. *A. moly*

ONION
(continued)

prefers a sunny, well-drained site. *A. aflatunense, A. cernuum, A. karataviense,* and *A. moly* are suitable for naturalizing. *Allium* may be left undisturbed in the garden for years until the presence of fewer blooms signals that bulbs are overcrowded. Remove flower stems after flowering. Protect bulbs with winter mulch north of Zone 5. Propagate by separating and replanting tiny bulblets after the foliage dies back, by planting the bulblets that appear amid flower clusters, or by sowing seed.

Selected species and varieties:

A. aflatunense (ornamental onion) produces deep purple, perfectly rounded 4-inch globes composed of densely clustered tiny star-shaped flowers appearing in late spring to midsummer on 2- to 4-foot stalks above 4-inch-wide leaves; Zones 4-8. *A. cernuum* (nodding wild onion) has loose clusters of 30 to 40 delicate pink or white flowers that dangle atop 8- to 18-inch stems in late spring above rosettes of grassy 10-inch leaves; it is most effectively planted in groups; 'Early Dwarf' grows 6 to 8 inches tall, forming neat clumps and producing deep lavender blooms with protruding stamens; Zones 3-8. *A. christophii* (stars-of-Persia) bears the largest flowers of the genus, appearing in late spring and early summer in spherical clusters 8 to 12 inches across, composed of many star-shaped amethyst blue flowers, each ½ inch wide, held above three to seven leaves on a sturdy 1½- to 2-foot stalk; Zones 4-8. *A. giganteum* (giant ornamental onion, giant garlic) has the tallest flower stalks of the genus, with 5- to 6-inch spherical clusters of deep purple to lilac-pink flowers borne in early summer atop 3- to 5-foot scapes that rise from stiff, gray-green basal leaves 2 inches wide and up to 30 inches long. They provide a stately accent for the rear of a border or center of an island bed, and are best planted in groups of three to five. Cut flowers may last up to 3 weeks; Zones 5-8. *A. moly* (lily leek, golden onion) has clusters of vivid yellow ¾- to 1-inch-wide star-shaped blooms appearing in mid- to late spring on 8- to 12-inch stems above a clump of 12-inch basal leaves; 'Jeannine' bears long-lasting 2- to 3-inch flowers on 1-foot stems above blue-green leaves.

ORNITHOGALUM
Ornithogalum

Light:	mostly sun
Plant type:	bulb
Hardiness:	Zones 5-10
Height:	6 inches to 2 feet
Soil and Moisture:	well-drained, moist
Interest:	flowers, fragrance
Care:	moderate

◄ Ornithogalum nutans

Ornithogalum bears star-shaped, often fragrant flowers in spring or summer with a distinctive tight "eye" of pistils at their centers. The attractive blossoms are most often white with a green stripe down the outside of each petal, though some types have yellow to orange petals. The flowers are carried in large clusters that are sometimes pendent but more often are facing upward in flat-topped bouquets above neat clumps of shimmering green, ribbonlike leaves. Ornithogalum looks beautiful naturalized in borders, beds, and rock gardens, or grown indoors as a potted plant.

Growing and care:

Outdoors, plant ornithogalum bulbs 4 inches deep and 2 to 5 inches apart in well-worked soil amended with rotted manure or compost. Keep soil evenly moist throughout growing season. North of Zone 8, treat tender species as annuals, lifting bulbs in fall for replanting in spring, or grow as container plants. Indoors, pot five or six bulbs 1 inch deep in a 6-inch pot. Propagate from seed sown in spring or by dividing bulbs and offsets in fall.

Selected species and varieties:

O. nutans (nodding star-of-Bethlehem) has fragrant, greenish white 2-inch flowers nodding along one side of 1- to 1½-inch stems from late spring to early summer; Zones 5-9.

PERSIAN VIOLET
Cyclamen

Light: mostly sun

Plant type: bulb

Hardiness: Zones 6-9

Height: 3 to 12 inches

Soil and Moisture: well-drained, fertile, moist

Interest: flowers, fragrance

Care: moderate

◀ Cyclamen hederifolium

Persian violet has distinctive, sometimes fragrant flowers with strongly reflexed petals swept back from a prominent center or eye. The petals are sometimes twisted, double, ruffled, shredded, or ridged, giving the delicate inch-long blossoms the appearance of exotic butterflies or fiery shooting stars. Each flower rises on a slender stem from a clump of long-lasting kidney- or heart-shaped leaves that are sometimes marbled green and gray above or reddish underneath. Allow hardy Persian violets to naturalize in wildflower gardens, rock gardens, and shady borders, where they often grow into low ground covers.

Growing and care:
Plant Persian violet's flat, cormlike tubers in summer or fall, setting them ½ inch deep and 4 to 6 inches apart. Provide an annual top dressing of leaf mold. Propagate from seed to reach blooming size in 3 years or by transplanting the self-sown seedlings in summer or fall.

Selected species and varieties:
C. hederifolium [also called *C. neapolitanum*] (baby cyclamen) has pink or white, sometimes fragrant flowers with a crimson eye on 3- to 6-inch stems above marbled leaves with toothed edges in winter.

PINEAPPLE LILY
Eucomis

Light: mostly sun

Plant type: bulb

Hardiness: Zones 8-10

Height: 1 to 2 feet

Soil and Moisture: well-drained, sandy, moist

Interest: flowers, foliage

Care: moderate

◀ Eucomis bicolor

Pineapple lilies are novel plants with dense bottle-brush spikes of tiny white starry flowers topped by a crowning tuft of leaflike bracts. The sturdy spikes rise from glossy rosettes of strap-shaped leaves in summer. Pineapple lilies blend well into borders, and when grown in containers are the conversation pieces of patio and deck gardens. They make long-lasting cut flowers.

Growing and care:
Plant outdoors in fall, setting bulbs 5 to 6 inches deep and 1 foot apart. Mulch plantings in Zone 8. North of Zone 8, grow pineapple lilies as container plants, setting bulbs just below the surface and allowing three to five bulbs per 1-foot pot. Propagate by removing bulb offsets that develop at the base of mature bulbs, or from seed to flower in 5 years.

Selected species and varieties:
E. autumnalis has spikes of ¾-inch greenish white flowers fading to yellow-green on 1- to 2-foot stems. *E. bicolor* bears greenish white flowers edged with purple on 2-foot stems. *E. comosa* (pineapple flower) has ½-inch greenish white, sometimes pinkish blossoms with purple throats on 2-foot stems.

PUSCHKINIA
Puschkinia

Light: mostly sun

Plant type: bulb

Hardiness: Zones 3-8

Height: 4 to 6 inches

Soil and Moisture: well-drained, moist

Interest: flowers, fragrance

Care: moderate

◀ Puschkinia scilloides var. libanotica 'Alba'

Puschkinia is a charming plant with profuse, softly colored flowers above rafts of glossy green leaves in spring. The slender wandlike stems hold oval buds that open into loose clusters of tiny flower bells that metamorphose into little, gently nodding stars. Puschkinia is a vigorous, easy-to-grow plant that naturalizes quickly, making it a sure bet for borders, edgings, rock gardens, or wildflower meadows.

Growing and care:
Plant bulbs in fall, setting them 2 inches deep and 6 inches apart in well-worked soil that has had some organic matter added to it. After flowering, top-dress with a light covering of compost or rotted manure. Group bulbs in small colonies for best effect. They bloom best when left undisturbed. Propagate by removing the small bulblets that grow alongside mature bulbs.

Selected species and varieties:
P. scilloides var. *libanotica* (striped squill) bears 1/2-inch bluish white flowers delicately striped with porcelain blue above 6-inch shiny green leaves in spring; 'Alba' has pure white flowers above dark green leaves in spring.

SPIDER LILY
Hymenocallis

Light: mostly sun

Plant type: bulb

Hardiness: Zones 6-10

Height: 1 1/2 to 2 1/2 feet

Soil and Moisture: well-drained, wet to moist

Interest: flowers

Care: moderate

◀ Hymenocallis caroliniana

Spider lilies add a dreamlike, ethereal atmosphere to the garden, with large, fragile-looking blossoms above deep green foliage. The large, fragrant white flowers are composed of six long grasslike petals surrounding a funnel-shaped cup. Spider lilies are excellent for wet meadows and bog gardens, or when planted along the shores of streams, ponds, and water gardens.

Growing and care:
Plant *H. caroliniana* bulbs 5 inches deep in loose soil high in organic matter and moisture. North of Zone 6 the bulbs can be planted in spring and lifted and brought indoors in fall for winter storage. Propagate by seed or division of bulb offsets.

Selected species and varieties:
H. caroliniana [also listed as *H. occidentalis*] is native to the southeastern and south-central United States. It grows 1 1/2 to 2 1/2 feet tall with a basal clump of shiny, light green strap-shaped leaves up to 17 inches long. White flowers 7 inches across are borne atop leafless stalks in clusters of up to six. Flowers appear in spring in the South and in summer in cooler regions.

SUMMER HYACINTH
Galtonia

Light:	mostly sun
Plant type:	bulb
Hardiness:	Zones 6-10
Height:	2 to 4 feet
Soil and Moisture:	well-drained, sandy, fertile, moist
Interest:	flowers, fragrance
Care:	moderate

◀ Galtonia candicans

Summer hyacinth produces bold spires of fragrant, nodding, snow white flowers accented by dark stamens from summer to fall. The blossoms are loosely arranged on stout stems above clumps of fleshy, narrow straplike leaves. Plant tall varieties at the back of flower borders, where they add late-season interest. Summer hyacinth naturalizes slowly into large clumps that provide years of enjoyment.

Growing and care:
Plant summer hyacinths in spring or fall, placing bulbs 6 inches deep and 1½ to 2 feet apart. Mulch bulbs in northern zones with 2 inches of leaf mold or compost in winter. North of Zone 6, lift bulbs in fall, allow to dry several hours, then remove tops and store for replanting the following spring. Propagate from seed to bloom in several years or by removing and replanting the few bulblets that may develop alongside mature bulbs.

Selected species and varieties:
G. candicans (giant summer hyacinth) has 2-inch fragrant white blossoms tinged with green on erect stalks to 4 feet tall in late summer. *G. viridiflora* has greenish flowers on 2- to 3-foot stalks above broad leaves in late summer to fall.

WILD HYACINTH
Brodiaea

Light:	mostly sun
Plant type:	bulb
Hardiness:	Zones 9-10
Height:	4 inches to 3 feet
Soil and Moisture:	heavy, moist to dry
Interest:	flowers
Care:	easy to moderate

◀ Brodiaea elegans

Wild hyacinths are loose, airy plants with brightly colored pink to violet flowers from spring to summer. These hardy wildflowers are native to the grasslands and plains in the West, where they have developed a tolerance for drought. *Brodiaea* have grasslike foliage and terminal clusters of ½- to 1½-inch tubular flowers on wiry stems. After flowering the plants go dormant, so place them where the foliage of other plants will fill in the space they leave. For best effect use wild hyacinths in groups of 12 or more in a perennial border, in a rock garden, or naturalized in meadows.

Growing and care:
B. elegans thrives in mostly sunny spots with poorly drained, heavy soils ranging from dry to moist. *B. pulchella* prefers mostly sunny places with poor, dry soils. Propagate by seed or offsets. Seedlings take 3 to 4 years to flower.

Selected species and varieties:
B. elegans (harvest brodiaea) has mounds of foliage up to 16 inches tall and violet to purple flowers that open in late spring to early summer on erect stems of about the same height as the foliage. *B. pulchella* [also called *Dichelostemma pulchellum*] (wild hyacinth) bears pinkish violet flowers in spring on stalks 2 to 3 feet tall.

AMERICAN PENNYROYAL
Hedeoma

Light: mostly sun	
Plant type: annual	
Height: 4 to 12 inches	
Soil and Moisture: well-drained, fertile, moist, sandy	
Interest: foliage	
Care: moderate	

◀ Hedeoma pulegioides

With aromatic mint-scented leaves growing along erect branching stems, American pennyroyal has been a popular plant for herb gardens for many years. The plant develops into low, bushy mounds with tiny flower clusters appearing where the leaves meet the stems from summer through fall. Use American pennyroyal as an edging, ground cover, or filler plant in informal borders. Sow it into lawns for fragrance, or allow it to trail gracefully over the edges of hanging baskets. Add dried leaves and stems to herbal potpourri; they are widely used as an herbal repellent for fleas and weevils. Although it figures in herbal medicine, its oil can be toxic.

Growing and care:
Start American pennyroyal seed indoors 6 weeks before the last frost or sow directly outdoors in early spring. Seed-grown plants take 2 years to reach flowering, but plants self-sow freely and seedlings transplant easily. To dry, pick stems while they are in flower and hang.

Selected species and varieties:
H. pulegioides (American pennyroyal, mock pennyroyal) has 1½-inch hairy oval leaves along square stems to 1 foot tall, and ¼-inch blue to lavender flowers.

ANGELICA
Angelica

Light: mostly sun	
Plant type: biennial, perennial	
Hardiness: Zones 3-9	
Height: 3 to 8 feet	
Soil and Moisture: well-drained, fertile, moist	
Interest: flowers, foliage, seed heads	
Care: easy	

◀ Angelica gigas

Tall columns of coarse-textured, licorice-scented leaves make angelica a bold border specimen or backdrop. In their second year, plants produce broad, flat clusters of tiny summer flowers followed by dramatic, rounded seed heads. Fresh angelica leaves are used to flavor acidic fruits such as rhubarb. The stems are steamed as a vegetable or candied for a garnish, and the seeds add sweet zest to pastries. The dried aromatic leaves can be used to scent potpourri. Angelica can cause dermatitis and should be eaten sparingly, as some herbalists believe it may be carcinogenic. Do not attempt to collect angelica in the wild, as it closely resembles poisonous water hemlock.

Growing and care:
Sow very fresh angelica seed in the garden in spring or fall. Remove flower stalks to prolong the life of the plants. Angelica self-sows readily; transplant seedlings before taproots become established.

Selected species and varieties:
A. archangelica (archangel, wild parsnip) grows to 8 feet tall with 6-inch-wide clusters of greenish white flowers. *A. gigas* reaches 6 feet with 8-inch clusters of burgundy flowers.

BORAGE
Borago

Light: mostly sun

Plant type: annual

Height: 2 to 3 feet

Soil and Moisture: well-drained, moist

Interest: flowers, foliage

Care: easy

◀ Borago officinalis

Borage is native to Europe and makes an attractive addition to flower or herb gardens, fresh flower arrangements, and summer salads. Both leaves and flowers are edible, with a refreshing cucumber-like flavor, and can be used to garnish salads or fruit cups. The plant has a somewhat sprawling habit that is best suited to an informal garden, where its soft-textured leaves and sky blue flowers add a cool, gentle touch.

Growing and care:
Sow seed directly in the garden at monthly intervals beginning 2 to 3 weeks prior to the last frost for continuous summer bloom. Allow 1 to 1½ feet between plants. Once established, plants will self-seed. Where summers are very hot, afternoon shade is recommended. Borage tolerates drought.

Selected species and varieties:
B. officinalis (talewort, cool-tankard) is a hardy annual with a rounded sprawling habit, bristly gray-green foliage, and succulent stems. Flowers are arranged in drooping clusters. Each is ¾ inch across and star shaped, with five petals. Though usually clear blue, they are sometimes light purple. Flower buds are covered with fine hairs.

CARAWAY
Carum

Light: mostly sun

Plant type: biennial grown as annual

Height: 2 feet

Soil and Moisture: well-drained, fertile, moist

Interest: flowers, foliage, seeds

Care: easy

◀ Carum carvi

Caraway is a delightful as well as useful addition to the herb garden, with feathery, aromatic carrotlike leaves and flavorful seeds. In late spring or early summer the plants send up branching flower stalks tipped with flat clusters of tiny white flowers followed by tasty seeds. Chop the leaves, which have a parsley-dill flavor, into salads, and cook the roots like carrots or parsnips. Use the anise-flavored seeds in breads and cakes, add them to meat, cabbage, and apple dishes, or crystallize them in sugar for an after-dinner candy to sweeten the breath and settle the stomach.

Growing and care:
Sow caraway in the garden in spring or fall and thin seedlings to stand 8 inches apart; once established, it self-sows. Snip leaves at anytime. Harvest seeds as flower clusters turn brown but before the seed capsules shatter. Hang to dry over a tray or cloth, and store the seeds in airtight containers. Dig 2-year-old roots to serve as a side dish.

Selected species and varieties:
C. carvi has ferny leaves up to 10 inches long and white flowers followed by ¼-inch dark brown seeds.

CHERVIL
Anthriscus

Light: mostly sun	
Plant type: annual	
Height: 1 to 2 feet	
Soil and Moisture: well-drained, moist	
Interest: flowers, foliage	
Care: easy	

◀ Anthriscus cerefolium

One of the fines herbes of French cuisine, chervil's finely divided leaves resemble parsley with a hint of warm anise flavor. Chervil is an ideal outdoor container plant. Chop fresh chervil into fish, vegetable, egg, and meat dishes. Use flower stalks in fresh or dried arrangements, and add dried leaves to herbal potpourri.

Growing and care:
Sow chervil seed in the garden for harvestable leaves in 6 to 8 weeks. Make successive sowings for a continuous supply of fresh leaves; seed sown in fall produces a spring crop. Remove flowers to encourage greater leaf production; alternately, allow plants to go to seed and self-sow, producing both early- and late-summer crops. Pick leaves before flowers appear, starting when plants reach 4 inches in height, and preserve by freezing alone or mixed with butter. Flavor fades when leaves are dried. Hang flower stalks to dry for use in winter bouquets.

Selected species and varieties:
A. cerefolium (chervil, salad chervil) produces 1- to 2-foot mounds of lacy bright green leaves topped by small, open clusters of tiny white flowers in summer.

COMFREY
Symphytum

Light: mostly sun	
Plant type: perennial	
Hardiness: Zones 3-9	
Height: 3 to 5 feet	
Soil and Moisture: well-drained, fertile, moist	
Interest: flowers, foliage	
Care: easy	

◀ Symphytum officinale

Comfrey forms bold clumps of coarse, hairy oval leaves useful as a backdrop in large borders or meadow gardens. From spring through fall, drooping clusters of funnel-shaped flowers are held on upright stems. Rich in nutrients, comfrey once figured prominently in herbal medicine but is now a suspected carcinogen and is recommended only for external use. Add dried and crumbled leaves to a bath as a skin softener. Steep leaves for liquid fertilizer, or add to the compost heap.

Growing and care:
Grow comfrey from root cuttings containing a growing tip, setting these divisions 6 to 8 inches deep and 2 to 3 feet apart. Choose sites carefully, as comfrey is difficult to eradicate once established. To control its spread, grow in large containers removed from other garden sites.

Selected species and varieties:
S. officinale (common comfrey) has deep green, rough-textured 10- to 20-inch basal leaves and ½-inch blue, white, purple, or rose tubular flowers. *S.* x *uplandicum* (Russian comfrey) is free flowering with blue or purple blossoms; 'Variegatum' has leaves marbled cream and green.

CORIANDER
Coriandrum

Light: mostly sun	
Plant type: annual	
Height: 1 to 3 feet	
Soil and Moisture: well-drained, fertile, moist	
Interest: foliage, seeds	
Care: easy	

◀ Coriandrum sativum

Coriander's pungent young leaves, commonly known as cilantro or Chinese parsley, are a staple in East Asian, Mexican, and Indian cuisines. With a hint of citrus, the round, ribbed seeds are used whole or ground in baked goods, curries, chutneys, and vegetable dishes. Add them to potpourri for a lingering lemon fragrance. The unpleasant odor of immature fruits earned coriander the nickname stinkplant; the characteristic agreeable fruity aroma develops as they ripen. Chop coriander roots into curries or steam them as a nutty vegetable.

Growing and care:

Sow coriander seed in spring and thin seedlings to stand 8 inches apart. Use fresh immature leaves for best flavor; cilantro loses flavor if dried. Collect mature seed heads and dry them in a paper bag to catch seeds. Dig roots in fall.

Selected species and varieties:

C. sativum has leaves that grow in small, scalloped fans resembling parsley when young, older leaves look ferny and threadlike, with flat, loose clusters of tiny white to mauve summer flowers; 'Long Standing' is a slow-to-bolt cultivar.

GERMANDER
Teucrium

Light: mostly sun	
Plant type: shrub	
Hardiness: Zones 5-9	
Height: 6 to 15 inches	
Soil and Moisture: well-drained, moist	
Interest: flowers, foliage	
Care: easy to moderate	

◀ Teucrium chamaedrys

Wall germander's spreading mounds of shiny evergreen foliage are covered from early to midsummer with spikes of small purple-pink flowers that add a perky cheerfulness to many types of gardens. Allow a specimen to spread in a rock or herb garden, or plant closely and clip into a low hedge resembling a miniature boxwood. The scalloped oval leaves release a faintly garlicky odor when bruised. Weave branches into dried wreaths. Wall germander once figured in herbal medicine but has fallen out of use.

Growing and care:

Grow wall germander from seed, from spring cuttings, or by division, setting plants 1 foot apart. Prune to shape in spring and deadhead to encourage bushiness. Provide protection from drying winter winds.

Selected species and varieties:

T. chamaedrys (wall germander) has square stems that trail then turn up to stand 10 to 15 inches high, lined with pairs of oval- to wedge-shaped ¼- to 1-inch leaves and tipped with whorls of ¾-inch white-dotted purple-pink flowers; 'Prostratum' has stems 6 to 8 inches tall spreading to 3 feet and pink flowers; 'Variegatum' has green leaves splotched white, cream, or yellow.

GIANT HYSSOP
Agastache

Light: mostly sun

Plant type: perennial

Hardiness: Zones 4-9

Height: 2 to 5 feet

Soil and Moisture: well-drained, moist

Interest: flowers, foliage, fragrance

Care: easy

◀ Agastache barberi 'Tutti-Frutti'

Giant hyssop is a bold addition to any garden, with clumps of erect stems lined with fragrant leaves and tipped with spikes of colorful flowers. The nectar-filled summer flowers are edible and make a delightful nibble. The blossoms also attract bees and butterflies and dry well for everlasting arrangements. Scatter the leaves in salads or infuse them for teas.

Growing and care:

Start giant hyssop seed indoors 10 to 12 weeks before the last frost, and set seedlings out 1½ inches apart to bloom the first year. Plant in soil that has been amended with some organic matter and water regularly during the growing season. Established plantings self-sow, or you can propagate by division in spring or fall every 3 to 5 years. Hang flowers upside down in bunches to dry.

Selected species and varieties:

A. barberi bears red-purple flowers with a long season of bloom on stems to 2 feet tall; 'Firebird' has coppery orange blooms; 'Tutti-Frutti' bears raspberry pink to purple flavorful flowers; Zones 6-9. *A. foeniculum* (anise hyssop, blue giant hyssop, anise mint, licorice mint) has licorice-scented leaves and purple-blue flowers on 3-foot stems; 'Alba' has white blossoms. *A. rugosa* (Korean anise hyssop) bears wrinkly mint-scented leaves and small purple flower spikes on 5-foot stems; Zones 5-9.

HOP
Humulus

Light: mostly sun

Plant type: perennial

Hardiness: Zones 3-8

Height: 10 to 25 feet

Soil and Moisture: well-drained, fertile, moist

Interest: flowers, foliage

Care: easy

◀ Humulus lupulus 'Aureus'

Hops are twining deciduous vines with coarse foliage like that of grapevines. They quickly clamber over trellises to form dense, textured screens. In summer female and male flowers appear on separate plants. Weave lengths of hopvine into garlands or wreaths for drying. Stuff dried female flowers, used as a bitter flavoring for beer, into herbal pillows to promote sleep. Blanch young leaves to remove bitterness and add to soups or sauces. Cook young side shoots like asparagus.

Growing and care:

Because female plants are more desirable than male ones and the gender of plants grown from seed is unknown for 3 years, it is best to grow hops from tip cuttings taken from female plants, divide their roots, or remove their rooted suckers in spring. Space plants 1½ to 3 feet apart. Cut hops to the ground at season's end.

Selected species and varieties:

H. lupulus (common hop, European hop, bine) has heart-shaped lobed leaves up to 6 inches across and female plants with paired yellow-green flowers ripening to papery scales layered in puffy cones; 'Aureus' has golden green leaves.

HORSERADISH
Armoracia

Light: mostly sun	
Plant type: perennial	
Hardiness: Zones 3-10	
Height: 2 to 4 feet	
Soil and Moisture: well-drained, moist to wet	
Interest: roots	
Care: easy	

◀ Armoracia rusticana

The pungent bite of fresh horseradish root grated into vinegar, cream, or mayonnaise for sauces and dressings is reason enough to grow this spicy herb. In spring, clumps of oblong leaves with ruffled, wrinkled edges grow from horseradish's fleshy taproot, followed by clusters of tiny white summer flowers. Chop fresh young leaves and toss in salads. Horseradish was used as a medicinal plant before it became popular as a condiment, and its dried leaves yield a yellow dye.

Growing and care:

Plant pieces of mature root at least 6 inches long in spring or fall. Set root pieces 3 to 4 inches deep and 1 to 2 feet apart in soil to which some organic matter has been added. Dig roots in fall and store in dry sand; slice and dry for later grinding, or grate into white vinegar to preserve. Horseradish can be invasive if not confined, as new plants grow from any root pieces left in the garden.

Selected species and varieties:

A. rusticana (horseradish, red cole) has thick, branching white-fleshed roots a foot long or longer with leaves to 2 feet and flower stalks to 4 feet; 'Variegata' has leaves streaked white.

HYSSOP
Hyssopus

Light: mostly sun	
Plant type: perennial	
Hardiness: Zones 3-8	
Height: 1½ to 3 feet	
Soil and Moisture: well-drained, moist to dry	
Interest: flowers, foliage	
Care: easy	

◀ Hyssopus officinalis

Hyssop's square stems are lined with narrow camphor-scented leaves and tipped with thick spikes of slightly flaring tubular flowers. The blue or white blossoms make attractive additions to herb gardens and attract bees, butterflies, and hummingbirds. Grow hyssops as bushy specimens or plant them closely for low hedges. Add the flowers to salads; or use the sage-like leaves to flavor poultry or stuffings. Use dried flowers and leaves in herbal teas or potpourri.

Growing and care:

Hyssop grows from seed to bloom in 2 years. Plants propagated from rooted cuttings or divisions taken in spring or fall will bloom in 1 season. Remove spent flowers to prolong bloom. Prune mature plants to the ground in spring. Shear into formal hedges for knot gardens or for use as edgings in formal gardens. Hyssop is sometimes evergreen in milder climates.

Selected species and varieties:

H. officinalis (common hyssop, European hyssop) has willowlike ¾- to 1¼-inch leaves and ½-inch blue-violet flowers on plants to 3 feet; ssp. *aristatus* (rock hyssop) produces fine leaves on 1½- to 2-foot plants; 'Albus' [also called 'Alba'] (white hyssop) has white flowers.

INDIAN BORAGE
Plectranthus

◀ Plectranthus amboinicus 'Variegata'

Light: mostly sun

Plant type: annual

Height: 1 to 3 feet

Soil and Moisture: well-drained, fertile, moist

Interest: foliage

Care: easy to moderate

The succulent, spicy leaves of Indian borage have a flavor reminiscent of a combination of thyme, oregano, and savory. In tropical areas where these herbs fail to thrive, cooks grow Indian borage as an attractive, tasty substitute. The plants are often allowed to ramble through the garden, forming an attractive ground cover, and in cooler areas are grown in containers. The leaves trail attractively from hanging baskets that are often hung just outside the kitchen door where the plants are always in easy reach. Use fresh leaves to complement beans, meats, and other strong-flavored dishes.

Growing and care:
Start Indian borage from tip cuttings or divisions in spring or summer. Plants stop growing at temperatures below 50°F and are quickly killed by even light frost. Pinch tips to keep plants bushy and contain their spread. Cut leggy plants back in spring. Feed potted plants monthly.

Selected species and varieties:
P. amboinicus (Indian borage, Spanish thyme, French thyme, soup mint, Mexican mint, Indian mint, country borage) has round gray-green leaves up to 4 inches across in pairs along thick stems, and whorls of tiny mintlike blue summer flowers in spikes up to 16 inches long; 'Variegata' has gray-green leaves edged in cream.

JOB'S-TEARS
Coix

◀ Coix lacryma-jobi

Light: mostly sun

Plant type: annual

Height: 3 to 4 feet

Soil and Moisture: well-drained, moist to wet

Interest: flowers, foliage, seed heads

Care: easy

Job's-tears produces long, narrow leaves clasping tall, jointed stems that create a lacy vertical accent as a border backdrop or temporary screen. When grown in containers the plants add a bold presence to patios and decks. In summer, arching flower spikes rise like froth above the foliage, and female flowers, enclosed in hard oval husks, hang decoratively in strings like dripping tears. Children enjoy stringing the small beads into bracelets and necklaces. Dry the stems for everlasting arrangements.

Growing and care:
Sow Job's-tears in spring when soil warms to 68°F; in colder climates, start seed indoors 2 to 3 months before last frost. Transplant or move established plants in spring or fall. Keep soil constantly moist while plants are growing. To dry, pick stems before seeds dry and shatter.

Selected species and varieties:
C. lacryma-jobi has leaves 2 feet long and 1½ inches wide on stems to 4 feet tipped with spiky flower clusters, male at the end, female at the base, encased in hard green husks that turn pearly white, gray, or iridescent violet as they ripen.

LAUREL
Laurus

Light:	mostly sun
Plant type:	shrub, tree
Hardiness:	Zones 8-10
Height:	4 to 40 feet
Soil and Moisture:	well-drained, moist
Interest:	foliage
Care:	easy to moderate

◀ Laurus nobilis

Laurel is an attractive evergreen plant with a handsome treelike form and aromatic leaves that emit a warm, spicy fragrance when crushed. In warm climates, bay laurel grows as a multistemmed shrub or tree to 40 feet. In northern areas the plant is frequently grown in containers, where it often reaches 4 to 6 feet tall. The glossy, leathery, aromatic leaves are prized by cooks and essential in bouquets garnis. Add leaves to potpourri, or dry branches for bouquets or wreaths.

Growing and care:
If planting outdoors choose a site protected from winds. To grow as standards, train plants to a single stem and prune frequently, rubbing off any new growth that appears along the trunk. Bring plants indoors before frost. Bay laurel can be propagated from seed or from hardwood cuttings but grows very slowly. Dry the leaves in a single layer in a warm, dark place; weigh down with a board to dry them flat. Store in airtight containers.

Selected species and varieties:
L. nobilis (bay laurel, bay, bay tree, true laurel) bears narrow 2- to 4-inch gray-green oval leaves; 'Angustifolia' (willow-leaved bay) has extremely narrow leaves; 'Aurea' has tapered golden yellow leaves.

LEMON BALM
Melissa

Light:	mostly sun
Plant type:	perennial
Hardiness:	Zones 4-9
Height:	1 to 2 feet
Soil and Moisture:	well-drained, moist
Interest:	foliage, fragrance
Care:	easy

◀ Melissa officinalis 'All Gold'

Lemon balm is a delightful herb with highly aromatic, citruslike foliage. The plant's fresh leaves are medium green and toothed, resembling mint, and add a lemony tang to salads, poultry or fish dishes, marinades, beverages, and vinegar. Dried leaves and stems are a potpourri ingredient.

Growing and care:
Sow lemon balm seed indoors about 8 weeks before planting out. Do not cover, as the seed needs light to germinate. Space plants 1 to 2 feet apart in well-worked soil that has had some organic matter added to it. Plant 'All Gold' in light shade to prevent leaf scorch, and shear 'Aurea' to prevent flower formation and greening of leaves. Lemon balm self-sows readily. Mature plants can also be divided in early spring. Contain the creeping roots by planting in bottomless pots at least 10 inches deep. Dry the leaves on screens.

Selected species and varieties:
M. officinalis (lemon balm, bee balm, sweet balm) bears 1- to 3-inch pointed oval leaves puckered by deep veins, and whorls of ½-inch white to yellow flowers in summer and fall; 'All Gold' has golden yellow foliage; 'Aurea' has green-veined yellow leaves.

LICORICE
Glycyrrhiza

Light: mostly sun	
Plant type: perennial	
Hardiness: Zones 5-9	
Height: 3 feet	
Soil and Moisture: well-drained, fertile, moist	
Interest: flowers, roots	
Care: moderate	

◄ Glycyrrhiza glabra

Licorice is a flavor that brings back fond memories of childhood. The herb that yields the flavoring spreads in broad clumps of erect branching stems lined with long leaves composed of paired 1- to 2-inch sticky yellow-green leaflets. In summer short flower spikes appear in leaf axils. The branching taproot contains glycyrrhizin, a compound 50 times sweeter than sugar and a source of the food flavoring. Dry root pieces to chew, or boil dried roots to extract the flavoring. Caution: Some people are severely allergic to glycyrrhizin.

Growing and care:
Licorice grows very slowly from seed. More often, it is grown from division of the crowns, rooted suckers, or root cuttings at least 6 inches long with two or three eyes. Space plants 1½ feet apart. Wait at least 3 years before harvesting roots; root pieces left behind will sprout the next year. Dry the roots in a shady location for up to 6 months and store in a cool location in air-tight containers.

Selected species and varieties:
G. glabra bears yellow-green leaflets and white to blue, sometimes violet, ½-inch flowers resembling tiny sweet peas on plants growing from a 4-foot or longer taproot branching into tangled mats.

LOVAGE
Levisticum

Light: mostly sun	
Plant type: perennial	
Hardiness: Zones 3-8	
Height: 3 to 6 feet	
Soil and Moisture: well-drained, fertile, moist	
Interest: foliage	
Care: easy to moderate	

◄ Levisticum officinale

Lovage is a vigorous herb with towering clumps of greenish red stalks covered with divided leaflets resembling flat parsley. The plants are excellent grown in borders as well as the herb garden. Lovage's hollow stems, wedge-shaped leaves, thick roots, and ridged seeds all share an intense celery flavor and aroma. Chop leaves and stems or grate roots to garnish salads or flavor soups, potatoes, poultry, and other dishes. Steam stems as a side dish. Toss seeds into stuffings, dressings, and baked goods. Steep leaves for herbal tea.

Growing and care:
Sow lovage seed in fall or divide roots in spring or fall, spacing plants 2 feet apart. Top-dress annually with compost or aged manure and keep well watered during dry spells. Harvest leaves two or three times a season. Deadhead to encourage greater leaf production, or allow flowers to ripen for seed. Dry leaves in bundles, or blanch and freeze.

Selected species and varieties:
L. officinale has deep green leaflets with toothed edges on branching stems to 6 feet topped with a flat cluster of tiny yellow-green spring to summer flowers.

MINT
Mentha

Light: mostly sun

Plant type: perennial

Hardiness: Zones 3-10

Height: 1 inch to 4 feet

Soil and Moisture: well-drained, moist

Interest: flowers, foliage, fragrance

Care: easy

◄ Mentha aquatica var. crispa

Mints are the backbone of many herb gardens, with richly colored, very aromatic foliage. These vigorous plants are very easy to grow and quickly spread into low mounds of attractive leaves. Tiny white, pink, lilac, purple, or blue summer flowers appear in spiky tufts at stem tips or in whorls where leaves join stems. Mints thrive in containers and can be potted for indoor use. Low-growing species make good ground covers for potted shrubs and quickly fill niches among paving stones; mow sturdy species into an aromatic carpet. Cooks prize the hundreds of mint varieties, which vary greatly in leaf shape, size, and fragrance. Fresh leaves are the most intensely flavored, but mint can also be frozen or dried. Use sprigs of fresh mint to flavor iced drinks and accent vegetable dishes. Mint sauces and jellies are a traditional accompaniment for meats; mint syrups dress up desserts; and crystallized mint leaves make an edible garnish. Steep fresh or dried leaves in boiling water for tea, or allow the infusion to cool into a refreshing facial splash. Add to bathwater for an aromatic soak. Mix dried leaves into herbal potpourri. Mints are a traditional herbal remedy, especially as a breath freshener and digestive aid.

Growing and care:
Plant divisions or rooted cuttings in spring or fall, setting them 8 to 12 inches apart. Provide apple mint with a protective winter mulch in colder zones. Restrain mint's aggressive spread by spading deeply around plants at least once annually or, more reliably, by confining plants in bottomless plastic or clay containers sunk with their rims projecting at least 2 inches above the soil and their sides at least 10 inches deep; pull out any stems that fall to the ground and root outside this barrier. Mints can also be restrained by growing them in patio containers. Established beds of peppermint, apple mint, and spearmint tolerate mowing. The leaves are most flavorful when cut before flowers appear; shear plants when buds first form to yield about 2 cups of leaves per plant, and continue to pinch or shear at 10-day intervals to prolong fresh leaf production. Dry the leaves flat on screens, or hang stems in bunches in a warm, well-ventilated area to dry, then rub the leaves from the stems. Crystallize leaves for garnishes by simmering gently in a heavy sugar syrup.

Selected species and varieties:
M. aquatica (water mint) bears heart-shaped 2-inch leaves on 1- to 2-foot stems; var. *crispa* (curly mint) has decoratively frilled leaf edges; Zones 5-10. *M.* x *gracilis* (gingermint) has shiny red-tinged leaves and stems, and is popular in Southeast Asian cuisine; Zones 3-9. *M.* x *piperita* (peppermint) characteristically bears 1- to 2-foot purple stems lined with intensely menthol-flavored deep green leaves yielding commercially important peppermint oil; var. *citrata* (orange bergamot) has a lemon fragrance and flavor; other varieties have aromatic overtones ranging from citrus to floral to chocolate; Zones 5-9. *M. spicata* (spearmint) produces wrinkled, pointed oval leaves 2 inches long with a sweet taste and fragrance lining 1- to 3-foot stems; Zones 3-9. *M. suaveolens* (apple mint, woolly mint) has hairy, wrinkled 2-inch leaves with a distinctly fruity aroma on 1- to 3-foot stems; 'Variegata' (pineapple mint, variegated apple mint) has creamy leaf edges and a pineapple scent; Zones 5-9.

MYRTLE
Myrtus

Light: mostly sun

Plant type: shrub

Hardiness: Zones 7-10

Height: 5 to 20 feet

Soil and Moisture: well-drained, moist

Interest: flowers, foliage

Care: easy to moderate

◀ Myrtus communis 'Variegata'

Myrtle's lustrous evergreen leaves, tiny flower buds, and white flowers with puffs of golden stamens share a spicy orange scent that has made the plant a favorite in wedding bouquets for generations. The plant has a mounding, upright habit ideal for massing into hedges. In colder areas myrtle is often grown as a container plant to accent patios in summer, and is then brought indoors over the winter. Weave fresh branches into wreaths. Toss fresh, peeled buds into salads. Use leaves and berries to flavor meats. Add dried flowers and leaves to potpourri.

Growing and care:
Start myrtle from seed sown in spring or from half-ripe cuttings taken in summer; plant in sites protected from drying winds. Myrtle will grow in light shade but prefers full sun. It tolerates severe pruning to maintain its size in containers.

Selected species and varieties:
M. communis (sweet myrtle, Greek myrtle) bears pairs of glossy 2-inch pointed oval leaves and creamy white ¾-inch flowers followed by blue-black berries; 'Flore Pleno' has doubled petals; 'Microphylla' is a dwarf ideal for containers; 'Variegata' has leaves marbled gray-green and cream.

PARSLEY
Petroselinum

Light: mostly sun

Plant type: biennial

Hardiness: Zones 6-9

Height: 1 to 2 feet

Soil and Moisture: well-drained, fertile, moist

Interest: foliage

Care: easy

◀ Petroselinum crispum var. neapolitanum

Whether bundled into a classic bouquet garni or chopped for use in sauces, eggs, vegetables, stuffings, or herb butters, parsley's classic deep green curly or flat leaves are as appealing to the eye as they are to the palate. The vitamin-rich sprigs freshen breath, and cooks around the world consider this herb a staple of the kitchen. The flatleaf types are more strongly flavored than curly varieties. Parsley is a biennial usually grown as an annual in the herb garden, as an edging plant, or in containers indoors or out.

Growing and care:
Soak parsley seed overnight before sowing to speed germination. Sow seed ¼ inch deep in soil warmed to at least 50°F. Thin seedlings to stand 4 to 6 inches apart. Begin harvesting leaves when plants are about 6 inches tall. Dry Italian parsley in the shade, oven, or microwave oven. Chop curly parsley and freeze in ice cubes for best flavor.

Selected species and varieties:
P. crispum var. *crispum* (curly parsley, French parsley) has highly frilled leaves on plants 1 to 1½ feet tall; var. *neapolitanum* (Italian parsley, flatleaf parsley) has flat, deeply lobed celery-like leaves on plants to 2 feet.

PATCHOULI
Pogostemon

Light: mostly sun

Plant type: perennial

Hardiness: Zone 10

Height: 3 to 4 feet

Soil and Moisture: well-drained, fertile, moist

Interest: foliage, fragrance

Care: moderate

◀ Pogostemon cablin

Patchouli's hairy triangular leaves contain a minty, cedar-scented oil valued in the making of perfume. Dried leaves gradually develop the scent and retain it for long periods in potpourri. In tropical gardens, patchouli forms mounds of fragrant foliage; elsewhere it is grown in containers to bring indoors when frost threatens.

Growing and care:
Patchouli rarely sets seed. Start new plants from tip cuttings or divisions in fall or spring. Outdoors where patchouli is not hardy, start tip cuttings to overwinter and treat plants as annuals, or grow in containers to move indoors. Feed potted plants weekly during spring and summer. Young leaves develop the best fragrance. Pinch plants two or three times each year to harvest young leaves and keep plants bushy. Dry leaves in a shady, well-ventilated area.

Selected species and varieties:
P. cablin [also classified as *P. patchouli*] has lightly scalloped leaves up to 5 inches long and half as wide in pairs along square stems tipped with 5- to 6-inch spikes of violet-tinged white flowers with violet filaments in fall.

PERILLA
Perilla

Light: mostly sun

Plant type: annual

Height: 1 to 3 feet

Soil and Moisture: well-drained, sandy, moist

Interest: foliage

Care: easy to moderate

◀ Perilla frutescens 'Atropurpurea'

The foliage of perilla adds color and fragrance to the herb garden or border, with mounds of wrinkled, aromatic burgundy leaves that contrast nicely when used as a filler among gray or white foliage. The leaves and seeds have a fragrance and flavor that blend mint and cinnamon, and yield an oil 2,000 times sweeter than sugar. Perilla is a staple in Japanese cuisine, where it is used fresh or pickled to garnish sushi and flavor bean curd. Spikes of flower buds are batter-fried for tempura. Leaves are used to color vinegar and fruit preserves. Add the dried seed heads to herbal wreaths.

Growing and care:
Sow perilla seed in spring, and thin seedlings to stand 1 foot apart. Harvest leaves anytime; gather flowers for tempura just as buds begin to form. Harvesting flower buds also encourages bushier growth. Allowed to produce mature seed, the plants self-sow readily.

Selected species and varieties:
P. frutescens 'Atropurpurea' (black nettle) has pairs of wrinkled oval leaves up to 5 inches long on square stems tipped with spikes of tiny white summer flowers in whorls, followed by brown nutlets.

PYCNANTHEMUM
Pycnanthemum

Light: mostly sun

Plant type: perennial

Hardiness: Zones 4-8

Height: 2 to 3 feet

Soil and Moisture: well-drained, moist

Interest: flowers, foliage, fragrance

Care: easy

◀ Pycnanthemum virginianum

A pleasingly sharp, peppery aroma fills the garden wherever pycnanthemum grows. The stout, square stems of this vigorous, mounding perennial herb are lined with whorls of very narrow aromatic leaves. In summer tufts of flowers appear at the tips of the stems and attract bees and butterflies to the garden. The plant is excellent in the herb garden or naturalized in wildflower meadows. As intensely flavored as it is fragrant, pycnanthemum is an excellent culinary substitute for true mint. Dry the dense flower heads for arrangements, or add dried leaves and flowers to potpourri.

Growing and care:

Pycnanthemum is easy to grow from cuttings or divisions of mature plants. Set plants out in spring or fall, spacing them 8 to 12 inches apart. Restrain their spread by spading around plants annually or by planting them in bottomless tubs and removing branches that root outside this barrier.

Selected species and varieties:

P. virginianum (Virginia mountain mint, wild basil, prairie hyssop) has smooth or slightly toothed, pointed, very narrow 1- to 1½-inch aromatic leaves and tiny white to lilac flowers in very dense, flat heads in summer.

SCENTED GERANIUM
Pelargonium

Light: mostly sun

Plant type: annual, perennial, or shrub

Hardiness: Zone 10

Height: 1 to 6 feet

Soil and Moisture: well-drained, fertile, moist

Interest: foliage, fragrance

Care: easy

◀ P. capitatum

Scented geraniums are a diverse group of plants, with more scents than a spice rack. When brushed or rubbed, the foliage emits a citrusy, floral, minty, or resinous perfume, depending on the species or cultivar. The kidney-shaped or broad triangular leaves are wrinkled, lobed, frilled, or filigreed to add texture to a border. Loose, open clusters of small white, pink, mauve, or lilac flowers on branching stalks add color in spring or summer. Outdoors year round where they can be protected from frost, taller species grow as border specimens or background shrubs or can be pruned into standards; sprawling types can be used as ground covers or trained against trellises. Elsewhere, scented geraniums are treated like summer bedding plants or grown in containers or hanging baskets; they also do well year round as houseplants. Use fresh leaves of citrus-, floral-, or mint-scented geraniums in teas and to flavor baked goods, jam, jelly, vinegar, syrup, or sugar; use resinous leaves to flavor pâté and sausage. Toss flowers into salads for color. Add dried leaves to floral or herbal potpourri. Infuse leaves in warm water for an aromatic, mildly astringent facial splash.

Growing and care:

Sow seed indoors 10 to 12 weeks before the last frost. While all scented geraniums do best in mostly sunny spots, lemon geranium, apple geranium, and peppermint geranium will tolerate a bit more shade. Too-rich soil

(continued)

tends to minimize fragrance. Remove faded flowers to encourage further blooming. In containers, scented geraniums do best when slightly potbound; repot only into the next larger size pot. Indoors, provide daytime temperatures of 65° to 70°F, about 10° cooler at night, with at least 5 hours of direct sunlight daily. Keep potted plants from becoming leggy by pruning them hard after blooming or in very early spring, then feeding with any complete houseplant fertilizer. To propagate scented geraniums, cut a branch tip at least 3 inches long just below a leaf node, dip into rooting hormone, and place in clean, moist sand to root; transplant into potting soil after 2 weeks. Pick scented geranium leaves for drying anytime and lay in a single layer on screens in a shady location.

Selected species and varieties:

P. capitatum (wild rose geranium, rose-scented geranium) is a spreading plant 1 to 2 feet tall and up to 5 feet wide with crinkled, velvety 2-inch rose-scented leaves and mauve to pink summer flowers. *P. citronellum* has lemon-scented 3½-inch-wide leaves with pointed lobes and pink summer flowers streaked purple on upright shrubs to 6 feet tall and half as wide. *P. crispum* (lemon geranium) has strongly lemon-scented, kidney-shaped ½-inch leaves and pink to lavender flowers in spring and summer on plants 2 feet tall and half as wide, whose leaves are traditionally used in finger bowls. *P.* x *fragrans* 'Variegatum' (nutmeg geranium) has small, downy gray-green leaves smelling of nutmeg and pine, and white spring to summer flowers lined with red on compact plants 12 to 16 inches tall and as wide. *P. graveolens* (rose geranium) has filigreed, rose-scented gray-green leaves and pale pink spring to summer flowers spotted purple on upright shrubs to 3 feet tall and as wide. *P. odoratissimum* (apple geranium) is a spreading plant 1 foot tall and twice as wide with small, kidney-shaped velvety, apple-scented leaves and red-veined white spring and summer flowers on trailing flower stalks. *P. tomentosum* (peppermint geranium) is a spreading plant to 3 feet tall and twice as wide with 4- to 5-inch peppermint-scented leaves and white spring to summer flowers.

SOAPWORT
Saponaria

Light: mostly sun	
Plant type: perennial	
Hardiness: Zones 3-8	
Height: 1 to 2 feet	
Soil and Moisture: well-drained, moist	
Interest: flowers, foliage	
Care: easy	

◀ Saponaria officinalis 'Rubra Plena'

Soapwort bears clusters of pale blush pink summer flowers scented with the aroma of raspberries and cloves atop clumps of erect stems. The flowers resemble ruffled funnels during the day, then open fully at night into casual, open bells. Toss flowers into salads or dry them for potpourri. Leaves, stems, and roots boiled in rainwater produce a soapy liquid prized for cleaning antique textiles. Soapwort once figured in herbal medicine but is now considered toxic.

Growing and care:

Sow soapwort in spring or fall, or divide mature plants in late fall or early spring. Avoid planting near ponds, as root secretions are toxic to fish. Plants self-sow invasively. Shear spent flowers to prevent seed formation and control spread. Shearing sometimes produces a second bloom. For liquid soap, boil sliced roots, stems, and leaves in lime-free water for 30 minutes and strain.

Selected species and varieties:

S. officinalis (bouncing Bet) has pointed oval leaves paired along sturdy stems and 1- to 1½-inch-wide pink flowers with single or double rows of petals; 'Rubra Plena' has double red petals that fade to pink.

SOCIETY GARLIC
Tulbaghia

Light: mostly sun	
Plant type: bulb	
Hardiness: Zones 9-10	
Height: 1 to 1½ feet	
Soil and Moisture: well-drained, fertile, moist	
Interest: flowers, foliage, fragrance	
Care: easy	

◀ Tulbaghia violacea

Society garlic is one of the most attractive plants in the herb garden, with large clusters of starry white, pink, or violet summer flowers on tall stalks above clumps of grassy evergreen leaves. Use society garlic's neat mound as a specimen in the perennial border, or grow the plant as an edging for garden beds or walkways. In cooler climates society garlic grows well as a potted plant and can be wintered on a sunny window sill. Use the flowers in fresh bouquets. The leaves, with an onion or garlic aroma and a mild taste that does not linger on the breath, can be chopped and used like garlic chives—as a garnish flavoring for salads, vegetables, and sauces.

Growing and care:
Propagate society garlic by removing and replanting the small bulblets growing alongside mature bulbs in spring or fall. Space plants 1 foot apart. For indoor culture, plant one bulb per 6- to 8-inch pot.

Selected species and varieties:
T. violacea has flat, grassy 8- to 12-inch leaves and ¾-inch white or violet flowers in clusters of eight to 16 blossoms on 1- to 2½-foot stalks; 'Silver Streak' has leaves striped cream and green.

SORREL
Rumex

Light: mostly sun	
Plant type: perennial	
Hardiness: Zones 3-8	
Height: 6 inches to 5 feet	
Soil and Moisture: well-drained, moist	
Interest: foliage, seed heads	
Care: easy	

◀ Rumex crispus

Sorrel is a very vigorous, persistent perennial that, once planted in the garden, often becomes a permanent resident. The slightly sour, lemony, arrowhead-shaped leaves add zest to salads and accent soups and sauces. Use fresh leaves sparingly, as the high oxalic acid content can aggravate conditions such as gout. Boil leaves for a spinachlike vegetable, changing the water once to reduce the acid content. Birds love the tiny seeds produced at the tips of the stalks.

Growing and care:
Sow sorrel indoors 6 to 8 weeks before the last frost, outdoors after the last frost, or divide mature plants and space 8 inches apart. Leaves become bitter in hot weather, but flavor returns with cooler temperatures. Pinch out flowering stalks to encourage leaf production and control invasive self-sowing. The plants self-sow prolifically and sometimes become more of a problem than a pleasure.

Selected species and varieties:
R. acetosa (garden sorrel, sour dock) bears narrow 5- to 8-inch leaves on clumps of 3-foot stems. *R. crispus* (curled dock) has extremely wavy, curly 12-inch leaves on plants 1 to 5 feet tall. *R. scutatus* (French sorrel) bears thick, broad shield-shaped leaves 1 to 2 inches long on trailing stems growing into mats 6 to 20 inches high and twice as wide.

SWEET FERN
Comptonia

Light: mostly sun	
Plant type: shrub	
Hardiness: Zones 2-6	
Height: 3 to 5 feet	
Soil and Moisture: well-drained, moist to dry	
Interest: foliage	
Care: easy	

◀ Comptonia peregrina

In the morning and evening, sweet fern perfumes the air in the wildflower garden or perennial border with a warm, sweet fragrance unlike any other herb. The plants form neat, tidy mounds of deep green foliage and fit well into borders and herb gardens alike. Sweet fern's lacy deciduous leaves are lightly covered with rusty brown hairs and resemble the fronds of a fern. The leaves make a delightful tea that was used by Native Americans as a medicine.

Growing and care:
Sow ripe sweet fern seed in fall, and overwinter in cold frames to transplant in spring. Otherwise, remove and transplant rooted suckers in spring or layer branches to develop rooted cuttings. Sweet fern can be difficult to transplant; to disturb roots as little as possible, dig up a large rootball when moving suckers or layered cuttings. Sweet fern grows best in loose, open soils and tolerates dry conditions.

Selected species and varieties:
C. peregrina has fans of narrow 5-inch pointed leaves with red-brown dangling male catkins and smaller round female flowers in summer followed by shiny conical brown nutlets in fall.

SWEET FLAG
Acorus

Light: mostly sun	
Plant type: perennial	
Hardiness: Zones 3-10	
Height: 1 to 5 feet	
Soil and Moisture: well-drained to heavy, wet	
Interest: foliage	
Care: easy	

◀ Acorus gramineus 'Variegatus'

Sweet flag is an aromatic herb with tangerine-scented leaves and cinnamon-smelling rhizomes. The plants thrive in wet soils along stream banks or in aquatic gardens and are easy to grow once established. Once used in herbal medicine, sweet flag is now considered hazardous. The spicy rhizomes are still gathered and used to scent potpourri.

Growing and care:
Sweet flag should be planted in soil that stays constantly wet, and thrives even when grown under 2 inches of water. It can be propagated from fresh seed sown soon after it is gathered or by division of the rhizomes in spring or fall. For potpourri collect rhizomes that are at least 2 to 3 years old in spring, wash well, slice, and dry; do not peel them, as much of their aromatic oil is in the outer layers.

Selected species and varieties:
A. calamus bears sword-shaped ¾-inch-wide leaves up to 5 feet tall and tiny yellow-green summer flowers. *A. gramineus* (Japanese sweet flag) has narrow leaves up to 20 inches long and a 2- to 3-inch spadix in summer; 'Ogon' has 12-inch leaves striped golden green and cream; 'Variegatus' has white-edged 1½-foot leaves only ¼ inch wide; Zones 7-10.

VALERIAN
Valeriana

Light: mostly sun

Plant type: perennial

Hardiness: Zones 3-9

Height: 3 to 5 feet

Soil and Moisture: well-drained, moist

Interest: flowers, fragrance

Care: easy

◀ Valeriana officinalis

Valerian is an attractive plant that is as beautiful as it is useful. The tall, vigorous plants bear small flat-topped tufts of tiny fragrant flowers in summer above a rosette of lacy fernlike leaves. Both cats and butterflies find the plants irresistible. The flowers have the scent of vanilla and honey and add soft texture to fresh floral bouquets. While some gardeners find the odor of the dried roots agreeable and add them to potpourri, others compare it to dirty socks. The roots yield a sedative compound used in herbal medicine. Add the mineral-rich leaves to compost.

Growing and care:
Sow common valerian seed in spring, or divide the creeping roots in spring or fall. Space plants 2 feet apart and mulch to conserve moisture. The plants thrive in cool, shaded locations and are weakened by hot, humid weather. Valerian spreads quickly and will self-sow if the flower heads are not removed.

Selected species and varieties:
V. officinalis (common valerian) has erect hairy stems lined with light green ferny leaves and flower stalks to 5 feet with tubular white, pink, red, or lavender-blue flowers in clusters up to 4 inches wide.

WILD CELERY
Apium

Light: mostly sun

Plant type: biennial grown as annual

Height: 1 to 3 feet

Soil and Moisture: well-drained, fertile, moist

Interest: foliage

Care: moderate

◀ Apium graveolens

The ridged stems, parsleylike leaves, and tiny seeds of wild celery all share the scent of the cultivated vegetable beloved as an aromatic culinary staple. While the stems and leaves are a bit too bitter for use in salads, they are excellent tossed into the cooking pot as a seasoning. Use wild celery sparingly, as it is toxic in large amounts.

Growing and care:
Sow wild celery seed in sites sheltered from drying winds. Thin out the seedlings to stand 12 to 16 inches apart. Water regularly to keep soil moist. In warm regions mulch around plants to keep soil cool. Gather leaves as needed and dry in a single layer in a shady, well-ventilated area. To obtain seed, pick flower heads as they begin to brown and store in paper bags until they dry and release seeds.

Selected species and varieties:
A. graveolens (wild celery, smallage) has rosettes of flat fan-shaped leaflets with toothed edges the first year, followed by elongated, ridged, branching stems tipped with small clusters of greenish cream summer flowers.

CAROLINA JASMINE
Gelsemium

Light: mostly sun

Plant type: woody vine

Hardiness: Zones 6-9

Height: 10 to 20 feet

Soil and Moisture: well-drained, moist

Interest: flowers, fragrance

Care: easy

◀ Gelsemium sempervirens

Carolina jasmine is a vigorous, twining evergreen vine with fragrant yellow funnel-shaped flowers in late winter to early spring. It is a favorite ornamental plant in the South. The tiered leaves provide fine texture to fences, trellises, or unsightly features, and the plant is also an excellent rambling ground cover. Planted at the base of a tree, it scrambles up the trunk. Tucked into the top of a retaining wall, it spills flowers and foliage over the side.

Growing and care:
Carolina jasmine grows best in soil well amended with rotted manure and compost but adapts to less fertile conditions. Best flowering occurs in mostly sunny locations. After a few years of growth the vines usually become top heavy and should be pruned back hard when dormant.

Selected species and varieties:
G. sempervirens (Carolina yellow jessamine, false jasmine, evening trumpet flower) is a vigorous grower with slender wiry stems bearing 1½-inch-long flowers singly or in clusters in the axils of narrow lance-shaped dark green leaves 1 to 3½ inches long that turn yellowish green or dull purplish in winter.

CHOKEBERRY
Aronia

Light: mostly sun

Plant type: ground cover

Hardiness: Zones 4-9

Height: 2 to 10 feet

Soil and Moisture: well-drained, moist to dry

Interest: flowers, foliage, fruit

Care: easy

◀ Aronia arbutifolia 'Brilliantissima'

Chokeberry is a shrubby ground cover whose thick tangles of woody stems bear a profusion of tiny cherrylike blossoms in spring. The snow white flowers yield to abundant clusters of glossy red berries that persist from fall through winter. The plant's dark green oval leaves turn bright scarlet in fall. Chokeberry is a vigorous grower producing plentiful suckers and dense stands, making it very effective for slopes, meadows, or shrub borders.

Growing and care:
Plant chokeberries in well-worked soil amended with some organic matter. The plants should be watered regularly in the months after planting, but once established are very drought tolerant. Fertilize lightly after flowering is completed in spring. Propagate from seed, from cuttings, or by transplanting rooted suckers.

Selected species and varieties:
A. arbutifolia 'Brilliantissima' bears ⅓-inch white spring-blooming flowers touched with red, followed by clusters of ¼-inch red berries on shrubs to 10 feet tall. *A. melanocarpa* (black chokeberry) is a very vigorous, fast-spreading shrub with dark green leaves turning bright red in fall, and white spring flowers followed by black berries.

831

CLEMATIS
Clematis

Light: mostly sun

Plant type: vine

Hardiness: Zones 3-9

Height: 6 to 25 feet

Soil and Moisture: well-drained, moist

Interest: flowers, foliage, seed heads, fragrance

Care: moderate

◀ Clematis x jackmanii 'Gypsy Queen'

Vigorous growth and large, spectacular flowers make clematis a favorite for growing on fences, trellises, or other structures. These hardy, leafy vines are covered with show-stopping fragrant flowers from late spring to fall, depending on the species. Masses of feathery seed heads add attractive accents after the flowers have faded.

Growing and care:
Plant clematis 2 to 3 inches deeper than it was growing in its container. Mulch in summer to keep roots cool, and again in late fall to protect from heaving in late winter. Propagate species from cuttings or seed, spacing plants 2 to 4 feet apart.

Selected species and varieties:
C. alpina (Alpine clematis) bears 1½- to 3-inch single lantern-shaped mauve or blue flowers in spring on 8-foot vines; Zones 3-7. *C. x jackmanii* (Jackman clematis) bears 4- to 7-inch deep violet flowers on 10-foot robust stems from late spring to frost; many cultivars are available, with flowers in shades of white, red, blue, and purple, some with single flowers, others with double; 'Gypsy Queen' has rich violet-red flowers; Zones 3-8. *C. paniculata* (sweet autumn clematis) bears 1- to 4-inch dainty white flowers on 25-foot vines in early fall. *C. texensis* (scarlet clematis) has leathery ¾-inch scarlet flowers in clusters from late spring until frost on 6- to 12-foot stems; Zones 6-9.

CLOCK VINE
Thunbergia

Light: mostly sun

Plant type: vine

Hardiness: Zone 10

Height: 3 to 6 feet

Soil and Moisture: well-drained, fertile, moist to dry

Interest: flowers

Care: easy

◀ Thunbergia alata

Clock vine is a perky climbing or trailing vine that produces masses of neat triangular leaves and cheerful-looking flowers throughout summer. Clock vine blossoms come in shades of deep yellow, gold, orange, and creamy white, each flower with a dark central eye. Plants are attractive in window boxes and hanging baskets, and are excellent as a fast-growing screen on a trellis or fence.

Growing and care:
Start seed indoors 6 to 8 weeks prior to the last frost, or sow directly outdoors after danger of frost has passed. Space plants 1 foot apart and provide support if you wish them to climb. Plants thrive where summer temperatures remain somewhat cool. Water during dry periods. If soil dries out the plants may stop flowering.

Selected species and varieties:
T. alata (black-eyed Susan vine) develops twining stems with 3-inch leaves with toothed margins and winged petioles. The solitary flowers are 1 to 2 inches across with five distinct rounded petal segments, usually surrounding a black or dark purple center; 'Susie' is a series with dark-centered flowers in three distinct shades of white, yellow, and orange.

CRIMSON STARGLORY
Mina

Light: mostly sun	
Plant type: vine	
Hardiness: Zones 8-10	
Height: 15 to 20 feet	
Soil and Moisture: well-drained, fertile, moist	
Interest: flowers	
Care: moderate	

◀ Mina lobata

This vigorous, fast-growing vine is native to Mexico and brings tropical color and form to sunny gardens. The attractive plant climbs by twining its reddish stem around supports. Throughout summer numerous red buds open to reveal tubular flowers that turn from orange to white as they mature. Plants provide an elegant light-textured screen or background for other flowers when grown on a trellis or fence. They can also be grown in containers.

Growing and care:
Start seed indoors in individual peat pots 6 weeks prior to the last frost, or directly in the garden after danger of frost has passed. Keep plants well mulched and supplied with abundant water. Fertilize when the first flower buds appear. Plants are hardy from Zone 8 south, but in warmer areas will benefit from midday shade.

Selected species and varieties:
M. lobata produces attractive dark green, three-lobed leaves along self-twining stems. The 1-inch flowers appear in showy long-stalked clusters, beginning as red boat-shaped buds that open orange, change to yellow, and eventually turn creamy white. All colors are present on a single cluster.

FIG
Ficus

Light: mostly sun	
Plant type: tender perennial vine	
Hardiness: Zones 9-10	
Height: 20 to 60 feet	
Soil and Moisture: well-drained, moist	
Interest: foliage	
Care: moderate	

◀ Ficus pumila

Related to the edible fig, this fig is grown for its rich green foliage rather than any fruit. Also known as creeping fig, this rambling vine rapidly covers walls or unsightly objects with a glossy mosaic of emerald-colored leaves. Particularly useful for covering masonry, fig's small, clinging roots, like those of English ivy, attach to brick, cement, or stucco. Young stems intertwine to create a dense network of branches. Creeping fig can also be grown in a container or as a houseplant.

Growing and care:
Creeping fig thrives with abundant water during the growing season. To promote bushiness pinch new shoots, and to maintain a neat, clinging habit remove the mature branches that extend away from the support. In late fall or early spring, thin plants to reduce density and maintain vigor. Although creeping fig is generally free of pests, woolly aphids can be a problem. Propagate by cuttings or layering.

Selected species and varieties:
F. pumila (creeping fig) produces numerous slender intertwined stems that crisscross to form a dense mat on a support, rapidly growing 20 to 60 feet, with 1-inch heart-shaped evergreen leaves; if allowed to develop, mature plants produce erect shoots with thickened 2- to 4-inch leaves and occasional 2-inch heart-shaped fruit; 'Variegata' bears white-mottled leaves.

GOTU KOLA
Centella

Light: mostly sun

Plant type: perennial ground cover

Hardiness: Zones 8-10

Height: 6 to 20 inches

Soil and Moisture: well-drained, moist to wet

Interest: foliage

Care: easy

◀ Centella asiatica

Gotu kola is versatile ground cover that is as much at home in a hanging basket as it is in the garden. The dainty scalloped-edged leaves line slender, trailing reddish green stems forming mats of soft-textured foliage. Tiny white or pink flowers hide beneath the leaves. Allow gotu kola to ramble, or grow it in patio containers. Its colorful trailing stems make it an ideal plant for hanging baskets.

Growing and care:

Sow gotu kola seed in spring or fall in moist or wet soil. Plants grow best in mostly sunny places where moisture is abundant. The plant roots easily as it grows along the ground, and these natural layers can be transplanted anytime; space them 1 to 2 feet apart. Gotu kola is sometimes invasive where conditions are favorable for its growth.

Selected species and varieties:

C. asiatica [also classified as *Hydrocotyle asiatica*] (gotu kola, tiger grass) has kidney-shaped 1- to 2-inch bright green leaves with gently lobed edges and white to pink flowers in summer.

GRAPE
Vitis

Light: mostly sun

Plant type: vine

Hardiness: Zones 5-8

Height: 20 to 50 feet

Soil and Moisture: well-drained, moist

Interest: foliage, fruit, bark

Care: moderate

◀ Vitis vinifera 'Purpurea'

Grapes are very vigorous, fast-growing vines that quickly cover arbors and trellises with a shady veil of green foliage. The plant's twining tendrils cling to just about any structure, providing nearly instant screens or canopies. The broad leaves, attractively lobed and incised, color brilliantly in fall. Older stems have shredding, peeling bark, while younger shoots carry clusters of blue-black fruit well into winter.

Growing and care:

Plant in deeply cultivated soil enriched with generous amounts of organic matter. Fertilize in spring a few weeks after flowering. When growing for shade or an arbor, cut canes back to a strong bud in winter to control spread. Propagate from cuttings.

Selected species and varieties:

V. amurensis (Amur grape) has 5- to 10-inch leaves that color crimson to purple in fall. *V. coignetiae* (crimson glory vine) is an extremely fast-growing vine—up to 50 feet per year—with 4- to 10-inch leaves turning scarlet in fall. *V. vinifera* 'Purpurea' (wine grape, common grape) bears 4- to 6-inch heart-shaped leaves that emerge reddish burgundy then mature to purple.

HONEYSUCKLE
Lonicera

Light: mostly sun

Plant type: woody vine

Hardiness: Zones 4-9

Height: 15 to 30 feet

Soil and Moisture: well-drained, fertile, moist to dry

Interest: flowers, foliage, fragrance

Care: easy

◀ Lonicera sempervirens

The rich, sweetly scented flowers of honeysuckle add a unique ambiance to any garden. The distinctive tubular blossoms are produced in great abundance along the fast-growing twining stems and are a magnet to hummingbirds. These vines are easy to grow and some may even become invasive if their growth is left unchecked. In the garden, honeysuckle provides a long season of bloom and can be trained to climb a trellis or fence, or to grow over old shrubs, providing colorful boundaries to borders and plantings.

Growing and care:
Plant honeysuckle in soil with abundant organic matter. Fertilize when flower buds first appear in spring, and prune immediately after flowering to maintain desired size. Provide sturdy supports for twining stems. Do not allow honeysuckle to twine around young trees, because it can cause girdling. Propagate by seed or cuttings.

Selected species and varieties:
L. sempervirens (trumpet honeysuckle) bears dark blue-green leaves and spring-blooming flowers; 'Alabama Crimson' is a twining vine to 20 feet with showy clusters of small, trumpet-shaped crimson flowers with bright yellow stamens; 'Sulphurea' is a 20-foot twining vine with a dense habit, evergreen oval leaves, and yellow flowers followed by ¼-inch shiny red berries in late summer and fall.

MAZUS
Mazus

Light: mostly sun

Plant type: ground cover

Hardiness: Zones 6-9

Height: 2 inches

Soil and Moisture: well-drained, moist, fertile

Interest: flowers, foliage

Care: easy

◀ Mazus reptans

A true ground hugger, mazus forms a dense, prostrate carpet with medium green oval leaves and one-sided clusters of charming rose to lavender flowers in late spring. The unusual blossoms have a white or yellow throat accented with polka dots. Mazus works well in rock gardens and borders, and since it tolerates occasional foot traffic, it makes an ideal plant for tucking between steppingstones.

Growing and care:
Set plants 12 to 15 inches apart in well-worked soil amended with rotted manure or peat moss. As mazus grows, roots develop along the stem, allowing it to compete well with weeds and grass. Propagate by dividing the plants in spring.

Selected species and varieties:
M. reptans has procumbent stems bearing inch-long coarsely toothed leaves that hold well into late fall or early winter, along with ½-inch-long flowers gathered into profuse lavender to purplish blue clusters, usually spotted with white or yellow in the center; 'Alba' has snowy white flowers.

ST.-JOHN'S-WORT
Hypericum

Light: mostly sun

Plant type: ground cover

Hardiness: Zones 5-8

Height: 1 to 1½ feet

Soil and Moisture: well-drained, moist to dry

Interest: flowers

Care: moderate

◀ Hypericum calycinum

St.-John's-wort has long-lasting sunny yellow flowers accented by a pincushion clump of central stamens. In fall the old flower stems hold interesting winged fruit capsules that persist into winter. The plant makes a stunning ground cover for open, mostly sunny slopes, and is an excellent addition to rock gardens or wildflower plantings.

Growing and care:
Plant St.-John's-wort in gravelly well-drained soil rich in limestone. In acid soils add ground limestone a few weeks before planting in spring. Space plants 1 to 1½ feet apart. Propagate by division in spring or by softwood cuttings in early summer. Provide extra water during dry periods. The plants may be short lived and should be divided every 4 to 5 years to rejuvenate them.

Selected species and varieties:
H. calycinum (creeping St.-John's-wort) produces 2- to 3-inch vivid yellow flowers with bright red anthers from summer to early fall, and creeping stems with dark green semievergreen leaves that turn purplish in fall.

WINTER CREEPER
Euonymus

Light: mostly sun

Plant type: ground cover

Hardiness: Zones 4-8

Height: 1 to 3 feet

Soil and Moisture: well-drained, moist

Interest: foliage

Care: easy

◀ Euonymus fortunei 'Emerald Charm'

Winter creeper is a versatile creeping shrub that is equally at home climbing a wall or spreading over the garden as a ground cover. The irregular mounds of glossy dark green leaves are perfect as an informal accent in the front of the shrub border, as a foundation planting, or in rock gardens. Winter creeper can also be trained as a climber on trellises or walls where the stout branches attract nesting birds.

Growing and care:
Plant winter creeper in loosened soil that has some organic matter. The plants grow well in full sun to full shade but prefer mostly sunny locations. Provide extra water during dry periods. Mulch in spring and fall to keep weeds down and conserve soil moisture.

Selected species and varieties:
E. fortunei is an evergreen ground cover with creeping stems covered with glossy, dark green leathery leaves; 'Dart's Blanket' is a salt-tolerant prostrate type growing 12 to 16 inches high with dark green leaves; 'Emerald Charm' grows to 3 feet with glossy green leaves; 'Gold Prince' grows in mounds 2 feet high with gold-tipped leaves that later turn all green.

BLUE OAT GRASS
Helictotrichon

Light: mostly sun

Plant type: ornamental grass

Hardiness: Zones 4-9

Height: 2 to 3 feet

Soil and Moisture: well-drained, moist to dry

Interest: foliage, flowers

Care: easy

◄ Helictotrichon sempervirens

Blue oat grass produces a dense clump of stiff, upright steel blue foliage and is a valuable addition to a rock garden or herbaceous border for both color and form. It contrasts well to perennials with green or silvery white leaves. The metallic blue color is also a lovely complement to the burgundy leaves of shrubs such as barberry 'Crimson Pygmy' or smokebush 'Royal Purple'. The flowers are buff colored and appear in graceful sprays above the leaves.

Growing and care:
Blue oat grass is easy to grow and develops its best color in dry, infertile soils. Space plants 1 to 1½ feet apart in an airy location with good air circulation. Cut back foliage to the ground in early spring before new growth begins. Propagate plants by division in early spring.

Selected species and varieties:
H. sempervirens forms a dense mound 2 to 3 feet high and equally wide, with light blue-gray leaves and flowers arrayed in drooping, one-sided 4- to 6-inch clusters on slender stems held above the foliage.

BRISTLE GRASS
Setaria

Light: mostly sun

Plant type: annual grass

Height: 2 to 5 feet

Soil and Moisture: well-drained, moist

Interest: foliage

Care: easy

◄ Setaria italica

Bristle grass is an ornamental grass from Asia with narrow linear leaves that have an agreeable though pungent odor when crushed. Cylindrical 1-foot-long seed heads appear in late summer to fall that gently bend among the arching leaves. Plants can be used as a background or summer hedge and are often cut for dried indoor arrangements.

Growing and care:
Bristle grass is a vigorous, easy-to-grow plant. Start seed indoors in individual peat pots 4 to 6 weeks prior to the last frost, or sow directly outdoors in early spring while soil is still cool. Transplant carefully, being sure not to disturb the roots and allowing 1 to 3 feet between plants. Water each week for a month to aid in rapid root growth. Once established, plants often self-seed and may become weedy.

Selected species and varieties:
S. italica (foxtail millet) produces rough-textured medium green leaves, each with a hairy basal sheath, and long-stemmed, dense flower spikes with green, purple, or brown bristles maturing into attractive seed heads in fall.

JAPANESE BLOOD GRASS
Imperata

Light: mostly sun

Plant type: ornamental grass

Hardiness: Zones 6-9

Height: 1 to 1 ½ feet

Soil and Moisture: well-drained, moist

Interest: foliage

Care: easy

◄ Imperata cylindrica 'Red Baron'

Japanese blood grass is a show-stopping addition to any garden, with ember red erect leaves that resemble flames flicking skyward. The slender leaf blades emerge green in spring and turn vivid red as summer advances to fall. The erect clumps of straplike leaves are particularly striking massed in a border, especially when mixed with coneflower and golden yarrow.

Growing and care:

Japanese blood grass will grow in a variety of conditions but attains the best color in mostly sunny sites. Plant plugs 1 foot apart in spring while soil is still cool. Keep soil evenly moist throughout the growing season. Fertilize lightly in spring. Remove any parts of the plant that revert to the solid green color of the parent species as they appear. Cut back to ground level in late winter or early spring before new growth begins. Propagate by division of clumps in spring.

Selected species and varieties:

I. cylindrica 'Red Baron' produces nonflowering clumps of ¼- to ½-inch-wide leaf blades that are green in spring and turn bright red in early summer through late fall.

LEMON GRASS
Cymbopogon

Light: mostly sun

Plant type: ornamental grass

Hardiness: Zones 9-10

Height: 2 to 6 feet

Soil and Moisture: well-drained, sandy, moist

Interest: foliage

Care: easy

◄ Cymbopogon citratus

Lemon grass is a clump-forming ornamental grass with abundant, flowing lemon-scented leaves. This easy-to-grow plant is as useful as it is ornamental, adding grace to borders and herb gardens as well as spicing up recipes. Steep fresh or dried leaves for a refreshing herbal tea. Lemon grass is also an excellent container plant for patios and decks, and is often grown on window sills in winter as part of a cold-season herb garden.

Growing and care:

Plant divisions of lemon grass in spring, spacing them 2 to 3 feet apart. Apply mulch both to conserve moisture in summer and to protect roots in winter. Where frost is a possibility, pot divisions in fall after cutting back to 3 inches and keep indoors over winter, watering only sparingly to prevent root rot. Provide moisture in extreme drought. Cut stems at ground level for fresh use, taking care when handling the leaf's sharp edges, and use the lower 3 to 4 inches for best flavor.

Selected species and varieties:

C. citratus (lemon grass, fever grass) has inch-wide aromatic evergreen leaves with sharp edges growing from bulbous stems in clumps to 6 feet tall and 3 feet wide.

MUHLY
Muhlenbergia

Light: mostly sun

Plant type: ornamental grass

Hardiness: Zones 6-10

Height: 1 to 4 feet

Soil and Moisture: well-drained, sandy, moist

Interest: flowers, foliage

Care: easy

◀ Muhlenbergia capillaris

The graceful foliage and airy flowers of these clump-forming perennial grasses make unforgettable mass plantings. In fall the softly colored seed heads complement the yellows and reds of the autumn garden. Plant muhly in mixed borders or rock gardens. The plants also look beautiful in meadows or on the upland shores of streams and ponds.

Growing and care:
Pink muhly adapts to moist or dry, sandy or clayey soil and tolerates occasional flooding or drought. Lindheimer muhly prefers moist, well-drained rocky soil, but it tolerates drought once established. Cut muhly grasses to the ground in early spring before new growth begins. Propagate by seed.

Selected species and varieties:
M. capillaris (pink muhly, hair grass) grows to 1½ to 3 feet with narrow, wiry, nearly evergreen leaves and 8- to 20-inch clusters of soft pink flowers on branching stems in early fall, followed by purplish seed heads; it is native to the eastern half of the United States. *M. lindheimeri* (Lindheimer muhly) produces clumps of narrow blue-green leaves 1½ feet long and purplish flower spikes on stalks up to 4 feet tall in fall, followed by silvery seed heads; Texas native; Zones 7-9.

SEDGE
Carex

Light: mostly sun

Plant type: ornamental grass

Hardiness: Zones 5-9

Height: 1 to 3 feet

Soil and Moisture: well-drained, fertile, moist

Interest: foliage

Care: easy

◀ Carex morrowii 'Variegata'

Sedge is a tough, very beautiful grasslike plant that thrives in a wide variety of gardening conditions. The neat mounds of gracefully arching narrow leaves make sedge useful in the foreground of edgings and rock gardens as well as sprinkled throughout mixed borders. It is also effective massed in large groups, where its soft texture and fluidity lend an airy, delicate touch to sunny landscapes.

Growing and care:
Plant sedge in moist, fertile soil that has been generously amended with organic matter. Space plants 12 to 15 inches apart. Sedge needs little care once established. Prune out any damaged leaves as they appear.

Selected species and varieties:
C. buchananii (leatherleaf sedge, fox-red sedge) has dense clumps of very narrow, reddish bronze leaves to 20 inches high; Zones 7-9. *C. morrowii* 'Variegata' (variegated Japanese sedge) has gracefully swirling 1- to 1½-foot-tall moplike mounds with leathery evergreen cream and green leaves ¼ to ½ inch wide; Zones 6-9. *C. pendula* (drooping sedge, giant sedge, sedge grass) produces mounds 2 to 3 feet high with bright green, furrowed, usually evergreen leaves ¾ inch wide and 1½ feet long.

SWEET GRASS
Hierochloë

Light: mostly sun

Plant type: ornamental grass

Hardiness: Zones 4-9

Height: 10 to 24 inches

Soil and Moisture: well-drained, moist

Interest: foliage, fragrance

Care: easy

◀ Hierochloë odorata

Sweet grass has delicate, gracefully arching leaves that have a soft lemon-vanilla smell. The dense tufts of bright green foliage gradually spread into wide mats, making a unique aromatic ground cover. In spring, tall flowering stalks bear loose clusters of brown spikelets above the leaves. Use sweet grass as an informal edging or allow tufts to spread in a meadow garden. Its creeping runners form mats of roots that help hold soil in steep or difficult locations. The leaves are often dried for use in potpourri, bundled into closet sachets, or woven into baskets and mats.

Growing and care:
Plant plugs or divisions of sweet grass in spring or fall, spacing them 15 to 24 inches apart. Fertilize lightly in spring. Sweet grass is a vigorous grower but can be restrained by planting in containers. Cut leaves at ground level and dry in bundles in a sunny location. For craftwork, boil the harvested green grass 10 minutes, then dry it in the sun for up to 1 week.

Selected species and varieties:
H. odorata (sweet grass, vanilla grass, holy grass, zubrovka) has thin, flat ¼-inch-wide leaves 10 to 20 inches long and pyramidal seed clusters on stalks to 2 feet.

WILD OATS
Chasmanthium

Light: mostly sun

Plant type: ornamental grass

Hardiness: Zones 5-10

Height: 2 to 4 feet

Soil and Moisture: well-drained, moist

Interest: flowers, foliage

Care: easy

◀ Chasmanthium latifolium

Wild oats is a versatile plant that offers easy-care four-season beauty to any garden. In spring bright green foliage appears, followed in summer by drooping panicles of green flowers. In autumn the plants ignite the garden with bright yellow-gold leaves. The panicles turn bronze and persist throughout winter, providing color and graceful movement. Wild oats is useful throughout the garden and is effective in mixed borders, specialty gardens, beside pools and streams, or massed in large groups.

Growing and care:
Unlike most ornamental grasses, *Chasmanthium* adapts well to mostly sunny spots, where the foliage attains its deepest colors. Plant in spring, spacing plants about 2 feet apart. Cut back to ground level before growth begins early in the following spring. Propagate by division or seed. It may self-sow.

Selected species and varieties:
C. latifolium (northern sea oats) is a clump-forming perennial grass from the eastern and central United States 2 to 4 feet in height with blue-green bamboolike leaves; its fall foliage is most intense in full sun. It bears oatlike spikelets of flowers on slender, arching stems in summer.

ABELIA
Abelia

Light: mostly sun

Plant type: shrub

Hardiness: Zones 6-10

Height: 3 to 6 feet

Soil and Moisture: well-drained, moist

Interest: flowers, foliage

Care: easy

◀ Abelia x 'Edward Goucher'

Abelia's fountainlike sprays of glimmering foliage lend airy grace and fine texture to borders and hedges. Tiny bell-shaped or tubular flowers bloom from early summer to frost. The small, pointed, richly green leaves are bronze when young and, after turning green through summer, often become bronze or bronzy purple again in fall. In the northern parts of its range abelia is semievergreen while in the South the foliage remains all year long.

Growing and care:

For best growth and flower production plant abelia in a location that gets a little afternoon shade. The plants thrive in loosened soil that has had some organic matter added to it. Water regularly from early spring to fall. Prune in late winter or early spring, removing wood more than 4 years old and trimming to shape.

Selected species and varieties:

A. x *grandiflora* (glossy abelia) is a rounded shrub 3 to 6 feet high (to 8 feet in the South) and equally wide, with small pinkish white flowers in summer. *A.* x 'Edward Goucher', the result of a cross between *A.* x *grandiflora* and *A. schumannii,* forms a 4- to 5-foot-tall shrub with equal spread bearing pinkish lavender flowers in summer. *A. schumannii* bears mauve-pink flowers amid downy, blunt-pointed leaves; Zones 7-10.

'ALBA SEMI-PLENA' ROSE
Rosa

Light: mostly sun

Plant type: shrub

Hardiness: Zones 3-7

Height: 6 feet

Soil and Moisture: well-drained, moist

Interest: flowers, fragrance

Care: easy to moderate

◀ Rosa 'Alba Semi-Plena'

Known also as White Rose of York, 'Alba Semi-Plena' is a very old variety. Its pure white semidouble flowers are 2½ inches across with a center of prominent golden stamens. The very fragrant blossoms appear in early summer with no repeat in fall. Elongated orange-red hips appear in late summer and fall. The foliage is gray-green. With sturdy, arching canes that develop a vase-shaped form, 'Alba Semi-Plena' can be grown as a freestanding shrub for a specimen or for use in borders, or it can be trained as a climber on a wall, a trellis, or a fence.

Growing and care:

Plant in well-worked soil to which organic matter has been added. Mulch in spring and again in fall around its root zone. Prune to desired shape after flowering is completed. 'Alba Semi-Plena' is very hardy and resistant to pests and disease.

Selected species and varieties:

R. 'Maxima' is a sport of 'Alba Semi-Plena' with even larger, very fragrant snow white blossoms; 'Suaveolens' is a near relative with pure white, intensely fragrant semi-double flowers in summer on canes reaching 6 feet.

ARBORVITAE
Thuja

Light: mostly sun

Plant type: shrub, tree

Hardiness: Zones 3-9

Height: 3 to 30 feet

Soil and Moisture: well-drained, moist

Interest: foliage

Care: easy

◀ Thuja occidentalis
'Hetz Midget'

Arborvitae's fine-textured evergreen foliage develops along dense pyramids of branches in shades of green, yellow-green, and blue-green. These versatile plants fit well in just about any part of the landscape or garden. They are especially useful as specimens, grouped in the shrub border, or massed into hedges or screens. Planted around ponds or streams arborvitae adds cool ambiance and color.

Growing and care:

Plants can be transplanted year round from containers or in balled-and-burlapped form. Set plants in well-worked soil amended with abundant amounts of peat or other organic matter. *T. orientalis* is less cold tolerant than American arborvitae. Propagate from cuttings.

Selected species and varieties:

T. occidentalis (American or eastern arborvitae, white cedar) has shiny green needles that turn brown in winter; 'Hetz Midget' is a dense 3- to 4-foot globe; 'Lutea' forms a golden yellow pyramid to 30 feet; 'Nigra' has dark green foliage on trees 20 feet high and 4 feet wide; 'Rheingold' has deep gold foliage on oval shrubs to 5 feet; Zones 3-7. *T. orientalis* [also called *Platycladus orientalis*] (Oriental arborvitae) has bright green or yellow-green young foliage maturing to dark green and holding its color through winter; Zones 6-9.

ASH
Fraxinus

Light: mostly sun

Plant type: tree

Hardiness: Zones 2-9

Height: 45 to 80 feet

Soil and Moisture: well-drained, moist to dry

Interest: foliage

Care: easy

◀ Fraxinus
pennsylvanica

Ashes are fast-growing shade trees with attractive green foliage that turns yellow or plum violet in fall. When the leaves drop they often crumble into tiny pieces requiring little raking. Small greenish yellow flowers are borne on separate male and female trees in spring. Paddle-shaped winged seeds on female trees hang from the branches in conspicuous clusters. The seeds germinate easily and may become a weedy nuisance in gardens. Select a male clone or a seedless variety for least maintenance.

Growing and care:

Though ashes prefer moist, well-drained soil, white ash tolerates moderately dry and slightly alkaline soils, and green ash adapts to wet soils and high salt. Plant in a location that allows this large tree to develop unimpeded.

Selected species and varieties:

F. americana (white ash) grows to 80 feet tall with an open, rounded crown and compound leaves, dark green above and pale below, that turn a rich yellow, then maroon to purple in fall; hardy to Zone 3; 'Champaign County' reaches 45 feet, with a dense canopy of leaves. *F. pennsylvanica* (red ash, green ash) grows 50 to 60 feet tall with an irregular crown half as wide, bearing shiny green leaves that may turn yellow in fall; Zone 3; 'Patmore', a seedless form, grows 45 feet tall, with a symmetrical, upright-branching crown; Zone 2.

BEAUTYBERRY
Callicarpa

Light:	mostly sun
Plant type:	shrub
Hardiness:	Zones 5-10
Height:	3 to 8 feet
Soil and Moisture:	well-drained, moist
Interest:	fruit
Care:	moderate

◀ Callicarpa americana

Beautyberry is an excellent description of this decorative, very ornamental shrub. Clusters of colorful ⅛-inch berries are gathered along beautyberry's arching stems for several weeks after the leaves have fallen in autumn. The oval, pointed leaves, arranged like ladders on either side of the stems, turn yellowish, sometimes pinkish, before dropping. Beautyberry is often used as a specimen, intermingled in the shrub border, or massed into an informal hedge.

Growing and care:
Prune to within 4 to 6 inches of the ground in early spring to create new shoots; only these produce flowers and fruit. Beautyberry is easy to grow from softwood cuttings or seed and is easily transplanted.

Selected species and varieties:
C. americana (American beautyberry) bears inconspicuous lavender summer flowers followed by magenta fruit clusters encircling stem tips; var. *lactea* produces white berries; Zones 7-10. *C. japonica* has violet to metallic purple berries; 'Leucocarpa' grows white berries after inconspicuous pink or white summer flowers; Zones 5-8.

BEECH
Fagus

Light:	mostly sun
Plant type:	tree
Hardiness:	Zones 3-9
Height:	50 to 70 feet
Soil and Moisture:	well-drained, moist, slightly acidic
Interest:	foliage, bark
Care:	easy

◀ Fagus sylvatica 'Atropunicea'

Beeches are long-lived trees with massive trunks and branches clad in smooth gray bark. In spring, as inconspicuous flowers form, silky green leaves unfurl, turning bronze or ochre in the fall. Nuts are small but edible and are enclosed in a small, spiny husk. Beeches have long horizontal branches that often sweep the ground and offer the landscape a classic form that is both bold and graceful.

Growing and care:
Plant beeches in soil that has been generously amended with organic matter. Water regularly until trees are established and during dry periods.

Selected species and varieties:
F. grandifolia (American beech) grows 50 to 70 feet tall and almost as wide, with light gray bark and toothy leaves 2 to 5 inches long, dark green above and light green below. *F. sylvatica* (common beech, European beech, red beech) is usually 50 to 60 feet tall and 35 to 45 feet wide, with elephant-hide bark, branching close to the ground; Zones 4-7; 'Atropunicea' ['Atropurpurea'] (purple beech, copper beech) has black-red new leaves that turn purple-green; 'Aurea Pendula' is a weeping form with yellow new leaves aging to yellow-green; 'Dawyck Purple' grows in a narrow column with deep purple leaves.

BIRCH
Betula

◀ Betula nigra

Light: mostly sun

Plant type: tree

Hardiness: Zones 2-9

Height: 40 to 70 feet

Soil and Moisture: well-drained to heavy, moist to wet

Interest: foliage, bark

Care: moderate

Birches are graceful trees with pliant, flowing branches, pendent flower catkins, and decorative bark. Their airy canopies are composed of medium to dark green finely toothed leaves that flutter in the slightest breeze and turn a warm yellow in fall. In spring the flowers, called catkins, hang like slender ornaments from the tips of the branches. Birches create a light dappled shade and are lovely in groups or singly as specimens.

Growing and care:

Although river birches can thrive in periodic flooding, most species need good drainage and grow best in loose, rich, acid loams. Paper birch and European white birch tolerate neutral soils, but river birch must have acid soil. Amend soil with peat moss, leaf mold, or finished compost. Add sand as well if the soil is heavy. Mulch to retain moisture and to protect from lawn-mower damage. All birches bleed heavily in late winter or early spring and pruning should only be done in summer or fall. Bottom branches on paper birch can easily be removed to create a high-branched specimen tree. Although river birch and paper birch are resistant to the bronze birch borer, European white birch is quite susceptible. Most birches live about 50 years.

Selected species and varieties:

B. nigra (river birch, red birch) reaches 40 to 70 feet with a spread almost equal to its height, usually multitrunked, with cinnamon brown bark, peeling when young and becoming deeply furrowed into irregular plates with age, and nearly triangular leaves to 3½ inches long that often show brief fall color; Zones 4-9. *B. papyrifera* (paper birch, white birch, canoe birch) is a low-branched tree with reddish brown bark when young aging to creamy white and peeling thinly to reveal reddish orange tissue beneath, growing 50 to 70 feet tall by 25 to 45 feet in spread, and bearing 2- to 4-inch roundish, wedge-shaped leaves turning a lovely yellow in fall; Zones 2-7. *B. pendula* [also listed as *B. alba*] (European white birch, warty birch, common birch) produces graceful, slightly pendent branches on a 40- to 50-foot-tall by 20- to 35-foot-wide tree with the bark on the trunk and main limbs changing slowly from whitish to mostly black on white with age; golden brown twigs; and slender branches bearing serrated, almost diamond-shaped leaves 1 to 3 inches long that hold later in fall than do the other species but often show little fall color; Zones 2-7; 'Dalecarlica' (cutleaf weeping birch, Swedish birch) has weeping, pliant branches that often sweep the ground and dangling, deeply lobed and sharply toothed leaves.

BUCKEYE
Aesculus

Light: mostly sun	
Plant type: tree	
Hardiness: Zones 3-7	
Height: 20 to 40 feet	
Soil and Moisture: well-drained, moist	
Interest: flowers, foliage	
Care: easy	

◀ Aesculus glabra

The buckeye is one of the harbingers of spring, coming into leaf before most other trees have broken bud. This low-branched, round-topped tree has deep green, very distinctive five-fingered compound leaves that turn a vibrant orange in fall. Its large greenish yellow spring flowers are held on long panicles and are sometimes difficult to see amid the foliage. The fruit is a brown seed capsule with a prickly cover, considered by some to be a good-luck charm. Buckeyes cast deep shade, discouraging most types of grass from growing beneath them. Plant them in a naturalized area or a mulched bed where leaf, flower, and fruit litter will not be a nuisance. The seeds are poisonous.

Growing and care:
A native to rich bottom lands and riverbanks, the Ohio buckeye prefers deep loam. Before planting, mix compost or leaf mold into the soil removed from the planting hole. Mulch well to conserve moisture and water regularly to avoid leaf scorch. Prune as needed in early spring.

Selected species and varieties:
A. glabra (Ohio buckeye, fetid buckeye) grows 20 to 40 feet tall with an equal spread, bearing medium to dark green leaflets 3 to 6 inches long that open bright green, followed by flower panicles up to 7 inches long, and later 1- to 2-inch oval fruit.

CEDAR
Cedrus

Light: mostly sun	
Plant type: tree	
Hardiness: Zones 6-9	
Height: 100 to 150 feet	
Soil and Moisture: well-drained, moist	
Interest: foliage	
Care: easy	

◀ Cedrus deodara

Cedars are magnificent specimen trees with massive sweeping branches smothered with soft blue-green foliage. Their beauty is magnified by their towering height, which can easily surpass 100 feet. Cedars are best used as specimen plants for large properties with enough room for the great trees to grow.

Growing and care:
Cedars need ample room to develop and should have a site protected from strong winds. Atlas cedar grows best in moist, deep loam but will tolerate other soils as long as they are well drained. A moderately dry site is best for deodar cedar.

Selected species and varieties:
C. atlantica (Atlas cedar) is a slow-growing tree eventually reaching 100 feet tall with an open and spindly form when young but maturing into a stately flat-topped shape with bluish green or sometimes green to silvery blue inch-long needles and 3-inch-long cones that take 2 years to mature; 'Glauca' (blue Atlas cedar) has rich, steel blue needles. *C. deodara* (deodar cedar) has a pyramidal form and is more attractive when young than Atlas cedar, becoming flat topped and broad with age, growing 40 to 70 feet tall with a nearly equal spread but sometimes reaching 150 feet, with light blue to grayish green needles up to 1½ inches long, a gracefully drooping habit, and 3- to 4-inch cones; Zones 7-8.

'CELESTIAL' ROSE
Rosa

Light: mostly sun

Plant type: shrub

Hardiness: Zones 3-8

Height: 5 feet

Soil and Moisture: well-drained, fertile, moist

Interest: flowers, fragrance

Care: easy

◀ Rosa 'Celestial'

In late spring 'Celestial' blooms with blush pink, sweetly fragrant semidouble blossoms wrapped around a center of yellow stamens. The fast-growing plants reach 5 feet in height with the pliant, arching canes well covered in blue-green foliage. 'Celestial' is excellent as an informal hedge, planted in large groups for a mass display in meadows or on hillsides, or as a specimen.

Growing and care:
Plant 'Celestial' in a location with a little bright shade in loosened soil amended with some organic matter. Water well after planting and during dry periods. Mulch in spring and again in fall to keep roots cool and conserve soil moisture. Prune as needed to shape. 'Celestial' is virtually pest- and disease-free and once established requires little care.

Selected species and varieties:
R. 'Great Maiden's Blush' bears large 2- to 3-inch pink, very fragrant double blossoms in late spring to early summer that fade to a whitish blush on arching 5-foot canes with abundant blue-green foliage; Zones 4-10.

CHERRY
Prunus

Light: mostly sun

Plant type: shrub, tree

Hardiness: Zones 4-10

Height: 3 to 50 feet

Soil and Moisture: well-drained, moist

Interest: flowers, foliage, fruit

Care: moderate

◀ Prunus subhirtella var. pendula

This huge genus contains some of the most decorative flowering trees and shrubs. The plants are used for everything from specimens to screens, foundation plants, and hedges, but are most prized for their fragrant, blush pink to white blossoms that produce a blizzard of color in spring.

Growing and care:
Plant these flowering trees in well-worked loam that has had abundant organic matter mixed in. Prune cherries only when necessary, removing crossed or ungainly branches. In warmer climates, provide afternoon shade for Carolina cherry laurel, even in winter. Common cherry laurel is tolerant of wind and salt spray. Laurels take pruning well. Water regularly until established, fertilizing lightly in spring as growth begins.

Selected species and varieties:
P. caroliniana (Carolina cherry laurel) is an evergreen oval-pyramidal shrub or tree, 20 to 30 feet high and 15 to 25 feet wide, with lustrous dark green, sharply tapered, sometimes spiny leaves 2 to 3 inches long and 1 inch wide hiding black fruits, and heavily scented white flower clusters to 3 inches long in early spring; Zones 7-10; 'Bright 'n' Tight' has smooth-edged leaves smaller than the species on a tightly branched pyramid growing to 20 feet tall. *P. laurocerasus* (common cherry laurel, English laurel) has lustrous, medium to dark green leaves

(continued)

2 to 6 inches long and a third as wide, slightly toothed and borne on green stems tightly branched on a broad 10- to 18-foot-tall evergreen shrub that produces heavily fragrant flowers in racemes 2 to 5 inches long, and purple to black fruit masked by the leaves; Zones 6-8; 'Otto Luyken' is a compact form 3 to 4 feet tall and 6 to 8 feet wide that blooms profusely and has dark green leaves 4 inches long and 1 inch wide; 'Schipkaensis' has shorter, slightly narrower smooth-edged leaves, to 5 feet high; Zones 5-8. *P. lusitanica* (Portuguese cherry laurel, Portugal laurel) has fragrant white clusters 6 to 10 inches long in late spring, and dark purple cone-shaped fruits on a bushy shrub or tree 10 to 20 feet high with evergreen leaves 2½ to 5 inches long; Zones 7-9. *P. mume* (Japanese flowering apricot) has pale rose flowers in winter, after which shiny green leaves and yellowish fruit appear on a tree to 20 feet; Zones 6-9 (to Zone 10 in California). *P. subhirtella* var. *pendula* (weeping Higan cherry) has pink single flowers that appear before the leaves on graceful, weeping branches on a 20- to 40-foot tree, followed by black fruit; Zones 4-9. *P.* x *yedoensis* (Yoshino cherry, Japanese flowering cherry) is a 40- to 50-foot tree that bears pink or white flowers in spring before or as the leaves appear, and black fruit; Zones 5-8; 'Akebono' has pink double flowers on a tree 25 feet high and wide.

CINQUEFOIL
Potentilla

Light: mostly sun	
Plant type: shrub	
Hardiness: Zones 2-7	
Height: 1 to 4 feet	
Soil and Moisture: well-drained, moist to dry	
Interest: flowers, foliage	
Care: easy	

◀ Potentilla fruticosa 'Abbotswood'

Cinquefoil's open five-petaled flowers resemble wild roses, and are held above spreading mounds of palmately compound silvery green leaves in summer. The plants are easy to grow and are effectively mixed into the shrub or perennial border. Cinquefoil is also useful massed onto hillsides or sprinkled in wildflower meadows, where its flowers sparkle like stars.

Growing and care:
Plant smaller cinquefoils 1 foot apart, larger types 2 feet apart. They flower best in mostly sunny places and with a not-too-rich soil. The plants generally need little care once established. Water during dry periods. Propagate by seed or division.

Selected species and varieties:
P. fruticosa (bush cinquefoil) grows 1 to 4 feet tall, 2 to 4 feet wide, with leaves that emerge gray-green then turn dark green, and 1-inch flowers from early summer to late fall; 'Abbotswood' grows to 2 feet with white flowers; 'Primrose Beauty' produces primrose flowers with deeper centers on 3-foot plants; 'Tangerine' grows 2 to 4 feet tall with yellow flowers flushed with orange and copper tones.

COTONEASTER
Cotoneaster

Light: mostly sun

Plant type: shrub

Hardiness: Zones 5-8

Height: 1 to 15 feet

Soil and Moisture: well-drained, moist

Interest: foliage, fruit

Care: easy

◀ Cotoneaster microphyllus

Cotoneasters are hardworking decorative shrubs with glossy evergreen foliage and brilliant red, hollylike berries from fall through winter. White or pink flowers, often quite small, appear in spring sprinkled along the stiff branches. Most cotoneasters spread at least as wide as their height, and are used as fast-growing ground covers that are ideal for slopes, rock gardens, and walls. Other species make interesting specimen plants for shrub borders.

Growing and care:

Bearberry cotoneaster is tolerant of most well-drained soils and is easily grown. Willowleaf and parney cotoneasters need moist, well-drained, acid to nearly neutral soil. Mature plants will tolerate drought, seashore conditions, and wind; dry or poor soil often produces the best fruiting. Cotoneaster is susceptible to fire blight, a blackened die-off of branch tips that, if not treated, is fatal to the plant; littleleaf cotoneaster may be more susceptible in the South. Other pests are borers, red spiders, and lace bugs. Prune only to control the plant's shape.

Selected species and varieties:

C. dammeri (bearberry cotoneaster) has a prostrate form 1 to 1½ feet high, and is an excellent ground cover because it roots wherever its branches touch soil. It spreads quickly to 6 feet wide, with white flowers up to ½ inch wide, a light crop of red berries, and narrow, 1-inch-long, lustrous dark green leaves that may become tinged with red-purple in winter; 'Skogholm' grows vigorously to 1½ to 3 feet high, spreading several feet each year. *C. lacteus* (red cluster-berry, parney cotoneaster) is a 6- to 10-foot shrub with a handsome fruit display persisting through winter and 2- to 3-inch-wide white flower clusters in spring, sometimes partly hidden by the foliage; Zones 6-8. *C. microphyllus* (littleleaf cotoneaster, rockspray cotoneaster) is a nearly prostrate shrub, usually 2 feet high or smaller, spreading up to 10 feet wide with ¼- to ½-inch-long glossy leaves, tiny white flowers, and red fruit; Zones 5-8. *C. salicifolius* (willowleaf cotoneaster) is a shrub with an arching habit, growing 10 to 15 feet tall with a smaller spread and producing narrow, willowlike leaves 1½ to 3½ inches long that are lustrous dark green in summer, becoming plum purple in winter. It bears flat 2-inch-wide white flower heads often masked by the foliage, and tiny, long-lasting bright red fruit; Zones 6-8; 'Autumn Fire' forms a 2- to 3-foot-high ground cover with 1½- to 2-inch very glossy leaves that turn reddish purple in winter, and scarlet fruit; 'Repens' has lustrous 1-inch leaves on a prostrate ground cover to 1 foot tall.

DOGWOOD
Cornus

Light:	mostly sun
Plant type:	shrub, tree
Hardiness:	Zones 3-9
Height:	15 to 30 feet
Soil and Moisture:	well-drained, wet to moderately dry
Interest:	flowers, foliage, bark
Care:	moderate

◄ Cornus florida

Dogwoods can turn the spring landscape into a fairyland of foliage and flowers, and transform fall into a bounty of leafy color and brilliant fruit. These classic, versatile plants offer four-season interest and are excellent additions to formal and informal plantings including wildlife gardens, where the trees attract songbirds throughout the year.

Growing and care:

Give flowering and pagoda dogwoods a moist, acid soil enriched with leaf mold, peat moss, or compost. Mulch to keep soil cool and moist. Kousa dogwood prefers loose, sandy, acid soil rich with organic matter. It is more drought tolerant and disease resistant than flowering dogwood. Although adaptable to a wide range of soil types, cornelian cherry prefers moist, rich sites and is probably the best performer of the dogwoods for the Midwest. Susceptible to the usually fatal anthracnose, which has killed many dogwoods on the East Coast, flowering dogwood has a better chance of staying healthy if stress is reduced by providing optimal growing conditions. The other dogwoods listed here appear not to be affected. For colder climates, the best bud hardiness in flowering dogwoods occurs in trees grown in those regions.

Selected species and varieties:

C. alternifolia (pagoda dogwood, green osier) bears strongly fragrant yellowish white flowers borne in flat clusters 1½ to 2½ inches wide on a horizontally branched tree growing 15 to 25 feet tall with a greater spread and tierlike habit, also bearing fruit that matures from green to red to blue-black; Zones 3-7. *C. florida* (flowering dogwood) is a small tree with a broad, artistically shaped crown, usually 20 to 30 feet tall with an equal or greater spread, producing white flowerlike bracts lasting 10 to 14 days in spring before the leaves emerge, followed in fall by small, glossy red fruits borne in clusters of at least three to four; Zones 5-9. *C. kousa* (kousa dogwood) is a multistemmed small tree 20 to 30 feet tall and wide with exfoliating gray, tan, and brown bark and attractive tiered branches, flowering in late spring after the leaves appear and lasting for up to 6 weeks, followed by pink to red roundish fruit up to 1 inch wide in late summer to fall, when the leaves turn reddish purple or scarlet; Zones 5-8; var. *chinensis* (Chinese dogwood) grows to 30 feet and has larger bracts than the species. *C. mas* (cornelian cherry, sorbet) is a multistemmed shrub or small, oval to round tree 20 to 25 feet tall and 15 to 20 feet wide, branching nearly to the ground, with attractive exfoliating gray to brown bark, bearing small clusters of yellow flowers for 3 weeks in early spring and bright red fruit in midsummer that is partly hidden by the lustrous dark green leaves, 2 to 4 inches long, that usually show little fall color; Zones 4-8.

ELM
Ulmus

Light:	mostly sun
Plant type:	tree
Hardiness:	Zones 4-9
Height:	40 to 70 feet
Soil and Moisture:	well-drained, moist
Interest:	foliage, bark
Care:	moderate

◀ Ulmus parvifolia

Exfoliating, mottled gray, green, orange, or brown bark is this graceful, durable shade tree's most outstanding feature. Lacebark elm has a spreading, rounded crown of medium fine, lustrous dark green foliage that holds late into fall, when it turns yellow to reddish purple. The trees make excellent specimens and add elegance when planted along long driveways.

Growing and care:
Lacebark elm grows best in moist, well-drained loams but adapts well to poor, dry soils, both acid and alkaline. Soil should be deep to accommodate the extensive root system. Growth averages 1½ feet per year. Prune to remove weak, narrow crotches as they appear. Although it is not immune to Dutch elm disease, it shows considerable resistance.

Selected species and varieties:
U. parvifolia (lacebark elm, Chinese elm, evergreen elm) grows 40 to 50 feet high and wide in most situations, usually with a forked trunk and drooping branches, bearing leathery, saw-toothed elliptical leaves ¾ to 2½ inches long and inconspicuous flower clusters hidden by the foliage in late summer to early fall, followed by ⅓-inch-wide winged fruits.

ENKIANTHUS
Enkianthus

Light:	mostly sun
Plant type:	shrub, tree
Hardiness:	Zones 4-7
Height:	6 to 30 feet
Soil and Moisture:	well-drained, moist
Interest:	flowers, foliage
Care:	easy

◀ Enkianthus campanulatus

Enkianthus is an easy-to-grow, very attractive shrub or small tree that offers up pendulous clusters of dainty flowers in spring and then delights with brilliant fall foliage. The plant is excellent as a specimen and is quite charming when tucked in the midst of a border of rhododendrons and azaleas.

Growing and care:
Plant enkianthus in spring or fall in well-worked soil that has been amended with peat moss. Water regularly until established. Mulch with pine needles in spring and again in fall.

Selected species and varieties:
E. campanulatus (redvein enkianthus), with a narrow, upright habit, grows to 6 to 8 feet tall in cold areas, to 30 feet in warmer climates, and has layered branches bearing at their tips tufts of 1- to 3-inch-long medium green leaves that turn bright red to orange and yellow in fall, and producing long-stalked clusters of pale yellow or light orange bell-shaped flowers with red veins in late spring as the leaves develop, the blooms sometimes persisting for several weeks; hardy to parts of Zone 4. *E. perulatus* (white enkianthus) grows 6 feet high and wide, with white urn-shaped flower clusters in midspring before the foliage appears, the bright green 1- to 2-inch-long leaves turning scarlet in fall; hardy to Zone 5.

EUONYMUS
Euonymus

Light: mostly sun

Plant type: shrub

Hardiness: Zones 4-8

Height: 4 inches to 70 feet

Soil and Moisture: well-drained, moist

Interest: foliage

Care: easy to moderate

◄ Euonymus alata 'Compacta'

Euonymus is one of the most popular shrubs for yards and gardens. The full, rounded bushes are covered with medium green leaves in summer that turn fiery red in fall. Inconspicuous flowers form in spring, and pink to red fruit capsules split to expose orange seeds in fall, which attract birds. The plants are ideal for mixed borders, specimens, hedges, specialty gardens, and woodland plantings.

Growing and care:
Plant euonymus in spring or fall in lightly worked soil amended with some organic matter. The plants grow well in conditions from sun to shade but achieve their best color and form in sunny and mostly sunny locations. Water regularly until plants are established. Prune out damaged or diseased wood as it appears.

Selected species and varieties:
E. alata [also listed as *E. alatus*] (winged euonymus, burning bush) is a slow-growing, wide-spreading, flat-topped shrub of variable height, usually 15 to 20 feet tall and wide, with soft green leaves 1 to 3 inches long that turn brilliant red in fall, yellow-green flowers in spring, and small red fruits borne under the leaves; Zones 4-8; 'Compacta' [also listed as 'Compactus'] (dwarf burning bush) grows 10 feet tall, its slender branches exhibiting less prominent corky ridges and forming a denser, more rounded outline; Zones 5-8.

FOTHERGILLA
Fothergilla

Light: mostly sun

Plant type: shrub

Hardiness: Zones 4-9

Height: 3 to 10 feet

Soil and Moisture: well-drained, sandy, moist

Interest: flowers, foliage

Care: easy

◄ Fothergilla major

This beautiful flowering shrub combines glossy, dark green foliage with delicate sprays of bottlebrush blossoms. The fragrant white flowers appear in spring and the blue-green leaves turn a brilliant yellow, orange, and scarlet in fall. Fothergilla works well massed, in borders, and in foundation plantings.

Growing and care:
Fothergilla thrives in most soil types but does not tolerate limy soils. The plants are virtually pest-free and require little care.

Selected species and varieties:
F. gardenii (witch alder, dwarf fothergilla) forms a dense mound 3 feet tall and 4 feet wide with zigzag spreading branches bearing 1-inch-long white spikes before the appearance of 1- to 2-inch-long wedge-shaped leaves that are dark green above and bluish white below; 'Blue Mist' has a feathery, mounded habit with glaucous, bluish leaves and subdued fall colors; 'Jane Platt' has narrow leaves and longer flower clusters than in the species; 'Mount Airy' has an upright habit, with profuse flowers and excellent fall color. *F. major* [also classified as *F. monticola*] (large fothergilla) has an upright growth 6 to 10 feet high with 2- to 4-inch white flower spikes tinged with pink, appearing with oval to roundish dark green leaves that show brilliant fall colors; Zones 4-8.

GARDENIA
Gardenia

Light: mostly sun

Plant type: shrub

Hardiness: Zones 8-10

Height: 1 to 6 feet

Soil and Moisture: well-drained, fertile, moist

Interest: flowers, foliage, fragrance

Care: moderate to difficult

◀ Gardenia augusta

Gardenias are classic warm-weather shrubs with rich evergreen leaves and linen white camellia-like summer flowers so intensely fragrant just one will perfume an entire room. While hardy only to Zone 8, this shrub is worth the effort to grow wherever conditions allow. Where it is not hardy it can be grown as a container plant.

Growing and care:

Plant gardenias in acid soil enriched with plenty of organic matter. They thrive in hot weather, and require monthly fertilizing during the growing season. Mulch to keep soil moist and protect the gardenia's shallow roots. Propagate by cuttings. Plants do poorly in overly wet or dry conditions.

Selected species and varieties:

G. augusta [formerly *G. jasminoides*] is an evergreen shrub 3 to 6 feet tall and wide with a dense, rounded habit, with 3- to 4-inch glossy oval leaves and double blooms up to 5 inches across; 'August Beauty' grows 4 to 6 feet tall with abundant 4- to 5-inch blooms; 'Radicans' grows to 1 foot tall and 3 feet wide with smaller foliage and flowers than the species.

HEBE
Hebe

Light: mostly sun

Plant type: shrub

Hardiness: Zones 8-10

Height: 2 to 5 feet

Soil and Moisture: well-drained, moist

Interest: flowers, foliage

Care: easy

◀ Hebe buxifolia 'Patty's Purple'

Native to New Zealand, hebes are rounded, leathery-leaved evergreen shrubs that produce spikes of lovely white, pink, red, lavender, or purple flowers 2 to 4 inches long at the ends of the branches from midsummer to fall. Their small glossy leaves, densely arranged on stems, make these fine-textured spreading shrubs good candidates for shrub borders, hedges, edgings, rock gardens, and perennial beds.

Growing and care:

Plant hebes in well-worked soil amended with organic matter. Mulch each spring and fall to conserve moisture and keep soil cool. Hebes thrive in cool coastal gardens, and need partial shade where summers are hot. Prune after flowering to avoid legginess.

Selected species and varieties:

H. 'Autumn Glory' is a mounding shrub 2 to 3 feet high and 2 feet wide with glossy dark green leaves 1½ inches long tinged with red when young, and dark lavender-blue flower spikes 2 inches long and sometimes branched, blooming profusely from midsummer through fall. *H. buxifolia* 'Patty's Purple' (boxleaf veronica) has 1-inch-long purple clusters and leaves scarcely ½ inch long, growing to 3 feet.

HYDRANGEA
Hydrangea

Light: mostly sun

Plant type: shrub

Hardiness: Zones 3-9

Height: 3 to 20 feet

Soil and Moisture: well-drained, fertile, moist

Interest: flowers, foliage

Care: easy to moderate

◀ Hydrangea macrophylla

Hydrangeas are longtime favorite garden plants that range from small to large, showy shrubs. The large, coarse-textured leaves combine with the bold flower clusters to add color and form to the shrub border. Many species have persistent flower clusters or attractive bark that keep them interesting throughout the seasons.

Growing and care:

Plant hydrangeas in well-worked, fertile soil that has been generously amended with organic matter. Mulch in spring and again in fall. Water well after planting and provide extra water during dry periods. The plants grow well in conditions ranging from full sun to full shade, but do best in mostly sunny places that offer midday shade. Prune *H. macrophylla* after flowering, and other species in late winter.

Selected species and varieties:

H. macrophylla (bigleaf hydrangea) grows 3 to 6 feet tall with 8-inch leaves and globular 5-inch flower heads in summer; Zones 6-9. *H. paniculata* 'Grandiflora' (peegee hydrangea) is a large shrub or small tree 10 to 25 feet tall with 1- to 1½-foot white to russet flower clusters in summer above dark green leaves; Zones 3-8.

'KÖNIGIN VON DÄNEMARK' ROSE
Rosa

Light: mostly sun

Plant type: shrub

Hardiness: Zones 3-8

Height: 4 feet

Soil and Moisture: well-drained, fertile, moist

Interest: flowers, fragrance

Care: easy

◀ Rosa 'Königin von Dänemark'

Aristocratic in appearance, 'Königin von Dänemark' (or 'Queen of Denmark') is a classic rose. Short, deep pink buds open to 2½- to 3½-inch light pink double flowers with slightly lighter pink petals toward the edges. The flowers are borne singly or in small clusters of three to five and are richly fragrant. The upright canes have abundant thorns and are covered with attractive blue-green foliage. The mature canes form an open, spreading shrub that is excellent as a hedge, screen, mass planting, or specimen. 'Königin von Dänemark' is also stunning as a background for the perennial border.

Growing and care:

Plant this easy-to-grow rose in well-worked soil amended with organic matter. Mulch around its root zone in spring and fall. In mass plantings or hedges set plants about 3 to 4 feet apart. Prune out older canes as needed. 'Königin von Dänemark' is a hardy, tough rose that is pest and disease resistant.

Selected species and varieties:

R. 'Madame Legras De St. Germain' bears very large, very fragrant, fully double white flowers in early summer on robust 7-foot canes with dark green foliage.

853

'MADAME PLANTIER' ROSE
Rosa

Light: mostly sun

Plant type: shrub

Hardiness: Zones 4-8

Height: 5 feet

Soil and Moisture: well-drained, fertile, moist

Interest: flowers, fragrance

Care: easy

◀ Rosa 'Madame Plantier'

A classic antique rose, 'Madame Plantier' has large, very double white flowers with a hint of cream at the edges of the petals. Borne in large clusters, the very fragrant 2½- to 3-inch flowers completely cover the plant in early to midseason. The vigorous, erect, nearly thornless canes reach to 5 feet tall with plentiful gray-green foliage. 'Madame Plantier' is charming trained against a wall or arbor and its free-flowing shape makes it attractive in mass plantings or informal hedges.

Growing and care:
Plant 'Madame Plantier' in well-worked soil well amended with rotted manure or compost. Mulch in spring and again in fall. Fertilize lightly in early spring as new growth appears. Prune to shape as needed and remove older canes periodically to ensure continued vigor. 'Madame Plantier' is a tough, good-looking plant that is virtually disease- and pest-free.

Selected species and varieties:
R. 'Blush Hip' has light pink double flowers on 5- to 6-foot smooth canes and gray-green foliage.

MAGNOLIA
Magnolia

Light: mostly sun

Plant type: shrub, tree

Hardiness: Zones 4-9

Height: 15 to 80 feet

Soil and Moisture: well-drained, moist

Interest: flowers, foliage

Care: easy to moderate

◀ Magnolia liliiflora

Magnolias are renowned for their masses of showy, often fragrant flowers that turn these graceful trees into living bouquets. In spring or summer the plants produce broad, cup- or star-shaped pure white to deep purple blooms that often ripen into ornamental conelike fruit with red seeds. Magnolias are either evergreen or deciduous, and make excellent specimen plants.

Growing and care:
Plant in spring or fall in soil amended with peat moss or compost. Fertilize in spring and mulch around the base of the trunk. Many species are susceptible to leaf spot, which defaces the leaves in late summer but does not damage the health of the plants. Water during hot, dry periods. Propagate by collecting fresh seed in fall and chilling for 4 months. Sow in spring.

Selected species and varieties:
M. liliiflora (lily magnolia) is a 15-foot multistemmed deciduous tree with medium green 6-inch elliptical leaves and narrow-petaled, lilylike, fragrant reddish purple spring flowers; Zones 5-8. *M.* x *soulangiana* (saucer magnolia) is a 30-foot deciduous tree with 6-inch dark green oval leaves, and large cup-shaped flowers in spring; Zones 5-9 *M. stellata* (star magnolia) is a deciduous shrub or tree to 20 feet tall with fragrant 4-inch white late-spring flowers tinged with pink; Zones 5-9.

MAPLE
Acer

Light: mostly sun	
Plant type: tree	
Hardiness: Zones 2-9	
Height: 6 to 75 feet	
Soil and Moisture: well-drained, moist	
Interest: foliage, flowers, bark	
Care: easy	

◀ Acer griseum

The maples are a diverse group of deciduous plants ranging from towering shade trees with brilliant fall foliage to small, picturesque specimens ideal as centerpieces for ornamental beds. Between the large and small maples are types well suited for specimen plantings around patios and decks. These lovely trees combine stately beauty with overall easy care, making them an invaluable part of any landscape or garden.

Growing and care:
Most maples can withstand occasional drought but turn color earlier in fall in dry conditions. Red maples thrive in wet, moist, or dry soil. Sugar and red maples prefer slight acidity but tolerate other soil types. *A. rubrum* 'Autumn Blaze' is said to be slightly more drought tolerant than true red maple cultivars. Paperbark maples tolerate a wide range of acid and alkaline soils. Japanese maples need highly organic loam, and the soil should be amended with peat moss or leaf mold before planting. Threadleaf maples should be planted in a sheltered location away from strong breezes, and provided with even moisture to avoid leaf scorch. Large maples have extensive, shallow root systems that crowd the soil's surface in search of water and nutrients, making it difficult to sustain significant plantings beneath them. All maples benefit from fertilizing in spring.

Selected species and varieties:
A. griseum (paperbark maple) is an oval- to round-crowned tree 20 to 30 feet tall with up to an equal spread, clad in very attractive exfoliating cinnamon brown bark and producing dark green to blue-green leaves with three leaflets that may turn red in fall; Zones 4-8. *A. palmatum* (Japanese maple) is a diverse group of small, slow-growing trees 15 to 25 feet tall with deeply cut leaves having five, seven, or nine lobes, and young stems that are reddish purple to green and become gray with age; Zones 5-8; 'Bloodgood' grows upright to 15 to 20 feet with maroon or reddish purple leaves that turn scarlet in fall, blackish red bark, and attractive red fruit; 'Dissectum' (threadleaf Japanese maple) is a small, pendulous, lacy shrub usually 6 to 8 feet tall, with drooping green-barked branches that bear very finely divided pale green leaves with up to 11 lobes that turn yellow in fall; 'Dissectum Atropurpureum' has lacy purple-red new leaves that fade to green or purple-green and turn crimson or burnt orange in fall, as well as tortuous branching that is most apparent in winter. *A. rubrum* (red maple, scarlet maple, Canadian maple) is a medium-fast-growing tree to 60 feet tall with ascending branches forming an irregular, oval to rounded crown and lobed green leaves yielding a dazzling fall color that is unreliable in the species but consistent among cultivars; 'Autumn Blaze' (*A.* x *freemanii*) is a fast-growing cultivar reaching 50 feet tall exhibiting superb orange-red fall color on its dense, oval to rounded crown; hardy to Zone 4; 'October Glory' has a round crown and vivid bright orange to red foliage in midfall, holding late into the season. *A. saccharum* (sugar maple, rock maple) is a truly stunning large shade tree reaching 60 to 75 feet tall with a spread about two-thirds that height in a symmetrical crown bearing greenish yellow flowers in spring and three- to five-lobed medium to dark green leaves that turn yellow, burnt orange, or scarlet red in fall; Zones 3-8.

MINT TREE
Agonis

Light: mostly sun

Plant type: tree

Hardiness: Zone 10

Height: 25 to 35 feet

Soil and Moisture: well-drained, moist to dry

Interest: flowers, foliage, fragrance

Care: easy

◄ Agonis flexuosa

The mint tree is a fast-growing, gracefully attractive evergreen for warm climates. Its leaves are long and willowlike, appearing in billowy masses along the strong branches. The foliage has a strong, minty aroma when crushed. In early summer small, white, pleasingly fragrant flowers appear. Mint tree is a versatile plant well suited for streetside use as well as specimen planting. In more northern zones it also makes a fine container plant.

Growing and care:

The mint tree requires a warm, nearly frost-free location and prefers a loose soil to which some organic matter has been added. Once the plants are established they are quite drought tolerant.

Selected species and varieties:

A. flexuosa grows to 35 feet, with an equal spread of deep 3- to 6-inch-long evergreen leaves that have a minty fragrance when crushed; small white, lightly scented flowers appear in early summer, followed by decorative woody seed capsules; attractive reddish brown, vertically fissured bark accents the foliage.

MOCK ORANGE
Philadelphus

Light: mostly sun

Plant type: shrub

Hardiness: Zones 4-9

Height: 4 to 12 feet

Soil and Moisture: well-drained, fertile, moist

Interest: flowers, foliage

Care: easy to moderate

◄ Philadelphus coronarius

Mock orange is an old-fashioned, highly decorative shrub that produces delightfully fragrant blooms in early summer that look and smell like orange blossoms. The plant has a rounded habit, forming thick clumps after many years. It is best planted in combination with other flowering plants in a mixed-shrub border or used as an informal barrier hedge.

Growing and care:

Mock orange is easily transplanted, fast growing, and not too particular about site. It will perform best in soil supplemented with abundant organic matter prior to planting. Once established it is tolerant of dry soils. Prune immediately after flowering to control size. Cut back stems that have borne flowers to encourage branching. To rejuvenate an old or overgrown specimen, cut back to the ground.

Selected species and varieties:

P. coronarius (sweet mock orange) is a large, very vigorous rounded shrub with ascending, arching branches, growing 10 to 12 feet tall and equally wide, often becoming leggy with age, exposing exfoliating orange-brown bark. It produces extremely fragrant white single flowers; 'Aureus' produces leaves that emerge bright yellow in spring and gradually turn yellow-green by midsummer, and may be useful as a border accent.

NEW ZEALAND TEA TREE
Leptospermum

Light: mostly sun
Plant type: shrub
Hardiness: Zones 9-10
Height: 6 to 10 feet
Soil and Moisture: well-drained, fertile, moist
Interest: flowers, foliage
Care: moderate

◀ Leptospermum
scoparium

The New Zealand tea tree is a fine-textured shrub with attractive evergreen leaves and small white, pink, or red flowers in winter, spring, or summer that put on a spectacular floral display. The plants are excellent for the shrub border, or informal hedges, or as specimen plants, where their show-stopping flowers and long, plentiful, twisting branches highlight the garden.

Growing and care:
The New Zealand tea tree is easy to grow in mild climates in a well-drained acid to neutral soil. It prefers some light shade, especially in areas with hot, dry summers. Warm temperatures combined with high humidity seem to weaken the plants and root rot often develops in poorly drained soils. Though it is somewhat drought tolerant, supplemental water should be supplied during dry periods or where the climate is hot. Prune as needed in early spring.

Selected species and varieties:
L. scoparium grows 6 to 10 feet high, slightly smaller in spread, with a rounded compact form. Leaves are dark gray-green and aromatic, profuse white flowers are $\frac{1}{2}$ inch across; 'Compactum' has a dense, mounding habit reaching just 3 feet high.

OAK
Quercus

Light: mostly sun
Plant type: tree
Hardiness: Zones 2-9
Height: 40 to more than 100 feet
Soil and Moisture: well-drained to heavy, wet to dry
Interest: foliage
Care: easy

◀ Quercus ilex

Oaks are large deciduous or evergreen trees with massive trunks and branches that can provide the dominant structure and framework for any landscape. The plants have a strong main trunk and usually stout horizontal branches supporting a broad canopy of dark green foliage. The leaves of deciduous forms often remain into winter. Small flowers form in spring, followed by acorns in late summer to fall that are sought out by many forms of wildlife. The acorns of red oaks require two years to mature.

Growing and care:
Oaks grow best in moist, deep soil, but most species fare well in a wide range of soil types. Holly oak can withstand inland drought and salt spray, but may become shrubby in exposed, seaside locations. Shumard red oak tolerates either wet or dry sites. A good oak for desert conditions, cork oak needs well-drained soil and is drought resistant once established; its leaves yellow in alkaline soil. Do not compact or change the elevation of soil within the oak's root zone, which usually extends far beyond the canopy's reach.

OAK
(continued)

Selected species and varieties:

Q. ilex (holly oak, holm oak, evergreen oak) reaches 40 to 70 feet high and wide, with leathery evergreen leaves, sometimes toothed and usually 1½ to 3 inches long, deep green above and yellowish to gray below; hardy to Zone 5. *Q. macrocarpa* (bur oak, mossy-cup oak) has a spreading crown of heavy branches and is usually 70 to 80 feet tall and at least as wide but has been known to top 100 feet. It bears 4- to 10-inch-long leaves, lobed near the stem, dark green above and whitish below, showing greenish yellow to yellow-brown fall color, and acorns, usually fringed, up to 1½ inches long; Zones 2-8. *Q. phellos* (willow oak) has narrow, slightly wavy willowlike leaves up to 5½ inches long, turning yellow, yellow-brown, and reddish in fall, on an oval crown 40 to 60 feet high and two-thirds as wide; Zones 5-9. *Q. robur* (English oak, truffle oak, common oak, pedunculate oak) has a short trunk that leads to a broad, fairly open crown, 40 to 60 feet tall with an equal spread under average landscape conditions (but it can reach 100 feet tall). It produces 2- to 5-inch-long rounded-lobed leaves that are dark green above and pale blue-green below, showing no fall color, and oblong acorns; Zones 4-8. *Q. shumardii* (Shumard's oak, Shumard red oak) grows 40 to 60 feet tall and wide, and is pyramidal when young but matures to a spreading crown, with russet-red to red fall color on deeply lobed and sharply pointed leaves 4 to 6 inches long and 3 to 4 inches wide; Zones 5-9. *Q. suber* (cork oak) is an evergreen tree 60 feet high and equally wide, with its trunk and main limbs clad in thick, corky bark, bearing coarsely toothed 3-inch lobeless leaves that are dark green above, fuzzy gray below; Zones 7-9.

OLEANDER
Nerium

◀ Nerium oleander

Light:	mostly sun
Plant type:	shrub
Hardiness:	Zones 8-10
Height:	6 to 20 feet
Soil and Moisture:	well-drained, moist
Interest:	flowers, foliage
Care:	easy

Oleander is a tough, easy-to-grow evergreen for warm climates that softens the summer months with sprays of long-lasting, beautiful flowers. The plants are closely branched with long, lance-shaped, willowy leaves that serve as a wonderful background for the fragrant, vividly colored blossoms. Oleander makes an excellent hedge, screen, or border and is very effective when used in mass plantings. It makes an easy-to-grow container plant that gives a tropical ambiance to patios and decks all summer long. All parts of the oleander are poisonous.

Growing and care:

Oleanders prefer a moist, well-drained soil but adapt to drier conditions. They tolerate drought, wind, salt spray, and air pollution. Prune in early spring to desired height and shape and to maintain dense habit.

Selected species and varieties:

N. oleander is usually 6 to 12 feet tall with an equal spread but may reach 20 feet, with upright stems, a bushy, rounded form, and 3- to 5-inch-long leathery leaves that remain dark green throughout the year. Fragrant flowers that form in terminal clusters are pink, white, or red and very showy, with a long blooming season; 'Casablanca' grows 3 to 4 feet tall with single white flowers; 'Little Red' has red flowers; 'Mrs. Roeddling' grows to 6 feet; its smaller leaves result in a finer texture; flowers are double and salmon-pink.

POMEGRANATE
Punica

Light: mostly sun

Plant type: shrub, tree

Hardiness: Zones 8-10

Height: 12 to 20 feet

Soil and Moisture: well-drained, moist

Interest: flowers, fruit

Care: easy

◀ Punica granatum

Pomegranates produce small, carnation-like flowers with crumpled petals in red, orange, pink, white, or yellow from early summer and sometimes into fall. The juicy yellow edible fruits up to 3 inches across that follow the floral display make these plants a worthwhile addition to any garden. Use pomegranates in shrub borders and groups, or grow in containers for a handsome small patio specimen.

Growing and care:

Easily cultivated, pomegranate makes its best growth in rich, moist loam but is adaptable to a range of other soils as long as they are well drained. Water well on planting and regularly for first growing season. Fertilize lightly when growth begins in spring and again after flowers fade. Prune after flowering is complete.

Selected species and varieties:

P. granatum grows 12 to 20 feet high, with an equal or lesser spread, bearing lustrous dark green leaves 1 to 3 inches long and 1 inch or less wide that unfurl bronzy and turn yellow in fall, and producing red flowers 1 inch wide; 'Legrellei' has double flowers with salmon-pink petals variegated with white.

PRIVET
Ligustrum

Light: mostly sun

Plant type: shrub

Hardiness: Zones 6-10

Height: 6 to 15 feet

Soil and Moisture: well-drained, moist to dry

Interest: foliage

Care: easy

◀ Ligustrum japonicum

Privet's glossy green leaves and dense, abundant branches have made it one of the most popular plants for all types of hedges. The plants adapt well to heavy shearing and are easy to grow, making them useful for hedges, screens, foundation plants, and even topiary specimens. White flowers, often considered malodorous, bloom in late spring or early summer, followed by black or blue-black berries.

Growing and care:

Privet is easy to grow and is virtually pest- and disease-free. Plant in spring or fall in soil that has had some organic matter added to it. Water regularly until plants are established. Prune or shear as desired for shape.

Selected species and varieties:

L. japonicum (Japanese privet, waxleaf privet, waxleaf ligustrum) is an upright, dense evergreen shrub 6 to 12 feet tall and up to 8 feet wide with 2- to 6-inch-high pyramidal flower clusters offsetting very dark green leaves 1½ to 4 inches long; Zones 7-10. *L. ovalifolium* 'Aureum' (California privet) has yellow leaves with a green spot in the center when planted in sun, heavily scented flower clusters 2 to 4 inches wide in summer, and shiny black berries on 10- to 15-foot densely arranged upright stems. It is semievergreen to evergreen in warmer climates.

REDBUD
Cercis

Light: mostly sun

Plant type: tree

Hardiness: Zones 4-9

Height: 8 to 30 feet

Soil and Moisture: well-drained, moist

Interest: flowers, fruit

Care: easy

◀ Cercis canadensis 'Forest Pansy'

Redbud is a small tree that graces the garden with four seasons of interest. In early spring the open branches are covered with white, pink, rose, or lavender flowers. Throughout summer the heart-shaped leaves are a lovely background to borders, and in fall attractive green seedpods turn brown and persist into winter.

Growing and care:

Eastern redbud needs some sun in late winter and early spring for the best flower production. In Zones 4 to 7, plant in spring; farther south, plant at anytime from fall to spring.

Selected species and varieties:

C. canadensis (eastern redbud) is a small tree with a spreading crown 20 to 30 feet tall, bearing 5-inch-wide leaves that turn a subdued yellow in fall; Zones 4-9; 'Alba' has white flowers; 'Forest Pansy' has red-purple leaves and pink-lavender flowers; Zones 7-9. *C. chinensis* (Chinese redbud) is a multitrunked tree 8 to 12 feet tall with upright growth and rose-purple flowers; Zones 6-9; 'Avondale' grows to 9 feet, with deep rose-purple flowers that bloom profusely. *C. reniformis* is usually 15 to 20 feet tall with glossy dark green leaves 2 to 4 inches wide and pale pink flowers; 'Oklahoma' has glossy leaves and wine red flowers; Zones 7-9.

REDLEAVED ROSE
Rosa

Light: mostly sun

Plant type: shrub

Hardiness: Zones 2-8

Height: 5 feet

Soil and Moisture: well-drained, moist

Interest: flowers, foliage, fragrance, fruit

Care: easy to moderate

◀ Rosa glauca

Redleaved rose is a charming, very hardy rose that adds four-season interest to any garden. This graceful, arching shrub has pliant, nearly thornless reddish purple canes covered with attractive blue-green leaves tinged with burgundy. In late spring the plant is smothered with clusters of small single pink blossoms with white bases surrounding a cluster of airy yellow stamens. In late summer the bush is decorated with small, dull red hips that persist into winter. Redleaved rose has a relaxed, rounded, arching habit and is a valuable addition to the perennial border or used as a specimen.

Growing and care:

Plant in a sheltered, cool location in soil amended with organic matter. Mulch in spring and fall and water regularly. Redleaved rose likes some high-afternoon shade, especially in warmer regions.

Selected species and varieties:

R. 'Carmenetta' is very similar to redleaved rose but is more tolerant of hot summers. The plants have large blue-green leaves and pink single flowers on canes reaching to 7 feet.

SLENDER DEUTZIA
Deutzia

Light:	mostly sun
Plant type:	shrub
Hardiness:	Zones 4-8
Height:	2 to 5 feet
Soil and Moisture:	well-drained, moist
Interest:	flowers
Care:	easy to moderate

◀ Deutzia gracilis

Slender deutzia has been prized by generations of gardeners for its long, graceful branches bearing pure white flowers in midspring. Like forsythia, it has a relatively short season of interest but is easy to grow and adaptable to most sites. Deutzia can be effectively used as a hedge, as a background for perennials, or in a mixed-shrub border. The plants are excellent for mass displays on slopes or woodland gardens.

Growing and care:
Plant in spring in moist, well-worked soil. Mulch around plantings in spring and again in fall. Provide extra water during dry periods. Prune out thick, older growth after flowering to keep plants vigorous. Plants can be propagated from softwood cuttings or by seed sown as soon as it ripens in late summer or fall.

Selected species and varieties:
D. gracilis grows to 5 feet tall and an equal width, with slender arching stems in a broad mounding habit, serrated leaves 1 to 3 inches long, and white flowers in erect clusters in spring that are effective for 2 weeks; 'Nikko' is a compact cultivar 2 feet tall and 5 feet wide with leaves that turn burgundy in fall.

SMOKEBUSH
Cotinus

Light:	mostly sun
Plant type:	shrub
Hardiness:	Zones 5-8
Height:	10 to 15 feet
Soil and Moisture:	well-drained, moist
Interest:	flowers, foliage
Care:	easy

◀ Cotinus coggygria
'Velvet Cloak'

An eye-catching accent plant, smokebush has glossy plum-colored fall foliage and abundant misty plumes of translucent flower heads from summer to fall. It is a wonderful specimen plant and adds soft texture to the shrub border. Smokebush is not only attractive, but is also easy to grow and pest and disease resistant.

Growing and care:
Plant smokebush in spring or fall in well-worked soil. Fertilize lightly in spring as leaves emerge and provide extra water during dry periods. Overfertilizing and overwatering encourage soft, leafy growth with few flowers and poor autumn leaf color.

Selected species and varieties:
C. coggygria (common smokebush, smoke plant, Venetian sumac, wig tree) is a loose and open multistemmed deciduous shrub 10 to 15 feet wide, bearing 1½- to 3-inch-long leaves that unfurl pink-bronze in midspring, mature to medium blue-green, and sometimes show yellow, red, and purple fall color and branched puffs changing to gray; 'Royal Purple' has purplish maroon leaves with scarlet margins, eventually turning scarlet all over; 'Velvet Cloak' has purple plumes and velvety dark purple leaves throughout the summer before changing to reddish purple in fall.

SNOWBELL
Styrax

Light: mostly sun	
Plant type: tree	
Hardiness: Zones 5-8	
Height: 20 to 30 feet	
Soil and Moisture: well-drained, moist, fertile	
Interest: flowers, bark	
Care: easy	

◀ Styrax japonicus

The delicate white bell-like flowers that dangle from the snowbell's wide-spreading branches are most visible from below, making this deciduous tree an ideal candidate to shade a patio or garden bench or to plant on slopes above walkways. The smooth, dark gray bark with interwoven orange colored fissures is attractive in winter.

Growing and care:

Plant in spring or fall in soil that has been generously amended with organic matter. Water well after planting and during dry periods. In northern areas do not plant in windy locations. Prune in winter if needed. Japanese snowbell is a remarkably pest-free plant.

Selected species and varieties:

S. japonicus (Japanese snowbell) is a dainty, low-branched tree whose crown is broader than its height, bearing medium to dark green pointed oval leaves 1 to 3½ inches long along the upper part of the branches; loose pendulous clusters of three to six slightly fragrant ¾-inch white flowers with prominent yellow stamens below the branches in late spring to early summer; and foliage that remains in place long enough to be killed by frost.

SOAPBERRY
Sapindus

Light: mostly sun	
Plant type: tree	
Hardiness: Zones 6-9	
Height: 25 to 50 feet	
Soil and Moisture: well-drained, moist to dry	
Interest: flowers, foliage, fruit, bark	
Care: easy	

◀ Sapindus drummondii

Soapberry is a versatile, very attractive tree with panicles of yellowish white flowers in late spring on graceful branches. The strong branches form a rounded crown of medium green compound leaves that turn gold in fall. Small yellow-orange berries, used by Native Americans to make soap, emerge in fall and persist through winter, finally turning black. The scaly orange-brown bark adds an interesting element to the garden in winter.

Growing and care:

Soapberry is tolerant of most soils but is especially at home in the poor, dry soils of its native Southwest. It is also tolerant of urban pollution and is insect and disease resistant. Easy to cultivate, soapberry needs little attention. Water well after planting.

Selected species and varieties:

S. drummondii (western soapberry, wild China tree) is either single stemmed or low branched, 25 to 50 feet tall with an equal spread, producing eight to 18 tapered, slightly curved leaflets, each 1½ to 3½ inches long, per 10- to 15-inch leaf, glossy above and fuzzy below. It sometimes produces abundant crops of ½-inch berries.

SOURWOOD
Oxydendrum

Light: mostly sun

Plant type: tree

Hardiness: Zones 5-9

Height: 15 to 30 feet

Soil and Moisture: well-drained, moist

Interest: flowers, foliage, fragrance, seeds

Care: easy

◀ Oxydendrum arboreum

Sourwood is a spectacular medium-size tree that provides four seasons of interest to the garden. Its young spring leaves are tinted bronze, turn glossy green in summer, then brilliant red in fall. Clusters of pendent, fragrant summer flowers cover the tree in a veil of perfumed petals, followed by feathery fans of narrow, pointed seed capsules that persist through winter. Honeybees make a delicious honey from the blossoms.

Growing and care:
Plant sourwood in soil that is rich in organic matter. Water well until plants are well established. Mulch to protect shallow roots and fertilize lightly in spring before flowers appear. Propagate from seed.

Selected species and varieties:
O. arboreum (sourwood, lily-of-the-valley tree, titi) is a pyramidal tree to 30 feet tall and about half as wide, with lustrous, pointed oval leaves 5 to 8 inches long and drooping 10-inch clusters of small, creamy white flower bells in summer. In fall the leaves turn into a fireball of reds, yellows, and oranges.

SPIREA
Spiraea

Light: mostly sun

Plant type: shrub

Hardiness: Zones 3-8

Height: 2 ½ to 8 feet

Soil and Moisture: well-drained, moist

Interest: flowers, foliage

Care: easy

◀ Spiraea x vanhouttei

Spireas are deciduous shrubs with abundant clusters of tiny, roselike flowers in tight panicles along the entire length of their stems in spring, or at the tips of their branches in summer. Each of the small pink or white flowers has five petals and a spray of stamens, often with colored anthers, at the center. Spireas are easy to care for and can be used as specimen shrubs, in shrub borders, or in beds.

Growing and care:
Spireas are vigorous plants well adapted to the mostly sunny garden. They grow well in all but the driest soil and benefit from added moisture during the growing season. Prune summer bloomers in late winter and spring-blooming varieties immediately after they flower.

Selected species and varieties:
S. japonica (Japanese spirea) is rounded, 5 to 6 feet tall, with 1- to 3-inch toothed, pointed leaves and 5- to 8-inch clusters of pink flowers in late spring and early summer; 'Little Princess' has deep pink flowers and blue-green leaves tinted red in fall on 2½-foot stems; Zones 4-8. *S. nipponica* (Nippon spirea) is compact, 3 to 5 feet tall, with 1-inch oval, blue-green leaves and an abundance of white flower clusters in midspring. *S.* x *vanhouttei* (bridal-wreath) grows 6 to 8 feet tall, spreading in vase or fountain fashion to a width of 10 to 12 feet with 1- to 2-inch white flower clusters in spring; Zones 4-8.

SPRUCE
Picea

Light: mostly sun

Plant type: shrub, tree

Hardiness: Zones 2-7

Height: 3 to 60 feet

Soil and Moisture: well-drained, moist, acidic

Interest: foliage

Care: easy to moderate

◀ Picea abies
'Nidiformis'

Spruces are a large group of very ornamental trees ranging from small shrubby forms to expansive giants. These needled, pyramidal evergreens are useful as windbreaks, screens, or single specimens. Smaller forms are good as accents in rock gardens or shrub borders.

Growing and care:
Plant spruce in well-worked soil that has been generously amended with peat moss or other organic matter. Water well at planting and during dry periods. Prune away brown galls that may appear at tips of branches. Shear to shape anytime when foliage is wet.

Selected species and varieties:
P. abies (Norway spruce) forms a fast-growing pyramid with drooping branches, 40 to 60 feet tall (it can reach 150 feet) and 25 to 30 feet wide. Its medium green foliage matures to dark green, bearing 4- to 6-inch cylindrical cones and often losing its form in old age; 'Nidiformis' (bird's-nest spruce) is a 3- to 6-foot-tall spreading mound. *P. glauca* (white spruce) is a tree that ages to a narrow, dense spire 40 to 60 feet tall by 10 to 20 feet wide, with ascending branches; Zones 2-6; 'Conica' (dwarf Alberta spruce) is a neat, very slow-growing (to 10 feet in 25 years) cone-shaped plant with light green foliage.

STEWARTIA
Stewartia

Light: mostly sun

Plant type: shrub, tree

Hardiness: Zones 5-9

Height: 10 to 45 feet

Soil and Moisture: well-drained, fertile, moist

Interest: flowers, foliage, bark

Care: moderate

◀ Stewartia
pseudocamellia

Stewartias add year-round charm and grace to the landscape, not only with their camellia-like flowers that bloom from mid- to late summer, but also with their colorful fall foliage and beautiful exfoliating bark. These stunning plants should be given a place of prominence in the landscape. The smaller types combine well with other flowering shrubs in mixed borders while the larger forms are best used as specimens.

Growing and care:
Stewartias are difficult to transplant and, once planted, should not be disturbed. Dig a large hole and add copious amounts of compost and peat moss to maintain an acid, organic soil. Stewartias require protection from drying winter winds and scorching summer sun. Provide extra moisture during dry spells. Once established, stewartias rarely need pruning.

Selected species and varieties:
S. koreana (Korean stewartia) is a pyramidal tree 35 to 45 feet tall with dark green foliage turning sunset red in fall, and 2- to 3-inch wavy-edged, creamy white flowers in late summer. *S. pseudocamellia* (Japanese stewartia) is an oval tree 20 to 40 feet tall with showy exfoliating bark, bearing 2- to 2½-inch white flowers with white filaments and orange anthers in summer, and 1½- to 3½-inch leaves that turn vibrant yellow, red, and purple in fall; Zones 5-7.

STRAWBERRY TREE
Arbutus

Light: mostly sun

Plant type: shrub, tree

Hardiness: Zones 7-9

Height: 8 to 12 feet

Soil and Moisture: well-drained, moist

Interest: flowers, foliage, bark, fruit

Care: easy

◀ Arbutus unedo

The strawberry tree is an excellent plant for the warm areas of the Southwest, providing garden interest throughout the year. The leaves are evergreen, the exfoliating bark is deep reddish brown, and the branches become attractively gnarled with age. Small urn-shaped flowers appear in 2-inch clusters in fall, and the orange-red berrylike fruit ripens the following season. Strawberry tree can be used as a hedge or a specimen, or to add variety to the shrub border.

Growing and care:
The strawberry tree tolerates a wide range of soil conditions as long as drainage is good. It requires watering only during periods of drought and is also tolerant of seaside conditions. Plant in a sheltered location away from drying winds.

Selected species and varieties:
A. unedo 'Compacta' is a slow-growing dwarf variety that eventually reaches 8 to 12 feet in height, producing dark green leaves, and bearing flowers and fruit almost continuously.

SUMAC
Rhus

Light: mostly sun

Plant type: shrub, tree

Hardiness: Zones 3-9

Height: 2 to 30 feet

Soil and Moisture: well-drained, moist to dry

Interest: foliage, fruit

Care: easy

◀ Rhus typhina 'Laciniata'

Sumacs are versatile, hardworking, easy-to-grow shrubs that add a tropical ambiance to landscapes and gardens. The plants spread rapidly to form dense thickets on steep banks and along walkways or roadsides, where they help stabilize the soil. Low-growing types are especially useful as ground covers or for fronting taller shrubs in a mixed border. Taller types should be limited to large-scale plantings. They are outstanding for their colorful fall foliage and bright red fruit, which is effective for many weeks.

Growing and care:
Sumacs prefer acid soil and do not tolerate poorly drained sites. They transplant easily and require minimal care, developing suckers and spreading rapidly to form colonies. Sumacs are virtually pest- and disease-free.

Selected species and varieties:
R. aromatica (fragrant sumac) grows from 3 to 6 feet tall, with glossy green trifoliate leaves turning red to reddish purple in fall; 'Gro-Low' reaches only 2 to 4 feet in height and is useful for the front of shrub borders, spreading to 8 feet wide with reliable orange-red fall color. *R. typhina* (staghorn sumac) is a 15- to 30-foot-tall tree with pinnately compound leaves that turn orange to scarlet in fall on velvety stems; 'Laciniata' (cut-leaf staghorn sumac) produces deeply dissected leaves that have a fine-textured appearance.

SWEET SHRUB
Calycanthus

Light: mostly sun

Plant type: shrub

Hardiness: Zones 4-10

Height: 6 to 12 feet

Soil and Moisture: well-drained, moist

Interest: flowers, fragrance

Care: easy

◀ Calycanthus occidentalis

Native to the United States and China, these delightfully unusual shrubs have distinctive segmented flowers with long, ribbonlike petals that have a pleasant fragrance reminiscent of tropical fruit. They are enjoyable additions to outdoor living areas or to foundation plantings, where the sweet fragrance of the flowers can drift through open windows. Sweet shrubs are medium size, with slightly rough dark green leaves and maroon-red flowers from midspring to summer.

Growing and care:
Sweet shrub should be planted in spring or fall. Prune as needed after flowering in summer. Propagate by dividing and transplanting suckers at the base of stems in fall. Fertilize lightly in spring as growth begins.

Selected species and varieties:
C. fertilis (Pale sweet shrub) grows 6 to 10 feet tall with 6-inch silvery green leaves and magnolia-like dark brown fragrant, flowers. *C. floridus* (sweet shrub, Carolina allspice) grows 6 to 9 feet tall and up to 12 feet wide with aromatic 2- to 5-inch leaves that turn bronzy yellow in fall, and 2-inch flowers with straplike petals that are usually burgundy-brown; 'Athens' has yellow flowers; 'Urbana' has an exceptionally sweet fragrance. *C. occidentalis* reaches 8 to 12 feet with slightly hairy 8-inch lance-shaped leaves and fragrant cinnamon-rose, narrow-petaled flowers; Zones 6-10.

VIBURNUM
Viburnum

Light: mostly sun

Plant type: shrub

Hardiness: Zones 4-9

Height: 3 to 12 feet

Soil and Moisture: well-drained, moist

Interest: flowers, foliage, fragrance

Care: easy

◀ Viburnum carlesii

Viburnums are easy-to-grow, extraordinarily attractive plants that add four-season interest to landscapes and gardens. These versatile plants offer snowy clouds of often intensely fragrant flowers in spring, beautiful summer and fall foliage, and colorful berries from autumn into winter. Viburnums are used as centerpieces for shrub borders, as screens, or as foundation plantings.

Growing and care:
Plant viburnums in loose, slightly acid loam soil amended with some organic matter. Fertilize in spring as growth begins and water regularly. Add a layer of mulch in spring and again in fall. Viburnums are remarkably pest- and disease-free and need little or no pruning.

Selected species and varieties:
V. carlesii (Koreanspice viburnum) has pink buds that open to white, domelike, enchantingly fragrant flower clusters 2 to 3 inches wide on a rounded, dense shrub 4 to 8 feet tall and wide, followed by ineffective black fruit in late summer; Zones 4-8. *V. plicatum* var. *tomentosum* (doublefile viburnum) has layered, tierlike horizontal branches on plants 8 to 10 feet tall and wide, with flat, pure white flower clusters; Zones 5-8; 'Shasta' grows 6 feet tall and 10 to 12 feet wide, with 4- to 6-inch, wide-spreading flower clusters so dense they obscure the dark green leaves.

WINTER HAZEL
Corylopsis

Light: mostly sun

Plant type: shrub

Hardiness: Zones 5-8

Height: 4 to 15 feet

Soil and Moisture: well-drained, moist

Interest: flowers, fragrance, foliage

Care: easy to moderate

◀ Corylopsis pauciflora

Winter hazel is one of the first shrubs to flower in spring, with abundant drooping panicles of sweetly fragrant flowers. Through summer the branches are thick with attractive green foliage. Winter hazel is excellent in the shrub border, set against a wall or structure, or planted in a woodland garden.

Growing and care:

Winter hazels grow best in a location with some spring sunshine for best flower formation. Protect from winter winds, sudden temperature dips, and spring frosts, which can easily kill flower buds. Work leaf mold, peat moss, or compost liberally into the soil before planting. There is usually no need to fertilize.

Selected species and varieties:

C. glabrescens (fragrant winter hazel) grows 8 to 15 feet tall with a similar spread, followed by toothy, pointed oval leaves 2 to 4 inches long and yellow flowers; Zones 5-8. *C. pauciflora* (buttercup winter hazel) grows 4 to 6 feet tall, with flowers in clusters of only two or three and leaves 1½ to 3 inches long; Zones 6-8. *C. sinensis* (Chinese winter hazel) is usually 5 to 8 feet tall but may grow to 15 feet, bearing blue-green downy leaves 2 to 5 inches long and flowers in 2-inch drooping clusters.

YEW
Taxus

Light: mostly sun

Plant type: shrub, tree

Hardiness: Zones 4-7

Height: 2 to 60 feet

Soil and Moisture: well-drained, moist

Interest: foliage

Care: easy

◀ Taxus x media 'Hicksii'

Yew is the ubiquitous evergreen plant seen in nearly every yard. With dense, very dark green needled foliage, the plants are easy to grow and provide a reliable, good-looking anchor to the landscape. Smaller forms make superb foundation plants or entrance shrubs. The plants can be left unpruned for an informal look or sheared into hedges and topiaries.

Growing and care:

Plant yews in soil lightly amended with organic matter. Water weekly until plants are established. Fertilize in spring when new growth appears. Prune or shear as needed to shape.

Selected species and varieties:

T. baccata (English yew, common yew) is a dense shrub or tree 30 to 60 feet high and 15 to 25 feet wide with a variable habit, often used as a screen or hedge; Zones 6-7. *T. cuspidata* (Japanese yew) grows from 10 to 40 feet tall with irregular, upright branches and abundant dark green needles; 'Densiformis' reaches 3 feet tall and 6 feet wide with very dark green foliage. *T.* x *media* is a cross between the English and Japanese yew with an extremely variable form, either a pyramidal tree or a spreading shrub 3 to 20 feet high, often with a central trunk; Zones 4-7; 'Hicksii' develops a columnar form to 20 feet tall in 15 to 20 years, narrow when young and becoming broader with age.

Plants for Mostly Shady Places

The plants that grow in mostly shady places live most of their lives in the shadow of other things. Towering trees or structures block the sun most of the day, yet these shade-loving plants thrive just the same. These plants of the shadows are a diverse group, with some preferring the less intense sun of early morning or late afternoon and shade for the remainder of the day, and others thriving in day-long dappled light or alternating hours of shade and sun. To grow plants in mostly shade, plan gardens that include plants of different heights, so the tiers of overlapping foliage can most efficiently use the light that is present. Enrich the soil with compost or rotted manure to increase fertility and moisture retention. And mulch the plantings in spring and fall to minimize the competition of weeds and to keep the soil cool.

COLEUS
Coleus

Light: mostly shade

Plant type: tender perennial grown as annual

Height: 9 inches to 2 feet

Soil and Moisture: well-drained, moist

Interest: foliage

Care: easy

◀ Coleus x hybridus 'Wizard Rose'

The vibrantly colored, heart-shaped opposite leaves of coleus grow on square stems and provide a long season of interest to borders in partially shaded sites. Leaves sport a wide variety of attractive patterns in colors that include chartreuse, green, orange, red, pink, bronze, and white.

Growing and care:

Start seed indoors or grow from leaf-stem cuttings overwintered indoors. Transplant outdoors after soil has warmed, allowing 8 to 12 inches between plants. Coleus are most colorful and grow best in partial shade, though some tolerate full sun if adequate water is supplied. Coleus is usually grown as an annual, but can be lifted from the garden in fall and repotted to be enjoyed as a houseplant through winter.

Selected species and varieties:

C. x *hybridus* has scalloped-edged leaves, usually 3 to 8 inches long, and upright pale blue flower spikes that are often removed to encourage growth; 'Fiji' series has fringed leaf margins in bright colors; 'Wizard' series grows to 10 inches in red, pink, and apricot shades with cream or green edges, and resists flowering.

COLLINSIA
Collinsia

Light: mostly shade

Plant type: annual

Height: 8 inches to 2 feet

Soil and Moisture: well-drained, moist to dry

Interest: flowers

Care: easy

◀ Collinsia heterophylla

Collinsia, also called Chinese houses, is a delicate annual wildflower of the western United States. The plants have very slender stalks topped with small clusters of snapdragon-shaped white, pink, blue, or purple flowers in spring. They are suited to rock gardens, woodland gardens, meadows, and borders, and are also easy to grow in containers.

Growing and care:

Sow seed directly in the garden in early spring while the soil is cool, in soil well amended with organic matter. Thin seedlings to stand 6 to 12 inches apart. Collinsia prefers areas with cool summers and partial shade. Once established the plants are moderately drought tolerant. Hot weather inhibits flowering. To extend flowering, remove faded blooms before seed can set. Propagate collinsias by seed; they often self-sow.

Selected species and varieties:

C. grandiflora (blue lips) grows 8 to 15 inches tall, bearing ³/₄-inch two-lipped flowers singly or in clusters in the leaf axils from mid- to late spring; the upper lip is white or purple and the lower lip is blue or violet. *C. heterophylla* (Chinese houses) grows 2 feet tall with blossoms arranged in tiers, and bright green foliage; the upper lip of the flower is lilac or white and the lower lip is rose-purple or violet.

FORGET-ME-NOT
Myosotis

Light: mostly shade

Plant type: annual, biennial

Height: 6 to 10 inches

Soil and Moisture: well-drained, moist

Interest: flowers, foliage

Care: easy

◀ Myosotis sylvatica
'Ultramarine'

Airy clusters of dainty flowers with prominent eyes open above the forget-me-not's low mounds of delicate foliage. Forget-me-nots provide a soft filler or a delicate border edging. They are particularly attractive in combination with spring-flowering bulbs such as tulips.

Growing and care:
Start seed outdoors in late summer to early fall for flowers the following spring. Enrich the soil with organic matter. Allow 6 to 12 inches between plants, and water during dry periods. Once established, forget-me-nots self-seed readily, performing like a perennial. Forget-me-nots do best in partial shade but thrive in mostly sun if plentiful moisture is available.

Selected species and varieties:
M. sylvatica (woodland forget-me-not, garden forget-me-not) produces 8- to 10-inch stems in clumps almost as wide, lined with soft, elongated leaves and tipped with loose clusters of ¼-inch yellow-centered blue flowers from spring through early summer; 'Ultramarine' is a dwarf, growing to 6 inches, with dark blue flowers; 'Victoria Blue' grows 6 to 8 inches, forming neat mounds and producing early flowers of gentian blue.

IMPATIENS
Impatiens

Light: mostly shade

Plant type: annual or tender perennial grown as annual

Height: 6 inches to 8 feet

Soil and Moisture: well-drained, moist

Interest: flowers, foliage

Care: easy

◀ Impatiens wallerana
'Super Elfin'

Massed as edgings or ground covers, impatiens brightens a shady garden with flowers in jeweled hues from summer through frost. These easy-to-grow plants are ideal when grouped beneath trees. Low-growing types are ideal for planters and hanging baskets.

Growing and care:
Plant *I. glandulifera* seed outdoors in fall. Start impatiens indoors 3 to 4 months prior to the last frost, or purchase bedding plants to transplant to the garden after all danger of frost has passed. Space *I. glandulifera* 2 feet apart, others 1 to 1½ feet apart. Impatiens grows best in partial to full shade, though some recently released varieties grow well in mostly sunny spots.

Selected species and varieties:
I. balsamina (garden balsam, rose balsam) grows to 3 feet, producing 1- to 2-inch flowers in mixed colors. *I. glandulifera* (Himalayan jewelweed) grows to 8 feet with 2-inch purple, pink, or white flowers in mid- to late summer. *I.* New Guinea hybrids (New Guinea impatiens) prefers more sun than other species and grows to 2 feet with showy, often variegated leaves, and flowers up to 3 inches across. *I. wallerana* (busy Lizzie) grows 6 to 18 inches tall with a compact, mounded habit and 1- to 2-inch flat-faced flowers available in many colors; 'Super Elfin' series bears flowers in assorted colors on wide-spreading plants.

MONKEY FLOWER
Mimulus

Light: mostly shade

Plant type: annual

Height: 10 to 14 inches

Soil and Moisture: well-drained, moist, fertile

Interest: flowers, foliage

Care: easy

◀ Mimulus x hybridus

Blooming from midsummer to fall, this native of both North and South America provides bright color to shady beds and borders. It fits well alongside a garden pond or stream and also makes an attractive container plant. Funnel-shaped two-lipped flowers are thought to resemble monkeys' faces.

Growing and care:

Start seed indoors 10 to 12 weeks prior to the last frost for transplanting to the garden after all danger of frost has passed. Space plants 6 inches apart. Plants benefit from the addition of organic matter to the soil. They require partial shade and ample moisture to thrive. In fall, plants can be dug and potted to continue flowering indoors over winter.

Selected species and varieties:

M. x *hybridus* has a mounded habit with glossy 2- to 2½-inch leaves and 2-inch tubular flowers in shades of red, yellow, orange, rose, and brown, usually with brown or maroon spotting or mottling.

PANSY
Viola

Light: mostly shade

Plant type: annual, perennial grown as annual

Height: 3 to 12 inches

Soil and Moisture: well-drained, moist

Interest: flowers

Care: easy

◀ Viola tricolor

Although many pansies are technically short-lived perennials, they are considered annuals because they bloom their first year from seed and their flowers decline in quality afterward, regardless of region. They may also be treated as biennials, sown in late summer for bloom early the following spring. Their vividly colored and interestingly marked flowers are borne over a long season, often beginning with the first signs of spring and lasting until the summer heat causes them to fade, although a bit of shade and water may encourage the blossoms to continue throughout most of the summer. The rounded flower petals overlap, and their patterns often resemble a face. Pansies are a good choice for planting with bulbs, combining well with the flower forms and providing cover for fading foliage. They are attractive when massed in beds, and useful as edgings or combined with other annuals in patio planters or window boxes.

Growing and care:

Sow seed outdoors in late summer for earliest spring blooms, or purchase transplants. Pansies started in late summer should be protected over winter in a cold frame or by covering plants with a light mulch or branches after the first hard frost. They can also be started indoors in midwinter to transplant to the garden in midspring. Germination can be enhanced by moistening and chilling the

(continued)

seed (between 40° and 45°F) for 1 week prior to planting. Space plants about 4 inches apart. Pansies prefer cool air and soil temperatures. In spring pansies can be grown in mostly sunny places if given ample water, and in shaded areas during summer. Remove faded blooms and keep plants well watered to extend flowering.

Selected species and varieties:

V. rafinesquii (field pansy) is a true annual that is native to much of the United States and grows 3 to 12 inches tall. Its ½-inch flowers are pale blue to cream, often with purple veins and a yellow throat. *V. tricolor* (Johnny-jump-up, miniature pansy) is a European native that has naturalized in much of the United States. It typically grows to 8 inches with a low, mounded habit and small, colorful flowers that have been favorites in the garden since Elizabethan times. The 1-inch flowers are fragrant, edible, and often used as a garnish. Colors include deep violet, blue, lavender, mauve, yellow, cream, white, and bicolors; 'Bowles' Black' bears blue-black flowers. *V. x wittrockiana* (common pansy) grows 4 to 8 inches tall and spreads to 1 foot. The 1- to 2-inch flowers are usually three toned in shades of purple, blue, dark red, rose, pink, brown, yellow, and white. Many varieties are available; 'Melody Purple and White' bears flowers with white and purple petals marked with deep violet-blue.

WISHBONE FLOWER
Torenia

◄ Torenia fournieri

Light: mostly shade

Plant type: annual

Height: 6 to 12 inches

Soil and Moisture: well-drained, moist

Interest: flowers

Care: easy

The blossoms of wishbone flower, also called blue-wings, have upper- and lower-lobed lips and are borne above a mound of foliage from midsummer to early fall. Because it thrives in shady locations, it is the perfect choice for a woodland bed or shady border. The plants are also well suited to hanging baskets and patio planters.

Growing and care:

Start seed indoors 10 to 12 weeks prior to the last frost; in Zone 9 and warmer, seed can be sown directly outdoors in early spring. Space seedlings 6 to 8 inches apart. Plants thrive in humid areas, and grow best in partial shade. In regions with cool summers the plants can be grown in mostly sunny locations.

Selected species and varieties:

T. fournieri (bluewings) has a rounded compact habit with neat oval leaves 1½ to 2 inches long. The 1-inch flowers appear in stalked clusters; each bloom displays a pale violet tube with a yellow blotch and flaring lower petal edges marked with deep purple-blue. The two fused yellow stamens resemble a poultry wishbone, hence the common name.

ARROWHEAD
Sagittaria

Light: mostly shade

Plant type: perennial

Hardiness: Zones 3-10

Height: 3 to 4 feet

Soil and Moisture: wet

Interest: flowers, foliage

Care: easy

◀ *Sagittaria latifolia*

Arrowhead, a perennial found throughout the United States and southern Canada in wet meadows, marshes, and ponds, has whorled clusters of showy flowers set off by large leathery leaves. The plants are easy-to-grow, reliable additions to water gardens, bogs, and marshes, and look especially nice planted along the shores of ponds and slow streams. Arrowhead produces edible tubers relished by ducks.

Growing and care:
Arrowhead grows best when its roots are submerged in shallow water, but it can also be grown in the wet soil of a bog garden. The plants are adaptable to a wide range of light conditions, from full sun to mostly shade. For a garden pool, plant arrowhead in containers, cover the soil with 2 inches of gravel, and submerge the containers. Propagate by seed or division in fall.

Selected species and varieties:
S. latifolia (wapatoo, duck potato) grows up to 4 feet tall with small, snow white flowers on leafless 1- to 3-foot stems from mid- to late summer. The arrow-shaped leaves are glossy green, dark and up to 16 inches long.

ASTILBE
Astilbe

Light: mostly shade

Plant type: perennial

Hardiness: Zones 3-9

Height: 8 inches to 4 feet

Soil and Moisture: well-drained, moist, fertile

Interest: flowers, foliage

Care: easy to moderate

◀ *Astilbe x arendsii* 'Rheinland'

The feathery plumes held above mounds of graceful, deep green to bronze fernlike foliage make astilbe an ideal filler in shady borders, or for use as a background accent or woodland edging, or near water elements in the landscape. The 8-inch to 4-foot stalks bear thousands of tiny five-petaled flowers that resemble white, pink, lavender, or red clouds when massed in the garden.

Growing and care:
Plant astilbes 1½ to 2 feet apart in moist soil, preferably in a cool, shady location. Water well and mulch if in full sun or average soil. Propagate by division every 3 to 4 years in spring or early summer. Feed plants each spring with a high-phosphorus fertilizer, and provide extra water during hot, dry periods.

Selected species and varieties:
A. x *arendsii* (false spirea) grows 2 to 4 feet tall with loose panicles of pink, white, red, or lavender flowers in summer; 'Fanal' combines rich bronze foliage with deep red flowers; 'Rheinland' has clear pink flowers on sturdy 2-foot stems; Zones 4-9. *A. chinensis* (Chinese astilbe) grows 8 inches to 4 feet with white, rose-tinged, or purple flowers; 'Pumila' has a dwarf habit with spires of mauve-pink flowers in late summer on 8-inch stems; Zones 3-8. *A.* x *rosea* (rose astilbe) 'Peach Blossom' has a compact form with sturdy 2-foot stems and feathery foliage beneath pale blush summer flowers.

BEARDTONGUE
Penstemon

Light: mostly shade

Plant type: perennial

Hardiness: Zones 3-8

Height: 1 to 3 feet

Soil and Moisture: well-drained, moist to dry, sandy

Interest: flowers, foliage

Care: easy to moderate

◄ Penstemon digitalis

Beardtongues are reliable soft-textured perennials with showy terminal clusters of brightly colored two-lipped summer flowers. Most species are native to the open woodlands and prairies of the Midwest. The plants are easy to grow if planted in a well-drained, sandy soil. Beardtongues are excellent for adding an airy, upright element to borders.

Growing and care:

Plant in spring after last frost in a well-worked soil that has been amended with sand and organic matter. Space plants 1 to 1½ feet apart. Water regularly while plants are actively growing. Mulch in regions with hot summers. When grown in full sun beardtongues produce the most flowers but are short lived. Plantings will last much longer when grown in a spot with mostly shade. Propagate from seed after stratification.

Selected species and varieties:

P. barbatus bears 1-inch slightly nodding red flowers on stems 1 to 2 feet high; 'Rose Elf' has stems to about 20 inches tall and plentiful clear rose blossoms in early summer; Zones 3-7. *P. digitalis* 'Husker Red Strain' [also listed under *P. smolliix*] has masses of bronzy red foliage and pearl white flowers on 3-foot stems; Zones 3-8. *P.* 'Evelyn' has upright 1½- to 2-foot stems and abundant shell pink flowers in summer; Zones 6-8.

BELLFLOWER
Campanula

Light: mostly shade

Plant type: perennial

Hardiness: Zones 3-8

Height: 1 to 2 feet

Soil and Moisture: well-drained, moist to dry

Interest: flowers

Care: easy

◄ Campanula portenschlagiana 'Resholdt's Variety'

Bellflowers are some of the most popular perennials and have long been stalwarts of beds, borders, and rock gardens. Their growth forms range from low cushions to tall, upright clumps. The color palette of the tubular or flaring flowers ranges from violet to blue to white. Flowers are borne in clusters or spikes from late spring through summer, with some species lightly reblooming in fall.

Growing and care:

In cool-summer regions bellflowers grow best in mostly sun, but still flower well in mostly shade. In regions with hot summers the plants should be given mostly shade. Space low-growing bellflowers 1 to 1½ feet apart, larger ones 2 feet apart. Propagate by seed or division; divide every 3 to 4 years to maintain vigor.

Selected species and varieties:

C. persicifolia (peachleaf bellflower) bears nodding 1-inch deep blue to white flowers on pliant 2-foot stems in summer and reblooms in fall; 'Grandiflora Alba' has large, pure white flowers; 'Summer Skies' has double white flowers accented with pastel blue. *C. portenschlagiana* (Dalmatian bellflower) has loose panicles of purple-blue star-shaped flowers in late spring and early summer above 4- to 8-inch mounds of coarse kidney-shaped leaves; 'Resholdt's Variety' has large, deep purple flowers on 6-inch stems; Zones 5-7.

BERGENIA
Bergenia

Light: mostly shade

Plant type: perennial

Hardiness: Zones 3-9

Height: 1 to 1¹⁄₂ feet

Soil and Moisture: well-drained, moist

Interest: flowers, foliage

Care: easy

◀ Bergenia cordifolia

Bergenias are noted for their large, showy rosettes of bold leathery leaves and 3- to 6-inch spikes of white, pink, or lavender-rose flowers in spring. In warmer climates the leaves are evergreen, while in the North they turn a dusky burgundy or bronze in the fall. Use bergenias in rock gardens, in beds and borders, as edging, or as a ground cover.

Growing and care:
Bergenias are very tolerant of cold, heat, and moist soil. A site that remains wet in winter may cause the roots to rot. Space plants 1 foot apart. They will spread quickly by rhizomes to form a thick ground cover. The plants are quite adaptable and thrive in fertile or poor soil and mostly sunny to mostly shady spots. Divide every 3 to 4 years to promote vigorous growth and flowering.

Selected species and varieties:
B. cordifolia [formerly listed as *Saxifraga cordifolia*] (heart-leaf bergenia, pig squeak) has clumps of 8- to 10-inch leaves with wavy edges and heart-lobed bases, and clusters of 1-inch pink flowers atop 10- to 18-inch stalks in early spring; 'Alba' has white flowers; 'Purpurea' has purple flowers. *B. crassifolia* (leather bergenia) has rounded leaves and lavender-pink flowers held high above bright green foliage. *B. stracheyi* (Strachey bergenia) has unwavy leaves edged with hairs, and white flowers in late winter or early spring; Zones 6-9.

BLEEDING HEART
Dicentra

Light: mostly shade

Plant type: perennial

Hardiness: Zones 3-8

Height: 4 inches to 3 feet

Soil and Moisture: well-drained, moist

Interest: flowers, foliage

Care: easy

◀ Dicentra spectabilis

Bleeding hearts have long panicles of ornate symmetrical flowers that dangle on arching stems above layers of soft, lacy foliage. The many Asian and North American species produce attractive flowers in spring and summer. In summer the gray-green foliage of most species fades as the plants become dormant. Bleeding hearts make excellent additions to woodland borders and mostly shady wildflower gardens.

Growing and care:
Bleeding hearts thrive in the dappled shade beneath tall trees. Plant *D. spectabilis* 2 to 3 feet apart and other species 1 to 2 feet apart. They will spread slowly by small tubers, self-sowing, or offsets. Propagate by division when plants are dormant.

Selected species and varieties:
D. canadensis (squirrel corn) reaches 6 to 10 inches with blue-gray leaves, and heart-shaped ¹⁄₂-inch white flowers in spring; Zones 3-7. *D. cucullaria* (Dutchman's-breeches) reaches 4 to 10 inches with yellow-tipped, double-spurred ¹⁄₂-inch fragrant white flowers in spring; Zones 3-7. *D. spectabilis* bears 1- to 1¹⁄₂-inch pink and white or all-white flowers from spring to midsummer on 2- to 3-foot stalks above feathery foliage; Zones 4-8.

BLUESTAR
Amsonia

Light:	mostly shade
Plant type:	perennial
Hardiness:	Zones 3-9
Height:	2 to 3 feet
Soil and Moisture:	well-drained, moist
Interest:	flowers
Care:	easy

◀ Amsonia tabernaemontana

Bluestar produces pale blue star-shaped blossoms that hang above the green foliage like clusters of shooting stars. Blooming in late spring and early summer, it is particularly effective combined with more brightly colored flowers. Its densely mounded willowlike leaves remain attractive throughout the growing season, providing a lovely foil for later-blooming perennials.

Growing and care:
Bluestars grow best in mostly shady places but thrive in mostly to fully sunny places as well. In poor to moderately fertile soil they rarely need staking; avoid highly fertile soil, which produces rank, floppy growth. The plants prefer to be undisturbed once established but should be divided every 3 to 4 years in spring or fall to keep them vigorous. Prune lightly to keep plants tidy. Provide extra water during dry periods.

Selected species and varieties:
A. tabernaemontana produces steel blue flowers in terminal clusters on stiff 2- to 3-foot-tall erect stems with densely occurring leaves 3 to 6 inches long that turn yellow in fall; var. *salicifolia* has longer and thinner leaves and blooms slightly later than the species.

BOWMAN'S ROOT
Gillenia

Light:	mostly shade
Plant type:	perennial
Hardiness:	Zones 4-8
Height:	2 to 4 feet
Soil and Moisture:	well-drained, moist
Interest:	flowers
Care:	easy

◀ Gillenia trifoliata

Bowman's root is a tall, delicate perennial with white star-shaped flowers often blushed with pink. The attractive dark green foliage accents the flowers, which emerge from wine-colored sepals in spring to summer and remain ornamental long after the petals drop. The plants are a useful addition to borders and are excellent when naturalized with flowering shrubs in meadows or woodland plantings.

Growing and care:
Plant in fall in soil that contains some organic matter. Space plants 2 to 3 feet apart and water regularly until plants are established and during hot dry periods. The plants thrive in mostly shady situations but also grow well in mostly sunny locations. Mulch well in spring and fall to keep roots cool and retain soil moisture. Cut back stems after flowering is completed. Plants often require staking. Propagate from seed, which is often quite difficult, or by divsion in spring or fall.

Selected species and varieties:
G. trifoliata [formerly *Porteranthus trifoliata*] bears five-petaled flowers 1 inch wide, in loose, airy clusters on wiry branching stems 2 to 4 feet tall above lacy leaves with toothed edges.

BUGBANE
Cimicifuga

Light: mostly shade

Plant type: perennial

Hardiness: Zones 3-8

Height: 3 to 7 feet

Soil and Moisture: well-drained, moist, fertile

Interest: flowers, foliage

Care: moderate

◀ Cimicifuga ramosa 'Brunette'

Bugbane is a distinctive perennial wildflower with airy columns of lacy leaflets topped by long wands of tiny, icy white frilled flowers in late summer to fall. These tall, graceful plants are excellent as accent specimens, naturalized in a woodland garden, or massed at the edge of a stream or pond.

Growing and care:
Plant bugbane in shady to mostly shady areas of the garden in soil enriched with organic matter. Fertilize lightly in spring and provide extra water during dry periods. Mulch to keep roots cool. Disturb established plantings as little as possible. Propagate by division in spring.

Selected species and varieties:
C. americana (American bugbane) has dense spikes of creamy blossoms on branched 2- to 6-foot-tall flower stalks in late summer to fall. *C. ramosa* (branched bugbane) bears 3-foot wands of fragrant white flowers on reddish stalks in fall; 'Atropurpurea' grows to 7 feet with bronzy purple leaves; 'Brunette' has purplish black foliage and pink-tinged flowers on 3- to 4-foot stalks. *C. simplex* 'White Pearl' has 2-foot wands of white flowers on branching, arched 3- to 4-foot flower stalks followed by round, lime green fruits.

COLUMBINE
Aquilegia

Light: mostly shade

Plant type: perennial

Hardiness: Zones 3-9

Height: 8 inches to 3 feet

Soil and Moisture: well-drained, moist to dry

Interest: flowers

Care: easy to moderate

◀ Aquilegia canadensis

Columbines are unique, very colorful flowers bearing complex erect or nodding blossoms with long spurs at the base of brightly colored petals. Their rounded, lacy blue-green foliage adds a soft accent to the garden. They are excellent additions to the wildflower garden, naturalized in meadows, or used in beds, borders, and rock gardens.

Growing and care:
Columbines thrive in organic-rich soil with even moisture and in a range of conditions, from full sun to full shade. All columbines self-sow, some prolifically. Propagate native columbines by sowing the small seed indoors in late winter. Do not cover seed, as light is needed to germinate properly. Leaf miners sometimes do cosmetic damage to the foliage.

Selected species and varieties:
A. canadensis (wild columbine) has graceful 2-foot stems bearing dainty, nodding crimson and yellow blossoms from spring to midsummer. *A.* x *hybrida* (hybrid columbine) bears large 3-inch spring-blooming flowers on 3-foot stems; 'Crimson Star' has 1½-inch flowers with red spurs, white central petal tips, and a projecting shower of elegant golden stamens; 'Dragonfly Hybrids' are 1 foot tall and range in color from red, yellow, or blue to various bicolors; 'McKana Giants' have oversize flowers borne on 2½-foot stems.

CORYDALIS
Corydalis

Light: mostly shade

Plant type: perennial

Hardiness: Zones 5-8

Height: 8 to 15 inches

Soil and Moisture: well-drained, moist

Interest: flowers

Care: moderate

◄ Corydalis flexuosa 'Blue Panda'

Corydalis are delicate woodland wildflowers bearing spikes of small, tubular flowers that hang from slender stems from midspring to summer. The fernlike foliage is similar to that of bleeding heart and remains attractive throughout the growing season. The plants are useful for edgings, rock gardens, and perennial beds.

Growing and care:
Corydalis grows best in light or dappled shade but tolerates deep shade well. For increased vigor, work organic matter such as compost, leaf mold, or peat moss into the soil before planting. Good drainage and even moisture are essential. If soil dries out in summer the plants may cease flowering. Apply an all-purpose fertilizer in spring. After 2 to 3 years, divide plants in early spring. Propagate from seed or by stem cuttings. Yellow corydalis self-seeds freely.

Selected species and varieties:
C. flexuosa 'Blue Panda' forms 8- to 12-inch-tall mounds of blue-green foliage accented with dense sprays of porcelain blue flowers from late spring until frost. *C. lutea* (yellow corydalis, yellow bleeding heart) is a bushy multi-stemmed plant 12 to 15 inches tall with slender spikes of ¾-inch-long yellow flowers held high above the blue-green foliage.

EPIMEDIUM
Epimedium

Light: mostly shade

Plant type: perennial

Hardiness: Zones 4-8

Height: 3 to 12 inches

Soil and Moisture: well-drained, moist, fertile

Interest: flowers, foliage

Care: easy

◄ Epimedium grandiflorum

Epimediums have sprays of waxy bicolored flowers with downward-curving spurs that appear in midspring before the small heart-shaped leaves emerge. New leaves are pale green or red as they unfurl, turn medium green in summer and bronze in fall, and remain throughout winter in warmer regions. Epimediums are popular plants for shady rock gardens. Planted in large groups, they can be used as a creeping ground cover for shady areas.

Growing and care:
Epimediums prefer moist, peaty loam, but tolerate drier soils once established. The plants grow best in mostly shady locations. Add compost or peat moss before planting 8 to 10 inches apart. Remove dead foliage in early spring before new growth starts. Propagate by division of rhizomes in late summer.

Selected species and varieties:
E. alpinum (red Alpine epimedium) produces 1-foot masses of reddish green leaves and slipper-shaped yellow and red flowers. *E. grandiflorum* (longspur epimedium, bishop's hat) grows 1 foot tall with 1- to 2-inch red-, pink-, lavender-, or white-spurred flowers with red sepals and 2- to 3-inch leaves; 'Nanum' is 3 inches tall; 'Rose Queen' has large, deep pink flowers and foliage that emerges reddish and turns dark green as it matures; 'White Queen' has white flowers.

FALSE SOLOMON'S-SEAL
Smilacina

Light: mostly shade

Plant type: perennial

Hardiness: Zones 3-7

Height: 2 to 3 feet

Soil and Moisture: well-drained, moist, fertile

Interest: flowers, foliage

Care: easy

◀ Smilacina racemosa

A member of the lily family, false Solomon's-seal bears pyramidal flower panicles in spring on gracefully arching stems with oval leaves that have prominent parallel veins. Colorful red berries that are a favorite of wildlife follow in late summer to fall. Native to moist woodlands, false Solomon's-seal is best used for wildflower gardens and for naturalizing.

Growing and care:

False Solomon's-seal thrives best in deep soil in cool, moist, shady to mostly shady locations, such as along a stream or pond or along woodland paths. Amend the soil with compost, leaf mold, or peat moss. Propagate by dividing the rhizomes in fall, allowing at least one bud per segment. Replant with the bud facing up. Mulch with leaf litter to overwinter.

Selected species and varieties:

S. racemosa bears 6-inch-long creamy white flower clusters in mid- to late spring on arching stems 2 to 3 feet tall. It produces pointed, oval to lance-shaped leaves to 9 inches long, and small, pea-size green berries that turn red in fall.

FOAMFLOWER
Tiarella

Light: mostly shade

Plant type: perennial

Hardiness: Zones 3-9

Height: 6 to 12 inches

Soil and Moisture: well-drained, moist

Interest: flowers, foliage

Care: easy

◀ Tiarella cordifolia

Foamflowers have spikes of white frothy flowers that bloom in midspring, and are native to moist woodlands and stream banks in eastern North America. These plants produce stalks that rise out of low-growing mounds of attractive, sharp-lobed, fuzzy heart-shaped leaves that are medium green in summer and reddish bronze or dark purple in fall, and remain visible over winter. They make an exceptional ground cover, edging, or rock garden plant for shady spots, and are especially effective when massed.

Growing and care:

Foamflowers require additional water during dry spells. They grow best in slightly acid soil with a high organic content. Space plants 1 to 1½ feet apart; they will spread quickly by runners. Propagate by digging and replanting runners in spring or fall, or by sowing fresh seed in the garden in fall.

Selected species and varieties:

T. cordifolia (Allegheny foamflower) has compact clusters of tiny ¼-inch-wide star-shaped, five-petaled white flowers with long white stamens on 6- to 12-inch-tall stalks above neat mounds of lobed leaves from midspring to early summer; 'Major' bears salmon-red or wine-colored blossoms; 'Marmorata' has maroon flowers and bronze leaves that become marbled with purple in winter; 'Purpurea' has purple flowers.

FOXGLOVE
Digitalis

Light: mostly shade

Plant type: perennial, biennial

Hardiness: Zones 3-9

Height: 2 to 4 feet

Soil and Moisture: well-drained, moist

Interest: flowers

Care: easy to moderate

◀ Digitalis x mertonensis

Foxgloves produce 2- to 3-inch spotted tubular flowers that crowd along a stiff stalk from late spring to early summer. These short-lived perennials or biennials overwinter as a clump of attractive light green leaves. Evocative of English cottage gardens, foxgloves provide strong vertical accents for beds and borders. They are most effective when planted in clumps. They grow well in coastal gardens and make excellent cut flowers if picked when partially open.

Growing and care:

Foxgloves tolerate mostly sunny to shady locations but prefer mostly shady spots in soil amended with some organic matter. Space established plants 1 to 1½ feet apart. Propagate by seed sown ¼ inch deep in late summer, by division in fall, or by transplanted self-sown seedlings in early spring.

Selected species and varieties:

D. ferruginea (rusty foxglove) produces a basal clump of narrow, deeply veined dark green leaves, each up to 9 inches long. A leafy 3- to 4-foot flower stalk rises from the clump, bearing dense clusters of small yellowish blooms that open from mid- to late summer. Each flower is ½ to 1¼ inches long, yellow-brown, and netted with a rusty red. Tiny hairs fringe the flower lip. *D. grandiflora* (yellow foxglove) is a perennial with brown-spotted yellow flowers on 3-foot stalks that needs partial shade; 'Temple Bells' has large flowers. *D. x mertonensis* (strawberry foxglove) is a perennial with dark strawberry pink flowers neatly layered on 4-foot stems that is grown as a cool-season annual in the Southeast. *D. purpurea* (common foxglove) produces a broad clump of large, rough-textured woolly leaves from which an erect flower stem with smaller leaves emerges in early summer. The flower stalks range in size from 2 to 5 feet. The 2- to 3-inch pendulous flowers are borne in a one-sided cluster up to 2 feet long. Their colors include purple, pink, white, rust, or yellow, and their throats are often spotted; 'Alba' grows to 4 feet with white flowers; 'Apricot' grows to 3½ feet with flowers ranging from pale pink to bold apricot; 'Excelsior' grows to 4 feet with blooms borne all around the stem rather than on one side, in shades of purple, pink, white, cream, and yellow; 'Foxy' grows 2½ to 3 feet, with flowers in pastel shades from rose pink to white appearing the first year from seed; 'Giant Shirley' grows 5 feet or more, producing strong stems with large mottled blooms in shades of pink.

GAY-FEATHER
Liatris

Light: mostly shade

Plant type: perennial

Hardiness: Zones 3-10

Height: 1½ to 5 feet

Soil and Moisture: well-drained, moist

Interest: flowers

Care: easy

◀ Liatris spicata

Gay-feathers are bold yet elegant plants with upright slender stalks topped with soft spikes of feathery flowers over clumps of grassy leaves. The 6- to 15-inch flower clusters open from top to bottom. They give a strong vertical accent to borders. Gay-feathers are superb for naturalizing in meadow gardens.

Growing and care:
Plant corms 3 to 4 inches deep in spring or fall in a well-worked soil amended with some organic matter. Space plants 1 to 2 feet apart in a sunny to mostly shady location. Propagate by separating and planting the tiny cormels that develop around mature corms.

Selected species and varieties:
L. ligulistylis has tufts of 3- to 5-foot stems with 1½-inch clusters of rosy purple flowers from summer to fall and deep green, narrow leaves. *L. spicata* (spike gay-feather, button snakewort) has clumps 2 to 5 feet tall and 2 feet wide with very narrow 3- to 5-inch tapering leaves on erect, stout stems, and purple or rose flowers from mid- to late summer; 'Alba' is pure white; 'Kobold' is a 1½- to 2-foot dwarf with dense heads of purple flowers tinged with burgundy.

GENTIAN
Gentiana

Light: mostly shade

Plant type: perennial

Hardiness: Zones 3-8

Height: 2 inches to 3 feet

Soil and Moisture: well-drained, moist to wet

Interest: flowers

Care: moderate to difficult

◀ Gentiana septemfida var. lagodechiana

Gentians are noted for their unique blossoms, which range from flaring bell-shaped forms of brilliant sapphire blue to more modest blue flowers that resemble unopened buds. The variability of this genus provides the gardener with plants that thrive in rock gardens, borders, or slightly alkaline fields.

Growing and care:
Gentians thrive in sunny to mostly shady locations in soil with abundant organic matter. Plant larger species 1 to 1½ feet apart and smaller ones 4 to 12 inches apart. Propagate plants by mixing the fresh seed with dry, fine sand and spreading the mixture on the surface of the garden in spring. The seeds need light to germinate, so do not cover with soil. Divide clumps in early spring.

Selected species and varieties:
G. acaulis (stemless gentian) bears 2-inch bell-shaped sky blue flowers spotted with yellow in spring above thick rosettes of 2-inch leaves and 4-inch stems; Zones 4-8. *G. andrewsii* (closed gentian, bottle gentian) has clusters of closed blue flowers in late summer and fall that become purplish with age; forma *albiflora* has white flowers; Zones 5-8. *G. septemfida* (crested gentian) has small terminal clusters of pleated 2-inch bell-shaped blue flowers from mid- to late summer on 8- to 12-inch stems with erect or arching clumps; var. *lagodechiana* has deep blue flowers on 6- to 8-inch stems.

GERANIUM
Geranium

Light:	mostly shade
Plant type:	perennial
Hardiness:	Zones 3-10
Height:	9 inches to 2 feet
Soil and Moisture:	well-drained, moist to dry
Interest:	flowers, foliage, fragrance
Care:	easy to moderate

◀ *Geranium sanguineum*

Geraniums have long been garden favorites for their bright five-petaled flowers in spring and summer and their spreading mounds of foliage. All have palmately lobed leaves, and some, such as *G. macrorrhizum*, which is the source of geranium oil, have strongly aromatic foliage. Geraniums are a versatile group of plants used in rock gardens and borders, as ground covers, or naturalized in meadows or woodland gardens. They sometimes are called hardy geraniums to distinguish them from the genus *Pelargonium,* also known as zonal geraniums.

Growing and care:

Plant geraniums in spring or fall, spacing them 1½ to 2 feet apart. Mulch after planting and fertilize lightly in spring. The plants flower best in mostly sunny locations but retain the best flower color in mostly shady spots. In regions with hot summers the plants need afternoon shade and supplemental water. Propagate geraniums by dividing clumps in spring every 3 to 4 years.

Selected species and varieties:

G. endressii 'Wargrave Pink' has 1- to 1½-inch bluish pink flowers with ragged 2- to 4-inch leaves divided into five segments and blossoming from spring to fall where summers are hot; Zones 4-8. *G. ibericum* (Iberian cranesbill) has 1- to 2-inch purple flowers from spring through summer on 1- to 1½-foot hairy stems clad with deeply lobed leaves; 'Album' has white flowers; Zones 5-8. *G.* x 'Johnson's Blue' has 15- to 18-inch leafy mounds with 1½- to 2-inch lavender-blue flowers traced with darker blue veins from spring to summer; Zones 5-8. *G. macrorrhizum* (bigroot geranium) produces 10- to 12-inch creeping stems bearing magenta flowers from late spring to early summer with very aromatic maple-shaped leaves that turn bright red in fall; 'Album' has white flowers; 'Bevan's Variety' has deep magenta flowers; Zones 3-8. *G. maculatum* (wild geranium, wild cranesbill, spotted cranesbill) has grayish maplelike leaves on 1- to 2-foot openly branched stems with 1-inch rose-purple to pale lilac flowers in late spring or early summer; Zones 3-7. *G.* x *oxonianum* grows 2 to 3 feet tall with slightly wrinkled, toothed leaves and pink summer flowers accented with darker-colored veins; 'A. T. Johnson' has pink flowers with a light silver cast; 'Rose Clair' has porcelain pink flowers in July on 1- to 2-foot stems; Zones 5-7. *G. psilostemon* (Armenian cranesbill) grows 1 to 2 feet tall with mounds of deeply toothed green leaves peppered in summer with bold magenta flowers marked with a prominent black eye; 'Bressingham Flair' has pink flowers on 1- to 3-foot stems; Zones 5-7. *G. sanguineum* (bloody cranesbill, blood-red cranesbill) bears solitary 1½-inch crimson flowers in spring and summer on 2-foot-wide mounds of gray-green leaves that turn red in fall; 'Album' has pure white flowers on 8- to 10-inch stems; 'Alpenglow' has dark green leaves and bright rose red flowers; 'Glenluce' bears clear pink blossoms on dense mounds of medium green leaves; var. *striatum* is a dwarf with soft pink flowers and purple veins; 'Splendens' is a vigorous grower with pearl-pink flowers accented with purple-red veins; Zones 4-9. *G. sylvaticum* (wood cranesbill) has crowded clusters of 1- to 1½-inch pinkish purple, violet-blue, or white flowers atop 1½- to 2-foot stems in late spring and summer; 'May-flower' has rich violet-blue flowers with white zones in the center; 'Nanum' has a low-growing habit and red flowers.

GOATSBEARD
Aruncus

Light: mostly shade
Plant type: perennial
Hardiness: Zones 3-7
Height: 1 to 6 feet
Soil and Moisture: well-drained, moist, fertile
Interest: flowers, foliage
Care: easy

◀ Aruncus dioicus

Goatsbeards bear dramatic 6- to 10-inch plumes of minute cream-colored flowers on 1- to 6-foot stems from midspring to early summer. After the flowers fade the tall mounds of deep green compound leaves provide a stately background for later-blooming plants. Goatsbeards are native to deciduous woodlands of the eastern and central United States and western Europe. The dwarf varieties often are mistaken for astilbes.

Growing and care:
Goatsbeards benefit from yearly additions of compost. The plants grow best in moist, fertile soil in light conditions ranging from mostly sun to mostly shade. Space plants 4 to 5 feet apart, and propagate by seed or from early-spring division of young plants.

Selected species and varieties:
A. dioicus (also listed as *A. sylvester*) has pinnately compound leaves bearing 20 or more 1- to 2½-inch dark green doubly toothed oval leaflets, and stems forming mounds up to 6 feet high with 4- to 16-inch-wide flower clusters borne at the tips of shoots and branches; 'Kneiffii' grows to about 3 feet high and has more finely divided foliage, giving it a more delicate appearance. *A. sinensis* is similar to *A. dioicus* but blooms a few weeks later and has more coarsely toothed leaves that are deep green overlain with light brown.

GOLDENROD
Solidago

Light: mostly shade
Plant type: perennial
Hardiness: Zones 3-9
Height: 3 to 4 feet
Soil and Moisture: well-drained, moist to dry
Interest: flowers, fragrance
Care: easy

◀ Solidago odora

Sweet goldenrod is an easy-to-grow perennial that artfully combines versatility with outstanding fall beauty. From summer into autumn, the tall, pliant stems are graced with delicate plumes of cheery yellow flowers and scores of smooth, lance-shaped green leaves that emit an anise fragrance when bruised. The blossoms add an airy touch to fresh or dried arrangements and have long been used to make a stunning yellow-colored dye for cloth. The leaves are used fresh or dried to make a soothing, anise flavored tea. Goldenrod is excellent in sunny to mostly shady wildflower meadows, herb gardens and rock gardens.

Growing and care:
Sow sweet goldenrod seeds or divide mature plants in early spring, spacing seedlings or divisions 12 to 15 inches apart. Goldenrod spreads rapidly and can be restrained easily by planting in large containers or surrounded with garden edging sunk into the soil. Shear plants to the ground in late winter or early spring before new growth begins.

Selected species and varieties:
S. odora (sweet goldenrod) bears slender single stems lined with glossy, narrow 2- to 4-inch smooth-edged leaves and tipped with one-sided 8- to 12-inch plumes of ¼-inch yellow flowers.

GOLDENSTAR
Chrysogonum

Light: mostly shade

Plant type: perennial

Hardiness: Zones 5-9

Height: 4 to 9 inches

Soil and Moisture: well-drained, moist

Interest: flowers, foliage

Care: moderate

◄ Chrysogonum virginianum var. virginianum

The deep green foliage of goldenstar provides a lush background for its bright yellow star-shaped flowers, which appear from late spring through summer. Its low-growing spreading habit makes it useful as a ground cover, for edging at the front of a border, or as an accent in a mostly shady rock garden.

Growing and care:

Goldenstar grows well in most soils with average fertility and produces more compact growth in poor soils. Mulch in spring and fall to retain moisture and keep soil cool. Flowering may stop during hot weather even if supplemental water is applied. For use as a ground cover, space plants 1 foot apart. Propagate by dividing the plants in spring in northern areas and in fall in warmer zones.

Selected species and varieties:

C. virginianum var. *virginianum* reaches 6 to 9 inches, with dark green leaves that are bluntly serrated along upright spreading stems, and flowers 1½ inches across that bloom throughout spring in warm areas, well into summer in cooler zones; var. *australe* is similar to var. *virginianum* but more prostrate.

HELLEBORE
Helleborus

Light: mostly shade

Plant type: perennial

Hardiness: Zones 4-9

Height: 2 inches to 1½ feet

Soil and Moisture: well-drained, moist

Interest: flowers, foliage

Care: moderate

◄ Helleborus orientalis

Hellebores have 2- to 3-inch cup-shaped flowers in subtle hues of creamy white, pink, and deep maroon nestled around attractive, deeply lobed evergreen leaves. They are valued for their late-winter or early-spring flowers, which appear when little else is in bloom. Hellebores are excellent for borders and paths and can be massed as a ground cover. The solitary blossoms make long-lasting cut flowers.

Growing and care:

Plant hellebores in spring in the North and in fall in the South, in full or partial shade, spacing them 1 to 2 feet apart. Mulch lightly in spring and again in fall. Give extra water during hot, dry periods. Propagate by seed or division in early summer, being careful not to damage the fragile roots. Plants also self-sow.

Selected species and varieties:

H. niger (Christmas rose) is 12 to 15 inches tall with nodding, creamy white flowers tinged with pink around prominent yellow stamens in late fall in the South and early spring in the North; 'Louis Cobbett' has white flowers stained with pink; Zones 5-8. *H. orientalis* (Lenten rose) is 15 to 18 inches tall with nodding clusters of two to six 2-inch cream, pink, maroon, or plum flowers from early to midspring; 'Queen of the Night' has blossoms with velvety deep red petals and a shower of bright yellow stamens.

HOSTA
Hosta

Light: mostly shade

Plant type: perennial

Hardiness: Zones 3-9

Height: 15 inches to 4 feet

Soil and Moisture: well-drained, moist

Interest: flowers, foliage

Care: easy

◀ Hosta 'Gold Standard'

Hostas are prized mainly for their spreading clumps of attractive foliage, which make them ideal for textural and color accents in perennial beds and borders. The plants bear trumpet-shaped flowers along strong stalks in summer in colors ranging from white to lavender. Hosta is excellent in borders or as a ground cover in mostly to fully shady places.

Growing and care:
Good drainage is essential, especially in winter. Although most hostas thrive in deep shade, variegated and blue forms need bright shade to hold their color. *H.* 'Francee' tolerates some sun. Remove flowers to improve foliage and prevent crossbreeding. Propagate by division in fall or early spring. Deer love to nibble hosta and plantings should be protected.

Selected species and varieties:
H. 'Francee' has dark green heart-shaped leaves with white margins, growing to 1½ feet tall, with lavender flowers on 2-foot stems; 'Gold Standard' grows to 2½ feet tall and has veined yellow leaves with green margins, and violet flowers; 'Krossa Regal' is 4 feet tall, with veined blue leaves up to 8 inches long and 5 inches wide, and lilac flowers atop 5-foot stalks. *H. sieboldiana* 'Frances Williams' grows to 3 feet tall, bearing foot-long crinkled leaves with yellow margins, and lilac flowers amid the leaves.

JOE-PYE WEED
Eupatorium

Light: mostly shade

Plant type: perennial

Hardiness: Zones 3-9

Height: 2 to 6 feet

Soil and Moisture: well-drained, wet to moist

Interest: flowers

Care: easy

◀ Eupatorium maculatum 'Atropurpureum'

These stately, robust natives to eastern North American wetlands display rounded clusters of small, misty, purplish pink or white flowers that attract honeybees, butterflies, and hummingbirds in late summer. Joe-Pye weed is ideal for planting near water elements or in bog gardens, or for naturalizing in wet meadows.

Growing and care:
Plant Joe-Pye weed in spring or fall in moist to wet soil in full sun to mostly shade. Space plants 2 to 3 feet apart. Divide clumps every 3 years in spring. Joe-Pye weed does not need mulching or fertilizing and is virtually pest-free.

Selected species and varieties:
E. maculatum (spotted Joe-Pye weed) bears flat-topped clusters of pink or purple late-summer flowers on 4- to 6-foot stems spotted with purple; 'Atropurpureum' has wine red flowers; Zones 3-6. *E. perfoliatum* (boneset) has loose clusters of antique white flowers from late summer to fall on 2- to 5-foot hairy stems piercing the base of the paired, stemless bright green leaves. *E. purpureum* (Joe-Pye weed) produces dome-topped clusters of pale pink to rose-purple flowers from late summer to fall on 3- to 6-foot green and purple stems above whorls of vanilla-scented leaves; Zones 4-9. *E. rugosum* (white snakeroot) grows to 5 feet with drooping terminal clusters of tiny white flowers from midsummer to early fall.

LADY'S-MANTLE
Alchemilla

Light: mostly shade

Plant type: perennial

Hardiness: Zones 3-8

Height: 4 inches to 1½ feet

Soil and Moisture: well-drained, moist, fertile

Interest: flowers, foliage

Care: easy

◀ Alchemilla mollis

Lady's-mantle carpets the ground with large cupped leaves that reveal silvery undersides when tipped by a breeze. Use the frothy clusters of tiny greenish flowers that rise above the semievergreen foliage in summer as fillers in fresh or dried arrangements. Young leaves are sometimes tossed with salads or added to tea; they also yield a green dye. Lady's-mantle was traditionally used in herbal remedies.

Growing and care:
Sow seed in spring; transplant divisions or the freely self-sown seedlings in spring or fall. Cut plants back hard to keep them compact; they recover readily. Plants can tolerate full sun in cool, moist northern areas. To dry, cut flowers just as they open and hang in bunches in a well-ventilated area.

Selected species and varieties:
A. alpina (Alpine lady's mantle) has broad leaves composed of pointed, lobed leaflets arranged like fingers on a hand and clusters of green flowers on creeping plants 4 to 8 inches tall, ideal for informal edgings. *A. mollis* [also called *A. vulgaris*] (lady's mantle) has scalloped fan-shaped leaves up to 6 inches across and yellow-green flowers on plants to 1½ feet tall.

LEADWORT
Plumbago

Light: mostly shade

Plant type: perennial

Hardiness: Zones 9-10

Height: 6 to 8 feet

Soil and Moisture: well-drained, moist

Interest: flowers

Care: easy to moderate

◀ Plumbago auriculata

Leadwort is a reliable large evergreen shrub that develops a mounded habit with long vinelike branches. Flowers are azure blue or white, and under ideal conditions they will appear year round.

Growing and care:
Leadwort is a mounding shrub and can be maintained through pruning as a dense, low hedge or foundation plant. If trained it will climb a trellis or wall, and it is also well suited as a tall ground cover for large, well-drained slopes. Leadwort thrives in full sun but tolerates light shade in hot areas; it tolerates coastal conditions as well but is sensitive to frost. Prune the oldest canes to the ground each year in early spring, and pinch new growth to encourage branching.

Selected species and varieties:
P. auriculata (Cape leadwort, Cape plumbago) grows 6 to 8 feet tall, spreading 8 to 12 feet or more. Leaves are 1 to 2 inches long, medium to light green, evergreen; flowers are 1 inch across in 3- to 4-inch clusters, blue or white. The main blooming season is from early spring through fall.

LEWISIA
Lewisia

Light: mostly shade	
Plant type: perennial	
Hardiness: Zones 3-8	
Height: 4 to 12 inches	
Soil and Moisture: well-drained, dry	
Interest: flowers	
Care: difficult	

◄ Lewisia cotyledon

Lewisias are low-growing perennials that inhabit rocky slopes and open woods of the western United States. They are excellent choices for rock gardens.

Growing and care:

Most lewisias prefer partial shade to thrive, yet *L. rediva* does well in mostly sunny locations. All species must have soil with excellent drainage. A mulch of gravel or stone chips 1 to 2 inches deep helps control crown rot. Keep soil moist but avoid wetting the foliage when watering. Starting plants from seed is often difficult and seedlings should grow for at least 1 year in containers before planting out.

Selected species and varieties:

L. columbiana (bitterroot) produces an evergreen rosette of flat, dark green leaves with branched clusters of pink-veined white or pink flowers on 4- to 12-inch stalks in spring; Zones 4-8. *L. cotyledon* (broadleaf lewisia) has neat rosettes of spoon-shaped leaves and loose clusters of white- or pink-striped flowers on 1-foot stalks in early summer; Zones 6-8. *L. rediviva* (bitterroot) has a rosette of cylindrical leaves that appears in late summer and remains green over winter. In early spring showy rose-colored flowers up to 2 inches across are borne on short stems. After flowering the plant goes dormant; Zones 4-8.

LOBELIA
Lobelia

Light: mostly shade	
Plant type: perennial	
Hardiness: Zones 4-8	
Height: 2 to 4 feet	
Soil and Moisture: well-drained, moist, fertile	
Interest: flowers, foliage	
Care: easy	

◄ Lobelia siphilitica

Lobelias are stunning perennials with strong, upright habits and bold flowers. The stout stems are covered with dark green leaves and topped with spikes of tubular flowers ranging from pastel blues to shocking scarlet. Lobelias are easy to grow and provide dynamic color to shady borders or woodland gardens.

Growing and care:

Plant lobelia in the garden in spring when soil is cool. Space plants 1 to 1½ feet apart in soil well amended with organic matter. Mulch around plants to keep roots cool and retain soil moisture. Provide extra water during dry periods. Propagate by sowing seeds in fall or by division in spring in northern areas and in fall in southern regions.

Selected species and varieties:

L. cardinalis (cardinal flower) is a strong-growing perennial usually 2 to 4 feet tall, but may reach 6 feet, with upright stalks of scarlet flowers in summer or fall; 'Compliment Scarlet' has vivid scarlet flowers on strong 3- to 4-foot stems in midsummer; Zones 5-8. *L. x gerardii* 'Verrariensis' has deep violet flowers along upright 3-foot stalks from mid- to late summer. *L. siphilitica* (great blue lobelia) is a perennial with blue tubular flowers on erect 2- to 3-foot leafy stems from late summer to early fall; Zones 4-7.

MARSH MARIGOLD
Caltha

Light: mostly shade

Plant type: perennial

Hardiness: Zones 3-8

Height: 10 inches to 2 feet

Soil and Moisture: moist to wet

Interest: flowers, foliage

Care: easy

◀ Caltha palustris

As its common name implies, the marsh marigold is an appropriate perennial for wet soils, where its clusters of brightly hued 2-inch yellow flowers provide an impressive display in spring. The flowers form on long stems that are held above the clump of lush dark green foliage. In addition to providing the perfect background for its flowers and subsequent seedpods, the mound of leaves remains attractive well into summer. It makes a good choice for edging a pond or water garden, or in a bog garden, where it can be kept constantly moist.

Growing and care:
While marsh marigold will grow in moist soil, it performs best in a wet location especially in the spring. Unlike many bog plants, it does not become invasive. Plants go dormant in late summer, after which some drying out of the soil can be tolerated. Propagate marsh marigold by division in early spring.

Selected species and varieties:
C. palustris (marsh marigold, kingcup) produces a 1- to 1½-foot mound of 3- to 4-inch-wide dark green leaves, and round green buds that open in midspring to 2-inch buttercup yellow flowers with five showy sepals borne on upright stems; 'Alba' bears single white flowers with bold yellow stamens; 'Flore Pleno' bears abundant double flowers that are showier than those of the species.

MASTERWORT
Astrantia

Light: mostly shade

Plant type: perennial

Hardiness: Zones 4-8

Height: 2 to 3 feet

Soil and Moisture: well-drained, moist, fertile

Interest: flowers

Care: easy

◀ Astrantia major

Masterwort is a charming, distinctive plant with long-blooming clover-shaped blossoms framed with a starry collar of bracts. The pink, violet, yellow, or white flowers appear in spring through summer and are held on strong stems well above the dark green deeply lobed foliage. Masterwort is a nice addition to cottage gardens or at the back of perennial borders. The plants make excellent cut flowers for fresh floral arrangements.

Growing and care:
Plant masterwort in well-worked soil that has some organic matter. Space plants 1½ feet apart. Provide extra moisture during periods of hot, dry weather. In warm, dry regions mulch plants in spring and fall. Propagate from seed sown in early spring or by division in spring or fall. Seed should not be covered, as it requires light to germinate. Of the two methods, division is usually preferred, as the seed can take up to 2 months to germinate.

Selected species and varieties:
A. major (great masterwort) bears unusual creamy white 2- to 3-inch blossoms tinged pink by the collar of purple bracts below the petals; 'Rosea' has rosy pink blooms suitable for drying and pressing; 'Sunningdale Variegated' has stripes of cream and yellow on lobed green leaves.

MEADOW RUE
Thalictrum

Light: mostly shade

Plant type: perennial

Hardiness: Zones 5-9

Height: 2 to 7 feet

Soil and Moisture: well-drained, moist

Interest: flowers, foliage

Care: moderate

◀ Thalictrum delavayi

These graceful plants are grown both for their clusters of airy, fluffy blossoms displayed over several weeks, and for their deeply cut, lacy foliage, which adds a soft accent to the garden the rest of the growing season. Plant either species of meadow rue listed below for a longer season of flowering in borders, rock gardens, and wildflower informal gardens. They also make good cut flowers.

Growing and care:
Meadow rues prefer morning sun and soil that never dries out. Space *T. aquilegifolium* 1 foot apart and *T. delavayi* 2 feet apart. Plants benefit from staking, especially if subjected to wind. Propagate by fresh seed sown in fall, or by division in spring.

Selected species and varieties:
T. aquilegifolium (columbine meadow rue) grows 2 to 3 feet tall with delicate, rounded dark green leaves and large clusters of creamy flowers with mauve centers in late spring and early summer; 'White Cloud' is slightly taller than the species, with dense foliage and clouds of white flowers. *T. delavayi* [also listed as *T. dipterocarpum*] (Yunnan meadow rue) is clump forming, growing 4 to 7 feet tall with showy clusters of lavender-blue or rose-purple flowers accented with bright yellow stamens in late summer and early fall; 'Hewitt's Double' has multi-petaled flowers.

MERRY-BELLS
Uvularia

Light: mostly shade

Plant type: perennial

Hardiness: Zones 3-8

Height: 10 inches to 2 feet

Soil and Moisture: well-drained, moist, fertile

Interest: flowers

Care: moderate

◀ Uvularia grandiflora

Merry-bells are robust woodland perennials with drooping, medium green leaves and elegant yellow or cream-colored flowers in spring. These hardy wildflowers are native to the moist forests of eastern North America, where they grow equally well in well-drained uplands and along streams and marshes. The plants spread quickly once established and are beautiful additions to wildflower gardens, especially when intermingled with plantings of spring beauty.

Growing and care:
Grow merry-bells in moist, shaded locations and incorporate organic matter into the soil prior to planting. Mulch with leaves in winter. Propagate by seed sown immediately after ripening or by division in fall—although the plants grow best if left undisturbed.

Selected species and varieties:
U. grandiflora (big merry-bells) have arching stems 1½ to 2 feet tall with lemon yellow flowers 1½ inches long. The petals are slightly twisted; Zones 3-8. *U. sessilifolia* (little merry-bells, wild oats) grows 10 to 15 inches tall with cream-colored inch-long flowers; Zones 4-8.

MONKSHOOD
Aconitum

Light: mostly shade

Plant type: perennial

Hardiness: Zones 3-8

Height: 2 to 4 feet

Soil and Moisture: well-drained, moist, fertile

Interest: flowers

Care: moderate

◀ Aconitum x bicolor 'Spark'

The vivid to somber hues of monkshoods and their glossy dark green deeply cut leaves make striking additions to any perennial border or naturalized area. Blooming in summer to fall when there are few other blue flowers in the garden, the tall spikes of flowers also make excellent cuttings. Caution: All parts of the plant are poisonous.

Growing and care:
Though monkshoods prefer shade as a rule, they especially need it during hot summer afternoons. They tolerate full sun only in constantly moist soil in cool climates. Add peat moss, compost, or leaf mold to soil before planting, and space plants 1½ feet apart. Taller varieties need staking. Divide clumps in spring or fall.

Selected species and varieties:
A. anthora has clusters of yellow flowers on 2-foot stems. *A.* x *bicolor* 'Spark' bears violet-blue flowers on 4-foot stems in mid- to late summer. *A.* x *cammarum* 'Bicolor' grows 2 to 4 feet tall with blue and white flowers. *A. carmichaelii* 'Arendsii' (azure monkshood) has large blue flowers on 3- to 4-foot stems. *A. napellus* (common monkshood, Turk's-cap) grows 4 feet tall with indigo blue flowers; 'Carneum' has pink flowers.

OBEDIENT PLANT
Physostegia

Light: mostly shade

Plant type: perennial

Hardiness: Zones 4-10

Height: 1½ to 4 feet

Soil and Moisture: well-drained, moist to dry

Interest: flowers

Care: easy

◀ Physostegia virginiana 'Vivid'

The wandlike stems of obedient plants, topped with conical spikes of delicate pink, lavender, or white flowers, grow in spreading clumps. The flower spikes have four vertical rows of tubular flowers that look like miniature snapdragons. *Physostegia* is called obedient plant because its flowers stay put when moved laterally, rather than springing back to their original positions. Obedient plants make excellent cut flowers, and are used as a filler in beds and borders or for naturalizing in wildflower meadows.

Growing and care:
Obedient plants tolerate most growing conditions but can be invasive when grown in sunny, moist borders because of their vigorously spreading stolons. They are best behaved in mostly shady locations or in meadows. Space plants 1½ to 2 feet apart. Propagate by seed or division in early spring or late fall.

Selected species and varieties:
P. virginiana (obedience) grows 2 to 4 feet tall with dense clusters of 8- to 12-inch two-lipped white, deep pink, or lavender-pink summer flowers and dark green, wavy-edged narrowly lance-shaped leaves; 'Bouquet Rose' has light pink flowers; 'Summer Snow' has pure white flowers in early summer; 'Summer Spire' produces deep pink flowers; 'Vivid' has dark green leaves beneath spires of bright pink flowers.

PATRINIA
Patrinia

Light: mostly shade

Plant type: perennial

Hardiness: Zones 5-9

Height: 2 to 6 feet

Soil and Moisture: well-drained, moist

Interest: flowers, seedpods

Care: easy

◀ Patrinia scabiosifolia

Patrinia produces large, airy sprays of sun yellow flowers late in summer and fall, followed by bright yellow seedpods on orange stems. This very ornamental plant is well suited to the middle or rear of a perennial border or a natural garden, where it combines particularly well with ornamental grasses. Patrinia flowers can be cut for long-lasting indoor arrangements.

Growing and care:
Plant patrinias in moist, well-drained soil in light shade. Taller types often require staking. Once established, patrinias are long-lived perennials that frequently self-sow. Deadhead spent flowers to limit seed production if desired. Seedlings can be transplanted to other areas of the garden in spring.

Selected species and varieties:
P. scabiosifolia is 3 to 6 feet tall, with ruffled, pinnately divided 6- to 10-inch leaves that form a large basal mound, and yellow flowers that form 2-inch clusters held well above foliage in late summer and fall; 'Nagoya' grows 2 to 3 feet with a compact habit and flowers that are almost fluorescent yellow.

PINK
Dianthus

Light: mostly shade

Plant type: perennial

Hardiness: Zones 4-8

Height: 3 to 24 inches

Soil and Moisture: well-drained, moist

Interest: flowers, fragrance

Care: easy

◀ D. gratianopolitanus 'Karlik'

Pinks are old-fashioned perennials whose fragrant, clove-scented flowers have been grown in gardens for generations. The cheerful blossoms come in a range of pastel shades above attractive, grassy blue-green foliage that is evergreen in mild climates. Pinks are reliable, easy-to-grow plants that are excellent in rock gardens, edgings, borders, or when massed in group plantings.

Growing and care:
Plant in well-worked soil that has had some organic matter added. Space pinks 1 to 1½ feet apart. Keep soil moderately moist but not wet. Cut stems back after bloom and shear mat-forming types in the fall to promote dense growth. Maintain vigor by division every 2 to 3 years. Propagate from seed, from cuttings taken in early summer, or by division in spring.

Selected species and varieties:
D. x allwoodii (Allwood pink) has single or double flowers in a wide range of colors that grow for 2 months above gray-green leaves in compact mounds 1 to 2 feet tall; 'Aqua' grows white double blooms atop 1-foot stems. *D. alpinus* (Alpine pink) is a dwarf variety of Allwood pink; 'Doris' grows very fragrant salmon-colored double flowers with darker pink centers on 1-foot stems; 'Robin' has coral red flowers. *D. barbatus* (sweet William) is a biennial species that self-seeds so reliably that it performs like a perennial; unlike other pinks, it

(continued)

produces flowers in flat clusters and without fragrance; 'Harlequin' grows pink and white flowers; 'Indian Carpet' has single flowers in a mix of colors on 10-inch stems. *D. deltoides* (maiden pink) bears ¾-inch red or pink flowers on 1-foot stems above 6- to 12-inch-high mats of small bright green leaves; 'Brilliant' has scarlet flowers; 'Flashing Light' ('Leuchtfunk') has ruby red flowers. *D. gratianopolitanus* (cheddar pink) has 1-inch-wide flowers in shades of pink and rose on compact mounds of blue-green foliage 9 to 12 inches high; 'Karlik' has fragrant deep pink fringed flowers; 'Tiny Rubies' has dark pink double blooms on plants just 4 inches tall. *D. plumarius* (cottage pink) has fragrant single or semi-double flowers 1½ inches across in shades of pink and white or bicolors above 1- to 1½-foot-high mats of evergreen leaves; 'Essex Witch' produces fragrant salmon, pink, or white flowers.

RODGERSIA
Rodgersia

◄ Rodgersia pinnata

Light: mostly shade	
Plant type: perennial	
Hardiness: Zones 5-7	
Height: 2 to 6 feet	
Soil and Moisture: well-drained, moist to wet	
Interest: flowers, foliage	
Care: easy to moderate	

Rodgersia is a coarse-textured perennial with tiers of dark green compound leaves, pliant stems, and billowy plumes of creamy white flowers. The feathery blossoms and rough-looking foliage add interest to the back of the shady border and look stunning when planted near water gardens, streams, and ponds.

Growing and care:

Space rodgersia 3 feet apart in soil that is very moist or constantly wet, such as at the edge of streams and ponds. In colder climates, provide winter protection by mulching. Propagate by division in early spring, leaving the soil intact around each section.

Selected species and varieties:

R. aesculifolia (fingerleaf rodgersia) has bronzy green coarsely toothed horse-chestnut-like leaves that are arranged like fingers on a hand and arise from 3- to 6-foot stems topped with creamy white or pink flower plumes; Zones 5-6. *R. pinnata* (featherleaf rodgersia) produces plumes of buff pink flowers that emerge from late spring to midsummer above bronze-tinted dark green leaves with finely serrated margins on 3- to 4-foot stems; 'Superba' has very large red flowers. *R. podophylla* (bronzeleaf rodgersia) has finger-shaped leaves that are green at first before turning to metallic bronze in summer, borne on 3- to 5-foot stems with yellowish white 1-foot plumes; Zones 5-6.

RUELLIA
Ruellia

Light: mostly shade

Plant type: perennial

Hardiness: Zones 4-9

Height: 1 to 3 feet

Soil and Moisture: well-drained, sandy, dry

Interest: flowers

Care: easy

◀ Ruellia caroliniensis

Ruellias are perennials found growing wild in open woods in the eastern United States. The plants produce decorative, deep green leaves and loose clusters of funnel-shaped flowers in shades of lavender, violet, or red. The plants blossom for a few weeks in summer and sporadically until fall. Ruellias add a delicate touch to wildflower meadows, herbaceous borders, and woodland edges.

Growing and care:
Plant in spring after soil has warmed. Ruellia prefers mostly sun to mostly shade while wild pertunia thrives in full sun to mostly shady spots. Space plants about 1½ to 2 feet apart. Water thoroughly, allowing soil to dry out between waterings. Ruellias prefer dry soils that are sandy or rocky but will adapt to other types of soils as long as they are not too moist. Propagate by cuttings taken in summer or by division in fall.

Selected species and varieties:
R. caroliniensis (ruellia) has clusters of two to four light purple flowers near the tops of unbranched stems 2 to 3 feet tall throughout summer; Zones 6-9. *R. humilis* (wild petunia) bears showy 2-inch lavender to purple flowers throughout summer and fall on compact bushy plants 1 to 2 feet tall.

SHOOTING-STAR
Dodecatheon

Light: mostly shade

Plant type: perennial

Hardiness: Zones 4-8

Height: 4 to 20 inches

Soil and Moisture: well-drained, moist to dry

Interest: flowers

Care: easy to moderate

◀ Dodecatheon meadia

Shooting-stars are elegant, dainty wildflowers that grow in moist, open woods, on prairies, and on rocky slopes. These perennials have a basal rosette of rich green leaves and leafless stalks bearing an array of showy flowers with sharply backswept petals. Shooting-stars are a nice addition to the woodland wildflower garden or the shady border.

Growing and care:
Shooting-stars are easy to grow if they are given the proper conditions. Give *D. dentatum* a moist, mostly shady site. *D. meadia* prefers light, sandy soil with abundant moisture while in bloom, in mid- to late spring and drier conditions in fall and winter. Grow *D. amethystinum* in moist, well-drained alkaline soil in partial shade. Mulch plants in spring and keep soil moist while plants are actively growing. Propagation by seed is quite difficult and new plants can most easily be obtained by division in fall.

Selected species and varieties:
D. amethystinum [also called *D. pulchellum*] (amethyst shooting-star) bears rose-crimson flowers on 8- to 16-inch stalks in late spring; Zones 4-7. *D. dentatum* (dwarf shooting-star) has white flowers with a purple spot at the base of the petals on 4- to 14-inch stalks above crinkled, toothed leaves. *D. meadia* (shooting-star) has white to deep pink flowers on stalks up to 20 inches; Zones 5-8.

SPIDERWORT
Tradescantia

Light: mostly shade

Plant type: perennial

Hardiness: Zones 3-10

Height: 10 inches to 3 feet

Soil and Moisture: well-drained, moist, fertile

Interest: flowers, foliage

Care: easy to moderate

◀ Tradescantia ohiensis

Found in open woods and on prairies, spiderworts are upright or trailing perennials whose flowers have three wide petals and showy stamens. The flowers can be blue, pink, or white and have three petals nestled among a cluster of buds atop a slender stem. The glossy green leaves provide a soft backdrop to other plants after the flowers have faded.

Growing and care:

Plant spiderworts in a shady spot in well-drained humus-rich soil. Space plants 1 to 1½ feet apart. Propagate by seed, stem cuttings taken at anytime, or division. Spiderworts are easy to grow, reliable, and virtually pest-free.

Selected species and varieties:

T. bracteata (bracted spiderwort) has clusters of blue-violet flowers surrounded by leaflike bracts on erect 10- to 16-inch stems with grasslike foliage in late spring to early summer; Zones 3-8. *T. ohiensis* (Ohio spiderwort) has blue flowers clustered at the tops of erect branching stems 2 to 3 feet tall from spring to summer in warm climates and summer in cooler zones; Zones 4-10. *T. virginiana* (Virginia spiderwort) bears blue to blue-violet flowers 1½ to 3 inches wide from spring to summer on a dense clump of branching stems up to 3 feet tall with narrow bright green leaves 1 foot long; Zones 4-10.

TOAD LILY
Tricyrtis

Light: mostly shade

Plant type: perennial

Hardiness: Zones 5-9

Height: 2 to 3 feet

Soil and Moisture: well-drained, moist, fertile

Interest: flowers, foliage

Care: moderate

◀ Tricyrtis hirta

Unusually shaped toad lily flowers point upward from the leaf base in white or pinkish sprays that arch above clumps of dark green leaves. The bullet-shaped flower buds open in summer or fall to reveal six thin, flaring, spotted petals that are joined at the base. The blooming season is relatively long, lasting up to 6 weeks. Toad lilies are a good choice for shady perennial borders, and woodland or shady rock gardens.

Growing and care:

Space rhizome pieces 1 to 1½ feet apart in humus-rich loam. Remove dead leaves in late fall. In Zone 7 and colder regions, mulch plants after the ground freezes to protect from heaving. Propagate by division in spring or fall.

Selected species and varieties:

T. formosana (Formosa toad lily) grows 1 to 2 feet tall with shiny 5-inch deep green leaves and clusters of 1-inch white to light pink flowers with yellow throats and dark purple spots at their tips; Zones 6-9. *T. hirta* (hairy toad lily) is hairy, growing 2 to 3 feet tall with 6-inch lance-shaped leaves and waxy 1-inch bell-shaped creamy white flowers spotted with red or purple; 'Alba' has pure white flowers; 'Variegata' produces dark green leaves with white veins.

TURTLEHEAD
Chelone

Light: mostly shade

Plant type: perennial

Hardiness: Zones 3-9

Height: 1 to 5 feet

Soil and Moisture: well-drained, wet to moist, fertile

Interest: flowers

Care: moderate

◀ Chelone lyonii

The unique, tubular white, pink, or rose flowers of *Chelone* resemble turtles' heads and have a puckered upper lip and a bearded lower lip. They are borne in a raceme atop straight, smooth 3- to 5-foot stems with dark green lance-shaped leaves. Turtleheads are native to marshes, stream banks, and moist woodlands of the eastern, southeastern, and western United States. They are ideally suited to bog gardens and wet spots in wildflower gardens and meadows.

Growing and care:
Turtleheads can be grown in ordinary garden soil enriched with compost or peat moss. Space plants 8 inches apart and add a layer of mulch in late spring. *C. glabra* benefits from staking or being planted with other tall species that it can use for support. *C. lyonii* is a native to the Southeast and tolerates drier conditions better than other species. Propagate turtleheads by spring division, summer cuttings, or seed planted in fall.

Selected species and varieties:
C. glabra (white turtlehead) grows 3 to 5 feet tall with clusters of 1½-inch white to pale pink late summer flowers and 6-inch lance-shaped leaves; Zones 3-8. *C. lyonii* (pink turtlehead) grows 1 to 3 feet tall with 4- to 7-inch dark green oval leaves and 1-inch rose-violet flowers from summer to fall.

VIOLET
Viola

Light: mostly shade

Plant type: perennial

Hardiness: Zones 3-9

Height: 2 to 10 inches

Soil and Moisture: well-drained, moist

Interest: flowers, fragrance

Care: easy

◀ Viola tricolor

Violets have dainty five-petaled flowers borne on thin stems. The flowers always have a prominent nectar-filled spur projecting back from the lower petal. These versatile plants often have attractive heart-shaped leaves that form low mounds. Their rainbow of colors and long season of bloom make them perfect for edgings or borders, and for growing in containers.

Growing and care:
Sow seed indoors 3 months before planting in the garden. Plant in spring or fall in soil rich in organic matter. Space plants 6 to 12 inches apart. Fertilize once a month from late spring to summer. Provide plants with full shade in areas with hot summers, and partial shade in cooler regions.

Selected species and varieties:
V. cornuta (horned violet, tufted pansy) grows 5 to 10 inches tall, bearing pale to deep violet-purple pansylike flowers in spring and early summer, and oval, toothed evergreen leaves; 'Alba' has white flowers; 'Atropurpurea' bears dark purple blooms with small yellow centers; 'Chantreyland' has pale apricot-orange flowers; 'Cuty' bears prolific bouquets of flowers in combinations of purple, white, and lavender; Zones 5-8. *V. tricolor* (Johnny-jump-up) grows 2 to 8 inches tall with ½-inch violet, blue, and yellow flat-faced flowers from spring through early summer.

AMAZON LILY
Eucharis

Light: mostly shade

Plant type: bulb

Hardiness: Zones 9-10

Height: 1 to 2 feet

Soil and Moisture: well-drained, moist

Interest: flowers, fragrance

Care: moderate

◀ Eucharis grandiflora

Amazon lilies are stunning, bold additions to any garden, with clusters of highly fragrant flowers that resemble daffodils. The blossoms rise from clumps of attractive, broad evergreen leaves with wavy edges. Amazon lilies thrive in regions with hot, humid summers where they are perfect for beds and borders. In northern regions the plants can be potted in containers and grown indoors.

Growing and care:
Outdoors, set bulbs with their necks at the soil line, spacing the bulbs 8 to 10 inches apart in a mostly shady location. The plants need high humidity and temperatures above 60°F to thrive, and they bloom best when crowded or potbound. Indoors, space bulbs 3 inches apart in pots, allowing three or four bulbs to each pot. To force, maintain bulbs at 80°F or higher for 4 weeks, then lower temperatures 10°F for another 12 weeks. Raise temperatures again to induce blooming. Propagate by removing and planting the bulb offsets.

Selected species and varieties:
E. grandiflora (Eucharist lily) bears clusters of large, drooping white flowers up to 5 inches across above leaves a foot long and 6 inches wide.

ARUM
Arum

Light: mostly shade

Plant type: bulb

Hardiness: Zones 5-9

Height: 1 to 1½ feet

Soil and Moisture: well-drained, moist, fertile

Interest: flowers, foliage

Care: easy

◀ Arum italicum 'Pictum'

Arum makes a good specimen plant for perennial borders and woodland areas. Because of its clumping habit it also makes a fine container plant. The broad arrow-shaped leaves emerge in fall and, in milder zones, remain all winter. Callalike flowers in shades of cream, green, or purple atop erect 1½-foot leafless stalks in spring or early summer and precede upright clusters of colorful berries. Caution: All parts of the plant are poisonous.

Growing and care:
Arum is easy to grow in mostly sun to mostly shady locations and thrives in well-worked soil amended with some rotted manure or compost. Set tubers about 3 inches deep and 8 to 12 inches apart. Once established the plants spread quickly. Top-dress lightly with compost in fall. To propagate divide large clumps in spring or fall.

Selected species and varieties:
A. italicum (Italian arum) bears creamy to yellow flowers in late spring followed by upright clusters of orange-red berries in summer on a 1- to 1½-foot-high clump of foot-long glossy green leaves with pale veins; 'Marmoratum' has very large leaves marbled in yellow-green; 'Pictum' (painted arum) has whitish green flowers with purple spots and red-orange fruit that appears after the dark green leaves, which are marbled with gray and cream, have faded away.

BLUEBELL
Hyacinthoides

Light: mostly shade

Plant type: bulb

Hardiness: Zones 5-10

Height: 15 to 20 inches

Soil and Moisture: well-drained, moist, fertile

Interest: flowers, foliage

Care: easy

◀ Hyacinthoides hispanica

The dainty bell-shaped flowers of bluebells are one of the joys of spring. The plants produce stout, strong stems from clumps of shiny green foliage topped with clusters of white, pink, or violet flowers. Excellent for naturalizing beneath trees, in mass plantings, and in borders with other bulbs, bluebells also make good container plants and are useful as cut flowers.

Growing and care:

Set plants in a mostly shady location that receives some early-morning or late-day sun. Amend soil with organic matter and plant 3 to 4 inches deep in the fall. Water regularly during dry periods, except in summer. Bluebells can be naturalized as far north as Zone 5. In colder areas, mulch heavily in winter, or dig the bulbs and replant in spring. Bluebells are vigorous growers and thrive even among the roots of trees. Bluebells spread quickly by self-seeding and can often become weedy. Propagate by division.

Selected species and varieties:

H. hispanica [also classified as *Scilla campanulata* or *Endymion hispanicus*] (Spanish bluebell) has 20-inch stems, each producing up to 15 flowers ranging from white to pink to violet above leaf straps that are 1 inch wide; hardy to Zone 5; 'Rose Queen' produces rose-colored flowers; 'White Triumphator' has white flowers.

DAFFODIL
Narcissus

Light: mostly shade

Plant type: bulb

Hardiness: Zones 3-10

Height: 6 to 20 inches

Soil and Moisture: well-drained, moist

Interest: flowers, fragrance

Care: easy

◀ Narcissus 'Carleton'

Daffodil is a huge group of spring-blooming bulbs that vary greatly in size, shape, and color. Each bloom has an outer ring of six petals called the perianth and a raised center called a corona, which may be a small cup, a large cup of medium length, or, when it is very long, a trumpet. Hybrids number in the thousands, and the genus is grouped into 12 divisions. There are miniature cultivars within almost every division. Used in rock gardens or borders or naturalized, daffodils give years of care-free early color.

Growing and care:

Plant large bulbs 6 to 8 inches deep, small ones 3 to 4 inches deep in well-prepared soil in fall, allowing time for the roots to become established before the ground freezes. Work peat moss or compost in for best results. After bloom, let foliage die down so the plant can build up nutrients for the next year's bloom. Propagate by dividing after foliage has died down. The chief pests are snails and slugs.

Selected species and varieties:

Division 1, Trumpet daffodils: 10 to 18 inches tall with one flower per stem with a trumpet-shaped corona; 'Beersheba' has white flowers on 15-inch stems; 'Lunar Sea' grows 18 to 20 inches tall with a yellow perianth and a white trumpet; 'Rijnveld's Early Sensation' has

(continued)

yellow winter blooms on 13-inch stems. *Division 2, Large-cupped daffodils*: Solitary flowers with the corona more than one-third but less than the full length of the petals; 'Carbineer' is bright yellow with an orange-red corona on 16-inch stems; 'Carleton' is fragrant, soft yellow with a frilled corona and broad perianth, 18 to 20 inches tall; 'Ice Follies' grows 17 inches tall with white petals and a corona that turns from yellow to white. *Division 4, Double daffodils*: One or more flowers on each 12- to 16-inch stem, with the petals, corona, or both doubled; 'Cheerfulness' is fragrant white with a corona flecked with yellow; 'Flower Drift' has ivory white petals and a yellow-orange corona; 'Yellow Cheerfulness' is fragrant yellow on yellow. *Division 6, Cyclamineus daffodils*: 8 to 14 inches tall with solitary yellow, white, or bicolored flowers having a long, wavy-rimmed corona and backward-flaring petals; hardy to Zone 4; 'February Gold', late-winter blooms with deep yellow petals and a yellow corona; 'Peeping Tom', all yellow, good for naturalizing; 'Tête-à-Tête', a miniature 6 to 8 inches tall, lemon yellow with a deeper yellow or orange corona; hardy to Zone 4. *Division 7, Jonquilla daffodils*: Delightfully fragrant flowers, as many as six to each 1-foot-tall stem; 'Pipit' has a fragrant white corona and pale yellow petals, to 15 inches; 'Sweetness' is 13 inches tall, very fragrant, all yellow; 'Trevithian', 17 inches with two or three very fragrant, deep yellow flowers per stem.

GIANT LILY
Cardiocrinum

◄ Cardiocrinum giganteum

Light:	mostly shade
Plant type:	bulb
Hardiness:	Zones 7-9
Height:	8 to 12 feet
Soil and Moisture:	well-drained, fertile, acidic
Interest:	flowers, fragrance
Care:	moderate

Giant lilies are massive plants with bold clusters of very large fragrant flowers as much as 6 inches long atop stout, thick stems. The long, narrow buds open into drooping flared funnels in tiers all around each stem. Glossy heart-shaped leaves up to 1½ feet long form a basal rosette and sparsely line each stem. Giant lilies grow best in filtered shade at the edges of moist woodlands and provide a dynamic presence when grown in borders and wildflower gardens.

Growing and care:
Plant giant lily bulbs in spring or fall with their tops just at the soil line, spaced 1½ feet apart. Giant lilies produce nonflowering shoots for several years before blossoming. The bulbs then die, leaving small bulblets, which will grow to flowering size in 3 to 4 years. Plant bulbs of different sizes to ensure blooms each year. Propagate by lifting and replanting bulblets after the main bulb flowers.

Selected species and varieties:
C. giganteum (heart lily) produces up to 20 nodding creamy white flowers suffused with green on the outside and striped maroon inside stout stems to 12 feet tall.

GRAPE HYACINTH
Muscari

Light: mostly shade

Plant type: bulb

Hardiness: Zones 4-8

Height: 6 to 12 inches

Soil and Moisture: well-drained, moist

Interest: flowers

Care: easy

◀ Muscari armeniacum 'Blue Spike'

Among the earliest of spring bulbs to brighten the garden, low-growing grape hyacinths rapidly spread into carpets of color. Their tiny flowers, less than ½ inch long, cluster in pyramidal tiers at the tips of slender stems above narrow grasslike leaves. The flowers are usually tubular, with their lips turned inward so that clusters resemble small bunches of grapes, or flipped outward like those of hyacinths. The fragrant blossoms are often attractively rimmed in contrasting color. Usually nodding, the flowers are occasionally so tightly crowded that lower blossoms hold upper ones facing out or up, giving the flowers a distinctive texture. Use grape hyacinths as edging plants, in beds or borders, or in wildflower or rock gardens, where they will naturalize quickly. They can also be forced for indoor bloom or used as cut flowers.

Growing and care:
Plant grape hyacinths from late summer to fall, setting bulbs 2 to 3 inches deep and 3 to 4 inches apart. The plants thrive in mostly shady locations but tolerate conditions ranging from mostly sunny to full shade. For indoor forcing, set bulbs 1 inch deep, allowing 10 to 12 bulbs per 6-inch pot. Grape hyacinths self-sow freely. Propagate by removing bulblets that grow around mature bulbs or from seed.

Selected species and varieties:
M. armeniacum (Armenian grape hyacinth) has dense clusters of 20 to 30 spring-blooming blue flowers with flipped white-rimmed edges nodding in overlapping tiers on 8- to 10-inch stems; 'Blue Spike' produces double-petaled long-lasting flowers; 'Cantab' has pale blue flowers blooming later than the species; 'Christmas Pearl', violet blooms; 'Fantasy Creation', soft blue double flowers; 'Saphir', long-lasting deep blue flowers rimmed with white. *M. aucheri* 'Tubergenianium' is a 6-inch dwarf with dense spikes of clear light blue blossoms at the top, shading to deep blue rimmed in white at the bottom. *M. azureum* [also called *Pseudomuscari azurea*] produces 20 to 40 cylindrical, open blue bells facing out and up on 8-inch stems; 'Album' is white. *M. botryoides* (common grape hyacinth, starch hyacinth) has overlapping tiers of nodding white, pink, violet, or blue flowers with white rims on 1-foot stems; 'Album' (Italian grape hyacinth) is a slightly shorter white cultivar. *M. comosum* [also called *Leopoldia comosa*] 'Plumosum' (feather hyacinth, tassel hyacinth) has dense clusters of light blue, violet, or fuchsia flowers with frilled threadlike petals on 4- to 6-inch stems. *M. latifolium* bears loose clusters of 10 to 20 flowers with flipped petals in spikes shading from light to dark blue on 1-foot stems. *M. neglectum* has dense clusters of 30 to 40 flowers with frilled white rims in spires shading from light to dark blue on 6-inch stems; 'Dark Eyes' is very dark blue; 'White Beauty' is white tinged pink.

NATAL LILY
Clivia

Light:	mostly shade
Plant type:	bulb
Hardiness:	Zones 9-10
Height:	1 to 1½ feet
Soil and Moisture:	well-drained, moist
Interest:	flowers, foliage
Care:	moderate

◀ Clivia miniata

A popular houseplant in Victorian times, the natal lily bears domed clusters of up to 20 trumpet-shaped 3-inch flowers in dramatic hues atop a single thick stalk flanked by pairs of broad, straplike evergreen leaves up to 1½ feet long. Bulbs may produce their long-lasting flowers twice a year under ideal conditions, and inch-long red berries follow the blossoms. *Clivia* can be grown outdoors in warm zones but bloom best as root-bound houseplants.

Growing and care:
Plant natal lilies outdoors in fall, in a location that receives mostly sun to mostly shade. Set the tops of the bulbous roots at the soil line, spacing them 1½ to 2 feet apart. Indoors, plant roots in 9-inch pots and leave undisturbed. Propagate from seed or by dividing the fleshy rootstocks after flowering.

Selected species and varieties:
C. x *cyrtanthiflora* (Kaffir lily) produces deep salmon-pink blooms. *C. miniata* (Kaffir lily) has scarlet blossoms with yellow-splashed throats; 'Aurea' grows golden yellow; 'Flame' is deep red-orange; 'Grandiflora' produces larger scarlet flowers.

RAIN LILY
Zephyranthes

Light:	mostly shade
Plant type:	bulb
Hardiness:	Zones 7-10
Height:	8 to 15 inches
Soil and Moisture:	well-drained, fertile, moist
Interest:	flowers
Care:	easy

◀ Zephyranthes
atamasco

Rain lily is a bulbous perennial wildflower native to the damp woods and bottom lands of the southeastern United States. The plants form colonies of thin, grasslike leaves decorated in spring with delicate funnel-shaped white or pink flowers. The plants are easy to grow and naturalize rapidly in rock gardens and lawns, or along paths.

Growing and care:
Sow seed in spring directly in the garden in rich, well-worked soil well amended with organic matter. Plant bulbs 3 inches deep in fall. The plants thrive in a range of light conditions, from full sun to mostly shade. Thin or space 3 to 6 inches apart. Plants grown from seed will flower in 3 to 4 years. Fertilize lightly in spring with a complete organic fertilizer. Provide extra water during dry periods. In northern areas bulbs can be lifted in fall and replanted in spring.

Selected species and varieties:
Z. atamasco (atamasco lily, rain lily) has showy funnel-shaped white flowers 3 inches long on leafless stalks about 1 foot tall in mid- to late spring. The flowers are sometimes tinged with purple and turn pink as they age. The thick, shiny, grasslike leaves form a clump 8 to 15 inches tall.

SNOWDROP
Galanthus

Light: mostly shade	
Plant type: bulb	
Hardiness: Zones 3-8	
Height: 4 to 12 inches	
Soil and Moisture: well-drained, moist	
Interest: flowers, foliage	
Care: easy	

◀ Galanthus nivalis

Among the earliest of spring-flowering bulbs, snowdrops often bloom while their leaves and flowers are still dusted with late-winter snow. The solitary pendent flowers have three outer petal-like segments that hang over a shorter green-tipped tube. The leaves are glossy green and straplike. Plant snowdrops in rock gardens, along pathways, or at foundations, or naturalize in lawns or under deciduous trees and shrubs.

Growing and care:
In late summer or fall, work peat moss or compost into the soil and plant bulbs 3 inches deep and 3 inches apart and mark their locations. The plants tolerate mostly sunny locations but do best in mostly shady spots beneath deciduous trees and shrubs. Snowdrop bulbs multiply quickly and can be divided every 3 to 4 years. Divide clumps of bulbs in late spring after the leaves have yellowed. To force snowdrops, plant four to six bulbs 1 inch deep in a 4-inch pot in late fall. Chill in the refrigerator for 6 to 8 weeks. Once returned to a warm spot, the bulbs will bloom in a few weeks.

Selected species and varieties:
G. nivalis bears nodding 1-inch single white flowers on 4- to 6-inch stems with narrow leaves; 'Flore Pleno' (double snowdrops) has glossy green, narrow foliage and 4- to 6-inch stems topped with double white nodding blossoms in early spring.

SNOWFLAKE
Leucojum

Light: mostly shade	
Plant type: bulb	
Hardiness: Zones 4-9	
Height: 6 inches to 1½ feet	
Soil and Moisture: well-drained, moist	
Interest: flowers, foliage	
Care: easy	

◀ Leucojum vernum

Snowflake is a perky little bulb with thin sprays of deep green leaves and nodding clusters of fragrant white flowers in spring. A native to woodlands, it thrives in the dappled light beneath forest trees and is perfect for wooded paths and wildflower gardens. Planted in masses snowflake quickly naturalizes, providing reliable annual displays. Once established the plants are best left undisturbed.

Growing and care:
Although they grow in average garden soil, snowflakes prefer sandy loam to which leaf mold, peat moss, or dried compost has been added. Plant bulbs 4 inches deep. Bloom may not occur the first year. Propagate by dividing, but keep bulbs moist while moving.

Selected species and varieties:
L. aestivum (summer snowflake, Loddon lily) grows 1 to 1½ feet tall with three to seven ¾-inch-long nodding flowers on each 1- to 1½-foot stalk, blooming in spring and early summer in the East but in late fall and winter in warm areas of the West; prefers mostly shade; 'Gravetye' [also known as 'Gravetye Giant'] produces 1½-inch flowers on 1½-foot stems. *L. vernum* (spring snowflake) is 10 inches tall with glossy green leaves and fragrant white flowers borne singly or in pairs on 4- to 6-inch stems in late winter or spring; prefers mostly shade; Zones 4-8.

SQUILL
Scilla

Light: mostly shade	
Plant type: bulb	
Hardiness: Zones 3-10	
Height: 6 inches to 2 feet	
Soil and Moisture: well-drained, moist, fertile	
Interest: flowers, foliage	
Care: easy	

◀ Scilla peruviana

Squill is one of spring's classic bulbs, carpeting the ground beneath taller bulb plants and shrubbery with a haze of tiny bells that open into dainty stars. Sometimes facing upward, sometimes dangling, the blossoms appear in clusters on slender stems clasped at the base by a few narrow ribbonlike leaves. Mass squill at the edge of borders, in rockeries, or in woodland gardens, where it will naturalize rapidly. Squill can also be forced for indoor bloom.

Growing and care:
Select squills from reputable breeders who propagate their own bulbs, as collection has endangered many species in the wild. Plant tender species outdoors in spring, setting bulbs with their necks at the soil line 8 to 10 inches apart. North of Zone 9, grow them as container plants, starting bulbs indoors in late winter for summer bloom. Plant all other squills outdoors in fall, setting bulbs 2 to 3 inches deep and 3 to 6 inches apart. Siberian squill even succeeds under evergreens, where other bulbs fail. The plants prefer mostly shady spots but grow well in conditions ranging from mostly sunny to full shade. Squills, particularly Siberian squill, self-sow easily. They can be propagated from seed to reach blooming-size bulbs in 3 years or by dividing small bulblets produced by mature bulbs in fall. The plants often naturalize in lawns and open woods.

Selected species and varieties:
S. bifolia (twinleaf squill) has loose upright clusters of up to eight tiny 1/2-inch pale blue flowers on 6-inch stems above two or three leaves in early spring; 'Rosea' is rosy pink; Zones 4-8. *S. litardierei* (meadow squill) has up to 30 tiny 3/16-inch blue flowers in a dense tuft on 8-inch stems in spring; Zones 5-8. *S. mischtschenkoana* [formerly *S. tubergeniana*] (Persian bluebell) has multiple 4- to 5-inch stems with sparse clusters of upturned 1 1/2-inch pale blue flowers striped darker blue, blooming late winter to early spring; Zones 5-8. *S. peruviana* (Peruvian lily, Peruvian jacinth, Cuban lily) has dense, domed 6-inch clusters of deep violet 1/2-inch flowers above evergreen leaves on 1 1/2-foot stems in summer; Zones 9-10. *S. scilloides* (Chinese squill, Japanese jacinth) has 1- to 1 1/2-foot leafless stems with clusters of up to 60 deep pink blossoms in summer followed by leaves in fall, sometimes persisting into spring; Zones 5-8. *S. siberica* (Siberian squill) bears sparse clusters of nodding 1/2-inch gentian blue flowers on 4- to 6-inch stems in early spring; 'Alba' is white; 'Spring Beauty' has large, deep blue flower stars; Zones 3-8.

BLOODROOT
Sanguinaria

Light: mostly shade

Plant type: perennial

Hardiness: Zones 3-9

Height: 3 to 8 inches

Soil and Moisture: well-drained, moist, fertile

Interest: flowers

Care: easy

◀ Sanguinaria canadensis

Bloodroot's very early-spring flowers emerge tightly clasped within kidney-shaped leaves. The waxy leaves, with deep lobes and scalloped edges, slowly unfurl to reveal a single flower resembling a tiny water lily. Allow the creeping rhizomes to spread slowly in woodland and rock gardens or under the shade of shrubs. The red-orange juice flowing in stems and roots was once used in herbal medicine and is now an ingredient in plaque-fighting toothpastes.

Growing and care:
Bloodroot grows best in shady locations beneath deciduous trees and shrubs but tolerates mostly sunny spots if ample moisture is available. Sow seed of the species in spring or fall or divide roots immediately after flowering. Set plants in soil well amended with organic matter, spacing plants 6 to 8 inches apart. *S. canadensis* 'Flore Pleno' must be grown from divisions, as it does not come true from seed.

Selected species and varieties:
S. canadensis (bloodroot) has grayish green leaves up to 6 inches across marked with radiating veins and 1½- to 2-inch flowers composed of a whorl of waxy, pointed white petals raised above leaves on 8-inch red stalks; 'Flore Pleno' [also called 'Multiplex'] has double whorls of petals.

SWEET CICELY
Myrrhis

Light: mostly shade

Plant type: perennial

Hardiness: Zones 3-8

Height: 2 to 3 feet

Soil and Moisture: well-drained, fertile, moist

Interest: flowers, foliage, fragrance, seeds

Care: moderate

◀ Myrrhis odorata

Sweet cicely is a handsome herb with tall stalks of finely cut leaves that perfume the garden with the aroma of anise and celery from spring to fall. As flavorful as they are fragrant, the fresh leaves can be used as a sugar substitute for tart fruits or to flavor salads, omelets, and soups. The soft white spring-blooming flowers are followed by tasty seeds that can be added either green or ripe to fruit dishes, salads, baked goods, and other dishes. The anise-scented taproot can be chopped into salads, served raw with dressing, or steamed as a vegetable.

Growing and care:
Because sweet cicely seed germinates erratically, the most reliable way to grow it is to divide mature plants in fall and plant the divisions. Set plants in well-worked soil that has been generously amended with compost or rotted manure. Space plants 2 feet apart. The plants do well in a range of conditions from sun to shade, though mostly shady spots are preferred. Harvest fresh leaves anytime, seeds either green or ripe. Dry leaves lose their taste but can be used for crafts. Dig roots for culinary use in fall.

Selected species and varieties:
M. odorata has fernlike leaflets along arching stems to 3 feet and flat clusters of tiny white flowers followed by ¾-inch upright, oblong, ridged green seeds ripening to brown-black.

ARDISIA
Ardisia

Light: mostly shade

Plant type: ground cover

Hardiness: Zones 7-10

Height: ²/₃ to 6 feet

Soil and Moisture: well-drained, moist, fertile

Interest: flowers, foliage, fruit

Care: moderate

◀ Ardisia crenata

Ardisia is a lovely low evergreen ground cover for shady areas with glossy dark green serrated leaves that are tapered at both ends and clustered at the ends of stems. Small star-shaped flowers are borne in racemes in summer, followed by bright red berries that persist into winter. Ardisia is a nice addition to wooded plantings, where the flowers, foliage, and fruit contribute four-season interest.

Growing and care:
Plant in a shady location in slightly acid soils. Amend soil with leaf mold, peat moss, or compost. Provide protection from harsh winter winds. Variegated forms are less cold hardy than the green ones.

Selected species and varieties:
A. crenata (Christmas berry) grows from 4 to 6 feet with lustrous foliage and bright red berries. *A. japonica* (marlberry) is a mat-forming ground cover 8 to 12 inches tall with lustrous 1½- to 3½-inch-long dark green toothed leaves that are pink when new. It bears white flowers in summer and red berries in the fall; variably hardy to Zone 7 but best in Zones 8-10; 'Hakuokan' is one of the largest cultivars and has broad, white leaf margins; 'Ito Fukurin' has light silvery green leaves thinly edged in white; 'Nishiki' has rosy pink leaf margins that turn yellow with age.

BAMBOO
Sasa

Light: mostly shade

Plant type: ground cover

Hardiness: Zones 7-9

Height: 2 to 8 feet

Soil and Moisture: well-drained, moist, fertile

Interest: foliage

Care: easy

◀ Sasa veitchii

Bamboo is a vigorous, easy-to-grow ground cover plant that displays long green leaves that jut out from tall cylindrical canes. A woody grass that develops rhizomes, bamboo can spread rapidly, functioning both as a ground cover and, for the taller species, as a screen. It is evergreen except in the coldest climates.

Growing and care:
Bamboo that is healthy and vigorous can quickly take over an area and restraints on its growth are essential. If foliage looks unkempt at the end of winter, prune plants to the ground. Propagate by division. The plants grow well in a range of conditions from sun to mostly shade.

Selected species and varieties:
S. palmata (palm-leaf bamboo, palmate bamboo) has leaves up to 15 inches long and 4 inches wide, medium green above and bluish green beneath, arising from narrow canes up to 8 feet tall and slightly more than ¼ inch in diameter; Zones 7-9. *S. veitchii* (Kuma bamboo grass, Kuma zasa) has purplish canes 2 to 4 feet tall, bearing leaves up to 8 inches long and 2 inches wide that are dark green above and bluish gray below, developing straw-colored, dry leaf margins in fall; Zones 8-9.

CHOCOLATE VINE
Akebia

Light: mostly shade

Plant type: vine

Hardiness: Zones 4-8

Height: 20 to 40 feet

Soil and Moisture: well-drained, moist to dry

Interest: flowers, fruit

Care: easy

◀ Akebia quinata

Chocolate vine is equally good at covering ground or walls, quickly twining around anything close at hand. With its semievergreen foliage, it offers multiseason interest to the landscape. Fruit pods, usually a bright, rich purple, dangle abundantly from the plant in fall; in spring, small fragrant flowers peep out from the new foliage. A good choice for a trellis or pergola, *Akebia* can also provide a cover for an eyesore in the landscape.

Growing and care:

A tough, vigorous plant, *Akebia* tolerates nearly any growing conditions, from sun to shade and moist soil to dry. Its growth is so robust it can easily choke out other plants, sometimes to the point of becoming invasive. Pruning is required to keep it under control.

Selected species and varieties:

A. quinata (five-leaf akebia) has attractive dark blue-green compound leaves with five leaflets, each to 3 inches long, nearly masking dark purple fragrant flower racemes that are hard to see from a distance. The flowers are followed by purple fruit pods up to 4 inches long that ripen in late summer; the leaves usually hold their color until the first hard freeze.

CLIMBING HYDRANGEA
Hydrangea

Light: mostly shade

Plant type: vine

Hardiness: Zones 4-7

Height: 60 to 80 feet

Soil and Moisture: well-drained, fertile, moist

Interest: foliage, flowers, bark

Care: easy

◀ Hydrangea anomala ssp. petiolaris

Climbing hydrangea is regarded by many plant experts as being the best vine, bar none. The plants are vigorous with very ornamental cinnamon-red bark, tiers of dark green leaves, and abundant clusters of linen white flowers from late spring to early summer. Climbing hydrangea is stunning when grown against buildings or along arbors, and songbirds find the ample branches excellent places to build nests.

Growing and care:

Climbing hydrangea thrives in a range of light conditions, from sun to shade but does best when grown in partial shade. To reduce the chance of transplant injury, purchase only container-grown plants. Plant in well-worked soil that has been generously amended with compost or other organic matter. Climbs easily up most supports and does best with east or northern exposures. Fertilize lightly in spring as growth begins.

Selected species and varieties:

H. anomala ssp. *petiolaris* (climbing hydrangea) climbs by root-like holdfasts to 80 feet with 6- to 10-inch-wide clusters of white flowers in late spring to early summer and broad, oval dark green leaves that cover the reddish brown, exfoliating bark.

DEAD NETTLE
Lamium

Light: mostly shade

Plant type: ground cover

Hardiness: Zones 4-8

Height: $^2/_3$ to 2 feet

Soil and Moisture: well-drained, moist

Interest: flowers, foliage

Care: easy

◀ Lamium maculatum 'White Nancy'

Dead nettle, so called because it does not sting like other nettles, is a vigorous, colorful ground cover with silvery foliage and flowers that bloom from late spring to summer. Several cultivars have been bred to be less weedy than the genus.

Growing and care:

Set plants 1 foot apart in moist, well-worked soil in spring or fall. Shear plants in midsummer to encourage a second flush of leafy growth. *L. galeobdolon* tolerates deep to bright shade. *L. maculatum* needs bright to partial shade. Once established the plants need little care and often self-sow.

Selected species and varieties:

L. galeobdolon [also listed as *Lamiastrum galeobdolon*] (yellow archangel) grows to 2 feet tall with coarse-toothed 3-inch-long leaves and bright yellow blooms with brown marks; 'Herman's Pride' is 1 foot tall with green and silver leaves and yellow flowers; 'Variegata' has variegated green and silver leaves and yellow flowers. *L. maculatum* (spotted dead nettle) is a spreading ground cover to 1½ feet high bearing small crinkled leaves; 'Beacon Silver' has greenish silver leaves with green margins and pink flowers; 'Chequers' is a heat-tolerant cultivar with dark green leaves bearing a silver center stripe and violet flowers; 'White Nancy' has greenish silver leaves and white flowers.

DUTCHMAN'S-PIPE
Aristolochia

Light: mostly shade

Plant type: vine

Hardiness: Zones 4-8

Height: 25 to 30 feet

Soil and Moisture: well-drained, moist

Interest: flowers, foliage

Care: easy to moderate

◀ Aristolochia macrophylla

Dutchman's-pipe is a vigorous twining vine with glossy dark green heart-shaped deciduous leaves up to 10 inches long. Hidden in the overlapping foliage are dark flowers that look like small pipes with fluted edges. Valued for its fast growth, *Aristolochia* is perfect for shading a porch, covering a trellis for privacy, or concealing an unsightly wall. The plant grows so quickly that it can cover a large trellis, arbor, or pergola in a single season.

Growing and care:

Aristolochia does well in bright to medium or partial shade. It tolerates any average garden soil but performs with more vigor if planted in a mostly shady spot with compost applied to its base in spring. Provide extra water during extended periods of dry weather. New plants need training during the first year. Propagate by division in fall.

Selected species and varieties:

A. macrophylla [also classified as *A. durior*] (pipe vine) has 4- to 10-inch heart- or kidney-shaped dark green leaves masking pairs of purplish brown, yellow-throated flowers in midspring to early summer and 2- to 3-inch-long ribbed capsules in fall.

DWARF MONDO GRASS
Ophiopogon

Light: mostly shade

Plant type: ground cover

Hardiness: Zones 6-10

Height: 2 to 14 inches

Soil and Moisture: well-drained, moist

Interest: flowers, foliage, fruit

Care: easy to moderate

◀ O. japonicus 'Nana'

Dwarf mondo grass forms moppy tufts of arching grasslike leaves that spread to create a ground cover in any kind of shade, from bright to dense. In appearance the plants resemble lilyturf, except dwarf mondo grass has flowers nestled within the shaggy foliage rather than above it. Clusters of small blue or black berries follow. Evergreen in the South, *Ophiopogon* is useful beneath trees and in borders and edgings.

Growing and care:

Although dwarf mondo grass tolerates average garden soil, it grows best when peat moss or leaf mold has been added. In colder climates the foliage tends to become shabby in appearance. Shear in early spring to promote new growth. Propagate by dividing in early spring.

Selected species and varieties:

O. japonicus (dwarf mondo grass) grows 6 to 14 inches tall with dark green leaves ⅛ inch wide or less and up to several bluish violet flowers per stalk; 'Kyoto Dwarf' is only 2 inches tall with narrow dark green leaves; 'Nana' is roughly half as tall as the species; Zones 7-9. *O. planiscapus* 'Nigrescens' (black dragon) has purplish black foliage 6 inches tall with pink or lilac flowers and black berries.

LILYTURF
Liriope

Light: mostly shade

Plant type: ground cover

Hardiness: Zones 4-10

Height: 8 to 18 inches

Soil and Moisture: well-drained, moist, fertile

Interest: flowers, foliage, fruit

Care: easy

◀ L. muscari 'Variegata'

The grasslike blades of lilyturf start out in tufts, gradually spreading until large clumps form. Ideal for use in edgings and rock gardens or as a ground cover, it also comes in variegated forms that provide textural accents. Flower spikes in purple or white bloom in late summer above the semievergreen foliage, followed by shiny black berries. In colder climates, the leaves look messy in late winter.

Growing and care:

Amend the soil with organic matter. Once established, lilyturf grows well in a wide range of conditions from sun to full shade but usually does best in mostly shady locations. Shear or mow the old leaves before new growth begins in spring. Propagate by division in spring.

Selected species and varieties:

L. muscari (big blue lilyturf) has tufts of straplike leaves 1½ feet tall and violet flowers; Zones 6-9; 'Gold Banded' is a compact form with wide yellow-edged leaf blades; 'Monroe's White' grows 15 to 18 inches tall with narrower leaf blades than the species and white flowers; 'Variegata' is 1 foot tall with creamy yellow leaf margins and lilac flowers; hardy to Zone 6. *L. spicata* (creeping lilyturf) grows 8 to 18 inches tall with leaves only ¼ inch wide and purplish white flowers.

MANDEVILLA
Mandevilla

Light: mostly shade

Plant type: vine

Hardiness: Zones 8-10

Height: 10 to 20 feet

Soil and Moisture: well-drained, moist, fertile

Interest: flowers, foliage, fragrance

Care: moderate

◀ Mandevilla x amabilis

Mandevilla is one of the most beautiful climbing vines, with abundant dark green leaves and prominet clusters of fragrant white, pink, rose, or salmon flowers. While hardy only in warm climates, mandevilla can be grown farther north as an annual or as a potted plant kept indoors over winter. The twining vine can be trained to climb a trellis, post, or arbor, where its trumpet-shaped flowers produce an elegant summer display set off by lush foliage. Some selections bear flowers that are extremely fragrant.

Growing and care:
Plant in soil with abundant organic matter. The plants do best in light shade but tolerate some early- or late-day sun. Keep plants evenly moist throughout the growing season. Pinch shoots to encourage bushiness, and remove faded flowers.

Selected species and varieties:
M. x *amabilis* [also listed as *Dipladenia* x *amabilis*] is a vigorous twining vine with evergreen leaves and abundant summer flowers opening pale blush pink and maturing to deep rose; 'Alice du Pont' has dark oval evergreen leaves and 4-inch-wide coral pink flowers in clusters throughout summer; Zone 10. *M. laxa* [also listed as *M. suaveolens*] (Chilean jasmine) has twining stems 15 to 20 feet long with oval deciduous to semievergreen leaves and 2-inch fragrant white flowers in summer.

MOSS PHLOX
Phlox

Light: mostly shade

Plant type: ground cover

Hardiness: Zones 3-9

Height: 3 to 6 inches

Soil and Moisture: well-drained, fertile, moist to dry

Interest: flowers

Care: easy

◀ Phlox subulata

Moss phlox is an easy-to-grow, hardy ground cover that produces vivid carpets of spring flowers. The plants produce dense clumps of needlelike semi-evergreen foliage that effectively choke out most weeds. From mid- to late spring, abundant white, pink, blue, lavender, or red flowers appear. Moss phlox makes an ideal planting for rock gardens and is especially attractive when allowed to cascade over stones or walls.

Growing and care:
Plant moss phlox in spring in well-drained soil that has some organic matter. Space plants about 12 inches apart. The plants do well in a wide range of light conditions from full sun to mostly shade and are maintenance-free once established. Moss phlox is easily propagated by layering or by division after blooming in late spring.

Selected species and varieties:
P. subulata (moss phlox, moss pink) has white, pink, blue, lavender, or red flowers above dense carpets of semievergreen foliage 3 to 6 inches tall and 2 feet wide; 'Emerald Cushion' grows to 3 inches tall with dark green foliage and pink spring flowers; 'Sky Blue' has deep green leaves and blue flowers in spring.

PACHYSANDRA
Pachysandra

Light:	mostly shade
Plant type:	ground cover
Hardiness:	Zones 4-9
Height:	4 to 12 inches
Soil and Moisture:	well-drained, moist, fertile
Interest:	foliage
Care:	easy

◀ Pachysandra terminalis

Pachysandra forms an attractive, vigorous ground cover that thrives in shady areas where other plants may not. Japanese pachysandra tolerates dense shade and competes well with shallow-rooted trees.

Growing and care:
Set the plants 1 foot apart in soil enriched with leaf mold or peat moss. Keep soil mulched until plants start to spread. Pachysandra thrives in fully to mostly shady locations and tolerates dense shade.

Selected species and varieties:
P. procumbens (Allegheny spurge) has flat gray-green or blue-green scalloped-edged deciduous to evergreen leaves, 2 to 4 inches long and 2 to 3 inches wide, sometimes mottled with brownish purple, that turn bronze in fall, and fragrant white or pinkish early-spring flower spikes 2 to 4 inches long. *P. terminalis* (Japanese pachysandra) has lustrous green, toothed evergreen leaves, 2 to 4 inches long and 1 inch wide, in clusters at the end of unbranched stems 6 to 10 inches high, with 1- to 2-inch spikes of white flowers in spring and insignificant white berries in fall; Zones 4-8; 'Green Carpet' has small, waxy green leaves and, at 4 inches, hugs the ground; 'Silver Edge' has green leaves edged with white.

VINCA
Vinca

Light:	mostly shade
Plant type:	ground cover
Hardiness:	Zones 4-9
Height:	6 to 12 inches
Soil and Moisture:	well-drained, moist
Interest:	flowers, foliage
Care:	easy

◀ Vinca major 'Variegata'

A workhorse for difficult shady areas, vinca provides mats of dark green evergreen foliage on interlaced vines that bear blue, lilac, or white five-petaled flowers 1 inch across in spring and periodically throughout summer. Vincas are useful as ground covers for shady banks and other areas, and as trailing additions to window boxes and planters.

Growing and care:
Vincas spread quickly in soil amended with organic matter. They tolerate poor soil, but will grow more slowly. In warmer climates they perform better in light to full shade. Plant them in spring or fall, spacing plants 6 to 12 inches apart. Mulch to conserve moisture. Vincas are easily propagated by division in spring, or by cuttings taken at anytime.

Selected species and varieties:
V. major has creeping or trailing stems with 1- to 3-inch-long leathery oval leaves and blue spring flowers; 'Variegata' has light green leaves with creamy white edges and is highly favored as an accent plant in baskets or containers; Zones 7-9. *V. minor* has glossy leaves to 1½ inches long on stems that form a mat 6 to 8 inches thick, and spring flowers in shades of blue or white; 'Alba' bears white flowers; 'Albo-Variegata' produces gold and green leaves and white flowers; 'Flore Pleno' has dark green leaves and purple-blue double flowers; Zones 4-8.

WINTERGREEN
Gaultheria

Light: mostly shade

Plant type: ground cover

Hardiness: Zones 3-10

Height: 4 to 6 inches

Soil and Moisture: well-drained, moist

Interest: flowers, foliage, fragrance

Care: moderate

◀ G. procumbens

Wintergreen slowly creeps along to form low mats of glossy aromatic evergreen foliage ideal as a ground cover and for use in rock gardens and wildflower gardens. Waxy summer flower bells dangle below the leaves, followed by fleshy red berries that remain on plants through winter. Brew freshly chopped leaves or berries for a refreshing wintergreen-flavored tea. Add a few berries to jams. Both leaves and berries yield an oil, now replaced by a synthetic formula, that was once used as a food flavoring and was applied externally to soothe sore muscles.

Growing and care:
Wintergreen thrives in mostly to fully shady places, though flowering is sometimes reduced in deep shade. Propagate wintergreen by divisions in spring or fall, or from cuttings taken in summer, spacing plants 1 foot apart. Mulch with pine needles or compost to conserve moisture. Harvest leaves anytime, berries when ripe.

Selected species and varieties:
G. procumbens (wintergreen, checkerberry, teaberry, ivry-leaves) has leathery 2-inch oval leaves on short erect stalks along trailing stems and ¼-inch white to pink flowers followed by edible red berries.

WOODBINE
Parthenocissus

Light: mostly shade

Plant type: vine

Hardiness: Zones 3-9

Height: 50 feet or more

Soil and Moisture: well-drained, moist to dry

Interest: foliage

Care: easy

◀ Parthenocissus tricuspidata

A tough, extremely fast climber that can easily scale 10 feet and more in a season, woodbine can make short work of covering walls, trellises, and slopes. Fastening itself to a structure with tendrils, it needs no support. Its dark green compound leaves turn purplish red to crimson in fall.

Growing and care:
Set plants 2 feet apart in spring in loosened soil amended with some organic matter. Once established woodbine can quickly become invasive and should be planted where it can spread freely. The plants do best in a wide range of conditions from sun to mostly shade and are tolerant of urban and seaside conditions.

Selected species and varieties:
P. henryana (silver-vein creeper) produces leaves with five leaflets up to 2½ inches long that are bluish green veined with white when young, with purple undersides, and turn red to reddish purple in fall; Zones 7-8. *P. quinquefolia* (Virginia creeper, American ivy, five-leaved ivy) has five leaflets up to 4 inches long, opening reddish bronze then turning dark green, then purplish to crimson in fall, with greenish white early-summer flowers and small blue-black berries on bright red pedicles that are visible after the leaves have fallen. *P. tricuspidata* (Japanese creeper, Boston ivy) bears lustrous three-lobed simple leaves; Zones 4-8.

BAMBOO
Fargesia

Light: mostly shade

Plant type: grass

Hardiness: Zones 5-9

Height: 10 to 15 feet

Soil and Moisture: well-drained, moist to dry

Interest: foliage

Care: easy

◀ Fargesia murielae

Bamboo is a vigorous fast-growing plant with distinctive tapered dark green leaves that flutter from purplish sheaths on slender reddish gray canes, which arch as they mature and spread to form mounded clumps. The plants provide dramatic color and vertical accent in ornamental beds, lending the garden a soft texture. Cut canes make good garden stakes.

Growing and care:

Plant in soil that has been loosened and amended with some organic matter. As clumps begin to develop above soil level, divide and replant. Clump bamboo is less invasive than umbrella bamboo.

Selected species and varieties:

F. murielae [also classified as *Thamnocalamus spathaceus*] (umbrella bamboo) has slender bright green canes to 12 feet tall, aging to yellow, and bending at the top under the weight of rich green leaves 3 to 5 inches long that turn yellow in fall before dropping; Zones 6-9. *F. nitida* [also classified as *Sinarundinaria nitida*] (clump bamboo, hardy blue bamboo, fountain bamboo) has hollow dark purple canes ½ inch in diameter and 10 to 15 feet tall (reaching 20 feet under optimal conditions) coated with a bluish white powder when young. After the first year the canes produce leaves to 7 inches long with bristly margins on one side.

CHAIN FERN
Woodwardia

Light: mostly shade

Plant type: fern

Hardiness: Zones 3-10

Height: 1 to 9 feet

Soil and Moisture: moist to wet, fertile

Interest: foliage

Care: easy

◀ Woodwardia fimbriata

Chain ferns come in distinctly different forms, each recalling the primitive grace that ferns in general are famous for. The netted chain fern spreads vigorously on branching rhizomes to form a spreading, lacy ground cover. Arising in a clump, the giant chain fern's spray of large arching fronds makes a dramatic statement in the shady garden.

Growing and care:

One of the easiest ferns to grow, the netted chain fern does best in soil that mimics its native habitat, the bogs and marshes of the East, although it can tolerate drier conditions. The giant chain fern prefers consistently moist, shady settings.

Selected species and varieties:

W. areolata (netted chain fern) has erect, deciduous fronds rising 1 to 2 feet high from creeping rhizomes. The sterile fronds are reddish green when new, turning glossy dark green with maturity and bearing netted veins; Zones 3-9. *W. fimbriata* (giant chain fern) has arching, evergreen fronds to 9 feet high arising upright in clumps from woody rhizomes; Zones 8-10.

CUP FERN
Dennstaedtia

Light: mostly shade

Plant type: fern

Hardiness: Zones 3-8

Height: 1 to 3 feet

Soil and Moisture: well-drained, dry to moist

Interest: foliage

Care: easy

◀ Dennstaedtia punctilobula

Cup fern is an easy-to-grow, low-maintenance plant that forms wide-ranging, dense mats of finely textured light green fronds. The delicate foliage smells like fresh-mown hay when crushed. A moderately fast-growing ground cover, it is particularly useful for slopes and rocky areas.

Growing and care:

Although cup fern grows best in slightly acid, loamy soils, it tolerates a wide range of soil conditions and, once it is established, can withstand summer drought. Give the plants plenty of room, setting them 2 feet apart. It requires little care but enjoys a springtime application of bone meal to the soil surface at the rate of 1 ounce per square yard. It spreads by slender, underground rhizomes; divide by separating the rhizomatous mats in spring.

Selected species and varieties:

D. punctilobula (hay-scented fern, boulder fern) has curved, pyramidal, very lacy fronds up to 3 feet long and 3 to 6 inches wide, covered with gland-tipped whitish hairs from which the scent emerges; the foliage turns yellow to brown in fall.

CYRTOMIUM
Cyrtomium

Light: mostly shade

Plant type: fern

Hardiness: Zones 7-10

Height: 1 to 2 feet

Soil and Moisture: well-drained, moist, fertile

Interest: foliage

Care: easy to moderate

◀ Cyrtomium falcatum

Cyrtomium is a medium-height, spreading fern with toothy, hollylike semievergreen fronds arranged in a circle and arching outward. Scattered amid rhododendrons or other evergreens in a shady location, the medium-fine, leathery glossy foliage adds textural interest to the shady landscape. In the North, it is often grown as a houseplant.

Growing and care:

Good drainage is particularly important in winter, when the cyrtomium can be subject to rot. Work leaf mold, peat moss, or compost into the soil when planting. In marginal zones, provide a site that is sheltered from winter winds and hard frost, and mulch heavily.

Selected species and varieties:

C. falcatum (Japanese holly fern) grows 1 to 2 feet tall, with leathery, dark green coarsely serrated fronds having four to 10 pairs of pinnae about 3 inches long. *C. fortunei* has erect fronds to 2 feet high and up to 10 inches wide with 12 to 26 pairs of pinnae that taper sharply and are a paler green and less lustrous than those of Japanese holly fern and not as serrated.

FLOWERING FERN
Osmunda

Light: mostly shade

Plant type: fern

Hardiness: Zones 2-10

Height: 2 to 6 feet

Soil and Moisture: well-drained, moist, fertile

Interest: foliage

Care: easy

◀ Osmunda cinnamomea

These stately deciduous ferns grow wild mostly in marshes and wet open forests, where they reach even greater heights, but they also adapt to the home garden. Spreading slowly on rhizomes, they make excellent background plantings in borders and rock gardens or against a wall. Cinnamon fern can be used to hide leggy shrubs. The plants prefer a partially shady location that receives some morning or late-afternoon sun.

Growing and care:
Flowering ferns thrive in soil consisting of 1 part loam, 1 part sand, and 2 parts leaf mold or peat moss. The interrupted fern needs fertile loam and slightly acidic conditions. Cinnamon and royal ferns can tolerate part sun if the soil remains wet, as by a stream or pond, but thrive in mostly shade elsewhere.

Selected species and varieties:
O. cinnamomea (cinnamon fern, fiddleheads, buckhorn) produces a 2- to 4-foot-tall fertile frond that looks like a cinnamon stick rising above light green foliage changing to gold in late summer before finally turning brown; Zones 3-9. *O. claytoniana* (interrupted fern) is 2 to 4 feet tall with tierlike new spring growth; Zones 2-8. *O. regalis* (royal fern) has 3- to 6-foot-tall fronds opening wine red then turning green, with 2- to 3-inch-long feathery leaflets that turn bright yellow in fall.

HAKONECHLOA
Hakonechloa

Light: mostly shade

Plant type: grass

Hardiness: Zones 5-9

Height: 1 to 1½ feet

Soil and Moisture: well-drained, moist, fertile

Interest: foliage

Care: easy

◀ Hakonechloa macra 'Aureola'

Hakonechloa is an easy-to-grow ornamental grass with warm-colored tapered blades that add a dynamic touch to walkways, borders, and rock gardens. This slow-spreading deciduous grass is stunning when planted in large groups on shady slopes or near water elements. Breezes rustling through the foliage produce soft textural effects. Hakonechloa is so adaptable it even grows well in containers, providing beauty to patios and decks throughout the summer.

Growing and care:
Plant in well-worked soil amended with some organic matter. Space plants 12 to 15 inches apart. Water regularly until plants are established and during extended dry periods. Hakonechloa thrives in partially shady locations with early-morning and late-afternoon sun, and should not be planted in locations that are excessively windy.

Selected species and varieties:
H. macra 'Aureola' (golden variegated hakonechloa) has a 1- to 1½-foot-high rhizomatous clump with an arching habit, consisting of bamboolike stems that display tapering 8-inch-long cream-colored leaves with bronzy green edges that usually spill over in the same direction and become buff colored in fall, as well as inconspicuous open panicles of yellowish green flowers that appear in late summer or early fall.

HOLLY FERN
Polystichum

Light: mostly shade

Plant type: fern

Hardiness: Zones 3-9

Height: 1 to 4 feet

Soil and Moisture: well-drained, moist, fertile

Interest: foliage

Care: moderate

◀ Polystichum munitum

The lustrous foliage of the holly fern provides evergreen beauty to rock gardens, borders, and edgings. These easy-to-grow plants thrive in the cool shade beneath deciduous trees.

Growing and care:

Holly ferns grow well in cool, rich, moist soil, although Christmas fern is tolerant of dry periods. Crown rot can be a problem; take special care to make sure the soil is well drained. Propagate by dividing in spring.

Selected species and varieties:

P. acrostichoides (Christmas fern, canker brake) is 1½ to 2 feet tall with dark green once-divided arching fronds that are widest at the base, developing multiple crowns. *P. braunii* (shield fern, tassel fern) has dark green twice-divided fronds to 2 feet long, tapering to the base and arranged in a vaselike circle; Zones 3-8. *P. munitum* (western sword fern, giant holly fern) is 2 to 3½ feet tall with long, narrow once-divided fronds; Zones 6-9. *P. setiferum* (soft shield fern, hedge fern, English hedge fern) has glossy semievergreen 1½- to 4-foot-long twice-divided fronds that are a rich medium green and soft to the touch; 'Divisilobum' has a very lacy habit with thrice-divided leaves; Zones 5-8.

OSTRICH FERN
Matteuccia

Light: mostly shade

Plant type: fern

Hardiness: Zones 4-7

Height: 2 to 6 feet

Soil and Moisture: well-drained, moist, fertile

Interest: foliage

Care: easy

◀ Matteuccia struthiopteris

Under average garden conditions, these magnificently feathery, medium green deciduous ferns easily tower to 3 feet—and even more in moist soil—making them excellent background plants. Vase shaped, they spread vigorously by way of stolons and can soon cover large areas. Fertile fronds are useful in dried flower arrangements.

Growing and care:

Ostrich ferns appreciate consistently moist locations and thrive in the partial shade of tall decidous trees, though they will tolerate mostly sunny locations if given ample moisture. They do best in moisture-retentive soil in cool climates and are not recommended for areas with hot summers. Easy to maintain and very vigorous, they can become invasive. Divide by cutting the stolons and digging up the new plants.

Selected species and varieties:

M. struthiopteris (ostrich fern) has upright plumelike, 3-foot-tall vegetative fronds with 30 to 50 pairs of feathery leaflets surrounding 1- to 2-foot-tall fertile fronds, which are olive green at first then change to light brown.

ALEXANDRIAN LAUREL
Danae

Light: mostly shade

Plant type: shrub

Hardiness: Zones 8-9

Height: 2 to 4 feet

Soil and Moisture: well-drained, moist

Interest: foliage, fruit

Care: moderate

◀ Danae racemosa

The lustrous rich green leaves of Alexandrian laurel and its gracefully arching habit lend elegance and texture throughout the seasons to formal as well as more casual gardens. Related to butcher's-broom, this laurel has bamboolike sheaves of rich emerald green stems and leaves. Small, easily overlooked flowers are followed by delightfully ornamental orange-red berries that appear in fall. The branches are often cut for use in holiday decorations and long-lasting indoor arrangements.

Growing and care:

Alexandrian laurel prefers light, open shade in a well-worked soil generously amended with rotted manure or compost. Winter sun can discolor the leaves. The plants are resistant to most pests and diseases and once established require little care. Propagate by dividing.

Selected species and varieties:

D. racemosa grows 2 to 4 feet high and equally wide, with long, pointed, rich green "leaves" that are actually flattened stems 1½ to 4 inches long and ¼ to 1½ inches wide. Inconspicuous greenish yellow flowers are followed by orange-red showy berries that are ¼ to ⅜ inch in diameter.

AZALEA
Rhododendron

Light: mostly shade

Plant type: shrub

Hardiness: Zones 3-8

Height: 2 to 12 feet

Soil and Moisture: well-drained, fertile, moist

Interest: flowers, fragrance, foliage

Care: easy to moderate

◀ Rhododendron occidentale

Azaleas are dramatic, elegant shrubs prized for their showy flowers and classic form. Azalea is one of the most popular blooming shrubs for shade and offers a range of colors, sizes, and hardiness to fit almost any garden. The plants are excellent as specimens, tucked into the shrub border, or naturalized into woodland or wildflower gardens. Mass plantings of azaleas are spectacular whether in a woodland setting or on the shore of a stream or pond.

Growing and care:

Plant azaleas in a sheltered site with morning and late-afternoon sun. Amend the soil with peat moss or other acidic organic matter. Keep soil moist and water deeply in dry periods and before the onset of winter. Azaleas are shallow-rooted plants and benefit from mulching in spring and fall. Prune in early spring, if needed, after blooming is completed.

Selected species and varieties:

Deciduous: Exbury and Knap Hill azaleas have an upright habit 8 to 12 feet tall and nearly as wide, with medium green leaves that turn yellow, orange, or red in fall, and flowers in pink, yellow, orange, rose, red, cream, and off-white; Zones 5-7; 'Gibraltar' has extra-large, brilliant orange ruffled flowers and orangy fall foliage; Zones 4-8. *Ghent azaleas* have a shrubby habit 6 to 10 feet tall with single or double flowers in yellow, white, pink,

(continued)

orange, red, and combination colors; generally hardy to Zone 5; 'Daviesi' has fragrant white flowers with yellow centers on a wide-growing multistemmed plant; 'Narcissiflora' has fragrant double yellow hose-in-hose blooms. *R. atlanticum* (coast azalea, dwarf azalea) is 3 to 6 feet high and wide, producing pinkish white flowers opening with or before blue-green leaves; hardy to Zone 6. *R. austrinum* [also known as *R. prinophyllum*] (rose-shell azalea, early azalea) is 2 to 8 feet tall with a densely branched spreading habit, bright green foliage that turns bronze in fall, and bright pink flowers that smell like cloves. *R. calendulaceum* (flame azalea, yellow azalea) has an open habit, 4 to 8 feet tall and wide, with flowers in a multitude of yellows, pinks, oranges, peach, and red, and medium green leaves changing to a quiet yellow or red in fall; Zones 5-7. *R. occidentale* (western azalea) is a native of the West Coast, with white or pinkish flowers, 1½ to 2 inches wide, in late spring and red or yellow fall foliage; Zones 6-7. *R. schlippenbachii* (royal azalea) grows 6 feet tall with an equal spread in a rounded upright habit, bearing large, fragrant, light to rose pink flowers that open with bronze foliage that turns yellow, orange, or red in fall; Zones 4-7. *R. vaseyi* (pink-shell azalea) has an upright form to 8 feet with rose-colored bell-shaped flowers appearing before medium green summer foliage that turns red in fall; Zones 5-8. *Evergreen: Gable Hybrids* grow 2 to 4 feet high and wide with glossy dark green 1-inch-long leaves and flowers in pink, red, lavender, and other colors; Zone 5; 'Rosebud' grows 4 feet high with double flowers similar to miniature roses in silvery deep pink.

BOXWOOD
Buxus

Light: mostly shade

Plant type: shrub

Hardiness: Zones 4-9

Height: 2 to 20 feet

Soil and Moisture: well-drained, moist

Interest: foliage

Care: easy to moderate

◀ Buxus microphylla 'Wintergreen'

Boxwoods are elegant evergreens with dense glossy green foliage that is perfect for shearing into hedges or topiaries. The plants are one of the most popular shrubs for formal gardens, and the branches are often used in holiday decorations.

Growing and care:
Plant in wind-protected areas and mulch to keep roots cool and moist. The plants grow well in a wide range of conditions, from sun to shade, with those grown in mostly shade being less subject to leaf scorch in winter. Plants grown in sun should be shaded until established.

Selected species and varieties:
B. microphylla (littleleaf boxwood) forms a very slow-growing mound 3 to 4 feet tall with an equal spread, producing medium green ⅓- to 1-inch-long leaves in summer that become yellowish to green-brown in winter; Zones 6-9; 'Tide Hill' grows slowly to 2 feet tall and 5 feet wide with foliage that stays green all winter; 'Wintergreen' has small, light green leaves. *B. sempervirens* (common boxwood) produces leaves ½ to 1 inch long on a slow-growing shrub 15 to 20 feet in height with an equal or greater spread; Zones 5-8; 'Suffruticosa' is very slow growing, dense, and compact, reaching 4 to 5 feet, with fragrant leaves; 'Vardar Valley' has a flat-topped habit, growing 2 to 3 feet tall with a 4- to 5-foot spread and dark blue-green foliage; Zones 4-8.

CAMELLIA
Camellia

Light: mostly shade

Plant type: shrub, tree

Hardiness: Zones 6-9

Height: 6 to 25 feet

Soil and Moisture: well-drained, fertile, moist

Interest: flowers, foliage

Care: moderate

◀ Camellia sasanqua 'Yuletide'

Camellia is one of the most beautiful of shrubs, with large, stunning red, white, or pink flowers resembling peonies set against deep glossy green leaves. Camellia is lovely as a specimen plant set where the magnificent blossoms can be viewed easily.

Growing and care:

Camellias do best in a location with some early- and late-day sun and a good deal of cooling shade. Plant in spring to allow cold hardiness to become established. Shallow-rooted camellias benefit from an application of mulch. Prune plants after flowering.

Selected species and varieties:

C. japonica (common camellia, Japanese camellia) forms a 15- to 25-foot-tall pyramid having 3- to 5-inch-wide flowers in midfall for some varieties, winter or early spring for others; Zones 7-9; 'Adolph Adusson' has red semidouble flowers 4 inches wide in late fall or early winter; 'Berenice Boddy' has light pink semidouble flowers with dark pink undersides in winter. *C. oleifera* and *C. sasanqua* Ackerman selections bear midfall flowers on a more cold-hardy plant 6 to 10 feet high; Zones 6-8; 'Snow Flurry' has white double blooms; 'Winter's Interlude' bears lavender-pink anemone-like flowers. *C. sasanqua* 'Yuletide' grows 6 to 10 feet tall, bearing 2- to 3-inch single red flowers with yellow stamens from fall to early winter.

DAPHNE
Daphne

Light: mostly shade

Plant type: shrub

Hardiness: Zones 4-9

Height: 3 to 5 feet

Soil and Moisture: well-drained, sandy, moist

Interest: flowers, fragrance, foliage

Care: difficult

◀ Daphne x burkwoodii 'Carol Mackie'

Daphnes are temperamental plants, but their intensely fragrant late-winter or early-spring flowers make them worthwhile to grow. They can be either deciduous or evergreen. Birds love the red berries that appear in summer. Daphne is a lovely plant for the shrub border or planted alone as a specimen. Caution: All parts of the plant are poisonous to humans.

Growing and care:

Plant daphne in spring or fall in a deep well-worked sandy soil that has had copious amounts of rotted manure or compost added. Once planted do not move. The plants do best in shady locations with some early- or late-day sun. Despite the best care, however, daphnes may suddenly die for unknown reasons.

Selected species and varieties:

D. x burkwoodii (Burkwood daphne) is 3 to 4 feet high with an equal spread, producing clusters of fragrant, creamy white to pinkish spring flowers and semievergreen foliage; Zones 4-8; 'Carol Mackie' has leaves with creamy margins. *D. mezereum* (February daphne) is 3 to 5 feet high and wide with lavender to rosy purple flowers that emerge in late winter to early spring before the semievergreen to deciduous leaves; Zones 4-8. *D. odora* (winter daphne) is 3 feet high, densely branched, and evergreen, growing extremely fragrant rosy purple flowers in late winter to early spring; Zones 7-9.

DEVILWOOD
Osmanthus

Light: mostly shade	
Plant type: shrub, tree	
Hardiness: Zones 7-10	
Height: 8 to 30 feet	
Soil and Moisture: well-drained, fertile, moist	
Interest: fragrance, foliage	
Care: easy	

◄ Osmanthus fragrans

Devilwood's clusters of tiny white four-petaled fall flowers may be mostly hidden by its foliage, but the fragrance is spectacular. Some species have hollylike leaves with spines that are gradually lost as the plant ages. Because of their density, these shrubs make good barrier plants. Others are useful as foundation plants, in borders, and as screens, but are especially valuable near walkways.

Growing and care:
Devilwood transplants easily into well-worked soil amended with some organic matter. The plants can be heavily pruned with no ill effect. Devilwood is easy to grow and is tolerant of urban conditions. The plants thrive in mostly shady locations and tolerate mostly sunny sites, though the foliage may become discolored.

Selected species and varieties:
O. x *fortunei* (Fortune's osmanthus) has an oval habit 15 to 20 feet tall with white flowers in fall; Zones 8-10. *O. fragrans* (fragrant olive) is the most fragrant form, a 15- to 30-foot shrub or tree that sometimes produces a spring bloom as well, with lustrous dark green spineless leaves; reliably hardy only in Zones 9-10. *O. heterophyllus* 'Gulftide' (holly olive, Chinese holly) has an dense upright form 8 to 15 feet high with glossy green leaves and prominent spines; 'Variegatus' slowly grows to 8 feet or so, with white margins on the leaves; Zones 7-9.

DROOPING LEUCOTHOE
Leucothoe

Light: mostly shade	
Plant type: shrub	
Hardiness: Zones 4-9	
Height: 2 to 6 feet	
Soil and Moisture: well-drained, moist, fertile	
Interest: flowers, foliage	
Care: moderate	

◄ Leucothoe
fontanesiana 'Rainbow'

With its clusters of creamy urn-shaped flowers, lustrous green leaves, arching branches, and spreading broad-mounded habit, *Leucothoe* looks stunning in the garden either as a specimen plant or planted in masses. The low forms make elegant ground covers.

Growing and care:
Plant *Leucothoe* in spring in a sheltered spot away from persistent winds. Add peat moss, leaf mold, or dried compost liberally to soil when planting, and mulch to keep roots cool. The plants grow best in mostly to fully shady locations but will tolerate mostly sun if kept well watered. Prune after flowering is completed.

Selected species and varieties:
L. davisiae (Sierra laurel) grows to 5 feet high with nodding upright panicles of flowers up to 6 inches long, borne above 1- to 3-inch leaves in late spring or early summer. *L. fontanesiana* (dog-hobble, drooping leucothoe) is 3 to 6 feet high and wide with arching branches of dark green 2- to 5-inch-long pointed leaves that turn red-bronze for fall and winter, and fragrant 2- to 3-inch flower clusters protruding from beneath the foliage in spring; 'Nana' is a dwarf 2 feet tall spreading to 6 feet; Zones 4-6; 'Rainbow' [also called 'Girard's Rainbow'] has leaves variegated in pink, yellow, cream, and green.

FIVE-LEAF ARALIA
Acanthopanax

Light: mostly shade

Plant type: shrub

Hardiness: Zones 4-8

Height: 6 to 10 feet

Soil and Moisture: well-drained, moist to dry

Interest: foliage

Care: easy

◀ Acanthopanax
sieboldianus
'Variegatus'

Five-leaf aralia is an excellent plant for difficult sites. The arching wide-spreading stems form the plant into a broad rounded shrub, but it can be sheared to produce a dense hedge. Its bright green compound leaves appear in early spring and persist late into fall. Slender prickles along the stems make *Acanthopanax* an effective barrier.

Growing and care:
Acanthopanax is easy to transplant and adapts well to all light conditions, from full sun to deep shade. It tolerates a wide range of soil types, from acid to alkaline and from sandy to clay, and it stands up well to air pollution and drought. As a hedge it can be heavily pruned or sheared to encourage compact growth and maintain the desired height. In an informal mixed planting, little pruning is necessary.

Selected species and varieties:
A. sieboldianus is an erect shrub with arching branches, five to seven leaflets per leaf, and light brown stems with slender prickles; 'Variegatus' stands 6 to 8 feet tall and has leaves with creamy white margins.

FUCHSIA
Fuchsia

Light: mostly shade

Plant type: shrub

Hardiness: Zones 9-10

Height: 1½ to 3 feet

Soil and Moisture: well-drained, moist

Interest: flowers

Care: easy

◀ Fuchsia x hybrida

The colorful pendulous blooms of fuchsia resemble brightly colored earrings, and dangle from stems that may reach 3 to 5 feet in length. It is grown most often in a hanging basket or container that can take advantage of its trailing habit. Fuchsia makes an effective standard when trained and pruned to develop an upright stem with a rounded crown of foliage and flowers.

Growing and care:
Plant fuchsia in a well-drained moisture-retentive potting medium and water regularly. Plants thrive in mostly to full shade. Fuchsia is subject to infestations of mites, whiteflies, mealybugs, aphids, and Japanese beetles. To overwinter plants, bring the container into a cool (40°F) area prior to the first hard frost, and water sparingly. In very early spring, cut back stems and increase watering. Plants can be moved outdoors after danger of frost has passed. Propagate by cuttings taken in spring or autumn.

Selected species and varieties:
F. x *hybrida* grows 1½ to 3 feet tall with a rounded to trailing habit, 2- to 5-inch-long pointed leaves, and pendent flowers, each with a 2- to 3-inch-long calyx tube and four sepals, and ½-inch-long petals, often in a contrasting shade, surrounding protruding stamens and styles; 'Crusader' bears flowers with a double violet corolla, white sepals, and a red tube; 'Pink Chiffon' bears double pink blooms.

HEAVENLY BAMBOO
Nandina

Light:	mostly shade
Plant type:	shrub
Hardiness:	Zones 6-9
Height:	2 to 8 feet
Soil and Moisture:	well-drained, fertile, moist
Interest:	flowers, foliage, fruit
Care:	easy to moderate

◂ Nandina domestica

Heavenly bamboo is an excellent plant for the four-season garden, with attractive flowers, foliage, and fruit. In spring the emerging leaves have a coppery hue and, as they are turning their summer color of blue-green, panicles of creamy flowers appear. In late summer and fall spectacular clusters of red berries appear that persist through winter. *Nandina* is excellent for foundations or borders, in masses, or as a specimen.

Growing and care:

Although *Nandina* grows best in acid loam, it tolerates a wide range of other soils and withstands drought. Winter sun helps redden foliage, and the plants thrive in full sun to full shade. Plant in groups to improve berrying. If left unpruned it becomes leggy; remove old canes or cut canes to various lengths to create a dense plant. Canes cannot be forced to branch.

Selected species and varieties:

N. domestica (heavenly bamboo, sacred bamboo) has an erect habit 6 to 8 feet tall with compound leaves having sharply tapered leaflets, each 1½ to 4 inches long and half as wide, 8- to 15-inch-long clusters of tiny white flowers with yellow anthers, and heavy panicles of ⅓-inch berries; 'Harbour Dwarf' grows to 2 to 3 feet, forming a graceful mound.

HEMLOCK
Tsuga

Light:	mostly shade
Plant type:	tree
Hardiness:	Zones 3-8
Height:	40 to 70 feet
Soil and Moisture:	well-drained, moist
Interest:	foliage
Care:	easy to moderate

◂ Tsuga canadensis

Hemlocks are softly pyramidal evergreens whose graceful drooping branches and small needles lend a fine texture to the shade garden. The plants can be allowed to grow into towering specimens or sheared into formal hedges and screens. They are excellent when massed along the shore of a pond or stream.

Growing and care:

Hemlocks thrive in a wide range of light conditions, from full sun to deep shade, but grow best in mostly shaded locations that are sheltered from strong winds. Plant in deep soil amended with organic matter. Mulch to keep soil moist and cool. Sunscald occurs at 95°F and above. Canadian hemlocks can be kept at 3 to 5 feet with shearing. Host to a number of pests, the hemlock has been besieged in parts of the East by the woolly adelgid.

Selected species and varieties:

T. canadensis (Canadian hemlock, eastern hemlock) has a tapering trunk 65 feet or taller, bearing medium green needles ¼ to ⅔ inch long and oval ½- to 1-inch cones on slender, pliant branches. *T. caroliniana* (Carolina hemlock) grows 45 to 60 feet tall, is more tolerant of urban conditions, and has darker green needles than those of Canadian hemlock and a stiffer form.

HOLLY
Ilex

Light: mostly shade

Plant type: shrub, tree

Hardiness: Zones 3-9

Height: 4 to 50 feet

Soil and Moisture: well-drained, moist, moderately acidic to neutral

Interest: foliage, fruit

Care: moderate

◄ Ilex 'Sparkleberry'

Evergreen hollies have lustrous broad-leaved foliage and often showy berries; deciduous hollies are attractive in winter, when they produce red fruits. Female hollies of both types produce red, black, and sometimes yellow berries if a male is nearby. The smaller hollies are useful for edgings and rock gardens, the medium-size varieties for foundation plantings and shrub borders, and the largest ones for screens and specimen trees.

Growing and care:
Evergreen hollies suffer when exposed to harsh sun, severe winter winds, and drought, and some hollies languish in heat and humidity. The plants prefer a sheltered, mostly shady site. If soil is either heavy or sandy, amend with organic matter such as leaf mold or peat moss. Water young hollies regularly. Female plants must have a male nearby for berries to form.

Selected species and varieties:
I. 'Apollo' grows 10 to 12 feet high and wide with reddish foliage aging to dark green. *I. crenata* (Japanese holly) has a dense rounded habit resembling boxwood, with dark green spineless leaves ½ to 1 inch long and black berries that are usually hidden under the leaves; Zones 5-8; 'Compacta' grows 5 to 6 feet tall and globular with leaves ¾ inch long; 'Convexa' is vase shaped and dense, to 9 feet tall and broader than its height, with ½-inch leaves; one of the hardiest of the species; 'Dwarf Pagoda' has tiny leaves ¼ inch wide and up to ½ inch long; 'Helleri' is a dwarf mound growing very slowly to 4 feet tall by 5 feet wide with small fine-toothed leaves; 'Hetzii' grows 6 to 8 feet tall and round with ½- to 1-inch leaves. *I. glabra* (inkberry, winterberry) is a multistemmed species 6 to 8 feet tall by 8 to 10 feet wide becoming loose and open with age, with ¾- to 2-inch-long spineless, spatula-shaped leaves and black fruit; 'Compacta' grows 4 to 6 feet high with denser branching than the species; Zones 4-9. *I. opaca* (American holly) grows 15 to 30 feet high, conical when young but later spreading, with dark green spiny evergreen leaves 1½ to 4 inches long and showy red or yellow fruit; 'Amy' has large lustrous leaves and large red berries; 'Cardinal', small light red berries and small, dark green leaves; 'Goldie', yellow berries and non-glossy leaves; 'Jersey Knight' (male) has a dense upright habit and dark green leaves; 'Old Heavy Berry' produces heavy yields of large red berries against large dark green leaves; Zones 5-9. *I. pedunculosa* (long-stalked holly) is a large shrub or small tree 15 to 25 feet high with wavy, shiny, smooth-margined leaves and berries on long stalks; Zones 5-7. *I.* 'Sparkleberry' has small red berries and nearly black bark. *I. verticillata* 'Winter Red' (winterberry, black alder) is a deciduous plant 6 to 10 feet tall and wide with 1½- to 3-inch spineless leaves and a profusion of red fruit on bare branches in early winter.

JAPANESE FATSIA
Fatsia

Light: mostly shade	
Plant type: shrub	
Hardiness: Zones 8-10	
Height: 6 to 10 feet	
Soil and Moisture: well-drained, moist	
Interest: flowers, foliage	
Care: moderate	

◀ Fatsia japonica

Abold, dramatic plant with a tropical effect, Japanese fatsia creates a rounded mound of deeply lobed dark green leaves up to 14 inches wide. In midautumn, round clusters of tiny white flowers form on long stalks, followed by round black fruit that persists through winter.

Growing and care:

Although *Fatsia* tolerates clay and sandy soils, it prefers light soils high in organic matter. The plants grow best in sheltered, mostly shady locations with some early- or late-day sun but also do well in full shade. Prune to control legginess. Fertilize in spring and after flowering.

Selected species and varieties:

F. japonica (Japanese fatsia, Formosa rice tree, paper plant, glossy-leaved paper plant) is a moderate to fast grower 6 to 10 feet high and wide, usually with an open, sparsely branched habit displaying lustrous evergreen leaves with seven to nine prominent lobes on 4- to 12-inch-long stalks, and flowers clustered in 1½-inch-wide spheres on white stalks, several spheres forming a showy, branched cluster. x *Fatshedera lizei* is an intergeneric hybrid between *F. japonica* 'Moseri' and *Hedera helix* 'Hibernica' with large, glossy, dark green leaves and slender stems that can be trained to a support.

JAPANESE ROSE
Kerria

Light: mostly shade	
Plant type: shrub	
Hardiness: Zones 4-9	
Height: 3 to 8 feet	
Soil and Moisture: well-drained, moist	
Interest: flowers, foliage	
Care: easy to moderate	

◀ Kerria japonica

Japanese rose sports abundant medium green leaves that serve as an excellent background for the vivid yellow springtime flowers. The foliage turns yellow in autumn and drops, revealing bare green stems that hold their color all winter. *Kerria* is excellent used in borders or massed at the edge of meadows.

Growing and care:

Kerria tolerates most soils and urban conditions but enjoys soil amended with organic matter. Excessive fertility produces reduced bloom. The plants grow best, and the yellow color of the flowers lasts longest, in mostly shady spots, though they also tolerate full shade. Remove winter-killed branches in early spring; other pruning should be done just after flowering. On 'Picta', remove any green shoots that emerge. Cut off old stems at the base every few years to maintain vigor.

Selected species and varieties:

K. japonica grows 3 to 6 feet tall with a greater spread of arching branches that bear glossy heavily veined coarse-toothed leaves 1½ to 4 inches long; 'Picta' [also known as 'Variegata'] is a dwarf clone growing to 3 feet tall with white-edged gray-green leaves and single yellow flowers; 'Pleniflora' [also known as 'Flora Pleno'] (globeflower kerria) grows semierectly 5 to 8 feet tall with very double pompom-like flowers 1 to 2 inches wide, more open in habit than the species.

LACE SHRUB
Stephanandra

Light: mostly shade

Plant type: shrub

Hardiness: Zones 3-8

Height: 1½ to 3 feet

Soil and Moisture: well-drained, moist

Interest: foliage

Care: moderate

◀ Stephanandra incisa 'Crispa'

Lace shrub, also called cutleaf stephanandra, is a tidy plant with a gracefully mounding habit of dense branches and plentiful attractive foliage. It may be grown on banks to prevent erosion or may be used as a low hedge or tall ground cover. Its thick foliage and low habit make it well suited to growing under low windows or among tall leggy shrubs in a mixed border.

Growing and care:
Plant lace shrub in moist, acid soil in a lightly shaded location. Add generous amounts of organic matter to the soil prior to planting to help retain moisture. Protect from breezy areas where drying winds can cause winter-kill of twig tips. Prune damaged or dead branches in spring as growth begins. The plant is easily propagated by simple layering of stems.

Selected species and varieties:
S. incisa 'Crispa' grows 1½ to 3 feet tall and 4 feet wide, and spreads by arching branches rooting readily when they touch the ground. Deeply lobed 1- to 2-inch-long bright green leaves turn reddish purple or red-orange in fall; inconspicuous pale yellow flowers appear in early summer.

MOUNTAIN LAUREL
Kalmia

Light: mostly shade

Plant type: shrub

Hardiness: Zones 4-9

Height: 2 to 15 feet

Soil and Moisture: well-drained, moist, fertile

Interest: flowers, foliage

Care: easy

◀ Kalmia latifolia 'Ostbo Red'

With its lustrous foliage and sometimes star-shaped flowers, mountain laurel is an exquisite plant for shady areas. The white, pink, or red blossoms appear in clusters in late spring, opening like little parasols. The flowers create a stunning display when the plants are massed along the shores of ponds or along paths.

Growing and care:
Although mountain laurel adapts to deep shade, it flowers best in mostly shady locations with some direct sunlight. Plants grown in sunny locations are more susceptible to leaf scorch in late winter and early spring. They do best in loose loam; add organic matter liberally to the soil when planting, and mulch to keep cool and preserve moisture. Remove flowers after they fade.

Selected species and varieties:
K. latifolia has a round habit, growing 5 to 15 feet high with 2- to 5-inch-long oval leaves. It flowers in clusters 4 to 6 inches wide in late spring to early summer; 'Bulls-eye' has deep purplish buds that open to creamy white flowers with a purple band; 'Ostbo Red', bright red buds that open to deep pink flowers; 'Raspberry Glow', wine red buds opening to raspberry pink blooms; 'Richard Jaynes', red buds opening to pink blooms that are silvery white inside; 'Silver Dollar', pink buds and large white flowers; 'Tiddlywinks' is a slow-growing dwarf 2 to 5 feet high with pink buds and lighter pink flowers.

OREGON GRAPE
Mahonia

Light: mostly shade

Plant type: shrub

Hardiness: Zones 5-10

Height: 10 inches to 12 feet

Soil and Moisture: well-drained, moist, fertile

Interest: flowers, fragrance, fruit

Care: moderate

◀ Mahonia bealei

Oregon grape's lemon yellow flowers in earliest spring can perfume a shady garden. The grapelike berries, maturing in summer, are covered with a blue bloom and are relished by birds. Stiff and formal in habit, *Mahonia* has leathery hollylike compound leaves that are blue-green in summer and purplish in winter.

Growing and care:

Plant *Mahonia* in spring in well-worked, acid soil that has been amended with abundant organic matter. The plants grow best in sheltered locations in mostly shade, though they will tolerate deep shade. Dry soils or too much sun will yellow leaves. Add a layer of mulch in spring and again in fall to retain soil moisture and provide extra water during dry periods.

Selected species and varieties:

M. aquifolium (mountain grape, holly barberry) has slightly fragrant flowers borne in terminal clusters 2 to 3 inches long and wide on upright stems on a 3- to 9-foot-tall shrub; Zones 5-8. *M. bealei* (leatherleaf mahonia) bears very fragrant flowers 6 to 12 inches wide and 3 to 6 inches long from late winter to early spring, and berries that turn from robin's-egg blue to blue-black on a 10- to 12-foot-tall shrub; hardy to Zone 7. *M. repens* (creeping mahonia) forms a spreading mat of stiff stems to 10 inches high with deep yellow flowers in 1- to 3-inch-long racemes.

PIERIS
Pieris

Light: mostly shade

Plant type: shrub

Hardiness: Zones 5-8

Height: 6 to 12 feet

Soil and Moisture: well-drained, moist, fertile

Interest: flowers, foliage

Care: easy

◀ Pieris japonica 'Variegata'

The ivory-colored clusters of pieris perfume the early-spring air with a subtle but unforgettable fragrance. New foliage, tinged with reddish bronze, unfurls and retains that hue for weeks before turning a lustrous dark green. Japanese pieris makes a beautiful four-season specimen, and also works well in foundations and borders.

Growing and care:

Japanese pieris grows best in well-drained soil well supplemented with leaf mold or peat moss. Mulch around plants with pine needles in spring and fall. Plant in a sheltered spot away from strong winds. Plants grown on northern exposures are less prone to winter leaf scald.

Selected species and varieties:

P. japonica (Japanese pieris, lily-of-the-valley bush) is an upright shrub 6 to 8 feet wide with spreading branches bearing rosettes of shiny leaves and slightly fragrant 3- to 6-inch-long flower clusters; 'Compacta' grows densely to a height of 6 feet with small leaves and prolific bloom; 'Crispa' has wavy leaves; 'Variegata' has leaves with creamy to silver margins.

PITTOSPORUM
Pittosporum

Light: mostly shade	
Plant type: shrub	
Hardiness: Zones 8-10	
Height: 10 to 12 feet	
Soil and Moisture: well-drained, moist	
Interest: flowers, foliage, fragrance	
Care: easy	

◀ Pittosporum tobira

Adense, impenetrable evergreen shrub whose flowers carry the scent of orange blossoms, pittosporum is used in foundation beds, drifts, barriers, hedges, and windbreaks. The round-tipped leaves are borne in rosettes at the ends of branches, lending a soft, clean appearance to the slow-growing symmetrical mound. A variegated form works well as a bright accent. Pittosporums may be left unsheared or pruned into formal shapes.

Growing and care:
Pittosporums tolerate soil from dry and sandy to moist clay, requiring only that the soil be well drained. They withstand salt spray and thrive in hot, humid climates and exposed locations.

Selected species and varieties:
P. tobira (Japanese pittosporum, mock orange) grows 10 to 12 feet high and nearly twice as wide, with leathery dark green leaves 1½ to 4 inches long and up to 1½ inches wide, and tiny five-petaled creamy white flowers in 2- to 3-inch clusters in spring, turning yellow with age and eventually becoming green to brown pods that split to expose orange seeds in fall.

RHODODENDRON
Rhododendron

Light: mostly shade	
Plant type: shrub	
Hardiness: Zones 4-8	
Height: 2 to 12 feet	
Soil and Moisture: well-drained, fertile, moist	
Interest: flowers, foliage	
Care: easy to moderate	

◀ Rhododendron 'P. J. M.'

Rhododendrons are the backbone of many shrub borders, with bold, mostly evergreen glossy foliage accented with striking clusters of elegant late-spring flowers. The plants are excellent in beds and borders, or allowed to naturalize in woodland and wildflower plantings, while dwarf forms add interest to rock gardens. Rhododendrons are stunning when planted in masses near ponds, allowing the beauty of the flowers to be reflected in the water.

Growing and care:
Rhododendrons need well-drained soil with plenty of peat moss or leaf mold. Set plant so that the top of the rootball is an inch or two above the surface of the soil. Mulch to conserve moisture and to keep roots cool. Water deeply in dry periods, particularly before the onset of winter. Evergreen types should be protected from hot afternoon sun and winter winds. Morning sun enhances bloom without stressing the plant. Foundation plantings run the risk of failing, because lime leaching from structural cement sweetens the soil; in these cases, increase soil acidity with aluminum sulfate. Unlike other members of this genus, royal azalea does well in near-neutral soil.

Selected species and varieties:
R. catawbiense (Catawba rhododendron, mountain rosebay, purple laurel) bears lilac-purple, sometimes purplish

(continued)

rose flowers in midspring, growing 6 to 10 feet tall and not as wide. *R.* hybrids: 'Blue Diamond' grows to 3 feet with lavender-blue flowers; hardy to Zone 7; 'Bow Bells' has bright pink flowers, rounded leaves, and bronzy new growth to 4 feet; hardy to Zone 6; 'Cilpinense' grows to 2½ feet with light pink flowers fading to white, its buds reliably hardy only in Zone 8; 'Moonstone' grows to 2 feet with pale pink flowers turning creamy yellow, reliably hardy to Zone 7; 'Ramapo' has blue-green new foliage and violet-blue flowers, 2 to 4 feet tall; Zone 5; 'Scarlet Wonder' grows 2 feet tall with bright red flowers and shiny quilted foliage; Zone 6. *R. mucronulatum* (Korean rhododendron) is a deciduous shrub with a rounded open habit, 4 to 8 feet tall and wide, with rosy purple flowers in late winter followed by 1- to 4-inch-long medium green leaves that are aromatic when crushed and turn yellow to bronzy red in fall. *R.* 'P. J. M.' grows 3 to 6 feet tall and wide with lavender-pink flowers borne profusely in early to midspring and dark green evergreen leaves 1 to 2½ inches long that turn plum in fall and winter.

SILVER-BELL
Halesia

Light: mostly shade

Plant type: tree

Hardiness: Zones 4-8

Height: 25 to 80 feet

Soil and Moisture: well-drained, fertile, moist

Interest: flowers, fruit

Care: easy

◄ Halesia monticola

Silver-bell is a handsome tree with strong upright branches smothered in spring with snow white dangling clusters of bell-shaped flowers. The attractive green leaves turn shades of yellow in fall. Green to brown four-winged fruits remain after the leaves have fallen. The furrowed and plated bark is gray, brown, and black. Silver-bell serves well as an understory tree but can also be used to create shade for other plants.

Growing and care:
Silver-bells do best in moist soil amended with organic matter. They are easy to grow and tolerate urban conditions well. The plants are pest- and disease-free.

Selected species and varieties:
H. monticola (mountain silver-bell) grows 60 to 80 feet tall with a usually conical habit displaying 1-inch-long flowers in two- to five-flowered clusters as the 3- to 6½-inch-long leaves begin to develop; 'Rosea' has pale rose-colored flowers. *H. tetraptera* [also classified as *H. carolina*] (Carolina silver-bell, opossumwood) is a smaller low-branched version of mountain silver-bell 25 to 40 feet tall with a rounded crown 20 to 35 feet wide consisting of ascending branches with 2- to 4-inch leaves, flowers ½ to ¾ inch long, and fruits 1½ inches long.

SKIMMIA
Skimmia

Light: mostly shade

Plant type: shrub

Hardiness: Zones 7-9

Height: 3 to 4 feet

Soil and Moisture: well-drained, moist

Interest: flowers, foliage, fruit

Care: easy

◀ Skimmia japonica

Skimmia forms a low mound of leathery leaves decorated in spring with clusters of flowers and in fall with bright berries that remain into the next spring. In order for a female bush to produce berries, a male bush, which produces larger flowers that are also fragrant, has to be located within 100 feet. Skimmia is beautiful in foundation plantings and in masses.

Growing and care:
Japanese skimmia may be planted in Zone 9 on the West Coast and north to Zone 7 on the East Coast if given a protected location. In hot climates, site it out of afternoon sun. Foliage may discolor in winter sun. Add 1 part peat moss or leaf mold to every 2 parts of soil to improve drainage. Fertilizing and pruning are not usually necessary.

Selected species and varieties:
S. japonica (Japanese skimmia) has a rounded densely branched habit, slowly growing to 3 to 4 feet tall and slightly wider, bearing bright green leaves 2½ to 5 inches long that are tightly spaced at the ends of branches, and producing 2- to 3-inch clusters of red buds that open to creamy white flowers on reddish purple stems.

SUMMER-SWEET
Clethra

Light: mostly shade

Plant type: shrub, tree

Hardiness: Zones 3-10

Height: 3 to 25 feet

Soil and Moisture: well-drained, moist to wet

Interest: flowers, fragrance

Care: easy

◀ Clethra alnifolia

Summer-sweet's fragrant 4- to 6-inch-long clusters of sweetly fragrant white or pink flowers appear in late summer. It is found throughout North America, with the most ornamental species native to swamps and wet woodlands of the eastern United States. Summer-sweet is often used as a specimen plant in mixed-shrub borders, or naturalized in moist woodland gardens.

Growing and care:
Plant summer-sweets in spring in well-worked soil amended with peat moss or compost. Mulch to keep roots cool and to retain moisture. Propagate in spring by transplanting offshoots that appear near the base of the stem.

Selected species and varieties:
C. alnifolia (summer-sweet, sweet pepperbush) grows 3 to 8 feet tall and 4 to 6 feet wide with 4-inch spikes of heavily scented snowy white flowers in summer and lustrous green leaves that turn gold in fall; 'Pink Spires' has rosy red buds opening to pastel pink flowers; Zones 3-9. *C. arborea* (lily-of-the-valley tree) is 20 to 25 feet tall with 3- to 4-inch elliptical evergreen leaves and 6-inch softly drooping clusters of fragrant white flowers in late summer and early fall; Zones 9-10.

SWAMP ROSE
Rosa

Light: mostly shade	
Plant type: shrub	
Hardiness: Zones 3-7	
Height: 4 to 5 feet	
Soil and Moisture: well-drained to heavy, wet to dry	
Interest: flowers, fragrance, fruit	
Care: easy	

◀ Rosa palustris

Swamp rose produces its fragrant dark rose pink single blooms intermittently throughout summer, providing a longer flowering season than most other species roses. Flowers are 2 inches across and are followed by oval orange-red hips in late summer through fall. Foliage is medium to dark green in summer, turning deep burgundy red in fall. The branches are long and graceful, forming a mounding shrub well suited for hedges and mass plantings.

Growing and care:
Plant swamp rose in a shaded location in soil that has some organic matter. The plants adapt to a wide range of conditions, and are at home in wet, marshy places as well as in drier ones. Prune out older canes to keep plants vigorous. Overgrown plants can be cut to ground level in fall or spring.

Selected species and varieties:
R. palustris var. *nuttalliana* has large flowers that appear from summer to fall. *R. palustris* var. *plena* is a variety of swamp rose with double rose pink flowers on canes about 5 feet high.

SWEETSPIRE
Itea

Light: mostly shade	
Plant type: shrub	
Hardiness: Zones 5-9	
Height: 2 to 5 feet	
Soil and Moisture: well-drained, fertile, moist to dry	
Interest: flowers, foliage, fragrance	
Care: moderate	

◀ Itea virginica

Sweetspire is a handsome shrub with creamy white, lightly fragrant summertime flowers and a colorful fall foliage display that is second to none. The blossoms are packed along cylindrical racemes that appear at the ends of slender twigs. The leaves are medium green in summer, turning brilliant shades of violet, red, and scarlet for weeks in fall. The plants thrive in the moist, fertile soils of wet meadows, of marshes, and along streams and ponds, making them perfect for naturalizing. They are also very drought tolerant and can be used effectively in the shrub border as well as dry woodlands.

Growing and care:
Plant sweetspire in moist to dry soil that has been liberally amended with organic matter. In dry locations keep soil moist until plants are established. Sweetspire can be propagated by division or sowing seed as soon as it ripens in fall.

Selected species and varieties:
I. japonica 'Beppu' is 2 to 5 feet tall with a spreading moundlike habit, spreading by suckers, with leaves that are rich green in summer and red in fall, and fragrant white flowers; useful as a ground cover. *I. virginica* 'Henry's Garnet' grows 3 to 4 feet tall and 4 to 6 feet wide, with green leaves that turn purple-red in fall, and fragrant white flowers in clusters up to 6 inches long; an excellent addition to mixed-shrub borders.

Plants for Places with Full Shade

The plants that grow in the dim light of shady places do not have to face the desiccating rays of the sun each day. Instead they have different obstacles to overcome. Shady places warm up more slowly in the spring and stay wet longer than sunny spots. For many shady places, trees or shrubs are already present and their spreading canopies block out the sun while their roots absorb moisture and nutrients. Very few plants thrive in full shade compared to the number of plants that prefer sun; but those that do well in full shade can give the garden years of beauty. To grow the best plants in shady places make sure the soil is well drained and amended with plenty of organic matter. Allow each plant an area free of competing roots, and your shady plantings can achieve their full potential.

Very few plants thrive in full shade, with no direct light to spur their growth. This is particularly so for annuals, which as a group need direct sunlight to fuel their rapid growth and short life cycle. Full shade conditions vary depending on the intensity of light. Full shade beneath a stand of mature pine trees is much darker than the full shade under honey locusts, willows, or apple trees. With this range of shade in mind, consider the conditions in your garden as you establish your full shade plantings.

Plants in this encyclopedia have been classified according to their preferred site and conditions. Because annuals do best with at least some sun they have been grouped in the other three sections of this encyclopedia. Yet even though full shade is not the best condition for annuals, there are some that do grow and blossom well there. These include: coleus, whose vibrant-colored leaves retain their brilliance longer when grown in shade; forget-me-not, which grows best in full sun to mostly shade but still flowers well when grown in very shady places; and impatiens, which ignites shade gardens with its vivid flowers from summer to fall.

BLUEBELLS
Mertensia

Light:	full shade
Plant type:	perennial
Hardiness:	Zones 3-8
Height:	1 to 3 feet
Soil and Moisture:	well-drained, moist to wet
Interest:	flowers, foliage
Care:	easy

◄ Mertensia virginica

These North American natives have long been grown in gardens for their springtime displays of pale blue trumpet-shaped flowers. Their leaves emerge in spring with a distinctive purplish sheen, and mature to pale blue-green. The flower shoots bear nodding clusters of pink buds that open to powder blue and fade to lilac. Bluebells enter dormancy shortly after flowering, and should be planted with companions such as ferns to fill in the vacant spaces. These plants are effective grown in large clumps in shady borders and rock gardens, or naturalized in deciduous woodlands or alongside streams.

Growing and care:
Propagate by sowing fresh seed in early summer, or by dividing the root mass immediately after flowers fade. It may be difficult to locate the dormant roots, so mark their locations to avoid damaging them later. Replant divisions 1½ feet apart, setting the plants so the crowns are even with the surface of the soil.

Selected species and varieties:
M. ciliata (mountain bluebells, Rocky Mountain bluebells) grows 1 to 3 feet high with a clumping habit, producing persistent smooth, succulent leaves and slightly fragrant ¾-inch flowers in late spring and summer; *M. virginica* (Virginia bluebells, Virginia cowslip) has 1½- to 2-foot shoots bearing thick elliptical leaves and clusters of 1-inch flowers in midspring; 'Alba' has white flowers.

DIPHYLLEIA
Diphylleia

Light:	full shade
Plant type:	perennial
Hardiness:	Zones 6-8
Height:	2 to 3 feet
Soil and Moisture:	well-drained, moist, fertile
Interest:	flowers, foliage
Care:	easy

◄ Diphylleia cymosa

Diphylleia is a decorative plant native to the eastern Appalachian Mountains. This easy-to-grow wildflower is useful for naturalizing in drifts under trees and large shrubs. Mammoth rounded, cleft leaves form the background for the cymes of white flowers with yellow stamens that appear in late spring or early summer. A month later, small powdery blue berries appear.

Growing and care:
Diphylleia is easily grown in settings that duplicate its native woodlands and does best beneath groves of tall deciduous trees. Work leaf mold, peat moss, or compost into the soil before planting. Mulch after planting with leaf mold to conserve soil moisture. Propagate by division in spring or by sowing seed at harvest.

Selected species and varieties:
D. cymosa (umbrella leaf) has 2- to 3-foot-tall stalks, and foliage that emerges copper colored before turning light green, consisting of only two leaves, each with a cleft dividing the leaf in half, each half with five to seven lobes. Flowers form above the foliage in flat-topped clusters, and berries appear later.

GOLDEN-RAY
Ligularia

◄ Ligularia stenocephala
'The Rocket'

Light: full shade	
Plant type: perennial	
Hardiness: Zones 4-10	
Height: 2 to 6 feet	
Soil and Moisture: fertile, moist to wet	
Interest: flowers, foliage	
Care: moderate	

Largely overlooked by many gardeners, golden-ray can be a valuable addition to shady gardens. The plants have large, boldly shaped leaves that accent the upright spikes of vivid yellow or orange flowers in summer. Golden-ray grows equally well in full or partial shade and in moist or wet soil. The plants form a coarse-textured ground cover that serves as a backdrop for the vivid flowers that seem to ignite shady areas.

Growing and care:
Because its enormous leaves lose large amounts of water, golden-ray does best in a cool spot where a continuous supply of moisture is assured. Propagate by division in spring or fall.

Selected species and varieties:
L. dentata (bigleaf golden-ray) has 20-inch-wide saucer-like leaves and daisylike flowers; 'Desdemona' has reddish leaves with purple beneath that turn bronze by summer on plants to 4 feet with reddish orange flowers; 'Othello' grows 3 feet tall with red-purple leaves and yellow-orange blooms; Zones 4-8. *L. stenocephala* [also listed as *L. przewalskii*] 'The Rocket' has clumps 4 to 6 feet tall with deeply cut leaves 8 to 12 inches wide and bright yellow flower spikes on black stems that emerge in summer and last longer than the species; Zones 5-8.

HARDY BEGONIA
Begonia

◄ Begonia grandis
ssp. evansiana

Light: full shade	
Plant type: perennial	
Hardiness: Zones 6-10	
Height: 2 to 3 feet	
Soil and Moisture: well-drained, moist, fertile	
Interest: flowers, foliage	
Care: easy	

Hardy begonia is a delightful addition to shady gardens. The plants produce masses of medium green to reddish bronze leaves shaped like small elephant ears. Slender stems rise above the foliage, each displaying loose, drooping clusters of pale pink blossoms in summer. Hardy begonias are excellent for shaded borders, for rock gardens, or as an edging along wooded paths. They can also be grown in pots or window boxes to add color to patios and decks.

Growing and care:
Plant hardy begonias in a shaded location in soil well amended with compost or other organic matter. For container growing plant in a soil mix made of equal parts potting mix and peat moss. Mulch around plants in spring and provide extra water during dry periods. North of Zone 8 cover with a layer of winter mulch.

Selected species and varieties:
B. grandis [sometimes classified *B. grandis* ssp. *evansiana*] (hardy begonia, Evans's begonia) has 2- to 3-foot branching stems with clusters of pale pink blooms in summer and large toothy leaves that are green with red veins above and red below.

LILY-OF-THE-VALLEY
Convallaria

Light: full shade	
Plant type: perennial	
Hardiness: Zones 2-8	
Height: 9 to 12 inches	
Soil and Moisture: well-drained, moist, fertile	
Interest: flowers, foliage, fragrance	
Care: easy	

◀ Convallaria majalis 'Albistriata'

Lily-of-the-valley's fragrant white flower bells are a welcome sight in spring. The tiny blossoms that line arching square stems clasped by a pair of broad green leaves add fragrance to nosegays or small bouquets. Lily-of-the-valley can be forced for indoor enjoyment. Caution: The plant is poisonous.

Growing and care:

Plant lily-of-the-valley pips in late fall, setting them 1 inch deep and 6 to 12 inches apart. In subsequent years, mulch with compost or aged manure in fall. The white variegated foliage of *C. majalis* 'Albistriata' tends to lose its color in deep shade. To force lily-of-the-valley, buy prechilled pips or hold pips in the refrigerator in a plastic bag for 8 weeks or more; pot with tips just below the surface and bring into a warm room to grow and flower. Propagate lily-of-the-valley by division in fall.

Selected species and varieties:

C. majalis has deeply veined 9- to 12-inch-long deep green leaves up to 4 inches across and five to 13 small, very fragrant flower bells followed by orange to red fall berries; 'Albistriata' [also called 'Striata'] has white, fragrant flowers above leaves accented with white veins.

MAY APPLE
Podophyllum

Light: full shade	
Plant type: perennial	
Hardiness: Zones 3-9	
Height: 1 to 1½ feet	
Soil and Moisture: well-drained, wet, fertile	
Interest: flowers, foliage, fruit	
Care: moderate	

◀ Podophyllum peltatum

This woodland wildflower bears large deeply lobed leaves up to 1 foot wide, and nodding six- to nine-petaled 2-inch-wide white flowers that arise in spring at the joint between two leaves. Flowers mature into 1- to 2-inch berries. The common May apple quickly spreads to form large colonies that may be invasive. The foliage dies down in summer. The seeds, stem, and root are poisonous, but the fruits are edible and used as food in parts of the southern United States.

Growing and care:

Often found in boggy, low-lying areas near woodland streams, May apple thrives in constantly moist soil to which leaf mold has been added. Propagate by dividing rhizomes in late summer or fall. Mulch with leaf litter in winter.

Selected species and varieties:

P. hexandrum (Himalayan May apple) has clumped stems 1 to 1½ feet tall, with six-petaled white to pink flowers that bloom before the three- to five-lobed 10-inch leaves unfurl. *P. peltatum* (common May apple, wild mandrake, raccoon berry) develops leaves before the flowers, which are often hidden by the foliage and are followed by yellow fruit.

PHLOX
Phlox

Light:	full shade
Plant type:	perennial
Hardiness:	Zones 3-9
Height:	5 to 14 inches
Soil and Moisture:	well-drained, fertile, moist
Interest:	flowers
Care:	easy

◀ Phlox divaricata
'Fuller's White'

Phlox is best known as a plant for sunny gardens, yet many prefer the soft light of shady borders and yards. The plants have attractive, five-petaled flowers in a variety of colors to brighten up woodland plantings or other shady places. Phlox is generally easy to grow and forms large clumps that slowly spread into colonies. Creeping phlox is especially suited for rock gardens or places where it can cascade over walls and stones.

Growing and care:
Plant phlox in well-worked soil generously amended with compost or other organic matter. Fertilize in spring as growth begins, and lightly after flowering is complete. Set plants 1 to 1½ feet apart. Provide extra water during dry periods.

Selected species and varieties:
P. 'Chattahoochee' has 1-inch-wide, deep violet flowers with purple eyes on a spreading tuft of stems to 1 foot tall; Zones 4-9. *P. divaricata* (wild sweet William) has semievergreen oval leaves beneath 1-foot-tall scapes topped with blue, purple, or white flowers; 'Dirigo Ice' reaches 14 inches with fragrant pale lavender flowers; 'Fuller's White' has white flowers. *P. stolonifera* (creeping phlox) has creeping 5- to 10-inch stems with evergreen leaves forming a mat with blue, pink, or white flowers; Zones 3-8; 'Blue Ridge' has pale blue flowers and lustrous foliage; 'Pink Ridge', pink flowers.

PRIMROSE
Primula

Light:	full shade
Plant type:	perennial
Hardiness:	Zones 3-8
Height:	2 to 24 inches
Soil and Moisture:	well-drained, moist, fertile
Interest:	flowers, fragrance
Care:	moderate

◀ Primula japonica
'Postford White'

Neat, colorful primroses produce clusters of five-petaled blossoms on leafless stems above rosettes of tongue-shaped leaves, which are evergreen in milder climates. More than 400 species of primroses in nearly every color of the rainbow offer the gardener a multitude of choices in height and hardiness for borders or shady woodland gardens.

Growing and care:
Space primroses 1 foot apart in moisture-retentive soil. Water deeply during dry periods. Japanese primroses require a boglike soil. Other species tolerate drier conditions. Polyanthus primroses are short lived and often treated as annuals. Japanese star primroses go dormant after flowering. Propagate primroses from seed or by division every 3 years in spring.

Selected species and varieties:
P. japonica (Japanese primrose) has whorls of white, red, pink, or purple flowers on 2-foot stalks; 'Miller's Crimson' has deep red blossoms; 'Postford White' has white flowers; Zones 3-6. *P.* x *polyantha* (polyanthus primrose) bears flowers singly or in clusters on 6- to 12-inch stems in a wide choice of colors; Zones 3-4. *P. sieboldii* (Japanese star primrose) has nodding heads of pink, purple, or white flowers on 1-foot stalks. *P. vulgaris* (English primrose) produces fragrant single flowers in yellow and other colors on 6- to 9-inch stems.

SAXIFRAGE
Saxifraga

Light: full shade

Plant type: perennial

Hardiness: Zones 7-9

Height: 4 inches to 2 feet

Soil and Moisture: well-drained, moist, fertile

Interest: flowers, foliage

Care: moderate

◀ Saxifraga umbrosa

An ideal plant for rock gardens, saxifrage's rosettes of leaves form a mat from which runners or stolons spread. The red threadlike runners of strawberry geranium, which is also grown as a houseplant, produce baby plants. Delicate flowers rise above foliage in spring.

Growing and care:
Saxifrages grow best in neutral, rocky soil but will tolerate other soils as long as they are very well drained but evenly moist. Generously enrich the soil with leaf mold or peat moss. Plant 8 to 10 inches apart in spring, and mulch lightly to overwinter. Apply an all-purpose fertilizer in spring. Strawberry geranium will tolerate some early- or late-day sun, while London-pride prefers full shade. Propagate by dividing after flowering.

Selected species and varieties:
S. stolonifera (strawberry geranium, beefsteak geranium) has 1½- to 2-foot branched stems bearing 1-inch-wide white flowers above 4-inch-tall clumps of round hairy leaves with white veins and red undersides, up to 4 inches wide. *S. umbrosa* (London-pride) has 1½-foot-high clumps of 2-inch-long oval leaves, pea green above and red beneath, with white, pink, rose, or bicolored flower sprays on 6-inch stems from late spring to early summer.

SOLOMON'S-SEAL
Polygonatum

Light: full shade

Plant type: perennial

Hardiness: Zones 4-8

Height: 10 to 36 inches

Soil and Moisture: well-drained, moist, fertile

Interest: flowers, foliage, fruit

Care: easy

◀ P. odoratum 'Variegatum'

Arching stems arise from rootstocks to bear 1½-inch-long greenish white bell-shaped flowers that dangle from the axils of parallel-veined green leaves in late spring. Black or blue fruits mature in fall. The plant spreads slowly by rhizomes to form a good ground cover for shade.

Growing and care:
Supplement soil with leaf mold, peat moss, or compost before planting. Propagate by division.

Selected species and varieties:
P. biflorum (small Solomon's-seal) grows to 3 feet tall or taller, bearing greenish white flowers with greenish lobes that usually hang in pairs below the stem in late spring to early summer, followed by blue berries. *P. commutatum* (Great Solomon's-seal) grows up to 6 feet tall with large, very coarse green leaves and clusters of yellow flowers in spring. *P. multiflorum* is 3 feet tall, bearing white flowers with greenish apexes, in clusters of two to six usually on the bottom half of the stem, and blue-black berries. *P. odoratum* 'Variegatum' (variegated Solomon's-seal) has 1- to 3-foot-tall stems bearing leaves with white margins and tips, with fragrant white flowers that have green spots in the throat along pliant, arching stems, followed by blue-black berries.

TOOTHWORT
Dentaria

Light: full shade	
Plant type: perennial	
Hardiness: Zones 4-9	
Height: 6 to 16 inches	
Soil and Moisture: well-drained, moist, fertile	
Interest: flowers	
Care: easy	

◀ Dentaria diphylla

Toothworts are low-growing perennial wildflowers native to rich woods and bottom lands in the eastern and central United States. They grow from rhizomes, producing loose clusters of small bell-shaped flowers in spring. After flowering the plant goes dormant and the leaves disappear.

Growing and care:

Toothworts do not tolerate much direct sun and thrive in the soft light of mostly shady woodlands. Plant in soil well amended with organic matter. Mulch lightly with shredded leaves in winter. Propagate by seed sown immediately after it ripens in fall, or by division in early spring or after the plant goes dormant in summer.

Selected species and varieties:

D. diphylla (toothwort, crinkleroot) grows 8 to 16 inches tall with deeply dissected leaves and loose clusters of white or pale pink four-petaled flowers from early to late spring; Zones 4-7. *D. laciniata* (cut-leaved toothwort) grows 6 to 12 inches tall with a whorl of deeply divided and coarsely toothed leaves halfway up each stem, and clusters of pink or white flowers above the foliage in spring.

TRILLIUM
Trillium

Light: full shade	
Plant type: perennial	
Hardiness: Zones 2-9	
Height: 6 inches to 1½ feet	
Soil and Moisture: well-drained, moist, fertile	
Interest: flowers, foliage	
Care: difficult	

◀ Trillium grandiflorum

Trilliums are elegant woodland perennials whose solitary, usually nodding flowers consist of three broad petals and three greenish sepals. Below each flower is a broad whorl of three leaves. The plants thrive in the rich soils and shade of open forests and make enchanting additions to woodland pathways and gardens.

Growing and care:

Plant container-grown trilliums in spring or early fall in rich soil well amended with organic matter. Add a layer of leaf mold mulch each fall and keep plants well watered throughout the growing season. Trilliums transplant poorly and established plantings should not be disturbed. Purchase only nursery-grown plants and avoid those collected from the wild.

Selected species and varieties:

T. cernuum (nodding trillium) is 1 to 1½ feet tall with nodding white flowers 1½ inches across with deep rose anthers; Zones 3-7. *T. erectum* (purple trillium) grows to 1½ feet tall with nodding or upward-facing maroon flowers 2½ inches across that have a musky scent; Zones 2-6. *T. grandiflorum* (large-flowered trillium) grows up to 15 inches tall with upward-facing long-lasting white flowers 3 to 4 inches across that turn red with age; Zones 3-8. *T. sessile* (red trillium, toadshade) grows to 1 foot tall with maroon, brown, purple, or yellow flowers whose petals point upward; Zones 4-9.

WILD SARSAPARILLA
Aralia

Light: full shade

Plant type: perennial

Hardiness: Zones 3-10

Height: 1 to 6 feet

Soil and Moisture: well-drained, moist, fertile

Interest: foliage

Care: easy

◄ Aralia racemosa

Wild sarsaparilla is a perennial that grows in open woods over much of the United States. Its large compound leaves partially obscure the fluffy flowers that appear in spring and impart a lush appearance to the shady garden. In late summer and fall the ripening berries attract birds to the garden. Wild sarsaparilla makes a good woodland ground cover.

Growing and care:

Plant *Aralias* in well-worked soil amended with generous amounts of rotted manure or compost. The plants require little care once they have become established. Wild sarsaparilla grows well in dryish upland soil or moist soil, while spikenard prefers a moist, fertile one. Mulch around plants in fall for winter protection and to conserve moisture. Propagate by seed or division in fall.

Selected species and varieties:

A. nudicaulis (wild sarsaparilla) reaches up to 1 foot in height with 6-inch doubly compound leaves, greenish white flowers from late spring to early summer, and purplish fall berries; Zones 3-7. *A. racemosa* (spikenard) grows 6 feet tall with leaves up to 2½ feet long and large clusters of tiny white flowers tinged with yellow or green in early to midsummer followed by purple berries; Zones 4-10.

YELLOW WAXBELLS
Kirengeshoma

Light: full shade

Plant type: perennial

Hardiness: Zones 5-8

Height: 3 to 4 feet

Soil and Moisture: well-drained, moist, fertile

Interest: flowers, foliage

Care: moderate

◄ Kirengeshoma palmata

Yellow waxbells is an unusual but charming late-blooming perennial that thrives in shady gardens. The plants produce large, maple-shaped leaves and loose clusters of nodding, funnel-shaped flowers that range from cream to apricot colors in summer and fall. The soft-colored flowers combine with the bold leaves to provide an eye-catching accent to woodland or shady meadow gardens. The plants are also useful in informal borders and shady rock gardens.

Growing and care:

Yellow waxbells need soil that has been liberally supplemented with compost, leaf mold, or peat moss, and that is cool and moist and slightly acidic. Water during dry spells, and mulch to retain moisture. Propagate by dividing every 3 to 4 years in spring or fall, though plants grow best if left undisturbed.

Selected species and varieties:

K. palmata produces nearly round, toothed leaves, each with up to 10 lobes, that arise from opposite sides of the stems and have an almost platelike appearance beneath clusters of 1½-inch-long cream to apricot bell-shaped flowers whose buds last for months before opening.

ARISAEMA
Arisaema

Light: full shade

Plant type: bulb

Hardiness: Zones 4-9

Height: 1 to 3 feet

Soil and Moisture: well-drained, moist

Interest: flowers, foliage

Care: moderate

◀ Arisaema triphyllum

Arisaemas produce a fleshy spike called a spadix nestled within an outer leaflike spathe that folds over the spadix like a hood. Glossy three-lobed leaves taller than the flower cluster persist throughout summer. The female flowers ripen to a cluster of attractive red fruit in fall. Use arisaemas in wildflower or woodland gardens or along stream banks, where they will slowly spread out and naturalize.

Growing and care:

Plant arisaema in fall, setting tubers 4 inches deep and 1 foot apart in soil that is constantly moist but not soggy. The plants do best in mostly shady locations but tolerate a range of conditions from mostly sunny to full shade. Cover with a light layer of mulch, such as leaf mold. Arisaemas can change sex from year to year, and a plant that bore fruit one year may not the next. Propagate by division in early fall.

Selected species and varieties:

A. dracontium (green-dragon) has a green spathe enfolding a 4- to 10-inch green or yellowish green spadix on a 1-foot stem. *A. sikokianum* bears an ivory spadix within a spathe that is deep maroon banded in green on the outside and ivory at its base on the inside, on a 1-foot stem. *A. triphyllum* (jack-in-the-pulpit, Indian turnip) has a green to purple spadix within a green to purple spathe striped purple, green, white, or maroon inside on a 1- to 2-foot stem.

BEAD LILY
Clintonia

Light: full shade

Plant type: bulb

Hardiness: Zones 2-9

Height: 4 to 20 inches

Soil and Moisture: well-drained, moist, fertile

Interest: flowers, foliage, fruit

Care: easy

◀ Clintonia andrewsiana

Bead lilies are woodland wildflowers with attractive flowers, foliage, and fruit to grace the garden from spring to fall. The plants have a basal rosette of very shiny emerald green leaves and thin but strong leafless stalks topped by a cluster of small lilylike flowers in spring. The pale yellow, white, or rose-colored spring blossoms yield to round, marble-size berries of indigo or blue from summer to fall. Bead lilies naturalize easily and are perfect for woodland gardens and paths and look charming planted near streams and ponds.

Growing and care:

Plant in mostly to full deciduous shade in well-worked fertile soil that has abundant organic matter. Bead lilies require cool, damp, shady locations, where they make excellent ground covers. Mulch in fall or early winter.

Selected species and varieties:

C. andrewsiana has 10- to 20-inch stalks of deep rose bell-shaped flowers followed by blue berries; Zones 8-9. *C. borealis* (blue bead lily) has greenish yellow flowers on 8- to 15-inch stalks followed by bright blue berries; Zones 2-7. *C. umbellulata* (speckled wood lily, white bead lily) bears white flowers with green and purple specks on 6- to 20-inch stalks followed by black berries. *C. uniflora* (bride's bonnet) grows 4 to 8 inches tall with white flowers and amethyst blue berries; Zones 4-8.

BLETILLA
Bletilla

Light: full shade

Plant type: bulb

Hardiness: Zones 5-8

Height: 8 to 20 inches

Soil and Moisture: well-drained, moist, fertile

Interest: flowers, foliage

Care: moderate

◄ Bletilla striata

One of the few orchids that can be grown outdoors, bletilla produces sprays of light rosy purple flowers in late spring or early summer just above broad, pointed, papery leaves that have prominent parallel veins. Bletilla is useful as a specimen, in group plantings, or as a container plant.

Growing and care:
Bletilla thrives in full, bright shade and rich moist loam in a loaction sheltered from strong winds. Work peat moss or compost into the soil, and plant no more than 2 inches deep. Water during dry periods; drought can result in diminished or no bloom the following spring. Propagate by dividing the pseudobulbs.

Selected species and varieties:
B. striata (Chinese orchid, Chinese ground orchid, hyacinth orchid, hardy orchid) grows 8 to 20 inches tall with nodding deep pink or rosy purple flowers up to 1½ inches across borne in terminal racemes of six to 10 above dark green pleated leaves; 'Alba' has creamy white flowers; 'Albostriata' has leaves bearing longitudinal white stripes that stay attractive throughout the season, and purple to rosy purple flowers.

CALADIUM
Caladium

Light: full shade

Plant type: bulb

Hardiness: Zone 10

Height: 1 to 2 feet

Soil and Moisture: well-drained, moist

Interest: foliage

Care: easy

◄ Caladium bicolor 'Aaron'

Exotic caladiums form clumps of intricately patterned translucent leaves that eclipse their insignificant flowers. The arrow-shaped leaves, rising continuously throughout summer, are vividly marbled, shaded, slashed, veined, and flecked in contrasting colors to brighten shady borders or decorate indoor gardens.

Growing and care:
Caladiums do best in full, bright shade but also grow well in mostly shady locations. Plant in spring when night temperatures remain above 60°F, setting the tubers 2 inches deep and 8 to 12 inches apart. North of Zone 10, lift and dry tubers in fall to replant the next spring. Provide high humidity and temperatures of 60°F or more. Propagate by division in spring.

Selected species and varieties:
C. bicolor [formerly *C.* x *hortulanum*] has foot-long arrow- or heart-shaped leaves; 'Aaron' has green edges feathering into creamy centers; 'Candidum' is white with green veining; 'Fannie Munson', pink-veined red edged in green; 'Festiva', rose-veined green; 'Irene Dank', light green edged in deeper green; 'June Bride', greenish white edged in deep green; 'Pink Beauty' is a pink dwarf spattered with green; 'White Christmas' is white with green veining.

941

FAWN LILY
Erythronium

Light: full shade	
Plant type: bulb	
Hardiness: Zones 3-9	
Height: 4 inches to 2 feet	
Soil and Moisture: well-drained, moist, fertile	
Interest: flowers, foliage	
Care: moderate	

◀ Erythronium 'Kondo'

Native woodland wildflowers, fawn lilies produce delicate, nodding lilylike blooms with petals curved back to reveal prominent stamens and anthers either singly or in small clusters. The flowers rise from pairs of pointed oval leaves that are often marbled or mottled in gray, brown, or bronze. Mass fawn lilies in woodland gardens or as a spring ground cover beneath deciduous shrubs, where they will naturalize into colonies.

Growing and care:
Plant fawn lilies in summer or fall, placing the corms 2 to 3 inches deep and 4 to 6 inches apart in a location that receives deciduous shade. Fawn lilies often take a year to become established before blooming. Provide adequate moisture in summer after flowers and foliage fade. Propagate from seed to bloom in 3 to 4 years or by removing and immediately replanting the small cormels that develop at the base of mature corms in late summer or fall.

Selected species and varieties:
E. citrinum has clusters of 1½-inch white or cream flowers with pale lemon throats on 10- to 12-inch stems; Zones 6-8. *E. dens-canis* (dogtooth fawn lily, European dogtooth violet) bears white to pink or purple single flowers 2 inches across with blue or purple anthers on 6- to 12-inch stems above leaves marbled brown and bluish green; 'Charmer' produces pure white flowers touched with brown at their base above leaves mottled with brown; 'Frans Hals' has royal purple blooms with a green throat; 'Lilac Wonder' is soft lilac with a brownish base; 'Pink Perfection', bright pink; 'Purple King', reddish purple with a white throat above brown-spotted leaves; 'Rose Queen', rosy pink; 'Snowflake', pure white; var. *japonicum* is a miniature only 4 to 6 inches tall with violet flowers tinged purple at the base; var. *niveus* is pale pink; Zones 3-8. *E. grandiflorum* (glacier lily, avalanche lily) has golden yellow flowers with red anthers in clusters on 1- to 2-foot stems. *E. revolutum* (mahogany fawn lily, coast fawn lily) bears 1½-inch white to pale lavender flowers aging to purple on 16-inch stems; 'White Beauty' is a dwarf producing 2- to 3-inch white flowers with yellow throats on 7-inch stems above leaves veined in white; Zones 3-8. *E. tuolumnense* (Tuolumne fawn lily) has 1¼-inch yellow flowers touched with green at the base on 1-foot stems above bright green 1-foot leaves; Zones 3-8. *E.* hybrids: 'Citronella' yields lemon yellow flowers on 10-inch stems; 'Jeannine', sulfur yellow blooms; 'Kondo', greenish yellow blossoms touched with brown at the base; 'Pagoda', pale yellow flowers with a deeper yellow throat on 10-inch stems.

ORCHID PANSY
Achimenes

Light: full shade

Plant type: bulb

Hardiness: Zone 10

Height: 1 to 2 feet

Soil and Moisture: well-drained, moist

Interest: flowers

Care: moderate

◀ Achimenes longiflora

Orchid pansy is a beautiful flower with the elegance of orchids and the cheerfulness of pansies. The large, 2-inch flowers have long, tubular necks and bloom amid fleshy, downy leaves on slender arching or trailing stems. Blossom throats are often splashed or veined in a contrasting color. Excellent as houseplants, orchid pansies can also be used outdoors in containers and hanging baskets on shady patios in locations with mild temperatures.

Growing and care:
Plant orchid pansy in spring, setting tubers 1 inch deep and 3 to 4 inches apart. Flowers appear 12 to 14 weeks after planting. Keep soil moist but not soggy, and fertilize while the plants are blooming. Gradually withhold water after flowering ceases. Store potted tubers over winter in dry soil, or lift and dry tubers in fall for replanting in spring. Propagate by dividing dormant tubers into ½-inch pieces just before repotting in spring.

Selected species and varieties:
A. longiflora has white, pink, red, lavender, or violet flowers, sometimes with contrasting throats, in midsummer amid whorls of hairy leaves on stems to 1 foot; 'Ambroise Verschaffelt' is white with a deep purple throat; 'Paul Arnold' has blue-violet blossoms.

SPRING-BEAUTY
Claytonia

Light: full shade

Plant type: bulb

Hardiness: Zones 4-9

Height: 4 to 12 inches

Soil and Moisture: well-drained, moist, fertile

Interest: flowers

Care: easy

◀ Claytonia virginica

Spring-beauties are low-growing perennials found in rich woodlands throughout much of the eastern and central United States. Their dainty flowers are pink or white with darker pink stripes on the petals and dark pink stamens. They are lovely planted in large drifts or scattered among other woodland flowers. The plants disappear shortly after flowering.

Growing and care:
Only purchase nursery-grown plants and refuse any collected from the wild. Spring-beauties thrive and spread rapidly in a moist soil with high-humus content in locations beneath deciduous trees. Incorporate generous amounts of organic matter into the soil prior to planting. They do well when planted among merry-bells and blue bead lilies. Propagate by corms or seed.

Selected species and varieties:
C. caroliniana (broad-leaved spring-beauty) grows from corms to produce two oval leaves, each 2 inches long. Throughout spring dainty pinkish flowers are borne in loose clusters along the upper portion of the 4- to 12-inch stems. *C. virginica* (narrow-leaved spring-beauty) is similar to the above species except that its leaves are slender and grasslike.

TUBEROUS BEGONIA
Begonia

Light: full shade

Plant type: bulb

Hardiness: Zone 10

Height: ⅔ to 1½ feet

Soil and Moisture: well-drained, moist

Interest: flowers, fragrance

Care: moderate

◀ Begonia Picotee Group

Tuberous begonias produce an abundance of large flowers over a long season of bloom with soft, waxy petals in vivid tones of red, orange, apricot, rose, pink, yellow, cream, or white, sometimes bicolored, on fleshy upright or trailing stems. Blossoms open in succession amid pointed, crenelated green to bronze foliage that is deeply veined, sometimes in contrasting colors. Their diverse flower forms have plain, frilled, or fringed petals that mimic the blossoms of roses, camellias, carnations, and other garden favorites. Thousands of hybrids offer almost limitless combinations of forms and colors for varying purposes. Upright tuberous begonias are striking when massed as bedding plants or grown as specimens in patio containers, whereas cascading forms are appealing when allowed to trail gracefully from hanging baskets.

Growing and care:

Plant tuberous begonias outdoors in spring for summer bloom, setting tubers 1 to 2 inches deep with their concave side up, 12 to 15 inches apart. The plants do best in filtered full shade, such as beneath deciduous trees. For potted plants, space three or four tubers evenly in each pot or hanging basket, with the top of the tuber at the soil line. For earliest flowering, start tuberous begonias indoors 6 to 12 weeks before planting outside. Keep soil constantly moist but not soggy. Prune small tubers to a single stem, larger ones to three or four stems, and pinch early buds to encourage more prolific flowering.

Provide support for upright forms. Fertilize while blooming with a dilute balanced houseplant fertilizer. North of Zone 10, lift tubers in fall after the first light frost, allow them to dry, and store them for replanting in spring. Propagate tuberous begonias from stem cuttings taken in spring; by dividing tubers, making sure to maintain at least one growth bud in each section; or from seed sown indoors in January to bloom in June.

Selected species and varieties:

B. x *tuberhybrida* flowers to 4 inches or more across, with hundreds of hybrids classified in 12 groups according to flower form and color. *Single Group*: Broad, flat-faced flowers composed of four enormous petals surrounding a central cluster of prominent stamens. *Crispa or Frilled Group*: Flat-faced flowers with large petals whose edges are ruffled or fringed, surrounding a colorful cluster of stamens. *Cristata or Crested Group*: Raised, frilled crests punctuating the center of each of several large sepals. *Narcissiflora or Daffodil-Flowered Group*: Double rows of petals in an arrangement that resembles a flat-faced narcissus. *Camellia or Camelliiflora Group*: Smooth petals of a single color arranged in overlapping layers like camellia flowers on upright plants. *Ruffled Camellia Group*: Overlapping layers of ruffled petals that conceal the stamens. *Rosiflora or Rosebud Group*: Center petals tightly furled like a pointed, unopened rosebud. *Fimbriata Plena or Carnation Group*: Finely fringed petals overlapping in double rows. *Picotee Group*: Double rows of overlapping petals edged in a narrow or broad band of a deeper shade of the main petal color. *Marginata Group*: Double rows of petals edged in a narrow or broad band of a contrasting color. *Marmorata Group*: Double rows of pink or rose petals dappled with white. *Pendula or Hanging-Basket Group*: A profusion of single- or double-petaled blossoms on trailing stems. *Multiflora Group*: Small single- or double-petaled blossoms on bushy plants with compact stems.

BEARBERRY
Arctostaphylos

Light: full shade	
Plant type: ground cover	
Hardiness: Zones 2-6	
Height: 6 to 12 inches	
Soil and Moisture: well-drained, fertile, moist	
Interest: flowers, foliage, fruit	
Care: easy	

◀ A. uva-ursi

Bearberry is a multifaceted plant with ornamental evergreen foliage that also has antibacterial properties, dainty spring flowers, and attractive red berries from fall to winter. The plants quickly spread into leafy mats that make an ideal ground cover to control erosion on difficult rocky or sandy banks. Dangling flower clusters lining the stems in spring are followed by bright red oval berries in fall. The berries attract various species of birds to the garden in fall and winter.

Growing and care:

Bearberry requires a sandy soil well amended with organic matter for best growth. The plants grow well in conditions ranging from full sun to full shade. Sow bearberry seed or set out rooted cuttings in spring, spacing plants 1 to 2 feet apart. Once established bearberry will tolerate dry conditions as long as it receives periodic deep watering. Propagate from seed, from stem cuttings, or by transplanting layered stems.

Selected species and varieties:

A. uva-ursi (common bearberry, hog cranberry, bear's grape, mealberry, kinnikinnick, sandberry, mountain box, creashak, trailing manzanita) has slender arching stems to 5 feet long, and produces ¼-inch urn-shaped red-tinged white flowers in spring, and clusters of red berries in fall through winter.

GINSENG
Panax

Light: full shade	
Plant type: perennial	
Hardiness: Zones 3-8	
Height: 6 inches to 3 feet	
Soil and Moisture: well-drained, moist, fertile	
Interest: foliage, fruit	
Care: difficult	

◀ Panax quinquefolius

Ginseng's thick roots send up a single thin stalk with leaves composed of several pointed leaflets arranged like the fingers on a hand. In late spring or summer, a short flower stalk carries a cluster of tiny yellow-green flowers above the foliage, followed by red berries. In woodland gardens, ginseng slowly spreads into a lacy ground cover. Ginseng's Greek name means "all ills," reflecting its root's fame as an herbal tonic in Oriental medicine. Roots are also used in herbal teas.

Growing and care:

Ginseng grows best in full shade and is often planted with goldenseal in shady woods. You can sow ginseng seed in spring or fall, but division and replanting of roots in spring is often more successful, as the seeds take a year to germinate. Provide organic mulch annually. When roots are at least 6 years old, dig them up in fall to use fresh or dried for teas.

Selected species and varieties:

P. pseudoginseng [also classified as *P. ginseng*] has 2- to 3-foot-tall stems with two to six leaves composed of toothed leaflets growing from a carrotlike root. *P. quinquefolius* (American ginseng) has stems 6 to 20 inches tall with leaves composed of 6-inch leaflets growing from a cigar-shaped root.

GOLDENSEAL
Hydrastis

Light: full shade

Plant type: perennial

Hardiness: Zones 3-8

Height: 6 to 12 inches

Soil and Moisture: well-drained, fertile, moist

Interest: foliage, flowers

Care: difficult

◀ Hydrastis canadensis

Goldenseal sends up solitary stems, each with a few broad, coarse leaves, and very slowly spreads into mats in woodland gardens. Tiny spring flowers develop into inedible fruits resembling raspberries in fall. Native Americans used goldenseal for body paint, as an insect repellent, and in various herbal medicines. Modern herbalists now consider it toxic, especially in large doses. In the past, inflated claims as to its medicinal powers led to overcollecting in the wild, and goldenseal is now endangered in many places.

Growing and care:
Grow goldenseal from pieces of rhizomes with leaf buds collected in spring or fall. Set pieces ½ inch deep and space them 8 inches apart. Protect with a winter mulch. Propagation from seed is difficult, as seed needs 18 months to germinate.

Selected species and varieties:
H. canadensis (goldenseal, turmeric) has deeply lobed, hand-shaped leaves up to 8 inches across, a single leaf at the base of each stem, and one or two at the top. It grows from thick, yellow-fleshed rhizomes with a licorice odor and petal-less ½-inch green-white flowers with fluffy stamens.

LUNGWORT
Pulmonaria

Light: full shade

Plant type: perennial

Hardiness: Zones 3-8

Height: 6 inches to 1½ feet

Soil and Moisture: well-drained to heavy, moist

Interest: flowers, foliage

Care: easy

◀ Pulmonaria saccharata 'Dora Bieleveld'

While grown primarily for their clumps of broadly oval hairy leaves mottled with silvery white spots, lungworts also bear clusters of blue or white trumpet-shaped flowers that nod from the tops of arching stems in spring. Lungworts are effective as coarse, slowly spreading ground covers. Their foliage emerges in early spring and remains green until fall. They can also be used as accents in shady borders and beds.

Growing and care:
Lungwort thrives in full shade and is tolerant of locations with some early-morning or late-afternoon sun. Set plants in soil well amended with organic matter and provide extra water during dry periods. Space plants 1 to 1½ feet apart. Cut flowering stems back as blossoms fade to promote vigorous growth. Propagate by seed or division in fall.

Selected species and varieties:
P. angustifolia has lance-shaped green leaves beneath sapphire blue flowers; 'Azurea' has pinkish blue buds that open to flowers of bright blue; 'Johnson's Blue' is a dwarf with sky blue flowers. *P. saccharata* (Bethlehem sage) has pink flowers opening to blue or white on 6- to 18-inch stems above mottled green and white leaves; 'Dora Bieleveld' has rosy pink flowers; 'Sissinghurst White' has early-flowering white blossoms and well-spotted leaves.

SPICEBUSH
Lindera

Light: full shade

Plant type: shrub

Hardiness: Zones 4-9

Height: 6 to 15 feet

Soil and Moisture: moist to wet

Interest: flowers, foliage, fruit

Care: easy

◀ Lindera benzoin

A dense, informal deciduous shrub with erect branches, spicebush offers three-season interest, fragrance, and flavor as a specimen or in a shrub border. Flowers bloom along bare branches of both male and female plants in early spring, followed by spicy-scented leaves. On female plants, leaves color and drop in fall to reveal small, bright scarlet fruits. Steep young twigs and fresh or dried leaves and berries for herbal tea. Add dried leaves and berries to woodsy potpourris, or grind dried berries as a substitute for allspice.

Growing and care:
Sow ripe spicebush seed in fall before it dries out, or hold at least 4 months in the refrigerator and sow in spring. Otherwise, start new shrubs from softwood cuttings taken in summer. Spicebush grows best in shady spots beneath deciduous trees but tolerates sun if grown in consistently moist soil. Collect twigs in spring, leaves throughout the growing season, and berries in fall, and use either fresh or dried.

Selected species and varieties:
L. benzoin (spicebush, Benjamin bush) bears fragrant, tiny yellow-green flowers in clusters that emerge before the 2- to 5-inch pointed oval leaves, which turn deep gold in fall, and ½-inch oval red fruits.

WILD GINGER
Asarum

Light: full shade

Plant type: perennial

Hardiness: Zones 3-8

Height: 6 to 12 inches

Soil and Moisture: well-drained, moist

Interest: foliage, flowers

Care: easy

◀ Asarum canadense

P airs of deciduous heart-shaped leaves on thin arching stems hide wild ginger's bell-shaped, maroon spring flowers growing at ground level. The attractive foliage, resembling that of cyclamen, grows along creeping rhizomes that develop into ground-covering carpets. While the edible roots are seldom used, they can substitute for fresh or dried ground ginger. Young leaves add flavor to salads, though they may cause dermatitis. Wild ginger figures in traditional herbal medicine.

Growing and care:
Wild ginger grows best in deep woodland shade but tolerates some dappled light. Sow wild ginger seed in spring, or plant divisions in spring or fall, cutting sections of rhizome with at least one pair of leaves. Set sections 1 inch deep in beds prepared with abundant leaf mold, compost, or other organic amendments, and space plants 1 foot apart. Wild ginger does especially well in sheltered areas in soil above limestone or marble bedrock. Keep new beds evenly moist. Once established, wild ginger becomes a low-maintenance weed-suppressing ground cover.

Selected species and varieties:
A. canadense (Canadian wild ginger) has broad, hairy dark green leaves up to 7 inches across on 6-inch-tall stems with inch-wide brown to purple flowers.

BUNCHBERRY
Cornus

Light: full shade	
Plant type: ground cover	
Hardiness: Zones 2-6	
Height: 4 to 8 inches	
Soil and Moisture: well-drained, moist	
Interest: flowers, foliage, fruit	
Care: moderate	

◀ *Cornus canadensis*

Bunchberry is one of the most charming native ground covers, with small, white to pinkish blossoms resembling flowering dogwood amid a sea of tidy bright green foliage. The flowers appear in spring and yield to a cluster of bright red berries in late summer. In fall the green leaves turn a vivid scarlet. Bunchberry thrives in shady, cool forests and carpets the ground beneath evergreens and deciduous trees alike. The plants make excellent ground covers for woodland gardens or a shady rock garden. They naturalize readily and grow well next to partridgeberry and wood sorrel.

Growing and care:
Plant in spring or fall in well-worked soil that has abundant organic matter. The plants do best in mountain areas or in cool, shady locations that stay evenly moist. Mulch with pine needles in fall. Bunchberry is easy to grow if its requirements are met and needs little attention once established.

Selected species and varieties:
C. canadensis is a beautiful ground cover with 4- to 8-inch creeping woody stems and four showy white bracts in late spring. In late summer and fall bright red berries and scarlet foliage appear.

IVY
Hedera

Light: full shade	
Plant type: vine	
Hardiness: Zones 5-10	
Height: 6 inches to 100 feet	
Soil and Moisture: well-drained, moist	
Interest: foliage	
Care: easy	

◀ *Hedera helix*

Ivies are perfect for carpeting shady banks and borders and, with their aerial roots, for climbing fences and posts. After climbing ceases at maturity, they produce yellowish green flowers 1½ to 2½ inches wide, and poisonous black berries.

Growing and care:
Though ivy tolerates a wide variety of soil types, it benefits from a good start: Enrich the soil with organic matter and keep the plants moist until they are established. Plant ivy in spring or fall, setting plants about 2 feet apart. Propagate by simple stem layering.

Selected species and varieties:
H. canariensis (Algerian ivy, canary ivy, Madeira ivy) has three- to seven-lobed dark green leathery leaves on dark red petioles; Zones 9-10; 'Variegata' has showy yellow or pale green streaks. *H. colchica* 'Dentata' (colchis ivy, fragrant ivy, Persian ivy) is a fast climber with slightly toothed leaves from 5 to 10 inches wide; hardy to Zone 6; 'Dentata-Variegata' has creamy yellow margins. *H. helix* 'Cavendishii' (English ivy) has three- to five-lobed leaves 2 to 4 inches wide with creamy white margins; 'Gold Heart' has triangular leaves with a gold center; 'Needlepoint' is a very dense slow grower with dark green leaves ¼ to 1 inch wide.

PARTRIDGEBERRY
Mitchella

Light: full shade

Plant type: ground cover

Hardiness: Zones 3-9

Height: 2 to 4 inches

Soil and Moisture: well-drained, moist, fertile

Interest: flowers, foliage, fruit

Care: easy

◀ Mitchella repens

Partridgeberry is a dainty low-growing evergreen native to woodlands and stream banks of the eastern and central United States. The small, dark green leaves often form glossy carpets that accent the pairs of pinkish white late spring flowers and scarlet fall fruit. It provides a fine-textured year-round ground cover for shaded areas and is a lovely addition to a rock garden. The plants naturalize easily and slowly spread into large colonies.

Growing and care:
Partridgeberry thrives in cool, moist, humus-rich soil in partial to full shade and is one of the few plants to thrive in the deep shade beneath conifers. Where snow cover is sparse mulch lightly with pine needles in winter. The easiest way to propagate partridgeberry is to take 6-inch stem cuttings in early spring; keep plants evenly moist in well-drained soil.

Selected species and varieties:
M. repens (partridgeberry, twinberry) has pairs of ¾-inch white to pinkish white flowers in late spring and bright red berries in fall. It has small, rounded, shiny dark green leaves with white veins on trailing stems up to 1 foot long that root as they creep over the ground.

SWEET WOODRUFF
Galium

Light: full shade

Plant type: ground cover

Hardiness: Zones 4-8

Height: 6 to 36 inches

Soil and Moisture: well-drained, moist

Interest: flowers, foliage, fragrance

Care: easy

◀ Galium odoratum

Sweet woodruff spreads into ground-covering mats with small clusters of white spring flowers above ruffs of leaves that become vanilla scented as they dry. Yellow bedstraw bears plumes of honey-scented yellow flowers from summer to fall. Weave fresh sweet woodruff stems into wreaths to dry or add dried leaves to potpourri. Use the dried flowers of yellow bedstraw to stuff herbal pillows.

Growing and care:
Sow woodruff seed in late summer or divide roots after flowering, setting plants 6 to 9 inches apart in a shady, moist location enriched with organic matter. Sow bedstraw seed or divide roots in spring, setting plants 9 to 12 inches apart. The plants do best in full shade but tolerate early- or late-day sun. To control these robust plants, set a container with the bottom removed in the soil; plant the seed or divisions in the can.

Selected species and varieties:
G. odoratum (sweet woodruff) bears open clusters of ¼-inch flowers and shiny 1½-inch leaves on 6- to 8-inch stems. *G. verum* (yellow bedstraw, Our-Lady's bedstraw) has elongated clusters of ¼-inch flowers and needlelike leaves on 1- to 3-foot stems.

ATHYRIUM
Athyrium

Light: full shade

Plant type: fern

Hardiness: Zones 4-7

Height: 1 to 3 feet

Soil and Moisture: well-drained, moist

Interest: foliage

Care: easy

◀ Athyrium nipponicum 'Pictum'

Athyriums are deciduous woodland ferns that thrive in a variety of light conditions, from mostly sun to full shade. Arising in clumps, the light green fronds are finely divided and grow upright or gracefully arched. These delicately textured plants work well as accents, space fillers, or background plants, or beside water. By late summer the foliage tends to look worn; it dies back in fall.

Growing and care:
Although lady ferns perform best in the slightly acid, rich loam of their native woodland settings, they accept a wide range of soil types and are among the easiest of all ferns to grow. Locate them out of windy areas, as the fronds are easily broken. The Japanese painted fern does well in partial to full shade, while lady fern prefers mostly sun to light shade.

Selected species and varieties:
A. filix-femina (lady fern) grows 2 to 3 feet tall with reddish, brownish, or tan stalks and erect, twice-pinnate fronds 6 to 9 inches wide and often wider. *A. nipponicum* 'Pictum' [also classified as *A. goeringianum*] (Japanese painted fern) is 1 to 1½ feet tall with divided fronds and gray-green foliage flushed with maroon on only the upper half of maroon stems.

MAIDENHAIR FERN
Adiantum

Light: full shade

Plant type: fern

Hardiness: Zones 2-10

Height: 8 inches to 3 feet

Soil and Moisture: well-drained, moist, fertile

Interest: foliage

Care: moderate

◀ Adiantum pedatum

Maidenhair ferns add airiness and texture to rock gardens and naturalized areas. Black or sometimes chestnut stripes accent the delicately etched green fronds. Slowly creeping on rhizomes, these mostly deciduous ferns form colonies.

Growing and care:
Maidenhair ferns do best in sites that mimic the moisture and shade of their native woodland settings. They thrive along woodland paths or in moist soils along the north side of buildings. Amend soil with leaf mold or peat moss before planting, and top-dress with bone meal every year. Propagate by dividing rhizomes in spring.

Selected species and varieties:
A. capillus-veneris (common maidenhair, duddergrass) has 1- to 2-foot-tall arching fronds; Zones 7-10. *A. hispidulum* (rosy maidenhair, Australian maidenhair) bears erect finely textured fronds, rosy as they unfurl, growing to 1 foot tall with hairy stripes; Zones 8-10. *A. pedatum* (northern maidenhair, five-fingered maidenhair) has slightly arching 10- to 18-inch-tall branched fan-shaped fronds, with chestnut brown stripes, spreading slowly; Zones 2-8. *A. venustum* (evergreen maidenhair) has medium green graceful, lacy arching fronds 8 to 12 inches long; Zones 5-8.

AUCUBA
Aucuba

Light: full shade

Plant type: shrub

Hardiness: Zones 7-10

Height: 6 to 10 feet

Soil and Moisture: well-drained, moist, fertile

Interest: foliage, fruit

Care: easy

◄ Aucuba japonica 'Variegata'

A rounded upright shrub with large leathery leaves that are often marked with flecks of gold or yellow, aucuba brightens shady areas. An excellent transition plant between woodland and garden, it is also useful for hedges and borders. If a male plant is nearby, female aucubas produce scarlet berries that last all winter but are often hidden by the foliage. Leaf color remains unchanged throughout the seasons.

Growing and care:
Aucuba prefers slightly acid loam but will tolerate other soils. Once established it withstands moderate drought. Full shade is best to maintain leaf color; direct sun, particularly in warmer climates, tends to blacken the foliage. Prune to control height and maintain shape.

Selected species and varieties:
A. japonica (Japanese aucuba, Japanese laurel, spotted laurel) has lustrous medium to dark green leaves 3 to 8 inches long and up to 3 inches wide that dominate tiny purple flowers borne in erect panicles in early spring, and ½-inch-wide bright red berries; 'Variegata' (gold-dust plant) is female and has deep green leaves heavily sprinkled with yellow.

HORNBEAM
Carpinus

Light: full shade

Plant type: tree

Hardiness: Zones 3-9

Height: 30 to 60 feet

Soil and Moisture: well-drained, moist to dry

Interest: foliage, bark

Care: easy

◄ Carpinus betulus 'Fastigiata'

A deciduous tree with crisp summer foliage, smooth gray bark, and a well-contoured winter silhouette, hornbeam (also called ironwood) makes a handsome specimen tree. Because it has dense foliage that takes well to pruning, however, it is often used as a hedge or screen. The dark green leaves may turn yellow or brown in fall. Hornbeam has extremely hard wood that was once used to make ox yokes.

Growing and care:
A highly adaptable and trouble-free plant, hornbeam tolerates a wide range of soil conditions. Plant in spring and keep well watered until established. European hornbeam prefers mostly sunny locations, while American hornbeam does best in full shade.

Selected species and varieties:
C. betulus (European hornbeam, common hornbeam) is pyramidal when young, maturing to a rounded crown, growing 40 to 60 feet tall under average conditions with a spread of 30 to 40 feet, bearing sharply toothed leaves 2½ to 5 inches long and 1 to 2 inches wide that remain unusually pest-free; 'Columnaris' has a densely branched steeple-shaped outline; 'Fastigiata' grows 30 to 40 feet tall with an oval to vaselike shape, and a forked trunk; Zones 4-8. *C. caroliniana* (American hornbeam) grows from 20 to 30 feet tall with a spreading canopy of toothed, roughly oblong leaves and smooth, gray bark.

SWEET BOX
Sarcococca

Light: full shade

Plant type: shrub

Hardiness: Zones 5-8

Height: 1½ to 5 feet

Soil and Moisture: well-drained, moist, fertile

Interest: foliage, fragrance, fruit

Care: moderate

◀ Sarcococca hookerana var. humilis

A handsome plant with year-round ornamental value, sweet box has shiny narrow leaves on its roundly mounded shape. In late winter to early spring, inconspicuous but fragrant white flowers bloom, to be replaced by shiny black or red berries that linger into fall. *Sarcococca* spreads slowly by suckers; the low form makes a good ground cover.

Growing and care:
Best grown in Zone 8 in the South and along the Pacific Coast, *S. confusa* and *S. ruscifolia* need shelter in Zone 7. Protect from winter winds. Add leaf mold or peat moss to the soil to improve drainage. Mulch to conserve moisture.

Selected species and varieties:
S. confusa has leaves to 2 inches long and ¾ inch wide on a densely branched shrub growing 3 to 5 feet tall and wide; Zones 7-8. *S. hookerana* var. *humilis* (Himalayan sarcococca) is 1½ to 2 feet tall and wide, blooming in early spring under 2- to 3½-inch-long and ½-inch-wide leaves. *S. ruscifolia* (fragrant sarcococca, fragrant sweet box) bears very fragrant flowers and red fruits on a 3-foot-high mound with an equal spread; Zones 7-8.

TERNSTROEMIA
Ternstroemia

Light: full shade

Plant type: shrub

Hardiness: Zones 7-10

Height: 6 to 15 feet

Soil and Moisture: well-drained, moist, fertile

Interest: flowers, foliage, fragrance

Care: easy

◀ Ternstroemia gymnanthera

L eathery leaves that open brownish red and mature to rich, glossy green clothe the gracefully arching branches of ternstroemia. In early summer small clusters of fragrant creamy white flowers put on a modest display. Small red berries turn black and last through winter. Primarily grown for its foliage, ternstroemia works well as a foundation plant or hedge; it can also be trained into a small tree.

Growing and care:
Although Japanese ternstroemia grows best in rich, slightly acid soil that stays moist, it tolerates occasional drought. Good drainage is essential. Given suitable conditions, the species is usually problem-free. Prune after flowering. Propagate by stem cuttings.

Selected species and varieties:
T. gymnanthera [sometimes confused with *Cleyera japonica*] (Japanese ternstroemia) grows 10 to 15 feet tall and wide with elliptical to oblong 2- to 6-inch-long leaves often arranged in whorls on the ends of branches and ½-inch flowers produced in clusters on the previous year's growth. Bloom and berries occur only on mature plants.

WITCH HAZEL
Hamamelis

Light: full shade	
Plant type: shrub, tree	
Hardiness: Zones 3-8	
Height: 6 to 20 feet	
Soil and Moisture: well-drained, moist	
Interest: flowers, foliage, fragrance	
Care: easy	

◄ Hamamelis japonica 'Zuccariniana'

Witch hazels brighten the fall and winter landscape with heavily fragrant yellow to red flowers on angular branches, sometimes appearing long after their colorful foliage has fallen. The two-valved dry fruit capsules explode, propelling the black seeds many feet away.

Growing and care:

Common and American witch hazels can tolerate heavy, poorly drained clay but grow best in well-drained, rich forest loams. Give Chinese and Japanese witch hazels well-drained acid soil to which organic matter has been added. Prune *H.* x *intermedia* to encourage dense branching.

Selected species and varieties:

H. x *intermedia* 'Arnold Promise' grows to 20 feet tall and wide with 1½-inch primrose yellow flowers in winter to early spring and gray-green foliage that becomes yellow, orange, or red in fall; hardy to Zone 5; 'Diane' grows 14 to 20 feet tall, bearing slightly fragrant orange-red flowers with purple-red calyxes and yellow-orange to red autumn foliage; 'Jelena' (sometimes called 'Copper Beauty') has copper-colored flowers and orange-red fall foliage; 'Primavera' has very fragrant prolific clear yellow flowers borne later than the species; 'Ruby Glow' bears coppery red to reddish brown flowers and orange-red fall foliage. *H. japonica* 'Sulphurea' (Japanense witch hazel) grows 10 to 15 feet high and wide with an open flat-topped habit, producing yellow flowers with red calyx cups in late winter and lustrous green leaves that turn yellow, red, and purplish in fall; hardy to Zone 5; 'Zuccariniana' has rich yellow flowers with a hint of green inside the calyx. *H. mollis* 'Goldcrest' (Chinese witch hazel) is an oval, broadly open large shrub or small tree 10 to 15 feet tall and wide with medium green leaves in summer that turn a vivid yellow to yellow-orange in fall and fragrant yellow flowers with red-brown calyx cups blooming for a long period in winter; reliably hardy to Zone 6; 'Pallida' has a spreading habit and lustrous leaves, with yellow flowers suffused with a blush of chartreuse in late winter; hardy to Zone 5. *H. vernalis* (American witch hazel) has a broad multistemmed rounded outline 6 to 10 feet tall with a greater spread, producing very fragrant yellow to red flowers from late winter to early spring and medium to dark green foliage in summer that turns golden yellow in fall; hardy to Zone 4; 'Carnea' has richly colored flowers with a red calyx and petals that are red at the base blending to orange at the tip. *H. virginiana* (common witch hazel) is a large shrub to small tree 20 feet tall and equally wide with angular spreading branches and fragrant yellow flowers that emerge in mid- to late fall, sometimes just as its 4- to 6-inch leaves have turned yellow.

Picture Credits

Images. 612: Jerry Pavia. 613: Jerry Pavia; © Walter Chandoha. 614: Jerry Pavia; Cynthia Woodyard. 615: Joanne Pavia; Thomas E. Eltzroth. 616: Jerry Pavia. 617: Jerry Pavia; Richard Shiell. 618: Peter Loewer; Jerry Pavia. 619: Joanne Pavia. 620: Jerry Pavia; Richard Shiell. 621: Jerry Pavia; Thomas E. Eltzroth. 622: Jerry Pavia; Thomas E. Eltzroth. 623: Jerry Pavia. 624: Jerry Pavia; Charles Mann. 625: Jerry Pavia; Thomas E. Eltzroth. 626: Thomas E. Eltzroth; Jerry Pavia. 627: Joanne Pavia; Mark Turner. 628: Jerry Pavia. 629: © Walter Chandoha. 630: Jerry Pavia. 631: Jerry Pavia; © Crandall & Crandall. 632: M. W. Carlton/National Wildflower Research Center; Steven Still. 633: Jerry Pavia. 634: R. Todd Davis Photography; Thomas E. Eltzroth. 635: Jerry Pavia. 636: Jerry Pavia; Steven Still. 637: Cynthia Woodyard; Jerry Pavia. 638: Michael Dirr; Steven Still. 639: Joanne Pavia; Joseph G. Strauch, Jr. 640: C. Colston Burrell; Richard Shiell. 641: Jerry Pavia; Joanne Pavia. 642: Richard Shiell; Steven Still. 643: Jerry Pavia; Richard Shiell. 644: Joanne Pavia; C. Colston Burrell. 645: Michael Dirr; Richard Shiell. 646: R. Todd Davis Photography; Joanne Pavia. 647: Jerry Pavia; Thomas E. Eltzroth. 648: Joanne Pavia; Richard Shiell. 649: C. Colston Burrell; John A. Lynch. 650: Joanne Pavia; Holly H. Shimizu. 651: Joseph G. Strauch, Jr.; Jerry Pavia. 652: Jerry Pavia. 653: © Roger Foley/design by Sheela Lampietti; Jerry Pavia. 654: Joseph G. Strauch, Jr. 655: Steven Still; C. Colston Burrell. 656: Mark Turner; Joanne Pavia. 657: David Cavagnaro; Steven Still. 658: Bill Johnson; David Cavagnaro. 659: Michael Dirr; Steven Still. 660: Virginia R. Weiler; Jerry Pavia. 661: Charles Mann; Joanne Pavia. 662: Joanne Pavia; Joseph G. Strauch, Jr. 663: Joanne Pavia; André Viette. 664: Joanne Pavia; Bill Johnson. 665: Joanne Pavia; Jerry Pavia. 666: Jerry Pavia. 667: Jerry Pavia; Brent Heath. 668: Thomas E. Eltzroth; © Saxon Holt. 669: Robert E. Lyons; Eric Crichton Photos,

Blanford Forum, Dorset. 670: © Saxon Holt; Jerry Pavia. 671: Jerry Pavia. 672: David Cavagnaro; Joanne Pavia. 673: Richard L. Doutt; © Michael S. Thompson. 674: Jerry Pavia. 675: Photos Horticultural, Ipswich, Suffolk; C. Colston Burrell. 676: Joanne Pavia. 677: Jerry Pavia. 678: J. S. Sira/Garden Picture Library, London; Richard Shiell. 679: © Michael S. Thompson; Photos Horticultural, Ipswich, Suffolk. 680: Jerry Pavia. 681: David Cavagnaro. 682: Brent Heath; judywhite. 683: Brent Heath; Thomas E. Eltzroth. 684: Andrew Lawson, Charlbury, Oxfordshire; Richard Shiell. 685: Richard Shiell; Jerry Pavia. 686: Jerry Pavia; Photos Horticultural, Ipswich, Suffolk. 687: Brent Heath; C. Colston Burrell. 688: Photos Horticultural, Ipswich, Suffolk; Brent Heath. 689: Brent Heath; Bill Johnson. 690: Dency Kane; Steven Foster. 691: Holly H. Shimizu; Dency Kane. 692, 693: Jerry Pavia. 694: Holly H. Shimizu; Thomas E. Eltzroth. 695: Holly H. Shimizu; Jerry Pavia. 696: Jerry Pavia; Dency Kane. 697: Joanne Pavia; Thomas E. Eltzroth. 698: Thomas E. Eltzroth. 699: Rita Buchanan; Richard Shiell. 700: Holly H. Shimizu. 701: Jerry Pavia; Joanne Pavia. 702: Dency Kane; Joanne Pavia. 703: Catriona Tudor Erler; Jerry Pavia. 704: Holly H. Shimizu; Jerry Pavia. 705: Jerry Pavia. 706: William H. Allen, Jr.; Jerry Pavia. 707: Richard Shiell. 708: Thomas E. Eltzroth; Holly H. Shimizu. 709: Richard Shiell. 710: Holly H. Shimizu; Jerry Pavia. 711: Joseph G. Strauch, Jr.; Photos Horticultural, Ipswich, Suffolk. 712: © Roger Foley; Thomas E. Eltzroth. 713: Thomas E. Eltzroth; Dency Kane. 714: Jerry Pavia. 715: Thomas E. Eltzroth; Jerry Pavia. 716: Deni Bown/Oxford Scientific Films, Long Hanborough, Oxfordshire. 717: Dency Kane; Jerry Pavia. 718: Jerry Pavia; Richard Shiell. 719: Richard Day/Daybreak Imagery; Carole Ottesen. 720: Jerry Pavia; Dency Kane. 721: C. Colston Burrell; Richard Day/Daybreak Imagery.

722: Michael Dirr; © Michael S. Thompson. 723: Jerry Pavia. 724: Thomas E. Eltzroth; Jerry Pavia. 725: Jerry Pavia; Peter Haring. 726: Jerry Pavia. 727: Peter Haring; Jerry Pavia. 728: © Crandall & Crandall; Anita Sabarese. 729: Charles Mann; © Crandall & Crandall. 730: Peter Haring; Jerry Pavia. 731: R. Todd Davis Photography; Joseph G. Strauch, Jr. 732: R. Todd Davis Photography; Thomas E. Eltzroth. 733: Richard Shiell; Peter Haring. 734: Michael Dirr; Dency Kane. 735: Jerry Pavia. 736: Richard Shiell; Jerry Pavia. 737: Jerry Pavia; Michael Dirr. 738: Jerry Pavia. 739: Peter Haring; Jerry Pavia. 740: Jerry Pavia; Bill Johnson. 741: Richard Shiell; Jerry Pavia. 742: Jerry Pavia; Richard Shiell. 743, 744: Jerry Pavia. 745: Richard Shiell. 746: Mike Shoup; Peter Haring. 747: David Cavagnaro; Peter Haring. 748: Richard Shiell; Jerry Pavia. 749: R. Todd Davis Photography. 750: Peter Haring; Thomas E. Eltzroth. 751: Lefever/ Grushow/Grant Heilman Photography, Inc.; © Runk/ Schoenberger/Grant Heilman Photography, Inc. 752, 753: Jerry Pavia. 754: Jerry Pavia; Cynthia Woodyard. 755: Jerry Pavia. 756: Thomas E. Eltzroth; Jerry Pavia. 757: Jerry Pavia. 758: Thomas E. Eltzroth; David Cavagnaro. 759: Jerry Pavia; Bill Johnson. 760: Jerry Pavia; Thomas E. Eltzroth. 761: Jerry Pavia; Joanne Pavia. 762: Jerry Pavia. 763: Thomas E. Eltzroth; Jerry Pavia. 764: Jerry Pavia. 765: Peter Loewer; Photos Horticultural, Ipswich, Suffolk. 766: Thomas E. Eltzroth; Jerry Pavia. 767-769: Jerry Pavia. 770: Joanne Pavia. 771: Jerry Pavia. 772: Jerry Pavia; Cynthia Woodyard. 773: Jerry Pavia; Thomas E. Eltzroth. 774, 775: Joanne Pavia. 776: Jerry Pavia. 777: Bill Johnson; Jerry Pavia. 778: Joseph G. Strauch, Jr.; Richard Shiell. 779: Richard Shiell; Steven Still. 780: Thomas E. Eltzroth; Joseph G. Strauch, Jr. 781: Bill Johnson; © Saxon Holt. 782: Richard Shiell; Jerry Pavia. 783: Jerry Pavia; Richard Shiell. 784: Jerry Pavia; Joanne Pavia.

785: Jerry Pavia. 786: W. D. Bransford/National Wildflower Research Center; Jerry Pavia. 787: Jerry Pavia; R. Todd Davis Photography. 788: Jerry Pavia; Carole Ottesen. 789: Jerry Pavia; Carole Ottesen. 790: Jerry Pavia; Steven Still. 791: Jerry Pavia. 792: Joanne Pavia; Carole Ottesen. 793: John A. Lynch; Virginia R. Weiler. 794: David Cavagnaro; Jerry Pavia. 795: Jerry Pavia. 796: Carole Ottesen; Thomas E. Eltzroth. 797: Joanne Pavia; Jerry Pavia. 798: Joseph G. Strauch, Jr.; Jerry Pavia. 799: Joseph G. Strauch, Jr.; Jerry Pavia. 800: Steven Still; Jerry Pavia. 801: John A. Lynch; Andy Wasowski. 802: Photos Horticultural, Ipswich, Suffolk; Bill Johnson. 803: Charles Mann; Jerry Pavia. 804: Brent Heath; Joanne Pavia. 805: Brent Heath; © Michael S. Thompson. 806: Robert E. Lyons. 807: © Michael S. Thompson. 808: Joanne Pavia; Jerry Pavia. 809: Joseph G. Strauch, Jr. 810: Brent Heath. 811: Leonard G. Phillips; Robert E. Lyons. 812: Jerry Pavia; Andy Wasowski. 813: Photo-Synthesis™; W. D. Bransford/National Wildflower Research Center. 814: Holly H. Shimizu; Jerry Pavia. 815: Jerry Pavia; Dency Kane. 816: Holly H. Shimizu; Joanne Pavia. 817: Richard Shiell; Jerry Pavia. 818, 819: Jerry Pavia. 820: Dency Kane; Holly H. Shimizu. 821: Jerry Pavia. 822: Jerry Pavia; Joanne Pavia. 823, 824: Jerry Pavia. 825: Rita Buchanan; Jerry Pavia. 826: Catriona Tudor Erler; Dency Kane. 827: Jerry Pavia. 828: Jerry Pavia; Joanne Pavia. 829: Jerry Pavia. 830: Harry Smith Horticultural Photographic Collection, Wickford, Essex; Jerry Pavia. 831: Jerry Pavia; Michael Dirr. 832: Charles Mann; © Walter Chandoha. 833: Richard Shiell; Jerry Pavia. 834: Catriona Tudor Erler; Mark Lovejoy. 835: Jerry Pavia; © Michael S. Thompson. 836: Robert E. Lyons; R. Todd Davis Photography. 837: Steven Still; © Michael S. Thompson. 838: Jerry Pavia; Richard Shiell. 839: Carole Ottesen; Jerry Pavia. 840: Dency Kane; Jerry Pavia. 841: Richard Shiell; Peter Haring.

842: Jerry Pavia; Michael Dirr. 843: Michael Dirr; Jerry Pavia. 844: © 1997 Alan & Linda Detrick. 845: Richard Shiell; Jerry Pavia. 846: Peter Haring; Jerry Pavia. 847: Joseph G. Strauch, Jr. 848, 849: Jerry Pavia. 850: Thomas E. Eltzroth; Jerry Pavia. 851: Richard Shiell; Jerry Pavia. 852: Derek Fell; Richard Shiell. 853: R. Todd Davis Photography; © 1997 Alan & Linda Detrick. 854: Peter Haring; Joanne Pavia. 855: Jerry Pavia. 856: Thomas E. Eltzroth; Jerry Pavia. 857: Thomas E. Eltzroth; Jerry Pavia. 858: Michael Dirr. 859: Richard Shiell; Jerry Pavia. 860: Joanne Pavia; © 1997 Alan & Linda Detrick. 861: Jerry Pavia. 862: C. Colston Burrell; Michael Dirr. 863: Joanne Pavia; Charles Mann. 864: Jerry Pavia; Joseph G. Strauch, Jr. 865: Michael Dirr; Richard Shiell. 866: Thomas E. Eltzroth; Jerry Pavia. 867: Jerry Pavia. 868, 869: Allan Mandell, Garden Photographer, Inc. 870: Jerry Pavia; Photos Horticultural, Ipswich, Suffolk. 871-873: Jerry Pavia. 874: Sally Kurtz; Thomas E. Eltzroth. 875: Jerry Pavia; David Cavagnaro. 876: © Crandall & Crandall; judywhite/New Leaf Images. 877: Jerry Pavia. 878: Steven Still; © 1997 Alan & Linda Detrick. 879: © Michael S. Thompson; Joseph G. Strauch, Jr. 880: Jerry Pavia; Joseph G. Strauch, Jr. 881: Joseph G. Strauch, Jr. 882: Charles Mann; Thomas E. Eltzroth. 883: Richard Shiell. 884: Jerry Pavia. 885: Jerry Pavia; Joseph G. Strauch, Jr. 886: Jerry Pavia; Bill Johnson. 887: Joanne Pavia; Richard Shiell. 888: Joanne Pavia; Jerry Pavia. 889: Jerry Pavia; Steven Still. 890: Bill Johnson; Carole Ottesen. 891: © Michael S. Thompson; © Crandall & Crandall. 892: Robert S. Hebb; Jerry Pavia. 893: R. Todd Davis Photography. 894: Virginia R. Weiler; John A. Lynch. 895: Jerry Pavia; Bill Johnson. 896: Richard Shiell; Jerry Pavia. 897: Eric Crichton Photos, Blanford Forum, Dorset; R. Todd Davis Photography. 898: C. Colston Burrell; Thomas E. Eltzroth. 899, 900: © Michael S. Thompson. 901: Rosalind Creasy; Carole Ottesen.

902: judywhite/New Leaf Images; Richard Shiell. 903: © Michael S. Thompson. 904: Joanne Pavia. 905: Jerry Pavia; © Michael S. Thompson. 906: © Michael S. Thompson; Jerry Pavia. 907: Jerry Pavia; Richard Shiell. 908: Richard Shiell; Jerry Pavia. 909: Richard Shiell; Jerry Pavia. 910: Jerry Pavia; Mark Turner. 911: Jerry Pavia. 912: Michael Dirr; © Michael S. Thompson. 913: Jerry Pavia. 914: Jerry Pavia; Robert E. Lyons. 915: Joanne Pavia; Jerry Pavia. 916: Michael Dirr; Jerry Pavia. 917: Jerry Pavia. 918: Richard Shiell; Jerry Pavia. 919: Jerry Pavia. 920: Michael Dirr; Jerry Pavia. 921, 922: Jerry Pavia. 923: Jerry Pavia; judywhite/New Leaf Images. 924: Steven Still; Jerry Pavia. 925: Jerry Pavia; Richard Shiell. 926: Richard Shiell; Jerry Pavia. 927: Robert E. Lyons. 928: Jerry Pavia; Joseph G. Strauch, Jr. 929: Mike Shoup; R. Todd Davis Photography. 930, 931: R. Todd Davis Photography. 933: David Cavagnaro; Michael Dirr. 934: judywhite/New Leaf Images; Jerry Pavia. 935: Deni Bown/Oxford Scientific Films, Long Hanborough, Oxfordshire; Carole Ottesen. 936: Joanne Pavia; Jerry Pavia. 937: Jerry Pavia. 938: Joanne Pavia; C. Colston Burrell. 939: C. Colston Burrell; Jerry Pavia. 940: Joanne Pavia; Jerry Pavia. 941: R. Todd Davis Photography; Jerry Pavia. 942: Joanne Pavia. 943: Brent Heath; Richard Day/Daybreak Imagery. 944: Robert E. Lyons. 945: Joanne Pavia; Tom Ulrich/Oxford Scientific Films, Long Hanborough, Oxfordshire. 946: Rita Buchanan; Joseph G. Strauch, Jr. 947: © Walter Chandoha; Jerry Pavia. 948: Mark Turner; Jerry Pavia. 949, 950: Jerry Pavia. 951: Jerry Pavia; Thomas E. Eltzroth. 952: Jerry Pavia; Thomas E. Eltzroth. 953: © Michael S. Thompson.

TIME® LIFE BOOKS

Time-Life Books is a division of **TIME LIFE INC.**

TIME LIFE INC.
PRESIDENT and CEO: Jim Nelson

TIME-LIFE TRADE PUBLISHING

VICE PRESIDENT and PUBLISHER	Neil Levin
Senior Director of Acquisitions and Editorial Resources	Jennifer Pearce
Director of New Product Development	Carolyn Clark
Director of Trade Sales	Dana Coleman
Director of Marketing	Inger Forland
Director of New Product Development	Teresa Graham
Director of Custom Publishing	John Lalor
Director of Special Markets	Robert Lombardi
Director of Creative Services	Laura McNeill
Senior Editor	Linda Bellamy
Technical Specialist	Monika Lynde
Production Manager	Carolyn Bounds
Quality Assurance	James D. King, Stacy L. Eddy

Produced by Gibson Design Associates, Charlottesville, Virginia.

Editorial Staff for
The Complete Garden Guide

Project Manager	Lynn McGowan
Proofreader	Celia Beattie
Indexer	Lina B. Burton
Picture Coordinators	Jennifer Callahan, Rebecca Mills
Cover Design	James Gibson, Gibson Design Associates
Cover Photo	Leonard G. Phillips

Pre-Press Services, Time-Life Imaging Center

Printed in U.S.A.
10 9 8 7 6 5 4 3 2 1

TIME-LIFE is a trademark of Time Warner Inc., and affiliated companies.

Library of Congress Cataloging-in-Publication Data
The complete garden guide: a comprehensive reference for all your garden needs / by the editors of Time-Life Books.
    p. cm.
      ISBN 0-7370-0614-5 (hardcover)
      1. Gardening. 2. Landscape gardening. I. Time-Life Books.
SB453 .C6416   1999
635--dc21   99-040070

Editorial Staff for
The Time-Life Complete Gardener

Editor: Janet Cave

Administrative Editor: Roxie France-Nuriddin

Art Directors: Cindy Morgan-Jaffe, Kathleen Mallow, Alan Pitts, Sue Pratt

Picture Editors: Jane Jordan, Jane A. Martin

Text Editors: Sarah Brash, Darcie Conner Johnston, Paul Mathless

Associate Editors/Research and Writing: Megan Barnett, Constance Contreras, Sharon Kurtz, Katya Sharpe, Robert Speziale, Karen Sweet, Mary-Sherman Willis

Senior Copyeditors: Anne Farr (principal), Donna D. Carey, Colette Stockum

Picture Coordinators: David Cheatham, Ruth Goldberg, Kimberly Grandcolas, David A. Herod, Betty H. Weatherley

Editorial Assistant: Donna Fountain

Contributors: Jennifer Clark, Catherine Harper Parrott (picture research); Vilasini Balakrishnan, Linda Bellamy, Cyndi Bemel, Susan S. Blair, Dena Crosson, Meg Dennison, Catriona Tudor Erler, Catherine Hackett, Adrian Higgins, Marie Hofer, Jamie R. Holland, Ann Kelsall, Bonnie Kreitler, Jocelyn G. Lindsay, Peter Loewer, Carole Ottesen, Rita Pelczar, Ann Perry, Warren Schultz, Roseanne Scott, Margaret Stevens, Marianna Tait-Durbin, Susan Gregory Thomas, André Viette, Cheryl Weber, Olwen Woodier (research and writing); Margery duMond, Marfé Ferguson-Delano, Jim Hicks, Bonnie Kreitler, Joyce B. Marshall, Gerry Shremp, Lynn Yorke (editing); John Drummond (art); Anne Sinderman (consultant).

Correspondents: Christine Hinze (London), Christina Lieberman (New York). Valuable assistance was also provided by Liz Brown (New York) and Judy Aspinall (London).